A CATHOLIC DICTIONARY

"To what shall we liken the kingdom of God? or to what parable shall we compare it? It is as a grain of mustard seed: which when it is sown in the earth, is less than all the seeds that are in the earth: and when it is sown, it groweth up, and becometh greater than all herbs, and shooteth out great branches, so that the birds of the air may dwell under the shadow thereof."
—Mark 4:30-32

A CATHOLIC DICTIONARY

Edited by

Donald Attwater

THIRD EDITION

"Knowledge is a fountain of life to him that possesseth it . . ."
—Proverbs 16:22

TAN BOOKS AND PUBLISHERS, INC.
Rockford, Illinois 61105

NIHIL OBSTAT:
    Georgius D. Smith, S.T.D., Ph.D.
    Censor deputatus

Imprimatur:
    E. Morrogh Bernard
    Vic. Gen.
    Westmonasterii
    die 10 Maii, 1946

NIHIL OBSTAT:
    Hubertus Richards, S.T.L., L.S.S.
    Censor deputatus

Imprimatur:
    ✠ Georgius L. Craven
    Epus. Sebastopolis
    Vic. Cap. Westmonasterii
    Westmonasterii
    die 30 Januarii, 1957

Library of Congress Catalog Card No.: 97-60871

ISBN-13: 978-0-89555-549-6
ISBN-10: 0-89555-549-2

Cover illustrations—*Top Row:* St. Peter's Basilica; St. Thomas Aquinas; statue of St. Joseph and the Child Jesus—photo: Alex LaSala. *Middle Row:* a Guardian Angel (from a painting by Heinrich Kaiser—photo: Victoria Ambrosetti); Tintern Abbey (Tintern, Gwent, Wales)—courtesy of the British Tourist Authority. *Lower Row:* Our Lady of Perpetual Help; Notre Dame de Paris (rear view)—courtesy of the French Government Tourist Office; Pope St. Gregory the Great (Barberini Palace, Rome).

Printed and bound in the United States of America.

TAN BOOKS AND PUBLISHERS, INC.
P.O. Box 424
Rockford, Illinois 61105
1997

"Herein, then, are to be found only facts and records, of one order or another, many of them purely external and accidental. But none, however small, without importance in its degree; for there is nothing in the Catholic Church without connexion, whether clear or obscure, with the love of God—and that love is the beginning and end of the whole matter."

—*From the Preface*

PUBLISHER'S PREFACE
To the 1997 Edition

IT is a pleasure to re-issue the esteemed CATHOLIC DICTIONARY edited by Donald Attwater. English-speaking Catholics have long been in need of just such a book as this, which is direct, clear, concise and accurate.

The reader will note that A CATHOLIC DICTIONARY was last published in 1961. The Church has seen many changes since that year, yet we believe this book remains an extremely valuable contribution to the Catholic world.

The articles on Catholic doctrine and on the principles of Catholic moral theology here give the timeless Catholic teachings which will remain valid and true forever. The articles on philosophy, theology and Church history, as well as those on Scripture, papal documents, etc. are similarly timeless.

On matters of discipline and liturgy, of course, many changes have taken place. In particular, the 21st Ecumenical Council—Vatican Council II—was held from 1962-1965; a new liturgy, in particular a New Order of Mass (*Novus Ordo Missae*), was introduced into the Latin Rite of the Catholic Church in 1970; and a new Code of Canon Law was promulgated by John Paul II in 1983.

In this edition a few of the most obvious points needing "updating" have been addressed in footnotes, with each footnote clearly marked as originating with the Publisher. But it was not feasible to footnote every instance where the current discipline differs from that set forth here. (On the whole, these are few). Readers should note in particular that any mention of Canon Law—such as, for instance, information on the offenses for which a Catholic incurs automatic excommunication—is based on the old Code of Canon Law (1917). (See p. 182 and elsewhere.) But even the apparently "outdated" disciplinary information included herein is of tremendous value, since it shows the mind of the Church and often records traditions that have been handed down for many centuries.

For examples, the reader may wish to look up REQUIEM MASS and EMBER DAYS. Both articles describe practices which one no longer finds in effect at the local parish, yet both set forth ancient Catholic traditions and the sound doctrinal reasons behind them. And who is to say that the Church as a whole may not at some time return to these traditions? One can already see the beginning of such a return taking place in regard to the Church's traditional liturgy—the "Tridentine" liturgy. In any case, all of A CATHOLIC DICTIONARY's 5,067 entries taken together show the Catholic Church as a masterpiece of order and structure, unsurpassed by anything else in the world. It is a miracle in itself!

To turn to another point, the reader of A CATHOLIC DICTIONARY may note here and there a certain "hard-headed" attitude regarding the history of various devotions, devotional objects, etc. That is, in these non-doctrinal matters, where Catholics are free to believe or not, this book sometimes tends toward a skeptical stance. For three examples, one may see the articles HOLY BLOOD OF BRUGES, HOLY BLOOD OF HALES, and HOLY COAT (p. 231). One can only say that the author of such articles is entitled to his opinion in these matters, but the reader is likewise entitled to *his* own opinion. One might also state that a somewhat hard-headed cast of mind is not necessarily a disadvantage in the authors of a dictionary—a work which is intended to pare things down to the essentials. In matters involving Sacred Scripture, on the other hand, one will find here not skepticism but rather respect for the historical truth thereof. (See, for example, GENESIS, HISTORICALNESS OF.)

The reader will also note that this book includes a number of entries relating to ecclesiastical places in Great Britain. This will be a help to English-speaking Catholics of the New World, putting them in touch with their English-speaking Catholic roots in Europe.

The book also includes a number of Eastern Catholic terms. Whereas Attwater was a Latin Rite Catholic, he was very familiar with the Eastern Rites, and in fact wrote a number of books on Eastern Catholic topics. These entries too are a fortunate inclusion, broadening A CATHOLIC DICTIONARY to cover—to some extent—the universal Catholic Church, not just her Western or Latin Rite.

The reader will note the excellent job of cross-referencing that has been done here, with numerous insertions of *q.v.* (or *qq.v.*—the plural) directing him to related entries.

Thus A CATHOLIC DICTIONARY is a great reference work—as well as a great book for just perusing and reading. Such a perusal could certainly go far toward providing the Catholic background which every educated Catholic should possess.

PREFACE

When this book was first planned in 1928 it was conceived as a simple dictionary of the technical words and phrases of the Catholic Church, of those which she has herself made, and of those general words which in a Catholic context do, or may, bear a special or exact meaning. But in the course of the preliminary work it was found desirable to extend its scope, the necessity for a more encyclopædic method becoming ever more apparent; and the book became a general work of quick reference to the signification of the words, terms, names and phrases in common use in the philosophy, dogmatic and moral theology, canon law, liturgy, institutions and organization of the Catholic Church. It looks primarily to present-day belief, practice, teaching, opinion, or as the case may require, and therefore history, exposition and apologetics are strictly secondary and subordinate, and biography has no place at all. The editor has worked with particular regard to the requirements of Catholic laypeople and with the hope of being useful to non-Catholic journalists and general enquirers.

Certain more detailed information is given about the Church in Great Britain and Ireland, and in a measure the United States, but it is hoped that undue space has not been devoted to matters purely local to those countries. On the other hand, an unusual but proper prominence is given to the liturgy of worship and to the Churches of the East.

It has been the editor's aim to avoid so far as possible direct affirmation or a tone of certainty about matters which are not certain. These are not easily to be entirely avoided; but it may safely be said that no doctrine on any matter has been ascribed to the Church (as distinguished from individual members) unless she in fact teaches it, and nothing which the Church herself teaches (and therefore demanding the assent of all her children) has been ascribed to any lesser authority. The editor will be grateful to all who, addressing him c/o the Publishers, will draw his attention to errors and omissions, or make suggestions and criticisms. A complaint about the first edition made by some Catholic reviewers was that the book was too scholastic in phraseology. There is substance in that criticism. But there has been so great a revival of Scholasticism in our time, and the Church has extended so eminent a measure of approval and encouragement to scholastic philosophy according to the mind of St. Thomas Aquinas, that extensive use of its phraseology was hardly to be avoided, strange as it may sometimes seem to those unfamiliar with it.

Non-Catholic users of this book are warned not to look therein for a complete statement or picture of Catholicism, even in broken and irregular outline. To do so would be something like seeking to learn about English literature by reading an English dictionary. No religion, except perhaps the most elementary, can be caught and confined within a mesh of words; and when those words are in the mechanical form of an alphabetical index the most that can be looked for is bare bones, and a dismembered skeleton at that—one whose bones have been laid out in order of size, as it were. Something may be done by reading or listening to the words of gifted writers, teachers and preachers to articulate that skeleton, to clothe it with flesh, to give it life, to breathe into it a soul and so to make of it a recognizable body, the Mystical Body of Christ. But the fact remains that no one, however holy, learned, experienced, sympathetic, good-willed, open-minded he may be, ever really understands the Catholic religion so long as he remains outside the visible body of the Church; it is impossible for him to see its component parts in their true proportion; he cannot recognize it in itself for what it is. To be able to do so is a free gift of God: it comes only with faith; but faith is open to all men, by Baptism and the will to believe.

For this reason: Christianity is a *life,* first and last and all the time; and so can be understood, or even properly apprehended, only by one who tries to live it; it is to minister to that life in the most obscure of her members that the Church of Christ exists; her affirmation of absolute truths, her moral and disciplinary law, her liturgy of public worship, her complex organization, all subserve that end. Baptism and faith are necessary for salvation, for by them alone are men given the freedom of that city wherein is life, temporal and eternal: the life of sanctifying grace of the individual and the corporate life of the Church inseparable therefrom; "I am come that they may have life and may have it more abundantly" (John x, 10).

Herein, then, are to be found only facts and records, of one order or another, many of them purely external and accidental. But none, however small, without importance in its degree; for there is nothing in the Catholic Church without connexion, whether clear or obscure, with the love of God—and that love is the beginning and end of the whole matter.

In arranging the words ordinary alphabetical order has been followed, without recourse to any fancy modification thereof. When a term consists of two or more words the editor has tried to index it according to custom and common sense; his object has been to put such terms under the letters in which the average reader is more likely to look for them: this has entailed inconsistencies, but such are adjudged preferable to an artificial and rigid arrangement.

Unless otherwise stated, references to canon law, customs and observances, and liturgical matters, relate to those of the Western or Latin church only.

Scriptural quotations and references and the numeration of the Psalms and the Ten Commandments are taken from Challoner's revision of the Rheims-Douay Bible and from Monsignor Ronald Knox's translation of the New Testament. For the Protestant variations in these, see the relevant notices within. References to St. Thomas are to the *Summa Theologica* unless otherwise stated. Encyclical letters and other papal pronouncements are quoted by their opening words, according to custom.

Generally speaking, the derivation of a word has only been given when it is not found in general English dictionaries, or when it is one of special interest or utility; for the last, the *New English Dictionary* of the Oxford University Press has, in the main, been relied on.

Cross-references are not always and invariably given, but only when such a reference is certainly necessary or probably useful.

Statistics have properly little place in a work of this sort; of those given, many are only approximate and given for the purpose of comparison. Events since 1939 have made statistics, conditions and ecclesiastical organization in some countries extremely fluid and uncertain, especially those countries under the control or influence of the U.S.S.R.

Among the many who helped in the production of the first edition, the following principal contributors wrote most (but not all) of the entries under the headings named:

THE BIBLE: Canon J. P. ARENDZEN, D.D., PH.D., M.A.

DOGMATIC THEOLOGY: The Rev. THOMAS E. FLYNN, PH.D., M.A. (now Bishop of Lancaster).

CANON LAW: The Rev. EDWIN N. OWEN, D.C.L.

PHILOSOPHY: The late Father AELRED WHITACRE, O.P., S.T.B.

MORAL THEOLOGY: The CATHOLIC ACTION SOCIETY, Heythrop College (now The Bellarmine Society).

MYSTICAL AND ASCETICAL THEOLOGY: Canon JOSEPH CARTMELL, D.D., PH.D., M.A.

THE VATICAN: Monsignor THOMAS F. CROFT-FRASER, Chief Master of Ceremonies of St. Peter's Basilica.

HISTORY, EASTERN CHURCHES AND LITURGY: The EDITOR.

The last three sections were specially revised by the Rev. H. E. G. ROPE, M.A., Father CYRIL KOROLEVSKY, and Dom BENEDICT STEUART, O.S.B., respectively.

A CATHOLIC DICTIONARY

"He said unto them: Therefore every scribe instructed in the kingdom of heaven, is like to a man that is a householder, who bringeth forth out of his treasure new things and old."
—Matthew 13:52

A

A IURE (Lat., by law). An ecclesiastical censure (*q.v.*) inflicted on account of a definite and permanent law requiring it, opposed to one inflicted *ab homine* (*q.v.*).

A POSTERIORI. Reasoning based on experience, from effects to cause, from deeds to laws, etc.; induction. Opposed to *a priori*.

A PRIORI. Reasoning independent of experience, and based only on principles of reason; deduction. Opposed to *a posteriori*.

AB HOMINE (Lat., by man). An ecclesiastical censure (*q.v.*) inflicted by a judge, generally on account of special circumstances, and intended to lapse with them, whether by a general provision or in a particular case; opposed to one imposed *a iure* (*q.v.*).

ABBÉ (Fr., abbot). i. An abbot.
ii. More commonly, the title of address in French-speaking countries for anyone who is entitled to wear the dress of the secular clergy. Therefore "Monsieur l'abbé" does not necessarily indicate a priest, or even a cleric in major orders.

ABBESS. The superior of an abbey (*q.v.*) of nuns in those orders of which the male members are governed by abbots; Franciscan nuns of the second order and of the third order regular also have abbesses. Appointment is by the election of the choir-sisters in secret ballot, and must be confirmed by their bishop, a prelate of the order, or the Holy See, according to circumstances. She must be forty years old and ten years professed. Except among the Franciscans the office is for life and the abbess may bear the ring, pectoral cross and pastoral staff, and receive the proper episcopal benediction after election. The abbess has complete domestic authority according to the rule and constitutions of her order, but no spiritual jurisdiction whatsoever, or any power bordering thereon. In the middle ages abbesses exercised practically all the temporal powers that then appertained to abbots as feudal lords of large territories and numerous tenants and vassals; they were summoned to royal councils in the reign of King John, and the abbesses of Wilton, Barking, Winchester and Shaftesbury were present at a council of the realm in 1277, and again in 1306, and on other occasions.

ABBEY. A canonically erected monastery of not less than 12 monks or nuns, governed by an abbot or abbess. There are in Great Britain (exclusive of Franciscan nuns) 20 abbeys: 9 of Benedictine monks, 8 of Benedictine nuns. 2 of Cistercian monks and 1 of Bridgettine nuns; in the U.S.A. there are some 30 abbeys of Benedictine and Cistercian monks. Abbeys of monks are exempt from episcopal jurisdiction, but most abbeys of nuns in Great Britain are subject to the bishop, except Stanbrook and those others which depend on the abbot president of the English congregation. In the past the extensive temporal possessions of abbeys gave their rulers great secular power; in England, before the Reformation, the principal of many great abbeys were St. Albans, Westminster, Glastonbury, St. Edmundsbury (Benedictine), Waverley, Fountains, Boxley (Cistercian), Bermondsey (Cluniac), Dorchester, Merton, Southwark and Bristol (Canons Regular). The abbots outnumbered the bishops among the lords spiritual, and together they modified the hereditary principle of the peerage to a very notable extent.

ABBOT (Syriac, *abba*, father). Ordinarily, the regular superior of an abbey of Benedictines, Cistercians, or other monks, or Canons Regular. He is elected for life (for 8 years in the English congregation) by the secret ballot of the professed members in holy orders of the community, and must be of legitimate birth, a priest, professed in his order and not under thirty years old. After election he must be blessed by a bishop according to the rite in the "Pontificale Romanum." The abbot is father, ruler and teacher of his monks, who owe him entire obedience; he has complete domestic authority according to the rule and constitutions of his order and spiritual authority as laid down in canon law. He may confer minor orders on his professed subjects, at certain times pontificate at Mass and at other services, and use *Pontificalia,* including the pastoral staff and throne, *i.e.,* all regular abbots are now mitred abbots; their ordinary insignia are the ring and pectoral cross. The qualifications and duties of an abbot are set out in the Rule of St. Benedict, cap. ii, and referred to throughout his rule, which is based on the abbot's personal responsibility and unlimited power to use his own judgment within the provisions of the rule: "Everything is to be done by the abbot's will" (cap. xlix); but he in all things must act for the salvation of souls, and must be kept up to the mark by his own conscience and not by a limiting council. In the east an abbot is called *hegumenos* or *archimandrite* (*qq.v.*).

ABBOT, BLESSING OF AN. Within three months of election an abbot must be sol-

1

emnly blessed by the bishop of the diocese within the boundaries of which his abbey is. The ceremony resembles liturgically the consecration of a bishop, but is in fact only a blessing in that it grants no further jurisdiction and confers no sacramental grace or character, nor is it in itself necessary for the exercise of the office, except for the conferring of minor orders. After the blessing he receives the homage of his monks at the abbatial throne. This blessing is also conferred on abbesses, other than Franciscan.

ABBOT, LAY. A layman who held an abbacy *in commendam* (*q.v.*).

ABBOT, SECULAR. A cleric who is not a member of a religious order but who possesses the title and benefice of an extinct monastic foundation. The rights and privileges vary. Also the superior of certain distinguished colleges of priests, *e.g.*, the canons of the church of Guadelupe (Mexico) and of several in Italy, and of secular abbacies-*nullius*, *e.g.*, San Martino al Monte Cimino in Italy and St. Alexander in Albania. The chapter of the basilica of Sant' Ambrogio at Milan is governed by a mitred abbot, who is count of Civenna, assisted by an archpriest.

ABBOT, TITULAR. An abbot who holds the title of an extinct abbey and so has neither subjects, jurisdiction, nor duties in respect thereof. The English Congregation O.S.B. thus perpetuates the titles of the former abbeys of Westminster, York, Glastonbury, St. Albans, St. Edmundsbury, Dunfermline, Abingdon, Reading, Colchester, Evesham and Tewkesbury; the Premonstratensian Canons, Barlings and Welbeck; and the Augustinian Canons, Waltham.

ABBOT GENERAL. A title given to the head of certain religious orders, *e.g.*, the Cistercians, the Lateran and Premonstratensian Canons, the Camaldolese, and the Cassinese Congregation of Benedictines of the Primitive Observance. See GENERAL.

ABBOT NULLIUS (DIOECESIS) (Lat., of no diocese). An abbot whose jurisdiction extends over the clergy (whether of his order or secular), people and churches of the district wherein his abbey is situated, such district being under the authority of no diocesan bishop. An abbot-*nullius* sometimes receives episcopal consecration, but even when he does not, his rights and powers closely approximate to those of bishops-in-ordinary; *e.g.*, he may administer the sacrament of Confirmation, consecrate churches and altars, and confer the tonsure and minor orders on seculars. He may be summoned to sit and vote decisively at œcumenical councils. There are 20 abbeys-*nullius*, of which one is in the United States (Belmont), one in Australia (New Norcia), two in Tanganyika (Ndanda and Peramiho) and one in Canada (Muenster), all Benedictine;

others are at Monte Cassino, Subiaco, St. Paul-outside-the-Walls of Rome, Einsiedeln (Benedictine), Tre Fontane at Rome (Cistercian) and St. Maurice d'Agaune (Austin Canons). Most abbeys-*nullius* are immediately subject to the Holy See.

ABBOT PRESIDENT. The presiding abbot of a congregation (*q.v.* iv) of the Order of St. Benedict. Their powers and periods of office vary, but all are bidden to respect the jurisdiction of the abbots: each is the ruling abbot of a house and simply "first among equals," except the abbot general of the Cassinese congregation P.O., who has no other charge and resides in Rome.

ABBOT PRIMATE. The representative head of the Benedictine Order, an office established in 1893, the holder "to reside at Rome for business directly concerning the well-being of the whole order." As such he has little power or jurisdiction. The office is attached to the abbacy of Sant' Anselmo, the international college of the order in Rome.

ABBREVIATIONS. See Appendix I.

ABDIAS. The Greek form of the Hebrew name *Obadiah* (Worshipper of Jahveh), whose prophetical book is the shortest of the Old Testament; it has only 21 verses and foresees chiefly the fall of Edom. Nothing is known of the prophet and his date is disputed; he is named in the Roman Martyrology, Nov. 19.

ABDUCTION. A diriment impediment (*q.v.*) which invalidates marriage, so long as she remains in his power, between a man and a woman whom he has carried off, or detained by force against her will and with a view to marriage. If the woman is restored to liberty and freely elects to marry her abductor, the impediment ceases.

ABERDEEN. A Scottish see, suffragan of St. Andrews, founded at Mortlach in 1063, transferred to Aberdeen in 1125, vacant from 1577 to 1878. It comprises the counties of Aberdeen, Banff, Caithness, Ross and Cromarty, Elgin, Kincardine, Nairn, Sutherland, part of Inverness, and the Orkney and Shetland Islands which, before 1472, were in the province of Trondhjem. This diocese includes the Enzie, a district where the faith has never died out; the church at Tynet was built in 1772, that at Preshome in 1789. Blairs College is the seminary for the whole province of Saint Andrews and was founded at Scalan in 1712. The patron of the diocese is Our Lady (of Help) of the Brig of Dee at Aberdeen. Gaelic name: Abaireadhain.

ABERDEEN, THE USE OF. A variation of the Sarum (*q.v.*) use of the Roman liturgy, proper to the diocese of Aberdeen and other parts of Scotland before the Reformation.

ABIOGENESIS. A compound Greek word signifying the same thing as spontaneous generation, or the origin of life from a non-living thing. This theory, understood strictly as the origin of life merely by the evolution of non-living matter, is opposed to the principle of causality (*q.v.*). But in the sense that the living in its lowest forms could be produced from the non-living by the agency of a superior cause it was held to be not only a possibility but a fact by the scholastics. Science rejects it as a fact.

ABJURATION OF HERESY. The act of renouncing heresy, unbelief or schism, obligatory on all apostates, heretics, and schismatics before they can be validly absolved from excommunication. Abjuration must be made before the local ordinary (*q.v.*) or his delegate and two witnesses, and is a necessary preliminary to the reception of a baptized adult convert. Unbaptized persons, and children under 14, have no abjuration to make when received into the Church.

ABLUTION. The washing of the thumbs and index-fingers of the celebrant at Mass after the communion, in order to remove any particles of the Blessed Sacrament that may be adhering thereto. The ablution is performed by the server pouring wine and water on to the thumbs and fingers of the priest, which are held over the chalice. The priest then drinks the wine and water (also called the ablution or the ablutions) and dries his lips and then the chalice with the purificator.

ABOMINATION OF DESOLATION, The (Matt. xxiv, 15; Mark xiii, 14). Something connected with idolatrous worship whose introduction into the Temple of Jerusalem would presage its destruction. What this something was, commentators are not agreed: it is commonly referred to the eagle-standards of the Roman army of Titus or to the heathen legions themselves. St. Jerome suggested the statue of Cæsar which Pilate placed in the Temple and which, to the Jews, would represent the emperor-worship of the Romans.

ABORTION. The expulsion of the fœtus from the womb before it is able to lead a separate life; to be distinguished from premature birth, *i.e.*, expulsion of a fœtus which is able to live separately, usually during the eighth and ninth months after conception. Accidental abortion is known as miscarriage. Artificial abortion directly sought for is a felony in English law, and is forbidden by the Church as a grave sin under pain of excommunication reserved to the bishop and of irregularity reserved to the Holy See; all who help to procure the abortion share in these penalties.*

ABRAHAM'S BOSOM. An expression used by St. Luke in his gospel (xvi, 22) to designate Limbo (*q.v. i,*) but often used by the Fathers and since for the state of the Blessed in Heaven. "The souls of men attain to rest after death only by the merits of faith. Now the first example of faith shown to men is Abraham, who was the first to sever himself from unbelievers and received a special sign of his faith. So the rest given to men after death is called 'Abraham's bosom'" (St. Thomas).

ABSENCE, ECCLESIASTICAL. A failure to fulfil the duty of residence at the place of their labours imposed by their office on bishops, parish priests and other clerics. Unlawful absence is punishable by canon law. Absence for a time is allowed for a just cause, *e.g.*, a pilgrimage, a reasonable holiday; or for a grave reason, *e.g.*, bad health, a duty imposed by authority, or an urgent requirement of charity. Parish priests have the right to two months' absence in a year, if a competent and approved substitute is provided, and unless the bishop for grave cause restricts it; for a bishop not more than 3 months' absence is allowed and then only provided the work of his diocese can be properly carried on. A priest is usually at liberty to absent himself for a few days without episcopal permission.

ABSOLUTE. i. That which exists of its own nature and is consequently independent of all else. There is only one absolute in this sense, *viz.*, God.

ii. What is perfect and complete in any line of being, as absolute beauty.

iii. Absolutely is opposed to relatively, and then it means a thing considered in itself alone, as opposed to a thing considered precisely as having reference to something else.

ABSOLUTION (Lat., *absolvere*, to loose from, to free, whence sometimes in the sense of to end, or finish). i. A judicial act whereby a priest remits the sins of a penitent who has contrition, has made confession and promises satisfaction. The minister must have jurisdiction, either ordinary, such as that of a bishop or parish priest over his subjects, or delegated, such as that of a priest who has received special faculties from a bishop. When in danger of death a Catholic may ask for and receive absolution from any priest, whether he has jurisdiction or not, or even if he is not in communion with the Holy See, *e.g.*, a priest of the Eastern Orthodox Church (canon 882). The forms of absolution (*q.v.*) are various; the words must be pronounced in the presence of the person to be absolved: thus valid absolution cannot be given, *e.g.*, by telephone. See also ABSOLUTION OF AN ACCOMPLICE; ABSOLUTION, CONDITIONAL; RESERVED CASES; JURISDICTION.

ii. Absolution from censures is a disciplinary act whereby a cleric, either in the confessional or outside of it, removes an ecclesiastical censure (*q.v.*) Such a penalty may be

---

* The 1983 Canon Law states new laws regarding automatic excommunications, including that incurred for abortion. To have the excommunication lifted, one would confess the sin to a priest in the Sacrament of Penance, and the priest would obtain any special authorization necessary for the lifting of the excommunication.—*Publisher*, 1997.

imposed either by an individual, *e.g.*, a bishop, and may then be absolved by himself, his successors, superiors or delegates; or by the general law of the Church in respect of certain crimes, when any confessor may absolve from it, unless it is a reserved case. It is not necessary that the person absolved should be present or even living.

iii. Absolutions for the Dead after a requiem Mass. These consist of a prayer, the *Libera, Kyrie, Paternoster*, versicle, response and a final prayer for the deceased. During the *Paternoster* the coffin or catafalque is sprinkled with holy water and incensed.

iv. The absolutions in the Divine Office are short prayers said before the lessons at Matins.

v. by way of . . . An indulgence (*q.v.*) applicable to the living is granted by way of absolution; that is, the Church, having full jurisdiction over the living Catholic, absolves him (provided his dispositions are perfect) from that amount of temporal punishment which in the eyes of God a given indulgence is satisfactory for (how much this is in any case we do not know; the terms of time used are an historical convention). *cf.*, Suffrage, i.

ABSOLUTION, CONDITIONAL. Absolution may and must be given conditionally if, were it given absolutely, the sacrament would be exposed to the danger of nullity, or if, were it denied, the penitent would be in danger of suffering grave spiritual loss.

ABSOLUTION, FORMS OF. There are two general forms of absolution, the indicative, "I absolve thee . . . ," as used in the Western church and the deprecatory, "May God, through me, a sinner, forgive thee . . . ," as used in general in the Eastern churches. Catholics of the Eastern rites are now usually absolved with the indicative form, sometimes borrowed from the "Rituale Romanum" and translated as required. The wording of the forms differs considerably between one Eastern rite and another, but in the Latin rite there are only small variations in some religious orders (*e.g.*, the Premonstratensian). The following is the usual form: "May Almighty God have mercy upon thee, forgive thee thy sins, and lead thee to everlasting life. Amen. May the almighty and merciful Lord grant thee pardon, absolution and remission of thy sins. Amen. May our Lord Jesus Christ absolve thee, and I by his authority absolve thee from every bond of excommunication (suspension), and interdict, so far as I can and you need. Therefore I absolve thee from thy sins in the name of the Father and of the Son and of the Holy Ghost. Amen. May the Passion of our Lord Jesus Christ, the merits of the blessed Virgin Mary and of all the saints, whatever good thou shalt have done and whatever evil thou shalt have endured avail thee for the forgiveness of sins, increase of grace and the reward

of life everlasting. Amen." Under certain circumstances the first two and last of these prayers may be omitted without affecting the validity of the absolution.

ABSOLUTION OF AN ACCOMPLICE. A priest guilty of a sin against the sixth (Protestant, seventh) commandment cannot validly absolve his accomplice except in danger of death; and even then the absolution would be illicit (*q.v.*), if another priest was available to whom the accomplice was willing to confess, and if no scandal would ensue from his or her so doing. A priest thus unlawfully attempting to absolve incurs excommunication very specially reserved to the Holy See.

ABSTINENCE. i. A moral virtue, subordinate to temperance, which regulates the use and enjoyment of food in the interest of soul and body.

ii. The refraining from eating flesh-meat or soup made from meat, and to be distinguished from fasting (*q.v.*), with which it may be combined. Abstinence is normally obligatory, for all who have completed their seventh year, on Fridays, ember days, Ash Wednesday, the Wednesdays or Saturdays of Lent, before noon on Holy Saturday, and the vigils of Pentecost, the Assumption and Christmas. If the vigil falls on a Sunday, there is no abstinence; and there is no abstinence upon a holiday of obligation. But in 1949 the Holy See decreed that, until further notice, the law of abstinence may be reduced by the ordinary (*q.v.*), for the faithful of the Latin rite, to all Fridays of the year and the following fasting-days: Ash Wednesday, Good Friday, and the vigils of the Assumption and of Christmas. The application of this decree varies in details in different countries and dioceses.*

ABSTRACT. In scholastic philosophy, abstract does not mean abstruse. It is opposed to concrete.

i. It signifies a perfection considered apart from its subject, as human nature, whiteness, etc.; the concrete would be Peter, white wall, etc.

ii. *To abstract* is an act of the mind whereby it considers (*a*) a perfection apart from its subject or apart from some other perfection which is in the same subject, as in white-hot metal heat may be considered apart from whiteness; (*b*) in the cognitive process it means the considering by the mind of the bare nature of a thing apart from all material conditions.

ABSTRACTION. With modern writers intellectual abstraction primarily signifies ignoring or omission of the attributes *not* attended to; with the schoolmen it was understood primarily to mean the positive side of the operation, the assumption by the mind

---

* The 1983 Canon Law states that abstinence from meat is required on Ash Wednesday and all Fridays of Lent, and abstinence from meat or another food "according to the prescriptions of the conference of bishops" on all other Fridays of the year unless they are solemnities, and that the bishops conferences can "determine more precisely" the observance of fast and abstinence and substitute other forms of

of the part selected, of the attributes which *are* attended to.

ABUNA (Arabic, our father). The head of the dissident Ethiopic Church. Abuna is metropolitan of Aksum and a Coptic (*i.e.*, Egyptian) monk, appointed and consecrated by the Coptic Patriarch of Alexandria.

ABYSSINIA. SEE ETHIOPIA.

ACACIAN SCHISMS. i. An important episode in the controversy over Arianism (*q.v.*). It takes its name from Acacius, bishop of Cæsarea in Palestine from 340 to *c.* 366, whose followers were sometimes known as Homœans.

ii. A schism named after Acacius, patriarch of Constantinople, between the Western and Eastern churches, lasted from 484 to 519. It was occasioned by the intrusion of usurpers to the sees of Antioch and Alexandria and the publication of the "Henotikon" (*q.v.*); the Eastern patriarchs at the direction of the Emperors Zeno and Anastasius I accepted this document, which was condemned by the Holy See as favouring Monophysism (*q.v.*). The breach was healed by the acceptance all round of the Formula of Pope Hormisdas (*q.v.*).

ACACIANS. A Semi-Arian sect, followers of Acacius of Cæsarea. They rejected the use of the terms "like" or "unlike" in "essence" or "substance," "consubstantial," etc., and said simply that the Son is *like* (ὅμοιος) the Father. They were therefore also called Homœans.

ACADEMIES, PONTIFICAL. Academy (the name of the garden in which Plato taught) means in this sense a learned society for the study of literature, art, etc. The principal are the Artists of the Pantheon, founded in 1542; the Arcadian, a literary society founded in 1690; the Theological (1718); of Liturgy and of Archæology, these two founded by Pope Benedict XIV; of the Catholic Religion, founded by Pope Pius VII in 1801; of the Nuovi Lincei refounded by Pope Pius IX in 1847 for the study of the physico-mathematical sciences; and of St. Thomas Aquinas, founded by Pope Leo XIII in 1879. Their subjects of study are indicated by the names. The Academy of Noble Ecclesiastics (*q.v.*) is a college.

ACCEPTED TEACHING OF THE CHURCH. A loose, and therefore dangerous, phrase; for it may imply that a formal teaching of the Church is not necessarily accepted by Catholics; and that is heresy. Or it may be used for pious belief (*q.v.*). *cf.* Magisterium.

ACCIDENT (Lat., *accidere*, to happen). i. A being that in the ordinary course of nature demands another as a subject in which to exist; *e.g.* colour in a wall. The essence of accident does not imply actual inherence

in a subject but aptitudinal (see below). Of accidents some are absolute and some modal: an absolute accident is a certain reality distinct from the substance in which it inheres and upon which it depends for its existence, as quantity, heat, etc.; a modal accident signifies not so much a reality as a state affecting the substance, as sitting, standing, etc.

ii. Eucharistic. After the substance (*q.v.*) of the bread and the substance of the wine have been converted into the Body and Blood of Christ at the consecration at Mass the accidents of bread and wine remain and are discernible by the senses. The fundamental accident is that of quantity, and in it inhere the shape, colour, brittleness or liquidity, taste and smell of the original substances. Hence it is as foolish as it is impious to suggest that our Lord's presence in the Sacrament should be tested by chemical experiment.

ACCIDIE (Gr., ἀκηδία, "don't care-ishness"). The capital sin of spiritual sloth, or regret for one's spiritual good, *e.g.*, regret for the gift of faith because of the troublesome obligations involved; in general a venial sin, but mortal if one explicitly regrets God's friendship or if the *accidie* leads to proximate danger of omitting a grave duty.

ACCLAMATION. i. One of the three ways of electing a pope. It consists in the electors unanimously proclaiming one name without proceeding to a vote. It is also called quasi-inspiration.

ii. A ceremony of greeting and invocation which takes place after the collect of the Mass at a papal coronation. It is also found in the coronation rites of secular princes, including that of the king of Great Britain. See also LAUDES.

ACCOMMODATION. i. The application by way of analogy of words of Holy Scripture to something not intended by the writer. Such accommodation is exceedingly common in the liturgy, *e.g.*, the lesson from the book of Wisdom in the common Mass of our Lady, or the introit of the Mass *Adjutor* of St. Joseph, from Ps. lxxix, and the lesson in the same Mass.

ii. That management or adaptation of truth which is sometimes demanded by the limitations of the hearer or by the stress of circumstances; an economy; a mental reservation (*q.v.*).

ACCOMPLICE. See ABSOLUTION; CO-OPERATION IN ANOTHER'S SIN; CRIME, ii.

ACCUMULATION OF PROBABILITIES. The view that faith ultimately rests on an accumulation of probabilities has been twice condemned by the Church; by Pope Innocent XI in 1679, and by Pope Pius X in 1907 (in the decree *Lamentabili*).

ACHADENSIS. The adjectival form of the name of the see of Achonry (*q.v.*) used in

---

penance; it also states that abstinence from meat is obligatory from age 14, but those under 14 are to be "educated in an authentic sense of penance." (Can. 1250-1253). A Pastoral Statement by the U.S. National Council of Catholic Bishops (Nov. 18, 1966) stated that abstinence is required on Ash Wednesday and all Fridays of Lent, and is "especially recommended" on all Fridays of the year. If in doubt one may check with one's pastor or the local chancery office.—*Publisher*, 1997.

the designation of its bishop in Latin documents. Noun, *Achada*.

ACHILLI TRIAL, The. An action for criminal libel and slander brought against Cardinal (then Father) Newman, in 1852, by Giovanni Achilli, an apostate Dominican and anti-Catholic propagandist, whom Newman had accused at a public meeting of five seductions and other crimes. All the evidence was abroad and Newman was deemed only to have substantiated his case in respect of Achilli's suspension for immorality; but such was the misdirection of the judge to the jury that *The Times* protested, and a new trial was applied for. This was refused, but a fine of only £100 was imposed.

ACHONRY (Lat., *Achadensis*). An Irish see, suffragan of Tuam; from 1603 to 1707 the see was vacant. It includes part of the counties of Mayo, Sligo and Roscommon. The bishop's residence, cathedral, and diocesan college are at Ballaghaderreen. The patron of the diocese is St. Nathy (Aug. 9), its first bishop, and the cathedral is dedicated in honour of the Annunciation. Irish name: Achadh Chonaire.

ACŒMETÆ (Gr. κοίμητοι, lit., the not-resters). Monks of large Eastern monasteries who sang the Divine Office in relays, thus keeping up a continuous service of praise. They flourished in the 5th and 6th centuries (*cf.* Laus perennis).

ACOLYTE. i. A cleric in the highest of the four minor orders of the Western church. His duties are to light the altar candles and to carry candles in processions, during the singing of the gospel, and on other liturgical occasions; to prepare wine and water for Mass; and generally to assist the ministers in the services of the Church. At his ordination the bishop hands to him an unlighted candle and an empty cruet, using words indicative of the office conferred and duties imposed.

ii. A lay man or boy who performs all or any of the duties of an acolyte.

ACT (Lat., *actus*). In scholastic philosophy *act* is not the same as *action* (*actio*). Act is the result of action, *i.e.*, the perfection attained by action. Properly speaking act cannot be defined since it is a first notion. It can, however, be understood by its opposite, which is potency; thus, in a piece of marble there is the potency to represent the king— the representation of the king is the *act* of the marble. Whence potency implies imperfection, act perfection.

ii. Human act. "Those acts are called human of which a man is master, and he is master of his actions in virtue of his reason and his will" (St. Thomas, I–II, i, 1). A human act is *voluntary* if it proceeds from the will with knowledge of the end to which it is directed; it is *free* if it proceeds from the will with that knowledge and also under

conditions in which it might not have proceeded. An act may be rendered less voluntary by ignorance, passionate desire or fear.

iii. Indifferent acts. It was claimed by Duns Scotus that certain deliberate acts could be performed which were neither good nor bad, and such acts are called indifferent. St. Thomas says such are possible in the abstract but not in the concrete; every individual deliberate act of this kind must be done for some end either good or bad: if for a good end, the act is good, if for a bad end, the act is bad.

ACT OF WORSHIP. The principal services of the Catholic Church, namely, the Mass and the Divine Office (*qq.v.*) are primarily acts of worship (and social, not merely individual, acts), and not a series of vocal prayers. The Mass is the offering of a sacrifice, literally and not figuratively; the Office is a world-wide and never ceasing service of praise, thanksgiving, and petition at which one assists whether in public or private. For this reason a verbal following and understanding of the Mass, or even of the language in which one is saying an office privately, is not obligatory to divine worship, which is directed to God and not to ourselves or one another. Nevertheless, the Church prefers that the Faithful should be instructed in these matters, that they may pray and sing with understanding as well as in spirit (1 Cor. xiv, 15), and for the avoidance of mere routine and ritualism.

ACTS OF THE APOSTLES, The. A canonical book of the New Testament written by St. Luke the Evangelist about the year 64. It narrates the progress of the Church in Judæa and Samaria by the ministry of SS. Peter, John, and Philip, and its spread to the Gentiles by St. Paul. In parts he writes as an eye-witness and participant; in other parts he uses first-hand evidence.

ACTS OF FAITH, etc. i. Voluntary and deliberate internal acts, expressive of faith in God and his Church, hope in God, charity, contrition for sin, resignation to God's will, etc. An act of contrition is perfect if it arises from the love of God, imperfect if it is prompted by, *e.g.*, fear of hell; either is sufficient as a condition for confession and absolution. An act of charity is the act by which we love God above all things for himself and our neighbours for his sake.

ii. The words in which the above internal acts may be outwardly expressed; they may be extempore, or formulas such as are found in prayer books, etc.

ACTS OF PAUL, The. A New Testament apocryphal writing, dating from after the middle of the 2nd century. It is heretical in its teaching on virginity, which it makes almost necessary to salvation, and in extending the ministry in some degree to women; the sign of the cross and prayers for the dead are referred to.

ACTA APOSTOLICÆ SEDIS (The Acts of the Apostolic See.) The official organ for the publication of decrees, decisions, pronouncements, encyclical letters, etc., of the Holy See; it also contains the decisions of the Roman Congregations, Tribunals, and Commissions; a diary of the Curia Romana; and notices of all ecclesiastical appointments and honours. Legislative acts of the Holy See are promulgated by their appearance in A.A.S., unless promulgation is otherwise provided for. The A.A.S. is printed chiefly in Latin.

ACTA MARTYRUM (The Acts of the Martyrs) i. The official records of the trial and execution of martyrs.

ii. Any account of their life and death written or purporting to be written by eye-witnesses or contemporaries, or founded upon such accounts. The value and degree of authenticity of the Acts of the Martyrs which have come down to us vary greatly; some are undoubtedly completely authentic; others are worthless, even as "pious tales." Between the two extremes is a large mass of mixed material which it has been the work of the Bollandists and others critically to examine and appraise. The collection of *Acta sincera* (authentic acts) made by the Maurist, Dom Ruinart, is now recognized by critics to contain a good many doubtful pieces.

ACTA SANCTÆ SEDIS (The Acts of the Holy See). A Roman periodical for the publication of papal documents; it was never more than quasi-official, and ceased publication upon the establishment of the *Acta Apostolicæ Sedis* in 1909.

ACTA SANCTORUM (The Acts of the Saints). i. The lives of the saints as published by the Bollandists (*q.v.*). There are three editions, which vary slightly in arrangement: the original, Antwerp, edition (1634–1794); the Venice edition (1764–70); and the Paris edition (1863–69). These extend only to the month of October. The series, still in progress at Brussels, has now reached the middle of November.

ii. Other collections of lives of the saints, *e.g.*, "Acta sanctorum Ordinis Sancti Benedicti" (of the Order of St. Benedict), "Acta Sanctorum Hiberniae" (of Ireland).

ACTION (Lat., *actio*). Opposite of passion or suffering (*q.v.*). It is an accident whereby a cause is constituted actually causing. It is transient if the effect is produced outside the cause, as *to write;* it is immanent if the cause is both the principle and the term of the action, as *to understand, to grow.*

ACTION FRANÇAISE. A royalist movement and school of political philosophy in France, initiated by Charles Maurras at the end of the 19th century. It appealed to local Catholic support by its authoritarianism, patriotism, doctrine of order, and defence of the Church, which it sought to use as a political tool; though some of the principles of its leaders were definitely anti-Christian and anti-social, it accused its opponents of religious unorthodoxy, and sought to exercise influence in purely ecclesiastical affairs. In 1914 five books of Maurras and his newspaper, *L'Action Française*, were condemned by the Holy Office; Pope Pius X approved the decree, but deemed it an inopportune moment for publication, which did not in fact take effect until 1926. Many Catholic members of the *Action* refused to submit, and in the following year the Holy Office issued a final condemnation which was confirmed by Pope Pius XI. Among the reasons for condemnation were that the *Action Française* taught both a false nationalism (*q.v.*) and that any civil polity other than a monarchy is incompatible with Catholicism (at any rate in France), and that it exalted politics above religion and the state above the Church. Many members of the movement continued to treat the action of the Holy See with defiance.*

ACTIONS-AT-LAW. An action to prosecute a spiritual right may be instituted in the ecclesiastical courts by any Catholic, except those deprived of this right by canon law. Such actions are tried in the first instance in the diocesan court, appeals being heard in the metropolitan and Roman courts.

ACTIVE LIFE. Pope St. Gregory the Great defines the active life thus: "To feed the hungry, to teach the ignorant, to correct the erring, to recall our neighbour to the path of humility when he becomes proud, to care for the sick, to dispense to all that which they need, and to provide for those entrusted to our care." The phrase "active life" is generally used in antithesis to "contemplative life" (*q.v.*), which is in itself of greater supernatural worth; but, according to St. Thomas, an active life may become strictly obligatory (*e.g.* to earn a living, to escape temptation, succour the needy) and so more meritorious than the other. Active life or active works does not refer to mere bodily activity, which may be employed in agriculture or the arts, but to external activities carried on away from the monastery, by the cure of souls, preaching, giving retreats, conducting schools, etc. Thus, the English and other Benedictines who serve parishes pursue an active life; the Cistercians, who farm the land attached to their monasteries, do not.

ACTIVE ORDERS. Those religious orders and congregations of men and women whose daily labours are the works of active charity, whether spiritual (preaching, hearing confessions, giving retreats, the cure of souls generally) or temporal (the care of the sick, schooling children, bringing up orphans,

---

* The papacy seems to have reconsidered the question of Action Française and its alleged offenses. Pope Pius XII officially lifted the condemnation on July 5, 1939.—*Publisher*, 1997.

etc.). Such are the Jesuits, the Redemptorists, the Passionists, the Christian Brothers, etc., among men, and the Sisters of Charity, the Little Sisters of the Poor, the Daughters of the Cross, the Ursulines, etc., among women. But see also MIXED LIFE.

AD ANGLOS. An apostolic letter addressed by Pope Leo XIII to the English people in 1895, inviting them to return to Christian unity and calling on God for "remedy, reconciliation and peace." Appended to the letter was the now familiar prayer to the Mother of God for England, her "dowry."

AD HOMINEM, ARGUMENTUM. A species of argument based upon the very principles (whether their truth be conceded or no) admitted by an opponent.

AD LIMINA APOSTOLORUM. To the threshold of the Apostles, *i.e.*, the graves of St. Peter and St. Paul at Rome The expression is generally used of a bishop's visit (*q.v.*) *ad limina.*

AD NUTUM SANCTÆ SEDIS. At the will of the Holy See, *e.g.*, one holding an office *ad nutum* is removable at the pope's pleasure.

ADAM. The Hebrew word for "man," used as a proper name for the first human being created by God. The connexion of the word with *adama*, the Hebrew for "soil," suggested in the Bible, is probably popular rather than scientific etymology: it is not likely that Hebrew was spoken in Paradise. See CREATION, FALL OF MAN.

ADAMITES. i. A 2nd-century sect, offshoot of the Gnostics, who met together for worship without clothes. It is uncertain whether they claimed a pre-Fall integrity, or whether they adopted a simplification of manners with an ascetic end. In either case they seem to have fallen into sensual practices.

ii. Similar sects in the Netherlands, Bohemia and elsewhere in the 13th and 14th centuries, who professed communism and practised promiscuity. There was a revival in the late 18th century which continued until 1849. See also BÉGHARDS.

ADDRESS, Modes of. See Appendix IV.

ADIUTORIUM NOSTRUM in nomine Domini. ℞. *Qui fecit cælum et terram.* (Our help is in the name of the Lord. Who made Heaven and earth.) This verse and response, accompanied by the sign of the cross, occurs at or near the beginning of several rites (Mass, Confirmation, Extreme Unction, Compline), and is the normal opening of solemn blessings (*e.g.*, of the dying, of women pregnant or after childbirth, of holy water, of sick children, of the people by a bishop or abbot) and of all ordinary blessings.

ADJURATION. A demand in the name of God, either in the form of a prayer or of a command, to do something or to refrain from doing something. Ritual adjuration is made over the salt and over the child (three times) at Baptism, and many times during the rite of Exorcism.

ADMINISTRATION of Ecclesiastical Property belongs in each diocese primarily to the bishop thereof. For this purpose he must join to himself not less than two persons (who must not be his close relatives) to form the diocesan council. The bishop has also to name councils for churches and shrines whose administration is not otherwise provided for. Such administrators have to use the same care which they would in dealing with their own property, and to render an annual account to the local ordinary. Religious orders are responsible for their own property, but if engaged in parochial work they must render accounts to the bishop of money and other property received for parochial purposes and how it was used.

ADMINISTRATOR APOSTOLIC. i. One, generally a bishop, appointed by the Holy See to govern a diocese (*a*) at the resignation, removal or death of its bishop (*sede vacante*) if there is no cathedral chapter; (*b*) when the bishop cannot do it himself because of infirmity, insanity, suspension, etc. (*sede impedita*). The appointment is usually temporary, and its rights and duties are set out in canon law, and the letters of appointment. When a diocese is divided, the bishop of the old one is often made administrator of the new, until a bishop is appointed thereto; and upon resignation a bishop sometimes administers the same diocese until his successor is named.

ii. An administrator appointed by the Holy See to govern or supervise any religious institution, such as a monastery, college or seminary.

ADMINISTRATOR OF A PARISH. Such an one may be appointed by a bishop under similar circumstances to those in which an administrator apostolic of a diocese is appointed. The priest delegated by a monastery or other religious corporation to take charge of a parish under its jurisdiction is in reality an administrator, being vicar for the corporation, which is the true rector.

ADMIRATIO (Lat., surprise). Disapproval aroused by another's action, which, though not sinful or giving scandal (*q.v.*), is unusual or improper.

ADMONITION. A penal remedy by which the ordinary (*q.v.*) or his delegate warns, publicly or privately, one who is in the proximate occasion of committing a crime, or on whom a grave and well-founded suspicion has fallen. Admonition is necessary before a censure can be validly inflicted, a religious expelled, or clerics prosecuted for certain offences.

ADONAI (Heb., my lord; really, my lords, in the plural of majesty). Several centuries before the Christian era Jews, out of reverence, had ceased to pronounce the sacred name of God, J H V H, proclaimed to Moses from the burning bush, and had substituted Adonai in its stead. To ensure this reading, later Jews put the vowel signs of this word under the consonants J H V H, and Christians later misread this as *Jehovah*. In the Septuagint J H V H is translated *kyrios*—lord; hence in English versions "the Lord" is usually put when the Hebrew text has J H V H and the Jews read "Adonai."

ADOPTION. i. In canon law. Where civil law recognizes legal relationship as resulting from adoption, the Church also recognizes such relationship, and attributes to it certain ecclesiastical effects, notably invalidity or unlawfulness of marriage. If civil law regards persons as incapable of valid marriage owing to legal affinity arising from adoption, such affinity constitutes a diriment impediment (*q.v.*) by canon law. If civil law regards such marriages as illicit, but not invalid, by canon law also they are illicit but valid.

ii. Supernatural. The effect of supernatural grace (*q.v.*), by which we become the children of God and co-heirs with Christ: "You have received the spirit of adoption of sons whereby we cry, Abba, Father" (Rom. viii, 15). This puts us into a new relationship with God. For this, some community of nature is requisite. In virtue of Christ's merits, those who are in a state of grace (*q.v.*) are made "partakers of the divine nature" (*q.v.*). This state is a mean between the natural sonship of Christ and the merely moral sonship which characterizes human adoption.

ADOPTIONISM. A heresy, which arose in Spain in the 8th century, claiming that Christ as man is only the adopted son of God. It thus asserted a double sonship in Christ, sonship as God and sonship as man, and so involved the Nestorian heresy (*q.v.*). A kind of Adoptionism was held by Abelard in the 12th century, and by others later, but they all repudiated the teachings condemned by Pope Hadrian and by the Council of Frankfort and two other synods between 785 and 798.

ADORATION. i. The word now often used in English to express those acts of divine worship which are directed to God only, and of which the characteristics are recognition of his perfection and omnipotence and our own complete dependence upon him (*latria, q.v.*). Veneration expressed for any person or thing worthy of, or thought worthy of, our reverence as rational creatures, *e.g.*, a saint, a relic (*dulia, q.v.*), is sometimes called adoration, but it is better to distinguish it by use of the word veneration therefor.

ii. The three fealties made to a newly elected pope are called *adoratio*, which in this connexion may be translated "homage." The first takes place immediately after election, when the cardinals kiss his foot and hand and receive the kiss of peace; the second is from all those who have accompanied the cardinals in the conclave; the third and most solemn takes place in the Sistine chapel of the Vatican and at the altar of St. Peter's.

ADORATION RÉPARATRICE NUNS. A congregation founded at Paris in 1848 which, by perpetual adoration of the Blessed Sacrament exposed, makes reparation for insults offered to it and for sinners generally. It includes a class of sisters who live outside the enclosure, but take regular part in the adoration. Their house in Chelsea is on the site of St. Thomas More's garden.

ADORATION OF THE CROSS, The. Part of the morning office of Good Friday. A crucifix is ceremonially unveiled, while *Ecce lignum crucis* (Behold the wood of the cross) is sung. Then clergy and people approach to venerate and kiss it. The choir sings certain "reproaches," mostly taken from the 4th book of Esdras and including a Greek-Latin dialogue, the Trisagion hymn (*q.v.*), repeated thrice; then an antiphon of adoration; and afterwards the hymn *Pange lingua gloriosi Lauream certaminis*, with a refrain *Crux fidelis* (O faithful cross . . .), and *Dulce lignum* (O dear wood . . .), alternately between each verse. The priest or deacon then goes to fetch the Blessed Sacrament for the communion service, while the choir sings anthems referring to the cross. The name "Adoration of the Cross" has been objected to for this rite on the ground that "adoration" implies *latria* (*q.v.*). It does not necessarily do so, but St. Thomas and others claim that on this occasion the cross is venerated with a "relative *latria*." However, the word "veneration" seems preferable.

ADULTERY. The completed act of carnal intercourse between persons of different sex, of whom one at least is married to someone else. It is a sin against both chastity and justice, and if both parties are married the offence is aggravated, for each one incurs a double sin of injustice. For a married person to give consent to his or her partner's adultery does not alter the sin, for marriage rights are inalienable. Under certain circumstances adultery is a diriment impediment to marriage (see CRIME). Adultery of a spouse entitles the injured partner to claim a judicial separation *a mensa et thoro* and in certain circumstances gives the right to refuse marital intercourse.

ADVENT (Lat., *adventus*, an arrival). The season leading up to the birth of Jesus Christ on Dec. 25, beginning on the Sunday nearest St. Andrew's Day (Nov. 30), which Sunday is the first day of the Church's year. The liturgy of Advent makes continual reference to the forthcoming event (especially by passages from the prophecies of Isaias), for which it prepares by penitential observances; *Te Deum* is omitted from Matins and *Gloria in excelsis* from Mass; purple vestments are worn and organs must be silent (except on Gaudete Sunday). The Office and Mass of the season must be said or commemorated daily, according to the rank of the feast which occurs. The law of fasting and abstinence in Advent is no longer in force. Except by permission of the ordinary, the solemn nuptial blessing may not be given at marriages from the beginning of Advent to Dec. 25 inclusive.

ADVOCATE. A clerical or lay lawyer who pleads causes before the Roman church courts. The facts of a case are established by the procurator, the advocate's function being only to plead the law before the judges. His fee is a fixed sum, whatever the result of the case, and the cases of the poor are undertaken free of charge. Consistorial advocates plead in canonization processes, they alone may plead in civil and criminal causes before the tribunals of the Vatican City, and they are usually summoned to sit at œcumenical councils, with a consultative vote. They are twelve in number, and their dean is always a layman.

ADVOCATUS DIABOLI (Lat., The Devil's Advocate). A slang name given to the Promoter of the Faith (*q.v.*) in the processes of beatification and canonization.

ADVOWSON (Lat., *advocatio*, the function of a patron). The right of presentation to a vacant benefice. In England such rights in respect of Anglican churches are often found in the hands of lords of the manor and other persons; a Catholic may become possessor of such an advowson by inheritance or otherwise, but he is prevented by the civil law from using his right of presentation. In such a case the right is exercised by the King.

AEQUIPROBABILISM. A system in moral theology which solves the problem of probability by insisting that the law must be obeyed unless the opinion favouring liberty is equally probable with that favouring the law. See PROBABILISM.

AËR (Gr., air). The large veil which, in the Byzantine liturgies, covers the *diskos* and chalice, each of which is covered separately by a smaller veil. With it the celebrant fans the eucharistic offerings while he says the Nicene Creed, and the deacon sometimes uses it for the same purpose instead of a *ripidion*.

ÆSTHETICS. The science of beauty (*q.v.*); that branch of philosophy which seeks to determine the nature of beauty and the modes of its apprehension. By many modern philosophers æsthetics is made a branch of psychology inasmuch as, denying its objective reality, they regard beauty as having no existence apart from the apprehending mind. But the divine beauty being the cause of all being, æsthetics is properly a branch of ontology.

ÆSTIMATIVE (Lat., *æstimare*, to form an estimate of). One of the four internal senses, whereby the desirable is instinctively distinguished from the baneful. See SENSES; INSTINCT; COGITATIVE SENSE.

ÆTERNI PATRIS. i. The apostolic letter of June 29, 1868, by which Pope Pius IX summoned the Vatican Council.

ii. An encyclical, issued by Pope Leo XIII on Aug. 4, 1879, directed to the revival of scholastic philosophy according to the mind of St. Thomas Aquinas. The pope called for a return to the study of the texts of the 13th-century scholastic writers, the rejection of unprofitable problems and false scientific theories, and a revivification, extension and perfection of the scholastic system. The notable revival of Scholasticism to-day, particularly the work of the late Cardinal Mercier, is a result of that encyclical.

ÆTESIS (Gr., αἴτησις, supplication). In the Byzantine rite, a litany such as those said by the deacon just before the Creed and the Our Father in the Liturgy, to which the people reply "Grant it, O Lord" at each petition.

AFFABILITY. A moral virtue, annexed to justice, by which a man is disposed to conduct himself appropriately to each and all of his fellow-men. It is often supposed that this quality is a product of education and training, but the virtue manifests itself with great frequency among the common people, and in inverse ratio to their amount of contact with other classes.

AFFILIATION. The uniting of lesser societies, confraternities, etc., to the greater ones, *i.e.*, primary unions, archconfraternities, with consequent participation by the former in the privileges, indulgences, etc., granted to the latter. No affiliation is valid without papal indult.

AFFINITY. The relationship arising from a valid Christian marriage, whether consummated or not. Affinity exists between the man and the blood-relations of the woman, and between the woman and the blood-relations of the man, but not between the blood-relations themselves. It is so reckoned that the blood-relations of the man are related by affinity to the woman, in the same line and degree as they are related by consanguinity (*q.v.*) to the man, and *vice versa*. Affinity in the direct line is a diriment impediment (*q.v.*) of marriage in any degree; in the collateral line it invalidates marriage up to the second degree inclusively. Affinity is a minor impediment in the second degree collateral; in all other cases it is major. The impediment is multiplied as often as the consanguinity whence it proceeds is multiplied, and also by a second marriage with a blood-relation of the deceased party.

AFRICA, THE CHURCH IN. The great church of North Africa was wiped out by the Moslem conquests in the 7th century, and in the northern and eastern parts Islam is today the religion that makes most progress among the heathen.

i. *Belgian Territory* (Congo). Estimated population 11 million; about 450,000 Catholics. Twenty-four vicariates and several prefectures, in charge of European missionaries and some African priests.

ii. *British Territory* (Nigeria, Rhodesia, Uganda, Kenya, etc.). Population over 37 million; over 3¼ million Catholics. There are about 30 vicariates, 2 Benedictine abbacies *nullius* (in Tanganyika), and a score of prefectures, in charge of various missionaries, especially the White Fathers. There is a considerable number of Negro clergy and religious in Central Africa, including one bishop. Mauritius and the Seychelles each forms an ordinary diocese, i.s.h.s. See also SOUTH AFRICA.

iii. *French Territory* (Algeria, Tunis, Ivory Coast, Madagascar, etc.). Combined population about 33 million; about 2¼ million Catholics. The first mission to Madagascar was early in the 17th century, and the proportion of Christians is there relatively high: ½ million in 3¾ million. Algiers is a metropolitan see with two suffragans; Carthage is an archbishopric with one suffragan. Elsewhere there are 22 vicariates and several prefectures, many in charge of the Holy Ghost missionaries. Indigenous clergy are not numerous.

iv. *Portuguese Territory* (Angola, the Azores, etc.). Population 8¾ million; over 1¼ million Catholics, three-quarters of them in the old dioceses. The metropolitan see of Loanda has suffragan sees for the Azores, Madeira, Cape Verde and São Thomé islands, all founded before 1520; there are also a prelature *nullius* and some missionary territories.

v. *Spanish Territory* (Guinea, etc.; the Canaries are accounted an integral part of Spain). Population about 175,000; 40,000 Catholics, forming the vicariate apostolic of Fernando Po.

vi. *Anglo-Egyptian Sudan.* Population about 6 million, Arab and Nubian Mohammedans in the north, heathen Negroes in the south. There are about 18,000 Catholics in 2 vicariates apostolic and a prefecture, with a patriarchal vicariate for a few Melkites at Khartum.

vii. *Other Territory.* In Libya there are about ¾ million people, with over 50,000 Catholics, nearly all of them Europeans. The mission was founded in 1643; there are

now 2 vicariates apostolic (Benghazi and Tripoli) and 2 prefectures. See EGYPT, ETHIOPIA, etc.

AFRICA, SOUTH, THE CHURCH IN. Under Dutch and English rule from 1652 to *c.* 1825 public profession of the Catholic faith was forbidden and clergy were not allowed to minister; civil disabilities on Catholics were finally removed in 1867, and all religions are now equal before the law. In the four provinces of the Union and Basutoland, Catholics are still a small minority, largely African converts, of about 700,000 in a total population of 11½ million; there are 4½ million non-Catholic Christians. The ecclesiastical organization is into 4 metropolitan sees and 17 bishoprics, with one abbacy *nullius.*

AFRICAN LITURGY, The. The liturgy of the formerly great church of North Africa, now disused for 1200 years. It derived from the primitive Roman usages, and is said to have influenced the present Roman rite and to have been the first to use Latin in its services. But very little indeed is certainly known about it.

"AFTER-CHRISTIAN." An inhabitant of Christendom and a descendant of Christian ancestors who, implicitly or explicitly, repudiates Christianity as a revealed religion. The term is specially used of such people in England and the United States where much contemporary educated public opinion regards religion in a merely humanitarian and pragmatic way.

AGAPE (Gr., brotherly love). The name given in ver. 12 of St. Jude's epistle to meetings of the Faithful such as are described in 1 Cor. xi, 20–2, 33–4. These meetings often included a meal and sometimes were followed by the Eucharistic celebration, the whole becoming one liturgical act, beginning on Saturday night and ending on Sunday morning. Tertullian (born *circa* 160) has left a full account of the *agape* in Africa in his day: it included prayer, a supper and the singing of psalms and hymns. These "love-feasts" were soon definitely separated from the Eucharist and became sources of disorder and scandal. St. Augustine and St. Paulinus of Nola complained of them, and the Councils of Laodicea (363) and *in Trullo* (692) had to forbid feasting in church. By the 8th century the *agape* had disappeared altogether.

AGAPETÆ (Lat. from Gr., ἀγαπηταί, beloved). i. Christian maidens who in the early days of the Church took a vow of chastity, but continued to live in the world instead of forming communities. Then arose the practice of their living in the houses of laymen who had taken the same vow, as housekeepers and for mutual encouragement. In spite of scandals and consequent forbiddance, the custom persisted into the 4th century.

The *agapetæ* must be distinguished from the *subintroductæ*, who were simply clerical concubines.

ii. A sect of the Gnostics who acted on the principle that "to the (self-styled) pure, all things are lawful."

AGE, CANONICAL. The age of reason, with its capacities and obligations, is assumed to begin about the end of the seventh year. Puberty begins with the fifteenth year in males and the thirteenth in females, but marriage is invalid below sixteen and fourteen respectively. Persons below the age of puberty cannot be required to take an oath and are excused from penalties *latæ sententiæ*. Sponsors and other witnesses should have reached their fourteenth year. A minor becomes of age and is bound by the laws of fasting from the end of his twenty-first year; this obligation ceases with the fifty-ninth year. A subdeacon must be at least twenty-one, a deacon twenty-two, a priest twenty-four and a bishop thirty. A religious noviciate cannot validly begin before the sixteenth year, and a year must elapse before profession; solemn or perpetual simple vows may not be taken before twenty-one. Abbesses and other superiors of nuns with solemn vows must be at least forty.

AGE OF DISCRETION. The time of life at which a human being becomes capable of making weighty decisions for himself, *e.g.*, as to whether he will live with his parents or elsewhere, what trade or profession he will follow. In English law it is fourteen. The expression has sometimes been used synonymously with "age of reason" (*cf.*, Pope Pius X's interpretation of cap. 21 of the Fourth Lateran Council). See AGE, CANONICAL.

AGE OF REASON. i. The time of life at which a human being begins to be morally responsible, normally at about seven years. At this age, then, Catholic children incur the obligation of confession, of hearing Mass, of abstinence (but not fasting) and may receive the sacrament of Extreme Unction; in the Latin rite they are not usually confirmed before this age. Holy Communion may be received when they have sufficient understanding, according to their years, of the mysteries of which the knowledge is necessary to salvation (*cf. Quam singulari*).

ii. An historical name for the 18th century in England and France, when Deism was set over against Revelation and Reason opposed to Enthusiasm.

AGE OF THE WORLD. The Bible tells us nothing of the age of the world, which must be left to scientific research. At first sight it seems to enable us to fix the date of the creation of Adam by adding up the ages of the Patriarchs. Several such attempts have been made but have failed because the three witnesses for the text, Massoretic, Samaritan and Septuagint, differ and are irreconcilable. Moreover the Biblical list of patriarchs is not guaranteed to be complete, nor is the precise significance of the ages assigned to them certain. Recent discoveries tend to push the date of man's creation further and further back, though not into the fabulous distance of some wild speculators.

AGES OF FAITH, The. A name by which some designate the middle ages (*q.v.*). By "ages of faith" is meant a period during which (European) society at large organized itself on Christian principles, building up a civilization and perfecting a culture which reached its zenith in the 13th century. It was axiomatic that God was man's last end and that the Church showed the way to that end. Man's understanding was rightly directed, but his will was as liable to deflection as at any other time. Thus there were many great sinners as well as many great saints; "the bulk of the population were not assiduously devout frequenters of the Sacraments or even of weekly Mass" (Belloc); and the religion, law and life of the middle ages were disfigured by any amount of wickedness, superstition and violent tyranny.

AGED POOR SOCIETY, The. A society instituted in 1708 and now having its headquarters in Westminster. It grants small pensions to poor aged Catholics and to old persons reduced from a superior station of society; and maintains an almshouse at Brook Green, Hammersmith.

AGGEUS. The Latin form of the name of the prophet Haggai (Festive), who gives it to a book of the Old Testament. In it he urges the Jews to the rebuilding of the Temple, which had been delayed for sixteen years after the return from Babylon in 536 B.C., and foretells for it greater glory than its predecessor, and that into that place the Messias, "the desired of all nations," should come. Aggeus is named in the Roman Martyrology on July 14.

AGGREGATION. The right enjoyed by an archconfraternity to affiliate to itself other confraternities of the same kind, imparting to them its indulgences and other privileges.

AGILITY. One of the four qualities attributed to the risen body by scholastic theologians; it implies ability to pass from place to place with great speed and otherwise to be a perfect instrument of the soul.

AGIOS O THEOS (Gr., Holy God). The first words of the Trisagion (*q.v.*).

AGLIPAYANS. A schismatic sect in the Philippine Islands, dating from 1902, named from their leader, Gregory Aglipay, a Filipino priest.

AGNETS (Slav. from Gr., ἀμνός, lamb). The first piece of bread cut from the *prosphora* (*q.v.*) at the preparation of the Liturgy in the Byzantine rite. As it is cut the celebrant says. "He was led as a sheep to the slaughter and as a spotless lamb, dumb before his shearers, so he opens not his mouth." The *agnets* is cut cross-wise on the under side (*i.e.*, the throat or heart) and pierced at the right side, the whole symbolizing that "the Lamb of God is sacrificed, who takes away the sin of the world for the life and salvation of the world."

AGNOSTICISM (Gr., ά, not; γνωστικός, knowing; *cf.* also ἄγνωστος, unknowable). The philosophy of the Agnostics, that is, of those who teach that the essences of things and in particular the first cause and final ends are absolutely unknowable. Agnosticism is a kind of Positivism (*q.v.*), having its origin in England (Spencer, Huxley), and its analogue in France (Comte, Littré; but whereas French Positivism ignores metaphysics, English Agnosticism endeavours to explain this ignorance. English Agnostics regard the first cause and final ends as objects of belief, not as objects of science or philosophy (*cf.* Fideism).

AGNUS DEI (Lat., Lamb of God). i. An invocation said aloud by the celebrant and sung by the choir just before the communion at Mass. The words, taken from those spoken by St. John the Baptist to our Lord (John i, 29) are: "Lamb of God, who takest away the sins of the world, have mercy on us." (twice), "Lamb of God, etc., give us peace." In the Lateran basilica the third response is the same as the other two, according to the custom of the time when the prayer was first used at Mass, about the year 700. In requiem Masses the responses to *Agnus Dei* are *dona eis requiem*, "give them rest" (twice), and *dona eis requiem sempiternam*, "give them everlasting rest."

ii. A sacramental consisting of a small disc of wax stamped with a figure of a lamb representing our Lord as victim. They are solemnly blessed by the pope on the Wednesday of Holy Week in the first and every seventh year of his pontificate. The making of any other agnus deis than these is strictly forbidden. In the prayers of blessing, the dangers of fire, flood and storm, plague, and of child-birth are referred to. They are often worn round the neck, and in the reign of Queen Elizabeth were among the things specially forbidden to be brought into England.

iii. An image of a lamb, usually haloed and bearing a cross or pennon, symbolizing the Blessed Sacrament and our Lord as victim.

AGRAPHA (Gr., not written). Sayings attributed to our Lord in other documents than the four Gospels. There are over seventy of these, but it is difficult, if not impossible, to establish the genuineness of most of them. They have no ecclesiastical authority, except ver. 35 of Acts xx.

AIR. The breathing of air, the sign of life (as God breathed on the face of Adam, God the Son upon his apostles, the Holy Ghost upon the infant Church), has from the earliest days been the most expressive ceremony of exorcism, whereby the spirit of darkness is expelled to make room for the spirit of light and life. It is used in the rites of Baptism, consecrating the holy chrism and oil of catechumens, and in blessing baptismal water.

AISLE (Lat., *ala*, a wing). i. A division of a church separated from the nave, and less often the quire as well, by an arcade of pillars and arches along its whole length; it may be on one or both sides of the nave and even, in big churches, continued round the east end.

ii. The passage between rows of pews or chairs. In this sense, aisle is from a confusion of *ala* with Old French *allée*—alley, and has led to the self-contradictory expression "the middle aisle," meaning the passage of the nave.

AKATHISTOS HYMNOS (Gr., The Standing Hymn, because it is always sung standing). An office in honour of our Lady sung on some days in Lent in the Byzantine rite. It has been translated into English, and Benedict XIV attached an indulgence to its recitation.

AKOLOUTHIA, The (Gr., sequence). Any Byzantine liturgical function, but particularly the Divine Office. This consists of corresponding hours to the Roman, namely, Mesonyktikon, Orthros (*qq.v.*); Prime (ὥρα πρώτη), Terce (ὥρα τρίτη), Sext (ὥρα ἕκτη), and None (ὥρα ἐννάτη), of similar construction with three psalms, prayers and hymns, and sometimes short additions called *mesoria*; *Hesperinos*, and *Apodeipnon* (*qq.v*): but its composition is entirely different. The psalms are sung through every week and there is a large number of rhythmic hymns (*kanons, kontakia*, etc.). The office is exceedingly long, and when sung takes about eight hours all together. Other Eastern churches all have their own offices which are referred to under the separate rites.

ALB (Lat., *tunica alba*, white tunic). A white linen vestment reaching from neck to ankles, with tight-fitting sleeves and confined by a girdle, put on after the amice (*q.v.*). It is principally used by the celebrant and ministers at Mass. It is permitted to ornament it with embroidery, apparels, or lace, but no decoration should detract from its character as a long white linen garment. The alb is probably derived from the under-tunic of the Romans and Greeks; it has now a symbolic significance of purity of heart.

ALBANIA, THE CHURCH IN. The population of Albania is about 1 million, of whom over three-fifths are Mohammedans.

There is an autonomous Orthodox church of about 185,000 members. Catholics number 100,000, mostly among the Gheg tribes in the north; their chief prelate is the archbishop of Skodra (Skutari), with four other dioceses and an abbacy *nullius* (*q.v.*). They are of the Latin rite; *cf.*, Italo-Greeks. Since 1943 all Catholic schools have been closed and all associations and the press suppressed, and a number of religious leaders executed.

ALBIGENSIANISM. A heresy that flourished in the south of France in the 12th and 13th centuries. It was a revival of Manichæism and part of the Catharist movement, which name it often bears. It taught the usual dualism, namely that there are two opposing principles, one good, the other evil, which created the spiritual and material worlds respectively; all flesh is in itself evil, all spirit good. Consequently our Lord did not have a real human body, and his earthly life was merely "appearance," and there could be no resurrection of the body. They rejected the sacraments, especially marriage, which was forbidden to their initiates, called the "perfect," among whom suicide was encouraged. The ordinary believers were simply so called and their morality was as loose as that of the "perfect" was strict. Initiation was by a rite called *consolamentum,* frequently administered at death.

ALCANTARA, THE KNIGHTS OF. A military order (*q.v.*) founded in Castile about 1177 to combat the Moors in Spain; it was successful, became wealthy and disorderly, and was curbed by Pope Alexander VI in 1494. Since the 16th century it has survived only as a lay order of honour.

ALCANTARINES. A name given (after St. Peter of Alcantara who supported them) to the Discalced Friars Minor, a branch of the Observant Franciscans founded in Spain at the end of the 15th century. In 1897 the name was suppressed when Pope Leo XIII abolished the divisions which had appeared in the course of the centuries among the Observants, and ordered them all to be known simply as Friars Minor.

ALEPH, BETH, etc. The letters of the Hebrew alphabet which are sung one by one before the verses of the Lamentations of Jeremias, at Tenebræ. They are merely indicative of the order of the verses, and are sung to a plaintive melody of five notes.

ALEPPINES (*Aleppo,* a town in Syria). A name distinguishing a congregation of Maronite Antonian monks, and another of Melkite Basilians.

ALEXANDRIA, THE CATHOLIC PATRIARCH OF. The only Catholic patriarch of Alexandria with jurisdiction is of the Coptic rite. The title and office were restored in 1895 by Pope Leo XIII who reserved to the Holy See the right of nomination. He has jurisdiction over the Catholic Copts of Egypt. The Catholic Melkite patriarch of Antioch also bears the title of Alexandria as a personal concession and administers the see by a vicar. There is also a titular patriarch of Alexandria of the Latin rite who resides in Rome.

ALEXANDRIA, THE PATRIARCHATE OF. An apostolic church, said to have been founded by St. Mark, and one of the five great patriarchates; among its bishops were St. Athanasius and St. Cyril. Since 567 there have been two unbroken lines of patriarchs, one for the Orthodox, who later followed Constantinople into schism from Rome, and one for the monophysites who refused to accept the Council of Chalcedon. There are now three bishops who bear the title of patriarch of Alexandria and exercise jurisdiction accordingly, namely the patriarchs (*a*) of the Catholic Copts, (*b*) of the dissident Coptic Church, (*c*) of the Orthodox, whose 125,000 subjects form an autocephalous unit of the Orthodox Eastern Church; about three-quarters of them are Greeks and the rest Syrians with a very few Egyptians.

ALEXANDRINE LITURGY, The. That one used in that patriarchate before the Council of Chalcedon and the monophysite schism, commonly called the Liturgy of St. Mark. It has been disused for many centuries, the Orthodox having substituted the Byzantine offices. But the Eucharistic Liturgy of the Coptic rite with one of its three *anaphoras,* named after St. Cyril of Alexandria, is derived from that of St. Mark and is still in use.

ALEXIAN BROTHERS, The. A religious congregation founded in Brabant in the 15th century. They conduct hospitals for the care of the aged, the infirm, epileptics, inebriates, the insane, etc. Their headquarters in Great Britain is at Twyford Abbey, Willesden, and they have hospitals in Germany, Belgium, the United States and elsewhere. Their name is taken from St. Alexius of Edessa. There are also Alexian nuns, chiefly in the Rhineland, who do similar work.

ALIEN PRIORY. A cell (*q.v.*) of a foreign monastery established in England to watch over the rights and revenues of the mother-house in respect of endowments (manors, tithes, etc.) in this country. Some alien priories were entirely dependent, others were conventual, paying a yearly tribute; they numbered at various times from 100 to 150 and were responsible for the sending of much money out of the realm, especially to the abbey of Cluny. These priories were all French; they came into being after the Norman conquest and were not alien until the Plantagenets began their long warfare with the French crown. In 1294 King Edward I seized all the alien priories and used their revenues in his war with France; the same policy was followed by his successors, and all alien priories were forcibly suppressed by King Henry V in 1414. Some houses formerly alien were united to English monasteries. Eton, Winchester, New College and All Souls at Oxford, and King's at Cambridge, among others, were partly endowed with the revenues of such priories.

ALIENATION. The making-over to another of property of the Church, whether by way of sale or otherwise, or the reduction of its value by mortgage, etc. Such alienation is forbidden except for just reason and under the circumstances and in the ways laid down by canon law.

ALITURGICAL DAYS. Those days of the year on which it is not permitted to celebrate Mass. Throughout the Latin rite there is, strictly, only one such day, namely Good Friday, except in the Ambrosian use wherein all Fridays of Lent are aliturgical. But in a sense Holy Saturday is aliturgical, since the one Mass permitted, at night, is of Easterday. In the Byzantine rite all the days of Lent are aliturgical except Saturdays and Sundays: that is, only the Liturgy of the Presanctified may be celebrated, and that is not a Mass.

ALL SAINTS' DAY. The feast (Nov. 1 in the Western church) on which are commemorated all the saints of God, canonized and uncanonized, known and unknown. It is a feast of the highest rank and was formerly often called All Hallows' in England. Religious orders have a feast of all the saints of their order later in the month. In the Byzantine rite it is kept on the first Sunday after Pentecost and on other days in other rites. "The feast of All Saints seems to me to be in some sort a greater than that of Easter or the Ascension. Our Lord is perfected in this mystery, because, as our Head, he is only perfect and fulfilled when he is united to all his members, the saints . . . it is glorious because it manifests exteriorly the hidden life of Jesus Christ. The greatness and perfection of the saints is entirely the work of his spirit dwelling in them" (M. Olier).

ALL SOULS' DAY (Nov. 2, or if that falls on a Sunday, then Nov. 3). The solemn "commemoration of all the Faithful departed in which the Church, their common Mother, after being careful to celebrate with due praise her children already rejoicing in Heaven on All Sâints' day, strives to help all those who still long in Purgatory by supplication to Christ, her Lord and Bridegroom, that they may quickly attain to the fellowship of the heavenly citizens" (The Roman Martyrology). Every priest is allowed to say three requiem Masses on this day, and each Mass has the indulgence of a privileged altar (*q.v.*). The Divine Office is also of the dead.

There are many local customs observed, such as the leaving of lights in the grave-yard during the previous night. In the Byzantine rite All Souls are commemorated on the 9th Saturday before and again on the 6th Sunday after Easter.

"ALL THE EAST, OF." A territorial designation forming part of the title of several patriarchs, Catholic and dissident. It has historical reference to the eparchy *Oriens* within the Roman prefecture of the East, which contained Palestine, Syria, Asia Minor and the land east to the Persian border. The primacy of Antioch over this territory was recognized by the first Council of Nicæa, and confirmed by the first of Constantinople.

ALLADENSIS. The adjectival form of the name of the see of Killala (*q.v.*) used in the designation of its bishop in Latin documents. Noun: *Allala*.

ALLATÆ SUNT. An encyclical of Pope Benedict XIV in 1755 addressed to missionaries in Asia Minor and Syria, instructing them on their relations with the Eastern Churches. In particular it forbids them to receive converted dissidents into the Latin or any rite but their own ("We desire most intensely that all should be Catholics, but not that all should be Latins"), and contains matter of oriental canon law which has been a precedent for legislation ever since.

ALLEGORICAL MEANING OF SACRED SCRIPTURE. This may be: (*a*) The literal (*i.e.*, grammatical, logical, historical) meaning expressed in a continued metaphor, *e.g.*, in the Canticle of Canticles; (*b*) the typical (*i.e.*, mystical, spiritual) meaning, when this refers to things to be believed (this is the commonest sense to-day); (*c*) either typical or literal when dealing with beliefs, especially concerning Christ and the Church. In a very ancient verse we find the meanings of Sacred Scripture divided according to subject matter: historical (facts), allegorical (faith), moral (conduct), anagogical (future life). The name comes probably from Gal. iv, 24 ("Which things are said by an allegory") where St. Paul teaches that Hagar and Sarah typified the two covenants.

ALLEGORY. A story illustrating one subject under the guise of another like to it. Allegory is extended metaphor.

ALLELUIA (Heb., "Glory to Him who Is"). An expression of joy and praise found in the Psalms, heard in Heaven (Apoc. xix, 1) and introduced into every liturgical use of the Catholic Church: it is of frequent occurrence throughout the Latin liturgies. After the epistle of the Holy Saturday Mass it is solemnly intoned, the celebrant singing it thrice, each time on a higher note, and throughout paschal time it is added to every antiphon, responsory and versicle, and is repeated several times in the introits and elsewhere at Mass. In times of mourning and penitence alleluia is omitted: *e.g.*, from Septuagesima to Holy Saturday, in the ferial Masses of Advent, on most vigils, and in Masses for the dead. In the Eastern liturgies it is used throughout the year and at requiems, and particularly during Lent. The Ambrosian rite uses the form *Hallelujah*. (See also ALLELUIATIC VERSE.)

ALLELUIATIC VERSE (or simply "the Alleluia"). In the Mass an alleluia is added to the gradual (*q.v.*) and followed by a verse, generally from the Psalms. It is in the form of a responsorial chant: *i.e.*, the alleluia is sung and repeated, then the verse is sung, and alleluia again sung. The alleluiatic verse is sometimes replaced by the tract (*q.v.*). As alleluia is the characteristic word of paschal time, the gradual is then omitted (except in Easter week) and to the verse is added another verse and a fourth alleluia.

ALLOCUTION, PAPAL. An address delivered by the pope to the cardinals in private consistory on a matter of contemporary importance. If the subject is one of general interest or effect the allocution is subsequently published; it often announces the papal policy in respect of dealings with a civil power.

ALMA REDEMPTORIS MATER ("Gracious Mother of the Redeemer"). The first of the antiphons of our Lady (*q.v.*). It is said or sung after the Divine Office from the first Vespers of the first Sunday of Advent to Compline of the Purification. The versicle, response and prayer which follow vary according to whether it is before or after the first Vespers of Christmas.

ALMONER. An archaic word for an archaic thing, namely, the official attached to the court of a king, prince, governor, ecclesiastic, etc., and charged with the distribution of his master's alms. An Anglican dignitary bears the title of Lord High Almoner to the King of England. In France the name (*aumonier*) is used for a chaplain, *e.g.*, to the army or a convent.

ALMS, GIVING OF. Any of the corporal works of mercy undertaken from motives of charity for the relief of our neighbour's necessity may be called almsgiving. Almsgiving is part of the universal law of charity and so is obligatory by the law of nature; each one is bound to give according to his means; and there is no class of the needy whom we are not bound to help: neither our enemies nor members of other religious bodies nor notorious sinners may be excluded from our charity. Moral theologians have distinguished several degrees of both necessity and ability to enable a man to gauge his obligation of almsgiving in particular cases. As a rule one is only bound to give alms from what is superfluous to the needs of oneself and family according to its state of life; some theologians claim that all such superfluous wealth should be distributed. Discretion should be used in giving; but it has ever been a characteristic of true Christian charity that it enquires not too closely as to the "deservingness of the case." The charge of indiscrimination is not serious, and among Christians to help the "deserving poor" is popularly esteemed justice rather than charity. Nor do the state or praiseworthy philanthropic institutions relieve us of our obligation; "the rich man cannot be excused from sin who makes it a practice never to give anything in alms on the plea that the poor can go to the workhouse, and that he pays his poor rate," and "a man who makes it a rule never to give alms to ordinary beggars certainly commits sin" (Slater, S. J.). "The precept of the divine law, 'There shall be no poor nor beggar among you,' does not forbid anyone to beg; but it does forbid the rich to be so mean that some men are forced to beg by necessity" (St. Thomas, II-II, clxxxvii, 5, ad 3). The Church lays down regulations governing the appeals of certain classes of beggars, such as mendicant religious.

ALMUCE. An ecclesiastical garment in common use before the Reformation. It consisted of a hood, made of cloth and lined with fur, and was used principally by canons as a protection for the head and neck when singing office in choir. It gradually developed a cape with two long pendants in front and, later, the fur was outside. It became a sign of ecclesiastical dignity, but in England it was worn also by parish priests. A form of it survives in Rome and elsewhere among the canons of some churches, *e.g.*, Arras, Chartres, Lucerne. Its use was revived in England by the Benedictine chapter of Newport while it existed from 1858 till 1916. The almuce must not be confused with the amice.

ALOGI (Gr., not-worders). A nickname given to certain heretics of the late 2nd century who rejected the Gospel and Apocalypse of St. John and denied the doctrine of the *Logos* (Word) therein contained. They were a reaction from Montanism (*q.v.*) which particularly upheld this gospel.

ALPHA AND OMEGA. The first and last letters of the Greek Alphabet ($A \Omega$). In Apoc. i, 8 they are used to designate the Eternal Father and in xxi, 6 and xxii, 13 God the Son, as eternal, self-existent, infinite being itself (*cf.*, i, 17 and Isaias xliv, 6; xlviii, 12).

ALPHABET, LITURGICAL USE OF. i. In the rite for the dedication of a church the consecrating prelate is directed to trace the Greek and Latin alphabets with the end of his pastoral staff in the ashes which have been strewn in the form of a St. Andrew's cross on the floor. This ceremony probably originally represented the formal taking possession of the church with the observances of Roman civil law.

ii. The Hebrew alphabet (Aleph, Beth, etc.) which occurs in the Tenebræ office.

ALTAR. An altar is that upon which sacrifice is offered. i. The Christian Sacrifice of the Mass, though not necessarily offered in a church or chapel, must always be offered on an altar, or an altar-stone (or antimension, *q.v.*), which is, in fact, a very small portable altar, and is sometimes so called. An altar or altar-stone must contain relics and be consecrated by a bishop or by a prelate having the faculties. Many of the altars in Great Britain and the United States are not yet so consecrated, and therefore they have to have an altar-stone, either let into or resting upon them in the centre, for use at Mass. Such an erection, however costly, large or imposing, is not strictly speaking an altar at all, but a table to support the true altar, which is the small consecrated stone. When an altar is consecrated (a fixed altar) the stone or *mensa* (*q.v.*) is then one unbroken piece forming the whole top of the altar. A shrine for a statue or picture, if it has no consecrated stone, is not an altar, however much like one it may look. A fixed altar consists of three parts: (*a*) the table or top of stone; (*b*) the supports, which may be a solid mass or consisting of a column or columns; (*c*) the sepulchre (*q.v.*). These three parts are the only essentials to a fixed altar. Altars now usually have one or more "shelves" at the back called *gradines* (*q.v.*). The high altar should stand clear of the east wall, and it has not less than three steps leading up to it. Side altars may stand against the wall and need only one step (the foot-pace or *predella*). Side altars are for the celebration of Mass when there are several priests: not to serve as image brackets or shrines. Altars, especially high altars, should be surmounted by a *ciborium* or a *baldacchino* (*qq.v.*). The Blessed Sacrament is reserved usually, but not necessarily, at the high altar; that altar remains *primarily* the place at which Mass is said, and accidentally the place where God dwells under the veil of bread. Inasmuch as the Blessed Sacrament may not be reserved at more than one altar, it is superfluous to have a tabernacle on more than one altar. The front of the altar should be covered by a hanging of good material (the frontal, *q.v.*). Every altar should have a title, that of the high altar being the same as that of the church.

ii. Eastern. In the Byzantine rite the altar is square, with a wooden top and surmounted by a *ciborium*. It is covered with a linen cloth reaching to the ground all round, with a silk or velvet covering above it. Usually there is left on the altar the cross, candlesticks, *antimension* (*q.v.*) and book of the Gospels. The *artophorion* (tabernacle) is sometimes on and sometimes behind it. There are no gradines, etc., and the altar is always clear of the east wall. There is only one altar in each church; if it is a large building with side-chapels and altars therein, each with its *iconostasis*, these are in effect separate churches. Only one Liturgy is celebrated at an altar in one day. The altars of other Eastern rites are on the same pattern, with variations, *e.g.*, the Copts have no cross, there is the curious Abyssinian *taboot* or ark (*q.v.*), and the Armenian altar is narrow with a number of gradines. In Catholic churches of these rites there is a tendency to imitate the worst examples of Latin altars; notably among the Armenians and in the four Syriac rites they are found with gradines piled with flower-pots and candlesticks.

ALTAR, DOUBLE. One so constructed that Mass may be celebrated at the eastern or western side at will, according to the disposition of the congregation, the crucifix and candles being in the midst and serving for both sides. Such are the high altars in the lower church of St. Francis at Assisi and in the abbey church of Ampleforth.

ALTAR, HIGH. The principal altar of a church, called in North America the main altar. It should be not less than 8 ft. in length, be built clear of the east wall (so that, *e.g.*, the consecrating bishop may move all around it), and must stand on at least three steps (there may be five or seven). The top step (foot-pace) should be as wide as the altar is long, and is the place of the celebrant; the middle step, of the deacon; the floor (*in plano*), of the subdeacon. The Blessed Sacrament is not necessarily reserved at the high altar. See ALTAR.

ALTAR, CONSECRATION OF AN. At least one fixed altar must be consecrated at the same time as a church. The bishop first anoints the sepulchre (*q.v.*) with chrism, and encloses relics therein; he then incenses the altar elaborately, passing around it three times; he then anoints the altar in the middle and at the four corners twice with oil of catechumens and once with chrism, incensing it after each unction; the *mensa* is then rubbed all over with the oil and chrism, incense burnt thereon, and the sign of the cross made with chrism on the chief parts of the altar. These ceremonies are accompanied by appropriate prayers and antiphons, and are used equally at the blessing of a portable altar or altar-stone.

ALTAR, GREGORIAN. An altar which has received the same privilege as St. Gregory's altar in the church of St. Gregory on the Cælian at Rome, namely, that of a plenary indulgence (*q.v.*) for the relief of a soul in Purgatory, gained by the celebration of Mass thereat without other conditions. Since 1912 this privilege will be conceded to no fresh altars. Gregorian altars other than the original at Rome are called such *ad instar*. As to the precise effect of this plenary indulgence, the Congregation of Indulgences has declared, "If the intention of the Church and the use of the power of the keys be considered, we must understand [by it] an indulgence that immediately delivers the soul from all the pains of Purgatory; but if the effect of the application is considered, then we must understand an indulgence the measure of which corresponds to the good pleasure and acceptance of divine mercy" (*cf.*, Altar, Privileged).

ALTAR, PAPAL. One upon which only the pope or his special delegate may celebrate Mass. The greater basilicas (*q.v.*) of Rome have each a papal altar.

ALTAR, PRIVILEGED. One at which a plenary indulgence may be gained for a soul in Purgatory by the celebration and application of a Mass. The privilege is either *local* (belonging to any priest at a particular altar) or *personal* (to a particular priest at any altar) or *mixed* (to certain priests at certain altars). To have the local privilege an altar must be permanent. Cardinals and bishops enjoy a personal daily privileged altar. Ordinaries may nominate *one* privileged altar (daily and perpetual) in cathedral, conventual and parish churches. On All Souls' day every altar (even a portable altar-stone) at which Mass is said is privileged; likewise all altars in a church during the Forty Hours, and altars at which there is perpetual Exposition. Masses of the Deceased Clergy Association in England are privileged. It is forbidden to exact an increase of stipend for a Mass at a privileged altar (*cf.*, Altar, Gregorian).

ALTAR-BREADS are the pieces of bread used in the Eucharistic Sacrifice. They are of two sizes, large for the use of the celebrant, and small for distribution in holy Communion. They are made of pure wheaten flour mixed with pure natural water and baked in an oven or between iron moulds. Bread thus made is unleavened or *azyme*. In most of the Eastern rites leavened bread and of different forms is used by both Catholics and dissidents. In the Latin, Armenian, Maronite and Malabar rites the altar-breads are round brittle wafers and have an image, generally of the Crucifixion or I.H.S., impressed on them. In the Latin church anyone may make altar-breads and they may be bought and sold in the ordinary way of commerce, provided they are pure and fresh. In the East the more ancient discipline prevails: in the Byzantine rite they are made sometimes by priests, their wives, nuns, etc.; in the Coptic, Syrian and Chaldean rites they should be baked on the day on which they will be used and in a special oven; while the Nestorian priest makes and bakes the bread himself as part of the preparation of the Liturgy. See also PROSPHORA.

ALTAR-CARDS. Three (though only one is prescribed) printed, painted or manuscript cards, sometimes framed, put upright on the altar at Mass to assist the memory of the celebrant at places where it is inconvenient to refer to the missal. They are laid flat or removed when Mass is not being said. A bishop uses the Pontifical Canon (*q.v.*) instead of altar-cards.

ALTAR-CLOTHS. Three white linen cloths which cover the altar at Mass; the topmost reaches the floor on either side. These have to be blessed by a bishop or other person with faculties, but between them and the altar is a waxed cloth (cere-cloth) which need not be blessed. In the event of the Precious Blood being spilled, it would be absorbed by these cloths before reaching the stone. Symbolically they signify the linen in which the dead body of our Lord was wrapped.

ALTAR-PIECE. A painting at the back of an altar, either by itself or part of a reredos.

ALTAR-STONE. i. A portable altar (*q.v.*) either used by itself or fixed into a permanent structure.

ii. The whole top (*mensa*) of a fixed and consecrated altar. This must be a single unbroken piece of stone; on it are cut five Greek crosses, one at each corner and one in the middle. The sepulchre of relics is generally cut in the *mensa* but sometimes it is in its support, if the support is solid. In the Byzantine rite the *antimension* (*q.v.*) may take the place of a consecrated stone. In the Syrian and Coptic rites the altar top is of wood.

ALTAR OF REPOSE. The altar, pedestal, or niche upon which the Blessed Sacrament is reserved from Maundy Thursday to Good Friday. After the Mass, the consecrated particles, contained in a ciborium covered with a white veil, are carried in procession, *Pange lingua* being sung, to a side-altar of the church, or to an adjoining chapel if such is available, and there deposited (not in a tabernacle), with a modest adornment of lights and flowers. When passing before the Host a double genuflection is made as though it were exposed. It is the custom for the people to visit the altar of repose for prayer and to provide that the Blessed Sacrament is not left unattended until at least midnight. On Good Friday it is borne back to the high altar for the communion service. The altar of repose must be distinguished from the mediaeval Easter sepulchre (*q.v.* ii), which represented Christ in the tomb, whereas the altar of repose is simply a place of reservation.

ALTRUISM (Lat., *alteri huic,* to this other). Altruism as a philosophy professes never to act for self, but for society. So that society flourish the Altruist is ready to be crushed and ruined, not in the matter of his pleasure only, but even in that of his own good. Selfishness, by which the Altruist means all manner of regard to self, is, upon his conscience, the unforgiven sin. It is opposed to Hedonism (*q.v.*). Be it said against the above doctrine: that the Altruist overlooks the fact that there is an inner being and life which is not referable to any creation outside himself but only to the Creator (*cf.,* Utilitarianism).

ALTUM DOMINIUM (Lat., supreme dominion). i. The right of the state to require private owners to part with land and other property for public purposes, a fair compensation being paid.
ii. The right of ultimate supreme administration of ecclesiastical property, inhering in the pope by virtue of his headship of the Church on earth. The ownership and ordinary administration of such property is vested in the individual and his successors or the corporation by whom it was acquired.

ALUMNUS (Lat., one nourished and brought up). i. An ecclesiastical student at a seminary or college.
ii. A child brought up and educated in a monastery, usually wearing the habit and participating to a certain extent in the monastic life, but not thereby committed to the ecclesiastical state. They are the modern equivalent to the children and boys (also called *alumni* or oblates) referred to in chapter xlv and elsewhere in the Rule of St. Benedict. There are alumnates at St. André, Maredsous, Montserrat, and other Benedictine abbeys. These institutions must be distinguished from monastic schools such as Downside or Collegeville.

AMAY. See MONKS OF UNION.

AMBITION. As a vice, ambition is the inordinate striving after or desire for honours and success. Its inordinateness consists in straining after that which is not deserved or for which one is not fit, or using unlawful means or letting ambition obscure the true welfare of oneself or others; otherwise, a due and modest ambition is not merely blameless but laudable.

AMBO (plural, *ambones;* from Gr. ἄμβων: a raised place). In early Christian basilicas, a small platform in the middle of the church, from the steps of which the epistle and gospel were sung. Afterwards there were two, on one side for the gospel and on the other for the epistle. So are they still to be seen in San Clemente and other churches of Rome. The ambo was also used for preaching, announcing edicts, etc. Its use was long ago superseded by the pulpit and lectern, but in some places ambones have come into use again, *e.g.,* at Ronquières in Belgium and at Ashford, Middlesex. In the Byzantine rite the gospel is often sung from an ambo on the north side of the church.

AMBROSIAN CHANT. The ecclesiastical chant proper to the Ambrosian rite. In the "Graduale Romanum," among the *alii cantus ad libitum novissime approbati,* there is a *Gloria in excelsis* of great simplicity and beauty taken from the Ambrosian books and the tune of *Veni Creator Spiritus* is of Ambrosian origin. The chant was originally strictly syllabic, *i.e.,* one or at most two notes to each syllable, and this is still so to a considerable extent.

AMBROSIAN HYMN, The. The name given in the Roman Breviary and elsewhere to the *Te Deum,* on account of a mistaken tradition that it was composed by St. Ambrose, or by him and St. Augustine together.

AMBROSIAN RITE, The. The ancient liturgy of the church and province of Milan. It is now much romanized, but some liturgiologists claim for it an independent Gallican origin. For practical purposes to-day it may be regarded as a use of the Latin rite (*q.v.*); how much it really owes to St. Ambrose is doubtful. It has very considerable differences from Roman usage and *formulæ* in the Mass, Divine Office and other services. Among those noticeable at Mass are a frequent Old Testament lesson which, like the epistle and gospel, is sung from an ambo in the cathedral of Milan; a different arrangement of the *Kyrie;* in the cathedral an offertory of bread and wine is made by lay-people; *Credo* is sung just before the preface; no bell-ringing at the consecration; the fraction is before the *Pater noster;* the *Agnus Dei* is said only at requiems; deacon and subdeacon kneel at either end of the altar; the sequence of colours is different, *e.g.,* black in Lent, when Fridays are aliturgical days; the old Roman Psalter (*q.v.*) is used throughout; almost every feast has its proper preface (*q.v.*). Pope Pius XI belonged to this rite, which is in use in most of the churches of the archdiocese of Milan and in some of Novara, Lugano and Bergamo.

AMBULATORY. i. The extension of the aisles of the quire of a church round the back of the high-altar, so making an uninterrupted processional path. Nearly all the great churches, ancient and modern, of England, are so arranged, *e.g.,* Canterbury cathedral, Buckfast abbey church.
ii. A covered gallery; one of the walks or sides of a cloister.

AMEN (Heb., certainly; so be it). The word was introduced or taken over from the usage of the synagogue into public and private prayer in apostolic times. Sometimes it merely marks the end of a prayer or hymn; or it is an expression of assent (as after the Creed) or of agreement (as after a petition). The Great Amen which the server or choir replies to the conclusion of the prayer *Nobis quoque peccatoribus* at Mass more particularly associates the people with the celebrant in the eucharistic action which he has just performed. It is pronounced *āmen* after English prayers etc., *ahmen* after those in Latin.

AMENDMENT, PURPOSE OF, is a necessary part of true contrition for sin; it is generally held that it need not be more than implicit, but in practice the determination to avoid sin should be explicit and real, and accompanied by a firm resolve to avoid the occasions of all sin, not merely those that are to be the subject of confession. The fact that such a resolution has been often broken in the past is no reason why it should not be sincerely made again, and if necessary to seventy times seven times; God asks for a resolve, not a guarantee.

AMERICAN CASSINESE CONGREGATION, The. One of the two American Benedictine congregations (*q.v.* iv). It had its origin in the monastery of St. Vincent (*q.v.*) at Beatty, Pa., founded by monks from Bavaria in 1846. St. Vincent's was made an abbey in 1855, and with its two priories formed into a new congregation, which now consists of the mother house and the abbeys of St. John, Collegeville (*q.v.*), St. Benedict, Atchison, Kan., St. Mary, Newark, N. J., Maryhelp (*q.v.*), St. Bernard, Cullman, Ala., St. Procopius, Lisle, Ill., St. Peter, Muenster (*q.v.*), St. Martin, Lacey, Wash., St. Gregory, Shawnee, Okla., St. Leo, Fla., St. Mary, Richardton, N. D., St. Bede, Peru, Ill., Holy Cross, Canon City, Colo., St. Anselm, Manchester, N. H., St. Andrew, Cleveland, and a priory in the Bahamas. The monks conduct a number of schools, seminaries and colleges, and minister in many parishes. The abbey of Lisle is concerned in Eastern work and some of its members are of Slav-Byzantine rite; this community has been entrusted with the ancient Bohemian monastery of Brevnov-Braunau, to help in the formation of a Czechoslovakian congregation.

AMERICAN COLLEGE. i. At Rome. A pontifical college for the training of aspirants for the priesthood from the dioceses of the United States, founded by Pope Pius IX, who gave the buildings. Its establishment was due particularly to the exertions of the then archbishops of Baltimore and New York, Kenrick and Hughes. The college, situated in the Via dell' Umiltà, was opened in 1859.
    ii. At Louvain. A college for the education of priests to work in the United States, founded in 1857, through the initiative of Mgr. Spalding, then bishop of Louisville, and Mgr. P. P. Lefevre.

"AMERICANISM." Certain modifications in Christian teaching as regards both faith and conduct advocated by some in order to increase conversions to the Church among the people of the United States. In an apostolic letter *Testem benevolentiæ* (1899) Leo XIII singled out the following opinions (among others) for condemnation: that spiritual direction is now less needed than in the past; that the natural virtues must be esteemed above the supernatural, and active virtues above the passive ones (so called); that the vows of the religious life are not in accordance with the requirements of human progress. These errors were, and are, to be met with outside the United States. "Americanism" is a misleading name, and in this sense it must not be confounded with the civil policy of the United States government and educational institutions.

AMICE (Lat., *amictus*, a garment). A rectangular vestment, made of white linen, about two and a half feet long by two feet wide, with two long strings. It is worn under the alb, covering the neck and shoulders, by priest, deacon and subdeacon at Mass. It probably originated as a scarf, wrapped as a protection round the neck, and before the biretta came into use it was pulled up over the head when going to and from the altar. This is still the custom among monks and friars, who use an amice shaped like their hoods. The amice has a tiny cross on it and was formerly often ornamented with an apparel (*q.v.*); this has survived in the Ambrosian and Dominican rites and in Spain, and has been revived elsewhere. Symbolically considered, the amice represents the "helmet of salvation" and "discipline of the tongue."

AMOS. A prophetical book of the Old Testament, named after its author, the earliest of the prophets of Israel or Juda whose words are extant. He was called by God in the first half of the 8th century B.C. to testify against Israel, whose idolatry, pride and luxury he describes; he sees in three visions her desolation, and prophesies the kingdom of the Messias in which the Gentiles also shall have part. He is named in the Roman Martyrology on March 31.

AMPLEFORTH. A Benedictine abbey of the English congregation near York, founded in 1608 at Dieulouard in Lorraine, organically the successor of the former community of Westminster, whose ancient arms it bears (see COAT OF ARMS). Its members were driven from France in 1793 and settled at Ampleforth in 1802; erected into an abbey in 1899. The monks conduct a large boys' school; other members of the community are engaged in parochial work.

AMULET. A small object on which is inscribed a charm, either in words or images, worn as a protection against evil. In so far as efficacy is attributed to anything other than the power of Almighty God, they are superstitious and as such forbidden to Catholics.

ANABAPTISTS, The (Gr., rebaptizers), were certain Protestant sects of the 16th century which denied the efficacy of infant baptism and therefore rebaptized (by immersion) such as had been baptized while children. They had other distinguishing beliefs, but the above was adopted by the Baptist sects of England and Wales, whose adherents were often called Anabaptists in consequence.

ANALOGION. In the Byzantine rite. i. A lectern.
ii. A table standing before the *iconostasis*, bearing a cross, candles and ikons, at which marriages and other ceremonies take place.

ANALOGY. Term applied to two or more things owing to the likeness, relation or order that exists between them and some primary object; there is an analogy, *e.g.*, between medicine, air and food in so far as these are related to man who is the subject of *health*, and to whose health medicine, air and food are related. Medicine, air and food are therefore said to be healthy by analogy. Analogous is opposed to univocal because the latter implies that a certain quality is to be found in two or more things *in the same sense* (as human nature is to be found in Peter, Paul and John), and not merely found as participated in a varying proportion or likeness or relation to some thing in which the quality is principally found, as in the above example of health. Because of the limitations of human nature, knowledge and perceptions, man knows the nature and perfections of God only analogically; *cf.*, Knowledge of God ii; Divine Perfection.

ANALYTIC (analysis means literally a pulling to pieces; and is opposed to synthesis, a building up). An analytic judgment is one whose predicate is contained in the notion of the subject, so that by pulling the subject to pieces the predicate (*q.v.*) should be found to be one of the parts, as *man is an animal*. On the contrary, a synthetic judgment is one whose predicate is not contained in the notion of the subject, the predicate therefore can never be discovered by analysing the subject, as *the wall is white*.

ANAMNESIS (Gr., calling to mind). The first of the three prayers (*Unde et memores*) which follow the consecration in the Mass. In obedience to our Lord's command the Church therein commemorates his passion, resurrection and ascension. There are similar prayers in other liturgies.

ANAPHORA (Gr., offering). A liturgical term for the canon of a eucharistic Liturgy, especially in the Eastern rites. The Latin, Armenian and Malabarese Liturgies have only one anaphora. In the Byzantine rite there are two, in the Coptic and Chaldean three, in the Ethiopic fourteen and the (West) Syrian sixty-four. Of these last only a few are used in practice (seven by Catholics). The Maronites have eight now printed in their books; the one most used is simply a form of the Roman canon. Anaphoras are named after different saints—*e.g.*, St. Basil, St. Peter, the Twelve Apostles, St. John Maro—by whom they are commonly supposed to have been written, but the attributions are thoroughly untrustworthy. They are used interchangeably, somewhat after the manner of the proper prefaces of the Roman Mass.

ANASTASIS, The. The Church of the Resurrection, commonly called the church of the Holy Sepulchre, at Jerusalem. Gr., ἀνάστασις, resurrection.

ANATHEMA. A Greek word originally signifying something set up as an object of consecration or execration, and so used in the Old and New Testaments. From the latter sense it came to mean a curse or ban, or sentence of reprobation. Finally it acquired the meaning of excommunication, the phrase *Anathema Maranatha* (1 Cor. xvi, 22) being used to signify the severest form of excommunication. In canon law *anathema* is the name given to excommunication inflicted with the full ceremonial of the "Pontificale Romanum," and is the word used instead of excommunication in the condemnatory doctrinal decrees of councils.

ANCHOR. The figure of an anchor was used in the Catacombs to represent the cross of Christ. It thus became a symbol of the Christian's hope.

ANCHORITE. A hermit. The word is used by St. Benedict in the first chapter of the Holy Rule. The mediæval "anchoress" or "ancress" was simply a female hermit. The word is often particularly used for one who confines himself to one room or dwelling, but see HERMIT.

ANCIENT OF DAYS, The. A title for Almighty God taken from the 7th chapter of the prophecy of Daniel, where it is used three times (vers. 9, 13, 22).

ANDREW, ST. One of the twelve apostles and the first disciple of Christ in point of time, brother of St. Peter. After our Lord's ascension he is said to have preached the gospel in Asia Minor and Greece and to have been martyred at Patras on Nov. 30, the day on which his feast is kept almost universally. He is honoured as the patron of Russia, Greece, and of Scotland, to which country some of his alleged relics were taken in the 6th century. He is twice named in the Mass.

ANGEL (Gr., ἄγγελος, messenger). One of the heavenly spirits, creatures of God who are employed by him as his messengers in the governance of the world. Angels are pure spirits, *i.e.*, they have nothing material about them and, unlike the human soul, they are not associated with matter. They are persons. They have by nature an intelligence more acute and a power greater than those of men. They watch over either individual men (guardian angels, *q.v.*) or societies of men, *e.g.*, nations, the Church.

ANGEL OF INCENSE, The. In the blessing of the incense after the offertory in the Roman Mass reference is made to "Blessed Michael the archangel standing at the right hand of the altar of incense." The name Michael here is a long-standing mistake for Gabriel: see ST. LUKE'S GOSPEL i, 11, 19.

ANGEL OF SACRIFICE, The. The explanation of "thy holy angel" referred to in the prayer *Supplices te rogamus* after the consecration at Mass is uncertain. Some refer it to an angel, St. Michael or another, who assists the celebrant; others regard it as a reference to the general idea that our prayers are presented in Heaven by angels (Apoc. viii, 3–5); others believe it to mean the Holy Ghost; yet others say that Jesus Christ himself, the "Angel of Great Counsel," is intended.

ANGEL OF THE SCHOOLS, The. A term applied to St. Thomas Aquinas.

ANGEL OF SYON, The. Bl. Richard Reynolds, Bridgettine of Syon House, Middlesex, martyred with the Carthusian priors, May 4, 1535; he must not be confused with his contemporary and fellow-religious, Richard Whytford, who called himself "the Wretch of Syon."

ANGELS OF THE CHURCHES, The, represented by stars in Apocalypse, i, 20. Presumably the bishops of the seven churches of Asia are there figured.

ANGELIC HABIT, The. A name given by Byzantine monks to the great habit. As there are three degrees in their monastic life, so there are three forms of the habit to correspond, namely the fore-habit, the little habit and the great habit. The last consists of an inner and outer *rason, mandyas,* (*qq.v.*) girdle, sandals, a veil, and special "scapular" with hood.

ANGELIC HYMN, The. The *Gloria in excelsis* (*q.v.*).

ANGELICAL SALUTATION, The. The Hail Mary, so called because the first part of the prayer consists of the words of the Angel of the Annunciation.

ANGELICO, The. The Collegio Angelico, the international theological college of the Dominican order at Rome. It was founded as a school, at their church of the Minerva, in the 13th century and received the right to confer degrees in 1580.

ANGELUS, The. A prayer in honour of the Incarnation, of which the English translation is as follows:

℣. The Angel (*angelus*) of the Lord declared unto Mary.
℟. And she conceived of the Holy Ghost.
  Hail Mary, etc.
℣. Behold the handmaid of the Lord.
℟. Be it done unto me according to thy Word.
  Hail Mary, etc.
℣. And the Word was made flesh.
℟. And dwelt among us.
  Hail Mary, etc.,

followed by the collect, "Pour forth, we beseech thee, O Lord, thy grace into our hearts; that we, to whom the incarnation of Christ thy Son was made known by the message of an angel, may by his passion and cross be brought to the glory of his resurrection. Through the same Christ our Lord. Amen." The angelus is said in the morning, at midday, and in the evening, when the angelus-bell is directed to be rung. This consists of three strokes followed by a pause three times, and then nine strokes, usually at about 6 a.m., noon and 6 p.m. The angelus is said standing on Saturdays and Sundays (with a genuflection at the third versicle) but kneeling at other times. During paschaltime it is omitted altogether and *Regina Cœli* is said instead, always standing.

ANGER. An emotion of warm displeasure demanding external expression in the infliction of punishment on the offender. To be angry in moderation and for a just cause is licit and often praiseworthy, *e.g.*, when parents are angered by their children's faults. The capital sin of anger is committed when one gives way to an anger out of all proportion to the offence; this is a venial sin, but it may lead to mortal sins of blasphemy, scandal, etc.; and when the punishment one wishes to inflict is immoderate; this is revenge (*q.v.*).

ANGLICAN CHURCH, The. i. Historically, *Ecclesia Anglicana*, the Catholic Church in England.
  ii. In current use, the Church of England (*q.v.*). The Anglican Communion is generally taken to include all Protestant episcopal churches deriving from the Church of England.

ANGLICAN ORDERS were declared invalid by Pope Leo XIII in the bull *Apostolicæ Curæ*, Sept. 18, 1896, owing to substantial defects in the rite of ordination used in the Church of England from the time of Edward VI and Elizabeth, and the corrupt intention (*q.v.*) of the persons ordaining, such rite and intention manifestly excluding the essence of the priesthood, *viz.*, the power to offer the

Sacrifice of the Mass, sacraments being invalid if the form used does not truly signify the effect intended by the Church. The pope declared that this bull was a final pronouncement on the matter, intended to close the controversy. Reordination of reconciled Anglican clerics has been the practice of the Church ever since Cardinal Pole (d. 1558).

ANGLICANISM. i. The body of Protestant episcopal churches deriving from and in communion with the Church of England (*q.v.*), including the churches of Ireland, Scotland (to be distinguished from the Established Presbyterian Church of Scotland), Wales, the United States, South Africa, etc., with their missions and dependences.

ii. The systems of faith and morals professed by these bodies. These it is impossible to summarize owing to the diversity of belief and (to a lesser degree) of conduct taught, permitted and tolerated in Anglicanism. From the definite "romanizing" of a section of the high-church party to the extreme liberalism of certain dignitaries and professors, many varieties of Christian thought can be found. They are usually very roughly classified as high-church, broad-church and low-church (*qq.v.*); but, as Father Humphrey Johnson has justly observed, there exists within the Church of England "a larger and more important party than any of these, though a less articulate one. This party serves as a cement between the others." According to the official Book of Common Prayer the articles of the three creeds are to be believed; the Bible contains all things necessary to salvation; Purgatory, indulgences, veneration of images and relics, and the invocation of saints are "vainly invented" and "repugnant to the word of God"; two sacraments necessary for salvation were ordained by Christ, Baptism and the Supper of the Lord; transubstantiation "is repugnant to the plain words of Scripture"; the "sacrifices of Masses . . . were blasphemous fables and dangerous deceits"; "the Bishop of Rome hath no jurisdiction in this realm of England," etc. These still represent the belief of many Anglicans.

ANGLO-CATHOLIC. A term applied to a large party in the Church of England and other Protestant episcopal churches, whose supporters approximate to Catholic faith and practice. The use of the term for convenience by some Catholic individuals and publications must not be construed as adhesion to belief in the Catholicity of the Church of England, which the name implies.

ANGLO-SAXON CHURCH, The. The English Church (*q.v.*) from its foundation by St. Augustine of Canterbury until the Norman conquest in 1066.

ANIMA CHRISTI (Soul of Christ). The opening words of a prayer to Christ in his passion, often ascribed to St. Ignatius Loyola, but in use for at least 250 years before his day. The Dominicans without adequate reason, call it a prayer of St. Thomas Aquinas, and use a somewhat more extended version than that found in ordinary prayer books and among the *Orationes post Missam*. The popular hymn "Soul of my Saviour, sanctify my breast" is a metrical version, by Fr. Maher, S.J., of the same prayer, and another translation, by Cardinal Newman, is printed in the *Raccolta*.

ANIMISM (Lat., *anima*, the soul). i. In general, a doctrine opposed to vitalism, occasionalism, pre-established harmony (*qq.v.*). It teaches that the soul is the principle of life in man and that it is at the same time the principle of man's sensitive as well as of his intellectual life without thereby ceasing to be spiritual and immortal. Thus taught Aristotle, and after him the Scholastics.

ii. The attribution of anthropomorphic will, passions and powers to material objects or to the lower animals, a belief common among human kind in all times and many places. It is advanced by some students of religion as the basis of all cults and the precursor of monotheism; the theory is now less popular and animism is seen to be often in direct conflict with or a perversion of monotheism.

ANNONCIADES, The. A small order of contemplative nuns founded by Bl. Joan of Valois in 1501; so called from their devotion in honour of the Annunciation.

ANNULMENT OF MARRIAGE. There is no such thing as the annulment of a consumated sacramental marriage. The expression is sometimes used inaccurately for the declaration of nullity (*q.v.*) of a union reputed to be a marriage but which upon examination is proved not to have been such.

ANNUNCIATION, The. i. The actual moment of the Incarnation, when the angel announced to our Lady that God the Son was to be born of her (Luke i, 26–38).

ii. The feast celebrating this event, observed almost universally on March 25, a date presumably selected because it is nine months before Christmas. It is accounted primarily a feast of our Lady, and is one of the three oldest. Formerly in some places (and still in the Byzantine rite to a certain extent) it was a feast of our Lord and called, *e.g., Conceptio Christi*.

ANOINTING. i. The application of oil to persons and things, a usage in the Church from the earliest times. In the Latin rite anointing is used at baptism, confirmation, the conferring of holy orders, the coronation of a king; and also in the consecration of churches, altars, etc., and in the blessing of the font on Holy Saturday and the vigil of Pentecost.

ii. Of the Sick. This is called in the

Western church the sacrament of Extreme Unction (*q.v.*). This name is a little misleading, for, according to the mind of the Church, the sacrament is not the immediate and last preparation for death (for this, the Commendation of a Soul, *q.v.*, is provided), but a means of obtaining health of soul and body and of making the faculties more alert and strong for the possible meeting with death.

ANTEPENDIUM. A Latin name (*ante*, before, and *pendere*, to hang) for that which in English is called a frontal.

ANTHEM. An English development of the word antiphon, now generally used of a verse or verses of scripture or other composition set to music, the singing of which is a characteristic of Anglican cathedral services; equivalent to a motet.

ANTHEM OF PUY, The. The hymn *Salve Regina*, so called on account of its popularity at the pilgrimage shrine of Our Lady of Le Puy in the middle ages.

ANTHROPOMORPHISM (Gr., ἄνθρωπος, man, μορφή, form). The ascription to the Supreme Being of human form and activities, with human passions and feelings. It designates the natural tendency of man to represent the Divinity as like to himself, having the same figure, senses, passions and powers. This tendency is to be found in all religions: but true religion does not think of God in this wise except in a metaphorical sense. Anthropomorphism attained its apogee with those Greeks who deified human nature and its passions. The true philosophy teaches that all human perfections which of themselves do not involve any imperfection are in God in a transcendental and infinite way; they are said to be in him not *univocally* but *analogously* (*q.v.*).

ANTICAMERA (SEGRETO), The (It., [private] ante-room). The room adjoining the pope's work-room, where cardinals and others of distinction await audience; those whose duty it is to attend therein. The *maestro di camera* (*q.v.*) has charge of the Anticamera.

ANTICHRIST. A designation of Christ's chief antagonist, who will precede his second coming and the end of the world, and whose activity will be directly connected with a widespread apostasy from the Christian faith. He will be an individual human personality, marked by utter lawlessness, self-deification, hatred of Christian truth, and rivalry with Christ through mock-miracles. He will cause the fall of many, but be destroyed by Christ. Scripture authority for his nature and work is found in 1 John ii, 18, 22; iv, 3; 2 John 7; and 2 Thes. ii: cf., Matt. xxiv, 5, 11, 24, and especially Apoc. xiii, 5ff. Several Old Testament texts also are regarded as prophetic of Antichrist: Isa. xi, 4; Jer. viii,

16; Ezek. xxxviii and xxxix; Dan. vii, 21. Jewish and Christian literature has by guess and inference enlarged on the scriptural portrait, sometimes with plausibility, sometimes with extravagance, the Jews, of course, only thinking of some great foe of Israel before the coming of the Messianic kingdom. Catholic exegesis does not allow that Antichrist be regarded as the mere symbol or embodiment of the anti-Christian spirit, but insists on the reality of his personality. Connexion of Antichrist with the papacy belongs to the aberrations of 16th-century religious warfare.

ANTICIPATION. The custom among those who are bound to the private recitation of the Divine Office of saying Matins and Lauds on the previous evening. Many clerics anticipate any time after 2 p.m. throughout the year; others do not anticipate at all.

ANTICLERICALISM. i. Opposition to Catholicism directed particularly against the lawful activities of the clergy. Anti-clericalism is usually secularist but is sometimes associated with Protestantism. It seeks by means of the civil law to suppress church schools and abolish religious teaching in all schools; entirely to secularize works of charity, such as hospitals; to suppress religious orders; to forbid public demonstrations of Christianity; to penalize the practice of religion by servants of the state, etc. France has been the home of anti-clericalism since the first quarter of the 19th century, and it is epidemic in Spain, Portugal, Italy; in all these countries it is a characteristic of the Freemasons, so that there masonry and anti-clericalism are synonymous.

ii. Lawful opposition to any improper pretensions of the clergy as such, or to an attempt of religious authority to operate outside its proper sphere.

ANTIDORON (Gr., a gift instead of [holy communion]). Pieces of bread taken from the loaves from which the particles required for consecration have been cut; during or at the end of the Byzantine, Armenian and Coptic liturgies these pieces of bread are distributed to the people, sometimes after having a separate blessing said over them. In the Byzantine rite it is blessed during the *anaphora* and is distributed by the priest after the Liturgy, with the words "May the blessing and mercy of the Lord come upon thee, always, now and for ever, world without end. Amen," and it is received in the right hand resting on the left—the primitive way of receiving the sacred Host. This *antidoron* is a sacramental from the devout reception of which may be obtained a special participation in the graces conferred by the holy mysteries, apart from actual communion. The custom was at one time common in the West. The French *pain bénit* (*q.v.*)

is a similar custom but not exactly equivalent.

ANTIMENSION (Gr., in place of a table). A piece of linen or silk, about eighteen inches square, on which are embroidered or painted the instruments of Christ's passion and entombment; sewn into it is a tiny bag containing relics of martyrs embodied in a kind of cement. It was used in the Byzantine rite primarily as a covering to an unconsecrated table on which the Liturgy was to be celebrated (just as the portable altar is used in the West); it is now used even on a consecrated altar. An antimension is consecrated by a bishop with a rite similar to that used for an altar. Priests of the Latin rite sometimes receive permission to celebrate on an antimension, *e.g.*, American chaplains in World War II.

ANTINOMIANISM (Gr., against the law). The doctrine that Christians are not bound by the moral law. It is a heresy as old as the Church and was written against by St. Paul and St. Peter, but it did not receive this name until the 16th century, when the doctrine of justification by faith alone was carried to this conclusion by some sects of Protestants. Antinomianism was specifically condemned by the Council of Trent (session vi, canons 19 and 20).

ANTIOCH, CATHOLIC PATRIARCHS OF. There are three with jurisdiction:
i. Melkite. Usually referred to as the Patriarch of Antioch, Alexandria, Jerusalem and all the East (he is also, amongst other things, "Father of Fathers, Shepherd of Shepherds, Bishop of Bishops and thirteenth Apostle"); in fact, Alexandria and Jerusalem are only titles and he is represented in those cities by vicars patriarchal. His jurisdiction extends over the Melkites inhabiting any part of what was, in 1894, the Turkish empire and Egypt. He is elected by the synod of bishops, residential and titular, and sends a detailed profession of faith to Rome; in sign of confirmation the pope sends him the *pallium* (which he only wears to be buried in). He is in the direct line of succession from the early bishops, so that the Orthodox patriarch is doubly in schism. He ordains all the bishops of the patriarchate and blesses the chrism for all.
ii. Syrian. The Patriarch of Antioch, the City of God, and of all the East, with jurisdiction over the Catholic Syrians throughout the former Turkish empire and Egypt. He is elected and confirmed like his Melkite brother (above). He alone has the right to consecrate bishops and the holy chrism for his church. The patriarchate was established in 1783, with residence at Sharfeh, but the see is now at Bairut; there are vicars patriarchal at Jerusalem and Alexandria.
iii. Maronite. The Patriarch of Antioch and all the East. Elected and with juris-

diction over Maronites as above. He has the right to consecrate all bishops of his rite and to name *chorepiskopoi*, etc.; to consecrate chrism for his whole church; and to reserve absolution for certain sins. He convenes a synod every three years and sends his representative to Rome every ten. The title of patriarch was confirmed to the Maronite primate in 1254, as an act of grace. He has a vicar patriarchal at Jerusalem.

ANTIOCH, THE PATRIARCHATE OF. An apostolic church, said to have been founded by St. Peter, the fourth of the great patriarchates, with its centre at Antioch in Syria, where we were first called Christians. After the council of Ephesus (431) nearly all the eastern part of the patriarchate adhered to Nestorianism and formed the Nestorian Church; in the next century Monophysism set up a rival line of patriarchs and formed the Jacobite Church; and later what was left of the patriarchate followed Constantinople into schism. In the course of centuries many of these schismatics, and others of the neighbouring patriarchates of Alexandria and Jerusalem, returned to unity and the Catholic patriarchate was reestablished in 1724. There are to-day three Catholic patriarchs of Antioch (*q.v.*) having jurisdiction, and there is a titular Latin patriarch, a relic of the Crusades, who adds his dignity to the court of Rome. There are also two non-Catholic patriarchs, one for the Orthodox and one for the Syrian-Jacobite Church (*q.v.*). The former with about 250,000 faithful, mostly Syrians, forms an autocephalous unit of the Orthodox Eastern Church (*q.v.*) in Syria and Mesopotamia, and has jurisdiction over 2 dioceses of Syrian Orthodox in the U.S.A., one in Brazil and one in Argentine. The *katholikos* of the Jacobites of Malabar (*q.v.*) is said to call himself "Patriarch of Antioch" without a shadow of right or reason.

ANTIOCHENE LITURGY, The. The original liturgy of Antioch, called "of the Apostolic Constitutions," said to be the oldest and most apostolic of all known liturgies. Its use was superseded by a modified form from Jerusalem, the "Liturgy of St. James" in Greek. After the monophysite schism the Orthodox gradually abandoned this for the Byzantine liturgy, which was itself derived from the Antiochene rite. The Jacobites evolved a form of the "St. James" in Syriac, the chief of the *anaphoras* of the West Syrian rite now in use.

ANTIPHON (Gr., ἀντιφωνή, answering voice).
i. A verse or words of scripture sung before and after the Song of the Three Children, *Benedictus, Magnificat, Nunc Dimittis*, etc., in the Divine Office; before and after each psalm at Vespers, Matins and Lauds; before the first and after the last psalm only at the Little Hours and Compline. The antiphons

at Vespers, Matins and Lauds are only doubled (*i.e.*, said or sung complete before and after each psalm, etc.) on a feast which is of double rank (the terms have no connexion); on lesser feasts and always in the other hours the first words only are said before the psalm, and the whole after it. See also ANTHEM.

ii. Any versicle or sentence sung by one side or part of a choir in response to the other. The singing of the psalms in alternate verses by two sides of a choir, or by choir and congregation, is antiphonal singing.

ANTIPHONS OF OUR LADY, The. Four chants in honour of our Lady, each with a versicle, response and prayer, sung according to the season of the year. They are *Alma Redemptoris Mater, Ave Regina Cælorum, Regina Cæli* and *Salve Regina*. The appropriate antiphon is said or sung after Compline in the Divine Office. When the office is said in choir the antiphon B.V.M. is sung kneeling, except on Saturday and Sunday, and throughout paschal-time. These antiphons are sometimes sung at non-liturgical services.

ANTIPHONAL CHANTS, The. The three chants at high Mass, the introit, offertory and communion, which are sung by the choir while other things are going on (*viz.*, the entrance or preparatory prayers, offertory, and cleansing of the vessels), as opposed to responsorial chants (the gradual and alleluiatic verse), which are sung for their own sake. The offertory was, however, originally a responsorial chant and in the Mass for the Dead is so still.

ANTIPHONER, ANTIPHONARY. A liturgical book containing the chant not only of the antiphons but of all sung parts of the Divine Office (psalms, hymns, etc.). It is designed for the use of canons, monks, and others bound to the public and solemn celebration of the office, and is also necessary to secular choirs.

ANTIPOPE. One claiming to be pope in opposition to a true pope canonically elected. There have been over twenty-five such, ten of them in the 12th century and most of them notoriously false pretenders. The last antipope submitted to Nicholas V, in 1449. The Clementine popes (*q.v.*) of the Great Schism are not called antipopes, owing to the historical uncertainty of their status.

ANTISEMITISM. Semite is the name given to most of the peoples mentioned in Genesis x as descended from Shem (Sem), the son of Noah, *e.g.*, Hebrews, Arabs, Syrians. But the word "antisemitism" is entirely confined to hatred and ill-treatment of the Jews, which would be better called "antijewishness." The attribution of any defect (or virtue) to the essence of any race, nation or group, and

discrimination against or penalizing of any body of people (as distinct from the just punishment of individual evil-doers), involve denials of Christian teaching on the unity and brotherhood (*q.v.*) of the human race and of the universality of The Fall (*q.v.*) and of God's grace, and are flagrant sins against justice and charity. Moreover, where the Jews particularly are concerned, Pope Pius XI reminded Christians that "Through Christ and in Christ we are the spiritual descendants of Abraham. Christians are not allowed to take any part in antisemitism. We recognize the right of everyone to defend himself and to take lawful measures to protect his legitimate interests: but antisemitism is forbidden. Spiritually we are Semites," *i.e.*, Jews.

ANTISTES (Lat., president, high priest). A title sometimes used for a bishop, *e.g.*, in the prayer *Te igitur* beginning the canon of the Mass.

ANTITYPE. The virtue, happiness, truth, person, event, etc., corresponding to a Biblical type (*q.v.*), *e.g.*, our Lady is the antitype of Eve; the Blessed Sacrament, of manna.

ANTONIANS. Eastern monks who take their name from St. Anthony the Abbot (*d.* 356) and follow his rule (*q.v.*). They take the usual vows, fast and abstain rigorously, may not smoke or eat meat. They sing the Night Office at midnight and the hieromonks are engaged in manual labour, parochial work and teaching; two-thirds of the religious are ordained. The habit is a black tunic, leather belt, small hood, and sandals. The superior (*reis*) of each house is elected by his monks, and the superior general may use the mitre and pastoral staff. The Maronite Antonians have three congregations (of Aleppo, the Baladite, and of St. Isaias) totalling about 750 monks; some live as hermits. The Chaldean congregation of St. Hormisdas has 3 monasteries and 100 monks. The Armenian Antonians were flourishing until 1871, when most of them went into schism; the Catholic remnant is now extinct. There are several houses of Maronite Antonian nuns.

ANTONY, ST., THE RULE OF. The monastic rule which forms the basis of the life of the Catholic Antonians (*q.v.*), the dissident Coptic monks of Egypt, and the Orthodox of Sinai. It was not written by Antony but has been put together from his written "Apophthegms" and oral instructions, and was intended for those living a semi-eremitical life rather than for cenobites.

APOCALYPSE (Gr., ἀποκαλύπτω, I uncover, reveal). A term widely used for a score or so of writings, both Jewish and Christian, written between two centuries before and three centuries after Christ, foretelling the future, and especially the Last Things, in the form of symbolic visions. Catholics apply it almost exclusively to the last book of the New Testament, the revelation of St. John (The Apocalypse, without qualification, always means this book), but sometimes to the visions in Daniel and Zacharias. Our Lord's description in the Synoptics of his second coming is sometimes called the Little Apocalypse by Protestant critics of the "eschatological school." The Apocalypse, according to tradition and internal evidence, was written towards the end of the reign of Domitian, *c.* 96. No interpretation of the many attempted by Catholic scholars is of faith.

APOCRISIARIUS (Lat., from Gr., ἀπόκρισις, answer). A general name given in early times to what we should now call nuncios and delegates, whether apostolic, patriarchal, episcopal, or other, especially to the papal representative at the court of the emperor in Constantinople. It is still used in the East.

APOCRYPHA (Gr., ἀπόκρυφος, hidden). Books erroneously held to be inspired and to be included in the canon of Scripture, but rejected as such by the Church, such as III and IV Esdras, III and IV Maccabees, Prayer of Manasses, 3rd Epistle to the Corinthians, the Gospel of James. Books styled "apocrypha" in Protestant editions of the Bible are not necessarily such in the eyes of the Catholic Church. (See CANON OF SCRIPTURE; DEUTERO-CANONICAL BOOKS; GOSPEL, APOCRYPHAL.) Any work of doubtful authenticity or certain falsity may be said to be apocryphal.

APODEIPNON (Gr., after supper). The last of the canonical hours in the Byzantine rite, corresponding to Compline. During Lent it is called Great Apodeipnon on account of its extra length during that season; it is joined with *Mesonyktikon* to form the vigil service of Christmas and Epiphany. Ordinarily it consists of Psalms l, lxix and cxlii, the Creed of Nicæa, *Trisagion* and Our Father, a *kontakion* according to the feast and final prayers.

APODICTIC. A term applied to demonstration (*q.v.*), a species of reasoning which deduces a conclusion from certain and evident premises; apodictical proof is distinguished from dialectical proof.

APODOSIS (Gr., conclusion). The end of a feast of our Lord or our Lady which has lasted more than one day, in the Byzantine rite. It corresponds to the Western octaveday, and in fact sometimes is an octave, but its length depends on the importance of the feast.

APOKATASTASIS (Gr., change of state). The doctrine of the final restitution of all rational creatures, including the Devil and his angels, to the grace and glory of God. This doctrine was held by Origen, Clement of Alexandria, St. Gregory of Nyssa and other theologians, but was condemned by the second Council of Constantinople in 553. *cf.*, Universalism.

APOLLINARIANISM. The heresy of Apollinaris, bishop of Alexandria (*d.* about 392), who taught that our Lord had no human intellect and that his flesh was of one substance with his divinity, brought with him from Heaven, so that God the Son actually died on the cross. In effect the heresy deprived Christ of both humanity and divinity.

APOLOGETICS. The science of the defence and explanation of the Christian religion. The word "apologetics" and the associated word "apologia" do not in any way imply defence of a system which must be apologized for in the ordinary sense, and must be distinguished from "apology," which in common speech has reference to some fault.

APOLYSIS (Gr., dismissal). The conclusion of a liturgical office in the Byzantine rite, consisting of an invocation of our Lord and his saints, after which the priest dismisses the people. There is a Great Apolysis after the Liturgy, *Orthros, Hesperinos* (*q.v.*) and the greater offices (baptism, marriage, etc.), and a shorter Little Apolysis at other times.

APOLYTIKION (Gr., that which delivers). The principal *troparion* (*q.v.*) of a feast in the Byzantine rite, often called "the *troparion* of the day." Each feast has its proper *apolytikion*, which is sung before the *apolysis* at *Hesperinos* and before the *hexapsalmos* at *Orthros*.

APOSTASY (Gr., desertion). i. Apostasy from the Faith (*a fide*) is the act by which a baptized person, after possessing the true Christian faith, totally rejects it. It differs from heresy and schism (*qq.v.*). The abandonment of Christianity by one who, though baptized in the Catholic Church, has been brought up from infancy in a non-Catholic sect, is not apostasy in the proper sense. The complete abandonment of the *practice* of the Faith is not apostasy, or even a presumption of apostasy. A person is an apostate whether he joins a non-Christian religion, as Judaism, Buddhism, Islam, or falls into unbelief, atheism, materialism, agnosticism, rationalism, indifferentism or "free-thought." Apostates from the Faith incur excommunication *ipso facto*, and other penalties. Penalties are incurred only for the *crime* of apostasy, not for the *sin; i.e.*, there must be some external act. Apostates remain subject to the laws of the Church.

ii. Apostasy from the Religious Life (*a religione*) is when a professed religious (male or female) of perpetual vows, whether solemn or simple, unlawfully leaves his or her community with the intention of not returning. An apostate remains bound by the rule and vows, and incurs *ipso facto* excommunication, reserved to the superior.

APOSTATE. One who, after possessing the Catholic Faith, totally rejects it (Apostasy, q.v., i). The Vatican Council condemned the proposition that Catholics are in the same position as those who have not received the Faith and so can regard as doubtful the Faith which they have already received on the Church's authority and withhold their assent until they have satisfied themselves of its credibility and truth by scientific demonstration; and it affirmed that Catholics can never have a just cause for changing or doubting their Faith. Some years earlier, Pope Gregory XVI emphatically repudiated the teaching of Hermes that positive doubt was the basis of all true theological enquiry.

APOSTLE (Gr., ἀπόστολος, one sent, a messenger). i. The name is given primarily to any one of the Twelve Apostles of our Lord who were in particular those called to be witnesses of him and to be sent out to preach his gospel, namely, SS. Peter, Andrew, James the Greater and John his brother, Thomas, James the Less the cousin of Jesus and Jude (Thaddeus) his brother, Philip, Bartholomew, Matthew, Simon Zelotes, and Matthias who filled the place of Judas Iscariot. It is extended in the New Testament to include Paul, Barnabas and others, and these, with Luke the Evangelist, are celebrated as apostles liturgically (but the last named is not mentioned in the canon of the Mass). The Apostles were the first bishops of the Christian Church and through them the bishops have ever since had the divine commission to teach all men and govern the Church, in union with the representative of their chief, St. Peter, and the God-given power to confect the sacraments necessary to the salvation of souls and the continuance of the Church.

ii. The first successful Christian missionary to a country is called its apostle. Such are: SS. Paul, of the Gentiles; Augustine of Canterbury, of England; Patrick, of Ireland; Columba, of the Picts; Felix, of East Anglia; Wilfrid, of Sussex; Birinus, of Wessex; Gregory the Enlightener, of Armenia; Frumentius, of Ethiopia; Boniface (Winfrid), of Germany; Anscar, of Sweden and Denmark; Cyril and Methodius, of the southern Slavs; Willibrord, of the Netherlands; Francis Xavier, of the Indies; Peter Claver, of the Negroes; Adalbert, of Prussia; etc.

iii. In the Byzantine rite the liturgical epistle is called "the apostle," being always taken from the apostolic writings; the same use was formerly common in the West.

iv. "The Apostle," without a name, generally refers to St. Paul.

APOSTLES OF IRELAND, THE XII. The name given by old Irish writers to twelve saints, pupils of St. Finian at Clonard, in the 6th century, namely: two Brendans (of Birr and Clonfert), Canice or Kenny, two Cierans (of Clonmacnois and Saighir), two

Columbas (of Terryglass and Iona), Laserian, Mobhi, Ninnidh, Ruadhan and Senach.

APOSTLES, THE LITURGY OF THE. The principal *anaphora* of the Chaldean rite (q.v.) which must be distinguished from the Ethiopic Liturgy of the Twelve Apostles and several *anaphoras* of the same name. The apostles are SS. Addai and Mari, said to have preached in East Syria and Persia.

APOSTLES' CREED, The. A brief statement of fundamental Christian truths, formerly attributed to the Apostles themselves. It is without doubt expressive of apostolic teaching, and there is some evidence that it is the amplification of a rule of faith used at Baptism in apostolic times. An early form is quoted by Tertullian (c. 200); nearly the present form is known from c. 525; the complete present form is found c. 750. It is used liturgically in the Roman rite of Baptism and of the ordination of a priest. In Eastern rites no liturgical use is made of the Apostles' Creed, but only of the Nicene Creed (q.v.) as authorized by the first Council of Constantinople.

APOSTLESHIP OF PRAYER, The. An association founded in France in 1844, whose object is the promotion of prayer for the intentions of the members in union with our Lord in Heaven. The practices of the association are the daily offering to God of one's good works, spiritual and material, the daily recitation of a decade of the rosary for the monthly intention recommended by the pope, and holy communion as an act of reparation on prescribed days. The association, which is under Jesuit direction, numbers many million members.

APOSTLESHIP OF THE SEA, The. A world-wide organization for the spiritual welfare of Catholic seamen. It co-operates with the Society of St. Vincent de Paul (q.v.) and other organizations in whatever works may conduce to its end: particularly in the visitation of ships, the enrolment of honorary port-chaplains, the provision of reading-matter and the establishment of sailors' institutes. The basis of the A.S. is the membership of seamen themselves, membership cards being in use in many languages; spiritual and material assistance is given by associate and active members. The work began in Great Britain in 1890 with the collection of literature; in 1896 visitation of ships and enrolment of sailors in a special branch of the Apostleship of Prayer (q.v.) was first carried out at Glasgow and the name "Apostleship of the Sea" was first used; in 1920 a Benedictine oblate with two secular tertiaries of St. Francis and a Jesuit started in Glasgow an organizing centre for the establishment of the work on an international basis.

APOSTOLIC CANONS, The. A collection of eighty-five ecclesiastical decrees drawn up probably during the 5th century but called apostolic because it was at one time believed that they were delivered by the Apostles to Pope St. Clement. They are concerned chiefly with the discipline of the clergy and contain a canon of the Sacred Scriptures.

APOSTOLIC CHURCHES. A term often applied to churches founded or governed by one of the Apostles in person, or reputed so to have been. Of those existing with varying degrees of dignity to-day there are the holy apostolic see of Rome, founded by St. Peter, Alexandria (St. Mark), Antioch (St. Peter), Jerusalem (St. James the Less), Athens (St. Paul), Cyprus (St. Barnabas). The Malabar Christians claim religious descent from St. Thomas and, certainly erroneously, the Armenians from St. Bartholomew, and Constaninople from St. Andrew.

APOSTOLIC COLLEGE. i. The Twelve Apostles as a body of men commissioned to be the common initiators of a certain work, namely, the "launching" of the Church of Christ.
ii. Those Roman institutions which are immediately subject to the Holy See and under its direction and protection, e.g., the College of Propaganda and certain national colleges, including the English.

APOSTOLIC CONSTITUTIONS, The. Eight books not of the apostolic age but probably compiled in the 4th century, being a revised and enlarged version of the "Didascalia Apostolorum" (q.v.). Their author's object was to give instruction in religion, morality and liturgy and they form a very valuable historical document. The Apostolic Canons are found added to MSS. of the Constitutions and both were compiled by the same author, but his identity is not known.

APOSTOLIC CONSTITUTIONS, The Liturgy of the, so called from being found in books II and VIII of the "Apostolic Constitutions" (q.v.). It is probably a tentative or specimen liturgy drawn up in the 4th century on the rather vague lines of the eucharistic liturgies in use during the first three centuries when, except for a sort of general skeleton or outline, they were in a fluid state; it may represent the original rite of Antioch. It has been attributed, quite wrongly, to St. Clement of Rome.

APOSTOLIC FATHERS, The. Those Christian writers who lived near enough to apostolic times to have had personal intercourse with the Apostles, or at any rate to have come within their near and unmodified influence. Their extant works are naturally very few; the principal are the "Didache," the "Letter of Clement," the seven letters of St. Ignatius of Antioch and the "Shepherd" of Hermas. These are mostly in the form of letters intended for individuals or local churches, such as those of Ignatius, six addressed to churches and one to Polycarp, written while being taken to Rome to suffer death for the Faith.

"APOSTOLIC KING." A title of the King of Hungary, used by the emperors of Austria. It was claimed in the 16th century, first used by Leopold I (d. 1705) and was formally granted to Maria Teresa in 1758, by Pope Clement XIII.

APOSTOLIC LETTERS. One of the divisions of writings emanating from the Curia Romana. An apostolic letter may be *simplex* (i.e., one drawn up in the pope's name), a *chirographum* (signed by the pope), an encyclical, or a *motu proprio* (qq.v.). The hierarchy of Wales was reorganized by an apostolic letter, *Cambria Celtica*, in 1916.

APOSTOLIC SEE, The. The episcopal see of Rome, founded by the Prince of the Apostles, Peter, and in virtue of his primacy the ultimate seat of authority for the whole Church of Christ. Other sees are of apostolic origin, notably Alexandria, Antioch and Jerusalem, but none of them had the authority of Peter's, and heresy, schism and the course of history have shorn them of most of the dignity and importance which as apostolic churches they ought still to enjoy.

APOSTOLIC UNION, The. A widespread association of secular priests with a simple rule of life intended to increase personal sanctification and the efficient discharge of parochial duties. The union promotes, so far as possible, common life among parish clergy, and it was greatly encouraged by Pope Pius X, who was himself a member.

APOSTOLICÆ CURÆ. A bull of Pope Leo XIII, issued in 1896, wherein it was declared that Anglican orders (q.v.) are invalid on extrinsic and intrinsic grounds. These were set out at length. The bull was the result of a papal commission specially set up to examine the question.

APOSTOLICAL SUCCESSION. i. The authoritative and unbroken transmission of the mission and powers conferred by Jesus Christ on St. Peter and the Apostles from them to the present pope and bishops.
ii. The uninterrupted substitution of persons in the place of the Apostles by the valid consecration of bishops and transmission of holy orders which the Orthodox and other Eastern churches share with the Catholic Church; but having severed communion with St. Peter's, the Holy See, they have thereby withdrawn themselves from apostolical succession in the full sense. Still less has it been maintained by such a body as the Anglican, which had its origin in acts whereby episcopal continuity was broken and subsequent consecrations vitiated. It must be noted that the phrase is frequently used by Protestants with imprecision; the apostol-

ical succession of the archbishops of Canterbury consequent on their possessing the titles, cathedral and endowments of, and a certain successive personal relation with, predecessors of unquestioned apostolicity, or of a minister who by a series of ordinations of one sort and another can link himself up with a Catholic bishop and so with the Apostles, is but a mechanical and external succession.

APOSTOLICITY. This is the mark (*q.v.*) of the Church which depends upon her apostolic origin. The Church has a three-fold apostolicity: (*a*) of doctrine, in that she teaches the same doctrine as the Apostles taught; (*b*) of mission or authority, in that she has inherited her mission and authority from the Apostles through a legitimate and uninterrupted succession of pastors; (*c*) of society, in that she is the same society as that of which the Apostles were the foundation.

APPAREL (Old Fr., *aparail*, from *apareiller*, to make to fit). A small oblong panel of embroidery on the cuffs and at the bottom, front and back, of an alb, and along the top of an amice. This characteristic mediæval ornament has again come into use of recent years; it has never been abandoned in the Ambrosian rite and in parts of Spain, but there the lower apparels are suspended by cords from the girdle instead of being sewn to the alb. The origin of apparels was to strengthen and protect the linen where it was most subject to wear.

APPARITION (Lat., presence) is the name sometimes reserved for certain kinds of supernatural vision, namely, those that are bodily or visible, and is often used for the manifestation of our Lady at Lourdes, of St. Michael on Monte Gargano, etc. Owing to the meaning of the word in popular use (ghost, spook), "appearing" better expresses these events.

APPEAL. i. As in civil so in ecclesiastical courts a party believing himself wronged by a judgment in a lower court may appeal to a higher tribunal. There is no appeal from the decision of the pope, and anyone appealing from the pope to a future general council is by that fact suspect of heresy and excommunicate. If a diocesan court pronounces a putative marriage to be invalid, the defender (*q.v.*) of the bond *must* enter an appeal.
ii. As from an abuse. An appeal from the ecclesiastical to the civil power on the ground that the first had encroached on the rights of the second, and *vice versa*. Such appeals were the cause of strife during the middle ages and after the Reformation were much abused on the part of the state, especially in France. *cf.*, Ecclesiastical Privileges.

APPELLANTS CONTROVERSY, The.   i. The Archpriest Controversy (*q.v.*).

ii. A controversy following the apostolic constitution *Unigenitus* (*q.v.*, ii), the publication of which was resisted strongly in France, where a number of bishops and their followers (The Appellants) appealed to a future general council; Cardinal Noailles, archbishop of Paris, did not submit till 1728.

APPETITE. An inclination towards something consequent upon knowledge. If the knowledge is of the sensitive order the appetite is called the sensitive appetite, in which the passions reside; if the knowledge is of the intellectual order it is called the intellectual appetite or the will.

APPETITE, IRASCIBLE (Lat., *irasci*, to get angry). Those passions (*q.v.*) whose objects are difficult of attainment because of certain obstacles that stand in the way are said to reside in the irascible appetite; anger is thereby aroused, hence such passions are called irascible.

APSE.   i. The semi-circular end characteristic of the early Christian churches. The bishop's throne was against the middle of the wall of the apse and the altar opposite to it in the forward part; the arrangement may be seen in many of the basilicas of Rome, *e.g.*, St. John Lateran, San Clemente, and is still normal in a church of the Byzantine rite.
ii. In romanesque and gothic church-building the semi-circular or polygonal termination to the chancel, aisles or transepts. The simple apse form is often complicated by projecting chapels which themselves are sometimes subsidiary apses.

AQUILEIA, PATRIARCHS OF. See GRADO and UDINE.

ARA CŒLI, The. (Lat., altar of heaven). The name by which is known the church of St. Mary on the Capitol in Rome and so called because, on the site of a chapel adjoining, the Emperor Augustus is said by tradition to have had a vision of our Lady enthroned in Heaven The church also contains a famous *bambino*.

ARABIA, THE CHURCH IN. Arabia is divided into several separate states, of which the total population is estimated at 7 million, solidly Mohammedan. The thousand or so Catholics form a vicariate apostolic, established in 1888 with headquarters at Aden. It is served by the Capuchin friars minor.

ARAMAIC. The Semitic language of Babylonia and of Syria, where it was superseded after the Moslem conquest by Arabic. From the time of the captivity in Babylon Palestinian Aramaic began to be spoken by the Jews instead of Hebrew, and was the language of Palestine at the time of our Lord's life on earth and consequently was spoken by him. Such words, found in the N.T., as *abba, talitha cumi, eloi lamma sabacthani* are *Aramaic.* The ancient Syriac, which is the liturgical language of the Syrian rites, is a dialect of Aramaic, so that Christians of these rites hear the words of our Lord in his own native tongue.

ARCH-. A prefix from Greek, ἀρχός, chief, used with such words as bishop, abbey, etc., to form titles indicating the principal bishop of a province, principal abbey of a congregation, etc.

ARCHABBOT. A title of honour given to the abbots of certain distinguished Benedictine monasteries, *e.g.,* Monte Cassino and St. Vincent's at Beatty, U.S.A. The archabbot of Montserrat (Brazil) is so called as president of that congregation.

ARCHANGEL. A spirit in the eighth rank of the nine orders of the celestial hierarchy. The Church honours three archangels by name: Michael, the captain of the heavenly host; Gabriel, the angel of the Annunciation; and Raphael, who by tradition moved the water of the pool of Bethsaida (John v, 1-4). According to Tobias xii, 15, there are four more, whose names are given in the apocryphal book of Enoch as Uriel, Raguel, Sariel and Jeramial.

ARCHBISHOP. i. In the Western church, the bishop of a diocese (archdiocese) who has authority, limited and defined by canon law, over the bishops of the dioceses of a defined territory (province). The bishops are suffragans and the archbishop is their metropolitan. An archbishop may have one suffragan only (*e.g.,* Cardiff) or many (*e.g.,* Westminster, five); some have no suffragans at all (*e.g.,* Hobart), it is then not a province nor is its archbishop a metropolitan (such is sometimes called a titular archbishop, *q.v.*). An archbishop must summon his suffragans to a provincial council once every twenty years and appeals from their courts are made to his; but his right of interference in the dioceses of his suffragans is strictly limited by law. He may grant indulgences (*q.v.*) of 100 days. An archbishop may not undertake the duties of his metropolitan office until he has received the *pallium.* The archbishoprics of England are Westminster (whose archbishop is "perpetual president of the assembly of bishops of England and Wales"), Birmingham and Liverpool; of Wales, Cardiff; of Scotland, Saint Andrews & Edinburgh, and Glasgow; of Ireland, Armagh, Cashel, Dublin and Tuam. There are 21 archbishoprics in U. S. A.

ii. In the Catholic Eastern churches nearly all the archbishops have no suffragans but often call themselves metropolitans none the less. The archbishops of Alba Julia (Rumanian), Lvov (Ruthenian) and Ernakulam (Malabarese) have suffragans. In practice, archbishop is the name often given to any bishop who is immediately subject to his patriarch; thus there are Melkite metropolitans, archbishops and bishops, but all appear to depend equally directly on the patriarch of Antioch and all get equally called archbishop. The position in the dissident Eastern churches is much the same. See METROPOLITAN, ii.

ARCHBISHOP, TITULAR. i. A prelate who has the rank and title of archbishop but without ordinary episcopal jurisdiction or specifically archiepiscopal duties. Such may be an ordinary archbishop who has retired, a coadjutor to a governing archbishop, a prelate entrusted with special duties, *e.g.,* as apostolic delegate, etc. *cf.,* titular bishop.

ii. An archbishop who has no suffragans (*i.e.,* is not a metropolitan, *e.g.,* Washington) but simply governs his own diocese (which is called exempt, or "immediately subject to the Holy See") is also called titular, but this use is unusual in English "Archbishop without suffragans" is a clearer expression.

ARCHBISHOP ELECT. One elected to an archiepiscopate who has not yet been consecrated bishop or, if he has been so consecrated, has not yet taken formal possession of his see.

ARCHCONFRATERNITY. One with the right to affiliate to itself by aggregation other confraternities of the same kind, imparting to them its indulgences and other privileges. The best known archconfraternities are the Guild of the Blessed Sacrament and the Rosary Confraternity.

ARCHDEACON. i. In the Western church this is nowadays not much more than a title of honour given sometimes to the first and sometimes to the second dignitary of some chapters. It is his duty to assist the bishop at certain pontifical functions, *e.g.,* an ordination, but even this office is often performed by the episcopal chaplain or other priest. In England the office of archdeacon was not revived with the hierarchy; in Ireland and Australia the title still exists and the holders bear the old title of "The Venerable." During the middle ages, when each diocese was divided into several archdeaconries, the office was an administrative one of great importance and power, with its own courts and jurisdiction. This was put an end to by the Council of Trent, and the archdeacon's place was to a great extent taken by the vicar general.

ii. In the East generally archdeacons are more common and have definite duties; moreover, they are usually really deacons, not priests. Among the Catholic Armenians he is an administrator without any jurisdiction, and holds a very similar position with the Nestorians, dissident Copts and Jacobites; or he may be the senior deacon in a monastery.

ARCHETYPE. The supreme model or exemplar, the inferiors of which are said to be participations or likenesses in varying proportions. Thus Beauty itself is the exemplar of all beautiful things, and the latter are said to participate in the beautiful in so far as each beautiful thing approaches more or less to the supremely beautiful or the archetype.

ARCHIMANDRITE (Gr., the ruler of a fold). i. An archimandrite in the Byzantine discipline is equivalent to a Benedictine abbot of an important monastery. Such an one may confer the subdiaconate and lectorate on his subjects, but has no right to *pontificalia* nor to officiate pontifically.

ii. In both Catholic and dissident churches of the rite it is now the custom to use the title as an honorary one, and there are both regular and (by an abuse) secular titular archimandrites. They have differing privileges and distinctions, most of them irregular. The Latin archimandritate of St. Saviour, now attached to the archbishopric of Messina, is a relic of Byzantine influence in Sicily.

ARCHIVES, DIOCESAN, contain records of all matters of an historical, general or personal importance, both in spiritual matters and administration; such as acts of synods, ordinations, dealings with property, summaries of parochial records of baptisms, marriages, etc. Archives are also kept by religious houses, but are necessarily of a more domestic nature.

ARCHPRIEST, ARCHPRESBYTER. i. Formerly the priest who assisted and took the bishop's place in public worship, as the archdeacon did in administration. They then became the chiefs of local centres of clergy, and are now more or less represented by the deans. The dignity of archpriest is retained at the Lateran, Vatican and Liberian basilicas; it is held by a cardinal who is bound to appoint a vicar. Certain important churches have an archpriest, *e.g.*, the former cathedral of Dol in Brittany. The title is often given to important parish priests in Italy, and to the heads of chapters of secular canons or to that member of the chapter holding the cure of souls dependent on it. In the province of Bari there is an archipresbyterate, Altamura and Acquaviva delle Fonte, immediately subject to the Holy See.

ii. In the East generally archpriests are more common and have definite duties; *e.g.*, with the Catholic Rumanians he is a sort of rural dean; among the Nestorians, a dean of the clergy of a town, and among the Armenians an overseer of churches in a district. Under the name of "protopope" the rank is very common in churches of the Byzantine rite for a rural dean or as a title of honour; an Italo-Greek parish-priest is nearly always a *protopapa*. In the rubrics of the Byzantine liturgies a bishop is frequently referred to as "archpriest," but distinguished as *archiereus* from the *protoiereus* or protopriest.

ARCHPRIEST CONTROVERSY, The. Also known as the Appellants Controversy. After the death of Cardinal Allen, in 1594, the Catholics of England were left without an ecclesiastical leader and superior. In 1598 the Holy See appointed George Blackwell archpriest over the secular clergy, with a council of twelve assistant priests. Some of the secular clergy, who disliked the influence of the Jesuits, challenged the appointment and sent two of their number to Rome. The appeal was dismissed. Blackwell's treatment of the appellants was so high-handed that thirty-three priests again appealed to Rome. The result was a draw. Blackwell was rebuked; dissociated from the Jesuits; and ordered to have three appellant priests on his council. But his jurisdiction was confirmed nor were Catholics forbidden to take political action against the state, as the appellants desired. The immediate result was a decree of banishment against Catholic priests, to which the appellants replied by an address of loyalty. Blackwell was superseded by George Birkhead, in 1608, and suspended in 1611 for contumaciously recommending the faithful to take an oath of allegiance to James I in a form condemned by the Holy See.

ARCOSOLIUM Lat., *arcus,* arch; *solium,* seat). An arched recess forming a burial-place in the catacombs; Mass was celebrated on the slab with which the grave was closed.

ARDAGH (*Ardachadensis*). An Irish see, suffragan of Armagh. In 1729 the diocese of Clonmacnois was united with it and the diocese now includes county Longford, most of Leitrim and parts of Offaly, Westmeath, Roscommon, Cavan and Sligo. The bishop's residence, cathedral, and diocesan college are at Longford. The patrons of the diocese are St. Mel (Feb. 6), its first bishop, and St. Cieran (Sept. 9), founder of the monastery and school of Clonmacnois in the 6th century; the cathedral also is dedicated in honhour of St. Mel. Irish name: Ard Achadh.

ARGENTINE, THE CHURCH IN THE. Population 13½ millions, the great majority Catholics, at least nominally; a quarter of the people are foreign immigrants, among whom religion tends to be specially cool. There are but few Indians. The state "supports the Roman Catholic religion," which the president and vice-president must profess. Purely civil marriage is recognized, but there is no divorce *a vinculo;* public education is secular, but voluntary religious instruction is provided for; there is an annual state grant towards the support of the clergy and maintenance of divine worship. The ecclesiastical hierarchy was reorganized in 1934: there are 7 metropolitan sees (Buenos Aires was established in 1620 and Cordoba in 1699), each with 2 suffragan dioceses.

ARGYLL AND THE ISLES (*Ergadiensis et Insularum*). A Scottish see, suffragan to Saint Andrews, formed in 1878 from the diocese of Argyll, founded about 1200, and that of the Isles, said to have been founded about 450 by St. Patrick and at one time united with Man under Trondhjem in Norway; vacant respectively from 1579 and 1553. It comprises Argyll, part of Inverness and the islands of Bute, Arran and the Hebrides where the faith has never died out (*e.g.*, on Benbecula, Eriskay, Barra, Vatersay). The bishop's residence and cathedral are at Oban. The patron of the diocese and of the cathedral is St. Columba. Gaelic name: Earra-Ghàidheal agus na h-Eileanan.

ARIANISM. The heresy of Arius (256-326), a priest of Alexandria who taught that the Word (*q.v.*) was not the equal of the Father, or true God, but merely a creature much more perfect than other creatures, who was used by God in his subsequent works of creation. The Son was thus inferior to the Father and of a different substance. Arianism was attacked by St. Athanasius, and condemned at the Council of Nicæa in 325. It was most widely spread and one of the most devastating heresies that ever afflicted the Church.

ARIDITY. The absence of consolation in prayer. It has many degrees, from the lack of sensible devotion to complete desolation. It is both dangerous and advantageous to the soul. On the one hand, it may lead to complete weariness in well-doing, and abandonment of the spiritual life; but on the other, when patiently endured, it fosters true devotion and fervour by making piety an affair of the will and not of the emotions. Aridity is sent by God to those whom he is leading to himself, in order to make them seek him only and not his consolations: hence it plays an important part in the night of the senses and the night of the spirit (*qq.v.*). But it is not always from God: it may be due to bodily health or to a careless spiritual life, in which case the remedy lies with the sufferer himself and with his bodily and spiritual physician.

ARISTOTELIANISM. The philosophic system of Aristotle (384-322 B.C.). First principles and essences are the object of philosophy. Upon these first truths, indemonstrable because of their self-evident truth, are based all our reasoning, the perfect form of which is the syllogism (*q.v.*). The universal exists in things from which it is abstracted by the mind. From an analysis of "being" in general he deduces the notion of *act* and *potency* (*qq.v.*); these latter ideas are essential to a theory which dominates the whole of his philosophy. Through its means he defines the nature of man (soul and body), the nature of body (matter and form), etc. The moral philosophy of Aristotle is at the same time most human and most noble. His natural theology is deficient in that he failed to understand that the prime mover was at the same time both the Creator and the Provider. The history of Aristotelianism is mixed up with the history of all philosophies.

ARK. i. The vessel built by Noe (Noah) as a refuge for his family and the beasts during the Flood.

ii. The Ark of the Covenant, carried by the people of Israel in their wanderings and then deposited in the Temple at Jerusalem, was a chest containing principally the Tables of the Law. From over the ark God communicated his will to Moses, and it came to be regarded as the guarantee of his abiding help. It disappeared after the fall of Jerusalem, in 587 B.C. In a figure of the litany of Loreto our Lady is addressed as Ark of the Covenant (*Fœderis arca*), that is to say, of the New Covenant between God and man. She was called *Arca* by St. Ambrose, St. Ephraem, and others; *Fœderis arca* was first employed by Richard of Saint Victor (*d.* 1173).

iii. A piece of liturgical furniture used in dissident churches of the Coptic and Abyssinian rites and called respectively *pitote* and *taboot*. The *pitote* is a wooden box which stands on the altar and shelters the chalice until the communion. The *taboot* is a box in which is kept the table of stone or hard wood which is laid upon the altar for the celebration of the Liturgy and which itself is also called *taboot*. The Abyssinians hold in great reverence the *taboot* of the cathedral at Aksum, asserting that it is the Ark of the Covenant, brought thither by Menelik I, son of Solomon and the Queen of Saba (Sheba); in other churches the *taboot* is honoured as a symbol of the title of the church.

ARMAGH (*Armacanus*). The primatial see of All Ireland, founded by St. Patrick about 450 and made an archbishopric in 1152, though its primacy was recognized from the first. It now includes the county of Louth, most of Armagh, and parts of Tyrone, Derry and Meath, and has 8 suffragan dioceses. The primate's residence, cathedral and diocesan college are at Armagh. The patron of the archdiocese is St. Maelmhaedhoc (Malachy, Nov. 3) and the cathedral is dedicated in honour of St. Patrick. Irish name: Ard Macha.

ARMENIA, THE CHURCH IN. In the years 1915-17 the Christians of Turkish Armenia suffered deportation and massacre at the hands of the Turks, and those of Azerbaijan and Russian Armenia were set on by the Turks and Kurds. Those left were recognized as forming a separate republic in 1918 and their independence confirmed by Turkey in 1920; but in the same year Armenia became a socialist soviet republic and the state of religion therein is now that of Russia in general. The number of Armenian Christians, Catholic and dissident, left in their country is a matter for speculation; numerous Armenians are scattered all over the world.

ARMENIAN CHURCH, The, was founded for all practical purposes by St. Gregory the Illuminator from Cæsarea in the 3rd–4th century, whence the term Gregorian is applied to it. At the beginning of the sixth century it repudiated the Council of Chalcedon (q.v.), and from that time the church of Armenia has been a national and very isolated church; it is not even in full communion with the other two monophysite churches, the Coptic and the Syrian-Jacobite. Reunion with Rome, proclaimed solemnly in 1198, was never complete and collapsed altogether in 1375, but the Armenian rite still shows much evidence of Latin influence. The Armenian orders and sacraments are valid. In addition to their alleged Monophysism they differ from the Catholic Church in their conception of Purgatory (to which they deny that name), but they pray for the dead; they reject all oecumenical councils after the third; they admit, but do not use, the sacrament of Extreme Unction; in practice they admit divorce, but forbid third marriages, and permit a deacon, priest or even bishop to marry after ordination, provided he relinquishes all sacred duties if he be a bishop or *vartaped*. They give the pope a primacy of honour among other patriarchs. The church is organized under two *katholikoi* and two patriarchs in the Near East, of whom the Katholikos of All the Armenians, at Etshmiadzin, is theoretically the supreme head; but the misfortunes of this scattered nation have greatly upset its ecclesiastical organization. The bishops and higher clergy (*vartapeds*) are always drawn from the monks, who are hardly more than secular clergy, often not even living in community. The faithful number between 2 and 3 millions. There are Gregorian Armenian churches in London and Manchester, and in the United States.

ARMENIAN RITE, The. The system and forms of worship and administration of the sacraments in use amongst the Armenians, both Catholic and dissident. The liturgical language is classical Armenian, and the eucharistic Liturgy is practically that of the Greek St. Basil translated, with Syrian and peculiar variations and with additions from the Latin Mass, e.g., the preparatory psalm *Iudica* and a *Confiteor*, and the last gospel from John i; it has only one *anaphora;* no water is mixed with the wine by the dissidents and, alone among dissident Eastern churches, they as well as Catholics use unleavened bread. The celebrant says the prayers in a low voice, while deacon and choir sing; the words of consecration are chanted aloud. The churches have no *ikonostasis* but a curtain (q.v.); the sanctuary is raised, with the altar towards the middle, and on the north side a niche in the wall to contain the bread, wine, chalice, etc., which are fetched therefrom in procession after the Creed. The liturgical chant is of peculiar beauty and is accompanied by bells and cymbals. The canonical hours are Midnight Office, Matins, Sunrise, Terce, Sext, None, Vespers, Peace (twilight) and Bed-time Prayers. Baptism is by triple pouring combined with immersion followed immediately by Confirmation and Communion—the priest dips his finger in the Precious Blood and passes it over the baby's lips; this last is now the practice only of the dissidents, among whom, too, only the married clergy are generally allowed to hear confessions. Alone among orientals, the Armenians have the four minor orders of the West. Among the dissidents there is little veneration of images, and they have only pictures in their churches. The Blessed Sacrament is reserved in a tabernacle on or behind the altar. Vestments are brightly coloured and never black; two peculiarities are that the celebrating priest wears a Byzantine episcopal crown and a high stiff embroidered collar called the *vagas*. Bishops use the Latin mitre and pastoral staff. Some 5% of the users of this rite are Catholics.

ARMENIAN RITE, CATHOLICS OF THE. There have been Armenians in communion with the Holy See ever since the temporary reunion of part of their church in 1198. They were organized in 1742. Those of the east are governed by the Patriarch-Katholikos of Cilicia, whose see is at Bairut, with five other bishops; those in other parts of the world (Russia, France, United States, Greece, Rumania) are under various ecclesiastical jurisdictions. Thirteen dioceses were destroyed at the murder of nine bishops, thousands of faithful, and dispersion of the rest, by the Turks in 1915–22. Married men may be ordained to the priesthood but this is being less and less used; they have a college at Rome. There is a number of monks (Mekhitarists, q.v.) and a congregation of nuns founded by Cardinal Hassun in 1852. Catholics use the same rite as the dissidents with a varying degree of uniformity: in Transylvania and elsewhere very hybrid liturgies are in use. Though they have the right to communion in both kinds it is not used. Holy water, the rosary, scapulars, the stations of the cross, Benediction, statues and seats in church are among the Western practices introduced into this rite. There are about 95,000 Catholic Armenians in various countries, and an unknown number in U.S.S.R. The priest Gomidas Keumurjian, martyred in 1707 by the Turks, was beatified in 1929.

ARMINIANISM. . The doctrines and following of Jacob Arminius (1560–1609) who revolted from Calvinism, denying its formulated doctrines of predestination, election and grace, on which matters the teaching of Arminius resembled that of the Council of Trent. The controversy is reflected in the 17th article of religion of the Church of England, and Arminianism was a popular term of abuse among English Puritans in the 17th century (Ferrar's establishment at Little Gidding was termed an "Arminian nunnery"); both the Baptists and Methodists were divided into Arminian and Calvinistic branches, but the Wesleyanism of Wesley was thoroughly Arminian.

ARMS OF CHRIST, The. The instruments of the passion of our Lord grouped together to form an emblem or symbol.

ART is deliberate skill employed in the making of things. Deliberate skill means that in which a rational mind is employed. Art is both intellectual and practical: it is of the mind and the mind directed towards making; it is a virtue of the practical intelligence. A work of art is therefore a thing for the making of which deliberate skill has been employed. The "fine arts" are those in which the mind is directed towards the making of a thing of beauty (q.v.) as distinct from a thing of physical utility. A useful thing may be beautiful but beauty is not specifically demanded of it.

ARTS, THE LIBERAL. The seven arts of the mediæval schools, viz., grammar, rhetoric, logic, arithmetic, music, geometry, astronomy. The first three formed the trivium course, the last four the quadrivium; the lowest forms in Catholic schools are often still called Grammar and Rhetoric. This nomenclature was first adopted by Marcian Capella in the 5th century.

ARTICLE OF FAITH (Lat., articulus, a joint). This expression has been used in several senses. Speaking of the Apostles' Creed the "Catechism of the Council of Trent" says that "as the members of the body are divided (sic) by joints, so also we properly and appropriately call an article whatever in the profession of faith is to be believed by us distinctly and severally from anything else"; some therefore confine the term to the truths contained in this creed (by so doing they do not, of course, imply that a Christian may reject other truths which are not articles of faith in this restricted sense). But ordinarily articles of faith include whatsoever the Church has defined or otherwise explicitly laid down for the belief of Christians. And he who, after due enlightenment, refuses his adherence to the revealed truths proposed by the magisterium (q.v.) of the Church, even on a single point, loses theological faith by that act. These articles must all receive the same kind and degree of assent, for all are equally true, the Resurrection with the Immaculate Conception, the Real Presence with Papal Infallibility.

ARTOPHORION (Gr., bread-carrier). The receptacle for the reserved Sacrament in the Byzantine rite, found on or behind the altar or elsewhere in the sanctuary. It may be like the Western tabernacle (though smaller), or a metal dove suspended from the ciborium. Among the dissidents little or no external reverence is paid to the reserved Sacrament, except when it is being actually carried to the sick.

ASCENSION, The. i. The departure of Jesus Christ in his glorified body from this world to the right hand of God the Father in Heaven, which took place in the presence of the Apostles forty days after his resurrection, traditionally on the Mount of Olives. The use of the word ascension does not involve the belief that Heaven is "somewhere up in the sky."

ii. A feast kept on the fortieth day after Easter Sunday to commemorate this event. After the gospel of the principal Mass the paschal candle is extinguished, symbolizing the departure of our Lord from his Apostles. One of the universal holidays of obligation (q.v.).

ASCETICISM (Gr., ἄσκησις, bodily exercise) is self-discipline in all its forms, particularly those voluntarily undertaken out of love of God and desire for spiritual improvement; its meaning is sometimes improperly limited to corporal austerity. It may be internal discipline applied to the mind, heart and will by purely internal effort, and at least a little of this is imposed on every Christian as a condition of salvation; or external, whether by the renunciations implied by the vows of poverty, chastity and obedience (these are imposed on none but undertaken by many) or by the various forms of bodily mortification and austerity (qq.v.) directed to making and keeping the appetites conformed to right reason and God's law. Asceticism is an integral part of Christian life, having its sanction in our Lord's life (which displayed virginity, poverty, fasting, obedience) and teaching. It is not an end in itself, discomfort of mind or body for its own sake, but a means towards personal sanctification, freedom of soul, and approach to God; its higher forms are entirely voluntary and based on the distinction between precepts and counsels (qq.v.): it seeks first the Kingdom of God and so attains to fullness of life. Austerity for its own sake, renouncement for the sake of renouncing, is at best an over-zealous exaggeration, at worst an error of Gnosticism and paganism.

ASH WEDNESDAY. The Wednesday after Quinquagesima Sunday, upon which begins the fast of Lent. It takes its name from the blessing and imposition of ashes (*q.v.*) peculiar to this day.

ASHES, THE BLESSING OF. After an antiphon, the officiating priest says four prayers, of which the first two ask for a blessing on the ashes, the third for compunction and the fourth for forgiveness for ourselves. The ashes are sprinkled with holy water and incensed, and then applied to the foreheads of the clergy and people with the words *Memento, homo, quia pulvis es et in pulverem reverteris:* "Remember, man, that thou art dust and to dust thou shalt return." Meanwhile appointed antiphons are sung, followed by a final short prayer. The ashes, made from the palms blessed on the previous Palm Sunday, symbolize the transience of human things, and the reception of them with humility is a sign of penance. Ashes or dust were significant of mourning among the Jews and have been used ritually in the Church from very early times, when they were sprinkled upon public sinners at the beginning of Lent. Blessed ashes are a sacramental. Ashes are also used in the consecration of a church. See ALPHABET.

ASPERGES, The. The ceremony of sprinkling the people with holy water before the principal Mass on Sundays. The celebrant sprinkles the altar, himself and his assistants, and then the laity, either from the quire-gates or passing down the church; meanwhile is said or sung the antiphon (from which the ceremony takes its name), *Asperges me, Domine, hyssopo et mundabor,* "Thou shalt sprinkle me with hyssop, O Lord, and I shall be cleansed," etc., followed by ver. 1 of Psalm l, *Gloria Patri* and the antiphon again. Returned to the altar, the celebrant sings versicles and a prayer asking that God's angel may "guard, cherish, protect, visit and defend" those present. The rite is at least as old as the 9th century and refers to the purified state in which we should assist at Mass. It is thus used only on Sundays, and during paschal-time the antiphons, etc., are replaced by *Vidi aquam.* It is used in the sick-room before all ministrations to the sick or dying, but not before a pontifical high Mass.

ASPERGILLUM. A short rod with a bunch of soft bristles or a perforated metal bulb at the end, used for sprinkling holy water on persons or things at the *Asperges* and blessings. Also called the *aspersorium* or *goupillon,* this last especially in France, it being commonly derived from *goupil,* a fox, from a supposed resemblance to or even use of the brush of that animal; there is little resemblance and the brush would be a very clumsy instrument; it probably comes from the same root as the English whip, wisp and wipe. A small branch of box, laurel or other shrub was the earlier usage, and is still seen in use occasionally (*cf.,* Hyssop).

ASPERSION. i. A valid but illicit (*q.v.*) manner of baptizing, *i.e,* by sprinkling the head with water. It was allowed in the Celtic church.

ii. Any sprinkling with holy water.

ASPIRATION (Lat., *aspirare,* to breathe). Literally, a prayer said in one breath, that is, an ejaculation (*q.v.*).

ASS, FEAST OF THE. A pseudo-liturgical development, taking its name from Balaam's ass, of a dramatic dialogue in church called *Processus Prophetarum,* in use at Paris, Beauvais, Sens, Laon, and other French churches, and of a celebration in memory of the ass which bore our Lady and the Holy Child into Egypt, on the day after the octave of the Epiphany. By the 13th century it had become a veritable abuse in such compositions as the Office of Pierre de Corbeil, and was put down with the assistance of a papal legate (*cf.,* The Feast of Fools and the Boy-bishop customs).

ASSENT. The judicial act of the mind which lies in the perception of the relation between subject and predicate; not to be confused with consent (*q.v.*), which is an act of the will. According to Cardinal Newman an assent to a proposition is real if the apprehension of the terms of the proposition is real, that is having "things" for its object; it is notional if the apprehension of the terms of the proposition is notional, that is having notions or abstractions for its object. In notional assent the mind contemplates its own creations instead of things; in real assent the mind is directed towards things represented by impressions which they have left on the imagination. The *assent of faith* is a true act of the intellect but under the command of the will.

ASSENT, EXTERNAL. i. A sensible act corresponding to the internal assent (*q.v.*), such as a confession of faith or the signing of a proposition. Sometimes this is demanded by ecclesiastical authority, *e.g.,* of one who is taking up an important office.

ii. May be opposed to internal assent and indicate the respectful silence which public order may demand of one who has grave reasons for doubting the truth of a non-infallible utterance of ecclesiastical authority.

ASSENT, INTERNAL. That act of the mind by which we accept a judgment or proposition as true. Such an act is necessitated by evidence internal or external, *i.e.,* by the clear manifestation of the truth to the mind, either by the apprehension of the terms of the proposition and their linking, or by authority. But it should also be made when doubt (*q.v.*) is obviously imprudent. Here there is room for the influence of the will. Truths of faith proposed by the infallible authority of the *magisterium,* actually exercising infallibility, demand absolute internal assent. But between this assent and doubt there are many grades of internal assent which may be demanded according to the circumstances of the pronouncement. Thus decisions of the Roman Congregations must commonly be met with internal assent; mere respectful silence is not sufficient, unless the subject is in a position to produce very grave reasons for such an attitude.

ASSESSOR. A cleric appointed to assist a judge in an ecclesiastical cause. He has no jurisdiction, nor is the judge bound to follow his advice. The assessor of a Roman congregation of which the pope himself is prefect is a prelate who arranges the work of the congregation and presents its reports to the pope. The similar official for a congregation having a cardinal prefect is called the secretary.

ASSISTANT AT THE PONTIFICAL THRONE. A member of the college of patriarchs (ex officio), archbishops and bishops who have been called by the pope to belong to the Papal Chapel. They rank after cardinals and in ceremonies are assigned a special place around the papal throne. When the pope lived at the Lateran palace they composed his court, and each assistant still receives the title "Count of the Apostolic Palace and Court of the Lateran."

ASSISTANT PRIEST. i. An assistant to a parish priest; a curate.

ii. The chief of the ministers of the bishop in pontifical functions. His principal duties are to hold open the books, indicate the place therein, carry the kiss of peace to the choir, etc. Abbots and protonotaries may have an assistant priest when they sing Mass pontifically, and one is permitted at the first Mass of a newly ordained priest celebrating solemnly and to certain regular prelates at high Mass, e.g., the minister general of the Friars Minor.

ASSOCIATION, RIGHT OF. An association or private society is formed within the state when several join together to attain as a common end the private advantage of the associates. The right to form such associations follows that natural impulse that man has to join himself with others as a necessary means to attain objects which without the collaboration of others would be impossible. The state is bound to protect natural rights, and unless the purposes of the association are evidently bad, unlawful or dangerous to the state, it cannot forbid their formation by the citizens; for both they and it exist in virtue of the like principle, namely, the natural tendency of man to live in society.

ASSOCIATION OF THE HOLY FAMILY, The. An active unenclosed institute of sisters founded at Bordeaux by the Abbé P. B. Noailles in 1820. It now consists of four separate branches: the Sisters of St. Joseph, who adopt and educate orphans; the Sisters of the Immaculate Conception (q.v. i); the Sisters of Hope, who nurse the sick; these all visit the sick poor in their homes; and the Solitary Sisters, who are enclosed and contemplative with perpetual adoration.

ASSOCIATIONS CULTUELLES (Fr., associations of worship). The Law of the Separation of Church and State published in France on Dec. 1, 1905, decreed that all churches and other ecclesiastical property connected with public worship should be put into the hands of associations cultuelles, to consist of from seven to twenty-five members, men or women, clerical or lay. The settlement of disputes was to lie with the council of state, which would be in a position to over-ride ecclesiastical authority. By an encyclical Gravissimo officii of Aug. 10, 1906, Pope Pius X forbade the formation of such associations cultuelles as being subversive of the divine constitution of the Church and calculated to lead to schism. The most important result of this and of subsequent laws is that the clergy have only the use of the church buildings and public worship is carried on therein on sufferance; they are esteemed the property of the state or of the local commune. However, in 1926 agreement was reached between the ecclesiastical and civil authorities for the establishment of corporate bodies, called Diocesan Associations, to help in the cost and maintenance of worship and for the administration of property which the Church might acquire in the future. These, unlike the associations cultuelles, are under the control of the bishop and conform to canon law. But the churches and other confiscated property have not yet been restored to these associations.

ASSOCIATIONS, PIOUS. Societies under direct ecclesiastical control formed with the approval of authority for the works of personal sanctification, charity, public worship, etc. They are usually divided into third orders (secular), confraternities and pious unions (qq.v.).

ASSUMPTION, The (Lat., assumere, to take to). i. The taking into Heaven of the soul and body of the Blessed Virgin Mary on the completion of her earthly life, by an anticipation of the general judgement (q.v.). After taking counsel with the whole Church through her bishops, Pope Pius XII in 1950 defined that the Assumption is divinely revealed; it is therefore now a dogma and article of faith (qq.v.). This of course does not mean that it is a "new dogma"; the Church teaches that this doctrine was implicit in the deposit of the faith (q.v.) from the beginning, and it has been held explicitly from early times; but until 1950 it was only a generally held belief, but one which it would have been impious and blasphemous to deny. It is generally held that our Lady died in the ordinary way of nature, and that the reunion of her body with her soul in Heaven took place shortly afterwards; her body was in any case preserved from corruption. It is uncertain whether our Lady died at Ephesus or Jerusalem.

ii. The feast of the Assumption is kept throughout the Church on Aug. 15 as a holiday of obligation. It is the principal of all our Lady's feasts and is the patronal festival of those churches dedicated in her honour without any qualification. It is also observed by the Orthodox and other dissident Eastern churches under the title of the Falling Asleep of the All-holy Mother of God.

ASSUMPTIONISTS. The common name of the Augustinians of the Assumption, also used of the Sisters, the Oblate Sisters and the Little Sisters of the Assumption (qq.v.).

ASSYRIAN CHURCH, The. A name first given to the Nestorian Church (q.v.) by the Anglican mission in Persia and Irak.

ASTERISK (Gr. star). An accessory used in the Byzantine liturgies, made of two pieces of metal crossed and bent into two semi-circles; a small star sometimes hangs from the intersection. It is placed over the *diskos* and serves to prevent the veil from touching the particles when the *diskos* is covered. A similar instrument is used to cover the paten when holy communion is brought to the pope at his throne when he celebrates pontifically.

ASTROLOGY. A pseudo-science which professes to judge the alleged occult influence of the stars upon human affairs. In the middle ages, Arabs and Jews were propagators of astrology, which began to be popular in the West after the Crusades. During the Renaissance period, Christendom was riddled with the superstition, which was believed in by popes, princes and peasants. It was eventually killed in Europe by the "Copernican system," but lingered on into the 18th century, and has had a popular revival in a crude form in our own day. In certain parts of England and Wales the name astrologer is popularly given to anyone reputed to have occult powers or knowledge. In ancient times astrology was far from being only a vulgar superstition: it had a definite part in science and philosophy and much of its subsequent popularity was due to Aristotle's theory that the movements of the stars are the efficient cause of earthly change.

ATHANASIAN CREED, The. An official statement of Christian doctrine principally in regard to the Holy Trinity and the Incarnation, probably composed during the life of St. Athanasius (d. 373) but not actually by him. It is sometimes called the *Quicumque vult* from its opening words. It has a place in the Latin liturgy, being said at

Prime on the feast of the Holy Trinity. Before the Office reforms that came into force in 1956 it was said more frequently.

ATHEISM (Gr., ἀ, not; θεός, God). The error of those who deny the existence of God. Practical atheism consists in living as if God were not. Speculative or theoretical atheism consists in the assertion that there is no God. It is probable that no one can in fact be a speculative atheist. The negation of God is rather in the heart than in the mind: "The fool hath said in his heart, there is no God" (Ps. xiii, 1).

ATHONITE. A monk (or other inhabitant) of Mount Athos (q.v.).

ATONEMENT, FRIARS OF THE. A branch of the third order regular of St. Francis, with its principal house at Graymoor, state of New York. It was founded as an organization of the Protestant Episcopal Church of the United States, together with nuns and tertiaries, the whole forming the "Society of the Atonement." In 1909 the society, led by its founder, Paul James Francis Watson, submitted as a body to the Holy See. Its organization was retained, the rule of the friars approximating to that of the Friars Minor, and after ordination Father Paul was appointed superior. The society works principally for the conversion of Protestants, publishing a journal called *The Lamp,* which has a large and influential circulation.

ATONEMENT, The. That act of reconciling (making "at-one") man to God, which Jesus Christ as mediator (q.v.) effected by his death for the redemption of man. This is the only theological term of English origin, but it is not used in all Catholic versions of the New Testament, e.g., in I John iv, 10.

ATTENTION. The act by which the mind, under the influence of the will, applies itself to one thing to the exclusion of others. A prayer may be so recited that mental distraction is excluded; this a case of internal attention. Material attention implies no more than a correct recital of the words; literal attention implies that the sense of the words is also observed. External attention excludes all obstacles to internal attention. To fulfil certain obligations, e.g., of hearing Mass, saying the Divine Office, external attention at the very least is required. But such obligations are imposed as means to ends, and for spiritual profit from such exercises it is necessary to strive after internal or true attention.

ATTRITION (Lat., *attritio,* a wearing-down by friction). Imperfect contrition (q.v.).

AUCOPOLITANUS. The Latin epithet for the bishop of Auckland in New Zealand.

AUDIENCE, PAPAL. In general, any reception accorded by the pope to an individual or group of individuals, from a Roman cardinal on business to a Spanish peasant on pilgrimage. Any stranger visiting Rome is enabled to pay a visit of respect and homage to the Father of Christendom. Private audiences are of course granted very sparingly, but public audiences, when a number of people are received together, are open to all. The usual procedure for those travelling "on their own" (as opposed to organized pilgrimages) is to present themselves, if possible with a letter of introduction, to the rector of the college of their nation in Rome, who makes the necessary arrangements. Non-Catholics, provided they are prepared to observe Catholic courtesies, are received equally with Catholics.

AUDITOR. An official who hears and draws up a record of an ecclesiastical cause, and reports to his superior; he cannot deliver judgment unless specially authorized. An auditor of the Rota (*q.v.*) is one of the college of judges of that tribunal. The Auditor of his Holiness is in charge of the department dealing with the appointment of bishops.

AUGUSTINE, RULE OF ST. St. Augustine of Hippo never drew up a detailed rule for the monastic life such as that of St. Benedict; his teaching on its general ascetic principles is found in several of his works, but especially in a certain letter addressed to a community of women in 423. St. Augustine's effect on the monastic life of the West is second only to that of St. Benedict, whose rule he influenced; and the rule of St. Augustine is the foundation of the constitutions, not only of the canons regular, but also of the Dominicans, the Trinitarians, the Mercedarians, the Knights Hospitallers and other orders. Chief among the few definite precepts of this rule are prayer in common and individual poverty—all personal property must be renounced before profession; its insistence on unity and charity in the practice of the common life makes it most adaptable to the various forms of religious life.

AUGUSTINIAN CANONS. See CANONS REGULAR OF ST. AUGUSTINE and OF THE LATERAN.

AUGUSTINIAN FRIARS. See HERMITS OF ST. AUGUSTINE.

AUGUSTINIAN NUNS. i. Nuns of the Order of Hermits of St. Augustine, whether directly subject to the Augustinian prior general, as are those of St. Rita's convent at Cascia, or under his special care, as those of St. Clare's convent at Montefalco and other Augustinian communities in Italy. They are enclosed and contemplative. Three congregations exist in Spain.

ii. Several other congregations are so referred to: the Augustinian Sisters of Meaux, the Augustinian Sisters of Penance, Sisters of St. Augustine, etc., some of which have houses in Great Britain and the United States.

AUGUSTINIAN RECOLLECTS. See HERMITS OF ST. AUGUSTINE (*c*).

AUGUSTINIANS OF THE ASSUMPTION, The. A religious congregation founded at Nimes in 1845 by the Abbé Emmanuel d'Alzon for the spreading of the Faith. It has missions in Africa, but its principal missionary work is in the Near East; it has seminaries, colleges, schools and churches of both the Latin and Byzantine rites in Turkey, Rumania and Bulgaria. It conducts a hospice for pilgrims at Jerusalem and the initiative of conveying large numbers of sick to Lourdes was first taken by it. There are organizations with schools and colleges in France, Belgium, the United States, Chili, England, and elsewhere. The congregation controls La Bonne Presse, a publishing house which produces annuals, periodicals, newspapers and books of value at all levels. This powerful congregation was particularly obnoxious to the French government and was the first to feel the full force of suppression in 1900, but it is now re-established in that country. It has over 1000 members. They recite the Divine Office in choir and maintain in their communities those Augustinian observances that are compatible with an active life of work for souls. Habit: wide-sleeved tunic, leather belt, cape and hood, all black.

AUGUSTINISM. The system of the doctrine of grace (*q.v.*) formulated by St. Augustine, bishop of Hippo (354–430). The essentials of the doctrine are the universal necessity of divine grace in every act that tends to salvation, the reality of the guilt of original sin, the divine election and predestination (*qq.v.*), but at the same time the complete liberty of the human will, and the reconciliation of these apparently conflicting doctrines. The name is sometimes wrongly applied to such doctrines as Predestinarianism (*q.v.*) for which their authors sought the protection of St. Augustine's name.

AUGUSTINUS, The. A posthumous work of Nicholas Jansen, published in 1640, wherein he claimed to expound St. Augustine's doctrine of grace. His theses were in 1649 summed up in five propositions which Pope Innocent X condemned in 1653; the Jansenists continued obstinately to maintain that these propositions were not to be found in the "Augustinus."

AUMBRY. A mediæval word meaning a cupboard, particularly one for keeping books. Aumbries are also receptacles made in the thickness of the wall of a church or sacristy to contain the holy oils, relics, sacred vessels, etc.

AUREOLE (Lat., golden). i. The gilt completely surrounding (often in *vesica* shape) figures of the three divine Persons, of our Lady, etc., in religious pictures, representing the glory attaching to those persons. It is the origin of the brass or plaster "rays" put around or behind statues and must be distinguished from the nimbus or halo (*q.v.*).

ii. In theology, a distinguishing reward given in Heaven to those who have contended heroically, *e.g.*, martyrs, virgins.

AURICULAR CONFESSION (Lat., *auris*, ear). Private personal confession, made "to the ear" of the confessor, as distinct from a public or open confession, or one that is made by several persons together in general terms. For confession to be auricular it is not necessary that it be spoken; for a good reason the sins may be written down and handed to the confessor saying that one accuses oneself of them. But confession by letter or by telephone is invalid, since the penitent must be present validly to receive the sacrament of Penance.

AURIPHRYGIATUS, AURIPHRYGIUS. Latin adjective meaning gold-embroidered; it has become the English word *orphrey* (*q.v.*).

AURORA, MASS OF THE (Lat., *aurora*, dawn). The name given to the second Mass of Christmas day, intended to be sung at dawn.

AUSTERITY. The practice of bodily mortifications and penances of any sort, or those mortifications themselves: it must be distinguished from asceticism (*q.v.*). Austerity is not an end in itself, practised for its own sake, but a means (necessary, but in very varying degrees) of advancement in virtue towards Christian perfection; austerity which does not tend to this end, or even retards it, is a vain and blameworthy observance. The practice of physical austerity is normally at the discretion of the individual (guided by his confessor), but a certain degree is imposed by the Church (fasting, abstinence). So far as imposed austerity is concerned the Eastern churches, Catholic or dissident, are (except in the matter of clerical celibacy) more severe than the Western church; especially in the monasteries, the fasts are most severe, but the observance of them among lay-people is not now always strict.

AUSTIN. An English abbreviation of Augustine, whence Austin Friars, Austin Canons, etc. (*cf.*, the street in the city of London where the first formerly had a friary).

AUSTRALIA, THE CHURCH IN. The first Mass was said in Australia by the Rev. James Dixon, a priest deported from Ireland, in 1803, but there was no freedom or progress for the Church until the arrival of Dom Bernard Ullathorne, O.S.B. (afterwards bishop of Birmingham), in 1833. In 1835 a vicar apostolic was appointed, and a regular hierarchy set up in 1842. The church now consists of 7 archdioceses with 17 suffragan sees, and 2 vicariates apostolic and a Benedictine abbey-*nullius* for missionary work among the aboriginal natives, New Norcia. The archbishoprics are Sydney, Adelaide, Brisbane, Melbourne, Perth, and Hobart. The faithful number about 1¼ million, in a population of 8 million. There is a delegate apostolic at Sydney for Australasia. All religions are now on an equal footing.

AUSTRIA, THE CHURCH IN. Population (in 1939) 7 million, of whom 90 per cent are Catholics, but many only nominally. Freedom for all religions is a fundamental law of the state. Salzburg is the primatial see, with one other metropolitan see (Vienna), 5 bishoprics and a Cistercian abbacy *nullius*. After March 1938 persecution of the Church by the nazis was second in intensity only to that of the Jews; from this ordeal Austrian Catholics seem to have come out purified and strengthened, and the former unhealthy tendency to a "tie-up" between churchmen and a particular political party is now at an end: but owing to the general political situation the outlook for the future is most dubious.

AUTHENTIC. In ordinary use the word authentic means genuine. But, commonly qualifying such words as edition or text, it may mean simply having a special authority and authorized for the use of the faithful; in this sense it is almost synonymous with "official." Thus the Vulgate (*q.v.*) is the authentic Latin version of the Holy Scriptures. This use of the word implies no guarantee of complete accuracy or inerrancy, but that it is substantially identical with the original.

AUTHENTICATION OF RELICS. Only those relics may be honoured with public veneration in churches which are approved as genuine by an authentic document of a cardinal, or the bishop of the diocese, or some other person to whom the faculty of authenticating relics has been granted by a papal indult. This authentication is not a guarantee of genuineness; it simply implies that it is not clearly spurious and that there is no substantial reason of which the authenticating person is aware why it should not be venerated.

AUTHORITY. An extrinsic criterion of truth. If the mind assents to a truth because it is forced to do so by the intrinsic evidence of the truth itself the assent is a *vision*, and is opposed to that adhesion of the mind to some truth because of the credibility of a master. The latter criterion is therefore extrinsic to the truth itself and it is called authority. Owing to this, to assent to a truth on authority is always a free act and so partly an act of the will—whereas vision is purely an act of mind and is not within our power of choice. Two qualities are essential in the master, namely, knowledge and veracity, and of these the mind must have no doubt. It follows that to assent to a truth because God has said it is to have attained metaphysical certitude.

AUTHORITY, CIVIL. The power wielded by the state (q.v.) over its constituent members in the pursuance of its end, supported when necessary by physical coercion. It is the natural means to the natural end of the state, and therefore comes from God. Most Catholic writers regard this authority as conferred immediately by God upon the state in such a way that its members may choose how it shall be exercised, viz., either by one, by a few, or by all of its members (monarchy, oligarchy, or democracy, q.v.), or by a combination of these (e.g., constitutional monarchy). Hobbes, Locke and Rousseau erroneously held that civil authority comes, not from God, but from the people consenting to delegate authority over them to one or more of their members; they thus confused the source of civil authority with its method of application. Since the state is a necessary society, juridically perfect in its own order, having for its end the complete temporal good of the individuals and families composing it, it has supreme authority in its own sphere, but must not act contrary to the natural or divine law, or encroach on the sphere of the Church's authority in spiritual matters.

AUTHORITY, ECCLESIASTICAL. The Church, as a perfect society, sovereign and independent, has supreme spiritual authority over her members, legislative, judicial and executive, by divine law. Her authority is independent of the civil authority of the state, and is of a higher order. Though instituted for a spiritual end, the Church has the right to use material and temporal means to secure that end, and in the use of such means as are necessary she has exclusive authority. The Church's authority, whether doctrinal or disciplinary, is in an ultimate analysis the authority of Jesus Christ himself and is exercised in his name by the "descendants" of the apostles as his ministers. And therefore this authority "secures the liberty of the individual Christian, by its impersonal and extra-personal character. It protects that liberty from the spiritual domination and claims to mediatorship of alleged leading personalities and sets Christ and the believer in direct contact with each other" (Karl Adam). Nor is it to be supposed that the Catholic has any more love for the principle of authority than others of the sons of Adam: but faith and reason telling him the profound and unassailable source and nature of true ecclesiastical authority, his

will is the more readily moved to compliance therewith.

AUTHORITY OF THE DIVINE OFFICE. The Divine Office cannot contain anything contrary to faith or morals, but neither is one bound to believe on its authority an historical statement contained therein, e.g., in the historical lessons (q.v.) of the second nocturn of Matins.

AUTHORITY OF PAPAL ACTS. Decrees and decisions of the Holy See, whether of the pope in person or of the Roman congregations, tribunals and offices (qq.v.), are to be accepted and obeyed by those for whom they are intended and to whom they are promulgated. Those acts of the Holy See which contain doctrinal teaching are to be received with internal assent, and not merely with external submission. All papal acts and decrees, including those of the Roman Curia, become binding immediately on publication in the Acta Apostolicæ Sedis, if no special date is fixed, and without need of episcopal promulgation, unless this is specially prescribed.

AUTHORITY OF PARENTS. Parents have by the law of nature such authority over the persons of their children as is necessary adequately to fulfil their obligation of caring for them until they can provide for themselves. In English law this is defined as a right of custody belonging to the father and the mother equally until the child shall be twenty-one years old or shall have married; but this right must not be exercised arbitrarily. The parent may use reasonable physical coercion to make his authority effective. In canon law his consent is not necessary to the validity, or even to the lawfulness, of the marriage of a child who has reached the canonical age (16 for a boy, 14 for a girl). Parental authority does not extend to any rights over the separate property of a child.

AUTHORITY OF SCRIPTURE, The, meaning of the Holy Bible (q.v.) is plenary and absolute, being the written word of God. The interpretation of the Scripture and promulgation of its authority is reserved to the teaching body of the Church as successors of the Apostles, to whom it was first committed. Its authority is equal with that of sacred Tradition, and there can be no conflict between them, as both consist of divinely guaranteed and revealed truths (cf., Inspiration).

AUTHORITY OF TRADITION. It is an article of faith from a decree of the Vatican Council that Tradition (q.v.) is a source of theological teaching distinct from Scripture, and that it is infallible. It is therefore to be received with the same internal assent as Scripture, for it is the word of God. Whereas much of the teaching of Scripture could not be determined without Tradition,

Tradition would suffice without Scripture; it is the safeguard of Scripture.

AUTHORIZED VERSION. The version of the Bible ordered to be made by King James I and published in 1611, based mainly on the so-called Bishops' Bible of Parker (1568) and modified by the use of Tyndale's, Coverdale's, Matthew's, Whitchurch's, the Geneva and the Rheims-Douay versions. It is the official English translation used in churches of the Anglican communion and favoured by English-speaking Protestants throughout the world.

AUTO DE FÉ (Sp., Port., *auto da fé*, act of faith). An assembly of the Spanish Inquisition (*q.v.*) at which those who wished to abjure their errors made a public recantation ("act of faith"); penances were imposed by the inquisitors, and they were reconciled to the Church. Those present who refused to recant were judged to be handed over ("relaxed") to the civil authority for sentence and punishment, which was carried out separately from the *auto de fé* and without ecclesiastical assistance.

AUTOCEPHALOUS CHURCH. A church whose chief bishop acknowledges the authority and jurisdiction of no other bishop over himself, so that he is the primate of an independent church. The term is used of the separate national churches which together make up the Eastern Orthodox Church. There has been an important increase in the number of these independent Orthodox churches in the past 100 years.

AVARICE. The inordinate love of wealth. It is in itself a venial sin, but a dangerous one because it so soon takes possession of a man and leads him into other and grievous sins. This is especially so at the present day when there are many unjust ways of becoming rich and when the possession of wealth gives so much power and worldly honour. St. Paul calls it "the root of all evil things" (1 Tim. vi, 10).

AVE MARIA. The first words of the Hail Mary (*q.v.*) in Latin, which runs: *Ave Maria, gratia plena; Dominus tecum: benedicta tu in mulieribus, et benedictus fructus ventris tui Iesus. Sancta Maria, mater Dei, ora pro nobis peccatoribus, nunc et in hora mortis nostræ. Amen.* The "*Ave* bell" is the bell rung for the Angelus (*q.v.*)

AVE REGINA CŒLORUM (Lat., Hail, Queen of the Heavens). The first line and title of the second of the antiphons of our Lady (*q.v.*). It is said or sung after the Divine Office from Compline of the feast of the Purification (Feb. 2) until Maundy Thursday, exclusive.

AVERROISM. The following by a school of Christian philosophers of the interpretation by Averröes (Mohammed ibn Roschd, 1126–98) of aristotelian thought. It involved the affirmation of the eternity of the world and the numerical unity of the intellectual soul in all men, and the denial of providence; and taught that philosophy was the supreme study of life, religion and its symbolic truths being only for the multitude. Averroism was condemned by the bishop of Paris in 1270.

AVIGNON POPES, The. i. Those legitimate popes, from Clement V (1305) to Gregory XI (1370), seven in all, who governed the Church from Avignon instead of Rome. They were all Frenchmen and the preponderating French influence of the papacy and the confusion in Rome and Italy that resulted were predetermining causes of the Schism of the West (*q.v.*).
ii. The Clementine as opposed to the Urbanist and Pisan (*qq.v.*) claimants to the papal throne during that schism.

AZYME (Gr., unleavened). A name given to the unleavened bread used in the Mass by the Western church. The Catholic Church has always taught that the use of either leavened or unleavened bread is valid in the Holy Sacrifice and, though it is the law of the Latin rite that unleavened bread be used, Catholics of most of the Oriental rites use it leavened, as was done originally at Rome. See BREAD, EUCHARISTIC.

AZYMES, FEAST OF THE (Exodus xii; Mark xiv, 1; Acts xii, 3). The Jewish feast of the Passover, during which unleavened (*azyme*) bread alone was eaten.

AZYMITES. A term of abuse for Christians of the Latin rite invented after 1053 by the Byzantines, the patriarch Michael Cerularius having made the use of *azyme* (the contrary being the Byzantine custom) one of his grievances against Rome.

B

BABINGTON CONSPIRACY, The. A plot, in 1586, to assassinate Queen Elizabeth and put Mary Queen of Scots on the throne, named from Francis Babington, one of the Catholic gentlemen concerned. It was to some extent fomented by the *agents provocateurs* of Walsingham, the minister of Elizabeth, who wished to implicate Mary Queen of

Scots in order to have excuse for her execution, she being heir presumptive and a Catholic. His object was attained, for the discovery of the plot frightened Elizabeth, who ceased to stand between her ministers and her cousin. It does not seem possible to exculpate Mary from complicity in the proposed murder of Elizabeth.

BABYLON, THE PATRIARCH OF, governs the Catholics of the Chaldean Rite. He is the Patriarch-Katholikos of Babylon of the Chaldees, resides at Mosul and has jurisdiction over the faithful of his rite throughout the world. The patriarch is elected by the synod of bishops, under the presidency of the apostolic delegate to Mesopotamia. The pope confirms the election and sends the *pallium*. The patriarch must make a profession of faith and of obedience to the Holy See and make a visit *ad limina* every ten years; he has vicars patriarchal for Egypt, Syria and elsewhere. The patriarchate dates from 1551; since 1834 the patriarchs have represented the original line of Nestorian *katholikoi*.

"BABYLONISH CAPTIVITY." A term, first used seemingly by Petrarch, for the exile of seven popes from Rome to Avignon, Clement V (1305) to Gregory XI (1370), in reference to the great exile of the Jews in Babylonia, 599–87 to 536 B.C.

BACHELOR. i. It is not necessary in the Western church that one promoted to the subdiaconate, diaconate or priesthood should be a bachelor. He may be a widower or a married man whose wife is professed in an order having solemn vows. But a married man who receives orders in good faith, but without a dispensation from the Holy See, may not exercise them. In the Eastern churches, both Catholic and dissident, the man ordained while a bachelor must remain unmarried.
ii. Bachelor is the lowest university degree in any faculty. In this sense the word is perhaps derived from Lat. *baccalaureus,* a corruption of *bacca lauri,* laurel berry, laurel being the emblem of distinction.

BAD FAITH. While anyone who acts against the dictates of conscience may be said to act in bad faith, the term is ordinarily restricted to those who, though convinced of the truth of the Church's teaching, remain outside her fold, and also to those in possession of property which they know to be another's. The possessor in bad faith of another's property is bound to restore it to the rightful owner, together with any gains which would naturally have accrued to him had it been left in his possession (but any gains which are due to his own industry he is justified in keeping); further, the possessor in bad faith is bound to repair whatever harm he foresaw would be caused to the true owner through his loss.

BALADITES (Ar., natives, rustics). Members of a Maronite congregation of Antonian monks, and of a Melkite congregation of Basilians.

BALDACCHINO (It., *Baldacco,* Bagdad, its place of origin). A canopy, suspended from the ceiling or attached to the wall in such a manner that it covers the altar. It may be of any material and should be ornamented with tapestry or other fabric. If there is a ciborium (*q.v.*), the baldacchino is not required. The necessity of one or the other is laid down in the "Ceremonial of Bishops" and the S.R.C. does not confine the requirement to high-altars and those where the Blessed Sacrament is reserved. When an altar is covered by a baldacchino or ciborium no smaller canopy is required for exposition and benediction of the Blessed Sacrament.

BALDAQUIN. The French and Spanish forms of the word *baldacchino* (*q.v.*), sometimes anglicized as "baldachin."

BALM, BALSAM. A fragrant, viscous fluid obtained from certain trees and plants, of which some is mixed with olive oil to make chrism. At the blessing of chrism in cathedral-churches on Maundy Thursday the balm is carried by a subdeacon in the procession after the ablution and is blessed by the bishop and mixed with a little oil before being poured into the oil of chrism after the exorcism and blessing. The balm itself is symbolical of the good odour of Christ, and mixing it with oil the union of the divine and human natures. In the Eastern churches several varieties of balm and other ingredients are used.

BALTIMORE (*Baltimorensis*). The oldest diocese in the United States, whose archbishop has perpetual precedence among the bishops of that country. In 1784 John Carroll, as prefect apostolic of the United States, made his residence at Baltimore, and became its first bishop when the diocese was set up in 1789. The see was made metropolitan in 1808, when its area was much reduced; its suffragan dioceses are Charleston, Raleigh, Richmond, Saint Augustine, Savannah and Atlanta, Wheeling and Wilmington. The archdiocese covers Maryland west of Chesapeake Bay. In the cathedral of the Assumption met three plenary councils of the American church (1852, 1866, 1884), and ten provincial synods have been held there. Among its bishops have been F. P. Kenrick, M. J Spalding and Cardinal James Gibbons. Baltimore is named from the Catholic founder of Maryland, Cecil Calvert, second Baron Baltimore.

BAMBINO (It., baby). A name often given to the image of the Holy Child in the Christmas crib, and to other similar images, such as that of the Child Jesus in the church of Ara Cœli, at Rome.

BANGOR, THE USE OF. The mediæval use of the Roman liturgy used in the diocese of Bangor and elsewhere in Wales before the Reformation.

BANKRUPTCY AND RESTITUTION. A bankrupt who has honestly complied with the formalities required by law and obtains an absolute discharge is at liberty to regard himself as free from his debts in conscience as well as in law.

BANNABIKIRA (Luganda "Daughters of Mary"). A congregation of African sisters founded in Uganda for the equatorial missions of the White Fathers by Archbishop Henry Streicher in 1909. Their work is religious instruction, teaching, nursing, etc. Black habit with blue veil; bare feet. This is one of the most flourishing congregations of indigeneous sisters in the foreign missions, and numbers over 400 members.

BANNERS. The carrying of banners, especially those of confraternities and guilds in processions, is a custom that grew in popularity in the middle ages. There is nothing to forbid departures from the general shape now in use, but the "Rituale Romanum" forbids them to be of a military or triangular form. Banners and flags may be blessed and admitted into a church if they are not those of an anti-Christian or condemned society and do not bear any forbidden or inappropriate device, but they may not be put inside the sanctuary or other place from which the laity are excluded during sacred services.

BANNS OF MARRIAGE (Lat., *bannum* from Teut., *bann*, a proclamation). The public ecclesiastical announcement of the names of persons intending marriage. The object of their publication is to discover impediments (*q.v.*), to avoid secret marriages, and to give interested parties an opportunity to intervene if they wish to do so. Banns must be published in the parish church of each place where the parties live, and also in other places if there is reason to suspect undisclosed impediments. Publication is made by reading out the names on three successive Sundays or holidays of obligation during Mass or any other service attended by a number of people, or they may, by permission of the ordinary, be posted on the notice board at the church door. If a person hearing the publication knows of an impediment, he is bound in conscience to reveal it to the clergy concerned. In a mixed marriage (*q.v.*) banns must not be published unless, for some reason, the bishop thinks it desirable. Publication of banns may be dispensed for a good reason.

BAPTISM, CEREMONIES OF. For valid Baptism it is necessary that ordinary water of any sort be applied to the person to be baptized in such a manner that it flows upon his head; it may be applied by infusion, immersion or aspersion (*q.v.*); one application of the water is sufficient for validity. At the same time must be pronounced, in any language and with the requisite intention, the words "I baptize thee (or 'This person is baptized') in the name of the Father and of the Son and of the Holy Ghost."

i. In the Western church, Baptism may only be lawfully conferred by infusion, and there should be three distinct pourings. At the solemn baptism of a child, it is first exorcized, signed with the cross and salt is administered ("the salt of wisdom" and a figure of heavenly nutriment); then, after another exorcism and a prayer, the child is taken into the church or baptistery, priest and sponsors reciting the Apostles' Creed and Our Father. After a third exorcism, the *ephphetha* (*q.v.*), and renunciations on behalf of the child, it is anointed with the oil of catechumens, and the sponsor makes affirmations of belief. The baptism proper follows, after which the child is anointed on the head with chrism, receives a white robe and lighted candle, and is dismissed in peace. The child throughout is called by its chosen Christian name, but there is no naming ceremony.

ii. In the Eastern churches. In all Eastern rites Baptism is by a triple immersion except that the Armenians, Syrians and Melkites combine a semi-immersion with infusion. It is followed immediately by Confirmation administered by the priest and among the dissident Armenians and Copts by holy communion under the species of wine. They all use anointings, except the Armenians who put a little chrism into the water. The Chaldean ceremony is notably modelled on the eucharistic liturgy. For the most part Catholics follow the same usages as the dissidents of their rite, but the communion of infants is forbidden, and the Maronites, Malabarese and Italo-Greeks have separated Confirmation from Baptism. The first two baptize just as in the Latin rite. A child is baptized in the rite of its father or of its Catholic parent (*e.g.*, in the case of a Latin Catholic woman married to a dissident Orthodox man).

BAPTISM, CONDITIONAL. Baptism may be given conditionally in certain circumstances if there is a serious doubt whether the baptism can be validly administered, and the doubt cannot be settled, *e.g.*, in the case of persons in danger of death and unconscious, and in the case of those who *may* have been already validly baptized. Conditional baptism is given privately with holy water, without the usual ceremonies. These should afterwards be supplied, except in the case of adult converts; these last are usually conditionally baptized in Great Britain and provide the commonest example of the practice.

BAPTISM, LAY. A lay person can baptize validly and in case of emergency (*e.g.*, when an unbaptized person is dying and no cleric can be obtained) is bound to do so. Anybody—man, woman, child, Catholic, Protestant, Jew—may do it, provided there is the intention to do what the Church does when baptizing, that the water is poured on the head of the person to be baptized, and that the requisite words—"I baptize thee in the name of the Father and of the Son and of the Holy Ghost"—are said at the same time. Though the sacrament is validly administered, it is gravely illicit for a lay person to baptize in other than cases of necessity. Midwives are required by canon law to know how to baptize in case of necessity.

BAPTISM, THE SACRAMENT OF (Gr. βαπτισμός, dipping in water). A sacrament (*q.v.*) of the New Law instituted by Jesus Christ, in which, as a result of washing with water accompanied by the words "I baptize thee in the name of the Father and of the Son and of the Holy Ghost," a human being is spiritually regenerated, and made capable of receiving the other sacraments. It imprints a "character" (*q.v.*) on the soul and admits the recipient to membership in the Catholic Church of Christ. The matter of baptism is natural water (remote) and its application so as to flow on the head (proximate); the form is the above or similar words (*e.g.*, in the Byzantine rite "The servant of God N., is baptized in," etc.). The ordinary minister is a priest but baptism by a lay person is valid (see BAPTISM, LAY). By it a child or adult is united to the visible body of the Church (by whomsoever the baptism was administered) and so remains until he performs any act (*e.g.*, adherence to a non-Catholic body) which involves his exclusion therefrom. Baptism by water, blood or desire (*qq.v*) is necessary to salvation.

BAPTISM OF BELLS. The rite for the blessing of a bell in the "Pontificale Romanum" is so elaborate that popular usage has improperly given to it the name of "baptism." It consists of the recitation of psalms, washing of the bell with holy water, anointing with oil of the sick and with chrism, putting a smoking thurible inside it, and reading the gospel of Luke x, 38-42. It is also given a name and has "god-parents."

BAPTISM OF CHILDREN OF NON-CATHOLICS may be lawfully performed, even if the parents object, provided the child is in danger of death and it can be prudently foreseen that it will die before attaining the use of reason. Outside this danger, children may be baptized if their Catholic upbringing can be guaranteed, and then only with the consent of at least one of the parents or guardians, if any, unless they have forfeited or cannot exercise their rights over the child.

BAPTISM OF THE INSANE may be lawfully performed if such a desire has been expressed in a lucid interval, or in imminent danger of death if, before losing reason, a desire had been manifested. Those who have been insane from birth, or since before attaining the use of reason, may at any time be baptized as infants.

BAPTISM OF THE UNBORN. If there is not a probable hope that a child can be baptized after birth, Baptism may be administered in the womb: in the case of a head presentation, on the head; in other presentations on the part presented, but then it has to be again baptized conditionally if it is living on complete delivery. Should the mother die in labour, the child is to be extracted from the womb and, if certainly living, baptized absolutely; if life is doubtful, conditionally. An aborted fœtus must also be baptized, unconditionally or conditionally according to circumstances.

BAPTISMAL GARMENT. The white robe, formerly worn by the newly baptized (*cf.*, Dominica in Albis, Low Sunday). Its place is now taken by a linen cloth, laid on the child's head with the words, "Receive this white garment, which thou shalt carry stainless before the judgement-seat of our Lord Jesus Christ that thou mayest have everlasting life." This cloth was sometimes termed a *chrismal*, and the expression "chrisom child" for one newly baptized is still occasionally used.

BAPTISMAL NAME. There is no obligation that the name given at Baptism should be that of a saint, but the Code of Canon Law requires that it be a Christian name, *e.g.*, Stella (Maris). The "Rituale Romanum" directs the priest to see that obscene, mythical and ridiculous names or those of false gods or heathen heroes be not given. Such a name as Achilles, common in Italy (*cf.*, Pope Pius XI, Achille Ratti) is made respectable by the martyr of that name. Fancy names are condemned by good sense and Christian tradition rather than by the law. It is a common custom to receive the name of the saint on whose day one was born.

BAPTISMAL REGENERATION. One of the effects of Baptism is our birth to the supernatural order (*q.v.*): "Unless a man be *born again* of water and the Holy Ghost . . ." (John iii, 5). Baptismal regeneration means that owing to the removal of sin by the sacrament and the infusion of first grace, the subject who has begun to live to nature now begins to live supernaturally. St. Paul speaks of Baptism as cleansing us, "giving us new birth" (Titus iii, 5).

BAPTISMAL VOWS is the name given to the renunciation of Satan, his works and his pomps made by the person to be baptized, or by his sponsors, at Baptism. They are, in fact, not vows but a promise. The solemn renewal of this promise is made publicly in common before Mass on Easter eve, and often at the end of a mission or retreat.

BAPTISMAL WATER. For the valid administration of Baptism, any sort of ordinary natural water may be used, fresh, salt, warm, cold, clean, dirty. But at least in solemn Baptism the water specially blessed for the purpose on Easter eve should be used. This special water may not be used for conditional Baptism.

BAPTIST. One who baptizes, "The Baptizer," and so used as an epithet for the first St. John (Luke iii, 1–22; vii, 28). In the East, however, he is commonly called The Forerunner (in Greek, *Prodromos*).

BAPTISTERY. i. A building set apart for the administration of the sacrament of Baptism. Many such buildings, the erection of which was common in earlier ages, are still in use, notably the one adjoining the Lateran basilica at Rome. There is no reason why separate baptisteries should not still be built.

ii. That part of a church containing the font and set apart for baptism. It should be a separate chapel, or at least railed off and the gate kept locked, and contain if possible a picture of the baptism of our Lord by St. John; its floor should be at least one step *below* the level of the church floor. After the high altar, the baptistery is the most important and sacred part of a church.

BAPTISTS, The. An important Protestant sect, first organized at the beginning of the 17th century. The Bible is their sole rule of faith and every individual has personal liberty of interpretation. They are named from the fact that they deny that infant baptism is a practice warranted by the Scriptures and since about 1640 they have denied the validity of any baptism except by the total immersion of adults, which is administered when the individual is aware and gives evidence of "conversion." They were early divided into Arminian and Calvinistic or "Particular" Baptists and also into the "open communion" sect which admitted non-Baptists to the Lord's Supper and the "close communion" which did not (now united). Their devotion to the person of our Lord and belief in the redemptive power of the Precious Blood is most edifying to all who have experienced it. *cf.*, Nonconformity.

BARNABITES, The. The popular name of the congregation of Clerks Regular of St. Paul, founded by St. Antony Mary Zaccaria in 1530 "to regenerate and revive love of divine worship and a properly Christian way of life by frequent preaching and faithful administration of the sacraments" in Lombardy. Their work is preaching, catechizing, giving missions, etc., with special reference to the epistles of St. Paul. They take the usual three vows of religion plus a fourth, not to seek positions of dignity nor to accept them except by order of the Holy See. The habit is a black cassock. They are not represented in Great Britain, Ireland or the U. S. A.

BAROQUE (Fr. from Span. *barrueco*, rough pearl). A flamboyant form of renaissance architecture in use during the 17th and 18th centuries; *e.g.*, San Carlo alle Quattro Fontane, Sant' Andrea del Quirinale, Santa Maria della Vittoria and many others at Rome, Santa Maria della Salute at Venice, Gesù Nuovo at Naples, the seminary church at Salamanca, Karlskirche at Vienna, Ignazkirche at Mainz.

BARTHOLOMEW, ST. Apostle, generally identified also with the Nathanael of St. John's Gospel, whose feast is kept by the Western church on Aug. 24. Nothing certain is known of his life; the tradition that he preached the gospel in Asia as far as India (some sought to identify him with the evangelizer of the St. Thomas Christians, *q.v.*), and suffered martyrdom in Armenia is quite unreliable. He is named in the canon of the Mass.

BARUCH (Heb., blessed). A deutero-canonical (*q.v.*) book of the Old Testament, taking its name from its traditional author, a disciple of Jeremias. It consists of confession of sins, a prayer for mercy, and exhortations first to righteousness and then to rejoicing. The last chapter is the letter of Jeremias. The sixth Prophecy on Holy Saturday (fifth on Whitsun Eve) is taken from Baruch iii.

BASIL, LITURGY OF ST. The Church of Constantinople had a liturgy of its own, derived from Antioch through Cæsarea, said to have been shortened and "edited" by St. Basil (*d.* 379); it was further modified by St. John Chrysostom and in that form was adopted by all the Orthodox churches. The original liturgy of St. Basil is still used both by Catholics and dissidents of the Byzantine rite on the Sundays of Lent (except Palm Sunday), Holy Thursday, Holy Saturday, the vigils of Christmas and the Epiphany, and on St. Basil's feast (Jan. 1). Its ceremonies differ not at all from those of St. John Chrysostom (*q.v.*); the chief differences in the text of the prayers are in those for the catechumens and the faithful, after the great entrance, and the whole of the *anaphora*.

BASIL, THE RULE OF ST., was drawn up for the use of his monastery in Pontus, in the form of questions and answers. They deal, in the main, with the virtues and vices, and aim at the inculcation of the religious spirit, obedience, poverty, contempt of the world; the rule was not legislative but supplementary to the way of life which was being actually pursued in his monastery.

The text of the rule makes much use of the words of Holy Scripture.

BASILIANS. i. A convenient designation for monks of Eastern rites in general, but inaccurate and one which they repudiate themselves. They profess no rule and there are no orders or congregations; each monastery has its own constitutions, and the life is what would be called in the West strictly contemplative: they sing very long offices, have long fasts, and undertake no outside work; many of them are not ordained, but no distinction is made in monastic status in consequence. They regard St. Basil as their patriarch rather than as a law-giver. Except among the Studites (*q.v.*) Catholic monasteries of men have all departed, in a greater or lesser degree, from traditional Eastern monachism in various important respects. And the Studites, as well as the Ruthenian (*q.v.*) Basilians referred to below, are now dispersed through the occupation of eastern Poland by the U.S.S.R. See also GROTTA-FERRATA.

ii. There are four congregations of Catholic Basilians more strictly so called; three are Melkite (the Baladite Shuwairites, the Aleppine Shuwairites, the Salvatorians) and one Ruthenian, called "of St. Josaphat." They have all, but particularly the last named, come under Western influence, and are organized with abbots-general (*protohegumenoi*), provincials, chapters, constitutions, etc. The life of the Ruthenian congregation is more that of clerks regular than of monks; they direct the Ruthenian college at Rome and have missions in Brazil, the United States and Canada. Their habit is a black tunic with cloth belt and *mandyas*. There is also a number of Ruthenian Basilian nuns in Europe and the United States. A large proportion of the hieromonks (*q.v.*) of the Melkite Basilians, who wear the regular Eastern dress, are engaged in parish work. There are also nuns in their congregations.

iii. A congregation of priests founded in 1800 by Mgr. d'Avian, archbishop of Vienne, to educate young men and prepare aspirants for the priesthood. They are now chiefly established in Canada.

iv. There was founded in 1559 a Spanish congregation of monks following the rule of St. Basil. It is now extinct.

BASILICA (Gr., royal). i. A name given primarily to certain ancient churches of Rome and elsewhere (*e.g.*, Bethlehem, Ravenna) which were built in the 4th century and later in a form chiefly derived from that of Roman public and private halls. The church was approached through a portico, beyond which was an open space with colonnades around it (the *atrium*) and on the far side an ante-room or *narthex;* the church itself was usually divided by columns into a nave and two aisles, with an apse at the end

with the altar at its opening and the bishop's throne against the wall beyond; on the near side of the altar were the *schola cantorum* and ambones (*qq.v.*).

ii. The greater or patriarchal basilicas at Rome are St. John Lateran, the archbasilica for the patriarch of the West (the pope); St. Peter's, for the patriarch of Constantinople; St. Paul's-outside-the-Walls, for the patriarch of Alexandria; and St. Mary Major's for the patriarch of Antioch. St. Lawrence's-outside-the-Walls is patriarchal for Jerusalem but is not always accounted major. Adjoining these churches were formerly residences for the respective patriarchs when in Rome. Each of the greater basilicas has an altar for the pope which none other may use without his permission. The churches of St. Francis and of Our Lady of the Angels at Assisi are also called patriarchal basilicas and papal chapels; each has a papal altar and throne.

iii. There are eleven churches in Rome that have the rank of minor basilica, and numerous others throughout the world (*e.g.*, the great churches at Loreto and Padua, the church of the Grotto at Lourdes, of Lough Derg in Ireland). It is simply a title of honour which gives certain ceremonial rights, *e.g.*, of precedence, to the clergy who serve it.

BASLE, COUNCIL OF. A council convened in 1431 under Pope Eugene IV. It is generally esteemed œcumenical until its transfer to Ferrara and Florence (1438-39), when those who remained at Basle constituted a rebellious synod which elected an antipope. The most important work of the Council of Basle proper was the reconciliation of the Hussites of Bohemia by certain concessions, principally that of communion in both kinds.

BAVARIAN CHAPEL, The. An embassy chapel (*q.v.*) in London, built by the Portuguese in 1730 and taken over by the Bavarian ambassador in 1747. It was rebuilt about 1788 and the same building is now the parish church of the Assumption and St. Gregory, in Warwick Street, Golden Square.

BEADLE (Old Eng., *bydel*, usher, announcer). An official who precedes a bishop or other dignitary, carrying a mace or wand, to clear the way and keep order.

BEADS. Various arrangements of beads on a string or chain are in use in the Catholic Church to help the memory in those devotions where repetition or set numbers of prayers are involved. In addition to the most common Dominican rosary (*q.v.*) there are those of St. Bridget, of the Seven Sorrows, of the Five Wounds, of the Immaculate Conception, the Camaldolese chaplet of our Lord, the Franciscan crown of our Lady, and the Byzantine rosary, used principally by monks. Lay-brothers in the older religious orders, Dominican tertiaries, and others who are prevented from saying the Little Office, have a "bead-office" of *Paters* and *Aves* instead. The expression "pair of beads" is of mediæval origin and simply means a set of beads, usually a rosary of five decades. The device of using beads for counting prayers is very ancient, and is not distinctively Christian; Hindus, Buddhists and Mohammedans use it. See BEDE.

BEARD. In the Western church clerics must be clean-shaven. The rule seems to have had its origin in the desire to distinguish clerics from laymen, and avoidance of the possibility of accident or inconvenience in drinking from the chalice has maintained it. However, Capuchin friars and Camaldolese monks wear the beard by rule, and nearly all foreign missionaries are bearded. The secular clergy of Albania are distinguished by large and impressive moustaches. Beards are worn by all the clergy of the Eastern churches, both Catholic and dissident; but the Malabarese shave, and the Ruthenian and many Catholic Rumanians have taken to the practice, especially in the United States. Many non-Catholic, and some Catholic, priests of the Byzantine rite grow their hair long as well.

BEATIFIC VISION, The. The immediate knowledge of God which constitutes the primary felicity of Heaven. The souls of the blessed see God directly and face to face, unveiled, clearly, openly, as he is in himself; and in this vision they equally enjoy God. This vision is supernatural, not proper to our human nature, so that the intellect of the blessed is supernaturally enlightened by the *lumen gloriæ*. The primary object of the Vision is God himself as he is, in all his perfections and in the three persons of the Trinity. The secondary object of the Vision includes all the mysteries that the individual soul believed while on earth, the sight, recognition and enjoyment of those loved on earth, and knowledge of the prayers and veneration addressel to them by those still on earth. The blessed have a distinct knowledge of individual things, exterior to God, whether actual or possible, and to the extent that God permits, seen either in God directly without the help of created mental image or seen in God as in their cause with the help of such image.

BEATIFICATION is the process by which enquiry is made into the sanctity of a deceased person and, upon proof thereof, permission accorded for his public veneration; this is usually limited to a particular country, diocese, or religious order and does not extend, without special permission, to the display of his image in church or to a Mass and Office in his honour. Beatification generally, but not necessarily, leads to canonization (*q.v.*), and both declarations can now be made only by the pope himself. But the initial enquiries are made by the local diocesan who reports to Rome and, if these are satisfactory, the cause or apostolic process is introduced and passes into the care of the Congregation of Sacred Rites, which subjects the life, writings and alleged miracles of the candidate to a most searching scrutiny; half a dozen or more stages are involved and so thorough is the enquiry that it usually lasts many years. The pope is the final judge and if he is favourable, the solemn beatification takes place in St. Peter's, when the brief is read, a picture of the *beatus* unveiled and venerated, and the new collect in his honour sung. He, or she, may henceforth be referred to as the Blessed so and so. The pope is not infallible in beatifying.

BEATIFICATION, EQUIPOLLENT, or Equivalent, is an authorization of public veneration of a martyr or confessor pronounced by the pope in consequence of the existence of certain special conditions named by Urban VIII in his decree on canonization (1634). So were beatified the English martyrs in 1888–95 on proof of existing public cultus, especially by the display of their pictures in the chapel of the English College at Rome, from 1580 onwards.

BEATITUDE. i. The state of the Blessed in Heaven (*q.v.*). "Beatitude is the ultimate goal of human life, and in a sense man can be said to possess it when he has a real hope of reaching it. We move towards this goal, beatitude, and come nigh to it by actions springing from the virtues and particularly from the gifts of the Holy Ghost" (*q.v.*, St. Thomas, I-II, lxix, 1). See BEATIFIC VISION; HEAVEN.

ii. "His, your Beatitude" or "Blessedness" is a form of reference or address proper to patriarchs in the East; in Rome its place is taken by "most Reverend Excellency."

BEATITUDES, The. The eight blessings, on the poor in heart, the patient, mourners, those that seek holiness, the merciful, the clean of heart, the peace-makers and the persecuted, pronounced by our Lord at the beginning of his sermon on the mount (Matt. v. 3-10). There is no specific difference between the acts here referred to and the ordinary acts of virtue; but they arise directly from the influence of actual grace (*q.v.*), prompting one to performance in correspondence with the gifts of the Holy Ghost (*q.v.*). The Beatitudes are rehearsed liturgically in the Liturgies of St. John Chrysostom and St. Basil.

BEATUS, *pl.* **Beati** (Lat., blessed). The official title of one who has been beatified. *Beatus* is also the epithet commonly used of canonized saints in the liturgy (*cf.*, the collects at Mass).

BEAUTY is conspicuous order in beings. Thoughts, deeds, and things are said to have beauty when, taken in themselves as beings, their orderliness is conspicuous, resplendent. "The beauty of God is the cause of the being of all that is" (St. Thomas, *De Div. Nom. Lect.* v). Chaos and disorder are privation of being. A beautiful thing is that which being seen pleases (St. Thomas, I v, 4 ad 1; "*Pulchra enim dicuntur quæ visa placent*"), because a rational mind cannot find satisfaction in what is disordered and therefore deprived of being. The adjective "beautiful" may be used of any thing that can be thought of as a being, even, *e.g.*, sensations, emotions, acts of virtue, but it can only be so used if the thing, sensation, etc., is taken intransitively, *i.e.*, as a being having its own proper order and not simply as a means to some other thing.

BEDA, The (Collegio Beda). The College of St. Bede, at Rome, began in 1852 as the Collegio Ecclesiastico. By 1857 the students were living at the English College, though their finances were separate and they had their own vice-rector. It was reorganized in 1898 as the Collegio Beda and in 1917 it was completely separated. It provides a special training for candidates for the priesthood who are ex-Anglican ministers or have found their vocation late in life, and for priests pursuing a course of higher studies in Rome.

BEDE. An Old and Middle English word for a prayer, which, through its association with rosaries, has survived in the word "bead." In its older form and meaning it is found in "bede-roll," *i.e.*, a list of persons to be prayed for, and other combinations, and also in "bidding-prayer" (*q.v.*).

BEDLAM. Corruption of the name Bethlehem. The original Bedlam was a general hospital conducted by religious and dedicated in honour of St. Mary of Bethlehem, founded in 1247 on the site now occupied by Liverpool Street Station in the city of London. In 1547 or earlier, it became an asylum for the insane, and still exists as such at Beckenham.

BÉGHARDS. Associations of laymen living in community without vows, which flourished during the 13th and 14th centuries, chiefly in Flanders and the Germanies. They were often associated with particular trades. Pantheistic and Antinomian errors combined with a rebellious spirit caused them to be several times condemned and they hardly survived the Reformation.

BÉGUINES. Laywomen who live in community, bound by temporary vows of obedience and chastity. Their residence is a *béguinage*, wherein each one or two inmates has a separate house; there is a chapel in common and the whole forms one enclosure. They keep their own property and leave the life at will. Those who are able, employ themselves in educational and charitable works. The principal *béguinage* to-day is at Ghent. Béguines are said to take their name from Lambert le Bègue who founded them in 1180, but their origin is much controverted. They were nearly suppressed through becoming involved in the errors of the Béghards.

BEING (Lat., *ens*). That which exists or can exist. Whatever is intrinsically contradictory neither has nor can have existence, as a square-circle, one equals two, etc.; such things are nonentities.

i. Real being (*ens reale*) is either actual or possible; if it exists it is actual; if it does not actually exist, and yet could exist, it is possible. Now a possible may be considered as possible in itself (*i.e.*, in so far as it contains no intrinsic repugnance); then it is called the absolute, or objective, or the metaphysically possible, as the geocentric theory of the universe, or a sea of milk; or it may be considered relatively with regard to a cause which absolutely speaking could bring it to existence; then it is called the relative possible: if therefore it can be shown that there is no such cause, then the production of such a thing is relatively impossible. Speaking of created causes, the relatively possible is either physical or moral, according as the cause is considered in itself or as accompanied by its customary circumstances and conditions; thus, it is physically possible for a man to learn philosophy without a master, but morally speaking this is not possible; it is, however, possible for him to acquire a few philosophic notions without a master.

ii. Mental being (*ens rationis*) is that which neither exists nor can exist in nature because it is wholly dependent on the conception of the mind, as genus, species, predicate, subject, precisely as such.

iii. Necessary and contingent being. Necessary being is that in whose very notion is contained the idea of existence; contingent being is that in whose notion is not contained the idea of existence: existence, therefore, may be present with or absent from contingent being. God alone is necessary Being, all things beside him are contingent. Contingent being therefore implies that if it exists its existence is not from itself but from another; hence all being whose existence is from another is contingent being.

BELGIUM, THE CHURCH IN. Most of the people of this country are at least nominally Catholics, but religion is complicated by political affiliations. The Church is not established by the state, and there is freedom for all religions. The country, with a population of over 8¼ million, forms one ecclesiastical province with 5 suffragan dioceses; the primatial metropolitan see is Malines (Mechlin). The apostolic nuncio at Brussels is also internuncio for *Luxemburg*. The people of this grand-duchy is almost entirely Catholic and forms a single diocese i.s.h.s. (*q.v.*), with a Benedictine abbacy *nullius*, Clervaux.

BELIEF. Assent of the mind to truths on the authority of a master. There is human belief and divine, according as the motive of the assent is human authority or divine. All belief is essentially an act of the will, seeing that the truth proposed for belief is not intrinsically but only extrinsically evident, that is, because the motive is extrinsic. In the case of divine faith a grace is necessary for this movement of the will, otherwise the act would not be supernatural. In the assent to a supernatural truth the mind is absolutely, that is, metaphysically, certain of the truth to which it assents, since the motive of the assent is divine revelation, the speech of God who can neither deceive nor be deceived. See AUTHORITY; EVIDENCE; ASSENT.

BELL. i. The principal use of church bells is to summon the faithful to divine service, a use which has been general since the 8th century. Other universal uses are for the daily *Angelus*, during the singing of the *Gloria in excelsis* at the Mass of Holy Saturday and Whitsun-eve, and at a funeral. In some places it is the custom to ring a *De profundis* bell at about 9 p.m., to toll when a person is dying (the passing-bell, properly so called) and again when he is dead, to chime during the *Gloria in excelsis* at the Midnight Mass of Christmas, during the *Magnificat* at Vespers on the feast of the Visitation, and to toll at the consecration in a principal Mass and even at Benediction of the Blessed Sacrament. No bells of any sort may be rung from the *Gloria* of the Mass of Maundy Thursday until the same on Holy Saturday; a wooden clapper may be used instead. It is a very old custom to ring the bells at times both of secular rejoicing and danger. Church bells are solemnly blessed by a bishop with a rite popularly called the baptism of bells (*q.v.*).
ii. At Mass. The use of a small handbell to direct attention to the most solemn parts of the Mass is a mediæval peculiarity of the Latin rite. The rubrics of the Missal direct its use only at the *Sanctus* and during the elevation of the Host and Chalice; it is also rung at *Hanc igitur*, and in many places it is the custom at *Domine non sum dignus*. Apparently it may not be omitted even at a private Mass at which no congregation is present; but it is not rung during solemn Mass in any of the patriarchal basilicas, during Exposition in any church and on a few other occasions. This usage has been adopted, quite unnecessarily, by some Catholics of Eastern rite.

"BELL, BOOK AND CANDLE." A common literary reference to excommunication or other ecclesiastical sentence. It derives from the ceremonies of the public and solemn promulgation (*anathema*) of the greater excommunication for which the "Pontificale" (the "book") still directs the assistance of twelve priests with candles; when the bishop has read the sentence these candles are thrown down as a symbol of the quenching of grace and joy in the offender's soul. The bell was presumably at one time used to add solemnity to the occasion. The ceremony seems to have now fallen into disuse.

BELMONT. i. A Benedictine monastery established in 1858, near Hereford, as the general noviciate and house of studies of the English congregation; it was also cathedral-priory (*q.v.*) of the former diocese of Newport, its mitred prior being provost of the diocesan chapter. Since 1916 it has been an abbey, with its own community. The monks conduct a school.
ii. The monastery of Our Lady of Help, also called Maryhelp Abbey, at Belmont, North Carolina, a house of the American-Cassinese Benedictine congregation. It was founded in 1884 and became an abbey *nullius* (*q.v.*) in 1910; from then until 1924 the abbot was a bishop and vicar apostolic of North Carolina. The monks conduct a senior seminary, college and school; the abbot has jurisdiction over 4 parishes and 2 dependent priories.

BEMA (Gr., tribune). A common name in the Byzantine rite for the part of the church beyond the *iconostasis*, *i.e.*, the sanctuary. In large churches it consists of three separate parts, each with an apse. In the middle is the altar, on the north the *prothesis* and on the south the *diakonikon*. Behind the altar is the episcopal throne with seats for the clergy on either side.

BENCH-RENT. A small sum of money offered in return for the right to occupy a certain seat in a church. Special places in church may not be reserved for members of the congregation except by express permission of the bishop. Where such permission is given, an offering for the use of the seat is customary.

BENE ESSE. The expression *ad bene esse* presupposes the *esse* (or being) of a thing to which is added the useful or the means of attaining some end; as knowledge is *ad bene esse* of a human being or the primacy of jurisdiction of the Roman pontiff is of the *esse* of the Church and not merely of its *bene esse*, as some heretics have maintained.

BENEDICAMUS DOMINO (Lat., Let us bless the Lord) is said at Mass instead of the usual formula of dismissal, *Ite, missa est*, when *Gloria in excelsis* has not been said, namely, in Masses of the Advent season, of the season from Septuagesima to Easter, on ferial days throughout the year and at most votive Masses; except that in requiem Masses *Requiescant in pace* (May they rest in peace) is said instead. The reason is uncertain but probably on these days other prayers formerly followed Mass so that the dismissal was not required; it has been suggested that at one time both were said. The formula also occurs at the end of all the hours of the Divine Office except Matins.

BENEDICITE, The. i. The canticle *Benedicite omnia opera Domini Domino*, "All ye works of the Lord, bless the Lord," often called the Song of the Three Children because it was sung by Ananias, Azarias and Misael in the furnace (Daniel iii). The first 20 verses are sung at Lauds as the fourth psalm on Sundays and feasts throughout the year, except from Septuagesima to Palm Sunday inclusive, when the remaining seven are sung. It is also included in the prayers provided in the missal for thanksgiving after Mass, and is said when returning from the grave after the burial of an infant.

ii. "Benedicite" is the ordinary word of salutation in a monastery.

BENEDICT, ST., THE HOLY RULE OF. The monastic rule followed by the Benedictines proper, the Cistercians, Camaldolese, Olivetans, Silvestrines and Vallombrosans (*qq.v.*), and in the past by the Cluniacs and several other extinct congregations. It was written in Latin by St. Benedict for his own monastery at Monte Cassino in the first half of the 6th century and became and remains the standard for all monks in the West. It consists of a prologue and 73 chapters which deal with the government of a monastery, ascetical principles, the Divine Office, interior organization, discipline, property, daily life, recruitment of subjects, appointment of the abbot, enclosure and community life. The principles governing the rule were the traditional ideas of St. Pachomius, St. Basil and St. John Cassian, but its detailed provisions were entirely original and directed to the attainment of moderation. "A monument of legislative art, remarkable alike for its completeness, its simplicity and its adaptability" (H. F. Dudden), which has been one of the chief civilizing factors of the western world; it "gave to a world worn out by slavery the first example of work done by the hands of free men" (Michelet). It provides for the life of men who wish to live in community and devote themselves entirely to God's service by self-discipline, prayer and work. They are to be essentially families, in the care and under the absolute control of a father (the abbot, *q.v.*); individually they are bound to personal poverty, abstention from marriage, and obedience to their superiors, and by the vows of stability and conversion of manners (*qq.v.*); a moderate degree of austerity is imposed by the night office, fasting, abstinence from flesh-meat, and restraint in conversation; their days shall be divided between reading and study and manual work of all kinds; in the forefront

is put corporate prayer, "the work of God"; St. Benedict legislated for bodies of laymen with one or two priests, the ordination of all choir-monks and the introduction of lay-brothers being a much later development.

BENEDICTINE. "Liqueur de safran, d'une finesse exquise, a l'arôme quintessencié d'angélique et d'hysope mêlés à des herbes marines," but (unlike Chartreuse) nothing to do with a monastic order. It is, however, made on the site of the great monastery of Fécamp in Normandy. "Trappistine" is also an ordinary commercial product.

BENEDICTINES, The. Monks and nuns of the order of St. Benedict, founded about 529. Strictly speaking, the Benedictine family does not constitute a single religious order; originally each house was entirely independent under its own supreme abbot and that principle is still adhered to in varying degrees. But the 4th Lateran Council (1215) legislated for the formation of associations of Benedictine houses and these congregations (*q.v.*) are in effect each one a true and separate order. According to the Rule of St. Benedict (*q.v.*) manual work is the principal occupation and the celebration of the Divine Office in choir the most important duty of monks. The Divine Office is celebrated daily, with more or less of solemnity, in every monastery; but with the custom of ordaining all monks (established since about 1000), and the appearance of lay-brothers, manual labour for choir-monks has almost disappeared. Instead, Benedictines have occupied themselves as missionaries, in study, and as schoolmasters, and education is their most characteristic activity to-day. But their activties vary from congregation to congregation and house to house, and the daily life of the monk varies accordingly. The congregations of Belgium and St. Ottilia are concerned with foreign missions; nearly all have schools (the English 9, the American-Cassinese 24, the Swiss-American 7, etc.). Many monks are engaged in ordinary parochial work. Only the monasteries of the Solesmes congregation have neither schools nor parishes and are rigidly devoted to a strictly ordered monastic life; but the same is true of other individual abbeys, including two in Great Britain, Buckfast and Prinknash (*qq.v.*). Of recent years the importance of the liturgy in Benedictine life has again come to the fore and they are the leaders of the liturgical movement (*q.v.*). (But historically the carrying out of the Mass and Office with great solemnity in choir pertains particularly to the canons regular.) The habit is a tunic, leather belt, scapular and hood, and shoes, with a full cowl in choir, all black (there are a few variations; *e.g.*, Monte Vergine, Prinknash, wear white). The noviciate is for one year, then triennial, followed by solemn vows; these are equivalently five—poverty, chasity, obedience, stability, conversion of manners (*qq.v.*). The degree of asceticism and strict observance varies from house to house. There are over 9,000 Benedictine choir-monks and laybrothers. In Great Britain there are five abbeys of the English congregation (*q.v.*) and Buckfast, Prinknash, Farnborough, Ramsgate and Quarr of other congregations. The United States has 21 houses of monks; Ireland has one priory. There were about 157 monasteries (including Cluniacs, *q.v.*) in England before the Reformation and 83 nunneries.

ii. The nuns of the order are strictly enclosed and normally contemplative, but some monasteries conduct schools. The houses are generally independent and subject to the bishop. Their chief work is the choral celebration of the Divine Office and their other occupations are both intellectual and manual; some houses have perpetual adoration (*q.v.*). In Great Britain there are abbeys at Stanbrook, Holme Eden, Talacre and Colwich (belonging to the English Congregation), Ryde, Frensham Hall, Oulton, Minster and Teignmouth; Atherstone, Princethorpe and Dumfries priories, and Kylemore in Ireland; and numerous houses of sisters in U. S. A. Habit: the same as the monks but with veil and wimple.

BENEDICTION, APOSTOLIC, The. The solemn public blessing with plenary indulgence (*q.v.*) which, before 1870, the pope pronounced from the balcony of St. John Lateran on Pentecost or Ascension day, from St. Peter's on SS. Peter & Paul, Maundy Thursday and Easter day, and from St. Mary Major's on the Assumption. The power to give this blessing and indulgence with a special formula is given to bishops and other prelates twice a year, to priests on special occasions and for general purposes, *e.g.*, Dominican tertiaries may receive it from their director, either as a body or individually, twice a year. All priests must give this blessing, with the formula from the "Rituale," to a sick person who is in danger of death; it conveys a plenary indulgence on the usual conditions.

BENEDICTION of the Blessed Sacrament. A short service, very popular in the Western church, consisting essentially of the singing of the hymn *Tantum ergo* with its prayer, followed by a blessing given to the people by making the sign of the cross above them with the Blessed Sacrament, either contained in the *ciborium* or displayed in a monstrance. It is usually added to Vespers or Compline or to non-liturgical public devotions. The custom came gradually into use from the 16th to the 18th century, and its forms are still very variable. In England the usual order is the exposition of the Host in a monstrance and its incensation while the hymn *O salutaris* is sung; the litany of Loreto or other litany, hymn, canticle, etc.; *Tantum ergo* while the Host is again incensed; the blessing with the Host (in

silence); the Divine Praises; the verse *Adoremus* and Psalm cxvi. This form is practically the same as that given in the first edition of "The Garden of the Soul" (*q.v.*) which was the first description of Benediction given in any English prayer book: the notable difference is that after the prayer were added two others, for the congregation and for the king. The laws governing the use of this service favour informal Benediction with the *ciborium;* the permission of the bishop, either particular or general, is required for the more usual form which involves exposing the Host in a monstrance. Benediction has been adopted by some of the Catholic Eastern churches, notably the Melkites, who have a special and impressive rite wherein the celebrant sings a triple deprecatory blessing at the moment of benediction. The apparent importance of this service in Catholic worship is adventitious; in certain great churches of Rome and elsewhere it is used very little and in the simplest possible form.

BENEDICTIONALE. A book containing various forms of blessing extracted from the Missal, the "Pontificale," the "Rituale," etc.

BENEDICTUS, The. i. The canticle of Zachary, *Benedictus dominus Deus Israel,* "Blessed be the lord God of Israel" (Luke i, 68–79), said daily at Lauds; when the office is sung with solemnity the altar, ministers, choir and people are incensed during the *Benedictus.* It is said or sung standing, in honour of the Incarnation, and with a sign of the cross at the first verse, the words being those of the Gospel. At the burial of an adult person this canticle is said as the body is deposited in the grave.

ii. The last part of the *Sanctus* at the end of the preface; "Blessed (*Benedictus*) is he that cometh in the name of the Lord. Hosanna in the highest" (Matt. xxi, 9). At high Mass it has become separated from its proper place and must, according to present ruling, always be sung after the consecration, the first part of the *Sanctus* having to be finished before the first elevation. Celebrant and people sign themselves with the cross at its first word.

BENEFICE (Lat., *beneficium,* a benefaction). An ecclesiastical foundation permanently constituted, consisting of a sacred office and the right of the holder to the annual revenue from the endowment. The four essential elements of a benefice are: (*a*) canonical erection, (*b*) an ecclesiastical office, (*c*) permanent endowment, and (*d*) the right of the incumbent to the revenue. Beneficed clergy have the free use of their income, as far as is necessary to live in a manner befitting their state, but they must spend what is superfluous for the poor or in good works. The benefice is distinct from the *fabrica,* or fund for the upkeep and repair of the church or other property. All parishes are to be erected into benefices wherever possible.

BENEFICIATUS. Any person holding an ecclesiastical benefice, but particularly a cleric having a benefice in a cathedral or collegiate church who is regarded as a member of the chapter, though not a canon and not called to its meetings.

BENEFIT OF CLERGY. An obsolete custom of English law whereby any tonsured person, monk, or nun, charged with a felony (except high treason or arson) could claim trial in the ecclesiastical, as opposed to the civil, court. Penalties were lighter and acquittals more frequent in the church courts, and in time the privilege was claimed by and conceded to all who could read, regardless of any real clerical status. From Henry II onwards the custom caused much friction between the ecclesiastical and civil powers, and it was somewhat modified by statute law. It persisted even after the Reformation, when the bishops of the new Anglican church were deprived of any criminal jurisdiction, first as a privilege of the educated in the civil courts, then as a means of evasion of extreme penalties by an increasing number of persons. Nevertheless, it was not finally abolished until the year 1827.

BENEMERENTE MEDAL, The. A decoration instituted by Pope Gregory XVI wherewith to recognize military valour and civil distinction and worth. It is awarded to both men and women.

BENIGNITY (Lat., *benignitas*, perhaps from *bene*, well; *genus*, born). One of the twelve fruits of the Holy Ghost (Galatians v, 22–3), called, in common speech, kindness. It need not be confined to the aged.

BEQUESTS FOR MASSES. When money is left for Masses it is for the bishop to determine how it is to be invested, and the number of Masses to be said. Bequests for Masses are valid in English law, according to a judgment of the House of Lords in 1919. From 1559 till 1791 the Mass was altogether illegal; in a case in 1835 it was argued that an unrepealed act of Edward VI, in 1547 described Masses for the dead as a "superstitious practice," and the Catholic Charities Act of 1832 did not recognize bequests for "superstitious purposes." Sir Charles Pepys, who tried the case, decided that this was the law, and that decision was followed by the courts until, in 1919, Lord Birkenhead, sitting as lord chancellor with four lords justices of appeal, decided that it was wrong in law and contrary to equity; one of his colleagues dissented from this judgment (*cf.*, sale of Masses).

BERAT (Ar., *bara'ah*). The document by which the Sultans of Turkey recognized a newly elected patriarch of Constantinople and others heads of Christian churches

throughout their territories. The custom was taken over from the emperors and involved an undue submission of Christian prelates to Moslem civil rulers. Large fees had to be paid for the delivery of the *berat;* it professed to confirm the recipient in his spiritual office and also made him the civil head of his "nation" (*millet*) and responsible therefor to the Sublime Porte.

BERENGARIUS, THE HERESY OF, was, that in the Blessed Sacrament the substance of the bread and the wine remain unchanged but become spiritually the true body and blood of Christ. Thus he denied transubstantiation (*q.v.*) while teaching (at any rate in a sense) the real presence (*q.v.*). The heresy is important chiefly because many have claimed that the elevation of the Host and Chalice after consecration at Mass was originally a protest against it, but this elevation was hardly known before 1200, and Berengarius of Tours died in 1088.

BERNARDINES, The. Members of several congregations of nuns with rules modelled on the primitive observance of Citeaux, since the 16th century. The surviving houses follow modified but severe rules, those of Anglet (Bayonne) observing perpetual silence. The Dames Bernardines, founded in 1799 by three Cistercian nuns driven out by the French Revolution, are enclosed and conduct schools for girls. White habit, with black scapular and veil; white choir cowl. The Bernardines have no connexion with the Cistercian order.

BETHARRAM FATHERS, The. The Priests of the Sacred Heart, a congregation of missionaries founded at Betharram, near Bayonne, in 1832.

BETROTHAL (Mid. Eng., *bitreuthian*, to make truth with, *i.e.*, to bind by promise). No promise of marriage or engagement is recognized by the Church as valid in either the external or internal forum (*q.v.*) unless made in writing and signed by the parties, and also by the rector of a parish or a local ordinary, or by two witnesses. Even then such promise gives no legal right to the celebration of the marriage, but only a right to damages for breach of promise. Betrothal is a prohibiting impediment (*q.v.*) to marriage with someone else until the betrothment is legitimately broken off.

BETTING AND GAMBLING. Betting is in itself lawful provided that the subject-matter of the bet is not sinful, that neither party is certain of the event, and that both parties understand the bet in the same way. Gambling on games of skill or of chance is lawful provided that both parties are willing to play, even though one of them realizes that he has no chance of success; that cheating and fraud are absent; and that the money staked is not required for payment of debts or to support themselves and their families. Gambling on the stock exchange is lawful unless unjust devices such as causing an artificial rise and fall of prices are employed. Betting and gambling are dangerous, for they easily lead to sin, misery and ruin of self and others. In 1590 Pope Gregory XIV found it necessary to restrain the sporting Romans by forbidding, on pain of excommunication, all betting on the results of papal elections, the duration of conclaves and the creation of new cardinals.

BEURON CONGREGATION, The. A Benedictine congregation founded in 1868, having its headquarters at the archabbey of Beauron, near Sigmaringen. The abbey at Erdington, Birmingham, belonged to it, but in 1922 its members migrated to Weingarten, disposing of the monastery to the Redemptorists. The great abbey of Maria Laach belongs to this congregation.

BEURON SCHOOL, The. The name applied to the workshops and studios (and, derivatively, to the works of art issuing therefrom) at the Benedictine archabbey of Beuron in Germany. The school supplies objects of ecclesiastical furniture, especially in painting and sculpture, which are in harmony with liturgical requirements, but at the the same time they conform to 19th-century pictorial sentiment. Characteristic Beuron work may, therefore, be said to fall between two schools; stiff and conventional in general lines, it is seen on closer acquaintance to be naturalistic and literary in sentiment. It is neither wholly liturgical, like the Mass which it is designed to complement, nor wholly sentimental, like the works of those artists whose admirers it is found to placate.

BEVERLEY (*Beverlacensis*). An Engish see erected in 1850, and suppressed in 1878, on the formation of the dioceses of Leeds and Middlesbrough *(qq.v.)*. Its pro-cathedral was the church of St. George at York.

BIBLE, THE HOLY (Gr., τὰ βιβλία, the books). A collection of writings divided into the Old Testament, consisting of 46 books written before the Incarnation of our Lord, and the New Testament, 27 books written since that time. These form the Sacred Scriptures *(q.v.)* which, says the Council of Trent (session iv), the Church "receives with piety and reverence . . . since the one God is the author of each [testament]." However, she does not support the fundamentalist view of the literal truth of every word, but teaches that the Bible is everywhere true in the sense intended by the individual sacred writer (see INSPIRATION; VULGATE, etc.). The books of the Bible are as follows. It should be noted that Protestant versions omit the deutero-canonical books *(q.v.)*, and name certain of the others as indicated in brackets below. Old Testament: Genesis, Exodus,

Leviticus, Numbers, Deuteronomy, Josue (Joshua), Judges, Ruth, four books of Kings (1 and 2 Samuel, 1 and 2 Kings), 1 and 2 Paralipomenon (1 and 2 Chronicles), 1 and 2 Esdras (Ezra, Nehemiah), Tobias, Judith, Esther, Job, Psalms, Proverbs, Ecclesiastes, Canticle of Canticles (Song of Solomon), Wisdom, Ecclesiasticus, Isaias (Isaiah), Jeremias (Jeremiah), Lamentations, Baruch, Ezechiel (Ezekiel), Daniel, Osee (Hosea), Joel, Amos, Abdias (Obadiah), Jonas (Jonah), Micheas (Micah), Nahum, Habacuc (Habakkuk), Sophonias (Zephaniah), Aggeus (Haggai), Zacharias (Zechariah), Malachias (Malachi), 1 and 2 Machabees. New Testament: The Gospels of SS. Matthew, Mark, Luke and John, Acts of the Apostles, the Epistles of St. Paul to the Romans, Corinthians (2), Galatians, Ephesians, Philippians, Colossians, Thessalonians (2), Timothy (2), Titus, Philemon, and Hebrews; the Epistles of SS. James, Peter (2), John (3) and Jude, the Apocalypse of St. John (Revelation).

BIBLE-READING has never been the subject of a general prohibition to Catholics. Decrees restraining the use of vernacular versions *(q.v.)* were first provoked in the 13th century by the excesses of Catharism, whose upholders sought support from the Scriptures. At the present day there are no restrictions put upon the reading of approved translations in any language; the faithful are, indeed, encouraged to it by the grant of indulgences, notably those published by Pope Pius X in 1914 for members of associations for the spreading of the reading of the Gospels; these included plenary indulgences on the usual conditions *(q.v.)* on nineteen certain feasts to those who should read the Gospels frequently, daily if possible, recommend such reading to others, and often make use of the prayer, "Grant, we beseech thee, O Jesus, that we may be obedient to the Holy Gospel."

BIBLIA PAUPERUM (Lat., Bible of the Poor). Picture-books illustrating New Testament events with their Old Testament types on the opposite page, much used for religious instruction in the 15th–16th centuries.

BIBLICAL COMMISSION, The. The Pontifical Commission for Biblical Studies. In 1902 Pope Leo XIII instituted a commission of cardinals, assisted by a number of consultors taken from different nations, experts in biblical matters, to issue doctrinal decisions concerning biblical questions. In 1907 Pope Pius X declared these decisions binding in conscience and to be received with internal and external assent. These decisions normally only obtain ordinary, not solemn, approval by the pope and are therefore not infallible pronouncements; hence they are in themselves reversible and do not call for the assent of divine faith. They call for that human faith and mental submission which is due to a religious authority which, though not infallible, yet enjoys such providential protection as God gives to the official utterances of the Church he founded. They are a stimulus and a guidance to further investigation. Decisions have been issued on such matters as tacit quotations and nonliteral histories, Mosaic authorship, the Fourth Gospel, Isaias, the first three chapters of Genesis, authorship and date of the Psalms, St. Matthew, SS. Luke and Mark and the Synoptic Problem, the Acts and the Pastoral Epistles, Hebrews, and on the second coming of Christ in the epistles of St. Paul.

BIBLICAL INSTITUTE, The Pontifical. A central college for students of the Holy Scriptures, established at Rome by Pope Pius X, in 1909, as a department of the Commission for Biblical Studies. Separated therefrom in 1928, and now one of the autonomies constituting the pontifical university for ecclesiastical studies. It has the faculty of conferring the doctorate in Sacred Scriptures.

BIDDING-PRAYER. A list of intercessions read out after the gospel at Mass in pre-Reformation days: in the first place for the pope, prelates and clergy, secular and regular; then for the realm and its prince, pregnant women, husbandmen, the harvest, the sick, pilgrims and benefactors; and lastly for the faithful departed, especially relatives, those buried in the churchyard and "the souls that have most need and least help." For all these the people were asked to say a *Pater, Ave* and *De profundis*, or other prayers. This was called "bidding the bedes," *i.e.*, praying the prayers. Our present custom of reading out, after the notices, the names of the lately dead and of others needing the prayers of their neighbours may be a survival of it.

BIGAMY. i. The contracting of a second or subsequent valid marriage in succession. The perfection of the sacrament of matrimony requires that it should be the marriage of one man with one woman. In a second marriage the union of Christ and his Church is less perfectly symbolized, and he who contracts such a marriage incurs irregularity (*q.v.*) for the reception of holy orders (*cf.*, 1 Tim. iii, 2).

ii. In its ordinary sense, if a married person attempts to contract another marriage, even with merely civil forms, the offender incurs infamy (*q.v.*), and if he or she does not separate from the unlawful partner may be excommunicated or put under interdict (*q.v.*).

BILOCATION. The personal presence of the same individual in more than one place at the same time. Bilocation is recorded of Antony of Padua, Catherine of Ricci and Philip Neri, among other saints; but these may have been appearances without any objective reality, or explainable in other ways, for the bilocation of a material body is a physical impossibility.

BINATION. The offering of Mass twice in the same day by the same priest, generally called in England duplication (*q.v.*).

"BINDING AND LOOSING." The power of binding and loosing exercised in the sacrament of Penance, conferred by Jesus Christ on the bishops and priests of the Church through the Apostles (Matt. xvi, 18); the supreme power of jurisdiction conferred on St. Peter and his successors (Matt. xvi, 19). Often called "the power of the keys" (*q.v.*).

BIOGENESIS. The theory that all living things have their source from living things only, as opposed to Abiogenesis (*q.v.*).

BIRETTA. A square cap with three ridges on the top and sometimes a tuft in the middle. It is worn by all the Western clergy, except monks and friars (excluding Conventual Franciscans), of all ranks on entering and leaving the church for service, and at certain times during those services, *e.g.*, during the singing of the Psalms of the Divine Office. The colour is black; but that of cardinals is red, of bishops, purple, and of Premonstratensian canons and Cistercian abbots, white. The biretta is also worn at times by regulars who are prelates, *e.g.*, by an abbot assisting at a ceremony in prelatical dress. Its use is not exclusively liturgical; it originated in a soft round cap to which the ridges were added to facilitate putting it on and off.

BIRITUALISM. The system whereby a Latin priest whose work, for missionary or other reasons, is among Catholics or dissidents of the Eastern rites uses as occasion may require the Liturgy and offices of those among whom he works; *e.g.*, the Benedictine professors at the Greek College in Rome. To it is now preferred the system of exclusive use of an Eastern rite ("adaptation"), which may be temporary and does not involve any change of rite.

BIRMINGHAM (*Birmingamiensis*). An English see erected in 1850, made an archdiocese in 1911, comprising Warwickshire, Oxfordshire, Staffordshire and Worcestershire, before the Reformation in the then dioceses of Worcester, Lincoln and Lichfield. A chief centre of the development of Catholicism in England in the early and middle 19th century. The first three Synods of Westminster were held at Oscott; the first Catholic public school (Sedgeley Park, 1763), the first church of the Sacred Heart (Old Oscott, 1820), the first house of perpetual adoration (Colwich, 1829) and the first post-Reformation cathedral and public statute of our Lady (St. Chad's, Birmingham, 1841) in England, and the centre of the Oxford Movement (*q.v.*) were all in this district. The church at

Stonor was consecrated in 1349, the missions at Radford, Spetchley Park, Worcester and Birmingham were founded in 1613, 1681, 1685 and 1689, and 8 others in the 18th century. The archbishops' house and cathedral (with relics of St. Chad) are at Birmingham, and the diocesan seminary at Oscott. The patron of the diocese is our Lady Immaculate; the cathedral is dedicated in honour of St. Chad, and is now a minor basilica (q.v.).

BIRTH CONTROL. A misnomer for the practice of carrying out sexual relations within or without marriage in such a way as to prevent conception. The Church condemns such practices as gravely contrary to the natural law. She sanctions only such true control as may be procured by abstinence from sexual relations. Artificial birth control is contrary to the natural law because it is a frustration of the proper end of the sexual act, which is procreation. Physical expression or consummation of love, the sealing and increase of affection by the mutual enjoyment one of another, are also objects of the act, but only proximate objects. To pursue such is good; but at the same time deliberately to avoid the ultimate end of the act, for the due attainment of which the proximate objects were ordained as a means, is unnatural, contrary to right reason, conduct unbecoming rational beings, and so morally wrong.

BIRTH, DEFECT OF. An impediment to ordination arising from illegitimacy (q.v.).

BIRTHDAY. From the 2nd century the Church has referred to the anniversary of their death as the birthday, into the better life, of her martyrs and saints. It is thus used in the liturgy, and the birthday according to the flesh is commemorated liturgically only in the case of two saints, our Lady and St. John the Baptist. Cf., NATIVITY.

BISHOP (Gr., ἐπίσκοπος, overseer). The supreme ecclesiastical ruler of a diocese. Bishops are the successors of the apostles, as the pope is the successor of St. Peter. For the affairs of their own dioceses they are responsible directly to the pope. They govern their flocks in the name of God as representatives of Christ; they are not delegates of the Holy See, though they are subject to its authority, but exercise their own powers by virtue of their office. They do not enjoy personal infallibility, but collectively, in union with the pope, they are infallible. They belong to the Teaching Church, the *Ecclesia Docens* (q.v.).

BISHOP, AUXILIARY. One appointed by the Holy See to assist a ruling bishop on account of his age, ill-health or the amount of work devolving on him. Such an one must be distinguished from a coadjutor and from a suffragan bishop. As no bishop may be consecrated without a title to a see, auxil-iary bishops are necessarily also titular bishops (q.v.).

BISHOP, COADJUTOR. One appointed with jurisdiction to administer the diocese of a bishop who is entirely incapacitated from performing his duties himself, e.g., because of insanity. The term is often applied to an auxiliary bishop (q.v.) to whom the Holy See has granted right of succession to the see which he is assisting, when it falls vacant, and such is its ordinary meaning in law.

BISHOP, RESIDENTIAL, DIOCESAN. A resident diocesan bishop exercising ordinary jurisdiction (q.v.) with all the rights and duties of his office in the diocese committed to his care, as opposed to an auxiliary or coadjutor bishop, vicar apostolic, etc.

BISHOP ELECT. One who has been appointed to a bishopric by the Holy See or whose canonical election thereto has been confirmed by the Holy See, but who is not yet consecrated and enthroned. He has full jurisdiction in his diocese, but of course cannot confirm, ordain, etc., in his own person until he has been consecrated.

BISHOP-IN-ORDINARY. A diocesan or residential bishop (q.v.).

BISHOP I.P.I. (Lat., *in partibus infidelium*, in the lands of the infidels). A name formerly given to a non-residential bishop consecrated to one of the numerous sees called *in partibus infidelium* because they had been abandoned owing to incursions of the heathen. As many of these now again have considerable Christian populations, Pope Leo XIII abolished the name and substituted *titular see* and *titular bishop* (q.v.) therefor.

BISHOP, TITULAR (formerly called bishop i.p.i., q.v.). A bishop consecrated for a see which, on account of the decay of Christian population, generally through the incursions of Islam, has been allowed to lapse. Such are appointed by the pope (in Eastern rites) by the patriarch) as auxiliaries to bishops-in-ordinary, as vicars apostolic, as an honour in recognition of distinguished services, etc.; a bishop-in-ordinary who resigns his see receives a titular see. Any jurisdiction exercised by a titular bishop is delegated: he has no ordinary jurisdiction even in his own see if he happens to visit it; he cannot perform any episcopal function unless authorized by his diocesan bishop or by the terms of his commission; but he has equal rights with other bishops at œcumenical councils if summoned thereto, though the pope is not bound to call titular bishops unless they are vicars apostolic. There are numerous titular sees, which include such places as Chalcedon (Kadi Keui), Capharnaum (Tell Hum), Sebaste (Sivasli), Nicaea (Isnik), Thessalonica (Salonika) and the seven sees of the Apocalypse; many of these sees are archiepiscopal.

In 1946 there were some 900 titular bishops, including 30 or more of Eastern rite.

BISHOPRIC. The office of bishop; often used as synonymous with see or diocese.

BISHOPS, APPOINTMENT OF. The pope appoints bishops at his own discretion in the Western church, but the exact circumstances of nomination vary. In a few dioceses the cathedral chapter or other body has the right of election. For a civil government to present or nominate a candidate is an irregular method of provision sometimes permitted by the Holy See, under varying conditions, to avoid worse evils. Such nomination does not confer the bishopric; collation is effected solely by institution of the Roman pontiff. The designation of persons by English chapters and bishops is for the guidance of the Holy See, and does not confer any right. The methods of appointment of Catholic bishops of Eastern rites vary greatly. In those churches which have a properly organized hierarchy the patriarch is chosen by the synod of bishops and confirmed by the Holy See. Melkite bishops are chosen by the clergy from among three candidates submitted by the patriarch of Antioch; he chooses titular bishops personally. A vacancy in a Syrian, Maronite or Chaldean see is filled by the synod of bishops, who choose either from a list submitted by the clergy and leading laity or at discretion; the choice must be confirmed at Rome. There is a tendency to dispense with the assistance of eminent lay people in these matters. Bishops for other Catholics of Eastern rites are elected in various ways in close touch with the Holy See.

BISHOPS, THE CONSECRATION OF, is performed by another bishop assisted by two co-consecrators (*q.v.*). It takes place during Mass which the elect concelebrates (*q.v.*) and consists of the preparation, begun before the Mass and concluded after the gradual with the Litany of the Saints; the consecration, including the imposition of hands with the words "Receive the Holy Ghost" and the anointing of the elect's head and hands during the singing of *Veni Creator;* the presentation of the pastoral staff, ring and Gospels, and the elect's offering of wine, bread and candles at the offertory, the mitre and gloves being given after the blessing; the conclusion, including the enthronement of the new bishop (if the consecration takes place in his own cathedral-church), *Te Deum,* his blessing of the people and liturgical greeting of his consecrator, the kiss of peace, and the Last Gospel.

BISHOPS, JURISDICTION OF. Bishops are the successors of the Apostles and by divine institution rule their dioceses with ordinary power under the authority of the pope. They have legislative, judicial and executive power. They cannot act against common law (*q.v.*), and have no jurisdiction over exempt (*q.v.*) religious as such; but subject to this a bishop can enact those laws which he considers for the good of his diocese and he is judge in the first instance in all ecclesiastical trials; he can punish lay people by censures and clerics by deprivation of office and censures (*q.v.*). He has supreme direction of his clergy, the conduct of divine worship, administration of ecclesiastical property, building of churches, erection of parishes, etc.; in addition to these and other powers which he has in his own right as a bishop, certain other powers, chiefly in the internal forum (*q.v.*), are delegated to him by the Holy See by faculties.

BISHOPS, OBLIGATIONS OF. It is the duty of bishops to rule their dioceses with legislative, judicial and executive power, to enforce the observance of canon law, safeguard the faith and correct abuses. Before institution they must make their profession of faith, and take the oath of fealty to the Holy See, within three months obtain consecration, and within four months take formal possession of their diocese by showing their letters apostolic to the cathedral chapter. Bishops are bound to reside in the diocese, and must not be absent from the cathedral at certain times of the year. Other duties are to preach in person, to offer Mass for the people on the prescribed days; to make the quinquennial report to the Holy See and the visit *ad limina* (*q.v.*); and to complete the pastoral visitation of the diocese every 5 years.

BISSEXTILIS, ANNUS (Lat., twice sixth year). A leap year, called *bissextilis* because there are two "sixth" days before the kalends (1st) of March.

BLACK. A liturgical colour. Black vestments are used at a requiem Mass and a black cope during the absolutions thereafter and at an interment; but if a requiem Mass is said in a church when the Blessed Sacrament is exposed therein purple is worn. When such a Mass is said at an altar whereon the Blessed Sacrament is reserved, the frontal and tabernacle veil must not be black but purple. Black is also used at the Mass of the Presanctified on Good Friday.

BLACK CANONS. Canons Regular of St. Augustine, so called because of the black cloak which they wear out-of-doors.

BLACK FAST. A fast-day on which only one meal was allowed, and that not till evening; in addition, meat, eggs, butter, cheese, milk and wine were forbidden. In Lent only bread, salt, vegetables and water were allowed. Such rigour is no longer found in the Western church, except in certain religious houses or due to individual piety.

BLACK FRIARS. The Dominicans, so called from the black cloak (*cappa*) and hood which they wear out-of-doors.

BLACK MADONNA. A statue or picture of our Lady which, either because of the material of which it is made or the manner in which it is painted or on account of age, is black in colour. The most famous is the statue of Notre Dame du Pilier in Chartres cathedral.

BLACK MASS. i. A requiem Mass, so called because black vestments are worn.

ii. A name given to the blasphemous and sacrilegious rites performed by certain apostates and infidels.

BLACK MONKS. The Benedictines, so called from their entirely black habit.

"BLACK POPE," The. A nick-name sometimes given to the superior general of the Society of Jesus on account of the excessive power and authority ignorantly supposed to be his; "black" because the Jesuits wear a black cassock and the pope a white one. He is elected by a general congregation of the society and has complete administrative power and spiritual authority within the society's constitutions, which he may for grave reason dispense but cannot change. He lives in Rome and has eight assistants of different nationalities.

"BLACKS AND WHITES." The two divisions of Roman patrician society from the setting-up of the Italian kingdom in 1870 until the recognition of the Vatican City in 1929. The Blacks were the loyal adherents of the Pope-King, and among their principal families were the Colonna, Orsini, Ruspoli, Sacchetti, Lancelotti, Massimo, Aldobrandini, Giustiniani-Bandini. For years no social intercourse of any kind took place between the two parties, but for some time before the conciliation they had been seeing quite a lot of one another.

BLAIRS. St. Mary's College at Blairs in the county of Kincardine, the principal seminary of Scotland. It was formed in 1829 by the fusion of the two little seminaries of Lismore and Aquhorties, the second of which had been founded at Scalan in Glenlivat in 1712.

BLASPHEMY. Speech, writings, gestures or thoughts which show contumely to or contempt for God or detract from his honour, whether such contumely, contempt or dishonour be intended or not. Intentional blasphemy is always a grave sin against religion; and efforts should be made if necessary to eliminate unintentional blasphemy from one's speech, etc. Blasphemy against God is committed indirectly by speech, etc., showing contumely and dishonour to or contempt for his Church, the saints or sacred things; the gravity of this sin depends on the kind of blasphemy.

BLASPHEMY OF THE SPIRIT, The (Matt. xii, 31-2; Mark iii, 29). "The sin against the Holy Ghost," that is, maliciously attributing to the Devil works that are manifestly of God. This sin shall not be forgiven because it implies a spirit of pride and degree of perversity normally incompatible with the repentance without which forgiveness is impossible. But St. Augustine explained this sin as final impenitence, which from its nature is unforgivable.

BLESS ONESELF, TO. To make the sign of the cross (*q.v.*) on oneself.

BLESSED. A beatus (*q.v.*). Such an one is referred to as, *e.g.*, Blessed John Jones, and must be distinguished from a fully canonized saint.

BLESSED IN HEAVEN, The. In Heaven (*q.v.*) the souls of the just enjoy eternal and unchangeable happiness in the possession of God in the Beatific Vision (*q.v.*)—essential beatitude; and in numerous other ways—accidental beatitude—of which one of the chief will be the reunion of the soul with the glorified body (*q.v.*) after the resurrection.

BLESSED SACRAMENT, The. A title of the sacrament of the Eucharist (*q.v.*) which indicates its supreme position among all the sacraments.

BLESSING. A rite by which the Church dedicates persons, places or things to a sacred purpose, or attaches to them a spiritual value, without consecration (*q.v.*). Any priest may give blessings, except those reserved to pope or bishop, and non-Catholics are capable of receiving them, with certain exceptions. No blessing is valid unless the prescribed formula is used. The chief blessings in use in the Church are: (*a*) of persons: an abbot, bride and bridegroom, dying person, woman before and after childbirth, children, people in general; (*b*) of places: a church, oratory, cemetery, house; (*c*) of things: baptismal water, bells, holy oils, vestments, altar linen, images. Among the numerous special blessings contained in the "Rituale Romanum" are those for a new house, a bedroom, a ship, pilgrims, food, gold, incense and myrrh and chalk at the Epiphany, a school-house, printing machinery, an aeroplane, an electric dynamo, a railway, a bridge, a child, bees, sick animals and others proper to religious orders or dioceses, *e.g.*, of a bonfire on St. John's eve (Tarbes). Pious objects blessed and indulgenced do not lose the blessing or indulgences by being broken and repaired, or by being given away or lent to others, but only by being totally destroyed or sold.

BLESSING OF ST. BLAISE, The, is given by touching the throats of the faithful with two crossed candles, blessed as prescribed, at the same time using the words, "May God deliver thee from trouble of the throat and from every other evil through the intercession of St. Blaise, the bishop and martyr. In the name of the Father and of the Son and of the Holy Ghost. Amen." This blessing may be given at any time or place but principally on Feb. 3, the feast of St. Blaise.

BLOOD, BAPTISM OF, is one of the two possible substitutes for Baptism (*q.v.*) of water and consists in suffering martyrdom for the Faith or for some Christian virtue, which infuses sanctifying grace into the soul and forgives sin. Martyrdom produces this effect by a special privilege, as being a supreme act of love in imitation of the passion of our Lord, but the martyr must have had attrition for his sins. Baptism of blood extends to infants. See DESIRE.

BLOOD, SHEDDING OF. i. Those who have committed voluntary homicide or effected an abortion, or who have co-operated in these crimes, who have mutilated themselves or others, or clerics who have unlawfully practised medicine or surgery with a death ensuing therefrom, incur irregularity (*q.v.*) for the reception or exercise of holy orders.

ii. Violation of a church (*q.v.*) is brought about by a voluntary homicide committed therein (even if actual death takes place outside and without effusion of blood), or by a considerable shedding of blood therein due to blows or other violence. Such acts in the porch, sacristy or tower do not constitute violation.

BLUE is no longer a liturgical colour, but it is used in Spain and Spanish America for the feast of the Immaculate Conception of our Lady. The same privilege has been extended to certain churches, *e.g.*, Downside Abbey. The idea that blue is peculiarly our Lady's colour is relatively modern, at any rate in England. Abbots of Sylvestrine monks are allowed blue *mozzetta* and *mantelletta*.

BLUE NUNS or Sisters. Several congregations are commonly so called on account of the colour of their habit or some part of it: *e.g.*, the Institute of Marie Reparatrice, the Sisters of the Temple, the Little Company of Mary.

BOAT. A vessel for holding incense before it is put into the thurible; so called from its shape.

BODILY DEFECT which makes it difficult, impossible, or lacking in decency for one to say Mass and fulfil the other functions of holy orders (*e.g.*, blindness, deafness, dumbness, a notable maimedness or deformity, inability to drink wine) constitutes an irregularity (*q.v.*) which, if it is certain, can only be dispensed by the Holy See. Such a dispensation is more easily obtained after ordination than before.

BODY. A composition of prime matter and form (*qq.v.*) essentially. Triple dimension (length, breadth, depth) mass, weight, colour, etc., are accidentals. The first notion of body is that it is something extended (*cf.*, extension ii)—but this is not the essence of body. Aristotle's theory, and also that of St. Thomas Aquinas and the great scholastics, is that it is essentially composed of matter and form, and that these two principles alone can explain the properties of body, such as activity, extension, etc.

BODY, GLORIFIED OR RISEN. The body which will be assumed by the just soul after the resurrection (*q.v.*); it will be a true body, having identity (some material identity is generally taught) with the earthly body, and be in some way spiritualized so that it is immortal and incorruptible. "Unstinted and complete restoration of all the sense life that makes us human beings is the true and primary meaning of the resurrection of the body" (Vonier). Scholastic theology attributes to the glorified body the qualities of impassibility, clarity, agility and subtlety (*qq.v.*), and teaches that it will be in the state of youth. The bodies of the reprobate will arise equally, to suffer eternally: they also will be identical, immortal and incorruptible.

BODY AND SOUL. Man is a composite of body and soul. Strictly speaking, it should be said that man is a composite of prime matter and soul. The soul is the substantial form (*q.v.*), and as such makes the prime matter in man to be body, to be human, to have activities, etc. If the soul is separated from the body, the body *ipso facto* ceases to be body and human body, etc.; it is only the incoming of new substantial forms which makes what was formerly prime matter in man to be what we call a corpse. The soul and the body are good and were made by God who is good, but the body has certain powers, which, owing to original sin, incline downwards rather than upwards. The passions reside in the lower part of our nature and these, unless restrained and kept in check by the powers of the soul, drag the soul down. The passions, since God implanted them in us, are good, but they must be in proper restraint; they are educated or trained by the cardinal virtues.

BOGOMILI, The. An important heretical sect which troubled southeastern Europe, especially Bulgaria, from the 10th to the 15th centuries. The name derives from that of its early leader, the priest Bogomil (probably a Slavonic form of "Theophilus"). Their beliefs were a fusion of those of the Paulicians and the Messalians (*qq.v.*), with a complete and peculiar mythology; its dualism was not absolute but gave a superior power to God. The relations between the Bogomils and the adherents of Albigensianism (*q.v.*) have not yet been fully examined.

BOHEMIAN BRETHREN, The. Now better known as the Moravians (*q.v.*).

BOLIVIA, THE CHURCH IN. The 3 million and more inhabitants of Bolivia are almost all Indians and mixed, most of them Catholics. The state "recognizes and supports the Roman Apostolic Catholic religion" and makes a small annual grant towards the support of the clergy and for the Indian missions, but the Church is not "established." There are 2 metropolitan sees, Sucre (founded at Charcas in 1551) and La Paz (1608), with 3 and 2 suffragans respectively; 3 vicariates apostolic and a prefecture are Indian missions.

BOLLANDISTS, The. The name given to the Jesuit editors of the "Acta Sanctorum" (*q.v.*), from John van Bolland who began the work, though he was not its originator, about 1630. It was interrupted by the French Revolution but re-established at Brussels in 1837, and still continues. The Bollandists, who never number more than about half a dozen, form one of the most learned groups of men. In addition to the "Acta," they publish "Analecta Bollandiana" and other scientific works of the first rank.

BOM (Port., good). Used as in "the church of the Bom Jesus" at Goa.

BON SECOURS (Fr., good help). Two congregations of nursing sisters bear this name, originating in Paris and Troyes respectively. They are trained nurses who give their services to the poor but accept payment from the wealthy.

BONA MORS, The (Lat., good death). i. "The Archconfraternity of our Lord Jesus Christ dying on the cross, and of the most blessed Virgin Mary, his sorrowing mother," founded at Rome in 1648 by Fr. Vincent Caraffa, S.J., to prepare Christians for a holy death.
ii. A popular service of devotion, having the same object.

BONSHOMMES (Fr., from Lat. *boni homines*, good men). A name popularly given to religious of the Grandmontine order (*q.v.*), to a minor order of friars (who may have been the same as the "Friars of the Sack," *q.v.*), and to a congregation of Portuguese canons, all now extinct.

BOOK OF HOURS. A mediæval prayer-book containing, principally, the Little Office of our Lady and the Office of the Dead, in Latin; often called in England a Primer (*q.v.*).

BOOK OF LIFE, The. A metaphor for the divine predestination (*q.v.*) to supernatural life. This predestination is absolute and complete concerning those of whom God knows that they will certainly die in a state of grace and will obtain eternal life. The term is thus used in Apocalypse (Revelation) xx, 15, and xxi, 27. It is incomplete concerning those who are now living in a state of grace and who may fall from it. For this use of the term *cf.* Luke x, 20, and Phil. iv, 3. So the Book of Life contains the names of those who are predestined to everlasting glory and whose names cannot be erased from it, but also the names of others in virtue of their predestination to sanctifying grace merely.

"BORN CATHOLIC." There is no such thing as a "born Catholic," for Baptism is the gate by which the Church is entered. The phrase is used in England to designate one born of Catholic parents and brought up in the faith, as distinct from one not so born and brought up who has embraced the faith. To be a born Catholic is a privilege rather than a virtue. "Cradle Catholic" is a better expression for the same thing.

BOSTON (*Bostoniensis*). One of the early dioceses of the United States, covering most of 5 counties in Massachusetts. The first Catholic church in New England was opened in Boston in 1788, and in 1808 the city became the seat of a diocese; the first bishop was John Louis Lefebvre. The see was made metropolitan in 1875, its suffragan dioceses being Burlington, Fall River, Hartford, Manchester, Portland, Providence, and Springfield. Among its bishops have been B. J. Fenwick and Cardinal William O'Connell. Boston is named from Boston in Lincolnshire, England; the name means "St. Botulf's stone."

BOWING, either by a simple inclination of the head, or medium, of the upper part of the body, or profound, from the waist, is the normal method of expressing reverence and respect throughout the Church. The occasions at which bowing is enjoined by the rubrics, on the ministers and those who assist at sacred ceremonies, are too many to enumerate; but apart from these a profound inclination should always be made towards the cross on a high-altar, or any altar at which Mass is being said, if the Blessed Sacrament is not reserved thereat. Certain of the religious orders (Carthusians, Calced Carmelites, Cistercians, Dominicans) and most Eastern rites use the profound bow instead of the genuflection (*q.v.*) liturgically (*cf.*, Metany).

BOY-BISHOP. A common custom, especially in England, during the middle ages was the "election" of a boy-bishop on St. Nicholas's day (Dec. 6). On the eve of Holy Innocents, dressed in mitre and cope, with the crook of his pastoral staff turned towards him (to show he had no jurisdiction!) and with other boys dressed in copes he went in procession to the Innocents' altar which he incensed. He then returned to his stall in choir, sang a blessing, and presided at Compline. The ceremony was associated with feasting and merry-making but was not subject to such abuse as the "feast of the Ass" *(q.v.)*.

BRAGA, USE OF, The. Certain liturgical peculiarities in the Roman rite, proper to the archdiocese of Braga, the primatial see of Portugal. Its Breviary resembles the Dominican, but with hymns according to the reform of Pope Urban VIII.

BRANCH THEORY, The. A theory maintained by many members of the Anglican churches, and to a certain extent officially held by their bishops, that the Church of Christ consists of three branches, the Roman, the Eastern Orthodox and the Anglican. How a church divided into three disagreeing members can display the unity which Christ declared his church to have, has not yet been explained by upholders of the theory.

BRAVERY. See FORTITUDE.

BRAZIL, THE CHURCH IN. Brazil is the largest country of South America and has over 46 million inhabitants, one-third of whom are Indians and many more of mixed Indian and Portuguese blood. Most are Catholic by profession, but for a great many this profession is merely nominal; there are numbers of German, Polish, Japanese, Turkish and other immigrants; Protestant organizations are active. Church and state were separated in 1891, and no religion may be either subsidized or molested; divorce *a vinculo* is not recognized, and church property is exempt from taxation. The primatial see is Bahia, founded in 1551; there are sixteen other metropolitan sees, with 56 suffragan dioceses; a feature of ecclesiastical organization in Brazil is the prelatures *nullius (q.v.)*, over a score of them, including a Benedictine abbacy, whose clergy are engaged in missionary work.

BREACH OF PROMISE of marriage canonically made (see BETROTHAL) is actionable in the ecclesiastical court to obtain damages, but not to claim the celebration of the marriage. Breach of a promise not made canonically is not actionable.

BREAD is principally used by the Catholic Church as one of the elements of the sacrifice of the Mass. Minor uses are as a sacramental *(q.v.)* e.g., bread blessed during the Liturgy *(antidoron, etc.)* or in honour of some saint, *e.g.*, St. Antony of Padua, and to cleanse the fingers after performing certain rites.

BREAD, BLESSED. See ANTIDORON and PAIN BENIT. There is a form for blessing bread and other food at Easter in the "Rituale Romanum."

BREAD, EUCHARISTIC. The altar-bread *(q.v.)*, used in the Western church and by the Armenians (both Catholic and other), Maronites and Catholic Malabarese, is unleavened *(azyme, q.v.)*. All the other Eastern churches, Catholic and dissident, use it leavened. The Nestorians and Jacobites mix with it salt and oil and some bread left from the previous Liturgy as well as the "holy leaven" *(q.v.)*; Catholic Chaldeans and Syrians add a little salt. Eastern altar-bread is generally in the form of small cakes (see PROSPHORA). A priest must always celebrate with the bread used in his own rite, wherever he may be saying Mass.

BREAKING OF BREAD, The, is now performed at the fraction *(q.v.)* in the Mass and corresponding actions in other liturgies. In the primitive Roman liturgy till about the 8th century it was broken into the *sancta (q.v.)*, the *fermentum (q.v.)* and a third part for communion of the celebrant, the people and those who were absent; a portion of this last was dropped into the chalice just before the consumption of the Precious Blood in papal Masses. This survives in all Masses now, but is done after the *Pax Domini.*

BREATHING. See AIR.

BREECHES BIBLE, The. The Geneva Bible *(q.v.)*, so called because Gen. iii, 7 was rendered, "they sewed fig leaves together and made themselves breeches."

BRENTWOOD *(Brentwoodensis)*. An English see formed in 1917 by division from the archdiocese of Westminster of the county of Essex, before the Reformation in the diocese of London. Its Catholic population is most dense in the eastern suburbs of London. At Ingatestone and Thorndon the Petre family kept the Faith alive through penal times; the mission of Stratford-by-Bow was founded in 1770. The Canonesses of the Holy Sepulchre have occupied King Henry VIII's mansion of New Hall near Chelmsford since 1799. The patrons of the diocese are Our Lady of Lourdes, St. Edmund of Canterbury, and St. Erconwald, founder of the former Benedictine nunnery at Barking; the cathedral is dedicated to the Sacred Heart and St. Helen.

BRETHREN OF THE LORD, The (Matt. xiii, 55). That these were cousins is in accordance with tradition and Biblical usage of the word "brother" *(cf.*, Gen. xii, 5 *et al.)*. Some hold that St. Joseph had been previously married and had children, which view is permissible and supported by some tradition; that the "brethren" were the children of Mary is incompatible with the Church's teaching of her perpetual virginity.

BREVIARIUM ROMANUM. "The Roman Breviary," that is, according to the general use of the Western church. *Breviarium Monasticum*, the breviary as used by the Benedictines; . . . *iuxta ritum sancti Ordinis Prædicatorum*, as used by the Dominicans;

. . . *Romano-Seraphicum,* as used by the Franciscans; . . . *ad usum insignis ecclesiæ Eboracensis,* as used in the former province of York, etc.

BREVIARY (Lat., a compendium). The book which contains all that is necessary to enable a cleric to recite the daily Divine Office (*q.v.*). It is usually printed in four volumes, one for each season of the year. Each volume contains the psalter, arranged for every day of the week; the hymns, prayers, antiphons, lessons, etc., proper to the season or movable feasts which may occur; the same for the feasts of saints; the same for saints who have no proper office, arranged according to whether they were martyrs, virgins, etc.; the Little Office of our Lady and Office of the Dead; any supplements that may be required for special or local feasts. A *"totum"* in one volume is now also published. In addition to the breviaries mentioned under "Breviarium Romanum" there are special ones for St. Peter's at Rome, the province of Milan, the church of Toledo, the Carmelites, the Carthusians, and others. Most of the Catholic Eastern churches still have their Divine Office scattered about several books, but the Maronites and Malabarese have well-arranged breviaries. The word is often used as a synonym for Divine Office.

BRIDGETTINE OFFICE, The, proper to the Bridgettine nuns, is an elaborated form of the Little Office of our Lady. The whole psalter is recited in the course of each week; each feria has its proper antiphons and three lessons at Matins taken from the "Sermo Angelicus" of St. Bridget; and there are proper hymns for each hour every day, except that the little hours share the same one on ferias. On feasts of our Lady the canticle *Benedicite* is sung, farced, at Vespers, and at the beginning of the same hour every day the two sides of the choir ask one another's pardon for offences.

BRIDGETTINES, The. Nuns of the Order of the Most Holy Saviour, founded by St. Bridget of Sweden in 1344, professing the rule of St. Augustine with special constitutions. They are enclosed and contemplative, conducting a crusade of prayer for the relief of the souls in Purgatory, with daily exposition of the Blessed Sacrament. Their habit is grey and they have a daily office proper to the order. The Bridgettines of the Recollection are a Spanish congregation with seven houses, and there are five others. One in England, at South Brent in Devon, has unbroken organic identity with the pre-Reformation Syon Abbey at Isleworth (*q.v.*). The order was originally founded for men as well as women in double monasteries (*q.v.*); an attempt in England to revive it for men separately was abortive.

BRIEF. A papal letter, signed by the secretary for briefs and stamped with an impression of the pope's ring; it is a less formal and weighty document than a bull (*q.v.*). The English hierarchy was restored by a brief, *Universalis Ecclesiæ,* in 1850.

BRIEFS TO PRINCES, SECRETARIATE OF. A Palatine secretariate whose business it is to draw up letters from the pope to kings, governors and other personages of importance. The secretary also composes consistorial allocutions (*q.v.*) and encyclicals (*q.v.*).

BRITISH CHURCH, The. The church established in what is now England and Wales before the mission of St. Augustine. There are several legendary accounts of its foundation but the actual facts are not known. In the persecution of Diocletian it gave the martyrs Alban, Julius and Aaron, and sent bishops to the synods of Arles and Rimini in the 4th century. St. Patrick was a product of this Romano-British church. After the Anglo-Saxon invasions it was utterly destroyed except in the north-west, Wales and Cornwall; from the middle of the 5th century contact with Rome was impossible. But there was close contact between Wales, Brittany and Ireland, and there ensued an era of great missionary monks and notable saints (*cf.*, Celtic Church and Rite); Gildas gives the other side of the picture. When St. Augustine came to the heathen English in 597, relations between the British "born-Catholics" and the Roman newcomers and their converts were not cordial; and the old British church in Wales was not absorbed by the church of Canterbury for another 450 years. See ENGLISH CHURCH.

BROAD-CHURCH. An old-fashioned but convenient label for the large body of Anglican Protestants who avoid the theology and zeal of the high-church on the one hand and the evangelicalism of the low-church on the other. "Broad'" may be referred both to the modernism of their theology and to their tolerance of any religious beliefs that do not involve ethical latitudinarianism. A large section of this party is now stiffened by a belief in the branch theory and continuity (*qq.v.*).

BROAD STOLE, The, is not a stole at all. See FOLDED CHASUBLE.

BROTHER. A title used (*a*) for novices and postulants in religious orders; (*b*) in formal documents, etc., for Dominican and other friars (*Reverendus pater, frater N. . . .*); (*c*) for lay-brothers; (*d*) for members of religious congregations whose members do not become priests. Secular tertiaries (*q.v.*) may and sometimes on formal occasions do use the title. The pope addresses a fellow bishop as "venerable brother."

BROTHERS. A collective name for the religious of congregations and institutes whose members do not receive holy orders, *e.g.*, the Alexian Brothers (nursing), the Brothers of the Christian Schools (teaching), the Brothers Hospitallers of St. John-of-God (nursing), the Xaverian Brothers (teaching).

BROTHERS OF THE CHRISTIAN SCHOOLS, The. The Christian Brothers, *q.v.*

BROTHERS OF ST. PATRICK. A teaching congregation founded by Daniel Delany, bishop of Kildare, at Tullow in 1808. It has spread to Austria and India.

BROTHERHOOD OF MAN. God "made, of one single stock, all the nations that were to dwell over the whole face of the earth" (Acts xvii, 26). But the brotherhood of man resides not only in the natural unity of the human race but also in the common fatherhood of God, in whose image man was made* and from whom all fatherhood is named. St. Paul further shows the unity and brotherhood of man from those links which bind us to God the Son incarnate, in whom "all created things took their being"; and especially from our common redemption through him, who gave us his commandment "that you should love one another as I have loved you" (John xv, 12).

BUCKFAST. A Benedictine abbey of the English province of the Cassinese congregation of Primitive Observance, at Buckfastleigh, in Devon. It was founded in 1882 by monks of Pierre-qui-Vire, banished from France, and was erected into an abbey in 1902. Its buildings are on the site of former Benedictine and Cistercian monasteries.

BUGIA. A small candlestick with a short straight handle. It is held with a lighted candle in it at the missal by the first chaplain in a bishop's low Mass, and by an acolyte in solemn functions at which a bishop assists. The use of the *bugia* is conceded to abbots, protonotaries apostolic and domestic prelates, and to certain regular prelates, *e.g.*, the minister general of the Friars Minor. The name is from Bougie, in Algeria, whence the wax for candles was once obtained. Also called a *palmatoria*.

BULGARIA, THE CHURCH IN. Of the 7 million people, 84 per cent belong to the Bulgarian Orthodox Church, an independent unit of the Eastern Orthodox Church, with a patriarch at its head. This is the official church of the nation, but its clergy are forbidden by law to "interfere in the affairs of such Christians as are not subject to them." The biggest minority is 13 per cent of Mohammedans. There are only about 45,000 Catholics, of whom 7,000 are of Byzantine rite, with an exarch (*q.v.*) at Sofia. The remainder, mostly of foreign origin, are of Latin rite and are organized in one diocese i.s.h.s. and a vicariate apostolic.

BULGARIAN HERETICS. A name used indifferently for the members of neo-Manichæan sects, Paulicians, Bogomili, Catharists (*qq.v.*). In a form now considered obscene the name has passed into common speech, throwing lurid light on the reputation of these heretics.

BULL, PAPAL. The most solemn and weighty form of papal letter, beginning "[Name], servant of the servants of God" and formerly always sealed with a lead seal (Lat. *bulla,* a boss or bubble). Anglican orders were condemned by a bull, *Apostolicæ curæ,* and the diocese of Brentwood was erected by a similar instrument, *Universalis Ecclesiæ procuratio,* in 1917.

BULLARIUM. A collection of bulls or other papal documents.

BURIAL, CHRISTIAN, is the interment of a corpse according to the Church's funeral rites (*q.v.*) in consecrated ground. If the grave is in a non-Catholic cemetery it is to be blessed at the time of the burial. The corpse, on the day of burial or before, should be taken to the church for the Office and Mass of the Dead. Among those who may not receive Christian burial are the unbaptized (except catechumens), and, unless they have shown some sign of repentance before death, apostates, members of non-Catholic bodies, suicides (*felo de se, q.v.*), those killed in a duel and those who have directed that their body should be cremated. Baptism is a necessary condition for ecclesiastical burial, but catechumens who die without baptism through no fault of their own are to be buried with the same rites as baptized persons.

BURSE. i. A square pocket or purse, about 12 inches square, made of cardboard covered with silk, in which the folded corporal (*q.v.*) is carried to and from the altar. In material and colour it should match the vestments.
ii. A free place in a seminary, college or other institution, supported by means of an endowment; the occupant is often selected by competitive examination.

BURSFELD UNION, The. A Benedictine congregation of monasteries in the Germanies formed in 1464; it flourished greatly until the Reformation and finally disappeared at the end of the 18th century. Their abbey of Lamspring was taken over by the English congregation in 1643 and is now represented by Fort Augustus Abbey.

BUSKINS. Ceremonial stockings reaching to the knee worn over his ordinary purple stockings by a bishop at pontifical Mass. They are of silk, embroidered with gold thread, and of the same colour as the other vestments.

---

* The term "fatherhood of God" is used here in a somewhat loose sense; the term is more precisely used in reference to the divine adoption of the Christian through Baptism and Sanctifying Grace.—*Publisher,* 1997.

BUSSOLANTI are the lay chamberlains on guard in the ante-rooms which lead to the pope's apartments; one of them, the sub-quartermaster, is always an architect. They wear a costume of crimson damask, rather like that of the *sediarii* who carry the *sedia gestatoria* (*q.v.*) in processions.

BUYING AND SELLING. A contract in which goods are exchanged for money. For such a contract to be just the seller must have the right to sell the goods and a just price (*q.v.*) must be charged and paid; in estimating this price consideration should be taken of any hidden defects which lessen the value of the goods; should, however, these defects be such as to render the goods substantially different from what the buyer intended to purchase, the contract is invalid.

BYZANTINE. The manner of church building and decoration, of Greek, Roman and eastern origins, of which the church of the Holy Wisdom at Constantinople (consecrated 562) was the archetype. It spread from Constantinople to Russia, Bulgaria, Serbia, Rumania, over Asia Minor, and in a lesser degree to Armenia and the Caucasus; and it had much influence in the west. With local exceptions, variations and modifications, it is still followed in the Byzantine rite as a sort of liturgical necessity; its purest form, both old and new, is well exemplified on Mount Athos; the cathedral at Westminster is a modern copying of Byzantine building and the only one on a large scale in the West.

BYZANTINE CHURCH, The. The church and patriarchate of Constantinople (*q.v.*, formerly Byzantium); the name is sometimes extended to include the whole Orthodox Eastern Church (*q.v.*).

BYZANTINE EMPIRE, The. The Roman empire in the East from the time that Constantine made Constantinople his capital until that city was finally captured by the Turks in 1453. From its geographical situation, language, manners and history it is sometimes called the Greek Empire. Its Church eventually became the separated Orthodox Church, which is still popularly called "Roman" in the Near East.

BYZANTINE RITE, The. The system and forms of worship and administration of the sacraments proper at first to the church of Constantinople, but now used by the whole of what is now the Orthodox Eastern Church (*q.v.*) and also by some Catholics. It includes three eucharistic Liturgies, that of St. John Chrysostom, of St. Basil and of the Presanctified (*qq.v.*), a Divine Office (*Akolouthia*, *q.v.*) of great length, and ceremonies for the administration of the seven sacraments (*qq.v.*). Its original language is old Greek, but it is used in many others as well, *e.g.*, Church Slavonic, Arabic, Rumanian, Georgian, Finnish, Albanian. It has its own chant, arrangement of church buildings, vestments (*qq.v.*) and other customs (*e.g.*, the sign of the cross is made from right to left), round statues and instruments of music are forbidden in church, communion is given with a spoon in both kinds. There is a definitive church arrangement. At the west end is the *narthex* (*q.v.*); then the nave. Stalls are arranged all around the walls; at the further end are stalls for the singers and between them and the *iconostasis* is the *analogion* (*qq.v.*): there are generally no other seats. On the left is the *ambo* (*q.v.*), on the right the bishop's stall. There may be a special gallery for women. Then the *bema* or sanctuary with the altar in the middle and the *prothesis* and *diakonikon* (*qq.v.*) on either side; the sanctuary is divided from the nave by the characteristic *ikonostasis* which completely hides the east end. Certain Catholic users of the rite have modified this arrangement, and in the United States and elsewhere seats for the people have been introduced, as well as statues. This rite is the most widespread after that of Rome and is followed by over 100 million Christians, of whom about 7 millions are Catholics.

BYZANTINE RITE, CATHOLICS OF THE, are those who use that rite and are subject to their own canon law, namely, the Italo-Greeks, and a number of Melkites, Ruthenians, Bulgarians, Georgians, Greeks, Hungarians, Rumanians, Russians and Yugoslavs. They are found in their countries of origin, U.S.A., Canada and elsewhere. They keep their rite and its customs in varying degrees of purity and in five languages, and are organized under bishops of the rite. All preserve the ancient customs of leavened altar-bread, communion under both kinds, the ordination of married men to the priesthood, baptism by immersion, etc. They have a number of monks and nuns (Basilians, *q.v.*). See also EASTERN RITES; BAPTISM; CONFIRMATION; etc.

C

CÆREMONIALE EPISCOPORUM. A liturgical book, "The Ceremonial of Bishops" *q.v.*).

CÆREMONIALE ROMANUM. A liturgical book, "The Roman Ceremonial" (*q.v.*).

CÆREMONIARIUS. The Latin term for a master of ceremonies (*q.v.*).

CÆSARIAN OPERATION. The delivery of a child, which cannot be born in the natural way, by surgical removal of the contents of the womb through incisions made in the abdominal and uterine walls. On account of the mutilation involved there must be some good reason, *e.g.*, the probability of thus saving the lives of both mother and child, to make it lawful. A woman in labour who cannot be delivered of her child alive is not bound to submit to this operation against her will; but the child must be baptized in the womb.

CAESAROPAPISM. A term used primarily of the relationship between Church and state in the Byzantine empire, wherein the Church tended to be a department of state, government-controlled; the emperor was esteemed to have a sacred and quasi-sacramental character: and so Caesar came almost to have the place of Pope (*Papa*). The use of the word is extended to cover any accepted domination of the ecclesiastical by the civil power, brought about by dependence of the Church on the state and too great a readiness to accept state assistance, whence follows state control. Caesaropapism has continued to have influence in the Orthodox Eastern Church right down to contemporary times (*e.g.*, in the pre-revolution Russian Church), other factors having arisen to perpetuate its force. See also ERASTIANISM.

CALATRAVA, ORDER OF. A Spanish military order founded in 1258 to defend the land against the Moors. It became powerful and wealthy, but has now ceased to exist except as an order of honour.

CALCED (Lat. *calceus*, a shoe). Certain religious are distinguished by this adjective, as wearing boots or shoes, from a branch of their order that goes barefoot or sandalled, *e.g.*, the Calced Carmelites.

CALDEY. A Cistercian monastery on the island of Caldey, off Tenby. This island was occupied by Celtic monks from about the middle of the 6th century and by Tironian Benedictines from about 1118 till 1534. In 1906 it was acquired by monks of the Church of England who, in 1913, became Catholics in a body (see PRINKNASH): these were succeeded in 1928 by Cistercians, chiefly from the Belgian abbey of Chimay. There are two pre-Reformation churches again in Catholic use on the island.

CALEFACTORY (Lat. *calefacere*, to make warm). The room in a monastery in which a fire was kept alight when necessary. The name is still sometimes used for a monastic common-room.

CALENDAR, KALENDAR, Ecclesiastical. A list of the days of the year with the feasts, saints' days, vigils, fasts, etc., noted as they occur. The liturgical seasons depending on the date of Easter, calendars necessarily vary in some respects from year to year. In the Western church every religious order and every diocese has its own calendar, and these

are subject to minor alterations on account of the requirements of the countries, congregations or towns in which they are being used. The Western calendars are all based on the general calendar of the Roman church (*q.v.*). Among the Easterns there is a variety of calendars with varying degrees of dissimilarity from that of the Roman church. Very few feasts are observed on the same day in every single Catholic church of the world but, excluding the few members of the lesser Eastern rites, there are over 100 feasts common to the Latin and Byzantine calendars and many of these are kept on the same or almost the same day. The calendars of the dissident orientals are substantially the same as those of Catholics of the same rite.

CALENDAR, ARMENIAN. The ecclesiastical calendar of the Armenian rite has only seven feasts on fixed dates, Christmas-Epiphany, Circumcision, Entry into the Temple (Purification), Annunciation, Birthday of our Lady, Presentation of our Lady, Immaculate Conception, all of which the Catholics keep on the same dates as in the West. All other feasts fall on a day of the week following a certain Sunday which depends on the date of Easter; during Lent and other fasts a saint's feast can be kept only on Saturday, and not at all from Easter to Pentecost; only certain feasts are observed on a Sunday. Therefore there are only about 130 saints' days in the year, and many of them are observed in groups, *e.g.*, the Egyptian Hermits, the Fathers of Nicæa, the Martyrs of Persia. The Catholics have adopted several Western feasts, *e.g.*, Corpus Christi. The dissidents alone in all the world still keep Christmas and the Epiphany as one feast, on Jan. 6. The annual reckoning is from B.C. 2492.

CALENDAR, BYZANTINE. This has no liturgical cycles corresponding to those of the Roman church year, but the period from the Sunday "before Septuagesima" to the Saturday after Whitsunday (*triodion* of Lent and *triodion* of Easter) stands apart as of special importance. Its feasts (of which a number fall on the same date as in the West) are divided into those of our Lord, our Lady and the saints, and there is one or more of these commemorated on every day of the year; they vary considerably in different countries. Sundays are named after the subject of the gospel of the day, *e.g.*, of the Prodigal Son (Septuagesima), of the Second Coming (Sexagesima). It consecrates days to many Old Testament saints (*q.v.*), and among its other special feasts are The Miracle of our Lady at Miasene (Sept. 1), the Earthquake of the Year 740 (Oct. 26, in thanksgiving for deliverance from it) the Ancestors of the Messias (Dec. 11), All the Fathers who were pleasing to God from Adam to St. Joseph (Sunday before Christmas), the Three

Holy Hierarchs (*q.v.*, Jan. 30), the feast of Orthodoxy (*q.v.*), the Image of our Lady of Kazan (July 8), etc. Feasts rank as greater of the first, second or third class, and lesser of the first or second class. The ecclesiastical year begins on Sept. 1. See JULIAN CALENDAR; FEAST; OCTAVE; SYNAXIS; VIGIL, etc., and Appendix II A.

CALENDAR, CHALDEAN. The Chaldeans divide their church year into ten unequal periods, from Advent to the general feast of the Dedication of the Church; there are only about 60 saints' days and feasts, and many of them are movable, occurring generally on Fridays (*e.g.*, the Four Evangelists on the 1st Friday after Epiphany, St. Damasus, 5th Friday after Pentecost): Corpus Christi, the Sacred Heart, Our Lady of Mount Carmel (under the name of Our Lady's Garment, *i.e.*, the brown scapular) and others have been adopted from the West. Among the special Chaldean feasts are the Syrian and Roman Doctors, St. Addai the Apostle, St. Mari, St. James of Nisibis (movable) and Our Lady of Seed-time (May 15). Though the Catholic Malabar rite is derived from the Chaldean, its calendar is that of the Roman church.

CALENDAR, COPTIC. For ecclesiastical purposes the Copts reckon their years according to the era of the Martyrs, from 284, the first year of Diocletian. They have seven great feasts of our Lord (Annunciation, Christmas, his Baptism, Palm Sunday, Easter, Ascension, Pentecost) and seven lesser (Circumcision, Miracle of Cana, Presentation, Last Supper, his Appearing to St. Thomas, Flight into Egypt and Transfiguration) which are mostly observed on different dates from elsewhere, and numerous feasts of saints. Some hundred feasts and saints' days are common to the Coptic and Roman calendars. The Birthday of our Lord, our Lady, and St. Michael (for the rising of the Nile and a good harvest) are supposed to be celebrated every month, as well as at other times. The Ethiopic calendar derives from the Coptic, but has several peculiar feasts (*e.g.*, Pontius Pilate) and extravagant customs; this has had to be stringently revised for Catholic use.

CALENDAR, SYRIAN. This is founded on the old calendar of the church of Antioch, and many of the dates are unusual, *e.g.*, the Visitation on the 6th Sunday before Christmas, St. Stephen on Jan. 8; to it the Catholics have added later and local feasts and several of Western origin, *e.g.*, Corpus Christi. Among their days of obligation are the Praises of the Mother of God (Dec. 26), St. Joseph, St. Ephrem and the titular of a church. From it is derived the Maronite calendar.

CALENDAR, THE GREGORIAN, is the Julian Calendar as adjusted by order of Pope Gregory XIII to make it accurate. Ten days were suppressed in 1582 and, beginning with 1700, the leap year was to be ignored at the beginning of every century, except once in every four hundred years. Protestants objected to this Roman innovation and it was not adopted in England till 1752. Its use was at once imposed on the whole Western church, and is now used by many Eastern Catholics as well; the other Eastern churches are gradually adopting it.

CALENDAR, THE ISLAMIC, computes years of 354 days from the Year of the *Hijrah* (flight of Mohammed from Mecca to Medina, July 16, 622 A.D.). Mohammedans are now (1948) in 1366-67 A.H.

CALENDAR, THE JEWISH, is reckoned from the creation of the world, which they date 3761 years B.C. 1948 is A.M. 5708-09.

CALENDAR, THE JULIAN, was instituted by Julius Cæsar in the year 708 of the Foundation of the City (45 B.C.). It divided the year into twelve months as at present, with an extra day in February regularly every four years. This gave the year eleven minutes too much and made necessary the Gregorian reform. The Julian reckoning is, however, still followed by the Catholic Bulgarians and Ruthenians, and by the Orthodox patriarchates of Jerusalem, Russia and Serbia, the Nestorian, Armenian, Jacobite and other churches (Rumania, Greece, Constantinople and other Orthodox churches have accepted the Gregorian reckoning for fixed feasts). These are all consequently thirteen days behind and the celebration of Easter and other feasts differs accordingly. Until 1924 the whole of the Orthodox Church used the Julian calendar. The church year begins on Sept. 1. Fairs and other local festivities in England are often found to be still fixed for dates according to the Julian calendar, and income-tax returns and national accounts generally are made up to April 5, *i.e.*, Old Lady Day.

CALENDAR OF THE ROMAN CHURCH, THE GENERAL (*See* Appendix II) is often referred to as "of the Universal Church," but in fact is not used by Catholics of Eastern rites, nor by some religious orders. In accordance with its name it originated in the calendar of the local Roman church, and in consequence contains a large number of feasts of native Roman saints, particularly of early martyrs; but in the past 350 years it has been extended and altered and now more merits the epithet universal: 20 or more feasts are of saints whom we should now call of Eastern rite, and a recent addition died only in 1897. Since the 16th century this calendar is used in all dioceses and congregations (except a few which have their own proper calendars) of the Western church, modified according to local requirements but in such a way that all the great feasts, of our Lord, our Lady, the principal saints and martyrs, etc., are celebrated on the same day. But a religious order with a large number of saints and *beati* will have a corresponding proportion of feasts peculiar to itself, *e.g.*, the Dominicans have about 70 such in the course of the year. A new and radically reformed calendar was approved for the Benedictines in 1915. The archdiocese of Westminster has over 30 special feasts of saints, some of which are fairly general in England but all nearly unknown elsewhere. The same variation takes place in the ranks of feasts (*q.v.*); *e.g.*, St. David (March 1) is of the highest rank in Wales, a double feast only in Birmingham, and not observed at all in Liverpool. Ireland and Scotland have both a number of local saints who do not appear in other calendars. When a church calendar is printed as such without explanation it is usually the general calendar of the Roman church, and to be of any practical use must be checked by and made to agree with the local *ordo* (*q.v.*). See FEAST; OCTAVE; VIGIL; YEAR, etc., and Appendix II.

CALIXTINES. A name given to the Utraquists (*q.v.*) on account of their badge, a chalice (Lat. *calix*).

CALUMNY is slander, the deprivation of another of his good name by imputing to him, behind his back, something injurious to his reputation of which the speaker or writer knows he is innocent. It incurs an obligation of making restitution so far as possible (*cf.*, Detraction).

CALVARY. i. The place of crucifixion of Christ (see below).
ii. A cross or crucifix mounted upon three steps.
iii. A crucifix, often life-size, with figures of our Lady and St. John.

CALVARY, MOUNT. The hillock on the west side of Jerusalem upon which our Lord was crucified. It was about 15 feet high. Together with the Holy Sepulchre near by it was buried with rubbish by the Emperor Hadrian and a grove or temple of Venus planted on the site. It had been brought within the circuit of the western wall of the city, as it still is, by King Agrippa I about A.D. 43. In 325 the Empress St. Helen had the sites uncovered. Constantine built a basilica and other buildings, Calvary being made to look tidy by being cut perpendicularly so as to make a cube with a flat top, 18 by 15 feet, and surrounded by porticos. In the 5th century a chapel was built on it. After other vicissitudes the diminished hill was included actually under the roof of the Crusaders' church of the Resurrection, and so it remains to this day. It is completely disguised by buildings and is apparently simply a chapel approached by steep stairs. Only about a quarter of the chapel actually rests on the hill of Calvary, the remainder being built up artificially. It contains three altars, two for the use of Catholics and one for the Orthodox, and an amazing bust of our Lady of Sorrows. See also GORDON'S CALVARY.

CALVINISM. The theological system of John Calvin (*d.* 1564) exposed in the four books of his "Institutes of the Christian Religion." The doctrine particularly associated with his name, but which he took from Luther and shared with the other reformers, is that God predestines some to everlasting life, others to damnation, nor does their predestination depend on their foreseen virtue or wickedness; the whole nature of fallen man is utterly corrupt, and justification with assurance of salvation can be effected only by faith; righteousness is imputed from without, it is not indwelling in the soul. Some of his followers maintained with Luther that this reprobation was a consequence of the Fall, and were called Infralapsarians to distinguish them from the true Supralapsarian Calvinists who held that the Fall was a consequence of God's decree of reprobation. The distinguishing notes of Calvinism were this absolute predestinarianism, the necessary permanence of grace, and the absorption of the state by the Church: all resulting from the misapplication of Calvin's central and true principle of the dependence of everything on God. He also taught Luther's sufficiency of the Bible, interpreted by personal interior revelation, and that the sacraments are a witness of grace, but only to the elect. Calvinism has been a tremendous influence in Protestantism, including the Anglican church in its earliest days, and two of its doctrines in particular are behind all subsequent religious disintegration: rejection of the hierarchical priesthood and loss of the doctrine of the Mystical Body, so that the individual soul becomes completely isolated; and the recognition of but one Will in the universe, and that divine Will directed to vengeance. The first has driven men to despair or to humanitarianism; the second, to infidelity and atheism.

CAMALDOLESE, The. An independent branch of the Benedictine order, founded by St. Romuald about 1012, having one congregation of cenobites (*q.v.*) and two of hermits, the founder's object being to establish the Eastern eremitical life in the West. The life of the cenobites is simply that of a strict interpretation of the rule of St. Benedict: Divine Office in choir, perpetual abstinence from meat, a long fast before Christmas, Matins and Lauds at midnight, considerable silence, manual labour. To this the hermits add seclusion in their cells, where they take their meals except on great feasts, perpetual silence except at recreation two or three times a week, very strict fasts and Friday abstinence on bread and water. There are five *cœnobia* and 15 groups of hermitages, all in Italy except one in Brazil and one in Poland,

The habit is like the Benedictine but white, with the scapular girdled; the hermits have a voluminous white cloak for out-doors. There are a few nuns of the order.

CAMAURO. A close-fitting red velvet cap, trimmed with white fur, worn sometimes by the popes.

CAMELODUNUM. The Latin name of the diocese of Northampton (*q.v.*). Adjectival form: *Northantoniensis*.

CAMERA, THE VENERABLE APOS-TOLIC (Lat. *camera*, chamber). The office entrusted with the administration of the property of the Holy See (excluding ordinary revenue, such as Peter's pence), especially during its vacancy; its offices are largely honorary. Its head is the Chamberlain (*q.v.*) of the Holy Roman Church, who has a staff of 8 clerics forming a college of prelates.

CAMERIERE SEGRETO (It.). Privy chamberlain (*q.v.*).

CAMERLENGO (It.). Chamberlain (*q.v.*).

CAMILLIANS, -ITES, The. The Ministers of the Sick (*q.v.*).

CAMPANILE (It.). A bell-tower or belfry especially of the Romanesque type common in Italy.

CAMPIFONTIS. Genitive (in the bishop's title) of *Campifons*, Latin translation of the name of the sees of Springfield, Mass., and Ill.

CAMPO SANTO (It. holy field). A cemetery, particularly one whose earth is reputed to have been brought from Jerusalem, *e.g.*, *dei Tedeschi* in Rome, and at Pisa.

CANADA, THE CHURCH IN. Mass was first celebrated in Canada probably about the middle of the 16th century; at the beginning of the 17th there were secular clergy and Jesuits among the colonists of Acadia (Nova Scotia), and in 1615 Champlain introduced Franciscan missionaries; the French Jesuits returned in 1633. In 1659 the jurisdiction of the archbishop of Rouen was taken away, and Mgr. Laval became vicar apostolic of New France; 15 years later the first episcopal see was established, at Quebec. The population is about 12 million, of whom Catholics are 6¼ million (over half of them French Canadians in the province of Quebec); over ¼ million are of Eastern rites. The Constitutional Act of 1791 guaranteed the civil and religious liberties of Catholics, and in 1851 the free exercise of any religion without distinction or preference was enacted. Large tracts of northern Canada are still mission territory: the early Christian history of the country was made glorious by the Jesuit missions and martyrs among the Indians, who with a few Eskimos today have some 90,000 Catholics. There are in Canada 15 archiepiscopal sees, *viz.*, Quebec (primatial),

Edmonton, Halifax, Kingston, Moncton, Montreal, Ottawa, Regina, Rimouski, Saint Boniface, Saint John's, Sherbrooke, Toronto, Vancouver, and Winnipeg. Their suffragans are 37 bishoprics, a Benedictine abbacy *nullius*, and 8 mission vicariates. There are an archbishop and 3 bishops for the Ruthenians. The Holy See has a delegate at Ottawa for Canada and Newfoundland (*q.v.*).

CANADIAN COLLEGE, The. A pontifical seminary for Canadian students established in Rome in 1887 by Cardinal Edward Howard and the Rev. F. L. Colin. It is in the Via delle Quattro Fontane, and is directed by the Sulpician fathers.

CANDIDA CASA (The White House). Whithorn in Galloway. See GALLOVIDIANUS.

CANDLEMAS DAY. The feast of the Purification of our Lady (Feb. 2), so called because the principal Mass is preceded by the blessing and distribution of candles (*q.v.*).

CANDLES are used in many rites and ceremonies of the Church, beginning with Baptism and ending with those round the coffin at a funeral. They are required on the altar for the due celebration of Mass, during the Divine Office according to the solemnity, and not less than twelve at Benediction. A candle is delivered to an acolyte at his ordination. They are used in liturgical processions (as at the singing of the gospel), in excommunications, at Tenebræ, at the blessing of the font, at the dedication of a church, and are offered to the bishop by the ordinands at the offertory of the Mass of ordination. They are blessed solemnly at the Purification; one must be before each consecration-cross of a church, and the lighting of the paschal candle is one of the most solemn of the Easter ceremonies. All candles used for liturgical purposes must contain a notable proportion of pure beeswax and be white, except in requiem Masses, when they should be unbleached. Candles are not used liturgically for the purpose of giving light but as a mark of joy and to show honour to God, holy things, or ecclesiastical dignitaries; they are recorded as being so used in the 4th century.

CANDLES, THE BLESSING OF, takes place before Mass on Feb. 2, even if the feast of the Purification has been transferred to the following day. The celebrant, in a purple cope, blesses wax candles with five prayers, sprinkling them with holy water and incensing them; while he distributes them to clergy and people *Nunc dimittis* is sung, with an antiphon between each verse, then another antiphon and a collect. Afterwards a procession is formed in which lighted candles are carried and three antiphons sung; these have been borrowed from the East (as has the whole ceremony), and the chant is of an unusual type. The candles are lighted again during the gospel and again from the consecration to the communion, unless the Mass be that of a Sunday and not of the Purification. The whole ceremony has reference to Simeon's words, "A light to enlighten the gentiles." The blessed candles may be lit in times of trouble or temptation, during thunderstorms, childbirth and at the hour of death.

CANDLES, LIGHTING ALTAR. Those on the epistle side are lighted first, beginning with the one nearest the cross and the others in turn; then those on the gospel side in the same order. In putting them out the process is reversed, beginning with the one furthest from the cross on the gospel side.

CANDLES AT MASS. Mass normally may not be said unless there are lighted candles upon the altar: at a priest's low Mass only two are allowed, unless it be a parochial or community Mass, or one said on a great feast, or at a wedding, etc., when there may be four or six; at a sung Mass on the same occasions, four or six; at a high Mass, four on doubles, during octaves, ferias of Lent and Advent, vigils and ember days, two on other ferias and simple feasts, six on doubles of the 2nd class and above (*Caer. Ep.* lib. I, d. xii, 24). A seventh candle is on the altar during a pontifical high Mass, if sung in the bishop's own diocese and not a requiem. The missal directs that an additional candle be lit on or near the altar, even at a private low Mass, from the *Sanctus* to the communion; this good custom is generally omitted except by the Dominicans. The rubrics give no encouragement to a lavish use of candles on liturgical occasions.

CANDLES, VOTIVE, are set up to burn before the Blessed Sacrament, relics, shrines or images. The origin of the custom is obscure, but from the earliest times a symbolism attached to the use of candles—notably in the case of the paschal candle. As the incense which sent up its cloud of fragrance was a symbol of prayer, so the candle consuming itself was a type of sacrifice. In the middle ages it was common for grateful persons to "measure themselves" to a particular saint; *i.e.*, a candle was set up of the same height or weight as the person who had received or desired some favour.

CANON is a word having a large number of ecclesiastical significances. It is the Greek κανών, a rule, *i.e.*, an unchangeable object by which is measured something that does or may change. See also KANON.

CANON (person). i. The chief category of canon is of members of a cathedral chapter (*q.v.*). Such a canon is appointed by the bishop with the advice of the other canons, and his canonry consists of a right to a stall in the cathedral quire, a voice in the chapter and a share of the chapter revenues (pre-

bend) when such is available; until he receives such prebend he is a minor canon. He is bound to reside in the cathedral city, sing the Divine Office in the cathedral, and assist the bishop in the government of his diocese. During an episcopal vacancy the chapter of canons succeeds to the bishop's ordinary jurisdiction, elects a vicar capitular (*q.v.*) and sometimes nominates the new bishop. But the rights and duties of canons vary from country to country and even from diocese to diocese. They form with the bishop the *senatus ecclesiæ*, but he is obliged to obtain their consent only in certain definite cases. They usually number eleven in an English or Scots diocese, presided over by the provost; there are no revenues attached to their canonries, so they are exempt from residence and Divine Office, except at a meeting one day in every month; they are, in fact, mostly rectors of the principal parishes. They have the right to recommend three candidates when the see is vacant. There are no cathedral canons in India (outside the Goanese province), Canada, Australia or the United States; in those Irish dioceses which have them they are little more than honorary. Canons are an institution peculiar to the Western church, but diocesan chapters are now found among he Ruthenians and the Catholic Rumanians. In England and Wales their choir dress is a black cassock with red buttons and trimmings, rochet and mozzetta, but canonical costumes vary greatly. Some chapters have astonishing privileges of dress, *e.g.*, those of Capua and Pisa wear a red *cappa magna* and mitre, those of Benevento and Malta all the *pontificalia*, those of Westminster and Salford the dress of the canons of St. John Lateran; the canons of Terni have the privilege of freeing a criminal condemned to death, on the feast of their patron, St. Juvenal.

ii. A member of a collegiate chapter (*q.v.*). His rights and duties are similar to those of cathedral canons, except that he assists in the administration of the college and has nothing to do with the government of the diocese. His principal business is assistance at divine service.

CANON, HONORARY. Before 1903 the making of honorary canons was forbidden in England. They are now found in several dioceses (*cf.*, titular canon).

CANON, LAY. A layman on whom a chapter confers a canonry as a mark of honour. The sovereigns of France were hereditary canons of St. John Lateran, of Angers, Poitiers and other cathedrals.

CANON, PONTIFICAL. A liturgical book containing the ordinary and canon of the Mass and certain forms proper to a bishop; it is used instead of altar-cards by bishops, abbots and protonotaries apostolic.

CANON, PRIVILEGE OF THE. The right of clergy and of religious, male and female, to personal inviolability, those who maliciously lay violent hands on them or grievously attack their liberty or dignity incurring excommunication *ipso facto,* reserved to the ordinary or to the Holy See according to the rank of the cleric (*cf.,* Privilege, ii). The name is an abbreviation of *privilegium canonis "Si quis suadente diabolo"* (If anyone moved by the Devil . . .), with which words the pertinent canon formerly began.

CANON, TITULAR. A titular dignitary, but one who is a true member of the chapter and entitled to a vote in its proceedings, as distinct from an honorary canon.

CANON COADJUTOR. A canon who performs the choir duties of a busy canon of a Roman basilica, with right of succession to the canonry.

CANON PENITENTIARY. One must be appointed in every diocese to hear confessions, with power to absolve from sins and censures reserved to the bishop.

CANON THEOLOGIAN. One must be appointed in every diocesan chapter. His business is to expound the Faith and to be an authority in theological and moral questions.

CANON OF HONOUR. A title of esteem bestowed by a bishop, usually on another prelate. The custom is unknown out of France and is not recognized by canon law.

CANON OF THE MASS, The, is the fundamental part of the Mass beginning with the prayer *Te igitur* after the *Sanctus* and ending with the Great Amen before the *Paternoster.* Its form is fixed, except for the prayers *Communicantes* and *Hanc igitur* (*qq.v.*). The whole of the canon is said by the priest in an inaudible voice, except the three first words of the last prayer, *Nobis quoque peccatoribus.* Everything from the beginning of the preface to the Amen before the Our Father forms one single eucharistic prayer and action, although in the present Mass it is broken up into several apparently separate prayers and parts, thus: five prayers precede the consecration, the first two of which are a petition for the acceptance of the sacrificial gifts, for blessings on the Church, the congregation and particular persons named (commemoration of the living), invoking in the third the merits of the saints. During the next prayer, *Hanc igitur,* by spreading his hands over the offerings the priest denotes that Christ sacrifices himself on the altar in our stead. The consecration *(q.v.)* is effected by the words of institution *(q.v.)* of the Eucharist as recorded by the Synoptic Gospels, 1 Cor. xi, and apostolic tradition; the priest elevates the Host and Chalice so that they may be seen by the people after their respective consecrations. Then follows the *anamnesis*

(q.v.), a prayer *Supra quæ,* another, claimed to be the *epiklesis (q.v.),* the commemoration of the dead, and a final doxology with the "little elevation" *(q.v.).* This canon as a whole can be traced back to the 4th century; in its present form it dates from the 7th. The canon of an Eastern Liturgy is usually called an *anaphora (q.v.).* The custom of saying the canon inaudibly arose from practical necessity during the singing of the *Sanctus* and has been perpetuated because it is a way of emphasizing its sanctity, dignity and impressiveness. This custom is disregarded at a Mass wherein priests are ordained and concelebrate, and has never obtained in the Eastern Liturgies so far as the words of institution are concerned.

CANON OF SCRIPTURE, The, is the list of inspired books of the Old and New Testaments *(q.v.).* Inclusion in the canon does not confer anything to the internal character of a book, but is only the Church's teaching of the fact of its antecedent inspiration *(q.v.).* The N.T. canon is the same as that at present commonly received among non-Catholic Christians; the O.T. canon contains in addition the deutero-canonical books *(q.v.).* These books and fragments are usually called Deuterocanonica, or of the second canon, not because their inspiration is in any way different from that of the others, but because the inspiration of the books at present in the Jewish Bible was definitely proclaimed by the Jewish authorities previous to Christ, whereas the inspiration of the Deuterocanonica, tentatively held but later rejected by the Jews, was definitely proclaimed in the Christian dispensation. The Protestant reformers, denying the infallibility of the Church, returned to the Jewish canon; the Council of Trent reaffirmed acceptance of the Christian one. Doubts expressed by individuals in certain places and periods about the canonical status of Hebrews, Apocalypse and some canonical epistles in the N.T., and the Deuterocanonica in the O.T., were thus declared incompatible with Catholic faith. See BIBLE.

CANONS, ECCLESIASTICAL, The, are rules, laws, decrees, definitions, concerning the Christian faith or life. Their exact nature varies according to circumstances and period. From the 4th to the 16th century the disciplinary decrees of councils and synods were called canons, but in the Councils of Trent and Vatican the name was confined to dogmatic utterances. The "Codex Iuris Canonici" *(q.v.)* contains 2,414 canons. In the Eastern churches the expression "against the canons" is the usual equivalent for "against the (canon) law."

CANONS REGULAR are priests bound by the vows of religion *(q.v.)* and living in community under a rule; secular, i.e., cathedral and collegiate, canons take no vows of poverty and of obedience and are now under no rule. Though they sing the Divine Office in choir and normally lead the life of monks, canons regular are at all times prepared to undertake the works of the active apostolate; they further differ from monks in that the taking of holy orders is an essential of their institute, whereas for monks it is accidental and was for long unusual. Their institution is traced by many authorities (*e.g.*, Pope St. Pius V) to the common life of the Apostles; but their origin is uncertain and, whilst there must have been a gradual development, it is only in the 11th century that they appear in full vigour. The institution is unknown in the East. The distinguishing mark of their dress is the white linen rochet.

CANONS REGULAR OF ST. AUGUSTINE are so called because they follow his rule (*q.v.*) which many canons regular adopted in the 11th century. They were very numerous before the Reformation, when they were known as Black Canons, from their cloaks, to distinguish them from the Premonstratensians (White Canons). They had over 150 monasteries in England and Wales, over 220 in Ireland, and about 25 in Scotland at the dissolution and served the cathedrals of Carlisle and Saint Andrews. They are now principally represented by the Canons Regular of the Lateran, of the Immaculate Conception and the Crosier Canons (*qq.v.*) and the congregations of St. Maurice d'Agaune and of the Great St. Bernard. These last are the "monks" who have charge of the hospices on the St. Bernard and Simplon passes and in Tibet. They were founded by St. Bernard of Menthon about 1004. Their habit is black, the rochet being represented by a linen band falling from the shoulders back and front.

CANONS REGULAR OF THE IMMACULATE CONCEPTION were founded in France by Dom Adrian Gréa, in 1866, with the object of restoring the primitive observance of the canonical life. They recite the Divine Office day and night, keep perpetual abstinence and very strict fasts, and combine this life with clerical duties and education. The congregation has spread to England, Canada and Peru. Habit: white tunic and rochet, black cloak, biretta.

CANONS REGULAR OF THE LATERAN of Our Most Holy Redeemer, The Sacred and Apostolic Order of, were those appointed to serve the Lateran Basilica, who were finally replaced by secular canons in 1483. They have now eight small provinces and an independent Austrian congregation. Their habit is a white cassock, rochet, and black biretta, and they are mostly engaged in parochial work. The English province has its novitiate at Bodmin, with six Cornish and one Dorset parish depending on it, and three other houses; it is governed by a titular abbot.

The Irish canons regular united with the Lateran congregation in 1699 but became extinct in 1829.

CANONS REGULAR OF PRÉMONTRÉ, The (Premonstratensians) are the most flourishing of the canons regular. They have four provinces, called *circaries*, and over 1,000 religious, and are now engaged in parochial, educational and mission work. The habit is a tunic, scapular, sash, cape, hood and biretta, all white, including the shoes and stockings. The English canons of the order belong to the circary of Brabant (Holland and Belgium); they have a house at Miles Platting in Manchester, a novitiate at Storrington, and several parishes. There is a Premonstratensian abbey with a college in U.S.A., St. Norbert's at West De Pere, Wisconsin. They are sometimes called Norbertine canons, after their founder St. Norbert (*d.* 1134). There are a few nuns of the order, strictly enclosed and contemplative. Special devotion to the Blessed Sacrament is a characteristic of the order, which had 36 houses of men in England at the Dissolution.

CANONESS. i. Secular canonesses, an institution peculiar to France and the Holy Roman Empire, were women of noble birth living more or less in community and bound to the Divine Office, but free to renounce their prebends and marry. At the Reformation many of these communities apostasized, with the result that houses of Protestant canonesses are still to be found in Schleswig and elsewhere in Germany. A few communities of Catholic secular canonesses survive also, as that of the Noble Ladies of the Hradschin in Prague whose abbess was always an archduchess of Austria (she had the right of crowning the Queen of Bohemia), and the two Bavarian chapters of St. Elizabeth and St. Anne, which admit widows as well as maidens. No French chapter survived the Revolution.

ii. Canonesses regular, analogous to canons regular and developed contemporaneously with them, belong to various congregations of which the best known are those of St. Augustine, of the Lateran, and of the Holy Sepulchre (*qq.v.*). They have convents in most parts of Europe, they are always enclosed and the choral recitation of the Divine Office is always their first work; many of their convents have schools attached. The characteristic of their habit is the linen rochet.

CANONESSES REGULAR OF ST. AUGUSTINE are represented in England by convents at Hull, Westgate and St. Leonards of canonesses who were driven from France. Each has a school attached. White habit and veil, with rochet.

CANONESSES REGULAR OF THE LATERAN have two wholly contemplative priories in England, at Newton Abbot (this community was founded at Louvain in 1609) and Hoddesdon, where there is perpetual adoration *(q.v.)*. The convents at Ealing and Haywards Heath have schools; the last is descended from the Windesheim congregation through the English priory founded at Bruges in 1629. White habit with black veil, pointed wimple and rochet; surplice on great feasts.

CANONESSES REGULAR OF THE HOLY SEPULCHRE, The, called Religious Regulars to distinguish them from members of the lay Order of the Holy Sepulchre *(q.v.)*, are of ancient but uncertain foundation; their present constitutions were approved by the Holy See in 1631. They are bound to choir office and a penitential life. They have a priory and boarding-school in England, at New Hall, near Chelmsford, that was founded for English women at Liège in 1642. Black habit and veil, sleeveless white rochet with red double cross, black cloak for choir on great occasions,

CANONICAL HOURS, The. The eight offices which form the Divine Office *(q.v.)*; they are distributed throughout the day and four of them, Prime, Terce, Sext, None, are named after the hours at or near which they are recited.

CANONICAL MARRIAGE. One celebrated according to the laws of the Church.

CANONICITY. The status of a book, or portion of a book, as a true part of the canon of holy Scripture.

CANONIZATION. A public and official declaration of the heroic virtue of a person and the inclusion of his or her name in the canon (roll or register) of the saints. Beatification *(q.v.)* having been accomplished, it must be proved that two miracles have been subsequently wrought at the intercession of the *beatus;* the tests and examinations are as rigorous as those which have gone before, and the miracles are discussed in three meetings of the Congregation of Rites; there are required two things to be proved: that the candidate was formally or equivalently beatified, and has worked two (or if equivalently beatified, three) miracles subsequent to beatification. The canonization is then carried out solemnly in St. Peter's by the pope in person, whereat the bull of canonization is read and a Mass sung in honour of the saint. Canonization involves that the saint not only may but must receive public honour; a day is appointed for his feast and a liturgical office composed therefor; his relics are publicly venerated, churches and altars dedicated in his honour, statues or pictures displayed in churches, and prayers to him made publicly. This judgment of the Church is infallible and irreformable. Owing to the amount of careful work involved and the

sumptuous scale of the final ceremony, canonization is an exceedingly costly process. This is probably the chief reason why so large a proportion of canonizations are of priests and religious, many of whom were public characters and whose cause is supported by the resources of a diocese, nation, or religious order. It must not be supposed that a person was not a saint because he has not been canonized (*i.e.*, declared or certified as such): some of our greatest saints were never formally canonized; but at least since the 12th century public veneration without the permission of the Holy See has been unlawful. The first solemn canonization was of St. Ulrich of Augsburg by Pope John XV in 993.

CANOPY. An honorific covering of various kinds. The name is applied indifferently to the altar *ciborium* and *baldacchino (qq.v.)*, to the *ombrellino (q.v.)* and to the canopy proper over the Blessed Sacrament; this is a rectangular piece of rich material supported by four or more poles and carried over the Blessed Sacrament and relics of the Passion during processions. Cardinals, bishops and abbots have canopies over their thrones. The veil of the tabernacle (*conopeum*) is also so called, but in this connection the word is generally applied to a temporary canopy above the throne of exposition.

CANOSSA. A castle between Modena and Parma where, in 1077, the Emperor-elect Henry IV where, who had been excommunicated for resisting papal reforms of simony, clerical incontinence and lay investiture, and for engineering revolts against the pope, did penance outside in the snow for three days and was then absolved by Gregory VII (Hildebrand). In the phrase "go to Canossa" the incident has become symbolical of the triumph of Church over state; but in fact it was a clever dodge of the emperor-elect whereby, by coming to the pope as a private person apparently penitent and so entitled to absolution, he avoided the deposition which would have followed his continued excommunication. He, in fact, incurred excommunication again in 1080, drove Gregory from Rome, and set up an antipope.

CANTATE SUNDAY. The fourth Sunday after Easter, so called from the first word of the introit. The custom of dating by the day of the week, before or after a certain Sunday distinguished by the first word of the introit, *e.g.*, Tuesday after *Aspiciens* (Advent Sunday), was very common in the middle ages (*cf.*, the Byzantine custom of distinguishing the Sundays after Easter by the subject of the liturgical gospel, the Sunday of Thomas, of the Holy Women, etc.).

CANTERBURY. The primatial city, the mother and head of the Church in England and Wales, from about 597 till the death of Cardinal Pole, the last archbishop, in 1558.

Its archbishop was Primate of All England with the right of consecrating all his suffragans, perpetual *legatus natus* of the Holy See, and first peer of the realm. Of 68 archbishops, seventeen are venerated as saints. The see remained in abeyance till it was put an end to by the establishment of a new hierarchy with its head at Westminster, in 1850. The name is now often used to stand for the Protestant Church of England as an official body.

CANTICLE. A sacred song whose words are taken from the Bible. Those in use at the Divine Office are the three evangelical canticles, the *Benedictus, Magnificat* and *Nunc dimittis* (*qq.v.*), sung daily at Lauds, Vespers and Compline respectively. The following are sung in the place of a fourth psalm at Lauds: on Sundays and feasts, the Canticle of the Three Children (Dan. iii); Monday, of David (1 Par. xxix, 10–12) or of Isaias (Is. xii), Tuesday, of Tobias (Tob. xiii, 1–10) or of Ezechias (Is. xxxviii, 10–20), Wednesday, of Judith (Jud. xvi, 15–21) or of Anna (1 Kings ii, 1–10), Thursday, of Jeremias (Jer. xxxi, 10–14) or of Moses (Exod. xv, 1–19), Friday, of Isaias (Is. xlv, 15–25) or of Habacuc (Hab. iii, 2–19), Saturday, of Ecclesiasticus (Eccl. xxxvi, 1–16) or of Moses (Deut. xxxii, 1–43). The canticles of thanksgiving in the Byzantine *Horologion* are nine: of Moses (two), Anna, Habacuc, Isaias, Jonas, the Three Children (two parts), and of our Lady and of St. Zachary in one; on certain days they are sung whole or in part at *Orthros*.

CANTICLE OF CANTICLES, The. The name, meaning "the song which is the best of all songs," given in the Vulgate and other Catholic versions of the Old Testament to that book called in Protestant versions "The Song of Solomon." It is in the form of a love-poem and epithalamium which the Church regards as an allegory of the relations between God and his Church, whether Jewish or Christian, and between Christ and the individual soul. It has always had a great attraction for mystical writers and is used in the liturgy in the offices of the Blessed Virgin Mary.

CANTIQUE (Fr.). A popular song or hymn of a folk sort and in the vernacular. The Jesuits, le Nobletz and Maunoir, during their missionary labours in Brittany in the 17th century, made a use of *cantiques spirituels* only paralleled by that of Wesley and his hymns in England and of "spirituals" among the Negro slaves; some of them were of an astonishing length. Such *cantiques* are a desirable adjunct to non-liturgical worship and are found in most countries of Europe except Great Britain and Ireland. But see HYMNS, VERNACULAR.

CANTOR. i. The precentor (*q.v.*).
ii. A leader of the choir who at solemn services sings at the lectern, dressed in a cope. There may be two, four or more of these cantors, who intone the antiphons, start the psalms and hymns, etc.

CANTORIS (Lat., of the precentor). The north side of a choir (place or persons) arranged for antiphonal singing (*cf.*, decani).

CAPITALISM. That system of industrial and commercial management wherein the owners of capital (*i.e.*, surplus wealth [*q.v.*] expressed in terms of money [*q.v.*]) lend their capital to manufacturers and traders and participate in the profits of the industry or trade. As participators in the business they are responsible partners and are called shareholders. The portion of it divided out is called the "dividend" or, loosely, "interest." As manufacturers and traders are unable to develop their businesses without borrowing capital and as lenders of capital (*capitalists*) have not necessarily any interest in the business concerned except their dividend, the tendency under the system is for manufacture and trading to be carried on solely for the sake of money; those who possess money or control capital become the real controllers, and all success and prosperity is expressed in terms of profit and loss. The difference between a capitalist and a money-lender is that the first becomes a shareholder in the business to which he lends, whereas the second is not concerned with the use to which his money is put. Modern large-scale business could not be developed or continued without the system of capitalism; but it is the destroyer of all small industries and of independent individual responsibility and control. The capitalist system is not in itself unlawful, but easily becomes the cause of abuses which the Church unequivocally condemns.

CAPITAL SINS. The chief or deadly sins (*q.v.*).

CAPITULAR MASS. The principal Mass celebrated daily by the canons in cathedral and collegiate churches wherein the Divine Office is said; it completes and crowns the daily liturgy and should where possible be a high or sung Mass. On certain days, two, or even three such Masses must be celebrated, by the requirements of the calendar. At Westminster Cathedral the capitular Mass is sung daily by the college of chaplains attached to the cathedral.

CAPITULUM (Lat.). i. A cathedral, collegiate or other chapter (*q.v.*).
ii. The Little Chapter (*q.v.*).

CAPPA (late Lat.). i. A cope (*q.v.*).
ii. A black large mantle with shoulder-cape and hood worn out of doors by the Dominicans, Trinitarians and Servites. A white cappa is worn in choir by the Premonstratensians.

CAPPA MAGNA (Lat., the great cloak). A garment of state worn in scarlet silk by cardinals and purple wool by bishops and permitted by privilege to some other prelates. It is a cloak covering the whole person in front, with a very long train and a large hood lined with fur or silk according to the season.

CAPPELLA ARDENTE (It., glowing chapel). A chapel wherein a dead body is lying awaiting burial, the coffin surrounded by burning candles; any place or part of a church where a body is so lying in state.

CAPPELLA PAPALE (It.). The Pontifical Chapel (q.v.).

CAPRANICA, The (It., *Almo Collegio Capranica*). The oldest college in Rome, founded by Cardinal di Capranica, in 1457, for 31 poor church scholars. By Pope Pius VII this number was reduced to 13 and paying students admitted. Benedict XV attached the college to the basilica of St. Mary Major and increased its numbers to 40.

CAPSULA. A round metal vessel with a short stem and a stand, wherein a large Host is reserved in the tabernacle for the purpose of Exposition and Benediction.

CAPUCHINESSES. A branch of the Poor Clares (q.v.) having the Capuchin constitutions and in some convents subject to the minister general of that order. They are chiefly in Italy, Spain and South America. Other Capuchin sisters are engaged in active work.

CAPUCHINS (from colloquial It. *scappuccini*, hermits). One of the three independent branches of the Franciscans (q.v.) initiated by Matteo da Bascio in 1525, who set himself to restore a literal observance of the rule of St. Francis (q.v.). They wear a coarse brown habit girded with a cord, a long pointed hood, sandals and beard; their conventual life is strict, the lay-brothers have to beg, and their churches are very plain; the Divine Office is recited without chant, with the night office at midnight. They do much mission work at home and abroad. They have two provinces, Mount Calvary and Pennsylvania, in the United States; the Irish province is officially entrusted with a crusade against the abuse of alcohol (Fr. Theobald Mathew belonged to the old Irish province); and there is an English province with friaries at Peckham, Pantasaph, Olton, Chester, Crawley, Penmaenmawr and Erith, and a house of studies at Oxford. The first Capuchins came to England in 1599 and were established there from 1617. They number altogether over 12,000 religious.

CARDIFF (*Cardiffensis*). The Welsh archdiocesan see, formerly the diocese of Newport, erected in 1916. The area covered is that of Herefordshire, Monmouthshire and Glamorgan, which formed the pre-Reformation diocese of Llandaff and part of Hereford. In several parts the Faith has never died out, e.g., at Abergavenny, Monmouth, Hereford, Courtfield, Llanarth and Usk; other old missions disappeared only during the last century. The Catholics are now nearly all Irish and English. The patron of the diocese is Our Lady Immaculate and the cathedral is dedicated in honour of St. David. Welsh name: Caerdydd.

CARDINAL (Lat. *cardo*, a hinge). A member of the Sacred College of Cardinals (q.v.), the counsellors and assistants of the pope in the government of the Church; he is a cardinal-deacon, cardinal-priest or cardinal-bishop (qq.v.), but this rank does not bear relation to his grade in holy orders, except that a cardinal-bishop is necessarily in episcopal orders. Until lately a cardinal might be a layman, but there had not been one who was not a priest since Antonelli (d. 1876), who was a deacon, and by the new Code of Canon Law he must be at least a priest. On account of their position as permanent advisers to the Holy See and holders of the exclusive right to elect the pope, cardinals now take precedence of all bishops, primates, and even patriarchs and and papal legates. Every cardinal has a title (q.v.) and serves on one or more of the Roman Congregations. A cardinal has numerous legal and other privileges, including the right to use mitre and crosier and to celebrate Mass pontifically, to receive all honours usually accorded to bishops, to be judged by none but the pope and temporally to rank with the princes of reigning houses. Unless he is the bishop of a foreign see, a cardinal is formally bound to reside in Rome. A cardinal may resign his dignity (cf., Cardinal Billot, in 1927) but can only be deprived of it for the most grave reasons. The chief badge of the cardinal is the red hat; they wear scarlet birettas and mantles (saffron while the Holy See is vacant) and the pectoral cross; members of religious orders retain the use of their proper habit. A cardinal is "His most Reverend Eminence" and "Most eminent Lord." See CARDINAL-PRIEST.

CARDINAL, CREATION OF A. All cardinals are nominated freely by the pope himself. The creation is effected by the delivery first of the scarlet skull-cap, and then of the scarlet biretta, usually by the pope in person. The red hat (q.v.) is given in a public consistory (q.v.) followed at a private consistory by the "opening of the mouth," whereby is signified the cardinal's duty of giving counsel, and the "closing of the mouth," whereby is signified his duty of keeping counsel. A title (q.v.) is also assigned and a sapphire ring bestowed. Sometimes a cardinal is created *in petto* (q.v.).

CARDINAL-BISHOP. The highest of the three ranks in the College of Cardinals (q.v.). Before the 8th century the popes had added the bishops of the neighbouring sees to Rome (suburbicarian sees) to the cardinal-priests of the city, with the duties of assistance and counsel. A cardinal-bishop is still the ordinary of one or other of these sees. A cardinal-bishop must be distinguished from one who is simply cardinal and bishop; e.g., the present Archbishop of New York is a cardinal-priest.

CARDINAL CANONS. Pope Callistus II, in 1120, erected seven canonries at Compostella whose occupants alone were allowed to say Mass at the shrine of St. James and who may wear the mitre and cassock, etc., of cardinal's scarlet.

CARDINAL-DEACON. The lowest of the three ranks in the College of Cardinals (q.v.). Amongst those who were labelled cardinals in consequence of their close association with the pope was the deacon of each of the seven regions into which Rome was divided; the deacons' duties were the care of the poor, the collection of acts of the martyrs and assistance at papal liturgies. When the regional division of the city became merely a name, the title cardinal-deacon was extended to other ecclesiastics as well. They were formerly headed by an archdeacon. The cardinal-deacons, 14 in number, are all priests and almost invariably live and exercise their functions in Rome.

CARDINAL DEAN. The Dean of the Sacred College (q.v.).

CARDINAL-PRIEST. The middle of the three ranks in the College of Cardinals (q.v.). The cardinal-priests represent the chief priests of each of the tituli or quasi-parish churches into which Rome was divided in the 4th–5th centuries. These principal priests were called presbyteri cardinales because they were permanently attached to their churches and to their bishop, the pope. For many centuries the name cardinal had not its present restricted use, but was applied to the principal clergy of many churches. The Roman cardinales were responsible for the maintenance of discipline and for assistance in the conduct of the liturgy at the four patriarchal basilicas. They were presided over by an archpriest. They gradually discharged ordinary ecclesiastical offices less and less and became more and more attached to the person of the pope as counsellors and assistants. After the 3rd Council of the Lateran (1179) the election of a pope was entrusted entirely to the three ranks of cardinals, without reference to the rest of the Roman clergy. The 50 cardinal-priests now include many bishops exercising ordinary jurisdiction in dioceses more or less remote from Rome.

CARDINAL PROTECTOR is a cardinal appointed to keep an eye on the interests of a particular religious order, congregation, church, nation, etc., but without any jurisdiction over them. The Franciscans were the first to have such a protector, and the office is now principally confined to religious institutes and colleges. The pope himself is protector of the Benedictine, Dominican and Franciscan orders, of the Byzantine monastery of Grottaferrata, of the collegiate chapter of SS. Celsus and Julian at Rome, of the Archconfraternity of the Way of the Cross, and of the Lombard Confraternity of SS. Ambrose and Charles. Portugal is the only nation that still has a cardinal protector.

CARDINAL SEES. The seven episcopal sees in the neighbourhood of Rome of which the bishops are cardinal-bishops (q.v.) in the Sacred College: namely, Albano, Frascati, Ostia, Palestrina, Porto & Santa Rufina, Sabina and Velletri. Ostia belongs always to the cardinal dean, who on attaining that dignity adds it to the see already in his possession.

CARDINAL VICAR, The, properly known as the Vicar of the City, is the vicar general of the bishop of Rome; he is a bishop with the authority of an ordinary (q.v.) and has a permanent auxiliary bishop called the vices-gerens. Unlike other vicars general, his office does not cease at the death of his bishop (cf., Vicariate of Rome).

CARDINAL VIRTUES, The, are the four great moral virtues, prudence, justice, fortitude and temperance (qq.v.): called cardinal because all the other virtues are related to or hinge upon them (Lat. cardo, a hinge); "as the door swings upon its hinges while remaining upright in its place. so should our human life be ruled by the four cardinal virtues." This enumeration of cardinal virtues has been taken over by Christianity from Plato and the philosophers of Greek antiquity. They are summed up by St. Thomas in his prayer: "Give me justice, to submit to thee; prudence, to avoid the snares of the enemy; temperance, to keep the just mean; fortitude, to bear adversities with patience."

CARDINAL IN CURIA (Lat., at the court). A cardinal who lives at Rome, as all cardinals who have not the government of a foreign diocese are bound to do. Though technically a cardinal in curia, Cardinal Newman was permitted to live in England.

CARDINALS, ORIENTAL. The cardinalate being an office fundamentally in relation to the local church at Rome, cardinals of Eastern rite have always been rare. There have been only 7 since the separation of the East, viz., Bessarion and Isidore of Kiev (Greek and Russo-Greek) after the

Council of Florence, Levitsky and Sembrat-ovich (Ruthenian) and Hassun (Armenian) in the 19th century, Tappuni (Syrian) in 1936, and Agaganian (Armenian) in 1946.

CARMEL. i. A mountain ridge running towards the sea on the north-west coast of Palestine, often called the Mountain of the Holy Elias (cf., 3 Kings xviii). It is the cradle of the Carmelite order, at whose monastery Christians, Jews and Mohamme-dans there unite to honour Mar Elias.

ii. Any Carmelite monastery, usually of nuns.

CARMELITE RITE, The, is the use of the Latin liturgy proper to the Carmelites but now only used by the Carmelities of the Old Observance, commonly called Calced. It is derived from the rite of the Holy Sepulchre (which name it bears) as used by the Latin church in Palestine in the 12th–13th cen-turies and somewhat resembles that of the Dominicans. Among its points of divergence from the Roman Mass are that at low Mass the bread and wine are prepared at the beginning (at high Mass between the epistle and gospel); the Psalm *Iudica* is said while moving to the altar; on greater doubles and higher feasts the introit is said three times; the bread and wine are offered together with one prayer; the celebrant extends his arms in the form of a cross after the consecration; some of the prayers are different, as before communion; *Salve Regina* is said before the last gospel except in Masses for the dead. There are also differences in the Divine Office (Pope Pius X's arrangement of the Psalter has not yet been adopted) as well as in the administration of the sacraments and in the burial service, wherein the divergence is very notable. Among the special feasts are those of Elias (who is named in the *Confiteor*) and Eliseus. The chant of the Carmelites is also peculiar to them alone. The Dis-calced Carmelites use the ordinary Roman rite.

CARMELITES, The, or Brothers of the Order of the most blessed Mother of God and ever virgin Mary of Mount Carmel, have claimed an organic descent from hermits liv-ing on that mountain under the direction of Elias and Eliseus. For practical purposes their history may be taken to begin in 1155, when a hermitage of western men was founded there by St. Berthold. The hermits spread to Europe and under a Kentishman, St. Simon Stock, modified their life and be-came mendicant friars. The reforming activ-ity of St. Teresa and St. John-of-the-Cross in the 16th century resulted in two inde-pendent branches of the order. (a) The Calced or Shod Carmelites (properly called "of the Old Observance") are the parent stem. They have modified their original rule, e.g., as regards fasting, abstinence, night office, and the like, but retain their mediæval

liturgy. They have six monasteries and a school in Ireland and are well established in U.S.A. In England they have one friary and in Wales conduct the junior seminary. (b) The Discalced, Barefooted or Teresian Carmelites say the Divine Office daily in choir, rising from bed for the night office, and mental prayer is also made in common, twice a day. Abstinence is perpetual and there are special fasts. The friars have monasteries in Ireland and the U.S.A., and in England houses at Wincanton and in Kensington. Both branches, in addi-tion to their monastic duties, are engaged on ministerial work, preaching, etc., and the Discalced have flourishing missions in the Near East, Iraq and Malabar. The mother-house on Mount Carmel is peopled by the Discalced. The habit is substantially the same in both branches, except that the Dis-calced wear sandals; brown tunic, scapular and hood, belt, with a white mantle, whence "White Friars." There are in all about 5,000 friars of this order. They had about 35 friaries in England at the dissolution.

ii. The nuns of the order, founded in 1452 with papal sanction under the "mitigated" rule then in force, spread rapidly, produc-ing among other saints Mary-Magdalen de' Pazzi (1607). From 1562 St. Teresa founded convents under the primitive (non-mitigated) rule, which are now far more numerous than the others. Among them, two kinds of con-stitutions are in force, differing but slightly, both approved by the Church, and both recognized as Teresian. The nuns live in poverty and have strict enclosure, limited numbers, perpetual abstinence and silence (except two hours' recreation), choir office, mental prayer, and manual work. There are four English foundations dating from penal times; the numerous modern founda-tions originate from Lyons and Paris. There have been convents in Ireland since 1700, and there is now a number in U.S.A. and Canada. Habit: same as the friars, with linen wimple and black veil. See also TERTIARIES ii.

CARNIVAL (Lat. *carnem levare*, to remove flesh-meat) is the three or more days which precede the beginning of Lent, observed as a time of dancing, feasting and merry-making generally. Owing to the excesses which often take place in Italy and elsewhere, the Blessed Sacrament is exposed in many places at this time. The equivalent to Carnival in Eng-land is Shrovetide.

CAROL. A vernacular hymn adapted for popular singing at a festival, usually but not necessarily Christmas, expressed in the sim-ple terms and metres that are associated with folk-music. There are now no genuine carols in popular use among English-speaking Catholics; and most of the compositions pass-ing as carols in the country at large, e.g., "O come all ye faithful" (*Adeste fideles*), are simply Christmas hymns. Nevertheless there are many carols available in print, mostly from pre-Reformation sources.

CAROLINOPOLITANUS. The Latin epithet for the bishop of Charlottetown, Canada.

CAROLOPOLITANUS. The Latin epithet for the bishop of Charleston, South Carolina.

CARTESIANISM. The system and philosophic tenets of René Descartes (1596–1650). Descartes, sometimes called the Father of Modern Philosophy, endeavoured to put forward a new method of search after truth, and by this method to give to the world a new philosophy. He sets out by doubting hypothetically of all truths. There is one truth, he says, of which it is not possible to doubt, namely the fact of my own thought and consequently of my own existence: "I think, therefore I am." The truth of this principle is due to its evidence; evidence therefore must be the criterion of all truth. Descartes does not precisely define what he meant by evidence; whether it be objective or subjective. Moreover, besides evidence of reason, there is evidence of authority, which he passes over, forgetting that man is not only capable of seeking after truth by his own rational power, but that he is also very much of a pupil and depends for much of his knowledge upon the teaching of a master. Further, to doubt of all truths, even hypothetically, involves also doubt in the principle of contradiction, which the *Cogito ergo sum* presupposes as true. In psychology, he professes an exaggerated spiritualism. Thought is the essence of the human soul, extension the essence of body: apparently he could not see that "to think" is only a property of the soul, just as extension is a property of body. In failing to pass beyond these properties he opened the way to the sensualism and positivism of Locke and Condillac. Further, for him, the union of soul and body is at best only accidental, and in this he reverts to Plato's doctrine. In comparative psychology, he asserts that animals are nought but wonderful machines constructed by the Divine Craftsman. In cosmology, he speaks of the whole material world as inert extension and infinite, subject to and diversified only by movement, hence his mechanicist conception of the universe. In ethics, he regards all moral laws as dependent upon the freewill of God. From this it follows that God, if he so willed, could change the decalogue. In theodicy, he endeavours to prove the existence of God from the idea itself of God. The idea of perfect being necessarily implies existence. Like St. Anselm's ontological argument, it is an unwarrantable passage from the ideal order to the real.

CARTHUSIAN RITE, The. The use of the Latin liturgy proper to the Carthusians is rarely, if ever, seen in a public church. The variations are many and some of them very notable, *e.g.*, the celebrant prepares the bread and wine before Mass, and reads all up to the gospel at the epistle side; the offertory of bread and wine is made both together; the canon is the same as that in the Roman Missal, but the ceremonies differ: right through, the arms are extended crosswise, except when the hands are employed; there are no complete genuflections and only a slight elevation of the Chalice; after the canon there are further variations both of words and acts and the Mass ends at *Ite missa est.* There is no high Mass; at the daily sung Mass a deacon assists, leaving his stall when necessary, wearing a cowl and putting on the stole, which he wears like the Byzantine *orarion*, as required; incense is used only on Sundays and certain feasts, the deacon incensing the altar during the offertory and the celebrant at *Orate fratres.* The Divine Office follows the general Benedictine arrangement in use among other monks; but the lessons of Matins are very long and no historical lessons are read. The liturgical chant has been preserved note for note from the 11th century and has a character of peculiar gravity and dignity.

CARTHUSIANS, The. i. An order of monks founded by St. Bruno at the Grande Chartreuse (*q.v.*) in Dauphiny in 1084. Their life is essentially that of hermits. On Sundays and feasts they meet in church for the Divine Office, in the refectory for two meals, for recreation, and once a week for a long walk; on other days conventual Mass, Vespers, and Matins and Lauds are sung in church and the rest of the time is spent by each monk in his cell, *i.e.*, a cottage with provision for prayer, reading, eating, sleeping, manual work and a tiny garden. Three offices, the Divine, of our Lady and of the Dead, are recited with the postures used in choir, and definite time is also allotted to mental prayer. Abstinence is perpetual and sleep is broken for nearly 3 hours by the night-office; the hair-shirt is always worn. The lay-brother's life is also very hard, but in community. The order has never required any reform. The habit is tunic, belt, scapular with hood and joined at the sides by bands, all white; head shaved all over but for a very narrow *corona* (*q.v.*). There were nine Charterhouses (*q.v.*) in England at the Reformation; the community of Sheen preserved its existence in the Low Countries till 1783: its last monk died in 1808. There is now a large one at Parkminster, Sussex, and 22 others in Europe, totalling about 750 religious.

ii. Nuns. These also are strictly enclosed and contemplative and follow the same rule as the monks, except that they have separate cells instead of cottages, eat together daily, to wear the *cilicium* is optional, and they do not walk outside their grounds. They retain the privilege of the consecration of virgins (*q.v.*). They have never been numerous and now number only 4 monasteries, in France and Italy; they are under the direction of the order and each has two monks attached who assist at all the offices from outside the church grille. Habit: similar to the monks but with a black veil and linen wimple.

CASE OF CONSCIENCE. Circumstances where action is called for, involving conflicting or uncertain principles; if no decision undisturbing to the conscience can be arrived at, the case is submitted to authority, normally the parish priest.

CASHEL (*Cassiliensis*). An Irish metropolitan see with 8 suffragan dioceses, founded in the 11th century. The archbishop has perpetual administration of the see of Emly, and the whole territory covers most of county Tipperary and part of Limerick. Since 1774 the archbishop's residence, cathedral and seminary are at Thurles. The patron of the archdiocese is St. Albert (Jan. 8), a former bishop, and of Emly St. Ailbe (Sept. 12); the cathedral is dedicated in honour of the Assumption. Irish name: Caiseal.

CASK. At the consecration of a bishop, after the offertory of the Mass the new bishop delivers to the consecrator two small casks of wine, two loaves of bread and two candles. The same is done by an abbot at his solemn benediction. It is a survival of the custom of the faithful making their gifts in kind at the offertory (*q.v.*).

CASSILIENSIS. The adjectival form of the name of the see of Cashel (*q.v.*) used in the designation of its archbishop in Latin documents. Noun: *Cassilia*.

CASSINESE CONGREGATION, The. i. A Benedictine congregation established from a reform at, and with the name of, St. Justina, at Padua in 1421; name changed in 1504. It was the first congregation to be modelled as an order (*q.v.*), as opposed to a federation of independent abbeys. Its chief houses are Monte Cassino and St. Paul's-outside-the-Walls of Rome, but it is now much reduced owing to Italian spoliation in the 19th century and to the formation of ii. (below) to which St. Justina now belongs.
ii. Of Primitive Observance. The largest of the Benedictine congregations, also called "of Subiaco" from its headquarters. Formed from i. (above) in 1872. Divided into 6 provinces: Italian, Belgian, English (Ramsgate, Buckfast, Prinknash, Farnborough), French, German and Spanish, with an abbot general and over 30 monasteries. It has no connection with the American Cassinese Congregation.

CASSOCK. The *vestis talaris*, a close-fitting garment reaching to the heels, fastened down the front with numerous small buttons; the ecclesiastical uniform of all clerics except those who, being members of orders or congregations, have a distinctive habit. The cassock of the pope is white, of cardinals red, of bishops and other prelates purple, and of everybody else black. For ordinary use cardinals, bishops and prelates have a black cassock with red or purple cincture, buttons and piping (*abito piano*). In Catholic countries it is by law the ordinary dress of the clergy; in England they are supposed to wear it always in the church and presbytery. The use of the cassock has been extended to laymen who serve in the sanctuary; in the English-speaking countries there can be no custom of sufficient antiquity to justify their use of any other colour but black; except that in churches of regulars it may follow the colour of the tunic of the order (*e.g.*, white among Dominicans) as approximating to that garment.

CASTEL GANDOLFO. An estate and mansion in the Alban Hills, near Rome, used as a residence by the pope during the hotter summer months. Its possession was confirmed to the Holy See by the Treaty of the Lateran, and the neighbouring Villa Barberini added thereto.

CASTI CONNUBII. An encyclical letter on Christian marriage published by Pope Pius XI, in 1930, in view of the present conditions, needs, errors and vices that affect the family and society.

CASTRATO (It., eunuch; pl. *castrati*). An adult male soprano whose voice was maintained at its youthful pitch by the requisite surgical operation. During the Renaissance and later such artificial soprani were very numerous and their employment was not discouraged, even in many church choirs. The custom is now entirely reprobated; the abuse of the employment of such singers was condemned by Pope Benedict XIV, and Clement XIV threatened with excommunication those who performed such an operation unless for lawful medical reasons. In speaking of women in choirs, the *motu proprio* of Pope Pius X on church music directs that "if high voices, such as treble and alto, are required, these parts must be sung by boys, according to the ancient custom of the Church."

CASUIST. One who applies general ethical rules to a particular case, weighs conflicting obligations, decides on lawful exceptions and valid distinctions. Any person faced with a moral problem and endeavouring to solve it according to the rules of good morality is thereby a casuist. The word is often ignorantly and maliciously used for a quibbler or for one who seeks "good reasons" for doing wrong.

CASUISTRY. The science of applied moral theology. From the general principles of morality the casuist determines what one ought to do in given circumstances and the innocence or amount of guilt to be attached to a given human act. In popular parlance the word has a debased meaning, *sc.*, quibbling, moral laxity, confusing issues.

CASUS (Lat., case). A problem, real or imaginary, arising in moral theology, canon law or ritual. Such cases are officially discussed at clergy conferences.

CATACOMBS. The subterranean cemeteries in which the Christians of Rome buried their dead during the first three centuries. They were designed like the burial-places of the Jews, and at first in association with the family vaults of patrician converts, so that, as burial-places, they enjoyed by Roman law immunity from disturbance. The presence of the bodies of the martyrs as well as their safeness caused them also to be used for the celebration of the divine mysteries. The bodies of the principal martyrs were translated to churches in the city during the 8th and 9th centuries. Over twenty-five of these cemeteries have been rediscovered, of which the principal are those of St. Callistus and of St. Sebastian, close to the Appian Way; of St. Agnes on the Via Nomentana; of St. Priscilla on the Salarian Way; and of SS. Nereus, Achilleus and Domitilla on the Via Ardeatina. The name is said to be derived from the church built over the cemetery of St. Sebastian, called *ad catacumbas* (probably from Gr., at the hollow), which was resorted to as the second burial-place of St. Peter. By the concordat of 1929 the disposition and maintenance of the Catacombs was reserved to the Holy See. There are other catacombs at Syracuse and in Malta.

CATAFALQUE (Fr. from It., a scaffold). A framework of wood completely covered with a black pall, with six candles burning around it. It stands just outside the communion-rail and symbolizes the corpse at a requiem Mass when the actual body is not present at the third, seventh, thirtieth and anniversary day. The absolutions (*q.v.*) are given at the catafalque as if the corpse were there.

CATECHETICS. The science of teaching Christian doctrine by word of mouth, especially to the young; it is part of the teaching office of the Church.

CATECHISM (Gr. κατήχησις oral instruction). i. Instruction in Christian doctrine by means of question and answer.

ii. A series of questions and answers summarizing Christian doctrine, formulated and published by authority. The best known catechism in England is the so-called "Penny Catechism," approved by the archbishops and bishops of England and Wales and directed to be used in all their dioceses. Its main divisions are faith, hope, charity, and the sacraments, with an appendix on the virtues and contrary vices, the Christian's

rule of life and the Christian's daily exercise. It forms the basis of religious teaching in all English Catholic schools and in the instruction of converts; but of late years there has been some questioning of its adequacy, and still more of the way it is sometimes used. In the United States the official Baltimore Catechism of 1885 is only one among many in use: a revision of this, in two parts according to age, was published in 1941. The first synod of Maynooth (1875) produced the "Maynooth Catechism" for use in Ireland. The "Catechism of the Council of Trent" or "Roman Catechism," published in 1566, is not really a catechism at all but a manual of Christian instruction for the use of the clergy. It is a document of high authority, being written by command of a general council and approved by many popes. Three quasi-official catechisms, for little children, for children and for grown-ups, were compiled by Cardinal Peter Gasparri and published in Rome in 1931. These have been translated into English and other languages.

CATECHIST. In the early Church one who instructed the catechumens and helped to prepare them for baptism. The name and duties are still retained by laymen in many foreign missions; *e.g.*, in the vicariate apostolic of Uganda native catechists in one year baptized 2,000 adults and 1,000 infants in danger of death, spiritually assisted 2,000 Christians dying without a priest and gave preliminary instruction to 8,000 heathen. Diocesan Catechist is a title conceded to qualified members of the Catholic Evidence Guild in his diocese by the Archbishop of Westminster and other English bishops.

CATECHUMEN (Gr. κατηχειν, to teach orally). A non-baptized adult under instruction to be received into the Church; a learner. Catechumens receive ecclesiastical burial if they die without baptism through no fault of their own (*cf.*, Baptism of desire). The catechumenate as an institution of long preparation for baptism still flourishes in certain foreign missions, *e.g.*, those of the White Fathers in Africa, where four years is the normal minimum time of instruction for adults; the catechumens occupy the porch or back part of the church, are excluded from Mass after the sermon, and a "discipline of the secret" (*q.v.*) in respect of the Church's rites and sacraments (other than Baptism) is enforced in their regard.

CATEGORICAL IMPERATIVE. In the Kantian philosophy this means the moral law in so far as the latter is impressed upon the conscience as an absolute duty. This doctrine is true so far as it goes, but it does not go far enough. The full notion of what a man *ought* is what he *must do under pain of sin.* Kant contends (and in this he is positively in error) that this imperative *Ought*, uttered by a man's reason, has the force of a law, made by that same reason. The doctrine is erroneous, inasmuch as it undertakes to settle the matter of right and wrong without reference to external authority; and inasmuch as it makes the reason in man his own legislator. No one can issue a command to himself, and without a law there is no obligation.

CATEGORIES. The Categories are the supreme *genera* under which are contained all our ideas of things. They are two in number, substance and accident; for either things are of such a nature that they exist of themselves in such wise that they have no need of a subject or support which sustains them, or they have need of such support. If they have no such need they are substances, as man, angel, tree; if they have need of a subject as a support they are accidents as colour, heat; these are nine in number, *viz.*, quantity, relation, quality, action, passion, place, time, position and habit (clothing, ornament, etc.).

CATHARISM (Gr. καθαρός, pure) is a general name for the dualistic sects which troubled Europe for 400 years from the beginning of the 11th century; the most important were the Albigensians (*q.v.*) in the West, and the Bogomili (*q.v.*) in the East. All the sects agreed in teaching that the material world was created by an evil principle, which some said was co-existent with God, while others regarded it as a rebellious creature; procreation was the supreme sin, since it resulted in another soul becoming clothed in matter. The teaching of the Cathari was a new religion rather than a heresy; it attacked the first principles of natural religion and ethics, and in its more fanatical forms was a danger not only to Christianity but to human society as such.

CATHEDRA (Gr., a chair). i. The stool, seat, chair or throne (*q.v.*) of a bishop in his cathedral-church.
ii. A liturgical term for the taking-up of the episcopal authority, *e.g.*, the feast of Cathedra Petri, Peter's Chair (*q.v.*).
iii. The seat of authoritative teaching. See EX CATHEDRA.
iv. The seat used by the celebrant at a Carthusian sung Mass; it is halfway down the sanctuary on the epistle side facing the deacon's lectern.

CATHEDRAL, CATHEDRAL CHURCH. The church of a diocese in which the bishop has his permanent episcopal throne or *cathedra* (*qq.v.*); usually and properly the cathedral is found in the town from which the diocese takes its name and wherein the bishop lives. A cathedral is not of necessity a large church, and there are sometimes larger and more beautiful parish churches in the same town, the cathedral being venerable for its old foundation and historical associations; but it must be consecrated, and

the date of its consecration and the feast of its titular are observed liturgically throughout the diocese. The cathedral is served by the chapter of canons whose duty it is to perform the liturgy therein daily; in the U.S.A. and elsewhere there are no canons, and in those Irish dioceses that have them they are not resident; in Great Britain, too, the canons are otherwise employed, but at Westminster Cathedral the whole liturgy is celebrated daily by a special college of chaplains. The cathedral is the mother church of the whole diocese, and its clergy have precedence, but in Great Britain the significance of the cathedral is somewhat obscured from the people, through the religious life of the diocese not centering round it so much as it does elsewhere. Architecturally the outstanding Catholic cathedrals in Great Britain today are Westminster and Oban (Argyll).

CATHEDRAL PRIORY. In the middle ages certain English cathedrals had a priory attached, whose monks served the cathedral and elected the bishop; they were governed by a cathedral prior who had all the powers of an abbot and was sometimes mitred and sat in Parliament. The arrangement was peculiar to England, and was perpetuated in the former diocese of Newport, of which the Benedictine priory church of Belmont, Hereford, was the pro-cathedral with a chapter of monks. In 1916 this diocese became the archdiocese of Cardiff and the English Congregation O.S.B. resigned its privilege. Including the cathedrals of the new foundation, there were thirteen cathedral priories, all except Carlisle (Austin canons) being Benedictine; their memory is preserved by titular prelates of the English Congregation who, without jurisdiction or duties in respect thereof, are the cathedral priors of Canterbury, Winchester, Durham, Bath, Chester, Coventry, Ely, Gloucester, Norwich, Peterborough, Rochester and Worcester (*cf.*, Abbot, Titular).

CATHEDRALS OF THE NEW FOUNDATION. Westminster, Gloucester, Chester, Peterborough, Bristol and Oxford were made dioceses by the schismatic king Henry VIII in 1541 and were recognized by the Holy See on the reconciliation in Mary's reign.

CATHEDRATICUM. An annual contribution to the support of a diocesan bishop payable from all churches or benefices under his jurisdiction; in countries where there are no proper benefices (*e.g.*, England) the amount payable, and by whom, is a matter of local legislation generally dealt with in diocesan synods.

CATHERINE-WHEEL. According to an unreliable tradition St. Catherine of Alexandria was a maiden martyr in that city about the year 310. The catherine-wheel (whether a fire-work, a somersault, a tavern sign, or a window) gets its name from the instrument of her attempted death, a spiked wheel, which broke at her touch, and so she was beheaded.

CATHOLIC. i. The word is derived from Greek and simply means universal. In combination with the word "church" it essentially merely indicates one of the marks (*q.v.*) of the Church, and was so used by St. Ignatius at the beginning of the 2nd century; but in the course of history it has come to be the distinguishing epithet of the Church of Christ and his faith: under other circumstances its place might have been taken by "apostolic" or "one." The use of the word in this distinguishing way became current and common in England only from the middle of the 16th century. In some mediaeval translations of the Creed *unam sanctam catholicam et apostolicam ecclesiam* is rendered "one holy apostolic church general."

ii. A Catholic is any person who, having been baptized, does not adhere to a non-Catholic religion or perform any act with the intention or effect of excluding himself from the Church. A "good Catholic" is one who practises his religion to the best of his ability (*cf.*, Anglo-Catholic, Roman Catholic; and see also SOUL OF THE CHURCH).

iii. Catholics normally call themselves Catholics without qualification, and are distinguished by the name alike in West and East (*cf.*, Roman Catholic, Orthodox); except for a body of High Anglicans, no other Christians use the name as a distinguishing title. But Catholics of the Byzantine rite sometimes call themselves Greek Catholics (*q.v.*), Chaldeans are so called, and Maronites always refer to themselves simply as Maronites—they avoid the name Catholic for the good reason that there is no such thing as a Maronite who is not a Catholic, and because in Syria the epithet particularly designates a Catholic Melkite.

iv. As an adjective, Catholic in this special sense should only be used of subjects of which Catholicity is predicable, *e.g.*, a man as man, a church, building, or catechism. To speak of a Catholic artist or grocer, Catholic poetry or truth is inaccurate and misleading: an artist or grocer who is a Catholic is a Catholic as a man (and this without reference to whether he paints only ecclesiastical pictures or supplies cheese only to the clergy); poetry may deal with a Catholic theme or be written by a poet who is a Catholic, but is not by that fact anything but poetry; truth is truth and it is improper to call the truth about the Catholic Church, Catholic truth (*q.v.*); (*cf.*, Catholic arithmetic, a Wesleyan judge, Quaker music, and, particularly, Catholic culture).

CATHOLIC ACTION. This expression, long current in Italy and elsewhere as a general term, was given a specific content and world-wide significance by Pope Pius XI. He defined Catholic Action as "the participation and collaboration of the laity with the apostolic hierarchy": in other words, it was a call to Catholic lay people themselves to get busy and not to leave everything to the bishops and other clergy. The scope of Catholic Action is very wide and varies from place to place: it can be manifested in worship, in study, in active apologetics, in the corporal works of mercy and in a dozen other ways; but there must be in a true sense religious ways; any political activity is absolutely forbidden to Catholic Action—that, said Pius XI, is its fundamental law. Its organization is as varied as its work: in some countries it is very highly organized, especially among younger people; in others, its organization is loose or non-existent, and in those circumstances Catholic Action is largely a personal ideal, an inspiration under which individuals and groups work for Christ according to the mind of the Church and with the direct encouragement of her pastors. In Italy, Catholic Action came particularly under the ban of the fascist regime, which *r*alled forth Piux XI's great encyclical *Non Abbiamo bisogno* in 1931.

CATHOLIC CHURCH, The, is the common name for the One, Holy, Catholic and Apostolic Roman Church which is the one Church of Christ (*q.v.*), and teaches the one completely true religion revealed by God for the solace and salvation of all mankind.

CATHOLIC APOSTOLIC CHURCH, The, is the unofficial name of a sect commonly known as Irvingites from Edward Irving (1792-1834), a Presbyterian minister who claimed supernatural enlightenment; he prepared the way for rather than founded the body. He claimed to revive the college of apostles and established a complex hierarchy with symbolical titles, Angel, Prophet, etc., and an imposing ritual. It is claimed that in their early days they manifested the gift of tongues. Their confession of faith is contained in the three ancient creeds; baptismal regeneration is taught and a spiritual (*i.e.*, not substantial) presence of our Lord in the consecrated elements, which are reserved on the communion-table; confession is optional and the sick are anointed. Their orders are not valid and the sect appears to be gradually disappearing, but it still has a number of churches in Great Britain.

CATHOLIC COMMITTEE, The. A committee formed in 1782 by prominent Catholic laymen to forward the cause of emancipation by disowning the Jacobites, by giving adherence to the House of Hanover, by disclaiming the deposing power of the pope, and by generally modifying the official attitude of the vicars apostolic and the clergy. It eventually merged in the Cisalpine Club (*q.v.*).

"CATHOLIC MAJESTY." A traditional title of the kings of Spain, formally granted by Pope Innocent VIII to Ferdinand, in 1491, in recognition of the taking of Granada and the expulsion of the Moors.

CATHOLIC–ORTHODOX. A term recently come into use to denominate themselves among Russian Catholics of the Byzantine rite. The name was used in a similar way by Pope St. Martin I (*d.* 649) and presumably may be extended to all Catholics of that rite. See ORTHODOX, ii.

"CATHOLIC TRUTH." Truth is one and absolute; the Catholic Church, and she only, has all the truths of religion (not necessarily all yet explicit and declared); all religions whatsoever have varying amounts of truth in them, some much, some little, which they share with the Church, but the Church alone has all. It being impossible to qualify truth except by way of classification of truths, the expression "Catholic truth" must be understood in the sense of "the truth about the Catholic Church, her life and teaching."

CATHOLIC UNIVERSITY OF AMERICA, The, at Washington, D. C., was founded in 1889 by the bishops of the United States, with money provided by Miss Mary Caldwell. Pope Leo XIII confirmed the statutes and empowered the granting of degrees. Mgr. John Keane, bishop of Richmond, was the first rector. It has faculties of philosophy, law, letters, natural science and the sacred sciences, with other departments; houses of studies for religious orders etc., have been established around the university, and there are affiliated institutions in other parts of the country. The governing body is a board of trustees deputed by the bench of bishops, and the chancellor is the archbishop of Washington *ex-officio*.

CATHOLICISM. The system of faith and morals revealed by God to man through Jesus Christ, who founded a catholic, *i.e.*, universal, Church as the depository of that revelation and as the common ark of salvation for all; the ecclesiastical system and organization of that Church. The principal articles of faith of Catholicism are: the unity of God in three divine Persons (the Holy Trinity); the fall of Adam and the resulting original sin of all mankind; that sanctifying grace was given to man at the beginning, lost by Adam, restored by Jesus Christ; the incarnation, passion, death and resurrection of Jesus Christ in whom are united two natures, human and divine; the one, holy, catholic and apostolic Church established by him; the immaculate conception, divine maternity and perpetual virginity of his mother, Mary; the real presence by transubstantiation of the body, blood, soul and divinity of Christ in the Eucharist; his institution of seven sacraments for our salvation; the absolute need of grace for salvation; purgatory, the resurrection of the body and everlasting life in Heaven or Hell; the primacy of jurisdiction and the infallibility of the pope of Rome; the Mass a true and proper sacrifice; the lawfulness of the veneration of saints and their images; the authority of Tradition and Scripture; the necessity for salvation of membership of Church, at least invisibly; the obligation of the moral law. The most obvious call of Catholicism on the attention of humankind is that it is the religion of God-become-man, and therefore it "calls for the whole personality, not merely pious feeling but also cool reason, and not reason only but also the practical will, and not only the inner man of the intelligence but also the outer man of the sensibility. Catholicism is according to its whole being the full and strong affirmation of the whole man in the complete sum of all life relations. It is the positive religion *par excellence*, essentially affirmation without subtraction, and in the full sense essentially thesis" (Karl Adam), as opposed to antithesis, conflict, contradiction and negation. Catholicism makes no claim to a monopoly of truth, goodness and beauty; it knows that man has an aptitude for the discovery of religious truths and moral values, that the True Light "enlightens every soul born into the world." But only in Catholic Christianity are religious truths found in their fulness, synthesized into a whole which gives a meaning to life, in God and his love for men. Catholic Christianity is the fulfilment of all those elements of truth found scattered and mixed with varying proportions of falsity, crudity and charlatanism throughout the myriad religions of man: it raises human beings to a supernatural state, making them "partakers of the divine nature."

CATHOLICITY. i. The universality of the Church (catholic meaning universal). This is one of the four marks of the Church. The Church is commissioned to teach all nations and all classes of persons: "Go ye into the whole world, and preach the gospel to every creature" (Mark xvi, 15), and to be the one ark of salvation for all. As a note it is found in the Catholic Church which sets out to teach the whole world, which is now in fact world-wide in extension and inclusion of men of all races and cultures, and whose universality is formal, *i.e.*, is accompanied by unity of faith and discipline.

ii. The word Catholicity is also applied to the teaching of the Church, which embraces the whole deposit of faith (*q.v.*) and all the necessary means of salvation.

CAUSÆ MAIORES (Lat., greater cases). Cases dealing with certain important matters, *e.g.*, the beatification and canonization of saints, absolution of certain grave sins, or concerned with important persons *e.g.*, the sovereigns of states, which by ecclesiastical law are reserved to the pope himself. Normally he judges such through delegates, whose decision must receive his confirmation.

CAUSALITY, PRINCIPLE OF. Whatever begins to be cannot itself be the reason of its inception. Hence the principle of causality is formulated thus: What begins to be has a cause.

CAUSE. i. That which effects something by its activity. In a wide sense it means that from which something originates or proceeds; in a strict sense it means that which gives being to another; in a less strict sense it means that which in any way whatsoever gives being or any mode of being to another. Cause and effect are correlative: an effect is that which begins to be; now that which begins to be cannot itself be the reason of its existence, hence this reason is called its cause.

ii. Cause is four-fold: material, that from which something is made, as marble is the material cause of a statue; formal, that owing to which a thing is of a certain specific character, as the soul is the (substantial) formal cause of the body whereby it is living and human, or as learning is the (accidental) formal cause whereby a man is learned; efficient, that which by its real activity produces something, as the artist who is the efficient cause of a statue; final, that which entices the efficient cause to act, as the gaining of money, love of the beautiful, etc., entices the artist to make a statue.

iii. Principal and instrumental cause. An important division of efficient cause. The first is that which produces an effect by its own power; the latter precisely as instrumental, that which produces an effect not by its own power but by a power communicated to it by the principal cause; in this case the effect is attributed not to the instrumental but to the principal cause. It should be noted that an instrumental cause when under the influence of the principal cause has an action proper to it which concurs in the production of the effect, otherwise it would not be employed by the principal cause.

iv. Exemplary. The ideal which an artist endeavours to realize in his work. This ideal is a true cause (see final cause above). In God the Divine Ideas according to which all things are made are called exemplary ideas or causes.

v. Of a servant of God. The preliminary enquiry and subsequent processes of beatification and canonization (qq.v.). A cause opens with an ordinary process under the bishop's jurisdiction in order to determine whether a sufficient case can be presented to the Roman authority, a tribunal formed of the Congregation of Rites with the pope as final judge. The process is divided into three stages: the informative, enquiring as to the general reputation of sanctity; de non cultu, showing the absence of previous public honour; and a careful examination of the writings left by the servant of God. When the congregation has satisfied itself as to the findings of the bishop's court the cause is introduced, and is then transferred to the jurisdiction of the Holy See. See BEATIFICATION; CANONIZATION.

CELEBRANT. The priest who actually says or sings Mass, as distinguished from the sacred ministers who only assist him. Often in the Byzantine rite and on certain occasions in the Latin rite, there is more than one celebrant (see CONCELEBRATION). He who officiates at Vespers and other services is sometimes called the celebrant.

CELEBRET (Lat., let him celebrate). A document signed and sealed by his bishop or religious superior stating that the owner is a priest and free to say Mass. Without such document permission to say Mass may be refused him in a church where he is a stranger.

CELESTIAL HIERARCHY, The. According to the general teaching of the Fathers and theologians, it is of nine choirs, namely, angels, archangels, virtues, powers, principalities, dominations, thrones, cherubim and seraphim, each rank being distinct and having status, dignity and powers of its own, all united in a harmony of praise and worship. Angels, archangels and cherubim are often mentioned in the Sacred Scriptures, the seraphim are described by Isaias (vi), and the others are referred to by St. Paul (Col. i, 16, Eph. i, 21). See ANGEL.

CELESTINES. i. A Benedictine "hermit" congregation founded by Pietro di Murrone (Pope St. Celestine V) about 1254. The rule was strict and the monks spread from Italy to France and Germany, but had no houses in England. Extinct since the 18th century.

ii. A small body of Franciscan hermits, protected by Celestine V. Suppressed in 1317. See FRATICELLI.

CELIBACY OF THE CLERGY. i. In the Western church marriage is prohibited to all clergy of the rank of subdeacon and upwards (but see BACHELOR). This is a matter of discipline which rests on a positive enactment of ecclesiastical law, which is rarely dispensed, except in the case of a subdeacon or deacon who relinquishes his orders; all who are ordained subdeacon by that very fact take a solemn vow of perfect chastity. It is grounded in the doctrine of the superior excellence of virginity and has been reinforced by the spiritual and temporal experience of many centuries: by it the clergy are left free for the things of God (cf., 1 Cor. vii, 32-3), and on countless occasions have been enabled to carry on under circumstances wherein wife and children would have made it impossible. At the beginning of the 4th century the Spanish Synod of Elvira ordered married clergy to live in continence, and this discipline spread throughout the Latin church; by the first Council of the Lateran (1123) marriage of the higher clergy was declared not only unlawful but invalid.

ii. Amongst Catholics of most Eastern rites the discipline of clerical marriage is that common to the East: married men may be ordained to the priesthood and retain their wives; if his wife dies the deacon or priest cannot remarry, nor can men ordained while bachelors afterwards marry; bishops must be single or widowers. There is a movement towards clerical celibacy among some Eastern Catholics (see the different rites). Of the 8,000 Eastern Catholic pastoral clergy in the world, about a half are married. *Cf.,* CUM DATA.

iii. Amongst the non-Catholic Easterns the discipline is as just stated and has been maintained, with periods of local relaxation, *e.g.,* among the Nestorians to-day, who permit marriage after ordination, and the dissident Syrians and Armenians who permit a widower priest to re-marry. The canon law of East and West, Catholic and dissident, therefore, agrees in this: that there can be no marriage of a deacon or priest *after* ordination, and that bishops must be single or widowers. Especially among the Orthodox, this means that bishops are principally selected from among the monks.

CELL. i. An outlying monastic house, either large or small, depending on a great abbey or priory, such as Brecon priory on Battle abbey, and Caldey priory on St. Dogmael's abbey. The alien priories suppressed in the 15th century were cells depending on foreign monasteries, as Craswell priory on the abbey of Grandmont (see also PRIORY).

ii. The separate room of a monk, friar, or nun, the cottage of a Carthusian, or the habitation of a hermit. A monastic cell is not a small and dark apartment but a decent room, furnished with such necessities as a bed, table, chairs, books, etc.

CELLAQUERCUS ET LEIGLINIUM. The Latin name of the dioceses of Kildare and Leighlin (*q.v.*). Adjectives: *Kildarensis et Leighlinensis.*

CELLARER. One of the obedientiaries (*q.v.*) of a monastery; now generally called the procurator (*q.v.*).

CELTIC CHURCH, The, is the term generally used to denote the Christian populations of Britain up to 597 (in Northumbria to 663) and of Wales, Scotland, Ireland and Brittany up to the 11th century. The British Church (*q.v.*) was formed during the Roman occupation; the real conversion of the Irish was effected by St. Patrick during the 5th century; and of the Picts and Scots by SS. Ninian, Columba and Kentigern between 400 and 600. When the British church declined after 410 there followed a period of intense missionary activity and the golden age of Celtic Christianity: Ireland sent Columba to Caledonia, Columbanus to Luxeuil and Bobbio, and SS. Gall, Fiacre and Fursey to Switzerland, France and elsewhere; between Brittany, Cornwall and Wales there was a continual coming and going of "sailor-monks" and bishops, whose names are found in place-names all over those countries, and the feasts of many of whom are still observed, *e.g.,* SS. Samson, Illtyd, Paul of Léon, Brioc, David, Petroc, Teilo, Tudwal, Cadoc. There is no reason to question the Catholicity of Celtic Christianity; it had seven sacraments, used rites of Catholic derivation, sent its bishops to Catholic synods. Its organization was loose and monastic (an abbot might, for example, be the religious superior of a bishop), and there were no fixed dioceses; it was with the adoption of the diocesan system of administration at the beginning of the 11th century that the Celtic church may be said to have disappeared in Ireland. In north England it coalesced with the church of Augustine after the Synod of Whitby in 663 (see MONACHISM, CELTIC).

CELTIC RITE, The. There was almost certainly no uniformity of rite throughout the Celtic church, and of those of the British and Scottish parts of it we have practically no knowledge. The "Bangor Antiphoner" and the Missals of Stowe and Bobbio, together with other MSS. and numerous isolated details, enable the general structure of the Irish Office and Mass to be seen, but after they had been subjected to direct Roman influence. The Celtic rite belonged to the Gallican (*q.v.*) family of liturgies, whose origin is unknown; the liturgical language was Latin. Its use was discontinued after the Synod of Cashel in 1172. The Celtic liturgy had the custom of kindling the new fire on Holy Saturday long before it was adopted by Rome in 855; Rome may have received it from Ireland. For the three customs of the Celtic rite which had a particular historical significance, see EASTER CONTROVERSY and WHITBY, SYNOD OF.

CEMETERY (Gr., sleeping-place). A piece of ground set apart for the burial of the dead, which for Catholics may be a separate enclosure or part of a general burying-ground, but consecrated in either case, except for a portion reserved for the burial of those to whom ecclesiastical burial is denied. All who die in communion with the Church have a right to ecclesiastical burial (*q.v.*); if no Catholic cemetery is available a grave in any one may be separately blessed. The churchyards of the pre-Reformation churches of Great Britain and Ireland are consecrated burying-grounds which have been profaned; legally they are on all-fours with any other non-Catholic cemetery but, other things being equal, they are very appropriate places for the burial of Catholics.

CENACLE, The (Lat. *cœnaculum,* a dining-room). The upper room in which took place the Last Supper, the manifestation of our Lord after the Resurrection, and the descent of the Holy Ghost; it was the first and mother of all Christian churches and up to the 4th century the cathedral of Jerusalem. Several churches have been built on the site (one of the best attested of all the Holy Places); the present building is largely due to the restoration by the Franciscans in 1342, but since 1551 it has been in the hands of the Moslems, who have turned it into a mosque.

CENACLE NUNS. The Institute of Our Lady of the Retreat in the Cenacle is an enclosed active congregation which gives facilities for retreats (*q.v.*) to women of all ranks of society and instructs catechumens; daily exposition.

CENSER. A vessel in which incense is burned, more commonly called a thurible (*q.v.*).

CENSOR [DEPUTATUS] (the title of a Roman magistrate). An official of the diocesan *curia* appointed to examine books, etc., which have been submitted for the *imprimatur* (*q.v.*) of the ordinary.

CENSORSHIP OF BOOKS. No book or printed matter dealing with religious or moral subjects may be published unless previously censored by ecclesiastical authority and permission granted. Clergy and religious require this permission even for secular subjects. Notice of such permission (*Imprimatur*) must be printed at the beginning or end of the book. This censorship is intended for the protection of the faithful from false teaching, and its scope is accordingly narrowed to a certification by the appointed censor that a given work contains nothing contrary to revealed and definite faith and morals and that it does not frivolously or inopportunely call in question the common teaching of theologians. To the same end the Church strictly forbids Catholics to read, keep, sell or give away without leave of the bishop any book, periodical, etc., which is dangerous to faith or morals, written in defence of heresy or schism, or published without due censorship.*

CENSURE. An ecclesiastical penalty by which a baptized person, guilty of a crime and contumacious, is deprived of certain spiritual benefits until, on the cessation of his contumacy, he is absolved. Censures may not be inflicted except for grave, external, and consummated crimes. Absolution must be given when contumacy ceases. There are three censures, excommunication, suspension and interdict (*qq.v.*).

CENTRE PARTY, The (Lat., *Centrum*). A former German political party to which, though not formally "confessional," most Catholics belonged. It was formed in 1870 and proved its value in the struggle of the Kulturkampf (*q.v.*), and continuously up to the time of the first Great War. There were other centre parties formed in the *Landtage* of Prussia, Bavaria, Baden, Würtemberg, Alsace-Lorraine, Hesse and Oldenburg.

CEREMONIAL, THE ROMAN, contains directions for the ceremonies of the election and coronation of the pope, the canonization of saints, the creation of cardinals, and of other papal functions and services. It is not classed as one of the official liturgical books.

CEREMONIAL, THE SACRED CONGREGATION OF. A Roman congregation (*q.v.*) which regulates papal ceremonies and sacred functions carried out by cardinals, and settles the precedence of cardinals and of envoys to the Holy See. It is quite distinct from the Congregation of Rites.

CEREMONIAL OF BISHOPS, The. A liturgical book divided in three parts containing: i. General detailed directions for pontifical functions and for everything connected with the Mass, together with the order of a synod. ii. Ritual directions for the singing of the Mass and Divine Office in cathedral and collegiate churches and for the ordering of special ceremonies in Holy Week and at other times, especially concerning the death and election of a bishop. iii. Directions for various extra-liturgical functions. The book is far from being concerned only with bishops and is required by priests as well.

CEREMONY. i. Any action, gesture, movement, or combination of them, used in divine worship and the administration and reception of the sacraments. Bodily ceremonies, like the public worship of which they are a part, are made necessary by the fact that man is a material as well as a spiritual creature. Some ceremonies are purely symbolical, such as the *ephphetha* (*q.v.*), salt, and other ceremonies of baptism which precede the actual pouring of water; genuflection, bowing, and the like, are obvious signs of respect. But most ceremonies have a practical origin, even though the reason for them has sometimes long since passed away; *e.g.,* when the chasuble was a large, ample garment, the lifting of it by the server at the elevation at Mass, which is still done, was desirable to take its weight off the celebrant's arms and keep it clear of his heels. The symbolical (sometimes fanciful) meanings attached to ceremonies are later additions often disguising their true significance, *e.g.,* the washing of the hands by the celebrant after the offertory at Mass, now representing purity of soul, was formerly rendered necessary by his having handled loaves of bread and jars of wine. The Roman church is eminently practical, she "never does anything for effect. A thing has to be done for its own sake, and she does it in a dignified, reverent and im-

---

* The 1983 Code of Canon Law states less strict requirements for the censorship of Catholic books: In general, the Church's approval is now required only for Scriptural texts, catechetical works, liturgical books, collections of ecclesiastical decrees or acts, prayer books, and books exhibited, sold or distributed in churches. (Canon 824ff.).—*Publisher,* 1997.

pressive way." Many ceremonies are accidental, their omission not affecting the validity of the thing to be done, so that for sufficient cause they may sometimes be deliberately left out, e.g., the baptismal ceremonies referred to. Others are absolutely essential, e.g., the pouring of water at Baptism itself, the anointings at Extreme Unction. The accidental ceremonies of the Eastern liturgies are more purely symbolical than those of the West; except the Carthusian, the Roman rite is the simplest and most straightforward of any liturgy in the Church.

ii. The complex of bodily movements and words which make up any single office, e.g., the ceremony of Confirmation. Such is better called a rite (q.v., i) or office.

CERTAINTY, THEOLOGICAL. The certainty attaching to a thesis which is a conclusion from a certainly revealed dogma by the mediation of a naturally certain truth. A thesis opposed to that which is theologically certain is said to be "erroneous."

CERTITUDE. A state in which the mind firmly adheres to some truth without fear of error. It is three-fold: metaphysical, when its opposite is inconceivable, as "$2 + 2 = 4$"; physical, when its opposite is conceivable, yet cannot be otherwise according to laws of nature, as "the earth revolves around the sun"; moral, when it should not be otherwise according to moral conditions, as "Mothers love their children." See EVIDENCE.

CERULARIUS, THE SCHISM OF. Michael Cerularius was patriarch of Constantinople from 1043 to 1058; he pursued an ecclesiastical policy which in 1054 led to his excommunication by the legates of Pope St. Leo IX. These legates handled the situation badly and it is possible that the excommunication was canonically invalid owing to Pope Leo's recent death; in any case it was directed only against Cerularius and two of his prelates: the Byzantine church as a whole and the other Eastern patriarchs were not (and never have been) excommunicated. But this event increased the separatist tendency of the Orthodox Eastern Church, which gradually grew and hardened after 1054, becoming finally definitive when Constantinople repudiated the Union of Florence (q.v.) in 1472.

CESSATIO A DIVINIS (Lat., suspension of divine service). A species of interdict imposed by an ordinary at his discretion forbidding for a time the holding of divine service in a given church or chapel, not on account of a fault of the clergy but as an act of reparation and grief for some outrage to which the building has been subjected.

CHALCEDON, THE COUNCIL OF. The fourth œcumenical council, held in 451. All the 630 bishops present were of the Eastern church except four; they plainly recognized the supremacy of the pope and the necessity for his confirmation of what they did. The council's great work was the definition regarding our Lord's nature and person, which condemned Monophysism (q.v.) and reaffirmed the condemnation of Nestorianism (q.v.): "We confess one and the same Jesus Christ, the only-begotten, in whom we acknowledge *two* natures without mixture, without change, without separation, without division . . . the attributes of either nature (human and divine) are kept intact and subsist in *one* person and one hypostatic union (q.v.). We confess not a (Lord) divided and separated in several persons, but one only Son, only begotten, the Word of God, our saviour Jesus Christ." This is the council that was rejected by the Copts, the Armenians and the Syrian Jacobites, most of whom have remained out of communion both with Rome and with the Orthodox Eastern Church ever since. By its 28th canon (which was not confirmed by the pope), this council made Constantinople, the imperial city, a patriarchate and confirmed its first place after Rome: herein was contained a germ of the schisms of Photius, Cerularius and the Eastern church (qq.v.). The fathers of this and the other five first œcumenical councils are commemorated in a feast of the Byzantine rite on the second Sunday in July.

CHALDEAN CATHOLICS are the descendants of former Nestorians who returned to the Church in the 16th century. They live chiefly in Mesopotamia and Persia, number about 96,000, and are governed by the Patriarch of Babylon (q.v.), under whom there are two ruling archbishops and five bishops. Historically, the Catholics of Malabar (q.v.) belong to this church, but are in fact organized separately. The secular clergy have a patriarchal seminary and one directed by French Dominicans at Mosul, where their liturgical books have been printed. About half the secular clergy are married. There is a congregation of Antonian monks with three houses including the famous Rabban-Hormizd. They use the Chaldean rite (q.v.), purged of the names of Mar Nestorius, etc., in the diptychs. The people are mostly peasants.

CHALDEAN RITE, The. The system and forms of worship and administration of the sacraments in use among the Chaldean Catholics, the Nestorians and, in a modified form, the Christians of Malabar (qq.v.). The liturgical language is Syriac and there are three eucharistic Liturgies, differing chiefly in the *anaphora;* that "of the holy apostles Addai and Mari" is most commonly used. Among the Nestorians is a curious custom called the Holy Leaven (q.v.). They receive holy communion under both kinds separately, but the Catholics now in one kind only. The peculiar usage of reuniting the two particles as if they had not been broken, after the fraction of the Host, was shared by the extinct Celtic rite: *Filioque* in the creed has been introduced by the Catholics; the words of institution are said or sung aloud. The churches have a solid wall between the raised sanctuary and nave reaching to the roof, with an opening in the middle; the altar is against the east wall; a baptistery adjoins the sanctuary. The Divine Office is divided into evening, night and morning prayer, to which the Antonian monks add the little hours. Baptism is by semi-immersion and pouring, the ritual being modelled on that of the eucharistic Liturgy, and is immediately followed by Confirmation. Men are separated from women in church; the altar is hidden by the wall, as above, but the curtain of the door in the middle is drawn back during parts of the Liturgy. The Nestorians have neither pictures nor crucifixes, but plain crosses only. Vestments are much the same as the Byzantine, except that the *phelonion* is rather like a cope without a hood. The rosary, scapular, way of the cross, and certain Western feasts are in use among the Chaldeans, but otherwise their rite has been little modified by Latin influence except in details and accessories. Bishops use the Latin mitre, staff, ring and cross. About 70% of the users of this rite are Catholics, but if the allied Malabarese are included, 96%.

CHALICE. i. The vessel used at Mass to contain the wine which by consecration becomes the blood of Christ. It is in the form of a cup with a stem, having a knop or knob and a base. It may be made of gold, silver or, in very poor churches, of tin, but silver and tin chalices must have the inside of the cup gilt. The chalice is consecrated with holy chrism by a bishop, and is desecrated by profanation or by damage sufficient to render it useless; re-gilding inside does not destroy consecration. A chalice may only be touched and handled by clerics, and by those layfolk authorized to perform the duties of a sacristan.

ii. The word chalice is often used to signify its contents.

CHALICE VEIL. A square piece of silk, of the same colour as the vestments, used to cover the chalice and paten on the way to and from the altar, and during Mass up to the offertory and after the ablutions. The Carthusians instead have a large corporal and draw one end over the vessels.

CHALK, THE BLESSING OF, is practised in some places, *e.g.*, Poland, after Mass on the Epiphany. The chalk is distributed to the faithful who with it write on their doors the names of the Magi, Caspar, Melchior and Balthazar, with an invocation.

The form of blessing is in the "Rituale Romanum."

CHALLONER'S BIBLE. The revisions of the Rheims-Douay Bible made by Bp. Challoner (N.T., 1749, 1750 and 1752; O.T. 1750). These versions "almost amounted to a new translation" (Newman) and "to call it any longer the Douay or Rhemish version is an abuse of terms. It has been altered and modified and until scarce any verse remains as it was originally printed" (Wiseman). Nevertheless this is what commonly passes as the Douay Bible and is the version generally used by English Catholics, (But see KNOX's VERSION). Challoner's alterations mostly took the form of approximations to the text of the Authorized Version of King James and the clearing up of obscure words and passages in the true Douay version.*

CHAM. A son of Noe (Noah), commonly called in English *Ham*.

CHAMBERLAIN (It. *camerlengo*). i. The chamberlain of the Apostolic Camera (*q.v.*) bears the title of Camerlengo of the Holy Roman Church; he is always a cardinal. He administers the revenues and property of the Holy See. On the death of a pope he becomes head of the Sacred College and is in charge of the administration of the Church; he assembles the conclave (*q.v.*) and takes charge of it until a pope is elected.

ii. The Camerlengo of the Sacred College is in charge of the property and revenues of the College of Cardinals and records the "acts," or business transacted, of a consistory (*q.v.*).

iii. The Camerlengo of the Roman Clergy is elected by the canons and parish-priests of the city as president of the local secular clergy.

CHAMBERLAINS, PAPAL PRIVY, are officials whose duties lie in and about the pope's apartments. They are divided into numerous classes, some of laymen, some of clerics, some of both. A supernumerary privy chamberlain is an honorary appointment made to clerics from all parts as a reward of merit; such an one in English-speaking countries is addressed as "The Very Reverend Monsignor N . . ."; they wear a purple cassock and *mantellone*. Supernumerary privy chamberlain "of sword and cape" is a corresponding honour for distinguished laymen who, when they are in Rome, may take a turn of duty in the Vatican. The lay chamberlains have a number of special costumes, of which the black 16th century court dress of "sword and cape" is the most becoming.

CHANCE. An effect that happens outside or alongside the intention of the cause (*q.v.*).

CHANCEL. The part of a parish church between the altar and the nave, so called from the *cancelli* (railings) by which it was

---

* For comparison with the Challoner Douay-Rheims version, we quote here Luke 1:26-28 from a facsimile edition of the 1582 Rheims New Testament. Despite the archaic spellings and typography, the wording is almost the same: "And in the fixt moneth, the Angel Gabriel vvas fent of God into a citie of Galilee,
(Continued on following page)

formerly enclosed, now replaced by the communion-rail. The chancel is for the accommodation of the choir, the part round the altar (the sanctuary) being reserved for the ministers. The word is not much used now, except archæologically, as modern churches rarely have chancels of sufficient size to admit a choir and so are simply sanctuaries. In conventual and other churches wherein the Divine Office is said daily, the large chancel is called the quire.

CHANCELLOR (Lat. *cancellarius*, a Roman legal official). i. The Chancellor of the Holy Roman Church is the cardinal at the head of the Apostolic Chancery (*q.v.*).
ii. The official in charge of a diocesan chancery (*q.v.*).

CHANCERY, THE APOSTOLIC. A Roman office whose sole duty now is to issue papal bulls for the establishment of new dioceses and chapters and similar matters. It was formerly an office of very great importance. Chancery is a shortened form of Chancellery (see above).

CHANCERY, DIOCESAN OR EPISCOPAL. The department of the diocesan *curia* (*q.v.*) which has the care and custody of official documents incidental to the administration of a diocese, including those issued by the bishop in his official capacity. These must be distinguished from the archives (*q.v.*). It also undertakes secretarial duties relating to the affairs of the diocese. The head of the department is the chancellor, who must be a priest. He is usually assisted by one or more secretaries or notaries, who may be laymen.

CHANGE. Passage from one form or perfection to another, from one state to another state. It may be substantial, from one substantial form to another: this implies a corruption or a generation; or accidental, a simple accidental transformation, as cold water to hot. See CONVERSION.

CHANT, ECCLESIASTICAL. i. The official chant of the Latin church is called Gregorian (*q.v.*). Various proper forms of this chant are in use, *e.g.*, the Ambrosian in the province of Milan, the Dominican by the Friars Preachers, the Carthusian by those monks. But they are all species of the genus plainchant (*q.v.*).
ii. Byzantine chant sounds very strange to Western ears. It has the eight modes, but the chant is enharmonic and has varying intervals. The Greeks, for example, sing ¼ or 5/4 tones, and the interval between two notes may change even in the same mode. In some melodies, a boy sings the dominant the whole time, and as the mode often changes in the same melody he changes his note accordingly as an instruction to the rest of the choir; this produces a buzzing or wailing background. But the Slavonic Byzantines (Russians, Ruthenians, etc.) and

Rumanians generally sing harmonized music, of great beauty.
iii. The other Eastern churches have their own music, all of similar enharmonic types, which the people often know by heart. No organs are allowed in the East, but see MUSICAL INSTRUMENTS. The Syrian chant is of a particular complexity as it has not been written down and the singers learn it from each other with endless variations. It is strictly rhythmical, and melancholy and monotonous to Western ears. Over 8,000 pieces of it have now been reduced to notation by the Benedictines directing the Syrian seminary at Jerusalem; some of these have been published in book form.

CHANTRY (Fr. *chanter*, to sing). i. The name given in the middle ages to the endowment of a priest in order that he might sing or say Mass for the soul of the endower or some other person named by him. It generally involved the carrying out of other duties, such as singing Office in choir and particularly of teaching school. Over one thousand chantries in England and Wales were suppressed and despoiled by Henry VIII and Edward VI.
ii. Abbreviation of chantry-chapel, wherein the chantry-priest said Mass. They were often formed inside or added on to large churches and sometimes contained the tomb of the founder (*e.g.*, William of Wykeham's in Winchester Cathedral), or were entirely separate buildings.

CHAPEL (late Lat. *cappella*, a little cloak [from the sanctuary in which was enshrined the cloak of St. Martin of Tours]). i. A partially enclosed portion of a larger church or a small addition to the main building thereof, containing an altar. Such side-chapels have often a special purpose, as for reservation of the Blessed Sacrament or to contain a shrine, tomb or relics. Each altar has its separate title, from which the chapel is named.
ii. A building set apart for public worship, but for the use of a community, family or individual and not for the faithful at large. See ORATORY.
iii. The Papal Chapel (*q.v.*).

CHAPEL-OF-EASE. A building in a remote part of a large parish, where the local faithful may hear Mass and receive the sacraments (Baptism and Marriage often excluded). It is served from the parish church, and is generally the germ of a new parish.

CHAPLAIN (literally, one who serves a chapel). i. The title given to the priest appointed to exercise the sacred ministry in an institution, such as a convent, orphanage or prison, usually with the cure of souls, or to minister to a special class of persons, *e.g.*, military and naval chaplains. The rector of the parish is often himself a chaplain; otherwise the chaplain, in the exercise of his office, is usually independent of the rector.

ii. Naval and military. Clergy appointed to minister to members of armed forces; they may be permanent or temporary, and in some countries receive the equivalent of a military commission. In Great Britain there are commissioned chaplains for the royal navy, army and air force; they are under the jurisdiction of an ecclesiastical superior who is a titular bishop. There are also officiating chaplains in home ports and military centers, drawn from among the local clergy. cf., EPISCOPUS CASTRENSIS.

iii. Cathedral. The canons of Westminster being non-resident, their choral duties are performed by a college of an equal number of chaplains or vicars. They wear the *mozzetta* in choir.

CHAPLET. A general name for the rosary and other devotions which are said with the help of beads. It literally means a wreath or crown, from Old French *chapelet* from *chape*, a cap.

CHAPLET OF ST. BRIDGET, The. A popular devotion (*q.v.*) in honour of St. Bridget of Sweden, associated with the Salvatorian fathers.

CHAPTER (Lat. *capitulum*, a chapter of a book). i. A daily meeting of religious (conventual chapter, *q.v.*) at which a portion of their rule is read, whence their greater assemblies (general, etc., chapters).

ii. A college of secular canons, *i.e.*, a cathedral or collegiate chapter (*qq.v.*).

iii. Biblical. The work of dividing the Bible into chapters was begun by Stephen Langton, archbishop of Canterbury, in about 1206, and was finished by Cardinal Hugh of St. Cher (*d.* 1263), who also divided each chapter into seven sections, lettered *a* to *g*. Verse divisions did not follow till the 16th century.

iv. Liturgical. See LITTLE CHAPTER.

CHAPTER, CATHEDRAL. The college of clerics instituted to carry out the sacred liturgy in the cathedral, to act as the bishop's council or senate, and to take his place when the diocese is vacant. The chapter consists of dignitaries and other canons (*qq.v.*). The first dignitary is usually styled Provost. Every cathedral chapter must have a canon theologian and a canon penitentiary. Only the Holy See can erect, alter or suppress chapters and appoint dignitaries. The bishop appoints to canonries.

CHAPTER, COLLEGIATE. A chapter of canons attached to a church other than a cathedral, for the more solemn celebration of the sacred liturgy. See COLLEGIATE CHURCH.

CHAPTER, CONVENTUAL, or OF FAULTS. A daily or periodical meeting of the religious in monasteries of strict observ-

ance, usually held after Prime. It includes the reading of the day's martyrology (*q.v.*), open self-accusation of faults against the rule (not sins) with the imposing of small penances therefor, and the discussion of matters affecting the daily life of the house. Among the Cistercians and Dominicans one religious may accuse another of a fault against the rule, but counter-accusations are forbidden. The modern Congregation of the Holy Cross has a weekly chapter of faults.

CHAPTER, GENERAL. A canonical conference of the provincial and other superiors and representatives of a whole religious order or institute, for the purposes of legislation, discipline, election of officers, etc.

CHAPTER, PROVINCIAL. A canonical conference of the superiors and other representatives of the local province of a religious order or institute.

CHAPTER-HOUSE. A hall set apart for the chapter of faults and other business in a monastery and for the meetings of the canons in cathedral and collegiate churches. *Confratres* and postulants are admitted, discourses and conferences given, announcements made and discipline maintained in monastic chapter-houses. Those of secular canons are more in the nature of board-rooms. Modern cathedrals and monasteries do not always have separate chapter-houses, but there are such at Quarr, Caldey and other abbeys in England.

CHARACTER. i. Psychological. The group of internal dispositions, issuing from heredity, environment, education or deliberately formed habits, which preside over one's habitual conduct.

ii. Theological. An indelible seal or mark on the soul, really and intrinsically inherent in the soul, produced by the sacraments of Baptism, Confirmation and Holy Order. It is a spiritual and supernatural power to receive or produce something sacred; thus the character of Order gives the power to consecrate the Eucharist.

CHARISMATA (Gr., divine gifts). A term used by St. Paul (Romans xii, 6; 1 Cor. xii, 4) to denote gifts, graces, granted by God primarily for the good of others rather than for the good of the person who receives the gift. Internal sanctity may manifest itself by such extraordinary gifts, *e.g.*, prophecy, the gift of tongues, but the *charismata* do not necessarily indicate sanctity, nor need they be the reward of merit. By theologians they are called *gratiæ gratis datæ* (graces gratuitously given) as opposed to *gratiæ gratum facientes* (graces making one acceptable). They were of more frequent occurrence in the early Church than they are to-day. St. Paul enumerates nine of them (1 Cor. xii, 8–10) which St. Thomas (I–II, iii, 4) distinguishes into three groups according as they are directed to the fulness of knowledge of divine things, to the power of miracles, to the power of expounding divine truth.

CHARITY. The infused virtue which enables us to love God above all things for his own sake, and to love for God's sake all those whom he has raised to his friendship or to whom he offers it. By charity we love the blessed in Heaven, the holy souls in Purgatory, and all men on earth, even our enemies. It is therefore seen that in its theological sense charity is of much wider range than in its common sense of good works and general amiability; indeed, these are the fruits of the virtue of charity rather than charity itself. Charity is not merely conterminous with the Christian life, it *is* that life (1 Cor. xiii).

CHARITY, ACT OF. Any act of the will which expresses the supernatural love of God. It is most commonly used of a form of words such as "O God, I love thee above all things and my neighbour as myself for thy sake"; but such words are not necessary for the act. When such an act has for its motive God's infinite goodness it is an act of perfect charity. This immediately blots out mortal sin, but it does not relieve the sinner of the obligation of confessing the sin. When the motive is self-regarding (*e.g.*, fear of Hell, gratitude to Christ) we have an act of imperfect charity. Acts of charity are of obligation sometimes during life after the age of reason.

CHARM (Lat. *carmen*, a song). A word, text, act or object, supposed to have occult power to avert evil or to bring something desired to pass. Their use is a superstition (*q.v.*) and as such is forbidden to Catholics.

CHARTER OF CHARITY, The (Lat. *Carta Caritatis*). The statutes governing the organization of the Cistercian order, drawn up by St. Stephen Harding in 1119, and confirmed by Pope Calixtus II. The Benedictine idea of separate monastic families was retained, but the abbot and convent of Citeaux was given a permanent pre-eminence and right of visitation of the other abbeys; Citeaux itself was to be visited by the abbots of its four daughter-houses, and each abbot was every year to visit the houses sprung from his own, as well as attend an annual general chapter at Citeaux. There were other provisions, and the whole system was the first example of an organized monastic congregation; in it the term "our order" is used as now understood for the first time.

CHARTERHOUSE. The name given in England to monasteries of the Carthusian order. It is a corruption of the French *Chartreuse*, where their first house was founded (*cf.*, It. *certosa;* Span. *cartuja*). The English school is so called from having been founded on part of the site of the London Charterhouse, whose last prior was martyred, with 15 of his monks, 1535-40.

CHARTOPHYLAX (Gr., keeper of the records). A chancellor; an official of the court of a bishop of the Byzantine rite. He has charge of the diocesan archives and questions of discipline are referred to him. The Italo-Greek bishop of Lungro has a *cartofilace*, and among the Rumanians he corresponds to a Western diocesan chancellor. Especially at Constantinople the office became one of great power, similar to that of a mediæval archdeacon in England.

CHARTREUSE, LA GRANDE. The mother-house of the Carthusians, in Dauphiny, founded by St. Bruno in 1084. It gave its name to the whole order and each of its monasteries. Its prior is *ex officio* general of the order and is the only head of an order who does not reside in Rome; after the monks were driven from La Grande Chartreuse he lived at the Charterhouse (*q.v.*) of Farneta, near Lucca. The liqueur, Chartreuse green and yellow, is now made at Tarragona by paid servants with the help and supervision of lay-brothers; the proceeds help to keep up the monasteries and maintain considerable charities. Before the dispersion from La Grande Chartreuse from that house alone 500 4-lb. loaves were distributed weekly, as well as other food and winter clothing in large quantities; a free hospital (100 beds) was built and endowed at St. Laurent-du-Pont; and a paper-mill was established to provide work for the poor. These works ceased when the "unprofitable servants" of the state were evicted by soldiers of the French Republic, on April 19, 1903. The monastery was returned to the monks in 1941.

CHASSE (Fr., shrine). An ark-shaped box or coffin, usually portable, to enclose considerable relics of a saint, such as that which contains the body of Bl. Oliver Plunket at Downside abbey-church or the relics of St. Chad in the cathedral of Birmingham.

CHASTITY. i. As a virtue it is that virtue which (*a*) excludes all indulgence of and all voluntary pleasure arising from the sexual appetite in the case of single persons; (*b*) controls the use of such appetite according to the dictates of right reason in the case of married persons. It is thus seen to be either absolute or relative: "a man's intercourse with his lawful wife is chastity," said St. Paphnutius before the Council of Nicæa; on the other hand, a married pair are at liberty to agree to live in absolute chastity. Chastity must be distinguished from celibacy, continence, purity, virtue (*qq.v.*).

ii. As an evangelical counsel, absolute chastity is voluntarily undertaken by the clergy of the Western church when ordained subdeacon, and by monks, nuns and other religious at profession in accordance with the terms of that profession. An act committed against chastity by one who has taken a vow of chastity, either by ordination, religious profession, or privately, is a twofold sin, against the virtue and against the vow.

CHASUBLE. The uppermost vestment worn by the celebrant at Mass, the distinctive sacrificial and priestly garment. Its general shape according to the pattern worn in Rome since the 17th century is that of two rectangles of silk roughly 46 ins. by 30 ins. with rounded corners, hanging from the shoulders, one in front and one behind, ornamented with orphreys (*q.v.*) forming a pillar at the back and a T cross at the front. Other patterns whose use has been revived are fuller, pointed in front and behind, ornamented with a Latin cross or Y orphrey; it may even be so ample as almost to reach the ground all the way round and so approximate to the primitive pattern which gave the chasuble its name, *casula*, a little house. It was originally the ordinary mantle or *pænula* worn by men in the Roman Empire which became proper to the clergy in the 6th century, and much reduced in size from the 13th to 18th; it now has several symbolical significances, chiefly of all-covering charity and of the yoke of Christ. The chasuble is worn only for the celebration of Mass and at processions of the Blessed Sacrament, and by none below the rank of priest, except that the deacon and subdeacon at high Mass in Advent and Lent and other penitential times wear it folded (*q.v.*) in front. See PHELONION.

CHAZRANION (Gr.). A straight stick of ebony with an ivory or silver knob borne by or before bishops and archimandrites of the Byzantine and other Eastern rites as an emblem of office.

CHERUBIKON (Gr.). "The Cherubic Hymn" intoned just before the great entrance in the Byzantine Liturgies, sung very slowly, broken off during the great entrance, and finished by the second choir when priest and deacon have returned to the sanctuary. It is said by the former three times in a low voice.

CHERUBIM (Heb. pl. of *cherub*). The second of the nine choirs or orders of angels (*q.v.*). St. Gregory the Great says that the word means " 'the fulness of knowledge,' and these sublime hosts are so called because they are filled with a knowledge which is the more perfect since they are allowed to behold the glory of God more closely" (*cf.*, Ezech. x). They kept the gate of Paradise after the Fall (Gen. iii, 24).

CHEVET. A series of chapels round the east end of a great gothic church (*e.g.*, Beauvais, with seven chapels, Le Mans with thirteen); this arrangement was rare in England. The middle chapel was usually that of our Lady (Westminster Abbey, Downside).

CHILDERMAS. An old English name for the feast of the Holy Innocents (Dec. 28).

CHILDREN, COMMUNION, ETC., OF. See INFANTS.

CHILDREN OF MARY. The name commonly given to members of the sodalities of the Blessed Virgin Mary which are numerous throughout the Christian world. These pious associations promote fidelity to religion and virtue of life by fostering devotion to the Mother of God.

i. At the beginning of the 12th century Bl. Peter de Honestis, a canon regular, founded the fraternity of Sons and Daughters of Mary at Ravenna; members wore a medal and a blue sash. St. Peter Fourier, canon regular, established a similar society in France about 1600. In 1864 the Sodality of the Children of Mary, under the patronage of the Immaculate Virgin and St. Agnes, was finally established and canonically erected in Rome under the care of the Canons Regular of the Lateran. This is for girls and women only.

ii. Other sodalities had their origin among pupils of the Roman College in the 16th century and were fostered by the Society of Jesus; they were not thrown open to women and girls until 1751.

iii. The Sodality of Children of Mary Immaculate was started in 1847 for young women attending the schools or workrooms of the Sisters of Charity; in 1876 it was thrown open to others. Their badge is the miraculous medal (*q.v.*).

CHILDREN'S CRUSADE, The. A body of 30,000 boys and girls of from ten to sixteen, led by a shepherd's boy, Stephen, which in June, 1212, set out from Vendôme for Marseilles, defying king, University of Paris, parents and priests, to capture Jerusalem. At the same time, 20,000 more, many of noble birth, under another shepherd, Klaus, left Cologne, and another body traversed Suabia towards the St. Gothard Pass. They were joined by a certain number of adults. The Marseilles contingent embarked on seven merchantmen; some perished at sea and the rest, through the treachery of the shipowners, were captured by Barbary corsairs and sold into slavery. Those under Klaus lost half their number on Mont Cenis; the rest were pillaged, kidnapped, beguiled, drowned, died of hunger and weariness; and Pope Innocent III turned the remnant back. The third party, similarly reduced, reached Brindisi, where the bishop dissuaded many of them, but many more were given free passages on ships—and sold as slaves or captured by the Moors. This extraordinary occurrence seems to have been part of the backwash from the scandalous misdirection of the Fourth Crusade; western Europe had been thoroughly worked up by Pope Innocent's appeal and the alleged vision of Stephen was a spark that lit a train.

CHILE, THE CHURCH IN. Population over 4½ million, mostly Catholics, but the proportion practising religion is small and political secularism is strong; there are a number of heathen Indians. The state pays a salary to the clergy in consideration of the ecclesiastical property confiscated in 1824, and in the following year Church and state were separated: more recently mutual relations have improved. Religious instruction is given in the public schools. The country forms 3 metropolitan provinces (the archbishopric at Santiago de Chile was founded in 1561), with 12 suffragan sees and 2 missionary vicariates.

CHILIASM. See MILLENNIUM.

CHINA, THE CHURCH IN. Christianity in its Nestorian (*q.v.*) form was established in China from Persia in the 7th century, but seems to have disappeared by the end of the 10th. The first Catholic mission was founded there by the Franciscan John of Monte Corvino (d. 1328); Matthew Ricci, a Jesuit, settled at Peking in 1601, and since then the Church in China has survived all opposition and persecution. There are now over 3½ million baptized Catholics, in an estimated population (including Mongolia, Tibet and Manchuria) of 450 million. The first Chinese priest and bishop was Gregory Lo, a Dominican (d. 1691). Although episcopal sees were set up at Peking and Nanking so long ago as 1307 and 1690 respectively, the Church in China had an entirely missionary organization until 1946. In that year an ordinary hierarchy was instituted, consisting of 20 metropolitan provinces with 79 suffragan sees; 38 missionary prefectures were organized apart from these circumscriptions. At that time, 28 of the dioceses were put in the exclusive care of Chinese clergy, 21 of them having Chinese bishops; of over 5000 priests, two-fifths were Chinese, and many nuns. The senior see is Peking, of which the first Chinese cardinal, Thomas Tien, became first archbishop. There are 16 senior seminaries in China, and 2 Catholic universities, with a university college and 1400 schools of all kinds. The Chinese government established diplomatic relations with the Holy See in 1943. Among the foreign missionaries working in China are representatives of most of the older orders, and Jesuits, Passionists, Lazarists, Salesians, Divine Word fathers and others, as well as Maryknoll, Maynooth and other missionary societies. There is no state religion and freedom has been guaranteed to Christians since 1912; the predominant religious philosophy is Confucian and Taoist; Chinese Buddhism also is important. Catholic missionaries are now forbidden by the ecclesiastical author-

ities to build churches in China in European architectural styles.

CHINESE RITES. A controversy carried on in China from 1643 to 1715 in which the Dominicans and other missionaries maintained that certain native customs, permitted to converts by the Jesuits and interpreted by them in a Christian sense, were idolatrous and inconsistent with the Faith. The case was decided by Pope Clement XI against the Jesuits and the customs forbidden. Earlier than this Pope Paul V had granted permission to the Jesuits to use the Chinese language for Mass, the Divine Office and the administration of the sacraments; the books were duly translated, and it is not clear why the permission was never put into effect.

CHIROTONY (Gr. χειροτονία, stretching forth of hands). The sacrament of Holy Order in the Byzantine rite; ordination.

CHIVALRY (late. Lat. *caballarius*, horseman). The system of mediæval knighthood with its religious, moral and social code; in return for a vow to fight in defence of religion and of the weak and oppressed the Church provided a ritual for the admission of a new knight into the "order." Chivalry represents the attempt of the Church in the early middle ages to tame a ferocious nobility by attaching a quasi-religious significance to the bearing of arms in warfare. It was only partly successful, producing gracious individuals such as St. Louis and Sir Walter Manny, and not being strong enough to make impossible wholesale atrocities such as those of the Fourth Crusade. Only by keeping peace (see TRUCE OF GOD), she found, could war be kept decent. Organized chivalry soon lost any definitely religious aspect and became a cult of honour and amorous devotion that was often as pagan as it was picturesque. The "Pontificale Romanum" still contains a rite for the blessing of a knight (*miles*), and the words used at the imposition of the sword well preserve the idea of Christian chivalry: "Receive this sword in the name of the Father and of the Son and of the Holy Ghost; use it in defence of thyself and of the holy Church of God, for the confusion of the enemies of the cross of Christ and of the Christian faith, and never unjustly to the injury of any man, so far as human frailty will permit: which may he deign to grant who with the Father and the Holy Ghost liveth and reigneth world without end."

CHOICE. See FREE WILL.

CHOIR, QUIRE (Lat. *chorus*, a band of singers). i. In cathedral, collegiate and conventual churches, that part of the building, usually west of the high altar, where the canons, monks or nuns have their stalls (*cf.*, chancel). Franciscans often have their choirs east of, *i.e.*, behind, the altar, as have the Benedictines at Ampleforth. To sing or say an office "in choir" is for the canons, etc., to do so together in the stalls with the appropriate ritual, as opposed to reading it privately.

ii. Those men and boys to whom is confided the singing of certain parts of the Mass, Vespers, etc., either independently or antiphonally with the congregation. They have a liturgical office and should therefore be attired in cassocks and surplices; they may be accommodated in the chancel (*q.v.*), a gallery or other convenient part of the church.

iii. By courtesy the name is extended to mixed bodies of men and women singers who, either because of necessity or of neglect of the regulations, are permitted to take the part of a liturgical choir. They must be accommodated in a gallery or in the body of the church and not wear ecclesiastical dress, and the males should be separated from the females (S.R.C. 4231). But in convents of women, whence male voices are excluded, the female voice enjoys every faculty granted to singers in general.

CHOIR-DRESS. The costume worn by the clerics present in choir at a sacred function. Secular priests wear a surplice over the cassock; bishops, and other prelates entitled to them, the *mozzetta* or *mantelletta* over the rochet and cassock; all wear the biretta. Monks wear a large cowl over their habit, and some friars have a cloak or *cappa* for choir use.

CHOIR-MONK. One professed "for the choir," *i.e.*, with the obligation of saying the Divine Office daily in choir, as opposed to a lay-brother. In the Western church all choir-monks must proceed to holy orders; only two monasteries have the privilege of professing men for the choir who may not intend to be ordained (Prinknash, Amay). Earlier monachism (*q.v.*) was essentially a lay life; it is still so to a great extent in the Eastern churches, Catholic and dissident. The older and some later orders of nuns are divided into choir-sisters and lay-sisters.

CHOIR-SCREEN. A solid stone construction separating the canons' or monks' quire from the nave in many mediæval cathedral and monastic churches; with the parclose-screens (*q.v.*) it made the quire self-contained and private. For lay people altars were provided outside, on either side of the screen-gates as in Westminster abbey-church and Notre Dame de Paris or, if the screen had no central doors, in the middle, as in Saint Alban's abbey-church. Usually the great rood was above this screen (Westminster), but at Canterbury it was to the west of it.

CHOIRS OF ANGELS, THE NINE, form the Celestial Hierarchy (*q.v.*).

CHOREPISKOPOS, CHOREPISCOPUS (Gr., a rural overseer). i. People with this title were found in the Western church to the 10th century. At first they received episcopal consecration; they performed the functions of the archdeacons who succeeded them.

ii. Among the Catholic Syrians, Chaldeans, and Maronites *chorepiskopos* is a title of honour; with the first named he often exercises the functions of a vicar general and with all he is entitled to certain pontifical insignia. It is an office also among the Nestorians and Jacobites. The Orthodox Church of Constantinople alone sometimes still confers episcopal consecration on *chorepiskopoi*, who are then auxiliary bishops in charge of a district of the city.

CHOSEN PEOPLE, The. i. The Jews of the Old Testament, who were chosen from among all peoples in virtue of a promise made by God to Abraham (Gen. xvii), and who became a privileged society. Their election did not imply necessarily worldly success, but supernatural privileges, especially the fact that the Redeemer was to come from among them.

ii. In a narrower sense the term is applied to such of them as were faithful to their calling, and who persevered in justice in time of trial (*cf.*, Is. lxv, 9 *et seq.*; Wisdom, iii, 9).

CHRISM, CONSECRATION OF. See BLESSING OF THE HOLY OILS. In the East the consecration of chrism (*q.v.*) is a sign of patriarchal authority, though now usurped by some autocephalous dissident churches. All the Catholic patriarchs of the East consecrate it for the bishops and clergy under their jurisdiction. Its composition, too, differs considerably; Constantinople uses over fifty ingredients, including olive oil, balsam, ginger, pepper, rose-water and wine.

CHRISM, THE HOLY. Olive oil with which a little balsam (*q.v.*) is mixed, and consecrated by a bishop at the blessing of the oils (*q.v.*) on Maundy Thursday. The chrism is used in the blessing of the baptismal font, at Baptism, Confirmation and the consecration of a bishop, and in consecrating churches, altars, chalices, patens and church bells. Anointing with chrism signifies the fulness and diffusion of grace, and it is held that such anointing is the matter (*q.v.*) of the sacrament of Confirmation. See also CONSECRATION OF CHRISM.

CHRISMAL, CHRISMATORY. An oil-stock or small metal vessel to contain the holy oils.

CHRISOM. An archaic word for the white linen cloth laid on the child's head at baptism after it has been anointed with chrism. "Chrisom child," a babe newly baptized.

CHRIST. The word is derived from Greek χριστός, meaning anointed one, a translation of the Hebrew *mashiah* (see MESSIAS). The

Christ was a title added to our Lord's name, Jesus, but even in the Bible the definite article is often omitted. See JESUS CHRIST.

CHRIST THE KING. A feast established by Pope Pius XI in 1925 to be celebrated on the last Sunday in October by the Western church. Its object is to reassert the authority of our Lord to rule all nations and of his Church to teach the human race, to bring men back to him, and so to establish "the peace of Christ in the Kingdom of Christ." Other feasts, e.g., the Epiphany, celebrate his kingly dignity, but this feast alone presents him in this aspect as our material object of worship. It is observed also by the Catholic Armenians, Malabarese and others.

CHRISTADELPHIANS, The (Gr., Brethren of the Lord). A Protestant sect founded in the U.S.A. by an English physician, John Thomas, in 1848. They teach the infallibility of the Bible as the sole rule of faith; that human immortality is conditional and will be bestowed upon responsible persons after the general resurrection; and that from his second coming Christ will reign visibly from Jerusalem. They reject the Holy Trinity, a personal Devil, Hell, and infant baptism. They have no regular ministry.

CHRISTENDOM in current usage means all those countries of which the inhabitants are wholly or predominantly Christian, though there is still a tendency to confine the word to Europe. Herein is a memory of its historical meaning, namely, of a polity which was accepted practically throughout Europe and in those nearer parts of Asia which had not yet been overcome by the advance of Islam. This polity was compounded of the religious, ethical, legal and social teaching of the Catholic Church, which both merged with and transcended the particular lives of each nation, state, country and province, so that over and above all their differences was what could be without vulgar rhetoric called "the conscience of Christendom." Nor did it operate only in the domain of conscience; such popes as St. Gregory VII (Hildebrand) and Innocent III sought, and to a certain degree succeeded, to make of Catholicism a political state as well, with the pope supreme over all. This objectifying of the kingdom of God on earth began with the emperor Charlemagne (742–814) and reached its height in the 13th century; it was threatened from the first, and then severely damaged, by the particularism of the Byzantine church; it declined, and disappeared at the Reformation. The counter-Reformation (q.v.) was a defensive and consolidating rather than a constructive movement. This mediæval concept of Christendom was the product of a certain time, form of civilization and order of society that have passed away; today Christendom has a personal rather than a territorial connotation.* What is a tem-

poral and spiritual loss can be made a spiritual gain in another direction; if it is now difficult or impossible to have the fulness of corporate Christian social life, that can lead souls to a greater appreciation and development of the common life of the Mystical Body of Christ. And the absence of a strictly delimited geographical Christendom removes one incitement to an attitude that emphasizes as "exclusive" the Gospel that is intended for all men equally. It is possible that a new religious culture will arise among Christians, one "not gathered and assembled, as in the middle ages, in a homogeneous body of civilization occupying a tiny privileged portion of the inhabited earth, but scattered over the whole surface of the globe —a living network of hearths of the Christian life disseminated among the nations within the great supracultural unity of the Church. Instead of a fortress towering above the lands, think rather of the host of stars strewn across the sky" (Maritain).

CHRISTENING. The traditional English word for baptism and the act of baptizing, i.e., making Christian. The manual for priests printed at Douay in 1610 still gives the vernacular baptismal formula as "I christen thee . . ." A Christian name is so called because it is the name given when one is christened.

CHRISTIAN. A name first given to the followers of our Lord at Antioch (Acts xi, 26). Since the rise of Protestantism the name has been used in so many different senses as to have become almost meaningless: it may indicate a Catholic or a Unitarian, or even be applied to an infidel who displays some virtue which is associated with Christ. It may reasonably be applied to the members of all the ancient churches, whether in communion with the Holy See or not, and to those Protestants who profess, explicitly or implicitly, the Nicæan creed in its traditional interpretation. The Church puts no definite official meaning on the word, as she does on Catholic.

CHRISTIAN BROTHERS. i. The Brothers of the Christian Schools, a congregation of laymen bound by the three religious vows, founded for the education of the poor by St. John Baptist de la Salle in 1684. Their training college at Reims was the first of such institutions for primary teachers in the world (1685). They have over 300,000 pupils throughout the world.

ii. The Irish Christian Brothers are a separate but similar institute founded in Dublin by Edmund Ignatius Rice in 1802. They have many schools in Ireland, England, Australia, India and North America.

"CHRISTIAN KING, MOST." A traditional title of the kings of France, assumed at least from the end of the 14th century and officially recognized by Pope Paul II in 1464.

---

* The essence of Christendom consists in the permeation of the social order by the Gospel, and this is always and everywhere to be sought, although the form it takes can differ in varying times and places. —*Publisher*, 1997.

CHRISTIAN NAME, *i.e.*, christening name, is, properly speaking, the name conferred at baptism. In current usage it is any name prefixed to the family name, whether assumed at baptism or any other occasion. See also BAPTISMAL NAME.

CHRISTIAN SCIENCE. The Church of Christ Scientist is a sect founded at Boston, Mass., in 1879 by Mrs. Mary Baker Eddy. Its most outstanding tenet is that ill-health is not real but simply the error of mortal mind, which is a false belief. If God is good, is real, then evil, the opposite of God, is unreal; God is all in all; and all is therefore good. The system, if one can so describe a theory never persistently applied, is based on pure Idealism (*q.v.*): "There is no life, truth, intelligence nor substance in matter" ("Science and Health, with Key to the Scriptures"). This book by Mrs. Eddy, in the writing of which she claimed divine illumination, is the official text-book of the sect and is a disorderly composition which owes all that is of practical value in the healing of disease to the teaching of P. P. Quimby, whose writings Mrs. Eddy plagiarized after his death. Quimby aimed at freeing man from sickness of body and soul by the method he supposed to have been used by Christ, *viz.*, exercising the patient's will and assurance. He founded the "New Thought" movement, which had numerous offshoots; its followers are chiefly in the United States. Undoubtedly many of the Christian Science cures are genuine, but their explanation must be sought for among forces whose potency Mrs. Eddy denied. The sect is remarkable for wealth and successful organization, rather than for the number of its adherents.

CHRISTIANITY is the religion of, the body of faith and morals taught by, the Catholic Church of Christ. The word may be properly extended to include the religious systems of the dissident Eastern churches and of some Protestant bodies. The current popular use of the word in an ethical, subjective sense, is to be deplored: it is stripping it of all objective or historical connotations (*cf.*, Christian).

CHRISTMAS, Christ's Mass, the common English name for the feast of the birthday of our Lord, attained its great popularity as a festival in the middle ages. A huge body of custom and belief grew up around the feast, especially of a convivial kind, much of which survived the Reformation, so that the Puritan parliament of 1644 abolished its observance and substituted a general market-day—with a fast. Nevertheless it retains its ancient character (in a rather debased form), as much in England as in any other country.

CHRISTMAS EVE. The vigil of the Nativity (*q.v.*).

CHRISTMAS TREE. Although the belief that certain trees and plants (*e.g.*, the Glastonbury thorn, *q.v.*) flowered on Christmas night and the parallel custom of using greenery for decoration were known in England before the 13th century, the Christmas tree (*Christbaum*), which even in Germany cannot be traced much earlier than the 17th, was only popularized in this country after 1840, under the auspices of Albert, Prince Consort. It is, however, mentioned fifty years earlier, in Mrs. Papendick's Journals (1789).

CHRISTOLOGY. The study of Jesus Christ, and the body of knowledge, theory and speculation concerning his natures, person, etc., with which such study is concerned.

CHRISTOPHER, IMAGES OF ST. Nothing is certainly known about St. Christopher, but the eastern story of the ferryman carrying the child Jesus is known throughout the world; east and west also share the belief that he who looks on an image of him shall not that day suffer harm: "After you have seen Christopher you go safely" (*cf.*, the wall-paintings opposite the doors of many old English churches, *e.g.*, at Breage and Poughill in Cornwall). The belief is perpetuated in the adoption of St. Christopher as a patron by motorists. The name is popularly interpreted as "Christ over [the water]"; actually it is from χριστός, Christ and φέρειν, to carry, *i.e.*, in the heart.

CHRISTOPOLITANUS. The Latin epithet for the bishop of Christchurch in New Zealand.

CHRONISTA (late Lat., narrator). A liturgical term for the deacon who sings the narrative portions of the four passions (*q.v.*) sung solemnly during Holy Week.

CHURCH (Gr. κυριακόν, the Lord's [house]; *cf.*, Ecclesia). i. A place of Christian worship (see below).
ii. The whole visible society in communion with the pope, the Church of Christ (*q.v.*).
iii. The Christians of a patriarchate or other delimitation, *e.g.*, the Western Church, the Maronite Church.
iv. The Christians of a particular diocese or, in the days before such were organized, of a single town or province, *e.g.*, the Church of Plymouth, of Corinth. These are exact meanings; the following uses are also sometimes met.
v. A single family of Christians (Rom. xvi, 5).
vi. The pastors of the Church (Matt. xviii, 17).
vii. Those who are in the clerical state and whose lives are devoted to the service of the Church.
viii. The name is properly extended to the ancient non-Catholic churches of the East, as was done by Pope Pius IX in his brief *Arcano divinæ providentiæ* of 1868, addressed to "the

Bishops of the Churches of the Eastern Rite who are not in communion with the Apostolic See"; but to Protestant religious organizations only by courtesy.

CHURCH (building). A church building is one set apart for ever for public Christian worship, namely for the offering up of the holy Sacrifice of the Mass, the singing of the Divine Office, the administration of the sacraments, and for the use of the faithful generally. In the West there is no single type of church building or uniformity of interior arrangement; in plan it may be anything from a plain rectangle to a circle or an irregular polygon with projecting chapels. The liturgical requirements of the Latin rite are relatively few and small; there must be at least one altar (*q.v.*) and in a small church there need not be more. This is placed at the east end (see ORIENTATION) and the celebrant says Mass with his back to the people except in certain Roman basilicas. The church must also be clearly divided into the nave for the accommodation of worshippers and the sanctuary for the altar and its ministers; some form of structural sanctuary (*q.v.*) is usual but even if there is none the altar must be railed off. In a parish church there must be a font and a confessional (*qq.v.*), but their disposition is not laid down. The characteristic of modern Latin church arrangement is the open altar; but mediæval quire- and rood-screens (*qq.v.*) are often still in place in north-west Europe and occasionally new ones are built. Seats for the accommodation of the laity are now usual in churches of the Latin rite, but are still the exception in Eastern buildings. For these, see each rite.

CHURCH, CONSECRATION OF A, is performed by a bishop, who must fast on the preceding day. He first makes a triple circuit of the exterior of the building, sprinkling it with holy water, each time striking the main door with his pastoral-staff and saying vv. 7–10 of Ps. xxiii in dialogue with the deacon within. The bishop and his ministers alone are then admitted and during the *Benedictus* he traces the alphabet (*q.v.*); Gregorian water (*q.v*) is then blessed and therewith he signs the main door and high altar, and sprinkles the altar, walls and floor as directed, and incenses them; after the relics have been fetched in procession and the main doorposts anointed with chrism, the altars are consecrated and the walls anointed at the consecration-crosses (*q.v.*); Mass is then celebrated. The anniversary of the consecration of a church is kept as a double feast of the first class with an octave.

CHURCH, NATIONAL. i. A local church which by the accidents of history has acquired an organization whose jurisdiction, and a rite whose use, are co-extensive and conterminous with a particular nation; such

are the Maronite, the Armenian, the Coptic, and the Ethiopic. In actual fact, each of these bodies, except the first, consists of two churches, one Catholic and one dissident.

ii. An entirely self-governing and self-contained church, co-extensive with a particular nation, state or race, and subject to no authority outside its borders. Such is the Protestant Church of England. Such an organization is at variance with the Catholic conception of the Church as a supra-national society and with the supreme pontificate and jurisdiction of the Holy See: and it is in practice incompatible both with unity and catholicity. The disruptive effects of national churches may be seen in the Orthodox Eastern Church where in one patriarchate alone (Constantinople) five national churches have become independent of their patriarch in the past century. Of which Solovyev says, "A clergy which wishes to be national, purely and simply, must, whether it like it or no, recognize the absolute sovereignty of the civil government. The sphere of national existence cannot have in itself more than one sole unique centre, the head of the state. . . . The episcopate of a particular church cannot claim the sovereignty of apostolic power except by forming a real connexion between the nation and the universal, supra-national Kingdom of Christ." The organization of the Catholic Church in this respect may be said to follow national lines, but roughly and loosely; *e.g.*, the Church in England and Wales is not a separate entity: it consists of four independent provinces, each directly subject to the Holy See, over the archbishops and bishops of which the Archbishop of Westminster presides merely as chairman, not as a primate of England with authority.

iii. A church building in a city appointed officially for, or commonly used by, the subjects of a foreign state residing in or visiting that city, where they can hear sermons and make confession in their own tongue, and possess a local national centre. In Rome the principal are: English, San Silvestro in Capite; Irish, Sant' Isidoro; American, Santa Susanna; French, San Luigi dei Francesi; German, Santa Maria dell' Anima and Santa Maria della Pietà; Portuguese, Sant' Antonio dei Portoghesi; Spanish, Santa Maria di Monserrato; Russian, Sant' Antonio Abate; Rumanian, San Salvatore alle Coppelle; Hungarian, San Stefano Rotondo; Armenian, San Nicola; Croatian, San Girolamo dei Schiavoni; Belgian, San Giuliano; Syrian, Sant' Efrem; Ruthenian, San Sergio. In London: Belgian, Notre Dame de Hal, Camden Town; German, St. Boniface, Adler St., E.; Italian, St. Peter, Clerkenwell Rd.; French, Notre Dame de France, Leicester Place; Lithuanian, St. Casimir, the Oval, E.; Polish, Our Lady of Czestochowa, Islington; Ukrainian,

CHURCH MILITANT, The. The members of the Church of Christ living on earth at any given moment; they are engaged in the warfare of earthly life.

CHURCH ORDER. A name given to collections of early treatises on Christian doctrine, discipline and worship. The ten principal Church Orders in their chronological sequence are: The "Didache" (2nd century), "The Apostolic Church Order," "Didascalia Apostolorum," "The Testament of the Lord," "The Egyptian Heptateuch," "The Ethiopic Statutes," "The Verona Latin Fragments," "The Canons of Hippolytus," "The Constitutions (or Epitome) of Hippolytus," and "The Apostolic Constitutions" (4th century).

CHURCH SUFFERING, The. The souls who at any given moment are detained in Purgatory (q.v.) till they are purified and fit for their "place of refreshment, light and peace" in Heaven.

CHURCH TRIUMPHANT, The. The souls in Heaven: together with the above two it forms the one Communion of Saints (q.v.).

CHURCH OF CHRIST, The. The visible religious society, distinct from the Synagogue, instituted directly by Christ, under one head, St. Peter and his successors, the popes, for the purpose of preserving and propagating his teaching, and of safeguarding and using the same means of salvation (sacrifice and sacraments, qq.v.). It has certain marks (q.v.) by which it may be known. It enjoys the indwelling of the Holy Spirit, and Christ has promised to be with it "all days, even to the consummation of the world" (Matt. xxviii, 20), so that it is indefectible. He has commanded all men to join the Church, which is the one ark of salvation for all.

CHURCH OF ENGLAND, The, is the official name of the official established religion of the realm of England; it is a form of Protestantism that evolved and took shape from 1535 onwards, and was definitely established by an act of parliament called the Act of Uniformity, which took effect from June 24, 1559, and by the Act of Supremacy of the same year which denied the ecclesiastical supremacy of the Holy See and vested all English ecclesiastical jurisdiction in the Crown. The Act of Uniformity imposed use of the Second Prayer Book of Edward VI on the clergy and attendance at its services on the laity. The primatial see of Canterbury was vacant, but all the bishops except one refused compliance with these acts and their sees were declared vacant. A new hierarchy was then formed, from the bishops of which subsequent Anglican orders (q.v.) are derived. In 1563 the new church adopted certain articles of religion, known as the Thirty-Nine Articles (q.v.) which confirmed its Protestant character and its dependence on the state; in practice, bishops of this church are nominated by the prime minister, who consults the ecclesiastical dignitaries. The Church of England is in possession of the buildings, properties and endowments which were provided for Catholic usages; the same is true of the Protestant Churches of Ireland and Wales, which are now disestablished, and of the Established Church of Scotland, which is presbyterian in organization. See also ANGLICANISM.

CHURCH OF ROME, The. By this name is signified:

i. In common usage, especially among non-Catholics, the Catholic Church as a whole as having its centre at Rome;

ii. The Roman patriarchate or Western church (q.v.);

iii. Accurately, the diocese of Rome (cf., Roman Church.)

CHURCH OF THE SEVEN COUNCILS, The. The Orthodox Eastern Church, as basing itself on the first seven œcumenical councils; the name is particularly used of the Orthodox Church of Constantinople.

CHURCH AND STATE. The relations of Church and state are based on the following principles: (a) Each is a perfect society, supreme in its own domain, the Church in spiritual things, the state in material and temporal things. (b) Each is juridically independent of the other. But because of the nobler end of the Church—the glory of God and the salvation of souls—the state is bound to further that end by refraining from all interference with the Church's legitimate authority and by aiding her positively. It is not enough for the state to hold aloof from the Church, although that may be the most to be hoped for in many modern states. The Church, on the other hand, fosters in her children reverence for the legitimate authority of the state. (c) The Church has absolute right, independently of the state, to those material and temporal things which are necessary to her spiritual end, e.g., church buildings, funds. (d) The Church is a society of a higher order than the state, so that in a conflict of rights over mixed matters the Church must prevail.

CHURCH UNITY OCTAVE, The. Eight days of prayer for the religious unity of all Christians and all men, held from the feast of St. Peter's Chair (Jan. 18) to that of the Conversion of St. Paul (Jan. 25). It was begun by Father Paul James Francis Watson at Graymoor, N. Y., while he was still an Anglican religious. It was blessed and encouraged by Pius X and following popes, and is now observed in many countries by increasing numbers of Catholics, Orthodox and Anglicans.

CHURCHES, CLASSIFICATION OF. Places of worship are either churches or oratories.

Churches are patriarchal, metropolitan, cathedral, collegiate, conventual or parish (*qq.v.*); basilica (*q.v.*) is a title of honour only. Public, semi-public and private are the three classes of oratory (*q.v.*)

CHURCHES, PRE-REFORMATION. In England and Wales the principal buildings of pre-Reformation date which are at present in use as public churches for Catholic worship are: St. David's, Caldey Island, about 12th century on older foundations, formerly an extra-parochial public church, restored to the Church in 1913; St. Illtyd's, Caldey Island, 12th-13th century on older site, monastic, restored to the Church in 1913; St. Etheldreda's, Holborn, built in 1297, private chapel of the bishops of Ely, restored to the Church in 1876; St. John's, Northampton, early 14th century, hospital chapel, restored to the Church in 1882; Holy Trinity, Stonor, consecrated 1349, private chapel and parish church. Other similar buildings, *e.g.*, St. Amand's, East Hendred, St. James's, Postlip Hall, are domestic oratories.

CHURCHING OF WOMEN. An act of thanksgiving after child-birth, the mother coming to church to receive the blessing contained in the "Rituale Romanum." No idea of purification whatsoever is contained in the rite, for in child-bearing is incurred no sort of taint. A mother is not bound but recommended to receive it; the common idea that she should not go to church for any purpose before being churched is a pernicious superstition. The woman kneels at the end of the church holding a lighted candle; the priest sprinkles her with holy water and recites Ps. xxiii, and then leads her to the altar-rails; here are said *Kyrie eleison, Paternoster* and certain versicles and responses, followed by a prayer for the good estate of mother and child and a final benediction. The blessing is not given in respect of illegitimate children.

CHURCHWARDEN. A layman appointed to assist in the administration of parochial church property. The use of the name is now confined to the Anglican body.

CHURCHYARD. The enclosure immediately surrounding a church, ordinarily used as a cemetery (*q.v.*).

CIBORIUM (Lat., from Gr., a cup). i. A metal vessel in which particles of the Blessed Sacrament for distribution in holy communion are reserved in the tabernacle; it is shaped very much like a chalice, with a lid. The inside at least must be gilt, and it is covered with a veil of silk.
ii. A canopy, of wood, stone or marble supported by four or more pillars, covering an altar. See BALDACCHINO.

CILICIA, THE PATRIARCH OF. The Patriarch-Katholikos of Cilicia of the Armenians governs the Catholics of the Armenian rite; he resides near Bairut in Syria. He is elected by the synod of bishops, the appointment being confirmed by the Holy See and the pallium conferred. The renewed patriarchate dates from 1742.

CILICIUM (Lat., haircloth). A penitential article of underwear, commonly called a hairshirt.

CIRCARY. The name given to a province of Premonstratensian canons. The circaries are Austria, Brabant, France, and Czechoslovakia.

CIRCUMCISION (Lat. *circumcidere*, to cut around). i. The removal of the foreskin of the penis as a religious rite is very ancient and widely spread, but its origin and significance are not clear. The practice existed in the Egyptian dynasties before 2400 B.C., and was probably an indication of priestly caste. Arabs and Jews ascribe its introduction amongst them to Abraham. God made it a sign of his covenanted priestly people (Gen. xvii, 10) and strictly enjoined it on Abraham's progeny. It was performed on boys at the eighth day after birth with a ritual flint knife, bestowal of name, godparents, formulas of prayer. Christ removed the obligation of circumcision, and the attempt by some to reimpose it on Christian converts failed owing to the Council of the Apostles (Acts xv), though for the sake of expediency Paul circumcised Timothy. Among Christians it still is practised by the Copts and Abyssinians, on the eighth day after birth and before Baptism; it has apparently no religious significance.
ii. A feast of the whole Church kept on Jan. 1, commemorates the subjection of the child Jesus to this rite of admission to the Covenant of God with Abraham, but it is referred to only in the gospel at Mass; the rest of the proper and the Office are a continuation of the Christmas feast. It is a holiday of obligation.

CIRCUMINSESSION (Lat. *circum*, around; *in.*, in; *sedere*, to sit, remain). i. The inexistence of the three distinct Persons (*q.v.*) of the Holy Trinity, each in the other.
ii. The mutual inexistence of the two distinct unmixed natures, human and divine, in Jesus Christ by virtue of the unity of his person.

CIRCUMSTANCES. Those external conditions which affect the quality of an action, namely: who (*e.g.*, if a man strikes his father and so adds impiety to injustice), what (*e.g.*, if a thief steals £10 it is worse than stealing 10 pence), where (*e.g.*, if one slays another in church and so adds sacrilege to murder), when (*e.g.*, if without dispensation or just cause one eats mutton chops on a Friday, and so makes a harmless action unlawful), by what means (*e.g.*, if one endeavours to obtain his just rights by unlawful means, as by telling lies), why (*e.g.*, if a man because he is starving takes bread which does not belong to him and so is blameless), and how (*e.g.*, if a parent corrects a mischievous child but roughly and without care). Aggravating and extenuating circumstances are those which increase or lessen the guilt of a sin but without changing the moral species of the act (*e.g.*, to steal a sixpence is a sin of theft but made venial by the smallness of the matter; but if it was the "widow's mite" that circumstance makes it mortal, though it still remains a simple theft). In confession it is obligatory to name circumstances which make a venial sin mortal or *vice-versa* and those which alter the specific nature of a sin (as in "who" and "where" above). In one act there may be several circumstances, each one of which increases or lessens its guilt.

CISALPINE CLUB, The (Lat. *cis*, on this side of; *Alpes*, the Alps). An association of some fifty influential Catholic laymen formed in 1791. They sought to forward the cause of English Catholics by adopting a more liberal policy towards the government than the official attitude approved by the Holy See—hence their name. The club had the support of one vicar apostolic, some clerics and a considerable number of laymen. It petered out after Emancipation in 1829.

CISTERCIAN RITE, The, since the proper missal of the order was revised in the 17th century, hardly differs from the Roman; it has its own "Rituale" and a Divine Office founded on that of the Monastic Breviary.

CISTERCIANS, The. Monks of the Order of Citeaux (*Cistertium*) founded at that place by St. Robert of Molesme, St. Alberic and St. Stephen Harding in 1098 for strict observance of the Rule of St. Benedict (*q.v.*). Now divided into two observances, Common and More Strict, vulgarly called Trappists, though they follow the primitive observance of Citeaux and not that of La Trappe (*q.v.*). The More Strict observance has perpetual silence (except for necessity) and abstinence from flesh, fish and eggs (except for the sick), no separate cells, night-office at 2 a.m., and manual labour for choir-monks as well as lay-brothers. Their work is pre-eminently farming, a trade of which they are masters; the Canadian abbey of La Trappe (*q.v.* ii) conducts a government agricultural college. The habit is a white tunic, black scapular with hood attached and confined by a belt, white cowl and hood in choir, great tonsure; the lay-brothers' habit is brown. This observance has 60 monasteries (with 3,500 monks) of which two—Mount Melleray and Roscrea abbeys (*q.v.*) and another are in Ireland, one in Scotland (Nunraw), twelve in North America and two, Caldey and Mount St. Bernard's, in England. The Common observance, whose life is considerably modified, has fewer monasteries and monks.

Before the Reformation there were 77 houses of Cistercian monks in England; to them England owes the development of its wool resources.

ii. Nuns. In both observances the nuns are strictly enclosed and contemplative. Those of the strict observance have the same rule as the monks, with silence, abstinence and much outdoor work. The habits of both choir-nuns and lay-sisters are similar to the men's, with linen wimple and black veil. Those of the strict observance have a priory in Dorsetshire at Stapehill, one in Ireland, one in U. S. A., and two in Canada.

CITEAUX, ORDER OF. The Cistercians (*q.v.*). The abbot general of the More Strict observance at Rome is now abbot of Citeaux, the monastery being governed by an auxiliary abbot. The first four houses which abbots visit Citeaux (see CHARTER OF CHARITY), are now La Grande Trappe, Port-du-Salut, Mellerey and Westmalle.

CIVIL ALLEGIANCE. That duty of love, reverence and obedience which every man owes to the state of which he is a member. Catholics no less than others are bound by allegiance to the lawfully constituted civil authority and this allegiance is not in itself in any way affected by the spiritual obedience which they owe to a "foreign prelate," *viz.*, the pope. But as the temporal and spiritual spheres sometimes overlap, and as civil governments sometimes legislate improperly in respect of spiritual or quasi-spiritual matters, it is by no means impossible for a Catholic to be faced by circumstances in which he must support the Church (God) against the state (Cæsar); moreover, "My country, right or wrong," is an immoral motto to which he cannot possibly subscribe. On the other hand, in the unlikely event of the Church improperly interfering within the sphere of the state, he is equally bound to support the state (*cf.*, Church and State, Civil Law, Patriotism).

CIVIL MARRIAGE. The act of the state declaring a man and woman husband and wife, and claiming thereby to make them such. The state has no juridical right to do this in the case of baptized persons. Its only authority is to register such marriages when validly contracted. Catholics are bound to have their marriages civilly registered. One contracted only according to the laws of the state is invalid if one or both of the parties are Catholics. Baptized non-Catholics using the civil form are validly married, not because the state has any power to marry baptized persons, but because non-Catholics are exempt from the Church's form of celebration. In England the civil act takes place immediately after the religious celebration. Where civil marriage is obligatory before the religious ceremony Catholics are permitted to fulfil the civil requirements on the understanding that by such act no marriage is intended. The state has the right to institute civil marriage for unbaptized persons as a condition of validity.

CLANDESTINITY (Lat. *clandestinus*, secret). A clandestine marriage is one that is null and void owing to the form of marriage prescribed by canon law being omitted, *viz.*, the presence of the rector of the parish or his delegate and two witnesses. Clandestine marriages are made valid by "re-marriage" with the prescribed form, or by a *sanatio in radice* (*q.v.*). A valid marriage may be effected before two witnesses and without the presence of the rector or any priest under certain circumstances, *e.g.*, if a dying person wishes to make a marriage of conscience (*q.v.*) and no priest is at hand; or if there is grave danger in delaying a marriage and it is foreseen that no priest will be available for at least a month: generally speaking, such a position can only arise in a missionary country or in times of persecution (*e.g.*, in Mexico, 1926-29).

CLAPPER (*crotalus*). A wooden clapper, similar to a watchman's rattle, is prescribed by the "Memoriale Rituum" to be used at the *Angelus* (and customarily is used for all the purposes of various bells) in the period from Maundy Thursday to Holy Saturday during which bells must be silent.

CLARENI, The. The Spiritual Friars (*q.v.*), from Angelo Clareno, their leader in the Marches.

CLARETIANS, The. The Missionary Sons of the Immaculate Heart of Mary, a congregation commonly called after their founder, Bd. Antony Mary Claret. They were established at Vichy in 1849 and now number over 4,000 members, with missions in Central America, Fernando Po, Africa and elsewhere. The American province has houses in U.S.A., Panama and England.

CLARITY, or LIGHT. A quality attributed to the risen body by scholastic theologians: by it is signified glory, beauty, shiningness.

"CLASS DISTINCTIONS." The Church recognizes the distinction of various ranks and orders in society, with their special duties and privileges, as a quality proper to humankind arising from the natural inequality of man with man, and that a claim to equal opportunity must be conditioned by equal ability. She reprobates class-warfare, whether occasioned by those of the upper classes who are overbearing and oppressive, or those of the common people who are jealous and vindictive.

CLASSIC, -AL (Lat. *classicus*, of the first class). In architecture, building according to the models of Greek and Roman antiquity, whether more or less strict imitations or planned and decorated according to the

forms evolved during the Renaissance, *e.g.*, St. Peter's and many others at Rome, the London city churches, Brompton Oratory, the Pantheon at Paris, the cathedral of Baltimore.

CLASSICS. The Church does not forbid the use of the classic writings of pagan antiquity in the education of youth, whether for the clerical or lay state. It is sometimes considered desirable to expurgate them in the interests of good morality. An attack on their use made by the Abbé Gaume in 1851 occasioned a European controversy which continued for fifteen years, and was decided against the innovators.

CLEMENCY. A moral virtue, allied to temperance, which moderates the imposition of punishment justly incurred.

CLEMENS-NON-PAPA (Lat., Clement—not the pope). A facetious name given to Jacques Clement, a composer of polyphonic ecclesiastical music, to distinguish him from Pope Clement VII, then reigning (1523-34).

CLEMENTINE EPISTLE, The. A letter of Pope St. Clement addressed to the Church of Corinth. It is one of the earliest extant Christian documents, not later than 97, and a valuable witness to the status of the Roman church at that date, for it purports to be an intervention in a local Corinthian dispute. It was at one time publicly read in churches both of the West and East, and there was question of its inclusion in the canon of Scripture.

CLEMENTINE INSTRUCTION, The. The regulations governing the Forty Hours' Prayer (*q.v.*) and the indulgences which may be gained thereat, as laid down by Pope Clement XII in 1736, modified by Pope Pius X in 1914.

CLEMENTINE LITURGY, The. An early form of liturgy found in the eighth book of the Apostolic Constitutions (*q.v.*). These and other early writings were erroneously attributed to Pope St. Clement I, and together with a genuine letter to the church at Corinth are known as the (Pseudo-) Clementine Writings.

CLEMENTINE POPES, The. Those claimants to the papal throne who resided at Avignon during the Schism of the West (*q.v.*). They called themselves Clement VII (1378) and Benedict XIII (1394) respectively, but they are not included in the lists of true popes. However, owing to their anomalous position they are not referred to as antipopes (*q.v.*), but as "called popes in their obedience."

CLERGY, The. Persons in the Church legitimately deputed to exercise the power of holy orders and jurisdiction. A person becomes a cleric by receiving the tonsure (*q.v.*, ii). All clerics must be permanently attached to a particular diocese or religious institute.

CLERIC, CLERK (derived from Gr.κλῆρος, a lot; but how or why is not known). i. Any member of the clergy, *i.e.*, one who has received the tonsure.

ii. In canon law clerical privileges, but not penalties, are extended to the following amongst others: professed monks and nuns, lay-brothers and sisters, tertiaries living in community.

CLERICS, OBLIGATIONS OF. All clerics are bound to lead exemplary lives, render obedience to their ordinaries, and undertake any ecclesiastical work reasonably required of them. They must wear the approved ecclesiastical dress, and must not neglect the studies proper to clerics. They are subject to restrictions in the matter of associating with women or dwelling in the same house with them. They are prohibited certain occupations, *e.g.*, trading; professions, *e.g.*, medicine, civil or military service, political office; and recreations, *e.g.*, hunting, games of chance. Ordinaries must see that all clerics under their care are regular in the celebration of Mass and practise frequent confession and daily meditation, visit to the Blessed Sacrament, recitation of the rosary, and examination of conscience. Subdeacons and upwards are bound by the law of celibacy and must recite the Divine Office daily. Priests must make a retreat at least every three years, and must take part several times a year in conferences of the clergy. For at least three years after ordination priests must submit annually to the junior clergy examinations.

CLERICALISM. Improper pretensions of clergy as such; attempted extension of ecclesiastical authority and influence beyond its proper sphere. By the enemies of the Church even the legitimate authority and activities of the clergy are called "clericalism" in a hostile sense. *Cf.*, Anticlericalism, i.

CLERKS REGULAR. Bodies of men bound by the religious vows and living in community under a rule, but engaged primarily in the active work of the ministry and not bound to office in choir, as distinct from the monastic and mendicant life. Such are the Barnabites, the Society of Jesus, the Somaschi, the Theatines (*qq.v.*) and others.

CLERKS REGULAR OF THE MOTHER OF GOD. A small congregation founded at Lucca in 1574 by St. John Leonardi. It is distinguished for the learning of its members, of whom the great Mansi was one.

CLERKS OF ST. VIATOR, The. A congregation founded by the Abbé Louis Querbes, which conducts schools of all grades. It consists of priests and brothers, between whom no distinction is made, with establishments in Canada, U.S.A., France, and Belgium.

CLIENT. In Latin *cliens*, a plebeian under the protection of a noble; hence, a person who puts himself under the care of, and has a corresponding reverence for, a particular saint in Heaven.

CLIFTON (*Cliftoniensis*). An English see, suffragan of Birmingham, erected in 1850. It covers the counties of Gloucester, Somerset and Wiltshire. The Arundells of Wardour kept the Faith alive during penal times and the mission there was established in 1776; Bristol, Gloucester and Bonham also in the 18th century. The bishop's residence and pro-cathedral (of the Holy Apostles) are at Clifton, a suburb of Bristol. The Franciscan convent at Taunton was established there in 1808. The patrons of the diocese are Our Lady Immaculate and SS. Peter and Paul.

CLOCERIA. The Latin name of the see of Clogher (*q.v.*). Adjective: *Clogherensis*.

CLOGHER (*Clogherensis*). An Irish see, suffragan of Armagh; it was administered by vicars practically from 1612 to 1727. It includes county Monaghan, most of Fermanagh and parts of Tyrone, Donegal, Louth and Cavan. The bishop's residence is the pre-Reformation episcopal palace at Clogher; the cathedral and diocesan seminary are at Monaghan. The sanctuary of Lough Derg is within the diocese. The patron of the diocese is St. Macartan (March 24), its first bishop, who is also titular of the cathedral. Irish name: Clochar.

CLOISTER. i. A covered passage enclosing a quadrangle (the garth), around which the buildings of a monastery are grouped. Hence a general term for monastic houses and life. In hot countries the inner sides of the cloister are often open arches supported on pillars. The cloisters were formerly often used for work-rooms and domestic purposes (*cf.*, those at Gloucester Cathedral), but now they are usually simply convenient passages where all parts of the house unite.

ii. Enclosure (*q.v.*).

CLONFERT (*Clonfertensis*). An Irish see, suffragan of Tuam. It includes parts of the counties of Galway, Roscommon and Offaly. The bishop's residence and cathedral are at Loughrea; he is assisted by consultors, without a chapter of canons. The patron of the diocese is St. Brendan (May 16), who is also titular of the cathedral. Irish name: Cluain Fearta.

CLONGOWES. Clongowes Wood College, the principal boys' school of the Society of Jesus in Ireland, at Naas, co. Kildare. It was founded from Stonyhurst (*q.v.*) in 1814, and itself has established other schools in Ireland and Australia.

CLONMACNOIS. A former Irish diocese now united with Ardagh, whose chapter has the double title.

CLOSED TIME. See FORBIDDEN TIME.

CLOTH OF GOLD may be used instead of white, red or green vestments, and cloth of silver instead of white only.

CLOTHING. The formal admission of an aspirant to canonical noviciate (*q.v.*) in a religious order or congregation by being solemnly clothed in the habit of the order. It cannot take place before the end of the fifteenth year either of a male or female.

CLOYNE (*Cloynensis*). An Irish see, suffragan of Cashel. It now covers the northern half of county Cork. The bishop's residence and cathedral are at Cóbh (Queenstown). The patron of the diocese is St. Colman (Nov. 24) who is also titular of the cathedral. The bishop of Cloyne and Cork from 1490 to 1492, Thaddeus MacCarthy, was beatified in 1895. Irish name: Cluain.

CLUNIAC. A monk of the Order or Congregation of Cluny.

CLUNY, THE CONGREGATION OF. An adaptation of the Rule of St. Benedict initiated by Abbot Berno of Gigny in 912. All its houses depended on the mother-house of Cluny, near Mâcon, whose abbot appointed the superiors of the other monasteries and in whose name all professions were made; it thus formed a great feudal organization, and the characteristic Benedictine family life was sacrificed. The daily life was grounded on the principle that the Divine Office is almost the only work for monks; church services were multiplied and carried out with much ritual and splendour. The reform flourished greatly for 250 years; its influence was potent beyond the walls of its monasteries and benefited the whole Church (it was the influence forming Pope St. Gregory VII); then it declined quickly, studies, teaching and manual labour almost disappeared, and Cluny itself disappeared entirely at the Revolution; but its influence is still discernible among the Benedictines. The Hungarian Congregation O.S.B., today somewhat resembles that of Cluny. There were only a few Cluniac houses left in England at the suppression.

COADJUTOR (late Lat. *coadiuvare*, to help). i. A formed (spiritual) coadjutor is in the third of the four classes into which the Society of Jesus is divided. He is bound by perpetual simple vows which have the legal effects of solemn profession. The fourth class is that of the solemnly professed. These two classes subsist together and do not lead one to the other. A somewhat analogous grade, called simply coadjutors, exists in the Institute of Charity.

ii. Unformed and formed temporal coadjutor are the two grades of Jesuit lay-brothers corresponding to the scholastics and coadjutors among the clerics. In the Institute of Charity also lay-brothers are called temporal coadjutors.

COAT-OF-ARMS. Cardinals, patriarchs, archbishops, bishops and certain other prelates display their coats of arms on their thrones, seals and elsewhere. They are forbidden to display on these coats crowns or other signs of a secular character or indications of noble birth, unless these belong to the essence and integrity of a family shield. The only exceptions are in the cases of members of the orders of St. John of Jerusalem and of the Holy Sepulchre, and of a secular dignity attached to a see. The coat of arms of the see of Westminster is that of the former primatial see of Canterbury but differently tinctured, namely: gules, an episcopal cross in pale or, ensigned with a cross patée of the second, surmounted of a pall argent, charged with four crosses formée fitchée sable, fringed of the second; and Heralds' College granted to Ampleforth Abbey the former arms of Westminster Abbey as being its organic successor (Per fesse dancetty or and azure a chief per pale gules and of the second charged on the dexter with two keys in saltire or and argent and on the sinister with a cross flory between five martlets of the first). The arms of the Vatican City are a tiara above two crossed keys, gold on red (*cf.*, Heraldry).

CO-CONSECRATORS. The two bishops who assist the officiating bishop in the consecration of a new bishop; under certain circumstances a missionary bishop may employ two priests for this purpose.

CODE OF CANON LAW, The. The common law of the Church is contained in the "Codex Juris Canonici" which came into force in 1918. It contains 2,414 canons. The code binds only the Latin church, not the Eastern churches, except when it deals with matters which, from the nature of the case, affect them also, *e.g.*, canon 864. Local laws must conform to the provisions of the code.*

CODEX (Lat.). A manuscript in book form, especially of the Sacred Scriptures. "The Codex" always refers to the "Codex Juris Canonici," the Code of Canon Law (*q.v.*).

CODEX ALEXANDRINUS. A Greek MS. of the two Testaments dating from about the 5th century and coming from Alexandria; in the British Museum.

CODEX AMIATINUS. An 8th century MS. of the Vulgate written by an English abbot, St. Ceolfrid, at Jarrow, for presentation to Pope St. Gregory II; now at Florence.

CODEX BEZAE. A 6th century Greek and Latin N.T. MS., given by Theodore Beza to Cambridge University in 1581.

---

* Pope John Paul II promulgated a new Code of Canon Law in 1983.—*Publisher*, 1997.

CODEX EPHRÆMI RESCRIPTUS is a palimpsest, having been written over with treatises of St. Ephrem the Syrian. It contains part of the Old and New Testaments in Greek and is now in the National Library at Paris.

CODEX SINAITICUS. A 4th century Greek MS. of the Bible found at the monastery of St. Catherine on Mount Sinai and now in the British Museum.

CODEX VATICANUS. The most important Greek MS. of the Bible, dating from the early 4th century; it is in the Vatican Library.

CO-EDUCATION in its strictest sense implies that both sexes are taught the same things together. This is the usual practice in the lower classes of elementary schools and in the universities. Traditional Catholic policy is opposed to its adoption in the higher classes of elementary schools and in secondary schools; for the advantages of economy and improved social intercourse are esteemed to be outweighed by adverse considerations, sc. physiological, vocational and moral.

CŒNOBITE (Gr., a common lifer). One of the four kinds of monk enumerated by St. Benedict in cap. i. of his rule; he lives in community under the rule of an abbot, as opposed to an anchorite or hermit who lives alone. Most monks are now cœnobites, but the Carthusians and some of the Camaldolese live an almost completely eremitical life. A monastery is therefore a *cœnobium*.

COGITATIVE SENSE (Lat. *cogitare*, to think). A name given by scholastics to man as equivalent to the æstimative sense (*q.v.*) in animals. It is a sort of instinct, or instinctive judgement, whereby man spontaneously knows in an unreflecting way what is hurtful to and what is good for his nature. Sometimes also called Particular Reason. See INSTINCT.

COGITO ERGO SUM (Lat., I think, therefore I am). Descartes took this as the first principle of philosophy. Doubting hypothetically of all, it seemed to him that this principle was the only one of which he could not doubt; upon it therefore he started to build his philosophy. The principle, however, presupposes others, such as that of contradiction, of identity, etc. See CARTESIANISM.

COGNITION. The union of a knowing faculty with a knowable object. Intellectual cognition is the union of a mind with being; sensitive cognition, the union of one of the internal or external senses with its proper object of the sensible order. This union is rendered possible not by the entrance into the knowing faculty of the object itself in its reality but by a representation thereof called, both in the intellect and in the senses,

an impressed species. The act of cognition is completed, at least in the intellect, by the formation of an expressed species, which is also called an idea.

COINCIDENCE (of feasts). See OCCURRENCE.

COITION. The act of sexual intercourse between a man and a woman. The act is good in itself but may be rendered unlawful by circumstances, *e.g.*, if the persons concerned are not man and wife. Spiritual writers and directors recommend that husband and wife should abstain from intercourse before receiving holy communion, as an ascetical exercise inducing greater recollection and single-mindedness; but it is by no means an obligation to do so and is clearly incompatible with daily communion.

COLETTINES. A branch of the Poor Clares (*q.v.*) founded by St. Colette, 1406-34.

COLLATERAL RELATIONSHIP is that which subsists between two persons who are descended from a common stock but not in the same line, *e.g.*, brothers, cousins. In consanguinity (*q.v.*) it annuls marriage to the third degree, but cousins may be dispensed; in affinity (*q.v.*) it annuls to the second degree, but both may be dispensed.

COLLATION. i. The light meal (8 or 10 oz. of food in England) which is allowed in addition to the full meal on fasting-days; it may be taken as luncheon or supper. The word "collation," so beloved of Victorian hostesses and caterers, is derived from the *Collationes* (conferences of spiritual writers or lives of the Fathers) which were read aloud at the hour when the above meal first came to be permitted in monasteries.

ii. The act by which an ecclesiastical superior appoints a fit person to a vacant benefice. In this sense the word is derived from Lat. *collatio*, a bringing together.

COLLECT. A short prayer (*oratio*), particularly that said before the epistle at Mass having direct reference to the feast, etc., of the day; it is repeated at Lauds, Terce, Sext, None and Vespers; at Prime and Compline the collect is invariable. Except on great feasts more than one is usually said, the others being commemorations (*q.v.*), for special objects (*e.g.*, the pope), or an *oratio imperata* (*q.v.*). The collects are sung at high and said aloud at low Mass. In addition to the proper collects for feasts of our Lord, the saints, and other occasions, the Missal contains similar short prayers (*Orationes Diversæ*) for every necessity of life; St. Alphonsus said that one of these prayers was worth a hundred rosaries. Collects are practically all addressed to God the Father. A common explanation of the word collect is that it "collects together" the prayers of the people (*cf.*, Good Friday Office), but the name really comes from *oratio ad Collectam* (the prayer at the Assembly), said by the pope when the clergy and people had assembled at a church on its station (*q.v.*) day, and repeated in the Mass which followed.

COLLECTION. The present custom of collecting money contributions from the faithful after the Creed seems to be a survival of the former custom of making offerings of bread, wine, candles, incense, etc., at the offertory (*q.v.*) of the Mass, the mediæval mass-penny being the link between the two. But the personal mass-stipend (*q.v.*) really takes the place of the old offerings.

COLLECTIVISM. A term used to designate that system of industry in which the material agents of production would be owned by the public collectively. It is usually confined to the economic aspect of Socialism (*q.v.*).

COLLEGE (Lat. *collegium,* a collection). i. An association of individuals for a common purpose and forming a corporation, *i.e.*, an artificial or moral person distinct from its component members. Every ecclesiastical college must be canonically erected with not less than three members; erection, change of status and dissolution can come only from the Holy See. Among such colleges are the College of Cardinals (*q.v.*) and the chapters of canons of cathedral and collegiate churches.

ii. An institution for higher education, especially professional or ecclesiastical (*cf.,* Seminary). A pontifical college is a seminary for the training of priests or missionaries, directly subject to the Holy See, *e.g.*, the English Colleges at Rome, Valladolid and Lisbon. Only those at Kandy (Ceylon), Scutari (Albania) and Columbus (U.S.A.) and the Armenian, Ethiopic, French, Lombard, Greek, Ruthenian, Spanish and Pio-Latino colleges in Rome have the word "pontifical" added to their name as a title.

COLLEGE OF CARDINALS, SACRED. This forms a corporation with a dean at its head and a chamberlain to administer its revenues, now small. In 1586 the number of cardinals was fixed at 70, namely, 6 cardinal bishops, 50 cardinal priests and 14 cardinal deacons, but the college is rarely full; in accordance with the Council of Trent it includes representatives of the principal Christian nations, which in Jan., 1946, were distributed thus: American 5, Argentinian 2, Armenian 1, Australian 1, Austrian 1, Belgian 1, Brazilian 2, Canadian 2, Chilian 1, Chinese 1, Cuban 1, Dutch 1, English 1, French 7, German 4, Hungarian 1, Italian 28, Peruvian 1, Polish 2, Portuguese 2, Spanish 4, Syrian 1. The preponderance of the Italians is due to the requirements of the government of the Church being seated at Rome. Of the above, nearly all belonged to the secular clergy; 6 were not in episcopal orders. A cardinal is not necessarily of the Roman rite; since 1856 there have been 2 Ruthenians, 2 Armenians and 1 Syrian. To the college of cardinals belongs the exclusive right and duty of administering the Holy See during its vacancy and of electing a successor, for which purpose it goes into conclave (*q.v.*). The primary function of the members is to act as a sort of privy council; they are in no sense a parliament; they also preside over the various Roman congregations and tribunals; and they are "protectors" of religious orders, colleges, etc.

COLLEGES, NATIONAL. Seminaries for the training of the clergy of various countries at Rome. Each college has its own premises in the city, as well as a summer house outside, and a distinctive dress. The following are the principal colleges with the date of their foundation: American (1859), Beda (English, 1898), Belgian (1844), Bohemian (1892), Brazilian (1929), Canadian (1888), Czechoslovakian (1929), Dutch (1931), Lithuanian (1947), English (1579), French (1853), German-Hungarian (1552), Irish (1618), Yugoslavonic (14th century; 1901), Lombard (1854), Polish (1866), Portuguese (1900), Scots (1600), South American (Pio-Latino, 1858), Spanish (1893). These all wear a cassock, sash and cloak for outdoors, mostly all black distinguished from one another by colours in the sash; but the Germans have a red cassock and the Scots a violet. The following colleges are for seminarians of particular rites rather than nationalities: Armenian (1883), Ethiopic (1919), Greek (1577), Maronite (1584; 1891), Russian (1927), Ruthenian (1897), Rumanian (1930). Ethiopians and Russians have cassock, sash, *rason* and *kamelaukion*, all black; Armenians, red sash, with *rason;* Greeks, blue cassock, red sash, black *rason* and *kamelaukion;* Maronites, black *rason;* Ruthenians, blue cassock and cloak, yellow sash. The religious orders also have their special colleges at Rome.

COLLEGES, ROMAN. The principal colleges beside the national are the Capranica, the oldest, founded by the cardinal of that name in 1457; the Roman Seminary (1565), divided into the greater and lesser seminaries, of which the first incorporates the former Seminario Pio, for students of Rome and adjacent dioceses; the Urban (1627), under the direction of the Propaganda Congregation; the Gregorian and Angelico universities; and the Academy of Noble Ecclesiastics (*qq.v.*). See also SAPIENZA, INSTITUTES and ACADEMIES.

COLLEGEVILLE. St. John's Abbey, Collegeville, Minnesota, is the American Benedictine monastery best known in other countries, on account of its work for the liturgical movement and in the promotion of social justice. It belongs to the American-Cassinese congregation, and was founded in 1856, with liberal help from King Ludwig I of Bavaria. The monks conduct St. John's

University, which includes a theological seminary, a college, and a boarding high-school, and have charge of an Indian mission in north Minnesota and a vicariate apostolic in the Bahamas. The abbey has several dependent priories.

COLLEGIATE CHURCH. One served by a college of secular priests, called canons because they form a chapter and sometimes live in common. Unless the church is parochial, their chief business is the celebration of divine worship; they are normally subject to episcopal jurisdiction. There are no such churches in England now, but there was a number before the Reformation, *e.g.*, the great churches at Beverley and Southwell; they are still found on the continent, especially in Italy, there being thirteen in Rome alone, the chief of which is St. Peter's itself. The minor basilica of St. Ambrose at Milan is a collegiate church served by a mitred secular abbot, archpriest, dean, 14 canons and 7 minor canons.

COLLEGIUM CULTORUM MARTYRUM. The Society for the Veneration of the Martyrs, founded in Rome in 1897, arranges Mass and other services in the catacombs on the feasts of the martyrs, when sermons on their lives are preached and conferences given.

COLOMBIA, THE CHURCH IN. Population 8¾ million, of whom nearly a half are Indians and Negroes and many of the rest mixed. Most of the people profess Catholicism, except for a number of heathen Indians. By the constitution "the Catholic Apostolic Roman religion is that of the nation, and the public authorities will protect it"; but the Church is not "established" and all religions are freely exercised. Public education is directed in accordance with the Catholic faith; there is no divorce *a vinculo;* the clergy are not liable for military service. The primatial see is Bogotá (founded in 1563), with 3 other archbishoprics, 12 suffragan dioceses, and a dozen vicariates and prefectures for the Indian missions. A concordat with the Holy See has subsisted since 1887.

COLOSSIANS, THE EPISTLE TO THE. A letter written by St. Paul while in prison at Rome to the Christians of Colossæ and neighbouring cities of Phrygia, and a canonical book of holy Scripture. It was directed against certain errors that had been taught among them and contains both dogmatic and moral teaching, including a clear statement of Christ as the one mediator and head of the Church, his Body (i, 13–20).

COLOUR BAR. A veto imposed by the state on: (*a*) Immigration of "coloured" races (*e.g.*, Chinese, Japanese) as in Queensland and California; this may be justified by circumstances; (*b*) intermarriage between whites and those who are even partially of Negro descent; the justification of such prohibition is disputed. As it is a purely civil enactment, the sacramental character of marriages contracted between Christians in disregard of this veto is not affected. Social and economic discrimination against a class or individuals merely on account of their race (as against the Negro in parts of U.S.A. and in South Africa) is an offence against both charity and justice, which aggravates ill-will, leads to violence on the part of the sufferers and lawless reprisals against them, and is based on principles directly opposed to the Christian doctrine of the unity of mankind. See ANTISEMITISM, BROTHERHOOD OF MAN.

COLOURS. i. Liturgical. White, red, purple or violet, green and black (*qq.v.*) are the ordinary colours of vestments. Cloth of gold and silver, and rose (*qq.v.*) on two Sundays, are permitted, and blue by privilege. The archdiocese of Lyons uses grey in Lent. In the Western church practice in this matter only became uniform in the 19th century; the Ambrosian rite still differs. The Roman sequence has been adopted by the Catholic Malabarese, and to a considerable extent by the Maronites and Ruthenians, but no other Eastern churches have special liturgical colours. The Byzantines use principally white. The origin and significance of these colours seem to be purely symbolic—red is obvious for martyrs, and so on.

ii. Papal. Yellow and white since 1808, when the French army of Italy adopted the former yellow and red. The flag of the Vatican City is white and yellow (nearest the pole) divided vertically and with the tiara and keys imposed.

COLUMBANUS, THE RULE OF SAINT, was written by the saint for his monasteries at Luxeuil and Bobbio. It was different in character from St. Benedict's (by which it was eventually superseded); the offices were much longer and the fasts more strict and the whole rule had a characteristic Celtic austerity.

COLWICH. An abbey of Benedictine nuns founded in Paris in 1652; they were driven out by the Revolution and settled in Staffordshire. They are enclosed and contemplative and were the first nuns in Great Britain to adopt perpetual adoration (in 1829), which they still practice. The house was originally a filiation from Cambrai (see STANBROOK), and in 1926 was reunited to the English congregation.

COMB, LITURGICAL. Combs of ivory, precious metal, or wood were in considerable use liturgically during the early middle ages. Their only survival is at the consecration of a bishop, when it is used to smooth the hair of the newly consecrated after the chrism with which he is anointed has been wiped from his head.

COMMA IOHANNINUM (Lat., The Johannine Clause). See the THREE HEAVENLY WITNESSES.

COMMANDERY. The manor or group of manors in charge of one or more knights of a military order. Such was the commandery of the Hospitallers at Clanfield in Oxfordshire. Those of the Templars were usually called preceptories, e.g., Garway in Herefordshire.

COMMANDMENTS, THE TEN, are the basic moral commands given by God to Moses (Exodus xix, 20–xx, 17; Deuteronomy v, 1–22), renewed and amplified by our Lord (Matt. v and xix). It should be noticed that all Protestants, except certain Lutherans, call "I am the Lord thy God . . . strange gods before me" the First Commandment, and join the 9th and 10th into one; therefore their references to Nos. 2 to 9 are one higher. The traditional Catholic order received from St. Augustine and based on the Hebrew text, is: First table: God; "I am the Lord . . . nor serve them"; 2, "Thou shalt not . . . vain"; 3, the Sabbath; Second table: Our neighbour; 4, honour parents; 5, murder; 6, adultery; 7, theft; 8, false witness; 9, adulterous desires; 10, envy. The Council of Trent (sess. vi, canon 19) condemned those who should say "that the Ten Commandments in no wise appertain to Christians"; they are binding on all mankind.

COMMANDMENTS OF THE CHURCH, The, are: 1, To assist at Mass and rest from servile work (q.v.) on all Sundays and holidays of obligation (q.v.); 2, to fast and abstain on the days appointed by the Church; 3, to go to confession at least once a year; 4, to receive the Blessed Sacrament at least once a year, and that about Easter time; 5, to contribute to the support of our pastors according to our means; 6, not to marry within certain degrees of kindred, nor to marry with solemnity at forbidden times (q.v.). These laws are binding under pain of sin, but certain circumstances excuse us from 1 (e.g., distance from a church, the demands of charity) and 2 (e.g., ill-health). Dispensations are given for marriage in the further collateral relationships.

COMMEMORATION. i. When there is occurrence (q.v.) between feasts and the Ordo (q.v.) indicates that the lesser feast is to have a commemoration, this is made at Mass by adding the collect, secret and post-communion of the feast to be commemorated after those prayers in the proper of the feast kept. Commemorations may also be made at (a) Lauds and (b) Vespers: after the collect is said, (a) the antiphon to the Benedictus of the commemorated office, then the versicle and response that would have been said after its hymn, and then its collect; (b) antiphon of Magnificat, versicle and response of Vespers hymn, and collect. The multiplication of commemorations at Mass or Office has now been abolished. On all feasts of St. Peter a commemoration is made of St. Paul, and vice versa. In the usage of the general Western calendar, there is a number of saints who have a commemoration but no separate Mass and Office, e.g., St. Christopher, St. Ursula. Since 1956, saints whose feasts were formerly simple (q.v.) are also observed in this way, e.g., St. Blaise, St. Silverius; but in some circumstances the Mass may be wholly of the saint. All these matters are indicated in the Ordo (q.v.) for the relevant year and place.

ii. A commemoration, or memento, of the living is made at Mass at the beginning of the canon, and of the dead before Nobis quoque peccatoribus; the celebrant adds what names he pleases to the prayers.

iii. In ordinary speech a saint or feast is said to be commemorated on a given day, whether it is liturgically observed or not. The Commemoration of all the Faithful Departed (Nov. 2), of St. Paul (June 30) and of Our Lady of Mount Carmel (July 16) is the official name of these feasts.

COMMENDATION OF A SOUL, The. Prayers recited by a priest or another beside a dying person, found in the "Rituale." After the last blessing and plenary indulgence have been given, a short form of the Litany of the Saints is said, followed by three prayers, sending forth the soul in the name of God and his saints, asking pardon for sins, and commending him to God; then a very ancient prayer for deliverance, in the form of a litany; then three more prayers of commendation and for forgiveness. Other prayers are provided which may be said by or for the dying person. Immediately after death, the responsory "Come to his aid, all ye saints of God" is said, followed by Kyrie eleison, Paternoster and a collect, and then a prayer for those present and De profundis. When the body is laid out, a crucifix should be put into its hands or upon its breast with the hands crossed; it is sprinkled with holy water; and a lighted candle is placed before it.

COMMENDATORE DI SANTO SPIRITO, The. The governor of the Hospital of the Holy Ghost, founded at the church of Santo Spirito in Sassia by Pope Innocent III in 1201 and confided to the Hospitallers of the Holy Ghost. The hospital is now secularized and the governorship is an honorary post bestowed at the will of the pope on a secular priest and carrying with it the titles of Abbot of Monte Romano and Baron of La Manziana.

COMMENDATORY ABBOT. A prelate or layman who holds an abbey in commendam (q.v.).

COMMENDATORY LETTERS are letters of introduction given to a priest going from one diocese to another; they testify to his ordination, freedom from censures, character and ability. Usually termed a *celebret*.

COMMISSARY APOSTOLIC. A delegate of the pope who has received authority to take evidence and pronounce judgement in a cause or to conduct some administrative matter. Appeal from his decision lies to the pope.

COMMISSARY PROVINCIAL. The provincial superior of the Friars Minor and Conventuals where there are not enough friars to form a real province; he is dependent on some other province. If dependent on the minister general he is called Commissary General (*cf.*, Minister ii).

COMMISSARY OF THE HOLY LAND. A Friar Minor whose duty it is to collect alms within a defined area for the maintenance of the Holy Places of Palestine, which by the special commission of the Holy See have been guarded by these friars, sometimes at the cost of their blood, for 700 years. There are over forty such commissariats, of which Great Britain forms one, with its headquarters at the Friary, Forest Gate. London, E.7. The proceeds of the collection for the Holy Places made throughout the Church on Good Friday are forwarded by the bishops to the local commissary.

COMMISSION, ECCLESIASTICAL. A body of clergy to which is confided some special work either by the pope or another bishop. The principal pontifical commissions are those for Biblical studies, for the revision of the Vulgate and for the interpretation of canon law. There are also in Rome commissions for Russian affairs, sacred archæology, historical studies, and the codification of Eastern canon law.

COMMIXTURE. The dropping of a small piece of the Host into the Chalice after the fraction (*q.v.*) and *Pax Domini* at Mass. The action is now symbolical of the union of the living Body and Blood in the glory of the risen Christ, and also of his union with his mystical body the Church; but it is a survival of primitive usage when, at a papal Mass, what remained of the third part of the Host after part had been assigned for the communion of the celebrant, etc., was dropped into the Chalice (*cf.*, *Fermentum, sancta*).

COMMON LIFE. A requisite of the religious life (*q.v.*), as opposed to the private or individual life of the secular clergy and laypeople on the one hand and to the strictly solitary life on the other. It involves submission to a rule and a common superior, community of goods and property, and daily life together, reciting the Divine Office in choir, feeding at a common table, etc. The degree of material communalism varies in different institutes: *e.g.*, the Carthusian daily life is almost solitary, whereas Cistercians, Poor Clares, and others, even sleep in a common dormitory.

COMMON LIFE, BROTHERS OF THE. An association of men and women who took no vows and earned their own livings, seeking Christian perfection in life in common. They were founded by Gerhard Groot, about 1380, and spread all over the Netherlands, founding free schools which restored learning in the land; with them were associated the canons regular of Mount St. Agnes and Windesheim. They did not survive the Revolution.

COMMON SENSE. i. Native or mother wit, "horse sense."

ii. Sometimes used for the common or universal consent of mankind to certain truths.

iii. *Sensus communis,* one of the internal senses whose function it is to differentiate between the reports of the various senses, or to reduce those reports to the unity of a common apperception.

COMMON TEACHING OF THEOLOGIANS. A doctrine which theologians of all schools in the Church teach as being not only true but binding in Catholic faith. Such common teaching is one of the channels of the ordinary *magisterium* (*q.v.*) and therefore infallible. For this, moral, not absolute, unanimity is necessary; contradiction from a group of weighty theologians would invalidate the binding force of the opinion of the rest. If all theologians deliver a doctrine concerning faith or morals as true or certain without saying that it is of Catholic faith, the denial of that doctrine by an individual would be stigmatized as rash.

COMMON OF THE MASS. The ordinary of the Mass (*q.v.*) and particularly those parts of it that are sung by the choir, namely, *Kyrie, Gloria in excelsis, Credo, Sanctus* and *Agnus Dei*, with various responses.

COMMON OF THE SAINTS (Lat. *Commune Sanctorum*). A division of the Missal and Breviary in which are found Masses and Offices for all those saints who have not special ones assigned to them, or who have only certain parts proper; the rest is then supplied from the common. It is divided into various classes, namely, vigils of an apostle; a martyr who was a bishop (2 Masses); a martyr not a bishop (2 Masses); several martyrs (4 Masses, one for paschaltime); any martyr in paschal-time; a pope; a confessor who was a bishop (2 Masses); a doctor of the Church; a confessor who was not a bishop (2 Masses); an abbot; a martyr who was a virgin (2 Masses); a virgin (2 Masses); other women martyrs; other holy women; the dedication of a church; common Masses of our Lady according to the time of year. When a class has several common

Masses they are distinguished from one another by the first words of the introit, *e.g.*, St. Simon Stock has the common Mass "of confessors not bishops *Os iusti*," with a proper collect.

COMMUNICANTES. The first word of the third prayer of the canon of the Mass, introduced by the direction *infra actionem*, "within the action," to remind the celebrant that here the *Communicantes* proper to the day is to be inserted; there are now only seven variants, namely, for Christmas, Epiphany, Maundy Thursday, Holy Saturday, Easter, Ascension, and Pentecost. The prayer calls on the blessed in Heaven to second our petition; our Lady, twelve Apostles and twelve martyrs are named. See SAINTS OF THE MASS.

COMMUNICATIO IDIOMATUM. "The communication of properties" between the Word and Christ the man. In virtue of the Hypostatic Union (*q.v.*) those things which are proper to the Word can be affirmed of Christ the man, and *vice versa*. But great care has to be exercised in the expression of the communication, if error is to be avoided. It is correct to say, for example, "The Son of Mary is God"; but it is wrong to say, "The humanity of Christ is divinity."

COMMUNICATIO IN SACRIS (Lat., joining in sacred actions). The act by which a Catholic actively and publicly joins in divine worship with non-Catholics. This is forbidden. Canon 1258 lays it down that a passive or merely material presence may be tolerated on account of the requirements of civil duty or honour or other grave reason (to be approved by the bishop in case of uncertainty); this has in view particularly non-Catholic weddings and funerals. It is usually judged that acting as bride's maid or groom's man is active assistance and therefore unlawful; while to be godparent at a non-Catholic baptism is absolutely forbidden. Even passive presence is unlawful if there be danger of causing scandal or harming one's faith. *A fortiori* it is forbidden to receive sacraments from non-Catholic ministers, even if they be objectively valid sacraments; but there are exceptions for these last when in danger of death (*Cf.*, Absolution i). The Holy See has been known to make other exceptions for specific cases in extraordinary circumstances.

COMMUNION, -VERSE. A variable antiphon said by the celebrant at Mass after the communion. It is all that remains of a psalm formerly sung during the people's communion, consequently the verse is usually from the psalms; in the Masses of Lent they are in succession from Psalms i to xxvi, with five exceptions, and there is a similar sequence from the 1st to 17th Sundays after Pentecost.

COMMUNION, FREQUENT. The Church exhorts her children to receive holy communion frequently, daily when possible; it may be received by anyone who is in the state of grace, has a right intention and is fasting from midnight. The Blessed Sacrament is a remedy for sin, not simply a reward of virtue. No one may receive twice on the same day, unless the second time be as Viaticum (*q.v.*); but a priest who has permission to say two Masses necessarily does so. "Confessors are to be careful not to dissuade anyone from frequent and daily communion, provided he be in the state of grace and approach with a right intention. A right intention consists in this: that he who approaches the holy table should do so, not out of routine or vainglory or human respect, but for the purpose of pleasing God and seeking this remedy for his weaknesses and defects" (Pope Pius X).

COMMUNION, HOLY. The reception and consumption of the sacrament of the Holy Eucharist or Blessed Sacrament whereby we participate in Christ himself and in his sacrificial work. "Our Saviour wished that this sacrament should be received as the spiritual food of souls, whereby may be fed and strengthened those who live the life of him who said 'He that eateth me, the same also shall live by me'; and as an antidote whereby we may be freed from daily faults and preserved from deadly sin. He would, moreover, have it to be a pledge of our glory to come and everlasting happiness" (Council of Trent. sess. xiii, canon 2). All those who are baptized and have the requisite intention may receive holy communion (*must* do so at least once a year); they must be in a state of grace (*q.v.*) and, normally, fasting from midnight, and fully to profit from the sacrament must have dispositions of charity. The Blessed Sacrament is the ordinary food of the soul. See INFANTS' COMMUNION; COMMUNION UNDER ONE KIND, etc.*

COMMUNION, MANNER OF RECEIVING. i. In the Latin rite the communicant kneels at the altar rails when the bell is rung before the priest's communion, holding the houselling-cloth or salver spread beneath his chin. After receiving the Precious Blood, the priest approaches the communicant with the Blessed Sacrament on the paten or in a *ciborium* (*q.v.*), takes a particle and makes a small sign of the cross therewith, and then puts it on to the extended tongue of the communicant saying, *Corpus Domini nostri Iesu Christi custodiat animam tuam in vitam æternam. Amen:* "May the body of our Lord Jesus Christ preserve thy soul to eternal life." The Dominican and other old uses have *custodiat te*, "preserve thee." At a papal solemn Mass the pope communicates at his throne.

ii. In the Byzantine rite the communicant approaches when the deacon appears at the

---

* See the footnote to FASTING COMMUNION for the current fasting rules.—*Publisher*, 1997.

holy doors (*q.v.*) with the chalice, saying, "Approach with fear of God, with faith and love." He stands before the celebrant, holding the veil of the chalice under his chin; the celebrant administers the Holy Body steeped in the Precious Blood from the chalice with a spoon (or by intinction), saying in the liturgical language, "The servant of God, N. . . ., receives the Precious and all-holy Body and Blood of our Lord, God, and Saviour Jesus Christ for the forgiveness of his sins and life everlasting. Amen." He retires, walking for a few paces backwards and making the sign of the cross.

iii. Other Catholic rites. In most of these the manner of receiving communion now approximates to Western usage, more or less closely. But the Ethiopians receive in both kinds (sometimes separately), and the Syrian celebrant "anoints" each of the pieces of the broken Host with a piece thereof that has been immersed in the Precious Blood and administers them to the laity thus. Some kneel, some stand, to receive; the latter is the primitive practice (*cf.*, the pope at his solemn Mass). All dissident orientals receive under both kinds in some form or another.

COMMUNION OUT OF MASS. It is allowable to receive holy communion at other times than at the time appointed during the celebration of Mass; but it is the mind of the Church that this should not be done except in cases of real necessity, for communion is an integral part of Mass and not a separate "devotion." The server or communicant says the *Confiteor* and the priest the absolution; then he displays the Host, saying the *Ecce agnus Dei* (John i, 29) and the *Domine, non sum dignus* (Matt. viii, 8); administers it; says an antiphon (*O sacrum convivium*) and prayer from the office of the Blessed Sacrament; and concludes with a blessing. In paschal-time the prayer is the post-communion of the Easter Mass.

COMMUNION, REFUSAL OF. Holy communion must be refused to such as are openly and publicly unworthy, *e.g.*, the excommunicated or under an interdict or manifestly infamous. If a person whom the priest knows (other than through the confessional, of course) to be in a state of private unrepented mortal sin asks privately for communion he must be refused; but if he presents himself publicly therefor, he cannot be refused unless it is possible for the priest to do so without giving scandal to others.

COMMUNION, SPIRITUAL. An earnest desire, especially during Mass, to receive the Blessed Sacrament when one is not able actually to do so; this desire is translated into the appropriate acts of love, thanksgiving, etc.

COMMUNION SERVICE. The Catholic Church has nothing corresponding to the communion service of Protestant bodies. The Mass is a sacrifice of which the communion of the celebrant is only a part, though essential; no communion of the people is necessary, though highly desirable. The prayers, etc., attached to communion "out of Mass" are not a service but simply give decency and order to an extra-liturgical proceeding. But the Good Friday rites now include what is in fact a communion service.

COMMUNION UNDER BOTH KINDS. The reception by the laity and not celebrating clergy of both the Body and the Blood, either separately or mingled together, was the ordinary practice of the whole Church until the 12th century. It is still the practice of all dissident Eastern churches and of the Catholic Byzantines, Syrians and Ethiopians. For the various manners of reception, see COMMUNION, MANNER OF RECEIVING.

COMMUNION UNDER ONE KIND, namely, of bread only, for the laity and not celebrating clergy, is the law throughout the Latin rite, together with the Maronites and Malabarese; with the Catholic Armenians, Copts and Chaldeans, it is usage but not law. The only exceptions are the deacon and subdeacon at a papal solemn Mass and the deacon in the Armenian and Maronite Liturgies; but of course the celebrant always communicates in both kinds separately. The danger of spilling the Precious Blood and other desecrations and the inconvenience and delay entailed by other methods, together with the activities of the Hussites (*q.v.*), were the principal reasons for this legislation being made definitive for the Latin rite at the Council of Constance (1415). Christ is received entire under either kind alone because, being risen from the dead, he is in the living state and so body and blood, soul and divinity must be united; "as much is contained under either species as under both; for Christ, whole and entire, exists under the species of bread and under each particle of that bread; and whole under the species of wine and under its separate parts . . . and they who receive under one species alone are deprived of no grace necessary to salvation" (Council of Trent, sess. xiii, xxi; *cf.*, John vi, 52, 59). Moreover, "the perfection of this sacrament is not in its use by the faithful, but in the consecration of the sacrament, and so there is no injury done to its perfection [by communion in one kind] inasmuch as the priest, and all in his person, offers and receives the Blood" (St. Thomas). The principle was recognized in both East and West from early times and was and is acted upon, *e.g.*, in Liturgies of the Pre-sanctified, and in the communion of infants under the species of wine, and in the primitive practice of communion at home. But of course a Western Catholic may communicate under both kinds in an Eastern Catholic church and *vice versa*, and that not merely on account of necessity but simply out of devotion.

COMMUNION OF SAINTS The. The unity under and in Christ of the faithful on earth (the Church militant), the souls in Purgatory (the Church suffering) and the blessed in Heaven (the Church triumphant); it is shared in by the angels and by those non-Catholics in good faith who belong to the Church invisibly. Prayer is of all the things of the spirit the one in which this communion or fellowship is most active: the living pray to God and the blessed on behalf of the suffering, and to God in honour of the blessed; the blessed intercede with God for the suffering and the living; the holy souls pray to God and the blessed for others; by virtue of his merits Christ intercedes continually for the living and the dead. Strictly speaking isolated prayer, or any other activity, does not exist for the Christian, in so far as he can do or suffer nothing without reference to other Christians; from this universality of purpose comes the infallible fruitfulness of Christian prayer. Within the Church militant the communion of saints (*i.e.*, redeemed ones) is exemplified in a special way by their participation in a common faith, reception of common sacraments, and acknowledgement of a common supranational authority, and that interdependence whereby every deed of each member affects for good or ill the whole body to which Christ "would have us, as members, be united by the closest bond of faith, hope and charity, that we might all speak the same things and that there might be no divisions among us" (Council of Trent, Sess. xiii, canon 2) (*cf.*, the Mystical Body and "Soul of the Church").

COMMUNION OF THE SICK. A special rite by which holy communion is taken to the sick-room and administered at the bedside of the sick person. One confined to the house by ill-health or infirmity may receive communion there as often as can be arranged provided he can keep the fast. Those who have been ill for a month and have no certain hope of a quick recovery may receive it on the prudent advice of the confessor once or twice a week after taking medicine or semi-liquid food by way of medicine or drink. The Blessed Sacrament should be taken publicly and with solemnity, but this is not done in many countries. Arrived in the sick-room, the priest says the *Asperges*, sprinkling all with holy water; communion is then administered with the usual preparatory prayers as used out of Mass (see above); the priest cleanses his fingers and the communicant drinks the ablution; then a prayer is said for health of body and soul and a final blessing given. See also VIATICUM.

COMMUNION WITH, TO BE IN. To be united and associated with in matters of religion, creed, worship or spiritual intercourse: thus all Catholics are in communion with the pope, the faithful on earth are in communion with the saints in Heaven. The conditions for members of the visible Church to enjoy communion and fellowship one with another and with the members of the Church triumphant and suffering are Baptism, faith and the absence of any separating censure, *e.g.*, excommunication (*q.v.*). The union is destroyed by heresy or schism.

COMMUNISM. The most logical and extreme form of Socialism (*q.v.*), outcome of the revolutionary theory of Karl Marx. The underlying philosophy is materialistic and determinist; the social order evolves through economic struggles between the classes in the direction of violent revolution and a dictatorship of the proletariat, to be followed by a "withering away" of the state and the substitution of a society where ownership of all things is common, where all will work voluntarily, and all take freely of goods produced according to his needs. As well as the abstract theory of Communism there must, since 1917, be considered the concrete attempt to apply its principles in the Union of Soviet Socialist Republics, where one aspect of it can be summed up in the words of Stalin: "Scientifically speaking, the dictatorship of the proletariat is a power which is restricted by no laws, hampered by no rules, and based directly upon violence." Whether in theory or practice, the Church utterly rejects Communism on account of its errors, notably: its atheistic materialism, its doctrine and practice of class-war, its denial of the rights and liberties of the human person, including the natural right to possess some measure of private property (in practice in the U.S.S.R. some private property is allowed), and its contempt for good morals under several heads. Communism has been repeatedly condemned by the Holy See, notably by Pope Pius XI in the encyclical letter *Divini Redemptoris* (*q.v.*). But the individual Catholic does well never to utter a condemnation of Communism without at the same time condemning those manifold injustices and abuses which help to pave the way for Communism in Christian lands.

COMPACTATA, The. The agreement by which the Council of Basle (1433) ended for a time the religious (Hussite) and political troubles in Bohemia and Moravia. Its chief provisions were for optional communion in both kinds, for liberty of preaching by priests under episcopal control, and for criminous clerks to be properly dealt with; individual secular priests might inherit or receive gifts, and similarly the Church might possess temporalities and exercise civil lordship over such possessions.

COMPANATION. See IMPANATION.

COMPANY OF JESUS, The. The Jesuits (*q.v.*), now called the Society of Jesus.

COMPANY OF MARY, The. A congregation to give retreats and conduct foreign missions, founded by St. Louis Grignion de Montfort in 1705. It is established in Canada, the United States, England and elsewhere, with missions in Nyasaland, Iceland, and other places.

COMPANY OF ST. PAUL, The. A religious institute (*q.v.*) founded by Cardinal Andrew Ferrari, Archbishop of Milan, in 1920, its particular object being to counteract the influence of communistic and other anti-religious organizations especially as exercised through social and educational institutions. Men (priests or lay) and women are equally eligible for membership; they reside in separate houses but meet for work. Priests must hold a degree in canon law, theology or other science; others must have a university degree or pass a test; all must be under 30 at entrance. Simple vows are taken and renewed annually; no religious habit is worn, and the members are encouraged to have ties of study, friendship and work outside the congregation so that they may not be cut off from the world but live in beneficent contact with it. Among their works (Opera Cardinal Ferrari) are a hospice in Rome, printing-presses at Bologna and Milan with several publications, rescue-homes, conducting of missions, schools and technical training-centres. Outside Italy, the company is established at Jerusalem, Paris and Buenos Aires.

COMPARATIVE RELIGION. A science which studies the nature and origin of religion in general, and the characteristics of religions compared with one another: *i.e.*, the comparative study of religion.

COMPASSION OF OUR LADY, The. The name given in certain dioceses and religious orders to the first feast of the Seven Sorrows of our Lady (*q.v.*).

COMPLINE (Lat. *Completorium*, the completion). The last hour of the Divine Office. It consists of a short lesson, *Paternoster* and *Confiteor*, three psalms with their antiphon, the hymn *Te lucis ante terminum*, a little chapter and short responsory, the canticle *Nunc dimittis*, with its antiphon, followed on certain days by *preces* (*q.v.*), lastly a collect and blessing. These are all invariable except that the psalms and their antiphon change each day of the week. In offices other than the Roman there are differences, *e.g.*, Benedictine Compline is quite invariable and omits the canticle, the Dominican has variations in the hymn and antiphons, and so on. Compline is the night prayer of the Latin church and is concerned with sleep and waking, life and death, sin

and grace. The equivalent office of the Byzantine rite is called *Apodeipnon* (*q.v.*).

COMPREHENSION. A term used in logic to signify the complex of notes which the idea of a thing represents; a "note" meaning whatever in an object is *per se* thinkable.

COMPROMISE. A method of electing a pope when voting is protracted and inconclusive; a small body of cardinals is commissioned to make a choice by which all will abide. It has not been used since the 14th century.

COMPUNCTION (Lat. *compungere*, to prick). A pricking of conscience, but used by ascetical writers to mean a definite remorse.

COMTISM. The system of philosophy of Auguste Comte (1798–1857), often called Positivism (*q.v.*).

CONCELEBRATION. The saying of Mass by several priests together, all consecrating the same bread and wine. Since about the 13th century the practice has gone out of use in the Western church, except at the ordination of a priest and consecration of a bishop; the new priest or bishop says the offertory prayers and the canon aloud with the officiant, and subsequently communicates at his hands (the new bishop in both kinds); it is used in the rite of Lyons also on Maundy Thursday. This usage is very common among all users of the Byzantine rite, Catholic or dissident. The senior in dignity officiates at the altar, the others all saying the prayers in a low voice; blessings, etc. are given by the chief celebrant; the words of consecration are said aloud in chorus; all communicate together. Any number of priests and bishops may concelebrate, and each one so doing offers the sacrifice really and truly. Concelebration is also used in some other Eastern rites.

CONCEPT. The representation through which the mind knows an object. If understood as the objective determination of the mind whereby the mind can know this or that, it is called tht *species impressa;* if understood as the reproduction by the mind within itself of the object understood, it is called the *species expressa.*

CONCEPTION. i. Active conception is the production of human life by the parental act of generation.

ii. Passive conception, or animation, is the infusion by God of the soul into the human embryo. It is to this that the term "immaculate conception" (*q.v.*) with reference to the Blessed Virgin Mary refers.

CONCILIAR THEORY. The idea that an œcumenical council is essentially superior to the pope. The theory first made its appearance in connection with the Great Schism of the West (*q.v.*) and was enunciated in a decree of the Council of Constance, which decree, however, was not confirmed by the Holy See. The theory was subsequently adopted by Gallicanism (*q.v.*) and was finally condemned at the Vatican Council in 1870.

CONCLAVE (Lat. *cum clave*, with a key). The assembly of cardinals for the election of a pope; also the place where the assembly meets. It takes place 15 days after the pope's death, when the cardinals are locked up in certain halls of the Vatican with their attendants; each cardinal has a separate "bedsitting-room." Voting takes place twice a day by secret ballot in the Sistine chapel into which none but cardinals are admitted; the checking of the votes is most stringent; and the daily ballots are continued till someone gets a two-thirds plus one majority. Election may also be by inspiration or compromise (*q.v.*). Theoretically any male Catholic, even a married layman, could be elected; in fact, all popes since Urban VI (1378) have been cardinals, and all since Adrian VI (1522) Italians. Immediately on election the pope selects a new name, receives the homage of the cardinals, is proclaimed to the people and gives his blessing to the City and to the World. Before his coronation (*q.v.*) he must be consecrated if he is not already a bishop, and afterwards take possession of and be enthroned in his cathedral-church of St. John Lateran. (This could not be done during the reigns of Leo XIII, Pius X and Benedict XV owing to the Roman Question, *q.v.*). His jurisdiction starts from the moment of his election.

CONCOMITANCE. Christ's Body is present in the Eucharist under the species (*q.v.*) of bread, and his Blood under the species of wine, by virtue of the words of consecration (*q.v.*). But under the species of bread his Blood is also present, and under the species of wine his Body, and under both species his Soul, by virtue of concomitance, *i.e.*, by virtue of the fact that a glorified, living body cannot be separated from blood and soul. This is natural concomitance. By supernatural concomitance the divinity is also present, by virtue of the hypostatic union (*q.v.*).

CONCORDANCE, BIBLICAL. An index to the Bible arranged alphabetically under the principal words used therein, enabling a wanted text or reference to be quickly found. They were invented in the 13th century by the Friars Preachers, friars John of Darlington, Hugh of Croydon and Richard Stavensby being three of the most prominent editors. The first English concordance was made before 1540; the best known is Alexander Cruden's (1st edn. 1736), which has been reprinted and abridged for popular use down to the present day.

CONCORDAT. A treaty between the Holy See and a sovereign secular state concerning the interests of religion. The spiritual welfare of Catholics is its sole object, and its signing tells us nothing about the Holy See's attitude to the government or political system of the state concerned. "The Concordat" indicates that of 1801 between Pope Pius VII and Napoleon Bonaparte, which re-established the Church in France; it was repudiated by the French government in its Law of the Separation of Church and State in 1905. The principal concordat of recent years is that made with Italy subsidary to the Treaty of the Lateran (*q.v.*). By this Italy recognizes the Catholic faith as the religion of the state and guarantees its free exercise; clerics in major orders and religious in solemn vows are exempt from military training and from combatant service on general mobilization; ordinaries, rectors and curates and others having cure of souls are exempt from non-combatant service as well; the secrecy of confession is recognized; persons promoted to episcopal sees shall be approved by the state; the right to present to ecclesiastical benefices belongs to the Church, but nomination to parochial benefices shall be approved by the state; incumbents of Italian benefices must be Italian citizens (these three provisions do not apply to Rome and the suburbicarian dioceses); the state recognizes marriage as a sacrament and indissoluble and the sole competence of ecclesiastical courts in nullity cases; cases of judicial separation are to be judged by civil courts; instruction in Christian doctrine is provided for in all public schools; the state recognizes religious orders and associations as juridical persons; the state will supplement the revenues of benefices which are insufficient to maintain the holder; the Holy See forbids the clergy and religious to take any part in politics, etc.

CONCORDAT OF WORMS, The, or *Pactum Calixtinum.* The agreement between Pope Callistus II and the Emperor Henry V by which the conflict over investiture was abated in 1122. Its promises were confirmed by the First Council of the Lateran.

CONCREATE, TO. A term used of the first production of a non-subsistent being from nothing. Thus prime matter was created with its substantial form; the term of creation being a complete subsistent being. In the creation of the angels infused knowledge (which is an accident and therefore nonsubsistent) was concreated with the angels.

CONCRETE. The opposite of abstract (*q.v.*); it means the real and the particular. Terms are concrete or abstract: the first expresses the subject and the form or quality as red, ardent, big; the latter expresses the quality as apart from its subject, as redness, ardour, bigness.

CONCUBINAGE. i. The state of two persons who, being free to marry one another, live together maritally and more or less permanently without being married. Up to the Council of Trent (in some countries, to *Ne temere, q.v.*), such a relationship was regarded as a clandestine but binding marriage on being made permanent.

ii. Any enduring liaison, whether the parties are free to marry or not.

iii. In Roman law, a recognized form of lesser or quasi-marriage; it might be either temporary or permanent.

CONCUPISCENCE (Lat. *concupiscere,* to desire). The general name given to any movement of the sensitive appetites towards whatever the imagination portrays as good or away from whatever it portrays as bad; hence desire, love, hate, are forms of concupiscence. In holy Scripture concupiscence usually means the desire of worldly things. But the word is used particularly of the insubordination of the sensual appetite against the dictates of reason and the general propensity of human nature to sin, in consequence of the Fall (*q.v.*). But this concupiscence must not be identified with original sin (*q.v.*), of which it is only a result.

CONCURRENCE OF FEASTS. The overlapping of two offices, one of which follows the other on consecutive days. It can only take place at Vespers, and when it occurs the relevant procedure is indicated in the *Ordo* (*q.v.*). See also COMMEMORATION, i; OCCURRENCE; RANK OF FEASTS.

CONCURSUS (Lat., an assembly). i. A method of appointment to vacant parishes and other benefices, by which candidates compete by examination, and the most successful candidate is given the office.

ii. Divine. That act by which God's energy flows into all the operations of creatures. It may be (*a*) mediate, and then it signifies the remote divine activity which gives and preserves created power of action; or (*b*) immediate, and then it signifies a proximate divine influx aiding the production of the created activity here and now. That there is such immediate *concursus* is the common Catholic teaching to-day; but the Thomists teach that it is prior in nature to the act, and the Molinists (*q.v.*) that it is simultaneous with it.

CONDEMNED AND FORBIDDEN (Lat. *damnanda et proscribenda*). The censure of a proposition in these terms merely implies a general forbidding and warning that it is dangerous. It does not necessarily follow that it is untrue wholly or even only in part.

CONDITIONAL ADMINISTRATION of Sacraments. The sacraments of Baptism, Penance and Orders may in certain circumstances be administered on a condition, which is then stated in the words of administration; *e.g.,* "If you are not baptized, I baptize you . . ." "If you are living, I absolve you . . ."

CONFECT, TO (Lat. *conficere,* to effect). A technical term to express the complete action, consisting of words, movements and intention, of bringing about a valid administration of a sacrament by the proper minister.

CONFERENCE, CLERGY. A monthly meeting of the secular priests, and others engaged in pastoral work, of a diocese or deanery. Problems in moral theology, etc., are propounded for discussion and solution; those unable to attend submit their answers in writing.

CONFESSIO (Lat., confession) was a name originally given to any tomb of a martyr; it is now applied to the crypt beneath the high altar where a martyr's relics are enshrined, chiefly in the Roman basilicas. Easily the most famous is that of St. Peter, which is often referred to simply as The Confessio.

CONFESSION. i. Sacramental. The auricular confession of sins to a priest in the tribunal of penance. All mortal sins committed after baptism must be confessed, together with those circumstances which alter the specific character of the sin. Confession must be made by all who have come to the use of reason, at least once a year. Venial sins, and mortal sins already confessed, are sufficient, but not obligatory, matter for confession. Confessors are officially warned against putting unnecessary or indiscreet questions to their penitents, especially when sins of impurity are concerned. See EXAMINATION OF CONSCIENCE. In ordinary circumstances confession can only be validly made to a priest with ordinary or delegated jurisdiction ("faculties") to hear confessions in that place. All priests on a sea-voyage who hold faculties to hear confessions from their own ordinary or from the ordinary of the port of embarkation or of any port at which they touch can hear the confessions of any of their fellow-passengers on the voyage. Confession to a heretical or schismatic priest with valid orders is lawful and valid in danger of death and in the case of a common error among the people, but not in any other circumstances.

ii. Annual. An obligation on all of years of discretion (*q.v.*), confirmed by the Fourth Lateran Council and now imposed by canon 906 of the Code of Canon Law; it may be made at any time and to any priest with the necessary faculties, and must be made with the proper dispositions. It is not obligatory on those who have not fallen into mortal sin, but is recommended. It must be understood that one confession a year is a minimum for those in mortal sin. A sacrilegious confession or one that is wilfully null and void does not satisfy the obligation.

iii. Sacrilegious. A sacrilegious confession is one in which the penitent wilfully conceals one or more mortal sins of which he is conscious, or has no contrition or purpose of amendment or intention of making satisfaction. By so doing he makes void the sacrament of Penance and commits an act of sacrilege, nor does absolution take effect even for those sins which he has confessed. To repair his sin it is necessary with the proper dispositions to confess the sacrilegious confession, the sins concealed, and the mortal sins of which he did accuse himself at the bad confession.

iv. Legal. A statement by one of the parties in a lawsuit against himself and for his adversary made before the judge in a court of law. If made freely and deliberately it relieves the other party of the obligation of proving the matter confessed.

CONFESSION OF AUGSBURG, The. A Protestant profession of faith in 21 articles, drawn up by Melanchthon to prepare the way for a general religious settlement and presented to the Emperor Charles V at the Diet of Augsburg in 1530. It has remained the chief symbol of Lutheranism, though Luther himself objected to it as a minimizing document which glozed over the fundamental differences between the Reformers and the Church.

CONFESSIONAL. An enclosed place, either structurally part of a church or constructed in a permanent or semi-permanent form within it, in which confessions are heard. It consists principally of a seat for the confessor, a place for the penitent to kneel, with a grating between them; except in cases of emergency it is forbidden to hear the confessions of women otherwise than in open church or to hear them without the grating. Confessionals have been obligatory in the Western church since the Council of Trent; they have been adopted in some of the Catholic Eastern churches. Vulgarly called "the box."

CONFESSIONS OF FAITH. Formulas of doctrine drawn up and promulgated by Protestant bodies from time to time. The best known are the Augsburg Confession (Lutheran), the Confession of Dort (Calvinist), the Scottish and the Westminster Confessions with the Longer and Shorter Catechisms (Presbyterian) and the Thirty-Nine Articles (Anglican). Among those of dissident Eastern churches the Orthodox Confession of Peter Mogilas (d. 1647) is one of the most important.

CONFESSOR. i. A canonized male saint who was not a martyr. For liturgical purposes confessors are divided into those who were bishops, those who were not, doctors of the Church, popes, and abbots.

ii. Any person who suffers ill-treatment for the faith's sake. In both these cases the word indicates one who has confessed or professed Christ publicly or in a notable manner.

iii. One who hears confessions. He must be in priest's orders and hold faculties (q.v.) from the bishop in whose diocese he is. In the confessional he has the place of our Lord for the reconciliation of sinners as well as being the minister of the sacrament; he is therefore spiritual father, teacher, counsellor and judge of his penitents.

iv. An extraordinary confessor is one appointed to hear the confessions of religious over and above their regular confessor. The novices in orders of men and all nuns are allowed by law an extraordinary confessor at least four times a year, and all religious concerned should present themselves to him at least to ask his blessing. If any religious, man or woman, asks for a special confessor in a particular case, the superior must grant the request without either enquiring the reason or showing displeasure thereat. Superiors of men do not ordinarily hear the confessions of their own subjects. Lay people are at liberty to confess to whomsoever they choose, provided he has the requisite faculties to hear confessions.

CONFIRMATION. i. Of an election, if required by law, must be sought from the competent superior within eight days. It must be granted in writing.

ii. In grace. A privilege commonly supposed to have been given to the Apostles after Pentecost. They were so deeply imbued with the grace of the Holy Ghost that *practically* they could not sin. This cannot be proved absolutely, but it is indicated in certain texts of Scripture, and is in harmony with the special office of the Apostles.

CONFIRMATION, THE CEREMONIES OF. i. In the Western church the sacrament of Confirmation is ordinarily administered by a bishop. After a general imposition of hands with a prayer for the gifts of the Holy Spirit, in the form of a litany, the bishop dips his thumb into chrism and, addressing each candidate (who is presented by his sponsor, q.v.), by the new name he has chosen, anoints him cross-wise on the forehead, saying in Latin, "N . . ., I sign thee with the sign of the Cross and I confirm thee with the Chrism of salvation. In the name, etc., Amen." Then, striking him gently on the cheek, he says, "Peace be with thee." The choir sings an antiphon, the bishop prays for the indwelling of the Holy Spirit, and gives a final blessing. Confirmation is received at the age of reason, preferably just before first communion; but in Spain it is often given immediately after Baptism and in Rome to every infant who seems in danger of death.

ii. All Catholics of Eastern rites are confirmed by the priest immediately after

Baptism except the Maronites, Malabarese, Ethiopians and Italo-Greeks. All anoint with chrism, generally on the eyes, forehead, nose, mouth, ears, etc., and without imposition of hands. The Byzantine formula is, "The seal of the gift of the Holy Ghost. Amen."

CONFIRMATION, THE SACRAMENT OF. A sacrament (q.v.) of the New Law in which a baptized person receives the Holy Ghost, is strengthened in grace and signed and sealed as a soldier of Jesus Christ. The minister in the Latin rite anoints with chrism (q.v.) and imposes hands, saying, "I sign thee with the sign of the Cross and confirm thee with the Chrism of salvation, in the name of the Father, and of the Son, and of the Holy Ghost." These words are the form of the sacrament; theologians are not agreed as to what constitutes the matter, but the common opinion is that it is the anointing and the imposition of the bishop's hand while he makes the sign of the cross on the person's forehead.* The ordinary minister of this sacrament is a bishop, but priests on foreign missions are frequently delegated to perform it, and it may be given to those in danger of death through illness by parish priests of a certain defined status; abbots and prelates *nullius* and prefects and vicars apostolic may confirm within their own sphere of jurisdiction, and cardinals anywhere. In the Eastern rites a priest is the ordinary minister of Confirmation; not by common law (according to the claim of the dissidents), but by delegation from the Holy See. In 1859 the Holy Office declared Confirmation by dissident priests valid (except where the privilege has been expressly withdrawn). It is of Catholic faith that all the sacraments were instituted by Christ himself, and therefore Confirmation; but it was not conferred until after Pentecost: for in it is given the fulness of the Holy Spirit, and this could not be till after his resurrection and ascension (John xvi, 7).

CONFITEOR (Lat., I confess). A form of general confession which occurs at the beginning of Mass, when the *preces* are said at Prime, and at the beginning of Compline. It is also said: by the server before holy communion is given, before administration of Extreme Unction, before the apostolic blessing of the dying, and before the publication of an indulgence at pontifical Mass. It also should be said, at least privately, before confession. The Dominican, Carthusian and Carmelite rites have forms of their own, very short (the last includes the name of Elias as founder); the Benedictines, Cistercians, Franciscans and Servites also introduce the name of their founder, Canons Regular the name of St. Augustine and discalced Carmelites that of St. Teresa into the ordinary Roman form. The name of St. Ambrose is added in the Milanese rite. It is always followed by two short deprecatory prayers

for mercy and absolution. In the East the Western form is used by the Malabarese, with the name of St. Thomas added. The Armenian is the only other Eastern rite having a *Confiteor* in the Liturgy, though the Maronites have a prayer somewhat resembling it.

CONFLICT OF LAWS. Particular laws are not abrogated by a new general law, unless special mention is made of them, but local laws may not derogate from common law already existing. For conflict of civil and ecclesiastical laws, see CHURCH and STATE and CIVIL ALLEGIANCE.

CONFRATER (Lat., associate). The mediæval name for the equivalent of the modern secular oblates (q.v.) of Benedictine monasteries, still used by some congregations O.S.B., e.g., the English. Membership of the confraternity is limited to those who have some special personal relation with the monastery, as friends, benefactors, etc.

CONFRATERNITY. In the strict sense, an association of the faithful erected by ecclesiastical authority for the exercise of some work of piety or charity and for the advancement of public worship. Women may be members of confraternities only for the spiritual benefits and indulgences obtainable. The Confraternities of the Blessed Sacrament and of Christian Doctrine are to be erected in every parish church. Confraternities which have the right of affiliating others to themselves are called archconfraternities. More loosely, a confraternity is any association of lay-folk canonically set up under ecclesiastical direction for pursuit of one or more of the activities tending to personal sanctification, but whose rules are not binding under pain of sin. This use of the term is inaccurate and misleading (cf., Pious Union).

CONGREGATION. i. Diocesan. A religious institute (q.v.) established by a bishop. When such has spread sufficiently and given evidence of vitality it applies for approval to the Holy See, which will, if deemed advisable, first issue a temporary approval, called the "decree of praise" (*decretum laudis*) and after further successful experiment grant final approbation. Congregations established by bishops remain diocesan so long as they have not received at least the decree of praise, but become pontifical directly it is received.
ii. Monastic. A term used in canon law to designate monasteries united under a common head. Such form a complete and independent organization, and the superior has no one above him except the Roman pontiff. The monasteries that compose it retain their independence and autonomy in all that pertains to the internal administration. Each one has its own noviciate and its subjects are ordained for the monastery (cf., iv).
iii. Religious. A religious institute (q.v.)

* Paul VI promulgated a new Form for the Sacrament of Confirmation: "Be sealed with the gift of the Holy Spirit."—*Publisher*, 1997.

in which the members take only simple vows. Such are the Lazarists, Passionists, Redemptorists, Marists, Rosminians, etc. (*qq.v.*) and numerous bodies of nuns. Even temporary vows suffice for real religious life provided they be public, that is, received by the superior in the name of the Church, and it be understood that they will be renewed when they expire, except for some unforeseen obstacle. This does not render renewal really obligatory, but the law demands stability at least in intention.

iv. O.S.B. Benedictine monasteries are divided into the following congregations: of Monte Cassino, English (*q.v.*), Swiss, Bavarian, Hungarian, Brazilian, Solesmes (French), American Cassinese, Beuron, Cassinese of the Primitive Observance, Swiss-American (*qq.v.*), Austrian, of St. Ottilia (for foreign missions), Belgian. The most of them are loose federations of autonomous equal monasteries (the autonomy of the monastic family in each abbey being the foundation of Benedictinism), one of whose abbots is president for a term. The abbeys of the Solesmes and Beuron congregations, however, must conform strictly to the discipline, customs, etc., of the eponymous mother-house; and the Cassinese P.O. is organized into provinces and has an abbot general who is not one of the ruling abbots. Each congregation, especially these three, is in effect a separate order (*q.v.*). A new Slavonic congregation was initiated for Czechoslovakia in 1945.

v. Roman. A body composed of cardinals and officials for the transaction of the headquarters business of the Church. Their decisions require papal approval and are then final, in any case for the individual; but they have not the force of a general law unless issued by a special papal mandate. These congregations are (*a*) of the Holy Office, (*b*) Consistorial, (*c*) of the Discipline of the Sacraments, (*d*) of the Council, (*e*) for the Affairs of Religious, (*f*) for the Propagation of the Faith (*Propaganda*), (*g*) for the Eastern Church (*h*) of Sacred Rites, (*i*) of Ceremonial, (*j*) for Extraordinary Ecclesiastical Affairs, (*k*) of Seminaries and of Universities of Studies (*l*) of the Fabric of St. Peter's. (*qq.v.*).

CONGREGATIONAL SINGING. The singing to Gregorian chant of the ordinary and responses of the Mass and the psalms and hymns of Vespers, Compline, etc., by the people, antiphonally, with the choir. It includes also Latin hymns and litanies at Benediction, processions, etc., nor does it exclude hymns in the vernacular. The revival of such singing was encouraged by Pope Pius X in II, 3 of his *motu proprio* on church music, and further encouraged by Pius XI. "It is most necessary that the faithful, not as outsiders or dumb spectators, should so take part in the sacred ceremonies that their voices alternate with those of the priest and choir according to the prescribed rules" (apostolic constitution *Divini Cultus*, 1928).

CONGREGATIONALISTS, The. A Protestant sect representing the Independents whose first leader in England was Robert Browne (*b.* 1550). The Gospels are their rule and basis of faith. Each congregation of communicants is autonomous, government resting with its members who elect their own ministers and are free from external control, recognizing no religious authority but Christ. The minister exercises the priesthood of his congregation by delegation. Especially in the U.S.A., this autonomy has been considerably modified by the formation of organized unions of the congregations. Their beliefs, originally Calvinistic, are now much diluted; but traditional Congregationalists have a firm hold on certain fundamental Christian doctrines and steadily maintain monthly communion at the Lord's Supper; this is what chiefly distinguishes them from some other Protestant bodies. See NONCONFORMITY.

CONGRUISM. A theory of grace developed by Suarez. According to it, God, wishing a salutary act to be performed by a certain soul, gives his grace under precisely those circumstances in which he infallibly knows, by his *scientia media*, that the soul in question will consent if grace be offered. This grace, since it is thus accommodated to future consent, is a "congruous grace."

CONJUGAL RIGHTS. The exercise of these is a right common to both husband and wife. Except by mutual consent neither may withhold him or herself from the other unless (*a*) from coition there is danger of death or serious sickness, (*b*) the requirement is unreasonable on account of the partner's madness or drunkenness, (*c*) the requirement is inordinate, *e.g.*, several times in one night, or (*d*) the partner has committed adultery. In (*a*) the exercise of conjugal rights is definitely illicit, but that a resulting pregnancy would be certainly fatal to the woman may not be lightly assumed.

CONNOCIA. The Latin name of the diocese of Clonfert (*q.v.*). Adjective: *Clonfertensis*.

CONNOR. An Irish see now united to that of Down (*q.v.*).

CONSANGUINITY. Blood-relationship, which is reckoned in canon law by lines and degrees. In the direct line there are as many degrees as there are generations. In the collateral line there are as many degrees as there are generations in the longer line. In the direct line marriage is invalid in any degree, whether generation is legitimate or natural. In the collateral line it is invalid to the third degree inclusive, the impediment being multiplied as often as the common root is multiplied. Marriage is never permitted if there is any doubt of the parties being related by consanguinity in the direct line or in the first degree of the collateral line. Consanguinity is a major impediment except in the third degree collateral, in which case it is minor.

CONSCIENCE. The judgement of reason concerning the lawfulness or unlawfulness of an act about to be or already performed or omitted. The dictates of a true or right conscience are in real conformity with the law of God; those of a false or erroneous conscience represent an action as good which is really bad, or *vice versa*. The conscience is doubtful when the judgment remains suspended concerning the lawfulness or unlawfulness of contemplated action; to act with a doubtful conscience is sinful (see PROBABILISM). A lax conscience habitually, and for the lightest of motives, judges to be right what is wrong and to be venial sin what is mortal sin. The clear voice of conscience, be it true or false, must always be obeyed; but for one, after his false conscience has been enlightened by authority or otherwise, to persist in his error and attempt to justify it by an appeal to his "conscience" is affectation, sinful, and a misuse of the word conscience (*cf.*, synderesis).

CONSCIENTIOUS OBJECTION. Refusal to take active and direct part in war on the ground of an objection of conscience. If the objection be that all war is essentially unjust, then the objector is contradicting the teaching of the Church (see WAR). But those are not the only possible circumstances. In the event of an undoubtedly unjust war, a Catholic would be bound in duty to refuse to take part in it, *i.e.*, he would have to be a conscientious objector. Or one who, while admitting the justice of a war, is convinced that he, on account of circumstances special to himself, is not justified in taking part or at least in actually fighting—such an one may, according to the circumstances, have a duty of conscientious objection. See also RESISTING EVIL.

CONSCIOUSNESS. A knowledge whereby the soul perceives modifications of itself. We not only feel and know but we know that we feel and know. There is a distinction between intellectual and sensitive consciousness. The latter is common to men and animals, and is that whereby modifications of the senses are known or felt; the former also gives knowledge of these, but primarily it gives knowledge of the modifications of mind and of will. Consciousness attests to the existence of internal modifications as facts actually existing in us only, and can tell us nothing of their nature, cause, etc.

CONSCRIPTION. Compulsory enlistment for military service, whether in war or peace. The state is entitled to resort to this drastic measure in the cause of self-defence, but provision must be made (as in Great Britain and the United States) for not forcing individual

consciences (even if mistaken consciences) or individual vocations (*e.g.*, clergy and monks). But the Holy See's understanding of the disastrous effects of conscription were expressed in Cardinal Gasparri's letter to David Lloyd George of Sept. 28, 1917: "Compulsory service has been for more than a century the real cause of innumerable evils; in the simultaneous abolition thereof lies the true remedy."

CONSECRATION. An ecclesiastical act by which a person or thing is definitely set apart for some religious office, state or use. It is superior to and more solemn than blessing, from which it must be distinguished. When the word is used without qualification, the consecration at Mass (*q.v.*) is generally meant.

CONSECRATION-CROSSES are twelve small crosses painted on or attached to the inside walls of a church, marking where at the consecration of the building the walls were anointed with chrism and so are an indication that the church has been consecrated. A bracket and candle are set before each cross, to be lit upon the anniversary of the consecration. The crosses may never be obliterated or removed.

CONSECRATION AT MASS. The action by which the celebrant changes the bread and wine into the body and blood of Christ. This happens when he takes the bread, saying, "This is my Body," etc., and the wine, saying, "This is the chalice of my Blood," etc., It is disputed among theologians as to how much of the usual form is necessary. In the dissident Eastern church, the *epiklesis* (*q.v.*) is considered necessary as well, but that is contrary to the teaching and practice of the Church. After consecration of the bread, the celebrant in the Latin Mass genuflects and adores, then raises the Host for the adoration of the people, then genuflects again; he acts similarly after the consecration of the wine. After consecration nothing whatever is left of the substance of bread and wine but in its stead the body and blood of Christ (and also in each respectively his blood or body, soul and divinity, present by concomitance, *q.v.*) under the outward accidents (*q.v.*) of bread and wine.

CONSENT. An act of the will, a voluntary complacence in something presented to it as good; consent must be distinguished from "assent," which is the intellect's recognition of something as true in the speculative order or as right in the moral order.

i. The consent necessary for the validity of a contract must be internal, *i.e.*, made with the intention of fulfilling the obligations involved: a fictitious consent vitiates the contract but leaves one liable to a claim for damages; it must be external, *i.e.*, manifested by some outward sign: silence can give consent in those contracts only whose nature admits of such consent, *e.g.*, the acceptance of a gift; it must also be mutual, *i.e.*, once the consent of one party has been given, the contract is sealed as soon as the other party gives his consent.

ii. In marriage. The consent of the parties is the essence of the marriage contract, and if it is lacking no human power can supply it. This consent is the act of the will by which each party gives and accepts the perpetual and exclusive right to those acts which are of their nature ordained for the generation of offspring. Substantial ignorance and error invalidate consent, but true matrimonial consent is possible even if the marriage is thought or known to be invalid. For the marriage to be valid consent must be legitimately manifested. The internal consent of the mind is presumed in law to conform to the words and signs exhibited in the celebration of marriage, but if either or both parties by a positive act of the will exclude either the marriage itself, or all right to the conjugal act, or any essential property of marriage, such marriage is null and void. Consent given under compulsion, or under grave fear in certain circumstances, is not valid for marriage.

CONSENT, COMMON. The agreement of, morally speaking, all men with regard to some opinion.

CONSENT, DEFECT OF. A diriment impediment (*q.v.*) invalidating marriage, consisting in the lack of free and deliberate consent to it of one of the parties. The most usual cause of such lack of consent is violence and fear (*q.v.*).

CONSENT OF THE FATHERS, UNANIMOUS. When the Fathers of the Church (*q.v.*) are morally unanimous in their teaching that a certain doctrine is a part of revelation (*q.v.*), or is received by the universal Church, or that the opposite of a doctrine is heretical, then their united testimony is a certain criterion of divine tradition. As the Fathers are not personally infallible, the counter testimony of one or two would not be destructive of the value of the collective testimony; so a moral unanimity only is required. This criterion is called the Unanimous Consent of the Fathers.

CONSISTORIAL CONGREGATION, THE SACRED, has for its charge the preparation of matter for consistories; the erection of dioceses, election of bishops, and whatever relates to dioceses of the Western church not subject to *Propaganda;* apostolic visitations; and the spiritual welfare of emigrants. The pope himself is prefect of this congregation.

CONSISTORY. An assembly of the cardinals summoned at the discretion of the pope. It may be private, semi-public or public, according as it is confined to the cardinals, cardinals and bishops, or cardinals, prelates and laymen. The function of a consistory is promulgation rather than deliberation. At a private consistory the pope names new cardinals and other formalities in connexion with their creation are carried out; the appointment or translation of bishops is announced; and the pope sometimes expresses his mind on a matter of public importance in an "allocution." In a public consistory the red hat is conferred on new cardinals. Formalities connected with beatification and canonization take place at all three varieties of consistory.

CONSOLATA FATHERS, The. A congregation of foreign-missionary priests founded at the church of the *Consolata* in Turin in 1901.

CONSTANCE, THE COUNCIL OF (1414-18). The sixteenth œcumenical council, which put an end to the Schism of the West by the election of Pope Martin V; it was only œcumenical (*q.v.*) in so far as its acts were confirmed by him. The council condemned the errors of Wyclif and Huss.

CONSTANTINE. The name of eleven emperors of Rome at Constantinople. Used by itself, the first, Constantine the Great, is always meant; for he greatly influenced the history of the world by (*a*) first the toleration and then the privileging of Christianity, (*b*) the summoning of the first œcumenical council, at Nicæa, and recognition of the supremacy of the Church in religious matters, and (*c*) moving the imperial throne to Constantinople. He himself was only a catechumen, who received Baptism on his deathbed; in the Byzantine rite he is venerated as a saint (May 21) with his mother St. Helen: "the holy, illustrious and great emperors, crowned by God and equal with the Apostles," and also in other Eastern calendars.

CONSTANTINIAN ORDER, THE SACRED. A military order (*q.v.*), fabled to have originated with Constantine the Great, whose members were bound to fight for the Faith and the Holy Roman Empire, to succour the distressed and to have a particular devotion to the Passion. The history of the order is obscure, and complicated by spurious documents. It still exists as an order of honour, having its headquarters at the church of St. Antony in Naples, which is served by a chapter of 40 knight-chaplains.

CONSTANTINOPLE, THE COUNCILS OF. The first (the second œcumenical council, 381) upheld the Faith against Arianism and Apollinarianism (*qq.v.*), and condemned the heresy of Macedonius, who denied the perfect Godhead of the Holy Ghost. The council added to the creed of Nicæa the words, "and in the Holy Ghost, the Lord and Giver of Life, who proceeds from the Father, who together with the Father and the Son is worshipped and glorified, who spoke by the prophets"; the creed then received practically its present form. This council is commemorated by a feast in the Armenian rite.

The second (the fifth œcumenical, 553) condemned the Three Chapters (*q.v.*).

The third (the sixth œcumenical, 680–1) put an end to Monothelism (*q.v.*) by defining the two wills in Christ, the human being subject to the divine. It also condemned Pope Honorius I (*q.v.*).

The fourth (the eighth œcumenical, 869) is said to have excommunicated Photius, the patriarch of Constantinople. It confirmed the Formula of Hormisdas (*q.v.*) by the signature of all the members. This was the last general council to be held in the East, but is repudiated by the Orthodox Eastern Church; and recent research by Catholic scholars, *e.g.*, Dr. Dvornik, has thrown doubt on the œcumenicity of this council.

CONSTANTINOPLE, THE LITURGY OF, was the Antiochene liturgy (*q.v.*) as used at Cæsarea in the 4th century, edited by St. Basil and again by St. John Chrysostom. With the further modifications of centuries it is still in use and usually referred to as the Byzantine rite (*q.v.*), which before the 12th century was imposed by Constantinople on the other Orthodox patriarchates, Alexandria, Antioch and Jerusalem.

CONSTANTINOPLE, PATRIARCHATE OF. The last in time of the great patriarchates was given a primacy of honour after Rome "because [Contantinople] is New Rome," the chief city of the Empire, while it was still a simple bishopric; its powers were greatly extended and made patriarchal by the Council of Chalcedon (Canon 28), but this second place was for long repudiated by Rome and not recognized by her officially till the 4th Council of the Lateran (1215). Before this, Constantinople had become in fact the great ecclesiastical power of the East, imposing its liturgy on the other orthodox patriarchates, and powerful enough to lead them all into definite schism during the middle ages, so forming what we know as the Orthodox Eastern Church (*q.v.*). After the capture of the city by the Turks in 1453 and the collapse of the brief reunion with Rome effected at Florence, the patriarchs of Constantinople nearly succeeded in extending their jurisdiction over all this church, but eventually their own huge patriarchate began to collapse; Russia became independent in 1589, Greece in 1833, Bulgaria in 1870, Serbia in 1879, Rumania in 1885, Albania in 1922, etc. The patriarchate to-day consists of only about 80,000 faithful in Turkey, mostly Greeks; at the Phanar (*q.v.*) is employed a large number of officials, but the patriarch has only a primacy of prestige in the Orthodox Church. He has, however, jurisdiction over Greek emigrants, with archbishops in London, Vienna, Sydney, America and elsewhere.

CONSTANTINOPLE, PATRIARCHS OF. There is no Catholic patriarch of Constantinople with jurisdiction. A Latin prelate at the Roman Court bears the title, a relic of the Crusades. In addition to the Orthodox patriarch (the "Archbishop of Constantinople, New Rome, and Œcumenical Patriarch"), a Gregorian Armenian primate has the title with jurisdiction, but few subjects since the first Great War.

CONSTITUTIONAL CLERGY, The. Those clergy who took the oath to maintain the civil constitution drawn up for the Church in France by the National Assembly in 1790. The constitution was condemned by Pope Pius VI as being detrimental to the freedom of the Church and the clergy forbidden to take the oath. The ensuing schism was not healed till the Concordat of 1801, by which time some of the constitutional clergy had abandoned the Faith entirely. Refusal to take the oath led to persecution by the government, which resulted in the flight to England (and elsewhere) of the *emigré* clergy, who did much to break down Protestant prejudice in this country.

CONSTITUTIONS. i. Papal. In the strict sense, those communications of general authority and applicability which the pope issues in his own name. In the wide sense, it includes also decrees of the Roman Congregations.

ii. Religious or monastic. The regulations governing religious institutes in the details of their life, the Rule (*q.v.*) being the general principles on which the society is based.

CONSUBSTANTIAL. Of one substance; applied to the three persons of the Blessed Trinity who are but one substance, thus, "The Holy Ghost is consubstantial with the Father and the Son."

CONSUBSTANTIATION. A Lutheran heresy concerning the Eucharist, according to which, after the consecration at Mass, the substances of bread and wine remain together with the newly present substance of Christ's Body and Blood: Christ is present *under* or *in* the bread and wine (and only till the end of the service), so that the sense of the words of consecration would be, "*Here* is my Body," etc., as opposed to "This is my Body," etc. The true doctrine is that the only substance present after the consecration is that of Christ.

CONSULTORS. i. Specialists, not necessarily living in Rome, who are attached to the Sacred Congregations in order to advise and give information to the members upon the matters in which they specialize.

ii. Diocesan consultors, from among the secular clergy and between 4 and 6 in number, must be appointed in all sees of the United States, Australia, and elsewhere, to assist and advise the bishop. Their duties are analogous to those of canons in England, canonical chapters not being erected in those countries.

CONSUMMATION by a completed act of physical union is necessary to the indissoluble completion of a marriage. A valid marriage before such consummation is only ratified (*ratum*), and is dissoluble under certain conditions, *e.g.*, impotence in one of the parties completely and certainly proved; religious profession automatically dissolves a ratified marriage.

CONTACT. (*a*) Physical or quantitative: the union of two bodies by extreme parts of each; (*b*) virtual: the union of two substances, one of which acts upon the other in such wise that the whole of the substance acted upon is touched. Physical contact, having reference only to extremes or superficies, must be extrinsic to what is touched; but virtual contact, which is proper to intellectual substances, effects that the substance touching is within what is touched. In this latter way an intellectual substance is united to a body by virtual contact.

CONTEMPLATION. An absorbing interest in some object, so that it is constantly thought about and engrosses the affections. In a religious sense it denotes (*a*) the contemplative life (*q.v.*), and (*b*) the prayer proper to the contemplative life, although not all contemplative religious attain it, nor is it confined by any means to such religious. It is a prayer which dispenses with reasoning or discourse and with distinct perceptions of God, and concentrates on him in a simple gaze and a wordless act of love. It is to be noted that the elements of general contemplation, mentioned above, are here found, *i.e.*, the mind and will engrossed by God, so that the genuineness of contemplative prayer is supported by the analogy of certain facts of ordinary experience. Many authors distinguish two kinds of contemplation: acquired, which is the prayer of simplicity (*q.v.*), and infused or passive, which is mystical union (*q.v.*); others refuse to admit any such distinction, and hold that the mystical life is a normal development of the interior life, and that therefore all souls are called, remotely, to it.

CONTEMPLATIVE LIFE. One of the forms of the religious life (*q.v.*), being a state, officially recognized by the Church, in which souls devote themselves to the objective worship of God and aim at attaining the prayer of contemplation (*q.v.*). It is an austere life, to ensure that detachment from creatures without which union with God is not possible. Much time is consequently devoted to prayer, and external activities are excluded (*cf.*, contemplative order). Pope Pius XI sums up the traditional teaching of the Church concerning this life: "All those who, according to their rule, lead a secluded life remote from the din and follies of the world, and who not only assiduously contemplate the divine mysteries and eternal truths and pour out ardent and continual prayers to God that his kingdom may flourish . . . but who also atone for the sins of other men, still more than for their own, by mortification, prescribed or voluntary, of mind and body—such must be said to have chosen the best part." But as all who follow this contemplative life are not contemplatives, so very many, whether clerical or lay, engaged in an active or semi-active life are contemplatives (*cf.*, mixed life), not only by being informed by the true spirit of divine contemplation, but also by attainment of that perfection of prayer. And in a yet more general sense, that man may be said to be contemplative who is concerned with ends rather than with means, with being rather than with becoming, with things rather than with appearances, who is contented, resigned, patient and incurious, who "recognizes but one cause in nature and in human affairs, and that is the First and Supreme," and whose apprehension of that cause tends to be passive, immediate, and independent of reasoning.

CONTEMPLATIVE ORDER. A religious order whose members are engaged in the objective worship of God to such a degree as to exclude the external works of the active life (*q.v.*), and all else that could be a hindrance to divine contemplation. Such are the Carthusian, Camaldolese and Cistercian monks, and Carthusian, Carmelite, Poor Clare, Dominican (second order), and some other nuns. What exactly constitutes the contemplative life is a matter of some dispute, but even in the above strict sense certain monasteries of Benedictine monks, and most of Benedictine nuns, must be called contemplative.

CONTINENCE. i. The virtue which restrains the will from consenting to strong movements of sexual desire.

ii. The abstinence, temporary or perpetual, voluntary or imposed by circumstances, from marital intercourse. If voluntary, it must be agreed upon by both the people concerned. The word is sometimes loosely used to express that chastity (*q.v.*) which must be observed by the unmarried.

CONTINGENT. i. Contingent being is that which does not contain within its notion the idea of existence, namely that to which existence belongs in such wise that without any contradiction existence can be absent. It is opposed to necessary being in whose idea existence is contained. All beings other than God are contingent. All contingent being is *ens ab alio*, and the converse. Moreover the ultimate reason or explanation of the existence of contingent being is necessary being.

ii. Contingent proposition, also called synthetic and *a posteriori*, is one whose predicate is not contained in the notion of the subject, as "Peter is black" (*cf.*, Necessary Proposition).

CONTINUITY THEORY, The. The claim that the Established Church of England has an unbroken organic continuity with the pre-reformation Church in this country and is an integral part of the Catholic Church; and that the episcopalian bodies deriving from the Church of England are also parts of the Catholic Church. This theory was always opposed by Catholic theologians and historians, and the condemnation of Anglican orders by Pope Leo XIII, in 1896, finally disposed of it for Catholics.

CONTRACEPTION. A barbarous but more accurate name for birth-control (*q.v.*).

CONTRACT. Ecclesiastical contracts follow the general rules of civil law for contracts which are in force in the territory, unless special rules are prescribed for particular cases. The Code of Canon Law contains regulations as to buying and selling, loans, gifts, investments, etc.

CONTRADICTION. A species of opposition (*q.v.*) between two propositions differing both in quality and quantity in such wise that it is impossible to affirm one without denying the other; *e.g.*, "All men are just" and "Some men are not just" are contradictory propositions. Contradiction differs from contrary (*q.v.*) in that two contrary propositions may both be false.

CONTRADICTION, PRINCIPLE OF. This principle is expressed thus: "It is impossible for a thing to be and not to be at the same time and under the same aspect."

CONTRARY. A species of opposition (*q.v.*) between things and in particular between propositions which exclude each other because differing in quality, that is, because one is affirmative and the other negative; *e.g.*, "All men are just" and "No man is just" are contrary propositions. Such propositions cannot both be true, but both may be false, as "All men are fools" and "No man is a fool."

CONTRITION (Lat. *contritio*, a wearing-down of that which is hardened). "Sorrow of heart and detestation for sin committed, with the resolution not to sin again" (Trent. sess. xiv, cap. 4). Once mortal sin has been committed, an act of contrition is necessary for salvation (this is of faith from Scripture and Tradition). To be effective contrition must be genuine, must comprise all mortal sin committed, must spring from a motive that has reference to God and include a hatred of sin as the greatest of evils (this is the common teaching of theologians). Contrition is termed perfect when it arises from the pure love of God; by perfect contrition

sin is forgiven even before it is manifested in the sacrament of Penance, though the obligation of confession remains. Imperfect contrition may be inspired by various motives, *e.g.*, the foulness of sin, the loss of eternal happiness, the fear of Hell and God's punishments. It must be genuine, include all mortal sins, have reference to God and be a detestation of sin above every evil. It is necessary and sufficient for the valid reception of the sacrament of Penance. See SORROW.

CONTRITION, ACT OF. A movement of the will expressing "sorrow and detestation in the soul over sin committed, accompanied by the purpose of not sinning again," as above. A form of words declaring such sorrow. Such an act prompted by pure love of God (the recognition of the wickedness of sin as an offence against God's infinite goodness) gives perfect contrition; a self-regarding motive (the passion of Christ suffered for our sins, the punishment of sin) gives attrition or imperfect contrition, as above. The act of perfect contrition blots out sin before the reception of the sacrament (though the obligation of confession remains). Hence it is necessary when a sinner who cannot go to confession has to be in the state of grace (*q.v.*) for some special reason, *e.g.*, the proximity of death, the administration of a sacrament, the attainment of the grace necessary for resisting a temptation. Any person who has sinned can make such an act with the aid of grace.

CONTUMACY (Lat. *contumacia*, haughtiness; from *tumere*, to be swollen [with pride]). i. A person is said to be contumacious who, without a just cause, fails to appear in court when legitimately summoned. It is for the judge to declare contumacy after full investigation, either at the instance of the other party or on his own authority.

ii. In regard to censures. Censures (*q.v.*) may be inflicted only on those who are contumacious. A person is contumacious who disregards the superior's admonitions or fails to obey his precepts. In censures *latæ sententiæ* (*q.v.*) contumacy is presumed unless a valid excuse is proved.

CONTUMELY is the use of words or gestures towards our neighbour in order to bring him into contempt, or, negatively, refraining from showing him the honour which is his due. It is a sin against justice as well as charity, and therefore requires that reparation be made according to the circumstances. Contumely (*vulgo*, insulting words and behaviour) must be distinguished from calumny and detraction (*qq.v.*).

CONVENT (Lat., a gathering). i. Used with the title abbot or prior means a monastic community in its corporate capacity, *e.g.*, the

Abbot and Convent of St. Gregory the Great at Downside.

ii. The buildings wherein lives a monastic community of monks, friars or nuns; the name is not given to the houses of the more recent congregations of men, Jesuits, Passionists, etc.

iii. In common speech, a house of nuns.

CONVENTUAL, used as an adjective, means pertaining to a religious community or to the monastic life. Conventual life is opposed to life in the world or as a parish priest; conventual seal is the seal of a community, whether of men or women; conventual church, the church of a monastery of monks or nuns.

CONVENTUALS. Those members of the Franciscan order who favoured the accumulation and holding of property in common and the use of income therefrom as in other orders, contrary to the Observants who insisted on St. Francis's prohibition thereof. Pope John XXII approved their policy in 1322. They are still called Friars Minor Conventual (*q.v.*).

CONVENTUAL MASS. The daily community Mass which must be said or sung in all conventual churches of regulars (*q.v.*) who are bound to the public recitation of the Divine Office.

CONVERSION (Lat. *convertere*, to turn towards). The passage of one thing into another.

i. Partial conversion is either substantial or accidental. The first implies the reduction of a substantial form into the potentiality of matter and the education into act from matter of some other substantial form. The second implies the same process except that the form "reduced" and the one "educed" is an accident. Total conversion is the passage of the entire substance (both matter and form) into another substance already existing on whose part there is no change whatsoever. This is transubstantiation (*q.v.*).

ii. Literally a "turning towards," used of a turning towards God or the Church of God —either, in the case of Catholics, from sin or a life of sin, or, for others, from previous heresy or unbelief. The latter indicates a turning to the Church from without and an acceptance of her doctrine and discipline.

iii. Forcible. Canon law expressly prohibits the use of force in the matter of faith (canon 1351), and this forbiddance was reiterated by Pope Pius XII in his encyclical *Mystici Corporis Christi.* "It is absolutely necessary," he said, "that conversion should come about by free choice, since no man can believe unless he be willing. . . . That faith without which it is impossible to please God must be the perfectly free homage of intellect and will. Should it therefore at any time happen that, contrary to the unvarying

teaching of this Apostolic See, a person is compelled against his will to embrace the Catholic faith, we cannot in conscience withhold our censure."

CONVERSION OF ENGLAND, The. A rallying-cry or "slogan" of common use among English Catholics. It must not be deduced therefrom that the Church attaches more importance to the conversion of England than to that of any other country, or that she addresses herself primarily otherwise than to individual souls.

CONVERSION OF MANNERS (Lat. *conversio morum*). Commonly understood to mean: "The rooting out of vices and the planting of virtues" undertaken in a special way by all who enter the religious life. But the phrase, which is taken from the Rule of St. Benedict, was originally *conversatio morum*, and was simply a synonym for "common life," "monasticity" (Abbot Chapman) as distinguished from secular life. Of such life the Benedictine monk makes a special vow at his solemn profession.

CONVERSUS (Lat.). A lay-brother (*q.v.*), *i.e.*, one who has undertaken conversion of manners (*q.v.*).

CONVERT. Any person who has reached the age of reason and who, never having been baptized or having been baptized and brought up in a non-Catholic sect, abjures his errors, submits to the Church and is received as a member, by baptism or by confession and absolution and the removal of censures, as the case may require. In England the term commonly indicates one who has been converted from Protestantism or indifferentism: on the Continent, especially in France, one who has been a Freemason, anticlerical or free-thinker, less often a Huguenot, being in any case one who has been brought up in a society wherein Catholicism is normal and understood; the two sorts of people are vitally different and failure to distinguish them leads to confusion.

CONVERTS, RECONCILIATION OF. Before adult converts from heresy or schism can be received into the Church they must abjure their errors and be absolved from excommunication by the ordinary (*q.v.*) or his delegate, in the presence of two witnesses. Conditional baptism is always administered to converts on their reception unless there is sure evidence of their valid baptism. No abjuration or absolution from censures is required from converts who have not been baptized, but in some dioceses in England and elsewhere the permission of the ordinary is required for their reception. In Great Britain the form of reconciliation is as follows: *Veni Creator Spiritus* is said or sung, followed by its prayer; the convert then kneels with his right hand on the Gospels and reads his profession of faith (the Creed of Pope Pius IV, *q.v.*) and abjuration of heresy; the Psalm *Miserere* (1) is then said and a prayer for absolution; here follow the Baptism or conditional Baptism if either be necessary, and the priest pronounces release from excommunication and imposes a small penance; unless the convert has just been baptized absolutely, confession and sacramental absolution then follow; *Te Deum* and a prayer are said or sung, and the convert is dismissed with a blessing and exhortation.

CO-OPERATION IN ANOTHER'S SIN may be (*a*) formal, by concurrence in the evil action and its accompanying evil intention of another; this is always sinful; or (*b*) material, by concurrence in an action but not in the evil intention with which it is done; this also is always sinful when the co-operator's action is in itself wrong, but if it is good or indifferent and if there is a sufficient reason for permitting the consequent sin of the other, material co-operation is lawful. Obviously many delicate cases of conscience arise under this head, which have to be decided each on its own merits; the main difficulty is in estimating the gravity of the cause which would justify material co-operation in another's sinful action. The guilt of another's sin may be caused or shared by counsel, advice, urging motives, demonstration; by command, express or implied; by consent; by provocation, ridicule, flattery; by concealment of the sin when there is an obligation to make it known; by being an active partner; by silence when expressed protest would be effective; and by defending the evil done. When the sin committed is an offence against justice, the co-operator is bound to try to make reparation if he was primarily responsible for the injury (*e.g.*, by command) or if, being more remotely responsible (*e.g.*, by advice), the principal has failed in his obligation of reparation.

COPE. A vestment in the form of a mantle reaching to the heels, open in front and held together on the breast by a clasp or flap (*morse*), with a flat shield-shaped attachment (once a hood) on the back. It is worn in processions, by the assistant priest at a pontifical Mass, by the officiant and his ministers at solemn Lauds and Vespers, and by the officiant at practically all solemn offices except Mass. On solemn occasions it is worn by cantors, even if they be laymen. Its origin is the same as that of the chasuble (*q.v.*), but for use outdoors in wet weather (*cf.*, its Latin name *pluviale*, a rain-coat).

COPTIC CHURCH, The. A Copt is simply an Egyptian (from Gr. αἰ[γύπτ]ιος), in actual use a Christian Egyptian. The church was founded at Alexandria by, it is said, St. Mark; practically the whole of it adhered to Monophysism (*q.v.*) after the Council of Chalcedon, and has so remained to this day. The Copts are in communion with the Syrian Jacobites, and in a sense with the Armenians. Coptic orders and sacraments are valid, but there is reason to fear that Baptism is not always validly administered. In addition to their heresy (if they really profess it) and denial of the supreme pontificate of the pope, they dispense bishops, priests and deacons from confession, give Extreme Unction to the healthy, allow divorce for adultery and other causes with freedom to remarry, and popularly hold very superstitious beliefs about Purgatory. The church is governed by the Patriarch of Alexandria, with 14 bishops who are chosen from among the monks, of whom there are seven monasteries; the patriarch exercises a very loose surveillance over the church of Abyssinia. The church numbers about a million members, mostly poor peasants, and the lower clergy are very poorly educated.

COPTIC MARTYRS, The. Those who suffered for the Faith in Egypt from 200 to 313, in the persecutions of Severus, Decius, Valerian, Diocletian and Maximinus. They are mentioned under five dates in the Roman Martyrology.

COPTIC RITE, The. The system and forms of worship and administration of the sacraments in use among the Copts, both Catholic and dissident. The liturgical language is Coptic, the former tongue of Egypt, interspersed with Greek and Arabic; the use of the latter is increasing. The eucharistic liturgy has three alternative *anaphoras*. On ordinary days Catholic priests celebrate in a low voice. A Coptic church should be divided by screens into narthex, women's part, men's part, choir and sanctuary which contains three altars in line, all built clear of the east wall; they are much decorated with carved wood, paintings and mosaic; the altar is never hidden by curtains but is commonly half-concealed by a screen (*haikal*). Before the offertory the bread and wine are carried in procession round the altar, there are 3 lessons in addition to the Gospel, the words of consecration are sung aloud, before the communion the people make a long act of faith. "I believe that this bread and this wine are the true flesh and true blood of Christ, born of the Virgin Mary . . ."; a great deal of incense is used and the people's association in the sacrifice is very close throughout. The Divine Office is said in Arabic; it consists of Vespers, Night-prayer, Matins, Dawn-prayer, Terce, Sext and None; bishops and monks have an extra "hour" (*satar*). Baptism by immersion is at once followed by Confirmation, with many anointings. Confession is hardly used by the dissidents; the Catholics usually communicate under the species of bread only; the bread is leavened. Extreme Unction properly requires a separate priest for each of the seven anointings but is actually administered by one. The vestments are Byzantine, with a *phelonion* like a cope without a hood; the dissidents add a linen wrapped round the head and neck rather like a large monastic amice. Catholic bishops wear the Latin mitre, ring and pectoral-cross. About 6.5% of the users of this rite are Catholics.

COPTIC RITE, CATHOLICS OF THE. These date from the 18th century, and Pope Leo XIII restored to this small but growing church (63,000 in 1947) a Patriarch of Alexandria; he has three suffragan bishops (Hermopolis, Assiut and Thebes). The Egyptian clergy conduct a senior and junior seminary. Celibacy was made obligatory on the clergy at the synod of Cairo in 1898 but the obligation is dispensed for priests converted from Monophysism. The patriarch and bishops are appointed by the Holy See. There is a congregation of Coptic nuns whose motherhouse is at Tahta.

CORAM CARDINALE, EPISCOPO (Lat., in the presence of a cardinal, or bishop). A Mass *coram cardinale*, etc., is one at which a cardinal or bishop does not celebrate but assists from his throne or a faldstool. At low Mass he receives the kiss of peace from the *instrumentum pacis* and at high Mass he blesses the water at the offertory and the people at the end, instead of the celebrant doing so. *Coram Sanctissimo*, in the presence of the Blessed Sacrament exposed in a monstrance.

CORBONA (Heb.). The treasury in the Jewish Temple for votive offerings (Matt. xxvii, 6); so, a *corban* was a consecrated gift (Mark vii, 11).

CORCAGIENSIS. The adjectival form of the name of the see of Cork (*q.v.*) used in the designation of its bishop in Latin documents. Noun: *Corcagia*.

CORD OF ST. THOMAS, The. A thin cord having fifteen knots, worn round the waist next the skin. It has reference to an incident in the life of St. Thomas Aquinas, and the wearers say fifteen Hail Marys daily in his honour for the maintenance of purity. It must be blessed by a Dominican or other priest having the necessary faculties.

CORDELIERS, The. A popular name in France in the middle ages for the Franciscan Recollects (*q.v.*).

CORINTHIANS, THE EPISTLES TO THE. Two letters to the Church in Corinth, written by St. Paul from Ephesus or Philippi about the year 54, and canonical books of holy Scripture. The first rebukes the dissensions and vices of the Corinthians and touches on many points of Christian doctrine, especially the resurrection; the second is far more personal: Paul justifies his own actions in their regard, deals with false apos-

tles, and recommends to their charity a collection on behalf of the poor Christians of Jerusalem.

CORK (*Corcagiensis*). An Irish see, suffragan of Cashel. It comprises the city and part of the county of Cork, where are the cathedral and bishop's residence; the diocesan college is at Farranferris. The patron of the diocese is St. Finbar (Sept. 25), its first bishop; the cathedral is dedicated in honour of our Lady. Irish name: Corcaigh.

CORONA (Lat., a crown). i. Five mysteries of the rosary (*q.v.*).
   ii. A circle of candles or other lights in a church, especially in the neighbourhood of the altar.
   iii. The rim or band of hair left round the head when tonsured.

CORONATION. i. Of a pope. This takes place after a Mass which the pope celebrates and during which he is solemnly blessed by three cardinal-bishops. The tiara (*q.v.*) is placed on his head by the senior cardinal-deacon. His reign dates officially from this day though he has full jurisdiction from the moment he accepts election. It formerly took place in St. John Lateran, but Leo XIII and Benedict XV were crowned in the Sistine Chapel, Pius X, XI and XII in St. Peter's.
   ii. Of a king. This, during the early middle ages, took on a quasi-sacramental character and included anointings with the oil of catechumens and chrism. The present coronation service of the realm of Great Britain is a modification and adaptation of the Catholic rite. The "Pontificale" contains a rite for the blessing and coronation of a king.
   iii. The coronation of an image requires papal sanction or the approval of the canons of St. Peter's if it is to be done publicly and with the rite approved by Gregory XVI in 1837. The crown (which in the second case is given by the canons, *e.g.*, our Lady's statue at West Grinstead) may be placed on a statue (*e.g.*, St. Anne d'Auray, Notre Dame des Tables at Montpellier) or affixed to a picture (*e.g.*, Our Lady of Perpetual Succour, and of Genazzano, crowned by Pope Innocent XI in 1676), but of course not every image with a crown has been crowned in this solemn sense. It is an ancient way of honouring the subject of any image which has greatly attracted devotion.
   iv. The Coronation of our Lady. A symbolical way of referring to the reception of our Lady into the presence of God at her Assumption (*q.v.*). It has been joined to and in some places has supplanted "the Glory of all the Saints" as the subject of meditation in the fifteenth mystery of the rosary. As a liturgical feast it is kept in Calabria (Aug. 17), Guatemala (May 18) and elsewhere.

Francia's picture of the subject is really an Immaculate Conception.

CORPORAL (Lat. *corpus*, a body). A piece of linen about 20 ins. square on which are put the Host and Chalice at Mass. When not in use it is kept in a burse (*q.v.*). It must be washed by a major cleric before being sent to a laundry. A corporal is also put beneath a vessel containing the Blessed Sacrament at any time, *e.g.*, on the "floor" of the tabernacle, and beneath the monstrance at Benediction.

CORPORAL WORKS OF MERCY, The, are seven: to feed the hungry, refresh the thirsty, clothe the naked, shelter the homeless, tend the sick, visit the imprisoned, and bury the dead.

CORPORATION. An institution, community, or group of persons to which legal status has been given by ecclesiastical authority. In law corporations rank as minors. Corporations are perpetual and exist *de jure* until suppressed, or until they have been nonexistent *de facto* for 100 years.

CORPUS CHRISTI (Lat., the Body of Christ). "The Solemn Feast of the most holy Body of our Lord Jesus Christ" to celebrate the institution of the Blessed Sacrament of which the commemoration on Holy Thursday has been obscured by other liturgical observances. It was established for the Thursday after Trinity Sunday by Pope Urban IV, in 1264, and its Mass and Office composed by St. Thomas Aquinas. The procession of the Blessed Sacrament now associated with this feast may take place on the feast itself and at any time of the day, but such a procession must be held on the following Sunday in any case. Most of the Catholic Eastern rites have adopted the feast; in Great Britain and Ireland it is a holiday of obligation.

CORRECTION, FRATERNAL. An admonition given to a sinner from the motive of charity to induce him to amend his ways; the obligation to give such admonition is laid down by the natural law and expressly defined by Christ (Matt. xviii, 15). It is grave under these three conditions: the sin to be rebuked must be certain, mortal and not repented of; there must be a reasonable hope that the admonition will do good and that no one else can or will give it; serious disadvantage to oneself will not follow. Great prudence must be observed in the discharge of this obligation.

CORRECTOR. The name of the general, provincial and local superiors of the Minim friars, so called because it is their business to correct first themselves and then those under them.

CORVOPOLITANUS. The Latin epithet for the bishop of Wagga-Wagga in Australia; it suggests that the place takes its name from a bird.

COSMOGONY. An account, true, theoretical or mythical, of the creation of the universe.

COSMOLOGY. The science of the universe, now usually of the inorganic world only.

COSTA RICA, THE CHURCH IN. This republic of over half a million inhabitants forms an ecclesiastical province, with one suffragan see and a vicariate apostolic. The Catholic is the state religion, without prejudice to others. In the upper law courts the judge is assisted by ecclesiastical assessors if a priest is charged with a crime.

COSTS of a trial in an ecclesiastical court must as a rule be paid by the loser, unless he is permitted to appear as a poor person. A table of costs must be drawn up by the provincial council or bishops' meeting. The judge may order the costs to be provisionally paid into court by the plaintiff before the action is heard. In certain circumstances costs are divided between the parties.

COSTUME, CLERICAL. See DRESS.

COTTA (It.). A common name for the short surplice (*q.v.*).

COTTOLENGO INSTITUTE, The. The Little House of Divine Providence (*q.v.*).

COTTON. See SEDGELEY PARK.

COUNCIL, DIOCESAN, is almost invariably referred to as a diocesan synod. It is a meeting of the chief clergy of his diocese summoned by a bishop at least every ten years to discuss the maintenance of the Faith and good order in the diocese. The members are only advisory, the bishop alone deciding and legislating; it is therefore not properly a council.

COUNCIL, NATIONAL, OR SYNOD. A council, which may be plenary or provincial (*qq.v.*) according to circumstances, of a whole nation or state. The last national council in England was the 4th provincial of Westminster, 1885: in Ireland, the 4th of Maynooth, 1927; in the United States, the 3rd of Baltimore, 1884. In 1928 a national council of the Armenians was convened at Rome and in 1929 of the Ruthenians.

COUNCIL, ŒCUMENICAL. A council, convened by the Holy See, of the bishops, and others entitled to vote, of the whole world, or a representative number of them. In addition to all bishops, residential or titular, right to vote is secured by law to all cardinals, abbots and prelates *nullius*, abbots primate or general, and the superior general of other monastic and mendicant orders and of clerks regular. Papal co-operation must be of the fullest extent to make a council œcumenical and its decrees have no binding authority until confirmed by the Holy See, but those at which the pope presides in person require no further confirmation. There is no appeal from the pope to an œcumenical council and if he dies during its course it is suspended until his successor reopens it. The decrees of such a council are infallible. It must be noted that the authority is not distinct from the ordinary *magisterium* (*q.v.*), but is merely a more solemn exercise of the same; also, the bishops are not delegates of their flocks (it is no parliament); nor is it an attempt to limit papal authority, for separate from that authority the council has no binding force as infallible. The following councils are regarded as œcumenical by the Catholic Church, only the first seven by the Orthodox Eastern Church, the first two by the Nestorians and the first three by the separated Armenians, Syrians and Copts. 1. Nicæa I, 325; 2. Constantinople I, 381; 3. Ephesus, 431; 4. Chalcedon, 451; 5. Constantinople II, 553; 6. Constantinople III, 680-1; 7. Nicæa II, 787; 8. Constantinople IV, 869; 9. Lateran I, 1123; 10. Lateran II, 1139; 11. Lateran III, 1179; 12. Lateran IV, 1215; 13. Lyons I, 1245; 14. Lyons II, 1274; 15. Vienne, 1311-13; 16. Constance, 1414-18 (in part only); 17. Basle-Ferrara-Florence, 1431-43; 18. Lateran V, 1512-17; 19. Trent, 1545-1563; 20. Vatican, 1869, adjourned 1870 and still unfinished. The first six are commemorated on a single feast in the Byzantine rite and some of them separately in several Eastern churches. *

COUNCIL, PLENARY, OR SYNOD. A council, of the ecclesiastical authorities, *i.e.*, residential archbishops and bishops, administrators of dioceses and vicars capitular, abbots and prelates *nullius*, vicars and prefects apostolic, of a given territory, usually a kingdom, state or nation. Such a council is presided over by a legate of the Holy See, which also confirms its acts before they may be promulgated. In its wider sense a plenary council of Latin America was held in 1899.

COUNCIL, PROVINCIAL, OR SYNOD. A meeting of the bishops of a province (*q.v.* i), convened by the metropolitan at least once in every twenty years, chiefly for the purpose of any necessary disciplinary legislation. Its acts must be approved by the Holy See before they are promulgated. The decrees of the provincial Councils of Westminster continue to have force in England and Wales though now divided into four provinces.

COUNCIL, THE SACRED CONGREGATION OF THE, deals with whatever relates to the holding of councils and conferences; with the observance of and dispensations from the commandments of the Church (*q.v.*); and makes regulations for the parochial clergy, canons, benefices, church property, pious associations, etc. With it is united the Congregation of Loreto which is responsible for the upkeep of that shrine and its pilgrimages. Decrees of plenary and provincial councils must be approved by the Sacred Congregation of the Council.

COUNSEL is a gift of the Holy Ghost and a fruit of prudence enabling one to see what is the right course in a given case and urging u to pursue it.

COUNSELS OF PERFECTION. The evangelical counsels (*q.v.*).

COUNSELS AND PRECEPTS. Precepts are rules of life and conduct necessary for all who wish to attain salvation, *e.g.*, the Ten Commandments. Counsels are rules of life and conduct for those who, not satisfied with the bare minimum, choose to aim at greater moral perfection by means of good works not commanded but commended as better than their opposites, *e.g.*, abstinence from lawful pleasures. Observance of the counsels is meritorious only if done from a supernatural motive. The distinction between counsels and precepts is denied by those who believe in justification by faith.

COUNT PALATINE, properly Count of the Apostolic Palace and Court of the Lateran, a title attached to many offices at the Roman court; must be distinguished from papal count, the most common pontifical title (*q.v.*) of nobility. Bishops assistant at the pontifical throne (*q.v.*) are counts palatine by right.

COUNTER-REFORMATION, The, is the name given to the Catholic movement of reform and activity which lasted for about one hundred years from the beginning of the Council of Trent (*q.v.*, 1545), and was the belated answer to the threatening confusion and increasing attacks of the previous years. It was the work principally of Popes St. Pius V and Gregory XIII and the Council itself in the sphere of authority, of SS. Philip Neri and Charles Borromeo in the reform of the clergy and of life, of St. Ignatius and the Jesuits in apostolic activity, of St. Francis Xavier in foreign missions, and of St. Teresa in the purely contemplative life which lies behind them all. But these were not the only names nor was it a movement of a few only; the whole Church emerged from the 16th century purified and revivified. On the other hand, it was a reformation rather than a restoration; the unity of western Christendom was destroyed; the Church militant led by the Company of Jesus adopted offence as the best means of defence and, though she gained as much as she lost in some senses, the Church did not recover the exercise of her former spiritual supremacy in actuality.

COURT. i. Ecclesiastical. The Church, as a perfect society (*q.v.*), has full judicial power over her members and so she has her courts of law. The court of first instance for ecclesiastical causes is the diocesan tribunal, the court of appeal being that of the metro-

---

* The 21st Ecumenical Council was Vatican Council II (1962-1965).—*Publisher*, 1997.

politan. Anyone may apply to have his cause tried in the Roman courts, either in first instance or by way of appeal, but the jurisdiction of the lower court is not suspended until the pope allows the trial of the cause in his own courts. There are three Roman courts, the Rota, the Penitentiary and the Signatura (*q.v*). The causes of clerics must always be heard in the ecclesiastical courts and not in lay courts, except by leave of the ordinary.

ii. Of the Vatican City. The civil and criminal court of first instance is a tribunal of three judges; from it appeal lies to the tribunal of the Rota (*q.v*.), the Signatura being the final court of cassation. Before all these courts only consistorial advocates may plead. The Sovereign Pontiff can refer any case at any stage to a special commission or exercise his supreme right of clemency, and an aggrieved person may appeal to him through the council of state.

COURT OF ARCHES, The. The principal ecclesiastical court of the former province of Canterbury which sat at the church of Our Lady of the Arches (St. Mary le Bow, Cheapside). This church was, with twelve other parishes, exempt from the jurisdiction of the bishop of London, and these "peculiars" were under the Dean of Arches who finally became the commissary of the Official. The court ultimately sat in Doctors Commons Hall. It was the appeal court of the Canterbury province, as the Chancery Court was that of York. An Anglican church-court bearing the same name provides a good example of the external and verbal continuity which is a characteristic of the Church of England.

COURT, DIOCESAN, PAPAL, etc. See CURIA, from which Latin word, meaning a senate, the English word "court" is derived through French *cour*, which is a confusion between *curia* and *cohors*, an enclosed yard.

COUSINS, MARRIAGE OF. According to the computation of canon law, first or cousins german and second cousins, being related by consanguinity in the 2nd and 3rd degrees collateral, cannot marry without dispensation on pain of invalidity. Dispensation from this impediment is commonly granted.

COVERDALE'S BIBLE. The first complete English Bible to be printed, made by Miles Coverdale, a "reforming" Augustinian friar, and published abroad in 1535.

COVETOUSNESS. The second of the seven deadly sins. See AVARICE.

COWL (*cuculla*). A long ample garment with wide sleeves, worn in choir by Benedictine, Cistercian and other monks and nuns; it is the same colour as the habit. Carthusians call their large joined scapular a cowl, the true cowl being worn only by the deacon at sung Mass. From the circumstance of its

having had a hood attached, the cowl is commonly erroneously confused with the hood (*q.v*.).

CRANIOTOMY. An operation by which the head of an unborn child is cut open and broken down if it presents an obstacle to safe delivery. The operation is licit only if the child is already dead; otherwise, even if thereby the mother's life would be saved, the sin of murder is committed.

CREATION. i. The production of a thing from nothing; this implies before production the negation of material from which a thing is made and indeed the negation of anything whatsoever of the thing to be produced. It is therefore the *entire* production of a thing. To create is an activity proper to God, and St. Thomas teaches the impossibility of any creature being used as an instrument by God to create.

ii. Of the world. In accordance with the first chapter of the book of Genesis, Catholics are bound to believe that the universe and everything in it was created by God; that it was created in time and not from eternity; that all things were created by God alone; and that all things created were good. Nothing is defined as to the order or period of creation. See GENESIS ii.

CREATIONISM. The true doctrine of the Catholic Church concerning the origin of the human soul, *viz.*, that each individual human soul is created from nothing immediately by God, at the moment of the conception of the body or at least when the body is sufficiently formed (*cf.*, Traducianism and Generationism). This doctrine is opposed to Plato who held that souls were created from all eternity and therefore existed before union with the body; to Leibniz, who held all souls were created at the beginning of time and were enclosed as seeds in matter which eventually evolve and become human; to Pythagoras and the Theosophists, who teach all souls existed from the beginning of time and pass from one body to another (Metempsychosis). As to the exact moment when the soul is infused into the body: Some say the infusion takes place in the instant of the conception of the *fœtus;* others (Aristotle, St. Thomas, and scholastics generally until the 17th century) hold the infusion takes place when the *fœtus* has taken the organic human shape. On this point Goudin, González and Frédault recede from the doctrine of St. Thomas.*

CREATURE. Any created person or thing. God made the human creature that it might know, love and serve him in this world and be happy with him for ever in the next; it has therefore no meaning, reason for existence or end outside of God. The Christian is continually warned against preferring a creature before the Creator, *e.g.*, by an inordinate attachment to another human being; but the more he knows God the greater

---

* With the advances in modern biology it has become ever more apparent that the human soul must be present from the first moment of conception.—*Publisher*, 1997.

will be his love for God's creatures on the one hand and the less the likelihood of his love becoming inordinate on the other. "No one desires to be loved except for his goodness; and when we love in this way our love is pleasing to God and in great liberty; and if there be attachment in it, there is greater attachment to God" (St. John-of-the-Cross).

CREDENCE (med. Lat. *credentia,* a side-table). A table or shelf in the wall at the epistle-side of an altar. On it are put the cruets, basin and towel required at Mass, and at high Mass the chalice, paten, altar-bread, etc., repose thereon, covered by the humeral-veil, until the offertory and after the ablutions.

CREDO (Lat., I believe). i. The first word of the Apostles' and Nicene creeds, used as a noun to indicate either of them: the second, in reference to the Creed at Mass; otherwise, generally, the first is meant.
ii. A musical setting of the Nicene creed.

CREED (Lat. *credo,* I believe). A formula of profession of faith, consisting of dogmas of revealed truth. Such are the Apostles' Creed and the Nicene Creed (*qq.v.*). The words are to be accepted in their natural sense (*cf.,* Modernism). Creeds in this historical sense originated as professions of faith at baptism. No one of the so-called "historic creeds of Christendom" is a complete and final statement of the Christian faith nor was such, nor intended to be such, even at the time of its first drawing-up.

CREED IN THE LITURGY. i. In the Roman rite the Nicene creed is said or sung at Mass only on Sundays, feasts of our Lord, our Lady, the apostles and evangelists, doctors of the Church, feasts of the first class and at solemn votive Masses. The custom of reciting it at the Eucharist was introduced first at Antioch in 476 but at Rome not till much later. The Apostles' creed is used at Baptism and at the ordination of priests, and formerly at the *preces.* The Athanasian creed is said at Prime on Trinity Sunday.
ii. All Eastern rites have the Nicene creed (or versions thereof) at every eucharistic liturgy, nor do they use any other creed. It is sung in the plural ("*We* believe . . .") by many orientals and in the Mozarabic Mass. The *Filioque* (*q.v.*) clause is omitted by all dissidents and some Catholics.

CREED OF POPE PIUS IV, The, is a profession of faith set out by that pope in a bull *Iniunctum nobis* in 1564. It affirms all the articles of the Nicene creed, the traditions of the Apostles, the sacraments, the sacrifice of the Mass, Purgatory, indulgences, the invocation of saints, and the Holy See. It is used in England in the rite for the reception of

converts, an article concerning the Vatican Council being added.

CREEPING TO THE CROSS, The. An archaic name for the Adoration of the Cross (*q.v.*) on Good Friday.

CREMATION. Destruction of the body after death by fire, the ashes usually being preserved; strictly forbidden by the Church, which enjoins burial of the body out of reverence to what was in life the temple of the Holy Ghost (1 Cor. vi, 19). Nevertheless, cremation is not intrinsically wrong, and so may be allowed by ecclesiastical authority for a grave reason, *e.g.,* public health. The Church legislates strictly against it, in addition to the above reason, because its practice has become associated with atheists and materialists who use it as a manifestation of their disbelief in human immortality and resurrection, and because it is a custom repugnant to Christian tradition and to the universal mind and practice of Christian people. There are other and legitimate means by which certainty that life is extinct can be provided (*cf.,* Will and Testament). *

CRIB. A manger with bars. i. The manger in which our Lord was laid after his birth in the stable at Bethlehem. Alleged relics of this wooden manger are venerated at the church of St. Mary Major in Rome.
ii. A representation of our Lord in the manger displayed in Catholic churches from Christmas eve until the octave of the Epiphany. It may consist simply of the figure of the Holy Babe or may include our Lady, St. Joseph, the Magi, animals, etc., and the figures may be diminutive or life size. In some churches the image of the Child is laid in the crib by one of the sacred ministers at the *Gloria* of the midnight Mass, or carried thereto in procession by the celebrant after Mass. The custom was instituted by St. Francis of Assisi at Greccio, at Christmas 1223, though not entirely unknown before.

CRIME. i. In canon law, an external and culpable transgression of a law to which a penalty is attached. Crimes are either public, notorious or occult. The Church, as a perfect society (*q.v.*), has the right to prosecute and punish delinquents. For a crime to be committed there must be either malicious intent or grave negligence. Culpability is lessened or extinguished by mental defect, ignorance, violence and fear. The commission of a crime gives rise to a criminal action for the infliction of the penalty, and a civil action for damages, if any. **
ii. Irregularity from crime (*ex delicto*) is the state of being incapable of receiving holy orders or exercising their functions (see IRREGULARITY) incurred by the following: apostates from the Faith, heretics, schismatics; those who have allowed themselves to be baptized by non-Catholics except in

---

* The 1983 Canon Law states that burial is earnestly recommended but that cremation is not forbidden "unless it has been chosen for reasons that are contrary to Christian teaching." (Can. 1176 §3). —*Publisher,* 1997.
** The 1983 Canon Law gives revised laws on "crime" ("Offenses and Penalties").—*Publisher,* 1997.

extreme necessity; those who have attempted marriage when they were already bound by marriage, orders or vows, or with a woman already bound by vows or marriage; those who have committed or co-operated in voluntary homicide or abortion; those who have mutilated themselves or others or attempted suicide; those clerics who have practised medicine or surgery forbidden to them and death has resulted; those who perform or attempt a function of an order which they have been forbidden by authority to exercise or when they have not received the order.

iii. As a diriment impediment (*q.v.*) to marriage. Marriage cannot be validly contracted (*a*) between persons who, with a promise of marriage to take effect if and when the consort of one, or both, dies, have committed adultery; the adultery must be complete and the promise real, unconditional and accepted; (*b*) between persons who have conspired and caused the death of the consort of one of them; and (*c*) between two persons who have committed adultery, of whom one (without conspiring with the other) has murdered his consort in order to be free to marry his accomplice in adultery. Any one of these constitutes the impediment of *crime*, but they do not affect the unbaptized. Dispensations are sometimes given for this impediment if the crime was not open and notorious.

CRIMINALS condemned to death, if in proper dispositions, are to be given absolution, Viaticum and the Last Blessing, but not Extreme Unction. They are required to make whatever reparation or restitution is due from them as far as possible.

CRIMINOUS CLERK. An historical term for those pleading benefit of clergy (*q.v.*) at the time of the struggle between St. Thomas Becket and King Henry II and thereafter.

CRITERIOLOGY. A part of logic which treats of the validity of those means or *criteria* whereby the mind attains truth. Of these criteria some are intrinsic, some extrinsic (as human authority): intrinsic are either subjective (as the cognitive faculties) or objective (as certain truths used as principles in reasoning). Criteriology examines the validity of all these.

CRITICISM, BIBLICAL. i. Textual. The use of scientific means to ascertain the actual text as it left the hands of the inspired writers.

ii. Higher. The ascertaining, mainly from internal considerations, of the sources upon which a biblical book has drawn, and the time and circumstances of its compilation. "Higher criticism" is often used in a pejorative sense because of the vagaries of some of its users.

iii. Historical. The study of the value of

biblical books as accounts of actual facts, whether from internal or external considerations.

CROAGH PATRICK. A mountain in Clew Bay in the archdiocese of Tuam whereon St. Patrick passed Lent in the year 441. It has been a place of pilgrimage without intermission ever since, the principal day being the last Sunday of July. The pilgrimage chapel, thrown down in penal times, was restored in 1905.

CROSIER, CROZIER. A common name for the pastoral staff (*q.v.*); sometimes erroneously given to the archiepiscopal cross (*q.v.*). It is derived from Med. Lat. *crocia*, a crook, confused with Old Fr. *crois*, a cross.

CROSIER CANONS. The Canons Regular of the Holy Cross are a small congregation founded by Bl. Theodore de Celles in 1211. Their habit is tunic, scapular, mozzetta and hood, with a red and white cross on the scapular; the colour varies from one country to another. These canons are best known for their faculty of blessing rosaries with the Crosier indulgence of 500 days for each bead. See also KNIGHTS OF THE CROSS.

CROSS. The most widespread and venerated (but not certainly the most ancient) symbol of the Christian religion, because upon a cross of wood our Lord died to redeem the world. Christ's cross was probably shaped as in Fig. 1, though it may have been as in Fig. 6; in the early days of the Church the cross was often symbolized as an anchor or disguised in a monogram.

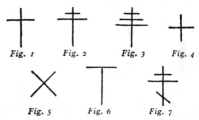

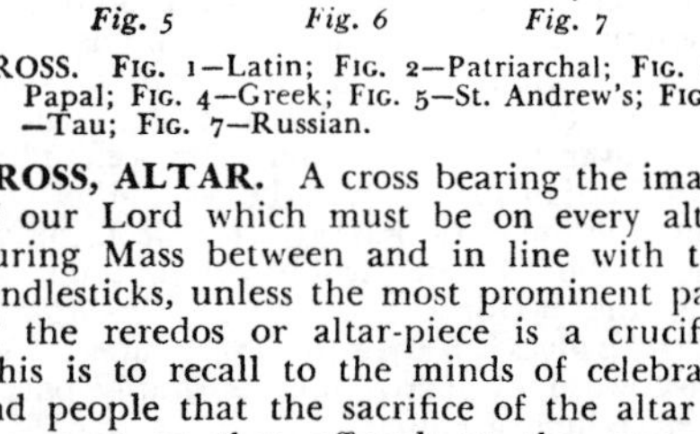

Fig. *1*   Fig. *2*   Fig. *3*   Fig. *4*

Fig. *5*   Fig. *6*   Fig. *7*

CROSS. FIG. 1—Latin; FIG. 2—Patriarchal; FIG. 3—Papal; FIG. 4—Greek; FIG. 5—St. Andrew's; FIG. 6—Tau; FIG. 7—Russian.

CROSS, ALTAR. A cross bearing the image of our Lord which must be on every altar during Mass between and in line with the candlesticks, unless the most prominent part of the reredos or altar-piece is a crucifix. This is to recall to the minds of celebrant and people that the sacrifice of the altar is the same as that offered on the cross of Calvary; it should therefore be visible to all. Formerly the cross and candlesticks were removed when Mass was not being said. This is still done in certain churches, *e.g.*, in Spain. Neither a crucifix at the top and part of the tabernacle nor a painting thereof on the altarcard are substitutes for the altar cross.

CROSS, ARCHIEPISCOPAL, is one similar to a processional cross and is borne before an archbishop, with the figure turned towards him, whenever he proceeds to or from an ecclesiastical function within his province; it does not take the place of a pastoral-staff. The display by archbishops of a double-barred cross in heraldic and other devices is common but improper.

CROSS, FEASTS OF THE. There are two feasts of the cross in the Roman calendar, the "Finding" on May 3, and the "Exaltation" on Sept. 14 (*qq.v.*). They are, with others, also observed in the East.

CROSS, GREEK. The equilateral cross (Fig. 4).

CROSS, HAND. A small hand cross is frequently used by bishops of all Eastern rites and by Syrian, Maronite and Armenian priests in giving both liturgical and extra-liturgical blessings. The only analogous custom in the West is that of blessing with the crucifix unscrewed from the processional cross after the stations of the cross on Good Friday.

CROSS, LATIN. The most familar form in the West, *crux immissa* (Fig. 1).

CROSS, PAPAL. i. The cross carried before the pope as before an archbishop.

ii. In heraldic and other devices, a cross with three bars (Fig. 3); it is, however, never shown behind the pope's coat of arms.

CROSS, PATRIARCHAL OR PRIMATIAL. A cross with two bars (also called Benedictine), used chiefly in heraldry. Among others, the primate of All Ireland (the archbishop of Armagh) wears a pectoral cross (*q.v.*) of this form (Fig. 2).

CROSS, PECTORAL. A small cross, containing relics, suspended round the neck by a chain or cord and worn outside the clothing (over the alb when vested). It is the emblem of a bishop but is also worn by cardinals, abbots, abbesses, protonotaries apostolic and others, especially canons of certain chapters which have the privilege. Bishops of the Byzantine rite wear such a cross over the *omophorion* when celebrating and Russian priests over the *phelonion*. Dissident bishops of Eastern rites (*e.g.*, among the Orthodox and Jacobites) now sometimes add the pectoral cross to the *enkolpia* or other badges of their ordinary dress. The cross worn by many nuns is simply part of their religious habit.

CROSS, PROCESSIONAL. A crucifix mounted on a long shaft of metal or wood. It is carried aloft at the head of all processions, with the figure turned forward, and is accompanied on either hand by an acolyte with a candle. At the burial of an infant the crucifix is detached from the shaft and carried so.

CROSS, RELICS OF THE TRUE. The cross of our Lord was found about 318 by the Empress St. Helen and within half a century portions of it had reached the furthest parts of the known world. The most striking evidence we possess of the existence of the main portion of the cross is found in the account which the pilgrim lady Ætheria has left of the solemn veneration of the relic on Good Friday in Jerusalem, *c.* 385. Many relics still exist, but usually they are so minute that, even taken with those that have disappeared but of which there is record, they are not sufficient to make up a whole cross of even 12 ft. by 8 ft. It was made of pine wood. Alone among relics, these may be carried beneath a canopy in processions and are genuflected to when exposed. The greatest relic of the kind in England is at Downside Abbey; there is a small one enclosed in the cross on the campanile of Westminster cathedral.

CROSS, RUSSIAN, has three bars of which the lowest represents the foot-rest and the topmost the title (Fig. 7).

CROSS-BEARER. He who carries the processional cross at the head of processions. On solemn occasions it is a subdeacon, vested in alb and tunicle; at other times a minor cleric or layman in cassock and surplice.

CROSS PRO ECCLESIA ET PONTIFICE (Lat., for Church and Pope). A minor decoration instituted by Pope Leo XIII as a reward for services to the Church. It is given to both men and women.

CROSS SALTIRE. The St. Andrew's cross (Fig. 5), so called because according to tradition the apostle Andrew was crucified on a cross of this shape.

CROSS TAU (Gr. ταῦ, equivalent of letter T). The T-shaped cross, also known as St. Antony's (the Hermit) cross (Fig. 6).

CROSS ON VESTMENTS. A tiny cross must be put near the top edge of the amice and a larger one in the middle of the stole and maniple; these are to be kissed when the vestment is assumed. All other crosses, even on the chasuble, are merely ornamental and superfluous. Nor is a cross required on the burse or veil.

CROWN, BAPTISMAL. A peculiarity of the Armenian rite. The crown is a wreath of plaited red and white ribands with a small cross attached, symbolizing the graces of the Holy Spirit. It is put on after the Confirmation which follows Baptism and is worn for eight days; it is then taken off, with a short prayer, by the priest.

CROWN, EPISCOPAL. A tall bulbous metal head-dress, richly ornamented, modelled after the imperial crown of Constantinople. It corresponds to the Latin mitre and is worn when celebrating the Liturgy by Byzantine (Catholic and dissident) and some other bishops. It is also worn by Armenian priests (Catholic and dissident) whose bishops wear the Latin mitre. Syrian Jacobite bishops have no liturgical headdress but a hood; others wear the Latin mitre.

CROWN, FRANCISCAN. A rosary of seven decades in honour of the seven joys of our Lady; also called the Seraphic Rosary.

CROWN, MARRIAGE. A metal crown or wreath which in all Eastern rites is placed upon the heads of the bride and groom during the ceremony of marriage. The wreath of flowers familiar in the West may be a survival or variation of the same custom, but was formerly held, especially in Germany, to be typical of virginity; why orange-blossoms are favoured for this is not certainly known: a likely suggestion is because of their fragrance and because they could be dried and so be available at any time of year; rosemary was formerly used in England. In Alsace, Luxembourg and other districts a newly ordained priest sometimes wears a wreath of flowers in place of a biretta when going to and from the altar at his first Mass.

CROWN, PAPAL. See TIARA.

CROWN, VIRGIN'S. One of the three articles handed to the candidate at the consecration of a virgin (*q.v.*) (*cf., Aureole* ii).

CROWN OF THORNS, The, with which our Lord was tortured during his passion is reputed to be preserved in Notre Dame at Paris. It is, in fact, only the rush foundation, to which no thorns any longer are attached. It was taken out of pawn, literally, by the Emperor Baldwin II and given to St. Louis of France, who built La Sainte Chappelle to contain it. At that time it still retained many of the thorns, but several of these were given away by St. Louis in golden reliquaries; one such reliquary is in the British Museum and it appears still to contain the thorn which it was made to enshrine. After the Revolution what remained of the relic or its rush foundation was brought to light through the compunction of one of the constitutional clergy. A feast in honour of the Crown of Thorns is kept at St. Peter's in Rome and by the Passionists on Friday after Ash Wednesday and by the Dominicans on April 24.

CRUCIFIX. A cross on which the figure of our Lord is painted, carved or otherwise represented. Whenever a cross is referred to in connexion with Catholic liturgy (*e.g.,* an altar cross) a crucifix is to be understood. The crucifix is now seen on the altars of all ancient churches except the Coptic and Nestorian, though in the East carving in the round is generally forbidden. But the use of the crucifix was not general before the 6th century, and the representation of our Lord suffering or dead is yet more recent; it began about the 13th century and only became general with the Spanish influence of the counter-Reformation. The traditional Catholic crucifix represented our Lord crowned, robed, alive, not hanging on but reigning from the cross.

CRUCIFIXION, The, of our Lord was the consummation of his redemption of the human race. It has always been the teaching of the Church that our Lord, as the man Jesus Christ, actually died upon the cross, not evading death by simulation or substitution, and in the same flesh came to life on the third day.

CRUELTY. i. The disposition to inflict suffering on others; or, negatively, indifference to the misery of others. Cruelty is a grave sin against charity.

ii. To animals. In his dealings with animals man must remember (*a*) that they are sentient (his reasonable needs may nevertheless be lawfully satisfied although this involves infliction of pain; but wanton infliction of pain satisfies no reasonable need and is sinful, because it is an outrage, not against the supposed rights of the animal (*q.v.*), but against the designed order of creation); and (*b*) that they are irrational (hence it is foolish to lavish excessive affection on them, sinful if thereby higher duties are neglected). It is lawful to take part in any sport in which pain is or may be inflicted on an animal (*e.g.,* fox-hunting), provided such pain is incidental to the sport and is not the object of the sport itself (*e.g.,* bear-baiting), and provided such pain is not disproportionate to the advantage in the way of recreation, etc. Bull-fighting has not been unanimously condemned by moral theologians, though Pope St. Pius V forbade it altogether. According to present regulations, the clergy are prohibited from being present thereat.

CRUETS. Two large phials or diminutive jugs and a small bowl made of glass, crystal or metal; the former to contain water and wine for use at Mass, the latter to receive the water from the celebrant's fingers at the *Lavabo.*

CRUSADE, THE FOURTH. The most important of the Crusades in so far as it had the most lasting results. Paid by the Doge of Venice to recapture for him the town of Zara (Dalmatia), the army proceeded thence by land to Constantinople and in 1204 sacked this second city of Christendom, massacring (including the co-emperor), burning and plundering; set up a Frankish emperor and a Latin patriarch; and seized all the Byzantine churches. The city was recovered by the Byzantine emperor Michael VIII Palaiologos in 1261. Pope Innocent III had preached this crusade against the Saracens and excommunicated the Venetians who had caused its diversion; but its terrors were remembered, and at the final schism in 1472 the Greeks said in effect "Rather the sultan's turban than the pope's tiara." Innocent III wrote to Cardinal Peter of Capua: "How will the Greek church be brought back to unity and her devotion to the Apostolic See renewed? The Latins have given an example only of perversity and works of darkness. It is natural that [the Greeks] should look down on them as curs. These soldiers of Christ . . . are drenched in Christian blood. . . ."

CRUSADE BULL, The. A papal bull granting to the faithful of the Spanish dominions certain privileges as a reward for their former crusades against the infidels. The privileges include a plenary indulgence to be gained on certain conditions and a dispensation from fasting and abstinence throughout the year except on certain days. The offerings of the faithful go to the endowment of churches and charities and a large proportion is absorbed by the state for the maintenance of clergy.

CRUSADES, The. i. Wars originally undertaken to deliver the Holy Places from the hands of infidels. Volunteers were enrolled by a vow and the receiving of a small cross. The Crusades proper began with the First in 1095 and ended with the Eighth in 1270. From 1099 to 1187 their object was attained and there was a Christian king of Jerusalem. Christendom lost the Holy Land through internal dissension, imperial jealousy and outbreaks of barbarity, such as those at Jerusalem in 1099 and Constantinople in 1204. Acre (Akka), the last place to be held, was lost in 1291. The Crusades increasingly belied their name and degenerated into little more than expeditions of aggrandizement and plundering; enmity with the Eastern emperor was aggravated to the lasting harm of Europe; and the Orthodox Church was treated with an indifferent contempt of which effects are still evident. The Holy Places were not relieved of the Turks until 1917, and then in the course of a secular war.
ii. The name is also given to subsequent wars with the Moslems both in the East and in Spain, and to such activities of secular arms as the war against the Albigensians in the 13th century.

CRUTCHED FRIARS, The, *i.e.*, crossed friars, were so called because each carried a stick with a cross upon it, afterwards exchanged for a cross sewn upon the habit. They were founded some time before the 12th century, followed the rule of St. Augustine and were suppressed in 1656. They had eight or nine houses in England, one of which gave their name to a street near the Tower of London.

CRYPT. The lower part, or "cellars," of a church, enclosed by the foundation walls, but sometimes built out above ground, causing the floor level of the choir to be raised, *e.g.*, at Rochester cathedral. They were, and

are, used for worship, but more particularly for burial; St. Thomas Becket was enshrined in Canterbury crypt until his translation in 1220.

CUBA, THE CHURCH IN. Population 4¼ million, mostly at least nominal Catholics. Clergy are exempt from military service. Purely civil (as well as religious) marriage is recognized by the state, but divorce is not. The 2 metropolitan sees, Havana and Santiago de Cuba, go back to 1787 and 1522 respectively; each has 2 suffragans.

CUIUS REGIO EIUS RELIGIO (Lat., Let the religion of each State follow that of its Prince). This Erastian principle, called the *ius reformandi*, was temporarily conceded to the German Protestant princes by the Peace of Augsburg (1555) and confirmed in the teeth of papal protest by the Treaty of Westphalia (1648). In accordance therewith the inhabitants of the Rhenish Palatinate had to change their religion four times in 60 years. But it was due to it that Germany was saved from a chaos like that of the French Wars of Religion, at any rate until the Thirty Years War; it made Protestantism politically respectable but refused any recognition to the Reformed. Theoretically the system would still be operative in the unlikely event of a Swiss canton changing its religion by a majority.

CULDEES, The (Irish *céli Dé*, companions of God). An institution of religious men that flourished in Ireland and Scotland from the 8th to the 11th century; at Armagh they lingered till the 16th. At first they were solitaries, but their life later approximated to that of secular canons living in community or to that of those canons regular who superseded them. To identify them with the monks of the Celtic churches (*e.g.*, at Iona) is quite incorrect. There was a Culdee community at York in the 10th century and at Ynys Enlli (Bardsey) in the 12th.

CULPA (Lat.). A fault, particularly those infractions of discipline that are confessed in the monastic chapter of faults (*q.v.*).

CULT, CULTUS, in a general sense is equivalent to worship (*q.v.*), adoration, veneration. But it is generally used with particular reference to the *hyperdulia* (*q.v.*) accorded to our Lady, the *dulia* (*q.v.*) given to the saints and the relative *dulia* to their relics, to pictures, etc. Thus the Iconoclast Controversy was one concerning the cult of images. The word is cognate with "cultivation" (*cf.*, the cult of the slim figure) and derives ultimately from Latin *colere*, to till.

CULTURE (from Lat *cultus*, worship, cognate with *colere*, to till: *cf.*, agriculture, cultivation). The complex of ways of thought, modes of living and historical setting that distinguishes a given people. Sympathies and conflicts of cultures have played an important part in the history of Christianity, and the Catholic Church has been a profound influence in the forming and modifying of cultures: so much so that attempts are sometimes made to identify the Church with this or that culture. But Christianity is not a culture, it is a religion; and its gospel transcends all systems bound up with a special period, nation, continent or culture because it is for every nation and every form of culture, itself being committed to none. European, Latin or "Anglo-Saxon" culture are no necessary part of the good news of Christ: the people of Uganda have as much right to what is good in their society as the French or the Americans or the English have to theirs. *Cf.*, Uniformity. It is sometimes stated that Catholic Christianity is a Graeco-Latin religion. "So huge an error is very significant. Those who make it, not realizing from what spirit they derive and oblivious of the divine transcendence of what constitutes the life of their life, end in practice by worshipping the true God in the same fashion as the Ephesians worshipped Artemis and primitive man worshipped the idols of his tribe. Christian universalism has to remind them that the Gospel and the Church, without doing harm to any particular culture or the state or the nation, dominate them nevertheless in an uncompromised independence and subordinate them to the eternal interests of the human being, to the law of God and the charity of Christ" (Maritain).

CULTUS DISPARITAS. A diriment impediment to matrimony, "difference of worship" (*qq.v.*).

CUM DATA. A decree of 1929 whereby the Holy See, at the wish of some American bishops, directed that only celibate Ruthenian (*q.v.*) priests should be admitted to or ordained in North America. This was a repetition of previous legislation, which had been modified in practice because it had been a factor in arousing strong discontent among some of the Ruthenians. "Cum data" did not affect the position of married oriental clergy already in the country.

CURATE (Lat. *curatus*, one having a charge; *cf.*, French *curé*, a parish priest). Strictly, one with the cure of souls, but in English usage a priest appointed to assist the rector of a parish (vicar co-operator). The ordinary nominates curates, after consulting the rector. A curate's duties are to assist and take the place of the rector in all parish work except what is specially reserved to the rector, to whose direction and vigilance he is subject. If the parish becomes vacant, the senior curate takes the place of the rector until an administrator (*œconomus*) or new rector is appointed.

CURE. A benefice or other ecclesiastical post carrying with it the cure of souls (*q.v.*).

CURE OF SOULS (Lat. *cura.*, care, charge). The pastoral care of the faithful. This belongs by ordinary law to the pope universally and to bishops and rectors of parishes in their own territories. Others may have the cure of souls as delegates or vicars of these. The cure of souls comprises the celebration of the *Missa pro populo* (*q.v.*), the administration of the sacraments, preaching and catechizing, and the care of the poor and the sick, and of children. The pastoral office necessitates personal residence in the territory.

CURIA, DIOCESAN. The court of a diocesan bishop, namely, those who assist him in administration, such as the vicar general, chancellor, ecclesiastical judges, etc., who act by the bishop's authority and for whose official acts he is responsible. The constitutions of diocesan *curiæ* vary.

CURIA ROMANA (Lat., The Roman Court). The totality of organized bodies which assist the pope in the government and administration of the Church, namely, the Congregations, the Tribunals and the Curial Offices (*qq.v.*), together with certain permanent commissions. In common speech the *curia* is taken to include the Pontifical Chapel and Family (*qq.v.*). The pope is responsible for all that is done officially by the *Curia* proper, as its members exercise his delegated authority.

CURIAL OFFICE. One of three departments of the *Curia Romana*, namely, the Chancery, Dataria and Camera Apostolica (*qq.v.*).

CURSING AND SWEARING. Cursing is calling upon God to inflict a spiritual or temporal injury on one's neighbour, oneself or any of God's creatures. This sin is primarily one of irreverence (against the virtue of religion, *q.v.*), but it may also be against charity. The gravity of the sin depends on the seriousness of the harm imprecated and on the deliberation used. Swearing is calling on God to witness to the truth of a statement. Such oaths are sinful whenever false or unnecessary, *i.e.*, calling on God to witness to the truth of a false statement, or of a true one when it is enough to make a simple affirmation. The sin is grave whenever grave irreverence, scandal or perjury are involved (*cf.*, Profanity).

CURSUS (Lat., course, order). The word is used in a variety of senses, *e.g.*, for the Divine Office (*cursus ecclesiasticus* or simply the *cursus*), for the Little Office B.V.M. (*cursus Marianus*), for the order in which the psalms are arranged in the Office, or for the rhythmic swing of earlier liturgical Latin.

CURTAIN. i. Of the tabernacle. See VEIL.
ii. In the Armenian liturgy. A large curtain is drawn completely hiding the sanctuary during the *prothesis*, before the great

entrance, and from the people's communion to the final prayer before the Last Gospel; a small curtain hides only the altar during the priest's communion. The large curtain remains drawn throughout Lent except during the liturgy of Palm Sunday.

CUSTODIAN OF THE HOLY LAND (Lat. *Custos Sanctæ Terræ*). The Most Reverend Father Custodian of the Holy Land and Guardian of Mount Zion is the superior of the Franciscan Friars Minor in Palestine, Syria, Armenia, Cyprus and Egypt. Until 1847 he governed all the Latin Catholics of Palestine, having episcopal jurisdiction, although not a bishop; since the return of the Latin patriarch to Jerusalem his jurisdiction is more limited, but he retains the right to *pontificalia*. He is always an Italian, resident in Jerusalem, and is assisted by a French custodial vicar, a Spanish procurator and five counsellors, one English, French, German, Spanish and Italian.

CUSTOM. i. In canon law. Established usage having the force of law. It obtains such force solely by consent of ecclesiastical authority. For custom to become law or release from law it must be reasonable and have a prescription of at least 40 years. It is not reasonable if expressly reprobated in law. Custom is the best interpreter of law. Particular customs are not abrogated by new general legislation to the contrary, unless specially mentioned. The Code of Canon Law of 1918 abrogated all contrary customs except immemorial ones and those expressly permitted.

ii. Liturgical. Legitimate liturgical customs create an obligation of observance along with that of the rubrics and decrees of the S.R.C. To be legitimate a custom must be reasonable, not expressly reprobated by authority, have a prescription both of extent and time (14 or 100 years or time immemorial, according to the case), and be accepted by the competent ecclesiastical authority. In practice many usages are dignified with the name and honour of customs that do not fulfil these conditions.

CUSTOS (Lat., custodians). A superior official of the Franciscans, having differing duties and responsibilities in each branch of the order. Among the Friars Minor a *custos regiminis* (governing custos) was in charge of a custody or small province and had the rights and duties of a provincial; he is now called a commissary. The name was also used for the member of a chapter who held the cure of souls attached to the church (corresponding to the French archpriest), and is still so used in some countries.

CYPRUS, THE CHURCH IN. The Church of Cyprus was founded by St. Paul and extended by St. Barnabas. Already in the year 431 it was recognized as independent of the metropolitan see of Antioch; and it is today an autocephalous unit of the separated Orthodox Church to which, except for a number of Moslems, practically all the Cypriots belong. There are a few Catholics of Latin rite and about 1,000 Maronites; the last named have a bishop, who lives in Syria where the greater part of his diocese is situated.

CZECHOSLOVAKIA, THE CHURCH IN. This state now consists of Bohemia, Moravia and Slovakia, whose inhabitants are Czechs and Slovaks, with minorities of German and Hungarian origin, about 14 million in all; 80 per cent are Catholics, but both Protestantism and secularism are strong. After the state was formed in 1918 there was a nationalist schism among the Czechs. There are 2 ecclesiastical provinces, Prague and Olomuc, with 4 suffragan dioceses and 5 others immediately subject to the Holy See, and a Byzantine-rite diocese of Ruthenians. Since world-war II there has been a certain discrimination against religion. Purely charitable and spiritual associations, as well as Catholic students' organizations and trade-union groups, have been declared illegal, and church schools confiscated; clergy, teachers and others have been arrested and deported on faked charges of subversive propaganda.

D

DALMATIC. The vestment proper to a deacon. It reaches to the knees at least, has wide short sleeves, and is open at the sides, and is of the same material and colour as the vestments of the officiating priest; it is ornamented with two narrow vertical strips (*clavi*) from the shoulders to the hem, joined at the bottom by two cross strips. It was introduced from Dalmatia (whence its name) to Rome as a secular garment in the reign of Diocletian and is called in the ordination service "the garment of salvation, the vesture of gladness and the dalmatic of righteousness." It is not worn at penitential times, its place being taken by the folded chasuble. It is also worn by a cardinal, bishop or abbot under his chasuble at pontifical Mass. A dalmatic is part of the coronation regalia of the sovereigns of England.

DAME (Lat. *domina*, mistress). The title of a professed Benedictine, Cistercian or Bridgettine nun (*cf.*, dom).

DAMES OF ST. MAUR, The. Officially called the Congregation of the Holy Child Jesus; founded by Fr. Nicolas Barré in 1678, to provide a special body of trained teachers and conduct schools; they have spread from Europe to the foreign missions. Semi-enclosed; Little Office B.V.M. in choir. Their habit is that of French widows of the 17th century; a black gown with train, silk collar and coif, veil out of doors.

DAMNATION (Lat. *damnum*, loss). The state of eternal punishment and reprobation (*q.v.*).

DAMNIFICATION (late Lat. *damnificare*, to inflict injury). The voluntary unjust causing of damage to the person, property, reputation or spiritual welfare of another, but without involving, as regards property, the taking of any out of the owner's possession. For such damage restitution (*q.v.*) must so far as possible be made, not only to the extent of the willed injury, but also to cover such further damage as was foreseen; and this whether or no the offender has "got anything" by his unjust act.

DANCE OF DEATH, The. i. A mediæval morality play displaying the inevitability of death and judgement for all from pope to peasant.
ii. The same theme represented by painting (*e.g.*, in the *campo santo* of Pisa) or by engraving (*e.g.*, those of Holbein's designs) in a series covering the different classes of people.

DANCING. Dancing in itself is an innocent recreation. It is sinful only if and when the dance itself is immoral or when one's own character or that of the company is such as to make dancing a proximate occasion of sin. Dancing by boys takes place before the high altar of the cathedral of Seville at Corpus Christi, the Immaculate Conception and Carnival. This seems to be the only example of strictly religious dancing that Catholics have retained, although some of the movements of the ministers in sacred ceremonies (*e.g.*, of celebrant, deacon and subdeacon at high Mass) are in the nature of a formal dance. There is, however, observed annually on Whit Tuesday at Echternach in Luxemburg a penitential procession in honour of St. Willibrord. Those taking part proceed with a peculiar hopping or dancing motion in time to a traditional tune. The observance is probably very ancient, though it is not known before 1553; it is now particularly by way of intercession against epilepsy and associated maladies.

DANIEL (Heb., God's judge). A book of the O.T. (certain parts being deutero-canonical, *q.v.*), named from its chief character and traditional author. He was carried off to the royal court at Babylon in 605 B.C., and his wisdom became proverbial (*cf.*, Ezek. xxviii,

3). The first part of the book is historical (the Three Children in the furnace, the judgement on Nabuchodonosor, Baltasar's feast, the lions' den); the second records Daniel's visions, looking forward to Christ and to Antichrist; the stories of Susanna and the elders and of Bel and the dragon are appended. Daniel is named in the Roman Martyrology on July 31, and the last prophecy on Holy Saturday is taken from his third chapter.

DARK AGES, The. The period, variously estimated, which followed the fall of the Roman Empire in the West (end of the 4th century) and preceded the middle ages, which reached their culmination in the 13th. Popular opponents of the Church sometimes stretch the term to cover as well the whole of the period up to the Protestant Reformation.

DARK NIGHT OF THE SENSES. The name given by St. John-of-the-Cross to the period of transition from meditation to contemplation (*qq.v.*). It is marked by increasing inability to think or make many acts in prayer, by distaste for self-analysis and for any definite scheme of acquiring virtues, by persistent temptation against chastity or faith, perhaps also by scruples, or by sickness and trials from others. The multiplicity and intensity of these painful conditions is a fair indication of the heights to which God will lead the soul, if she is generous. It is called a night of the senses, because the soul is being made to dispense with the assistance and comfort even of the interior senses in time of prayer and to seek God by pure faith, which is a way of darkness and obscurity; also, because the creature is suffering through the seeming paralysis of its faculties and the many trials to which it is subjected.

DARK NIGHT OF THE SPIRIT. The soul that has passed through the dark night of the senses (*q.v.*) and attained contemplation, has still another purgation to undergo, far more intimate and searching, in immediate preparation for the spiritual marriage (*q.v.*). St. John-of-the-Cross calls it the dark night of the spirit. It generally comes after several years of contemplation, and itself lasts several years, with intermissions. It is purgative contemplation, sterile to the last degree, the soul experiencing acute desolation, because she seems to be abandoned by God, and at the same time feeling an intense yearning for him, which only serves to increase her pain of loss. It is the very brilliance of the divine light shed upon the soul that causes suffering: its strength blinds her, so to say, so that she has no consciousness of it; but it also illumines her to the very depths and makes her fearfully aware of her misery, helplessness and defects.

DATARIA, THE APOSTOLIC (Lat. *datio*, a giving). A curial office consisting of a

Cardinal Datary, with a subdatary, prefect and officials, whose competency is confined to the examination of candidates for papal benefices, drawing up documents for their collation, exacting the charges attached thereto and satisfying the claims of those with rights to pensions or other emoluments.

DAUGHTERS OF THE CROSS, The. An unenclosed congregation founded in 1832 by Mother Marie-Thérèsè Haze at Liège. They undertake any works of mercy in hospitals, prisons, schools, etc. Black habit. There are other congregations of this name, including that founded by St. Andrew Fournet and St. Elizabeth Bichier des Ages at Maillé in Poitou in 1806, for education and nursing.

DAUGHTERS OF OUR LADY HELP OF CHRISTIANS, The. The sister congregation of the Salesians, founded by St. John Bosco. They do much the same work for girls as the Salesians do for boys, and help the Salesians in their work also. They are found throughout the world.

DAUGHTERS OF WISDOM, The. (Fr. *Filles de la Sagesse*). Founded by St. Louis Grignion de Montfort in 1703 for all kinds of good works. Unenclosed; Little Office B.V.M. in choir. Grey habit, linen coif, neckerchief and apron; black cloak with hood in choir and outdoors.

DAWN, THE MASS AT. The second Mass of Christmas Day. Its proper refers to the worship of the shepherds and the flooding of the world with the light of the Prince of Peace. The station for this Mass was the church of St. Anastasia, who was martyred on Dec. 25, whence the commemoration of her in this Mass. The church was probably originally dedicated in honour of the *Anastasis* (Resurrection).

DAY HOURS (Lat. *Horæ Diurnæ*). i. All the "hours" of the Divine Office except Matins. With certain exceptions, at Prime and Compline, they all begin with Our Father and Hail Mary said in silence, then *Deus in adiutorium . . . (q.v.)*, followed by *Alleluia* or, from Septuagesima until Wednesday in Holy Week, *Laus tibi, Domine, rex æternæ gloriæ* ("Praise to thee, O Lord, king of eternal glory"); they end after the collect with *Dominus vobiscum: R. Et cum spiritu tuo. Benedicamus Domino: R. Deo gratias. Fidelium animæ per misericordiam Dei requiescant in pace. Amen* (The Lord be with you: And with thy spirit. Let us bless the Lord: Thanks be to God. May the souls of the Faithful through the mercy of God rest in peace); the Our Father in silence, if no other hour follows immediately. *See* each hour for its order.

ii. A book containing the same for all the year. usually with the addition of the Little Office B.V.M., the Office of the Dead, Gradual and Penitential Psalms, the commendation of a soul, other prayers and certain litanies and blessings.

DE AUXILIIS CONTROVERSY, The. A theological dispute in the 16th–17th century between the Dominicans and the Jesuits concerning the *auxilia* or helps of grace. Clement VIII appointed a commission which heard both sides and deliberated for nine years without coming to a conclusion. How divine Providence can assist man through grace and yet leave the freedom of the will inviolate is still unexplained: but the fact remains.

DE CONDIGNO (Lat., out of worthiness). This is the denomination of one kind of merit *(q.v.)*, in which the reward is due either (*a*) in justice, in that the deed is in itself adequate to the reward; or (*b*) in fidelity, in virtue of a promise of such a reward for the deed although it is beyond its natural deserts. Thus a workman merits his pay *de condigno*. So in the sphere of grace *(q.v.)* the good works of the just merit grace and eternal life *de condigno*.

DE CONGRUO (Lat., out of suitability). Another kind of merit *(q.v.)*, in which there is no absolute claim to the reward, either in justice or in fidelity, although it is recognized that such reward is becoming. Thus if a successful business man gives a park to his native city, he does not establish a claim to any "honour," but no one is surprised, least of all himself, when he receives a knighthood. So, in the sphere of grace *(q.v.)* the sinner can merit justification *(q.v.) de congruo*, but not *de condigno (q.v.)*.

DE HÆRETICO COMBURENDO (Lat., concerning the burning of a heretic). An Act of Parliament, 2 Henry IV c. 15, directed against the Lollards *(q.v.)*. "Whereas . . . diverse false and perverse people of a certain new sect . . . do perversely and maliciously . . . preach and teach these days openly and privily divers new doctrines and wicked heretical and erroneous opinions, etc. If any person upon the said wicked preachings, etc., be before the bishop convicted and do refuse duly to abjure . . . then the sheriff [or mayor, etc.] shall receive the same persons and cause them to be burnt before the people in a high place that such punishment may strike fear to the minds of others." Certainly it appears that Wycliff's teachings were a danger to the peace of the realm (*cf.*, Oldcastle's activities); but the Act was sponsored by Henry IV to gain the support of the Church in England, he being notoriously a usurper, and many of the higher clergy fearing the rapacity of Parliament and the evangelical fervour of some of the common people; nevertheless it was only the promulgation in England of the then common law of Christendom. So, though this was the only statute on the subject in force from Henry IV to Edward VI, and again under Philip and Mary, heretics had been burned before 1401, and were again after its respective repeals under Edward VI and Elizabeth.

DE LA SALLE BROTHERS, The. The Christian Brothers (q.v.).

DE NUMERO PARTICIPANTIUM (Lat., of the number that takes part). An active as opposed to a titular office, e.g., a protonotary apostolic d.n.p.

DE PROFUNDIS (Lat., Out of the depths). Ps. cxxix, of which these are the opening words. It is one of the Penitential and Gradual Psalms (qq.v.), and in the Divine Office is said at Vespers on Wednesdays and of the Dead, and at the second Vespers of Christmas. It is the prayer for the dead used more than any other, and is said for their repose on both liturgical and extra-liturgical occasions. In some places it is the custom so to say it at the ringing of a bell about 9 p.m., daily; there is an apostolic indulgence of 100 days attached to this practice.

DEACON (Gr. servant). The second of the major orders and the third of the hierarchical orders.

i. In the Western church the duties of the deacon are to minister at the altar and to preach. His offices are in practice chiefly ceremonial; he sings the gospel at high Mass and assists the celebrant generally: incenses him and the choir, hands him the altarbread, pours wine into the chalice which he offers with the celebrant, removes and replaces the pall, receives the kiss of peace and gives it to the subdeacon, etc. He can also administer holy communion and baptize solemnly with permission in case of necessity. The order is bestowed by the laying-on of the bishop's hands with appropriate words ("Receive the Holy Ghost . . .," etc.); also the stole, dalmatic (q.v.) and gospel-book are delivered.

ii. In the Eastern churches, especially the Byzantine, many deacons never proceed to the priesthood but assist as curates in the parishes; such is called a "deacon of office." The services of a deacon are theoretically necessary to a celebration of the Liturgy, though in fact his place is often taken to a certain extent by a minor cleric or a layman, but not, as in the West, by another priest. The liturgical dress of the Byzantine deacon is the sticharion, epimanikia and orarion (qq.v.), and the ripidion is his badge of office.

DEACONESS. An institution of the early Church which set aside certain widows and maidens of mature age to assist at the instruction and baptism of women, to wait on the bride at marriage, visit the sick and prisoners, etc. Their "ordination" by an epis-copal laying-on of hands gave them an official standing in the Church, which by abuse in certain places seems to have obtained almost the recognition of holy orders (condemned by the 19th canon of the Council of Nicæa). The office was extinct in the West by the 10th century, but remained longer in the East, where its ecclesiastical pretensions were even more exaggerated (cf., Consecration of a Virgin).

DEAD, BAPTISM OF THE, which was practised by some heretical sects, is condemned by the Church as meaningless, superstitious and sacrilegious, for the dead cannot profit thereby.

DEAD, MASS FOR THE. The souls detained in Purgatory can be aided by the suffrages of the faithful, but especially by the acceptable sacrifice of the altar (Council of Trent, sess. xxv). Any Mass can be offered for the dead, but *the* Mass for the Dead has a special liturgy containing beautiful and appropriate prayers, including the hymn *Dies Irae*. It also has a proper preface, which summarizes the grounds of Christian resignation in face of death.

DEAD, PRAYERS FOR THE. It is an article of faith (q.v.) that the souls in Purgatory can be helped by our prayers (Council of Trent, sess. xxv). The practice of praying for the dead, of which there are traces in the Old Testament (cf. II Macabees xii, 46), is established in the oldest Christian tradition. It was familiar to Tertullian and Augustine, and is clearly exposed in the inscriptions of the Catacombs and in the most ancient liturgies. It is a universal custom amongst Catholics, who are in the habit of saying special prayers (many of them enriched with indulgences, q.v.) for the departed; Ps. cxxix, De Profundis (Out of the depths), is the most common of such prayers.

DEADLY SINS, THE SEVEN. A more popular but less accurate name for the capital sins, viz., pride, covetousness, lust, anger, gluttony, envy, sloth. They are the source of all sins, since the inordinate attachment to any temporal good may give rise to inordinate ways of pursuing or enjoying it.

DEAN (Lat. decanus, one having authority over ten). i. The usual name for the chief dignitary of a diocesan or collegiate chapter, as in Ireland and France; but sometimes second to the provost. He is appointed by the Holy See but he has no greater powers than the other canons, except in certain German dioceses. He is president of the chapter meetings and has a casting vote, has right of precedence, and certain liturgical duties. In some monasteries the prior is called dean (cf., Rule of St. Benedict, cap. xxi), and the name is given to the president of the professors of a faculty in a university.

ii. Rural. A senior priest who has the

oversight of a group of parishes. His duties and rights vary from diocese to diocese, but always include the summoning and presiding at periodical (generally monthly) meetings of the clergy of the deanery (cf., Vicar Forane).

iii. The senior member of any body, e.g., commonly of diplomatic representatives. In this sense the French form *doyen* is often used.

DEAN OF THE SACRED COLLEGE, The, is the senior cardinal-bishop, who becomes bishop of Ostia but retains also the see previously held. He has the usual rights and duties of the president of a body; he consecrates a new pope if the elected is only a priest and presides at his coronation (he is generally assistant priest at the Mass), and has the privilege of the *pallium* at all functions.

DEATH is the extinction of life in the body, through the departure of the soul, and takes place when the body is no longer adapted to life. Death of the soul is a figure of speech, meaning that the soul is turned away from its true end, God, by mortal sin; the soul cannot die, but in its state of disembodiment, from death until the general resurrection, its activties are curtailed.

DEBT. The discharge of a just debt is an obligation of justice. If by the passage of time its recovery has been barred at civil law, it still remains a debt in conscience and must be paid.

DEBT, MARRIAGE. An expression for the sexual intercourse due between husband and wife, borrowed from 1 Cor. vii, 3. See CONJUGAL RIGHTS.

DECADE. A fifth, or one mystery, of the ordinary rosary *(q.v.)*, consisting of one Our Father, ten Hail Marys and one Glory, with meditation on one or other of the mysteries; the corresponding beads on a rosary.

DECALOGUE, The. The Ten Commandments *(q.v.)*.

DECEASED WIFE'S SISTER. The diriment impediment of affinity in the first degree of the collateral line exists between a man and his deceased wife's sister. It is an ecclesiastical impediment which the Church can and often does dispense.

DECEIT. Any concealment, perversion or denial of the truth expressed for the purpose of misleading another, though not necessarily to gain any advantage. It is to be distinguished from fraud *(q.v.)*. This is always a sin against the virtue of truth; it may also be a sin against charity (e.g., using deceit to avoid helping another in need), or against justice (e.g., should the deceit harm another in his person or in his possessions).

DECLARATION, THE ROYAL. The profession made upon accession to the throne of England by all sovereigns from William III to Edward VII which, in offensive terms, repudiated the Mass, transubstantiation and veneration of our Lady and the saints. A harmless formula was substituted in 1910, largely owing to the efforts of Baron Braye. It must be distinguished from the coronation oath, which is to maintain the "Protestant reformed religion as established by law."

DECLARATION OF NULLITY. If a marriage is invalid owing to a diriment impediment or lack of consent or defect of form, it is for the Church alone to declare such nullity *(q.v.)*. The state has no right to decree the invalidity of marriage in the case of baptized persons. Nullity causes of first instance are dealt with in the diocesan courts, either summarily or with full judicial procedure, according to the class of case, appeals being heard in the metropolitan or Roman courts. The Defender of the Marriage Bond must always be present at the hearing of a nullity suit.

DECLARATIVE forms of absolution *(q.v.)*, as opposed to the deprecatory, are used in the Western, Armenian and other churches.

DECOLLATION (Lat., beheading). An imperfectly acclimatized word sometimes used for the feast of the Beheading of St. John the Baptist on Aug. 29.

DECORATIONS, PONTIFICAL, conferred usually on lay people who have distinguished themselves in a temporal manner in the cause of Christ, are titles of nobility, orders of knighthood *(qq.v.)* and minor decorations (medals and crosses).

DECREE. An ordinance, edict or decision set forth by ecclesiastical authority. The decrees of a pope or of a general council are universally binding; those of a Roman congregation in a specific case are binding on those concerned, but not necessarily on others; those of a national or provincial synod must be approved by the Holy See before being put into force. The personal (as opposed to synodal) decrees of a bishop lapse with his death.

DECRETALS. Decisions of the popes given in various forms on matters of discipline, i.e., canon law, but not always binding on the whole Church. The earliest decretals (more often called constitutions) were letters to bishops in reply to questions or reports, which had the force of law, so that all bishops of the Western church had to have collections of them. They were collected and collated by a Camaldolese monk, Gratian, in the middle of the 12th century *(Decretum Gratiani)*. But The Decretals generally indicates the collection of laws made by St. Raymund of Peñafort in 1230-34 by order of Pope Gregory IX, and subsequently added to and worked over by numerous commentators. All these cumbersome and confusing works were swept away when the new Codex Iuris Canonici (*q.v.*) came into force in 1918. "Decretist" was formerly a name for a doctor in canon law and "decretalist" for one particularly learned in St. Raymond's collection.

DECRETALS OF PSEUDO-ISIDORE, The. See the FALSE DECRETALS.

DEDICATION, FEAST OF THE. i. The anniversary of the dedication of a consecrated church is observed therein as a double feast of the first class with an octave. A candle should be burned before each consecration cross on the feast itself during the whole day beginning at first Vespers. Some dioceses and religious institutes celebrate the dedication of all consecrated churches on the same day (*e.g.*, throughout Ireland on Oct. 23; throughout the Order of Preachers on Oct. 22; throughout the diocese of Clifton on Oct. 16). The dedication of a cathedral church is always celebrated separately and by all churches in its diocese as a double of the first class with an octave (regulars with a proper calendar omit the octave). The feasts of the dedication of the major Roman basilicas, St. John Lateran (cathedral of the world; Nov. 9), St. Peter's and St. Paul's (Nov. 18), and St. Mary Major's (Our Lady of the Snow, Aug. 5) are observed throughout the Western church.

ii. A Jewish festival, also known as the feast of the Machabees and of Lights, instituted by Judas Machabeus in memory of the purification of the Temple in 164 B.C., after its pollution by Antiochus Epiphanes. It is observed on Dec. 12.

DEDICATION OF A CHURCH, The, is the setting of it apart for divine worship. This may be done by a simple blessing or by solemn consecration. All churches, public- and semi-public oratories, must be at least blessed, with the rite of prayers, aspersions and Mass provided in the "Rituale," by a bishop or a delegated priest. In case of pollution it may be reconciled by a priest. A church so blessed has no right to the liturgical feast of the Dedication (*q.v.*). Consecration (*q.v.*) must be performed by a bishop.

DEDICATIONS OF CHURCHES. It is commonly said that such and such a church is dedicated to our Lady or to St. Antony or to the Assumption, etc., and custom allows the expression, but in fact every church is dedicated to God and to God only; the names by which they are known are the names of those saints or mysteries of religion in whose honour or under whose patronage they are dedicated; *e.g.*, the cathedral of Canterbury was dedicated to our Lord only (Christ Church), that of Southwark is now dedicated to God in honour of St. George. Dedications of new churches to-day are generally chosen on account of popular devotion or

local association. In England the Sacred Heart, our Lady, St. Joseph and St. Patrick are the most popular and St. Michael, St. Peter, the two St. Johns and St. Anne are common. Among local saints are Lawrence of Canterbury (Sidcup), Mildred (Minster), Werburg (Chester), Aldhelm (Sherborne), Felix (Felixstowe), Petroc (Padstow), Ia (Saint Ives), Piran (Truro), Tudwal (Barmouth), Teilo (Tenby), Samson (Caldey and Guernsey islands), Godric (Durham), Maughold (Ramsey), Herbert (Windermere), Walstan (Costessey), Richard (Chichester). See TITULAR, *i.*

DEDUCTION. An argumentation whereby the mind proceeding from a knowledge of universals draws a conclusion concerning one of the particulars. The process is based upon the principle, *Dictum de omni; dictum de nullo:* whatever is affirmed of a universal (or class) is affirmed of all contained under that universal or class; and whatever is denied of a class is denied of all particulars contained under that class. See SYLLOGISM, INDUCTION.

DEFECT, IRREGULARITY FROM (Lat. *ex defectu*), is the state of being incapable of receiving holy orders or exercising their functions (see IRREGULARITY) incurred by the following: the illegitimate; those with bodily defect; the bigamous; those lacking "lenity"; the infamous; those who are or have been epileptics, insane or possessed (*qq.v.*). See also IMPEDIMENTS TO ORDINATION.

DEFENDANT. In canon law judicial trials must take place in the ecclesiastical court of defendant's domicile. The defendant when summoned must attend either in person or by procurator. The judge may require personal attendance. Culpable failure to appear when cited constitutes judicial contumacy, and the trial may proceed with the defendant absent. In criminal causes the defendant must have an advocate, either of his own choice or appointed by the judge. Defendant may appeal against adverse sentence, such appeal to be lodged within 10 days.

DEFENDER OF THE BOND [OF MARRIAGE] (Lat. *Defensor Vinculi [Matrimonii]*). Such an one is appointed in every diocese and his presence is necessary at every case in which the validity of a marriage is called in question; his business is to sustain the marriage by all lawful means. If the court declares the marriage null, he *must* appeal to the higher court; if the second court upholds the nullity he is not bound to appeal again, but may do so. But in a few cases where certain facts are certainly and clearly proved (*e.g.*, that the reputed marriage took place in a registry office, the parties being Catholics), the defender may consent to a declaration of nullity without appeal.

DEFENDER OF THE FAITH (Lat. *Fid[ei] Def[ensor]*). A personal title conferred on King Henry VIII by Pope Leo X, in 1521, in acknowledgement of the king's services to religion in writing a defence of the seven sacraments and papal supremacy (*Assertio Septem Sacramentorum*) against the teachings of Luther. It is still used as part of the style and titles of the sovereigns of England by virtue of an Act of Parliament of 1543. The same title was bestowed on King James V of Scotland by Pope Paul III.

DEFINITION. i. An answer to the question, "What is it?" 1. (*a*) Nominal definition: that which explains what a thing is by a term, as the first cause is a nominal definition of God (distinct from etymological, which explains the origins of a term). (*b*) Real definition: that which explains what is the essence or nature of a thing in itself, as: "Man is a rational animal." 2. (*a*) Intrinsic: that which explains what a thing is by its inherent principles, as: "Man is a composite of organic body and a rational soul." (*b*) Extrinsic: that which explains what a thing is by principles, not inherent, but to which it is somehow related, as: "The human soul is created by God in his own image, for eternal bliss." 3. (*a*) Essential: that which explains what a thing is by those intrinsic principles which constitute it and distinguish it from all else. It is either physical (or natural) if it explains a thing by its real constituent principles, as: "Man is a composite of organic body and a rational soul": or it is metaphysical if it explains a thing by its genus and difference, as: "Man is a rational animal." (*b*) Descriptive: that which explains a thing otherwise than by constituent principles. It is twofold: Proper, which explains a thing by its attributes or properties, as: "Man is *an animal* capable of laughter"; Accidental, which explains a thing by the enumeration of certain accidents, as: "Man is a biped that walks erect," etc. Rules of definition: (1) A definition must be clearer than the thing defined. Thence three corollaries: (*a*) the defined should be excluded from the definition; (*b*) a definition should give the proximate *genus* of the thing defined and its ultimate difference; (*c*) a definition must not be negative. (2) A definition should contain neither more nor less than what the defined contains, so that the definition and the defined should be convertible, as: "Man is a rational animal: every rational animal is a man."

ii. Theological. A formal statement of doctrine, concerning faith or morals, made by the pope as universal teacher, or by an œcumenical council (*q.v.*) in union with him. Such a statement may be prepared by a long process of purely human work, but when it is finally issued it is guaranteed infallible. Hence it is definitive: there is no appeal against it either now or hereafter. It binds all the faithful at all times, and is not subject to revision. A definition is not the statement of a new belief, but a declaration that the doctrine in question has always been a part of the deposit (*q.v.*) of faith. Sometimes the doctrine has been explicitly held from the beginning and is defined to allay subsequent controversy or the attacks of heretics (*e.g.*, the definition of the divinity of our Lord in 325); or it may that, having hitherto been implicitly believed as contained in other truths explicitly believed, it must now be held explicitly by all (*e.g.*, the definition of the Council of Chalcedon that our Lord is *in* two natures). Truths have generally become explicit before definition, *e.g.*, the Immaculate Conception.

DEFORMITY, as irregularity. See BODILY DEFECT.

DEFRAUDING HUSBAND OR WIFE. One who without just cause withholds conjugal rights (*q.v.*) from his or her partner (1 Cor. vii, 3–5), such being a grave offence against justice.

DEFRAUDING LABOURERS OF THEIR WAGES. A sin which cries to Heaven for vengeance (*cf.*, James v, 4); its most usual form is for the employer to take advantage of the needs of his employees to sweat or underpay them. He is bound to make restitution (*q.v.*).

DEFRAUDING THE STATE. See PENAL LAW.

DEGRADATION. An ecclesiastical vindicative penalty by which a cleric is deposed from his office, deprived perpetually of the clerical habit, and reduced to lay estate. It can only be inflicted for crimes for which such penalty is expressly laid down in canon law, or when a cleric, already deposed and unfrocked, still continues to cause grave scandal for one year. Degradation is either verbal, by simple edict, but having immediate juridical effect, or real, when carried out in solemn form according to the "Pontificale Romanum." The use of the latter is of very rare occurrence, and its last recorded use is believed to be in 1853 when a priest was publicly degraded in Poland, handed over to the civil power, and banished to Siberia for murder. After his death it was discovered that he suffered innocently on behalf of another, of whose guilt he knew only under the seal of confession. Reduction to lay estate cannot deprive a priest of the sacerdotal character and he continues to be bound to celibacy and recital of the Divine Office.

DEGREES OF HUMILITY, The. An ascetical prescription of the Rule of St. Benedict (cap. vii) whereby the monk "will presently arrive at that love of God which, being perfect, casteth out fear; whereby he shall begin to keep, without labour, and as it were naturally and by custom, all those precepts which he had hitherto observed through fear." The degrees are (a) that a man, always keeping the fear of God before his eyes, avoid all forgetfulness (e.g., that he is always beheld from Heaven by God); (b) that a man love not his own will; (c) that a man for the love of God submit himself to his superior in all obedience; (d) that if in this obedience hard and contrary things are done to him, he should embrace them patiently; (e) not to hide from one's abbot any of the evil thoughts or sins committed in secret; (f) to be contented with the meanest and worst of everything and to esteem himself a bad and worthless labourer; (g) that he should not only call but believe himself lower and viler than all; (h) to do nothing except what is authorized by the common rule of the monastery; (i) to refrain his tongue from speaking, keeping silence until a question be asked him; (j) not to be easily moved and prompt to laughter; (k) when a monk speaketh, to do so gently, gravely, with few and reasonable words; (l) that the monk, not only in his heart but also in his very exterior, always show his humility to all. Some of these rules necessarily refer only to monks, but in principle they represent Christian teaching of humility for all. The first four degrees relate to the will, the second four to the intellect, and the remainder to the outward man. Of them St. Thomas says, "Humility subsists essentially in the appetite . . . but its regulating power lies in the knowing faculty . . . and out of the interior dispositions of humility spring certain external manifestations. . . ."

DEISIS (Gr. δέησις, petition). i. An impetratory prayer, e.g., the clauses of the great and little *synapte* and of the *ektenes* in the Liturgy and other services of the Byzantine rite.

ii. An image of our Lord in judgement, our Lady and St. John Baptist, sometimes found in the apse of a Byzantine church and nearly always in the place of honour on the *iconastasis* (cf., the carvings of the Last Judgement at the principal entrance of certain Western cathedrals, e.g., Amiens).

DEISM. A word, unknown to antiquity and to the middle ages, designating the system of those who admit a God and yet reject his revelation. It is a form of rationalism, developed mainly in England in the 18th century by Shaftesbury, Tindal and Bolingbroke (cf., Theism).

DEITY. In ordinary language means the same as God, but in theology there is a distinction between God and Deity: although they are in reality one and the same, yet their signification is different. God is concrete and signifies the divine essence in the possessor, and, as such, can stand for a divine person; Deity is abstract and signifies

the divine essence as an abstract form, that is, as apart from the possessor, and as such cannot stand for a divine person.

DELATION. Denouncement, as when a dangerous book is delated to the Holy Office or a teacher of heresy to his bishop. See DENUNCIATION.

DELEGATE, APOSTOLIC. A papal representative in a country having no regular diplomatic relations with the Holy See. His duties are purely ecclesiastical, being to watch over the state of the church in the territory assigned, and to keep the Holy See informed in regard thereto. He may give final decisions in appeals from diocesan and metropolitan courts, saving the right of appellants to elect to appeal direct to Rome first. Delegates apostolic are also appointed temporarily for special undertakings. They have precedence over all ordinaries except those that are cardinals. In 1947 the permanent delegations were: African missions, South Africa, the Antilles, Australasia, Belgian Congo, Bulgaria, Canada and Newfoundland, Palestine, Great Britain, Pakistan, Ethiopia, Greece, Indochina, Indonesia, Iraq, Japan, Mexico, Persia, the Philippines, Syria, Turkey, and the United States.

DEMIURGE (Gr. δημιουργός artisan). A word used by Plato to designate the Maker of the Universe, afterwards taken over by the Gnostics, Marcionites, Paulicians and other heretics to indicate the imperfect God of the Old Dispensation or the evil power who was responsible for matter, such being their teaching.

DEMOCRACY. A system of government in which the sovereign power is vested in the people as a whole and is exercised directly by them or by representatives chosen by them. It is generally agreed that to deserve the epithet "democratic," in such a government the people must have some effective control over what their representatives do, and minorities of all kinds, political, religious, racial, must enjoy equality of treatment with the majority, freedom of expression and action, and not suffer from any discrimination. There is nothing sacred about democracy as such: there can be bad and oppressive democracies as well as good ones; if the voice of the people is sometimes the voice of God, it can at other times be the voice of the Devil. The Catholic Church does not undertake to decide which is the best among diverse forms of government; she condemns any which is unjust, irreligious or immoral in its action. Individual Catholics who claim that a good democracy is the form of government most in consonance with Christianity do so because they believe it is the most likely (or least unlikely) to respect human rights (q.v.). For example, "To express his own views of the duties and sacrifices imposed on him, and not to be compelled to obey without being heard—these are two rights of the citizen whose expression is implied in the term democracy" (Pope Pius XII). See PRINCE; SOVEREIGNTY OF THE PEOPLE.

DEMON (Gr. δαίμων, deity). A name commonly given to the fallen angels or evil spirits satellite to Satan, who is The Demon (*cf.* Devil).

DEMONIAC. A person possessed by a demon or evil spirit. The Gospels give several instances of persons thus possessed and healed by Christ (Matt. x, 1; Mark iii, 10; Luke ix, 1, 10, 17). The suggestion that these persons were simply epileptics, or sufferers from some similar complaint, and that the reference of Christ and of the Apostles to demons is due either to ignorance of natural phenomena or to accommodation to popular illusion, must be rejected by Catholics. See POSSESSION.

DEMONSTRATION. An argumentation which deduces a conclusion from certain and evident premisses. Demonstration therefore necessarily implies that the premisses are indemonstrable, either immediately or mediately. (*a*) Demonstration *propter quid:* that which deduces its conclusion from principles which are self-evident *per se nota* and absolutely first or are the proper and adequate reason of the conclusion demonstrated, as when the eternity of God is deduced from his immutability. (*b*) Demonstration *quia* proceeds (1) either from principles which are not absolutely first, as when a cause is known from its effects (for these are not absolutely or in themselves prior to the cause); or (2) proceeds from principles which are not the proper and adequate reason of the conclusion, although the latter is inferred with certainty, *e.g.*, if the eternity of God is demonstrated from the fact that God is Necessary Being. (*c*) Demonstration *a priori:* that which proceeds from cause to effects, from the universal to the particular; it may be either *propter quid* or *quia* (see above). (*d*) Demonstration *a posteriori:* that which proceeds from effects to cause, from particulars to the universal. (*e*) Direct demonstration proves a thing to be or not to be from positive principles manifesting to the mind a thing in itself in which we see its truth. (*f*) Indirect demonstration concludes a thing to be or not to be because otherwise absurdities would follow.

DENMARK, THE CHURCH IN. Catholicism was proscribed in Denmark from the Reformation till 1849 when freedom and political equality were extended to all faiths, Lutheranism remaining the state religion. The country, wherein the prestige of the Church increases rapidly, forms one diocese, with its see at Copenhagen; it numbers about 35,000 Catholics in 4 million people. The principal Danish see was formerly Roskilde.

DENOMINATION. A religious body (usually Christian), considered simply as a category into which a given person is classified, without reference to its religious implications.

DENUNCIATION of crime to the ecclesiastical authority is of obligation on all the faithful if grave harm would otherwise result to religion or public morals. Denunciation may be made in writing or orally to the ordinary, chancellor, rural dean or rector of the parish, and the denouncer must provide evidence for the Promotor of Justice. Malicious and frivolous denunciations are to be ignored; also anonymous denunciations which appear to have no solid foundation. Any of the faithful may and should, if necessary, denounce books against faith and morals to the ecclesiastical authorities, and the name of the denouncer is not to be revealed. Any of the faithful may denounce an invalid marriage. The crime of solicitation in confession must be denounced by the penitent, under penalty of excommunication, but false denunciation is a sin reserved to the Holy See and incurs excommunication likewise specially reserved to the Holy See.

DEO GRATIAS (Lat., Thanks be to God). A formula of thanksgiving frequently used throughout the Latin liturgies.

DEONTOLOGY. The branch of moral philosophy which deals with the science and study of duty and moral obligation, such as is adverted to in the expression "I ought."

DEPOSING POWER, The. The right of the Holy See under certain circumstances to depose sovereigns and absolve their subjects from allegiance. "Though certain popes have sometimes exercised this deposing power in extreme cases, they did so in accordance with the public law of the time and by the agreement of Christian nations, whose reverence for the pope as the supreme judge for Christ extended to his passing even civil judgement on princes and nations. But the present state of affairs is entirely different, and only malice can confound things and times so altered. . . . No one now thinks any more of the right of deposing princes which the Holy See formerly exercised; and the Supreme Pontiff even less than anyone" (Pope Pius IX to the Academy of the Catholic Religion, 1871). In the bull *Unam sanctam* Pope Boniface VIII declared in 1302 that "unbelieving kings and princes can in certain circumstances be deprived of the dominion which they have over believers, by sentence of the pope," and in mediæval Europe such power was freely admitted and in certain cases exercised. The last attempt to use it was directed against Queen Elizabeth of England by Pope St. Pius V's bull of deposition (*q.v.*). In 1818 the Holy See prescribed for bishops in Great Britain and her dominions a new form of the oath to be taken before consecration; it includes a clause (which goes back to 1793) declaring that nothing in the oath is at variance with allegiance to the Crown of these realms.

DEPOSIT OF FAITH, The. That body of revelation, containing truths to be believed and principles of conduct, which was given by Christ to the Apostles, to be preserved by them and their successors, with the guarantee of infallibility, for the guidance of the Church. It embraces the truths of both Scripture and Tradition. Some of its articles are explicit in Scripture, *e.g.*, the Word was made flesh; and others are implicit, *e.g.*, the Immaculate Conception (*q.v.*). It closed with the death of the last surviving apostle. It is entrusted to the infallible *magisterium* (*q.v.*) of the Church to preserve, unfold and defend the deposit. The word is found in 1 Tim. vi, 20, *Depositum custodi*, "Keep safe what has been entrusted to thee." It was not in common use before the 16th century, though the idea has always been familiar to the Church. The term is consecrated by the Council of the Vatican (sess. iii, cap. 4): "And the doctrine of faith which God revealed is proposed, not as a mere philosophical discovery to be elaborated by human minds, but as the divine deposit delivered by Christ to his spouse, to be by her faithfully guarded and infallibly declared."

DEPOSITION. i. An ecclesiastical vindicative penalty by which a cleric is suspended for life from office, dignities, pensions, etc., and is rendered incapable of further preferment. The ordinary is to make some provision out of charity for those without means of livelihood. Deposition can only be inflicted in cases of great gravity expressly mentioned in law. A pope cannot be deposed from his office. An heretical pope necessarily ceases to be head of the Church, for by his heresy he is no longer a member thereof; in the event of his still claiming the Roman see a general council, improperly so called because without the pope, could remove him. But this is not deposition, since by his own act he is no longer pope. In other forms of wrong-doing he remains a member of the visible Church and does not differ from any other sinful ruler whose lawful commands must be obeyed. The Holy See can depose a bishop for a grave crime, the pope only or his delegate being competent to try him. The pope can also depose a bishop at will, but it must be for some very grave reason and for the good of the Church—as after the Concordat of 1801, when Pope Pius VII removed all the bishops of France from their sees. Patriarchs of Eastern rites have the power to depose a subject bishop

guilty of crime without reference to the Holy See.

ii. Burial. Used in the "Martyrology" for the day of death of a saint.

iii. An image of the removal of our Lord's body from the cross.

DEPOSITION, BULL OF. A bull of Pope St. Pius V, *Regnans in excelsis*, 1570, whereby Elizabeth, "pretended Queen of England," was declared excommunicate, deprived of the kingdom which she claimed, and all her subjects discharged from their allegiance; this because she claimed headship of the Church in England (this was mis-stated), had adopted Calvanism (this was mistaken), oppressed Catholics and coerced her subjects into heresy and repudiation of the Holy See, contrary to her coronation oath. All who should obey her were involved in the excommunication, but the operation of the bull was later suspended until English Catholics could be released from the impossible position in which this put them. The bull seems to have been issued under the erroneous belief that the bulk of the people were wholeheartedly devoted to the Faith; it resulted in increased oppression for the faithful Catholic minority and the aggravation of those controversies about oaths and tests which vexed and weakened their body from the oath of obedience of 1606 until Emancipation in 1829. The suspicion which it helped to cast on the civil loyalty of Catholics has persisted to this day. See DEPOSING POWER.

DEPOSITION, or REPOSITION, MASS OF. The Mass celebrated at the end of the Forty Hours' devotion, when the Blessed Sacrament ceases to be exposed and is returned to the tabernacle.

DEPOSITION OF OUR LADY, The. A former name for the feast of the Assumption.

DEPRECATORY forms of absolution (*q.v.*), as opposed to the indicative, are in use in most of the dissident Eastern churches (except the Russian) and are valid as they express the idea of judicial pronouncement.

DERIA. The Latin name of the see of Derry (*q.v.*). Adjective: *Derriensis*.

DERRY (*Derriensis*). An Irish see, suffragan of Armagh, founded in the 13th century; it was administered by vicars for most of the 17th century. It comprises nearly all county Derry with parts of Donegal and Tyrone. The bishop's residence, cathedral and diocesan college are at Derry; there is no chapter of canons. The patrons of the diocese are St. Colmkille (Columba, June 9) and St. Eugene (Aug. 23) who is also titular of the cathedral. Irish name: Doire.

DESCENT INTO HELL, The. The fifth article of the Apostles' Creed is: "He [Christ] descended into hell." Of this the Church teaches that at his death the soul of Christ went to Limbo (*q.v.*) where the souls of the just were detained until he should have opened the Kingdom of Heaven to them, which was done at his ascension (*cf.*, Eph. iv, 9; 1 Peter iii, 18–20).

DESECRATION is the deprivation of the sacred character inhering in a place or thing on account of its having been consecrated or solemnly blessed. A fixed altar is desecrated if the *mensa* is separated from its support, and any altar or altar-stone if a large or anointed part is broken off or if the relics are removed or the sepulchre opened, except by authority for a legitimate purpose. A chalice or paten is desecrated by profane usage or by damage sufficient to make it useless; regilding does not desecrate. A church is desecrated if the greater part of the outer walls are destroyed at any one time, or if additions are made at one time exceeding in extent the original building; temporary conversion to profane usage does not involve desecration unless there is also violation (*q.v.*). Objects which may or should receive a blessing are not liable to desecration but may suffer loss of blessing (*q.v.*) and of indulgences attached. A church may be deliberately abandoned to decent profane purposes; the Acts of the Church of Milan (Part I, p. 135) contains a form of liturgical procedure.

DESERT. An institution peculiar to the Carmelites consisting of a monastery in a retired place with a small resident community, to which other friars might retire for a year at a time to live almost as hermits. The life resembled that of Carthusians but was even more severe and more time was devoted to mental prayer. To-day of over twenty "deserts" only one remains in use, at Rigada near Santander, Spain. The first desert was founded by the Discalced friars in 1592; the institution never flourished among the Calced.

DESIGN, THE ARGUMENT FROM. The 5th argument of St. Thomas for the existence of God. It runs thus: All things in the world act for a common end which is the good, the unity and the beauty of the universe. Wherefore it is evident that they tend towards and attain that end not by chance but intentionally. But many of these things are void of any knowledge whatsover: wherefore they cannot of themselves direct themselves to the aforesaid end. They are therefore directed to this end by a governing mind, just as an arrow is directed to a mark by an archer. Therefore there exists a cause which directs and governs all things. This cause is God.

DESIRE. A craving, a yearning, a feeling of want; the mental state of uneasiness awakened by the representation of an absent good. Desire is not free unless consented to or ratified (*cf.*, Passions).

DESIRE, BAPTISM OF, is one of the two possible substitutes for Baptism (*q.v.*) of water. When it is not possible thus to be baptized, an act of perfect contrition or pure love of God will supply the omission. Such acts are a perfect and ultimate disposition calling for the infusion of sanctifying grace, and at least implicitly include a desire and intention to receive Baptism of water should occasion offer. Infants are not capable of Baptism of desire. An heathen, believing, even though in a confused way, in a God whose will should be done and desiring to do that will whatever it may be, probably has Baptism of desire. It may reasonably be assumed that vast numbers of persons unbaptized by water have thus been rendered capable of enjoying the Beatific Vision. See BLOOD.*

DESOLATION. i. The absence of consolation, sensible or spiritual; hence the same as aridity (*q.v.*).

ii. Applied especially to the intensest kind of aridity, in which the soul is not only dry but feels herself abandoned by God, and so shares the anguish of our Lord on the cross, when he cried: "My God, my God, why hast thou forsaken me?" It is the trial proper to the dark night of the spirit (*q.v.*).

iii. Of our Lady or Maria Desolata. A popular devotion (*q.v.*) in honour of the sorrows of Mary observed in some churches, especially those of the Jesuits, on Good Friday evening.

DESPAIR. A wilful rejection of hope (*q.v.*) in that one judges the duties necessary to obtain eternal life impossible to fulfil. Despair is a mortal sin when it arises from distrust of God's goodness and fidelity; venial when due to melancholy or to fear of one's own weakness.

DESTINY. In Catholic philosophy destiny means the ordering of secondary causes that they produce their effects in accordance with the divine providence. It is understood by the Fatalists to be a blind necessity binding all things and all their activities. Such a view destroys free-will (*cf.*, Fate).

DESTROYER OF HERESIES. "Rejoice, O Virgin Mary, for thou alone hast destroyed all heresies." This acclamation, which forms part of the tract of the common Mass of our Lady after Septuagesima and is used elsewhere in the liturgy, refers to her divine motherhood, belief in which is incompatible with false belief about the person of her Son (*cf.*, Nestorianism, Theotokos).

DETACHMENT. An ascetic indifference to creatures (*q.v.*), not absolute but relative to the affection had for God and divine things. True detachment consists not in a negation of affection for creatures (all of which have their part in God) but rather in an enlightened and just sense of proportion; it is

---

* See also NECESSARY TO SALVATION and NECESSARY, NECESSITY.—*Publisher*, 1997.

exercised in respect of material success, wealth, "good fortune," not because these things are not good in their kind and degree but on account of their difference in kind and relative unimportance in the destiny of the human being considered as a whole. But detachment of will is the hardest, most necessary, and most meritorious detachment; the fully detached person leaves *himself* unreservedly in God's hands, "not as I will but as thou wilt": he asks nothing and refuses nothing. Recollection (*q.v.* i.) and detachment are closely allied.

DETERMINATION OF BEING. That which modifies in any way whatsoever some other thing. Thus: an idea is a determination of the mind, virtue a determination of the soul, colour of a wall, etc.

DETERMINANTS OF MORALITY. Those conditions which determine the goodness or badness of an action, namely, the formal object, the end in view, and the circumstances. For a good action, all these must be good; one evil vitiates the whole act.

DETERMINISM. The doctrine that teaches every effect is determined in its causes so that everything comes to be necessarily. It does not exclude spontaneity of action or a certain deliberation but it excludes freewill in that the doctrine suppresses all contingency. Intellectual determinism teaches the irresistible influence of motives; physiological, the irresistible influence of the passions; mechanical, explains the highest grades of life by the mechanicist theory.

DETRACTION covers those sins commonly referred to as uncharitable talk; it is unjustly depriving another of his good name behind his back, either by calumny (*q.v.*) or by saying that which is true; in the latter case there is no right to publish what is true against him without just cause if it is not publicly known, for every man has a right to his good reputation so long as he can retain it. But for a just cause (*e.g.,* the public good, or to protect the innocent) the secret sin of another may be made known. The degree of seriousness of detraction is in accordance with the harm done to the person detracted and the malice of the speaker; being a sin against justice as well as charity it leaves an obligation of making restitution as far as possible. He who by listening to detraction encourages it actively or passively sins equally with the detractor.

DEUS IN ADIUTORIUM meum intende. R̴. *Domine, ad adiuvandum me festina.* (O God, come to my assistance. O Lord, make haste to help me.) The first words of Psalm lxix, used at or near the beginning of all the hours of the Divine Office, accompanied by the sign of the cross. They are followed by the *Gloria Patri* which, when the Office is sung, is sung slowly to enable

stragglers to take their proper places in the choir before its end; otherwise they are late and must make satisfaction (*q.v.*). It is omitted from Maundy Thursday till None on Holy Saturday, inclusive, and in the Office of the Dead.

DEUTERO-CANONICAL BOOKS. Those books of the O.T. whose place in the canon (*q.v.*) was not admitted till after that of the other books. They are Tobias, Judith, Wisdom, Ecclesiasticus, Baruch, 1 and 2 Machabees, ver. 4 of chap. x to the end of Esther, and Daniel, ver. 24 of chap. iii to ver. 3 of chap. iv and chaps. xiii and xiv. Their authority is equal with that of the other books of the Bible and is so admitted by all the Eastern dissident churches, except that Greek and Russian Orthodox theologians have now for some time been questioning it. Protestants have always rejected them (see APOCRYPHA), because they are not included in the Hebrew Bible of the Jews.

DEUTERONOMY. The fifth book of the O.T. and last of the Pentateuch. Its Greek name means "the second law," because it largely consists of a recapitulation of the history of Israel and repetition of the laws of the covenant, to which others are added; it ends with the death of Moses. It is called in Hebrew by its opening words *Elle haddebarim.* Its author was Moses (see PENTATEUCH). The eleventh prophecy on Holy Saturday (third on Whitsun Eve) is taken from Deuteronomy (xxxi).

DEVELOPMENT OF DOCTRINE. The process, under the infallible guidance of the Holy Spirit, by which the contents of the Deposit of Faith (*q.v.*) are explicitly drawn out. That all the truths of the deposit should be thus explicitly taught and believed from the beginning was not humanly possible. Some were contained implicitly or obscurely in the primary truths (*e.g.,* the Immaculate Conception, *q.v.*); others were enshrined in the practice of the Church rather than in formularies (*e.g.,* rebaptism of heretics forbidden). In course of time these might be questioned or denied. Theological discussion would follow. Finally they would be defined by the infallible Church as of divine faith (*q.v.*) and a part of the original deposit.

DEVIL (Gr. διάβολος, slanderer). i. A name commonly given to those angels who with Lucifer or Satan (The Devil) rebelled against God. So far as their natural characteristics are concerned they in no wise differ from the other angels; they are purely spiritual beings who by their own act have lost supernatural grace.
   ii. The Devil, or Satan. The chief and leader of the rebelling angels and so of the evil spirits which they now are. The nature and circumstances of their sin is a matter of speculation, but St. Thomas teaches that it was a sin of pride. "Since a spirit is imma-

terial his fall cannot have been due to fleshly or material desires but only to spiritual ones; in these there can be no sin save of insubordination, or pride which resided in an undue desire to be 'like to God,' in that he sought as the ultimate goal of his happiness something to which he could attain by his own natural powers, turning away his desires from that supernatural happiness which comes from the grace of God. Or, if he wished to find his happiness in such likeness to God as is due to grace, then he sought it by the powers of his own nature . . ." (I, lxiii, 3). Suarez and other theologians have suggested that God revealed the coming of the Incarnation, that the angels foresaw that they would have to abase themselves before God the Son in the form of a creature lower than themselves, and that so some rebelled. By bringing about the fall of our first parents, he involved the whole human race in ruin, from which it was rescued by the sacrifice of Calvary. The Devil, "goes about, roaring like a lion, to find his prey" (I Peter, v, 8), and with his following will not be bound in Hell until the last day. Nevertheless all temptation and consequent sin must not be attributed to him directly, for fallen human nature is vulnerable also to the suggestions of the world and the flesh. It is of divine faith that the Devil and his wicked companions were created by God, that they were good and by their own fault fell into sin, that the Devil tempted man to his fall, that the devils still tempt and persecute mankind. It is certain that they are pure spirits and as such have an intelligence of a high order, and that they have a will now obstinately bent to evil. All this demands that they should be persons, i.e., intelligent individuals responsible for their own activities.

DEVIL'S ADVOCATE, The (Lat. *Advocatus Diaboli*). A popular name for the Promoter of the Faith (*q.v.*).

DEVOLUTION. When a patron has failed to exercise, or has exercised improperly, his right of presentation to a benefice, the right is transferred, for that occasion only, to an ecclesiastical superior who presents by right of devolution. Chapters having the right to elect a bishop are allowed by custom a second choice if their first was canonically void; if it does not elect within three months the Holy See appoints.

DEVOTION. i. "A will to give oneself readily to the things that pertain to the service of God" (St. Thomas, II-II, lxxxii, 1). It is the chief act of the virtue of religion and is acquired by earnest meditation on the love of God for his creatures, particularly as manifested in the incarnation and passion of his Son.

ii. Another name for consolation, sensible or spiritual, i.e., for emotions felt in the service of God. It is sensible when the senses themselves are directly moved, e.g., in the gift of tears, when it is *felt*, and spiritual when its source is in the will (cf., the peaceful joy of the prayer of quiet). Such devotion has its dangers: it may engender a wrong view that the love of God, unless in some way felt, is not real: it may give rise to vanity and spiritual pride, as though one were already a saint: it may lead to spiritual gluttony, i.e., a craving for the "sweet things" of God, instead of for God himself: also it may be counterfeited by nature or by the Devil. But it has also great advantages. It encourages the soul in the service of God, and is a powerful aid to the will in well doing. The opposite of devotion is aridity (*q.v.*).

iii. A particular attraction towards some particular mystery or personage of the Christian faith.

iv. A prayer; a formula of worship directed towards or in honour of some particular personage or mystery of the Faith; one of the popular devotions (*q.v.*).

DEVOTIONS, MONTHLY, dictated by popular taste, have received a certain amount of ecclesiastical recognition and corresponding exercises often take place in the churches on some such plan as the following: Jan., the Child Jesus; Feb., the Holy Trinity; Mar., St. Joseph; April, the Holy Ghost; May, our Lady; June, the Sacred Heart; July, the Precious Blood; Aug., the Heart of Mary; Sept., the Seven Sorrows of our Lady; Oct., the Guardian Angels or Holy Rosary; Nov., the souls in Purgatory; Dec., the birth of Christ.

DEVOTIONS, POPULAR, are spontaneous pious movements of the Christian body towards this or that aspect of the faith, sanctified individual, or historical event, approved by authority and usually expressed in authorized vernacular formulas and observances. They are very numerous; among the most notable are devotion to the Blessed Sacrament and to the Sacred Heart (*q.v.*) (these must be distinguished from devotion to Jesus Christ pure and simple), to our Lady (especially as immaculately conceived, and as having appeared at Lourdes, *qq.v.*), to St. Joseph, to St. Antony of Padua (at whose intercession it is claimed lost articles are found); the use of the rosary and other chaplets of beads; of the stations of the cross; of the monthly devotions; the wearing of scapulars and medals; the observance of the Nine Fridays (*qq.v.*), etc. It would appear that such devotions, good in themselves, have a somewhat disproportionate part in the lives of many, for the approval and encouragement which they have received must be distinguished from the solemn obligation which the Church imposes on clergy and laity in varying degrees to make use of her official public worship. Most of the popular devotions are susceptible of use in public as well as private, and the introduction of these exercises, individualistic and calculated to be popular in the same ratio as they appeal to the emotions, as a regular feature of church services has resulted in a reaction, the liturgical movement (*q.v.*), towards the truly corporate worship and nurture of the intelligence provided by the services of the Roman church. The use of the epithet "popular" suggests a misleading contrast, the liturgy being primarily and essentially designed for popular worship. Among Eastern Catholics some devotions of Western origin have become considerably popular; but to dissident oriental Christians they are unknown.

DEVOTIONS, WEEKLY. A special dedication for each day of the week has received liturgical recognition by the assignment of votive masses (*q.v.*) as follows: Mon., of the Holy Trinity; Tues., of the Angels; Wed., of St. Joseph, of SS. Peter & Paul or of the Apostles; Thur., of the Holy Ghost or of the Blessed Sacrament; Fri., of the Cross or of the Passion; Sat., the special Masses and Office of our Lady.

"DEVOUT FEMALE SEX, The." An expression occurring several times in the Common and Little offices of our Lady. It signifies nuns, the Latin *devotus* meaning "devoted" in the strict sense, *i.e.*, bound by vow.

DIAKONIKON (Gr., of the deacon). i. In a Byzantine church the part of the sanctuary to the south of the altar; here priest and deacon vest at a table at the beginning of the liturgy and the sacred vessels and books are kept in closed cupboards.

ii. The book containing the deacon's part for the Liturgy, *Orthros* and *Hesperinos*.

iii. In the plural, *Ta diakonika*, the prayers in litany form recited by the deacon, *e.g.*, the *ektenes* (*q.v.*).

DIALECTICS. The science which treats of the rules by which the mind in its search after truth may judge rightly or proceed correctly; a department of logic.

DIALOGUE MASS. A low Mass at which the responses ordinarily made by the server are spoken aloud by the congregation in chorus, according to earlier custom. The people sometimes recite the Creed, Gloria, etc., as well. To introduce the practice of the dialogue Mass into a public church the permission of the bishop is necessary.

DIAMPER, SYNOD OF. A council of the Syro-Indian Christians of Malabar summoned by the Portuguese archbishop of Goa, Menezes, in 1599. In correcting the liturgical books and customs they were arbitrarily and improperly altered to make them conform to Portuguese ideas of propriety, and the Malabarese were submitted to Latin ordinaries; the state of affairs then inaugurated lasted

for 300 years and in 1653 there was a disastrous schism which still partly subsists.

DIASPORA (Gr., exile). The name given to the state of dispersion of the Jews consequent on the forced emigrations and deportations to which they were submitted by their various conquerors, culminating in the capture of Jerusalem by Titus in A.D. 70; also given to the countries where they lived and to the Jews so dispersed.

DIATESSARON (Gr., from four). i. A gospel narrative made up from the four canonical Gospels by a convert called Tatian, who afterwards became a gnostic, probably between 160 and 180.

ii. Any harmony of the Gospels.

DICASTERY, -ERIUM (Gr., δικαστήριον, court of justice; from the Athenian jury which gave sentence as well as verdict). An office or collection of departments such as that of the congregations, etc., forming the Roman Curia, sometimes called the Pontifical Dicastery.

DIDACHE, The (Greek). "The *Teaching* of the Twelve Apostles," a treatise written before the end of the 2nd century, rediscovered in 1875. The first part is moral, the second disciplinary and liturgical: it describes Baptism, gives prayers for communion, and speaks of a hierarchy of apostles, prophets, teachers, bishops and deacons. By some of the Fathers the Didache was valued only after the Bible. It is a valuable witness to the teaching and practice of the early Church, *e.g.*, "Meet together on the Lord's Day and break bread and give thanks, having confessed your transgressions, so that your sacrifice may be pure. Let not anyone that is at variance with his neighbour join you until they are reconciled, that your sacrifice be not defiled. For this is that sacrifice that was spoken of by the Lord, 'In every place and time offer me a pure sacrifice . . .'"

DIDASCALIA APOSTOLORUM. A treatise on the public life of the Church written in the 3rd century, at one time believed to be the work of apostolic times. Baptism (by immersion, with anointings), Penance, the Eucharist and the reconciliation of sinners are mentioned, the Old Testament is freely quoted, and the supreme authority of bishops is clearly recognized.

DIES IRÆ (Lat., day of wrath). The opening words of the sequence (*q.v.*) proper to requiem Masses, whereby the hymn is known. It must be said at the three Masses of All Souls' day and in funeral Masses; at other requiems it is optional. Moreover it must be said by the celebrant and sung by the choir at all high Masses of requiem, nor may any of the 19 stanzas be omitted. The hymn is usually attributed to Friar Thomas of Celano, O.S.F. (*c.* 1200–55), and has been translated into English nearly 250 times.

DIFFERENCE OF WORSHIP, RELIGION. A diriment impediment (*q.v.*) to marriage arising when one of the parties has been baptized in the Catholic Church or converted thereto and the other is an unbaptized person. It can be dispensed for a grave reason but similar guarantees must be given as in cases of mixed religion (*q.v.*), from which this impediment must be distinguished. See MIXED MARRIAGE.

DIFFINITIVELY. A mode whereby certain spiritual substances are said to be in place, as the soul in the body. It implies that the soul is *here* in such wise that it is nowhere else. See PLACE.

DIFFINITORS are elected by the general and provincial chapters to assist the general and provincial superiors of the Augustinian Hermits, Carmelites and Franciscans, in the government of their order or its provinces. Among the Dominicans the elected representatives of the provinces sent to a general chapter are called diffinitors, the general chapter being alternately one of diffinitors and priors provincial, then diffinitors only, then priors provincial only, and so on. In some dioceses there are diffinitors to assist the rural deans.

DIGNITARY. A member of a cathedral or collegiate chapter who has a precedence of honour and formerly also a certain jurisdiction; such are promoted from among the canons by the Holy See. The usual dignitaries are the provost and dean, sometimes the archpriest and archdeacon, any one of whom may be the head of the chapter, according to its constitution.

DIKERION (Gr., two-candlestick). One of the two candlesticks held by a Byzantine bishop when he blesses the people. It has two branches and a candle in each, either crossed or bent to make a single flame; it is held in the left hand and represents the two natures of Christ (*cf., Trikerion*).

DILATI (Lat., the deferred). The forty-four English martyrs not yet declared venerable, their cases being put back for further consideration. Thirty-seven of these are known to be confessors of the Faith who died in prison, but it is not decided if their deaths were resulting from the imprisonment.

DIMISSORIALS, LETTERS DIMISSORIAL. A permission and authorization granted by an ecclesiastical superior to his own subject to receive holy orders outside the superior's jurisdiction. Dimissorials are ordinarily given by (*a*) the pope, to any candidate and addressed to any bishop; (*b*) a bishop to his own subjects; (*c*) abbots and other exempt religious superiors to their own subjects, normally addressed to the bishop in whose diocese the monastery is.

DIOCESE (Gr. διοίκησις, administration). The territory governed by a bishop. The pope alone can erect, alter, divide, unite or suppress dioceses; these powers he exercises chiefly through the Consistorial Congregation. Abbeys and prelacies *nullius* rank in law as dioceses. A diocese must be divided into parishes and deaneries. In every diocese there must be a *curia*, consisting of the vicar general, official, chancellor, promoter of justice, defender of the marriage bond, synodal judges and examiners, secretaries, etc. Every diocese normally has also a chapter of canons to help the bishop in the government of the diocese, and to rule it in his stead when the see is vacant. All secular clerics must be attached to a diocese. There are (1947) in the Western church 1400 dioceses, of which 1 (Rome) is papal, patriarchal and pre-eminent; 4 have the honorary title of patriarchal sees; over 300 are metropolitan sees, 30 archbishoprics without suffragans, about 1000 suffragan bishoprics, and 90 bishoprics immediately subject to the Holy See; the Eastern rites have 66 dioceses, of which 6 are patriarchal, 20 are called metropolitan (most of them have no suffragans) and 40 are bishoprics. (The *Annuario Pontificio* gives 92 dioceses of Eastern rite, but many of these, in the former Turkish empire, are without pastors or people.)

DIPLOMATIC CORPS. The following countries have diplomatic representatives at the court of the Supreme Pontiff: ambassadors: Argentine, Belgium, Brazil, Chile, Colombia, Eire, France, Italy, Peru, Poland, Spain, Bolivia, Ecuador, Portugal, Dominican Republic; ministers: Great Britain, Austria, Czechoslovakia, Costa Rica, Haiti, Yugoslavia, Liberia, Monaco, Nicaragua, Rumania, San Marino, Salvador, Venezuela, Cuba, Guatemala, Honduras, Panama, China, Egypt, Finland, Lebanon, Holland, Uruguay, India and the Knights of Malta. The legation of the United States, established in 1852, was discontinued in 1868; but the President of the United States now has a personal representative at the Vatican, with the rank of ambassador.

DIPTYCHS (Gr., twice folded). Two tablets connected by a hinge, having on the one the names of the living to be commemorated at Mass and on the other the names of the dead. Their use was established very early; discontinued in the Latin church in the 12th, and in the East in the 15th, century (the Catholic Syrians still have an analogous custom). The names of the pope, patriarch, bishop, emperor, benefactors, were always found on the diptychs of the living: to remove a name therefrom was equivalent to excommunication or breaking of communion, and was a frequent occurrence in ecclesiastical strifes. The names were read aloud by a deacon from the *ambo (q.v.)* or in a low voice to the celebrant or simply said or adverted to by the celebrant himself. The mementoes *(q.v.)* of the living and the dead in the Roman Mass are a different expression of the purpose fulfilled by the diptychs in the East. In the Liturgy of St. John Chrysostom the names of the dead are said in a low voice by the priest, and by the deacon when he incenses the altar, after the consecration, followed by a memento of the living. the pope, the ordinary, etc., each bishop having a special form, *e.g.*, "Remember, O Lord, N . . . the very pure and most holy, our teacher, lord and shepherd, the all-honoured bishop of Bairut and Gabail, who governs Phœnicia of Sabel and of the Lebanon, for many years." This is a modest example.

DIRECTION, SPIRITUAL. The guidance of souls to sanctity. It is in God's designs that men should find their pedagogues to Christ among their fellow-men; thus he sent the convert Saul to Ananias to learn the divine Will. The solitaries in the deserts and the founders of religious orders were spiritual directors to the disciples who gathered round them: their principles of direction were the Sacred Scriptures and their own rich spiritual experience. Direction is necessary for all souls seeking holiness, and it has always been recognized as a most difficult office. "To guide a man seems to me to be the art of arts and the science of sciences" (St. Gregory Nazianzen); "There are fewer than can be imagined who are fitted for this office" (St. Francis of Sales). There are required in the good director knowledge, though not experience, of the whole of ascetical and mystical theology, prudence, insight into human nature, a large-hearted charity, strength of character and a strong adherence to supernatural ideas: he must remember that he is but the instrument of the Holy Ghost, who is the real director of souls. The person directed should be very frank with his director, and very obedient. Direction also belongs to the office of a confessor, since, besides being a judge, he is also a teacher and physician of souls.

DIRECTIVE. See PRECEPTIVE.

DIRECTOR, SPIRITUAL. One who directs souls (see DIRECTION), but not necessarily in the sacrament of Penance. It is common for an individual to resort to one priest for direction and to another for confession; indeed, one may, with proper safeguards, submit oneself for direction to a person not in holy orders.

DIRGE was formerly used technically to indicate a public recitation of Matins and Lauds of the Office of the Dead, from *dirige*, the first word of the first antiphon at Matins, hence its modern meaning of lament or solemn burial hymn *(cf., Placebo)*.

DIRIMENT IMPEDIMENTS are obstacles arising either from natural law or the law of the Church which prohibit marriage between the persons affected and make null and void any attempted marriage between them *(cf.,* prohibiting impediments). They are: insufficient age, previous marriage subsisting, consanguinity, affinity, spiritual relationship, adoption, public honesty, solemn vows, sacred orders, difference of worship, crime of a particular kind, impotence, error, imbecility, violence and fear *(vis et metus)*, abduction, clandestinity *(qq.v.)*. Lack of consent, whether intentional or due to ignorance, or error, or grave fear, or unfulfilled condition, is equivalent to a diriment impediment, as is clandestinity, *i.e.*, the omission, culpable or not, of the form of celebration required for a valid marriage. The Church alone has the right to declare authentically when the natural or divine law invalidates marriage, and to make other diriment impediments for baptized persons. No one can dispense from diriment impediments but the pope, and those who are given this power by common law or papal indult. Impediments of the natural law can never be dispensed.

DISABILITIES OF CATHOLICS, in Great Britain. Those remaining after the Relief Act of 1829 (Emancipation, *q.v.*) were removed by the Act of 1926 with the exception of the following legal incapacities still remaining: No member of the reigning house who is, or has married, a Catholic, can be king or queen of England; Catholics are excluded from the office of Regent, and perhaps of Lord Chancellor and Keeper of the Great Seal; nor can one be High Commissioner of the Anglican Church or of the Presbyterian Church of Scotland, occupy posts in their ecclesiastical courts, or divinity professorships at Oxford, Cambridge or Durham, or certain Anglican scholastic appointments; nor present to an Anglican living. The incapacity of Catholic priests to sit in the House of Commons is shared by Anglican clergymen.

DISCALCED (Lat. *dis*, without; *calceus*, shoe). An epithet, "barefooted," applied to certain religious orders and congregations which are distinguished by the wearing of sandals, *e.g.*, the Discalced Carmelites, the Discalced Clerks of the Holy Cross, etc. (Passionists), the Discalced Augustinians.

DISCERNMENT OF SPIRITS. Man's will, while remaining free, is subject to the influence of motives. In matters of morality and spiritual progress it is subject to impulses which may emanate from God, the Devil or native concupiscence. The power, or the act, discriminating among these various sources is called the Discernment of Spirits. It may be an acquired gift, or one infused by God. As infused, it is one of the *charismata (q.v.)* mentioned by St. Paul (1 Cor. xii, 10). Psychological and moral rules for the discernment of spirits are given by many ascetical writers; "The Exercises of St. Ignatius" present a classic example. The basis of all such rules is found in Gal. v, 19-23, where St. Paul distinguishes between the works of the flesh and the fruit of the spirit.

DISCIPLE (Lat. *discipulus,* a pupil). One of the Twelve Apostles; or any one of the early believers in our Lord, particularly in the body of 72 (or 70) followers referred to in Luke x, 1; as St. Bede the Venerable says, "In the Apostles we have the episcopal character, in the seventy-two Disciples that of priests." In the Byzantine rite several feasts of these are kept by name (Ananias, Aquila, Sosipater, etc.) during the course of the year, and in other Eastern rites, *e.g.,* the Chaldean, they are commemorated in a common feast.

DISCIPLES OF THE LORD, The. A congregation of native priests, founded in 1928, for missionary work in China and the first religious institute of that nationality. The initial formation of the congregation was entrusted to the Redemptorists, and the first ordinations were carried out in 1929 by Bishop Ch'eng, vicar apostolic of Suanhwafu.

DISCIPLINE. A small whip or scourge of cords variously arranged, used for self-inflicted mortification *(q.v.).* Its use is prescribed in the more austere religious orders and congregations; among the Cistercians, for example, it is self-administered on most Fridays of the year after the night-office for the space of a *Miserere.* Its voluntary use should be submitted to the advice of a prudent director.

DISCIPLINE, ECCLESIASTICAL. See GOVERNMENT, JURISDICTION, CENSURE, etc.

DISCIPLINE OF THE SACRAMENTS, SACRED CONGREGATION OF THE. A Roman congregation *(q.v.)* concerned with legislation (other than ritual) for administration and reception of the sacraments, and dispensations from impediments to, and questions as to the validity of, marriages and ordinations.

DISCIPLINE OF THE SECRET, The. (Lat. *Disciplina Arcani*), was the custom during the first five centuries of concealing entirely from unbelievers the more sacred rites and doctrines of the Church, lest blasphemy, profanation or persecution should ensue; and of enlightening catechumens *(q.v.)* slowly and by degrees, to test their fervour and for the avoidance of ill instruction. This does not imply an inner circle of initiates into esoteric knowledge, for all catechumens were fully instructed by the time they came to Baptism, Confirmation and first Communion on Holy Saturday. Reminders of this discipline, which it is now believed soon became largely conventional, are the symbols (*e.g.,* the fish,

the lamb, the shepherd) seen in the Catacombs, and the division of the Mass and other liturgies into "of the Catechumens" and "of the Faithful," the saying of the Our Father silently, etc. In recent times a form of this discipline has been revived in the African missions of the White Fathers and elsewhere.

DISCURSION. An act whereby the mind from a truth known proceeds to the knowledge of some other truth.

DISESTABLISHMENT. The reduction or release of a church from a state of establishment *(q.v.),* such as was effected in France in 1905, although in so far as the Faith had only been recognized by the state as that of the great majority of Frenchmen the Church in France was not fully established. The expression is more familiar in connexion with the disestablishment of the Protestant churches of Ireland (1869) and of Wales (1920).

DISKOS (Gr., quoit). The Byzantine paten *(q.v.);* a metal dish with a rim, larger and deeper than the Western paten, and in Russia often provided with a foot; it is never placed on the chalice. The Catholic Rumanians and Ruthenians now often use a Latin paten.

DISMISSAL from a religious institute *(q.v.)* consequent on misbehaviour may be by sentence of law when guilt has been established by trial or *ipso facto* on declaration of the fact of guilt by the competent superior. The offences which involve dismissal *ipso facto* for a religious, whether male or female, are public apostasy from the Faith, flight with a person of the opposite sex, and attempted marriage, even civil.

DISPARITY OF CULT. Difference of worship *(q.v.).*

DISPENSATION i. The relaxing of a law in special circumstances. It can be granted by the legislator, his successor or superior, and their delegates. No one but the pope can dispense from common law unless the law itself allows it or a faculty is obtained from the pope. Ordinaries can dispense from diocesan laws, and in particular cases from provincial laws. Dispensations must not be granted without a just cause, and they are to be interpreted strictly. Rectors of parishes can dispense in particular cases from the observance of Sundays and holydays and of fast and abstinence days.

ii. For marriage. No one but the Holy See can dispense from matrimonial impediments, unless the law itself allows it, or a faculty is obtained from the pope. In danger of death and certain other emergencies local ordinaries (and, if these cannot be consulted, rectors of parishes and confessors) can dispense from all impediments of ecclesiastical law except the priesthood and affinity in the direct line.

Dispensations for mixed marriages can only be obtained if the necessary promises (*q.v.*) are made. Among the causes ordinarily accepted as sufficient for granting a dispensation (taking into consideration the seriousness of the impediment) are: the advancing age of the woman, to put an end to strife (between nations, about inheritance of property, etc.), to legitimize offspring, to validate an invalid union entered into in good faith, to avoid a civil marrige, to remove scandal or remedy concubinage. Impediments of the natural law can never be dispensed.

iii. Of vows. Local ordinaries and certain religious superiors can for a just cause dispense their subjects from all vows except those reserved to the pope, provided such dispensation does no injustice to other persons. No one else can dispose from a vow without a faculty from the pope (*cf.*, Vow).

DISPERSION OF THE APOSTLES, The. A feast of this name commemorating the departure of the Apostles on their missionary journeys is observed on July 15 in some dioceses (*e.g.*, Westminster) and missionary institutes.

DISPOSITION. i. The variable inclinations to, aversions from, feelings and capabilities, accorded to each individual by nature. See TEMPERAMENT.

ii. According to St. Thomas, matter is the subject of dispositions, as distinguished from the habits (*q.v.*) of the intellect and the will. Disposition is the more easily changed.

iii. An attitude or certain conditions of mind and will that may be necessary for the valid or lawful fulfilment of an office or acceptance of a benefit or gift. Definite dispositions are thus required for the valid and lawful administration or reception of the sacraments. To be "in good dispositions" is to desire to do that which God would have us do; more particularly, to make a humble confession and receive the sacraments devoutly after falling into sin and at the hour of death.

DISSENTER. One who dissents from the general religious belief of a country, but generally an English Protestant who does not belong to the Church of England. See NONCONFORMITY. A relief bill which was drafted for Parliament in 1789 proposed to give to English Catholics the official name "Protesting Catholic Dissenters," which a number of Catholics of that day were willing to accept.

DISSIDENT. An epithet now commonly applied to the separated and heretical Eastern churches to distinguish them from Catholic bodies of the same rite, *e.g.*, there are Catholic Copts and dissident Copts.

DISSIMULATION. Attempting to hide the truth from others by a course of action from which they are likely to draw a wrong inference; allowable for proportionally grave reasons.

DISSOLUTION OF THE MONASTERIES, often referred to simply as The Dissolution. In 1536 the English Parliament prayed King Henry VIII to take all the property of monasteries having an income under £200 a year "that it should be converted to better uses and the unthrifty persons so spending the same be compelled to reform their lives"; in 1538-40 all the other monasteries were similarly suppressed by means of forced and illegal surrenders of their property. As soon as a house was surrendered the commissioners broke its seal and assigned pensions to its members, plate and jewels were reserved to the king, roofs stripped and the lead and furniture and all else saleable sold and proceeds paid into the Court of Augmentation; the lands by degrees were alienated from the crown by gift or sale. It is estimated that there were 6,000 monks, canons and friars, and 2,000 nuns, with a very large number of lay dependents. Most of the religious received pensions and many of them benefices, but the amount of unemployment among the servants must have been considerable. There were about 815 religious houses of all kinds, of which 186 were greater monasteries.

DISTINCTION. The negation of identity. (*a*) Real distinction: a lack of identity independently of and antecedently to the mind's consideration. A real distinction may be: (1) entitative, as between thing and thing; (2) modal, as between a thing and a mode affecting it, *e.g.*, a man and sitting; (3) virtual, as in a thing we distinguish diverse formalities because the thing which is really one can produce different effects, *e.g.*, although the human soul is essentially one, it is nevertheless triple by its power or virtue because it can produce whatever a brute animal, plant, or stone can effect, *viz.*, sensitive life, vegetative life, and extension. This distinction is not so much a distinction as the ground of a distinction. (*b*) Logical distinction: a lack of identity due solely to the mind's consideration and wholly dependent on that consideration. (1) It is *ratiocinantis* if a thing does not afford the mind any proximate foundation for such a distinction, *e.g.*, the distinction between a subject and predicate; (2) it is *ratiocinatæ* if a thing affords the mind a proximate basis for distinguishing diverse formalities within it. This is the same as a virtual distinction (see above).

DISTRACTION. Lack of due attention at prayer. When voluntary, it is a venial sin of disrespect. When involuntary, it does not deprive the prayer of merit; indeed, the imaginative disturbance may be the occasion of an increase of merit, especially when the distraction is persistent, because then the will has to make much more deliberate and sustained efforts to keep united with God, than when the prayer goes easily. A prayer full of distractions is, however, deprived of the fruit of sensible or spiritual consolation. A distracted life will involve distracted prayers. It is therefore incumbent on men to practise silence, solitude and recollection so far as their state of life permits.

DISTRIBUTISM. The theory that the political, economic and personal freedom proper to man without distinction of class or race can only be maintained when property in the means of production is widely distributed. Distributists hold that large concentrations of wealth or property are bad, and they seek to promote the revival of ownership of land, workshops, etc., by individuals and are generally opposed to monopolies and amalgamations. They hold that the "small-holder," small shop-keeper, the peasant and the artist-craftsman are the normal men and that Capitalism (the rule of the money-lender) and Industrialism (the rule of the machine) can be deliberately undermined and gradually abolished. Distributism has no religious affiliation but its theory is claimed to be in special harmony with Catholic teaching as to the nature of man and his needs.

DIVINATION. i. The act of foretelling the future or discovering the unknown through the aid of evil spirits. This is a species of superstition (*q.v.*) and is always a grave sin against the virtue of religion (*q.v.*).
ii. "Dowsing." The act of discovering metals or water hidden in the earth by means of divining rods. This is not superstition; the power of discovery is to be attributed to the natural powers possessed by the person or rod.

DIVINE. i. An old-fashioned word for a theologian.
ii. A student in a seminary who has completed his course of philosophy and is studying theology.

DIVINE, The. So is generally translated the title *theologos* accorded to St. John the Evangelist; the noun "divine" having gone somewhat out of use, "theologian" might be better. The same epithet is given to St. Gregory Nazianzen.

DIVINE OFFICE, The, is the service of prayer and praise, psalms, lessons, hymns, etc., ancillary to and distinct from the sacrifice of the Mass, which all priests and certain other clerics are obliged to recite daily (see below), which is said or sung in choir by monks, friars, many nuns and some others, and in which the laity are exhorted to take part according to their ability and opportunity. It is also recited or sung daily in the choirs of cathedrals by the canons; but not in missionary or quasi-missionary countries such as England or the U.S.A., where there are either no canons or they are non-resident.

The cathedral of Westminster, where the office is said in choir by the attached clergy, is an exception. The typical and most widely used office is that found in the Roman Breviary; all other Latin offices, Monastic, Ambrosian, Carmelite, etc., approximate to it more or less closely. Throughout this work all references to the Divine Office or any part of it refer to the Roman office, unless otherwise stated. It is believed all to have developed from the primitive *synaxis* (*q.v.*) but has for many centuries consisted of the present seven hours, namely, Matins and Lauds (which in the Roman Breviary are regarded as one hour for all practical purposes), Prime, Terce, Sext, None, Vespers and Compline (*qq.v.*). These are distributed throughout the day and normally take up all together about 1½ hours when said privately; sung in choir they take much longer. See also AKOLOUTHIA.

DIVINE OFFICE, OBLIGATION OF THE. In the Western church, all priests, deacons and subdeacons and all religious, male and female, solemnly professed in orders that have office in choir, are bound to recite the Divine Office daily, unless prevented by sickness, by other imperative duties or unless lawfully dispensed. When not said aloud in choir, it must be read privately but with at least silent articulation of the lips. A right intention and at least external attention (*q.v.*) are required, but the Church strongly urges that the prayers should be said with intelligence and internal devotion: "So assist at the office that our mind and our voice may accord together" (Rule of St. Benedict, cap. xix). Their daily office is obligatory also upon all Catholic priests of Eastern rites, but those of the Byzantine are not held to any fixed amount owing to the great length of their office. No dissident orientals have this obligation, except in the monasteries.

DIVINE PRAISES, The. A series of imprecations of praise which may be said after Benediction of the Blessed Sacrament before the Host is replaced in the tabernacle; each one is said by the priest in the vulgar tongue and repeated by the people. They are: "Blessed be God, Blessed be his holy Name, Blessed be Jesus Christ, true God and true man, Blessed be the name of Jesus, Blessed be his most sacred Heart, Blessed be Jesus in the most holy Sacrament of the Altar, Blessed be the great Mother of God, Mary most holy, Blessed be her holy and immaculate Conception, Blessed be the name of Mary, virgin and mother, Blessed be Saint Joseph, her chaste spouse, Blessed be God in his angels and in his saints." They originated in a shorter form at the end of the 18th century as an act of reparation for blasphemy and profanity.

DIVINE RIGHT OF KINGS. A theory of sovereignty which in its moderate form asserts kingship to be a divinely instituted form of government and in its extreme form holds individual kings to be, by immediate divine ordinance, rulers of their particular subjects. The theory has no logical foundation. It probably originated in the "sacring" of the Eastern and Western emperors at their coronation, and in the consequent sacrosanct character attributed to them. The idea was taken up later by national monarchs in their struggles with other domestic powers and against the papacy and its doctrine of the supremacy of spiritual over temporal power. It was developed after the Reformation partly in opposition to the doctrine of the deposing power (*q.v.*) of the pope and was controverted by Suarez and other contemporary theologians.

DIVINE SAVIOUR, SOCIETY OF THE. The Salvatorians (*q.v.*).

DIVINE SERVICE, The. i. The name ordinarily given to the eucharistic Liturgy by the Ruthenians.

ii. A general term for acts of public liturgical worship.

DIVINE WORD, SOCIETY OF THE. A missionary congregation founded at Steyl in Holland, by Father Arnold Janssen, in 1875. Its principal missions are in China, where in 1933 it was given charge of the Catholic University of Peking; the first rector thereof appointed by the society was the American Father Joseph Murphy. The society is particularly distinguished in the field of anthropology and comparative religion.

DIVINI REDEMPTORIS. An encyclical letter of Pope Pius XI published in 1937, pointing out the errors of communism (*q.v.*), notably its atheistic materialism, its doctrine of class-war, its denial of the rights and liberties of the human person. After expounding the pertinent Christian teaching, the pope concluded that the essential errors of communist theory and practice are so enormous that Communism is intrinsically evil and that Catholics may not collaborate with it under any pretext whatever.

DIVINITY OF CHRIST, The. Christ's Godhead. In virtue of the hypostatic union (*q.v.*) Christ is a divine person. It does not mean merely that he was a messenger from God, or that he was a man of outstanding virtue with a mission to redeem his fellowmen (Socinianism, Unitarianism), still less that he was a superman, or that he was divine in the sense that Bach, Shakespeare and Giotto were "divine." It means that Christ is truly God, the son of God by nature. It follows that Mary is mother of God.

DIVINO AFFLATU. An apostolic constitution published by Pope Pius X, in 1911, whereby the reform of the Divine Office ordered by the Vatican Council was inaugu-rated. It consisted principally of a rearrangement of the Psalter, which was so distributed that all the psalms may be recited each week, and with about an equal length for each day's office. This was a return to ancient practice. It was also provided that the Mass and Office of Sunday and of ferias in Lent should not normally be superseded by the feast of a saint.

DIVORCE. Divorce, in canon law, signifies the dissolution of the marriage bond (*divortium plenum, a vinculo*), or the permanent separation of the parties, the bond remaining (*divortium semi-plenum*): for the latter see SEPARATION. A valid Christian marriage, if consummated, cannot be dissolved (as to the bond) by any human power or for any cause except death. A non-consummated marriage between two baptized persons, or between a baptized person and one unbaptized, is desolved *ipso facto* by the solemn religious profession of either party, and also by papal dispensation for a just cause at the request of either or both parties. Marriage between two unbaptized persons, even if consummated, is dissolved by the Pauline Privilege (*q.v.*), and by papal dispensation for a grave cause (*cf.*, Indissolubility of Marriage). In the non-Catholic Eastern churches the indissolubility of marriage is recognized in principle, but is not commonly acted on in practice.

DIVORCE, CIVIL, in so far as it implies the right to marry again, is contrary to the divine law of the indissolubility of marriage, which binds all mankind, both baptized and unbaptized. Where a marriage is null by canon law the parties may apply for a civil divorce with the leave of the ordinary. For a grave spiritual reason, *e.g.*, to secure the Catholic education of children, the ordinary may permit a Catholic to apply for a civil divorce, regarding it as a separation only. Apart from this case, it is a disputed question whether a judge may pronounce a civil divorce or a lawyer apply for it, in a solely legal capacity. It is probable that such act is not so intrinsically evil as never to be justified, but circumstances would seldom admit of it, owing to scandal and the danger of partaking in another's sin. The replies of the Holy Office on this point still leave room for doubt. It is certainly unlawful for a Catholic to vote for a divorce law in a legislature.

DIVORCE A TORO ET MENSA (Lat., from bed and board). The name given in canon law to what in civil law is called a judicial separation. To avoid confusion with divorce *a vinculo* (*q.v.*) it is better to call it a separation (*q.v.*).

DOCETISM (Gr. δοκεῖν, to seem). The assertion that Jesus Christ was not a man, but only seemed to have a human body and to lead a human life, whence it is also called

Illusionism. Docetic teaching has been characteristic of many heresies from the days of the Apostles themselves, *e.g.*, Gnosticism, Manichæism, Paulicianism (*qq.v.*).

DOCTOR (Lat. *docere,* to teach). i. A teacher, as in Doctor of the Church (*q.v.*)

ii. A holder of the highest university degree in any faculty, which was at first primarily a qualification and authorization to teach. Only theological faculties that are so authorized by the Holy See may confer the doctorate in theology and canon law. Every bishop, canon penitentiary, canon theologian and some others must be a doctor of theology or canon law, or at least a licentiate. The doctoral *insignia* are the cap and ring which, however, must not be worn on liturgical occasions. In the faculty of Arts the Doctor is called Master but some universities have introduced a higher degree in this faculty with the title of Doctor of Philosophy.

DOCTOR ANGELICUS (Lat., The Angelic Doctor). St. Thomas Aquinas, a friar preacher, 1225-74.

DOCTOR COMMUNIS (Lat., The Common Doctor), *i.e.*, the teacher for all times, all places and all people, St. Thomas Aquinas (*cf.*, Doctor Universalis).

DOCTOR ECSTATICUS (Lat., The Exalted Doctor). Denis the Carthusian (van Leeuwen), 1402-71.

DOCTOR EXIMIUS (Lat., The Excellent Doctor). Francis Suarez, Jesuit, 1548-1617.

DOCTOR GRATIÆ (Lat., The Doctor of Grace). St. Augustine of Hippo, 354-430.

DOCTOR IRREFRAGABILIS (Lat., The Unanswerable Doctor). Alexander of Hales, a friar minor, *c.* 1180-1245.

DOCTOR MARIANUS (Lat., Our Lady's Doctor). St. Anselm of Canterbury, 1033-1109.

DOCTOR MELLIFLUUS (Lat., The Honeysweet Doctor). St. Bernard of Clairvaux, Cistercian, 1090-1153.

DOCTOR MIRABILIS (Lat., the Marvellous Doctor). Roger Bacon, a friar minor of Oxford, 1214-94.

DOCTOR SERAPHICUS (Lat., The Seraphic Doctor). St. Bonaventure, a friar minor, 1231-74.

DOCTOR SUBTILIS (Lat., The Subtle Doctor). John Duns Scotus, a friar minor, 1270-1308, from whose name the "superior" humanists of the 16th century gave us the word "dunce."

DOCTOR UNIVERSALIS (Lat., The Universal Doctor). St. Albert the Great, a friar preacher, 1206-80, so called because of the extent and scope of his knowledge (*cf.*, Doctor Communis).

DOCTOR OF THE CHURCH. An ecclesiastical writer, noted both for the greatness of his learning and the holiness of his life, whose feast has been extended to the whole Western church with a Mass and Office either of his own or of the common of Doctors. The Byzantine church honours, on Jan. 30, "our holy fathers, universal doctors, the three holy hierarchs Basil the Great, Gregory the Theologian (Nazianzen) and John Chrysostom" to whom the Roman church added St. Athanasius and the Western saints Ambrose, Augustine, Gregory the Great and Jerome: these are the great Greek and Latin doctors. Since 1568 the following have been declared Doctors of the Church by the Holy See (date is that of death): SS. Thomas Aquinas (1274), Bonaventure (1274), Anselm (1109), Isidore (636), Peter Chrysologus (450), Pope Leo the Great (461), Peter Damian (1072), Bernard (1153), Hilary (*c.* 368), Alphonsus Liguori (1787), Francis of Sales (1612), Cyril of Alexandria (444), Cyril of Jerusalem (386), John the Damascene (780), Bede the Venerable (735), Ephrem the Syrian (378), John-of-the-Cross (1605), Peter Canisius (1597), Albert the Great (1280), Robert Bellarmine (1621), Antony of Padua (1231).

DOCTRINE. That which is taught. Christian doctrine ordinarily means that body of revealed and defined truth which a Catholic is bound to hold, but is often extended to include those teachings which are not of faith but are generally held and acted upon. Occasionally the word indicates these last only, "the teachings of theologians," as distinct from "the faith taught by the Church."

DOGMA (Gr., ordinance). A truth directly proposed by the Church for our belief as an article of divine revelation. The vulgar notion of a dogma, as an arbitrary doctrine imposed nobody quite knows why, is thus seen to be at fault; the content of a dogma is truth revealed by God and therefore must be believed: it is not assumed to be true because many believe it.

DOGMATIC FACT. A truth, not revealed, but so intimately connected with revelation that it cannot be denied without imperilling some dogma, *e.g.*, our Scriptures are genuine; Pius XII is the legitimate successor of St. Peter in the primacy. Concerning such facts the Church is infallible in her judgements.

DOLOURS OF OUR LADY. See SORROWS OF OUR LADY. Dolour is a word of only poetical or facetious use in English.

DOM. i. The title given to professed monks of the Benedictine, Carthusian and Cistercian orders and to Lateran, Premonstratensian and other canons regular: *e.g.*, the Rev. Dom A. . . . B. . . ., O.S.B. In the Cassinese congregation O.S.B. the title is also conceded to novices. It is contracted from Lat. *dominus*, master, and in the form of *don* is applied in Italy to all clerics except friars and clerks regular *(cf.,* Dame).

ii. A name for a cathedral in Germany.

DOMESTIC PRELATE. An honorary distinction conferred by the Holy See on clergy in any part of the world; the recipient is thereby constituted a member of the Pontifical Family *(q.v.)* with certain ornamental privileges; *e.g.,* his dress approximates to that of a bishop outside his diocese and he has the use of the *bugia* at Mass. His style in English is Right Reverend Monsignor. These prelates are an ancient institution which perhaps had its rise in the notaries appointed by Pope St. Clement to collect the acts of the martyrs.

DOMICILE. Place and fact of permanent residence in the eyes of the law. In canon law it is acquired by residence begun in a parish or diocese with the intention of remaining there permanently, or by actual residence for ten years, and is lost by departure therefrom with the intention of not returning. A wife's domicile is that of her husband, but if legally separated she may establish her own. The domicile of minors is that of their parents or guardians. A domicile makes the person the subject of the ordinary of the diocese and of the rector of the parish in which it is situated.

DOMINATIONS, DOMINIONS (Eph. i, 21, etc.). One of the choirs of the celestial hierarchy *(q.v.).*

DOMINE, NON SUM DIGNUS . . . (Lat., Lord, I am not worthy . . .). An adaptation of the words of the centurion (Matt. viii, 8), said by the celebrant before his communion, and again before the communion of the people, with a triple striking of the breast. They did not find an authorized place in the Roman Missal till 1570, and are still not used by Carthusians and Dominicans.

DOMINIC, THE RULE OF ST. St. Dominic left no rule in the ordinary sense. The Dominicans follow the Rule of St. Augustine with added constitutions which regulate the life, work and organization of the order; these were founded on the statutes of the Cistercians and of the Premonstratensian canons, and as adapted by St. Dominic provided for a compact and united religious body, with fixed rules and governed on elective principles—the first of its kind. He bound his friars to corporate poverty (modified in 1475) and to the monastic laws of silence, fasting, office in choir, common life and the three vows, at the same time providing wide power of dispensation for the better fulfilling of the order's primary objects of teaching and preaching. Until 1250, indeed, the Dominicans were regarded as canons and wore the rochet. From time to time this rule has been modified, especially by way of addition, at general chapters of the order.

DOMINICA. The name given to Sunday in the liturgical books of the Latin rite; *dies Dominica* means the Lord's day.

DOMINICA IN ALBIS (DEPOSITIS). The Sunday next after Easter, or Low Sunday; called as above in the liturgy because formerly on this day the newly baptized laid aside their white garments *(cf.,* the hymn at Vespers).

DOMINICAL LETTER, The. The Sunday letter for any year is that one of the first seven letters of the alphabet which occurs opposite the first Sunday of the year when the first letter is put opposite the first day, the second opposite the second day, and so on. Its use in the calendar is to show the days of the month on which the Sundays will fall in any year. Leap years have two dominical letters; one for Sundays in January and February, the other for the rest of the year.

DOMINICAN REPUBLIC, THE CHURCH IN THE. This state (Santo Domingo) is the eastern part of the island of Hispaniola and the oldest settlement of European origin in America; its capital was founded by order of Columbus, and it became an episcopal see in 1513. Its inhabitants number 1½ million, of Spanish and Negro origin, especially the latter. They are nominally all Catholics, and freedom of action is guaranteed to the Church by the constitution. The country forms a single diocese, the archbishop of Santo Domingo having no suffragans.

DOMINICAN RITE, The. The use of the Latin liturgy proper to the Dominicans, approved by Popes Clement IV and St. Pius V. The chief differences from the Roman use in the celebration of Mass are: at low Mass the chalice is prepared by the celebrant at the altar before the Mass begins, at high Mass at the bench after he has read the gospel; versicle *Confitemini* is said instead of psalm *Iudica;* short *Confiteor; Gloria* and *Credo* are begun at the middle of the altar and continued at the Missal; the host and chalice are offered together; the canon is the same as the Roman, but the celebrant's arms are extended cross-wise from after the consecration till the words *Hostiam puram,* and there is some variation in the prayers after; *e.g.,* the *Agnus Dei* is said after *Pax Domini* and *Domine non sum dignus* is said only at the people's communion, which is given with the words *custodiat te* instead of *custodiat animam tuam.* Archæologically this liturgy is of great interest as approximating closely to the Sarum use *(q.v.).* The differences in the Divine Office are slight, the principal being the retention of the hymns in their form of before the "reform" of Pope Urban VIII *(q.v.).* After conventual Mass and all hours of the Office *Salve Regina* is sung, with three prayers; after Compline there is *Salve* with a procession, and a commemoration of St. Dominic. The chant, in conformity with the whole rite, is mediæval and differs in detail from other editions. The office is recited or sung quickly but clearly. The calendar observes a large number of feasts of *beati* proper to the order, and the Sundays after Pentecost are reckoned after the octave of Trinity Sunday.

DOMINICANS, The. The Order of Preachers was founded by St. Dominic in 1215 for the salvation of souls, especially by means of preaching. They are mendicant friars whose active work is rooted in monastic observance (see DOMINIC, RULE OF ST.), and whose preaching of truth involves commensurate study. The order is the guardian of scholastic theology and philosophy, is found established near all the chief seats of learning and has numerous foreign missions. There are also nuns of the order (Preacheresses, *q.v.*), and a third order (*q.v.*). The English province has nine friaries and 2 boys' schools, and missions in Grenada and South Africa; there is a separate Irish province and three provinces in the U.S.A. There were over 50 priories in England at the Reformation. The order is the fifth of the religious orders numerically, with about 6,000 religious. Habit: stockings, tunic, scapular, *mozzetta* and hood, all white; belt; black *cappa* with *mozzetta* and hood for church and out-of-doors (whence Black Friars); great tonsure; lay-brothers' scapular, black.

DOMINION (Lat. *dominium,* ownership [in theology]). A term used by John Wyclif to express that spiritual authority and material ownership which he denied to sinful clerics. He taught that both obedience and material support should be withheld from unworthy clergy and that the civil powers should deprive such of their property; this developed into the doctrine that the clergy had no right to have temporal possessions or exercise coercive jurisdiction at all.

DOMINUS VOBISCUM. ℞. Et cum spiritu tuo (Lat., The Lord be with you. And with thy spirit). A very ancient form of Christian salutation, now embodied in the liturgy of the Western church, where it is of frequent occurrence; the response is made by the server, the choir, or ideally, by the whole congregation. It is used eight times during Mass and before the principal collect of each hour of the Divine Office (and before numerous other liturgical prayers), even when said privately, because the Office is said in union with and on behalf of the whole Church. But lay-people and clerics below the rank of deacon never use this formula, substituting therefor *Domine, exaudi orationem meam.* ℞. *Et clamor meus ad te veniat* (O Lord, hear my prayer. And let my cry come unto thee.) See PAX VOBIS.

DONATION OF ADRIAN, The. See LAUDA-BILITER.

DONATION OF CONSTANTINE, The. A forged document dating probably from the end of the 8th century, purporting to be an act of the Emperor Constantine the Great conferring on the Pope of Rome supremacy over all patriarchs and bishops of the world and sovereignty over the city of Rome, all Italy and other provinces and cities of the Western parts. It was accepted as the explanation of an accomplished fact; its authenticity was not questioned till the 15th century, and its falsity not universally admitted for another hundred years. Neither the spiritual supremacy nor the claim to temporal power of the Holy See depend in any way on this document, though in the past it has been used as evidence to support them. See also FALSE DECRETALS.

DONATISM. A schism taking its name from Donatus of Casa Nigra, its leader, which began at Carthage in 311 and devastated the Church in Africa for a hundred years. It arose out of the appointment of Cæcilian as bishop of Carthage, whom the party of Donatus claimed to have been consecrated by a *traditor* (*q.v.*) and so invalidly. The schismatics held the heretical doctrine that sacraments administered by an unworthy minister were invalid and that sinners could not be members of the Church. The Donatists had over 270 bishops and the support of a body of fanatics called Circumcellions, *i.e.,* those who wandered among the cottages, *circum cellas,* of the countryside, terrorizing the Catholics by brigandage; violence on both sides resulted. The schism was overcome by the work chiefly of St. Optatus and of St. Augustine of Hippo.

DOOM (Old Eng. *dóm,* sentence of law). A representation of the Last Judgement sometimes painted in the space between the chancel-arch and the roof of English pre-Reformation churches (*e.g.,* in the guild chapel at Stratford-on-Avon). Doom was formerly the common word for the Judgement (*cf.,* crack of Doom, Doomsday).

DOOR-KEEPER, or PORTER. The lowest of the minor orders in the Western church. The office has been known at least since 251, and its duties, now nominal, are "to ring the bells, open the church and sanctuary, and open the book for the preacher." At ordination the keys of the church are delivered to him with the instruction: "So behave as having to account to God for the things kept under these keys."

DOOR-MONEY. A small voluntary contribution made for its upkeep on entering a church. The faithful are to be given free entrance to the ordinary services in church, and all customs to the contrary are reprobated. A place or box for voluntary offerings may be placed at the door, but no payment may be exacted (canons 1181, 1263).

DOORS, HOLY. i. The doors at the basilicas of St. Peter, the Lateran, St. Paul and St. Mary Major, which are kept walled up except during the years of Jubilee. The opening and closing of these doors (at St. Peter's by the pope, elsewhere by cardinals commissioned as legates *a latere*) are the most distinctive ceremonies of the Holy Year (*q.v.*), and can be traced at least to 1450. The expulsion from Paradise, the reconciliation of penitents (penance is a door to Heaven) and the idea of sanctuary seem all to have contributed to give meaning to these symbols. It is not, however, necessary to enter the basilicas by their holy doors to gain the Jubilee indulgence (*q.v.*). At ordinary times the doors are closed by two partitions of brick, between which are deposited medals and a commemorative parchment.

ii. The doors in the middle of the *iconostasis* (*q.v.*) of a Byzantine church, which are only used for liturgical purposes. The upper part is open, but furnished with a curtain which is drawn across at the more solemn parts of the Liturgy. On the south of the doors is a picture of our Lord, on the north of our Lady. They are often erroneously called the Royal Doors (*q.v.*).

DOORS, ROYAL. The western part (*narthex*) of a Byzantine church is walled off from the nave to which admittance is given by doorways corresponding to those of the iconostasis (*q.v.*); the middle are the Royal Doors.

DORMITIO B. M. V. (Lat., The Falling Asleep of the Blessed Virgin Mary). A name for the feast of the Assumption, and the title of the Benedictine church on Mount Zion.

DORTER. An obsolete name for a monastic dormitory.

DOSSAL, DORSAL (Lat. *dorsum,* back). A curtain hung at the back of an altar by way of reredos or adornment.

DOUAY (also spelt Douai, Doway). i. The name in its Catholic association ordinarily refers to the English College founded at that town in Flanders by (Cardinal) William Allen in 1568; it was removed to Rheims from 1578 till 1593; and after a troubled but glorious history came to an end at the French Revolution, being refounded in England at Crook Hall (now Ushaw) and Old Hall, Ware. This college was the first seminary to be established in accordance with the decrees of the Council of Trent. It sent hundreds of seminary-priests to England, of whom more than 160 gave up their lives and are commemorated as the Blessed Martyrs of Douay on Oct. 29 in the diocese of Westminster and on the 30th in Hexham and Newcastle. There were also Irish and Scots colleges and English Franciscan and Benedictine houses in the town; the last named only left in 1903, and is now at Douai Abbey, Woolhampton.

ii. The Abbey of Our Lady and St. Edmund at Woolhampton, Berkshire, commonly called Douai Abbey. It was founded at Paris, in 1615, as a restoration of the royal abbey of St. Edmundsbury (suppressed in 1539) and was benefited by King James II and King Louis XIV. In 1818 it was revived at Douai and in 1903 transferred with its school to England in consequence of the French laws against religious orders. It was erected into an abbey in 1899. It belongs to the English Benedictine congregation, and its monks conduct a large school; other members are engaged in parish work.

DOUAY BIBLE. The translation of the Bible into English done at the English College, Douay, and at Rheims, and published, the N.T. in 1582, the whole in 1609-10, more properly called the Rheims-Douay Bible (*q.v.*). Its use was superseded in Great Britain by Challoner's revision (*q.v.*), which is commonly called the Douay Bible. A revision made in 1859 by Mgr. F. P. Kenrick, archbishop of Baltimore, is commonly used in the United States, but other versions are in use.

DOUBLE. The principal term used in distinguishing between feasts according to their liturgical rank. In the 5th century, when the bodies of the martyrs had been removed from the outlying cemeteries to the churches of Rome, the custom arose of saying a double office on certain days, one the fixed and regular office of the day, the other a special office in honour of the saint whose feast it was. The custom is obsolete centuries ago, but the word remains and has nothing to do with the "doubling" of the antiphons (*i.e.*, reciting them in full before and after each psalm). See RANK OF FEASTS.

DOUBLE EFFECT. The principle of effect operates where there is question of abstaining from a certain action because in addition to a good effect it will produce a bad. Such an action is lawful, provided that the action is not wrong in itself, that the doer intends and desires the good effect but not the bad, that the good effect is produced independently and not by means of the bad (else evil means would be used to produce a good end, which is forbidden), and that there is a weighty reason for allowing the bad effect.

DOUBLE OF THE FIRST CLASS, etc. See RANK OF FEASTS.

DOUBLE MONASTERY. One which sheltered both monks and nuns, usually under the supreme command of the abbess; they met only in the church, where they were separated in two choirs, for the liturgical offices. Such was St. Hilda's abbey at Whitby, and the Benedictine house whose church, St. Helen's, still stands off Bishopsgate, London. The order of Fontevrault, the

Bridgettines and the Gilbertines were specifically founded as orders of double monasteries, but in the last named the prior was always superior. These institutions were common up to the end of the middle ages and Bridgettine double monasteries continued in Poland until the middle of last century. They are now all extinct.

DOUBT. i. The suspension of judgement in presence of the two parts of a contradiction; a withholding of assent to either side. It is positive if it is due to sound reasons on both sides (weights in both pans of the balance); it is negative if the suspension is due to the absence of grave reason from both sides (no weight in either pan).

ii. In conscience. Since it is unlawful to perform an action without a moral certainty, even though imperfect, of the action's lawfulness , it is clearly wrong to act if the conscience is doubtful as to whether the action is right or wrong. The kind and degree of sin thus committed is then in accordance with the nature of the doubt. But see PROBABILISM.

iii. In law. Laws and penalties do not bind if there is a reasonable doubt of their existence or obligation, but in doubt as to the justice of a law or penalty it must be held as binding till the doubt is removed. If the law is certain, and the doubt is one of fact which cannot be settled, the ordinary can dispense from common law except in those cases in which the pope is not wont to dispense.

iv. In marriage. The validity of a marriage already contracted must be upheld in case of doubt until its nullity is established. But the Pauline Privilege (q.v.) enjoys the benefit of the doubt. If a doubt arises as to the existence of an impediment before the marriage, and the doubt cannot be settled, the priest must refer the case to the bishop.

DOUILLETTE (Fr., a padded gown). A straight black outdoor coat, reaching to the ankles, and with deep cuffs, worn by clergy over the cassock or habit.

DOVE. i. A common Christian symbol of the Holy Ghost, who appeared in the form of a dove at our Lord's baptism; of the Church, indwelt by the Holy Ghost; of peace and hope, etc.

ii. The most common form for the early and mediæval pyx (q.v.), and still often the form of the Byzantine artophorion (q.v.).

DOWN AND CONNOR (Dunensis et Connorensis). An Irish see, suffragan of Armagh. It consists of two ancient dioceses finally united in 1451 and now comprises the county of Antrim, most of Down and the Liberty of Coleraine in Derry; it includes the sacred city of Downpatrick, where Patrick, Brigid and Colmkille were buried. The bishop's residence, cathedral and diocesan college are at Belfast. The patron of the united dioceses is St. Maelmhaedhoc (Malachy, Nov. 3) and the cathedral is dedicated in honour of St. Patrick. Irish name: Dún agus Conaire.

DOWNSIDE. A Benedictine abbey near Bath, the senior house of the English congregation. It was founded at Douai in 1606; the monks were expelled in 1795 and were sheltered at Acton Burnell in Salop and came to Downside in 1814; erected into an abbey in 1899. The monks conduct a large school for boys; other members of the community are engaged in parochial work.

"DOWRY, OUR LADY'S." A complimentary name given in former times to the realm of England (cf. "The Island of Saints and Scholars," Ireland in the 6th-8th centuries). According to Thomas Arundell Archbishop of Canterbury the name was already well known in 1399: "We the English, being the servants of her special inheritance and her own dowry, as we are commonly called, ought to surpass others in the warmth of our praise and devotion [to our Lady]" (Wilkins, Concilia, III, p. 246).

DOWRY OF RELIGIOUS. In convents of nuns a postulant must bring with her the dowry required by the constitutions or by legitimate custom. The dowry is to be transferred to the community before the clothing, and on the death of the nun it becomes the property of the community. During the lifetime of the nun the money is to be invested and only the interest used. The dowry is to be returned to the nun if she leaves the order, whatever be the cause.

DOWSING. See DIVINATION, ii.

DOXOLOGY. A formula of praise (Gr. δόξα, glory). The greater doxology is the Gloria in excelsis (q.v.), the lesser, or simply the doxology, is Gloria Patri (q.v.) In Eastern rites a doxology is added to the Our Father, e.g., in the Byzantine the words "for thine is the kingdom and the power and the glory, Father, Son and Holy Ghost, now and for ever, and world without end," of which a variation has become usual among Protestants (cf., 1 Pet. iv, 14). Such an addition is already noted in the Didache (q.v.).

DRAGONNADES. One of the means employed to enforce the provisions of the revocation of the Edict of Nantes (q.v.). It consisted in the quartering of dragons (mounted infantry, whence "dragoon") on Huguenots, who had to provide them with beds, fire and light and submit to "discomfort." The order was grossly abused by the troops, who were rarely punished. A similar system was in use after the Restoration for breaking the spirit of the Covenanters in the Scottish lowlands.

DREAMS, INTERPRETATION OF. Attempting to obtain insight into the future from the stream of thoughts and fancies that flow through the mind during sleep. It is an act of superstition (*q.v.*), gravely sinful if the aid of evil spirits to teach by dreams is desired, or if one makes dreams a constant guide of his actions; but to be influenced by them occasionally in matters of small importance would be but venially sinful, as in this case a firm faith in the efficacy of dreams is ordinarily lacking. Though knowledge of its intrinsic malice is often absent, the act exhibits a want of confidence in divine Providence. That God has taught by means of dreams is clear from the Bible; but to trust a dream, one must be morally certain of its divine origin.

DRESS, CLERICAL. i. The official dress of the secular clergy of the Western church is a black cassock with or without cincture, with a long cloak and hat for outdoors; the face should be clean shaven and a small tonsure on the crown of the head. In Great Britain, the U.S.A. and other countries, this is not insisted on, but the cassock is enjoined for the church and house.

ii. The Catholic Eastern clergy have a black gown, to which the Chaldeans add a turban and the *rason* (*q.v.*), the Ruthenians a tall round cap of their own, the Maronites a turban or cap, the Syrians the *kamelaukion* (*q.v.*), the Byzantines the *rason* and the *kamelaukion* etc. See HAT, i. The Malabarese wear Roman clothes, biretta and all, (*cf.*, BEARD).

DROIT DU SEIGNEUR (Fr., right of the lord). An alleged mediæval "right" whereby the lord held his vassal's bride at his own disposal on the night of her marriage. There is no reliable evidence for any such custom. It has been suggested, but without much probability, that this fable may have arisen from a misunderstanding of the pious custom called the "Tobias night," when a couple passed the first, or even the first three, nights of their marriage in a state of virginity, "as was confirmed by the example of Tobias" (Tobias viii, 4) and approved by religion.

DROMORE (*Dromorensis*). An Irish see, suffragan of Armagh. In 1705 the Bishop of Dromore was the only bishop in Ireland and he was in prison. The diocese includes parts of the counties of Down, Armagh and Antrim. The bishop's residence, cathedral and diocesan college are at Newry. The patron of the diocese is St. Colman (June 7), its first bishop, and the cathedral is dedicated in honour of St. Patrick. Irish name: Drom Mhór.

DRUNKENNESS. The state produced by excessive use of strong drink. It is either complete or partial. In the former state a man cannot distinguish between right and wrong and has no control over his actions, *i.e.*, he is deprived of the use of reason; to drink foreseeing that such drunkenness will result is a mortal sin. Should the loss of control stop at walking unsteadily, "seeing things," vomiting, etc., the drunkenness is partial and is usually a venial sin; it can become mortal through aggravating circumstances, *e.g.*, grave scandal, serious loss to oneself or one's family. A man is responsible for those sins committed during a drunken bout which experience tells him he is likely to commit.

DRUZES, THE. A sect that broke away from Islam in the 11th century. They live mostly in the Jebal Druze of the Lebanon, are of a fierce and warlike disposition, and the secular enemies of the Maronites (*q.v.*).

"DRY MASS" (Lat. *Missa sicca*) is not a Mass at all, but a recitation of the prayers of the Mass omitting the essentials, offertory, consecration, communion. It was once a very common practice upon occasions when Mass was impracticable, *e.g.*, at afternoon funerals, at sea (*Missa nautica*), for hunting men in a hurry (*Missa venatoria*), when no fasting priest was available, or out of devotion. The custom is still observed by the Carthusians, each of whom says a dry Mass (*officium Missæ*) of our Lady daily in his cell after Prime of the Little Office B.V.M. The rite of blessing of palms on Palm Sunday closely resembles a "dry Mass."

DRYNESS, SPIRITUAL. See ARIDITY.

DUALISM (Lat. *duo*, two). i. A philosophic and religious system according to which the universe is the work of two co-eternal and opposed principles, the one good, the other bad. See MANICHÆISM.

ii. A word also applied to those systems which teach a duality of beings irreducible among themselves: as God and the world; thought and extension. In this sense Dualism is opposed to Monism (*q.v.*).

DUBLIN (*Dublinensis*). An Irish see, founded in 1038 and made metropolitan in 1152. It now comprises the county of Dublin, most of Wicklow and parts of Kildare and Wexford, has 3 suffragan dioceses, and the archbishop bears the title of Primate of Ireland. The diocesan college is at Clonliffe. The chapter consists of a dean, precentor, chancellor, and two archdeacons (of Dublin and Glendalough), with 10 presbyteral, 4 diaconal and 8 subdiaconal prebends. Within the diocese are the national seminary at Maynooth, and All Hallows' missionary college conducted by the Lazarists. The patrons of the archdiocese are St. Kevin (June 3) and St. Lorcan (Lawrence) o'Toole (Nov. 14); the pro-cathedral is dedicated in honour of our Lady. Irish name: Baile Átha Cliath.

DUEL. A prearranged fight with deadly weapons between two persons, usually in the presence of witnesses called seconds, undertaken for the purpose of settling a private dispute, avenging an insult, etc. Duels are always unlawful when engaged in to decide a private quarrel because the danger to life involved is directly willed, and the combatants, their seconds and other assistants incur *ipso facto* excommunication whose absolution is simply reserved (*q.v.*) to the Holy See; this is even incurred by spectators who by their intentional presence associate themselves with the crime, by public officials who favour or do not try to prevent it, and by parties in a duel which is arranged to stop short of death or serious injury. Seriously to challenge or to accept is a grave sin, even if no duel result.

DULIA. The reverence and homage paid to saints and angels on account of their supernatural excellence and union with God. To be distinguished from the adoration of God (*latria, q.v.*) and the special honour paid to Mary (*hyperdulia, q.v.*). From the Greek δουλεία, the saints being the δουλοί, servants, of God.

DUNBOYNE ESTABLISHMENT, The. A department of Maynooth College providing a 3-years' course of higher ecclesiastical studies for picked students. It takes its name from a bequest of John Butler, 12th Baron Dunboyne, who was bishop of Cork but apostatized in 1787; he repented before his death in 1800 and left property in Meath to the college.

DUNENSIS ET CONNORENSIS. The adjectival form of the name of the see of Down and Connor (*q.v.*) used in the designation of its bishop in Latin documents. Noun: *Dunum et Connoria.*

DUNKELD (*Dunkeldensis*). A Scottish see, suffragan of Saint Andrews, founded before 1115, vacant from 1585 till 1878. It now includes in addition the old dioceses of Dunblane and Brechin and comprises the counties of Clackmannan, Angus, Kinross, Perth and part of Fife. The bishop's residence

and cathedral of St. Andrew are at Dundee. The patron of the diocese is St. Columba. Gaelic name: Dún-Chaillinn.

DUPLICATION, or BINATION. The celebration of two Masses by the same priest on the same day. Except on Christmas day and All Souls' day, when a priest may say three Masses, no priest may say more than one Mass a day without a papal indult or a faculty from the local ordinary. The latter may grant the faculty only if, through the scarcity of priests, a large number of persons would otherwise miss Mass on a day of obligation. The bishop may never permit more than two Masses by the same priest. When a priest says more than one Mass, the ablutions are not consumed till the last Mass.

DURATION. Permanence in being, with or without succession; with succession it is Time, without succession it is Eternity (*qq.v.*).

DURHAM, THE USE OF. The version of the Roman liturgy in use at the cathedral of Durham until the Reformation; it differed but little from that used at York and throughout the north of England.

DUTY. i. For general meaning see OBLIGATION.

ii. In a special sense duty, more usually duties, means attendance at Sunday Mass and frequentation of the sacraments, especially with reference to confession and to the Easter obligation.

DYING, PRAYERS FOR THE. See COMMENDATION OF A SOUL.

DYNAMISM (Gr. δύναμις, force, power). The system which explains matter by intrinsic and even immanent forces and not by extension and movement. Exaggerated Dynamism even identifies matter with force (Leibniz, Newton). Dynamism is opposed to Mechanicism (*q.v.*).

E

EARTH, BLESSED. It is the custom at funeral services which have of necessity to take place in private and at the house of the deceased, to put blessed earth into the coffin while the canticle *Benedictus* is said (*cf.*, the very ancient custom, still invariably observed by English Protestants, of throwing earth upon the coffin when it is in the grave; among Catholics it has been supplanted by the sprinkling of the coffin with holy water).

EARTHLY PARADISE, The. The Garden of Eden (*q.v.*).

EAST INDIES, PATRIARCH OF THE. A title of the Archbishop of Goa (Portuguese India), who is also called Primate of the

Orient; it has no significance except as a mark of honour bestowed by Pope Leo XIII in 1886. The see is simply metropolitan with 4 suffragans and certain privileges.

EAST INDIES (DUTCH), THE CHURCH IN THE. During the earlier Dutch occupation Catholic missions were not allowed, and the first missionaries began work only in 1808. Today there is a small Catholic minority in a population of many million Mohammedans, Buddhists and animists. These Indonesian islands are now independent.

EASTER (etymology uncertain; St. Bede derives it from *Eastre*, a forgotten dawn-goddess; see PASCH). The English name for the Sunday of the Resurrection of our Lord, "the feast of feasts," and "most solemn of all solemnities," for the Resurrection is the keystone of the Christian faith and hope; the rejoicing thereat is extended liturgically over 56 days, paschal-time (q.v.). The Mass for the day is really the second Mass of the feast: according to Ambrosian usage, two Masses are prescribed, one for the newly baptized and one for the feast (see HOLY SATURDAY). The whole octave was formerly kept as a holiday of obligation (q.v.); Monday and Tuesday are now feasts of devotion (q.v.) and Monday is a civil holiday in England, Wales and Ireland. The Masses of the week are notable for the sequence *Victimæ Paschali* (q.v.) and many references to the newly baptized of Holy Saturday. Meat, eggs and other foods formerly forbidden in Lent are blessed, and there are still numerous local customs, some of pagan origin. The special observances of the Byzantine rite include a procession overnight which leaves the church in darkness; the Resurrection is announced outside; a ceremony called "the Assault of Heaven" takes place at the doors; and the procession re-enters the brilliantly illuminated church; the greeting "Christ is risen." Ŗ. "Truly he is risen," is exchanged, guns are fired, bells rung, and fireworks set off; the crosses of the clergy and the Gospels are venerated and the Liturgy of St. John Chrysostom then begins.

EASTER CONTROVERSY, The. Disputes about the day on which Easter should be kept arose at the end of the 2nd century and again at the time of the first Council of Nicæa in 325 (see QUARTODECIMAN), but the above name is generally given to the triple disagreement between the native British Christians and St. Augustine of Canterbury. The three points at issue were: (a) that the Britons were still keeping the old Roman paschal cycle of 84 years (with the addition of a few mistakes of their own) instead of the cycle of 19 years adopted at Rome in 525; it was a question of reconciling the Jewish lunar year with the Roman solar year; (b) the Britons wore the tonsure (q.v.) peculiar to Celtic Christians; (c) there was something alleged to be wrong (we do not know what) with their baptismal rite. Both sides attached importance to these things and, though St. Augustine did not try to impose the Roman rite and customs in other matters and there was agreement about doctrine, the dispute was carried on until the Synod of Whitby (q.v.).

EASTER DUTIES. The obligation to receive holy communion at least at Easter time; in Great Britain, generally between Ash Wednesday and Low Sunday; Ireland, between Ash Wednesday and the octave of SS. Peter and Paul; the U.S.A., between the first Sunday in Lent and Trinity Sunday. This communion should be made if possible in one's parish church (if made elsewhere, one's parish-priest should be informed) and in one's own rite. Annual confession (q.v.) is usually made at the same time.

EASTER EGGS may possibly be a "baptized" pagan custom, since they are an obvious symbol of fertility. But an utilitarian explanation seems more likely: during Lent, eggs were forbidden in early times as articles of diet, so when Easter came, the eggs which had accumulated, lamb's flesh, etc., now once more available, were specially blessed, partly perhaps with a view to restraining gluttony after long deprivation (cf., Pancakes). In many places it is still the practice to paint the eggs and bring them to church in decorated baskets for a blessing before or after Mass. Chocolate eggs and such-like fooleries are a degeneration of no significance. Blessings for eggs, bread and the lamb at Easter are provided in the "Rituale Romanum."

EASTER VIGIL. See HOLY SATURDAY.

EASTER, DATE OF. Easter Sunday is the first Sunday after the full moon which occurs on or next after March 21; it therefore always falls on some date between March 22 and April 25 inclusive. This date for its observance was fixed by the Council of Nicæa in 325. In the dissident Eastern churches the rule for finding Easter is the same, but they continue to follow the Nicene regulation that it must always fall after the Jewish Passover; in addition many of them follow obsolete calendars (q.v.); in consequence the dates of the feast do not often coincide either among themselves or with the West. There is probably no theological or canonical objection to a fixed Easter, but it would be an innovation which many people would regret as a quite unnecessary rejection of ancient custom. Accumulation of convergent probabilities points to Sunday, April 9, A.D. 30, as the historical date.

EASTERN CHURCH, The. i. The term used officially at Rome to designate the Catholics of the Eastern rites as a body.

ii. Historically, the Patriarchates of Constantinople, Alexandria, Antioch and Jerusalem before the schism.

iii. Often inaccurately used by both Catholics and others for the Orthodox Eastern Church to-day. See EASTERN CHURCHES.

EASTERN CHURCHES, The, are either Catholic (see EASTERN RITES, CATHOLICS OF THE) or dissident, that is, non-Catholic. The dissidents are: (a) that body of independent national churches which together form the Orthodox Eastern Church (q.v.); and (b) the Nestorian, Armenian, Coptic, Ethiopic and Syrian Jacobite churches (qq.v.). These churches have it in common that they were all, at one time or another, parts of the

Catholic Church and that they all now deny the supreme authority of the Holy See, with other errors added thereto. They all teach the Real Presence, the Eucharistic Sacrifice (the Mass), confession, veneration of our Lady and the saints, prayers for the dead, and other doctrines and practices which are usually regarded as distinctively Catholic; and all (with the doubtful exceptions of the Copts and Ethiopians) have valid orders and sacraments, so that a dying Catholic may be absolved by and receive communion from one of their priests (as did certain Catholic Japanese during their war with Russia). The dissident Eastern churches must therefore be sharply distinguished from any of the Protestant bodies. Of late years the Church of England has sought a *rapprochement* with the Orthodox churches. Dissident Eastern Christians number about 48 million, excluding Russia.

EASTERN CONGREGATION, THE SACRED, was established as a separate body by Pope Benedict XV in 1917, having previously been a special congregation of Propaganda. To it are reserved all matters of every kind concerning persons, rites or discipline of Eastern churches, including those which in matter or person likewise affect Latins, and also those concerning Latins alone in certain Eastern countries (*e.g.*, Greece, Egypt). The pope himself is prefect of this congregation.

EASTERN RITES, CATHOLICS OF THE, are divided into those of the Byzantine rite (*q.v.*), Catholic Armenians, Chaldeans, Catholic Copts and Ethiopians, Maronites, Catholic Syrians, and those of Malabar (*qq.v.*). Except the Italo-Greeks (*q.v.*), all these bodies are composed of individuals or groups or their descendants who have, mostly in the 16th and 17th centuries, returned to Catholic unity from the corresponding non-Catholic church of their rite, and are often called Uniates (*q.v.*). They are as fully and completely Catholics as those of the West. They keep their own liturgies, canon law and customs not by concession but by right, as Latins hold theirs; in these things they differ greatly among themselves and from the Western church, but in faith, morals and obedience to the Holy See there is no difference. Nor are they a "half-way house" between the Latin and dissident Eastern churches; they simply represent what, before the schisms, were the great Eastern patriarchates (*q.v.*) of the Catholic Church; they do not belong to the Latin part of the Church any more than did St. John Chrysostom, St. Athanasius or St. Ephrem: "The Church of Christ is neither Latin nor Greek nor Slavonic, but Catholic; all her children are equal in her sight" (Pope Benedict XV). Of all Christians of Eastern rites, 4.5% are Catholic; of all Catholics, 2.5% are of Eastern rites; they number over 8 millions in all, of whom nearly one million are in North America, mostly Ruthenians.

EASTERN STUDIES, THE PONTIFICAL INSTITUTE FOR (The Oriental Institute). Founded by Pope Benedict XV in 1917, is a house of studies for oriental clergy, whether Catholic or dissident. Western clergy may also follow the course, which is for three years, in theology, canon law, liturgy, sacred and profane history, archæology, etc. It is now one of the autonomies constituting the pontifical university ("the Gregorian") for ecclesiastical studies, and is under the direction of Jesuits.

EBIONITES, The. An heretical sect known chiefly in Palestine from the 1st to the 4th centuries. They denied the divinity and virgin birth of our Lord; observed the Jewish Law and in consequence regarded St. Paul as an apostate and rejected his authority; and used only one Gospel, attributed to St. Matthew. Their Judaism was modified later and the sect mostly became a form of Gnosticism (*q.v.*).

ECCE HOMO (Lat., Behold the man, John xix, 5). An image of our Lord, often the head only, crowned with thorns.

ECCLESIA (Gr. ἐκκλησία, assembly). The word used in the Septuagint to translate the Heb. *qahal*, meaning the children of Israel as a religious body, and in the New Testament for the Church of Christ as opposed to the Synagogue of the Jews. It has now a number of modified significations, all of which are rendered in English as "church" (*q.v.*, German *kirche* and other Teutonic forms).

ECCLESIA ANGLICANA. The English Church (*q.v.*), a common name for the Church in England in papal and other documents (including *Magna Carta*). So also *E. Scotica* for the Church in Scotland, *E. Gallicana* for the Church in France, etc.

ECCLESIA DISCENS (Lat., The Learning Church). The body of the faithful who accept the infallible teaching of the *Ecclesia Docens* (*q.v.*).

ECCLESIA DOCENS (Lat., The Teaching Church). The successors of the apostles in their office as teachers, *i.e.*, the pope in person, and the body of bishops in union with the pope.

ECCLESIASTES (Heb. *Qoheleth*, the Preacher). A book of the Old Testament. According to both Jewish and Christian tradition it was written by King Solomon, in view of the luxury to which he had given himself (3 Kings x, xi, 1–8). "Vanity of vanities, and all is vanity" is his text throughout; the disappointments of earthly life can only be met by mortification, patience and wisdom, that is, the remembrance of God and observance of his commandments.

ECCLESIASTIC. A cleric, person in holy orders, especially of the superior ranks.

ECCLESIASTICAL TITLES ACT, The (14–15 Victoria, c. 60). A measure passed through Parliament in 1851 in consequence of the reestablishment of a Catholic hierarchy in England in the previous year. It made it a penal offence for a Catholic bishop to adopt and use the name of any place in Great Britain as his territorial title; it declared all acts done under such titles to be null and void and property bequeathed to such persons to be forfeited to the Crown. The bill was never put into force and was repealed in 1871; the first prelate to ignore it, by signing himself on a public document "William, Bishop of Hexham," was Mgr. Hogarth (1786-1866). The Relief Act of 1829 had provided that Catholic bishops were not to use territorial titles borne by Anglican bishops and in England this has been studiously avoided; Anglicans have not used the like courtesy, e.g., Liverpool, Southwark.

ECCLESIASTICUS (Lat., from Gr., The Preacher). A deutero-canonical book (q.v.) of the Old Testament, properly known as "The Wisdom of Jesus the son of Sirach." It is rejected from Protestant versions of the Bible but included in their Apocrypha (q.v.). It is known in its entirety only through a Greek version; of the Hebrew original only about a half has been discovered. It contains dogmatic and moral teaching centring around the eternal and creative wisdom of God, and the wisdom of man which consists in submission to him. Nothing is known of Joshua ben Sira but he probably wrote about 200 B.C.

ECLECTICISM (Gr. ἐκλέγειν, to choose). A philosophic system which consists in choosing what is good in each system, thus endeavouring to harmonize all systems, at least in some way. Eclecticism differs from Syncretism in that the first chooses with discernment, the latter on the contrary embraces the irreconcilable and incompatible.

ECONOMICS. A science which investigates the general laws which, in a given state of society, govern the production of goods and services, their distribution among men, the methods by which this distribution is carried out, and the various ways in which goods and services are used or consumed. There are no "iron laws of Economics" which coerce the human will and render nugatory the natural laws of morality; and the science should conduct its investigations and present its conclusions with due regard to moral law when it conflicts with economic phenomena.

ECONOMY (Gr. οἰκονόμος, steward). The art of orderly management in any sphere; hence political economy, domestic economy the economy of nature, doctrinal economy (i.e., its judicious presentation so as to suit individual needs and conciliate prejudices), the economy of Redemption (i.e., the orderly plan actually adopted by God), etc.

ECSTASY (Gr. ἔκτασις, the state of being put out of one's senses). A very vivid act of contemplation accompanied by the alienation of sense life. A state in which the soul is rapt in God and receives wonderful spiritual illumination: so intense is the prayer that the soul goes out of the body, as it were, the senses are inhibited, and the vegetative functions slow down. The body is not injured, but rather strengthened, by the experience. Sham ecstasies are marked by injury to the nerves, sometimes by unseemliness, and by a complete absence of spiritual profit. Ecstasies do not as a rule last long. It does not seem necessary to ecstatic prayer that the senses should be alienated, for the great Western mystics of the "Benedictine centuries" furnish no evidence of such bodily phenomena; in any case the alienation is not miraculous, but merely the natural result of the transports of the soul.

ECUADOR, THE CHURCH IN. Four-fifths of the 2½ million people in the Republic of The Equator are Indians and half-caste, mostly Catholic by profession except for a number of Indians. Ecuador was the only state in the world to protest officially against the seizure of Rome from the Holy See in 1870, and moreover voted a subsidy to the pope; but since 1895 it has become semi-secularist. Church and state have been separated, ecclesiastical property put under state control (not confiscated, however), new religious orders forbidden, and foreigners not allowed to hold higher ecclesiastical offices; public education is secular. But there is freedom of worship for all religions, clergy are exempt from military service, and diplomatic relations were re-established with the Holy See in 1937. The country forms one metropolitan province (the archbishopric, Quito, was founded in 1545), with 6 suffragan sees and several vicariates and prefectures in the Indian missions.*

EDEN, THE GARDEN OF. The home of our first parents. Its situation is not certainly known but it is generally said to have been between the rivers Euphrates and Tigris. Here Adam and Eve dwelt in a state of original justice, immortality and integrity (qq.v.) until the Fall (q.v.).

EDICT OF MILAN, The. The announcement by which the Emperor Constantine in 313 granted freedom in the exercise of their religion to Christians and all others.

EDICT OF NANTES, The. An act of King Henry IV of France in 1598, closing the seventh of the Wars of Religion. It accorded to the Huguenots, among other things, full liberty of private worship; complete control of 200 towns, some fortified, with right of

---

* For ECUMENICAL, see OECUMENICAL.—*Publisher,* 1997.

public worship therein and in 3,000 domains of the higher nobility and other places; special departments in the courts to try their cases; and access to all public offices. Thus, in effect, was set up a Protestant state within the state. King Louis XIV, bent on religious unity, and with the support of the Gallican hierarchy, interpreted the edict in the strictest sense and began to encroach on its provisions; irritation was caused by the continued persecution of Catholics in England and elsewhere; and the edict was formally revoked in 1685. Profession of the "so-called Reformed Religion" was made a legal offence; children had to be baptized and brought up Catholics; converted pastors were to receive a pension; a Protestant was at liberty to remain such but might not engage in even private collective worship. The revocation was imposed with violence and cruelty, the alternative to conversion being imprisonment and loss of goods; thousands of refugees fled to England, Holland and elsewhere; others took up arms in the Cevennes and other parts and were hunted down. The responsibility for the revocation and what followed rests with the king personally; Pope Innocent XI had approved of the general scheme for a "general conversion," but except in matters strictly spiritual the pope was almost powerless in the France of Louis XIV and Gallicanism.

EDIFICATION (Lat. *ædificare*, to build up). An expression used by St. Paul to denote the building-up of the Mystical Body of Christ, his Church, by the diverse gifts given to some and by the good example of charity given by each one to another (Eph. iv, 12, 16). The word is often now used in the less noble way of indicating the emotional reaction of an individual to an action or other thing which he considers devotional; "disedifying" too often simply means that the speaker doesn't like it (*cf.*, Scandal).

EDUCATION (Lat. *educere*, to bring out, develop). The provision of suitable instruction to fit the child for the duties of adult life. Catholics have always held that intellectual education must not be separated from religious and moral instruction. This complete education is primarily the grave duty of the parents, who are consequently strictly forbidden to send their children to a non-Catholic school, even though no religion is taught there. Not even the bishop can dispense from this prohibition when there is positive danger of the children's perversion; if such danger is absent and no suitable Catholic school is available, the bishop alone has power to dispense. It is no part of the normal function of the state to teach. It is entitled to see that citizens receive education sufficient to enable them to discharge the duties of citizenship in its various degrees, and may therefore take means to safeguard the efficiency of education. To parents too

poor to pay for the education of their children, it is the duty of the state to furnish the necessary means from the common taxation of the whole community. But in so doing the state must not interfere with parental responsibility, nor hamper the reasonable liberty of parents in a choice of a school for their children. Where the people are not all of one creed, there must be no differentiation on the ground of religion. Where there is need of greater school accommodation the state may, in default of other agencies, intervene to supply it; but only "in default of, and in substitution for and to the extent of, the responsibility of the parents" of the children who need this accommodation. The teacher is always acting *in loco parentis*, never *in loco civitatis*, though the state may take reasonable care to see that teachers are efficient. Thus a teacher never is, and never can be, a civil servant, and should never regard himself or allow himself to be so regarded. Whatever authority he may possess to teach and control children, and to claim their respect and obedience, comes to him from God through the parents and not through the state, except in so far as the state is acting on behalf of the parents. The above principles (which were reaffirmed in Pope Pius XI's encyclical to the bishops of Italy, Dec. 31, 1929) are not in entire accordance with those of the present system of universal compulsory schooling. The Church affirms that instruction in the Christian faith, and not in profane subjects, is the first essential of the right ordering of human life.

EDUCTION. The action of drawing forth a form from the potentiality of matter; *e.g.*, the artist draws forth, in somewise, the shape of a statue from the marble. In the same way, *servatis servandis*, a substantial form (*q.v.*) is educed by an agent capable of doing so from the potentiality of prime matter (*q.v.*).

EDWARDINE ORDINAL, The. The rites for the ordination of bishops, priests and deacons drawn up during the reign of Edward VI by certain Protestant prelates with the approval of Parliament, and published in 1552 for use in England. It is on the insufficiency of the forms in this ordinal that the invalidity of Anglican orders (*q.v.*) primarily depends. Additions to these forms were made in 1662 but, even if they were sufficient, it was then too late; ordinations by the 1552 rites had been regarded by the Holy See as invalid from the very beginning.

EFFECT. That which begins to be. See CAUSE.

EGYPT, THE CHURCH IN. Egypt (Misr) has a population of 17 million, 92 per cent Mohammedan, and Islam is the official religion of the state; but all faiths may be freely practised. The largest Christian body is the separated Coptic Church (*q.v.*) and there is the Orthodox patriarchate of Alexandria (*q.v.*). Catholics number about 227,000 half of whom are orientals of various rites and the rest (mostly European foreigners) of the Latin rite. Catholics of the Coptic rite (*q.v.*) have a patriarchal and 3 episcopal sees; the Armenian and Maronite rites have each a diocese; the Melkites, Syrians, and Chaldeans (*qq.v.*) all have patriarchal vicars. The Latins are organized in 1 diocese and 2 vicariates apostolic.

EIKON. See ICON.

EILETON. A square of linen serving, in the Byzantine rite, the same purpose as a corporal (*q.v.*). When not in use the *antimension* is wrapped in it.

EJACULATION. A prayer consisting of a few words only which can be repeated often and at any time (*e.g.*, "Jesus, mercy! Mary, help!" "My Lord and my God!"); many ejaculations have indulgences (*q.v.*) attached to them.

EKPHONESIS (Gr., lifting of the voice). The final words of a prayer said or sung aloud when the previous part has been said silently; such are the words *Per omnia sæcula sæculorum* (For ever and ever) at the end of the "secret" (*q.v.*), and elsewhere in the Mass. The *ekphonesis* enables the people to know where the celebrant has got to, and is used in all liturgies, particularly the Byzantine and Armenian.

EKTENES (Gr., extended). In the Byzantine rite, a series of supplications for various classes of people recited by the deacon, the choir and people responding *Kyrie eleison* (*q.v.*) once or thrice to each petition. Such a litany is said at *Hesperinos*, *Orthros* (*qq.v.*), and in the Liturgy, when the celebrant's corresponding prayer ends with an *ekphonesis* (*q.v.*).

ELECT, THE. Those chosen by God either (*a*) for the grace of faith and the true religion (the most common sense), or (*b*) for eternal glory. See ELECTION, i.

ELECTION. i. Theological. A divine decree antecedent to Predestination (*q.v.*) by which God intends to give to the predestined eternal glory and the graces and merits necessary for the attainment of that glory. According to St. Thomas, it is an act of the will, whereas predestination is an act of intelligence. The predestined are the objects of a true election on the part of God. St. Thomas teaches (I, xxiii, 4) that "Predestination of its very nature presupposes election, and election love. The reason is that predestination is a part of Providence," which orders things to an end, and thus involves the previous willing of that end (election).

ii. In canon law. Where the provision of an ecclesiastical office is in the hands of a collegiate body, such provision is made by election, by the ballot of those entitled to vote. The election must be held within three months of the vacancy, and the person elected must accept or renounce within eight days. Election often requires confirmation by a superior. The pope is elected by the Sacred College of Cardinals; election of a bishop by a chapter is now rare.

iii. Papal. The third Lateran Council enacted that a pope should be elected by the cardinals alone, and that two-thirds of the votes of the cardinals present were necessary to the validity of the election. The general rules applicable to the election are set out in the constitution *Vacantis Apostolicæ Sedis* of Pope Pius XII in 1945. See CONCLAVE.

ELECTORS, IMPERIAL. Those in whom was vested the power of electing the Holy Roman emperors: originally all the princes generally; from the 13th century the Archbishops of Cologne, Trier and Mainz, the King of Bohemia, the Elector Palatine, the Electors of Saxony and Brandenburg; an Elector of Bavaria was added in 1648, one of Hanover in 1692, one each for Würtemberg and Hesse in 1801. The Golden Bull of the Emperor Charles IV at the Diet of Nürnberg in 1356 finally settled the number and the precedence of the electoral college and was henceforth regarded as a fundamental law of the Empire until the Peace of Westphalia (1648).

ELECTRIC LIGHT (or gas) may be used for the lighting of churches, but not as an element of the services nor with theatrical effect. It is forbidden to be used in connexion with candles on the altar or as a substitute for the candles prescribed to be before the Blessed Sacrament or sacred relics exposed; nor may it be used to light up the interior of the tabernacle or of the place where the Blessed Sacrament is exposed by putting lights therein. It may be used instead of a sanctuary lamp in extreme necessity at the discretion of the ordinary.

ELEEMOSYNARY. Concerned with, dependent upon, alms. From Greek ἐλεημοσύνη (*i.e.*, compassionateness) is the Latin *eleemosyna* (whence the above word), which in Old English became *ælmysee* and is now *alms*.

ELEMENTS, EUCHARISTIC. The bread and wine used in the consecration at Mass. The word "elements" is used by St. Jerome for food and drink; but it is also used for the matter (*q.v.*) of a sacrament. Either leavened or unleavened bread, made of wheat, is valid matter; but, for lawfulness, unleavened bread must be used in the Latin rite and leavened in most others. The wine must be the juice of the grape, unmixed with any other liquor in notable quantity.

ELEVATION, THE LITTLE. At the end of the prayer *Nobis quoque peccatoribus* which precedes the *Paternoster* at Mass the celebrant, after three signs of the cross with the Host over the Chalice and two between the Chalice and his breast, lifts the Chalice and Host together a few inches above the altar to express the offering up of the sacrifice of praise. It may originally have been an invitation to those around to adore, as the gesture was known at least 300 years before the elevation at the consecration. Its equivalent is properly the only elevation in Eastern liturgies, and is more solemnly carried out.

ELEVATION OF THE HOST, The, for adoration immediately after its consecration at Mass is a relatively recent custom first observed at the end of the 12th century in the diocese of Paris as a protest against the erroneous teaching that our Lord's body was not present until after the consecration of the chalice. The celebrant is instructed to lift the Host so that the people can see it; they therefore are intended to look at it and adore. The elevation of the Chalice was not the rule until the end of the 16th century, and is still not done by the Carthusians who, moreover, do not genuflect completely at the consecration. See also ELEVATION, LITTLE. There are normally no corresponding elevations in Eastern rites; see HOLY THINGS TO THE HOLY. But the Catholic Armenians, Malabarese and others tend to adopt forms of the Western practice.

ELEVEN THOUSAND VIRGINS, The. Nothing at all is known of these maidens beyond the fact that they were martyrs at Cologne before the 4th century. Their number, "eleven thousand," is purely fabulous; early mediæval calendars vary between five and eleven, units, not thousands. The Roman Martyrology has on Oct. 21, "At Cologne, the birthday of SS. Ursula and her companions, martyrs," etc. According to one legend they were British maidens, fleeing from the Saxons, who fell into the hands of the Huns.

ELEVEN BISHOPS, The. Those bishops of the Church in England who were ejected from their sees by Queen Elizabeth and died in prison or under other restraint between 1559 and 1578, namely, Tunstall of Durham, Boyle of Lichfield, Oglethorpe of Carlisle, White of Winchester, Pate of Worcester, Poole of Peterborough, Bonner of London, Bourne of Bath and Wells, Thirlby of Ely, Turberville of Exeter, and Heath of York. The last survivor of the old hierarchy was Goldwell of Saint Asaph, who escaped from England and died in Rome in 1585; he became vicegerent of Rome and was the only English bishop at the Council of Trent.

ELIAS. The great prophet of the Old Testament, who appeared at our Lord's transfiguration. In some versions of the Bible he is called Elijah. He is mentioned in the "Roman Martyrology" on July 20,

on which day Catholics, Orthodox, Jews and Moslems together honour him on Mount Carmel; the Carmelites have a liturgical feast in his honour on that day, they regarding him as their founder or at least as their spiritual father. *See* III Kings xvii—IV Kings ii.

ELIJAH. The Hebrew form of the name of the prophet Elias.

ELISEUS. A Hebrew prophet, the successor of Elias, called in some versions of the Bible, Elisha. He is mentioned in the Roman Martyrology on June 14, on which day the Carmelites keep his feast with proper Mass and Office.

ELISHA. The Hebrew form of the name of the prophet Eliseus.

ELOHIM. One of the three common names used in the Heb. Old Testament for God, the others being *El* and *Eloah*. Its meaning is uncertain.

ELPHIN (*Elphinensis*). An Irish see, suffragan of Tuam. It comprises parts of the counties of Roscommon, Sligo and Galway. The bishop's residence and cathedral are now at Sligo. The patron of the diocese is St. Asicus (April 27), its first bishop, who is also titular of the cathedral. Irish name: Aill Finn.

ELVIRA, THE COUNCIL OF. A synod of Spanish bishops held in the 3rd-4th century, important because it was the first to impose celibacy on bishops, priests and deacons (canon xxxiii).

EMANATION. The process of coming from another. That which emanates is of the substance of the one from which it emanates. Emanatism is the theory that created things are emanations of God; they are, therefore, particles, as it were, of the substance of God. This is Pantheism (*q.v.*).

EMANCIPATION, CATHOLIC. The removal of those disabilities under which the Catholics of Great Britain and Ireland lived during penal-times (*q.v.*). This was the work of four parliamentary measures. (*a*) 18 George III c. 60 (1778) which enabled Catholics who took a prescribed oath of loyalty legally to inherit and purchase land; the clergy could no longer be prosecuted at the instance of common informers; the penalty of life-imprisonment for keeping a school was removed; (*b*) 31 George III c. 32 (1791) renewed the oath; those who took it were free from prosecution for saying or hearing Mass, for being clergy or religious, or for otherwise exercising their religion; Catholic schools were made legal; the legal and military professions were opened to Catholics, but they could not be officers, judges or king's counsel; (*c*) 33 George III c. (1793) admitted Irish Catholics to the franchise, bar, army, navy and universities, and put them almost on a level with Protestants; (d) 10 George IV c. 7 (1829), The Roman Catholic Relief Act again imposed an oath (abolished in 1871), but admitted English Catholics once more as full members of the state; nearly all disabilities were done away with and most public offices were opened to Catholics; they could sit in Parliament and vote at elections. This was not a measure of justice to a tiny minority in England (some 500,000) and to a big majority in Ireland so much as an act of expediency wrung from an unwilling government and an unsympathetic country by fear of the then Irish situation. Catholics were still disqualified from presenting to Anglican livings and from holding the offices of regent, lord chancellor of Great Britain or Ireland, lord lieutenant of Ireland, and commander-in-chief of the military forces; marriages before priests were still invalid at law; Catholic soldiers and sailors were still bound to attend Protestant church-parade; Catholic charities were superstitious usages. Bishops were forbidden to assume the titles of ancient sees; religious (Jesuits were mentioned by name) resident in the country were ordered to register themselves, and such coming into the country from abroad were guilty of misdemeanour; religious celebrations and dress in public were forbidden. None of these last three restrictions were seriously enforced, though the third was invoked at the time of the Westminster Eucharistic Congress in 1908. All but a few existing disabilities (*q.v.*) were removed by an Act of 1926.

EMBASSY CHAPEL. A chapel attached to the household of a foreign ambassador. Owing to their extra-territorial status these were immune from the operation of the penal laws (*q.v.*) in England, and were in consequence much resorted to by London Catholics in the 17th and 18th centuries. The best known were the Bavarian, Sardinian and Spanish chapels (*qq.v.*).

EMBER DAYS (derivation uncertain). The Wednesday, Friday and Saturday following the first Sunday in Lent, Whitsunday, Holy Cross day (Sept. 14), and St. Lucy's day (Dec. 13), which are days of fasting for the special sanctification of the four seasons, and for obtaining God's blessing on the clergy, for whose ordination the Ember Saturdays are specially set apart. They are of very ancient use but uncertain origin. The propers of the Masses reflect the season in which they occur; those for Wednesday keep the old custom of two lessons before the gospel and the ones of Saturday have six lessons. At capitular high Mass these are sung by the canons in turn.

EMBLEM. A device or badge associated with a person or thing in pictorial or other representation; it must be distinguished from a symbol, which itself represents some-

thing else, *e.g.*, a triangle for the Holy Trinity, whereas an emblem (except in a few special instances) cannot stand alone. Common emblems of saints are: an anchor, Philomena and Rose of Lima; an arrow, Sebastian, Ursula, Teresa and others; an axe, Bartholomew, Matthew and Peter Martyr; a bell, Antony the Abbot and Benedict; boy in a boat, Nicholas; a bull, Luke, Blandina and others; carpenter's square, Joseph, Thomas and Jude; a chalice, John Evangelist, Bruno and others; a child, Augustine of Hippo and Hilary; cross, John Baptist, Helen and others; crown of thorns, Agnes, Catherine of Siena and others; a dragon, Margaret, George; a dog, Hubert and Roch; a dove, Ambrose, Gregory, David and others; an eagle, John Evangelist and Augustine; fetters, Vincent de Paul and others; a flowering staff, Joseph; a gridiron, Lawrence; the infant Jesus, Christopher and Antony of Padua; a hind, Giles; a hive, Bernard and Ambrose; a hog, Antony the Abbot; a Host, Ignatius Loyola and others; an instrument of music, Cecily; keys, Peter; a lamb, John Baptist and Agnes; a lily, Joseph, Aloysius and others; a lion, Mark and Jerome; long hair, Agnes, Mary Magdalene and Mary the Egyptian; a monstrance, Clare, Norbert and others; a pen, Augustine, John Chrysostom, Thomas Aquinas, and others; a raven, Paul the Hermit, Benedict; a rosary, Dominic; roses, Elizabeth of Hungary, Teresa of Lisieux and others; a saw, Joseph and Simon; a skull, Jerome and Bruno; a snake, our Lady, Patrick and others; a ship, Peter, Ursula and others; sheep, Joan of Arc, Genevieve, Brigid and others; scallop shell, James the Greater; spiked wheel, Catherine of Alexandria; a star, Dominic; a stag, Hubert and Eustace; stigmata, Francis of Assisi, Catherine of Siena and others; a sword, Paul, Catherine of Alexandria and others; saltire cross, Andrew; tiger, Irenæus; vase, Mary Magdalen and Remi; wreath of flowers, Dorothy, Rose and many others. It is not by any means always possible to recognize an image of a saint by its emblem, as some are common to many, but a combination of two or three emblems will often give the clue. Certain emblems are proper to classes, *e.g.*, the palm to martyrs, a church-building to founders of churches, a book or pen to founders of orders, doctors and evangelists, a crown to royal persons, etc.

EMBOLISM (Gr. ἐμβαλλειν, to throw in). An insertion or addition. The word is applied particularly to the prayer inserted immediately after the *Paternoster* at Mass, beginning, "Deliver us, we beseech thee, O Lord," which is an amplification of the last petition of the Lord's Prayer. A similar addition is found in all other liturgies, except the Byzantine and Ethiopic.

EMINENCE. "Your Eminence," "His Eminence," "Most Eminent," "Most reverend

Eminence," is the mode of address proper to cardinals and to them only, with the sole exception of the Grand Master of the Knights of St. John of Jerusalem.

EMINENT. A mode (*q.v.* i) in which a perfection is said to be contained in something in a higher way; *e.g.*, the vegetative soul is contained eminently in the spiritual soul because, although not contained there formally as such and distinct from the spiritual soul, nevertheless the latter can do everything a vegetative soul can do. On the other hand a perfection can be contained in something both eminently and formally. See below.

EMINENTLY. An important distinction is to be made between the words "eminently," "formally," "virtually." It is possible to conceive, *e.g.*, of an effect in its cause in three ways: (1) under another form, but in a superior way; thus knowledge in man is eminently in God; (2) under the same form, and thus the human nature of a child is formally in its parents; (3) simply in the potency of another, that is virtually; thus is the oak in the acorn.

EMLY (*Emeliensis*). An Irish see now in the perpetual administration of the archbishop of Cashel (*q.v.*).

EMMANUEL, "Which being interpreted is, *God with us.*" A name given to our Lord in prophecy (Isa. vii, 14, viii, 8) and referred to by St. Matthew (i, 23). The church of the vicar apostolic of Natal at Durban is dedicated to Christ under this title, a very uncommon usage among Catholics.

EMOTION (Lat. *emovere*, to move). Complex feeling (*q.v.*) inducing a state of consciousness formed by the fusion of minor feelings.

EMPEROR, The, formerly referred to in the Roman liturgy was the ruler of the Holy Roman Empire (*q.v.*). The prayers for him on Good Friday and in the *Exsultet* are now replaced by prayers for the rulers of states. From 1530 until the dissolution of the Empire in 1806 the Holy See recognized its rulers only as "emperors elect," as during that time no one of them presented himself for imperial coronation at Rome.

EMPIRICISM (Gr. ἐμπειρία, experience). A theory which accentuates the assumption that all our mental possessions are a product of purely sensuous experience.

EMPLOYERS, DUTIES OF. The Christian religion teaches that "owners and employers must not regard their work-people as their slaves; . . . that work is not a thing to be ashamed of . . . but an honourable calling; . . . and that it is shameful and inhuman to treat men as chattels or to look on them as so much muscle and physical power whereby money may be made. . . . The employer is bound to see that the worker has time for his religious duties; that he is not exposed to evil influences and dangerous occasions; and that he be not led away to neglect his home and family or to squander his earnings. [He] must never work his employees beyond their strength or employ them on work unsuited to their sex or age. His great and chief duty is to give everyone a fair wage . . . to make one's profit out of another's need is condemned by all laws, human and divine. . . . The rich must religiously refrain from cutting down workmen's earnings, whether by force, fraud or usurious dealing" (Pope Leo XIII, *Rerum novarum;* cf., servants, living wage).

ENCÆNIA. i. A Jewish feast commemorating the re-dedication of the Temple after it had been desecrated by Antiochus Epiphanes. *cf.*, Ps. xxix and John x, 22.

ii. A feast commemorating the dedication on Sept. 13 and 14, 335, of the basilica of the Resurrection built by Constantine between Calvary and the Holy Sepulchre. It was formerly a very great solemnity and is still kept in the Byzantine rite on Sept. 13.

ENCLOSURE. (*a*) That part of a monastery or convent which has been canonically enclosed as the residing place of the religious. (*b*) The restriction imposed by the law regarding this material enclosure. The extent of building enclosed is arbitrary and governed by requirements; thus the quire of the church is nearly always enclosed but the nave not, and there are usually public rooms at the entrance to the monastery itself: but the boundaries of the enclosure must be clearly indicated.

i. Male religious may not leave their enclosure without permission of their superior, but permission is freely given as occasion requires. Laymen may enter a monastery of men when invited to do so, but women are strictly excluded; both she who enters and the religious admitting her *ipso facto* incur excommunication absolutely reserved to the Holy See. But queens and similar personages with their retinues and notable benefactresses with a papal indult may claim admittance.

ii. Female religious with solemn vows (*q.v.*) are more strictly enclosed. No professed nun may leave the enclosure except with a papal indult, or being in danger of death, or on account of other very grave evil. No one, male or female, clerical or lay, may enter their enclosure; offenders and those who admit them incur excommunication as above. There are the following necessary exceptions: the bishop or superior of the order or their delegates when making a visitation; the confessor, to minister to the sick or dying; reigning sovereigns, their consorts; cardinals, and their attendant court; physicians and workmen when required. Under varying conditions a nun professed in solemn vows may receive visitors in the "parlour" where conversation takes place through a large grating (grille), which may be curtained. The laws for nuns with simple vows (q.v.) are less rigorous unless the rule of their institute involves the strict enclosure; but even then they are not protected by the excommunications and other legislation of the papal enclosure of the solemnly vowed. Enclosed nuns engaged in active work freely meet outsiders within the limits of their school, hospital, etc.

ENCYCLICAL. An encyclical letter is one addressed by the pope to the patriarchs, primates, archbishops, bishops and other ordinaries of the whole Church or, less often, to the hierarchy of a particular country (e.g., the letter of Pope Leo XIII "to the English" in 1895). Of late years the Roman pontiffs have more and more expressed their minds in this form of utterance: e.g., Pius IX in *Quanta cura* which accompanied the Syllabus (q.v.) of 1864; Leo XIII in *Æterni Patris*, on the philosophy of St. Thomas, *Immortale Dei* on Christianity and the state, *Rerum novarum*, on "the condition of the working classes," *Providentissimus Deus*, on the study of the Bible; Pius X in *Pascendi*, which condemned Modernism; Benedict XV in *Maximum illud* on the need for "native clergy" (q.v.), *Humani generis*, on preaching, and five on peace; Pius XI in *Mortalium animos* on the unity of the Church, in *Orientalium rerum* on the Eastern churches, and in *Quas primas* on the kingship of Christ; Pius XII in *Mystici Corporis Christi* on the mystical Body of Christ. Encyclicals are not necessarily infallible documents, though the pope could choose to speak *ex cathedra* by means of them if he wished to do so; but if they contain doctrinal teaching Catholics are bound to give to them interior as well as exterior assent and obedience.

ENCYCLOPÆDISTS, The. The contributors to the "Encyclopédie, ou Dictionnaire raisonné des sciences, des arts et des métiers . . ." edited by Diderot and d'Alembert between 1751 and 1765; among them were Rousseau, Grimm, Voltaire, the Baron d'Holbach, Condorcet, Buffon, Turgot. The name is particularly given to the group called "the philosophers" who gave the "Encyclopédie" a twist towards infidelity, freethinking and rationalism and whose general writing and teaching prepared the mind of France for the irreligion of the Revolution.

END (Lat. *finis*). That for the sake of which something is done. (a) *Finis qui:* the thing intended; *finis cui:* the subject for whose benefit the thing is intended; *finis quo:* the attainment or use of the thing intended. (b) *Finis operis:* the thing to which an action tends of its own nature (e.g., an alms given relieves the poor); *finis operantis:* the thing to which an agent directs an action (e.g., an alms given for vainglory). (c) Proximate, intermediate and ultimate (or last) ends are self-explanatory. (d) Primary end; the end which principally moves an agent to act and which is of itself sufficient; secondary, the end which of itself is not sufficient but yet attracts an agent to act; e.g., the primary end of marriage is procreation of children, a secondary end is for instance the comforts of a home, etc. (cf., Motive, Intention).

END JUSTIFIES THE MEANS, The. A false doctrine which teaches that sinful means may lawfully be used to produce a good effect, often—but wrongly—ascribed to the moralist Busembaum (d. 1678) and other Jesuits. It has been repeatedly condemned, from St. Paul onwards (Rom. iii, 8); no sinful act whatever may be committed that good may come.

END OF THE WORLD, The. That this world shall have an end, when Jesus Christ shall come again in glory to judge both the living and the dead, is taught by the Church as a matter of revealed truth. As to when or how this will happen, she teaches nothing. The events accompanying the end of this world are referred to in many places of the New Testament (e.g., Matt. xxiv, xxv, 31-46; Luke xxi, 5-28; the Apocalypse), but as to their time or order nothing is known. Of them our Lord said, "Of that day and hour no man knoweth, neither the angels in Heaven, nor the Son, but the Father" (Mark xiii, 32); but "that these things will happen we must believe, but how or in what order experience will show us better than any human intelligence can clearly discover."

ENDOWMENT. The endowment is an essential element of an ecclesiastical benefice and of all pious foundations. It is for the ordinary (q.v.) to determine the amount of endowment necessary. The regular offerings of the faithful may be reckoned as endowment, and in case of necessity parishes may be erected without endowment. Funds for endowment must be safely and fruitfully invested by the ordinary.

ENDS OF THE MASS, The Four, for which it is daily and always offered, are: adoration, the worship of Almighty God; thanksgiving; reparation for the sins of the world; and petition for all the needs of the world.

ENERGUMEN (Gr., worked up; cf., energetic). A demoniac, one possessed. The name was commonly used of these unfortunates in the early Church, when they formed a distinct class among Christians.

ENERGY. i. In Aristotle ἐνέργεια is opposed to δύναμις as act (q.v.) is opposed to potency (q.v.).

ii. Principle of the Conservation of. . . . This consists in affirming that in a closed system (that is, one upon which forces external to the system do not act) the total sum of energy is invariable whatever transformations may take place within that closed system.

ENGAGEMENT. See BETROTHAL.

ENGLAND AND WALES, THE CHURCH IN. The hierarchy of the Catholic Church in this country was restored in 1850 (cf., English church, Penal Times, Wales) and in 1908 it ceased to be a missionary country (q.v.) in the technical sense. It now consists of four provinces: Westminster (whose archbishop is perpetual president of the bishops of the country), with the suffragan sees of Brentwood, Northampton, Nottingham, Portsmouth, and Southwark; Birmingham, with the archdiocese of Birmingham and three suffragan sees, Clifton, Plymouth, and Shrewsbury; Liverpool, with the archdiocese of Liverpool and five suffragan sees, Hexham and Newcastle, Lancaster, Leeds, Middlesbrough, and Salford; and Cardiff, an archdiocese with one suffragan see, Menevia. Catholics number about 3 million which is 7 per cent. of the total population; a number of these are foreigners and a large number are Irish; statistics are not obtainable but the number of Catholics in England with two English parents and four English grandparents cannot be a very large proportion of the total. The general population of the British Commonwealth is about 540 million, of whom some 27 million are Catholics. Great Britain also possesses in Europe, Gibraltar, a diocese i.s.h.s., of which most of the civil population are Catholics; and the islands of Malta and Gozo, each a diocese: of their 290,000 people, 96 per cent. are Catholics and canon law has the force of civil legislation in their government.

"ENGLISH ATHANASIUS, The." John Milner (1752-1826) titular bishop of Castabala and vicar apostolic of the Midland District, so called on account of the vigour of his preaching, and polemical writing, whether against Protestants or those Catholics of whose concessions in order to gain emancipation he disapproved.

ENGLISH CHURCH, The, was founded by St. Augustine on the impetus of Pope St. Gregory the Great in 597; he erected his primatial see at Canterbury and received the *pallium* (q.v.) in 601. It failed to absorb the remains of the British church (q.v.) until the Norman conquest. It was organized particularly by the seventh archbishop, St. Theodore, a Greek. For over 900 years it was in communion with the Holy See, acknowledging its primacy of jurisdiction and supremacy in all spiritual matters, and was an integral part of the Catholic Church. At the accession of King Henry VIII it consisted of the province of Canterbury, whose archbishop was primate of All England, with suffragan sees at Bath and Wells, Chichester, Ely, Exeter, Hereford, Lichfield and Coventry, London, Lincoln, Norwich, Rochester, Salisbury, Winchester, Worcester, and the four dioceses of Wales (q.v.); and the province of York, whose archbishop was primate of England, with two suffragan sees, Carlisle and the prince-bishopric of Durham. In 1534 by the action of all its bishops bar one (St. John Fisher, of Rochester) in acknowledging the king as supreme head of the Church in England, this church, the mother of numerous canonized saints and countless holy men and women, went into schism. From 1553 to 1558 it was reconciled under Queen Mary. In 1559 all the bishops living except one refused the new oath of supremacy; they died, some in prison, were not replaced, and the English church ceased to exist as an hierarchically organized body. It was simply a remnant. See PENAL TIMES.

ENGLISH COLLEGE, THE VENERABLE, at Rome for the preparation of English candidates for the priesthood had its origin in a pilgrims' hospice founded in 1362, the seminary being actually founded in 1579—the third oldest of the national seminaries in Rome—to supply missionaries for Elizabethan England. Forty-two of its students were martyred and six died in prison. There are to-day about 60 students who pursue most of their studies at the Gregorian University; they are supported by their respective dioceses, though most of them contribute something themselves, and there are a certain number of burses held by winners of scholarships. The college is under the immediate protection of the Holy See. See also BEDA; DOUAY; LISBON; VALLADOLID.

ENGLISH CONGREGATION, The, of the Order of St. Benedict has abbeys at Downside, Ampleforth, Woolhampton (Douay), Fort Augustus and Hereford (Belmont); priories at Ealing, Worth and North Berwick; and two priories in the U.S.A. at Portsmouth, R. I., and at Washington, D. C.; and abbeys of strictly enclosed nuns at Stanbrook, Holme Eden, Talacre, and Colwich. The work of the congregation is primarily educational: Downside, Ampleforth and Douay have large schools attached and the other houses also have schools; the monks serve a number of parishes in different parts of the country. Ampleforth and Downside have houses of studies at Oxford and Cambridge respectively. It is the senior congregation (q.v.) of the order (1215: 1336) and in 1500 had 24 mitred abbots and 18 others ranking as peers; continuity with this predissolution congregation was maintained through one monk, Dom Sigebert Buckley (d. 1609), through whom Ampleforth Abbey is the canonical and legal successor and representative of the former abbey of Westminster. The congregation has over 600 religious. There are other monasteries of Benedictines (q.v.) in England, not of this congregation.

ENGLISH LADIES, The. The Institute of Mary (*q.v.*).

ENGLISH MARTYRS, The. By this name is indicated not all and sundry of the English and Welsh people who were martyrs of the Church but those who were put to death for the Faith between the schism of King Henry VIII and 1681. Of these, 2 have been canonized, St. John Fisher, cardinal and bishop of Rochester and St. Thomas More, chancellor of the Realm; 197 have been declared Blessed, including 85 secular priests, 41 laymen, Margaret Pole, Countess of Salisbury, and 3 other lay-women, 15 Benedictines, 18 Carthusians, 4 Franciscans, 1 Augustinian, 1 Bridgettine and 26 Jesuits. 116 others (*Prætermissi*) have had their cause introduced at Rome and are called Venerable; they are called officially the Ven. George Haydock and his Companions. Forty-four other cases (*Dilati*) have been put back for further examination. The 360 whose names are actually before the Holy See are by no means the only faithful ones who suffered death during this period; the proceedings for 242 others (priests, religious and lay-people) have been begun, and there are yet others whose history is obscure or whose death may have been primarily due to other than religious considerations. The last actually to die in prison for the Faith was Fr. Matthew Atkinson, Franciscan, in 1729, after 30 years' imprisonment. The feast of the Blessed English Martyrs is observed in England on May 4, and individuals and groups are commemorated on various dates in different dioceses.

ENGLISH MYSTICS, The. Certain pre-Reformation mystical writers whose works have been classed together as those of an English "school" rather on account of a common indefinable "flavour" than for any other reason. The principal and their chief writings are Richard Rolle of Hampole (*d.* 1349) "The Amending of Life," "The Fire of Love," "Contemplations of the Dread and Love of God"; Walter Hilton (*d.* 1396), "The Scale of Perfection"; Mother Julian of Norwich (*d. c.* 1415), "Revelations of Divine Love"; the author of "The Cloud of Unknowing" (14th century). Though he belongs to another age, Fr. Augustine Baker, O.S.B. (1575-1641), is generally counted among the English mystics.

ENGLISH POLYPHONISTS, The. A number of composers of ecclesiastical and other music in polyphony of the 16th century, of whom the principal were William Byrd (*c.* 1543-1623), Thomas Tallis (*c.* 1514-85) and John Taverner (*c.* 1475-1535). These three remained faithful to the Church and wrote much music for her liturgy, which has in our own time been brought back into use, notably by Sir Richard Terry at Westminster Cathedral; and their popery did not prevent the first two from receiving royal and other official musical appointments.

ENGLISH POPE, The. Adrian IV, 1154-59, the only Englishman so far who has occupied the Holy See. His name was Nicholas Breakspear, he was born at Abbot's Langley in Hertfordshire, and is said to have been refused admittance to St. Alban's Abbey as an unpromising subject. He joined the Augustinian canons regular at Avignon and as cardinal-bishop of Albano was sent as legate to Scandinavia, where he earned the title of "Apostle of the North." To him is attributed the bull *Laudabiliter (q.v.)*.

ENKOLPION (Gr., that worn on the breast). A round or oval medallion, suspended from the neck, bearing a representation of our Lord or our Lady and often containing relics. Bishops of the Byzantine rite wear one and sometimes two *enkolpia* as well as the pectoral cross.

ENS. Being (*q.v.*) in the abstract *(cf.,* Entity). This word was coined by the scholastic philosophers as a particle of the Lat. verb *esse,* to be, in imitation of the participle formation *absens* from *abesse.*

ENTELECHY. (Gr. ἐντελέχεια from ἔχειν, to have), in the philosophy of Aristotle signifies act (*q.v.*) or form (*q.v.*) in opposition to potency and matter. Thus the soul is the entelechy of the body.

ENTHRONEMENT OF THE SACRED HEART, The, in the home is the recognition of the sovereignty of Jesus Christ over the Christian family affirmed, outwardly expressed, and made permanent by the solemn installation of an image of the Sacred Heart in a place of honour in any home, accompanied by a prescribed act of consecration.

ENTHRONIZATION of a bishop is his solemn taking possession of his cathedral-church by seating himself upon the episcopal chair and receiving the homage of his clergy. It may be done at the end of the consecration rite, if that takes place in his own cathedral; otherwise it takes place separately upon the first convenient occasion. But a bishop elect has jurisdiction from the moment that he informs his chapter of his appointment.

ENTITY (Lat. *entitas,* from *ens* [*q.v.*].) The concrete of being. In being it is possible to to distinguish two formalities, *viz.*, a *subject* having, or affected by, existence, and *existence* by which the subject is affected. The first is being in the concrete and is called thing or *res;* the second is being in the abstract and is called being simply or *ens.* The first is a noun, the second a participle.

ENTRANCE, THE GREAT, in the Byzantine liturgies is the bringing of the bread and wine for the sacrifice from the *prothesis* (*q.v.*). At the *Cherubikon* the celebrant carrying the chalice and the deacon carrying the *diskos* (*q.v.*) and thurible, preceded by acolytes with cross, lights and *ripidia* (*q.v.*), leave the sanctuary by the north door, go down that side of the church and up the middle and so to the altar by the holy doors; priest and deacon saying alternately, "May the Lord God remember us all in his kingdom, always, now, and for ever, world without end." In the Armenian liturgy a similar "entrance" is made but around the altar, and there are approximations in other liturgies.

ENTRANCE, THE LITTLE, in the Byzantine liturgies. The celebrant, with deacon carrying the gospel book and acolytes as above, leaves the sanctuary by the north door and comes to the middle of the church where he says a prayer and blesses the holy doors silently, kisses the gospel-book, and all approach the altar through the holy doors. There is a similar "entrance" in the Armenian liturgy and approximations in other rites.

ENVY, one of the deadly sins, is sadness because of another's good, especially if it is regarded as a lessening of one's own. It is a sin against charity, whereby we should be pleased at the good of others, and in a matter of weight is mortal. That acute form of envy popularly called jealousy is particularly dangerous, for it often leads to brooding upon our own sufferings, to fomenting ill-will against our neighbour, to underhand revenge by word or deed, or even to open violence.

EPACT (Gr. ἐπακταὶ ἡμέραι, intercalated days). The excess of the solar over the lunar year, the common solar year of 365 days containing 12 moons and 11 days, expressed in the number of days of the moon's age on Jan. 1, required to be known in calculating the date of Easter.

EPARCHY. Formerly the province (Gr. ἐπαρχία) of a metropolitan but now used in the East to signify a diocese.

EPHESIANS, THE EPISTLE TO THE. A letter written by St. Paul, probably to other churches besides that of Ephesus, at a time when he was in prison, and a canonical book of holy Scripture. It consists of dogmatic and moral teaching addressed to converted pagans.

EPHESUS, THE COUNCIL OF. The third œcumenical council (*q.v.*), 431, which declared our Lady to be the Mother of God (θεοτόκος: *Dei genitrix*) she having borne the Word (*q.v.*) from God, who had become flesh, the Word being united substantially to flesh; and condemned Nestorianism (*q.v.*) which denied this doctrine in consequence of its teaching two persons in Christ. This council is commemorated by a feast in the Armenian and Coptic rites.

EPHPHETHA, THE CEREMONY OF, is part of the rite of solemn Baptism. The priest wets his right thumb with spittle from his mouth and touches therewith, in the form of a cross, each ear of the person to be baptized, saying, "Ephphetha, that is to say, Be opened"; and touching his nostrils says, "For a savour of sweetness." It is the ancient rite of "the opening of the ears" which conferred on catechumens the right to be initiated into the Christian mysteries: now the opening of the ears to hear God's word and of the nostrils to the atmosphere of divine grace are signified.

EPIEIKEIA (Gr., mildness). Equity; the interpretation of a law whereby it is held not to bind in a particular case because some special hardship would result. Such interpretation can never be applied to divine law, whether positive or natural, and for the common good it is not permitted in respect of some ecclesiastical laws, *e.g.*, those regarding the binding power of diriment impediments to matrimony (*cf.*, Dispensation).

EPIGONATION (Gr. ἐπιγουνίς, thigh). A lozenge-shaped piece of stiff material, about 12 ins. x 10 ins., with a cross or image embroidered on it, suspended by a corner at the height of the right knee by a ribbon attached to the girdle or shoulder. It is worn only by the pope in the West (*subcinctorium*, *q.v.*), but is an eucharistic vestment of all Eastern bishops (except those who use Latin vestments), archimandrites and other dignitaries. Its origin is uncertain; it now symbolizes the spiritual sword of justice.

EPIKLESIS (Gr., invocation). A prayer to God the Father, or to the Son, or to both Persons, begging them to send down the Holy Spirit (or, occasionally, the Word) on the bread and wine at Mass in order that these may be changed into the body and blood of Christ, and to implore for the recipients the salutary effects thereof. It is found in all the liturgies of the East, and many writers maintain there are traces of it in the Latin rite before and after the consecration, in the prayers *Quam oblationem* . . . and *Supplices te* . . . of the canon, or elsewhere. The Byzantine form, following the *anamnesis* and used alike by Catholics and Orthodox, is: "We offer to thee this reasonable and bloodless sacrifice, and we pray, beg and beseech thee to send down thy Holy Spirit upon us and upon these gifts here present. And make this bread the sacred body of thy Christ; and make that which is in this chalice the precious blood of thy Christ: changing them by thy Holy Spirit." Non-Catholic Eastern churches, following the Orthodox, now teach that the consecration is effected not by the words of institution (*q.v.*) alone but with the *epiklesis*, that the body and blood of Christ are not present till it has been said; but this effect certainly takes place at our Lord's words of institution. Liturgies are celebrated in time, and display both dramatic anticipations and retrospections.

EPIMANIKIA (Gr., upon the sleeves). Embroidered over-sleeves which tighten the sleeves of the Byzantine *sticharion* (*q.v.*) at the wrists. They are a liturgical vestment of all Eastern rites.

EPIPHANY, The (Gr. ἐπιφάνεια, manifestation), is the name of a feast of the first rank and a holiday of obligation observed throughout the Christian world on Jan. 6, which commemorates the manifestations of our Lord, (*a*) to the gentiles in the persons of the Magi, (*b*) of his divinity made at his baptism in Jordan and (*c*) of his power shown in the miracle of Cana. In all Eastern rites it is the baptism that is chiefly celebrated and some give the miracle a separate feast; in the Latin rite the Magi have the greatest prominence in both Mass and Office of the feast, but the baptism is the chief theme of the Mass of the octave: all three are referred to at Matins, Lauds and Vespers. In cathedrals and other big churches the dates of the movable feasts of the year are solemnly announced at Mass. Until the 4th century the birth of our Lord was also celebrated on this day in the East; it is so still by the dissident Armenians. It is customary in the East, with reference to the baptism, to bless waters—sea, lake, river—with much ceremony on this day; a corresponding blessing appears in the "Rituale Romanum" but its use appears to be forbidden by S.R.C. 3792 ad xv. This feast no longer has a vigil or octave; but its octaveday is observed as a commemoration of the Lord's baptism. In the East the feast is called the Theophany (*q.v.*).

EPISCOPACY (Gr. ἐπίσκοπος, overseer). i. The bishops of the Church as a body.

ii. The doctrine that there is an order superior to the priesthood, that of bishops, whose special duty it is to govern their flocks, both clergy and laity, to consecrate churches, altars, etc., to ordain bishops and priests and to confirm. That there is such an order is an article of faith defined by the Council of Trent (sess. 23, can. 7): If any one say that bishops are not superior to priests, or that they have not the power to confirm or ordain, or that the power which they have is common to them and to priests . . . let him be anathema.

EPISCOPAL, -ALIAN, CHURCH. Any Christian body organized with bishops on an hierarchical principle and teaching that such organization is divinely appointed; but the term is used particularly and almost solely for Protestant bodies so organized, and their members are called Episcopalians. The term is used chiefly in Scotland to distinguish the Anglican from the Presbyterian church of that country, and in the U.S.A. to designate the Anglican church in North America.

EPISCOPATE. i. The office of a bishop.

ii. The period of time during which a given bishop rules.

iii. The bishops of a province, country or church.

EPISCOPUS CASTRENSIS, called in English an army bishop. A titular bishop (*q.v.*) appointed by the Holy See as ordinary of the military chaplains and armed forces of a given state in peace and war. The first British army bishop was appointed in 1917 and now has jurisdiction over all arms. The military ordinary of Italy has jurisdiction as well over all religious, male and female, working in military hospitals.

EPISTEMOLOGY (Gr. ἐπιστήμη, knowledge) is that branch of philosophy which is concerned with the theory of the origin, nature, grounds, method and limits of knowledge.

EPISTLE. i. Biblical. One of the twenty-one books of the New Testament written as, or in the form of, letters to individuals or churches. Those of St. Paul (fourteen) are called by the name of the group or person to whom they were addressed; the others, by the name of the writer. These last are called Catholic or General Epistles because they were intended for the Church at large, though in fact 2 and 3 John are addressed to individuals. The Pastoral Epistles are those to Timothy and Titus in which they are instructed in the duties of the episcopal office.

ii. Liturgical. The first of the two scriptural lessons at Mass is called the epistle because generally taken from one of those books, but it is sometimes from the Acts, Apocalypse or one of the sapiential books of the Old Testament. At high Mass the epistle is sung by the subdeacon; under certain circumstances it is permitted to a minor cleric and in churches of Carthusian nuns is sung by a consecrated nun at the choir-lectern and in solemn papal Masses is sung in Greek as well as Latin. The subdeacon mounts the *ambo* (*q.v.*) if there be one; otherwise he stands on the south side of the sanctuary facing the altar (but in the Lyons rite he sits, facing the people). In the Byzantine rite "the Apostle" (as the epistle is called) is read from the steps of the *iconostasis*, facing the altar. On feasts, the portion chosen to be read has reference or is appropriate to the occasion celebrated: those of fast-days are Old Testament lessons (*cf.*, the week-days of Lent), but two of every three liturgical epistles are taken from those of St. Paul. In Eastern liturgies it is sung by a reader who is often a layman (but the Maronites and Malabarese have adopted the Roman custom).

EPISTLE-SIDE. That end of the altar or side of the sanctuary at which the epistle is said or sung at Mass, namely, the south or right-hand side facing the altar.

EPISTLES OF THE CAPTIVITY, The. The four letters, to the Ephesians, Colossians, Philemon and Philippians, written by St. Paul while he was in prison, probably during his first imprisonment in Rome, though some have claimed at Cæsarea. It is likely that the first three were written and sent off at one time; the last stands by itself.

EPISTOLARY, -ARIUM. A book containing the liturgical epistles, for the use of the sub-deacon at high Mass.

EPITAPHION (Gr. τάφος, tomb). In the Byzantine rite, an ornamented bier representing the tomb of our Lord. On Good Friday the figure is taken from the cross and laid on the *epitaphion* with flowers, grave-clothes and spices (The Burial of Christ). In the evening it is carried in procession round and out of the church, sometimes through the town (The Funeral of Christ), and then laid on the altar while *troparia* modelled on the last five verses of Matt. xvii are sung.

EPITRACHELION (Gr. τράχηλος, neck). The stole worn by a priest of the Byzantine rite whenever he fulfils a liturgical office. It is a strip of silk, about 5 ins. wide, with the two ends fastened together in front for most of their length, leaving a loop through which to pass the head; it reaches in front almost to the feet and is ornamented with crosses and fringe. Other oriental priests wear a similar stole. (*cf.*, Orarion).

"EQUAL TO THE APOSTLES." An appellation given to certain saints in the Byzantine calendar, *e.g.*, Mary Magdalen, Constantine and Helen, Vladimir. It is merely an example of the oriental liking for high-sounding titles and means no more than that they are regarded with very great veneration (*cf.*, the Orthodox Patriarch of Alexandria, who is Thirteenth Apostle and Judge of the World).

EQUALITY. i. Of man. All men are essentially and spiritually equal; no man is preferred before another, or of greater value than another, in the sight of God, on account of any advantage or superiority; the salvation of the slave is as important as that of the emperor, of the imprudent man as that of the prudent. Every human being whatsoever has therefore certain fundamental natural and spiritual rights (*q.v.*). But extrinsically and in the natural order there is clearly inequality between man and man, they being born with varying abilities, characteristics, physical, mental and spiritual capacities and natural gifts. (*cf.*, "Class-distinctions").

ii. Of man and woman. See WOMEN; WIFE; HUSBAND; FEMINISM.

EQUIPOLLENT. Equal in force, equivalent. See BEATIFICATION.

EQUIVOCATION (Lat. *æquivocus,* equal voiced). i. In logic. A word having two or more equivalent meanings, *e.g.,* sole: the fish, and part of a boot. Used in sophistic (*q.v.*) argument thus: Light is opposed to darkness, But feathers are light, Therefore feathers are opposed to darkness. An idea cannot be equivocal.

ii. The use of words or expressions susceptible of two or more meanings, either in themselves or in conjunction with their circumstances. The intention of conveying a wrong impression is usually implied. Equivocation should in general be avoided; it is permissible only on the same conditions as mental reservation (*q.v.*) with which it is often synonymous.

ERA, THE CHRISTIAN. The reckoning of time from the year of the birth of Christ, *A* [*nno*] *D* [*omini*] (Lat., the year of the Lord), 1; years before that are *A* [*nte*] *C* [*hristum*] or B [efore] C [hrist]. The system is due to Dionysius Exiguus, a monk at Rome in the early 6th century; he computed the birth of Christ to have taken place in the year of the foundation of the city of Rome (A.U.C.), 753, and made that his A.D. 1; this calculation was probably several years too late but it does not matter for chronological purposes, and anyway it is too late to do anything about it now. Other Christian eras are that "of Diocletian" or "of the Martyrs" reckoned from A.D. 284 (this was the one superseded by the Dionysian era in the West but is still used by the Coptic Church); the Indiction, a period of fifteen years, of which the first began in Sept. A.D. 312; and the Byzantine, which reckoned from the creation, put at 5508 B.C.

ERASTIANISM. The subordination of church to state, so called from Erastus (Thomas Lieber, 1524-83), a Protestant theologian who taught that the Christian prince had received from God the same power as the magistrate in the Jewish dispensation. Erastianism is entirely opposed to Catholic teaching (see CHURCH AND STATE) but has often afflicted the Byzantine (Orthodox) Church, formerly in its head and now particularly in its members, and also the Church of England from time to time. See CÆSAROPAPISM.

ERECTION, CANONICAL. The setting up and giving canonical status by competent ecclesiastical authority of a religious organization or body; *e.g.*, the Holy See alone erects dioceses, cathedral-churches, abbeys of monks or nuns, archconfraternities; a bishop or religious order may erect a confraternity, a seminary or a convent.

EREMITE. See HERMIT. Eremitical: pertaining to a hermit.

ERGADIENSIS ET INSULARUM. The adjectival form of the name of the see of Argyll and the Isles (q.v.) used in the designation of its bishop in Latin documents. Noun: *Argathelia et Insulæ.*

ERRONEOUS (Lat. *erronea*). A proposition condemned as erroneous is one which contradicts a truth deduced from two premisses of which one is an article of faith and the other naturally certain.

ERROR. i. And salvation. Invincible error (q.v.) is no bar to salvation.* But error concerning a matter of faith or of conduct will imperil salvation if (a) it can be corrected by moral diligence, or (b) if it is due to a direct refusal to see the truth (affected error). Thus, if a Catholic were to practise birth control, protesting that in spite of what was said by priests he did not believe that it was wrong, he would be in a state of sin, and, dying in that state, he would lose his soul.
ii. In canon law. A mistaken judgment of a vital sort concerning the nature of the contract or with regard to the individual with whom it purports to be made (e.g., his identity) is an invalidating circumstance in a marriage. But such error must be a substantial element affecting valid consent.

ERROR, INVINCIBLE. Error is ignorance of the truth combined with a positive holding of a false opinion. It is invincible when it is not attributable to any lack of moral diligence, i.e., when the subject either entertains no doubt; or, if he has a doubt, does not advert to the necessity of resolving the doubt by enquiry; or if, on making enquiry, he is unable to arrive at the truth. Thus, a person brought up in Protestantism may be in invincible error regarding, e.g., the infallibility of the pope. Invincible does not mean that the error is objectively invincible.

ERROR, TOLERATION OF. The Church is not, and cannot be, indifferent to error in doctrine. Being infallible, she is certain of the truth. She is commissioned to teach the truth to all men. She is bound to preserve her children from error; and this she does by checking the first appearance of error, condemning error by her infallible pronouncements, forbidding the faithful to take part in the services of a false religion, framing an index of prohibited books. But while she condemns objective error, she does not condemn those outside her fold who are in invincible error (q.v.). "Love men, destroy errors," said St. Augustine. And Pius IX wrote in an encyclical of Aug. 10, 1863, "Far be it from the children of the Catholic Church in any way to be enemies to those who are not bound to us by the ties of the true Faith and charity."

ESCHATOLOGICAL SCHOOL, The. That school of Protestant biblical scholars who teach that our Lord believed the end of the world to be imminent and that the kingdom of God would descend from Heaven in his own generation. This false teaching involves the conclusion that he cannot have intended to found a church and that any authority given to his apostles was simply personal (cf., Second Coming).

ESCHATOLOGY (Gr. τὰ ἔσχατα, the last things) is that branch of theology which is concerned with death and the last things, the destruction and renewal of the world, the eternal reign of Christ when all men are judged and all things fulfilled, etc. It is the most difficult part of Christian dogma; very little has been defined regarding it and theologians are very cautious in their treatment; more popular writers and preachers do not always emulate them.

ESDRAS. A priest and doctor of Israel, called in Heb. *Ezra* (help). Two books of the Bible bear his name (the second is also called Nehemias, after its author). The first book, written by Esdras himself, narrates the return of the Jews from their Babylonian captivity, the rebuilding of the Temple and the putting away of their wives by those who had married foreign women in defiance of the law; Nehemias follows on with the rebuilding of the city, especially its walls, and the repentance of the people for their past transgressions, and their promise to God: but the relative chronology of these events is very uncertain. Esdras is named in the Roman Martyrology on July 13. Two books of the uncanonical apocrypha (q.v.) are called III and IV Esdras: IV furnishes several well-known texts to the Latin liturgy, e.g., "Eternal rest give to them, O Lord."

ESOTERICISM (Gr. ἐσωτερικός, interior). The holding of secret doctrines by certain schools of antiquity (e.g., the Pythagoreans), such doctrines being imparted only to a small number of select disciples.

ESPOUSAL (Lat. *sponsalia*). Betrothal (q.v.). In the passage of time and the decay of the custom of solemn betrothal, the word has come to be used as synonymous with wedding (cf., Spouse).

ESPOUSALS OF OUR LADY, The. A feast of our Lady celebrating her betrothal to St. Joseph, kept in some places on Jan. 23. A commemoration of St. Joseph is made in the Mass.

ESSE. See BEING; BENE ESSE.

ESSENCE. That whereby a thing is what it is; that whereby a thing is constituted in a determinate species; that whereby a thing is distinguished from other things; that which is the root and the subject of properties attributed to a thing. An essence, as essence,

---

* See also NECESSARY TO SALVATION and NECESSARY, NECESSITY.—*Publisher*, 1997.

is necessary, immutable, indivisible and negatively eternal. See each of these, and EXISTANCE; SUBSTANCE; NATURE.

ESSENES. One of the three chief Jewish sects from the 2nd century B.C. to the end of the 1st A.D. They were strict "communists," observant of the natural virtues and austere of life; they had an esoteric doctrine which is still unknown. Having the same Judaic origin and a strict ethical system, Essenism had in some points a superficial likeness to Christianity.

ESTABLISHMENT, CHURCH. The recognition by the civil power of a particular religion as the official religion of the state, usually involving the grant of civil privileges and temporal assistance by way of endowment or otherwise to that religion and its ministers. The best-known example still subsisting is the Protestant church of England, which is frequently referred to as The Establishment or The Established Church. The Catholic Church is now established in this sense only in Italy and Spain and certain republics of South America. It is common for the national autonomous churches forming the Orthodox Eastern Church to be in some measure established. Such establishment is in many ways advantageous to religion and, other things being equal, facilitates the proper relations between church and state (*q.v.*). But there is danger of the state coming to regard the Church as under obligation to it and endeavouring to bring it into subservience and, especially in recent times, of nationalizing it to an extent incompatible with Catholicity. This is emphasized by the history of the Orthodox national churches.

ESTHER. An historical book of the Old Testament, of which chapter x to the end is deutero-canonical (*q.v.*). It records the plot of Aman to destroy the Jews throughout Persia and its frustration by Esther ("star"), the Jewish wife or concubine of King Assuerus, and her uncle Mardochai, the Jews by permission of the king exercising a bloody justice upon their persecutors. This deliverance was celebrated by a festival, called *Purim* ("of lots," because Aman's day of massacre was so selected), which is still observed by orthodox Jews. Esther is commemorated by a liturgical feast in the Coptic and Ethiopic calendars on Dec. 21.

ESTONIA, THE CHURCH IN. The Estonians are predominantly Lutheran. The few thousand Catholics, mostly foreigners, were in 1939 in charge of an administrator apostolic. Estonia is now part of the U.S.S.R.

ETERNAL LIFE. It is the teaching of the Church that every individual human being is destined to eternal life in the next world, the just to enjoy the Beatific Vision in Heaven, the reprobate to the punishment of Hell (*qq.v.*). The gospels witness to this teaching in unequivocal terms (*e.g.*, Mark x, 30; John iii, 15; Matt. xxv, 41). "The beatitude of the saints is called eternal life because by it they enjoy God and are made, in a sense, sharers in the divine Eternity which transcends all time. Hence the continuance of their blessedness is not broken up by the succession of past, present and future; so that the blessed have no hope of the continuance of their happiness, for they have it in itself and there is no such concept as 'the future.'" (St. Thomas, II-II, xviii, 2 ad 2).

ETERNAL PUNISHMENT is the lot of those who die in deliberate unrepented mortal sin, that is, of those who having free will have freely chosen evil and not withdrawn their choice. They are lost by their own choice; they have deliberately rejected Infinite Love. "The duration of punishment corresponds to the duration of the fault considered not so much as an act but as a stain; so long as that remains the debt of punishment remains. The bitterness of the punishment corresponds to the gravity of the fault. Now an irreparable fault of its very nature endures for ever, hence to it is due eternal punishment" (St. Thomas, I-II, lxxxvii, 4). *Cf.*, HELL.

ETERNITY. i. Positive eternity. That which measures the duration of an absolutely immutable being. Eternity therefore essentially excludes beginning, end and succession, but is something essentially positive although sometimes defined by negative terms; it is "the perfect and simultaneous possession of the wholeness of life without beginning or end" (Boethius). This is absolute eternity, proper to God alone. Spiritual substances are said to be endowed with relative or participated eternity, in the sense that once being brought to existence they will never cease to exist although the absolute power of God could deprive them of such existence.

ii. Negative eternity is that the truth of which prescinds from time. All essences are negatively eternal because they are immutably and indivisibly what they are; *e.g.*, it is always true (in the past, present or future) that the three angles of a triangle are equal to two right angles.

ETHICISM. A word coined to express the idea that religion is principally, if not entirely, a system of morals, or even simply an aspiration and endeavour to give effect to natural goodness—"If one does one's best to act fairly to all men, that is the best religion." This sign of decay of the religious temper is found increasingly in all forms of Protestantism; and ethical considerations are improperly used as a criterion of criticism and judgement in other human activities, *e.g.*, art.

ETHICS. A practical science which investigates the laws of right conduct with reference to the natural end of man. General ethics seeks the criterion of good and evil in human acts from the standpoint of natural reason, while the conclusions arrived at are applied in Special ethics to the various circumstances of human life and the diverse conditions of men.

ETHIOPIA, THE CHURCH IN. The very mixed population of Ethiopia or Abyssinia is estimated to be between 6 and 8 million, of whom half are non-Christians (Mohammedans, etc.). The remainder mostly belong to the separated Ethiopic Church (*q.v.*). After deplorable events in the 16th and early 17th centuries, the country was closed to Catholic clergy till 1839. Catholics now number about 50,000, of whom ⅖, organized into 5 vicariates apostolic and several prefectures, are converts from heathenism and are of the Latin rite. The remainder, mostly in Eritrea, are of the Ethiopic rite (*q.v.*), with a bishop (at Asmara) and lower clergy of their own nationality. There is also a number of Italians in Eritrea. A college for seminarists of this rite was re-established in Rome in 1919; some of the clergy are married. There are now Catholic monks of this rite, who have been trained by the Cistercians. An Ethiopic priest, Michael Gabra, martyred in 1855, was beatified in 1926.

ETHIOPIAN CHURCH, The. Ethiopia (Abyssinia) was first evangelized, by St. Frumentius, towards the middle of the 4th century. From the first it was associated with the Church of Alexandria, and followed Egypt into the monophysite schism. It still closely resembles the Coptic Church (*q.v.*), and till 1936 its primate, *abuna* (*q.v.*), was always an Egyptian monk appointed by the Coptic patriarch. The Ethiopian Church is not yet organized into proper dioceses and parishes. Monks are numerous, but their standard is very uneven. The pastoral clergy are extremely ill-educated, and little respected by the people; because of the carelessness with which ordinations are sometimes conducted there is doubt if Ethiopian orders, and consequently sacraments, are valid. Confirmation and Last Anointing are no longer used, and Penance usually only at death. The religion of the people is riddled with superstition and their standard of Christian life is deplorably low. Altogether the Ethiopian Church is probably the most backward of Christian bodies, a state of affairs largely due to its historical circumstances, cut off by Islam from the rest of Christendom for century after century. Among its special characteristics are the observance of some Judaic customs and a taste among the monks for fantastic theological speculations.

ETHIOPIC RITE, The. The liturgy and usages of the Ethiopians are practically those of the Coptic rite translated into Ge'ez (*qq.v.*). Many of the churches, often built of mud and thatched, are round, divided by high partitions into 3 concentric circles, with the altar in the middle. Characteristic vestments are the sort of tippet with 5 long pendants over the chasuble, and the picturesque crown worn by bishops and others. Catholics of the rite at present use only its eucharistic liturgy and pontifical services; for the rest they have the Roman rites, translated into Ge'ez, pending the revision and publication of the proper offices. The dissidents' services are characterized by the singing accompanied by rattles, cymbals, bells and drums, by processions, and even by dancing.

ETSI PASTORALIS. A bull of Pope Benedict XIV, in 1742, with primary reference to the Italo-Greeks (*q.v.*) ordering them "to keep studiously and carefully the habits, institutions, rites and customs which they have received from their Greek fathers"; forbidding "latinization" or interference; recognizing the ordination of married men; ordering that there shall be no precedence based on rite, etc. On the other hand, it legislated definitely for privileges for the Latin rite, which provisions subsequent legislation has cancelled.

EUCHARIST, THE SACRAMENT OF THE (Gr. εὐχαριστία, thanksgiving). A sacrament of the New Law in which, under the appearances of bread and wine, the body and blood of Christ are truly, really and substantially present, as the grace-producing food of our souls. Moreover, "it is very true that as much is contained under either species as under both; for Christ, whole and entire, exists under the species of bread, and under each particle of that species; and whole under the species of wine, and under its separate parts" (Council of Trent, sess. xiii, cap. 3; and *cf.*, stanza 10 of *Lauda Sion Salvatorem* in the Mass of Corpus Christi). The holy Eucharist is the *living* Christ; as a living body is not without its blood, or living blood without a body, so Christ is received whole and entire under either form of bread or wine. The use of the word "eucharist" has its origin in our Lord's giving thanks at the Last Supper (Matt. xxvi, 27, etc.), it is used in a general sense in the *Didache* (*q.v.*) and definitely for the Blessed Sacrament by St. Ignatius in his letter to the church of Smyrna (about 107). The matter of the sacrament is bread and wine; the form is the words of consecration. The special sacramental effect is the spiritual nutrition of our souls analogous to the effect of food in our bodies. Mass can be said and the Eucharist consecrated only by a bishop or priest, who is also the ordinary minister for administering holy communion. But a deacon may be delegated to do this last, and in case of urgent necessity (*e.g.*, danger of death without Viaticum) a layman may administer it to himself or to others.

EUCHARISTIC ADORATION. Worship given to Christ present in the Blessed Sacrament, outside of Mass and holy communion. This was a development in the Western church of the 11th and subsequent centuries, which received the encouragement of the Church in the establishment of the feast of Corpus Christi (1264) and the approval of the Forty Hours' prayer, Benediction and perpetual adoration (*qq.v.*). It has been even more marked in private devotion, expressing itself in "visits to the Blessed Sacrament" and the popularity of exposition (*q.v.*). But the profit to be derived from prayer before the reserved Sacrament must not be regarded as part of the sacramental virtue of the Eucharist in its proper sense; its efficacy as a sacrifice is bound up with the act of the Mass and as a sacrament with the act of eating, and does not extend beyond these (*cf.*, Reservation).

EUCHARISTIC CONGRESS. An international gathering, presided over by a papal delegate, which by means of solemn services and other religious exercises, together with addresses and discussions, gives honour to the sacrament of the altar and increases devotion thereto. The first was at Lille in 1881, and they have been held since then in, among other places, Paris, Jerusalem, Lourdes, Rome, London, Quebec, Chicago, Dublin and Sydney. These congresses are organized by a permanent committee. Similar congresses of a national character are also frequently held.

EUCHARISTIC HEART OF JESUS, The. A feast observed in Rome and some other dioceses on Thursday following the octave of Corpus Christi. Its object is to commemorate our Lord's love for mankind as manifested in the holy Eucharist and to encourage the faithful by frequent and ever more worthy reception of that sacrament to kindle a like love in themselves. It was instituted by Pope Benedict XV, "for our Lord Jesus Christ, in the boundless love with which his sacred heart burns, guards those who follow him in that same heart, living in them as they in him, who is our sacrifice, our fellow man, our food, our viaticum and our earnest of the glory that shall be." Pope Leo XIII established a confraternity under the same name to offer worship and thanks to the Sacred Heart for the sacrament of his love.

EUCHARISTIC LITURGY OR SACRIFICE, The. Generic terms for the eucharistic services of the Church, called the Holy Mass in the Latin church and usually the Divine Liturgy in the Byzantine churches (Ruthenian, Divine Service; Chaldean, Syrian, Coptic, Malabar, The Offering; Maronite, Holy Sacrifice). There are five or six chief eucharistic services in use in the Church, with several minor varieties, but each is a true eucharistic liturgy and the same holy sacrifice as the others.

EUCHOLOGION (Gr., prayer-book). A liturgical book of the Byzantine rite containing the text of the three eucharistic liturgies, the ceremonies and prayers of the priest and deacon at the Divine Office and for the administration of the sacraments, sacramentals, blessings, etc. It is a combination of Missal, Pontifical and Ritual, and is often abridged into the "Little Euchologion." The word has been sometimes used in French, *eucologe*, for a sort of *paroissien* (*q.v.*), *e.g.*, one published at Reims in 1865.

EUDEMONISM (Gr. εὐδαιμονία, happiness). The theory in ethics according to which happiness is the last end of man; it is opposed to Hedonism, which makes pleasure the end of man.

EUDISTS, The. The Congregation of Jesus and Mary, a society of secular priests founded by St. John Eudes in 1643 for the direction of seminaries. After reconstitution in 1826 their principal work has lain in colleges and missions. The congregation is modelled on that of the Oratory and no vows are made.

EUGENICS. The science which aims at improving the well-being of the human race by studying the factors which affect bodily and mental health, with a view to the encouragement of the beneficial and the elimination of the harmful. Statistics are adduced to show that the chief obstacle is the marriage of the unfit, leading to an increase of hereditable evils such as insanity, venereal disease, and possibly addiction to drink. The Church has nothing but praise for the aim of eugenics and has no objection to the positive methods proposed as a remedy of the evil, *e.g.*, granting diplomas to the fit, endowing them to encourage the rearing of a large family, providing healthy homes, educating public opinion; but she cannot approve of the negative methods suggested by some eugenists, *viz.*, "birth control" (*q.v.*), compulsory sterilization (*q.v.*) of degenerates. Compulsory segregation would imply a prohibition of the marriage of the unfit; this runs counter to present ecclesiastical law which, while not encouraging their marriage, does not forbid it; the alleged facts do not justify an interference with their right to marry. When eugenists go astray, it is because they forget or deny that spiritual well-being is of far greater importance than material, and that even a tainted existence is better than no existence at all.

EULOGIA (Gr., a blessing). A name given to any object that has been blessed, but particularly to bread. In very early times blessed bread seems to have been given as a substitute to such as could not receive communion (*e.g.*, public penitents), "for the health of mind and body, and as a protection against disease and the snares of all enemies" (*cf.*, *antidoron* and *pain bénit*. The word is also used for the Blessed Sacrament itself).

EUNOMIANISM. The heretical teaching of Eunomius and Aëtius during the second half of the 4th century. It was an exaggerated Arianism (*q.v.*), affirming that the Son is unlike the Father in will as well as in substance.

EUSEBIUS, THE CHRONICLE OF. A work of Eusebius Pamphili, bishop of Cæsarea (*c.* 260-*c.* 340), "the father of church history." It consists of two parts, the "Chronography," an "outline of history" down to A.D. 225, and the "Canons," chronological tables with historical notes. The Babylonian story of the Creation and the Flood is found in this chronicle. But the "Eusebian Canons" usually refers to ten tables of corresponding or parallel passages in the gospels, drawn up by him.

EUTHANASIA. A gentle and easy death; a euphemism devised to express the direct and deliberate painless killing, or hastening of the death, of one in great pain. This is murder, which nothing can excuse. It is of course lawful to give drugs to relieve pain temporarily but not with the intention that death shall take place while the state of unconsciousness continues. See also UNFIT.

EUTYCHIANISM. An extreme form of Monophysism (*q.v.*), professed by the followers of Eutyches, a Greek archimandrite (378-*c.* 455). To the monophysite teaching that the human and divine natures in our Lord are identical, he added further errors, of which the principal was that our Lord had two natures before the hypostatic union (*q.v.*) which at his incarnation were fused into one—the exact contrary of the truth. The alleged monophysite churches, especially the Armenian, have always repudiated the Eutychian exaggerations: indeed, he is denounced by name by Armenian bishops at their consecration.

EVANGEL (Gr. εὐαγγέλιον, the reward given to a bringer of good tidings). An archaic name for the good news or gospel of Jesus Christ, especially as recorded by one of the four writers of a biblical gospel, hence called the Evangelists.

EVANGELIARIUM. A book containing the liturgical gospels for the use of the deacon at high Mass.

EVANGELICAL. Appertaining to the Gospel, but used particularly of those Nonconformists and a section of the Church of England who maintain that the essence of the Gospel consists in the doctrine of salvation by faith; good works and two sacraments only having no saving efficacy in themselves. Evangelicalism exhibits a firm hold on some of the fundamentals of Christianity (*e.g.*, the

Atonement), but as the name denotes, it recognizes no rule of faith outside the Bible; the average discourse from an Evangelical pulpit could appropriately be preached almost word for word by a Catholic priest.

EVANGELICAL COUNSELS, The, are voluntary poverty, perpetual chastity and entire obedience. Their observance is not necessary to salvation; they are a rule of perfection put forward to be voluntarily taken up by those who find in themselves the vocation to do so. They are not perfection itself, but instruments for its attainment, for maintaining and strengthening love of God and one's neighbour.

EVANGELIST. i. One of the authors of a canonical gospel, namely, Matthew, Mark, Luke or John. Evangelists have each a proper Mass, but their Office is the common of Apostles with special lessons.

ii. In apostolic times the name seems to have been given to missionaries of the gospel. So to-day among Protestants an itinerant preacher is called an evangelist.

EVE. The name of the first woman, from Heb. *havvah*, life, living; "because she was the mother of all living." (Gen. iii, 20).

EVE (of a feast). See VIGIL.

EVENSONG. An English name for Vespers, now applied only to the evening service of the Anglican Church. It was still in use among English Catholics in 1812, if not later.

EVIDENCE. A certain manifestation of a truth. Objective evidence is the clearness of a truth itself which, precisely owing to its clearness, compels the mind's assent; it is the ultimate criterion of truth. Subjective evidence is the clear perception by the mind of a truth thus manifested; this is called *certitude*. Intrinsic evidence is the same as objective. Extrinsic evidence: a truth not intrinsically evident may become manifest by some credible authority which latter is extrinsic to the truth itself.

EVIL (Mid. Eng. *uvel;* a word of uncertain derivation). i. Notion of evil. It is opposed to good and to perfection. It is not a pure negation of being, but a negation of good; it is the absence of a perfection that is due, in one word a privation, and as such (that is in itself) it is not real; it is, however, real in so far as it presupposes the good which it limits; *e.g.*, blindness of itself is not a reality, nor is sin, but blindness is in the body and sin in the soul. Evil then is founded on the good.

ii. Species of evil (*a*) Metaphysical. Leibniz calls the absence of greater perfection (although not *due* according to the nature of a thing) metaphysical evil. Strictly speaking, this is not an evil at all, for it is not a privation but a simple limitation. (*b*) Physical: the privation of a physical good, as blindness in a man. (*c*) Moral: The privation of some moral good. There is also a distinction between evil of fault (*culpa*) and evil of punishment (*pœna*); the first is a disorder in the free will, and is the cause of the second, which is a privation of good, resulting from the fault.

iii. Manichæism (*q.v.*). From the above notion of evil it is manifest that a supreme evil the cause of all evil, such as the Manichæans held, is self contradictory, for since evil is a privation a total privation would be absolute nothing.

iv. Origin of evil. Evil is caused by the good but accidentally. The good cannot of itself, and as such, be the cause of evil, but only in so far as evil is joined to or accompanies its action: good alone can be a cause because what is good is being; evil in itself is a negation and cannot therefore be a cause. In short, evil is an accidental effect of good— a bad effect conjoined to a good effect; thus the eagle killing and eating its prey is a good, but to this effect, good in itself, an evil effect is conjoined, *viz.*, the destruction of some animal. Good is the accidental cause of evil: On the part of the cause in two ways: (*a*) if the principal cause lacks sufficient power to produce the entirety of its effect, *e.g.*, a sick man on account of weakness cannot walk; (*b*) if the instrumental cause is defective, *e.g.*, bad writing due to a broken pen. On the part of the effect in two ways also: (*a*) owing to a lack of proper disposition in the matter, as damp wood won't burn; (*b*) if the perfection to be produced is incompatible with some other perfection, *e.g.*, to make an oak table demands the destruction of an oak tree. God does not cause evil but he permits it that good may ensue. The present universe demands that many things must fail for the good of the whole: there would be no room on this earth for the present generation if former generations had not died, etc. God is not the cause of sin, but he permits sin that human free will may be safeguarded. For the Christian, original sin is the ultimate reason of moral evil in the world, and man's free will is the proximate reason.

EVIL, MATERIAL. i. Those physical, mental, or social conditions, regarded in themselves and without reference to their possible origin in the personal sins of men, which are the cause of pain and suffering *e.g.*, disease, poverty, unemployment, war.

ii. The inability of one element of nature to attain its full perfection, owing to the restraining influence of another element: the oppression of nature, "red in tooth and claw."

iii. Material sin (*q.v.*).

EVIL, MORAL. The deviation of the will from the dictates of conscience. Should this evil set of the will lead to any act, the act too is said to contain moral evil. Consequently,

moral evil is nothing positive, but is essentially negative.

EVIL, THE PROBLEM OF. The difficulties expressed in the question: "Why does God, who by his nature is infinite, omnipotent and good, permit the existence of the moral evil of sin and the evils of mental and physical pain among his creatures in a world which he himself created and maintains in being," and in the question arising therefrom: "Why, foreseeing the abuse of free will by humankind, did he create man at all or create him thus?" It would seem that no complete solving of this mystery is possible in this world; but reason and revelation show the lines upon which a satisfactory answer may be found. It can be proved that God is infinitely good and powerful, and the problem of evil cannot be stated in such a way as to show any absolute contradiction of these attributes. We must accept the mystery then. A difficulty does not make a doubt, especially when we realize the incapacity of the human intellect to comprehend the infinity of God. Out of physical evil God can draw good. That he often does so is obvious to the reflecting mind, and faith teaches that pain and trial when accepted in loving conformity with the divine will are the surest way of attaining that union with God which is the basis of a happy eternity. Even the sufferings of animals can be the occasion of the good of a nobler order in man. God's glory is the end of creation, and it was to his glory to make human beings free agents. But if men are free some men will surely abuse their freedom and sin, in spite of the fact that they have clear guidance and sufficient grace to avoid it. But we must take it that a world containing free agents, even though there is widespread sin in it, is a greater glory to God than a world in which there would be no possibility of free action and moral virtue (*cf.*, Evil, iv).

EVIL EYE, The. A superstitious belief, prevalent in almost every part of the world long before the Christian era, that the gaze of certain peculiarly endowed persons has a baleful influence, bringing ill luck to those upon whom their eyes may rest. This result may occur apart from any intention of causing harm. In southern Italy this superstition of the *jettatura* is widespread, and the common people often wear some amulet or other to counteract it.

EVIL-SOUNDING (Lat. *male sonans*). A proposition is said to be evil-sounding and offensive to pious ears when it is, if compared with common belief, opposed to piety and reverence, or, while being true, is expressed unbecomingly.

EVOLUTION, EVOLUTIONISM (Lat. *evolvere*, to roll). i. Words signifying development or progress, in particular of living beings among which are distinguished ontogenetic and phylogenetic evolution. The first is the development of the individual from the state of the fecundated *ovum* to the state of adult; the second is the transformation of one species into several others which derive in diverging ways.

ii. Transformism, or Evolutionism, means the theory of the transformation of species only, but evolution is a more general and universal theory which is applied to the physical world, to the realm of ethics, to man and to society (Spencer). *Absolute* evolutionism is not justified by physical science which has established without doubt the stability of species, without ever discovering veritable specific transformations; moreover, it is condemned by metaphysics which refuses to admit that effects can be more perfect than their efficient causes; and "extreme" evolution denies the special act of creation of life, attributing the whole process to a natural development from inorganic matter. The doctrine of the natural development of all the species of the animal and vegetable world from a few primitive types created by God is *moderate* evolution. Catholics are free to believe in moderate evolution, excluding the evolution of man. Animals, as distinguished from man, are devoid of reason. Hence the animal soul, *i.e.*, the principle which gives an animal life, is essentially material. Hence, man's soul, though depending on material things for its activities, being essentially spiritual, the evolution of man *as a whole* from the lower animals is impossible. Some Catholic writers at the end of the nineteenth century and others in recent years have advocated the theory of the evolution of the human *body*. The Church has not issued any formal teaching on the subject, but certain writers in the last century were asked to withdraw books in which they had advocated a theory which excluded any direct divine intervention in the formation of Adam's body. The animal origin of his body seems difficult to harmonize with the historical account in Genesis (the same applies *a fortiori* to the formation of Eve); on the other hand, it must be borne in mind that Holy Scripture does not profess to give a *scientific* account of the origin of things. Inasmuch as the scientific arguments in favour of this human evolution make the theory probable but not certain, the conservative attitude taken up by Catholic theologians is natural and justifiable.*

EX CATHEDRA. The pope is said to speak *ex cathedra* when "exercising his office as the shepherd and teacher of all Christians, he, in virtue of his supreme apostolic authority, defines a doctrine concerning faith or morals to be held by the whole Church" (see his INFALLIBILITY). The *cathedra* (*q.v.*) being the official episcopal throne, the word is used figuratively of an official pastoral utterance of the most solemn kind.

EX OPERE OPERANTIS (Lat., from the work of the worker). A term used in describing the effects of prayers, good works, sacred signs or ceremonies (sacraments or sacramentals, *q.v.*), and indicating that the effect depends upon the sanctity of the minister or the dispositions of the subject.

EX OPERE OPERATO (Lat., from the work wrought). A term used in describing the primary effect of a sacrament, to indicate that the grace is conferred in virtue of the sensible sign instituted by Christ for this end, so that, if the sacrament is validly confected, its effect is objectively infallible and independent of the merits or virtues of minister or recipient. This does not mean that such dispositions are without effect, for (a) they always increase the fruits, (b) they sometimes are necessary for the validity of the sacrament, *e.g.*, of Penance, and (c) they are always, in adults, a condition of the actual conferring of the grace of the sacrament.

EX VOTO (Lat., out of a promise). An offering made in pursuance of a vow or as a token of gratitude. The silver hearts, etc., sometimes seen round statues are *ex votoes;* the crutches, etc., hung up in the grotto at Lourdes were given *ex voto* (*cf.*, Votive Candles).

EXALTATION OF THE CROSS, The. A feast kept on Sept. 14 (Holy Cross Day), commemorating the return of the True Cross to Jerusalem by the Emperor Heraclius in 627 after retaking it off from the Persians, who had carried it off thirteen years before. It may have had an earlier origin in Constantine's vision (see LABARUM). It is one of the great feasts of the Byzantine rite, the World-wide Exaltation of the Holy and Life-giving Cross, on the same date, which is connected with the finding of the cross by the empress St. Helen and the commemoration of the Dedication of the Basilica of the Resurrection of Jesus Christ our God (*i.e.*, the church of the Holy Sepulchre at Jerusalem) on the previous day.

EXAMEN, particular or general, is an examination of conscience of devotion (*i.e.*, not enjoined, as before confession) made daily or at other intervals to enable one more easily to correct faults and progress in virtue. The particular examen concentrates on some one failing to be avoided or virtue to be strengthened; the general is concerned to keep track of all sins and weaknesses.

EXAMINATION OF BISHOPS consists of a series of questions concerning obedience, the episcopal life and the Christian faith which are put to a bishop elect when he makes his profession of faith before consecration.

EXAMINATION OF CONSCIENCE has in ordinary circumstances to be made by the penitent before going to confession in order

---

* 1.) The theological meaning of the term "probable" is not "likely," but rather "possible." See p. 404 below. 2.) In the encyclical *Humani Generis* (1950) Pope Pius XII gave guidelines and strong cautions regarding the theory of the evolution of the human body. 3.) The theory of evolution appears less scientifically tenable with each passing year.—*Publisher*, 1997.

to ascertain of what sins he must accuse himself and be sorry for since he last received absolution. He must use such reasonable care as he would in any other matter of grave importance to remember at least all mortal (*q.v.*) sins since his last confession; otherwise he is incapable of receiving absolution. Sins which are forgotten come under the absolution, but if remembered afterwards must be mentioned at the next confession; the same with *bona fide* errors. If the penitent cannot remember the exact number of *times* he has committed a serious sin, *e.g.*, if he has sinned repeatedly over a long period, it suffices to say "about — times" or "about — times a day, week," etc.

EXARCH (Gr. ἔξαρχος, a ruler). i. In the Eastern churches is now properly a head of a church whose position is between that of a patriarch and a metropolitan. The primates of the Orthodox churches of Cyprus and Sinai are exarchs, but do not use the title. But the title is also used for patriarchal vicars, analogous to vicars apostolic, and others. In this sense an exarch is a priest or bishop charged by the proper high authority with a special mission, generally temporary. The name has been given to the heads of the Russian and Greek Catholics of the Byzantine rite, and is the title of the Melkite patriarchal vicar for Jerusalem. The bishops of the Ukrainians and Rusins in the United States of America are, and are now called, exarchs.

ii. The civil governor of a large or important province of the Roman empire, *e.g.*, the exarchs of Ravenna.

EXCARDINATION is the transfer of a cleric permanently from the jurisdiction of one bishop to that of another.

EXCELLENCY. "His Excellency," "Your Excellency." The official Roman style of address and reference for all archbishops, bishops, and certain other prelates. In some countries (*e.g.*, Great Britain) a customary local style is used instead.

EXCLUSION, RIGHT OF, or VETO. The supposed right claimed by certain rulers of states to name a person whom they wished to exclude from election to the papacy. This right, which was never approved by the Holy See, was definitely reprobated and prohibited by Pope Pius X in the constitution *Commissum nobis*, Jan. 20, 1904.

EXCOMMUNICATION. An ecclesiastical censure which excludes a person from the communion of the faithful, with consequent disabilities and deprivations. Excommunicates are of two kinds: *vitandi* (*q.v.*) are those excommunicated by the Holy See expressly as such by name or those who lay violent hands on the person of the Roman Pontiff; all others are *tolerati*. Excommunicates lose the right of attending divine service and receiving the sacraments. If clerics, they are forbidden to administer the sacraments, except in certain specified circumstances for the benefit of the faithful. They have no share in indulgences or in public prayers and Masses; but the faithful should pray privately for them and priests may apply Mass privately for them. The chief crimes which incur a special censure and excommunication *latæ sententiæ* (*q.v.*) are: throwing away the sacred Host or otherwise treating it with specified grave irreverence, laying violent hands on the pope, a priest pretending to absolve his female accomplice in sin, direct violation of the seal of confession (these are very specially reserved, *q.v.*, to the Holy See); those who having professed the Catholic faith apostatize, profess heresy and go into schism, appealing from the decision of the pope to an œcumenical council, deliberately citing a cardinal, apostolic nuncio or delegate, or one's own ordinary as defendant before a civil court without leave of the Holy See, forging apostolic decrees, letters or other papal documents, falsely accusing a priest to his superiors of solicitation in the confessional (these are specially reserved to the Holy See); granting or publishing indulgences for money, joining the Freemasons or other societies which work against the Church or lawful civil authority, citing any bishop or abbot or prelate *nullius* before a court as above, violating the laws of monastic papal enclosure, conversion of ecclesiastical property to one's personal use, duelling, attempted marriage by or with a person under a solemn vow of chastity, simony (these are simply reserved to the Holy See); attempt by a Catholic to contract marriage before a non-Catholic minister as such, agreeing before marriage that all or any of the children shall be brought up outside the Church, making, selling, distributing or exposing false relics, laying violent hands on any cleric or religious whatsoever, procuring abortion (these are reserved to the bishop or other ordinary); publishing without leave of the ordinary notes and comments on the holy Scriptures, compelling anyone against his or her will to receive holy orders, to enter a religious institute or, being therein, to be professed, failing to report it to the ordinary within a month if one has been solicited in the confessional (these being reserved to nobody, the offender can be reconciled by any priest in confession, and outside of it by anyone having jurisdiction over him). *

EXEAT (Lat., he may go out). A letter of excardination (*q.v.*), without which a priest may not be permanently attached to a diocese other than his own.

EXECRATION. Desecration (*q.v.*).

EXEGESIS (Gr., explanation). The investigation and expounding of the true sense

---

* This list is based on the 1917 Code of Canon Law. The 1983 Code of Canon Law lists far fewer crimes for which one incurs automatic (*ipso facto*) excommunication (Canon 1364 ff.), e.g., apostasy, heresy, schism, throwing away the sacred species (consecrated Host or Precious Blood) or taking or retaining them for a sacrilegious purpose, using physical force against the Roman Pontiff, procuring a successful

(q.v.) of the Sacred Scriptures, that is, the truth actually conveyed by them.

EXEGETE. One who deals in exegesis; an expounder of the holy Scriptures.

EXEMPLARISM. The theory of Plato according to which God formed the world from a pre-existent matter in accordance with the ideas or types (see ARCHETYPE), which are eternally present in the divine Mind. These ideas or types form the intelligible world which the human mind contemplates or rather resembles when it withdraws from the senses. The theory is against the doctrine of creation and the true theory of the origin of ideas.

EXEMPT. i. Religious. Those religious (q.v.) who are subject to their own superiors only, and not to the local ordinary. Members of all religious orders of solemn vows (except nuns not subject to a regular superior) are exempt, also by special privilege some congregations of simple vows. Exempt religious are, however, subject to the local ordinary in many matters affecting their relations with non-religious, e.g., in parochial work.

ii. Diocese. A diocese which is not under the metropolitan authority of any archbishop but is immediately subject to the Holy See; e.g., those of Switzerland, and others in Italy, Yugoslavia, Gibraltar, etc. An archdiocese whose archbishop is not a metropolitan is also called exempt; e.g., Winnipeg, Udine, Athens, Panama and others.

EXEQUATUR (Lat., he may perform). The right claimed by civil rulers, or for them by jurists, to examine papal bulls, etc., and decide whether or no they shall be admitted to take effect in their territories. The 41st proposition condemned by the syllabus of Pope Pius IX was that: "the civil power, even when exercised by an infidel ruler, has an indirect and negative power over religious affairs; it therefore possesses not only the right called that of *exequatur,* but also that of appeal as from an abuse, so-called" (q.v.) (cf.. Provisors).

EXEQUIAL MASS is the requiem Mass said at a funeral (Lat. *exsequi,* to follow, finish). It is followed by the absolutions (q.v.) and procession to the grave.

EXERCISE (Lat. *exercere,* to keep at work). An act of worship or form of devotion or meditation, especially such as have the training of the soul as their object, e.g., the Spiritual Exercises of St. Ignatius Loyola. The modern use of the word is in accord with the primitive conception of the Christian as an "athlete of the Lord" (1 Cor. ix, 24-26).

EXISTENCE. The ultimate act of essence (q.v.). That whereby a thing is outside its

causes. Thomists affirm and Suarezians deny that this ultimate actuality or existence is really distinct from the reality of the essence in created things. This is a recondite discussion, but it has an important bearing on the question as to what ultimately constitutes a supposit or person (qq.v.) and makes it differ really from an individual nature; it is thus vital to the theological exploration of the Hypostatic Union. In God existence and real essence are absolutely identical. The classic proofs for the existence of God are five in number and are formulated by St. Thomas in the "Summa": (a) The fact that all things *move* cannot be ultimately explained unless there be a prime mover: this is God. (b) All causes must themselves be caused or uncaused; the ultimate uncaused cause is God. (c) All contingent beings presuppose necessary beings; necessary beings are themselves the reason of their necessity or not; if not, their necessity is *derived* ultimately from an absolute necessary being. This is God. (d) All degrees of perfection demand ultimately the absolute perfection of which they are participations, and which is their reason. These degrees exist, therefore the supremely perfect exists. This is God. (e) (the argument from design). All things tend towards an end which is the good of the universe. Innumerable things are void of intelligence, and cannot therefore direct themselves to the aforesaid end. The intelligence directing them is God.

EXODUS (Lat., going out). The second book of the O.T., so called because it relates the going-out of the Children of Israel from Egypt; it describes their wanderings in the Sinai desert, the giving of the Ten Commandments, the making of the covenant between God and his people, the setting up of the altar and institution of a priesthood and a liturgy. In Hebrew it is called *Veelle semoth,* its opening words. Its author was Moses (see PENTATEUCH). The fourth and ninth Prophecies of Holy Saturday and the second of Whitsun Eve are taken from Exod. (xiv, xv, xii).

EXORCISM (Gr. ἐξορκἰζω, to put on oath). i. The driving out of evil spirits in cases of demoniacal possession (q.v.) by adjuration (q.v.). Such exorcism must be performed by a priest with express permission of the bishop, and with the rite provided in the "Rituale Romanum." Exorcism is rarely necessary in civilized lands, but foreign missionaries are sometimes called on to use it.

ii. Lesser exorcisms, which do not imply a state of possession, are used in the ceremonies of Baptism (q.v.), and in blessing certain objects, e.g., water, salt.

EXORCISM, THE RITE OF, begins with the litany of the Saints, the Our Father secretly, two prayers for the one possessed and an admonishment of the unclean spirit; then

abortion. Accomplices in an offense may also incur the excommunication. Clerics are subject to automatic excommunication for additional offenses. Proper Church authorities can attach an automatic excommunication to additional offenses. Certain circumstances exempt a person from automatic excommunication. The 1983 Code likewise states new laws for the lifting of excommunications.—*Publisher,* 1997.

is read one or more passages from the Gospels (from John i, Mark xvi, Luke x or xi) and the exorcist (priest or bishop) prays for the requisite power for himself; he then puts the end of his stole round the neck and his right hand on the head of the possessed and, after a short prayer invoking the name of God, pronounces "with great faith" three long exorcisms of the demon, accompanied by signs of the cross and the first two followed by prayers. These are repeated if necessary, and there are also recommended to be recited as required the Our Father, Hail Mary, Apostles' Creed, the *Magnificat*, *Benedictus*, Athanasian Creed, and various psalms. A prayer is added that the released victim be not again afflicted.

EXORCIST. The second of the minor orders, of which the duties are "to cast out devils, to warn the people that non-communicants should make room for the communicants, and to pour out the water needed in divine service." At ordination he receives the "book of exorcisms" (usually the "Pontificale" or "Rituale"), but all the above duties are now obsolete so far as the exorcist is concerned (see EXORCISM); the order is only a step to the priesthood. In the Orthodox Eastern Church the exorcists are not ordained; anyone, lay or cleric, who has the gift may, and does, use exorcism. This was the practice of the early Church.

EXPECTATION OF OUR LADY'S CHILD-BEARING, The. A feast kept in Spain and other places on Dec. 18. The name sufficiently explains it.

EXPERIENCE (Lat. *experiri*, to go through). The actual perception of an object or the retention of such perception in the memory.
  i. The experience of any fact of religion: thus the experience of God in the mystical union (*q.v.*).
  ii. The experience of the soul-satisfying nature of some religious doctrine or practice, which is too often wrongly accepted as adequate proof of its truth or supernatural significance. This is the basis of pragmatism (*q.v.*) in religion.

EXPLICIT. See IMPLICIT.

EXPOSITION (of the Blessed Sacrament) is the open displaying of the Blessed Sacrament for a period of time in such a way that it may be seen by the people, who honour God and satisfy their devotion by praying before it. Private exposition, when the tabernacle is opened so that the ciborium containing the Host may be seen, may be held at any time for a just reason without reference to the bishop. Public exposition, when the Host is displayed in a monstrance, requires an important reason, particularly one affecting the public welfare, and consent of the bishop, except on the feast of Corpus Christi.

There are certain rules laid down providing for the solemnity with which exposition must be surrounded. At the beginning of exposition *O Salutaris* is sung and the Host incensed; at the end *Tantum ergo* is sung and all is done as at Benediction. This custom of extra-liturgical devotion arose in the middle ages and has become increasingly popular since the 16th century, but the Church has shown a restraining rather than a yielding disposition in its regard. (See BENEDICTION; FORTY HOURS; PERPETUAL ADORATION.)

EXPOSITION, MASS OF. The Mass celebrated at the beginning of the Forty Hours (*q.v.*) devotion when the Blessed Sacrament is exposed.

EXPOSITION OF RELICS is the display of relics of saints (under certain circumstances of *beati*) upon an altar or elsewhere for the veneration of the faithful. They must be contained in their reliquaries and at least two candles must burn on the altar; but they may never be exposed on the same altar as that on which the Blessed Sacrament is being exposed.

EXPRESS; TACIT. Express and tacit mention, consent, permission, etc., normally have the same force in canon law, except that the first is the more easily capable of proof. But frequently the law itself requires express mention, etc., in which case tacit does not suffice.

EXPULSION OF PENITENTS, The. The ancient discipline of expelling public penitents from the church on Ash Wednesday is still provided for in the "Pontificale Romanum" by a rite of Gallican origin extended to the Roman liturgy about 1290; it fell into desuetude during the middle ages, and has not been restored in spite of the recommendation of the Council of Trent. The ceremony consists of the imposition of ashes and the hair-shirt (the sack-cloth and ashes of Israel), the penitential psalms, litanies and prayers, and the leading of the penitents out of the church by the bishop, who shuts the door on them, saying, "Thus are you to-day banished from the threshold of your mother the Church because of your sins and wickedness, as the first man, Adam, was driven out of Paradise because of his transgression." St. Thomas distinguishes this expulsion as solemn penance from the earlier public or canonical penance. Their reconciliation took place on Maundy Thursday. When the imposition of ashes was extended to all the people, this expulsion was symbolized by the Lenten veil (*q.v.*), of which the Passion-tide veiling of images is probably a survival.

EXSULTET, The. The Paschal Praise or so-called blessing of the paschal candle on Holy Saturday, beginning with this word. It is, in fact, not a blessing but a hymn of praise, sung by a deacon. The first part or prelude announces that he will sing the praise of the paschal candle, symbol of the Eternal Light; the second part, in the form of a preface, is a lyrical apostrophe of the glory of the night of the Resurrection. The *Exsultet* ends in a prayer for pope and bishop and all the people of God. The metrical *cursus* of the *Exsultet* is remarkable, and with its chant it forms one of the most glorious passages of the whole Latin liturgy. The paschal candle is blessed and lit before the *Exsultet* is sung; five incense grains, tokens of Christ's wounds, are fixed in it, and the date of the year cut thereon.

EXSURGE DOMINE. A bull of Pope Leo X issued in 1520 condemning forty-one errors of Martin Luther on penance, indulgences, the authority of the Holy See, the Church and councils, on good works and on Purgatory.

EXTENSION. i. In logic the word is used of an idea which is able to represent the many or the few.

ii. In things. That property of a substance which has parts outside parts. It is often confused with quantity, of which it is only a property: hence the distinction between internal extension and external. The first is the distribution of the parts of a substance within itself (quantity); the latter the distribution of these parts in place in triple dimension of length, breadth and depth (property of quantity).

EXTERN SISTER (Lat. *externus,* outward). A member of certain strictly enclosed orders of nuns (*e.g.,* Carmelites, Poor Clares), who lives within the convent but outside the enclosure. Extern sisters answer the door, go shopping, and act generally as the outside agents of the nuns, but must be distinguished from the lay-sisters proper within the enclosure. They have a distinctive dress and are sometimes called *tourières,* "turn sisters."

EXTRA ECCLESIAM NULLA SALUS (Lat., outside the Church there is no salvation). See SALVATION OUTSIDE THE CHURCH.

EXTRA-LITURGICAL WORSHIP denotes those services, etc., of a popular character which, though carried out by the faithful together and in a public church and led by the clergy, are not provided for in the Church's official books of worship; *e.g.,* Benediction, the Stations of the Cross. See POPULAR DEVOTIONS.

EXTRAORDINARY ECCLESIASTICAL AFFAIRS, THE SACRED CONGREGATION OF. A Roman congregation (*q.v.*) having the consideration of matters submitted to its examination by the pope through the cardinal secretary of state, especially those connected with civil law or with agreements made with civil powers.

EXTREME UNCTION, CEREMONIES OF. After the *Asperges* (*q.v.*) the priest says three prayers for peace, health, safety and the guardianship of angels for all who dwell in the house; then the *Confiteor* (*q.v.*) and an exorcism. Then with his thumb he anoints the sick person with the oil of the sick on his eyes, ears, nostrils, closed lips, hands (the backs in the case of a priest or bishop; otherwise the palms) and feet, repeating a prayer each time: "Through this holy anointing and his most tender mercy, may the Lord pardon thee whatever sins thou hast committed by [sight, etc.]. Amen." The rite concludes with three prayers for health of soul and body for the sick man, the first referring to the words of St. James's epistle, v, 14, 15. In the Byzantine rite this sacrament is administered (if possible, in the church) by 1, 3, 5, or 7 priests, who themselves bless the oil, with 7 lessons, 7 gospels, and 7 prayers, and each priest repeats the 7 anointings; this form is commonly curtailed. Brow, nostrils, cheeks, lips, breast and both sides of the hands are anointed with a prayer for the healing of soul and body. Catholics of the Armenian and all Syriac rites use the Roman, or very similar, ceremonies. Among those dissident Orientals who still use this sacrament it is called simply "anointing," and no danger of death is necessarily required for its administration: sometimes it may even be received by a quite healthy person as an act of devotion, to avert sickness and to obtain remission of sins. Through misunderstanding, partly due to the use of the word "extreme," they accuse the Catholic Church of giving it only to the actually dying. This sacrament is no longer used by the dissident Armenians, Abyssinians and Nestorians.

EXTREME UNCTION, THE SACRAMENT OF (*i.e.,* "Last Anointing"). A sacrament of the New Law in which, by anointing with oil and the prayers of the priest, health of soul and (sometimes) of body is conferred on a baptized person who is in danger of death through sickness. The oil must be specially blessed (oil of the sick, *q.v.*) and the prayers of the priest must have a particular form. The health of the body is an effect to be expected only when God sees it to be profitable to the soul. The proximity of death from any cause other than sickness does not provide an occasion for the use of the sacrament. It is administered to those sick persons of whose death fears are entertained, *i.e.,* if there is a danger of death. It is called "extreme," or last, not because it is given as a preparation for death (indeed, rather does it look hopefully for health of body as well as soul), but because it follows in order of time the anointings made at Baptism, Confirmation and holy Orders. Anointing the sick with oil is referred to in Mark vi, 13, but the specific direction for the sacrament is in James v, 14, 15. With Confirmation and Matrimony it has less important reference to salvation than the other sacraments, with which the evangelists were more concerned. The sacrament can only be administered by a bishop or priest; several priests may each perform one or more anointings, as is usual in the Eastern rites. Its remote matter is the oil and the proximate matter the anointing, each organ having its special form, as above.

EZECHIEL (Heb., strengthened by God). A book of prophecy of the Old Testament, taking its name from its author who was carried off from Jerusalem to Babylonia in 598 B.C.; traditionally he was slain for rebuking idolatry. The symbolical vision recounted and its general allegorical form make the book very obscure; but it consists principally of prophecies of the destruction of Jerusalem and of the neighbouring nations and promise of the restoration of Israel by God's grace and the coming of a new Kingdom. The seventh prophecy on Holy Saturday (sixth on Whitsun Eve) is taken from Ezechiel (xxxvii). Ezechiel is named in the Roman Martyrology on April 10.

EZRA. The Hebrew form of Esdras (*q.v.*).

F

FABRIC OF ST. PETER'S, THE SACRED CONGREGATION OF THE VENERABLE. A Roman congregation (*q.v.*) to whose care is committed the fabric of St. Peter's basilica of the Vatican; it also controls the School of Mosaic and the Petrine Museum.

FABRICA. The *fabrica* of a church, institution, foundation, etc., is the building itself and its material accessories. The funds of the *fabrica* are distinct from the revenue of a benefice, which belongs to the incumbent. Provision is made in canon law for a council, which may include laymen, to administer the *fabrica* of churches.

FACULTY. i. A power to do; the fourth species of quality. The mind and will, *e.g.*, are powers by means of which the soul thinks and wills. No substance is immediately operative, hence the need of powers or faculties through which it acts. This is proved because act and potency are in the same supreme genus, and since the act is an accident so must that which produces the act be an accident and not a substance. Hence the need of a faculty which is an accident.

ii. The professorial staff and *magistri* of a given department of learning in a university (formerly the branch of learning itself), whose head is the dean. The Four Faculties are Arts, Theology, Law and Medicine, but modern universities have invented others.

FACULTIES. The powers or rights granted to bishops by the Holy See, or to priests by their ordinaries, to enable them to exercise certain acts of jurisdiction outside their ordinary competence; especially the delegated jurisdiction in the internal forum, *i.e.*, to hear confessions and administer the sacrament of Penance, granted to confessors who have not this power by ordinary law.

FACULTIES OF THE SOUL. Those qualities or properties by which the human soul is enabled to act, the proximate principles of human activity, namely, imagination, memory, understanding, and will (*qq.v.*).

FAITH. i. The object of belief; the sum of the truths taught by the Catholic religion.

ii. A theological virtue (*q.v.*) by which our intellect is disposed to assent firmly to all the truths revealed by God, because of the infinite truth and wisdom of God who can neither deceive or be deceived. The words of St. Paul (Heb. xi, 1), Faith is "that which gives substance to our hopes, which convinces us of things we cannot see" make a convenient definition of faith, and all other definitions are a development of this. "If you would reduce the words to the form of a definition, you might say: Faith is a habit of the mind by which eternal life is begun in us, in that it makes the intellect assent to things which appear not. . . . The fact that it is called evidence (*argumentum*) distinguishes faith from opinion, suspicion and doubt, in which there is no firm adhesion of the intellect to anything; the fact that it is 'of things which we cannot see,' distinguishes it from knowledge and understanding, by which a thing becomes apparent. The fact that it 'gives substance to our hopes' distinguishes the virtue of faith from faith in common acceptance, which is not ordained to any hoped-for happiness" (St. Thomas, II-II, iv, 1). "Since faith rests upon infallible truth and the contrary of a truth can never be demonstrated, it is clear that the arguments brought against the faith cannot be strict demonstrations, but difficulties that can be answered" (St. Thomas I, 1. 8c), or in the words of Cardinal Newman, "Ten thousand difficulties do not make one doubt."

iii. Justifying. Faith is necessary for justification, but it must be true faith and not merely the confidence which Luther depended upon: "If anyone say that justifying faith is nothing else than confidence in the divine mercy which remits sins on account of Christ . . . let him be anathema" (Council of Trent, sess. vi, can. 12, *de justificatione*); "Go out all over the world and preach the gospel to the whole creation. He who believes and is baptized will be saved; he who refuses belief will be condemned" (Mark xvi, 15, 16). And for salvation this faith must be informed by charity.

FAITH, The. The system of belief and conduct taught as revealed truth by the Catholic Church of Christ, often used as a synonym for the Church itself. The Faithful are the members of the Church or any group of them: formerly, particularly as distinguished from catechumens (*cf.*, Mass of the Faithful), and this usage is still current in those foreign missions wherein the primitive catechumenate has been revived.

FAITH, ACT OF. A supernatural (*q.v.*) act of the intellect making a firm assent to truth revealed by God, on the authority of God himself revealing; sometimes used of the form of words in which this act is expressed. We are obliged to make an act of faith: When we realize for the first time that God has made a revelation and that we are bound to believe it; often during life; after a fall into heresy; when it is the necessary means of resisting a temptation against faith; when a new definition of faith is proposed. "An act of faith can be meritorious in so far as it is subject to the will and this not only as regards its use but also as regards assent. For the action of reason can precede faith, as when one will not, or will not at once, believe unless human reason can be adduced, and this lessens the merit of faith. But reason can also follow the will to believe. For when one has a prompt will to believe, he loves the truth he believes and ponders it and welcomes any reasons which can be found to support it. And in this sense human reason does not lessen but increases the merit of faith" (St. Thomas, II-II, ii, 10).

"FAITH WITH HERETICS, NO." There is no such principle, and never has been. It is a figment of imagination taking origin from the acts of the Council of Constance (July 6, 1415) which condemned the heretical and dangerous principles of John Huss. Huss was deposed and degraded, and handed over to the civil authority, by which he was burned at the stake. All this was in face of a safe-conduct granted to him by the Emperor Sigismund. The alleged principle is derived from the words of the decree: "A safe-conduct notwithstanding, it is permissible to a competent ecclesiastical judge . . . to proceed against [heretics] and punish them . . . if they pertinaciously refuse to forsake their errors, even if, in reliance on the safe-conduct they have come to a place of judgement to which otherwise they would not have come; and he who makes the promise (*i.e.*, issues the safe-conduct) as long as he has done all in his power, has no further obligation in the matter." In short, the council refused any authority of the emperor to over-ride ecclesiastical jurisdiction.

FAITH AND MORALS. Between faith and morals are three essential links: (*a*) Every moral obligation has its roots in the will of God as seen in the natural law; but man's reason is so blinded and his will so perverted by passion and prejudice that divine revelation was necessary to give him a correct knowledge of the natural law. (*b*) Absence of faith involves the absence of the sharpest spurs to duty, *sc.*, love of God, hope of Heaven, fear of Hell. (*c*) The Christian revelation imposed the moral obligation of believing in its content, receiving the sacraments, believing and obeying the Church. But "Faith is illuminative, not operative; it does not force obedience, though it increases responsibility; it heightens guilt, it does not prevent sin" (Newman).

FAITH AND REASON. To know a truth by reason is to see the truth because of its intrinsic evidence which is immediate if the truth be a first principle, mediate if the truth is a conclusion deduced from that principle. To know a truth by faith is to give assent to it not because of intrinsic but of extrinsic evidence, that is, on account of some reliable authority which tells us of the truth. If the authority is human the assent to the truth is called human faith, if divine it is divine faith. Divine faith and reason cannot contradict one another, because truth cannot be opposed to truth. On the other hand reason helps faith and faith perfects reason. The resources of philosophic speculation are most useful to faith when there is question of truths accessible to reason; on the other hand the body of philosophic doctrines, to which in its entirety human reason would rarely attain, is easily discovered for reason by the aid of faith, even though, consequently, reason may hold this body of truths on purely rational grounds. The philosophy that the Church teaches does not derive its scientific value from the fact that it is Christian, but from the fact that it is true in itself. Catholic philosophy is constructed in such wise that its full accord in fact with theology appears as a necessary consequence of the rigorous demands of reason itself rather than as the accidental result of a wished-for harmony.

FAITH AND WORKS. Faith without good works (*q.v.*) is useless; through such good works as man does by the grace of God and the merits of Christ, he truly obtains increase of grace and merits eternal life. *

FAITHFUL COMPANIONS OF JESUS, The. An unenclosed congregation of sisters founded by the Countess de Bonnault d'Houet at Amiens in 1820. They conduct schools of all classes and have many houses in Great Britain. Their constitutions are

---

* Meritorious good works that "count" for Heavenly reward are only those performed by a Christian in the state of grace (Sanctifying Grace, *q.v.*), that is, as a living branch on the Vine which is Christ (cf. *John* 15:4-6). Such works are not merely human acts, but supernaturalized acts. See PARTAKERS OF THE DIVINE NATURE. Upon committing a mortal sin, a Christian loses Sanctifying Grace and the

(*Continued on following page*)

founded on the rules of the Society of Jesus. Black habit.

"FAITHFUL MAJESTY, MOST." A title of the kings of Portugal, granted to John V by Pope Clement XI in 1717 in recognition of his services against the Turks.

FALDA. A garment of white silk with a train, worn over the cassock and peculiar to the pope on occasions of solemnity.

FALDSTOOL. A four-legged chair with arms but no back. It is used both as a seat and as a *prie-dieu* by a bishop officiating outside his own diocese, or within it when he is not using his throne, *e.g.*, he occupies it before the altar when confirming or ordaining. Other prelates with a right to *pontificalia* (*q.v.*) may use it.

FALK LAWS. The May Laws (*q.v.*), called after the name of the jurist appointed by Bismarck to be Prussian minister of worship, who drafted and prepared them.

FALL OF MAN, The. The rejection of a supernatural life involved in the transgression by the first man of a special direct precept revealed by God, and the subsequent deprivation of his supernatural and preternatural gifts, sanctifying grace, potential immortality, impassibility, integrity, etc. (*qq.v.*). The Fall, does not involve an intrinsic corruption of human nature; nature as such was left intact,* but was shorn of those gifts which God had bestowed over and above the needs and requirements of nature, that is to say, the supernatural grace of which our First Parents were deprived had been a free gift of God, not due to man as man. These privileges were lost not only for Adam, but also for his descendants, so that neither he nor his progeny could have attained their supernatural end, *i.e.*, the vision of God, but for the merits of the Redeemer promised at once after the Fall. Catholics may not interpret the Fall merely as the gradual deterioration by sins of individuals, but are bound to hold one great historic sin of our first parents involving the disinheriting of all their children but for the Second Adam, Christ.

FALLEN NATURE. The state of fallen nature, redeemed by Jesus Christ, or of original sin (*q.v.*), is the condition in which all men are born. It differs from the state of pure nature (*q.v.*) in that before Baptism we suffer from the privation of supernatural grace which God had bestowed on Adam; in our natural powers in the two states there would be no difference. It does not mean that human nature is, or ever was, essentially "bad, desperately wicked, depraved, corrupt, utterly abominable"; such doctrine was a popular heresy of Protestantism. Baptism does not reduce us to the state of pure nature but restores us to the supernatural state from which Adam, and the human race in him, fell.

FALLING ASLEEP OF MARY, The. i. Another name for the feast of the Assumption (*q.v.*).

ii. "Transitus Mariæ," a 4th–5th century apocryphal work telling, with great embellishment of wonders, of the death and assumption of the Blessed Virgin. In it she is referred to as our Lady and the Mother of God, she is sinless, unblemished in body and soul, the interceder with her Son, venerated by men and angels, an agent of miracles; and incense, altar and sacrifice are spoken of in reference to Christian worship. There are ancient versions in Greek, Latin, Syriac, Arabic and Sahidic, which vary considerably.

FALSE, The. Difformity or disagreement between the mind and a thing.

FALSE DECRETALS, The. A number of forged papal letters, purporting to be of the popes of the first six centuries, written by and included in a collection of canon law made by one who called himself Isidore Mercator, about 850. They cover the whole field of Christian doctrine and discipline and lay particular stress on the rights of the episcopate and of the Holy See, but contain nothing that was an innovation at the time they were written. They were accepted as genuine and used by canonists throughout the middle ages; but from the middle of the 15th century came under suspicion, and have been repudiated by all canonists since 1628.

FALSE WITNESS. Perjury; the making upon oath a statement known to be untrue; always a grievous sin against religion (*q.v.*). Should the perjury cause harm to another, the additional sin of injustice would involve the obligation of reparation (*q.v.*). The Eighth Commandment has in view any harm done to another by our words.

FALSE WORSHIP is worship that is not in accordance with truth, *e.g.*, that of the Jews, which was superseded by Jesus Christ; or if a layman should pretend to celebrate Mass. Or it may be false by way of excess, as when an infallible effect is attributed to wearing a medal (*q.v.*) or to saying a prayer on 30 consecutive days or to receiving holy communion on nine consecutive first Fridays, such fixed periods of time being customs approved by the Church as assisting people to the due performance of acts of devotion, the degree of whose efficacy depends wholly on God's will and the person's dispositions.

FALSO-BORDONE. Faux-Bourdon (*q.v.*).

FAME, defect of, as irregularity. See INFAMY.

FAMILIAR. A lay servant employed by and living in a monastery, seminary, etc., or attached to a bishop's household.

FAMILY, The. The first, fundamental and most natural type of society, composed of

---

ability to perform meritorious good works—until he receives Sanctifying Grace back again by proper repentance.—*Publisher*, 1997.

* Human nature was "wounded" in the Fall—with consequent "darkening" of intellect and weakening of will.—*Publisher*, 1997.

father, mother and children; it is the basis of all human society and exists for the good of its individual members; the state exists for the common good of the totality of individuals and families which compose it. It is "the society of a man's house, a society limited in numbers, but no less a true society anterior to every kind of state and nation, invested with rights and duties of its own totally independent of the civil community" (Pope Leo XIII). The right and duty of the parents is to provide sustenance, training and education for their children; this involves the acquisition of private property, as a necessary right and duty also; and a certain degree of permanence in association, which is provided for by the indissolubility of marriage. Conversely, adult children are bound to the support and care of their aged or indigent parents. So long as the members are able and willing adequately to perform their duties, a family is entitled to be free from domestic interference by the state. Like the marriage on which it is founded, the family reflects the union of Christ with his Church, and illustrates the priesthood of the faithful, by an exercise of which in the sacrament of Matrimony the man and woman join themselves together to form a new unit of society. (cf., Parents.)

FAMILY PRAYERS. It is in accordance with the mind of the Church that the members of a family should meet together at least once a day for the purpose of worshipping Almighty God. It is deplorable that this custom is so little used nowadays, at any rate in English-speaking countries.

FAN. A very early liturgical accessory of which the object was to keep flies, etc., away from the sacred vessels. Its only survival in the West is in a few churches in southern Italy, but it is kept in the Eastern rites (ripidion, q.v.). See also FLABELLUM.

FANON. i. A vestment peculiar to the pope at solemn Mass. It is a cape with a hole for the head to go through, and consists of two oval pieces of white silk, striped with red and gold. It is put on like a monastic amice, but with the lower piece over the shoulder of the alb, and the upper drawn out over the chasuble. Also called the orale.

ii. The silken cloth formerly tied to a crosier for cleanliness (sudarium, q.v.).

FARCING (Lat. farcire, to fill up). The repetition of a scriptural text or other words between the verses, or between every two verses, of a psalm, canticle, etc. It was a practice so much developed as to become an abuse in the middle ages; the Kyrie at Mass, particularly, was often farced with texts fitted to the notes of the long neums (q.v.), and Gloria in excelsis treated in the same way. The name farcing is sometimes given to the way in which the invitatory and Ps. xciv (Venite exsultemus Domino) are recited at the beginning of Matins, and, extra-liturgically, in processions, etc., to, e.g., a double Alleluia after each verse of the Magnificat. In the use of Braga the antiphon is repeated several times between the verses of this canticle on great feasts, and the Bridgettine nuns so sing the Benedicite at Vespers on feasts of our Lady. To sing thus was sometimes called triumphare antiphonas, or to sing triumphaliter, "with triumphal solemnity," and is not really farcing at all; the repetition of an antiphon is simply a return to or survival of the original antiphonal or responsorial usage. True farcing was entirely mediæval and is now quite abolished in the Roman rite; but the Carmelite use has farced Kyries before the prayer at Lauds of Tenebræ.

FARNBOROUGH. A Benedictine monastery at Farnborough in Hampshire. It was founded in 1895 at the invitation of Eugénie, exiled empress of the French, who provided a monastery not far from her own house and is now with the Emperor Napoleon III and the Prince Imperial buried in the crypt of the church. The care of the imperial mausoleum was originally entrusted to the Premonstratensian canons but was transferred to Solesmes Benedictines. Their abbey was dissolved in 1947 and the monastery became a dependency of Prinknash Abbey (q.v.).

FAST (Old Eng. fæsten, an observance). i. The act of fasting (q.v.).

ii. A period during which the Church enjoins that fasting shall be observed. The principal fast throughout the Church is that of Lent (q.v.). Many religious orders have special fasts (e.g. every Friday or from Holy Cross till Easter). Other fasts in the Eastern rites are: of the Apostles, 4–42 days; of our Lady, 7–14 days; of Christmas, 12–40 days; and Ninive (q.v.). These extra fasts are of monastic origin and though some dissidents observe them scrupulously, for most Catholics they are now reduced to a few days of abstinence from flesh-meat and other special foods.

FAST, NATURAL, is the refraining from all food, liquid or solid, from midnight, such as is required for the lawful reception of holy communion. But see FASTING COMMUNION.

FAST DAYS in England and Wales and North America are normally all the days of Lent except Sundays until Holy Saturday evening; the ember days; the vigil of Pentecost; and the vigils of the Assumption and Christmas, except when these feasts fall on a Monday. For the days on which abstinence must be added to fasting see ABSTINENCE. Detailed regulations vary according to countries and dioceses.*

FASTING is concerned with the quantity of food eaten and so must be distinguished from abstinence (q.v.). The law is that on a

---

* The 1983 Code of Canon Law states that fasting is obligatory on Ash Wednesday and Good Friday, and that Lent is a penitential time throughout the universal Church. The U.S. National Conference of Catholic Bishops stated on November 18, 1966 that "self-imposed observance of fasting on all weekdays of Lent is strongly recommended."—*Publisher,* 1997

fast day only one full meal may be taken
and that aftei noon. Drink is not limited,
but such liquids as soup count as food.
Custom allows 2 or 3 oz. of dry bread or
similar food at breakfast and 8 or 10 oz. of
food at collation (q.v.), or according to local
usage. * Fasting is only imposed on those
who are over 21 and under 59, but severe
work, whether manual or mental, sickness
and debility excuse from the obligation; in
cases of doubt a dispensation may be asked
for from the parish-priest. Fasting is far
more rigorous and lasts for longer periods in
all Eastern churches. It is an act of penitence and physical mortification imposed by
the Church for exercise in temperance and
the health of souls.

FASTING COMMUNION. A natural fast
from food and drink is obligatory before
holy communion, from midnight, except in
danger of death, or to save the sacrament
from irreverence, and in certain other circumstances.**The swallowing of something
in the nature of food or drink is necessary to
break the fast; hence involuntarily to swal-
low a piece of paper, or a little toothpaste,
or a piece of food dislodged from the teeth,
or to smoke a pipe or take snuff, etc., does
not break the fast; nor does the deliberate
drinking of plain water. This natural fast
may be modified on account of working at
night or in other severe conditions, long distance from church, long wait for food after
communion, communion after 9 a.m., in bad
health, and at evening Mass. The nature
of the modifications varies. A confessor
should be consulted in each circumstance
(but not every time so long as the condition
lasts), except in the case of communion at
evening Mass: for this, food may be taken 3
hours before, and non-alcoholic drink one
hour before. There are special and stringent
rules about all alcoholic drink. The reason
of this law is religious reverence, which from
early days required that the Body of Christ
should be the first food taken in the day; it
was a universal custom already in the days
of St. Augustine (d. 430). There is the
further reason of avoiding profane revelry,
and especially possible over-drinking, before
going to the Lord's table.

FATALISM. The doctrine that all effects
are produced by a blind necessity (see DES-
TINY). Not to be confused with Determinism
(q.v.).

FATE (Lat. *fatum*, a prediction). In its
Christian sense, the ordering of secondary
causes by God so that they produce their
effects in accordance with the divine providence.

FATHER is by right the title of a mendicant
friar but in speech is extended to all priests
of the regular (q.v.) clergy. In English-
speaking countries and Portugal it is used in
address and reference for all Catholic priests

(in England this custom is hardly 70 years
old; secular priests were "Mr." and "sir," as
they still are at Ushaw); in Catholic countries secular priests are *Monsieur l'abbé, monsieur le curé,* or as the case may be, *signor,
don,* etc. (cf., *Dom*). All priests of Eastern
rites are "Father."

FATHER OF HERESIES, The. Simon
Magus (Acts viii, 9–24), who according to tradition persevered in his evil ways. He gives
its name to the crime of simony (q.v.).

FATHER OF LIES, The. The Devil. See
John viii, 44. This is a very common figure
of speech in the East, where a man is often
thus addressed from a notable characteristic
or the goods he deals in, *e.g.,* a baker,
"father of loaves."

FATHER OF ORTHODOXY, The. St.
Athanasius, so called because of his inflexible
opposition to Arianism (q.v.).

FATHERS OF CHARITY. See INSTITUTE OF
CHARITY.

FATHERS OF THE CHURCH, The, or
simply the Fathers. i. All those writers of
the first twelve centuries whose works on
Christian doctrine are considered of weight
and worthy of respect. They include Clement of Alexandria, Tertullian, Origen, Palladius, Maximus the Confessor.

ii. More strictly, those teachers of the first
twelve, and especially of the first six, centuries, who added notable holiness and complete orthodoxy to their great learning. The
chief are, the Doctors of the Church (q.v.)
up to and including St. Bernard; St. Clement
of Rome (1st cent.); SS. Ignatius of Antioch,
Justin, Irenæus, Polycarp (2nd cent.); SS. Cyprian, Dionysius (3rd cent.); SS. Optatus and
Epiphanius (4th cent.); St. Vincent of Lerins
(5th cent.); St. Cæsarius of Arles (6th cent.).
The authority of these fathers is great
though not unlimited; but when they show
a morally unanimous consent on a point of
doctrine it is considered decisive.

FATHERS OF THE DESERT, The. The
monks and hermits of the Egyptian deserts
in the 4th century from whom all Christian
monasticism derives. The most famous were
SS. Antony, the father of all monks, Paul,
the first hermit, Pachomius, Hilarion and
Epiphanius and Palladius, their historian.
In the Nitrian desert of northern Egypt in
the 4th century there were 5,000 monks presided over by St. Antony. These were either
strictly hermits who met only on Saturdays
and Sundays for worship, or else semi-hermits
living in twos and threes. There was no
common rule, but aspirants learned from a
senior and the elders exercised an informal
authority. Arising partly from this individualism was their characteristic of astonishing physical mortifications (fasting, vigils,
etc.), which were uncontrolled and encouraged by the example of one another—com-
petitions in feats of endurance, in fact.
When not engaged in prayer or reading they

---

* The current regulations are not specific as to amount of food taken at the 2 smaller meals, but these
must not together equal the full meal (which is not restricted as to time of day). Food may not be
eaten between meals, but liquids are allowed, including milk and juice.—*Publisher,* 1997.
** In 1953 Pius XII reduced the Communion fast to 3 hours from solid foods and alcoholic beverages

worked at such trades as weaving and basket-making. In southern Egypt, St. Pachomius organized the monks into monasteries, under a rule; they had fixed daily times for church services and worked at all the common trades, the smith's, the tanner's, agriculture, the carpenter's, etc., and could add to the general austerities at will. All Christian monachism, Eastern and Western derives from these fathers—who of course were not normally priests.

FATHERS OF ST. EDMUND, The. A congregation of missionary priests founded by Father J. B. Muard in 1843. Their headquarters are at the former Cistercian abbey of Pontigny where the alleged body of St. Edmund of Canterbury is enshrined.

FATHERS OF ZION, The. The Priests of Our Lady of Zion are a small congregation founded by a converted Jew, Father Theodore Ratisbonne, at Paris in 1855. Their special concern is prayer and work for the conversion of Jews.

FAUX-BOURDON (Fr., false base. This and It. *falso-bordone* have ousted the Middle English form *faburden*). The accompanying of a melody (*cantus firmus*) in thirds and sixths, except the first and last notes, in which the highest part took the octave and the middle part the fifth of the tenor, or variously. This three-part form of polyphony was extensively used in churches in the later middle ages. It is now permitted to be employed in singing the psalms and canticles of the Divine Office, alternately verse for verse with the unisonous chant; it may even be used for a whole psalm provided the principle of choirs chanting verses alternately is preserved; to sing a psalm *di concerto* is absolutely forbidden.

FEAR. A disturbance of the mind produced by an evil threatening oneself or someone associated with oneself. It is absolutely grave, if it would daunt a brave man. A relatively grave fear may arise from something slight in itself, but of real foreboding to a timid person. Fear cannot destroy a voluntary (*q.v.*) act, unless it is so vehement as temporarily to upset the balance of reason. A mortal sin, when it arises from something evil in its very nature, is not condoned because of fear, but its imputability may be decreased, according to circumstances. The fear of death would not excuse a Christian from the sin of denying his Faith. But *positive* laws do not, as a rule, bind in the presence of grave fear; so, fear of relapse into sickness might excuse from the obligation of Sunday Mass. Acts and contracts made under fear, though valid in their nature as contracts, are often by positive law made invalid or liable to be rescinded. Thus consent to marriage extorted by grave fear is invalid. See VIOLENCE AND FEAR.

FEAR OF GOD. Fear of punishment of sin, which though good in itself is evil for us (*cf.*, Fear). Sin results in separation from God, and so it can be said that God can, and should, be feared. "The object of fear is evil. When, therefore, a person turns from God because of some evil he fears, such fear is called human or of this world. But sometimes a man turns to God and clings to him because of fear. Now in this case the evil is either the evil which is punishment or that which is sin. If then one turns to God and clings to him through fear of punishment his fear will be servile: if through fear of sin, his fear will be filial, for children fear that which offends their father" (St. Thomas, II–II, xix, 2). But, says St. Gregory, "We do not render true service to God so long as we obey from fear and not from love."

FEAST. A special day set apart for the liturgical commemoration of the Holy Trinity, of some event or mystery (*q.v.*) in the life of our Lord, our Lady, the angels or the saints, or of some other event of religious importance. Feasts are classified as (*a*) immovable, which occur on fixed days (*e.g.*, those of saints), or movable, which depend on the date of Easter (*e.g.*, Pentecost); (*b*) (holidays) of obligation (*q.v.*) or feasts observed only liturgically, including those of devotion (*q.v.*); (*c*) of universal celebration (so called; really only universal to the Western church) or of local celebration, proper to religious orders, countries, dioceses or other places; (*d*) according to their rank (*q.v.*). Feasts are also divided into primary or secondary within their own rank. Primary are the principal mysteries of religion and any ordinary saint's day (*e.g.*, Pentecost, St. Lawrence); secondary are accessory to or derived from some other feast (*e.g.*, the Stigmata of St. Francis, the Holy Name of Mary, the Exaltation of the Cross). Thus a feast of our Lord may give way to that of a saint, *e.g.*, if the Sacred Heart (movable) occurred on the Birthday of St. John Baptist (June 24).

FEAST, PROPER. A feast is proper to a certain place if it is of the titular saint of the church, of the primary or secondary patron of the place, or of a saint whose body or other considerable relic is preserved there, or of one who has some special relation with the church, locality or body of persons. A feast proper in this sense is preferred, other things being equal, to a feast in the general calendar of the Roman Church, with certain exceptions. Each diocese of the British Isles has a number of proper feasts which either are not celebrated at all or have lower rank in the general calendar. The principal ones observed in most English dioceses are SS. Cuthbert (March 20), the Blessed English Martyrs (May 4), Dunstan (May 19), Alban (June 22), John Fisher and Thomas More (July 9), Wilfrid (Oct. 10), Edmund of Canterbury (Nov. 16). SS. Kentigern (Jan. 14),

---

and 1 hour from other beverages (water did not break the fast); in 1964 Paul VI reduced the fast again to 1 hour from both food and drink, except for water and medicine, which may be taken at any time. —*Publisher*, 1997.

Columba (June 9) and Ninian (Sept. 16) are proper feasts throughout Scotland, and there are numerous native saints celebrated in Ireland and some in Wales.

FEAST OF DEVOTION. One which was formerly a holiday of obligation (*q.v.*) but is so no longer; it is observed with some solemnity and Mass is said for the people. The feasts of devotion in England and Wales are the Purification (Feb. 2), St. Gregory the Great (Mar. 12), St. Joseph (Mar. 19), the Annunciation (Mar. 25), St. George (April 26), the Finding of the Cross (May 3), St. Augustine of Canterbury (May 27), the Birthday of St. John Baptist (June 24), St. Anne (June 26), St. Lawrence (Aug. 10), the Birthday BVM (Sept. 8), St. Michael (Sept. 29), the Immaculate Conception (Dec. 8), St. Stephen (Dec. 26), the Holy Innocents (Dec. 28), St. Thomas Becket (Dec. 29), St. Silvester (Dec. 31), Monday and Tuesday of Easter and Whitsun weeks and all feasts of apostles except SS. Peter and Paul, which is a holiday.

FEAST OF OUR LADY. A day upon which the public worship of Almighty God has special reference to an event in the life of the Blessed Virgin Mary or to some other event or quality connected with her. There are seventeen such feasts celebrated throughout the Western church, namely: The Annunciation (Mar. 25), the Appearing of the Immaculate Virgin at Lourdes (Feb. 11), her Assumption (Aug. 15), her Birthday (Sept. 8), the Dedication of the Basilica of St. Mary Major (Aug. 5), her Immaculate Conception (Dec. 8), Our Lady of Mount Carmel (July 16), her holy Name (Sept. 12), her Presentation in the Temple (Nov. 21), her Purification (Feb. 2), our Lady of Ransom (Sept. 24), the Holy Rosary (Oct. 7), her Seven Sorrows (Friday after Passion Sunday and again on Sept. 15), her Motherhood (Oct. 11), her Immaculate Heart (Aug. 22), the Visitation (July 2) and Mary the Queen (May 31). There are numerous others observed only in some dioceses or churches (some feast for our Lord or our Lady can be found for nearly every day in the year), *e.g.*, her Expectation, her Miracles, her Purity, her Girdle and Veil at Blachernæ, our Lady Help of Christians, of Good Counsel, of Perpetual Succour, of Guadalupe, of Kazan, of Czestochowa, Refuge of Sinners, Queen of All Saints and Mother of Fair Love, of Grace, of the Meadows, of Sowing, of the Harvest, etc. (*cf.*, Shrines).

FEAST OF OUR LORD. A day upon which the public worship of Almighty God has special reference to an event in the earthly life of Christ or to some other event or aspect of a mystery connected with him. There are fourteen such feasts observed throughout the Western church, namely: his Ascension, his Birthday (Dec. 25), his Circumcision (Jan. 1), Corpus Christi, the Exaltation (Sept. 14), and Finding (May 3) of the Cross, the Dedication of the Basilica of St. Saviour or the Lateran (Nov. 9), Easter, the Epiphany (Jan. 6), his Holy Name (Jan. 2), his Precious Blood (July 1), his Sacred Heart, his Transfiguration (Aug. 6), and Christ the King (last Sunday of Oct.). Of those celebrated only in some places the feasts of the Passion (*q.v.*) are the principal; others are, our Holy Redeemer, the Flight into Egypt, the Finding in the Temple, his Baptism, the Raising of Lazarus, the Good Shepherd, etc.

FEAST OF NINE LESSONS. Any one above the rank of simple feast, as having nine lessons at Matins. Simple feasts and ferias have three.

FEAST OF PRECEPT. A holiday of obligation (*q.v.*).

FEASTS, CARDINAL, are those which have a series of Sundays connected with them, namely, Epiphany, Easter and Pentecost.

FEBRONIANISM. The exaggeratedly Gallican teaching of Bishop John Nicholas von Hontheim, calling himself "Febronius" (1701–90). He maintained, *inter alia,* that the power of the keys (*q.v.*) was lodged in the whole body of the faithful, though it was to be exercised only by the clergy; that every bishop had unlimited power of dispensation, condemnation of heresy, administration, etc., in his own diocese; that the Holy See was not superior to the rest of the bishops as a body or to a general council; and that the bishops should restrain the activities of the Holy See. These doctrines were condemned by Popes Clement XIII and Pius VI but achieved popularity at the courts of certain Catholic sovereigns and led to "Josephinism" (*q.v.*).

FEELING. i. Sense of touch.

ii. Pleasurable or painful aspect of any conscious state.

iii. Complex mental excitement not distinctly cognitive.

iv. An impression or vague cognition (*q.v.*) whose grounds are not distinctly apparent.

v. The word "feelings" is popularly used to denote a state or attitude of consciousness in the formation of which emotions and sensitive affections play an important part. Because human experience depends so largely on sensation, feelings exert an immensely powerful influence on consciousness and psychological life in general; but since they are conditioned by health, weather, fatigue, etc., our feelings are not completely under our own control. They are not, therefore, of themselves, a reliable medium for the valuation of the actions and events of our lives. The value and goodness of these should be estimated by the use of reason (*q.v.*), "for the perfection of things should be measured by their nature alone, and things are not more or less perfect because they flatter or wound our senses" (Spinoza).

FELO-DE-SE (Anglo-Latin, a felon concerning oneself). A self-murderer; self-murder, when the action is done deliberately by a sane person, as opposed to suicide while of unsound mind.

FEMINISM. The claim by and for women that the female sex should be regarded and treated in all respects in the same way as the male sex. The Church teaches that no pursuit or occupation should be denied to woman as woman unless it hampers or destroys her natural *rôle* in the human economy; and also that her complete spiritual equality with man does not imply identity of function or activity. Thus women are by divine law ineligible for holy Orders; the man is the natural and responsible head of a family. Generally speaking, the philosophical connotations of popular feminism are incompatible with Catholicism, "which is pro-feminine but anti-feminist." But the spectacle of the mediæval abbess with all the powers of a secular landlord, holding manorial courts with right of gallows, liable to be summoned to Parliament, governing houses of men, sitting and voting in the imperial Diet (*cf.*, Wilton, Barking, Shaftesbury, Gandersheim, Fontevrault), has not been paralleled in modern times. See WOMAN.

FENABORENSIS. The adjectival form of the name of the see of Kilfenora (*q.v.*) used in the designation of its bishop in Latin documents. Noun: *Fenabora*.

FERENDÆ SENTENTIÆ, CENSURE. A censure (*q.v.*) imposed by the sentence of a judge (*cf.*, *latæ sententiæ*).

FERETORY (Lat. *feretrum*, a bier). i. A large portable reliquary (*q.v.*).
ii. That part of a church specially set apart for an important shrine of a saint. In the great churches of the middle ages this was usually behind the high altar (*e.g.*, St. Edward's shrine in Westminster Abbey).

FERIA (Lat., originally meaning holiday, free-day). i. The liturgical name for all days of the week except Sunday (*Dies Dominica*) and Saturday (*Sabbatum*), thus: Monday, *feria Secunda*; Tuesday, *f. Tertia*; Wednesday, *f. Quarta*; Thursday, *f. Quinta*; Friday, *f. Sexta*; the second, third and so on days. The *feriæ* are major or minor. The major are the week-days of Advent and Lent, Rogation Monday and September ember days, which have precedence over a simple feast in the Roman calendar; the Mass and Office of Ash Wednesday and the first three days of Holy Week are privileged and never displaced. The above are the ordinary names for the days of the week in the vernacular of Portugal (*Domingo, Segundo feira,* etc., *Sabado*).
ii. A week-day on which no feast or vigil is observed.

FERIA QUARTA CINERUM (Lat., The Fourth Day, of Ashes), *i.e.*, Ash Wednesday.

FERIA QUINTA IN CŒNA DOMINI (Lat., The Fifth Day, at the Lord's Supper), *i.e.*, Maundy Thursday (*q.v.*).

FERIA SEXTA IN PARASCEVE (Lat., The Sixth Day of the Preparation [of the Jews for the Sabbath], the liturgical name for Good Friday.)

FERIAL. Of the week-day.

FERMENTUM (Lat., leaven). The second of the three portions into which the Host was broken in the primitive Mass. It was carried by deacons from the bishop's Mass to the other churches of the city and dropped into the chalice by the celebrant at the *fractio panis* (breaking of the bread) of his Mass. In Rome it was sent from the pope's Mass to those of the cardinal priests. Thus was symbolized the unity of the holy Sacrifice in place—that it is always and everywhere one and the same (*cf.*, Sancta)—and the union subsisting between the bishop and his flock.

FERNS (*Fernensis*). An Irish see, suffragan of Dublin. It includes most of the county of Wexford and part of Wicklow. The bishop's residence is at Wexford and his cathedral at Enniscorthy. The patron of the diocese is St. Aedan (Jan. 31), in whose honour the cathedral is dedicated. Irish name: Fearna.

FERRAIOLA (It.). A short cape, reaching half-way to the elbows, appurtenant to the cassock.

FERRAIOLONE (It.). A large black cloak worn over the cassock; it is *de rigueur* for secular priests at papal audiences.

FERRARA-FLORENCE, COUNCIL OF. See FLORENCE.

FERULA (Lat., a rod). i. The wand with which the minor priests penitentiary (*q.v.*) lightly strike penitents. Pope Benedict XIV granted an indulgence of 20 days for the observance of this rite.
ii. A staff with a short transverse top, forming a cross *tau*, with which clergy and lay-folk used to support themselves during long offices in the days before sitting was conceded. Such a staff is the emblem of St. Antony the Abbot and is still used in choir by the Maronite monks of his rule, and also by dissident Ethiopian and Coptic monks.

FÊTE-DIEU (Fr. God's festival). The common French name for the feast of Corpus Christi.

FIDEI DEFENSOR (Lat., Defender of the Faith) (*q.v.*).

FIDEISM (Lat. *fides,* faith). The doctrine that faith is the foundation of philosophy. Fideism properly so called bases all philosophic certitude upon divine revelation; it is therefore a kind of traditionalism (*q.v.*). There is also a fideism which maintains that we assent to first truths in virtue of a natural faith. The error of fideism consists in this, it asserts that human reason is wholly incapable of attaining any truth whatsoever apart from revelation.

FIFTEEN TUESDAYS, DEVOTION OF THE. The reception of holy communion on fifteen successive Tuesdays preceding the feast of St. Dominic (Aug. 4), in honour of that saint. This pious practice originated in Florence in 1631 when that city was visited by the plague; Tuesday was the day in 1233 on which his body was translated at Bologna, and fifteen refers to the mysteries of the rosary. The observance of the practice to implore a spiritual or temporal good has spread beyond Italy.

FIGURE (Lat. *figura,* shape). i. A species of quality which is a modification of a material substance resulting from the limits affecting the superficies of quantity. Figure is the same as shape, the latter word being applied to artificial objects, the word *form* being used of natural objects.
ii. Of a syllogism. The apt disposition of terms as regards subjection and predication.
ii. A type (*q.v.* ii).

FILIOQUE (Lat., And from the Son). The clause in the Nicene creed which affirms the double "procession of the Holy Ghost" (*q.v.*) The word *Filioque* was first added to the creed in Spain in the 6th century and it spread in the Western church, except at Rome. This custom became the object of attack, was defended by many local synods, was forbidden by Pope Leo III in deference to the Greeks, and finally allowed by Pope Benedict VIII (1012-24). This implied no change of doctrine; it was merely a disciplinary matter, the variations being due to the necessity of defending an attacked dogma, the desire to conciliate the Greeks and the fidelity due to a decree of the Council of Ephesus which made the Nicene creed a definitive expression. Of course such a decree would not bind the *Ecclesia docens* to limit itself when need for more explicit expression arose, but could only be designed to exclude either contradictory teaching or irresponsible developments of the formula. There was no question of the doctrine but only of the necessity of adding its expression to the liturgical creed; in the Catholic Eastern churches the equivalent words may be omitted except when scandal would be thereby occasioned but, except for some of the Byzantines (including the Greek and Russian churches at Rome), most of them use it. It does not appear printed in the Cath-

olic editions of Byzantine liturgical books published by authority at Rome. This addition was one of the five complaints put forward to justify the schism of Photius (*q.v.*) and became not so much the stone of offence as the shibboleth between the Catholic and Orthodox churches. That the theological differences involved were capable of adjustment was shown at the Council of Florence, and theologians on both sides claim that this is so still. But there has been much aggravation and the Orthodox teaching is less clearly defined and agreed upon than the Catholic, so that it is difficult to ascertain their exact doctrine; the official Orthodox catechism in English flatly denies the "double procession." None of the other dissident orientals say the *Filioque,* or presumably believe in the double procession of the Holy Ghost, but the doctrine has not come up for their consideration as it has in the West.

FINALITY. The causality of ends, or the order of final causes. That there is finality in nature and that it is universal is evident; hence the principle: "Nature does nothing in vain" (Aristotle), in other words, God had an end in view when he created things.

FINDING OF THE CHRISTIANS, The. A feast proper to Japan on Mar. 17, commemorating the discovery by Fr. Bernard Petitjean, in 1865, of a number of Japanese Catholics, descendants of the survivors of the massacres of 1638, from when until 1832 the Church had been apparently dead in Japan. They of course had no clergy and had baptized and taught their children from generation to generation.

FINDING OF THE CROSS, The. A feast in the Western Church on May 3, commemorating the finding of the True Cross in a pit near Calvary by the empress St. Helen in 326. The apparent actual dates of the events marked by the feasts of the Finding and Exaltation of the Cross (Sept. 14 and May 3 respectively) have become exchanged in liturgical observance. In the Byzantine rite it is commemorated with the Exaltation (*q.v.*) These feasts of the cross seem originally to have had associations with the *Labarum* (*q.v.*) with the dedication of the church of the Holy Sepulchre, and with the vision of the cross accorded to St. Cyril of Jerusalem in 351; the last is commemorated by the Byzantines on May 7.

"FINDING'S KEEPING." This popular saying does not hold good in Christian morals (nor in the civil law of England). One who finds property may lawfully elect to leave it where it is; but if he takes charge of it, he is bound to look after it and use ordinary means to discover the owner. His title in the property found is good against everybody except the owner and if he does not turn up within a reasonable time this title becomes absolute in morals (but not at English law).

FINITE. That where perfection is limited; a created thing; that whose existence is really distinct from its essence.

FINLAND, THE CHURCH IN. The Finns are nearly all Lutherans, but there is a small autonomous Orthodox church, whose members are mostly Karelians. The few Catholics, about 1,000, form a vicariate apostolic.

FIRE. The use of fire is confined in Christian worship to the blessing of the new fire on Holy Saturday and to burning candles (qq.v.), particularly at the celebration of Mass. The first is an observance which spread from the Celtic ritual; the second derives from the Roman law whereby certain civil magistrates were preceded by lighted torches. This was adopted by the pope and afterwards by other bishops, who were preceded by seven acolytes with candles; these were eventually put on, instead of around, the altar, reduced to six for symmetry in the 15th century, and left there—but there are still seven when a bishop pontificates.

FIRE, HELL. A common name for the secondary and positive punishment of Hell, which theologians agree is real and exterior to the victim. But though not a metaphor, the agent called fire is only analogous to earthly fire, for its action is reserved for pure spirits, human souls and, after the resurrection, risen bodies; moreover, being eternal, it must burn without consuming.

FIRE, THE HOLY. A ceremony peculiar to the Orthodox and Armenians in the church of the Holy Sepulchre on Holy Saturday. The patriarchs of the two churches retire into the chapel of the Angel, whence they pass out fire through two windows to the awaiting people, who believe it to be miraculously kindled. The clergy concerned do not affirm its miraculousness, nor do they deny it —and perhaps wouldn't be believed by their flocks if they did. In 1834 over 400 people were killed in the rush for the fire. The Holy See denounced these proceedings so long ago as 1238. A less abused form of the same ceremony takes place at Constantinople.

FIRST CAUSE. A nominal definition of God. All causes other than God are called secondary causes (q.v.), which cannot act except under the real influence of the First Cause.

FIRST FRIDAY. See NINE FRIDAYS.

FIRST PRINCIPLES. Self-evident truths from which conclusions are derived either mediately or immediately. They are called axioms and are indemonstrable, as the principle of the contradiction, of identity, etc., the whole is greater than its part, that which begins to be has a cause, etc.

FIRST VESPERS. The celebration of a feast properly begins the day before at Vespers, so that first Vespers is that office said on the eve, while second Vespers is said on the day itself. Because of the multiplication of feasts, the second Vespers of one sometimes coincides with the first Vespers of the following (concurrence, q.v.). Which Vespers then is said is indicated in the Ordo (q.v.). In practice now, first Vespers is said or sung only for every Sunday and for double feasts of the 1st and 2nd class.

FISH, The. The chief of the symbols of the early Church, representing our Lord and, in association with loaves of bread, the Blessed Sacrament. It was derived from the Gr. word for fish, ἰχθύς, of which the letters form the initials of the title Ἰησοῦς Χριστός Θεοῦ Υἱός Σωτήρ, "Jesus Christ, Son of God, Saviour."

FISTULA (Lat., tube). A tube of gold by means of which the pope receives the Precious Blood, standing at his throne, at a solemn papal Mass. Its use was formerly more common.

FIVE WOUNDS, The, in the feet, hands and side of our crucified Lord, were a favourite object of devotion and frequently represented in the decoration of the middle ages. The device was adopted as the standard of the Pilgrimage of Grace (q.v.). The feast of the Five Wounds is observed in some places on the fourth Friday of Lent.

FIVEFOLD SCAPULAR, The. Five scapulars (q.v., iii), those of the Holy Trinity, Carmelites, Servites, Immaculate Conception and the Passion, upon a single pair of bands and worn as one.

FLABELLUM (Lat., fan). A ceremonial fan, made of ostrich plumes, with a long staff, one of which is carried on either side of the pope whenever he is borne in procession in the sedia gestatoria (q.v.) robed in pontifical vestments; if he is wearing rochet, mozzetta and stole the flabella are not carried. Their origin was the usual practical purposes of a fan.

FLAGELLANTS (Lat. flagellum, a scourge). Groups of fanatical persons who performed and administered exaggerated physical penances in public. They appeared in several times and places during the middle ages; particularly in Italy in 1260, in 1348 when the popular movement spread to Germany and north-west Europe and was definitely organized into heretical sects, and again during the Council of Constance. Although individuals (e.g., St. Vincent Ferrer) made use of the flagellant movements for legitimate religious ends, authority generally did not encourage them and definitely condemned their excesses. But after the Reformation modified processions of penance were taken up, especially by the Jesuits, and became a widespread custom which in places persists still; in Latin America penitential societies of flagellants are said to exist in face of the opposition of the Church. Beating with a rod was formerly used as a punishment in monasteries and was recognized as a suitable way of dealing with erring clerics. This is no longer so, but self-flagellation in moderation and for reasons of devotion is not forbidden. See DISCIPLINE.

"FLAMINIAN GATE, FROM OUTSIDE THE." The pastoral letter written by Cardinal Wiseman, first archbishop of Westminster, to the Catholics of England at the restoration of the hierarchy (*q.v.*) in 1850. It was naturally composed in a tone of jubilation and congratulation, and precipitated the uproar against "papal aggression" which the restoration occasioned.

FLECTAMUS GENUA (Lat., Let us bend our knees). Said by the deacon (or priest) before the litany collects at the office of Good Friday and in certain penitential Masses, the subdeacon (or server) replying *Levate* (Rise up), the words being accompanied by corresponding movements. Originally, the priest having announced the object of the prayer (as on Good Friday), the people knelt and prayed in silence for the intention, standing again when the priest offered the petitions of all aloud in the collect.

FLOOD, The. The Biblical story is accepted as historical throughout and not as fact embroidered with legend. A great destructive flood in the Euphrates valley is admitted by all and its date, though at present unknown, may in the future be roughly fixed by further excavation and research. There is no official teaching on the extent of the Flood, but its geographical universality is held by only a few Catholic scholars, and even its ethnological universality is no matter of faith, though it is the common opinion. Affinity between the Biblical and Babylonian accounts is admitted, but not as proof of dependence of the former on the latter. The existence of two sources combined in the Mosaic account is admitted as a possible but not often as a proven fact.

FLORENCE, THE COUNCIL OF. A continuation of the œcumenical Council of Basle, transferred to Ferrara in 1438 and to Florence in 1439. It effected a reunion not only with the Orthodox Church but also with the Armenians, the Copts and some of the Syrian Jacobites, but it never became operative among most of the churches concerned. The reunion was disliked by the Orthodox at large and political considerations had played too big a part in bringing it about. The Orthodox patriarch of Constantinople formally repudiated it in 1472; nevertheless, in the patriarchates of Alexandria, Antioch and Jerusalem the union appears to have subsisted till the Turkish conquest at the beginning of the sixteenth century, in the Russian province of Kiev for longer.

FLOWERS, ALTAR. It is allowed to use natural or artificial flowers or sweet-smelling branches for the decoration of the altar, especially on festival days, but they must be removed when Mass or Office of the season is said in Advent, Lent and other penitential times, and at requiem Masses. Nor may they be put upon the altar-table itself. In 1932 the cardinal vicar forbade the use of artificial flowers in any church in Rome. It is usually considered more dignified to dispense with them entirely, but the lavish decoration with flowers of the church, of shrines and of images on the feast of the saint represented is a graceful and appropriate practice. The presence of girls scattering flowers before the Host at processions of the Blessed Sacrament is not prescribed by the rubrics, but is common and permitted, provided they do not walk between the clergy and the sacred Host.

FLOWERS, BLESSING OF. In the appendix of the "Rituale Romanum" is a form for blessing flowers and fruit on the feast of the Assumption. It is in common use in Poland.

FLOWERS, FUNERAL. The use of flowers, in the form of wreaths and otherwise, at the funeral of an adult is discouraged though not positively forbidden by the Church. They are hardly in accordance with the solemnity of the occasion and their cost is more properly devoted to stipends (*q.v.*) for Masses for the benefit of the deceased. At the burial of children who have not attained the age of reason, the use of flowers is customary and appropriate.

FOLDED CHASUBLE, The, has two forms: (*a*) a chasuble shortened or pinned up in front, worn by deacon and sub-deacon at high Mass in great churches during Advent, Lent and other penitential seasons; (*b*) a chasuble rolled up, or more often simply a broad strip of silk, worn over the left shoulder and under the right arm by the deacon from before the epistle to the communion at penitential seasons; in its strip form it is generally referred to as a broad-stole or *stolone*. These are a survival of the time when the chasuble was habitually worn by others besides priests, and deacon and subdeacon disposed them as above to facilitate their movements. They are a visible reminder of the great age of the penitential Masses.

FONT. i. The permanent receptacle for baptismal water, at which Baptism is normally administered. The "Memoriale Rituum" provides that it should consist of a large bowl to contain the water and a small one in its rim to receive the surplus from the child's head, both bowls having drains which run into the earth; they should normally be made of stone and lined with metal; and must be covered with a lockable lid. The base of the font should be *below* the level of the baptistery floor and in big churches this should entail a descent of at least three steps —thus showing resemblance to a sepulchre (Rom. vi, 4); moreover, the font should be surmounted by a *ciborium* (*q.v.*).

ii. A holy-water stoup (*q.v.*) is sometimes called a font.

FONT, THE BLESSING OF THE (more accurately, of Baptismal Water), takes place at the Easter vigil on Holy Saturday. After a collect the officiant sings a long preface modelled on the primitive eucharistic prayer. He recalls first the marvels done by God through water; he then divides the water cross-wise, invoking the Holy Ghost for its spiritual fruitfulness and exorcising the evil one, touches it with his hand, and makes the sign of the cross thrice in blessing; he again divides the water, throwing some of it towards each quarter of the globe, referring again to God's wonders therewith; he breathes thrice cross-wise thereon, asking a blessing, and three times dips the foot of the paschal-candle therein, singing each time "May the power of the Holy Spirit come down into the water of this font"; again he breathes thrice, in the form of the Greek letter ψ, and concludes the preface. The priest then pours into the font some oil of catechumens, then chrism, then both together, all cross-wise and with a short prayer at each pouring (*cf.*, the Armenian custom of putting chrism into the water at every baptism). If there are any to be baptized, he then baptizes them. Finally, the blessed water is carried in procession and poured into the font. This rite is no longer repeated on the vigil of Pentecost.

FONTEVRAULT, THE ORDER OF. An order of nuns following the Rule of St. Benedict, consisting of the abbey of Fontevrault and dependent priories (three in England). The rule was supplemented by constitutions provided by the founder, Robert d'Abrissel (*d.* 1116). The mother-house and most of the dependents were double monasteries (*q.v.*), and the monks were very strictly subordinated to the nuns. From its reform in 1475 till the Revolution Fontevrault was one of the most distinguished abbeys of France, a refuge for the royal and a school for their daughters; a few houses of nuns of the order still exist as a teaching congregation with mitigated rule.

"FOOL FOR CHRIST'S SAKE, A." The self-lowering of Jesus Christ, meditated upon by simple loving souls, has given birth to a special kind of asceticism in the East (and not unknown in the West), the way of the "fool for Christ's sake" (in Greek *salos*, in Slavonic *yurodiv*). Such a one was the 6th-century Egyptian St. Simeon the Fool, mentioned in the Roman Martyrology on July 1.

FOOLS, THE FEAST OF. Pseudo-liturgical observances associated with the feast of the Circumcision which were considerably abused in Western Europe in the middle ages, and not finally put down till the 15th century (*cf.*, Feast of the Ass).

FOOT-PACE. The English name for the *predella*, the single platform on which a side altar stands, or the third or highest step if it is a high altar. The server at low Mass should not kneel on the foot-pace, even if it is the only step and the floor is uncomfortable.

FORBIDDEN BOOKS. See INDEX.

"FORBIDDEN TIMES." From the beginning of Advent till Christmas day, and from Ash Wednesday to Easter Sunday, inclusively, during which time marriages may not be solemnized with nuptial Mass and Blessing. This does not mean that the marriage itself may not be celebrated, and for a just cause the bishop may permit the solemnities. Marriage may be contracted on any day of the year and the nuptial Mass and Blessing supplied after the lapse of the forbidden times. See COMMANDMENTS OF THE CHURCH.

FORCE, or violence, is the use of a greater external force than can be resisted in order to make another do something against his will. If he who is forced resists to his utmost but is overcome, he is blameless in respect of the resulting action; if his resistance is only partial, he is guilty in proportion. Such coercion is not necessarily physical (*cf.*, Violence and Fear). See also WAR, RESISTING EVIL, etc.

FORDHAM. A Catholic university in New York, having its origin in a college founded by Bishop Hughes in 1841. It was taken over by the Jesuits in 1846, and during the subsequent hundred years of its history it has steadily grown in numbers and prestige, and many of its alumni have been distinguished in ecclesiastical and civil life. It has faculties of arts and sciences, law and medicine, social service, business and graduate schools, and a teachers' college. Fordham is the largest Catholic institution of higher education in the United States.

FORGIVENESS. The taking back into favour of one by whom we have been slighted, disobeyed, robbed, or in any way injured. Forgiveness is a necessary fruit of Christian charity, and if the offender has expressed sorrow or otherwise tried to make amends is due in justice. But if one is in the position of having the right to inflict punishment (*e.g.*, as a parent), forgiveness does not necessarily involve the remission of punishment.

FORGIVENESS OF SINS. The complete removal of the guilt and stain of sin (though there may remain a debt of punishment, which is not sin). It is not merely a cloaking of the sin: "If any man assert that everything which has the true and proper nature of sin is not removed by the grace of Christ, but that it is only erased or not imputed, let him be anathema" (Council of Trent, sess. v, can. 5). It is of faith that all sins can be forgiven by the sacrament of Penance (q.v.). The Montanists taught falsely that grave post-baptismal sins (especially adultery) could not be forgiven; the Novatianists said the same of apostasy; and the Donatists said it of the sin of yielding the sacred books to the persecutors. No sin is forgiven without sorrow.

FORGOTTEN SINS. See EXAMINATION OF CONSCIENCE.

FORM in scholastic philosophy means "perfection" and is that partial principle whereby a thing is what it is and is denominated such and such.

i. (1) Substantial form: the substantial act or perfection of prime matter; it is therefore an essential part which together with prime matter (q.v.) as the other essential part constitutes a thing or places it in a determinate species; as, the human soul. (2) Accidental form: any perfection added to a thing already essentially constituted, as knowledge in man (see ACT).

ii. The *form of a sacrament* is one of the three essentials of the making of a sacrament (q.v.). It consists of words, which determine the matter (q.v.), that is, give signification to the sacramental use to which the matter is being put. A substantial change in the form invalidates a sacrament, as does a small change if it is due to the heretical or perverse intention of the minister.

FORMALLY. Used of a perfection considered precisely as such. (See EMINENTLY.) Opposed to Materially (q.v.). See also SIN, FORMAL.

FORMALISM. i. The endeavour to pass off as corresponding to reality a maze of useless distinctions.

ii. A word sometimes used to designate Kant's theory of ethics according to which an action is good because obligatory, and not, as it ought to be, the converse.

iii. In religion. An excessive preoccupation with the external aspects of worship or external observances of devotion or with the abstract content of religion; a lack of correspondence between an outer apearance of religion and the inner dispositions or set of the will; a concern for the letter of the Christian law combined with neglect of its spirit; an emptying out of faith and charity, leaving only an exterior husk of "religiosity." This form of religious degeneration, condemned so fiercely by Jesus Christ in the person of the Pharisees, is one of the most dangerous corruptions; "Faith is eaten away by the cancer of formalism, that is, routine church-going, parrot-like recitation of prayers, unthinking use of sacraments . . . you have a religion laid waste."

FORNICATION is a completed act of sexual intercourse between a man and woman who are not married but are free to marry. It is under all circumstances a grave sin and intrinsically wrong.

FORT AUGUSTUS. A Benedictine abbey of the English congregation in Invernessshire, founded in 1876, representing the monasteries of Lamspring in Hanover (suppressed there in 1803) and of St. James's, Ratisbon, the few survivors of whose communities it incorporated. In 1882 it became an independent monastery, immediately subject to the Holy See and was made an abbey in 1888; it is now reaggregated to the English congregation. The monks conduct a school. Priories at Washington and Portsmouth, R. I., U.S.A., have been established from this monastery.

FORTITUDE. A cardinal virtue and one of the gifts of the Holy Ghost (qq.v.), whereby man is inclined to face those evils which he most dreads and to resist the motions of mere recklessness; it involves the control, not the absence, of fear. It is "to enter upon arduous tasks [whether spiritual or temporal] with as good a will as upon matters that are easy, that you may not bow beneath adversity nor be lifted up by prosperity. It is humility without pride in success or despair in failure." Potentially allied to this virtue are magnificence, magnanimity, patience and perseverance (qq.v.).

FORTUNE-TELLING. Predicting or pretending to predict the future by means of palmistry, crystal-gazing, ihterpreting dreams, etc. This is superstition (q.v.); a grave sin against religion (q.v.) if the aid of evil spirits is invoked; usually a venial sin, if the means used are thought to be apt in themselves for foretelling the future, since the act usually implies a want of confidence in divine providence. Fortune-telling is permissible if indulged in for amusement, provided no trust is put in the means used.

FORTY HOURS' PRAYER, The. The solemn exposition of the Blessed Sacrament for the space of 40 hours, more or less, being the time our Lord lay in the tomb, continuous adoration being maintained by relays of watchers. The usual practice is to arrange that the exercise is taken up from church to church so that the exposition is so far as possible continuous in the diocese. Canon 1275 orders that this devotion shall be held once every year in all churches where the Blessed Sacrament is habitually reserved; if this cannot be done without serious inconvenience or with the necessary solemnity, then the exposition shall be at least for several consecutive hours on certain days. A high Mass of the Blessed Sacrament is sung at the initial exposition, a Mass for peace on the second day, and a Mass of the Blessed Sacrament when it is returned to the tabernacle (in some places low Masses are permitted), and there must be a procession with the Host at the first and third Masses. Although this is an act of extra-liturgical worship, originating in the 16th century, it is governed by a large body of regulations, laid down by Pope Clement XII in 1736, the Clementine Instruction. In some dioceses (*e.g.*, those of the United States) exposition may be discontinued during the night, and the processions omitted at the discretion of the pastor. Originally this was an intercession for peace (*cf.*, the second Mass), but it is now regarded more particularly as an act of reparation for the sins of men.

FORUM (Lat., a public place; whence, a judicial court). The sphere in which the Church exercises her jurisdiction, especially her judicial authority. The forum is of two kinds: external, to deal with matters affecting the public welfare of the Church and her subjects; internal, to deal with matters which concern the private spiritual good of individuals, especially in the direction of their consciences. The Church exercises her jurisdiction of the internal forum chiefly in the tribunal of Penance. The internal forum is itself of two kinds, the sacramental forum, when the jurisdiction is exercised in the actual administration of the sacrament (the forgiving or retaining of sins); and the non-sacramental forum, when it is exercised apart from this. The papal tribunal in matters of the internal forum is the Sacred Roman Penitentiary. An act of jurisdiction exercised in the external forum is valid also for the internal forum but not *vice versa*.

FORUM, PRIVILEGE OF THE. The exemption of clerics from lay courts in all causes, whether civil or criminal, unless with leave of the competent ecclesiastical authority. Permission of the pope is required in the case of cardinals, legates, bishops, etc., and of the local ordinary (*q.v.*) in the case of other clerics, before an ecclesiastic may be cited in a civil court. The ordinary must not refuse permission without a grave cause, especially if the plaintiff is a lay person.

FORUM COMPETENS (Lat., the proper court). The sphere of jurisdiction belonging to the particular authority in the Church qualified to deal with certain matters or persons, especially judicially. In the external forum the *forum competens* in causes of first instance is the court of the local ordinary, in causes of appeal that of the metropolitan.

FOUNDATION MASSES. Those for which the stipends are received from endowments canonically established for this purpose. It is for the local ordinary or provincial council

to determine what sum is required to establish a foundation Mass, and how such sum is to be invested and administered. If in the course of time the endowment proves insufficient to provide adequate stipends for the number of Masses founded, the Holy See may reduce the number of Masses to be said, but no inferior authority has power to do this.

FOUNDATION-STONE, THE BLESSING OF THE, of a new church must be performed by a bishop with the rite provided in the "Pontificale Romanum." It includes the setting of a four-square corner-stone, the blessing of it, the altar site and those of the foundations with holy water specially made at the beginning, the naming of the titular saint, and the singing of Psalms lxxxiii, cxxvi, l, and lxxxvi, the litany of the Saints and *Veni Creator Spiritus*.

FOUR HOLY CROWNED ONES, The. Martyrs who are honoured in the Western church by a commemoration on Nov. 8. They were scourged to death in Rome in 303, and thus commemorated because their names were not discovered until many years later: so says the Roman Martyrology, but their story is uncertain.

FOUR HORSEMEN, The (Apoc. vi, 1-8). The first probably represents Christ, the king and conqueror; the others being War, Famine and Plague, the powers of the earth that oppress his Church and people.

FOUR LAST THINGS, The, are Death, Judgement, Heaven, Hell (*qq.v.*). That branch of theology which deals with them is called Eschatology.

FOURTH GOSPEL, The. A decree of the Biblical Commission (*q.v.*) of May 29, 1907, declared the fourth gospel to be the work of John, the son of Zebedee, and forbade Catholics to regard that gospel as wholly or partially allegorical or doctrinally symbolical, or to consider the words of our Lord recorded there as theological compositions of the evangelist put in our Lord's mouth though not strictly and truly his. It is the common opinion that St. John wrote the gospel in extreme old age (*c.* 90-100) and that he chose in Christ's life such words and deeds as prove Christ's assertion of his divinity. Such a purpose sufficiently explains the difference in contents and tone between this and the preceding gospels. Three of the propositions condemned by the decree of the Holy Office *Lamentabili* of July 3, in the same year (Nos. 16, 17, and 18) were to the effect that John's narratives and discourses were mystical and theological meditations without historical truth; that he exaggerated the miracles further to glorify the Incarnate Word; and that John is a witness, not to Christ, but to Christian life and thought in his day.

FOXE'S "BOOK OF MARTYRS." "The Acts and Monuments of the Martyrs," by John Fox (commonly Foxe), which purported to set out the sufferings of numerous Protestants at the hands of Catholics, and especially under Queen Mary I in England. In 1571 Convocation of the Church of England directed that copies of the book should be available in all cathedrals and in the houses of bishops and other dignitaries and until recently (and sometimes still) the book was used in good faith for anti-Catholic controversial purposes. The Protestant historian James Gairdner, in his "History of the English Church in the 16th Century," has demonstrated that Fox was dishonest and worthless as a witness in the matter of the cruel excesses of that reign.

FRACTION, The, or breaking of the Host, the Sacred Bread, takes place in the Latin Mass between the Lord's Prayer and the *Agnus Dei.* During the ending of the prayer *Libera* (the embolism, *q.v.*) the celebrant uncovers the chalice, takes the Host and breaks it in half and puts the portion in his right hand on to the paten; he then breaks off a small piece from the portion in his left hand and puts the remainder also on to the paten; with the small piece in his right hand he makes the sign of the cross three times over the chalice, saying, *Pax Domini sit semper vobiscum:* "May the peace of the Lord be always with you"; he then drops the small piece into the Sacred Blood in the chalice, saying the prayer *Haec commixtio:* "May this mingling and hallowing of the body and blood of our Lord Jesus Christ avail us that receive it unto life everlasting. Amen" (the commixture, *q.v.*). This repetition of the breaking of the bread performed by our Lord at the Last Supper caused the name *Fractio Panis* to be given to the whole sacrifice among the early Christians. See FERMENTUM and SANCTA. In the Byzantine liturgies the celebrant after the Lord's Prayer breaks the *agnets* (*q.v.*) into four parts with the words "Broken and distributed is the Lamb of God, Son of the Father, who is broken but not divided, ever eaten but never consumed, and who sanctifies those who participate." The parts having been arranged cross-wise on the paten, the top one is dropped into the chalice, and the *zeon* (*q.v.*) is then poured in.

FRANCE, THE CHURCH IN. France has a population of 42 million, most of whom are nominally Catholic; but it is estimated that, especially in urban areas, a good half of them are indifferent or positively anti-religious. In 1905, the government abrogated the concordat with the Holy See of 1801, church and state were separated, and a period of spoliation and oppression ensued. After world war I the position of the Church greatly improved and there was a notable revival of religion, with a strong intellectual element (see J.O.C. MOVEMENT, ASSOCIATIONS CULTUELLES, and ACTION FRANCAISE.) The 1901 Law of Associations (*q.v.*) has not been repealed, but numerous communities returned to France after 1918 and remain, on sufferance but unmolested. All clerics are liable for military service. Diplomatic relations with the Holy See were restored in 1921. The archdiocese of Reims has a primacy of honour in the north and Lyons in the south, and there are 15 other metropolitan sees, with a total of 68 suffragans; the dioceses of Metz and Strasbourg are i.s.h.s. The independent principality of *Monaco* forms a separate diocese, i.s.h.s.

FRANCIS, THE RULE OF ST. There are three Franciscan rules, for the friars, the nuns (Poor Clares) and the lay tertiaries (*qq.v.*). The definitive rule for the friars is that of 1223. Various interpretations and constitutions in regard to it have been made from time to time by the Holy See. It is followed by the Friars Minor and the Capuchins; the Conventuals keep it according to the constitutions of Pope Urban VIII (1628) which sanctioned certain modifications especially with regard to poverty. In accordance with it, boots or shoes may be worn only in case of necessity, the Divine Office is said daily in choir, all Fridays are fasting days, there must be corporate as well as individual abandonment of all property, the particular evangelical work of the brothers is preaching, and provision is made for the conduct of missions to the heathen; Franciscan life is summed up as being "to observe the holy gospel of our Lord Jesus Christ by living in obedience, without goods, and in chastity." Pope Nicholas III, in 1279, decreed that the clause about property should be understood in the sense that the brothers were to have no more than the "moderate use" of things necessary, without any ownership therein (*cf.,* Syndic Apostolic).

FRANCISCAN MISSIONARIES OF MARY, The. An institute of sisters with simple vows following the rule of the third order of St. Francis and subject to the minister general of the Friars Minor, founded in India in 1877 by Mother Mary de Chappotin de Neuville. They undertake any work in the missions in any part of the world, particularly on behalf of women in *purdah* or *harem* countries. All their chapels have daily exposition of the Blessed Sacrament. The congregation has over 5,000 members. White habit, scapular, cord and veil; black veil and grey cloak outdoors.

FRANCISCANS, The, are the friars minor founded by St. Francis of Assisi in 1209. They form one Order of Friars Minor, divided into three distinct and independent branches, of which one is known simply as Friars Minor, another as Friars Minor Conventual and the other as Friars Minor Capuchin (*qq.v.*). The Friars Minor and Capuchins are the second and third largest religious orders in the Church. The order had 64 houses in England, where they were known as Grey Friars, at the Reformation and the province was re-established at Douay in 1625. The personality of their founder and his doctrine of poverty have left a permanent impress on Catholicism; as missionaries these friars have gone to the ends of the earth; and to them is due the popularizing of such devotions as the stations of the cross and the Christmas crib. The life in certain secluded friaries in Umbria and Tuscany still approximates closely to that of the earliest friars. See FRIARS MINOR; CONVENTUALS; CAPUCHINS.

ii. The nuns are called Poor Clares (q.v.), and there are several congregations of sisters of the third order (q.v., ii) regular. There are many other congregations following the rule of the third order of St. Francis in all parts of the world, most of which have no other connexion with the order.

FRANCIS XAVIER'S HYMN. "O Deus, ego amo te," a hymn mistakenly attributed to St. Francis Xavier, best known in English in Caswall's version, "My God, I love thee, not because I hope for Heaven thereby."

FRANKINCENSE (Matt. ii, 11). A particular gum used in the compounding of incense, from Old Fr. *franc encens,* finest incense.

FRATER (Lat., brother), or *fratry.* An obsolete name for a monastic dining-hall or refectory.

FRATICELLI (It., little friars). A name formerly given in Italy to members of any mendicant order but historically reserved for various ill-defined rigorist, often also schismatical and heretical, bodies which appeared during the 13th-15th centuries. Some of them infiltrated into certain discontented rigorist parties which had broken away from the Franciscan order. They professed an extreme poverty and, *inter alia,* the Wycliffite error that sin deprives the clergy of their sacerdotal powers and jurisdiction, and lords spiritual and temporal of their temporal authority, and claimed that the popes after John XXII were spurious. Considerable violence was used in their suppression. Called in France *frérots.*

FRAUD. An artifice, trick or other action performed with the intention to deceive in order that the doer may obtain an advantage to which he has no right; a sin against justice. It is to be distinguished from deceit (q.v.). "To use fraud to sell a thing above its just price is altogether sinful, being the misleading of another to his loss" (St. Thomas).

FREE CHURCHES, The. The name assumed by, and in common speech often granted to, those bodies which originated with the dissenters (q.v.) from the Church of England, as being free from the authority of prelates or princes.

FREE LOVE, *i.e.,* sexual relations outside of marriage, is contrary to the natural law and therefore necessarily forbidden by the Catholic Church.

FREE WILL. See LIBERTY.

FREEDOM OF MAN. Inasmuch as he is born endowed with free will, every man may be said to be born free; but in the sense that he cannot be bound to obedience to another without his own consent the maxim is fallacious. The natural dependencies of mankind on parents, on each other, on the state, on God, carry with them corresponding duties, obediences, subjections, from the obligations of which man is not able to free himself. But man is a responsible being, and it pertains to his perfection *freely* to choose good and reject evil: accordingly it is a duty (and a problem) of lawful authority of whatever kind to exercise the minimum of coercion compatible with right order and the public good. *Cf.,* LIBERTY.

FREEDOM OF THOUGHT. The profession of many agnostic, or even sceptical, thinkers who claim to use their intelligence in the solution of all problems without reference to any authority, law, dogma, or even *a priori* principle. As we know it to-day, the school originated in England at the end of the 17th century, when there was a sect of "Freethinkers." This soon acquired a philosophic colour, and Hume and Bolingbroke professed it and, as free-thinkers, attacked Christianity. Voltaire took it up and popularized the teaching in France. Although it is world-wide, France has perhaps been its most fertile seed-ground, and there its promoters have been among the most dogmatic of persecutors of religion. Complete freedom of thought is obviously a chimæra. Where there is certainty there must be determination of the intellect. No one can be free of the laws of logic or free of truth: a civilized man cannot believe that the moon is made of green cheese. Neither can anyone who hopes to attain truth be free of authority: life is not long enough, for one thing. What he can do, and should do, is to investigate and establish the basis of the authority to which he gives credence. In fact, nobody does reject all authority; most free-thinkers are content to reject the authority of God, and of the Church which safeguards God's revelation.

FREEDOM OF WORSHIP. The inalienable right of all men to worship God according to the teaching of the Catholic Church. No state can justifiably prevent the exercise of this right; and indeed it has a duty to foster this true worship, since God's supremacy calls for man's acknowledgement in worship, and Christ established one form and content of public worship in establishing one only Church, to which all are commanded to submit. But to avoid greater evil or to achieve a higher good, public authority can tolerate false religions, so long as they do not teach open immorality.

FREEMASONRY (the origin of this word is a matter of dispute; in its present sense its use dates from the foundation of the Grand Lodge of England in 1717). Membership in and the activities of an international fraternity, ostensibly for mutual help and brotherly association, called the Free and Accepted Masons, having an elaborate ritual and system of secret signs. The fact that the Freemasons' is a secret society (q.v.) is alone sufficient to make membership illegal for Catholics. Over and above this, it has received numerous papal condemnations, beginning with the constitution of Clement XII, *In eminenti*, in 1738, wherein it was declared that certain associations calling themselves Freemasons and other names made profession only of natural religion (*i.e.*, Deism, q.v.), independently of any creed; that their objects and proceedings were completely secret, which secrecy was enforced by an oath; that in the opinion of competent judges many members of such societies were discredited as unprincipled; and that several civil governments had already suppressed them as a public danger. As the society spread, subsequent pronouncements were an amplification of this one. According to Pope Leo XIII, the ultimate aim of Freemasonry is "the overthrow of the whole religious, political and social order based on Christian institutions and the establishment of a state of things based on principles of pure naturalism," and this is undoubtedly true in Italy, France and other countries. In England Freemasonry is more definitely of a philanthropic and convivial character—has, indeed, the reputation of being a respectable middle-class amusement; but it is opposed to the common good in so far as men may be preferred to positions of responsibility on account not of their fitness but of friendship and patronage, and because of the potentiality for mischief of such an uncontrolled secret society. But it, equally with "continental Masonry," comes under Canon 2335, which punishes with excommunication simply reserved to the Holy See those who become members of the Freemasons' and other societies that work against the Church or lawful civil authority.*

FREE-THINKER. One who accepts no authority outside himself in the matter of religious belief, referring all to the unaided human reason; a rationalist or secularist. See FREEDOM OF THOUGHT.

FRENSHAM ABBEY. An abbey of Benedictine nuns founded at Brussels by Lady Mary Percy in 1599, from which derive or are related the present convents of Stanbrook (Cambrai, 1625), Oulton (Ghent, 1624), Colwich (Paris, 1652), Teignmouth (Boulogne, 1652, and Dunkirk, 1662), Kylemore (Ypres, 1665) and Atherstone (1842). The Brussels nuns were driven out by the Revolution in 1794, went to Winchester, and settled at East Bergholt in Suffolk, in 1857; in 1948 they migrated to Frensham Hall, Shottermill, in Surrey. They are enclosed and contemplative.

FRIAR (Old Fr. *frere*, a brother). A member of one of the so-called mendicant orders. "Friar" is not synonymous with "monk," they are as different as artillery from infantry; the life of a monk is normally passed within the walls of his monastery; a friar has his headquarters in a friary but his work is of the active ministry and may take him to all parts of the earth; a friar is a member of a highly organized, widespread body with a central authority to which he is professed; a monk's allegiance is to the abbot of an autonomous individual monastery. Moreover, there is no limit to the amount of property which monks may hold as a corporation; originally friars might have none, even in common, but this was modified by the Council of Trent. The "four mendicant orders of the common law" are the Dominicans, Franciscans, Carmelites and Augustinians (qq.v.); the lesser friars are the Servites, Trinitarians, Mercedarians, Minims, Brothers of St. John of God and the Order of Penitence (qq.v.).

FRIARS (ORDER) OF ST. AUGUSTINE. See HERMITS OF ST. AUGUSTINE.

FRIARS MINOR, The. The largest of the three independent branches of the Franciscan (q.v.) order, and the second most numerous order in the Church (over 20,000 professed religious). They observe the unmitigated rule of St. Francis (q.v.) and are engaged more particularly in preaching and the sacred ministry, especially to the poor and in foreign missions; in China, North Africa and the Custody of the Holy Land (which includes Syria and Lower Egypt) they have been established since the 13th century. England is a separate province, with headquarters at Forest Gate (London) and a dozen other friaries; it also has a mission territory in India. There is a province for Ireland, and five for the United States. The habit is a dark brown tunic, confined by a rope girdle, with a round hood; mantle for winter; bare feet and sandals, great tonsure.

FRIARS MINOR CAPUCHIN. See CAPUCHINS.

FRIARS MINOR CONVENTUAL, The. One of the three independent branches of the

---

* Although the 1983 Code of Canon Law does not lay down the penalty of *ipso facto* (automatic) excommunication for joining Freemasonry, Canon 1374 states: "One who joins an association which plots against the Church is to be punished with a just penalty; one who promotes or moderates such an association, however, is to be punished with an interdict." Moreover, it remains true that "The faithful who belong

Franciscans (*q.v.*). They follow the rule of St. Francis modified in certain respects by Pope Urban VIII, particularly with regard to the holding of property. The habit is a black tunic with a white cord, a large double hood pointed behind and falling over the shoulders at the side, biretta and shoes. They number over 4,000 religious, who are engaged in giving missions, preaching, etc. and in the three U.S.A. provinces they serve parishes. They have a friary and three other churches in England and are in charge of the basilicas of St. Francis of Assisi and St. Antony at Padua where those saints are buried.

FRIARS PREACHERS. The Dominicans (*q.v.*).

FRIARS OF THE SACK, so called from their coarse, shapeless habit, were a minor order of friars of Italian origin who came to England about 1257. They were dispersed on the continent after the Council of Lyons (1274) but remained in England until the dissolution of the monasteries.

FRIARY. A community of any one of the orders of friars and the house in which they live. It is now applied almost exclusively to Franciscan houses.

FRIDAY ABSTINENCE. See ABSTINENCE, DAYS OF.

FRIENDS, THE SOCIETY OF (commonly called Quakers) is a small but influential Protestant body formed by the followers of George Fox in the mid-17th century. Their chief characteristic has been called "The Doctrine of the Inner Light," a perception of the divine immanence in their own hearts and minds: they claim no special revelation. They have no formal profession of faith, but their doctrinal statements cover the truths of the Apostles' Creed, though for many their traditional meanings are by now much modified; their attitude to the Sacred Scriptures is that of "reverent and honourable esteem" —the rule of faith is in a man's heart rather than in a book. Though certain among them are called ministers, they have no clergy set apart, they reject all sacraments as ordinarily understood, and have no rites of worship: they meet together in silence and whosoever is moved by the Spirit to pray aloud, exhort, rebuke, give praise, is at liberty to do so. They refuse to take oaths (as unnecessary) and are rigidly opposed to all war. Quaker spirituality has considerable points of resemblance to Catholic mysticism, and their morality is quite lofty, *e.g.,* "Where debts have not been paid, the Society holds that no legal discharge liberates the debtor from the obligation to pay them in full, should it ever be in his power to do so (*cf.,* Debt herein), and in the meantime declines to accept his contributions for religious or benevolent purposes;" in so far as they hold that "no human tribunal can be an adequate judge of any man's conscience," they deny the state any jurisdiction in spiritual matters. The Friends form as it were a religious order within Protestantism; and their numerous large-scale works of mercy have evoked the admiration of the whole world.

FRONTAL. The English word for the *antependium* or *pallium,* a piece of material hanging over and completely covering the front side of an altar. The Missal and the Ceremonial of Bishops suppose that at any rate high altars will be so ornamented during Mass. It may be made of any material and of any colour, but it should follow the colour of the day's feast; nevertheless, a black frontal is forbidden on an altar at which the Blessed Sacrament is reserved, so on such purple must be used at requiem Masses. It is forbidden to decorate the black frontal with a skull or similar images. Being properly the vestment of the altar, it may surround three or all four sides; nor is there anything to prevent the altar-cloth itself being prolonged to the ground in front, with or without embroidery and colours, as is done at Ravenna. It has always been allowed that a very precious altar front does not require a frontal; but such are rare. Most "artistic" altars should have a frontal out of consideration for sensitive worshippers, if for no better reason.

FRUITS OF THE HOLY GHOST, THE XII, are charity, joy, peace, patience, benignity, goodness, longanimity, mildness, faith, modesty, continency, chastity (*qq.v.;* Gal. v. 22). The precise meaning of the words of St. Paul is a matter of discussion. It would appear that these fruits are acts produced by virtue, not the virtues or habits themselves: a harvest of the spirit, worked on by grace, and done joyfully and with peace of soul.

FRUITS OF THE MASS, The, are said to be three-fold: the general fruit in which all the faithful share, the special fruit which is applied to those for whom the Mass is said ("the repose of the soul of N . . ." "the private intention of Mrs. X . . .") and the more special fruit, inalienable from the celebrant himself. The whole efficacy of the Mass is derived from our Lord's sacrifice on the cross, and in so far as it is a "sacrifice of worship and thanksgiving" its effect is unlimited—man worships God in a god-like way. As a sacrifice of impetration and propitiation (*qq.v.*) its general fruit is only relatively unlimited—limited by the will of God as regards the Church at large and by the dispositions of the faithful actually present; a Mass confers actual grace (*q.v.*) on a given assistant thereat to the extent among other things of his good disposition and pur-

to Masonic associations are in a state of grave sin and may not receive Holy Communion." (Declaration on Masonic Associations by the Sacred Congregation for the Doctrine of the Faith, Nov. 26, 1983.)— *Publisher,* 1997.

ity of intention, not in a mechanical fashion; its special fruit is, in practice, strictly limited to the person or persons for whom the Mass is said (so that a priest may not say one Mass in discharge of two different stipends) and they profit therefrom passively. The *objective* efficacy of the Mass is always the same and independent of the worthiness of the celebrant; but its *subjective* efficacy is conditioned by the spiritual state of the Church at large, of the celebrant himself, and of all who assist thereat: so that the fruits resulting from the sacrificial activity of the Church are reduced if the pope be wicked, the clergy unspiritual or the layfolk apathetic; they are increased by the personal holiness of the celebrant or the fervour of a large congregation, by ceremonies carried out with loving care and chant sung with understanding and devotion.

FRUSTULUM (Lat., a little bit). The morsel of solid food, 2 or 3 oz., allowed as breakfast on fasting days, usually called in English a *pittance*.

"FULL OF GRACE." These words, spoken of our Lady by the angel Gabriel (Luke i, 28) and repeated thousands of times daily by loving Christians, do not mean that she was endowed with grace to the fullest extent possible or that she had all possible effects of grace, but simply that she had the grace necessary to fulfil her calling, to be the mother of God made man—in itself sufficient to exalt her far above all others, angels or men.

FUNDAMENTAL AND NOT-FUNDAMENTAL ARTICLES. A distinction invented by Protestant theologians in the 17th century, whereby they taught that explicit belief in certain articles of faith was necessary to salvation and essential to Christianity, whereas acceptance and teaching of other, non-essential, articles was not required. This doctrine has persisted and is held by many Protestants to-day. It is diametrically opposed to the teaching of the Catholic Church which is that, while certainly some truths are more important to be known than others, nevertheless the Christian is not at liberty to deny or question any truth whatsoever which has been revealed by God. The Church has never considered the definitions of the faith as "provisional" or "optional truths," but as acquired and obligatory verities and facts (*cf.*, Article of Faith). The matter was again referred to by Pope Pius XI in his encyclical *Mortalium animos*.

FUNDAMENTALISM. The name given in the United States to that form of Protestantism (now almost disappeared in Great Britain) which regards holy Scripture as a complete, sufficient and final authority: its words being interpreted literally (especially such passages as Gen. i and ii, but always excepting Matt. xxvi, 26-8) and to the exclusion of any doctrine not plainly contained therein.

FUNERAL RITES. At the house, or meeting it at the churchyard gate, the priest, vested in a black cope, sprinkles the body (*i.e.,* coffin) with holy water, saying Ps. cxxix (*De profundis*) with an antiphon and, while the body is being conveyed to the church, Ps. l (The *Miserere*). After entering the church the responsory *Subvenite* is sung with its verse, and if the Office of the Dead and requiem Mass are to be said or sung, they immediately follow. After Mass is said the prayer *Non intres,* "Enter not into judgement with thy servant, O Lord," and the responsory *Libera me,* "Deliver me, O Lord, from everlasting death," with its versicles, *Kyrie eleison* and the Lord's Prayer, while the priest sprinkles the body with holy water and incenses it, thrice on each side; he then says a prayer for the deceased, that he may have everlasting joys. While the body is being carried to the grave *In Paradisum* (*q.v.*) is sung; if necessary, the grave is blessed, it and the body being again sprinkled and incensed; otherwise, the body is at once laid therein while the *Benedictus* (*q.v.*) is said with the antiphon "I am the Resurrection and the Life," followed by *Kyrie eleison,* the Lord's Prayer, and a prayer for the fellowship of the deceased with the choirs of angels. There are sometimes added the *Subvenite* and other prayers in English, followed by a prayer for those present. While returning to the church, *De profundis* is again said. Both in the church and in the grave the body of a priest should be disposed with its head towards the altar, *i.e.,* the east, but of a lay person in the reverse position. The body of a priest is buried in Mass vestments (purple or black), and other clerics according to their order. The burial of a child who has not attained the use of reason is a rite of totally different character. See under INFANTS.

FUNGIBLE COMMODITY (Lat. *fungi* [*vice*], to serve [instead of]. Goods which are intended for consumption and that are replaced (*e.g.,* in repaying a loan) by similar but not identical goods, *e.g.,* a pint of beer. Money considered as a means of exchange, but not when considered as laid-up capital, is a fungible commodity, ceasing to be of any use to the owner when he has used it (*i.e.,* exchanged it for goods). See MUTUUM.

FUTURE (Lat. *futurus,* about to be). That which will come to existence, but is now within its causes.

G

GABBATHA (Aramaic, called Hebrew in John xix, 13, because it was the language spoken by the Jews). The place where Christ was condemned. Our Lord was interrogated by Pilate in the inner court of the *prætorium*. The Jews did not enter it because, containing leavened bread, to do so would on that day have made them legally unclean; they therefore stayed in the outer court, "in the place that is called *Lithostrotos* (*q.v.*), and in Hebrew *Gabbatha*" (John xix, 13). The traditional site of the *prætorium* is on the northwest of the former Temple at the Antonia fortress on the hill Bezetha, *Gabbatha* being east of the convent of Our Lady of Zion. This site is disputed.

GALATIANS, THE EPISTLE TO THE. A letter written by St. Paul to the Church in Galatia in Asia Minor, forming a canonical book of Holy Scripture. It was written against some judaizers there who were teaching that observance of the Mosaic Law was necessary to the perfection of Christianity; they had argued away the apostolic authority of St. Paul, whose reply is correspondingly personal.

GALILEE. A large porch at the entrance to a church, such as the one at the west end of Ely cathedral, which contains two chapels, and at Durham and Lincoln cathedrals. A suggested explanation of the name is that the porch, being less sacred than the rest of the building, is as Galilee to Judæa (*cf.*, Matt. iv, 15)—which seems a bit fanciful.

GALILEO'S CASE. One of the alleged failures of papal infallibility. In 1616 and again in 1633 the Holy Office of the Roman Inquisition, led astray by excessive doctrinal caution, condemned as formal heresy the then novel scientific teaching of Galileo Galilei that the sun is the centre of the universe and immovable and that the earth moves with an annual and diurnal motion. The popes Paul V and Urban VIII sanctioned this condemnation. It is not claimed for the decisions of Roman congregations that they are infallible; infallibility is a personal, incommunicable gift pertaining to the pope. The pope may approve a congregation's decree without making the contents his own, or he may approve it in a special manner and identify himself personally with it: in neither case does that render the decree infallible. Such a decree could only come within the sphere of infallibility if it was re-promulgated by the pope *ex cathedra* and under the other conditions which the doctrine of papal infallibility (*q.v.*) requires. In the case of Galileo the popes neither did nor attempted to do this.

GALLICAN LITURGIES. i. The liturgical rites of Gaul from the earliest times to the 8th century. The Mozarabic and Celtic rites (*qq.v.*) were allied thereto.

ii. A frenchified version of the Roman rite used by the Normans in Sicily and southern Italy.

iii. The former French diocesan uses, of which survivals are still found at Bayeux and elsewhere.

GALLICANISM. i. The teaching set forth in a document called "The Gallican Liberties," set out in four propositions drawn up by the clergy of the Church in France in 1682. The first proposition denied that St. Peter and his successors received any power from God extending to temporal and civil affairs, declared princes to be subject to no ecclesiastical power in temporal matters, and denied the deposing power of the pope (*q.v.*); the second declared the supremacy of œcumenical councils over the pope; the third affirmed the force and validity of the laws, customs and constitutions of the Gallican and other local churches; the fourth declared that the pope has the principal share in questions of faith and that his decrees regard all the churches and every church in particular, but that his judgement is not irreformable unless the consent of the Church be added. Gallicanism first appeared at the beginning of the 15th century, and was widely professed in France and Flanders during the 17th and 18th (it spread to Ireland for a short time and was not unknown in England); it was checked at the Revolution and the 2nd, 3rd and 4th of the above propositions were condemned by the Vatican Council. It is now professed only by the heretical sect of the Old Catholics (*q.v.*).

ii. Secondarily, the name is used to designate any tendency to stress and exalt the prerogatives of a local (national) church at the expense of the authority of the Holy See.

GALLOVIDIANUS. The adjectival form of the name of the see of Galloway (*q.v.*) used in the designation of its bishop in Latin documents. Noun: *Gallovidia, Candida Casa*.

GALLOWAY (*Gallovidianus*). A Scottish see, suffragan to Saint Andrews, founded at Whithorn, vacant from 1558 till 1878. It comprises the counties of Dumfries, Kirkcudbright, Wigtown and Ayr. The bishop's residence is at Maxwelltown and St. Andrew's cathedral is at Dumfries. The patron of the diocese is St. Ninian. Gaelic name; Gallaobh.

GALVIENSIS ET DUACENSIS. The adjectival form of the name of the see of Galway and Kilmacduagh (*q.v.*) used in the designation of its bishop in Latin documents. Noun: *Galvidia et Duacum*.

GALWAY AND KILMACDUAGH (*Galviensis et Duacensis*). An Irish see, suffragan of Tuam. Galway was made an episcopal see in 1831 and in 1883 Kilmacduagh was permanently united to it, and its bishop made perpetual administrator of the diocese of *Kilfenora*, since 1750 administered by Kilmacduagh. The whole territory now consists of a district in the counties of Galway and Clare with one parish in Mayo. The bishop's residence and pro-cathedral are at Galway. The patrons of the dioceses are St. Nicholas (Dec. 6), St. Colman (Oct. 29) and St. Fachanan (Aug. 14); the cathedral is dedicated in honour of the first named. Irish name: Gaillimh.

GAMBLING. See BETTING.

GARDEN OF THE SOUL, The. A prayerbook compiled by Bishop Challoner (1691-1781), first published in 1740. So great was its popularity and influence that it has given rise to the term "Garden of the Soul Catholic," to designate one who displays the solid and unostentatious piety of penal days in England combined with a certain imperviousness to ideas foreign to that time and place. This name has reference to the earlier and authentic editions of the book, which consisted principally of liturgical prayers in English and a brief treatise on the spiritual life. So varied have been the additions, subtractions and alterations in the subsequent countless editions that the book to-day is unrecognizable; a comparison of an early edition with any recent one is a most instructive exercise.

GARTH (Old Norse *garthr*, a yard). The open space, grass lawn or otherwise, enclosed by the four walks or sides of a cloister. In the Carthusian and other orders dead brethren are sometimes buried in the garth.

GATE OF HEAVEN (Lat. *Ianua Cæli*). A title given to our Lady in the litany of Loreto; she was the gate whereby Christ came to open Heaven to man and at her intercession the gates of Heaven are opened to the souls in Purgatory. The first recorded use of the expression is by St. Peter Damian; the same idea occurs in the *Alma Redemptoris* and *Ave Regina*.

GATES OF HELL, The. (Matt. xvi, 18). The word translated "hell" is *Hades*, the equivalent in the Greek Testament of the Heb. *Sheol*, "the place of departed spirits." That the "gates of hell" shall not prevail against the Church therefore means that it is to last for all time; or the expression may simply be a synonym for the powers of darkness and evil.

GAUDETE SUNDAY. The third Sunday of Advent, from the first word of the introit, "Rejoice." It is a day of liturgical rejoicing in a penitential season: vestments of rose-colour may be worn, deacon and subdeacon wear dalmatic and tunicle (instead of folded chasubles), the organ may be played and the altar adorned with flowers.

GE'EZ. Classical Ethiopian, the liturgical language of the Abyssinian rite. It is a Semitic tongue, closely allied to Arabic. It ceased to be spoken before the 13th century. The various dialects, Tigré, Amharic, are probably descended from a sister language of Ge'ez. Pending the revision of their own liturgical books the Catholic Abyssinians formerly used the Roman Mass in Ge'ez, as they still do the "Rituale Romanum."

GEHENNA is the Gr. form of the Heb. *Gehinnom*, the valley [of the sons] of Hinnom, on the south side of Jerusalem where the city refuse was burnt and Moloch had been worshipped. Our Lord uses the name to signify Hell, "where their worm (pain of loss) dieth not, and the fire (pain of sense) is not extinguished" (Mark ix, 42-47).

GELASIAN SACRAMENTARY, The. "The Book of the Sacraments of the Roman Church," a sacramentary (*q.v.*) of the 7th or 8th century compiled for use in Gaul. Its ancient attribution to Pope Gelasius I is erroneous. It contains proper Masses for Sundays and feasts, a common of saints, votive and requiem Masses, ordination and dedication rites, the blessing of the font and of the holy oils, etc., according to the use of Rome with Gallican additions, *e.g.*, proper prefaces.

GEMARA (Heb., completion). One of two commentaries, the Palestinian or the Babylonian, on the *Mishna* (*q.v.*) completing the *Talmud*.

GENEALOGIES OF JESUS, The, are found in St. Matthew's gospel i, 1-17, and St. Luke's iii, 23-38, Matthew tracing it from Abraham to Joseph, Luke from Joseph or Mary to Adam. Between David and Zorobabel, Matthew has 15 names, Luke 20, and all differ save one; between Zorobabel and Joseph, Matthew has 10, Luke 17, and all differ. The objections to Luke's line being from Joseph are met by postulating that Joseph was physically the son of Jacob but legally (see *Levirate*) of Heli, and that Salathiel was physically the son of Neri, but by adoption of Jechonias (*cf.*, Jeremias xxii, 24-30). If it be maintained that Davidic descent through Mary is also necessary (as the O.T. prophecies seem to require), tradition has always held that she was so descended; and it has further been maintained that Luke's line is traced from her, she being descended from David's son Nathan and St. Joseph from David's son Solomon. That Christ was descended from David is not disputed, but the above and other difficulties presented by the Biblical genealogies have not yet been solved by exegetes. That our Lady's father is always called Joachim is of little significance; our knowledge of it depends on the apocryphal Gospel of James.

GENERAL. The colloquial term for the superior general of an order or congregation; it is really an adjective qualifying another noun—master general, provost general, superior general, etc., as the case may be. The unity and centralized government of the friars required the innovation of a supreme chief for each order whom the Franciscans call minister general, the Dominicans master general, and the Augustinians and Carmelites prior general. The congregations of canons regular have abbots general, as do the Cistercians, but the only Benedictine congregations which have generals in the proper sense are those of Solesmes, Beuron and the Cassinese of Primitive Observance (superior general, archabbot and abbot general respectively). A general of exempt (*q.v.*) religious has ordinary spiritual jurisdiction over his subjects and may absolve reserved cases (*q.v.*) *pari passu* with a diocesan bishop; they may themselves reserve certain cases and have the right to vote if summoned to œcumenical councils. Most of these generals are elected for a term of years, as are the superiors general of more recent congregations (but that of the Jesuits for life).

GENERAL CONFESSION. A repetition of all previous confessions either of one's life or over a considerable period of time. It may be made necessary by previous confessions having been wilfully incomplete or lacking in true penitence, or by the confessor having been without jurisdiction. Such a general confession is customary before first communion, ordination, monastic profession, etc., and may be allowed in order to remove doubts and scruples in respect of past sins. Except for such or other good reasons, the making of a general confession is strongly discouraged by ascetical writers and confessors as being an occasion of scrupulosity and generally harmful.*

GENERATION. The passage from non-being to being. (*a*) In a wide sense: the origin of a form from potentiality. Strictly: the origin of a living thing from the substance of another living thing in likeness of nature. (*b*) Active: the act of the generator; passive: the inception of the generated. (*c*) Univocal: that in which generator and generated are of the same species; equivocal: that in which generator and generated are of diverse species. (*d*) Substantial: the production of a new substantial composite; accidental: the eduction of an accident from the potentiality of a substance.

GENERATIONISM. The false theory that the soul of the child comes from the soul of the parents (*cf.*, Traducianism and **Creationism**).

GENESIS. The first book of the Jewish and Christian holy Scriptures, so called because it treats of the creation and beginning of the world and relates the early history of the people chosen by God to receive his revelation and fulfil his mission. In Hebrew it is called *Beresith*, its opening word. Its author was Moses (see PENTATEUCH and below). The first three prophecies on Holy Saturday and the first of Whitsun Eve are taken from Genesis.

GENESIS, HISTORICALNESS OF. The Biblical Commission (*q.v.*) on June 30, 1909, declared that the first three chapters of Genesis contain an account of real facts corresponding to objective reality and historical truth and are not fiction derived from ancient mythologies and cosmogonies, purged of their polytheism and adapted to monotheism. Catholics cannot hold that they contain allegories or symbols destitute of a foundation of objective reality and used to inculcate religious and philosophical truths under the appearance of history, or that they contain legends, partially historical and partially fictitious, freely composed for instruction and edification. The literal historical sense may not be doubted when facts narrated in these chapters are connected with the foundation of the Christian religion, *e.g.*, the creation of all things by God at the beginning of time, the separate creation of man, the unity of the human race, the original happiness of the First Parents in a state of righteousness, integrity and immortality, the transgression of the divine precept at the instigation of the Devil, the casting out from that state of innocence, the promise of a future Redeemer, etc. But it is not necessary to take in the literal sense all individual words and phrases where expressions are obviously metaphorical or anthropomorphical and when common sense and necessity demand the abandonment of the literal meaning. In the first chapter especially no rigid scientific precision must be sought: the author did not intend to give a scientific exposition of the origin of the world but a popular description suitable to the capacity of men of that time and in their common speech. This decision, though not an utterance of infallible authority, is the norm which regulates all Catholic exposition of these chapters and influences the interpretation of the following seven. See also QUOTATIONS, CREATION ii.

GENEVA BIBLE, The. An English version of the Bible, being a revision of the Great Bible and Tyndale's versions, published under Calvinistic auspices at Geneva in 1560.

GENTILES, The, in the Bible, means any who are not Jews. Not being of the Chosen People, the word (*Goyim* in Hebrew) is often

---

* In his *Introduction to a Devout Life*, St. Francis de Sales recommends a General Confession when one seriously begins a devout life (Part I, chap. 19), and making a General Confession is part of doing the Spiritual Exercises of St. Ignatius Loyola.—*Publisher*, 1997.

used in contempt and dislike or as a warning (Jer. xiv, 22; Rom. ii, 24). St. Paul was the Apostle of the Gentiles (Eph. iii, 1-12), since whom the word has for Christians often designated those who are neither Christian nor Jew.

GENUFLEXION (Lat., *genu,* a knee; *flectere,* to bend). The momentary bending of one knee (the right) so as to touch the ground; the body should be held erect and the sign of the cross not made. This is one of the two normal ceremonial reverences (*q.v.*) of the Western church; it has to a great extent superseded the profound bow, general before the 16th century, still preferred by some religious orders, and almost universal in the East; at the English Convent of Canonesses regular at Bruges the young gentlewoman boarders were still in the 17th century instructed to curtsey to the Blessed Sacrament. All genuflect when passing before an altar at which the Blessed Sacrament is reserved or is lying upon the corporal during Mass, or upon which a relic of the True Cross is exposed, and to the unveiled cross throughout Good Friday. The clergy (excluding prelates) and assistants during liturgical functions genuflect to the altar-cross and to a bishop enthroned. Directions differ as to whether the server at low Mass should genuflect to the altar cross; the S.R.C. (4193, 1) says he should. There are various occasional genuflexions, *e.g.,* at the *Incarnatus* in the Creed and at the end of the Last Gospel at Mass, at *Veni, Sancte Spiritus* in the gradual at Whitsuntide, during the *Te Deum,* towards the end of the Epiphany gospel, etc. The genuflexions at the consecration in Mass are relatively recent and are still not fully used by the Carthusians. A double genuflexion consists in kneeling on both knees, bowing the head and rising; it is made only before the Blessed Sacrament when it is exposed. See KNEELING.

GENUS (Lat., a race, plural *genera*). i. In logic. The one something which is univocally predicated of the many specifically distinct, as the determinable part of their essence.
ii. In biology. A collection of like species which are dissimilar from others of the same zoological family.
iii. In metaphysics. A constitutive note, determinable by a difference.

GENERIC DIFFERENCE. A difference of genus as between plant and stone, the former of which is living, the latter non-living.

GENTILUOMO (It., gentleman). See MAGISTRATUS.

GEORGETOWN. The oldest Catholic institution of higher learning in the United States is Georgetown University at Washington, D. C., founded by John Carroll (afterwards first bishop in the United States) in 1789.

Its first president was the Rev. Robert Plunket. Since 1805 it has been under the direction of the Jesuit fathers. Power to grant degrees was accorded in 1815 (by Congress) and in 1833 (by the Holy See), and it was formally incorporated in 1844. It has faculties of arts, law, medicine, foreign affairs, commerce and dentistry.

GEORGIA, THE CHURCH IN. Georgia is a republic of the U.S.S.R., south of the Caucasus, having 3½ million inhabitants. Their national church is an ancient autocephalous member of the dissident Orthodox Church, with a katholikos at its head. Before the revolution there were 32,000 Catholics of the Latin rite, 8,000 of Armenian rite, and a handful of Byzantine rite. Nothing is known of them now.

GERMANY, THE CHURCH IN. In 1939, one third of the 69 million inhabitants of Germany were Catholics, 5 million of them living in Bavaria. Those who have not been deported from east of the Oder-Neisse line are now under Polish rule, which will involve a modification of German hierarchical organization; this in 1939 consisted of the metropolitan sees of Cologne, Bamberg, Breslau, Freiburg, Munich and Paderborn, with 18 bishoprics. The dioceses chiefly affected by the partition are Breslau, Danzig, and the Ermland, with the prelature of Schneidemühl. The concordat entered into by the government of the Third Reich in 1933 abrogated the then existing concordats of the Vatican with Bavaria, Prussia and Baden. It is yet too early to judge the effects of the nazi regime and of world-war II on the Church in Germany.

GESTA (Lat., deeds). A word sometimes used after the 5th century for accounts of the life and death of martyrs, instead of *acta, passio,* etc.

GETHSEMANE (Heb., oil press). The place where our Lord suffered the agony "in the garden" and was seized by the Jews. It lies at the foot of the mount of Olives on the east side of Jerusalem, across the brook Kedron; part of it has been enclosed by the Franciscan fathers and another part by the Russian Orthodox whose emperor Alexander III built a church thereon in the Muscovite manner. Other places connected with the Agony are shown in the neighbourhood.

GETHSEMANI. The abbey of Our Lady of Gethsemani, in Kentucky, the senior Cistercian monastery of America. It was founded in 1848 by Dom Eutropius Proust, with monks from the monastery of Melleraie in Brittany; two years later it was made an abbey—the first in North America. In addition to farming, the monks conduct a boys' college. There have been Cistercians in America since 1802, when French monks made a foundation at Pigeon Hill, not far from Baltimore.

GHETTO (perhaps from It. *Giudecca*, Jewry). The quarter of a town reserved for Jews; residence therein was formerly compulsory at the instance of either civil or ecclesiastical authority. In England called Jewry (*cf.*, Old Jewry in the city of London).

GHOST (Old Eng., *gást*, a spirit). Catholic theology has nothing to say against the possibility of a ghost, in the sense of an apparition of one dead. It is within the providence of God to permit departed souls to appear on earth to fulfil some good purpose, *e.g.*, to give help or warning, or to obtain prayers. The Church also fully recognizes the possibility of apparitions or illusions caused by diabolical agency. Because of this common meaning of the word "ghost," the expression "Holy Ghost" for the third Person of the Trinity is sometimes objected to. It is certainly archaic, going back in English to the earliest times, and there is a tendency nowadays to prefer "Holy Spirit."

GIFTS OF THE HOLY GHOST, THE VII, are wisdom, understanding, counsel, knowledge, fortitude, piety and the fear of the Lord (Is. xi, 2 [*qq.v.*]). These gifts are habits by which the intellect (first four) or the will (last three) is disposed and ready to receive and act upon the light and assistance of the Holy Ghost. They must be distinguished from the virtues (*q.v.*) (which dispose the faculties to acts recommended by reason), and from the actual grace (*q.v.*) which they receive; they reside permanently in the soul with habitual grace (*q.v.*) and are lost with it.

GILBERTINES, The. An order of canons and nuns, with lay brothers and sisters, founded by St. Gilbert, parson of Sempringham, Lincolnshire, about 1135. It was the only purely English order the Church has known. Most of the monasteries were double (*q.v.*), the canons following the rule of St. Augustine, with additions, and the nuns the Cistercian recension of the rule of St. Benedict. The habit was black, with a scapular, hood and white cloak. The order was governed by a master or prior general who had complete control. It was very successful at first but at the dissolution had only four greater monasteries; there were twenty-one lesser houses and one in Scotland. No attempt has been made to restore the order. The body of St. Gilbert is in the church of St. Sernin at Toulouse, whither it was taken by King Louis VIII.

GILD, GUILD (Old Eng., payment). i. An association for commercial, social and religious purposes. Merchant gilds were established in all the towns of England, Wales and Ireland (except London) in the 13th-14th centuries and were open to all who could pay the fees. Their rules provided for charity and neighbourliness among members, for the conduct of gild business, and general regulation of trade for the benefit of the town and the gild, especially by strict supervision of the quality of goods exposed for sale. Craft gilds were, in England, an overflow from the merchant gilds when these became too big and complex to be managed, and were for the workers in each particular trade or craft. Each trade was restricted to members of the gild which was thus able to guarantee good work by insisting on proper apprenticeship, the use of good materials, etc., and by punishing adulteration and other frauds. These gilds were voluntary lay associations whose principles, consciously or not, were thoroughly grounded in Christian notions of justice; their trade was pervaded by a morality strange to-day: neither buyer nor seller was to take advantage of the other's necessities, but payment was to be a fair return for the labour expended upon honest work. On their strictly religious side, processions, miracle-plays, corporate attendance at Mass, the distribution of alms, and suffrages for the dead of the gild were common to most of them; some first came into existence as religious or *frith* (peace) gilds. Merchant gilds declined in the 14th century, and the craft gilds were damaged by an increased exclusiveness and oligarchical tendencies. In 1545-47 King Henry VIII appointed commissioners to seize such property of the gilds as was held for religious and charitable purposes; the commissioners exceeded their legal powers and the gilds never properly recovered. The gild system in varying forms was also spread over France, Flanders, the Germanies and Italy. It was a characteristic product of the middle ages, but now as dead as mutton.

ii. A name for a confraternity, *e.g.*, the Guild of the Blessed Sacrament.

GIRDLE, or cincture, is a long rope of linen or hemp, tasselled at the end, with which the alb is confined at the waist. It may be the colour of the other vestments but is usually white. Its practical use is to control the loose alb; symbolically it refers to sacerdotal purity.

GIROVAGI (Lat., wanderers around). The fourth kind of monk named by St. Benedict in his rule: "Who spend all their lives-long wandering about divers provinces, staying in different cells for three or four days at a time, ever roaming with no stability, given up to their own pleasures and to the snares of gluttony. . . ."

GLAGOLITIC. An ancient Slavonic alphabet, whose invention is often wrongly attributed to St. Jerome. It was until 1927 used in the liturgical books of those Catholics of Yugoslavia who have the Roman rite in Old Slavonic. The Byzantine users of this language print their books in the Cyrillic alphabet, invented from the Greek letters by the disciples of St. Cyril, apostle of the Slavs, for ecclesiastical purposes; it is probable that the Glagolitic characters, certainly older, are really those of Cyril. *Cf.*, SLAV RITE ii.

GLASTONBURY THORN (*Cratægus præcox*). This variety of the common thorn flowers in the spring at the usual time, and again, under certain conditions, at midwinter. If November and December are mild, the second crop of flowers, which are formed at the beginning of October, open out fully about Christmas. The age of the tree has a great deal to do with this winter flowering. Young trees will form their buds in October but seem to lack the strength to open them in the cold of winter; really old trees put forth their flowers readily about Christmas time, provided the two previous months have been fairly mild. The tree appears to be nothing more than a sport from the common thorn, which has been grafted on to a stock of the same, and retains all the peculiarities of the sport. The proof of this is, that seeds from a Glastonbury thorn always produce common thorns, and the double-flowering variety can only be obtained from cuttings or grafts. The plant bears its name from having previously been localized on Wearyall Hill at Glastonbury, where legend attributed it to a flowering of Joseph of Arimathea's staff. The original tree was destroyed by Cromwellians in 1653 but not before slips had been taken from it, from which all subsequent Glastonbury thorns are sprung. The fact that a Glastonbury thorn did not blossom on Dec 25, 1752, new style, was taken by many people as a divine direction that Christmas should be celebrated according to the old style, Julian calendar.

GLASGOW (*Glasguensis, Glasgoviensis*). A Scottish see founded by St. Kentigern (Mungo) about 543, made metropolitan in 1492 and vacant from 1603 till 1878 when it was revived as an archdiocese without suffragans. Made metropolitan again in 1947, with 2 suffragan dioceses, Motherwell and Paisley. It comprises the county of Dumbarton and parts of Lanark and Stirling. The archbishop's residence is at Bearsden and the cathedral of St. Andrew at Glasgow. The diocesan seminary is at New Kilpatrick, Bearsden. The Lourdes shrine at Carfin is a great place of pilgrimage. The patron of the archdiocese is St. Kentigern (Jan. 13). Gaelic name: Glaschu.

GLEBE (Lat. *gleba*, soil). The land attached to a parochial benefice as part or whole of the endowment for the support of the parish-priest. In England those glebe lands which have not been alienated are, of course, in the hands of the clergy of the Established Church or the holders of their livings; the English Catholic clergy have no glebe, or any other endowment as a rule.

GLORIA IN EXCELSIS DEO (Lat., Glory be to God on high). i. The Angelic Hymn or greater doxology, from its opening words. A hymn of praise to the three Persons of the Holy Trinity, consisting of ver. 14 of Luke ii with additions of Greek origin. It was at first proper to the midnight Mass of Christmas, but it is now said or sung in practically all Masses except those that are penitential or for the dead, *i.e.*, at which purple or black vestments are worn, and on ferias out of Easter time. When the *Gloria in excelsis* is intoned on Maundy Thursday, Holy Saturday and Christmas night all the bells of the church, great and small, are rung, and in the cathedral of Lucca flames are kindled thereat whenever the archbishop pontificates. Celebrant and people sign themselves with the cross at the last clause. It is not sung in any of the Eastern eucharistic liturgies, but the Byzantines use an amplified form at *Orthros* (*q.v.*) on Sundays and greater feasts, and the Copts say it at Extreme Unction.

ii. A musical setting of the same ("Gloria").

GLORIA PATRI, et Filio, at Spiritui sancto. Sicut erat in principio et nunc et semper et in sæcula sæculorum. Amen: (Glory be to the Father, and to the Son, and to the Holy Ghost. As it was in the beginning, is now, and ever shall be, world without end. Amen.) This brief hymn of praise has been used throughout the Western church (but with a quite different form in the Mozarabic rite) since the 7th century. It is always recited at the end of each psalm of the Divine Office, and in numerous other places; its most notable omissions are after the psalms of the Office of the Dead, and during the last three days of Holy Week. Its use is not so common in the East, where the words "as . . . is" are omitted.

GLORIOUS MYSTERIES, THE V, of the rosary (*q.v.*) are: the resurrection of our Lord, his ascension, the coming of the Holy Ghost at Pentecost, the assumption of our Lady, her coronation in Heaven together with the glory of all the saints. The coronation has only relatively recently been added to, but often supplants, the last mystery. In England in the 18th century "our Lady's eternal felicity and that of all the blessed in the Kingdom of Heaven" was named and meditated upon.

GLORY. i. The praise and splendour belonging to anyone on account of his known excellence.

ii. In God, who is all excellence, there is perfect knowledge of his own goodness, and therefore perfect glory.

iii. The glory of the blessed is their participation of the divine glory. This consists in the vision and love of God, for which their intellect must be perfected by a supernatural habit (*q.v.*) which renders them proximately capable of seeing God intuitively (*i.e.*, directly, without the intervention of creatures). This habit is the "Light of Glory."

GLORY, FORMAL. St. Thomas (I–II, ii, 3) borrows Augustine's definition of glory (he here attributes it to Ambrose): *clara notitia cum laude, i.e.,* "an outstanding knowledge of a person's goodness, with consequent praise of the person." The fundamental goodness in the person on account of which he is praised is "objective" glory. This is the foundation of the knowledge which engenders the praise, *i.e.,* of the "formal glory." The formal glory of God is the knowledge and praise of his goodness by intelligent creatures. The rest of God's creatures can contribute to his objective glory only, for though they manifest God's goodness, they cannot offer him a conscious meed of praise.

GLOSS (Gr. γλῶσσα, [foreign] speech). The name of a Scripture commentary, consisting of a chain of quotations from the early fathers, doctors and divines. It was compiled by Walafrid Strabo (*d.* 849) and remained for 600 years the standing authority in exegesis. This, the Ordinary Gloss, was followed some 150 years later by the Interlinear Gloss, made by Anselm of Laon, and later still by others which, however, never obtained equal standing. The word originally denoted marginal, interlinear or foot notes, consisting of one or more words explicative of an obscure word in the Bible text. When such words through copyists' errors have slipped into the text itself, they are still designated "gloss."

GLOVES, made of silk and decorated, are worn by cardinals and bishops of the Latin rite up to the offertory at pontifical Mass (except a requiem). A bishop is invested with them at his consecration but they seem always to have been purely ornamental.

GLUTTONY. Inordinate indulgence in food or drink; usually a venial sin, but mortal if serious injury to health or if complete drunkenness (*q.v.*) results.

GNOSTICISM (Gr. γνῶσις, knowledge). The generic name of a group of heretical systems which flourished in the first three centuries of the Christian era, and which had one common element of teaching, *viz.,* that salvation is by knowledge, the possession of the few. They were of pre-Christian origin, and had come into contact with the religions of Egypt and India as well as with Judaism. They indulged in magic, they assimilated much Christian phraseology and corrupted many Christian dogmas. All matter was a corruption of the divine; Christ was an æon, an intermediary of God with matter; existence was an evil to be escaped from by knowledge. Basilides, Valentinus, Bardesanes, Tatian and Marcion were prominent gnostics; Irenæus was their most conspicuous antagonist.

GOA, PATRIARCH OF. See EAST INDIES.

GOD. i. "The Supreme Spirit, who alone exists of himself, and is infinite in all perfections" (Catechism). He is utterly distinct in reality and essence from all other things that exist or can be conceived, all of which, if they exist, get their existence from him, "the first cause uncaused." God is *eternal,* without beginning or end or succession; *all-knowing,* even of man's most secret thoughts; *immeasurable,* being at once in Heaven, on earth, and in all places that are or can be; *just,* rendering to everyone according to his due, in this world or hereafter; *almighty,* for he can do whatever he wishes by the simple act of his will; *merciful,* for he wants the sinner not to die, but to be converted and live. He is *all-good,* untouched by the breath of any evil or imperfection, and his *beauty* is the cause of the being of all that exists. See KNOWLEDGE OF GOD II; PERFECTION, DIVINE; IMMANENCE; TRANSCENDENCE; OMNIPOTENCE; OMNISCIENCE; KNOWLEDGE; LOVE; CREATION, etc.

ii. As a person. The one God is not one person (*q.v.* ii) but three, so it were better to speak of God as personal, *i.e.,* as having the perfection "personality." If he had not this perfection we could not attribute to him his actions, we could not say, *e.g.,* that God creates, loves, rewards, punishes, provides. It is a widespread modern error to consider God as some impersonal evolving life-force.

GOD THE FATHER. The first Person of the Blessed Trinity (*q.v.*), who is of no one, but of whom is the Son begotten, and from whom with the Son, by a common spiration (*q.v.*), the Holy Ghost proceeds.

GOD THE HOLY GHOST. The third Person of the Blessed Trinity (*q.v.*), proceeding from the Father and the Son by an eternal procession (*q.v.*), a person distinct from the Father and the Son but uncreated, omnipotent and co-equal and co-eternal with them. See HOLY GHOST, etc.

GOD THE SON. The second Person of the Blessed Trinity (*q.v.*), the only begotten of the Father by an eternal generation (*q.v.*), a person distinct from the Father and the Holy Ghost but uncreated, omnipotent and co-equal and co-eternal with them, who became incarnate and is known as Jesus Christ (*q.v.*). See DIVINITY OF CHRIST; WORD, etc.

GOD'S ACRE. A fancy name for a church-yard, originally used with reference to the church-yard as a sanctuary for the living, not as a burial place for the dead.

GODPARENTS, -CHILDREN. See SPONSOR.

GOLD, MYRRH AND INCENSE may be blessed on the feast of the Epiphany with a form provided in the "Rituale Romanum."

GOLDEN BULL. i. A name given to several papal bulls, either because they were sealed with gold or on account of the importance of their contents; *e.g.*, of Sixtus IV, granting privileges to the Franciscans (1479); of Clement XI, making the royal collegiate chapel at Lisbon of metropolitan cathedral rank (1716); of Benedict XIV, confirming the privileges of the sodalities of our Lady (1748).

ii. A name for the confirmation of the States of the Church by the Emperor Frederick II in 1213, and also for the law of the Emperor Charles IV providing for the mode and rights of election of the Holy Roman emperors (1356); this last was a fundamental law of the Empire until the Peace of Westphalia in 1648.

GOLDEN LEGEND, The (Lat. *Legenda Aurea*), called by its author, Bl. James de Voragine, O.P. (*floruit* 1270), simply "The Legends of the Saints." A collection of stories that achieved extraordinary popularity in the middle ages; they are nearly worthless as history but make one of the most readable books of devotion ever written. A modernization of the first English edition (printed by Caxton in 1483) is published by Messrs. J. M. Dent & Sons in pocket volumes.

GOLDEN MASS. A Mass of our Lady formerly celebrated in some places with very great pomp, especially in cathedral churches, on the ember Wednesday in Advent. The custom is still observed in the collegiate church of St. Gudula at Brussels on Dec. 23.

GOLDEN NUMBER, The. That number from 1 to 19 which indicates the place of a given year in the lunar (metonic) cycle of 19 years. It is important in fixing the date of Easter, the moon's phases in every nineteenth year occurring on the same day of the month.

GOLDEN ROSE, The. An ornament made of gold in imitation of a spray of roses, one rose containing a receptacle into which is poured balsam and powdered musk. This device is solemnly blessed by the pope on *Lætare* Sunday. The blessing refers to the rose as a sign of spiritual joy and asks that the Church may bring forth fruit of good works and "the perfume of the ointment of the Flower sprung from the root of Jesse" (*i.e.*, our Lord). The golden rose thus blessed is solemnly conferred from time to time on sovereigns and others, churches or cities distinguished for their services to the Church. The latest to receive it was the Queen of the Belgians in 1925 on the occasion of her silver wedding. That presented by Pope Pius IX to the Empress Eugénie in 1856 is preserved at Farnborough Abbey, Hampshire. The custom was instituted before the 11th century.

GOLDEN RULE, The. Do as you would be done by. It was formulated by our Lord (Matt. vii, 12): "Do to other men all that you would have them do to you," and again in Matt. xix, 19, and elsewhere, "Thou shalt love thy neighbour as thyself." In the negative form it occurs in the book of Tobias iv, 16, "See thou never do to another what thou wouldst hate to have done to thee by another," and in the *Didache* (*q.v.*), "[Love] thy neighbour as thyself, and all things whatsoever thou wouldst not have befall thee do not thou to another." It is one of the first principles of the moral law, not confined to Jews and Christians; it was known, for example, to Confucius and Plato, Isocrates and Aristotle.

GOLDEN SEQUENCE, The. The sequence for Pentecost, *Veni, Sancte Spiritus* (*q.v.*).

GOLGOTHA. The Aramaic name for Mount Calvary (*q.v.*), meaning a skull, perhaps from its shape, though "head" is a common name for a hill in several languages, *e.g.*, Welsh *pen, moel;* Arabic, *rás.*

GONG. The use of a gong instead of a little bell at the altar during Mass is condemned by the S.R.C., 4000, 3, and authorities agree that this applies to gongs of any sort. A single, small hand-bell (*parva campanula* or *tintinnabulum*) is prescribed.

GOOD, The. That which is desirable; an end; whatever is capable of perfecting something. The good is the proper object of the will.

i. (*a*) Virtuous good: the perfection which a man is capable of receiving or acquiring in accordance with his moral nature. (*b*) Useful: an effective means of obtaining some end. (*c*) Delectable: a good that brings delight because of its agreement with the nature of the seeker.

ii. (*a*) True: a good which in fact perfects the seeker. (*b*) Apparent: a good which a seeker thinks to be perfective of himself, but which in reality is not so.

GOOD, THE HIGHEST or SUPREME. A nominal definition of God who is absolutely desirable; every desire can be perfectly realized in him.

GOOD FAITH. One who conscientiously believes that his statements or beliefs are true and actions honest is said to be in good faith, even though mistaken in this belief. Guilt is not imputed to one in good faith, even if, as a matter of fact, he is not acting rightly. Many outside the true Church are in this state. One may, in good faith, hold property to which one has no right, because, *e.g.*, it is not known that the property is stolen.

GOOD FRIDAY. The English name for Friday in Holy Week on which is commemorated the passion and death by crucifixion of Jesus Christ. It is, of course, a day of fasting, abstinence and penitence, but there is no obligation of resting from servile work or of attending the Church's offices— but it would be a grave fault to absent oneself out of contempt or indifference. Apart from the special case of Holy Saturday, it is the only day of the year upon which Mass may not be celebrated. The Good Friday Office (*q.v.*) takes place in the afternoon, between 3 o'clock and 6. One or more other services, of an extra-liturgical and unofficial character, are usually held for the devotion of the faithful, *e.g.*, the stations of the Cross, the Three Hours (*qq.v.*). The 7th century Spanish custom of shutting up the churches and having no service at all on Good Friday was forbidden by the 4th synod of Toledo. The Good Friday rites were drastically reformed by Pope Pius XII in 1956.

GOOD FRIDAY OFFICE, The, is made up of four distinct parts, the readings, etc., the solemn prayers, the adoration of the Cross, and the communion-service: the first part is the Mass of the catechumens (*q.v.*) in its early and simplest form. At about 3 p.m., the priest and his ministers prostrate themselves before the bare altar. The first lesson, sung by a lector, is Osee vi, 1-6, and is followed by a responsory from Habacuc iii, referring to the judgment of God upon the last day, and a collect; the subdeacon sings the second lesson (Exod. xii, 1-11) which speaks of the paschal lamb, and is followed by a second responsory, a cry of the betrayed Messias, from Ps. cxxxix. The passion (*q.v.*) according to St. John is then solemnly sung. Then follow prayers for all sorts and conditions of men in the form of a litany: the object of the petition is first announced by the priest (*Oremus pro . . . "Let us pray for . . .*"), the deacon calls on the people to kneel (*Flectamus genua, q.v.*) and, after a pause for silent prayer, he signals them to arise (*Levate!*); the priest then prays aloud as mouthpiece of the people, collecting together their petitions. The Church, the pope, the clergy and people, civil authorities, catechumens, the avoidance of physical evils, heretics and schismatics, the Jews, and the heathen are thus in turn prayed for. The form of these prayers is unchanged since at least the 4th century; they are probably the ordinary "prayers of the faithful" which once preceded the offertory at Mass. The adoration of the Cross and communion-service (formerly the Mass of the Presanctified, *qq.v.*) follow. In the Byzantine rite, in addition to the Liturgy of the Presanctified, the special services of the day are the representational deposition of Christ in the morning and funeral of Christ in the evening (see EPITAPHION)..

"GOOD KING WENCESLAS." St. Wenceslas (Vaclav) was a duke of Bohemia who promoted the evangelization of his country, and was slain in a political plot by his brother in the year 929. He is the patron saint of Czechoslovakia. The carol "Good King Wenceslas" does not indicate an ancient

English devotion to him: the words were written by the hymnodist J. M. Neale in the 19th century, to fit an old tune.

GOOD SHEPHERD, The. The Christian symbol of our Lord as the good or beautiful shepherd (John x, 11), carrying a lamb of the flock was known in the catacombs and has persisted to this day; but devotion to him as the good shepherd has been entirely supplanted by that to the Sacred Heart which is indeed a wider version of the same thing. The second Sunday after Easter is Good Shepherd Sunday, on account of its gospel at Mass, John x, 11-16; a feast of our Lord as good shepherd is kept in some places on that Sunday or the previous day, and on the Saturday after Low Sunday or on Sept. 3 a feast of our Lady Mother of the Good Shepherd.

GOOD SHEPHERD NUNS. The enclosed religious of Our Lady of Charity of the Good Shepherd at Angers, an offshoot of the Sisters of Our Lady of Charity of the Refuge (*q.v.*). Similar work, to which it adds the conduct of general reformatories, homes for inebriates, communities of penitents. White tunic and scapular, blue girdle, black veil.

GOOD THIEF, The, who on the cross confessed Christ. Nothing is known for certain of him except what is narrated in the gospels; apocryphal writings call his name Dismas. His feast is kept in some places (*e.g.*, diocese of Salford, March 26), and he is named in the Roman Martyrology on March 25.

GOOD WORKS. All works involved in the observance of the precepts and counsels (*q.v.*), though the term is usually reserved for the latter, and comprises all that falls under the three broad headings of prayer, fasting, almsdeeds. Good works are not the cause of justification. We are made just by the sanctifying grace of infused charity; but if we love God efficaciously above all things we necessarily act accordingly, and thus good works are necessary to salvation. But good works must also precede justification in an adult. The Council of Trent requires for justification, besides faith, acts of fear, hope, initial love and sorrow. In this sense also, therefore, good works are necessary to salvation as prerequisite.

GOOD OF MARRIAGE, THE THREE-FOLD, without which matrimony is impossible: (*a*) the good of the offspring, consisting in their procreation, up-bringing and education; (*b*) the good of mutual faith, which consists in the unity of marriage and faithfulness; (*c*) the good of the sacrament, consisting in an indissoluble and holy union, signifying the union of Christ with his Church.

GORDON RIOTS, The. Serious civil disturbances in London lasting from June 2 to

9, 1780. They arose out of a demonstration against the first Catholic Relief Act (1778) organized by Lord George Gordon, a somewhat crazy eccentric. The No-Popery mob which supported his petition to the House of Commons got out of hand and fell upon the Sardinian and Bavarian embassy chapels (the latter still stands in Warwick Street); for a week off and on chapels (including Moorfields, Wapping and East Smithfield) and houses were plundered and burned, the persons and residences of those favourable to Catholic relief were set upon (the aged Bishop Challoner only just escaped and died later, partly from shock), Newgate prison was fired and 300 felons set free, prisoners were released from other prisons; the Thames bridges were seized and the Bank of England twice attacked. The rioting was eventually put down violently and with considerable bloodshed by troops on the initiative of the king. The number of Catholics and others who lost their lives one way or another is not known, nor the precise amount of damage done to property; a second Great Fire was only narrowly averted. Twenty-one of the ringleaders were hanged, but Gordon was indicted on a wrong charge and escaped scot-free. St. George's cathedral, Southwark, now stands on the ground where the mob first assembled.

GORDON'S CALVARY. A small hill outside the north wall of Jerusalem close to the Damascus Gate wherein are two caves having the appearance of eye-sockets (in one of them Jeremias is reputed to have written his lamentations). A Jewish tradition was said to identify this skull-like hill as Golgotha and the identification was taken up very enthusiastically by General Gordon; a tomb in a garden on the west side is alleged to be the true sepulchre of Christ. These sites became a sort of rallying-ground for Protestants during the late 19th century, and they were acquired and are now held by influential English trustees; but this enthusiasm has somewhat cooled as a result of more critical research. See CALVARY; HOLY SEPULCHRE.

GOSPEL (Old Eng. *god spell*, good tidings). i. The life and teaching of Jesus Christ as recorded by the Evangelists, and the books wherein it is set down, namely the Gospels according to Matthew, Mark, Luke and John. These are the only gospels for which the Church vouches by including them in the canon of Sacred Scripture, but the word is also used to designate other records of the acts and words of Christ even though manifestly spurious (see below).
ii. The whole of the teaching of Christianity at any given moment, whether contained explicitly or implicitly in the deposit of faith, recorded by Scripture or tradition or made clear by definition (as in the expression "to preach the gospel").

GOSPEL, APOCRYPHAL. An early written narrative concerning our Lord, having no authority and of doubtful or no value either as a record of events or as a witness to his teaching. The names of over fifty such are known, of which the principal are the "Pseudo-Matthew," "Protoevangelium of James," and the gospels of Nicodemus, Peter and Thomas (*qq.v.*). So far as is known, no apocryphal gospel of which there is any record is so old as to be among the writings referred to in Luke i, 1.

GOSPEL, THE LAST, is the prologue of St. John's, i, 1-14, which is read from the altar-card by the celebrant at the gospel-side of the altar at the end of Mass. At the third Mass of Christmas the last gospel is Matt. ii, 1-12, and on Easter eve and Palm Sunday it is omitted, unless palms have not been blessed, when it is Matt. xxi, 1-9. It was formerly a practice of private devotion to say John I, 1-14 after Mass, and was only made a definite part of the liturgy by Pope St. Pius V in 1570; at a pontifical Mass it is still said by the bishop while he unvests. Of Eastern liturgies, only the Armenian has a last gospel (John i, 1-18; in paschal-time, xxi, 15-20), which practice was taken directly from that of Western priests with whom they came into contact in the middle ages.

GOSPEL, LITURGICAL. i. The singing or reading of the gospel after the gradual at Mass, and the part of the gospels sung. After receiving a blessing from the celebrant the deacon carries the book in procession with lights and incense to the north side of the sanctuary; where there is no *ambo* (*q.v.*), that is, nearly everywhere, the subdeacon holds open the book, while the deacon incenses it and then, facing north, sings the appointed passage. Afterwards the subdeacon takes the book for the kiss of the celebrant. At low Mass the book is moved by the server from the epistle to the gospel-side of the altar (in imitation of the deacon's position), and the sacred passage is there read by the celebrant. When the passage is announced (*Sequentia*, or *Initium* . . . The Continuation, or The Beginning of . . .) the deacon or priest makes a sign of the cross on his forehead, mouth and breast, that the gospel truth may be in his mind, his mouth and his heart; the people do likewise and stand erect during the singing or reading. On feast-days the gospel narrates the event or has other reference to the feast; the selection of passages for other days is very ancient but the principle, if any, underlying the selection is not known. When the pope sings Mass, the gospel is chanted twice, in Latin and Greek. All Eastern liturgies accompany the gospel reading with special ceremony; the Byzantine much resembles the Roman usage.
ii. The Last Gospel (see above).
iii. In the Roman rite the gospel at Matins is now reduced to its opening clause, the

following lessons (7th-9th) being from a homily expounding the rest of it. But in the Monastic Breviary the whole of the gospel of the day is read after the *Te Deum*. Among Carthusian nuns if no priest is present at Matins a nun assumes the stole and reads this gospel.

GOSPEL OF NICODEMUS, The, or "The Acts of Pilate," an apocryphal book compiled probably in the 5th century. It is a highly elaborated and fanciful account of the trial, death and resurrection of our Lord, culminating in the conversion of Annas, Caiphas and the Sandhedrin upon hearing an account of his ascension. This book gives the names of the two thieves (Dismas and Gestas), of Pilate's wife (Procla), of the centurion (Longinus), of the woman with an issue of blood (Bernice or Veronica), and others.

GOSPEL OF PETER, The. An apocryphal book first mentioned *c.* 191. The existing fragment departs from the canonical gospels in several particulars and shows traces of Docetism (*q.v.*).

GOSPEL OF THOMAS, The. An apocryphal book, originating among the gnostics, and one which professed to correct the ignorance on the boyhood of our Lord. It is chiefly a record of prodigies of the crudest and most puerile kind. From it was derived the Arabic "Gospel of the Infancy," still popular among the Nestorians.

GOSPEL-SIDE. That end of the altar or side of the sanctuary at which the gospel is said or sung at Mass, namely, the north or left-hand side facing the altar.

GOSPELS, DATES OF THE. We have no certain information on this point. Generally speaking Catholic scholars assign St. Matthew's to about A.D. 50 and St. Luke's before 60, with St. Mark's between them; St. John's between 90 and 100. Mark and Luke cannot be dated after the beginning of the siege of Jerusalem; the Greek version of Matthew may have followed them.

GOSSIP. An old English name for a sponsor at baptism, from *godsibb* meaning "God-relation." The word gossip in this sense was in use among Catholics in parts of England up to at least the beginning of the 19th century. The transferred meaning of the word is a melancholy reflection on the habits of sponsors, which it is to be hoped is not justified.

GOTHIC ARCHITECTURE (Gothic, originally used in the 17th century as a term of contempt for that which was not classic). The manner of building, Franco-Norman in origin, used roughly from the end of the 12th to the end of the 16th century in France and England, and for not so long and to a lesser degree in other parts of western Europe. It is commonly divided into styles (Early English, Decorated, Perpendicular, etc.), but these are arbitrary divisions, for by a series of imperceptible transitions the manner of building was continually modified and altered at the will of the workmen. The distinguishing characteristic of this building to the lay-observer is the pointed arch and the system of stone vaulting thereby made possible. Gothic was not an ecclesiastical style—contemporary barns, bridges and houses were built by the same workmen in the same way. From the fact that it was entirely the creation of Christian men and owed nothing directly to pagan models, this sort of building has been represented by enthusiasts as the only one suitable for Catholic churches, at least in Western Europe. Even were this true, we should still be faced with the difficulty that gothic, as a system of building, has been out of use for 300 years and, as a system of ornament, is dependent upon the existence of intellectually responsible workmen such as contemporary industrial organization does not produce. Perfectly plain and unornamented gothic building is possible where stone is readily available; but it is the ornamental accompaniments of mediæval gothic which make it popular and these are not obtainable under modern conditions except in lifeless copies.

GOTHIC REVIVAL, The. The revival in England of the use first of the ornament and then of the system of building characteristic of gothic architecture (*q.v.*) begun by wealthy *dilettanti* such as Horace Walpole in the 18th century, popularized æsthetically by Ruskin and ethically by the Anglican Camden Society and A. W. Pugin, the most capable of its early practitioners and a Catholic, and extended to other things as an attractive form of decoration by Sir Walter Scott and others. The revival had a great but far from unchallenged popularity among English Catholics, and its influence is still strong, especially among the clergy; Milner's church, old St. Peter's at Winchester, represents its beginning and such churches as St. John's at Norwich and St. Philip's at Arundel its goal. The general popularity of the revival lasted until the beginning of the 20th century.

GOTHIC RITE, The. Another name for the Mozarabic rite (*q.v.*), referring to the period of the Visigothic kingdom in Spain.

GOTHIC VESTMENTS. A term commonly used for vestments whose shape differs from that of modern Roman (*q.v.*) patterns, resembling those of the past at any stage of development from the catacombs to Pugin, excluding the Renaissance. The expression is misleading; the Gothic rite had no vestments peculiar to itself, nor did those worn in gothic churches differ from those worn at the same time in the basilicas of Rome. It is a difference of time, not of style or of place. Gothic vestments have a fuller, sometimes pointed, chasuble, and longer and narrower stole and maniple with the ends little or not at all splayed. They are worn by Benedictines and Dominicans practically everywhere, and are in increasingly common use in many countries.

GOVERNMENT. i. Civil. See AUTHORITY, CIVIL.

ii. Ecclesiastical. The Church, as a perfect society, has supreme authority over her subjects, legislative, judicial and executive, in all matters pertaining to her spiritual end. The supreme authority over the universal Church belongs by divine institution to the pope individually, and to the bishops collectively (œcumenical council) in union with the pope. Also by divine institution bishops have authority in their own territories, dependently on the pope. The pope in the government of the universal Church is assisted by cardinals, either as a body (the Sacred College), or distributed in the Roman Congregations, Tribunals, and Offices. The bishop in his diocese is assisted by the cathedral chapter, officials of the diocesan curia, and rectors of parishes.

GRACE (Lat. *gratia*, favour). i. Strictly, a supernatural (*q.v.*) gift of God to an intellectual creature, bestowed with a view to eternal life. In 1713, in the bull *Unigenitus*, Pope Clement XI condemned the Jansenist proposition that "no grace is given outside the Church."

ii. Sometimes, broadly, any gift freely given by God irrespective of a relation to man's supernatural end. So creation and conservation are sometimes called graces.

GRACE, ACTUAL. Any supernatural (*q.v.*) and transient aid by which God enlightens the mind or assists the will to produce supernatural acts. It affects the faculties of the soul (intellect and will), whereas habitual grace (*q.v.*) affects the very substance. Such grace may be given either immediately ("No man cometh to me, except the Father . . . *draw* him," John vi, 44), or mediately, on the occasion of a reading of Scripture or the hearing of a sermon, from a joy or a sorrow, a dream, a sunset, or a song.

GRACE, BAPTISMAL. The particular grace bestowed in the sacrament of Baptism for the securing of the special effect of the sacrament. Every sacrament gives such a sacramental grace, which is not distinct from sanctifying grace (*q.v.*), but is a special aspect of it. Baptism produces sanctifying grace for the first time in the soul at the moment in which it remits original sin (*q.v.*), and any actual sin which may be there, and the punishment due to actual sin. With sanctifying grace, it bestows the infused virtues, the gifts of the Holy Ghost and a title to those actual graces (*qq.v.*) which will enable the recipient, now spiritually regenerated, to live the Christian life worthily.

GRACE, EFFICACIOUS. That grace to which the will freely consents, so that the grace always produces its effect. As to its exact nature there is a famous dispute between Thomists and Molinists (see MOLINISM). It is an article of faith that this grace does not necessitate the will, although its result is inevitable.

GRACE, ELEVATING. That grace which gives the power of eliciting supernatural (*q.v.*) acts. This must itself be supernatural, otherwise it could not be the source of supernatural effects.

GRACE, HABITUAL. An absolutely supernatural (*q.v.*) quality, intrinsically and permanently inhering in the soul, by which we are made friends of God, adopted sons, coheirs with Christ, "partakers of the divine nature" (*q.v.*). It is a created and finite habit, not to be identified with the Holy Ghost indwelling in the souls of the just; fixed in the soul, it is no mere imputation of the merits of Christ, no mere "garment" (the Protestant error). When Scripture so speaks of it, this is merely to indicate that it has an external origin in the merits of Christ.

GRACE, ILLUMINATING. That actual grace (*q.v.*) by which God enlightens the minds of men to help them towards eternal life. It is necessary for the repairing of the injury of ignorance wrought by original sin (*q.v.*); also for the sake of the rousing of the will, according to the adage of the schools, *Nihil volitum nisi præcognitum* (Nothing is willed unless it is previously known). It may take the shape of some natural mental experience which God puts in one's way *e.g.*, a sermon; or it may be an immediate divine enlightenment, as in the case of Lydia (Acts xvi, 14) "whose heart the Lord opened to attend to those things which were said by Paul."

GRACE, IMPUTED. The heretical teaching of some of the Reformers regarding the nature of habitual grace (*q.v.*) which results from justification (*q.v.*). Having taught that justification was a mere judicial declaration of the non-imputability of sin, they went on to say that the merits of Christ were positively *imputed*, so that the sinner was *cloaked* in the grace of Christ.

GRACE, INTERIOR. Anything which is grace in the strict sense of the word, and which therefore affects the soul interiorly, as does habitual grace, for example. It is opposed to natural gifts of God, like divine *concursus* (*q.v.*), and to the exterior graces, *e.g.*, sermons, which merely dispose the soul for grace.

GRACE, IRRESISTIBLE. The supposedly irresistible efficacy of divine aid, by which, according to Calvinism, man, though free from any physical necessity, is forced to well-doing. Jansenism taught that, in his fallen state, man was moved irresistibly, though freely, by the greater of the two delectations to which he is subject, that of Heaven (grace) or that of earth (concupiscence). This is heresy. The Council of Trent declares: "If anyone shall say that the free will of man, moved and excited by God, does not co-operate by assenting to God's excitation and call, so as to dispose and prepare himself to obtain the grace of justification, and that he cannot refuse if he will, but like an inanimate object does absolutely nothing and merely remains passive, let him be anathema" (sess. vi, can. 4).

GRACE, NATURAL. A purely natural gift of God to which we have no claim. Our very existence and our various natural powers and perfections are graces in this sense. Pelagianism (q.v.), professing to accept the doctrine of grace, restricted it to this use.

GRACE, PREVENIENT. Actual grace enlightens the mind and fires the will with a view to the work of salvation. In this stirring of the will there are two moments: the first of these is a grace which moves the will spontaneously, unfreely, making it incline to God, and this is a "prevenient grace." The heavenly inspirations may be accepted freely or rejected freely by the aroused will. If they are accepted it is in virtue of a further grace (or the same grace under a different aspect) which is called "consequent" or "co-operating grace."

GRACE, SACRAMENTAL. The particular grace produced by each sacrament, e.g., regeneration by Baptism, increase of charity by the Eucharist. There is difference of opinion among theologians as to its nature, but it is commonly held to be habitual grace (q.v.) with special reference to the object of the sacrament, and a title to actual graces when the need of them arises for the more perfect fulfilment of the end of the sacrament.

GRACE, SANCTIFYING. Another name for habitual grace, which makes the soul holy.

GRACE, SUFFICIENT. The grace which for lack of co-operation by the receiver goes without the effect for which it was bestowed, and thus is opposed to efficacious grace (q.v.). It must not be imagined that there are graces which of their very nature are divorced from their effect.

GRACE, SUBSTANTIAL (otherwise, Uncreated Grace). The Holy Ghost dwelling personally in the souls of the just: "The love of God has been poured out in our hearts by the Holy Spirit, whom we have received" (Rom. v, 5); "Do you not understand that you are God's temple, and that God's Spirit has his dwelling in you?" (1 Cor. iii, 16).

GRACE, HIS, YOUR. The usual mode of address and reference to archbishops in some English-speaking countries.

GRACE AT MEALS (Lat. gratiæ, thanks). The asking of a blessing on the food before meals and making a thanksgiving therefor after seems to have been regarded as an obligation by Christians from the very earliest times and is mentioned in the New Testament, e.g., Acts xxvii, 35. In English-speaking countries the custom has not yet fallen into the desuetude of family prayers, but tends to become more and more a "private devotion." In seminaries, monasteries and elsewhere the forms provided in the Breviary are used, differing slightly for dinner and supper and at certain seasons of the year; in other places the short prayers for before and after dinner extracted from these longer forms are said. The Rule of St. Benedict (cap. xliii) prescribes penalties for those who are late for grace, which include the docking of their wine.

GRADINE (also called predella, retable, scabellum). The shelf, or one of several shelves, at the back of an altar, on which are put the cross, candlesticks, etc. An altar being by definition a table and not a sideboard, gradines are not in accordance with liturgical principles; they had their origin in the exuberance of neo-classical designers, and their use has become customary throughout the Western church and in several of the Eastern churches. In certain great churches (e.g., the major basilicas of Rome, Westminster and New York cathedrals, Downside abbey, Quarr abbey) and an increasing number of smaller ones the high altars at least are quite flat.

GRADO & AQUILEIA, PATRIARCHS OF. The honorary titles of the metropolitans of Grado and of Aquileia in the early middle ages, transferred in 1451 to the bishop of Venice, and in 1751 changed to Patriarch of Venice. They originated in a 6th century schism of the metropolitans of Illyricum who first resided at Aquileia. These were the first of the minor patriarchal (q.v.) titles of the West. See also UDINE.

GRADUAL (Lat. gradus, a step, of the ambo on which it was originally sung). Two verses from the psalms, other Holy Scripture or occasionally, from an ecclesiastical composition, sung after the epistle at Mass; joined to it is the alleluiatic verse (q.v.), and the whole is usually referred to as the gradual. The gradual proper represents the psalm which used to be sung after the first of the two lessons before the gospel, the alleluiatic verse that which was sung after the second lesson (cf., e.g., Mass of Wednesday in Holy Week). During paschal time, except Easter week, the gradual proper is dropped and instead are sung two verses preceded by "alleluia" twice and each followed by it once.

The alleluiatic verse is sometimes displaced by a tract (q.v.), and in five Masses the whole gradual is followed by a sequence (q.v.). The gradual has the most elaborate of all the chants of the Mass, being the only one sung independently of any action. For "The Gradual"—a book—see GRADUALE ROMANUM.

GRADUAL PSALMS, The. Fifteen psalms, namely, nos. cxix-cxxxiii, which in Hebrew bear a superscription which is variously rendered as "gradual canticle," "song of degrees," "song of ascents." In the Breviary they are arranged in three sets of five, with a collect for each set, of which the first is for the dead, and they were formerly of obligation on certain days in reciting the Divine Office; this has been abolished, but these psalms, all of which are expressive of trust in God, still have a certain eminence of honour. Their name has been variously explained, some scholars attributing it to their being sung on steps of the Temple, others to their use on pilgrimages up to Jerusalem, etc.

GRADUALE ROMANUM (Lat., The Roman Gradual). A liturgical book containing all the chants required for the Mass, both ordinary and proper, throughout the year, as used generally in the Western church. Various religious orders and dioceses have their own "Graduale."

GRAFFITO (It., plural graffiti). Drawing or writing scratched on a wall, etc. Scribbling on monuments is no new vulgarity and Christian graffiti of the far past are now of much value as evidence for archæologists and historians: e.g., those in the catacombs and those of Crusaders in the basilica of Bethlehem.

GRAIL. An obsolete English word for the gradual (q.v.).

"GRAIL, THE." A movement founded in Holland in 1921 by Father James van Ginneken, S.J. (d. 1945). Its motive power is an organization of lay women who devote their whole lives to the lay apostolate after a training of 3 years or more. Their work includes the training of girls to become "leaders" in Catholic life, a training that is cultural as well as apostolic. Other work is among non-Catholics, particularly in the foreign missions. The movement has spread from Holland to Germany, Great Britain, the United States, Australia and New Zealand. In these countries the means of training vary according to national needs, but the spirit is the same throughout.

GRAIL, THE HOLY (possibly from late Lat. gradalis, a dish). A mediæval term for a fabulous vessel which was supposed to be either the cup or dish of the Last Supper. The Grail legend was the centre of the Arthurian and other mediæval romances which, however, are susceptible of other origins. In the 12th century the Grail was associated with St. Joseph of Arimathea, who was said to have preserved therein water in which the dead body of Christ had been washed and brought it to England (Glastonbury) in the year 64. Among the relics of the cathedral of Valencia is the Holy Chalice, the bowl of which is carved from a single sardonyx; this is reputed to be the original cup, which another story finally deposits at Montserrat; St. Joseph is supposed also to have visited Spain (with St. James), but the Bollandists reject the story. Similarly at Genoa, in the treasury of the cathedral, is the Holy Dish, a sexagonal green glass vessel plundered from Cæsarea in 1101, and alleged to have been not only used at the Last Supper, but to have been given to Solomon by the Queen of Sheba. For reasons of workmanship neither relic can possibly be authentic.

GRAND PENITENTIARY, The. The president of the Roman tribunal called the Apostolic Penitentiaria (q.v.). He is a cardinal-priest and master in theology or doctor of canon law, and must either discharge his duties in person or through a substitute who must be a cardinal similarly qualified.

GRANDMONT, THE ORDER OF. An extinct French religious order, of Benedictine hermits, founded by St. Stephen of Muret about 1100 with its mother-house at Grandmont in Normandy. Its customs were very severe, but from 1224 were relaxed and the order deteriorated rapidly; a primitive observance branch was formed in the 17th century, but in 1787 it came to an end. Of the three English houses, Craswall in Herefordshire (fl., c. 1222-1464) is one of the loneliest and least known monastic ruins in England.

GRATITUDE is a moral virtue, annexed to justice, which disposes one to remembrance and appreciation of kindness received and prompting to return it in any suitable manner.

GRAVE. When a Catholic is to be buried in ground that has not been consecrated, the grave is blessed with a prayer, holy water, and incensation immediately before the coffin is lowered. If for some reason the priest cannot accompany the body to the grave, the custom is that he shall bless earth and put some into the coffin.

GREAT BIBLE, The. An English version of the Bible, edited by Miles Coverdale at the order of Thomas Cromwell, and published in 1539: so called on account of the size of the volume, but later editions were called Cranmer's Bible. It must not be confused with Coverdale's Bible, published four years earlier.

GREAT CHURCH, The. The official name of the Orthodox Church of Constantinople, with reference to the Hagia Sophia (q.v.). Though reduced to insignificance in size, weakened in authority and damaged in prestige, it still takes precedence of all Orthodox churches.

GREAT COUNCIL, The. The fourth council of the Lateran and the twelfth œcumenical council, 1215.

GREAT HABIT, The. The Angelic Habit (q.v.).

GREAT LAURA, The. The senior monastery of Mount Athos (q.v.); but the name sometimes refers to the monastery of Mar Saba, 10 miles south-east of Jerusalem, and one of the oldest inhabited monasteries in the world, founded by St. Sabas in 491. St. John Damascene, St. Theodore of Edessa and St. John the Silent were among its monks. The buildings, perched on the side of a cliff, were restored by the Russian government in 1840 and re-peopled with monks of the Orthodox Eastern Church, members of the Brotherhood of the Holy Sepulchre, but leading a strictly monastic life.

GREAT O'S, The. The Greater Antiphons (q.v.) to the Magnificat during the week preceding Christmas Eve. They begin respectively: O Sapientia (O Wisdom!), O Adonai et Dux domus Israel (O Day-Star and Leader of the House of Israel!), O Radix Jesse (O Root of Jesse!), O Clavis David (O Key of David!), O Oriens (O Light-bringer!), O Rex gentium (O King of Nations!), O Emmanuel (O God-with-us!). There were formerly other Great O's of which one, O Virgo virginum (O Maiden of maidens!), is the Magnificat antiphon at second Vespers of the feast of the Expectation of Our Lady's Child-bearing (q.v.). They are sung with special solemnity, being repeated in full both before and after the Magnificat, although the days are ferial; in churches of monks, canons, nuns, etc., the first on Dec. 17 is intoned by the superior, that of the next day by the sub-superior and so on. In some churches the first, O Sapientia, is sung between every two verses of the Magnificat, and the bells rung. Formerly Dec. 17, especially in monasteries, was marked by a special recreation in connexion with this antiphon, and in some monasteries this is still done.

GREAT RELICS, The. Three principal relics of the passion of Christ preserved in St. Peter's at Rome, namely, the point of the spear which pierced his side, the Veronica (q.v.) and a piece of the True Cross. They are kept in a balcony above the statue of St. Veronica beneath the dome, and are offered for public veneration only on Easter Sunday, the last four days in Holy Week and a few other fixed days each year, and also on certain extraordinary occasions, such as the closing of the Holy Door in the years of Jubilee.

GREAT SCHISM, The. A name given to the controversy regarding the succession to the papacy, 1378-1417, generally called the Schism of the West; it is less often given to the Schism of the East (qq.v.).

GREAT SILENCE, The. The silence observed in monasteries which follow the Rule of St. Benedict from after Compline until after Prime the next morning. It is imposed by cap. xlii of the rule, and may only be broken in case of urgent and grave necessity. It is also observed in other orders e.g., among the Poor Clares from Compline until the conventual Mass, and in a mitigated form by most modern congregations.

GREAT WEEK, The (Lat. Hebdomada Maior, literally, the Greater Week). The liturgical name for Holy Week (q.v.). Also called Hebdomada indulgentiæ, of reconciliation (of penitents), H. luctuosa (Sorrowful Week), H. muta (Silent Week; no bells or organ), H. nigra (Black Week), etc.

GREATER ANTIPHONS, The (Lat. Antiphonæ Maiores). The antiphons to the Magnificat at Vespers on the seven days preceding Christmas-eve, often called the "Great O's" (q.v.), because each begins with that interjection.

GREATER DOUBLE (Lat. Duplex maius). The rank of feast (q.v.) next above a double and below a double of the 2nd class.

GREATER LITANIES, The (Lat. Litaniæ Maiores or Romanæ). A procession, in which the litany of the Saints is sung, followed by a rogation Mass, now regarded as a prayer for the harvest; it is observed on April 25, St. Mark's day, but has nothing to do with that feast. The observance differs in no way from the Lesser Litanies (q.v.); it may be called major as being of greater age than the others, and is called Roman to distinguish it from those others which originated in Gaul. It was instituted to supplant a heathen festival, the Robigalia, on the same date.

GREATER MONASTERIES. Those in England having an annual income of more than £200, suppressed by King Henry VIII in 1538-40.

GRECA (It., Greek). The black clerical overcoat (douillette) is so called in Rome, as having some fancied resemblance to the Byzantine rason (q.v.).

GREECE, THE CHURCH IN. The population of Greece (Hellas) is about 7 million. The Orthodox Church is the established Church of the Greek people (see GREEK CHURCH i), and activities opposed to it are forbidden; but other recognized faiths are tolerated by law. There are some 50,000 Catholics, mostly in the islands and of remote foreign origin, some of their sees going back to the Crusades. They have a somewhat confused ecclesiastical organization;

the principal see is Athens, an archbishopric without suffragans; other important sees are Corfu and Naxos, with 4 other dioceses and a vicariate apostolic. The faithful have been completely hellenized for centuries. There is a handful of "pure" Greek Catholics of the Byzantine rite, who are the object of much suspicion and dislike to the state church authorities; they are under an episcopal exarch at Athens. There are also some Catholics of Armenian rite, with an ordinary.

GREEK. Up till the middle of the 3rd century the services of the Roman church were in the Greek tongue, not classical Greek but ἡ κοινή γλῶσσα, the common language, practically the Greek of the New Testament. A minute relic of this may possibly be found in the use of the words *Kyrie, Christe, eleison* (*q.v.*); the brief dialogue beginning *Agios o Theos* on Good Friday was probably introduced through the influence of Greek colonists at Rome in the 7th-9th centuries. The language is still given a certain pre-eminence after Latin at Rome; at solemn papal Masses the epistle and gospel are sung in both languages. Old Greek is the original language of the Byzantine rite and is used by the Italo-Greeks and some other Catholic Byzantines. Among the dissident Orthodox it is used by the churches of Constantinople, Greece, Cyprus and Sinai, and to a certain extent in Palestine, Egypt and the U.S.A. All the Eastern rites except the Chaldean have a number of Greek words and phrases imbedded in them, the Coptic the most.

GREEK CATHOLICS. A name commonly used by and of the Ruthenians, Rumanians, Melkites, Italo-Greeks, and other Catholics of the Byzantine rite (*qq.v.*). The usage is convenient as distinguishing them from Catholics of the Latin rite (they in this sense say they are not "Roman" Catholics, but is to be discouraged in so far as it suggests a separation from the centre of unity at Rome; moreover, the name is inaccurate, for few of them are Greek by race or use that tongue liturgically. The name then should be confined to the small body of Catholics in Turkey and Greece who use the Byzantine rite in Greek. Such terms as the "United Greek Church" cannot be too strongly reprobated; there is no such thing, and their use results in such absurdities as "Greek Ruthenian Roman Catholics." It should be noted that the dissident Orthodox, even the Greek-using ones, never call themselves Greek Catholics.

GREEK CHURCH, The. i. The fourth largest and one of the most important of the autocephalous units making up the Orthodox Eastern Church; it separated itself from the patriarchal jurisdiction of Constantinople in 1833. It is the Church of the Greek people, and its chief hierarch is the Archbishop of Athens and All Greece. Of recent years a fine spiritual movement called *Zoe* (Life) has made progress among them. The Greeks are prone to be rather bitterly hostile to Catholicity, in part due to their harrowing experiences of "Frankish" aggression, whether in the 13th century (Fourth Crusade) or the 20th (Italy, Germany).

ii. The above is the only body that ever describes itself, or can be correctly described as, the Greek Church; but the term is often extended to the patriarchate of Constantinople, with the churches of Greece and Cyprus; historically also to the patriarchates of Alexandria, Antioch and Jerusalem; and even to the whole Orthodox Eastern Church, for which there is no sort of justification at all.

GREEK FATHERS, The. Those Fathers of the Church (*q.v.*, ii) who belonged to the Eastern church and wrote and taught in the Greek tongue. The principal are Athanasius (*d.* 373), Basil (379), Cyril of Jerusalem (387) Gregory Nazianzen (390), Gregory of Nyssa (*c.* 395), John Chrysostom (407), Cyril of Alexandria (444), and John Damascene (749).

GREEK RITE. A term frequently and incorrectly used to designate what is in fact the Byzantine rite (*q.v.*). There is no Greek rite analogous to the Latin rite (*q.v.*); the Byzantine rite is properly used in many languages, of which Greek happens to be the original—as it was of the now Latin rite of Rome.

GREEN. The liturgical colour of vestments used on Sundays (unless the office of a feast is said) and ferias from the octave of the Epiphany until Septuagesima and from the octave of Corpus Christi until Advent.

GREGORIAN ARMENIAN CHURCH, The. The church of Armenia as founded by St. Gregory the Illuminator. The epithet is used only of the separated Armenians to distinguish them from the Catholics—though both bodies derive from Gregory.

GREGORIAN CHANT. A name distinguishing that species of ecclesiastical plainchant (*q.v.*) normally used by the Western church from the Ambrosian, Mozarabic and other species of plainchant. Gregorian chant has sub-species or varieties, such as those in use with the Carthusians and Dominicans, and is found in varying editions, *e.g.*, Ratisbon, Vatican, of which the last must be regarded as the authentic one.

GREGORIAN MASS. One celebrated at a Gregorian altar (*q.v.*).

GREGORIAN SACRAMENTARY, The. A sacramentary (*q.v.*) of the 8th century (791) amplified from one arranged by Pope St. Gregory I, sent by Pope Adrian I to Charlemagne as an example of the Roman usages. It contains the ordinary and propers of the Mass and the rite of ordination, and has undergone local modification and addition, *e.g.*, the supplement of Alcuin; no unsupplemented example now exists.

GREGORIAN UNIVERSITY, THE PONTIFICAL, or Roman College, one of the autonomies of the central pontifical university for ecclesiastical higher studies. It was founded by St. Ignatius Loyola and St. Francis Borgia and constituted by Pope Julius III in 1552, confirmed and established by Pope Gregory XIII in 1582. It has faculties of theology, canon law, philosophy, church history and missionary work, and normally numbers a couple of thousand students. The college is directed by Jesuit fathers, and is to be distinguished from the Roman Seminary.

GREGORIAN WATER. Water with which is mixed ashes, salt and wine. In accordance with a prescription of Pope St. Gregory I it is blessed by the bishop at the consecration of a church (*q.v.*), and is used for sprinkling the altar, walls, etc.; it is also used at the reconciliation (*q.v.*) of a consecrated church.

GREGORY DIALOGOS, THE LITURGY OF ST. The name by which the Liturgy of the Presanctified (*q.v.*) of the Byzantine rite is known, it being supposed without any evidence that it was drawn up by him who wrote The Dialogues, *i.e.*, Pope St. Gregory the Great. It is by confusion with Gregory Nazianzen, but neither did he compile the liturgy.

GREMIAL-VEIL (Lat. *gremium*, lap). A rectangular veil laid over the knees of the bishop when seated during the singing of the *Kyrie, Gloria* and *Credo* at pontifical Mass, and during the distribution of ashes, candles or palms and the anointings at confirmation, ordination, etc. At Mass it is of the same material and colour as the vestments, on other occasions of white linen. Its object is to keep the vestments clean and free from drops of oil, ashes, etc. This lap-cloth was formerly used by all the ministers at high Mass, and is still by the Dominicans (*mappula*) and by the celebrant only among the Carthusians and Calced Carmelites.

GREY FRIARS. The name formerly given in England to the Franciscan friars minor on account of the grey or indeterminate colour of their mediæval habit. A Franciscan bishop still wears a grey *mantelletta*.

GRILLE. i. The metal or wooden grating prescribed by canon law to be between the priest and the penitent making confession: it is the essential part of a confessional box.
ii. The wooden or metal grating in the parlour of every convent of strictly enclosed nuns at which visitors may be interviewed. It varies in size from an aperture in a wall a few feet square to a large screen dividing a room into two parts. In some orders (*e.g.*, the Carmelite) it is covered by a shutter, and in some by a thin opaque veil, except when a nun is talking to a parent, brother or sister; in others (*e.g.*, the Benedictine) it is never so veiled. There is also a large latticed screen dividing the nuns' choir from the altar of the chapel, with an aperture at which holy communion is given.

GROTTAFERRATA. The only Eastern monastery that has remained in unbroken communion with the Western church from ancient times. It was founded in Calabria before 980, and since 1004 has been at Grottaferrata, near Rome. The monks are Italo-Greeks of the Byzantine rite; their particular work is learned studies, and they print liturgical books of various Eastern rites. The monastery was made an abbey *nullius* (*q.v.*) in 1937.

GROTTO OF THE NATIVITY, The. The place of our Lord's birth at Bethlehem. It is one of a series of caves, now made subterranean by the superimposition of the basilica built by the Emperor Justinian. At its altar only Orthodox and Gregorian Armenian priests are allowed to minister; Catholics have an altar of the Manger, six paces away. The authenticity of this holy place has never been seriously disputed.

GUARDIAN. i. One having the custody of the person or property or both of an infant, lunatic, etc. A cleric is no longer forbidden to act as guardian.
ii. The superior of a Franciscan friary. He is elected for three years.

GUARDIAN ANGEL. An angel appointed by God to watch over every soul born into the world. This is the general teaching of theologians, and is in accordance with many events narrated in the Bible (*cf.*, Matt. xviii, 10), but it has not been defined by the Church and so is not of faith. The functions of the guardian angel are to lead the individual to Heaven by defending him from evil, helping him in prayer, suggesting good thoughts, etc.; the angel acts upon the senses, and the imagination, but not directly upon the will—the co-operation of the human being is required. The approval of the Church of devotion to our guardian angels was expressed by Pope Clement X when the local feast in their honour was extended to the whole of the Western church and fixed on Oct. 2.

GUATEMALA, THE CHURCH IN. Population 3¼ million, mostly at least nominal Catholics. Since 1879 religious orders are illegal, but sisters are tolerated in hospitals and other institutions. State schools are all secular. The country forms the province of Santiago de Guatemala (see founded in 1534) with 2 suffragan dioceses.

GUEST-MASTER. An obedientiary (*q.v.*) of a monastery who must be "a brother whose soul is possessed with the fear of God" (Rule of St. Benedict, cap. liii).

GUILD. See GILD.

GUILT. In a general sense guilt is the measure in which one is responsible for a sinful act. In theological language the primary consequences of sin are its guilt and its stain. The guilt of mortal sin lies in the complete aversion of the soul from God, its stain in the accompanying loss of sanctifying grace. The guilt of venial sin is diminution of the soul's splendour in God's sight; it has no stain.

GUIANA, THE CHURCH IN. The combined population of the 3 Guianas is about 550,000, of whom a fifth are Catholics. The people are very mixed, and include a large proportion of Asiatic labourers and descendants of escaped Negro slaves, as well as a number of convicts. British, French and Dutch Guiana each forms a separate vicariate apostolic, the mission at Cayenne going back to 1643.

GUNPOWDER PLOT, THE. A plot to kill King James I and the Prince of Wales by blowing up the House at the meeting of Parliament on Nov. 5, 1605. Eight principal Catholic gentlemen, who had been disappointed at the failure of the king to lighten the penal burden of Catholics, were concerned; of whom Robert Catesby was the chief and Guy Fawkes the best known. Owing to the efforts of Francis Tresham and Lord Mounteagle to stop the plot and secure the escape of the conspirators it was discovered, and those concerned (13 in all) either killed in flight or executed. It is frequently asserted that certain Jesuits, particularly Fr. Henry Garnet, were privy to this plot. It is maintained that Garnet had no knowledge of it outside confession, except in vague general terms of "some attempt for the relief of the Catholic cause," and the case for his complicity has not been substantiated; he was nevertheless executed. The laws against recusancy were made more severe by 3 James I c. 4 and carried out more strictly; and until 1859 the Book of Common Prayer contained a service of thanksgiving for the king's escape.

GYNÆCEUM (Gk., γυνή, woman). The part of a Byzantine or other Eastern church sometimes set apart for the accommodation of women; e.g., latticed gallery at the west end of the nave, extending round the aisles, reached by a separate door from the narthex or from outside, or it may be an aisle or other part of the church partitioned off. The traditional Christian custom of separating men and women during public worship is, on the whole, still observed in all Eastern rites, Catholic and dissident; but among many orientals in Europe and America this discipline is relaxed. It is still occasionally observed in churches of the Latin rite.

H

HABACUC (Heb., Embrace). A prophetical book of the Old Testament, consisting of a colloquy between the prophet and God on the wickedness of the people and their coming punishment at the hands of the Chaldeans, ending with a hymn of praise and trust in God. Habacuc is named in the Roman Martyrology on Jan. 15.

HABIT (Lat. habitus, from habere, to have). i. An acquired discipline or modification of the soul, made constant and fixed by use. A habit once acquired becomes itself the principle of activity so that acts are produced readily, easily and with pleasure; once acquired it is with difficulty lost and in this it is opposed to disposition (q.v.), which is easily lost. Habits, both good and bad, are therefore usually acquired by repetition of the same acts; they are eventually lost by cessation of those acts.

ii. The clothes or uniform proper to a religious order. A distinctive habit appertains to all orders and congregations of nuns, to all monks and friars, and to some of the more recent congregations of men; the Jesuits are a notable exception. Generally speaking the tunic, belt or girdle, hood and scapular (qq.v.) are common to all men's habits, with a large cloak for use in choir or out-of-doors; sandals are exceptional. Most habits in colour are variations in black, brown and white, but a few are more bright, e.g., the Sylvestrine Benedictines (blue), Redemptorist nuns (blue and red). In certain countries the wearing of the religious habit by men outside their monasteries has gone out of use; this is notably the case in Great Britain and the United States, though there are now no longer any provisions of the civil law to prevent it; certain monasteries in England have rectified this. Monks and friars who become bishops are still bound to their proper habit, and their prelatical dress is black or white instead of purple. The habit of secular tertiaries (q.v.) is a true religious habit but it may not be worn in public except in rare circumstances by permission of the bishop and the order concerned. The assuming of the habit is the outward and visible sign of the undertaking of the religious life, hence the term "clothing" (q.v.).

HACELDAMA (Aramaic, the field of blood). The potter's field, bought to be a burying-place for strangers with the price of Judas's treachery (Matt. xxvii, 3-8), being the same wherein he had hanged himself (Acts i, 18-19). It is situated at the east end of the Wadi ar-Rababi (Valley of Hinnom) on the south side of Jerusalem, and is a desolate place used for the burial of pilgrims almost to our own day.

HAGGAI. The Hebrew form of the name of the minor prophet Aggeus.

HAGIA (Gr., holy things). The rubrical name in the Byzantine rite for the sacred Elements after consecration.

HAGIA SOPHIA, The. The church of the Holy Wisdom at Constantinople (Gr. ἡ ʻΑγία Σοφία; often barbarously and misleadingly called Saint Sophia). Architecturally one of the greatest and most important churches in Christendom, and for long second only to St. John Lateran and St. Peter's in ecclesiastical importance. Built under the Emperor Justinian in 532-7; the cathedral of the patriarch of Constantinople; after the capture of the city by the Turks in 1453 turned into a mosque, and since 1934 a museum.

HAGIOGRAPHY (Gr. ἅγιος, holy). Writing of and research into the lives of the saints. The Hagiographic Books are those of the Hebrew Scriptures not included under law or prophets.

HAGIOLOGY. Books and other records treating of the lives and legends of saints and holy people. Owing to popular imagination, the excessive credulity of some writers and the inadequate critical equipment of others, this word is sometimes used in a contemptuous sense.

HAGULSTADENSIS ET NOVOCASTREN-SIS. The adjectival form of the name of the see of Hexham and Newcastle (q.v.) used in the designation of its bishop in Latin documents. Nouns: *Axelodunum, Novum Castrum.*

HAIL MARY, The, also known as the Angelical Salutation and *Ave Maria,* the most familiar of all prayers addressed to the Blessed Virgin. It consists of three parts, of which (a) and (b) are scriptural (Luke i, 28, 42) and (c) added by the Church: (a) "Hail, Mary, full of grace, the Lord is with thee, blessed art thou amongst women (b) and blessed is the fruit of thy womb, Jesus. (c) Holy Mary, mother of God, pray for us sinners now and at the hour of our death. Amen." (a) and (b) were first used as a formula of devotion during the 12th century and various petitions were added at will; the present form was fixed in 1568. The form used at the beginning and end of each hour of the Little Office B.V.M. in the Dominican rite consists of only (a) and (b) and this salutation still survives elsewhere here and there, e.g., in the Bridgettine office. It is used in numerous popular devotions but never in the liturgy, wherein all prayers are addressed to Almighty God. But the first two, scriptural, parts are sung in certain Masses and as an antiphon in offices of our Lady. The full Hail Mary is unknown in the Eastern churches except among Catholics (in various forms) and the dissident Jacobites in Malabar; but the Ethiopians say it just before the gospel of the Liturgy, with the final clause "Pray and intercede for us with thy beloved Son that he forgive our sins." The Hail Mary occurs in many forms of devotion, often frequently repeated.

HAIR. In the West the clerical state has always been distinguished by a shaving of part of the head in some form or other (tonsure [q.v.]). In the East, the opposite is the custom, the hair is let to grow long, but among the Orthodox in Europe and America the clergy have begun to cut their hair and even shave their faces; these hitherto were signs of canonical degradation or suspension. Nuns in both East and West keep their heads cropped.

HAIR-SHIRT. A garment woven of goat's or other hair worn next the skin as a mortification. It varies in shape and size from a chest-protector or a girdle to a waistcoat and is of common use among religious of both sexes; nor is its use confined to them. For Carthusians and Discalced Carmelites it is prescribed by rule.

HAITI, THE CHURCH IN. Population about 3 million, 95 per cent poor peasants, mostly Catholics but many nominal; the Negro element is predominant among the people. There is said to be only 1 priest to every 17,000 souls. By the concordat of 1860 with the Holy See the Church is specially protected by the state, which pays a small salary to the clergy. Bishops are named by the government, but may be refused by the Holy See. Haiti forms a metropolitan province, with 4 suffragan dioceses. The first offering of Mass in the New World is said to have been at Point Conception in Haiti (Hispaniola) on December 8, 1493 by Father Juan Perez, friar minor, on the second arrival of Columbus there.

HALF-HOLY DAYS. Feasts on which the faithful were bound to assist at Mass but not to abstain from servile work. They now exist in only a few dioceses, e.g., of Utrecht, where the Presentation, Birthday and Immaculate Conception B.V.M. are so observed.

HALO (Gr. ἅλως, disk of the sun) or *nimbus.* In representations of sacred persons, a circle or solid disk surrounding the head. It is a pre-Christian device to indicate majesty or power and is now symbolical of virtue and grace. A halo with a cross on it is usually reserved for Jesus Christ and the Lamb of God, but may be used for God the Father or the Holy Ghost; emblems are sometimes added to the halo, *e.g.*, a star for St. Dominic. It is prohibited to represent with the halo anyone who has not been beatified or whose *cultus* has not been recognized by the Church in some other way.

HANC IGITUR. The first words of the prayer following the *Communicantes* in the canon of the Mass, asking God to accept our oblation and to dispose our days and end in peace. As he says it, the celebrant spreads his hands over the bread and wine to which he refers to show that Christ sacrifices himself for us by taking upon himself the burden of our sins. This gesture, which emphasizes the sacrificial character of the Mass, was not introduced till the 15th century; Carmelites, Carthusians and Dominicans make an inclination instead, according to previous custom. The *Hanc igitur* is varied slightly on Maundy Thursday, Holy Saturday, Easter and Pentecost, with their octaves, and at the consecration of a bishop.

HANDMAIDS OF MARY. A congregation of Ruthenian (*q.v.*) sisters, founded in 1892 by the archimandrite Jeremiah Lomnitsky, for teaching, nursing, care of orphans, etc. They were formerly the most numerous women religious of Byzantine rite, but presumably they are now dispersed in Galicia; they are, however, established in Canada and Brazil among the immigrant Ukrainians.

HAPPINESS. A bringing of the soul to act according to the habit of the best and most perfect virtue, that is, the virtue of the speculative intellect, borne out by easy surroundings, and enduring to length of days (Aristotle). This perfect happiness cannot be attained in this life; the definition represents an ideal to be approximated to, not attained. Yet man desires perfect happiness: this desire is natural, springing from the rational soul: on earth man may attain to contentment, and to some happiness, but not to perfect happiness: consequently nature has planted in man a desire for which on earth she has provided no adequate satisfaction. Now "nature does nothing in vain." What is it that man desires above all finite being? It is God. Man's ultimate happiness is to see God. But no created intelligence by its own natural perception can attain to see God as he is. By an act of gratuitous condescension God has invited man to this beatific vision—revelation informs us of this. Happiness in this life consists in so acting as to acquire the habit of lifting the mind to God in whose vision and possession the perfect happiness hereafter consists.

HAPPINESS, CELESTIAL, is the last end of man and consists in the sight and possession of God in the Beatific Vision (*q.v.*) in which his very being will be one with our intelligence in the order of knowledge, with a consequent and corresponding love and delight in the will. See HEAVEN.

HARKIRKE, The (Old Eng. *hár*, old; *circe*, church). A penal times (*q.v.*) burying-ground for Catholics provided by William Blundell on his estate at Crosby Hall, near Blundellsands, for the which charity he was fined £2,000. Twenty-seven priests and many laypeople rest therin.

HARROWING OF HELL, The. The ancient English popular term for the descent of our Lord into Limbo (*q.v.*). It was a popular subject in the mediæval mystery-plays and the earliest known English play of the kind bears this name, though it actually deals with the apocryphal visit of our Lord to the Hell of the Lost.

HAT. i. Ecclesiastical. In countries where the decencies of ecclesiastical dress are strictly regarded, the rite, if not the obedience, of a cleric is indicated by the sort of hat he affects out-of-doors. Some form of the broad-brimmed low-crowned hat of beaver or felt, with halyards according to rank, should be, but is not, a characteristic of Catholic priests of the Latin rite; but nobody but a Byzantine or Syrian wears the *kamelaukion* (*q.v.*), an Armenian the round black pointed cap (with a veil, if celibate), a Copt his Egyptian-looking black cylinder, a Chaldean or Maronite his respective sort of turban. *Cf.*, Heraldry.

ii. In church. In accordance with 1 Cor. xi it is the Christian custom that laymen should be uncovered in church and women covered. In the West as regards men and the East as regards women this is carefully observed; but in some Eastern countries (*e.g.*, Egypt) the *tarbush* or *kufiyeh* is kept on by men and in some parts of Catholic countries of the West women often do not cover the head, especially out of service time. The lace veil or *mantilla* is alike the most becoming and most convenient head-covering for women in church and is of obligation at papal audiences.

HATRED. Strong dislike or ill-will towards anyone. Hatred of enmity is directed towards the person himself, hatred of abomination towards his qualities. Hatred of God of either kind and hatred of enmity towards our neighbour are mortal sins; hatred of abomination of our neighbour's wickedness or evil qualities is not necessarily sinful. That involuntary state which is ordinarily signified by the declaration "I don't know why, but I can't stand so-and-so," arises from incompatibility of character and disposition and not from ill-will and may be blamelessly indulged to the extent of avoiding the person's company in order to prevent friction; but if ill-will enters either into the feeling or consequent action a state of enmity is involved, which is sinful to the extent of the ill-will.

HEAR MASS, TO. A common expression meaning to be present at Mass for the purpose of worship, and in particular in order to fulfil the Sunday obligation. Its use is often condemned on the ground that it suggests that the part of the people is merely to be present and attend passively; "to assist at Mass" is the better phrase. The obligation of hearing Mass on Sundays and holy days binds all Catholics over seven years of age. The obligation is satisfied by hearing Mass in any church or public or semi-public oratory, or in the open air, and according to any Catholic rite, Latin or oriental. Hearing Mass in private oratories does not satisfy the precept without a papal indult, with the exception of private cemetery chapels. Bodily presence is necessary in the place where Mass is celebrated, or in its immediate precincts. Mass must be heard with attention and devotion, but any form of prayer satisfies the obligation.

HEARSE (Fr. *herse*, a harrow). i. A wooden framework supporting the pall (or hearsecloth) over a coffin in church and supplied with spikes for candles (whence the name). It was formerly in common use but is now only sometimes seen at the funerals of distinguished people; the name has been transferred to the 4-wheeled vehicle in which a coffin is carried.

ii. The triangular frame bearing the *Tenebræ* (*q.v.*) candles is still called a hearse; one candle is fixed at the apex and seven on either of the adjacent sides.

HEART OF MARY, THE IMMACULATE.
i. Devotion to her heart is a special form of devotion to our Lady. Her physical heart is venerated because united to her person, and as the seat of her love (especially of her divine Son), virtues and inner life; such devotion is an incentive to a like love and virtue. The devotion is analogous to that to the Sacred Heart of Jesus (*q.v.*) and was first considerably fostered by St. John Eudes in the 17th century.

ii. A feast of the Most Pure Heart of Mary was first granted in 1799; it was later observed in many places on various dates. Finally, a new feast, called "of the Immaculate Heart of Mary," was added to the Western calendar for August 22 by Pope Pius XII.

HEARTH-PENNY. An old name for Peter's Pence (*q.v.*).

HEATHEN, The, are those who profess any religion other than Christianity (Catholic or non-Catholic), Judaism or Islam. The Jews and Mohammedans worship the One God and, though infidels, must on no account be classed as heathen. The word is synonymous with "pagan," but it is good usage to reserve the latter word for the heathen of classical antiquity. Etymologically it is of Old English derivation, meaning "dweller on the heath," apparently a loose rendering of *paganus*, through a misunderstanding of its

derivation—a misunderstanding that persisted till our own day. See PAGAN.

HEAVEN. The place and state of perfect and eternal happiness. It consists primarily in the sight of God face to face, termed the Beatific Vision (*q.v.*): this sight involves the spiritual possession of him and the love of him to the utmost of the creature's power. Other joys will be the sight of Christ's humanity, companionship with our Lord, angels and the saints, and the understanding of the wonders of creation. After the Last Judgement the risen body (*q.v.*) will share in the joys of the soul. The bliss of Heaven is not equal in degree for all but differs according to their merits. God will indeed be seen without intermediary by all but, being infinite, he can be seen, though directly, yet with differing intensity by different spectators. The blessed recognize one another and love one another in God. In Heaven the will of man is fixed on its ultimate end and hence can fail no longer and the bliss of Heaven can never end.

HEBDOMADARY, ARIAN (Gr. ἐβδομάς, a week). In a church of monks, canons or others bound to recite the Divine Office in choir, the priest or religious appointed in turn for a period of one week to sing the daily conventual or chapter Mass, to begin all the hours of the Divine Office, sing their collects, give the necessary blessings, etc.

HEBREW BIBLE, The, of the Jews consists of the entire Old Testament with the exception of the deutero-canonical books. It is divided into the Law, *Torah* (Genesis, Exodus, Leviticus, Numbers, Deuteronomy); the Prophets (*Nebiim*), including the historical books; and the Writings, or *Hagiographa* (*Kethubim*).

HEBREWS, THE EPISTLE TO THE. A letter addressed by St. Paul to Christian Jews, probably those of Jerusalem, and a canonical book of holy Scripture. In it he exalts and explains the priesthood of Jesus Christ and supersession of the old covenant by the new, and fortifies them against backsliding into Judaism. The Pontifical Biblical Commission allows the opinion that, though the matter is due to St. Paul, it has been cast into its present form by another.

HEDGE-PRIEST. An archaic expression for an illiterate and unbeneficed priest of a low status who wandered about the country.

HEDGE-SCHOOL. The name given to the informal schools conducted by Catholics throughout Ireland during the 18th century and early part of the 19th. They were carried on in roadside cabins or literally under hedges and in ditches, in the Gaelic tongue, and Latin, English, reading, writing and figuring were taught to all and sundry; the general fee was 3s. 3d. (Irish) a quarter. There were similar schools for adults. These schools were illegal and the masters proscribed; by 1731 over 550 of them had been suppressed, but they continually sprang up again in opposition to the state-aided proselytizing institutions called Charter schools.

HEDONISM (Gr. ἡδονή, pleasure). A false ethical theory which contends that pleasure is the last end of man (cf., Eudemonism).

HEGUMENOS (Gr. ἡγούμενος, leader). The common name for the head of a monastery of Eastern (Basilian) monks, equivalent to abbot. He is elected by the monks, and appointed, blessed and installed by the bishop or patriarch. He has, subject to the canons and the rule of each house, complete control over the monastery and its dependencies, and is usually assisted by a council of seniors. He rules for life unless deposed for misbehaviour. Even if his monastery is exempt from episcopal jurisdiction he has no rights corresponding to those of a Western mitred abbot. See ARCHIMANDRITE.

HELL is the place and state of eternal punishment (q.v.) which consists, primarily, in the deprivation of the enjoyment and sight of God face to face (pain of loss) and, secondarily, the infliction of positive punishment by an external objective agent, called fire (q.v.), which is a physical reality though unlike earthly fire (pain of sense). This punishment is not equal for all, but corresponds to the sinner's aversion from God and conversion to creatures. Only those are punished in Hell who depart this life with personal, grave, deliberate and unrepented sin. The number of lost is unknown and the loss of no individual person has been revealed. After the Last Judgement the bodies of the lost will share in the punishment of their souls. It is of faith that their punishment will never end.

HELLENISM. A term used particularly of Greek philosophy and literature, and of their considerable influence upon Western civilization. Hellas and Hellene are the classical names for Greece and a Greek (their use was revived in that country in the 19th century).

HELPERS OF THE HOLY SOULS, The. An institute of women founded in 1856 by Eugenie de Smet, helped by St. John Baptist Vianney, to pray, suffer and work for the benefit of the souls detained in Purgatory. They are unenclosed, visit the sick and poor and abandoned, conduct orphanages, etc., and work on foreign missions. Their dress is that of a French *bourgeoise* of 1850; black dress, cape and cap, with cloak and veil outdoors.

HELP OF CHRISTIANS (Lat. *Auxilium Christianorum*). A title of our Lady added to the litany of Loreto by Pope St. Pius V after the battle of Lepanto. A feast of our Lady under this invocation for May 24 was instituted by Pope St. Pius VII at the end of

his captivity by Napoleon I and is observed in many places, including the dioceses of Shrewsbury and Menevia of which our Lady is patron under this name.

HENOTIKON, The (Gr., unification). i. A document drawn up by Acacius of Constantinople and published by the Emperor Zeno in 482 with the object of settling the controversy between Catholics and the monophysites. It did not satisfy the latter, was condemned by the Holy See, and led to the Acacian Schism (q.v.).
   ii. An edict in 571 of the Emperor Justin II which finally closed the controversy of the Three Chapters (q.v.).

HEORTOLOGY (Gr. ἑορτή, festival; λόγος, knowledge). The science and study of the origins, history and meaning of ecclesiastical feasts and celebrations.

HEPTATEUCH, The (analogous form to Pentateuch). The first seven books of the Bible: Genesis, Exodus, Leviticus, Numbers, Deuteronomy, Josue, Judges.

HERALDRY, or armory, is the science of the devices whose primary use was to be displayed as distinguishing marks on the banners, shields, surcoats, etc., of fighting men. As such it would appear to have no ecclesiastical aspect or interest; but in fact the extension of the application of armorial bearings to such pacific objects as seals, and the status of higher ecclesiastics in the European feudal system of the middle ages, caused a definite ecclesiastical heraldry to emerge. Though a mediæval spiritual lord was, in theory, not a man-at-arms, the heralds did not assign to him anything instead of the military shield, corresponding to the woman's lozenge: nevertheless an oval cartouche for clerics has been in very general use in Italy, France and Spain. The use of coats-of-arms by bishops and others is provided for by the Western church, but it is a meaningless archaism and ecclesiastical heraldry (like all heraldry, debased already by the Renaissance) is thoroughly degenerate; in the U.S.A. it is an absurdity. The Heralds' College of London refuses to recognize the arms of Catholic sees in England (as distinct from the personal arms of their bishops) for technical reasons; those of the archdiocese of Westminster were granted by a papal brief. In place of crests and as a badge the arms of ecclesiastics are surmounted by a mitre (if a bishop or abbot) or by a flat hat, red with 15 tassels a side if a cardinal, for a patriarch, archbishop or bishop, green, with 15, 10 or 6 tassels respectively, and black with 6 tassels for generals of orders, 3 for provincials and abbots, and 2 or 1 for simple priests. The use of these tassels (*houppes*) is not uniform. The Armenians are the only non-Catholic Eastern ecclesiastics who use heraldic devices (cf., Coat-of-arms).

HEREDITY. A name given to the system which explains man as a moral being and as a physical being by qualities transmitted from parentage. It cannot however be maintained that intellectual and moral qualities can be transmitted to descendants by blood. The Law of Heredity is "A law in virtue of which ascendants transmit certain physical qualities, and speaking of man, certain intellectual and moral qualities to descendants." This "law" is applied to all living beings. To explain by heredity all the qualities of man not excepting virtues and vices is to deny man's free will and even the spiritual nature of the soul.

HEREFORD, THE USE OF. The version of the Roman liturgy in use in the diocese of Hereford during the middle ages. It resembled that of Sarum (*q.v.*).

HERESIARCH. An originator or founder of a heresy, *e.g.*, Arius, Eutyches, Luther.

HERESY (Gr. αἵρεσις, choice, sect; in its origin the word had no bad connotation). As a sin heresy consists in the formal denial or doubt by a baptized person of any revealed truth of the Catholic faith; as a crime it consists in the outward and pertinacious manifestation of the sin. Heresy differs from apostasy and schism (*qq.v.*). Anyone guilty of the crime of heresy incurs excommunication *ipso facto*, specially reserved to the Holy See in the internal forum (*q.v.*); in the external forum the local ordinary can absolve under conditions specified in law, and then any approved confessor can absolve the sin. The sin of heresy is not reserved by common law apart from the crime, but the commission of the crime involves the reservation of the sin because of the censure. Heresy which is not formal, that is, material heresy (*q.v.*), is neither a sin nor a crime, but material heretics are subject to certain disabilities in canon law, *e.g.*, exclusion from the sacraments, from ecclesiastical burial, church patronage, sponsorship, benefices, etc. *Cf.*, Heretic.

HERESY, MATERIAL. Heresy which is the outcome of ignorance and accompanied by no obstinacy of the will, *e.g.*, the heresy of a Protestant who has never suspected that his own is not the true religion (*q.v.*). It is without guilt so long as there is no doubt in the heretic's mind regarding his false position. It is opposed to *formal heresy*, which is the deliberate denial or doubt of a revealed truth.

HERETIC. One who, having been baptized and professing Christianity, pertinaciously rejects or doubts any article of faith determined by the authority of the Catholic Church. An unbaptized person or one who repudiates Christianity is therefore not a heretic, nor in this strict sense are most Protestants and other non-Catholic Christians, for, never having professed certain truths of the Faith, they cannot reject or doubt them. In so far as they maintain material heresy (*q.v.*) they are material heretics but incur no guilt thereby. It can hardly be doubted that the vast majority of non-Catholic Christians are in good faith and labouring under invincible ignorance (*q.v.*).* It is amusing to note, in this age when many people boast that they are heretics and resent any stigma of orthodoxy, that the Church refuses them both the name and the odium attaching to it (*cf.*, Apostasy, Heresy, Schism, Schismatic).

HERETICAL (Lat. *hæretica*). A proposition condemned as heretical is thereby convicted of being directly opposed to a truth revealed by God.

HERMENEUTICS (Gr. ἑρμηνεύω, interpret). The principles which govern the right interpretation of the Sacred Scriptures and associated, therefore, with the science of exegesis (*q.v.*).

HERMESIANISM. The theological errors of the Rev. George Hermes (1775-1831), the principal of which concerned the relation of reason to faith. His views were condemned by the Holy See in 1835, again in 1847, and again at the Vatican council, sess. iii, c. 5, 6.**

HERMIT (Gr. ἐρῆμος, desert). One who lives alone and devotes himself primarily to the exercises of religion in order the better to know, love and serve God. Anchorite, or anchoret, means the same thing, but for convenience it may be used to distinguish one who lives entirely solitary and alone, a member of no order and subject to no rule but what he imposes on himself: leaving "hermit" to indicate a member of one of the recognized eremitical orders. Anchorites and hermits were the precursors of all Christian monasticism (see the FATHERS OF THE DESERT who, in turn, looked back to Elias and John the Baptist), and the solitary life in both forms was part of the normal life of the Church for many centuries. To-day, partly owing to the desire of authority to keep them in hermit communities, partly to changed social and economic conditions, anchorites are practically non-existent; and the hermit life is confined principally to the Carthusians and the Camaldolese (*qq.v.*). The latter permit experienced hermits to become recluses in a strict sense, usually temporarily but sometimes for life. The desert (*q.v.*) monasteries of the Carmelites are practically extinct and the Hermits of St. Augustine (*q.v.*) are no longer hermits. There are hermitages in the neighbourhood of Maronite (*q.v.*) monasteries (Antonian), each of which is occupied by two monks, of whom one is a priest; necessities are brought to them from the monastery, but they do not normally receive visitors and keep almost perpetual silence; they eat once a day (never

---

* This is one opinion. Of course, only God can rightly judge whether a given non-Catholic is or is not in good faith.—*Publisher*, 1997.
** See also APOSTATE.—*Publisher*, 1997.

meat), wear a hair-shirt always and are bound to a certain number of hours of manual work daily. See also HERMITS OF ST. PAUL.

HERMIT OF KNARESBOROUGH, THE HOLY. Robert Flower, son of a burgess of York, born about 1160, died *c.* 1218, having passed his life as a hermit in various places but chiefly in a cave on the banks of the Nidd near Knaresborough. He had a great reputation for sanctity and is commonly referred to as Saint Robert but has never been canonized nor does his name appear in any known calendar; he has been confused with both St. Robert of Newminster (*d.* 1159) and Robert Grosseteste, Bishop of Lincoln (*d.* 1253).

HERMITS OF ST. AUGUSTINE, The. An order formed by Pope Alexander IV, in 1256, by the union, under the Rule of St. Augustine, of several existing societies and congregations of hermits. Shortly afterwards most of its members forsook the contemplative for the active life and the order became one of friars. It had a large number of houses (32 in England) before the Reformation and Revolution. It now consists of three independent branches. (*a*) The Calced form the main body. They have 18 provinces, including one for the United States and one for Ireland, which has 3 small priories in England. (*b*) The Discalced are found in Italy and Germany and their life is more austere. They wear sandals, have strict fasts and silences, never sing a high Mass. They preserve a trace of the hermit origin of the order, each province having a "house of recollection" to which friars can retire and live contemplatively. (*c*) The Recollects are a Spanish reform with missions in the Philippines, Brazil, Venezuela, Colombia and elsewhere, and one small house of refugee friars in the diocese of Plymouth. The work of the whole order (about 3,800 religious in the three branches) is in teaching, study, foreign missions and the cure of souls; only those teaching or living in the houses of recollection are dispensed from parochial work. The habit is a black tunic with a hood and girdle, and a large cowl for choir use. Since 1567 the Augustinians have been the fourth of the greater mendicant orders; they must be distinguished from the Canons Regular of St. Augustine (*q.v.*), also often referred to as Augustinians.

HERMITS OF ST. JEROME, The. An order founded in 1380 by Bl. Peter Gambacorti. Their principal work was study and exegesis of the Scriptures, and the life was eminently one of retirement. The great Spanish province, which formerly had the Guadalupe, Belen, Escurial and 55 other monasteries, was proscribed and dissolved in 1836. The remnant of the order came to an end in 1933, but an attempt is being made to revive it at Parrall, near Segovia.

HERMITS OF ST. PAUL, The, have existed in the neighbourhood of Cordoba since 1309. They have occupied their present enclosure since the 17th century. They are all laymen, each one occupying a separate three-roomed hermitage; the superior, his assistant and the chaplain (a secular priest) live together. They say daily the Little Office of our Lady; meet in chapel thrice for spiritual reading, etc., and in the refectory for meals; they pray, meditate, work and read according to rule; there is a long community walk once a month, when talking is allowed; sleep is broken from 2 a.m. to 4 a.m. for Matins, etc.; perpetual abstinence. Simple vows only are taken, renewable every year. The hermits at present number only a few.

HERODIANS, The, with whom the Pharisees took counsel (Mark iii, 6) were a political party whose members outwardly conformed to Judaism but who, as partisans of the Idumæan kings, were a leaven (Mark viii, 15) of religious scepticism and moral laxity.

HEROIC ACT OF CHARITY, The, is that a member of the Church on earth, either using a set formula or simply by an act of the will, offers to God for the holy souls in Purgatory all the indulgences which he gains and all the satisfactory works which he performs in his life-time and all the suffrages that may be offered for him after his death. It is an offering as to the acceptance and application of which by God in any given case nothing is known; it is heroic because the offerer is willing to take upon himself the undiminished pains of Purgatory to benefit his neighbour. Priests who make this act may gain a plenary indulgence for a soul at choice each time they say Mass, and laymen whenever they receive communion, on the usual conditions. The act is revocable at will.

HESPERINOS (Gr. ἑσπερος, evening). The service of Vespers in the Divine Office of the Byzantine rite. It is sung in the afternoon or evening and is the first hour of the following day's office. It falls into three parts, the ordinary office beginning with an invitatory followed by Psalm ciii; then come diaconal litanies and psalms, the last two with six *troparia* (*q.v.*) of the day; during the second part is sung the thanksgiving hymn *Phos Hilaron* (*q.v.*), which is the centre to which all parts of the office converge; the office finishes with the Song of Simeon, the *Trisagion*, the Our Father, a *troparion* of the day and a prayer to our Lady. Normally Hesperinos is sung in every Byzantine church on Saturday evenings.

HESYCHASM (Gr. ἡσυχία, quiet). A theory of mysticism upheld by the Orthodox Eastern Church in defence of a system of contemplation first practised by the Athonite monks in the 14th century. The ascetic training, according to its upholders, led to the beholding of the uncreated light of God, which accompanied the Transfiguration. It was taught that this "light of Tabor" and all divine operation is distinct from the divine essence. To combat this doctrine and the pantheistic developments of Hesychasm, its opponents used the teaching of St. Thomas and the scholastics, thus aggravating anti-Western feeling and widening the scope of the controversy. In 1351 a synod approved the doctrines of Hesychasm and canonized its defender, Gregory Palamas, as a doctor of his church. An Orthodox monk who reaches a high degree of contemplation is still called a *Hesychast,* but the name does not necessarily mean more than "one who observes quiet."

HEXAHEMERON, The (Gr., six days). The history of the six days of creation as described in Gen. i. A Catholic need not believe that these days were periods corresponding to our spaces of 24 hours; he may, for example, hold that each was a considerable period of time. See GENESIS, HISTORICALNESS OF.

HEXAPLA, The (Gr., six-fold). The name given to Origen's edition of the Old Testament in Hebrew and Greek, because it was arranged in six columns, according to the number of versions used. Certain parts being in seven or eight columns caused it to be called also *Heptapla* or *Octapla.*

HEXAPTERYGON (Gr., six-winged). Another name for the *ripidion* (*q.v.*).

HEXATEUCH, The (analogous form to Pentateuch). The first six books of the Old Testament: Genesis, Exodus, Leviticus, Numbers, Deuteronomy, Josue.

HEXHAM (*Hagulstadensis*, more correctly *Hagustaldensis*). An English see created in 678, suppressed about 821, revived in 1850; the name of Newcastle (*Novocastrensis*) was added in 1861. Suffragan of Liverpool. Covers the counties of Northumberland and Durham, and so includes the former palatine see of Durham. The parishes of Croxdale and Biddlestone are continuous with pre-Reformation times, Birtley, Swinburn and Durham were established in the 17th, and 15 others in the 18th century. The bishop's residence is at Tynemouth and his cathedral at Newcastle. There is a Carmelite convent founded at Lierre in the Low Countries in the 17th century, and one of Poor Clares founded in France in the 17th century. The patrons are our Lady Immaculate and St. Cuthbert (whose body is said to be hidden in the cathedral of Durham).

HIERARCH. Any exalted member of a hierarchy but especially an archbishop or patriarch. The Byzantine rite has on Jan. 30 a feast of the Three Holy Hierarchs (SS. Basil the Great, Gregory Nazianzen and John Chrysostom).

HIERARCHICAL ORDERS, The, are the episcopate, priesthood and diaconate. They are termed "honours" by the Fathers and early ecclesiastical writers: *cf., honorum dator* in the text of the ordination of deacons.

HIERARCHY, THE CELESTIAL, is usually accounted of nine choirs; angels (*q.v.*), archangels, virtues, powers, principalities, dominations, thrones, cherubim and seraphim. The last three are turned especially towards God in worship; the first two are his ministers, virtues and dominations his servants, principalities and powers agents of strength (*cf.,* Gen. iii, 24; Is. vi, 2-7; Ezech. x; Eph. i. 21; Col. i. 16; 1 Peter iii, 22).

HIERARCHY, ECCLESIASTICAL (Gr. ἱερός, sacred; ἄρχος, ruler). The organization of the ranks and orders of the Christian clergy in successive grades. This may be considered i. as the hierarchy of Order, whose powers are exercised in worship and the administration of the sacraments, and ii. as the hierarchy of Jurisdiction, whose power is over the members of the Church.

i. The orders of bishop, priest and deacon are of divine institution; the subdiaconate and minor orders (*q.v.*) are of ecclesiastical institution and have grown out of the diaconate. The rank of abbot (*q.v.*) is not an order; he is simply a priest (who is privileged by law to confer minor orders on his own subjects). The forms of blessing by which certain ecclesiastical ranks are conferred in the Eastern churches approximate to ordination rites but do not make these ranks separate ecclesiastical orders: *e.g.,* that of a *kummus* among the Copts, the Armenian *vardapet,* and the *chorepiskopos* of the Syrians and others.

ii. In the hierarchy of Jurisdiction the papacy and episcopate are alone of divine institution. Cardinals, patriarchs, exarchs and primates derive their powers (other than episcopal) by delegation expressed or implied from the Holy See; metropolitans and archbishops from their patriarch, exarch or primate (that is, in the West immediately, in the East mediately, from the pope); archdeacons, vicars general, vicars forane, rural deans, pastors and rectors from their diocesan bishop. (See also PRELATE-NULLIUS; TITULAR BISHOP; VICAR APOSTOLIC, etc.) By virtue of his primacy, supreme authority over the whole church belongs to the Supreme Pontiff or Pope, who is also Patriarch of the West, Primate of Italy, Metropolitan of the Roman province and Bishop of Rome; these offices must be clearly distinguished one from another. Diocesan bishops administer their dioceses by divine right, and may be subject to an archbishop or other hierarch or directly subject to the Holy See; but they are not provincial governors representing a central authority and exercising delegated powers; they are under the pope, but not as delegates or nuncios: they represent not him but

Christ: thus each diocese is properly a church (*cf.*, Vatican Council schema on the constitution of the Church). In common speech "the hierarchy" denotes all the diocesan bishops of a nation or province.

HIEROMONK (Gr. ἰερομόναχος, priest-monk). An Eastern monk who has been ordained to the priesthood. In Eastern monasticism the majority of monks have no holy orders, and the distinction between choir-monks and lay-brothers (*qq.v.*) is unknown. This is to a certain extent true also of some Catholic oriental religious congregations.

HIERONYMITES, The. See HERMITS OF ST. JEROME.

HIERURGIA. A sacred action or rite; the Mass.

HIGH-CHURCH. The term applied to those members of the Church of England and other Protestant episcopal bodies whose beliefs, practices and conception of the Church of Christ approximate in varying degrees to the teaching of the Catholic Church. The party had its beginnings in the 17th century with such men as Laud and Andrewes, who were opposed equally to the Holy See and to Calvin but were enthusiastic for what may be called a "high standard of Christian authority and belief"; in 1833 the Oxford Movement (*q.v.*) began, openly trying to establish the Catholicity of the Church of England and in twelve years bringing an entirely new spirit and life into that body; since then the high-church party has continued to grow and prosper and become more diversified in its shades of faith and practice. Its right wing, to a certain extent the whole party, now call themselves Anglo-Catholics (*q.v.*); they claim that the Church of England can give to its children all that the Roman Church gives to hers, except communion with the Apostolic See.

HIGH MASS. The ordinary English name for *Missa solemnis*, in which the celebrant is assisted by a deacon and subdeacon. This is the normal (but not most common) way of celebrating Mass. High Mass also requires the presence of a choir and of a certain number of servers or acolytes, and the use of incense. The choir or people sing the common and the proper of the Mass (*qq.v.*), except as below: the subdeacon sings the epistle; the deacon the gospel and *Ite missa est*, or its substitute; the celebrant intones the *Gloria* and *Credo*, sings the collects, preface, *Paternoster*, post-communion prayers and *Dominus vobiscum*, etc.: he also recites the whole of the Mass including the parts sung by others, except *Ite missa est*. Other characteristics are: the solemn singing of the gospel (*q.v.*), the incensation of the altar after the preparatory prayers, and of the offerings, altar, ministers, choir and people before the *Lavabo*, and the giving of the *Pax*

or kiss of peace. Daily conventual and collegiate, and parochial Masses on Sundays and great feasts, should be high Masses when possible; failing the necessary ministers, etc., a sung Mass (*q.v.*) is desirable. Except in parochial churches the Capuchins do not have high or sung Mass.

HIGH PLACES (Eph. vi, 12). Not the exalted offices of the state or church or the pagan altars built on hills often referred to in the Old Testament, but the upper places of the air, as being, at any rate metaphorically, the dwelling-place of the evil spirits against whom St. Paul was warning the Ephesians. The rendering of the passage in the original Rheims version, though not sonorous like "the spirits of wickedness in the high places," is less ambiguous and a literal translation of the Vulgate: "The spirituals of wickedness in the celestials."

HILDEBRAND. The name of Pope St. Gregory VII before his elevation to the papacy, by which name he is still frequently called.

HILLEL AND SHAMMAI. Two Jewish rabbis of opposite schools living immediately before the birth of Christ. Shammai represented the rigorist, Hillel the liberal tendency of Jewish thought. By Jewish and modernist writers Hillel has been put forward as a rival to Christ, without any justification in whatever remains of his words and activities; he was apparently a man of ability and kindly disposition but never broke the bonds of Jewish legalism and servitude to the letter of the Law.

HISPANO-GALLICAN RITE, The. The Mozarabic Rite (*q.v.*).

HOLIDAY OF OBLIGATION (Old Eng. *háligdæg*, holy day). A feast-day on which Catholics are bound to assist at Mass and to refrain from servile work. In the Western church these days are: all Sundays, Christmas, Circumcision, Epiphany, Ascension, Corpus Christi, Assumption, SS. Peter and Paul, All Saints, the Immaculate Conception and St. Joseph. The last two are not observed as holidays in England and Wales; Ireland has St. Patrick's day instead of St. Joseph; the Epiphany, Corpus Christi, Peter and Paul and St. Joseph are not kept in the United States. Each Eastern rite has its own feasts of obligation. The Byzantine "Horologion," for example, names 45 in addition to Sundays; in practice these are much reduced, *e.g.*, the Melkites nominally keep about 30 since the Council of Ain Traz in 1835.

HOLINESS (Old Eng. *hál*, whole). Holiness or Sanctity denotes union with God. i. The sanctity of dedication or consecration, whereby a person or thing is pledged to God's service or is the object of his special protection and pleasure, *e.g.*, churches, days, water, relics, priests, the married state.

ii. Moral holiness, or union with God through morally good acts. Sanctifying grace is its indispensable basis; for grace unites man to God by allowing him to share in the divine life, and is always accompanied by infused virtues and the gifts of the Holy Ghost. Mortal sin alone destroys holiness, for it alone deprives the soul of grace. Progress in holiness, even to an heroic degree, is made by keeping the commandments, the doing of good works and the practice of virtues.

HOLINESS, YOUR, HIS. A title of respect and honour reserved to the pope in the West. Its use in the East is more common: the Melkite patriarch of Antioch and several of his metropolitans and bishops are "most holy" in the Liturgy, the Orthodox patriarch of Constantinople is "his All-Holiness," and so on.

HOLLAND, THE CHURCH IN. For historical reasons the Kingdom of The Netherlands is commonly regarded as a Protestant country, but in fact, of its over $8\frac{1}{2}$ million people, 36 per cent is Catholic; and the religious life of this minority is peculiarly strong and influential. In theory all religions are equal before the law, and in fact most inequalities are now abolished. Clerics are not liable for military service and receive small salaries and pensions from the state. With certain exceptions, organized manifestations of religion are forbidden in public. What is now Holland was mostly in the care of vicars apostolic from about 1600 to 1853. The country now forms 1 ecclesiastical province, with its metropolitan see at Utrecht and 4 suffragan dioceses.

HOLME EDEN. An abbey of Benedictine nuns founded at Kilcumein in Scotland by the first abbot of Fort Augustus, Dom Leo Linse, in 1891. It became an abbey in 1909, was aggregated to the English Congregation O.S.B. in 1918, and in 1921 removed to Holme Eden, near Carlisle.

HOLOCAUST. From Gr. ὅλος, whole, καυστός, burnt, meaning a sacrifice wholly consumed by fire, and in that sense can best be rendered in English as "burnt-offering." The term is used particularly of the burnt-offerings of the Jews, but it is also extended to any whole and complete sacrifice, whether literal or figurative.

HOLY ALLIANCE, The. A treaty signed in 1815 between the tsar of Russia, Alexander I (Orthodox), the king of Prussia, Frederick William III (Lutheran), and the emperor of Austria, Francis I (Catholic), in which King Louis XVIII of France, and George, prince regent of England, subsequently joined. The principles of justice, love and peace were affirmed in relation to both internal and external affairs, their peoples were entrusted to them by God, Christian morality must

obtain in politics, and they would not make war on one another. This "sublime mysticism and nonsense" had little political influence, but together with other treaties and the policy of Prince Metternich it helped for eight years to revive a sense of the unity and common responsibility of the states of Europe.

HOLY BLOOD OF BRUGES, The. A relic believed to be drops of the actual blood of Christ collected by St. Joseph of Arimathea when he washed the sacred body for burial. It was given by Baldwin, king of Jerusalem, to Count Dietrich of Alsace and by him to the city in 1150. The solemn procession in which it is carried in May every year was instituted in 1303 in thanksgiving for the delivery of the city from the French by Jan Breidel and Pieter de Coninck. Other alleged relics of the Precious Blood are preserved at Weingarten Abbey in Würtemberg and in the cathedrals of Sarzana, Mentone and Mantua. These relics may receive veneration but not divine worship (*cf.*, Precious Blood).

HOLY BLOOD OF HALES, The. An alleged relic of the blood of our Lord kept at Hales Abbey. It was denounced by the Reformers as a gross and wilful fraud; it is known that the relic was given to the abbey, and another to Ashridge in Buckinghamshire, by their founder, Richard of Cornwall, who probably got it from Constantinople after its sack in 1204. The authenticity of these relics, though honestly believed in, is more than questionable.

HOLY COAT, The. A piece of material preserved at the cathedral of Trèves (Trier) and alleged to be the seamless garment worn by our Lord at his passion. Its written history goes back only to the 12th century, but tradition claims it to have been sent to Trèves by St. Helen. Argenteuil in France also venerates a holy coat; its supporters say it is *the* seamless garment, and that Trier's is simply *a* garment of Christ. This relic is traced to Charlemagne and there is not much to choose between the two traditions.

HOLY CROSS COLLEGE. The oldest Catholic college in New England, founded in 1843 by the second bishop of Boston, B. J. Fenwick, and the Rev. James Filton. It is directed by the Jesuit fathers.

HOLY CROSS DAY. Sept. 14, the feast of the Exaltation of the Cross.

HOLY CROSS, THE CONGREGATION OF THE. A society of priests and lay-brothers under simple vows engaged on foreign missions and in the education of youth. It was formed by the fusion of two bodies, of brothers and priests, founded in 1820 and 1835 respectively in France. The motherhouse and chief centre of activity is now at the University of Notre Dame, Indiana, U.S.A.

HOLY FACE, The. Devotion to the Holy Face of our suffering Lord became widespread in the early middle ages through the story of the Veronica and the *Volto Santo* (*qq.v.*) of Lucca. It received renewed impetus from Léon Dupont, the "holy man of Tours," who in 1850 founded the confraternity of the Holy Face whose members make reparation for the blasphemies and insults offered to Christ. It is represented on many Eastern icons and in the Russian Orthodox Church particularly is a common object of the people's veneration.

HOLY FAMILY, The. The child Jesus, with his mother Mary and foster-father Joseph. The Holy Family is a popular subject of devotion and has given a name to a confraternity and other associations and to several congregations of religious; in some places· the month of March ·is dedicated in its honour. A feast of this name was instituted by Pope Leo XIII in 1893 and extended to the whole Western church in 1921; it is observed on the Sunday within the octave of the Epiphany. On account of the flight into Egypt it has been observed by the Copts from early times, and under several different titles during the year, but especially on May 24.

HOLY FATHER, MOST (Lat. *Beatissime Pater*). A title of address and reference to the pope, as spiritual father of all Christians.

HOLY GHOST, The. The third Person of the Blessed Trinity (*q.v.*), consubstantial (*q.v.*) with the Father and the Son, from both of whom he proceeds by a common spiration (a movement of the will tending towards the beloved object). He is "sent" by the Father and the Son on the mission (*q.v.* iv) of accomplishing the work of salvation in the souls of men. The Holy Ghost came down upon the apostles on the day of Pentecost, confirming them in their faith and filling them with the fulness of all gifts that they might preach the gospel and spread the Church throughout the world. He sanctifies us by his graces and by the virtues he infuses, and enlightens and moves us so that, if we co-operate with grace, we may attain to everlasting life. The Holy Ghost continually gives life and comfort (he is The Comforter; John xiv, 16) to the Church by his ever-present help, and by his gifts guides her infallibly in the way of truth and holiness.

HOLY GHOST FATHERS, The. A congregation arising from the union in 1848 of societies founded in Paris in 1703 by the Abbé C. F. Poullart des Places and at Amiens in 1844 by the Ven. Francis Paul Libermann. It undertakes the direction of home and foreign missions, seminaries, and colleges. Its numerous missions are principally in Africa.

HOLY HAND, The. A relic of Bl. Edmund Arrowsmith, S.J., martyred in 1628, preserved in the church of St. Oswald at Ashton-in-Makerfield. It is reported to be the occasion of remarkable cures of sickness and disease. A similar relic of Bl. John Kemble is in St. Francis Xavier's church, Hereford.

HOLY HELPERS, THE XIV. A devotion popular for many centuries in Germany to the early martyrs George, Blaise, Erasmus, Pantaleon, Vitus, Christopher, Denis, Cyriacus, Achatius, Eustace, Giles, Margaret, Catherine and Barbara (the names vary) who were (and are) invoked against many common ills and as patrons of many occupations. A church has been dedicated in their honour at Baltimore, and permission given to certain places to keep a feast in their honour on August 8 and other dates.

HOLY HOUR, The. A devotion consisting of exposition of the Blessed Sacrament for the space of one hour to enable the faithful to meditate before it, especially upon the Passion. Hymns, litanies and other prayers are sometimes sung, and the exposition is terminated by Benediction.

HOLY INNOCENTS, The. The children murdered by order of King Herod as recorded in St. Matthew's gospel ii, 16-18. Their number is not known, but it cannot have been large, legends to the contrary notwithstanding. The Western church keeps their feast on Dec. 28, and their Mass has peculiarities: though they are venerated as martyrs purple vestments are worn and the *Gloria* and *Alleluia* omitted, but on the octave-day, and when the feast falls on a Sunday, red and the *Gloria* are prescribed. All Eastern rites honour them liturgically under the name of The Holy Children, but on various dates. At Bethlehem, where their feast is a holiday of obligation, the friars and children of the choir visit their altar under the basilica every evening and sing the hymn from Lauds of the feast, *Salvete, flores martyrum*, "Hail, blossoms of the martyrs."

HOLY MAID OF KENT, The. Elizabeth Barton, first a farm girl at Court-at-Street and then a Benedictine nun of St. Sepulchre's, Canterbury. From 1525 she claimed to have supernatural visions and in particular to be informed of the divine wrath against King Henry VIII on account of his adultery. In 1533, with two secular priests, two Franciscans, and a Benedictine, her supporters, she was arraigned for high treason, attainted, and put to death at Tyburn in the following year. Her character and revelations have been the subject of disagreement; contemporary evidence supports that she was "reputed among many people of this realm to be a very holy woman, inspired by God."

HOLY MAN OF LILLE, The. A layman, Philibert Vrau (1829-1905), so called on account of his religious, social and charitable works in that city. He was one of those concerned in bringing about the first eucharistic congress. With his brother-in-law, Camille Feron-Vrau, his cause of canonization has been introduced at Rome, where they are called "the frock-coated saints."

HOLY MAN OF TOURS, The. A layman, Léon Dupont (1797-1876) who in 1850 founded the confraternity of the Holy Face (*q.v.*) whose members pledge themselves to works of reparation.

HOLY NAME OF JESUS, The. i. The name Jesus is the Latin form of the Gr. Ἰησοῦς, derived from the Heb. *Jehoshua* (Josue), Aramaic *Yeshu*, and means "Jahweh is salvation." It was given to our Lord by the direction of God himself (Luke i, 31, Matt. i, 21), but was not a unique name, *e.g.*, it was borne by the son of Sirach, author of "Ecclesiasticus," and by a helper of St. Paul (Col. iv, 11). It is a common name in the Arabic-speaking East and is given as a baptismal name in Spain.

ii. Honour is given to the Holy Name as a symbol representing our Lord himself, and this since apostolic times (Phil. ii, 9-10); when it is pronounced in the liturgy all bow the head or otherwise acknowledge it, nor need this practice be confined to public worship. But a definite devotion in honour of and directed towards the name was the work of two Franciscans, SS. Bernardine of Siena, and John Capistran in the 15th century. As a result a liturgical feast of the Holy Name was granted to their order, and in 1721 this was extended to the whole Western church. It is observed on the Sunday following Jan. 1, but on Jan. 2 when the first Sunday of the year falls on the 1st, 6th or 7th. The dying are directed to pronounce the Holy Name at least inwardly when receiving the "last blessing" (*q.v.*). Devotion to the Holy Name is widespread among the Orthodox of Russia, whence it was introduced from Mount Athos.

HOLY OFFICE, THE SACRED CONGREGATION OF THE, was erected in 1542 as a continuation and supersession of the Universal Roman Inquisition (*q.v.*), and since 1917 has taken over the work of the suppressed Congregation of the Index. Its business is the protection of faith and morals, the judging of heresy, dogmatic teaching as to the sacraments and indulgences, impediments to marriage with non-Catholics, questions affecting the eucharistic fast, and the examination and prohibition of books dangerous to faith or otherwise pernicious. Many of the offices of this congregation are always filled by Dominicans, whose order was prominently associated with the Inquisition. The prefect of this congregation is the pope himself, who presides in person when decisions of great importance are announced; but it must not be supposed that such approval renders the decisions infallible.*

HOLY OILS, The, are three, Oil of Catechumens, of the Sick, and Chrism (*qq.v.*). They are kept, each in its separate vessel, locked in an aumbry or cupboard, in the wall of the sanctuary on the gospel-side, whose door is covered with a purple veil. They should only be handled by clerics.

HOLY OILS, BLESSING OF THE, takes place in cathedral-churches at a special Mass on Maundy Thursday. The bishop is assisted by twelve priests, seven deacons and seven subdeacons. Just before the Lord's Prayer the oil of the sick (*q.v.*) is brought in and blessed, with an exorcism and a prayer that it may be healthful to soul and body. The consecration of the holy chrism (*q.v.*) is after the communion; and then the oil of catechumens is blessed, the bishop and priests first breathing over it, with an exorcism and a prayer that those who come to Baptism may, so to say, be made slippery to sin thereby. The oil is then saluted, *Ave, sanctum Oleum!* (Hail, holy Oil!), by the bishop and priests, who kiss the mouth of the vessel; it and the chrism are then removed in procession to the sacristy.

HOLY PLACES, The. The places in Palestine connected with the life, death and resurrection of Jesus Christ. They are principally the Holy Sepulchre, Calvary, the Upper Room, the site of the Temple, Gethsemane, the Via Dolorosa, the church of the Assumption and the sanctuary of the Ascension at Jerusalem; the grotto of the Nativity at Bethlehem; the church of the Visitation at Ain Karim; the church of the Annunciation at Nazareth; the river Jordan where our Lord was baptized; the hill of Transfiguration (Tabor); and the sea of Galilee. To these is generally added the sanctuary of Matariah, near Cairo, where the Holy Family rested during the flight. The shrine of Elias on Mount Carmel, the sepulchre of the Patriarchs at Hebron (Al Khalil) and the tomb of Rachel are also greatly venerated, and there are lesser shrines marking almost every recorded incident of our Lord's life. The authenticity of each of these localizations has to be judged on its own merits; some are clearly guesses, others had their origin in mere commemorative chapels, others in sectarian jealousy; but the most important are well supported by tradition and archæology. The Friars Minor have had the custody of these holy places on behalf of the Western church since the 13th century, but the premier and some exclusive rights in the church of the Holy Sepulchre, the basilica of Bethlehem, and other places have been exercised by the Eastern Orthodox (*vulgo* Greeks) since the Byzantine schism; and a bad general state of ill feeling and quarrel-

---

* The Holy Office is now called the Sacred Congregation for the Doctrine of the Faith.—*Publisher*, 1997.

someness has been aggravated by the claims of Gregorian Armenians and others as well as by the Mohammedans.

HOLY SATURDAY. The eve of Easter, a day of mourning for Christ in the tomb, until the vigil of the Resurrection in the late evening or during the night. The vigil office consists of the blessing of the New Fire, the procession of the Paschal Candle into the unlit church, the singing of the *Exsultet* (*qq.v.*), four Old Testament lessons (see PROPHECIES), the litanies of the Saints, in two parts, the blessing of the font (*q.v.*), baptisms (if any), the renewal of baptismal promises, the first Mass of Easter, and Lauds. At the *Gloria in excelsis* of the Mass all bells are rung, the organ is played, images unveiled and festal hangings displayed; "Alleluia" is solemnly sung after the epistle; there is no introit, offertory, *Agnus Dei*, communion-verse or last gospel. Lauds consists of one psalm (cl), the *Benedictus* and a collect. The fire and candle refer directly to the risen Christ, the lessons and blessing of baptismal water to those who are to be baptized during this vigil and may make their first communion at this Mass (formerly there was a last scrutiny of catechumens). The people renew their baptismal promises standing, holding lighted candles, and in the mother-tongue; they say the Lord's Prayer together, and are then blessed with the new holy water. The Lenten fast ends today, *Regina cæli* is said instead of the Angelus, and the people's houses are blessed. In the Byzantine rite, the Liturgy of St. Basil is sung at midnight, with special observances, including the reading of prophecies and a procession outside the church; when it returns with candles into the unlit church the gospel is sung as usual, and, when the Resurrection is solemnly announced, the bells are rung and the people greet one another: "Christ is risen! Truly he is risen!"

HOLY SEE, The. The episcopal see of Rome, but generally used as a term to indicate the pope as supreme pontiff, together with those associated with him in government at the Church's headquarters.

HOLY SEPULCHRE, THE BROTHER-HOOD OF, was organized in the Orthodox patriarchate of Jerusalem in the 16th century to look after the holy places, to provide an efficient higher clergy, to administer property and to judge causes. Its president is the patriarch, all members of the holy synod belong to it, and it runs the patriarchate. There are about 150 members (called hagiotaphites, ἅγιος τάφος, holy tomb), who live principally in four monasteries and are the heart of the predominant Greek influence in Palestinian Orthodoxy.

HOLY SEPULCHRE, THE CHURCH OF THE (properly called the Church of the Resurrection), so called because it encloses all that remains of the tomb of our Lord, situated 140 ft. north-west of the hill of Calvary. The natural rock was cut away all round and the cave thus isolated, and a circular building (the *Anastasis*) erected around it by Constantine the Great. In 1009 the roof and upper parts of the rock walls of the tomb were destroyed by the Khalif Hakim-bin-amr-Illah; the remnants are completely hidden by an exceedingly ugly little building put over them by the Orthodox after the fire of 1808. This sepulchre was the objective of the Crusaders, and the church which now shelters both it and Calvary (*q.v.*) was built by them; it was terribly messed about in the 1808 restoration. The quire of the canons is now the Orthodox cathedral, and the Friars Minor have their quire in a large side-chapel; the dissident Copts, Syrians and Armenians also share the building. Numerous other holy sites are shown therein, but they are mostly only commemorative chapels. The authenticity of this chief pilgrim shrine of Christendom was strongly attacked in the 19th century, but its genuineness is well substantiated. In Jerusalem and churches of the Friars Minor elsewhere there is a feast of the Holy Sepulchre on the second Sunday after Easter, commemorating the Resurrection; and a feast of the dedication of the church in 335 is held on Sept. 13 in the Byzantine rite.

HOLY SEPULCHRE, GUARDIANS OF THE. The Friars Minor, about a dozen in number, who occupy the friary adjoining the church of the Holy Sepulchre in order to officiate in the church, watch over the sanctuaries and minister to pilgrims. The office is onerous, the friary being small and unhealthy, and access to it cut off at night. The duty is taken in three monthly turns by friars from the neighbouring larger friary of St. Saviour, where they have a pharmacy, boys' orphanage, printing-press, book-binding, joiner's and cobbler's workshops, a smithy, a mill, a library and a large parish church to keep them busy.

HOLY SOULS, The. The souls of the just detained in Purgatory (*q.v.*). It is part of the duty of Christians to pray for these members of the Church Suffering, both individuals and as a body, that they may be speedily admitted to Heaven; the Council of Trent declaring that they are aided principally by the Sacrifice of the Mass. All or any of our good works, however, may be offered for their benefit, the Heroic Act (*q.v.*) being particularly meritorious. It is taught by some theologians that the Holy Souls pray to God both for themselves and for us, and in practice the faithful follow the opinion of those theologians who maintain that we may hopefully invoke their prayers on our behalf. Nevertheless the Church does not direct us so to do as in the case of the saints. The month of November is particularly set apart for devotion to the Holy Souls.

HOLY SPIRIT, The. The Holy Ghost (q.v.).

HOLY THINGS TO THE HOLY (Gr. τὰ ἅγια τοῖς ἁγίοις). An ancient formula reminding the faithful of the pure conscience required for the worthy reception of holy communion. It is found in every Catholic eucharistic liturgy, except the Roman and its derivatives. The people answer "One only is holy, one only is Lord, Jesus Christ in the glory of God the Father. Amen," or similarly. The words are accompanied by a lifting-up of the Holy Bread (and in some rites the Chalice), which has caused this ceremony to be approximated to the Roman elevation, but it is actually a counterpart of our *Agnus Dei* before communion. In the Mozarabic Mass *Sancta sanctis* is said in connexion with the commixture (q.v.).

HOLY THURSDAY. The Thursday before Easter, Maundy Thursday (q.v.); also an old name in England for Ascension Day.

HOLY WATER. Water blessed by a priest according to the form in the "Rituale Romanum." It is a sacramental whose principal use is at the Sunday *Asperges* (q.v.) and it is employed in nearly every blessing which the Church gives. Holy water is taken (*i.e.*, the tips of the fingers are dipped in and the sign of the cross made) as a symbolic washing and act of recollection on entering a church; it is now the universal custom to do so again on leaving it, but the practice is rather meaningless. It may also be used on going to bed and getting up, in moments of temptation, and on numerous other occasions. Washing with water is a natural symbol of spiritual cleansing, and its hallowing is particularly directed to its use against the assaults of spiritual enemies, *cf.*, the exorcisms and prayers of the blessing. It is a constant reminder of our Baptism and its devout use blots out venial sin. The use of holy water is known in some Eastern rites but is not so frequent as in the West.

HOLY WATER FONT. A receptacle for holy water, usually called in English a stoup (q.v.).

HOLY WEEK. The week immediately preceding Easter Sunday in which is recalled the memory of our Lord's last days and passion before the resurrection. The liturgical prayers and ceremonies of the week not only re-enact these events, but are a summary of fundamental theology; in particular they show Jesus Christ as the triumphant Messias and the suffering Redeemer; in every sense Holy Week is the centre of the Christian year. Palm Sunday commemorates the entry into Jerusalem, Maundy Thursday the institution of the Holy Eucharist, and the liturgy is marked by restrained rejoicing; Monday,

Tuesday, Wednesday and Good Friday, in particular, are days of mourning; Holy Saturday night marks the transition to joy at the consummation of the Lord's redeeming work. The passions from the gospels are read on Sunday, Tuesday, Wednesday and Friday, on which day Mass may not be celebrated, nor on Saturday before the evening. The fact that Easter was at first the only properly appointed time for conferring Baptism also greatly affects this week: hence the blessing of oils on Maundy Thursday and of the font on Holy Saturday, and numerous details of the services throughout the week. During the eight days preceding Holy Saturday only those may be baptized who are in danger of death. All Eastern liturgies have Holy Week observances peculiar to themselves. In the Byzantine rite the Liturgy of St. Basil is celebrated on Thursday and Saturday, and of the Presanctified on the other weekdays; on Palm Sunday and the first three days, the whole of the four gospels, or at least several chapters, are read through ceremonially, and the reading is followed by *Orthros* of the following day, called from a *troparion* the Prayer of the Bridegroom. (See the different days.) In the East, Holy Week is called Passion Week.

HOLY WOMEN. A liturgical division of female saints for whom there are common Masses; they were married, widows or penitents as distinguished from virgins. There is further division into Virgin Martyrs and Holy Women Martyrs.

HOLY YEAR. One during which the Holy See grants an extraordinary plenary indulgence (of the jubilee, q.v.) to all throughout the world who shall visit Rome in order to venerate the tombs of the Apostles and the see of Peter, practically all other indulgences being suspended. Since 1475 this has occurred every 25 years. It begins with the opening of the holy doors (q.v., i) on the Christmas eve of the previous year and ends with the closing of the same twelve months later. The idea of a year of special celebration at fixed periods is referred to by Moses (Lev. xxv, 10-15); the first Christian holy year recorded is 1300, and was associated with the beginning of the century; the period was reduced from 100 years to 50, to 33, and finally to 25 by Pope Paul II.

HOLYWELL (Treffynnon). A well in Flintshire at the place of the martyrdom of St. Gwenfrewi (Winefride). It is the only pre-reformation shrine in Great Britain (except-ing possibly that of St. Edward in Westminster Abbey) to which pilgrimages have never ceased, and miraculous cures happen there to our own day. On St. Winefride's day in 1629, 1,400 pilgrims and others were present; King James II visited it in 1687; the Protestant Bishop of Saint Asaph complained in 1713 that "great resort is had to Holywell by pilgrims, as they call them, from all the different quarters of the kingdom, and even Ireland." The well is the property of the Duke of Westminster, who lets it to the town, which sub-lets to the Catholic authorities.

HOMICIDE. The killing of one human being by another acting in a private capacity. This is murder (q.v.) if done with malice aforethought. Homicide may be justifiable in cases of defence against violent aggression (cf., self-defence, war); the aggressor's death is not intended as such, but is the unfortunate effect of repelling the aggression. Homicide which is caused by culpable carelessness is itself culpable.

HOMILETICS (Gr. ὁμἰλειν, to have intercourse with). The art and science of preaching, whether sermons, homilies, catechetical instructions, or other religious discourses.

HOMILY. An informal discourse on a passage of Sacred Scripture, directed particularly to uncovering its spiritual lessons. It is the oldest form of preaching and was extensively used by the Fathers. An appropriate extract from one of their homilies is always appended when a (abbreviated) lesson from one of the Gospels has been read at Matins.

HOMOIOUSION (Gr., of like substance). The keyword of Semi-Arianism (q.v.), which contended that the Son was like the Father in substance, but not identically one with him in substance or nature. This is contrary to the orthodox doctrine of the unity of the divine nature in the three Persons of the Blessed Trinity.

HOMOOUSION (Gr., of one substance, consubstantial, q.v.). This is the accepted meaning since the Council of Nicæa in 325, where the word was adopted as the touchstone of orthodoxy against Arianism (q.v.). It had been rejected at the Council of Antioch (264-272) because it was there interpreted as "of one *person*" and later there was equivocation over the first part of the word, and it was rendered as "of *like* substance."

HONDURAS, THE CHURCH IN. Honduras has a population of nearly a million, most of them Indians and half-castes, with a number of Negroes. Catholics predominate but secularism is strong; ecclesiastical property has twice been confiscated, and religious orders and congregations are forbidden by law. The country forms an ecclesiastical province, with one suffragan see and a vicariate apostolic. *British Honduras* is a crown colony forming a separate vicariate apostolic (of Belize), served by the Jesuits. Its population of 59,000 are mostly Negroes, over a half being Catholics.

HONORIUS, THE CONDEMNATION OF POPE. An alleged failure of papal infallibility. Sergius, Patriarch of Constantinople, wrote to Pope Honorius I (625-38) telling him of the reconciliation of followers of Monophysism (q.v.) by the use of the formula that there was "one will and one energy in Christ"; that its orthodoxy had been challenged; and asking for a ruling. Honorius neither defined nor condemned: he insisted that Christ was perfect God and perfect man, and wished any reference to one or two energies (or operations) to be dropped; and admitted that "there being only one principle of action, or one direction of the will in Christ, therefore there must be one will also." This was the heresy of Monothelism (q.v.), unless he meant by "one will" simply a perfect concord of the human and divine wills. But in any case infallibility (q.v.) is not involved, for he did not make an *ex cathedra* decision; his reply was not a clear statement for the acceptance of the whole Church and he wrote, "We must not wrest what they say into church dogmas." In the sixth œcumenical council (iii Constantinople, 680-1), Monothelism was condemned and Pope Honorius anathematized by name for having followed the heretical lead of Sergius. This anathema Pope St. Leo II confirmed only in the sense of a condemnation of his predecessor for "hedging" and neglecting to denounce heresy outright when he ought to have done so.

HONOUR. The open recognition of another's worth or dignity. It is the first of the external goods which man has a right to enjoy and one is bound in justice to give honour where honour is due (Rom. xiii, 7). "Like the esteem of human glory honour is good (and may lawfully be sought) on condition that charity is its principle and the love of God or the good of one's neighbour its object" (St. Thomas). Honour is impugned by insult, but it is never allowable to use violence on another who is attacking one's honour or good name, even if other effective means of preserving it or of obtaining reparation are not available.

HOOD. That part of the habit of a monk or friar which forms the covering for the head. It is popularly but wrongly called the cowl (q.v.). All western monks except Benedictines of the English congregation, and some friars, have a pointed hood, others are round; it is attached to the tunic, the scapular, or to the short cape. At one time the hood was the ordinary head-dress of religious, but its use is now chiefly liturgical, all monks and friars (except Friars Mᵐᵒʳ) wearing the flat clerical hat out-of-doors. The prelates' *mozzetta* has a hood which since the use of the biretta is merely an ornamental miniature (cf., the piece of silk, once a coif, on a judge's wig).

ii. A hood, generally black with a number of little crosses, is worn both liturgically and ordinarily by Syrian and Maronite bishops and *chorepiskopoi*. When other head-gear is required it is put on over the hood. The white linen "amice" of dissident Coptic priests is another form of this hood, as is the veil of Byzantine and Armenian prelates: they are all of monastic origin.

HOPE is the desire for a future good which though hard to attain is not impossible of attainment. As a supernatural virtue it is that disposition of the soul which enables it to aspire towards God as its last end and towards all the means, spiritual and temporal, necessary to the attainment of that end; knowing that neither means nor end can be achieved by its own efforts unaided by the grace of God and that co-operation with that grace is necessary. Hope, though a theological virtue, is not directed towards God solely but only primarily and directly; indirectly, to the Beatific Vision (*q.v.*). Secondarily it looks to the resurrection and all good, both spiritual and temporal, and the like happiness and blessings for others. Hope in the infinite goodness, power and faithfulness of God is necessary to salvation, for it is in itself an indispensable means to that salvation, and the habit (*q.v.*) of hope is infused into infants at Baptism; the denial of this necessity was one of the errors of Quietism (*q.v.*). The sins against hope are despair and presumption (*qq.v.*). In the object of hope, God, and the supernatural means provided, Grace, we have complete certitude added to hope; for the rest, there cannot be certitude because of the weakness and malice of the human will.

HOPE, ACT OF. i. A confident and unhesitating expectation, resting upon God's most faithful promises, of eternal happiness to be obtained by the divinely appointed means. We hope for the enjoyment of God himself, and for all the aids necessary to attain this. Also we can hope for these benefits for others.
    ii. A form of words expressing this act.

HORÆ DIURNÆ (Lat., day hours). A book containing the Day Hours (*q.v.*) of the Divine Office. *Horæ*: this, or a Book of Hours (*q.v.*).

HORMISDAS, THE FORMULA OF. A document drawn up by Pope St. Hormisdas, the signing of which by the Eastern prelates in 519 ended the Acacian Schism. It affirms clearly that the Catholic religion is kept immaculate by the Apostolic See of Rome, that the perfection and wholeness of that religion lies in communion with that see, and that those are out of communion who do not agree with that see; and condemns Nestorius, Eutyches, Acacius and others by name. At the eighth œcumenical council (iv Constantinople) Eastern and Western bishops subscribed this formula, it was confirmed at the "reunion councils" of Lyons

(1274) and Florence (1439), and frequently referred to at the Vatican Council.

HORNS OF THE ALTAR. The projections on the altar of the Most High in the Temple at Jerusalem (Exod. xxvii, 2, *e.g.*). The name has been carried over to indicate the four corners of the Christian altar, the word "corner" being derived from, and "horn" cognate with Lat. *cornu*, a projection.

HOROLOGION (Gr., hour account). A liturgical book of the Byzantine rite containing the common prayers of the Divine Office, the *troparia* (*q.v.*) for each day of the month, a number of hymns (*kanons*), and the ecclesiastical calendar.

HORTUS CONCLUSUS (Lat., an enclosed garden). A figure of our Lady, from the Canticle of Canticles iv, 12: "My sister, my spouse, is a garden enclosed. . . ."

HOSANNA. A Hebrew shout of triumph and rejoicing arising from words in Ps. cxvii, 25, meaning "save [us], we pray." It was used by the crowd at our Lord's entry into Jerusalem (St. John xii, 13). It occurs in the liturgy during the *Sanctus* at Mass and during the blessing of palms and the procession on Palm Sunday.

HOSEA. The Hebrew form of the name Osee.

HOSPITAL. Radically the word (from Lat. *hospes*, a guest) simply means any charitable institution for the care of the poor or afflicted (*cf.*, asylum, meaning a refuge or shelter). The numerous hospitals of the middle ages were for the benefit of the aged, pilgrims, foundlings, orphans and others, as well as for the sick, and were usually (but not always) under ecclesiastical control. The religious, male and female, who served them were, and are, called hospitallers.

HOSPITALITY. The Christian duty of hospitality, imposed particularly on bishops and beneficed clergy by the Council of Trent, has always been most notably exemplified by the monastic orders. The Rule of St. Benedict (cap. liii) directs: "Let all guests that come be received like Christ himself . . . let special care be taken in the reception of the poor and of strangers, because in them Christ is more truly welcomed." "At the arrival or departure of all guests, let Christ—who indeed is received in their persons—be worshipped in them by bowing the head or even prostrating on the ground. . . . Let the abbot pour water on the hands of the guests"— these are still the observances of some Cistercian houses; and all monasteries have a guesthouse or special quarters set apart. Every bishop at his consecration promises to show kindness and mercy to the poor, to strangers, and to all who are in want, for the sake of the name of the Lord. In the Casa Nuova of the Friars Minor at Jerusalem (which, however, is principally a hospice especially for pilgrims) guests are entertained free of all charge for ten days.

HOSPITALLERS, THE KNIGHTS. A powerful and wealthy military order (q.v.), the Knights Hospitallers of St. John of Jerusalem, which began in 1092 with the building of a hospital for pilgrims in that city. They followed a rule founded on that of St. Augustine. Local establishments were usually called commanderies; there were 53 in England and their grand prior was first baron of the realm. From 1309 to 1523 they were known as Knights of Rhodes, where the grand master ruled as a temporal sovereign, and from 1530 to 1798 as Knights of Malta. The decadence of the order after 1571 was as great as its power and splendour, the vows were ignored, and it was forcibly suppressed in many countries. It is still a religious and secular order of the Church (see KNIGHTS OF ST. JOHN).

HOSPITALLERS OF ST. JOHN-OF-GOD, The. An order for the care of the sick founded by St. John-of-God at Granada in 1540. The members are for the most part laymen but priests are received as the needs of the order and its patients require; they have solemn vows and follow the rule of St. Augustine, reciting the Little Office B. V. M. daily in choir, and take a fourth vow, to serve the sick for life. They conduct over 100 hospitals. Habit: tunic, belt, scapular and round hood, all black. Called in Italy *Fate bene fratelli*.

HOST (Lat. *hostia*, a victim). i. The consecrated eucharistic Elements, particularly the species of bread (e.g., the elevation of the Host).

ii. An unconsecrated altar-bread (q.v.). See also BREAD, PROSPHORA.

HOT CROSS BUNS. Small round cakes, marked with a cross and made of simple ingredients, to be eaten on Good Friday. This English custom of eating buns on that day cannot be traced back for more than two or three centuries; in some parts of the country a superstition has grown up that these buns, preserved until they are quite hard, are beneficial when used medicinally. Their only connexion with Catholic practice lies in the fact that for long years after the Reformation pious Protestants still observed Good Friday as a day of penance by eating salt fish, etc.; the same conservative spirit seems to have introduced these plain buns marked with a cross as another form of fasting diet suitable for the occasion.

HOTEL, MAISON, DIEU (Fr., house of God.). A name frequently given to the hospitals established and conducted by religious during the middle ages; such was the *maison-dieu* still existing (as a museum), and so called, at Ospringe, near Faversham. The

name is sometimes still given to hospitals, e.g., at Paris and Quebec.

HOT WATER, Liturgical use of. See ZEON.

HOUR. One of the eight divisions of the Divine Office or Canonical Hours, so called because prescribed to be recited at or about definite times.

HOUSEHOLD OF THE POPE. See the PONTIFICAL FAMILY.

HOUSE, THE BLESSING OF A, may take place at any time with the form given in the "Rituale Romanum." All the houses of a parish should be blessed at Easter, with water taken from the font before the oil is put in, and with a special form consisting principally of the antiphon *Vidi aquam* (q.v.), and a prayer referring to the preservation of the houses of Israel in Egypt. There is also a special blessing for a new house, and for houses on the feast of the Epiphany.

HOUSE OF GOLD (Lat. *Domus aurea*). A title given to our Lady in the litany of Loreto; its first recorded use is by Cardinal Isidore (of Kiev), in 1463.

HOUSELLING-CLOTH (from *housel,* an obsolete English word for the Blessed Sacrament). A white linen cloth attached to the altar-rails in churches of the Latin rite; is held beneath the chin by communicants to catch the Sacred Host if it should be dropped. Instead or in addition must now be used a shallow metal dish, passed from hand to hand or held under each person's chin by the server or sacred minister.

HUGUENOTS. The historical name (originating in a nickname derived from Ger. *eidgenoss,* confederate), for the Protestants of France, followers of Calvin. In the 16th-17th centuries they numbered from one-tenth to one-fifteenth of the population, a large proportion of whom were wealthy and influential people; they called themselves Les *Réformés,* the Reformed, but were officially known as Les *Prétendus Réformés,* The So-called Reformed. At the Revolution they numbered about 430,000 and were reorganized as a body and recognized by the state in 1802. To-day there are about half-a-million Calvinists and small minorities of Lutherans and Independents, who exercise an influence far beyond that of their numbers, partly owing to their wealth. They show the same tendency to disintegration and to the liberalizing or abandonment of Christian doctrine as do Protestant bodies elsewhere.

HUMANISM. i. The intellectual development of the 14th-16th centuries in Europe which sought to base all art and learning on the culture of ancient Greece and Rome. Humanism opposed itself to Scholasticism. The movement was nursed by the Church;

such popes as Nicholas V, Pius II and Leo X were its champions, and such men as Cardinal Bessarion, Cardinal Nicholas of Cusa, Erasmus, Vives, and Pico della Mirandola among its leaders. But Humanism was well named; its enthusiasm was not tempered by control, it produced Carlo Aretino and Machiavelli as well as Dean Colet and St. Thomas More, and it helped to pave the way for the Reformation. In the event, Scholasticism returned and again flourishes. Among the legacies of Humanism are the insubordination of the state, whether represented by a dictator or a soviet, arising from its classical doctrine of collective morality as opposed to personal morality; and the substitution of class distinctions for differentiation by function. "Humanism . . . was mundane, pagan, irreligious, positive" (J. A. Symonds). See RENAISSANCE.

ii. In its more extended meaning, deriving from the above, Humanism is devotion to human interests or a system concerned with real or supposed human interests without reference to God or divine things; the belief in the self-sufficiency of the natural man, and of human values (cf., Pragmatism). But see PERSON, i.

HUMANITY. i. Human nature whereby man is man; the abstract of the concrete man; the idea of humanity is therefore a universal idea.

ii. The human race, mankind: the idea of humanity is then a collective idea.

iii. A virtue implying feelings of benevolence.

iv. In the plural, humanities, signifies scholarship, especially Latin and Greek classics.

v. The Religion of Humanity rejects the supernatural, and is concerned chiefly with the advancement of man's material welfare (Comte).

HUMANITY OF CHRIST, The. The human nature assumed by the second Person of the Blessed Trinity at the incarnation. It was a perfect human nature, "made of a woman, made under the law" (Gal. iv, 4), with body, soul, and human will, human affections and human passions (utterly exclusive of anything that could be construed as vice or sin). Christ loved, sorrowed, was angry; he felt the treason of Judas and the defection of his disciples; he "grew bewildered and dismayed" in Gethsemane (Mark xiv, 33); he suffered under the torments of his passion; he died.

HUMANITARIANISM. i. The philosophical and religious system of Auguste Comte (1798-1857), commonly called Positivism (q.v.).

ii. Any popular or personal version of the positivist "religion of humanity" whose chief object is the natural happiness and material comfort of human beings. It is generally associated with belief in a benevolent Deity

which tends to degenerate into a mild Pantheism (q.v.); this may account for the apparent perversity by which humanitarians are often unreasonably concerned about the "happiness" of the lower animals, sometimes at the expense of the convenience of human beings.

HUMERAL-VEIL (Lat. humerus, a shoulder). A veil of silk about 8 ft. by 3 ft., usually fringed and ornamented in the middle. It is worn at high Mass by the subdeacon when he carries the sacred vessels from the credence table to the altar and while he holds the paten at the foot of the steps; by the priest carrying the Blessed Sacrament in procession, giving benediction therewith or taking it as viaticum to the sick, and when a relic of the True Cross is carried in procession. It is worn round the shoulders like a shawl and the ends cover the hands only, if the Host is in a monstrance; any other vessel is covered entirely. Its colour is white, but at Mass it matches the other vestments, and is red for relics of the Cross.

HUMERALE. The name given to various shoulder coverings, predecessors of the amice, omophorion, pallium, rationale, etc. (qq.v.).

HUMILIATI (It., The Humble Ones). A penitential association of lay people founded in the 11th or 12th century. Their orthodoxy became compromised and for a time they were forbidden to preach. Early in the 13th century some of the members formed a regular religious order, the male branch of which was suppressed by Pope St. Pius V in 1571. There are still five houses of the nuns in Italy, also called Hospitallers of the Observance, engaged in nursing. Those who remained lay people were called the Third Order (depending on the others), the first instance of its kind.

HUMILITY. A moral virtue (q.v.) prompting in its possessor an appreciation and external expression of his true position with respect to God and his neighbour; opposed, therefore, both to pride and to immoderate self-abjection. As pride devastates the Christian character, so humility builds it up, or rather, is an absolutely necessary prerequisite and the first of the virtues to the extent that it removes the greater obstacles to faith, upon which all rests. But affected humility is odious and the virtue does not require that a man should depreciate his ability against his knowledge; for, says St. Thomas, "that a person should recognize and appreciate his own good qualities is no sin" and "humility consists in keeping oneself within one's own bounds"; to do this one must know those bounds, neither narrower nor wider than they really are.

HUNGARY, THE CHURCH IN. Though Hungary is commonly esteemed a "Catholic country" a third of its 9 million people are

Protestants of old standing, Jews and secularists. After world-war I the last-named element was responsible for the spoliation of many ecclesiastical institutions and properties; the same thing now is happening again, under Communist influence, for the Church was still a big landowner and the economic and social contrast between higher and lower clergy rather unhealthily marked: all are now being reduced to the same level of want. In 1939 all religions were in theory equal before the law, but there were certain restrictions on Judaism, and the Catholic Church still had a somewhat privileged position: *e.g.*, the bishops were all *ex-officio* senators; but the adherents of Calvinistic Protestantism are extremely influential. The primatial see is Esztergom, with 1 other metropolitan see, 1 archbishopric without suffragans, 7 other dioceses, and an abbacy *nullius*. There is also a diocese of 150,000 Catholics of Byzantine rite, who are mostly of Ruthenian and Rumanian origin but are now magyarized. (Hungarians call their country Magyarorszag and themselves Magyars.)

HUSBAND. The husband is the head of the family by natural law, and obedience (*q.v.*, iv) and loyalty are due to him from his wife. Nevertheless, he is a senior partner, not a master, and his wife a companion, not a servant (Eph. v. 22-23). He sins if he treats her with harshness or neglect; if he refuses her reasonable desire for marital intercourse; and if he withholds that love, consideration, and deference to her reasonable wishes which are her due. In cases of dispute in matters affecting them both (*e.g.*, where and how the children shall be educated), his reasonable decision must prevail, but may not be enforced arbitrarily or roughly; "harmony, which is an effect of charity, does not imply unity of opinion but unity of wills" (St. Thomas). He is bound to support his wife, children and step-children. His rite decides that of his children, except when he is a non-Catholic and his wife a Catholic (*cf.*, Wife, Parents).

HUSSITES. Name given to the followers of John Hus or Huss (1369-1415), who professed the errors of the Wycliffites (*q.v.*) in Bohemia. But their chief characteristic was Utraquism (*q.v.*) and their principal leaders John Ziska and Andrew Procopius. The movement was complicated by political considerations and war broke out between the Bohemian peasantry and the Emperor, Pope Martin V instituting a crusade against the Hussites; it was pursued with savagery on both sides for fifteen years. Sects of the Hussites fought among themselves, and embraced extravagant heresies, *e.g.*, the abolition of the liturgy, denial of Extreme Unction, auricular confession and Purgatory, the adoption of communism and sexual promiscuity. The less extreme of the Hussites were reconciled by the granting of communion in both kinds

and other concessions by the Council of Basle and later by the preaching of St. John Capistran (1385-1456); the successors of the more extreme are now known as Bohemian Brethren or Moravians (*q.v.*).

HYBRIDISM, LITURGICAL. The modification of Eastern liturgies, principally by the adoption or imposition, complete or adapted, of formulas, ceremonies and usages borrowed from the Roman rite. Many Catholics of the Eastern rites have suffered from this process. The most extreme examples are the Armenians of Transylvania and of Lvov, the Maronites and the Malabarese. The Copts, Ruthenians, Armenians, and Italo-Greeks have a number of such modifications and regard them as their proper usages; others are less affected and show a tendency to return to liturgical purity. This hybridism has a definitely discouraging effect on the reunion of the corresponding non-Catholics of these rites; Pope Benedict XIV forbade such innovations in 1743, Pius IX proclaimed the absolute equality of all Catholic rites in 1867, and lately the Syrian and Ethiopic rites underwent a reform in which Western intrusions were removed (*cf.*, Uniatism).

HYLOMORPHISM. The scholastic theory of matter and form (*q.v.*), in Greek ὕλη and μορφή respectively.

HYMN (Gr. ὕμνος, a religious song). A sung metrical composition in honour of God, of his saints, or otherwise of a religious character; briefly, a religious song. Hymns are either liturgical or non-liturgical (see below).

HYMN-BOOK. The hymns of the various rites of the Catholic Church being prescribed to be sung at appointed places in the liturgies, they are there printed and no separate collection of hymns is necessary. In the sense of an official book of vernacular hymns, the Church has not, and by the nature of the case cannot have, such a thing. Many countries have an officially authorized book of such hymns and tunes. In England it is the "Westminster Hymnal," in the U.S.A. the Baltimore "Manual of Hymns"; but many others are in use, *e.g.*, the "Catholic Hymnal" (ed. O'Farrell), "Armagh Hymnal" (ed. Leslie), "Dominican Hymnal," the "Book of Hymns" (ed. Ould).

HYMNS, LITURGICAL, are those appointed for use in the liturgy and consist principally of some 175 hymns with their tunes which form part of the Divine Office. The best known are *Lucis Creator optime* (Sunday at Vespers), *Te lucis ante terminum* (at Compline), *Ave maris Stella* (Vespers of Our Lady), *Iesu, dulcis memoria* (Vespers of the Holy Name), *Iste Confessor* (Vespers of the Common of Confessors), *Pange, lingua, gloriosi* (Vespers of Corpus Christi), *Stabat Mater dolorosa* (Lauds, Vespers and Mass of the VII Sorrows B.V.M.), *Veni, Creator* (Vespers and Terce of Pentecost and other occasions). It should be noted that the Office hymns underwent a "reform" by Pope Urban VIII (*q.v.*) which accounts for variant versions in some Breviaries. *Adoro te devote* (from the thanksgiving after Mass), *Dies iræ* (at requiems), *Lauda Sion* (Corpus Christi), *Victimæ paschali* (Easter), *Veni, Sancte Spiritus* (Pentecost), *Gloria, laus et honor* (Palm Sunday), are found in the Missal. Certain prose compositions, *e.g.*, the *Te Deum, Gloria in excelsis, Exsultet,* are always called hymns. Liturgical hymns may be sung at other times, *e.g.*, at Benediction or processions.

HYMNS, NON-LITURGICAL, are either in Latin or other liturgical language, *e.g., Veni, veni Emmanuel* (Advent), *Adeste fideles* (Christmas), *O filii et filiæ* (Easter), *Concordi lætitia, Stabat Mater speciosa, Omni die dic Mariæ* (of our Lady), etc., or in the vernacular language of the country. In England these may be divided into (*a*) hymns which are simply religious verse, good or bad, *e.g.*, "Lead, kindly Light," "Praise to the Holiest," "Sweet Sacrament Divine," "O thou undaunted daughter of desires," "God of mercy and compassion," "Immaculate Mary, our hearts are on fire," "I, the Ark, that for the graven Tables," "Ah me, how calm and deep," "Daily, daily"); (*b*) popular hymns in a more exact sense, such as carols (*q.v.*), folk-hymns, and compositions showing similar characteristics to these, *e.g.*, "Hierusalem, my happy home," Fr. Postgate's hymn, "Behold a silly tender babe." The first class now prevails exclusively in practice; but in those countries where the popular tradition has never been broken the second is still in common use, especially in country districts, *cf.*, the *noëls* of France. Non-liturgical hymns are an adjunct to the more formal worship; their use is common in England but they can hardly be called truly popular and in quality and variety they have suffered the same decay and neglect as other religious and ecclesiastical art.

HYPAPANTE (Gr., The Meeting [of our Lord and his mother with Simeon and Anna]), the name given to the feast of the Purification in the Byzantine rite; it has a vigil and an octave. It formerly had the same name, *Occursus Domini*, in the Latin rite. Copts call it "The Presentation" and Arabs and Armenians "The Entry of our Lord into the Temple." The Melkites alone of their rite bless candles, at *Hesperinos* (Vespers).

HYPERDULIA. The special homage paid to Mary on account of her supreme dignity as Mother of God, and her consequent unique holiness and nearness to God. It recognizes that she is a creature, and so it differs from *latria* (*q.v.*); but a creature holier and nobler than any angel or saint, and therefore worthy of a greater reverence than the *dulia* (*q.v.*) paid to them. It implies a loving reverence for God's mother and ours, and a confidence in her power and benevolence.

HYPNOTISM (Gr. ὕπνος, sleep). Artificial production of a state resembling deep sleep in which the subject acts only on external suggestion. According to the more probable opinion, many of the phenomena of mesmerism (*q.v.*) and hypnotism are based on natural processes, and as a consequence neither mesmerism nor hypnotism is to be absolutely condemned. These practices, however, should not be used by anyone just for curiosity, on account of the evils both physical and moral which can arise from their use. Scientists and doctors are allowed to make experiments for the furtherance of science and for the healing of certain maladies, provided they do not seek or expect anything preternatural, and provided proper safeguards be used and the consent of the patient obtained.

HYPOCRISY (Gr. ὑπόκρισις, acting of a part), is the feigning of virtues and qualities that one does not possess. It is a fruit of pride and partakes of the malice of lying; pretence in some form is necessary, for the mere concealment of one's sins is not in itself hypocrisy. The common notion that it is hypocrisy for a man to make public profession of a religion and its moral code without reference to his *bona-fide* failures, whether public or private, to live up to it, is an ebullition of ethicism (*q.v.*).

HYPOSTASIS. The Greek word (Gr. ὑπο, under; στάσις, position) for a supposit (*q.v.*). A complete substance, master of its own acts, and incommunicable. If this completely subsisting substance is of an intellectual nature it is called person (*q.v.*), whereas animals, trees, stones, etc., are called hypostases or supposits.

HYPOSTATIC UNION, The. Hypostasis means person or individual, and the hypostatic union is the union of the two distinct natures of God and man in the one person of Jesus Christ. Christ is true God and true man, consubstantial (*q.v.*) with the Father according to his godhead, consubstantial with us according to his humanity. The two natures are inseparably united, without confusion; they do not lose their distinction by their union, but what is proper to each is conserved; but they are united in one person and one subsistence. There are consequently two wills, and two operations.

HYPOTHESIS (Gr., foundation). A supposition made to explain certain facts, without reference to its truth, used as a starting-point for investigation. Hypothesis is most useful in natural sciences, as is evidenced by the discoveries of Copernicus, Kepler, Galileo, Newton and others. To be good, or preferable to others, an hypothesis must have these conditions: it must not be incompatible with any observed fact, but explain all facts in some wise; and it must be the most simple of possible hypotheses, or at least be the one which explains phenomena in the best way. An hypothesis does not become a *thesis* until it is shown that all other hypotheses are wrong.

HYSSOP. Leafy twigs of a shrub, either marjoram or the thorny caper, used for sprinkling in the Jewish rites of purification; (*cf.*, the beginning of the *Asperges*).

I

I. H. S. See MONOGRAM.

I. S. H. S. See EXEMPT ii.

ICELAND, THE CHURCH IN. The Danish penal laws against Catholics were in force from the Reformation till 1874, when freedom of worship was granted. There are now about 500 Catholics among 120,000 Lutherans, the island being a vicariate apostolic in charge of priests of the Company of Mary. The vicar apostolic has the episcopal title of the old Icelandic see of Holar.

ICON, EIKON (Gr. εἰκών, an image). The name may be applied to any image, but in practice is confined to the flat paintings which take the place of statues in Eastern churches. Among the Byzantines, especially the Greeks and Russians, the icons are often protected by a covering of metal on which the outline of the picture is stamped or engraved and which is cut away to show the face and hands; except on modern very cheap "commercial" icons the whole of the picture is painted underneath and the metal is removable; it is inexact to reserve the name, icon to those having such a metal shield. The characteristics of all icon-painting (except the Coptic) derive ultimately from the post-Iconoclasm Byzantine painters and have been preserved to this day. Yet Western influences can be traced, possibly very early in Russia, and "Our Lady of Perpetual Succour" (not popular versions of it), apparently a purely Byzantine icon, known in Russia as Our Lady of the Passion, is believed by some to be of Western origin. Eastern churches are full of icons (except those of the Nestorians, who have given up the use of all images, as the Jacobites tend to do), and that of the saint of the day is usually displayed on the *analogion*. Icons play a more conspicuous part in worship than do statues in the West; they are repeatedly incensed, kissed, carried in procession, and otherwise reverenced, those of our Lord and our Lady on the *iconostasis* (*q.v.*) especially; these are kissed before communion and before them the priest and deacon prepare for the Liturgy. Some Catholic churches of Eastern rites have now statues as well as or even instead of icons, a liturgically corrupt practice.

ICONOCLASM (Gr. Εἰκονοκλασμος, image-breaking). The heresy that the veneration (relative worship) of holy images is unlawful. About 726 the Emperor Leo the Isaurian published an edict which led to the destruction of images and persecution of their defenders. In 787 the seventh œcumenical council (ii Nicæa) defined that "both the figure of the sacred and life-giving cross, as also the venerable and holy images . . . are to be placed suitably in the holy churches of God . . ." but that the honour paid to them is only relative for the sake of their prototypes: they are to receive veneration, not adoration; that is the faith of the Catholic Church and of the now separated Orthodox. But in 814 Iconoclasm broke out again at the instigation of the Emperor Leo the Armenian and his successors, and the persecution of orthodox Catholics and destruction of monasteries and images lasted till the Empress Theodora became regent in 842. St. John the Damascene and St. Theodore the Studite were the principle defenders of the orthodox teaching and practice. The custom in the East of using icons and mosaics but not round statues or other carved images seems to be a back-wash of Iconoclasm.

ICONOGRAPHY, CHRISTIAN. The representation of God, his saints, etc., by means of pictures, statues, mosaics or any other made images. Iconology is the study and knowledge of these images.

ICONOSTASIS (Gr., picture-stand). In churches of the Byzantine rite, a solid barrier between the sanctuary and the nave, consisting of from one to five or more rows of icons. It is pierced by three doors, the middle one with double half-doors closed by a curtain, and the whole screen is generally covered with icons: our Lord on the right and our Lady on the left of the middle (holy) doors are essential. A common arrangement is St. John Baptist and the patron-saint beside the south and north doors respectively which have St. Michael and St. Gabriel on them; the Annunciation on the holy doors; above, a row representing liturgical feasts; above that, the apostles; again above, a row of prophets with a cross or calvary-group at the very top. The whole is gilt and painted and lamps burn before the principal paintings. All Orthodox churches have an *iconostasis* (Slav ones richer and taller than the Greek); so do Catholic Byzantine churches when they can afford them. The Ruthenians sometimes have open screens which do not hide the altar, and most of the Italo-Greek churches have none at all; the same is true of America. This characteristic adornment, which in part is now really a liturgical necessity, is sometimes called the *templon*; it took on its present form in the late middle ages, developing from the barrier of columns such as may be seen in the cathedral of Torcello and S. Maria in Cosmedin.

IDEA (from Gr. ἰδεῖν, to see). Mental representation of an object. In scholastic philosophy an idea represents *directly* the universal nature, or the *quod quid est*, of a thing stripped of its individuating notes: thus the particular is known only indirectly and, as it were, by reflection. See SPECIES.

IDEALISM. i. Rationalistic Idealism denotes the view that the world is governed by an idea or plan. Aristotle and theistic philosophers are idealists in this sense, though they may believe in the existence of a real material world.
  ii. Phenomenal Idealism means the theory that denies all material reality. Idealism in the first signification is opposed to a purely mechanical theory of the genesis and conservation of the world; in the last to realism (*q.v.*), or the assumption of the existence of a real extra-mental world.
  iii. In its colloquial sense, an ideal is an exalted object to be striven for, *e.g.*, a high standard of personal conduct, or an entirely just ordering of society: hence "idealism", for living under the inspiration of such objects. Because idealism in this sense is apt to waste itself in ineffectual aspiration or high-flown talk it has incurred the contempt of some. Unjustly: for when vague idealism appears as a useless substitute for practical action, this is a degeneration; Christianity is by excellence the teaching that holds up high ideals before its followers and urges them to try to live in the light of such perfections.

IDENTITAS MYSTERII (Lat., sameness of mystery). A term referring to two feasts whose object is the same person, *e.g.*, the Sacred Heart and the Crown of Thorns.

IDENTITY, THE PRINCIPLE OF. Every being is its own nature.

IDEOLOGY. Name given by d'Alembert, Tracy and other disciples of Locke and Condillac to that part of philosophy which treats of "being" and general ideas, such as the Transcendentals, the Categories, etc. But latterly the word has come into popular use to indicate any philosophy, world-view or set of ideas, especially political.

IDES. The eighth day after the nones (*q.v.*); 15th of March, May, July and October, 13th of other months. Part of the Roman system of dating, still sometimes used in ecclesiastical documents.

IDIORRHYTHMY (Gr., one's own arrangements). The life of an Orthodox Eastern monastery in which the monks live either apart or as members of a family of 7 or 8, presided over by a *proestos*. Each receives fuel, wine, some food and a little money, but for the rest must support himself, and is not deterred by any vow of poverty. They meet in church to sing the office and dine together on great feasts. The whole monastery is administered by the council of *proestoi*. Nine of the Mount Athos monasteries are idiorrhythmic and must be distinguished from an ordinary monastery, which is a *cœnobium*.

IDLENESS. i. The state of having nothing to do or of doing nothing.
  ii. A vice disinclining one to work. Man is bound to occupy his time with work in order to earn a livelihood for himself and dependents or to prevent the Devil from finding work for him. Idleness is not the capital sin of sloth (*q.v.*).

IDOL (Gr. εἴδωλον, image, a phantom). Any person or thing, other than God, usually an image of some kind, to which divine worship is paid. The images in Catholic churches are not idols because divine worship is not given to them. The "graven things" forbidden by Exodus xx, 4-5, are precisely idols as above, and not images in themselves.

IDOLATRY. The giving of divine worship to anyone or anything but God; in itself, the greatest of mortal sins. Even material idolatry, whereby on account of fear or some other reason mere external worship is given to a creature with no intention of worshipping it, is a grave sin. To worship God in a wrong way (*e.g.*, by joining seriously in the worship of the Jews) is also a form of idolatry. Catholics are sometimes accused of idolatry in respect of the Blessed Sacrament, our Lady and the saints, relics and images: they do indeed worship the Blessed Sacrament—because it is God under the appearances of bread; to our Lady and the saints they give a veneration and honour which may be properly accorded to those who are human like ourselves but immeasurably exceed us in virtue, and are moreover now in very truth at the right hand of God; to images is given honour which refers to those whom they represent: God is worshipped through the image, which itself can neither hear nor help.

IGNORANCE. The absence of knowledge in one capable of such knowledge. Ignorance is vincible or invincible (*qq.v.*) according as it could or could not have been dispelled by a reasonable exercise of moral diligence. It is *crass* ignorance if next to no attempt has been made at self-enlightenment. Ignorance is *affected* if the means of finding out what one ought to know are deliberately and purposely neglected, precisely in order that one may not know it; so that, for instance, one may sin more freely. Ignorance must be distinguished from nescience and error (*qq.v.*). Voluntary and vincible ignorance of such matters as the truths of faith necessary to salvation or the duties of one's state of life is in itself sinful. Ignorance does not invalidate any act that is otherwise valid.

IGNORANCE, INVINCIBLE. The lack of an element of knowledge, which is not to be ascribed to want of due diligence on the part of the subject. Thus a man educated in Protestant surroundings would probably be invincibly ignorant of the Immaculate Conception. Since such ignorance cannot be dispelled by the use of ordinary diligence, it is in itself free from blame and no bad action done as a result thereof can be a formal sin; the doer not knowing its malice it is involuntary and not imputable to him.

IGNORANCE, VINCIBLE. Ignorance is a lack of the knowledge of the truth. It is vincible when it is due to want of reasonable effort in investigation. It is opposed to invincible ignorance (*q.v.*). One who does a wrong action in vincible ignorance is less blameworthy than if he had full knowledge; nevertheless, he is not excused thereby for, though he does not will the evil in itself, he wills its cause and so sins.

ILLATIVE SENSE. That supposed faculty of the mind which perfectly integrates all the subtle and elusive elements of judgement and reasoning and gives to their conclusions a life-value which is larger than the logical value of the conclusion of a syllogism. The name was invented by Cardinal Newman in his "Grammar of Assent" and the idea is an integral part of his epistemology; but the whole of his epistemology has been adversely criticized by scholastic philosophers.

ILLEGITIMACY. i. The condition of those born out of wedlock. A bastard becomes legitimate in canon law upon the marriage of its parents if they were free to marry one another at the time the child was conceived, or born or at any time in between: otherwise it can only be legitimized (1) by a dispensation from the diriment impediment granted either by "ordinary power," or by "power delegated" through a general indult, except in the case of adulterous or sacrilegious offspring; (2) by a particular rescript of the Holy See. Legitimation by subsequent marriage is now the law in most civilized countries, but not in many states of the U.S.A. In the case of a "marriage" actually canonically null and void because of a diriment impediment unknown to one or both of the parties, the children are legitimate; and they are esteemed so in cases of doubt (*e.g.,*

foundlings) unless and until the contrary is proved.

ii. Illegitimacy (defect of birth) is an irregularity (*q.v.*) preventing the reception or exercise of holy orders. It ceases by legitimation, by dispensation (granted by the Holy See, or by bishops and others in virtue of delegated authority), and by solemn religious profession.

ILLICIT. Unlawful, forbidden. Illicit must be distinguished from invalid; *e.g.*, it is illicit for a Catholic lay person to baptize a baby (except in case of necessity), but such illicit baptism is valid, *i.e.*, the baby is truly baptized. This distinction is of particular importance in marriage cases. A diriment impediment (*q.v.*) makes an attempted marriage invalid and of no effect; *e.g.*, if a man goes through a marriage ceremony with his first cousin, without dispensation, it is invalid, no marriage. A prohibiting impediment (*q.v.*) makes a marriage illicit (and if entered into without dispensation, with deliberation and full knowledge, a sin), but it is valid, a true marriage; *e.g.*, if a Catholic marries a baptized non-Catholic without dispensation, the marriage is valid but illicit.

ILLUMINATI. i. An heretical Spanish sect of the 16th–17th centuries which claimed that it is possible to reach a mystical state in which the very essence of God is contemplated.

ii. An influential secret society to destroy revealed religion, founded in Germany in 1776. See ILLUMINISM.

ILLUMINATIVE WAY, The. The second stage of the spiritual life, following on the purgative way (*q.v.*). In it "man principally aims at progressing in good, and this endeavour belongs to proficients, who chiefly strive to strengthen charity by increasing it" (St. Thomas, II–II, xxiv, 9). It is spiritual adolescence, and consists in following Jesus Christ, the light of the world, in the earnest pursuit of holiness. The soul is no longer weak in charity, but definitely virtuous. In prayer the will is readily stirred to affections without many reflections; indeed, according to Suarez, affective prayer is characteristic of this state.

ILLUMINISM. In general, the claim to possess special enlightenment, put forward by the founders of many sects and their followers. Specially, the teaching of an esoteric sect founded and secretly established with consummate ability by Adam Weishaupt (1748–1830), a professor of canon law in the University of Ingolstadt. Its object was to overthrow every kind of government, civil, ecclesiastical and paternal, and to restore what Weishaupt considered the primitive state of absolute liberty and equality. He stuck at nothing in his enterprise, initiating his disciples into all manner of deceit with a readiness to commit any crime for the cause, on the plea that the end justified the means. His plotting was discovered and many of his disciples were punished by the Elector of Bavaria, but Weishaupt escaped to Ratisbon where he carried on a pamphlet war. Later he sought the protection of the Duke of Saxe-Gotha. The sect gradually declined in the first quarter of the 19th century, but not before it had infected many of the clergy with rationalism. With a view to its destruction the Holy See signed concordats with Bavaria in 1817 and with Prussia in 1821. The founder was reconciled with the Church before his death.

IMAGE. A sculpture, painting, etc., of our Lord, our Lady or other of the saints, or of some other person. Properly speaking an image is not a naturalistic portrait or representation of the person designated though it may incidentally be such; essentially it is heraldic, symbolic and conventional. It does not seek to create an illusion; it is part of the furniture of a church or house, or shrine, either architecturally (*e.g.*, the sculptures on the west porch of Chartres) or liturgically (*e.g.*, the crucifix on an altar) or devotionally (*e.g.*, the statue of St. Antony in many churches). Images are properly to be regarded as a complement to the liturgy; as the liturgy is public worship, so an image is something publicly venerated. A sentimental or realistic character being inappropriate to a thing publicly owned and used, "likeness to nature" is of no importance compared with religious and dogmatic significance.

IMAGE OF GOD, The. "Man is said to be in the image of God, not according to his body, but according to that by which man excels other animals. Wherefore after the saying 'Let us make man to our image and likeness,' it is added 'and let him have dominion over the fishes of the sea,' etc. (Gen. i, 26). But man excels all animals by his reason and intellect. Wherefore, according to intellect and reason, which are incorporeal, man is in the image of God" (St. Thomas, I, iii, 1 ad 2).

IMAGES, VEILING OF. Before the first Vespers of Passion Sunday all the crosses, pictures, statues, etc., of a church are covered with unadorned purple veils. Those of the cross are removed on Good Friday and the others at the *Gloria in excelsis* on Holy Saturday; the stations of the cross need not be covered. This is an obvious sign of mourning and also may have reference to the words "He hid himself" in the gospel of Passion Sunday; but the former covering of the whole rood-screen with a "Lenten veil" (*q.v.*) at the beginning of Lent is probably its true origin. The Maronites and Melkites also have this custom, but the latter do not cover their *ikons* until Vespers on Palm Sunday.

IMAGES, VENERATION OF. A relative honour or *cultus* is to be paid to sacred images and relics, inasmuch as they relate to Christ and the saints. Public veneration is not to be paid to images other than those in traditional use in the Church, of which the bishop is the judge. The blessing of images for public veneration is reserved to the ordinary, who may delegate it to others. No sacred pictures may be printed or reproduced for public veneration or distribution without being submitted to previous ecclesiastical censorship. Of the veneration of images the Council of Trent says: "The images especially of Christ, of the Virgin Mother of God, and of other saints, are to be had and kept in churches and due honour and reverence paid to them; not because it is believed that there is any divinity or power in them or that anything may be asked from them, or that any faith may be put in them as the heathen used . . . but because the honour shown to them is referred to the prototypes which they represent; so that, through these images which we kiss and before which we bow with bared heads, we worship Christ and honour the saints whose likeness they display" (sess. xxv) (*cf.* also, Idolatry, Invocation of Saints). With the permission of the ordinary, images of those holy ones who have been neither canonized nor beatified may be displayed on the walls or windows of churches (except over altars) provided no religious veneration is publicly shown to them.

IMAGES-NOT-MADE-WITH-HANDS (Gr. εἰκόνες ἀχειροποίηται). Certain images of our Lord are so called as having been imprinted by contact with his sacred face, *e.g.*, the Veronica and the Mandeylion (*qq.v.*), or otherwise miraculously made. Several such images are, or were, venerated in Russia, of which the best known was the wonder-working icon in the chapel of the Little House of Peter the Great at Petrograd, and another venerated by the Georgians at Tiflis.

IMAGINATION. A faculty which retains and reproduces representations of absent material objects: one of the four internal senses. The representation or phantasm of the imagination differs from the act whereby we perceive a real object such as a horse: the former is invariably very faint in intensity as compared with the latter; it is also of an unsteady and transitory character as compared with the representation of a real object which is characterized by permanency and stability. The greatest difference between the two is the reference to objective reality by the latter which is absent from the former. The word Fancy is sometimes used to mark the activity of the imagination as exercised in the production of comic or even of beautiful things; it is confined to the sphere of the unreal, whilst imagination may represent the actual.

IMBOMON, The (Gr., raised place). The round chapel built at the place on the Mount of Olives from whence our Lord went back into Heaven. The first was built about 350, the present building by the Crusaders; in it the Franciscans sing Mass and Office on the feast of the Ascension, camping round about from the vigil.

IMMACULATE CONCEPTION, The, of the Blessed Virgin Mary. i. The doctrine that our Lady "in the first instant of her conception was, by a singular grace and privilege of Almighty God in view of the merits of Jesus Christ the Saviour of the human race, preserved exempt from all stain of original sin" (q.v.). It must be noticed that, contrary to a common error, this doctrine has nothing to do with the virgin-birth of Christ; nor does it involve a virgin-birth of Mary; she was physically conceived and born in the ordinary way. But her soul at the first moment of its creation and infusion into her body was clothed in sanctifying grace (q.v.) which to every other child of Adam is only given in the first instance after birth and, since Christ, at Baptism (though it is generally held that Jeremias and St. John Baptist received it before birth, but not at conception); the stain of original sin was not removed but excluded from her soul. "It was altogether becoming that as the Only Begotten had a Father in Heaven whom the seraphim extol as thrice holy, so he should have a mother on earth who should never lack the splendour of holiness." In 1854 Pope Pius IX declared by the bull *Ineffabilis Deus* (from which all quotations in this paragraph are taken) that it "is a doctrine revealed by God and therefore must be believed firmly and constantly by all the faithful." This was a declaration that it had always formed part of the Apostolic Faith, though for long and by individuals hitherto believed only implicitly (q.v.). Even after the schism this doctrine was taught explicitly by some dissident Eastern theologians but was officially repudiated by Anthimos VII, patriarch of Constantinople, in 1895, and the Orthodox Eastern catechism in English denies it; but it seems probable that most dissident orientals hold the doctrine implicitly.

ii. The feast of "the Child-begetting of the Mother of the Mother of God" was observed in the East before the 8th century and is kept by all Eastern churches. It was apparently not observed in the West much before the 11th century, under the title of the "Conception of Our Lady." "Immaculate" was added, and a new Mass and Office provided in 1863; it is kept on Dec. 8 and is a double of the 1st class with a vigil and octave, and is a holiday of obligation (but not in England).

IMMANENCE (Lat. *in manere*, to remain within). i. The property of an activity, the principle and term of which are the same.

See ACTION. An immanent act is therefore opposed to transitive, which passes to something external. Immanent is also opposed to transcendent (q.v.). In Spinozism and Pantheism God is immanent to the world, and not (as in Catholic philosophy) transcendent—often called the "Philosophies of Immanence."

ii. Divine. The dwelling of God in creatures. The term is used in two ways: (a) Its legitimate use is to express the fact that in God we live and move and have our being, that he has made us with all our faculties, and that we have the constant aid of the divine *concursus* (q.v.); furthermore, that in a distinct and supernatural way he is in the souls of the just. This indwelling of God in the souls of the just is the object of a quasi-experimental knowledge of God to the mystics, whose souls are most intimately united with him, and who in virtue of a refined faith and the gifts of the Holy Ghost have a mystical "contact" with him. (b) This second legitimate sense of a supernatural indwelling is on one side of the border which, when crossed, gives the illegitimate use. Immanence is then the positive aspect of Modernism (q.v.), the doctrine that we are in some sort emanations of the divine substance, and that the only way to get a knowledge of God (q.v.) is by our subconscious mind. This is opposed to divine transcendance (q.v.), which is the complement and safeguard of the true doctrine of immanence, and, indeed, to the direct teaching of the Vatican Council.

IMMEDIATELY SUBJECT TO THE HOLY SEE, DIOCESE. See EXEMPT DIOCESE. Usually contracted into i.s.h.s.

IMMERSION. A method of baptism by completely immersing the candidate in water. Most Eastern rites, Catholic or dissident, practise immersion or semi-immersion. The *Rituale Romanum* prints the rite for baptism by immersion, whether of infants or adults, for use where (if anywhere) that is still the custom in the Western church. See BAPTISM CEREMONIES, ii.

IMMORTALITY. That attribute in virtue of which a being is free from death. A being is incorruptible if it does not contain within itself a principle of dissolution; it is indestructible if it can resist every external power tending to destroy it. If the indestructible and incorruptible being is endowed with life it is called immortal. Annihilation is always possible to God by the mere withdrawal of his conserving act.

IMMORTALITY OF ADAM, The. Ultimate death was the natural lot of Adam and Eve. God, however, conditionally promised them the preternatural gift of immortality; the condition was not fulfilled and immortality was withheld (Gen. ii, 16-17; iii, 19). The

Council of Trent (canon i, sess. 5) condemned those who denied that "the offence of this prevarication incurred the wrath and indignation of God and therewith *death*, with which God had previously threatened him."

IMMORTALITY OF THE SOUL. That attribute in virtue of which the human soul is free from death. That the soul is immortal is proved thus: (*a*) The human soul is incorruptible both *per se* and *per accidens*. See INCORRUPTIBILITY. (*b*) The human soul cannot be annihilated either by itself or by any created being. Annihiliation is the reduction of something to nothing. But this cannot be the effect of any positive action for every positive action terminates in a positive reality. Any positive act, other than creation, therefore can only cause a change in the soul. Therefore any action whether of the soul itself or of any other creature can effect merely a change in the soul. It follows therefore that annihilation can be effected by God alone who created and conserves the soul in being by the withdrawal of his sustaining or conservative act. (*c*) The human soul does not perish at death. The moral law commands us to do right and avoid wrong; but God is a wise, just and holy legislator; he must therefore have fortified this law with a perfect sanction. Now there is no such perfect sanction in this life. Therefore the soul must exist for at least some time after death, so that the present deficiencies of the practical order shall be set right. If there is no retributory state, then the moral life of man is an hallucination. Other arguments to establish that the soul does not perish at death can be drawn (1) from the desire of perfect happiness which is unattainable in this life, and (2) from the universal judgement of mankind in the belief of a future life, a judgement that cannot lead man into error since it springs from man's rational nature. (*d*) There is no ground for supposing that the soul will ever perish, for no reason can be given why God should annihilate it. The end for which God conserves the soul in existence is his own extrinsic glory. But this remains for ever. Therefore the act of conservation should be everlasting. The only conceivable grounds to the contrary are (1) the incapacity of the soul to act apart from the body and therefore its inability to love and praise God (now against this it can be urged that since it is proved the soul lives at least some time after death it is capable of experiencing reward or punishment, it must therefore be endowed with mind and will, and so is capable of contributing to the glory of God); and (2) the unworthiness of the souls of the wicked to exist (but against this it can be urged that they can continue for all eternity to glorify by their punishment the offended majesty and justice of God).

IMMOVABLE FEASTS are those which are fixed for a certain day in the month. Some of them are liable to be transferred to another day or even ignored liturgically in certain circumstances, *e.g.*, if Corpus Christi falls on May 30, the feast of St. Felix is not celebrated that year or when March 25 occurs in Holy Week the Annunciation is put off until after Easter.

IMMUNITY (Lat. *immunis*, free from public service). i. Exemptions granted by law in favour of ecclesiastical persons, places or property; *e.g.*, the immunity of clerics from military service or service on juries, of churches from profane use, of ecclesiastical buildings from taxation (*cf.*, Privilege ii).

ii. The rights conceded by international law to the premises and persons of the diplomatic agents of foreign powers accredited to a state, particularly the right of extraterritoriality. By the Treaty of the Lateran these immunities were granted to papal properties within Rome and its environs but outside the Vatican City (*q.v.*) and also to the buildings occupied by the Dataria, the Chancery, the Holy Office, the Congregations of the Eastern Church and of Propaganda and the Vicariate of Rome and any others on Italian territory in which the Holy See might establish its administrative and judicial bodies. The right of immunity is extended to all churches in Italy during the time at which the pope is assisting therein at ceremonies not open to the public.

"IMMURING OF NUNS." To wall up living nuns (or anybody else), in the sense of depriving them of air and so putting them to death, has never been a punitive practice of the Catholic Church or of any of her institutions. The fable probably originated with the technical terms for imprisonment in the local inquisitions (*e.g.*, *murus strictus seu arctus* for "solitary confinement") and was popularized in England by Sir Walter Scott (in "Marmion"), Mrs. Browning (in "The Lay of the Brown Rosary"), and by other innocent writers or unscrupulous controversialists. But that mediæval ecclesiastical prisons were often scandalous places and their punishments crude and severe cannot be denied; nor that the Holy See and its legates were active in putting down these abuses when they were able. Moreover, there has been confusion with the voluntary *inclusi* (*q.v.*); and in some places monastic offenders were enclosed in the same way, but not necessarily for life.

IMPANATION. The error concerning the real presence of Christ in the Eucharist taught by Oseander, a disciple of Luther, *viz.*, that the bread is not changed into the body of Christ, but that after the consecration both substances are present unchanged in the one individual—a sort of hypostatic union.

IMPASSIBILITY. Freedom from suffering. It is the common teaching of theologians that Adam and Eve had this condition before the Fall, but it has not been defined by the Church. It need not mean that they could not feel any pain, but only that they were free from those evils which are due, directly or indirectly, to the fallen state of human nature. Complete impassibility, freedom from suffering, defect and corruption, will be a quality of the risen bodies of the just.

IMPECCABILITY. Inability to sin. Occasionally confounded with infallibility (q.v.), with which it has nothing to do, and with sinlessness. The man Jesus Christ was the only impeccable man in the history of the world; theologians assert that our Lady, who was certainly sinless, was impeccable, not by nature but by divine privilege.

IMPEDIMENTS TO MARRIAGE are obstacles which render a marriage either unlawful (illicit, q.v.) or invalid. They are divided into (a) diriment and prohibiting impediments (qq.v.) and (b) impediments of the divine or natural law and those of ecclesiastical law. Impediments of the natural law (e.g., that one of the parties is already married) never change and can never be dispensed. Impediments which are the result of the discipline of the Church (e.g., holy orders, difference of worship) are subject to change and some operate only in the Western church; moreover they are dispensable, but certain of them (e.g., priesthood) are never subject to dispensation because of their extreme gravity.

IMPEDIMENTS TO ORDINATION. In addition to the perpetual impediments called irregularities (q.v.) the following classes of men are debarred from ordination until the impediment ceases or is dispensed: sons of non-Catholics so long as their parents remain in error, husbands of wives (never dispensed ordinarily, see BACHELOR), those holding an office forbidden to clerics, slaves, those bound to military service, neophytes recently baptized or reconciled, and those labouring under infamy of fact (q.v.).

IMPENITENCE, FINAL. The sin against the Holy Ghost committed by one who, at the hour of death, wilfully remains impenitent of his grievous sins.

IMPERFECTIONS are of two kinds: negative, when, moved to perform a good action which one is not bound to do, one fails to do it; positive, a violation of God's known will in a matter that does not strictly oblige us, e.g., non-observance of his rule by a secular tertiary (q.v.), the observance of which is desired by God but does not bind under pain of sin. An imperfection, then, is not a sin.

IMPETRATION (Lat. impetrare, to obtain), or petition, is prayer appealing to the goodness of God and asking for the spiritual or temporal welfare, in general or particular, of ourselves or others. Distinguish from propitiation (q.v.).

IMPLICIT. In common speech implicit is used, generally in connexion with "faith" or "trust," to mean absolute, unreserved and even openly expressed. Theologians use the word more accurately: e.g., an implicit truth is one contained, and perhaps concealed, in other explicit or clear and definite truths, and an explicit belief in the second involves implicit belief in the first. Thus, the age-long explicit doctrine that the pope as the successor of St. Peter is supreme teacher, who has ever kept the Faith pure and with whom all must be in communion, contained implicitly the doctrine of papal infallibility (not defined explicitly until 1870).

IMPOSITION OF HANDS. The ceremonial laying of the hands, or analogous movement, on a person or thing, usually to convey some spiritual quality or power, is of common use in the Church. (a) At confirmation it takes place at the beginning of the rite and again in the act of anointing, the second imposition jointly with the anointing being the essential matter (q.v.) of the sacrament in the general view of theologians. (b) In the ordaining of deacons there is an imposition of hands, and of priests, three, and again in the consecration of a bishop. The laying-on of hands in these three ordination rites is alone the matter (q.v.) of the respective orders. At the ordination of a priest, all the priests present lay on their hands after the bishop. In the Eastern rites also imposition alone forms the matter of Orders. (c) In other rites and blessings (e.g., Baptism, Exorcism) and at the Hanc igitur (q.v.) at Mass.

IMPOTENCY. The inability of a person of either sex to have complete sexual intercourse. It is a matrimonial impediment of the natural law if it precedes the celebration of marriage and if it is of its nature permanent, whether it is absolute or relative, and whether known to the other party or not. In doubt of impotency, whether a doubt of law or a doubt of fact, marriage is not to be impeded. It must be distinguished from sterility (q.v.), which is not an impediment. Either party can claim nullity of marriage by reason of impotency, and special procedure is provided in canon law for the trial of such cases.

IMPRIMATUR (Lat., let it be printed). The word by which a bishop or his delegate licenses a book for publication (see CENSORSHIP OF BOOKS); the licence itself.

IMPRIMI POTEST (Lat., it may be printed). The words by which the general, provincial or other prelate of a religious order or his delegate approves of the publication of a book by a member of the order. It is required in many orders in addition to the episcopal licence (*imprimatur*).

IMPROPERIA. The Reproaches in the Office of Good Friday, sung antiphonally by two choirs and recited by the celebrant and his ministers. They are addressed by Christ to all men in the person of the Jews, reciting his mercies and their ingratitude; the first three have as refrain the *Trisagion* in Greek and Latin, and the remaining nine ver. 3 of Micheas vi. They are concluded by an antiphon, "We worship thy cross," etc. The name often refers to musical settings of the Reproaches, especially those published by Palestrina in 1560.

IMPROPRIATION. The making over of tithes (*q.v.*), due to a parish-church, to a religious house or other corporation or to an individual, ecclesiastical or lay. The impropriator or patron then became rector and was bound to provide a vicar for the church with an adequate stipend. This proceeding was very common in England from the 12th century onwards and is the basis of the distinction between rectors and vicars in the Church of England to-day, the vast number of monastic impropriations having passed into lay hands; it also enables a Catholic landowner to find himself lay-rector of an Anglican church with the right to present an incumbent to the living—but exercise of the right is barred to Catholics (but not to Jews) by the civil law.

IMPUTABILITY (Lat. *imputare*, to reckon). i. The ascription of the guilt of sin to the sinner. Imputability may be lessened by lack of full advertence to the sinfulness of the act and by diminished consent of the will; material sin (*q.v.*) is not imputable at all. From the nature of the case, the subjective malice of sin and its consequent degree of imputability can ordinarily be estimated with absolute certainty and accuracy only by the infinite knowledge of God.
ii. The heretical Protestant doctrine of justification (*q.v.*) as the remission of sin by the imputation of the righteousness of Christ: that justified man is only declared and reputed just, whereas in fact he is really made so.

IN ARTICULO MORTIS. Lat., at the moment of death.

IN CŒNA DOMINI. i. A papal bull so called because it was issued annually on Maundy Thursday, the day "of the Lord's supper." It excommunicated, generally and by name, heretics, renegades, corsairs and other criminals, and certain offenders against the rights of the Church and of the Holy See.

These excommunications were reserved (*q.v.*) to the pope. It was first published in 1364, suppressed in 1773 and abrogated in 1869 by the bull *Apostolicæ Sedis* which revised the whole law of censures.
ii. *Feria quinta in cœna Domini*. Maundy Thursday (*q.v.*).

IN COMMENDAM [DEPOSITUM] (Lat., given in trust). i. A benefice held *in commendam* was one which, being without an occupant, was temporarily put under the care of another ecclesiastic who drew its revenues. So obvious a measure of convenience was used very early, but is unknown to-day except in the case of certain cardinals *in curia*.
ii. The common historical meaning of the phrase is with reference to abbeys and other religious houses of which the revenues were granted to an ecclesiastic not a member of the order concerned, or to a layman, for his own use, another person being appointed acting superior. The beneficiary was supposed to regard the abbey as recommended (*commendatus*) to his care. This was an abuse already in the 8th century and was responsible more than any other single cause for spiritual and material decay in monasteries, which became a temporal part of the feudal system; it was at its worst in the 13th and 14th centuries, and in France continued till the Revolution—Cardinal Richelieu held 20 abbeys; S. Germain-des-Prés had princes and a king among its commendatory abbots. In England, at any rate after William I, this abuse was unknown among the monasteries; Wolsey holding Saint Albans *in commendam* was the first and only example (*cf.*, Pluralism).

IN FIERI. A scholastic expression designating the passage from potency to act (*q.v.*), and is opposed to *in facto esse* which expresses "being" or the term of the passage.

IN GLOBO (Lat., in a lump). The condemnation of a number of propositions all together as false, evil-sounding, scandalous, heretical, etc., without indicating the degree of error attached to each proposition, as was done, *e.g.*, in the constitution *Unigenitus* (*q.v.* ii).

IN NOMINE PATRIS et Filii et Spiritus Sancti (Lat., In the name of the Father and of the Son and of the Holy Ghost). (*a*) The formula used in Baptism. (*b*) With the addition of *Amen* a formula of sanctification which accompanies the sign of the cross (*q.v.*) used before undertaking prayer, preaching or any other work, spiritual or temporal. It is thus used at the beginning of Mass, where it has immediate reference to those prayers up to the introit which really are a preparation. It is also used liturgically as a part of other formulas, *e.g.*, of absolution (with a sign of the cross over the penitent), in the prayer of exorcism, immediately before anointing the sick, and in mingling salt at the making of holy water (in both cases with three signs of the cross). The phrase is more than the mere labelling of an act as specifically Christian; "name" is taken in its more extended sense, of a living person (cf., the Eastern prayer, "Remember, O Lord, thy servants . . . every one by his own name . . ."), and the speaker in some sort and according to whether he be priest or lay person thus announces his participation in the priesthood of Christ and that all good activities of a Christian are in their measure a co-operation with God.

IN PARADISUM. The first words of an antiphon "May the angels lead thee into Paradise," sung while a body is carried from the church to the grave for burial.

IN PARTIBUS INFIDELIUM (Lat., in the lands of the unbelievers). Every bishop must have a see, but there are certain of them (e.g., auxiliaries to diocesan bishops) whose relation to their see must necessarily be titular or honorary. To each of these, then, is assigned a former residential see which has been abandoned, transferred or otherwise come into disuse, generally on account of the incursions of the Arabs. Such bishops and sees were formerly called *in partibus infidelium,* but many of the sees having now again a considerable Christian population Pope Leo XIII, in 1882, abolished the designation and substituted that of "titular" bishop or see (q.v.).

IN PETTO. It is at the discretion of the pope to appoint cardinals and inform the Sacred College in consistory that he will announce their names at some future time. Such are said to be reserved *in petto* (It., in the breast). Unless and until they are announced publicly, they have no rights or duties; but upon this declaration they have precedence and proceeds of their office from the date of appointment *in petto.* It is claimed that Dr. John Lingard, the historian of England, was thus created cardinal, in 1826, by Pope Leo XII, who died before announcing the fact.

IN PLANO (Lat., on the level). A technical rubrical term for the floor of the sanctuary as distinct from the steps leading to the altar.

IN PRINCIPIO (Lat., in the beginning). The opening words of St. John's Gospel, sometimes used to denote the first fourteen verses thereof which are normally the Last Gospel at Mass.

IN SE (Lat., in itself). An expression used to imply that a thing is looked at *in itself,* absolutely, or as such, without reference to anything extrinsic.

INCARDINATION. The correlative of excardination (q.v.).

INCARNATION, The. The assumption of human nature by the second Person of the Blessed Trinity, God the Son. "And the Word was made flesh, and dwelt among us" (John i, 14). The Incarnate God had a true human body, a true human soul and a true human will; his two natures, divine and human, are united in one person; as God he was invisible, incomprehensible, timeless; as man he became visible, comprehensible, living in time; he was in all things like us save in sin: but did not in any way cease to be God. This union of two natures is called the Hypostatic Union (q.v.).

INCENSATION, INCENSING. The act of imparting the odour of incense by swinging the thurible in such a manner that smoke is given off. In the West this is done by a short, sharp swing from the middle of the chains; in the East, by swinging the thurible by the extremity of the chains.

INCENSE (Lat. *incensum,* a thing burnt). A vegetable gum or combination of gums in the form of grains or powder which on being burnt gives off an aromatic smoke; both smoke and substance are called incense. Its use in pre-Christian worship is certain but the period and practical reason (if any) of its adoption by the Church is unknown; it is mentioned in the 5th century. Symbolically it represents the consuming zeal of the Christian, the good odour of virtue and the going-up of prayer and good works to God, and to offer it before a person or thing is a mark of honour thereto. During high Mass there are several incensations, of the altar (twice), of the gospel-book, of the celebrant and ministers, choir and people, of the bread and wine, and at the consecration; it is also used at solemn Lauds and Vespers, certain blessings (e.g., ashes, palms), Benediction, processions, and absolutions for the dead. It is burnt by means of a portable thurible (q.v.). All Eastern rites make great use of incense; e.g., the Maronite, even when the Liturgy is said and not sung, and in the Armenian liturgy the deacon swings the thurible towards the people whenever the celebrant blesses them. Some Latin uses restrict the use of incense; the Capuchins have it at conventual low Mass on certain feasts. Unburnt incense is put with the relics into the sepulchres (q.v.) of altars, and five large grains are affixed to the paschal candle (q.v.). These last represent probably the spices mingled in the winding-sheet of Christ. Incense may not be used at sung Mass without an indult.

INCEST. Sexual intercourse between those related by blood or by marriage; a sin against both chastity and piety. Between relatives by blood to the third degree and by marriage to the second is incest by either natural or ecclesiastical law; between a parent and child incest is against the natural law and is distinct in malice from that of the other relationships. Incomplete acts incur this guilt.

INCLUSUS (Lat., one enclosed). A monk, nun or other person who with permission of ecclesiastical authority was voluntarily walled-up in a cell, an aperture, of course, being left by which food could be introduced and communication take place. This custom, now obsolete, has helped to give rise to the myths of "immuring of nuns" (*q.v.*). An *inclusus* could be dispensed from his undertaking.

INCORRUPTIBILITY OF THE SOUL. Essential corruption (*per se*) is the dissolution of a being into its component principles, as the death of a man. But the soul is a simple or indivisible substance (*q.v.*). Therefore it cannot corrupt *per se*. A being is said to corrupt *per accidens* when it ceases to be indirectly, because of the destruction of the subject on which it depends. But the soul is a spiritual substance (*q.v.*). Therefore it cannot corrupt *per accidens*, since it does not intrinsically depend on the body for its existence.

INCUMBENT (Lat. *incumbere*, to devote oneself to). The holder of an ecclesiastical benefice, especially parochial.

INDEFECTIBILITY. The quality of unfailingness in the Church, her constitution and ministration, promised by Jesus Christ in the words "Behold, I am with you all through the days that are coming, until the consummation of the world" (Matt. xxviii, 20). Her indefectibility is seen externally by her triumph over the most terrible trials and dangers and her abounding life and health after nineteen hundred years of history; internally it has preserved her supernatural life and channels of grace intact through all the dangerous possibilities arising from human indifference, carelessness and ill-will. This special providence of God is technically called *assistentia;* we are aware of it both by faith and sight, but the manner in which it works is a matter of speculation.

INDEX OF FORBIDDEN BOOKS, The (*Index Librorum Prohibitorum*). The list of books condemned because heretical, dangerous to morals or otherwise objectionable, published by authority of the Holy Office (*q.v.*). The rules governing the prohibition of books in general apply to those on the Index, even if they would not otherwise fall under the prohibition; the Holy Office takes cognizance only of books denounced to it. The Index is of universal application, and a permit of the Holy Office is required to read or retain books named in it; ordinaries can give permission in urgent cases for a particular book. Translations are condemned equally with the originals. Very few English books are on the Index, whose latest edition contains about 5,000 titles, each of which is distinguished either as entirely condemned or as forbidden until corrected. The prohibition of books extends to any that are harmful to faith or morals, whether on the Index or not; those selected for this public condemnation are usually on account of local, particular or personal circumstances (many most harmful books are not so noticed); from time to time books are removed from the Index. The object of this discipline is simply to defend the religion of the faithful from unnecessary sources of danger, whether proximate or remote; those who have a good reason for reading a forbidden book or books (*e.g.*, because their profession requires it, to be able better to defend the Faith, etc.) can easily get permission to do so; but curiosity is not a good reason. The *Index Expurgatorius* is a list of passages deleted from certain books, after which they may be freely read and circulated. It is often confused with the above.*

INDIA, THE CHURCH IN. The combined population of India, Burma, and Ceylon is over 400 million, the prevailing religions being Hinduism, Buddhism and Islam. All faiths are equally respected and protected by the law and enjoy complete freedom. Catholics number about 5 million, being over three-fifths of the Christian population. The first Christians of India were those called "of St. Thomas" (*q.v.*) whose descendants still live in Malabar; the Western church first came in the persons of the Portuguese in 1498 and missionary work has continued ever since. Portuguese ecclesiastical policy led to a serious schism, still represented by the Malabar (*q.v., c*) Jacobites. The former *padroado* (*q.v.*) districts in western India have an almost exclusively Indian and Eurasian pastoral clergy, and the clergy of the Syro-Malabar and Malankarese rites (*qq.v.*) is entirely Indian, so that the total number of indigenous bishops and priests is over 2,000; there are as well many Indian religious of both sexes. Apart from the old Portuguese foundations of Goa, Cochin and Mylapore, the Latin hierarchy was established in 1886, but its bishops (except in the Goan province) still depend on the missionary Congregation *de Propaganda Fide*. There are 9 metropolitan sees (Goa with the honorary title of Patriarch of the East Indies) with 43 suffragan dioceses (Ceylon forming 1 province with 6 sees). Burma is divided into 3 vicariates apostolic; and there are half-a-dozen prefectures, including that of Kafiristan and Kashmir, which includes the independent state of Afghanistan from which Christian missionaries are excluded. The Malabarese and Malankarese, who also do mission work among their heathen fellow countrymen, have 4 and 2 dioceses respectively.

INDIAN MISSIONS. This expression often refers to Catholic missions among the Indians native to the United States. Before the

---

* The *Index of Forbidden Books* has no longer been published since the Second Vatican Council (1962-1965), but the obligation remains of not reading anything dangerous to one's faith or morals.—*Publisher*, 1997.

Republic they were chiefly cared for by Spanish and French missioners. There are 360,000 Indians and Eskimos, of whom nearly one-third are Catholics. There are some 400 mission centers, served principally by members of religious orders.

INDICTION, THE ROMAN. The number of a year in a cycle of 15 years, a method of dating said to have been first used by Constantine the Great. There were several ways of reckoning it. For ecclesiastical purposes Pope St. Gregory VII fixed Jan. 1, 313, as the date of starting. The indiction is still noted in the Roman calendar.

INDIFFERENT ACT. An indifferent act is one which is morally neither good nor bad. Though such an act is theoretically possible, most theologians agree that in the concrete no act can be indifferent, since the morality of an act depends not only on the act itself but also on the end in view and the accompanying circumstances; this end must be good or bad.

INDIFFERENTISM. i. The denial that the worship of God and the practice of true religion is a duty of man. This indifferentism is of varying degrees and expressed in different maxims: "There is no God"; "Man cannot know if there be a God"; "One religion is as good as another"; "It does not matter what you believe so long as you act well"; "The only useful function of religion is to keep the lower classes in order."

ii. The neglect of religious practice, not necessarily arising from contempt of religion but from indifference or uncertainty. This is very common and much of it is but little culpable, for the printed sheet and the spoken word have corrupted minds and simple folk know not which way to turn amid a multitude of conflicting teachers.*

INDIVIDUAL (Lat. *individuus*, indivisible). A being undivided in itself and divided from every other.

INDIVIDUALITY, -ATION, PRINCIPLE OF. What precisely makes a being to be *this* being, or what is the precise ultimate reason of the *thisness* of a being; *not* what is the efficient cause of the individual, or what intrinsically constitutes the individual, or what are the outward signs by which one individual is distinct from another. Thomists, relying on the distinction between matter and form (*q.v.*), place the principle of individuality in the *material component* of bodies, not in the *form;* it is "matter affected by quantity," *materia quantitate signata.* Owing to this, Thomists after St. Thomas teach that each angel is *specifically* distinct and that two angels can never be individuals of one species since the angels are void of all matter. Other scholastics think the ultimate principle of individuality is to be placed in the whole concrete nature of a thing; others

again, with Scotus, posit a formality of *thisness* only "formally" distinct from the substance; while yet others regard the "existence" (*esse*) of the thing as a sufficient ultimate explanation of individuation.

INDIVIDUATING NOTES. The characters or qualities which distinguish one individual from another. Not to be confused with the principle of individuation.

INDIVIDUALISM. A doctrine which exaggerates the liberty and rights of the individual to the exclusion of the rights of the family and of society.

INDO-CHINA, FRENCH, THE CHURCH IN. The gospel was first successfully preached in Tongking in the early years of the 17th century by Jesuit missionaries. To-day there are over 1¼ million Catholics in an estimated population of 23 millions. There is a large body of indigenous clergy and nuns, whose history goes back for two centuries. The country is organized in 16 vicariates apostolic.

INDONESIA, THE CHURCH IN. See EAST INDIES, DUTCH.

INDUCTION. i. A reasoning or argumentation which proceeds from particulars to the universal, from parts to the whole, from phenomena to laws, from effects to causes, from signs to the signified, from the contingent to the necessary, etc.: it is the opposite of deduction or the syllogism (*q.v.*) which proceeds from the universal to the particular, etc. If, *e.g.*, we find each particular cat we have seen likes fish, we conclude that all cats like fish. Induction is either complete or incomplete according as all particulars are known or only a limited number; in the latter case a particular may be found which would nullify a universal law.

ii. In canon law. The personal introduction of an incumbent to take formal possession of his benefice, by authority of the superior who instituted him. Induction must take place within the time and in the form prescribed; otherwise the benefice can be declared vacant.

INDULGENCE (Lat. *indulgentia*, remission). The remission before God of the temporal punishment (*q.v.*) due to those sins of which the guilt has been forgiven, either in the sacrament of Penance or because of an act of perfect contrition, granted by the competent ecclesiastical authority out of the Treasury of the Church (*q.v.*) to the living by way of absolution, to the dead by way of suffrage (*q.v.*). Indulgences are either plenary (*q.v.*) or partial. Partial indulgences remit a part of the punishment due for sin at any given moment, the proportion of such part being expressed in terms of time (*e.g.*, 30 days, 7 years).**The precise meaning of these time periods has never been defined; their use is a relic of the former penitential discipline of

---

* See NECESSARY TO SALVATION and NECESSARY, NECESSITY.—*Publisher*, 1997.
** Partial indulgences are no longer measured in terms of specific time periods, but are designated simply by the words "partial indulgence."—*Publisher*, 1997.

the Church (*cf.*, Penance), out of which the granting of indulgences arose and in which the time-periods had their natural and practical significance; but the modern indulgence, though less precise and practical, is no less effective. To the pope, by divine authority, is committed the dispensation of the whole Treasury of the Church; inferior authorities in the Church can grant only those indulgences specified in canon law: cardinals may grant 200 days, archbishops 100, bishops 50. No one may apply indulgences to other living persons, but all papal indulgences may be applied to the souls in Purgatory unless otherwise stated. Indulgences attached to prayers are lost by any addition, omission or alteration; those attached to objects of devotion (rosaries, etc.) only cease when the objects themselves cease to exist or are sold. It being absolutely necessary to the gaining of an indulgence, however small, that one should be in a state of grace, it is readily seen that the vulgar and uninformed notion of an indulgence as a "permission to sin" is wide of the mark. For this crude misunderstanding the use of the word "indulgence" is itself partly responsible, and the increasing revival of use of the traditional English term "pardon" (*q.v.*) is welcome. See also SALE OF INDULGENCES; USUAL CONDITIONS.

INDULGENCES, APOSTOLIC. Indulgences, plenary or partial, attached to crucifixes, rosaries, medals and other images, etc., blessed by the pope personally or by his delegate. The indulgences can be gained only by the first person to whom the blessed object is given and depends upon the saying of certain prayers or the doing of certain works of charity (visiting the sick or poor or prisoners) or other good deeds; each indulgence according to its nature can be gained only on certain days and those which are plenary require the usual conditions (*q.v.*) as well. These indulgences are not attached to fragile objects or to those made of base metals.

INDULT (Lat. *indultum*, a concession). A faculty granted by the Holy See to bishops and others to do something not permitted by the common law of the Church, *e.g.*, to a priest in charge of a foreign mission to administer the sacrament of Confirmation. The name is also given to the permission to say Mass at sea, for a religious to be secularized, for a prelate to use *pontificalia* (*q.v.*), and suchlike licences. Distinguish from a dispensation (*q.v.*).

INDUSTRIALISM is that method of organizing the business of manufacture in which labour and responsibility are subdivided and standardized. It depends upon Capitalism (*q.v.*) and the extensive use of machinery and aims at mass production, *i.e.*, production of the largest possible number of identical articles. The costs of production are thus reduced to a minimum and, according to the degree of competition (reduced as much as possible by the organization of monopolies), profits are raised to the highest point. Without this system many things, *e.g.*, motor cars, telephones, could not be produced at a price within the means of any but the very rich. It also results that joy in labour is not the portion of the workman (*cf.*, Eccl. iii, 22) and responsibility is practically non-existent (*i.e.*, no individual workman can be held responsible for any individual article made). For pleasure and amusement the workman is forced to rely upon non-working time alone and, while conveniences and utilities are multiplied exceedingly, artistic responsibility in ordinary workmen is completely destroyed and the sense of beauty becomes the exclusive possession of students and connoisseurs.

INEFFABILIS DEUS. The bull of Dec. 8, 1854, whereby Pope Pius IX declared the doctrine of the Immaculate Conception (*q.v.*) to be of faith.

INFALLIBILITY. Incapability of teaching what is false. It has always been believed that the Catholic Church of Christ is divinely kept from the possibility of error in her definitive teaching in matters of faith and morals, and this was expressed by the Vatican Council (sess. iii, cap. 4), "the doctrine of faith which God has revealed has not been proposed as a philosophical discovery to be improved by human talent, but has been committed as a divine deposit to the Bride of Christ [the Church] to be faithfully guarded and infallibly interpreted by her." This infallibility resides (*a*) in the pope personally and alone (see below); (*b*) in an œcumenical council (*q.v.*) subject to papal confirmation (these infallibilities are distinct but correlative); (*c*) in the bishops of the Church, dispersed throughout the world, teaching definitively in union with the pope. This is not a different infallibility from (*b*) but is the ordinary exercise of a prerogative (hence called the "ordinary *magisterium*") which is manifested in a striking manner in an œcumenical council. This ordinary *magisterium* is exercised by pastoral letters, preaching, catechisms, the censorship of publications dealing with faith and morals, the reprobation of doctrines and books: it is thus in continuous function and embraces the whole deposit of faith. Infallibility does not involve inspiration (*q.v.*) or a fresh revelation; the Church can teach no *new* dogma but only "religiously guard and faithfully expound" the original deposit of faith (*q.v.*) with all its truths, explicit and implicit (*q.v.*); nevertheless, infallibility extends to indirect and secondary doctrines and facts whose connexion with revealed truths is so intimate as to bring them within its scope.

INFALLIBILITY OF THE POPE. The Vatican Council (1870) declared "it to be a dogma of divine revelation that when the Roman Pontiff speaks *ex cathedra*—that is, when he, using his office as shepherd and teacher of all Christians, in virtue ot his apostolic authority, defines a doctrine of faith or morals to be held by the whole Church—he, by the divine assistance promised him in blessed Peter, possesses that infallibility with which the divine Redeemer was pleased to invest his Church in the definition of doctrine on faith and morals, and that, therefore, such definitions of the Roman pontiff are irreformable in their own nature and not because of the consent of the Church." Note that this infallibility refers only to teaching concerning faith or morals, and then only when the pope speaks officially as teacher addressing the whole Church with the intention of obliging its members to assent to his definition (and this intention must be manifest, though not necessarily expressed); that neither impeccability nor inspiration (*qq.v.*) are claimed; that infallibility is personal to the pope and independent of the consent of the Church. This doctrine the Vatican Fathers declared to be "a tradition handed down from the beginning of the Christian Faith," that it was implicit (*q.v.*) in the teaching of the Church up to that time. Infallibility does not by any means do away with the necessity of study and learning, but simply under certain conditions guarantees that the conclusions drawn from study and learning are free from error; the pope's knowledge is not infused into him by God: he gains it just as does any other man, but he is assisted, watched over, by the Holy Spirit so that he does not use his authority and his knowledge to mislead the Church at the times and under the conditions stated above.

INFAMY. A stigma attaching in canon law to the character of a person. It is of two kinds: *infamia facti* (of fact) or loss of good name by reason of crime or evil conduct, and *infamia juris* (of law) or stigma attached by common law to certain persons as a vindicative penalty, *e.g.*, to those who profane the Blessed Sacrament, lay violent hands on the pope or his legate or a cardinal, desecrate dead bodies in their graves, take part in duels, or commit simultaneous bigamy. Infamy of fact is a temporary impediment to the reception or exercise ot holy orders; infamy of law is an irregularity (*q.v.*) therefor.

INFANCY in canon law is the state or period of childhood up to the age of seven years completed. Infants are considered in law not to have the use of reason even if in fact they possess it, unless otherwise stated. Adults without the use of reason (*e.g.*, the insane) are reckoned as infants.

INFANTS, ANOINTING OF. Children may validly and lawfully receive Extreme Unction only if they have come to use of reason, even though not yet seven years old. If there is a reasonable doubt whether the age of reason has been reached, Extreme Unction is to be administered conditionally.

INFANTS, BAPTISM OF. Infants are to be baptized very soon after birth, but no definite rule as to time is laid down by canon law. Non-Catholic infants in danger of death may be baptized even against their parents' wishes. Otherwise they may be baptized only if at least one parent or guardian consents, and there is an assurance that they will be brought up in the Catholic faith. Foundlings, *i.e.*, abandoned infants whose parents are unknown, are to be baptized conditionally if no evidence as to their baptism is available. Though in early times it was often not carried out in practice, it is the continuous tradition of the Catholic Church from the Apostles (*cf.*, Acts xvi, 15, 33; 1 Cor. i, 16; Col. ii, 11–12) onwards that our Lord intended the sacrament of Baptism to be conferred on infants equally with adults (*cf.*, Luke xviii, 15; John iii, 5; though it is not claimed that it can be explicitly proved from holy Scripture). The engagements made on their behalf they would be in any case bound to undertake on growing up; as to their lack of actual faith, it is paralleled by their lack of actual sin, as says St. Augustine: "He who has sinned by another [Adam] believes by another." The Council of Trent anathematized those who should say that little children, lacking actual faith, are not among the faithful after baptism, or that they are to be rebaptized on reaching years of discretion, or that it is better to omit baptism than to confer it on those not believing by their own act.

INFANTS, BURIAL OF. Baptized children who have died before attaining the use of reason (and also all those of whatever age who have been insane all their life) are buried with a rite notably different from that of adults; it has no note of mourning, the priest and his assistants are vested in white, and flowers may properly be strewn on the coffin; the processional cross is carried without its long handle. After sprinkling the corpse with holy water the priest says Ps. cxii with an antiphon, while it is being carried to the church Ps. cxviii, and on arrival Ps. xxiii, *Kyrie eleison* and the Our Father in silence; then follows another sprinkling and a prayer that we may all be joined with the blessed children in Heaven. The "Rituale Romanum" says nothing about a Mass to be celebrated on such occasions; but the Mass of the day or an unprivileged votive Mass of the Angels may fittingly be said or sung. While going to the grave Ps. cxlviii with an antiphon is said and at the cemetery *Kyrie eleison*, the Our Father in silence and a prayer for the salvation of all mankind. After another sprinkling and incensation, the coffin is lowered into the grave and a prayer in the vernacular for those present may be added. On leaving the grave the Song of the Three Children (Dan. iii) is said. Unbaptized children are buried without liturgical rites in a special part of the cemetery.

INFANTS, COMMUNION OF. In danger of death, holy communion may and should be given to children provided they realize that it is different from ordinary bread, and that they reverently adore it. Otherwise a fuller knowledge of Christian doctrine and a careful preparation are required before children may be admitted to the sacrament. The responsibility for this rests on the parents or guardians, the rector of the parish and the confessor. See QUAM SINGULARI.

INFANTS, CONFESSION OF. Children are bound to go to confession at least once a year when they have come to the use of reason. This obligation does not arise before the age of seven years, but children may be admitted to the sacrament before that age if they have sufficient use of reason.

INFANTS, UNBAPTIZED. The Church has always taught that unbaptized children*are excluded from Heaven but has defined nothing as to their positive fate. It is the general teaching of theologians that they enjoy a state of perfect natural happiness (limbo, q.v.), knowing and loving God by use of their natural powers and without grief at lack of the Beatific Vision. The Church has never taught that they are condemned to the Hell of the demons and the reprobate; on the other hand, Heaven is a reward in no way due to their human nature as such.

INFIDEL, MARRIAGE WITH AN. This comes under the impediment of mixed religion or difference of worship (qq.v.) accordingly as whether the infidel concerned is baptized or not.

INFIDELITY as a sin against faith is of three kinds: (a) positive: rejection of the Faith of Christ by one who has received knowledge of it together with sufficient grounds for belief; (b) privative: the neglect to examine the claims of the Church on the part of one who recognizes the necessity of such examination; (c) negative: the state of one who has no opportunity of learning the Faith or who does not advert to the necessity of enquiry. (a) is a grave sin, (b) is a sin according to the degree of negligence, (c) is not sinful. Technically, a baptized person cannot be an infidel, but in common speech those are called infidels who, whether they have been baptized or not, do not accept Christianity as a divine revelation; those who accept it as such but in an erroneous form are called non-Catholics (q.v.) (cf., Heathen).

INFINITE. That to whose perfection there is no limit. The word itself is negative and means "not finite"; the finite meaning that to whose perfection there are limits: but the idea underlying the negative word is positive.

The infinite is either absolute or relative: the first is that which has no limits in every order of perfection, the latter which has no limits in any one particular order of perfection. The distinction between the finite and the infinite is ultimately resolved to this: the finite is a real composition of essence and existence (qq.v.), which latter are therefore really distinct in a created thing, whereas in the infinite these two are identical. The infinite must not be confused with the indefinite which is sometimes called the infinite in potentia, because this latter is that which actually has limits but to which no limits can be assigned, e.g., a number of men is always actually a limited number, but it is possible to increase that number without end, in other words it is always possible to add to any given number. Hence to add finite to finite can never give the idea of the infinite but only of the indefinite.

INFINITY OF GOD. Infinity means the absence of limits. There is no limit to the perfection of God in whom is the fulness of all being. "The Catholic Church believes and confesses that God is . . . infinite in intellect and will and all perfection" (Vatican Council, sess. iii, cap. 1).

INFORM (Lat. *informare*, to give shape to). Said of a form (substantial or accidental) which gives being to (or informs) a recipient, as the soul informs the body, giving it being and life and making it human, or as colour gives being (accidental) to a wall.

INFRA ACTIONEM. See COMMUNICANTES.

INFULÆ (Lat., fillets). The two lappets depending from the back of a mitre; in the singular, *infula* sometimes means the mitre itself.

INFUSION (Lat. *fundere*, to pour). The method of baptism by pouring, used in the Latin and other churches. Sometimes and more accurately called affusion.

INGRESSA. The entrance, the name of the introit in the Ambrosian rite, consisting of antiphon and psalm verse.

INHERENCE. Said of accidents (q.v.) which in the ordinary course of nature demand a subject in which to inhere. Inherence, therefore, implies imperfection, viz., the incapability of existing apart from a subject.

INNOCENCE, ORIGINAL. The state of man before the Fall (q.v.) as enjoying the supernatural gift of sanctifying grace (q.v.). Baptismal innocence is the state of one who has received such grace by Baptism and has never lost it, even temporarily, by the commission of actual sin.

INORDINATE ATTACHMENT. See CREATURE.

INQUISITION (Lat. *inquirere*, to look into). An ecclesiastical tribunal for the discovery,

---

* That is, unbaptized children who have not reached the age of reason.—*Publisher*, 1997.

punishment and prevention of heresy, first instituted in southern France by Pope Gregory IX in 1229. Hitherto heresy had been dealt with by the secular power at the instance of the bishops, but the spread of Catharism (q.v.) provoked new procedure. The Inquisition was generally administered by the Dominicans, but was not founded or even formulated by St. Dominic. The institution was based on the principle that truth must be upheld and promoted in the interests of secular no less than ecclesiastical justice; error must be abandoned or uprooted. The Inquisition was punctilious in its adherence to law; but after full allowance has been made for "other times, other manners," some of its procedure and punishments must be set down as utterly unreasonable and in consequence cruel. In France it became a semi-political tribunal which disappeared in the 16th century; it was never established in England or the Germanies; for Rome and Spain see below. *

INQUISITION, CANONICAL. The private judicial investigation to be made before anyone is summoned to appear in an ecclesiastical court in a criminal action. The inquisitor is usually one of the synodal examiners (q.v.). He must make his report to the ordinary, and he may not act as judge in the trial of the cause.

INQUISITION, THE HOLY ROMAN AND UNIVERSAL, had its origin in the appointment by Pope Gregory IX (1227-41) of judges (inquisitors) to deal with heresy in any part of Europe, but particularly with anti-social Albigensianism in southern France, where it seems to have been an oppressive, if not ferocious, tribunal. A particular Roman Inquisition to safeguard faith and morals was erected by Pope Paul III in 1542 as the supreme doctrinal tribunal for the whole world. It was noted for a lenience not characteristic of similar courts elsewhere. It is now known as the Congregation of the Holy Office (q.v.).

INQUISITION, THE SPANISH, was set up by King Ferdinand and Queen Isabella in 1478, empowered by Pope Sixtus IV. Its object was to proceed against lapsed converts from Judaism (Maranos), crypto-Jews and other apostates whose secret activities were dangerous to Church and state, and it was extended to the Christian Moors (Moriscos), who were in danger of apostasy. It established itself in Spanish America and from about 1550 till well on in the 17th century it was keeping Spain clear of Protestantism. It also inflicted punishment for such offences as masquerading as a priest to deceive the people, bigamy, encouraging polygamy, perjury, forging, and shamming revelations. As early as 1480 complaint was made to Rome of the excess of the Holy Office of Spain and its first hundred years of existence were its worst, though the subsequent suppression of Prot-

estantism has received more attention. Both its cruelties and the number of death-penalties inflicted have been exaggerated, but were sufficiently scandalous to excite horror. It has not been established that it was other than a primarily ecclesiastical tribunal, though much under the influence of the civil power; but it acted independently, and often in defiance, of the Holy See. The unholy severity of both the Spanish and French Inquisitions was tempered by the fact that they flourished in days before police and other organization and procedure was in a state of efficiency which may itself involve inhumanity. Early in the 19th century the Inquisition was for a time revived as part of a political movement to restore royal absolutism in Spain. Its last victim was a village schoolmaster who was hanged in 1826.

INSANITY, together with epilepsy and possession, render the subject irregular for the reception or exercise of holy orders. But if the affliction was temporary and he is now certainly free, he can apply for a dispensation, or if already ordained may resume his functions. The perpetually insane cannot contract marriage.

INSIGNIA (from Lat. signum, a sign). Badges, ornaments or garments distinctive of rank. Those of a bishop in the Western church are, according to the occasion, the buskins, sandals, pectoral cross, dalmatic and tunicle, mitre, gloves, ring, pastoral staff, rochet, mozzetta, cappa magna, skull cap, morse, mantelletta and gremial veil (qq.v.); to these an archbishop adds the cross and pallium. Those peculiar to the pope are the falda, subcinctorium, fanon, tiara, and sedia gestatoria (qq.v.); ordinarily he wears a white cassock and skull cap, with red shoes, and in choir a rochet, red mozzetta (white in Easter week) and a stole. The insignia of a Byzantine bishop are the veil, mandyas, pastoral staff, dikerion and trikerion, sakkos, omophorion, enkolpia and crown or mitre (qq.v.). An Armenian archbishop is preceded by four symbols of office: the metropolitan cross, the episcopal crosier, the vartabed's staff and the heraldic emblem of his diocese.

INSPIRATION of the Holy Scriptures. Inspiration is a direct divine charismatic influence on the mind, will and executive faculties of the human writer by which he mentally conceives, freely wills to write, and actually writes correctly all that God intends him to write and nothing else, so that God is truly author of the book produced. This divine influence does not demand awareness in its recipient and is of necessity hidden from other persons. It is only known through divine revelation given to the Church, which is the sole guarantor of the fact. It carries with it absolute absence of error, God's infinite veracity being incompatible with error of any kind. This does not necessarily involve rev-

---

* Worthy of note is the fact that the 17th-century "witch"-burning hysteria did not occur in those Catholic countries which had an organized apparatus for intelligent investigation of alleged religious crimes.— *Publisher*, 1997.

elation or the bestowal of truths hitherto unknown, therefore facts of natural science and history can be expressed subject to the limitations of human knowledge, so long as such expression excludes all statement of error. Inspiration does not vary in degree; it is equal in all books and in all parts thereof, and it guarantees absolute inerrancy and divine authorship throughout. As inspiration is no mechanical force, but acts through the mind and will of the human writer in a human way, the human author's style, diction and mental outlook naturally remain in the book produced, though God is the author of all that is written and man only the instrument of his hand.

INSPIRATION, QUASI. See ACCLAMATION, i.

INSTALLATION. The induction of a newly appointed canon to his stall in the cathedral or collegiate church, when a profession of faith must be made and oath to observe the capitular statutes taken. The ceremony is performed by the dean or provost, or the bishop himself, in the presence of the chapter. The word is occasionally used for canonical induction or institution (*q.v.*) generally.

INSTINCT. A natural aptitude which guides animals in the unreflecting performance of complex acts useful for the preservation of the individual or of the species. Reason supposes a judgement and a choice; instinct is a blind impulse which naturally impels animal nature to act in a determinate manner.

INSTITUTE, RELIGIOUS. i. Canon law calls a "religion" or religious institute in general a society of men or women approved by ecclesiastical superiors, in which the members in conformity with the special laws of their association take vows, perpetual or temporary but to be renewed when they expire, and by this means tend to evangelical perfection. It must be a society in the strict juridical sense, a collegiate moral person, governed by the laws laid down for such persons. To become a religious institute in the full canonical sense it must receive positive and formal approval from the legitimate authority, that is, the Holy See or the bishop. As a condition for such approval each institute must have its rule or constitution determining its mode of government, the rights and duties of the members. Each member must take the vows of religion publicly, that is, in the hands of the legitimate superior, who receives them in the name of the Church. Institutes are principally divided into orders and congregations (*qq.v.*) and are clerical or lay. Canon law considers as clerical those in which at least a notable proportion of the members are priests, *e.g.*, Dominicans, Jesuits; lay, when according to its constitutions the great majority of its members must be brothers and only a few receive holy orders, even if

these occupy the more important positions in the congregation, *e.g.*, the Hospitallers of St. John-of-God. In 1943 there were in the Church 61 such institutes of men, with over 100,000 members, and 732 of women, with about half a million members.

ii. For an early example of what is called a *secular institute,* see COMPANY OF ST. PAUL.

INSTITUTE OF CHARITY, The. A religious congregation founded by the Abate Antonio Rosmini-Serbati in 1828. Its primary object is the sanctification of the souls of its members by charity, in the sense of love of God—the one thing necessary. And since love of God implies also the love of man, its members prepare themselves by prayer, purification of conscience and the striving after the necessary virtues to undertake works of neighbourly charity of every kind, whether spiritual, intellectual or corporal. It has the usual religious vows and includes priests, clerics who do not go on to the priesthood and lay-brothers. It has no special habit. At present it has charge of parishes, colleges and schools, and directs other undertakings founded for the good of the faithful. The flourishing English province was founded by Fr. Luigi Gentili in 1835; they have a school for boys at Ratcliffe and among their churches is St. Etheldreda's, Ely Place, London, restored to the Church by these fathers in 1876. They have also establishments in Ireland. The nuns of this institute are called Sisters of Providence (*q.v.* i).

INSTITUTE OF MARY, The (Fr. *Dames Anglaises;* Ger. *Englische Fräulein;* Loreto Nuns). Founded by Mary Ward at Saint-Omer in 1609, suppressed in 1629, revived 1633 and established in London 1639: the first active and unenclosed religious institute of women, with simple vows and no choir office. Its London and Yorkshire houses were for 150 years the only convents in Great Britain; the present Bar Convent at York was founded near Fountains in 1642 and transferred to Micklegate Bar in 1686. The work of the congregation is the education of girls. It numbers over 5,000 members, divided into several independent provinces, including many convents in Ireland. Full black habit with white cuffs and head-dress; thin black veil.

INSTITUTE OF PERPETUAL ADORATION. A society founded in 1856 by Anne, Countess de Meens, for perpetual adoration, making vestments, etc., for poor churches, and instruction in Christian doctrine. Unenclosed; no habit, but a simple mourning dress with crape cap.

INSTITUTES, ROMAN. The Biblical Institute and the Institute for Promoting Eastern Studies (*qq.v.*) are units of the Pontifical Gregorian University; there are also institutes of Sacred Music and of Christian Archæology.

INSTITUTION, in canon law, is the provision of an ecclesiastical office or benefice by the local ordinary or other competent authority to the candidate who has been presented or nominated by the patron or other person to whom this right belongs. Candidates legitimately presented are to be instituted within two months, and institution is followed by induction (*q.v.*, ii).

INSTRUCTIO CLEMENTINA (Lat., The Clementine Instruction). The regulations governing the Forty Hours prayer (*q.v.*) published by Pope Clement XII in 1736.

INSTRUMENTUM PACIS (Lat., instrument of peace). The *pax* (*q.v.*, ii).

INSTRUCTION. The catechetical instruction of children and adults is one of the most important duties of pastors. Rectors of parishes are bound to give instruction to children both before and after their reception of the sacraments. For this purpose they may make use of the Confraternity of Christian Doctrine which must be established in every parish. They are also bound to explain their religion to adults on all Sundays and holidays of obligation. Parents, guardians, sponsors, masters and mistresses are bound to see that those under their charge receive catechetical instruction. No convert from heresy may be received into the Church until he has received instruction in Christian doctrine and its moral law adequate to the needs of his age, education, intelligence and general circumstances.

INSTRUMENTS OF THE PASSION. The cross, nails, hammer, and other material accessories of our Lord's death, sometimes represented in pictorial and other decoration.

INTEGRITY (Lat. *integer,* whole, untainted). The total absence of concupiscence (*q.v.*), by preternatural gift (*q.v.*) of God, a quality of Adam and Eve before the Fall; their whole sensitive and imaginative life and activity was completely under the control of and ruled by their reason. According to St. Thomas, their enjoyment of the pleasures of sensitive life was consequently more intense than ours, their natural faculties being purer and therefore keener.

INTELLECT (Lat. *intus legere,* to read within). Broadly speaking, intellect is the faculty of thought. Under thought is included attention, judgement, reflection, self-consciousness, the formation of concepts, and the processes of reasoning. The intellect is partly passive (νοῦς παθητικός, *intellectus possibilis*) and partly active (νοῦς ποιητικός, *intellectus agens*). These different names denote merely different aspects of the same power. The *intellectus agens* is the power whereby the universal is abstracted from sensible

(*q.v.*) things; *intellectus possibilis* is the power of perceiving the universal thus abstracted and of judging and reasoning. This faculty is suprasensuous because it performs operations beyond the scope of the senses; for its formal and direct object is the universal, the immaterial, the absolute, whereas the object of the senses is always particular, concrete and material. The intellect is really distinct from the soul, of which it is a power and through which the soul acts.

INTELLECTION, PRINCIPLE OF. That from which the act of intellectual knowledge comes. The person knows by means of his intellect, which in turn depends on abstract notions derived from objects of sense. Any of these elements may be called a principle of intellection.

INTELLECTUALISM. Word applied to certain systems whose endeavour is to reduce all things to knowledge as to their ultimate basis. Opposed to Voluntarism, which seeks to explain things by having recourse to the will or the freedom of the will as to their basis. Thomism is severely intellectualist, whereas Scotism is voluntarist.

INTELLIGIBLE. Term applied to all things that can be perceived by the mind. The intelligible world is opposed to the sensible world. The former means the world of ideas, and also all realities such as can be known by the mind through the means of ideas: essences, substances, causes, God, the soul, the true, the beautiful, the good, etc. The intelligible world is the object of philosophy; the sensible world the object of the physical sciences.

INTENTION. i. The tendency of the will towards some end through some means. One acts with intention when the will directs one's activities towards a definite end. An intention is actual when it is here and now made, virtual when it is no longer attended to yet still exerts its influence on the resultant activity; it is habitual if, while no longer exerting a positive influence, it has never been retracted. An interpretative intention is one which has never been actually made but would have been had the person thought about it (*cf.,* Motive, End). If an act is such that it produces two effects so interconnected that the will cannot choose one without the other, the effect primarily intended is "willed in itself," the effect not intended is "willed in its cause." If the latter effect be evil, the action may not be performed unless there be a proportionally grave reason and provided that the good effect does not come about by means of the bad.

ii. Order of Intention. Opposed to Order of Execution. That which is *first* in the order of intention is *last* in the order of execution. The object or the end an agent has in view is the first cause of his action, and at the same time the last end.

iii. In conferring the sacraments the minister must have at least a virtual intention of doing what the Church does, and the recipient's intention must be at least habitual (see above). Anglican orders (*q.v.*) were rejected by Pope Leo XIII because of defect of intention (and defect of form), but intention here does not mean the internal intention of the minister but the external intention, *i.e.*, the internal intention as manifested externally in the rite. It is the intention of the rite rather than that of the minister which the pope had in mind.

iv. An object for which a person prays and asks others to pray; the particular blessing asked of God in response to any good work: it may be spiritual or temporal, on behalf of ourselves or others, living or dead, particular or general (*e.g.*, the conversion of England). A private intention is such an object whose nature is unexpressed; a Mass intention is that for which a Mass is offered, by a person assisting thereat or one who has arranged for the Mass to be said, but more usually referring to the intention of the sacrificing priest himself. Prayer for "the pope's intentions" is one of the usual conditions for gaining a plenary indulgence (*q.v.*).

INTERCESSION is the praying by one person on behalf of another, following the word of St. Paul, "I desire therefore, first of all, that supplications, prayers, intercessions, and thanksgivings be made for all men" (1 Tim. ii, 1). See MEDIATION; INVOCATION OF SAINTS; HOLY SOULS. A Great Intercession forms part of every eucharistic liturgy. This liturgical intercession is a prayer for all ranks and orders in the Church, living and dead, and for all men, wherein the celebrant names those for whom he wishes particularly to pray and a commemoration of the saints is made. There are often two intercessions, of which the first, in the form of a litany, comes after the Liturgy of the Catechumens and is called the Prayers of the Faithful. In the Roman Mass it consists of the second part of the prayer *Te igitur*, the commemoration of the living and the *Communicantes* before the consecration and the commemoration of the dead and *Nobis quoque peccatoribus* (*qq.v.*) before the Lord's Prayer. In the Byzantine Liturgies it follows the *epiklesis*. See also INVOCATION.

INTERCOMMUNION. i. The deliberate and knowing administering of a sacrament (real or supposed) by a minister of a religious body to a member of another religious body not in communion with that of the minister; *e.g.*, as has occasionally happened, by an Orthodox Eastern priest to an Anglican or *vice versa*.

ii. An agreement between two religious bodies whereby each extends its privileges of membership to the other's members without reference to dogmatic and other differences between the bodies. Such intercommunions are manifestations of Panchristianity (*q.v.*), and may neither be used by Catholics nor extended to non-Catholics. See COMMUNICATIO IN SACRIS.

INTERDICT. An ecclesiastical censure by which members of the Church, while remaining in the communion of the faithful, are excluded from participation in certain sacred offices, and from the reception or administration of certain sacraments. An interdict may be general or particular, local or personal; a special limited form of the last named is interdict *ab ingressu ecclesiæ*, by which the offender is forbidden to celebrate divine offices in church, to assist at them, or to receive ecclesiastical burial. Interdicts follow the general rules of censures as to infliction and absolution. An interdict on a state or diocese can only be imposed by the Holy See, but on a parish, or other local or personal infliction, by a bishop.

INTEREST. See USURY; MUTUUM.

INTERNAL ACTS AND LAW. Internal acts are not subject to human laws in the external forum, except indirectly, in so far as they are necessarily implied in the performance of an external act, *e.g.*, hearing Mass with attention. Internal acts must conform to the teaching of the Church, but are not subject to the discipline of the Church except in the internal forum of conscience. The Church does not, and cannot, legislate, pass judgement, or take disciplinary action in regard to internal acts, so long as they remain purely internal. As to whether the Church could at least make directive laws for such acts, it is disputed. The more common and probable opinion denies that she could do so.

INTERNUNCIO, APOSTOLIC (Lat. *inter*, between; *nuntius*, messenger). A papal representative having charge of a legation in a foreign country with the same powers and privileges as a nuncio, but without his dignity. See LEGATE; NUNCIO.

INTERPELLATIONS (Lat. *interpellare*, to interrupt). The questions put by the bishop or his delegate to the non-Catholic party in a case of the Pauline privilege (*q.v.*), namely, "Are you willing to embrace the Faith and be baptized?" and "Are you at least willing to live peaceably with your partner without contumely to the Creator?" Probably both questions are normally necessary for the validity of a second marriage, but either or both may be dispensed from by the Holy See for a good reason. The interpellations are to be made by authority of the convert's ordinary, or, if this cannot be done, privately by the convert, but in such a way that evidence can be produced.

INTERPRETATION. i. Of the Sacred Scriptures. See SENSE OF . . .

ii. Of canon law. No one is authorized to

give an *authentic* interpretation of ecclesiastical laws except the legislator himself or his successor, or persons delegated for this purpose by either of these. Authentic interpretation has the same binding force as the law itself. Judicial interpretation has not the force of law, and only binds the persons and affects the causes for which it is given by the judge. In interpreting laws consideration must be given to the literal meaning of the words, the context and parallel texts, the purpose of the law, the intention of the legislator, the principles of equity, the style and practice of the Roman court, and the teaching of approved canonists. There is a pontifical commission at Rome for the interpretation of canon law.

INTERPRETATION, PRIVATE. A cardinal principle of the Protestant Reformation, *sc.,* that the Bible being the sole rule of faith, each man has the right to base his beliefs and practice on the meaning he chooses to give to the Bible's teaching. Its insufficiency is clear from four considerations: the impossibility of practising it during apostolic times when the New Testament was non-existent and faith had to come by hearing (Rom. x, 17; 1 Thess. ii, 17); the incompatibility of private interpretation with faith, the former being a proud act of judgement, the latter a humble act of submission; the incapacity of the many to read, or, at least, to form a true judgement on such difficult matters (2 Pet. iii, 16); the paramount influence of education and environment, rendering it impossible to form a truly private interpretation. Historically, the impracticability of private interpretation has been implicitly admitted by Protestants in every Confession of Faith, in their acquiescence in definite forms of church government, and in the establishment of state religions.

INTERPRETER. If a priest and penitent know no language in common, recourse may be had, with the penitent's permission, to an interpreter; he will be bound by the seal of confession equally with the priest. But if the penitent cannot find a confessor who can understand him, he is not bound to make use of an interpreter, but may make his confession as best he can, by signs expressing sorrow for his sins; for one is only obliged to confess to the priest alone.

INTERSTICES (Lat. *interstitium,* an interval). The canonical intervals of time that must elapse between the reception of the various ranks of holy order. Those between the minor orders (*q.v.*) are at the discretion of the bishop; between acolyte and subdiaconate, one year; between subdiaconate and diaconate, three months; between diaconate and priesthood, three months. Minor orders may not be given with the subdiaconate, or two sacred orders on the same day, or tonsure (*q.v.*) and one minor order together, or all

the minor orders at one time. No one may receive the tonsure before beginning his theological course, the subdiaconate before the end of its third year, or the priesthood before the middle of the fourth. Regulars (*q.v.*) must be solemnly professed before receiving the subdiaconate, unless they have a privilege to do so after simple profession.

INTINCTION (Lat. *intingere,* to dip in). A method of giving holy communion by dipping the sacred Body in the precious Blood and so administering it. It was formerly very common; in the East from the 9th till the 18th century, when it gave place to the use of the spoon; in the West from the 7th to the 11th century. The Syrians, both Catholic and Jacobite, closely approximate to the custom, by "anointing" the species of Bread with the Blood at the fraction, and administering them with the fingers. In recent years the practice of intinction has revived among the Catholic Melkites and is spreading to other Byzantines.

INTRANSIGENCE (Lat. *in,* privative; *transigere,* to agree). Refusal to compromise on a matter of principle. The word is of French political origin, but often applied to the attitude of the Holy See in the face of attempts to harm religion, especially by unjust interference with ecclesiastical rights, which must be maintained for the good of souls. It is sometimes used with a depreciatory intention, those who thus use it having confused intransigence with intractability, *vulgo* stubbornness.

INTROIT (Lat. *introitus,* entrance). The first variable portion of the Mass, consisting of an antiphon (usually from the psalms), a psalm-verse, *Gloria Patri,* and the antiphon repeated. It is really the beginning of Mass (the previous prayers are preparatory), and so is preceded by the sign of the cross. At high Mass the *Graduale* directs that it be sung by the choir during the procession from the sacristy, which recalls its origin in a complete psalm formerly sung during this procession. Proper Masses are distinguished one from another by the first word of the introit: *e.g., Lætare* (4th Sunday of Lent), *Quasimodo* (Low Sunday), *Requiem* (of the Dead), *In medio* (common of Doctors). In Masses of more recent composition the introit often has reference to the occasion, *e.g.,* those of Christ the King, of St. John Baptist de Rossi (May 23).

INTUITION. Direct knowledge of an object, or the act whereby the mind perceives a truth immediately evident.

INVENTION. A word sometimes used in English calendars to designate certain feasts, *e.g.,* the Invention of the Cross, of the Head of St. John Baptist, etc. It is derived from Lat., *invenire,* to find; and having regard to current meanings of invention, "finding" is the better word to use.

INVESTITURE (Lat. *investire*, to clothe). The term used in the middle ages to designate the act by which a sovereign granted their titles, possessions and temporal rights to bishops, abbots and other spiritual lords. It led to appointment to sees and prelacies by lay princes and nobles, the keeping of sees vacant, and other abuses. The forbidding of lay investiture by Pope Gregory VII in 1075 precipitated a conflict between the Holy See and the emperors, which lasted until the Concordat or Agreement of Worms in 1122. It was by insistence on free canonical investiture against King Henry I that St. Anselm of Canterbury became a confessor of the Faith.

INVITATORY, -ORIUM. Ps. xciv, with an antiphon said six times and the half three times, said at the beginning of Matins and serving as an introduction to the whole office of the day; the antiphon varies according to the day and season. In the Roman Office it is omitted on the Epiphany (when Ps. xciv forms part of the 3rd nocturn), and on the last three days of Holy Week.

INVOCATION OF SAINTS. It is the teaching of the Church that God enables the saints to hear and see the needs of those on earth; that they present our petitions before the throne of God; and consequently, that we may pray to them. This is part of the doctrine of the communion of saints (*q.v.*). "We employ two forms of prayer, differing in the manner of address; for to God we say properly, 'Have mercy on us, hear us': to the saints, 'Pray for us' . . . the greatest care must be taken by all not to attribute to any other that which belongs to God" (Catechism of the Council of Trent), though this is a matter of the intention rather than of the words used. Invocation of our Lady and other saints does not supplant prayer to God, but is by way of reinforcement thereto, as when one asks a friend for help in confirmation of one's own efforts in any matter. Therefore no Catholic is formally bound to pray to the saints; the Council of Trent (sess. xxv) only requires him to acknowledge that it is "good and useful" so to do. The Mass is, of course, offered to God only and, barring particular exceptions such as the litany of the Saints, the prayers of the liturgy are all addressed to him directly.

IPSO FACTO (Lat., by that very fact). A phrase used when expressing that a certain consequence automatically follows a certain action or set of circumstances; *e.g.*, a priest who with full knowledge of the crime and its penalty directly violates the seal of confession incurs excommunication *ipso facto*, by that very fact, automatically, without sentence of law.

IPSUM ESSE. An expression applied to God alone, who is Being Itself, whose essence is existence.

IRAK, THE CHURCH IN. Irak (Mesopotamia) has a population of 3½ million, mostly adherents of Islam (*q.v.*), both Sunnis and Shi'ahs being represented. Of the Christian minority, a few are Nestorians and Jacobites (*qq.v.*) but the majority, about 150,000, are Catholics, mostly Chaldeans (*q.v.*). There are 5 Chaldean dioceses (1 patriarchal, of Babylon); 2 dioceses of Syrian rite (*q.v.*); and 1 of Latin rite with 2 mission territories. The Chaldean patriarch is *ex-officio* a member of the senate of Irak, and the relations of Catholics with the Moslem civil power have been much less unsatisfactory than those of the badly treated Nestorian "Assyrians."

IRELAND, THE CHURCH IN. The total population of Ireland is about 4,270,000, of whom 90 per cent are Catholics in Eire and 33 per cent in the partitioned area. All religions are free throughout the country, but Catholics are seriously discriminated against in the north. The Catholic Church is not established in Eire, but it is the religion of the state, which maintains an ambassador at the Vatican; there is a papal nuncio in Dublin. The unity of ecclesiastical organization is not affected by political division: the primatial see is in fact situated in Northern Ireland. The early Irish ecclesiastical divisions were not episcopal dioceses in the strict sense; the present diocesan divisions derive from the synods of Rathbreasail (1118) and Kells (1152). The Church in Ireland has unbroken continuity with the Celtic church founded by St. Patrick and his predecessors in the fifth century, and the diocesan hierarchy survived the Reformation intact, though in 1705 the bishop of Dromore was the only one left and he was in prison. It has four provinces and twenty-three dioceses under the primatial see of All Ireland at Armagh, namely: Armagh, with its archdiocese and eight suffragan sees, Meath, Derry, Dromore, Down & Connor, Kilmore, Clogher, Ardagh & Clonmacnois, Raphoe; Dublin (whose archbishop has the title of Primate of Ireland), with Kildare & Leighlin, Ossory, Ferns; Cashel & Emly, with Cork, Killaloe, Limerick, Waterford & Lismore, Cloyne, Ross, Kerry; Tuam with Achonry, Galway & Kilmacduagh, Elphin, Clonfert, Killala (*qq.v.*). The cathedrals and other buildings of the ancient Irish church are in Protestant occupation. The cause of the beatification of 260 Irish martyrs of the 16th-17th centuries has been introduced at Rome.

IRISH COLLEGES abroad for the training of candidates to the priesthood are at Rome (1628), Paris (1605) and Salamanca (The College of the Noble Irish, founded under the patronage of King Philip II in 1592; absorbed the Seville and Compostela colleges in 1769). Several other colleges were founded in Belgium, France and Spain during the penal times but have now ceased to exist.

IRISH MARTYRS, The. Those natives of Ireland who are alleged to have died for the Faith between 1537 and 1714. The cause of the beatification of 260 individuals or groups of these was begun in 1904, and the first instalment of evidence introduced at Rome in 1920. They include 15 archbishops and bishops, 37 secular priests, 151 regulars, 51 laymen and 6 women. Oliver Plunket, Archbishop of Armagh, executed at Tyburn in 1681, was beatified in 1920.

IRON VIRGIN, The. A large hollow figure carved with the head of a woman, lined with spikes, and having doors through which a victim could be put inside. It was for long supposed to be a mediæval instrument of torture, and its use was attributed to the Inquisition (which was never established in Germany) and to the Jesuits (who did not exist in the middle ages). It is now known to be a sham, constructed in the 19th century by somebody of morbid tastes.

IRREFORMABLE (Lat. *reformare*, to change). Unchangeable. Irreformability is a quality of certain acts of the pope and of the Church, *e.g.*, a solemn definition of an article of faith.

IRREGULARITY. A canonical impediment, of its nature permanent, rendering unlawful, though not invalid, the reception or/and the exercise of the sacrament of orders. Irregularities are of two kinds, *ex delicto*, arising from the commission of certain grave crimes, and *ex defectu*, arising from defects which are not crimes. The chief irregularities *ex delicto* are apostasy, heresy, schism, murder, abortion, usurpation of sacred orders, bigamy (simultaneous), marriage attempted by one bound by holy orders or religious vows, or with a woman bound by religious vows, guilty reception of heretical baptism. Among irregularities *ex defectu* are illegitimacy, grave bodily deformity or disablement, insanity, epilepsy, and second marriage. There are also temporary impediments (*q.v.*) which are not irregularities. Ignorance of irregularities does not excuse from them. Irregularities require a papal dispensation, but ordinaries can dispense their own subjects from irregularities *ex delicto* as long as the crimes were not open and notorious, except those arising from murder and abortion.*

IRREMOVABLE OFFICES in canon law are those from which the holders cannot be removed except by judicial procedure in an ecclesiastical court.

IRVINGITE. A member of the sect commonly supposed to have been but not in fact founded by Edward Irving, called the Catholic Apostolic Church (*q.v.*).

ISAIAH. The Hebrew form of the name of the prophet Isaias.

ISAIAS (Heb., Jahweh is salvation). One of the greatest of the prophets, who died probably about 690 B.C. His book in the Bible is a collection of prophecies, uttered during many years and on many different occasions. They are all in Hebrew verse with the exception of chapters xxxvi-xxxix, which are historical and in prose. It contains a number of Messianic prophecies which makes it a gospel before the Gospel. The Biblical Commission (*q.v.*) in 1908 issued a declaration defending the unity and the truly prophetic character of the book. Isaias is traditionally believed to have died a martyr under the wicked king Manasses and is named in the Roman Martyrology on July 6; the fifth and eighth prophecies on Holy Saturday, and the fourth on Whitsun Eve are taken from his 54th, 55th and 4th chapters.

ISLAM. The infinitive of an Arabic verb meaning "to commit oneself [to God only]," and in use is equivalent to "monotheism"; preceded by the definite article *al* it signifies that religion often called in English Mohammedanism, from the name of its prophet Mohammed ibn Abdallah (*c.* A.D. 570-632). It was compounded of primitive Arabian and Sabæan religion, Judaism, and monophysite and other heretical Christianity and is expounded in the Koran (*q.v.*), the Hadith and the Sunna which contain the sayings and doings of the prophet. The principal dogmas of al-Islam are the unity of God, the unique office of Mohammed (which does not exclude lesser prophets, *e.g.*, Moses, Abraham, Jesus Christ), the existence of angels and demons (*jinn*), predestination of good and evil by God, and an eternal Heaven or Hell after the general judgement. Its obligations, the five pillars of Islam, are Affirmation (faith), Worship (*salat*) five times daily (preceded by ceremonial cleansing), Alms-deeds (*i.e.*, particularly the official tribute, *Zakat*), Fasting, and Pilgrimage to Mecca. There is a general duty to join in a holy war (*jehad*) for the defence or aggrandizement of Islam when called upon, *e.g.*, by the Sultan of Turkey on Nov. 27, 1914. Polygamy is legal, but limited to four wives; divorce is practised and circumcision enjoined; every Friday there is public worship at noon; pig-meat, wine, images of men and animals (especially in the round) and usury are among things forbidden. There is no sacrifice or priesthood in Islam. There are numerous ritual, theological and political sects, of which the principal, arising from the disputed succession to Mohammed, is that of the *Shi'ahs* in Persia and India: in reference to them the orthodox are the *Sunnis*. Theoretically the civil and religious guardianship of the Mos-

---

* The 1983 Code of Canon Law states new laws regarding "Irregularity."—*Publisher*, 1997.

lem world resided in the *khalifat* (successor) but his office was abolished by the Turkish republic in 1924. Moslems number about 210 millions and no other people are more impervious to the teaching of Christianity. Conversion means complete social ostracism and often persecution; in a Moslem state the religious and civil power are practically one; and in an unorganized and indirect way Islam is a great missionary power. In Turkey the dominance and establishment of Islam has been done away with, but in Africa its advance among the heathen is continuous.

ISRAEL, ISRAELITES (Heb. *yisrael*, striver with God; Gen. xxxii, 28). i. The descendants of the patriarch Jacob or Israel; later called the Jews (*q.v.*).

ii. The Kingdom of. The ten tribes who revolted from King Roboam and established a separate kingdom between Dan and Beth-el. In 721 B.C. they were carried into captivity by the Assyrians, since when these tribes have been "lost," *i.e.*, absorbed in the populations of Babylonia, Persia and among the Syrian colonists in Palestine.

ISSOUDUN FATHERS, The. The missionaries of the Sacred Heart, a congregation of foreign-missionary priests founded at Issoudun, Indre, France, in 1854.

ITALA VETUS. The Old Latin version of the Bible in use in the Western church until its place was taken by St. Jerome's Vulgate (*q.v.*). In 383 he made a first revision of the psalms which was in use liturgically until the reform of Pope St. Pius V. Under the name of the "Roman Psalter" it is still retained by the canons of St. Peter's and in the Ambrosian rite; and its text is followed in the invitatory psalm at Matins and throughout the Roman missal, *e.g.*, the introits. Very divergent views are held by scholars as to what the history of the Itala version was, beyond its being a literal word-for-word rendering into Latin from Greek without literary pretensions (*e.g.*, Ps. cxxv). The whole New Testament of our present Vulgate is this version as revised by St. Jerome, and Wisdom, Ecclesiasticus, Baruch and Machabees in the Old are almost, if not quite, untouched by him; the rest he newly translated.

"ITALIAN MISSION, The." A name for the Catholic Church in England, first used by Dr. Benson, archbishop of Canterbury (*d.* 1896), the notion being that since the 16th century Catholics, particularly the clergy, are a body of people commissioned by an Italian bishop (the Pope of Rome), and with no canonical rights in this land, to seduce the people of England from their allegiance to the "English branch of the Catholic Church," *i.e.*, the Protestant Church of England. It is a rhetorical expression no longer much used. The real Italian mission, in fact, was in 597, when St. Augustine landed in Kent with forty other foreign monks sent from Rome by Pope St. Gregory the Great to convert the heathen English.

ITALO-GREEKS, more accurately called Italo-Greek-Albanians or Italo-Albanians, are Catholics of the Byzantine rite (*q.v.*) in Calabria and Sicily, with colonies in the U. S. A. They are descendants of Albanian refugees of the 15th and 16th centuries, among whom were some Greeks, and represent a revivification of the Greek Christians who inhabited those parts (*Magna Græcia*) from its evangelization. They form two dioceses, one in Calabria and the other in Sicily. Their clergy are trained at the Greek College in Rome. Of a formerly flourishing monasticism, only the ancient abbey of Grottaferrata, near Rome, remains (the Latin archbishop of Messina is called "Archimandrite of St. Saviour," in memory of another one). They use the Byzantine rite, in Greek; but have adopted Western popular devotions, together with some of our feasts, round statues, Benediction, *etc.* They use their own version of the Byzantine chant. A few of the clergy are married. They number about 50,000 in Europe.

ITALY, THE CHURCH IN. The population of Italy was estimated to be 45½ million in 1947. Practically all the people are baptized into the Catholic Church; but in 1940 Cardinal Lavitrano declared that only a third of the Italian people regularly assist at public worship and only 12 per cent of the adult men receive communion at Easter. It has been estimated that one-fifth of the adults are consciously opposed to the Church. Any other religion may be freely exercised. The position of the Church is regulated by the provisions of the concordat (*q.v.*) made between the Holy See and the Italian government in 1929. The Italian ecclesiastical circumscriptions underwent much modification in 1818, many dioceses being suppressed or permanently united to others; nevertheless Italy still has, both absolutely and relatively to population, more than twice as many diocesan bishops as any other country. The pope is primate of the Italian church and metropolitan of the Roman province, with 7 suburbicarian (*q.v.*) sees and 15 others in the conciliar region of Lazio depending on him. There are 38 other metropolitan sees, with 145 episcopal sees suffragan to them, 16 archbishoprics without suffragans, 47 bishoprics i.s.h.s., 9 abbacies *nullius*, and 3 prelatures nullius. Three of the metropolitan provinces are in Sardinia and 4 in Sicily; 2 dioceses are of Italo-Greeks (*q.v.*). The independent republic of *San Marino* is divided between the dioceses of Montefeltro and Rimini. See also LATERAN TREATY.

ITE, MISSA EST: Deo gratias (Lat., Go, dismissal is made. ℟. Thanks be to God). The liturgical phrase which gives its name to the Mass (*q.v.*). Until about the 12th century the service actually ended at these words. They are now followed by the prayer *Placeat tibi,* the blessing, and the last gospel, which were formerly private devotions of the celebrant (*cf.,* the preparatory prayers at the beginning), and this aspect of them is noticeable at high or sung Mass when this dismissal is sung aloud, and the rest takes place in a low voice. It is replaced by *Benedicamus Domino* in ferial and most votive Masses and on Sundays in Septuagesima, Lent, and Advent; and by *Requiescant in pace* at requiems, because these used always to be followed by the absolutions (*q.v.* iii) and other prayers.

ITINERARY, —ARIUM. A form of blessing for a cleric about to undertake a journey, printed at the end of the Breviary. It con-sists of the *Benedictus* with an appropriate antiphon, the Lord's prayer, versicles and four collects. There are variations; *e.g.,* the Dominicans have an antiphon atter each verse of the *Benedictus* and five collects.

IUDICA PSALM. Ps. xlii recited by celebrant and server at the beginning of Mass; an expression of awe at approaching God's altar and of confidence in his mercy. On account of its joyful character it is omitted in Passiontide and Masses for the dead. The Dominicans say instead ver. 1 of Ps. cxvii (as was done in the old English uses of Sarum, York, Bangor and Hereford), and the Carthusians ver. 3 of Ps. cxl.

IUDICA SUNDAY. A name given to Passion Sunday from the first word of the introit, taken from Ps. xlii, which is not said in its usual place at the beginning of Mass.

IUS REFORMANDI. See CUIUS REGIO.

J

JACOBITE. A member of the Syrian Jacobite Church (*q.v.*) or of the third largest body of Christians in Malabar (*q.v., c*). The name comes from the bishop *Jacob* al-Baradai (6th century). It has also been given to the followers of Prince James, son of King James II of England, because Heb. *Ya'aqob* = Gk. *Iakobos* = It. *Giacobbe,* later *Giacomo* = Eng. *James.*

JAHVEH is probably the correct pronunciation of the sacred name of God J H V H, mistakenly pronounced Jehovah (see ADONAI). The occurrence of this name in certain sections of the Pentateuch was supposed to indicate different authorship from that of sections containing Elohim (*q.v.*) as designation of the Deity, hence *Jahvist.* Research has no difficulty in showing the inconclusiveness of such a method of argument.

JAMES (THE GREATER), ST. Apostle and elder brother of St. John (the sons of Zebedee), the feast of whose martyrdom by the sword is kept by the Western church on July 25, and in the Byzantine rite on April 30. The tradition that he preached the gospel in Spain and that the relics enshrined at Compostela are his is now generally rejected outside that country. He is named in the canon of the Mass. St. James the Less is commemorated with St. Philip (*q.v.*).

JAMES, THE LITURGY OF ST. A modified form from Jerusalem of the primitive Antiochene liturgy which it superseded. After the monophysite schism the heretics continued to use it in Syriac, and the Catholics in Greek until it was supplanted by the Liturgy of Constantinople. The Syrians, Catholic and Jacobite, still use a form of the Syriac version, and the Maronites a derivative thereof; and the Orthodox of Zakynthos and Jerusalem now again use the Greek St. James once a year, on the saint's feast.

JANSENISM. The heresy propounded by Cornelius Jansen (1585-1638), bishop of Ypres. It was promulgated originally in his "Augustinus," a work which purports to give the doctrine of St. Augustine. It denied the freedom of the will, the possibility of resisting grace, and that Christ died for all men, and maintained that it was not possible for man to keep some of God's commandments. Pope Urban VIII condemned the "Augustinus" in 1642, and in 1653 Innocent X condemned as heretical five propositions which embodied Jansen's errors. The heresy took a great hold in France, and later centred round the nuns of Port Royal (*q.v.*). Many of the heretics showed a great piety and asceticism; but Jansenism was harsh, and its harshness pervaded much theological teaching for over a century.

JANSENIST CHURCH OF HOLLAND, The. A small body (about 10,000) representing a schism caused at Utrecht by French and Dutch ecclesiastics and laymen who refused to submit to the bull *Unigenitus* (1713) condemning Jansenism (*q.v.*). They are organized under an archbishop at Utrecht, with two suffragans. They call themselves "Old Roman Catholics" and till recently preserved all the doctrine (except the Immaculate Conception, Papal Infallibility, and their heresy), discipline and customs of the Roman church; they now have abandoned compulsory clerical celibacy, say Mass in the vernacular, and are allied with the "Old Catholics" (*q.v.*). Their orders and sacraments are valid.

JANUARIUS, THE MIRACLE OF ST. The liquefaction of what is said to be the solidified blood of St. Januarius (a martyr at Pozzuoli under Diocletian) when the glass phial containing it is brought near to the relic of his head and prayer made to God. This marvel usually happens in public eighteen times in each year in the cathedral of Naples. The event has frequently been tested and examined, and no satisfactory explanation by natural causes has yet been suggested. Similar liquefactions of other blood relics are reported to take place elsewhere in the Neapolitan province and of an alleged relic of the blood of St. Pantaleon at Constantinople.

JAPAN, THE CHURCH IN. St. Francis Xavier landed in Japan in 1549 and within a hundred years there were nearly 2 million Catholics; these nearly all disappeared during the persecutions of the early 17th century (but *cf.*, The Finding of the Christians). Since the re-establishment of missions in the 19th century Catholic progress, contrary to the case in China, has been less than Protestant. In a population of about 70 millions only some 100,000 are Catholics. An ordinary hierarchy was set up in 1891; there is now the metropolitan see of Tokyo with 5 suffragan dioceses, 2 vicariates and several prefectures. The Jesuits have a university at Tokyo. The laws against Christianity were abolished in 1873, all religions are free and equal, Christian churches, etc., having the same civil privileges as the temples of Shintoism, the national religion. A number of the Catholic clergy and religious are Japanese, but many are still European. Nagasaki, destroyed by atomic bomb, was the cradle of the Church in Japan; four-fifths of its Catholics perished. There is a small Japanese dissident Orthodox church.

JEALOUSY (through Old French from Lat. *zelosus*, zealous). In its most usual meaning jealousy is resentment or ill-will towards another because of some good he enjoys or may enjoy, generally a temporal good: see ENVY. The biblical expression "a jealous God" (Exodus xx, 5) illustrates an earlier shade of meaning in the word; God's love will tolerate no unfaithfulness in the beloved object.

JEHOVAH. See ADONAI; JAHVEH.

JEREMIAS (Heb., Appointed by Jahveh). i. The author of the Old Testament book of prophecy bearing his name and of the Lamentations. The Hebrew form of his name is Jeremiah, and the English form Jeremy. He was sanctified from his mother's womb, to be "a prophet unto the nations" (Jer. i, 5). "Jeremiad" is a popular name for a lamentation or warning, from the characteristics of his utterances. He lived and predicted at the end of the 7th and beginning of the 6th century B.C., and traditionally was stoned to death by the Jews. He is mentioned in the Roman Martyrology on May 1.

ii. His prophecies. These form a canonical book of the Old Testament and are chiefly resolved into short prophecies against the Jews and false prophets, the two great prophecies of the fall of Jerusalem, prophecies of the return from Babylon, and against Egypt and other lands, particularly Babylon itself.

JERUSALEM (Heb., City of Peace). The Holy City of God, the religious and political capital of the Jews; the scene also of the passion and resurrection of Jesus Christ and so no less significant to Christians. It is used by exegetes as a type of the Church militant, of the just soul, and of Heaven, and this last has particularly caught the imagination of Christians. It is thus celebrated in many hymns, both liturgical and vernacular, *e.g.*, *Cœlestis urbs Jerusalem, Urbs Sion aurea*, "Hierusalem! my happy home," *O quanta qualia*.

JERUSALEM, THE COUNCIL OF. The meeting of apostles and presbyters with SS. Paul, Barnabas and others to decide whether Gentile converts were bound by Mosaic law (Acts xv, 4-29). The dogmatic decision given by St. Peter declared Gentiles not so bound. St. James, wrongly supposed to be of the opposite opinion, accepted St. Peter's ruling and proposed a working scheme in a limited district to avoid collision with Jewish feeling. A letter was sent to converts in Antioch, Syria and Cilicia enjoining abstention from idol-offerings, blood of animals, things strangled and fornication. The last was probably included lest new converts, being declared in principle free from Mosaic legislation, should follow the common Gentile opinion that sexual converse by mutual consent between the unmarried was a matter of indifference, or at worst venial. In its doctrinal aspect the decree of the council is infallible and unchangeable; its disciplinary enactments were never universal and soon fell into desuetude (Acts xv).

JERUSALEM, THE LATIN KINGDOM OF, was established by the Crusaders in 1099, and lasted until 1187. There were nine kings from Godefroi de Bouillon to Gui de Lusignan, but the title was kept by those who carried on the kingdom round St. Jean d'Acre until 1291, and persisted in the house of Savoy until 1870. The kingdom was organized completely on the lines of European feudalism (there was a duchy of Antioch, county of Edessa, lordship of Sidon, etc.), and the church was similarly reorganized without any attention to the rights of the Eastern bishops. Hence appeared Latin patriarchs in Jerusalem and Antioch, five Latin archbishoprics and eight episcopal sees which, except as titles, disappeared with the kingdom. The crown was elective and its government seems on the whole to have been a good example of Christian administration, wise, just and moderate.

JERUSALEM, THE LITURGY OF. The Liturgy of St. James (*q.v.*).

JERUSALEM, PATRIARCHATE OF. The fourth in time and last in importance of the five great patriarchates, extending only over Palestine and Sinai, and not recognized as such until the Council of Chalcedon in 451. Previously its bishop had been subject to the metropolitan of Cæsarea Palestinæ. From 637 until 1917 (except for the period of the Latin kingdom) its Christians were subject to a Moslem government. Its patriarchs led their people into schism, following Constantinople and the other Orthodox churches, finally after 1453. It remains an autocephalous unit of the Orthodox Eastern church with a patriarch, three resident metropolitans, ten titular archbishops, all Greeks, and about 45,000 Syro-Palestinian faithful; these last are always trying to get rid of their Greek prelates who monopolize the government and interests of the church. This church exercises principal control in the churches of the Holy Sepulchre and of the Nativity and other holy places.

JERUSALEM, THE PATRIARCHS OF, are to-day three in number. So far as the Catholic Church is concerned the patriarchate is in abeyance, though the title is borne by the Melkite patriarch of Antioch, who administers the see by a vicar. There is a Latin patriarch whose see was established during the crusades but titular from 1187 till 1847, when it was made resident upon the return of the Orthodox patriarch, whose predecessors had long lived at Constantinople: his jurisdiction is over the Latins of Palestine, Transjordania and Cyprus and in fact he does not differ from any other Latin archbishop without suffragans. There are two dissident patriarchs, of the Orthodox and of the Armenians.

JESSE-WINDOW. A stained-glass window in which is represented the characters in the genealogical tree of our Lord, springing from Jesse, the father of King David.

JESU'S PSALTER, commonly but incorrectly called "The Jesus Psalter." A form of devotion containing fifteen principal petitions, which ten times repeated make 150, for graces necessary to the spiritual life; every five petitions have an antiphon and are followed by Our Father, Hail Mary and *Credo*, and the ten repetitions of each petition are followed by a varying number of verses em-

broidering it, written in rhythmical prose. It was probably composed by Richard Whytford, a Bridgettine ("The wretch of Syon," *c.* 1467-*c.* 1558), and is found in primers as well as separately in the 16th and subsequent centuries. Since the 17th century and in modern English prayer-books it appears in a debased and shortened form.

JESUATS. A nick-name, from their frequent use of the Holy Name, given to the lay congregation of Apostolic Clerks of St. Jerome founded for the care of the sick by Bd. John Colombini before 1367; they were suppressed in 1668. They must not be confounded with the Jesuits (*q.v.*), who happily are still with us. The *Jesuatesses,* founded by Bd. John's cousin, Bl. Catherine, as a penitential congregation survived till 1872.

"JESUITESSES." The Jesuits do not undertake the permanent direction of nuns and there is not nor has there been any corresponding congregation of women, though the institutes of many modern congregations of nuns are based on the Society's rules. The name "Jesuitesses" was given by its opponents to the first congregation of Mary Ward (The English Ladies, or Institute of Mary, *q.v.*).

JESUITS, The. The Society, at first called Company, of Jesus, an order of clerks regular founded by St. Ignatius Loyola in 1534. Whilst the primary end of the Society is to be at the call of the pope for whatever work is required, its chief apostolic labours are the education of youth and foreign missions. In addition to their numerous schools and colleges for lay pupils, Jesuits are in charge of a number of seminaries in Rome and elsewhere and such pontifical institutions as the Gregorian University, and are strongly represented on Roman congregations and commissions; outstanding in their scholarship is the work of the Bollandists (*q.v.*); and they are responsible for mission territories in many parts of the world (including Alaska). They have a number of priests of Byzantine rite, working chiefly among Russians and other Slavs. The solemn vows of religion are taken by a special section of the priests when they make their second profession or, as is said, "take their last vows," to which is added a fourth, of special obedience to the Holy See to go wherever sent on missions. The training undergone is long, arduous and varied. A devoted spirit of obedience, versatility and efficiency are characteristic of the Society. Its rules are contained in the "Institutum Societatis Jesu," especially the constitutions as drawn up by St. Ignatius himself; in view of fables current about the society, it may be noted that these rules are not secret (*cf.*, MONITA SECRETA). The Society is divided throughout the world into provinces, governed by provincials under the father general residing in Rome. The English province conducts the boarding-colleges of Stonyhurst, Beaumont and Mount St. Mary's, as well as secondary day schools, numerous parishes, and retreat houses in Great Britain, and missions in British oversea territory. Ireland and Canada has each its own province, and there are four in the United States, where the Society's educational establishments are very numerous, including Fordham University in New York, Marquette at Milwaukee, Loyola at Chicago and New Orleans, and Georgetown. It is the largest of the religious orders, having about 28,000 members. No distinctive habit was prescribed, but members of the English province wear a black gown with a length of cloth hanging from each shoulder ("wings") something like that of a solicitor, originating in the dress of the students at the University of Paris in St. Ignatius's time; it was formerly worn over the *soutane*, as it is still at Ushaw College.

JESUITS, SUPPRESSION OF THE. An administrative measure of Pope Clement XIV in 1773, forced on him for political reasons by the sovereigns of Europe. The ostensible reason was that the Jesuits were disturbers of the public peace, but the brief of suppression refrained from stating that the numerous charges were proved. The Society survived in Russia, the Empress Catherine refusing to allow the bishops to promulgate the brief. In 1801 Pope Pius VII approved them there, in 1804 he restored the Society in Naples and in 1814 everywhere.

JESUITS' BARK. Quinine *(cinchona)*, so called because it was introduced into Europe from South America and its use popularized by missionaries of the Society of Jesus in the 17th century.

JESUS. See HOLY NAME.

JESUS CHRIST. The Son of God made man for us; the Word, begotten of the Father from all eternity, who took flesh and was born of the Virgin Mary by the power of the Holy Ghost; who lived in Galilee and Judæa, preached the Kingdom of God, did miracles and founded the Church; who suffered under Pontius Pilate, and died on the cross, a willing victim for the sins of the world; who was buried and, on the third day, rose from the dead, and forty days later ascended into Heaven where he now sits on the right hand of the Father; who also is really and corporeally present in the Blessed Sacrament: and is the Way, the Truth and the Life of all Christians.

JEWS, The (Heb. *y'hudah*, Judah, one of the twelve Hebrew tribes and the name of one of their two kingdoms). The children of Israel (Jacob) and the people chosen by God to receive his revelation. After their rejection of Jesus Christ, the Messias whom

they awaited, the final ruin of their nation was brought about by the destruction of Jesusalem by the Romans in 70 and the crushing of the revolt under Bar-Kokba in 132-5. Since then they have been dispersed throughout the world *(diaspora)*, a state of affairs on which their new "national home" in Palestine has had no appreciable effect. They form a number of more or less well-defined bodies according to their countries of adoption: *e.g.*, the *Sephardim* are Spanish and Portuguese, the *Ashkenazim* from northern Europe, the *Chasidim* (Pious), a south Russian sect; all orthodox Jews are now Pharisees *(Perooshim)*. The Jews were the Church of the Old Dispensation or Covenant (See JUDAISM). They have often been subjected to attempts at forcible conversion by local ecclesiastical authorities while always enjoying a notable degree of consideration and protection from the Holy See. Barnage, their Protestant historian, testifies that "Of all sovereigns, there has been scarcely one whose rule over the Circumcised has been more just than that of the popes." Before the nazi massacres there were estimated to be 15¾ millions of Jews in the world, of whom the largest single colony is New York (2 million). The great obstacles to conversion of Jews have been the attitude of "closed mind" towards Christianity adopted by them since the fall of Jerusalem, and Christian loss of interest through lack of access; in addition is the aggravating of prejudice against Catholicism by "anti-Semitism" *(q.v.)* and by non-Catholic Christians, in spite of the conspicuously fair attitude of some Jewish writers.

JOB (Heb., one persecuted). A book of the Old Testament, called after the name of its principal character. The prologue relates the sufferings of Job permitted by God to try his constancy; three friends attempt to console him (his greatest trial of all) attributing his misfortunes to his sins; they argue with one another; the remedial and testing functions of affliction and the mystery of God's ways are set forth by a fifth party, Elihu, and confirmed by God; in an epilogue Job is vindicated and delivered. In the original Hebrew this book, except for the prologue and epilogue, is in poetic form, and both for instruction and edification it is one of the most remarkable in the Bible; all the lessons at Matins in the Office of the Dead are taken therefrom. The writer of the book, its date and the time at which Job flourished, are all unknown; he is named in the Roman Martyrology on May 10.

J.O.C. MOVEMENT, The. *Jeunesse Ouvrière Chrétienne*, Young Christian Workers. A movement founded in Belgium by Canon Cardijn between 1919 and 1924. Its aim is the reinstatement of the concept of work as itself an apostolate, a collaboration of man with God; and the leading of the workers to Christ from within by the life and activity of workers themselves. The movement is highly organized, from local nuclei of "militants" upwards to the national organization. In Belgium membership grew in 10 years from under 500 to 100,000 young men and women, with numerous reviews and other publications; and it has had a strong observable effect on the country's industrial workers, most of whom supported anti-religious political bodies. It had a similar success in France, and before 1939 had spread to other countries, including Austria, Yugoslavia, Canada and Great Britain. The strong religious element in early trade-unionism in the last-named country was among Canon Cardijn's direct inspirations for his own work.

JOEL (Heb., Jahveh is strength). A prophetical book of the Old Testament named after its author, a contemporary of Osee (*q.v.*) and the earliest of the prophets of Juda. He foretells the Assyrian invasion under the figures of natural calamities, exhorts to repentance, and promises the blessings and coming of the Messias in Zion. He is named in the Roman Martyrology on July 13.

JOHN, ST. i. Apostle and evangelist, known as the Theologian or Divine and The Beloved Disciple, whose feast is kept throughout the Church, in the West on Dec. 27. To him was committed the care of his all-holy Mother by Christ on the cross. He was the author of the gospel which bears his name, of three canonical epistles, and of the Apocalypse, and was the only one of the twelve apostles who was certainly not called to martyrdom, dying at Ephesus about the year 100 at a great age. The feast of St. John before the Latin Gate kept in the Western church on May 6 (he has a feast in the Byzantine rite two days later) commemorates the dedication of a basilica at the place by the Porta Latina of Rome where, according to an old but unreliable tradition, he was thrown into a vat of boiling oil by order of the Emperor Domitian and was delivered unharmed. He is named in the canon of the Mass.
ii. His gospel. This was written in Greek, probably between 90 and 100, in order that "you may believe that Jesus is the Christ, the Son of God, and that believing you may have life in his name"; and it differs from the other gospels in that this is presented from a definitely theological point of view, whence the writer has been called "the divine" or "theologian." Since the end of the 18th century rationalistic critics have strongly called in question the authorship and authenticity of this gospel, and the papal decree *Lamentabili* and the Biblical Commission (*q.v.*) in 1907 condemned certain of their views.
iii. His epistles. Three letters of St. John are in the canon of Scripture, all probably written from Ephesus. The 1st and longest, addressed to Christians at large, continues the lesson of his gospel; vv. 7 and 8 of cap. v. furnish the controversy of the Three Heavenly Witnesses (*q.v.*). The 2nd has only 13 verses and is addressed probably to a local church; the 3rd (14 verses) to one Gaius, of whom nothing is known.

JOHN CHRYSOSTOM, LITURGY OF ST. The eucharistic liturgy commonly used in the Byzantine rite. After a long preparation (*proskomide, q.v.*) the priest goes to the altar and the deacon to the front of the *iconostasis*, which is his usual place because he acts as interpreter between the celebrant and people; when there is no deacon, the celebrant alone says the prayers and carries out the ceremonies. The first part of the Liturgy (of the Catechumens) consists broadly of the great litany (*synapte* or *eirenika*) the singing of psalms (*typika*) with antiphons, the little entrance (*q.v.*), the epistle, the gospel, the *ektenes* (*q.v.*) and the prayers for the catechumens. The liturgy of the Faithful begins with prayers for the people; then follows the *cherubikon* (*q.v.*) and great entrance (*q.v.*), the kiss of peace in pontifical celebrations, the doors of the *iconostasis* are shut and the creed is sung. The *anaphora* begins with a preface; the words of the consecration are said aloud; then follow the *epiklesis* (which the Orthodox regard as a necessary part of the consecration), the mementoes of the dead and the living, the Lord's Prayer, the elevation and fraction, the communion and thanksgiving, distribution of *antidoron* and the dismissal. Throughout the Liturgy the celebrant says other prayers silently while the choir or deacon is singing; it takes about two hours and is celebrated by the Orthodox on Sunday and feasts only; most Catholics of the rite have introduced a form equivalent to low Mass; concelebration (*q.v.*) is common, especially as not more than one celebration a day is supposed to take place at any altar. This Liturgy is a modification attributed to St. John Chrysostom (*d.* 407) of the Liturgy of St. Basil, and has been further altered since his time; together they form the most authentic expression of the Church's original liturgical tradition.

JOHN-OF-GOD, THE ORDER OF ST. See HOSPITALLERS OF.

JOHN OF JERUSALEM, THE ORDER OF ST. See HOSPITALLERS and KNIGHTS OF ST. JOHN.

JONAS (Heb. *Jonah*, a Dove, or the Murmurer). The only prophet who came out of Galilee (*cf.*, John vii, 52) and the only one of the prophets of Israel sent to preach to the Gentiles, as recounted in the Old Testament book which bears his name. It records rather than prophesies, but his being swallowed and cast out by a great fish is a type of the death and resurrection of Christ: cf., Matt. xii, 38-41, upon which passage Catholic exegetes principally base their contention that the events narrated were objective facts. Jonas is named in the Roman Martyrology on Sept. 21, and the tenth prophecy on Holy Saturday is taken from his 3rd chapter.

JOSEPHINISM is the principle that the state has complete supremacy over the Church which it controls in accordance with what it judges to be the best interests of the nation. It is the ultimate issue of Gallicanism and Febronianism (*qq.v.*) and is named after the Emperor Joseph II (1765-90) who put it into practice.

JOSEPHITES. A teaching congregation founded in Belgium in 1817; the Congregation of St. Joseph.

JOSUE (Heb. *Joshua*, the same name as *Jesus*, saviour). The leader of the children of Israel appointed by Moses to succeed him, who gives his name to a canonical book of the Old Testament. This book relates the passing of the Israelites over Jordan into the promised land, the conquest of Canaan, and its partition among the tribes. It was written either by Josue himself or soon after his time. He is, with Gedeon, named in the Roman Martyrology on Sept. 1.

JOY. A fruit of the Holy Ghost (*q.v.*) which helps one to serve God cheerfully. St. Thomas says "Joy is not a virtue distinct from charity, but an act or effect of charity (love)." Among the four necessities for canonization enumerated by Pope Benedict XIV is that the candidate should have displayed an expansive joy in his life and influence, however melancholy his natural temperament may have been.

JOYS OF MARY, The, as an object of devotion are variously enumerated (five, seven, twelve or more); the most usual now are the Annunciation, Visitation, Nativity, Epiphany, Finding in the Temple, Resurrection, Ascension. One old English carol has suckling her Son, Jesus curing the lame, curing the blind, reading the Bible, raising the dead, the Resurrection and the Ascension. The Franciscans have a feast of the Joys on Aug. 22 (with a proper sequence), which is also observed in Portugal, Brazil and elsewhere on the Monday after Low Sunday, with special reference to the Resurrection.

JOYFUL MYSTERIES, THE V, of the rosary (*q.v.*) are: the annunciation of Gabriel to our Lady, the visitation by our Lady of St. Elizabeth, the birth of our Lord, his presentation in the Temple, and the finding of the child Jesus talking with the doctors.

JUBÉ. The name given in France to the rood-loft or choir-screen (*qq.v.*), from the formula *Jube, domne, benedicere* used before singing a liturgical lesson, which suggests a possible former use of the rood-loft.

JUBILATE SUNDAY. The third Sunday after Easter, from the first word of the introit at Mass.

JUBILEE (word of Hebrew derivation but uncertain origin; see Lev. xxv, 10-55). A plenary indulgence (*q.v.*) granted by the Holy See with special solemnity for a definite time, together with special faculties to confessors. The lesser or extraordinary jubilee is granted on a special occasion, such as the 50th anniversary of the pope's ordination, as in 1929; but the term ordinarily refers to the greater indulgence associated with the Holy Year (*q.v.*). This is gained by confession, communion and prayer at the Roman basilicas of St. Peter, St. Paul, the Lateran and St. Mary Major for the pope's intentions (these at the last jubilee were: peace, the conversion of non-Catholics, a just settlement of the affairs of the Holy Land); certain classes of people (*e.g.*, in 1925, invalids, working people, religious, and others unable to travel far) gain the indulgence at home on conditions laid down by the local bishops. During the continuance of the jubilee all indulgences (with a few exceptions, *e.g.*, of the dying) granted in favour of the living are suspended, though they may be gained for the dead; confessors chosen for the jubilee confession have power to absolve from all ordinary reserved sins and censures; but special faculties of absolution held by bishops and priests are suspended in respect of those who are able to go to Rome. In the year following a holy year the jubilee is extended to the whole world (in 1926, for twelve months). By unique privilege the ordinary jubilee indulgence may be gained at the cathedral of Compostela (which also has its holy door, *q.v.*) every year wherein the feast of St. James the Greater falls on a Sunday.

JUBILUS. The joyful melody to which is sung the final "a" of the second and third alleluias, after the gradual (*q.v.*) in the Roman Mass; any long final neum (*q.v.*) of a joyous nature.

JUDA, THE KINGDOM OF. The two tribes of Juda and Benjamin which remained faithful to King Roboam at Jerusalem, from whom the Jews of to-day are descended.

JUDAISM. The religion revealed by God to Israel, now represented by the Catholic Church which receives the promised Messias, Jesus Christ, and admits the Gentiles of all nations to his covenant. In ordinary use is meant the religion of the Jews who rejected the Messias. Since the destruction of the Temple in A.D. 70 they have no altar and no sacrifice (*cf.*, Osee iii, 4), and worship consisting of prayer and reading the Law is conducted in the synagogue by a *rabbi* (*q.v.*, really a "moral theologian"). The orthodox

Jews, those who believe in one God who rewards and punishes, the words of Moses and the prophets, the immutability of the Law of the Pentateuch, who observe that law and the festivals, who look for the coming of the Messias, the restoration of Israel, the resurrection of the dead and the emptying of Hell (*sheol*), decrease in numbers; since the 18th century liberal Jews have again and again "restated" their revelation until it is now for many emptied of almost all Judaic content.

JUDAIZERS. Those members of the early Church who claimed that the Mosaic law was still binding either on Jewish Christians or on all (*cf.*, Acts xv, Gal. ii). They were principally divided into the Nazarenes and the heretical Ebionites. Coptic and Ethiopian Christians still observe certain Jewish rites but apparently without religious significance.

JUDE, THE EPISTLE OF ST. A short letter in the canon of Holy Scripture written to the Church at large, and convert Jews in particular, urging them to beware of erroneous dogmatic and loose moral teaching in their midst. It has so much in common with 2 Peter that one must have owed to the other, but which to which is not known. *Cf.*, Simon and Jude.

JUDGE, ECCLESIASTICAL. Judicial power in the Church belongs to the pope universally and to the bishop in his diocese. The local ordinary is the judge in causes of first instance, and the metropolitan the judge of appeal. A diocesan judge, called the official, usually acts for the bishop. Others, called synodal judges or examiners, try certain causes. In some trials a collegiate tribunal of three or five judges is required. The judge alone exercises judicial power in all causes, whether civil or criminal, there being no jury system in church courts. The judge is bound to follow the rules of procedure laid down in the Code of Canon Law, Book iv.

JUDGES. A canonical book of the Old Testament which relates the history of Israel under the rule of the judges, *i.e.* nonhereditary rulers, noteworthy among whom were Gedeon and Samson, illustrating how the fortunes of Israel fluctuate according to their faithfulness to the covenant with God. Its authorship is attributed to the prophet Samuel.

JUDGEMENT. The mental act by which something is asserted or denied. In the judgement alone is logical truth (*q.v.*) to be found: in the primitive act of apprehension there is contained an implicit affirmation that the object perceived exists, but in judgement alone, which is consequent upon simple apprehension, is that affirmation (or negative) explicit. Analytic judgement is that whose predicate is contained in the notion of the subject, as: man is rational, $2 + 2 = 4$. Synthetic judgement is that whose predicate is not contained in the notion of the subject, as: the horse is brown. It will be seen that analytic judgements are necessary and universal and that synthetic have no such character and are therefore called contingent.

JUDGEMENT, INTELLECTUAL. i. An act of the mind discovering the logical *nexus* between two abstract ideas and perceiving that one is contained (or not) in the extension or the comprehension of the other.

ii. A judgement of our neighbour's intellectual capacity. This is sometimes a duty, and then we must judge according to the facts, whether he be a fool or a philosopher. But sometimes these judgements are unnecessary and dictated by pride or prejudice, and so sinful.

JUDGEMENT, MORAL. A judgement of the morality of an action, whether our own or our neighbour's. A confessor has to exercise such a judgement on his penitent in the tribunal of penance (*q.v.*), and a superior may have to judge his subject. But too often men arrogate to themselves the right to judge their neighbour's conduct and motives, and sin thereby. "Judgement is only lawful according as it is an act proceeding from justice and for this three things are required: it must flow from an inclination for justice, come from a superior authority, and be pronounced according to the rules of prudence; if defective on any of these points the judgement will be faulty and unlawful" (St. Thomas II-II, lv, 2). Our Lord warned against rash judgements in Matt. vii, 1, 2.

JUDGEMENT, PRIVATE. Luther rejected the teaching authority of the Church, maintaining that private individuals were competent to get all the guidance they needed from their own reading of the Scriptures, and that the claim of the Church to teach was an intrusion on the liberty of conscience. This is called the right of Private Judgement.

JUDGEMENT OF THE SOUL. i. Particular. This takes place immediately after the death of each person and irrevocably settles the soul's salvation or damnation, even though it may have to undergo temporal punishment in Purgatory.

ii. General. This takes place after the final Resurrection, when the body will share in the reward or punishment of the soul, and when the righteousness of God's ways will be manifestly vindicated before all creation.

JUDITH (Heb., Jewess). A deutero-canonical (*q.v.*) book of the Old Testament, which is therefore not found in the Hebrew and Protestant Bibles. It is an historical work, narrating the stratagem whereby a beautiful widow, Judith, killed Holofernes, general of the Assyrians, and enabled the Israelites to drive off the invaders: so illustrating God's care for his people and his use of the weak to confound the strong. The Copts and Ethiopians commemorate Judith by a liturgical feast on Sept. 12.

JURISDICTION is the power belonging to the Church, as a perfect society, of ruling her members for the attainment of her spiritual end. This power is of divine institution and includes legislative, judicial and executive authority. It can only be exercised by clerics. Jurisdiction is either ordinary, attached to an office; or delegated, committed to a person apart from an office (see below). It is exercised either in the external or in the internal forum (q.v.). Jurisdiction in the internal forum is necessary as well as Orders for the validity of sacramental absolution. The pope's jurisdiction is universal; that of inferior authorities can only be exercised on their own subjects in their own territories. In the case of a common error or a positive and probable doubt, either of law or of fact, the Church supplies the necessary jurisdiction, in both the external and internal forum, to make the act valid.

JURISDICTION, DELEGATED. Jurisdiction which is committed to a person and not attached to an office. Anyone who has ordinary jurisdiction may delegate it wholly or partially to another, unless expressly forbidden by law. A delegate may not subdelegate unless he is a delegate of the pope, or is delegated by an inferior ordinary (q.v.) for all cases. Delegated jurisdiction depends entirely on the terms of the mandate. Jurisdiction may be delegated either to an individual or to a group, and to the latter either as a collegiate body acting together or to any single member. Delegated jurisdiction ceases when the mandate has been fully carried out, when the time fixed has expired, by revocation of the authority delegating, or by renunciation of the delegate, if accepted. It does not cease with the jurisdiction of the authority delegating except where this is expressly stated in law.

JURISDICTION, ORDINARY. That which is attached by the law itself to an ecclesiastical office, as distinct from delegated jurisdiction which is committed to a person apart from an office. It is called proper, if the office belongs to the holder in his own name, e.g., a diocesan bishop; and vicarious, if held in the name of another, e.g., a vicar apostolic. One who holds ordinary jurisdiction can delegate it wholly or partially to another, except where the law expressly disallows this. Ordinary jurisdiction does not cease with that of the person who conferred the office, but it ceases with the loss of the office to which it is attached, and is suspended by legitimate appeal in the matter appealed from. Ordinary jurisdiction may be for the external or internal forum (q.v.) or both.

Those with ordinary jurisdiction in the external forum are called Ordinaries. Ordinary jurisdiction in the internal forum belongs to the pope and cardinals universally, and in their respective territories to bishops and rectors of parishes and their legitimate substitutes, and to canons penitentiary; also to superiors of exempt religious (q.v.) over their own subjects. Those with ordinary jurisdiction in the internal forum can absolve their subjects anywhere, even outside their own territory.

JURISDICTION OF DISSIDENT CLERGY. Absolution given by priests of the dissident Eastern churches to their people is not invalidated by lack of jurisdiction. The Church has never required a general confession from Eastern dissidents who are being reconciled (if their previous confessions were invalid this would be absolutely necessary); and Catholics are forbidden to confess to dissident priests because of its unlawfulness (communicatio in sacris), no mention being made of invalidity. The reunion with the Orthodox and other churches effected by the Council of Florence has never been officially repudiated by the Holy See, which presumably has not withdrawn the jurisdiction then conferred (cf., Confirmation).

JUS PRIMAE NOCTIS. See DROIT DE SEIGNEUR.

JUST PRICE. That price at which, in justice, goods should be bought and sold, which does not depend merely on the agreement of the parties. It is the common local value of the thing sold, estimated by the judgement of those who are fully cognizant of the production, distribution and other conditions affecting the value of the article in question: e.g., a market price is usually a just price. A just price is general, not exact, and has a highest and a lowest limit within which justice is satisfied. Fancy prices for rare or unique objects are not unjust; but a higher price must not be asked on account of the special need of the buyer, though it may be because of that of the seller. "The institution of buying and selling is for the common good of both parties, each of whom wants what the other has got. Now a transaction designed for the common advantage of both should not bear harder upon the one than the other; therefore the contract between them should be upon the principle of equality of thing to thing. Now the quantity of a thing that serves human use is measured according to the price given for it, for which purpose we have the invention of money. Therefore if either the price exceeds the quantity of the value of the thing, or conversely the thing exceeds the price, the equality of justice will be destroyed. And therefore to sell a thing dearer or buy it cheaper than it is worth is a proceeding in itself unjust and unlawful" (St. Thomas, II-II, lxxvii, 1).

JUSTICE. i. The cardinal moral virtue which inclines one to give whatever is due to God, to one's neighbour, to oneself. By its extent and implications one of the most important and far-reaching of the virtues, for with charity it should govern man's relations with his fellows; it must be distinguished from charity, for justice involves what is *due* to another by right. It includes many other virtues, notably religion, obedience, truthfulness, gratitude, liberality, piety.

ii. More frequently the term is limited to legal and to distributive justice, which refer respectively to what is due from us to the state and from the state to us; and to commutative justice, which inclines one to give another his due as a man irrespective of who he is. Thus to infringe another's rights by damage to his property, theft, calumny, detraction, adultery, etc., is to sin against justice (*cf.*, Restitution).

iii. Sanctifying grace, as in the expression "state of justice," for "state of grace" (*q.v.*).

iv. Righteousness in general, as in Matt. vi, 33. Where most English versions of the Bible translate δικαιοσύνη "righteousness," the Douay version renders it "justice," following literally the Vulgate *iustitia*. Recent Catholic translators, notably Mgr. Knox, have abandoned this confusing practice.

v. Original justice. The state of Adam before the Fall (*q.v.*) when he enjoyed the preternatural qualities and gratuitous gifts of justice (*i.e.*, principally, sanctifying grace), integrity and immortality (*qq.v.*). It was conferred on him not only personally but as the head and representative of the whole human race, and lost both for him and for us at the Fall (*cf.*, Pure Nature, Fallen Nature).

JUSTIFICATION. In its active sense, Justification is the act of God declaring and *making* a person just; in its passive sense, it is the change in a soul which passes from the state of sin to that of sanctifying grace (*q.v.*) or justice. At the time of the Reformation the following Protestant errors became current: (*a*) Faith alone is the necessary disposition for justification; (*b*) justifying faith is a mere confidence in the divine mercy; (*c*) justification is separable from sanctification; it is a mere judicial declaration that the sinner will not be punished, and that sanctification itself is but a cloaking of sin and an extrinsic imputation of the merits of Christ.

JUSTIFICATION BY FAITH. Faith (and that, true faith, not merely fiduciary) is a necessary condition of justification. That faith alone justifies is a heresy of Luther condemned by the Council of Trent (sess. vi, can 9 *de justificatione*): "If any one shall say that the wicked man is justified by faith alone, meaning that no other thing is required to co-operate for obtaining the grace of justification, and that it is not necessary for him to be prepared and disposed by the movement of his will, let him be anathema."

JUSTIFICATION BY WORKS. Justification by faith alone is not possible. Other dispositions of the soul, works done under the influence of grace such as fear, hope, charity, hatred of sin, are necessary. Such is the clear doctrine of Scripture: "Do you see that by works a man is justified, and not by faith only? . . . . Faith without works is dead" (James ii, 24, 26).

K

KALEMAUKION (Gr. κάμηλος, being originally made of camel hair; there are several spellings). The hat characteristic of the clergy of the Byzantine rite. It is black, cylindrical and has a flat brim at the top; minor clerics and all Russian clergy wear it without a brim; monks and bishops cover it with a veil falling on to their shoulders. Its use is both liturgical and as an ordinary head covering. It is also worn by the Syrians, Catholic and Jacobite, and it may have been the origin of the papal tiara.

KALENDS. The first of the month in the old Roman calendar, still sometimes used in ecclesiastical documents. As the Greek calendar is different, the phrase "The Greek Kalends" is equivalent to saying—never.

KALOGEROS (Gr., good old man). The colloquial term for a monk in the Near East.

KAMISION. The garment worn by minor clerics and acolytes in the Byzantine rite. It is a long ungirdled tunic of linen or silk, with wide sleeves, white, red or other colour; embroidered at the bottom, neck and sleeves. Often called *sticharion* (*q.v.*).

KANON. In the Byzantine Divine Office is a rhythmical composition consisting of 2, 3, 4 or 9 odes, divided into *troparia* (*qq.v.*), having a certain relation to the scriptural canticles (*q.v.*). Most *kanons* are acrostic; the initial letters of the *troparia* make a verse having reference to the feast. Every Sunday and feast has its proper *kanon*.

KANTISM. A philosophy evolved by Emmanuel Kant (1724-1804) which embraces a "Critique of Pure Reason" and a "Critique of Practical Reason." The former treatise consists of an examination into the origin, extent and limits of knowledge. The first step in philosophy must be criticism, as opposed to dogmatism, on the one side, and scepticism on the other. By criticism Kant means an attempted scrutiny into the range and validity of our knowledge. Dogmatism, he maintains, assumes while scepticism rejects, alike unwarrantably, the veracity of our faculties. Kant's *Criticism* results in the denial of everything transcending experience. The "Critique of Practical Reason" seeks to restore in the form of *belief* what he has previously demolished as rational cognition: though the existence of God, the immortality of the soul, and the freedom of the will, are incapable of proof, if not replete with contradictions, yet their admission is exacted by the needs of our moral nature.

KARSHUNI. Arabic written in Syriac characters, used by Maronites and other Syrians for the rubrics in their liturgical books. It is used also for the lessons, Lord's Prayer and other prayers in Jacobite liturgical books, and sometimes in those of the Catholic Syrians and Maronites as well. There is a Karshuni version of the Bible.

KATHISMA (plural, *kathismata*). One of the 20 parts into which the Psalter is divided in the Byzantine Divine Office.

KATHOLIKON. The chief church of a monastery of the Byzantine rite; *cf.*, the former choir of the Latin canons in the church of the Resurrection at Jerusalem, now the *katholikon* of the Orthodox patriarch.

KATHOLIKOS (Gr., universal delegate). The title of the heads of the Nestorian, Georgian and Armenian churches. Originally it meant a primate who was more than a metropolitan and less than a patriarch (the first known *katholikos,* at Seleucia-Ctesiphon, was the patriarchal delegate of Antioch); now *katholikos* and patriarch are indistinguishable, though apparently the Armenians put the first named first, for they are organized under two *katholikoi* and two patriarchs and it is the *Katholikos* of Etshmiadzin who has the primacy of honour. The Catholic patriarchs of Babylon and Cilicia are sometimes called the patriarchs-katholikoi of Chaldeans and Catholic Armenians respectively, and the title is historically exact.

KELLION. A small monastery of Byzantine monks, 3 or 6 usually, dependent on a mother-house; several *kellia* are sometimes grouped together with a common church to form a *skete.*

KELLS, THE SYNOD OF. Several plenary and provincial councils of the Irish church are so called. The principal was held in 1152, presided over by a papal legate, at which the primacy of Armagh was confirmed, *pallia* conferred on Dublin, Cashel and Tuam, and numerous small and indeterminate dioceses suppressed. The present Irish diocesan system dates substantially from this synod.

KENOSIS (Gr., emptying or despoiling). i. An heretical theory of the Incarnation constructed by certain Protestant divines, according to which God the Son, in becoming man, discarded his divinity and certain divine attributes, particularly his omnipotence and omniscience, and assumed in their stead human gifts and infirmities, so that he was unaware of his divinity until after the resurrection; or, in a modification of the theory, that he did not exercise omnipotence and omniscience, so that he was sometimes unaware of his divinity. They base their theory on two texts of St. Paul: Phil. ii, 7, "[Christ Jesus] emptied himself, taking the form of a servant," and 2 Cor. viii, 9, "being rich, he became poor." They think that thus they can give a better account of the texts which concern the human nature, the growth in knowledge, the supposed ignorance of the time of the end of the world. Such a theory is obviously irreconcilable with the true doctrine of the Hypostatic Union *(q.v.).* The true meaning of the two basic texts is that Christ emptied himself, not by laying down his divinity, but by concealing it under the form of a man ("taking the form of a servant"), and that, though he was rich as God, he appeared in poverty as man.

ii. Any abasement, reduction to a lower state, or transformation into an inferior condition.

KENOTIC. Pertaining to the heretical doctrine of *kenosis (q.v.),* or to any abasement, *e.g.*, the kenotic theory of sacrifice in the Mass which claims that the exclusion of our Lord's natural, human, visible, tangible quantity, beauty and general appearance by the mode of presence in the Eucharist constitutes the sacrifice.

KERRY AND AGHADOE (*Kerriensis et Aghadoensis*). An Irish see, suffragan of Cashel, formed some time before the 12th century by the union of the dioceses of Ardfert and Aghadoe, which should strictly be its name as Kerry is not a town but a county; it was vacant practically from 1610 to 1703. It now includes all Kerry and part of county Cork. The bishop's residence, cathedral and seminary are at Killarney. The patron of the diocese is St. Brendan (May 16), who is also titular of the cathedral. Irish name: Ciarraighe.

KILDARE AND LEIGHLIN (*Kildarensis et Leighlinensis*). An Irish see, suffragan of Dublin, formed by the union of two ancient dioceses in the 17th century. It includes the county of Carlow and parts of Kildare, Offaly, Leix, Kilkenny, Wicklow and Wexford. The bishop's residence, cathedral and ecclesiastical college are at Carlow, and he is assisted by diocesan consultors, without a chapter of canons. The patron of the combined dioceses is St. Brigid (Feb. 1), whose monastery was at Kildare and whose pilgrim-fire was kept burning day and night in a kiln until the Reformation; the cathedral is dedicated in honour of our Lady. Irish name: Cill Dare.

KILFENORA (*Fenaborensis*). An ancient Irish see, suffragan of Cashel, now perpetually administered by the bishop of Galway. Irish name: Cill Fiomabhra.

KILLALA (*Alladensis*). An Irish see, suffragan of Tuam. It comprises parts of the counties of Mayo and Sligo. The bishop's house, cathedral and diocesan college are at Ballina. The patron of the diocese and titular of the cathedral is St. Muredach (Aug. 12), its first bishop. Irish name: Cill Alaidh.

KILLALOE (*Laonensis*). An Irish see, suffragan of Cashel. It now includes parts of Clare, Tipperary, Limerick, Galway, Offaly, and Leix. The bishop's residence, pro-cathedral and diocesan college are at Ennis. The patron of the diocese is St. Flannan (Dec. 18), its first bishop; the pro-cathedral is dedicated in honour of our Lady. Irish name: Cill Da Lua.

KILMACDUAGH (*Duacensis*). An ancient Irish see now united to Galway (*q.v.*). Irish name: Cill Mac Duach.

KILMORE (*Kilmorensis*). An Irish see, suffragan of Armagh, of ancient foundation but taking its present name only after 1454. It includes county Cavan and parts of Leitrim, Fermanagh, Meath and Sligo. The bishop's residence, pro-cathedral and diocesan college are at Cavan; there is no chapter of canons. St. Phelim (Aug. 9) is patron of the diocese, and the pro-cathedral dedicated in honour of St. Patrick. Irish name: Cill Mhor.

KINDNESS. "Benignity"; a fruit of the Holy Ghost prompting its possessor to assist others by word and deed.

KING, PRAYER FOR THE. The Roman Missal no longer provides for the insertion of the name of the Christian prince in the canon of the Mass, but it gives a commemoration *pro Rege*, praying for his health in soul and body and assistance in his duties. In Great Britain it is customary to say or sing after the principal Mass on Sunday a prayer for "N. our king . . . with the queen his consort and the royal offspring"; under a republic the collect of the votive Mass for peace is said.

KING OF THE ROMANS. The title of the prince elected emperor of the Holy Roman Empire (*q.v.*) during his predecessor's lifetime. He retained it after his coronation as king of Germany until he had received the imperial crown from the pope. No German king assumed the style of emperor previous to being thus crowned in Italy until the time of Maximilian I (1493).

KING'S EVIL, The. Scrofula, so called because it was said to be cured at the touch and intercession of the kings of France and England. This power of touching for the evil was traditionally conferred on the kings of France by. St. Remi, and first exercised in England by St. Edward the Confessor. In its final form the king touched the sufferer, while deprecatory prayers were said, and invested him with a medal of St. Michael ("touch-piece"). It appears beyond doubt that this ceremony was sometimes the occasion of cures. The last English prince to touch was Henry, Cardinal Duke of York (*de iure* King Henry IX), and the last French king, Charles X, at the hospital of St. Marcoul at Reims, after his consecration in 1824.

KINGS, BOOKS OF. In Catholic versions of the Bible those books are called the 1st, 2nd, 3rd and 4th of Kings which in Hebrew and Protestant versions are called 1st and 2nd Samuel and 1st and 2nd Kings respectively. Books I and II relate the story of Samuel and his anointing of Saul as first king of Israel; his unsuccessful reign, and the establishment of the royal and messianic house of David after the taking of Jerusalem and the setting up of the Ark in Zion. The 3rd and 4th books are a separate work, but take up the story where the 2nd left off; they narrate the death of David and the succession of Solomon, and the history of Israel and Juda under their kings until the destruction of Jerusalem by Nabuchodonosor. The authors of these books are unknown, though the Jews attribute the second two to Jeremias.

KINGDOM OF GOD, The. i. In the Old Testament, the Kingdom of God is the Jewish people: they were his people and he was their king, for whom the earthly king was but a vicegerent. It also means the governance of Israel by God. Later, taught by the prophets, the Jews began to look forward to a kingdom that was to come. This expectancy was keen at the time of our Lord's appearance, John having preached that the Kingdom of God was at hand.

ii. In the New Testament, our Lord's own teaching is full of references to the Kingdom of God (or Kingdom of Heaven in St. Matthew, in deference to the reluctance of the Jews to pronounce God's name). The phrase has several distinct meanings: the spiritual rule of God, the kingdom of grace, the future kingdom of Heaven, the kingdom of Christ (with insistence that this is a spiritual, not a temporal, rule), the Church. The spiritual rule of Christ over men, his supreme sovereignty over princes and peoples, is emphasized by the liturgical feast of Christ the King. The Kingdom of Heaven proclaimed by our Lord is not a purely celestial thing, *in futuro;* it began in this world at the Incarnation, it is here and now, existing as a spiritual power, the ruling of God, in the body of the Church; but will be perfected and come to its fulness only hereafter: "At present, we are looking at a confused reflection in a mirror; then, we shall see face to face" (I Cor. xiii, 12).

KISS, as a mark of honour. i. Liturgical. The altar is kissed nine times (including whenever he turns his back to it) by the celebrant at Mass as symbolizing Christ, he kisses the gospels and the paten, the server kisses the cruets at the offertory (but not in requiem Masses), etc. The hand of the celebrant or officiant and the article handed are kissed by the minister whenever he gives or receives anything from him; but such kissing is omitted when Mass is celebrated *coram Sanctissimo.* When receiving blessed palms or candles, the faithful kiss first the article and then the priest's hand; when receiving holy communion from a bishop or abbot his ring is kissed first: this is a survival of the old kiss of peace at this point. The prelate kisses the feet which he washes at the *Mandatum* on Maundy Thursday. In a papal Mass the pope's foot is kissed by the Latin and Greek deacons and by cardinals and others on certain occasions connected with his election (adoration, *q.v.*). ii. Extra-liturgical. In private audiences the pope's foot (*i.e.,* the cross on his right shoe) may be kissed by the visitor; bishops kiss his knee as well; this sign of respect for the Vicar of Christ was formerly given to other patriarchs and even to temporal sovereigns. The ordinary mark of honour to a cardinal, bishop or abbot is to bend the knee and kiss his ring. Relics are kissed ceremonially in church by way of veneration. The kissing of holy images, shrines, etc., is far more common in the East than in the West; it is simply the natural extension of the instinct to kiss the picture of a lover or parent, which is not strange to us.

KISS OF PEACE, The, or **Pax.** i. At Mass. A token of brotherly love surviving from the liturgy of the earliest times, taking place in the Mozarabic and Eastern rites at the beginning of the liturgy of the faithful, and in the Roman and other Latin liturgies after the *Agnus Dei.* The celebrant kisses the altar whereon the body of Christ lies and then puts his hands upon the deacon's arms and they incline their heads slightly, left cheek to left cheek, the priest saying *Pax tecum* (Peace be with thee), and the deacon responding *Et cum spiritu tuo* (And with thy spirit). It is then given to the subdeacon and by him to the canons, choir, monks, or other occupants of the stalls. It is omitted in requiem Masses and on Maundy Thursday and Holy Saturday. At pontifical Mass the bishop gives it to his first five ministers. In the West it is no longer given to the laity except, by means of an *instrumentum pacis* or *pax* (*q.v.* ii), to sovereigns, chief magistrates, and other privileged persons, such as the lord mayor of Dublin in that city. In the Byzantine rite the kiss of peace is confined to the officiating clergy at pontifical and concelebrated Liturgies; in the Armenian rite the people still give it to one another, somewhat after the Roman manner; the Chaldeans, Syrians, Copts, and Maronites convey it to one another by a touching of hands.

ii. Other liturgical uses. A newly consecrated bishop receives the kiss of peace from the other bishops present and a newly ordained priest from his ordainer. In a Byzantine ordination the ordained gives the kiss to all the clergy present. In mediæval uses it was given to the groom and by him to the bride at a nuptial Mass.

KNEELING is, generally speaking, a practice confined in the liturgy to penitential times, *e.g.,* during the collects and post-communions during Lent, during the litanies when not sung in procession. It is only since the middle ages that it has become customary during the consecration and the singing of *Incarnatus* in the Creed. The rubric directs that those assisting at low Mass kneel all the time except at the gospel. In extra-liturgical services (*e.g.,* Benediction) kneeling is the usual posture, and special *cultus* of the Blessed Sacrament has modified the rule that to bow while kneeling is superfluous. In most Eastern liturgies kneeling is practically unknown.

KNIGHT, PAPAL. A member of one of the six pontifical orders of knighthood (*q.v.*), *e.g.,* a knight of the Order of St. Gregory the Great.

KNIGHTS OF COLUMBUS'S "OATH," The. A bogus oath alleged by both ignorance and malice to be taken by members of the Knights of Columbus, a fraternal and philanthropic society of Catholics in the U.S.A. The "oath," of a grandiloquent and bloodthirsty character, appears to have originated in the Low Countries in the early part of the 18th century to discredit the Jesuits, but some claim to have traced it to England in the 17th century or even to 1580; it was resurrected and edited for political purposes in Pennsylvania in 1912. It was denounced as false and libellous by a committee of Congress in 1913.

KNIGHTS OF THE CROSS. The Sacred Military Order of Cross-bearers with the Red Star, founded as hospitallers by Bl. Agnes of Bohemia at Prague in 1237. Reorganized in 1694 and now commonly known as Crosier Canons of the Red Star. There are now very few members, who are engaged in teaching and parochial work; the general and grand-master resides at Prague.

KNIGHTS OF ST. JOHN, The. The Sovereign, Sacred and Military Order of St. John of Jerusalem, commonly called Knights of Malta, is the organic descendant and representative of the Knights Hospitallers (*q.v.*). Alone among the orders of chivalry it still retains a small nucleus of members (Knights of Justice) who take the vows of religion and are professed for the service of the poor and the defence of the faith; the principal other degrees are Knights of Honour and Devotion, who must have certain qualifications of noble birth, and Knights of Magistral Grace, not so qualified; the grand cross is sometimes accorded by the grand master of the order to princes who are not Catholics, *e.g.*, to King Edward VII. Charitable work is carried on in various hospitals, the British association of the order being connected with the Hospital of St. John and St. Elizabeth in London. As a sovereign order the knights have a diplomatic representative at the papal court; this was in abeyance from 1832 till 1930. These veritable Knights of St. John must be distinguished from the Knights of the Hospital of St. John of Jerusalem in England, a famous charitable organization which has no connexion with the ancient order beyond the occupancy of its former headquarters at Clerkenwell.

KNIGHTS OF MALTA. The name of the Knights Hospitallers (*q.v.*) during their sovereign occupation of Malta (1530-1798). Their former conventual church is now the co-cathedral of that diocese. The name is still used commonly for the Knights of St. John.

KNIGHTS OF RHODES. The name of the Knights Hospitallers (*q.v.*) during their sovereign occupation of Rhodes (1309-1523).

KNOP (Middle English survival). The knob or rounded protuberance in the middle of the stem of a chalice to facilitate holding it securely.

KNOWABILITY OF GOD. See KNOWLEDGE OF GOD, ii.

KNOWLEDGE. i. An intellectual virtue (*q.v.*). See SCIENCE.
ii. A gift of the Holy Ghost (*q.v.*) which enables us to appraise the spiritual value and utility of created things.
iii. Conjectural. It was asserted by Gregory of Valencia (*c.* 1550-1603) that God has only a conjectural knowledge of the conditioned future. This is contrary to the doctrine of St. Thomas, and was condemned by the board of theologians in the Congregation *de Auxiliis*. Of the future, conditioned or otherwise, God has a certain knowledge.
iv. Theories of. Protagoras and the ancient sceptics taught that the human mind

was the measure of things; others that the mind knows only relations; others, as Hume, Kant, Locke, that the essences of things are outside the reach of the mind. Thus the relativity of human knowledge is held by Sceptics, Criticists, Positivists and Agnostics. The points of agreement and opposition between various theories of knowledge regarding the origin and nature of primary truths and ideas may be summed up as follows: (*a*) The evolutionist maintains (1) the existence of obscure innate ideas or cognitions, as (2) an organic inheritance, (3) from a previous living being, (4) of a lower grade, (5) but originally acquired by sensuous experience, (6) during a vast period, and therefore of eminent validity within the field of possible experience. (*b*) Plato upheld (1) innate ideas or cognitions, as (2) faint spiritual vestiges (3) of a previous life, (4) of a higher grade, but (5) not derived from sensuous experience, (6) and therefore of eminent validity. (*c*) Descartes and Leibnitz defended (1) innate ideas or cognitions as (2) divinely implanted in the mind in a potential condition, (3) and therefore of eminent validity. (*d*) Kant holds (1) innate forms, (2) antecedent to and conditioning all experience, (3) and therefore formally necessary within the field of possible experience, but (4) of no real validity as applied to things-in-themselves. (*e*) Associationism denies innate ideas in any form, and ascribes the necessity of these special cognitions to the continuous experience of the individual's own life. (*f*) Intuitionism, the true theory, teaches indeed that the mind is endowed with a native faculty for the apprehension of such verities, but it denies that they are purely subjective contributions. They have their origin in experience, but neither their necessity nor universality (*q.v.*) is based upon mere iteration of experience; on the contrary, the mind is compelled to enounce a truth as necessary and universal not by any *a priori* form or innate idea, but by the objective necessity of the relation which is seen to hold in reality.

KNOWLEDGE, INFUSED. Knowledge independent of sense, and dependent on ideas directly poured in by God. It is the knowledge natural to angels who, having no bodies, cannot be dependent on sense impressions. Man's natural knowledge is all derived originally from sense impressions, and however far it goes it clings to sense imagery. Infused knowledge will be enjoyed by our souls in the Beatific Vision (*q.v.*). It is sometimes supernaturally granted to holy men on earth. It was one of the branches of the knowledge of Christ.

KNOWLEDGE OF GOD. i. God knows and apprehends himself completely. He also knows all things outside himself, whether they be past, present, or future, even such future things as depend upon man's free will.

It is commonly taught that his knowledge includes all possible essences, and all the things which might have happened but which, as a matter of fact, will not happen (futuribles). All these things he knows of himself and in themselves, in a single glance, in the one permanent and unchanging act in which he sees himself.

ii. Regarding our knowledge of God, the Vatican Council lays down the following: "If anyone say that God, one and true, our Creator and Lord, cannot be certainly known by the natural light of human reason from the things that are made, let him be anathema" (sess. iii, can. I *de revelatione*). So, by reason alone, it is possible to know God's existence with certainty. He is the first cause uncaused of all the things of our experience. He is the designer of the order of nature. Moreover, we know his nature and attributes to some extent. We observe the perfections of creatures, and attribute them in various ways to God, but always remembering that they are in him in a more eminent way, for all we see of natural perfection is but a pale image of the splendour of the divine perfections; and we always deny all limits to his perfections. Because he is simple (*q.v.*) all his perfections are identified with his essence and because he is infinite our knowledge of him can only be analogical. Thus we make for ourselves a true, but inadequate, notion of God. This knowledge of God by natural reason is confirmed and amplified by revelation (*q.v.*). In condemning the errors of L. E. Boutain, in 1840, Pope Gregory XVI said, "However feeble and obscure the reason is rendered by original sin, there remain in it, however, enough clarity and strength that it may lead us with certainty to [the knowledge of] the existence of God, of the revelation made to the Jews through Moses and to Christians by the worshipful God-man."

KNOWLEDGE OF JESUS CHRIST. i. As God, he always had the complete knowledge of God (*q.v.*).

ii. As man, he had: (*a*) the knowledge implied in the Beatific Vision (*q.v.*); (*b*) infused knowledge (*q.v.*); (*c*) experimental knowledge, such as is proper to man, acquired by the use of sense and intellect. This would increase from day to day. It was perfect of its kind, and was not liable to error.

"KNOW-NOTHINGISM." A prolonged outbreak of anti-Catholic and anti-foreigner agitation in the U.S.A., from 1851-58. It received its name from a society whose members, in accordance with an oath, "didn't know," when questioned about its personnel, activities, etc. Know-nothings were allied to a Native American Party and believed that "All men are created equal, except Negroes and foreigners and Catholics," especially Catholic foreigners and Catholic Irish. They promoted rioting, plunder, arson, bloodshed and murder in various parts. Know-nothingism was swallowed up in the anti-slavery agitation and its organization collapsed after a split over the nomination of candidates to the presidency; the majority united with the Republicans.

KNOX'S VERSION. An English version of the New Testament made between 1939 and 1943 by Mgr. Ronald A. Knox at the request of the archbishops and bishops of England and Wales. In 1945 it was authorized for public use in the churches of those countries.

KONTAKION. A hymn of the Byzantine rite recalling in an abbreviated form the subject of the day's feast; it is sung after the sixth ode of the kanon at the little hours and the Liturgy.

KORAN, The (Ar. *qur'an*, recitation). The holy scriptures of al-Islam consisting of the revelations of God claimed by Mohammed. The collection was made by his scribe Zaid ibn Thabit after his death and contains 114 *suras* or chapters; they include materials of different dates but appear to be arranged in order of length, beginning with the longest (except the first *sura*). The book is written in Arabic in a sort of rhymed prose, and is regarded as being verbally inspired by God and thus is the final authority in matters of faith, morals, worship and law, prescriptions for which are found mixed up with eschatology, history, fables and prophecies, all of which subserve a moral end. The Old and New Testaments with their apocrypha are among its sources. The legislation with regard to women, and other matters, contrasts sharply with the actual development of Moslem practice.

KOREA, THE CHURCH IN. Christianity was known in Korea (Chosen) through books in the middle of the 18th century and its first apostles were Korean laymen; the first missionary priest, a Chinese, arrived in 1795 and found 4,000 neophytes already there. Though slow, progress in Korea is relatively considerably greater than in Japan: Catholics number about 96,000 and over 100 of the clergy are Koreans. There are 3 vicariates and 4 prefectures. In 1948 the country was still cut in two by Russian occupation of the northern part.

KU-KLUX-KLAN. The fancy name of a secret society in the southern states of the U.S.A. representing a well-warranted reaction against the outrages of the Carpetbaggers, *i.e.*, Northerners sent into the South by the Republican party after the Civil War of 1861-65 to administer affairs, which, in association with newly enfranchised Negroes, they did chiefly for their own profit. After World War I it was revived as an anti-Catholic organization, with a great parade of secrecy, fantastic costumes and comic titles.

KULTURKAMPF, The (Ger., culture-war). The attempt by Prince Bismarck and the government to make the Catholic Church in Prussia independent of Rome and completely subject to the state, with the object of strengthening the Protestant imperial power. It began in 1871 with some minor legislation; in 1872-73 the Jesuits and some other religious orders were subjected to laws which caused them to leave the country and education was secularized; in 1873 the May Laws (*q.v.*) were passed and the resulting struggle lasted until their gradual repeal or supersession between 1880 and 1891. Until 1879 these laws were administered with energy; numerous bishops and priests were fined and imprisoned; over 1,000 parishes were without priest and sacraments; seminaries, monasteries, charitable establishments were closed; clergy were punished for administering Viaticum and other sacraments; attempts were made to intrude "official" parish priests and to form schismatical churches. It took place principally in Prussia (at one period all the bishops were governing their dioceses from abroad) and spread to Bavaria, Baden and Hesse; politically the Catholic defence was led by Ludwig Windthorst and the newly formed Centre Party (*q.v.*). The expression *Kulturkampf* is now used in general for any extended attempt on the part of a state against the position, freedom of function and influence of the Catholic Church.

KUMMUS. The abbot of a monastery of the Coptic rite. The title is also given as an honorary one to distinguish secular priests (*cf.*, Archimandrite).

KYLEMORE. A monastery of Benedictine nuns in co. Galway in Ireland. During Queen Elizabeth's reign a Benedictine convent was founded in Brussels by three English nuns; a daughter house was planted out at Ghent in 1664, which in turn started a house at Ypres in 1685 for Irish women. During World War I this Ypres house was destroyed, and its community returned to Ireland in 1921, settling at Kylemore. The dames of this convent conduct a boarding-school for girls.

KYRIALE, The. A liturgical book containing principally the chant of the ordinary of the Mass, together with a number of kyries, credos, etc., for use at will. It gives eighteen different plainchant Masses, each one of which is distinguished by a number and a Latin name (*e.g.*, no. VIII, *de Angelis*), and assigned to a particular rank of feast or season of the year; but any one of them may be used upon any occasion if convenience or the capability of the choir requires it, and on feasts the various parts of different Masses may be combined. The names of these Masses are taken from the texts with which the neums of the *kyries* were formerly farced.

KYRIE ELEISON (Gr., Lord, have mercy). i. *Kyrie eleison* (thrice to the Father), *Christe eleison* (thrice to the Son), *Kyrie eleison* (thrice to the Holy Ghost): an invocation said alternately by celebrant and server, and sung by the choir at high Mass after the introit. It is said not to be a direct survival of the time when the Roman liturgy was in Greek but the remnant of a later litany (*cf.*, the Masses of Holy Saturday and the vigil of Pentecost).

ii. A musical setting of the same.

iii. The same but with three invocations only occurs constantly in the Roman liturgy, usually in association with the Lord's Prayer, *e.g.*, at the *preces* in the Divine Office and in many blessings.

iv. *Kyrie eleison* alone (*Christe eleison* is peculiar to the Latin liturgy) is used freely in all Eastern rites (sometimes translated into the liturgical language), particularly as the invocation following each petition of a litany.

L

LA (GRANDE) TRAPPE. i. An abbey in the diocese of Séez founded in 1122 and from 1147 belonging to the Cistercians; in 1664 a stricter observance of the rule was established by the Abbot de Rancé (who had been its abbot *in commendam*), and thence sprang the Trappist reform in the Cistercian order, which was adopted by many of the monasteries of France.

ii. The monastery of Our Lady of the Lake of the Two Mountains, at La Trappe in the diocese of Montreal, is the senior Cistercian abbey of Canada. It was founded in 1881 through the enterprise of Dom John Chouteau, abbot of Bellefontaine in France, and Father Rousselot, of Montreal, with monks from Bellefontaine; it was made an abbey in 1891. The monks conduct an agricultural school which is officially recognized by the government and affiliated to Montreal University.

LA SALETTE. A pilgrim shrine in the diocese of Grenoble, where our Lady is alleged to have appeared to two children in 1846. The genuineness of the vision has been most seriously disputed. The shrine gives its name to a congregation of missionary priests, founded there in 1852 by Mgr. Philibert de Bruillard. Their headquarters is now Turin.*

---

* The apparition of Our Lady at La Salette has been approved by the Church and is now generally recognized as genuine, forming one of the four greatest approved Marian apparitions of the 19th and 20th centuries, along with Lourdes, Fatima and Rue du Bac (the Miraculous Medal).—*Publisher,* 1997.

LABARUM (Lat.). The imperial standard of the Emperor Constantine the Great, whereon Christian symbols superseded the Roman military ones in accordance with his alleged vision of the cross. It included the monogram ☧ and the motto Τούτῳ νίκα conquer by this [sign]) on a purple banner, depending from the cross-bar. After the victory of the Milvian Bridge, when Constantine defeated his rival Maxentius in 312, it was adopted throughout the army in place of the eagle standards.

LABOUR. Work (*q.v.*), bodily or mental; imposed on all for the maintenance of life by the direct arrangement of Providence. The Church teaches that seeking one's bread by labour, including bodily labour, is honourable, and she adduces the example of Christ himself. Furthermore, she teaches that there is no necessary opposition between the wealthy and the working men, rather are they designed by nature to live in harmony for their mutual advantage. Capital cannot do without labour, or labour without capital. It is, however, contrary to Christian principles to treat the labourer as a tool to be bought in the cheapest market. In the wage-system as such, or in Capitalism (*q.v.*), there is nothing essentially unjust, but justice demands that adequate wages, based on human requirements, should be the first charge on the profits of industrial enterprise.

LACE and its imitations may be used for the decoration of albs, rochets and cottas, but as these garments are essentially made of linen or linen and cotton, its use is restricted, and in some sacristies entirely dispensed with. C.S.R. 3804, xii, concedes lace on albs from the girdle downwards only on more solemn days and for dignitaries, and in England canons are restricted to 12 in. on their rochets; a depth of 3 in. on cottas is usual in Rome. The rochets of Canons Regular of the Lateran and of canonesses are without this adornment.

LACTICINIA (Lat. *lac*, milk). Milk and foods made from milk, *e.g.*, cheese, distinguished from flesh-meat and eggs. *Lacticinia* were formerly forbidden on the fasting-days of Lent, but this is no longer the case; their consumption is still restricted and often entirely forbidden on the numerous fast days of all Eastern rites.

LACUS SALSI. Genitive (in the bishop's title) of *Lacus Salsus*, Latin translation of the name of the see of Salt Lake, Utah.

LADIES OF MARY, The. An enclosed teaching congregation, founded at Alost in 1817. Black habit, blue scapular and girdle. The nuns of this congregation are called Madame.

LADY ALTAR. An altar dedicated in honour of the Blessed Virgin Mary, generally with a statue or picture of her; it is commonly in a conspicuous place on the gospel side of the church. If the whole church, and consequently the high altar, is dedicated in her honour, there is often a lady altar as well.

LADY CHAPEL. The chapel within a church which contains the lady altar. In large gothic churches it was frequently situated behind the high altar: in a *chevet* on the continent or a square-ended retro-choir in England (Chester, Hereford).

LADY DAY. The feast of the Annunciation on March 25; the name has now associations other than religious. *Lady-day in Harvest*, or Marymas, was the feast of the Assumption, August 15.

LÆTARE MEDAL. A gold medal presented annually on *Lætare* Sunday by the University of Notre Dame, Indiana, to a lay Catholic American of distinction.

LÆTARE SUNDAY (Lat., rejoice). The fourth of Lent, so called from the first word of the introit. Being mid-Lent Sunday the altar may be decorated, the organ played and rose-coloured vestments (with dalmatic and tunicle) worn; *cf.*, *Gaudete* Sunday. On the following Wednesday catechumens formerly received the *aperitio aurium* (opening of the ears; *cf.*, the *Ephphetha* ceremony) and the *traditio symbolorum* (teaching of the creed, Our Father and gospels) in preparation for Baptism on Holy Saturday. On this day the Golden Rose (*q.v.*) is blessed. Also called Refreshment Sunday (see its gospel) and Mothering Sunday (*q.v.*).

LÆTENTUR CŒLI. A bull of Pope Eugene IV in 1439, being the decree of union with the Orthodox Eastern Church, brought about by the Council of Florence. The Orthodox accepted the lawfulness of the use of *azyme*, consecration by the words of institution, Purgatory (without material fire), procession of the Holy Ghost from the Father and the Son as from one principle (without adding it to the liturgical creed) and the primacy of the Holy See (without prejudice to the rights of other patriarchs).

LAICIZATION. i. The reduction of an ecclesiastical person or thing to a lay status; *e.g.*, the lawful turning over of a church building to secular purposes, the degradation (*q.v.*) of an erring priest (which does not, however, deprive him of his priestly orders). ii. The deprivation by the civil power of ecclesiastical control and influence in any institution where that control or influence should be operative, *e.g.*, the primary schools of France in 1882; and the compulsory secularization of ecclesiastical property, *e.g.*, monastic properties in Italy in 1866.

LAITY, The. Those who have membership in the Church without authority. The distinction of clergy and laity is of divine institution, although not all grades of clergy are divinely instituted. Lay persons cannot exercise the power of orders or jurisdiction, but they may be religious (q.v.) and rule their brethren in religion with dominative power, which is not jurisdiction. The laity have the right, legally enforceable, to receive from the clergy those spiritual aids to salvation due to them in accordance with ecclesiastical discipline. They are exhorted to join approved associations, and are forbidden to belong to condemned or dangerous societies. No lay association has any ecclesiastical status unless erected or at least approved by the competent ecclesiastical authority. Non-Catholics may not be members of a Catholic association which has a religious significance or implication, or which claims ecclesiastical sanction. Spiritual associations of lay persons are of three kinds: Third Orders, Confraternities and Pious Unions (qq.v.). The word is first used in the Clementine Epistle (q.v., and see LAYMAN).

LAMB. A very early symbol of the Christian soul after death (cf., the Good Shepherd). Later the symbolism was transferred to our Lord himself (John i, 29) and the lamb, distinguished by a halo and in association with the cross, has remained the most common symbol of the eucharistic Victim. The expression Lamb of God referring to the Blessed Sacrament occurs in the Latin, Byzantine and Syriac liturgies. See also AGNETS.

LAMENTABILI. i. A decree of the Holy Office on July 4, 1907, in which, inter alia, the works of Loisy and Houtin and 65 heretical propositions of Modernism (q.v.) were condemned, of which the last was characteristic: 'Catholicity to-day cannot be reconciled with true science if it is not transformed into a non-dogmatic catholicism, i.e., into a wide and liberal Protestantism." This was preliminary to the encyclical Pascendi (q.v.) of the following September.

ii. A letter addressed by Pope Pius X to the bishops of Latin America in the interests of the Indians of Peru and elsewhere.

LAMENTATIONS. i. The Lamentations of Jeremias, a book of the Old Testament in which the prophet mourns over the destruction of Jerusalem and the Temple and the miseries of his people.

ii. Part of the same sung as the lessons of the first nocturn of Matins (Tenebræ) on Thursday, Friday and Saturday of Holy Week.

LAMMAS DAY (Old Eng. hlafmæsse, loaf Mass). An archaic name for the feast of St. Peter-in-Chains (Aug. 1), formerly observed as a sort of early harvest thanksgiving, loaves of the new corn being blessed at Mass. Latter Lammas means never (cf., Greek Kalends).

LAMPS, usually consisting of a hanging glass vessel filled with olive oil in which a burning wick floats, are used in the Catholic Church as tokens of honour. At least one such lamp must burn day and night before the Blessed Sacrament, and it is fitting that there should be one before the high altar, even if the Sacrament is not reserved thereat; extra lamps of this kind may be lit on great feasts to total any odd number. Similar lamps may be burned before other altars, shrines, images, etc. The sanctuary-lamp must be fed with olive oil or beeswax; in case of necessity permission may be given to substitute other oil or even electric light (q.v.). Lavish use is made of honorific lamps in Eastern rites, but (except among Catholics) not with reference to the reserved Sacrament; even in the West this use of a lamp was not made obligatory till the 16th century.

LANCASTER (Lancastrensis). An English see, suffragan to Liverpool, formed in 1924 out of the dioceses of Liverpool and Hexham; its territory is Westmorland and Cumberland and Lancashire north of the Ribble, before the Reformation in the dioceses of Carlisle and York. Claughton-on-Brock and Fernyhalgh have continuity with the pre-reformation parishes; St. Mary's at Preston was established in 1605 and 19 other parishes started as 18th-century missions (one quarter of the total number). The patrons of the diocese are our Lady of Lourdes and St. Cuthbert; the cathedral is dedicated in honour of St. Peter.

LANCE, THE HOLY. i. Several relics throughout the world purporting to be parts of the spear with which our Lord's side was pierced on the cross, the most famous being at St. Peter's in Rome. The authenticity of none of them is established.

ii. A feast of the Holy Lance and Nails was instituted by Pope Innocent VI in 1354; it is observed in certain places on the Friday after the first Sunday in Lent.

iii. A liturgical knife, two edged like the point of a lance and the handle ending in a little cross. It recalls the lance which pierced our Lord and is used during the preparation for the Byzantine liturgies to cut the prosphora (q.v.).

LAND, PRIVATE OWNERSHIP OF. The right of an individual to possess land is included in his general right to possess private property (q.v.). Although the earth was given for the use of the human race, no part of it was assigned to anyone in particular, the limits of private possessions being left to be fixed by man's own industry and the laws of individual nations. The primary and sufficient title to ownership is occupancy. To-day many favour nationalization of land: there would appear to be no ethical objection to such a policy, provided it were shown necessary to the good of the commonwealth and that just compensation were paid so far as possible.

LANGUAGE OF THE CHURCH. Latin (*q.v.*) is the official language of the Catholic Church in so far as it is the one whose use is hallowed by tradition and confirmed by experience in the headquarters work of the Church in the city of Rome. It is the language in which doctrine is defined and anything affecting the Church at large is recorded; all official acts of the Church are in that tongue and normally it is used in all correspondence and business with the Holy See and Curia. That an universal church must have an official language is obvious; that this language is Latin is the result not of deliberate choice but of historical circumstances. See LITURGICAL LANGUAGE.

LAODICEAN. A term of reproach used of one who is lukewarm in faith or practice (or derivatively in other matters), from Apoc. iii, 14-16.

LAONENSIS. The adjectival form of the name of the see of Killaloe (*q.v.*) used in the designation of its bishop in Latin documents. Noun: *Laonia*.

LAPSED CATHOLIC. A somewhat loose term applied to anyone who has fallen away from Catholic faith or practice. It may be applied to a one-time Catholic who has fallen into apostasy, heresy, or schism (*qq.v.*), or who has ceased to manifest by external practice of Mass, sacraments, etc., the profession of the Catholic religion. Whether or not such a person has incurred formal excommunication depends on the extent of his knowledge and perversity. If he has, it may be necessary to have recourse to the Holy See or the local bishop before sacramental absolution can be given.

LAPSUS (Lat., lapsed). The name given in the 3rd century to those who fell away from the faith under stress of persecution, as distinct from apostates who did so willingly. *Lapsi* were principally divided into *thurificati*, who had offered incense at pagan shrines; *sacrificati*, who had sacrificed or partaken of pagan sacrifices; and *libellatici*, who gave to or received from the magistrate a declaration (*libellus*), false or true, that they had performed the required acts of idolatry.

LAST BLESSING, The. A blessing with plenary indulgence to be given to a departing soul. Any priest has faculties to impart it and the formula of Pope Benedict XIV must be used. It may not be given to the excommunicated, the impenitent or those manifestly dying in mortal sin. The sick person should, at least interiorly, pronounce the Holy Name with acts of contrition and of submission to God's will.

LAST SACRAMENTS, The. Extreme Unction and Viaticum (*qq.v.*); other ministrations to the dying are often included in the term.

LAST SUPPER, The. The meal taken by Jesus Christ with his disciples on the evening of his betrayal at which he instituted the Blessed Eucharist both as a sacrifice and as a sacrament; as the first it is completed on Calvary and perpetuated in the Mass and other eucharistic liturgies, as the second it is given in holy communion; by this new rite the sacrifices of the Old Law were superseded and for ever done away with.

LAST THINGS, The. Death, Judgement, Heaven, Hell.

LATÆ SENTENTIÆ, CENSURE. A censure (*q.v.*) incurred by the very fact of committing a crime (*cf., Ferendæ sententiæ*).

LATERAN, The. i. The church of our Most Holy Saviour, commonly called of St. John Lateran, the cathedral-church of the pope as bishop of Rome. Inscribed over its entrance is: *Omnium urbis et orbis ecclesiarum mater et caput*: "The Mother and Head of all churches of the City and of the World"—which it is. From 1870 until the settlement of the "Roman Question" in 1929 the pope was unable to use his cathedral. Above the high altar are enshrined the reputed heads of SS. Peter and Paul. The cathedral chapter consists of a cardinal archpriest, a vicar, 19 canons and 20 *beneficiati;* there are 8 benefced chaplains and 12 other benefced clerics, and a college of 6 penitentiaries, Friars Minor.

ii. The Palace of the Lateran, adjoining the church, the residence of the popes from the beginning of the 4th century until the beginning of the 14th; it is now used as the Pontifical Museum of Christian Antiquities. The original palace, formerly that of the family of the *Laterani*, was given to the Holy See by the Emperor Constantine.

LATERAN, COUNCILS OF THE. The 1st (the ninth œcumenical council, 1123) was the first general council to be held in the West. It ratified the Concordate of Worms and declared the marriages of clerics and of the closely related to be null.

The 2nd (the tenth œcumenical, 1139) condemned Arnold of Brescia and passed thirty canons on morals and discipline, condemning simony and usury.

The 3rd (the eleventh œcumenical, 1179) condemned the Albigensians and Waldensians; decreed that only cardinals should elect a pope and that two-thirds of the votes were required for election; forbade the ordination of clerics who have no proper means of support and the demanding of money for the administration of the sacraments, burial or admission to a monastery.

The 4th (the twelfth œcumenical, 1215), the greatest of the Middle Ages and sometimes cited simply as the Lateran Council, condemned the errors of Abbot Joachim on the numerical unity of the Holy Trinity; defined the Incarnation and other mysteries against the Albigensians; forbade the establishment of new religious orders; confirmed the necessity of at least annual confession and communion for all; legislated against pluralism; and defined the doctrine of the Real Presence, using the expression "transubstantiation."

The 5th (the eighteenth œcumenical, 1512-1517) defined the authority of the pope over all councils; condemned the error that the intellectual soul is mortal or is only one in all men; provided for the ecclesiastical supervision of *montes pietatis* (pawnshops); forbade the printing of books without the episcopal *imprimatur*. Numerous other lesser councils have been held at the Lateran.

LATERAN, THE TREATY OF THE. A treaty made between the Holy See (Pope Pius XI) and the Kingdom of Italy (King Victor Emmanuel III) on Feb. 11, 1929, and ratified on the following June 8, whereby "was adequately assured to the Holy See all that was necessary to provide due liberty and independence for the spiritual government of the diocese of Rome and of the Catholic Church in Italy and throughout the world. It therefore declared the 'Roman Question' (*q.v.*) to be definitely and irrevocably settled and done away with and recognized the Kingdom of Italy under the dynasty of the House of Savoy and with Rome as its capital" (art. 26). By this treaty Italy recognizes the *de iure* and *de facto* international sovereignty of the Holy See with its absolute sole jurisdiction over a state called the City of the Vatican (*q.v.*) and guarantees its freedom and independence; certain public services (railway, post-office, etc.) are supplied by Italy; the person of the pope is inviolable and sacred, and cardinals enjoy the honours of princes of royal blood, and wherever resident in Rome are Vatican citizens; certain other ecclesiastics residing outside the City are given immunities; the Vatican and Italy have ordinary diplomatic relations; in a particular case or as a general rule the Italian government will see to the punishment in its own territory of crimes committed in the City, which in turn will extradite immigrant Italians accused of acts considered criminal by both states; ecclesiastical sentences on clergy and religious in spiritual and disciplinary matters shall have full juridical effect in Italy; the Holy See wishes to remain outside the rivalries and conferences of other states, unless appealed to in its spiritual capacity; the Vatican City is therefore a permanently neutral and inviolable territory; the Law of Guarantees (*q.v.*) and cognate legislation is abrogated, etc. Associated with this treaty was a domestic concordat and a financial convention whereby the Italian state paid to the Holy See the sum of 8⅓ million pounds in cash and 11 million pounds in Italian state bonds, which was accepted in restitution for material damage consequent on the loss of the States of the Church (*q.v.*). The treaty and concordat were incorporated in the constitution of the new Italian republic after World-War II.

LATERAN CANONS, The. i. The chapter of secular canons of the cathedral-church of St. John Lateran at Rome.

ii. The Canons Regular of the Lateran (*q.v.*).

LATIN (the former language of the inhabitants of *Latium*, the province of Italy wherein Rome is situated). i. Official use. Latin superseded Greek as the official language of the Western church during the 3rd century, being first used for liturgical purposes in Africa. Ecclesiastical Latin had its origin not in the classical literary but in the popular speech, it was well established by St. Jerome's "Vulgate," and its development for many centuries was that of a living language, conditioned by pastoral, missionary, liturgical, legal, philosophical, theological, political and other practical requirements. At the Renaissance attempts were made to purify this language on the lines of long-dead classical usage; the results were not always happy (*cf.*, the reformed hymns of the Roman Divine Office), but some desirable reforms in terminology and a new standard of correctness took effect. It remains the official language of the Church (*q.v.*), and of the Western liturgies but, especially in English-speaking countries, the local vernaculars are in increasing use for some occasional offices, for extra-liturgical worship and in the training of the clergy. In the Roman and other international colleges Latin maintains its position for instruction and textbook purposes.

ii. Liturgical use. The use of a single "dead" language for public worship throughout the Western church (and the use of other dead or obsolete tongues elsewhere) is not a piece of arbitrary legislation but an historical development which is preserved on account of its consonance with the nature of that worship: the Mass is a sacrifice, primarily an act to be done, not a prayer to be said, and it is done in and with the proper hieratic forms, of which the hieratic language is one. (Similarly with the administration of the sacraments, and even the Divine Office is primarily a corporate act of worship rather than a series of prayers.) Certain practical advantages also accrue (*e.g.*, uniformity of celebration, fixity of meaning), but these must not be over-stressed, seeing that the Church has never demanded uniformity (*q.v.*) of liturgical language (*q.v.*), nor does she forbid vernacular (*q.v.*) liturgies.

LATIN-AMERICAN COLLEGE, The. The College of St. Joseph founded at Rome in 1858 by Pope Pius IX and Mgr. Joseph Eyzaguirre, a Chilean, for students for the priesthood from those countries of the New

World where Spanish and Portuguese are spoken. It is directed by the Jesuit fathers.

LATIN, ECCLESIASTICAL, PRONUNCIA-TION OF. The pronunciation used by the Western church is sometimes distinguished as the Italian pronunciation; none other is authentic for ecclesiastical and liturgical purposes. Vowels: Every vowel, even a final e, is pronounced; a = *ah* as in "rather"; e = *ay* as in "day"; i = *ee* as in "sweet" when long, as in "pit" when short; o, when long, as in "fort," nearly as in "not" when short; u = *oo* as in "tool" when long, as in "pull" when short. Diphthongs: æ and œ = *ay* as in "day"; au = *ow* as in "now." Consonants: Every consonant except h is sounded; c = *k* before a, o, u, au, and h; c = *ch* as in "cherry" before e, i, æ and œ; g, as in "gate" before a, o, u, and au; g = *j* as in "journey" before e, i and æ; gn = *ni* as in "union"; i = *y*; sc = *sk* before a, o, u and h; sc = *sh* as in "show" before e, i and æ; ti = *tsi* before a and o; xc = *ksh* before e, i and y; z = *ds*; h in *nihil* and *mihi* becomes *k*.

LATIN CHURCH, The. That part, the overwhelmingly larger part, of the Catholic Church which uses the Latin liturgies and is subject to the bishop of Rome as patriarch as well as supreme pontiff. Synonymous with Latin rite (*b*), Roman church (ii), Western church, Western patriarchate (*qq.v.*).

LATIN LETTERS, SECRETARIATE OF. A Palatine secretariate in which are drawn up the less formal and less solemn letters addressed by the pope to various personages.

LATIN RITE, The. A term used officially in many documents and popularly in some parts of the world (and adopted in this work) to designate, (*a*) the system and forms of worship and administration of the sacraments used in the Latin tongue, and (*b*) the Catholics who use the same. In the second sense it is synonymous with Latin church, Patriarchate of the West, Western church (*qq.v.*). Liturgically the term is useful rather than accurate: actually, there are two Latin rites in use, the Roman and its derivatives, and the Gallican represented by the Ambrosian and Mozarabic liturgies; for practical purposes these may be regarded as variations of the Latin rite of which the Roman rite (or use, *q.v.*) is the pattern and parent and most widely used. Other Latin uses are those of religious orders (Carmelite, Carthusian, Dominican, *qq.v.*) and of dioceses (Bayeux, Braga, Lyons, *qq.v.*); other orders and places have minor variations, of which the Monastic Breviary, used by all Benedictine monks, is the most important. The eucharistic liturgy of this rite is called the Mass (*q.v.*) and its canonical prayer the Divine Office (*q.v.*); its forms for administering the sacraments, its churches, vestments, etc., are referred to under their proper headings. To the rule that the terms Western church and Latin rite (*b*) are inter-changeable there are two tiny exceptions: some Catholics in Yugoslavia have the Roman rite in Old Slavonic and the Italo-Greeks (*q.v.*) use the Byzantine rite. To a large majority of people the Latin rite, quite inaccurately, represents the whole Catholic Church.

LATINIZATION. i. The modification of Eastern liturgies by Latin usages, *e.g.*, *azyme*, Roman vestments, separation of Confirmation from Baptism, etc., the importation of Western popular devotions and ascetical practices, and the imposition of specifically Western provisions of canon law among Catholics of Eastern rites. Legislated against particularly by Pope Leo XIII in his constitution *Orientalium dignitas*.

ii. The exertion of purely Western influence over Catholics of Eastern rites and over oriental dissidents by schools, seminaries, missionaries, etc.; and the direct or indirect inducement of converts from Orthodoxy and other orientals to embrace the Latin rite (*cf.*, *Orientalium dignitas*, change of rite).

LATITUDINARIANISM (Lat., *latitudo*, breadth). False tolerance in religious matters. In English the word has been chiefly used of those tendencies in Protestantism which later became frankly Modernist, and the term is somewhat old-fashioned.

LATRIA (Gr., the status of a servant; *cf.*, *dulia*). That supreme homage and religious worship which is due to God alone in acknowledgement of his being our Creator, our first beginning and last end, of his sovereign dominion and infinite goodness. Relative *latria* is paid to images of the Sacred Heart, to crucifixes, and to such other religious objects as are exclusively connected with a divine person. The homage does not rest in the symbol (that would be idolatry), but goes to the associated Person. *Latria* differs from *hyperdulia* and *dulia* (*qq.v.*) not in degree but in kind, accordingly as their objects are respectively the Creator and the creature.

LATROCINIUM (Lat., brigandage). The name given to the Robber Synod of Ephesus (*q.v.*) by Pope St. Leo the Great.

LATTER-DAY SAINTS, The. The official name of the sect commonly called "Mormons," principally established in the state of Utah, U.S.A. It has a basis of Christian orthodoxy but is chiefly known for the material organization and success of its members and for the teaching and practice of polygamy; this has now been abandoned officially. The founder of the sect was Joseph Smith (murdered in 1844), who embodied certain spurious revelations in the *Book of Mormon* (1830).

LATVIA, THE CHURCH IN. Population about 2 million, of whom over a half are Lutherans and about a quarter Catholics. In

1939 the country formed a metropolitan province, with one suffragan diocese. Latvia (Lettonia) is now a republic of the U.S.S.R.

LAUDA SION. The sequence, from its opening words, of the Mass of Corpus Christi, written by St. Thomas Aquinas; it is the supreme example of theological poetry. There are several versions in English, of varying quality.

LAUDABILITER. An alleged bull of Pope Adrian IV, of about the year 1159, granting the overlordship of Ireland, as a fief of the Holy See, to King Henry II of England and his successors. Its name is often given to the whole series of documents bearing on the donation of Adrian. Though the subject of very much controversy, the authenticity of the donation and bull seems very probable. The kingship of Ireland was recognized to Mary I and Philip in 1555, the English sovereigns having called themselves only Lords of Ireland until Henry VIII.

LAUDES (Lat., praises). i. Another name for *tropes* (*q.v.*).
ii. An extra-liturgical ceremony in honour of a bishop, abbot, etc., consisting of the singing of acclamations and greetings; the custom is almost obsolete. But see ACCLAMATION.

LAUDS (Lat., praises). The second hour of the Divine Office in the Latin rite, taking its name from Psalms 148, 149 and 150 which formerly always formed part of it and in which the word *laudate* ("praise ye . . .") often occurs. It is the office of dawn, but by those who recite it privately and in cathedral and collegiate churches it is generally said with Matins overnight; in monasteries it is sung at various hours of the early morning, immediately after Matins. It consists of four psalms and a canticle, with their antiphons, followed by a little chapter, hymn and versicle (all variable); then the *Benedictus* (*q.v.*) with its antiphon (sung with the same solemnity as *Magnificat* at Vespers); *preces* (*q.v.*) on certain days, collect of the day, commemorations (if any) and conclusion. It is followed by the antiphon of our Lady (*q.v.*) according to the season. There are two sets of psalms for each day of the week at Lauds; the second of these (*Ad Laudes,* II) is used in Lent and certain other penitential days. The aspect of morning prayer is clearly marked in the office, it sees in the rising sun a type of the Resurrection and seems veritably to shout praises to God. The equivalent office of the Byzantine rite is called *Orthros* (*q.v.*).

LAURA (literally, an alley). The Greek name for a monastery wherein the monks lived in separate huts or cells around the church (*cf.,* the Carthusians). The particular form of early monasticism which the name indicated has long ceased to exist, but *laura* remains as the ordinary name for any big monastery of the Byzantine rite.

LAUS PERENNIS (Lat., endless praise). The custom of singing the Divine Office by relays of monks so that the praise of God never ceases in the monastery. It first appeared in the West about 522 at Agaunum in Switzerland and was much practised in Celtic monasteries, but is now no longer practised anywhere, though the custom of perpetual adoration (*q.v.*) approximates to it. Also called the Perpetual Psalmody (*cf.,* *Acœmetæ*).

LAVABO (Lat., I will wash). The first word of Ps. xxv, 6-12 which the celebrant says while washing and drying his fingers after the offertory at Mass, used as a name for the ceremony. The water is poured upon his fingers and caught in a bowl by the server. The *Lavabo* originated in the practical necessity of cleansing the fingers after handling loaves of bread, etc.; it now signifies that purity with which the mysteries should be approached. When the celebrant is a bishop he washes his hands again after the ablutions (*q.v.*).

LAVAL UNIVERSITY at Quebec was founded in 1852 under charter of Queen Victoria and canonically set up by Pope Pius IX. It has faculties of arts, law, medicine and theology, and schools in other disciplines; other Canadian educational institutions are affiliated to it. The chancellor and visitor is the archbishop of Quebec *ex-officio*. The formerly affiliated college of Montreal is since 1919 an independent university, of which the archbishop of Montreal is *ex-officio* chancellor.

LAW is used in a twofold sense: (1) *lex,* a rule of reason for the common good promulgated by authority; (2) *jus,* the system of such rules in orderly arrangement. Law is natural or positive, the latter divine or human; human law is either ecclesiastical or civil. Internal acts are not subject to law except indirectly, as being implied in the external act prescribed. Laws affect only the future unless expressly made retroactive. They are usually territorial, but may be personal apart from territory. Laws are simply prohibitory, and not invalidating, unless this is expressly or equivalently stated. Law is "an ordinance of reason that aims at the common good," it is imposed on the community so that good order may result from a common method of action; arbitrary legislation, "law-making for law-making's sake" or in order to satisfy an itch for exercising authority or for interfering with other people, is a perversion and abuse. "In so far as it [law] deviates from right reason it is called an unjust law. In such a case it is no law at all, but rather a species of violence" (Pope Leo XIII), for the first requirement of law is that it should be just.

LAW, CANON. i. The body of laws formulated by the Church for the discipline of her members, now contained in the "Codex Juris Canonici." Canon law binds all baptized persons over seven years of age, unless specially exempted. It is of two kinds, common law, binding universally, and particular law, binding locally. It comes into force by promulgation (*q.v.*). Catholics of Eastern rites (*q.v.*) have their own canon law, and are not subject to the laws of the *Codex*, in accordance with canon I which says that its laws bind only Catholics of the Latin church except in those points which of their very nature affect also the Eastern churches.
ii. Catholics of Eastern rites. These are governed by the canons of early councils and subsequent special legislation, whether of the Holy See or of councils of the different churches whose acts have been approved; *e.g.*, the constitution *Orientalium dignitas* of Pope Leo XIII; the Armenian plenary council of Rome in 1911; the Syrian council of Sharfeh in 1888; the Maronite council of Dair Saîdat al-Luaizeh in 1736; the 3rd Melkite council of Ain Traz, 1835; the Ruthenian councils of Zamosc in 1720 and 1891; the Coptic council of Cairo in 1898, etc. The provisions of the "Codex Juris Canonici" affecting orientals are chiefly canons 1, 542, 622, 782, 804, 881, 955, 1004 and 1099. A commission for the codification of Eastern canon law was set up in Rome in 1930. An arbitrary and incomplete compilation of Byzantine canon law was printed at the Phanar (*q.v.*) in 1800, the *Pidalion* ("rudder").

LAW, CIVIL (Lat., *civis*, a citizen). The state as a perfect society has full legislative power in all material and temporal matters, provided that it does not enact anything contrary to natural, divine or ecclesiastical law. Civil law is binding in conscience on all subjects of the state, including ecclesiastical persons, apart from certain clerical privileges. Whether a particular law binds under sin depends on the intention of the legislator, which may be known from the nature of the case or from the circumstances. Civil law that legislates on spiritual matters has no binding force, unless sanctioned or tolerated by ecclesiastical authority. Historically, the Civil Law is equivalent to Roman Law (*cf.*, Municipal).

LAW, COMMON. The law of the Church generally in force in all dioceses, and contained in the "Codex Juris Canonici." No local law is valid which derogates in any way from common law.

LAW, DIVINE. i. Eternal: "The Divine Reason or Will of God, commanding the observance and forbidding the disturbance of the natural order of things" (St. Augustine); called "the natural law" when perceived through the light of reason. Total ignorance of its primary precepts (*e.g.*, "Evil must be avoided") or continued ignorance of its secondary precepts (*e.g.*, "Thou shalt not steal") is impossible.
ii. Positive: precepts known through Revelation. These fall into three classes: (*a*) moral—a more explicit determination of the natural law; (*b*) ceremonial—with respect to the sacraments and the Mass; (*c*) juridical —with respect to the constitution and authority of the Church.

LAW, ETERNAL. The law of God directing the whole universe to its end, existing from all eternity in the divine mind as the correlative of creation, and comprehending all created things, rational and irrational, spiritual and physical, concerned as well with the properties of matter as with human acts.

LAW, HUMAN. Law is divided into natural and positive, and positive law is either divine or human. Human law is either ecclesiastical or civil, and is null and void if and in so far as it detracts from natural or divine law.

LAW, INTERNATIONAL, or LAW OF NATIONS. The system of laws generally agreed between nations and in force in the states adhering to such agreement. It is founded on the natural and divine law, and on the elements of civil law common to civilized states. All that is not natural and divine law depends for its authority on pacts between the states, and there must always be something defectible in such law until a supra-national power can be evolved, exercising authority by its own right, and not depending for the validity of its power on voluntary adhesion. Whether such evolution is possible or even desirable is much disputed, but international law, even if defectible as such, is valuable in promoting uniformity of civil law in the various states.

LAW, MUNICIPAL (Lat. *municipium*, a free town). A term used in canon law for the local laws of a particular state as opposed to the Roman civil law which in times past was the common law of most of Christendom (England, Wales and Ireland were notable exceptions).

LAW, NATURAL. We use the word "law" in two senses which are not so independent of each other as they are sometimes taken to be. When we speak of the law of gravitation, for example, we are alluding to a particular case of *the constant and uniform mode of operation which is found in all individuals of a special nature when placed in like circumstances*: this we call a law of nature, a physical law. When we similarly refer to the constant mode of *being* of things, the unchangeableness of their essence, we call this a metaphysical law of nature. But we also use "law" to express that *ordering of reason to the common good which is promulgated by one in authority*, *e.g.*, the law against rioting. If that law has received expression in words or such sensible signs, it is called a positive law. But if it is manifested by our own nature it is called a natural law. Thus, man's reason teaches him that he may not steal, that he is forbidden to steal not merely by a positive command of the decalogue (q.v.) but by an obligation manifested in his very nature. This "natural law" like the "law of nature" can be studied in its subjects. It is not necessarily shown by the uniformity of their behaviour, for man is free and his freedom is often abused to break the law. But it can be studied in his appetites and faculties. From them we can learn, not what a man is constrained to do, but what he *ought* to do. Both laws are a reflection of the original plan of the divine wisdom which co-ordinates all the elements of the universe for its perfection, and which we call the "eternal law."

LAW, PENAL. i. A positive law which is not binding under pain of sin but only under pain of the penalty attached. The state has power to make laws that bind in conscience and the infringement of civil laws often involves the transgression of a moral precept, in which case such laws are binding in conscience for that reason. Otherwise they may be presumed purely penal, unless the civil authority makes clear its intention of binding the citizens' conscience. This is considering the matter strictly from the point of view of sin and is not to be construed as an irresponsible encouragement or condonation of law-breaking; all citizens should scrupulously obey the just laws of their country. It is a very probable opinion and one supported by the authority of Blackstone that the positive laws of Great Britain are purely penal (*cf.*, Taxation).

ii. Any one of the legal enactments passed between 1559 and 1722 whereby it was sought to cripple and render incapable of action the Catholics of Great Britain and Ireland and if possible to get rid of their religion in those countries. There were over 20 of these acts in England alone and characteristic provisions were: £100 fine and a year's imprisonment for saying or hearing Mass; fine of £20 a month for not attending the Anglican church; high treason to be or make a convert—the ordinary penalties for treason were hanging, drawing and quartering, loss of property and attaint of blood (23 Eliz. c. 1, 1581); high treason for a Jesuit or seminary priest (q.v.) to be within the realm and a felony to shelter him (27 Eliz. c. 2, 1585); all convicted recusants (q.v.) to communicate once a year in the Anglican church or forfeit £20 for first offence, £40 for the second, £60 for the third and imposing an oath (condemned by the Holy See) under the penalties of *Præmunire* (q.v.) (3 Jas. I, c. 4, 1605); Catholics forbidden to hold an army commission or any other public or municipal office, or to be executors or guard-

ians, lawyers, physicians or apothecaries and every convicted recusant was disabled from prosecuting or defending any action in the civil courts and fined £100 if found within 10 miles of London (3 Jas. I, c. 5); by imposition of two oaths and a blasphemous declaration, Catholics were prevented from sitting in Parliament (30 Chas. II, c. 2, 1678); any bishop or priest exercising his office or Catholic keeping a school to be imprisoned for life, £100 reward for the simple apprehension of any priest or the conviction of a Catholic for sending children to be educated abroad, and no Catholic who refused the oaths and declaration could purchase or inherit land—it passed to the Protestant next-of-kin who need not account (11 and 12 Will. III, c. 4, 1699); a tax to raise £100,000 was levied on Catholics (9 Geo. I, c. 18, 1722) (*cf.*, Emancipation). The last priest to die in prison was Matthew Atkinson (Hurst Castle, 1729); the last to be tried for his life for exercising his sacred office, the Hon. James Talbot (Old Bailey, 1769); the last to be imprisoned for life for the same, John Baptist Moloney (Croydon, 1767); the last prosecution for celebrating Mass was in 1771; the last to be fined for not attending the Protestant church were two Yorkshire labourers and their wives, whose goods were distrained on to pay the fine in 1782.

LAW, POSITIVE. Law that is freely enacted and made known by an act, spoken or written, of the lawgiver, opposed to natural law (q.v.). It is either divine, imposed directly by God, or human, and human law again is either civil or ecclesiastical (generally called "canon law"). Positive human law arises either by statute cr other enactment or by long-standing custom (prescriptive law), but in most civilized countries customary laws have now been re-enacted by promulgation of a code: a notable exception is the Common Law of the realm of England.

LAW OF ASSOCIATIONS, The. The law of 1901 which resulted in the suppression of most of the monasteries and houses of religious orders and congregations in France and the confiscation of their property. Religious associations were ordered to ask for a special authorization to carry on, which in most cases was done. In 1902 all petitions of "teaching, preaching and [so-called] commercial congregations" were rejected together, and the law extended to those which had been authorized in 1886. In two years over 13,000 schools were closed and hospitals, orphanages and asylums deprived of their staffs and support. The law is still in force but after the war of 1914-18 large numbers of the congregations returned without hindrance. In 1929 bills were passed through the Chamber to facilitate the re-establishment in France of the headquarters of certain missionary congregations—a political move not free from disturbing significance.

LAW OF GUARANTEES, The. The law by which the government of Italy, in 1871, regularized to its own satisfaction the position of the Holy See whose states it had seized. Its main points were: that the pope's person was sacred and inviolable; he was entitled to royal honours and protection; an annual sum of 3¼ million *lire* was at his disposal; the Vatican and Lateran palaces and the villa Castel Gandolfo remained his property and were extra-territorial (St. Peter's was a national monument except when the pope was actually in it); the pope or conclave of cardinals had complete freedom of communication with the outside world; freedom of assembly of the clergy. The Holy See always refused to recognize this law, maintaining its sovereignty by divine right as against a statutory concession of the Italian state as to one of its subjects, which might be repealed at its will; in particular in 1872 Pope Pius IX rejected the proffered income, which none of his successors touched. The law was abrogated by the Treaty of the Lateran in 1929.

LAWFULNESS AND VALIDITY. Validity must be distinguished from lawfulness. See ILLICIT.

LAXISM. A system in moral theology which contends that a doubtfully probable opinion favouring liberty dispenses one from fulfilling an obligation. Laxism was condemned by Pope Innocent XI in 1679.

LAXTON. Blackfriars School, the lay boys' school of the English Dominicans, founded at Bornhem in Flanders in 1659 by Father (later cardinal) Thomas Howard, o.p. After the French Revolution it was reopened at Carshalton in Surrey, moved to Hinckley in Leicestershire in 1825, to Hawkesyard in Staffordshire in 1898, and finally to Laxton Hall in Northamptonshire in 1924. A preparatory branch was opened at Llanarth Court, Monmouthshire, in 1948.

LAY-BROTHER -SISTER. A member of a religious order who is neither in holy orders nor bound to the Office in choir (*cf.*, Choirmonk, Nun) but whose duties are in manual labour and the material affairs of the monastery. They are true members of their order, but their noviciate is generally longer and conditions of profession different; their habit usually varies slightly from that of the choir-religious; and they occupy separate quarters. Their formal religious duties are daily Mass and a short office of prayers. The proportion of lay-religious in a monastery varies with the order and country; with the Cistercians it is large, with Benedictines in England very small, in Germany large, and so on. Besides the necessary vocation, the qualification of a lay-brother is that he should be master of a trade or a good unskilled workman rather than a person of literary education; they are sometimes supplemented by paid servants. Lay-religious are clerics in the extended sense of the term and enjoy clerical immunities. The institution was not known before the 10th century, when the ordination of monks was gaining ground and manual work losing it.

LAY COMMUNION. An early penitential discipline whereby clerics guilty of certain sins were reduced to lay status. The term is practically obsolete, but loss of clerical status is still involved in degradation (*q.v.*).

LAY CONFESSION. An humble accusation of one's sins to a lay person (*a*) as an exercise of humility and for the purpose of receiving direction from a prudent person or (*b*) when dying without the ministration of a priest available. (*a*) Can only rarely be advisable or prudent; (*b*) is undoubtedly useful for ensuring the necessary degree of contrition for one's sins. But it must be clearly understood that neither confession is sacramental, that there is no question of a lay-person's inability to give absolution, and therefore neither can take the place of confession to a priest when that is possible.

LAY-SCHOOL. This term indicates, not simply a school conducted by lay-people, but one wherein the instruction is entirely and *ex professo* without reference to religion (*cf.*, Lay-state, Lay-morality, etc.). It is sometimes applied to state schools or private schools as opposed to those conducted by ecclesiastics or under their supervision. It is no part of the normal function of the state to teach. But if there are not sufficient schools already existing, it may provide and conduct schools of its own, provided they satisfy the legitimate requirements of parents, especially in the matter of religion. Such schools must not be favoured at the expense of other properly conducted schools.

LAY STATE, The. An expression indicating an ideal of the 19th century expressed in the phrase "a free church in a free state." Such a conception of the relation between church and state (*q.v.*) is not in accordance with Catholic teaching, and moreover favours the emergence of the "jurisdictional state" which holds itself supreme even in spiritual matters. But under present conditions, when the religious beliefs of Christian peoples are varied and their organizations have received a definitely legal form and indifference is endemic, the complete separation of church and state is tolerated as an expedient arrangement. Its inconveniences are sometimes modified by a concordat (*q.v.*).

LAYING-ON OF HANDS. See IMPOSITION.

LAYMAN, -WOMAN (Gr. λαός, the people). One who has not received the tonsure or any holy order and is not a religious to whom a clerical status is extended; a member of the body of the faithful.

LAZARISTS, The, or Vincentians. The Congregation, or Priests, of the Mission founded by St. Vincent de Paul in 1625, named from the College of St. Lazarus, where they were established. Founded as missioners to rural districts and for the education of the clergy, they now have missions, seminaries and colleges in all parts of the world; they also conduct diocesan seminaries and colleges. They are secular priests bound by simple vows, the usual vows of religion plus one of stability, and wear ordinary clerical dress. They direct a training college and have churches in England, the fathers belonging to the Irish province; there are two provinces for the United States, where the fathers conduct De Paul University in Chicago and Niagara University in New York state.

LAZINESS. See SLOTH.

LEAGUE, The. An organization founded by the Catholics of France under Henry of Guise in 1585 to combat the Huguenots and prevent the accession of Henry of Navarre to the French throne.

LEAVEN, HOLY. The Nestorian Church emphasizes the continuity of the Eucharist by the unity of the bread used. Each time it is baked it is leavened not only with some dough from the last baking but also with a small portion of the "holy leaven" which is handed on from age to age in each church. The account of this, handed down, it is said, from their apostles Mar Addai and Mar Mari, is that "at our Lord's baptism St. John caught the water that fell from his body in a vessel, and before his death he gave it to his disciple John the son of Zebedee to keep it till required. At the Last Supper our Saviour gave one loaf to each disciple, but to St. John he gave two and bade him eat one and keep the other for the holy leaven. When the soldier pierced the side of our Lord on the Cross there came out water and blood, and St. John saw them—the blood the sign of the mysteries in the Church and the water the sign of regeneration. John . . . took the blood in the loaf . . . and the water in the vessel which the Baptist had given him" mixed them all together and divided it among the Apostles. This leaven is renewed with a special office by priest and deacon on Maundy Thursday: what remains in the vessel is mixed with dough, salt and olive oil, and leavens the whole. Nestorians count this leaven (*malka*, king) as one of the sacraments and no Liturgy may be celebrated without it. They say that the reason why Westerners anathematize Nestorius is that when he fled from Constantinople he took all the holy leaven with him and left the rest of the world without it. The whole legend is baseless.

LEBANON, THE CHURCH IN. See SYRIA.

LECTERN (Lat. *legere*, to read). A high movable reading desk, of wood or metal, standing in the middle of the choir of cathedral and other churches wherein the Divine Office is recited. Its principal purpose is to support the chant-books of the cantors, and the liturgical lessons, prophecies, etc., are sung thereat. The book-rest is often in the form of an eagle's outstretched wings, or may be double and revolving. A light folding lectern is used to support the gospel-book at high Mass. See AMBO; MISSAL-STAND.

LECTIO BREVIS. The Short Lesson (*q.v.*).

LECTION. A portion of the Holy Scriptures, of the writings of the Fathers, or of other ecclesiastical composition, appointed to be read in the services of the Church. See LESSON.

LECTIONARY, -ARIUM. A book containing the lessons (*q.v.*) appointed to be read at Matins, either those extracted from the Breviary or those proper to a particular place or body of persons; also a book containing the epistles and gospels for Mass.

LECTOR, or Reader. i. The second of the minor orders (*q.v.*) of the Western church. It has been known since the 2nd century, the duties (now obsolete) being to "intone the lessons, to bless bread and all firstfruits." At ordination a lectionary is handed to him. At a sung Mass (*q.v.*) a lector should sing the epistle, vested in a surplice; the first lesson of the Mass of the Presanctified may also be sung by him, and the epistle at high Mass if no subdeacon is present.

ii. All Eastern churches have an office of lector, whose business it is to sing the epistle and other lessons, though some (Jacobites, Nestorians) now omit the ordination. In some big churches of the Byzantine rite he performs his duties resting in that order for life (*cf.*, the deacon).

iii. The first theological degree in Dominican schools. The course is of seven years and the degree, Lector of Sacred Theology, qualifies the holder as a professor. It is equivalent to Doctor of Divinity. The addition *Præs.* to S.T.L. indicates that the lector has been presented for the Mastership in Sacred Theology, having fulfilled the academic conditions and passed the final examination.

LEEDS (*Loidensis*). An English see formed in 1878 at the suppression of Beverley, and now suffragan to Liverpool. It consists of the West Riding of Yorkshire, with part of York, formerly in the archdioceses of York. There are some very old Catholic missions in the diocese (Broughton Hall, Carlton, Hazlewood) and several established in the 17th and 18th centuries. The Bar Convent of the Institute of Mary was established at York in 1686, the first since the Reformation. The patrons of the diocese are our Lady of Perpetual Succour, St. Wilfrid (bishop of York) and St. Francis of Sales; the cathedral is dedicated in honour of St. Anne.

LEGATE (Lat. *legare*, to send). An ecclesiastic representing the Holy See and having a varying degree of its authority. The principal varieties are *legatus natus*, nuncio and internuncio (*legati missi*), *legatus a latere* and apostolic delegate (*qq.v.*). The Holy See has the right to send legates, with or without ecclesiastical jurisdiction, to any part of the world. They have the title "Excellency" and, even if not bishops, take precedence of all ordinaries who are not cardinals; they are responsible only to the Holy See for their acts; if they have a territory assigned to them they are the ecclesiastical superiors of all, even metropolitans, therein and can summon provincial or national synods, consecrate bishops and churches, absolve from censures, etc.; but with respect to the ordinaries their jurisdiction is chiefly appellate.

LEGATUS A LATERE (Lat., legate from the side). That is, a peculiarly confidential one, of the pope: a cardinal envoy sent on a mission of particular importance or delicacy, armed with special powers.

LEGATUS NATUS (Lat., born legate). One who is legate of the Holy See by virtue of the office which he holds. The former archbishops of Canterbury were *legati nati*, and the honour is still attached to certain sees, *e.g.*, Reims, Gniezno-Poznan, Salzburg, but since about the 12th century the distinction has involved only honorary privileges, of dress, etc.

LEGEND (Lat. *legere*, to read). (*a*) A popular traditional tale which may be true, false or a mixture; (*b*) historically, one of a collection of such stories, about a saint or other religious subject, collected together in the middle ages and then generally regarded as true; (*c*) popularly, as in (*a*), but the tale almost necessarily false. The Church proposes no such legends for the belief of the faithful, who may reject or accept them in accordance with the result of scientific examination of their source, evidence, etc.: nevertheless, pastors and teachers are at liberty to use them for purposes of instruction and edification, with proper precaution, even if uncertain or manifestly false (*cf.*, Lesson, Historical).

LEGION OF MARY, The. An association of lay people whose object is to help the clergy in their work for the sanctification and saving of souls. It was founded in Dublin in 1921, and spread rapidly after 1928 to Great Britain, the Americas, India and other parts of the world. It undertakes any work approved by the ecclesiastical authorities (*e.g.*, religious instruction; visiting the sick, the aged, prisons, lodging-houses; running clubs; distributing printed matter) except the collecting of money and the giving of material relief. It has a distinctive organization, its parts titled from the terms of a Roman military legion.

LEGITIMACY is presumed by canon law of all children born of a marriage unless the contrary is proved beyond doubt. The children of a putative marriage are legitimate. Legitimacy is required for the reception of holy orders. See ILLEGITIMACY.

LEGITIMATE MARRIAGE. A valid marriage between unbaptized persons.

LEGITIMATION by subsequent marriage can only take effect in canon law in respect of natural children born of parents who, either at the conception or at the birth or at any time between, were free validly to marry one another. The pope at his discretion can declare legitimate any child born out of marriage. See ILLEGITIMACY.

LENITY. Mildness (*q.v.*).

LENT (Old Eng., *lencten*, the spring season). The English name for Quadragesima (*q.v.*), the period of forty days from Ash Wednesday to Holy Saturday (excluding Sundays) observed as a preparation for the passion, death and resurrection of our Lord and as a time of penitence, prayer and fasting, spiritual and physical. Forty is the number of days of the Flood, of years of the Israelites' wandering, of the days of the fast of Elias, of Moses on Sinai and of our Lord in the desert. Formerly it was a time of preparation for the baptism of catechumens and for the reconciliation of penitents: both have left their mark on the liturgy of the time. During Lent the faithful must observe the law of fasting (*q.v.*) unless dispensed or excused, and are encouraged to special almsdeeds and practices of worship, and to refrain from dancing, etc. Solemnization, as distinct from celebration, of marriages is forbidden in Lent. Each day has its special Mass (composed in the 7th and 8th centuries), very few feasts are observed (none on Sundays), private votive Masses are forbidden and requiems (except for a funeral, etc.) are allowed only on the first free day in each week; at Mass and Office of the season the organ is not played, purple vestments with folded chasubles (*q.v.*) are worn, *Gloria in excelsis* and Alleluia are omitted, the tract of Ash Wednesday is said on every Monday, Wednesday and Friday; there is a special preface, etc. In the Eastern rites the duration and observances of Lent vary. In the Byzantine rite the severe fast (meat, *lacticinia*, eggs, fish, oil, wine, are forbidden) lasts forty-eight days; on Sundays the Liturgy is St. Basil's and all week-days except Saturdays are aliturgical, *i.e.*, the Liturgy of the Presanctified or none at all is celebrated.

LENTEN VEIL. A curtain hung between the people and the altar during Lent in the middle ages, symbolizing the expulsion of sinners and penitents from the Church according to ancient discipline. Its colour was at first white and afterwards purple; but it remained white in England and was black in Germany. It probably survives in the veiling of images during Passiontide, and may be seen in variations of its original form in some churches of Westphalia, Spain and Sicily; in the last it is hung some way off the floor and so no longer hides the altar. It is also used in Cistercian churches and in the rite of Braga.

LEONINE CITY, The. That part of Rome, formerly suburban, surrounded with a fortified wall by Pope St. Leo IV (847-55) to defend the Vatican basilica against the Saracens.

LEONINE SACRAMENTARY, The. The oldest known Latin sacramentary, erroneously attributed to Pope Leo I, containing parts of the propers of a number of Masses dating from the 4th to the 7th centuries, many of the prayers of which are still in use.

LEONINE UNION, The. Four branches of the Franciscans, the Observants, Recollects, Reformed and Alcantarines united into one body by Pope Leo XIII in 1897. To these Pius X, in 1909, gave the name of Friars Minor of the Leonine Union to distinguish them from the other friars minor, Capuchin and Conventual, but this name has never come into use, either popularly or in official documents; they are called simply Friars Minor. The Recollects, etc., were never juridically independent branches of the order but were subject to the (somewhat restricted) power of the minister general of the Observants.

LESSER LITANIES (Lat. *Litaniæ Minores* or *Gallicanæ*). The singing of the litany of the Saints in procession on the Rogation Days (*q.v.*) (*cf.*, Greater Litanies).

LESSER MONASTERIES. Those in England having an annual income of less than £200, suppressed by King Henry VIII in 1536.

LESSON (Lat. *legere*, to read). A portion of the Bible, from the Fathers, or other ecclesiastical writings, appointed to be read:
i. At Mass, namely the epistle and gospel (*qq.v.*). Formerly there were three, the first being from the Old Testament. This is still so on certain penitential days (*e.g.*, Ember Wednesdays), and on some other days (*e.g.*, Ember Saturdays) there are four or five lessons before the gospel. This O.T. lesson is still part of the Mozarabic Mass (from the Apocalypse in paschal time) and is of frequent occurrence in the Ambrosian and some Eastern rites; during penitential times their number is increased. See PROPHECIES.
ii. At Matins. On simple feasts and ferias there are three lessons, all from the Bible, or with one historical lesson (*q.v.*), or all from a homily, according to the day. When there are three nocturns ("nine-lesson feasts"), those of the first are scriptural, the second generally historical, the third are always from a homily on the gospel of the day. The Monastic Breviary has four lessons to each nocturn (*q.v.*).
iii. At other offices. The Little Chapter and Short Lesson (*qq.v.*) of the day hours are really short lessons. Certain other rites, *e.g.*, the Commendation of a Soul, have appropriate scriptural lessons.

LESSON, HISTORICAL. One (on feasts of 9 lessons, all three) of the lessons of the second nocturn of Matins which narrates the life of the saint of the day or other historical matter, *e.g.*, an account of the seizing of the cross by Chosroes and its return by Heraclius (Exaltation of the Cross), the miraculous fall of snow (Dedication of St. Mary Major), the bull *Ineffabilis Deus* of Pope Pius IX (octave of the Immaculate Conception). Historical statements found in these lessons are not bound to be believed on the authority of the Divine Office; indeed, that a stringent revision of these lessons is required was agreed at the Vatican Council.

LETTONIA. See LATVIA.

LEVIRATE (Lat. *levir*, brother-in-law). The Jewish law by which a dead man's brother or next-of-kin had to marry his widow "and raise up seed for his brother . . . that his name be not abolished out of Israel" (Deut. xxv, 5-10) (*cf.*, Ruth iii and iv; Matt. xxii, 23-27).

LEVITATION. A word invented about 1875, from Lat. *levis*, light [of weight], to designate certain spiritistic phenomena; now applied also to occurrences among the saints and others of the raising of the human body from the ground, its suspension in the air without visible prop, and sometimes of its movement in the air actuated by no apparent physical force. Such levitation is recorded of over two hundred persons, usually during prayer but under various conditions, generally gently and to the height of about 2 ft. St. Joseph of Cupertino (*d.* 1663) and St. Alphonsus Liguori (*d.* 1787) are notable examples. Certain of these cases are supported by evidence which appears definitely to establish their genuineness, nor is a natural explanation forthcoming. In such events, if true, may be seen a special mark of God's favour whereby it is made evident even to the physical senses that prayer is a raising of the heart and mind to God: they have no other significance.

LEVITE. A descendant of the Jewish patriarch Levi, the men of whose tribe were hereditary ministers to the priests of the Tabernacle and Temple; hence the name is used figuratively for a Christian cleric below the order of priest, especially a deacon, *e.g.*, in the *Exsultet*.

LEVITICUS. The third book of the Old Testament, so called because it contains the ritual and other laws of the Jewish priests and their assistants from the tribe of Levi. It records the consecration of Aaron and his sons as the first priests and general prescriptions for moral and ceremonial purity. In Hebrew it is called by its first word, *Vaikra*. Its author was Moses. See PENTATEUCH.

LEX ORANDI, LEX CREDENDI. A form of the axiom of Pope St. Celestine I, *Legem credendi statuit lex orandi*: "The rule of prayer determines the rule of faith," that is, the liturgy of worship is a chief instrument in the tradition of true doctrine. For example, the bull *Ineffabilis Deus*, in defining the doctrine of the Immaculate Conception, makes frequent reference to liturgical texts and observance in support thereof. Nevertheless, "liturgical recognition" must not be regarded as a dogmatic decision; *e.g.*, there is a Mass and Office of the Holy House of Loreto and of the apparition at La Salette, but no Christian is bound to belief in either of these marvels.

LIBELLUS MARTYRUM (Lat., certificate of the martyrs). A writing delivered by one in prison or otherwise suffering for the Faith to a repentant *lapsus* (*q.v.*) upon presentation of which the bishop at his discretion granted peace to, *i.e.*, reconciled, the penitent, even though his canonical penance was not ended. It was in effect an indulgence (*q.v.*), the penitent profiting by the merits of the confessor.

LIBER PONTIFICALIS (Lat., The Book of the Popes). A collection of biographies of the popes from St. Peter to Stephen V (*d.* 891). Those up to Boniface II (530-2) were written all together about that time and a great deal of spurious matter included; those which follow were written shortly after the death of each pope or group of popes but are of unequal value. From Victor II (*d.* 1055) till Eugene IV (*d.* 1447) similar biographies were again undertaken by various authors.

LIBER USUALIS. A liturgical book containing the proper Masses and all the hours of the office except Matins and Lauds for all Sundays of the year and for feasts which may displace the Sunday office, together with their chant.

LIBERA, The, generally refers to the responsory beginning *Libera me* (Deliver me, O Lord, from everlasting death) sung at funerals after the Mass and before the absolutions. But it may indicate the prayer *Libera nos*, the embolism (*q.v.*) of the Lord's Prayer at Mass.

LIBERALISM. A group of errors regarding the relation between Church and state, divine law, ecclesiastical law and various articles of belief. In various forms it contends that all laws are derived from the authority of the state (Absolute Liberalism); or, while granting a juridical authority to the Church, it denies that the Church is in any way supreme or superior to the state and, maintaining that her authority is over consciences only, lays down that she has no external or social authority (Moderate Liberalism); or, granting the Church's independence and supremacy, it lays down that her power should not be pressed. Its origin goes back to the liberal elements in pre-Revolution French society, and it has issued in Modernism (*q.v.*). It has been frequently condemned by a succession of popes from Pius IX to Benedict XV. Liberalism in this and other unacceptable forms must not be confused with the advocacy of those things which properly pertain to a free man or such political bodies as the Liberal party in Great Britain.

LIBERIA, THE CHURCH IN. The number of people in this Negro republic is estimated at about 1¼ million. There are some 7,000 Catholics and the country forms a vicariate apostolic, in charge of the Lyons missionaries.

LIBERALITY is a moral virtue, annexed to justice, which manifests itself in what is commonly called "generosity." It may be exercised either by rich or poor and, though properly in respect of material goods, in the free use of spiritual or intellectual gifts (*cf.*, Munificence).

LIBERIAN BASILICA, The. The patriarchal basilica of St. Mary Major, otherwise known as our Lady-of-the-Snow (*q.v.*) and as St. Mary *ad Præsepe* because of the alleged relics of our Lord's crib preserved therein; founded by Pope Liberius in 366.

LIBERIUS, THE CASE OF POPE. An alleged failure of papal infallibility. It is held as proved by some eminent historians that Pope Liberius (*d.* 366) approved of the condemnation of St. Athanasius, the opponent of Arianism, by Arian bishops, and himself subscribed a semi-Arian (*q.v.*) profession of faith: these acts being the consideration on which he was allowed to return to Rome by the Emperor Constantius who had banished him. Whether Liberius did these things, and whether that or the wishes of the Roman people was the cause of his return from exile, are matters of dispute. But even if the allegations are proved, infallibility was not involved. He was an exile in the emperor's power at the time; he made no doctrinal definition; and did not attempt to impose any belief on the Church. All the circumstances required for an exercise of infallibility (*q.v.*) were lacking.

LIBERTY. The power of choice. There is internal liberty and external; the first is freedom from all necessity or of all determinism in virtue of which man would of necessity wish whatever he wishes; the second is freedom from external necessity or force. There is liberty of contradiction (*i.e.*, freedom to do or not to do) and liberty of contrariety (*i.e.*, freedom to do this or to do that). The first is essential to free-will, the latter not. Liberty to sin is not essential to free-will for it is an abuse of free-will and is therefore not of the perfection but of the imperfection of free-will. The internal liberty (see above) of man is proved in psychology and in ethics. Its demonstration is drawn from three main sources: from the consciousness that the will is free; from the moral conscience, because of *duty* which demands freedom of the will; from the absurd consequences resulting from the negation of free-will. The truth of human free-will is based ultimately on the rational nature of man, upon the flexibility of his mind and of his will: just as the mind does not adhere invincibly to all conclusions, neither does the will to any one particular good (*cf.*, Freedom).

LIBERTY, DEFECT OF. Any one of the simple impediments (*q.v.*) to ordination constitutes defect of liberty, making a man irregular for the reception of holy orders unless and until the condition ceases to exist.

LICENTIATE. An academic degree granted by universities for proficiency in theology, philosophy, canon law, etc.; the holder is also called a Licentiate. The degree ranks below that of Doctor or Master, and usually above that of Bachelor.

LIE. A statement made at variance with the mind of the speaker. To tell a lie is intrinsically wrong because opposed to man's rational and social nature; it can therefore never be justifiable (*cf.*, equivocation, mental reservation). A jocose lie (*i.e.*, one told in jest) is no lie if the untruth is quite evident; otherwise it is a venial sin. An officious or "white" lie (*i.e.*, one told in order to prevent harm or to obtain some advantage to oneself or one's neighbour) is a venial sin unless grave harm is caused. A malicious lie is one deliberately told with intent to injure another; this is a venial or grave sin in accordance with the harm intended.

LIFE. Life consists in spontaneous and immanent (*q.v.*) movement. A living thing is not only the principle of its movement (spontaneity in a wide sense), but also the term (spontaneity in a strict sense, which includes immanence). It follows that the vital principle is distinct from matter as it is from chemical and physical forces. There are three degrees of life: vegetative, sensitive, and intellectual. The highest life is God who moves himself and all creatures without himself being moved by anything; he is Pure Act and possesses life without limits.

LIGAMEN (Lat. a bond). An existing marriage whereby either party is debarred from contracting another marriage.

LIGHT. i. The Church makes use of two kinds of ceremonial lights, namely, candles and lamps (*qq.v.*). "Lights" usually indicates candles.

ii. Intellectual. The *intellectus agens* or active intellect which lights up the material world in so far as abstracting therefrom the universal or essence it makes that world intelligible.

LIGHT OF GLORY (Lat. *Lumen gloriæ*). That principle which strengthens and elevates the mind so that it may be able to look upon God face to face.

LIMBO (Lat. *limbus,* hem, edge). i. The Limbo of the Fathers. A place and state of rest wherein the souls of the just who died before Christ's ascension were detained until he opened Heaven to them; referred to as "Abraham's bosom" (Luke xvi, 22) and "Paradise" (Luke xxiii, 43) and notably in Eph. iv, 9, and 1 Peter iii, 18-20.

ii. The Limbo of Children. It is of faith that all, children and adults, who leave this world without the Baptism of water, blood or desire (*qq.v.*) and therefore in original sin are excluded from the vision of God in Heaven. The great majority of theologians teach that such children and unbaptized adults free from grievous actual sin enjoy eternally a state of perfect natural happiness knowing and loving God by the use of their natural powers. This place and state is commonly called Limbo.* *Cf.*, Infants, Unbaptized.

LIMERICK (*Limericiensis*). An Irish see, suffragan of Cashel, founded some time before the 12th century. It includes most of the county of Limerick and a small part of Clare. The bishop's residence, cathedral and diocesan seminary are in the city of Limerick. The patron of the diocese is St. Munchin (Jan. 2) and the titular of the cathedral St. John Baptist. Irish name: Luimneach.

LINCOLN, THE USE OF. The mediæval use of the Roman liturgy used before the Reformation in the diocese of Lincoln. Practically nothing is known of it; the local customs were written down in 1265 but none of the books seem ever to have been printed.

LIQUEFACTION. The becoming liquid of solid matter, alleged of certain blood-relics of saints, *e.g.*, of St. Januarius (*q.v.*).

LISBON. One of the cities where priests were trained for the English mission. The college of SS. Peter and Paul was founded in 1622 and is still a seminary for English students. The Irish College has ceased to exist.

LISBON, PATRIARCH OF. Title conferred on the archbishop of Lisbon in the 18th century. His powers are simply metropolitan, with certain privileges.

---

* The traditional teaching of Catholic theologians on Limbo is that Limbo is only for unbaptized children under the age of reason, and that the final destination of all who have reached the age of reason is either Heaven or Hell.—*Publisher*, 1997.

LITANY (Gr. λιτανεία, prayer). A form of prayer consisting of alternate brief invocations and petitions in two parts, said or sung antiphonally between priest, deacon, or cantors, and people. Only those litanies which are contained in the Breviary or in the more recent editions of the "Rituale" may be recited publicly; they are the litany of the Saints, of our Lady (qq.v.), of the Holy Name, of the Sacred Heart and of St. Joseph. Of these, only the first is used liturgically and is therefore frequently referred to simply as The Litany or The Litanies. The *Kyrie eleison* is a relic of former litanies used in the Roman Mass, and in all Eastern rites litanies remain an outstanding feature of the eucharistic liturgies. In the Ambrosian rite litanies are sung at Mass every Sunday in Lent instead of *Gloria in excelsis*.

LITANY OF OUR LADY, or OF LORETO. A litany commonly sung during Benediction of the Blessed Sacrament and on other extra-liturgical occasions. It consists principally of 49 invocations of our Lady, with the prayer "Pray for us"; the first 19 are addressed to her as Mother and Virgin, each with a separate epithet, "of Christ," "loving," "faithful," etc.; the next 13 are remarkable terms, symbolic of her office, power or virtues, "Mirror of justice," "Tower of David," "House of gold," etc.; then follow four common titles, and twelve addressed to her as Queen, "of angels," "of all saints," etc. The litany ends with the collect from the common Mass of our Lady, and the antiphon *Sub tuum praesidium* is often added. The litany had its origin at the sanctuary of Loreto and began to spread towards the end of the 16th century. The titles used in this litany are sometimes criticized as extravagant and in-novations; it may therefore be noted that most of them can be found or paralleled in the writings of the Fathers of the first six centuries.

LITANY OF THE SAINTS, The, is sung on the occasion of the Greater Litanies, Roga-tion days, at special penitential or interces-sory processions, when conferring major orders, consecrating a bishop, blessing an abbot or abbess, during the Forty Hours de-votion, and on other occasions. A special shortened form is in use only on Holy Satur-day and the vigil of Pentecost, and another in the commendation of a departing soul. The full form consists of the usual beginning addressed to the Persons of the Blessed Trin-ity; then, each with the response *Ora pro nobis* (Pray for us), three invocations by name of our Lady, three of Archangels, St. John Baptist, St. Joseph, sixteen of apostles and evangelists, seven of martyrs, seven of doc-tors and bishops, five of founders of orders, seven of women, each class being followed by one or two invocations addressed to the class in general; then seven petitions for deliver-ance from spiritual and temporal evils and ten in the name of the mysteries of the life of Christ; then follow seventeen petitions on behalf of the Church and her members; then Our Father silently; Ps. lxix; versicles and responses; and a series of ten final collects, drawn from various parts of the liturgy. Some religious orders, *e.g.*, the Dominicans, have their own proper version of this litany.

LITERAL SENSE. See GENESIS; QUOTATIONS; SENSE OF THE SCRIPTURES.

LITHOSTROTOS (Gr.). A paved place (John xix, 13) (*cf.*, Gabbatha).

LITHUANIA, THE CHURCH IN. The estimated population is 2 million, of whom three-quarters are Catholics. In 1939 they formed 1 province, with its metropolitan see at Kaunas, with 4 suffragan dioceses. The country is now incorporated in the U.S.S.R., and in 1946, of 7 bishops-in-ordinary and auxiliary, 1 had been murdered, 3 had disap-peared, and 3 were in exile.

LITTLE BROTHERS OF MARY, The. See MARISTS, ii.

LITTLE CHAPTER, The (Lat. *Capitulum*). A verse which follows the psalms at Lauds, Prime, Terce, Sext, None and Vespers and the hymn at Compline. It is taken from the Bible and followed by *Deo gratias*. It is in fact a very short lesson, and so is not found at Matins which has its own system of les-sons. It is variable according to the season, etc., except at Prime and Compline.

LITTLE CLAIRVAUX. A Cistercian mon-astery in Nova Scotia, the earliest existing of its order in the New World; founded by Dom Vincent de Paul in 1825. In 1900 the community was transferred to the monastery of Our Lady of the Valley at Lonsdale, R. I.; but three years later Little Citeaux was re-opened by some Cistercians from Brittany.

LITTLE COMPANY OF MARY, The. A congregation of sisters founded at Notting-ham in 1877 to care for the sick and the bodies of the dead and to keep up continual prayer for the dying and dead. Unenclosed: Little Office B.V.M. in choir; no lay-sisters. Black habit, blue veil; white choir cloak.

LITTLE FLOWER, The. A name com-monly given to St.-Teresa-of-the-Child-Jesus, canonized in 1925, only 28 years after her death.

LITTLE HOURS, The. i. The shorter hours of the Divine Office or of the Little Office B.V.M., namely, Prime, Terce, Sext and None, of which the last three are alike in structure and length.

ii. The Little Office B.V.M. as a whole.

LITTLE HOUSE OF DIVINE PROVI-DENCE, or Charitable Cottolengo Institute. An institution founded, in 1828, at Turin by St. Joseph Cottolengo for corporal works of charity of every kind. It is equipped with hospitals, workshops, schools, almshouses, refuges, orphanages, etc., conducted by several religious institutes and several thousand persons are supported without any endowment. The most abandoned and wretched are particularly sought after and the activities of the institute have spread to British East Africa, Palestine, Switzerland and elsewhere.

LITTLE OFFICE. A form of prayer modelled on, and a miniature of, the Divine Office, but practically invariable and in honour of some particular saint or mystery of the faith. The most commonly used now are "of our Lady" (*q.v.*) and "of the Immaculate Conception"; without qualification, the first is always meant.

LITTLE OFFICE OF OUR LADY, or of the Blessed Virgin Mary. According to the Roman Breviary, this consists of Matins (Invitatory and its psalm, hymn, three psalms according to the days of the week, the Lord's Prayer, three lessons from Ecclus. xxiv, *Te Deum*); Lauds (Ps. xcii, xcix and lxii, the canticle *Benedicite*, Ps. cxlviii, little chapter, hymn, *Benedictus*, with its antiphon, collect and commemoration of the saints); the Little Hours (each with the same hymn and with three psalms, little chapter and collect); Vespers (Ps. cix, cxii, cxxi, cxxvi and cxlvii, little chapter, the hymn *Ave Maris Stella*, *Magnificat* with its antiphon, collect and commemoration of the saints; and Compline (three psalms, hymn, little chapter, *Nunc dimittis* with the antiphon *Sub tuum* and collect). There are small variations during Advent. Some religious orders, *e.g.*, the Bridgettines, Carthusians and Dominicans, have Little Offices proper to themselves; those of the first two are quite unlike any other. The Little Office is obligatory on members of some orders on certain days (on Carthusians every day) in addition to the Divine Office; it is the usual daily office of some lay-brothers and sisters and of many congregations of active nuns; it is the normal office obligatory on tertiaries, secular and regular; and forms the daily prayer of numbers of lay-folk. The Books of Hours and Primers of the past consisted principally of this office.

LITTLE ORATORY, THE BROTHERHOOD OF THE. An institution attached to each house and church of the Congregation of the Oratory (*q.v.*) and forming an integral part of the whole. It is a confraternity of laymen, called the Brothers, who meet on Saturdays and Sundays especially for prayer and spiritual instruction; they also undertake such works as visiting the sick and ministering to the needs of the poor. The "Little Oratory" was St. Philip Neri's primary work, out of which the Congregation of Priests of the Oratory grew.

LITTLE SISTERS OF THE ASSUMPTION. A congregation of unenclosed nuns founded by Fr. Étienne Pernet, A.A. and Mother Mary of Jesus (Fage) in 1864, to nurse the sick and in any other way help the poor in their homes. Black habit. Distinguish from the Sisters of the Assumption.

LITTLE SISTERS OF THE POOR, The. Founded by Jeanne Jugan and others in Brittany, in 1840, to shelter and provide for the homeless poor of both sexes over 60 years old. They make a daily collection of alms, clothing and broken food; no lay-sisters. They number over 6,000 members throughout the world and are responsible for many thousands of old people; many homes in the United States, Great Britain and Ireland. Black habit.

LITURGICAL BOOKS. i. The principal books of the Latin rite are the Missal, the Breviary, the "Rituale Romanum," the "Pontificale Romanum," the "Ceremonial of Bishops," the "Martyrology" and the "Memoriale Rituum" (*qq.v.*); among others, required only for singing purposes, are the "Antiphoner," the "Graduale," the "Kyriale" and the "Liber Usualis" (*qq.v.*) Of the making of other books, of extracts, etc., for convenience, there is no end.

ii. In the Eastern churches the offices are still arranged in a number of separate books, each containing only those parts required by individuals, *e.g.*, the celebrant, the deacon, the choir, as in the West before about the 11th century. The chief Byzantine books are the *Euchologion, Horologion, Menaion, Typikon* (*qq.v.*) and the *Pentekostarion, Triodion* and *Oktoechos* or *Parakletike* for the use of the choir. The Maronite and Malabar rites have a missal arranged on the Roman pattern.

LITURGICAL LANGUAGE. The Church has no single official liturgical language, though Latin has a certain precedence of honour on account of its being proper to the Holy See and its extensive use. It is used in worship throughout the Western church, except for tiny groups in Yugoslavia, Calabria and Sicily. The other languages used, in the approximate order of their numerical extension, are: 1. Church Slavonic, by the Ruthenians, Russians, Serbs and Bulgarians of the Byzantine rite; 2. Rumanian; 3. Syriac, by the Syrians, Maronites, Chaldeans and Malabarese; 4. Arabic, by the Melkites; 5. Magyar; 6. Armenian; 7. Greek; 8. Coptic, by the Egyptians; 9. Ge'ez, by the Ethiopians; 10. Malayalam, by the Malankarese; 11. Georgian. Latin has a huge numerical majority, owing to missionary energy and the Eastern schism; Greek has an almost equal place of honour, but Slavonic comes second numerically; Syriac is greatly regarded by its users as approximating to the Aramaic spoken by our Lord. Of the above, Latin and 8 and 9 are dead languages; 1, 3, 6, 7 and 11 are classical or old forms, only partly understood by the people; 2, 4, 5 and 10 are spoken tongues (vernacular, *q.v.*). Originally services were held in whatever was the spoken language. In the East this was Greek, but soon Aramaic (Syriac) and Coptic were used as well. At Rome most of the earlier converts were Greek-speaking; this was superseded by Latin in the 3rd century. When Christianity reached the rest of Italy, Spain and Gaul, Latin was spoken by nearly all; this gradually developed into Italian, Spanish, French, etc., but the written language of the liturgy remained fixed and slowly and imperceptibly became a dead language so far as the ordinary people were concerned. See LANGUAGE OF THE CHURCH; LATIN; GREEK.

LITURGICAL MOVEMENT, The. The activity in the Western church which seeks to restore intelligent participation, first, in the sacrifice of the Mass, then, in the other offices of the Church (as distinguished from popular devotions, *q.v.*), as the principal and ordinary way of common prayer of the faithful at large. It is based on the principles that Christianity is essentially the religion of the worship of the Lord Jesus Christ; that the Church provides her services for our use and sanctification; and that "the active participation in the most holy Mysteries and in the public and solemn prayer of the Church is the primary and indispensable source of the true Christian spirit" (Pope Pius X).

LITURGICAL WORSHIP consists in the public use of an act of worship of Almighty God, in a form laid down by the Church, in the name and on behalf of the whole Christian people and accomplished or presided over by an accredited minister who is specially deputed by the Church to carry out the worship which she as a society renders to God; it is the social exercise of the virtue of religion. In an extended sense it includes the private use of public worship, *e.g.*, nuns singing Office in their private chapel, an individual reciting it to himself on the top of a bus; for in such cases the worshipper is acting in union with the Church at large and performing one of the Church's own actions. Liturgical worship is not simply association in prayer; it takes its dignity and supreme efficacy from our being members of the Mystical Body of Christ and from our conscious association with that Body and its Head in offering worship to God. It consists principally of the Mass, the Divine Office and the Sacraments. *Cf.*, Prayer.

LITURGY, The (Gr. λειτουργία a public duty or work; used in the Septuagint and New Testament, *e.g.*, Luke i, 23, for the Temple service). i. The forms of prayer, acts and ceremonies used in the public and offi-

cial worship of the Church, principally in the offering of the Eucharistic Sacrifice, the singing of the Divine Office and the administration of the Sacraments, and the use thereof. This must be distinguished from the public use of popular devotions (*q.v.*).

ii. In particular, the Eucharistic Sacrifice itself, always called "The Mass" in the Western church but usually "The Holy Liturgy" or "The Offering" in Eastern churches. In this work, this sense is distinguished from i. above by the use of a capital L, or sometimes the added adjective "eucharistic."

iii. Rarely, some other particular service, *e.g.*, the liturgy of Baptism, better called the rite or office of Baptism.

LITURGIES, THE EUCHARISTIC (see ii. above), now in use in the Catholic Church are: i. Latin. (1) The Roman Mass, derived from a primitive Roman rite, with major variants used by the Carmelites, Carthusians and Dominicans, and several minor variants. (2) The Ambrosian Mass and the Mozarabic Mass, both probably of Gallican derivation.

ii. Non-Latin. (1) The Byzantine Liturgies of St. John Chrysostom and of St. Basil, with their daughter the Armenian Liturgy, and (2) the West Syrian Liturgy of St. James, with its variant the Maronite Liturgy. These derive from the primitive rite of Antioch. (3) The East Syrian Liturgy of the holy Apostles Addai and Mari, with two others, and its variant the Liturgy of Malabar. (4) The Coptic Liturgies of St. Basil, of St. Gregory Nazianzen and of St. Cyril, derived in part from the primitive rite of Alexandria, with the daughter Liturgy of the Ethiopians. In a more scientific terminology, (2) are referred to as the Antiochene rite and (4) as the Alexandrian rite.

LIVERPOOL (*Liverpolitanus*). An English see created in 1850, erected into an archdiocese in 1911. It now embraces western Lancashire south of the Ribble, and the Isle of Man, which before the Reformation were under the jurisdiction of the bishops of Lichfield and Sodor & Man. It is the most heavily Catholic-populated district in Great Britain, and large numbers belong to families who have never lost the faith; Little Crosby is cent. per cent. Catholic and 21 of the parishes were established as missions in the 16th and 17th centuries (Standish in 1574). The diocesan seminary is at Upholland. The patrons of the diocese are our Lady Immaculate, St. Joseph and St. Kentigern, and the new cathedral will be dedicated to Christ the King.

LIVING. The common English word for a parochial benefice, now only used in the Church of England.

LIVING WAGE. The remuneration which, according to circumstances, enables a whole-time male wage-earner to support himself and his family in reasonable and frugal comfort. Every workman has a right to a living wage; this is "a dictate of natural justice more imperious and ancient than any bargain between man and man. If through necessity, or fear of a worse evil, the workman accept harder conditions because an employer or contractor will give him no better, he is made the victim of force and injustice" (Pope Leo XIII. *Rerum novarum*).

LOCI THEOLOGICI (Lat., theological places). The repositories whence theologians derive their arguments. The chief among them are Scripture and Tradition. These natural, internal sources are supplemented by subsidiary, artificial or external sources (*e.g.*, history), which are in themselves independent of revelation.

LOCUTIONS, SUPERNATURAL. (*a*) Words heard by the ear but produced supernaturally; (*b*) words produced supernaturally in the imagination; (*c*) thoughts communicated directly to the intellect. The words are very clearly understood, compel attention, convey an assurance of their truth and remain long in the memory. They may enrich the soul in an instant with very extensive or penetrating knowledge, or work sudden and important changes in conduct. They leave an effect of peace and recollection. Imaginative and aural locutions may, of course, be counterfeited by the Devil, or be the result of a neuropathic condition. Such pseudo-locutions can be detected by their nature or effects: incoherence, disquietude of soul, no spiritual influence for good, positive harm. Locutions, like visions, are not at all essential to the spiritual life.

LOGIA. i. A Greek term for the Sayings of our Lord supposed to have existed in a separate and distinct collection, possibly compiled by St. Matthew and embodied later partially in the present first gospel and partially in the third. There is no convincing evidence for the existence of such a document, and Catholics are directed by the Biblical Commission to accept the present Greek text of the first gospel as substantially identical with the Aramaic text written by St. Matthew. The early 2nd century commentary by Papias on the Lord's *Logia* probably refers to the four gospels.
ii. *Logia Iesu.* The name given by Grenfell and Hunt to seven or eight Sayings of Christ, found in 1897 at Oxyrhynchus on a papyrus of the 2nd or 3rd century. Their value as authentic utterances of Christ is uncertain.

LOGIC (Gr. λόγος word, thought). Logic deals (*a*) with those operations of the mind which take for granted the correctness of the materials supplied from without and regulates the disposal and development of those materials (Formal Logic); (*b*) with those operations by which is ensured the correctness of the materials supplied and their correspondence with the external realities which they represent (Material Logic). Thus in general (*i.e.*, including both formal and material logic) it may be defined as "The science which directs the operations of the mind in its knowledge of truth."

LOGOS. Gr., Λόγος. Word (*q.v.*).

LOGY. A suffix from Gr. λόγος meaning "science."

LOIDENSIS. The adjectival form of the name of the see of Leeds (*q.v.*) used in the designation of its bishop in Latin documents. Noun: *Loidis.*

LOLLARDS (Middle Dutch, *lollærd*, a mumbler, mutterer). A nickname for the Wycliffites (*q.v.*), by which they were commonly known; the reason for the name is obscure.

LONGANIMITY (Lat. *longus*, long; *animus*, spirit). Longsuffering, forbearance; a fruit of the Holy Ghost (*q.v.*). Longanimity is patience exercised over a considerable period of time; patience is exercised in respect of that which is trying in itself, longsuffering in respect of its continuance.

LONGINUS. Traditionally the name of the soldier referred to in John xix, 34; he is mentioned in the Roman Martyrology on March 15.

LORD. The Lord Bishop of N——, my Lord, his Lordship, etc., are the usual modes of address and reference to bishops in English-speaking countries, except the United States. The same are extended to abbots on more formal occasions (and abbesses, other than Franciscan, are Lady Abbess), but this seems to be going out of use and "Father Abbot" is now usually said in personal intercourse. "Lord" in this connexion is simply the translation of the Latin *dominus* (master, ruler, sir) which has a less specialized connotation than the English word; but its use has been affected by the fact that mediæval bishops, and often abbots and abbesses and other prelates as well, were peers of the realm (usually barons) and so temporal lords; *cf.*, the Eastern usage where a bishop (or celebrating priest) is addressed liturgically and often ordinarily as Δέσποτα (O ruler), or by an equivalent term.

LORD'S PRAYER, The (Lat. *Oratio Dominica*). The prayer taught by our Lord to his apostles (Matt. vi, 9-13; Luke xi, 2-4), generally called by Catholics "the Our Father" (*q.v.*).

LORETO, THE HOLY HOUSE OF (It. *Santa Casa*). A small building, about 31 ft. by 13 ft. enshrined within the basilica at Loreto, near Ancona, said to be the house of our Lady at Nazareth, transported first in 1291 to Illyria and in 1294 hither, on each occasion by the ministry of angels. The tradition has been approved by many popes and saints and numerous miracles are recorded there; but the most recent research tends to show that the tradition is mistaken and rests on some unexplained misunderstanding. As in the case of the reputed relics of St. Katherine at Mount Sinai, "angels" was probably originally a metaphor for "monks." The marvel is mentioned in the Roman Martyrology on Dec. 10, on which day a feast of our Lady of Loreto is observed in some places. There is a nice appropriateness in the fact that our Lady under this title is the patron saint of airmen. The Roman congregation which had charge of the affairs of this venerable shrine is now united to the Sacred Congregation of the Council.

LORETO NUNS. The name given in Ireland to sisters of the Institute of Mary.

LOS VON ROM (Ger., Away from Rome). An anti-Catholic and pan-German movement begun in Austria in 1897, and continued in a modified form until the collapse of the monarchy in 1918. The name has been extended to any similar movements or parties among the German-speaking peoples. The purpose of the original movement was to weaken Catholicism in Austria for political objects, and it was taken advantage of by Protestants and Old Catholics (q.v.) for extreme proselytizing. Large subsidies from German Protestant organizations made possible the publication and distribution of tracts and the building of preaching-stations and meeting-houses even in small villages. The Catholic counter-movement did not get properly under way until 1903; it emanated from the abbey of Emmaus at Prague and brought about the reorganization of the *Bonifatius Verein* to carry on the work.

LOST SOULS, NUMBER OF. God has given no revelation as to the number or proportion of lost souls, nor is there any common teaching of theologians on the subject. The Church tells us infallibly the names of numerous persons who are in Heaven; she does not say, and forbids her children to maintain, that any particular individual is in Hell.

LOTTERY. If properly conducted the organization of or taking part in a lottery is morally blameless, prohibition by the civil law notwithstanding.

LOUGH DERG. See ST. PATRICK'S PURGATORY.

LOUISVILLE (*Ludovicopolitanus*). One of the early dioceses of the United States, established at Bardstown, Kentucky, in 1808 and transferred to Louisville in 1841. Its first bishop was B. J. Flaget. It was made metropolitan in 1937, the sees of Covington, Nashville, and Owensborough being assigned to it as suffragans.

LOURDES. A town in the department of Hautes Pyrénées, between Tarbes and Pau, where, between Feb. 11 and July 16, 1858, our Lady appeared on eighteen occasions to a peasant girl, St. Bernadette Soubirous. It subsequently became the most famous pilgrim shrine of the present day. The archives of the Medical Bureau (see below) contain the records of several thousand cases; at a moderate estimate it may be said with certainty that these include some three to four hundred cures which medical science cannot explain. Of these, a few have been declared miraculous by the bishops of various dioceses after definite canonical enquiry. There are also undoubtedly many cures which are never reported to the bureau and others at the various shrines of our Lady of Lourdes throughout the world. These material favours are insignificant beside the spiritual potency of Lourdes, which as a purely religious sanctuary is one of the greatest ever known. It receives over a million pilgrims a year, of which only a small proportion, averaging 15,000, are afflicted in body. The feast of the Appearing of our Lady at Lourdes is observed throughout the Western church on Feb. 11.

LOURDES MEDICAL BUREAU, The. The examination of sick people who claim to have been cured at Lourdes, during the procession of the Blessed Sacrament, in the baths (the water of which does not contain any therapeutic property), or elsewhere, is conducted at the Bureau des Constatations Médicales by unpaid and independent doctors who happen to be in Lourdes and who have registered their names at the bureau. The president is the only medical man permanently attached to the bureau and he is appointed by the bishop of Tarbes and Lourdes. His function is to preside at the examinations and discussions concerning alleged cures, made among the doctors at the bureau, the majority of whom accompany some pilgrimage and are present only for three or four days. Any doctor, of any nationality, any belief or no belief, is free to enter the bureau and make whatever enquiries he likes, and be present when any case of alleged cure is being investigated. The individual concerned is interrogated at the B.C.M. as to the history of his malady, the circumstances of the alleged cure, etc., as are any friends or witnesses who have accompanied him. The medical certificates of the case are closely scrutinized, and the patient examined, usually by four doctors chosen by the president from amongst those who have registered their names. If any specialist for the particular malady in question is present, he is of course asked to examine the patient. These doctors draw up a report, which is read out to all the medical men present, and a discussion takes place. Then the president, after summing up the salient points, puts the following questions, which must be answered by a simple Yes or No. (1) Did the disease really exist? (2) Is there a complete cure or only an evident amelioration? (3) Is there need to wait before coming to a decision? (4) Can the cure be attributed to a natural process? The first reports are provisional, and, if anything is subsequently discovered, it is noted in the official organ in which particulars of all the certified cures are published. The B.C.M. does not certify any cure as miraculous, that pertaining to the ecclesiastical authorities; it concerns itself with purely medical questions.

LOVE. i. The adhesion of the will to an object which is presented by the intellect as good. It manifests itself in solicitude for the other's welfare, delight in his presence, desire for his approval. Though it resides in the rational will, it under certain circumstances reacts strongly on the sensory faculties. It is that state in which "correspondence of wills makes of two one spirit. Nor is it to be feared that inequality of the two who are parties to it should make this concurrence of wills in any way imperfect or weak: for love knows not reverence. Love takes its name from loving, not from honouring. Let him who is struck with fear or astonishment or dread or admiration be satisfied with honouring, for all these feelings are absent in him who loves. Love is filled with itself, and where it has come it overcomes and transforms all other dispositions" (St. Bernard, "On the Canticle." lxxxv, 12-14).

ii. The theological virtue of charity (*q.v.*). See LOVE OF GOD.

iii. Of man and woman. A complex disposition or state of feeling centring round the natural appetite, whereby a being seeks that which is its good; it includes an intellectual element, an instinctive impulsion towards procreation, a sensitive attraction to the object desired, and certain emotive forces. Sexual love, as all the appetites, must be governed according to right reason.

iv. Of benevolence. Either love of complacence (*q.v.*) or, more usually, love of complacence joined to friendship, so that each of the two friends loves the other because of the beloved's own inherent lovableness, irrespective of his being a source of good to the lover.

v. Of complacence. Love shown another because of his own inherent lovableness, irrespective of his being a source of good to oneself.

vi. Of concupiscence. Love shown to another inasmuch as he is a source of good to oneself. Love of God because he is our present help or future reward is such love; it in no way excludes love of benevolence (*q.v.*) but frequently leads to it.

LOVE OF ENEMIES. Love of those who have injured or hate us is implied in the general precept of charity and expressly commanded by Christ (Matt. v, 44). The precept is positive, in so far as it binds us to forgive our enemies and show them at least the common marks of Christian charity; negative, in so far as it forbids us to curse or hate them, wish them evil, exclude them from our customary salutations, commerce and prayers (*cf.*, Hatred, Revenge). Serious breach of this precept is a mortal sin.

LOVE OF GOD. i. The theological virtue of charity (*q.v.*). Habitual charity is a virtue, immediately infused by God along with sanctifying grace, inclining the will to exercise actual charity, i.e., to love God above all things with the love of benevolence (*q.v.*), and to love one's neighbour as oneself for God's sake. Loving God above all things means that the intellect appreciates God as worthy of the highest love and that the will prefers him to all other things accordingly. Habitual charity is an indispensable means of salvation, for it is inseparable from sanctifying grace; it can be destroyed by mortal sin only. The exercise of actual charity is man's paramount duty, imposed by the natural law and by divine precept, "Thou shalt love the Lord thy God" (Matt. xxii, 37); acts of charity should be made frequently during life and especially at the hour of death. The precept is violated indirectly by every mortal sin, directly by spiritual sloth (*q.v.*) and by hatred of God.

ii. For us. The existence of all creation and of each and every creature depends on the love of God which wills its existence; if God ceased to love any creature it would thereby cease to be. But God does not withdraw his love even from those who deliberately and knowingly reject it, who therefore exist after death in a state of eternal punishment (*q.v.*), loved but not loving.

LOVE OF OUR NEIGHBOUR is of divine precept, both positive (Matt. xxii, 39) and natural; for our neighbour is any intellectual creature who like us is capable of divine adoption and eternal beatitude, whom Christ wishes to be in some way morally identified with himself. The precept implies acts of internal love and external beneficence, including fraternal correction, the giving of alms, and assisting our neighbour in his necessity even at inconvenience to ourselves. Thus if only by our help he can avoid damnation, we must risk life and limb to render that help, and in general the detriment we should be ready to undergo should be in proportion to his needs and the nearness of his relationship with us, sc., whether parent, relation, neighbour or fellow man; but we are never justified in committing the smallest sin to relieve our neighbour even in his utmost need.

LOW-CHURCH. The popular name given to the evangelical party in the Church of

England which maintains the essential Protestantism of that institution, adheres to the doctrinal and devotional formulas of the Book of Common Prayer, and regards the Bible as the ultimate rule of faith. The Church Missionary Society is one of the best known and most characteristic manifestations of this school of Anglicanism.

LOW MASS. The ordinary name in England and elsewhere for *Missa privata* or *plana*; it is a modified form of high Mass and the most common way in which Mass is celebrated. The celebrant is assisted by, normally, one server or acolyte, who is generally a layman or boy, and there is no choir; the prayers, therefore, which do not vary from those of high Mass, are all spoken by the celebrant, in two tones of voice, clear, and inaudible: the collects, epistle, gospel, post-communion, etc., aloud, the canon secretly. The ceremonies differ from high Mass in so far as there is no deacon or subdeacon, all is done at the altar, and there is no incense. Normally two candles only are alight on the altar, and a third during the canon. Low Mass is sometimes accompanied by the singing of Latin or vernacular hymns or chants or even by the recitation of prayers aloud; these are extra-liturgical and so far as the Mass is concerned are as if they were not. Low Mass has been in use only since the early middle ages, and is still foreign to Eastern Liturgies; but nearly all the Catholics of Eastern rites have adapted their liturgies to admit of an equivalent form of celebration, notably the Maronites, the Malabarese, and the Armenians.

LOW SUNDAY. The English name for the Sunday next after Easter. Its origin is uncertain: perhaps the Sunday "below" Easter day.

LUCERNARIUM (Lat., the office of lights). A primitive evening office, the parent of Vespers, at which all the lamps of the church were lit and a hymn sung; *cf.*, the blessing of the fire and lighting of the paschal candle on Holy Saturday. The responsories at the beginning of Ambrosian Vespers are still called *lucernaria,* and the hymn "Hail, gladdening light!" is the central point of *Hesperinos* (*q.v.*). *Cf.,* Acts xx, 8.

LUCIFER (Lat., light-bearer; the Lat. translation of the Gr., φωσφόρος, which in the O.T. renders the Heb. *Helel,* shiner, the name of the planet Venus, the morning and evening star). Usually understood as the proper name of Satan, the chief fallen angel, because of Christ's saying, "I saw Satan like lightning falling from Heaven" (Luke x, 18), combined with Isaias xiv taken as a description of the pride and fall of Satan.

LUCIUS LEGEND, The. The story that a Romano-British king, Lucius, wrote to Pope St. Eleutherius in the year 167, asking for missionaries to be sent to Britain, which was done. This tale is not heard of before the sixth century, and later amplifications embroider it considerably. Scholars regard both Lucius and the event as apocryphal (Britain has probably been confused with Britium in Mesopotamia). But this and other fables (*e.g.,* of St. Joseph of Arimathaea at Glastonbury) suggest that Christianity reached the Isle of Britain very early.

LUDOVICOPOLITANUS. The Latin epithet for the archbishop of Louisville, Ky.

LUKE, ST. i. Evangelist and martyr, whose feast is observed throughout the Church, nearly everywhere on Oct. 18. He was a Greek of Antioch, a physician by profession, and the companion of St. Paul during the greater part of his missions and his captivity at Rome. He wrote the Acts of the Apostles and the gospel which bears his name, having in view the need of educated Gentile converts of an historical background for their faith. He is venerated as a martyr, but we have no particulars of his death. The tradition that Luke was a painter is relatively late, and none of the numerous pictures of our Lady attributed to him seems to be older than the 6th century.

ii. His gospel. This was written in Greek before the year 70 when, as he himself tells us in i, 1, other accounts of the life of our Lord were already in existence; these, as well as the testimony of "those first eye-witnesses who gave themselves up to the service of the word," he doubtless used. The question of the relationship between his and Matthew's and Mark's narratives is called the "synoptic problem" (*q.v.*). Eighteen parables and six miracles are recorded only by Luke, who gives prominence to our Lord's teaching on prayer, to the women who were associated with him, and to his eternal priesthood. In 1913 the Biblical Commission (*q.v.*) declared Luke, a physician, to be the author of the gospel that bears his name, and that he wrote according to the preaching of St. Paul and other sources. The authorship, inspiration and canonicity of chapters i and ii, and xxii, 43-4 may not be doubted, nor that the *Magnificat* (i, 46-55) was spoken by our Lady and not by St. Elizabeth.

LUKEWARMNESS. See TEPIDITY.

LUMEN CHRISTI (Lat., the Light of Christ). Words sung thrice by the deacon on Holy Saturday when carrying the newly lighted paschal candle through the darkened church; the people respond "Deo gratias!" The triple taper formerly used was originally a precaution against the draughts of the church.

LUNETTE or LUNULA (Lat. *luna,* the moon). A crescent-shaped device or a double circle of gold or metal gilt, by means of which the Host is held securely and upright when exposed in a monstrance.

LUST. i. Any passionate enjoyment or desire.

ii. An inordinate appetite for venereal pleasure, indulgence of which is one of the seven deadly sins.

LUTHERANISM. The religious system founded by Martin Luther (1483-1546), an apostate Augustinian friar and author of the Reformation in Germany. Its leading ideas are justification by faith alone, radical corruption due to original sin, necessarianism, imputed grace, consubstantiation, the worthlessness of good works, private judgement (*qq.v.*). It is really a misnomer to call it a system, for there is a lack of method and coherence in Lutheranism which desystematizes it. Nearly two-thirds of the Lutherans of the world are still to be found in Germany; the remainder are chiefly in Norway, Sweden, Denmark, Finland and the U.S.A.; in the first three countries they form the state church. Rationalizing has been a disintegrating influence, but of recent years a "high-church" element has appeared.

LUXURY. i. The possession and use of everything which will gratify the sensitive appetites. This is not in itself sinful, but it may involve sins of excess and against justice and charity, for self-indulgence commonly blinds one to the rights and needs of others.

ii. Sinful indulgence in venereal pleasure (*q.v.*). This is an archaic usage of the word, now rarely heard in this sense.

LYONS, COUNCILS OF. The 1st (the thirteenth œcumenical council, 1245), was concerned with the excommunication of the Emperor Frederick II and other semi-political matters, imposed a levy on all benefices for three years to finance a new crusade, instituted the wearing of red hats by cardinals, etc. The 2nd (the fourteenth œcumenical, 1274) was a reunion council which, with the political aid of the Eastern emperor, effected the reunion of the Orthodox Eastern Church; it was repudiated again by Constantinople eight years later. The council also passed measures of canon law, including legislation of great importance for conclaves, some of which is still in force.

LYONS, THE FATHERS OF (Fr. *Missions Africaines de Lyon*). A congregation of secular priests founded there in 1856. They have mission territories in Africa, and missions to the Negroes of the United States. A few of these missionaries use the Coptic rite in Egypt.

LYONS, THE RITE OF. Certain liturgical peculiarities preserved in the archdiocese of Lyons. Among others at Mass are different preparatory prayers, sequences for Christmas, Epiphany, Ascension, and many other feasts, and special prefaces for Advent, St. John Baptist, All Saints and others; the bread and wine are offered together at the offertory; a "little elevation" during the Our Father, etc. Second Vespers of Easter is celebrated with great solemnity and a procession (as with the Carmelites and in other French dioceses, *e.g.*, Chartres); the *Magnificat* is sung three times. During Lent the liturgical colour is ashen, *i.e.*, grey. The canons of the cathedral wear mitres on doubles of the 1st and 2nd class, of the same colour as the vestments. This was the liturgy used by St. John Vianney, the *curé* of Ars.

M

MACE. A short heavy staff, usually of metal and ornamented with heraldic devices, carried before ecclesiastical and other personages and corporations (*e.g.*, a bishop, a chapter) as a sign of authority. The precentor's staff, still seen in some great churches (*e.g.*, at Solesmes), is a sort of mace.

MACHABEES, THE BOOKS OF, are four in number. The first two are deutero-canonical (*q.v.*) and were declared to be authentic parts of the canon of Scripture by the councils of both Florence and Trent. They are so called because they narrate the history of Judas Machabeus and his brothers in their leadership of the Jews against Antiochus Epiphanes and his successors in their endeavour to wipe out the Hebrew nation and religion, between 175 and 135 B.C. The second book, by a different writer, repeats some of the same events with more detail and with special reference to the worship of the Temple. Neither the authors nor dates of composition of these books are known. The two books called III and IV Machabees are apocryphal works not included in the canon of holy Scripture; Protestants reject all four.

MACHABEES, THE HOLY. Martyrs whose feast is observed throughout the Church, on Aug. 1 in the Western church by a commemoration in the office of the day. They were seven young Jews, who with their mother and their preceptor, Eleazar, refused to conform to the anti-Jewish rites of Antiochus Epiphanes in the 2nd century B.C. They are the only saints of the Old Testament who are honoured liturgically throughout the Western church. Their alleged relics rest beneath the altar of San Pietro in Vincoli at Rome.

MADONNA (It., my lady). A picture, statue or other image of the Blessed Virgin Mary; our Lady herself.

MAESTRO DI CAMERA (It., master of the room [of the pope]). The principal chamberlain who has authority over all other chamberlains and charge of the personal service of the pope. He makes all arrangements for audiences and pontifical ceremonies, and is custodian of the ring of the Fisherman (*q.v.*).

MAFRIAN (Syriac, the fructifier, a personal epithet that has become an official title). An office peculiar to the Syrian Jacobite Church formerly consisting in a primacy of jurisdiction under the patriarch over the dioceses of Arabia and Persia. But the "Mafrian and Katholikos of the East" is now only a titular bishop, a sort of vicar general and auxiliary to the Jacobite patriarch of Antioch.

MAGDALEN. A euphemism for a reformed and penitent prostitute, from the common notion that St. Mary Magdalen had been a harlot. Technically, the name was formerly given to members of religious congregations of penitents, and now to those in homes for the reclamation of prostitutes and other unfortunates. St. Mary Magdalen (*i.e.*, of Magdala, a town on the sea of Galilee; formerly called in English *Mawdleyn*) is venerated in the West as The Penitent and in the East as The Myrrh-bearer (Mark xvi, 1; *cf.*, the Three Marys). Her life has been the subject of numerous legends, of which the best known takes her to Provence and buries her at La Sainte Baume. That she is to be identified with the public sinner of Luke vii, 37, is the more probable view; that she became the pattern of the contemplative life (Luke x, 38-42) has always been the tradition of the West, though disputed by some of the Greek fathers.

MAGDEBURG CENTURIATORS, The. A group of historians who undertook to write the history of Christianity in the interests of Protestantism and of the particular views of their leader, Matthias Vlacich; their name is due to the first five volumes, published at Magdeburg, having each dealt with one century. Thirteen Latin volumes, covering the same number of centuries, appeared between 1559 and 1574. They were answered by Cardinal Baronius.

MAGI. A Median-Persian caste from whom the ministers of the Mazdean religion were taken and hence practically identical with Persian priests and prophets. The number of Magi, "the wise men," who saw the star (*q.v.*) in the east and visited the infant Christ at Bethlehem is not known, but they are usually depicted as three; mediæval legend gives them the names of Gaspar, Melchior and Balthasar, the first representing the Hamitic, or black, races. It is uncertain whether they found the prophecy in the books of the Zoroastrian religion or in the Jewish scriptures (in Num. xxiv, 17), as Jewish colonies were spread throughout Persia since the 7th century B.C. The Mazdean religion was the nearest approach to monotheism then known and its ministers were a respected class.

MAGIC (Turanian *imga*, profound, whence Old Persian, *magus*, a sorcerer). The power or practice of producing marvellous physical effects either through the invocation of evil spirits (this is black magic—a very grave sin of superstition, *q.v.*) or through means which are generally thought to be disproportionate to the effects they produce (this is white magic, which varies in its seriousness according to the gravity of the matter and the extent of the disproportion). The Church has always known the possibility of black magic (*cf.*, Witchcraft) and strictly forbidden its exercise to her children; but its incidence varies greatly with times and places and she does not lightly assume the activity of evil spirits at the request of men. In reference to the comparative study of religion, magic is found to be a corruption of religion, epidemic during the decay of civilizations.

MAGISTERIUM (Lat. *magister*, a master). The Church's divinely appointed authority to teach the truths of religion, "Going therefore, teach ye all nations . . . teaching them to observe all things whatsoever I have commanded you" (Matt. xxviii, 19-20). This teaching is infallible: "And behold I am with you all days, even to the consummation of the world" (*ibid.*) The solemn *magisterium* is that which is exercised only rarely by formal and authentic definitions of councils or popes. Its matter comprises dogmatic definitions of œcumenical councils or of the popes teaching *ex cathedra*, or of particular councils, if their decrees are universally accepted or approved in solemn form by the pope; also creeds and professions of faith put forward or solemnly approved by pope or œcumenical council. The ordinary *magisterium* is continually exercised by the Church especially in her universal practices connected with faith and morals, in the unanimous consent of the Fathers (*q.v.*) and theologians, in the decisions of Roman Congregations concerning faith and morals, in the common sense (*q.v.*) of the faithful, and various historical documents in which the faith is declared. All these are founts of a teaching which as a whole is infallible. They have to be studied separately to determine how far and in what conditions each of them is an infallible source of truth.

MAGISTRATUS. A layman who attends on a bishop at pontifical functions and at Mass may minister the ewer, basin and towel when the prelate washes his hands. There are often two *magistrati* in attendance.

MAGNA CARTA (Lat., the Great Charter). An instrument imposed on John, king of England, in 1215 designed to curb the power of the Crown for the advantage of the baronage. It was to a considerable extent the work of Cardinal Langton, archbishop of Canterbury, and provided *inter alia* for the freedom of the Church in England (*Ecclesia Anglicana*) from lay interference (especially in the matter of election of bishops), and that bishops and abbots should sit in the common council of the realm; it confirmed the competency of ecclesiastical courts to deal with matters of probate and intestacy, a state of affairs that subsisted almost to our own day.

MAGNANIMITY (Lat. *magnus*, great; *animus*, spirit). The just esteem of oneself as worthy of honour, combined with the consciousness that that worth is due to the mercy of God. It is a moral virtue allied to fortitude, for it has no fear of undeserved dishonour, knowing both supernatural rectitude and human worthlessness.

MAGNIFICAT, The. The canticle of our Lady (Luke i, 46-55), from the first word of the Latin version, *Magnificat anima mea Dominum*, "My soul doth magnify the Lord," said daily at Vespers; when the office is sung with solemnity the altar, minister, choir and people are incensed during this canticle. It is recited or sung standing and with a sign of the cross at the first verse, the words being those of the Gospel. On certain occasions (*e.g.*, feast of the Visitation), and in certain places (*e.g.*, Lyons, on Easter Sunday), the *Magnificat* is accompanied by the ringing of bells and other solemnities. In the Byzantine rite it is sung at *Orthros* (Lauds).

MAGNIFICENCE or Munificence, is a moral virtue to be attained only by those who are wealthy, whether in material goods, ability or virtue. It consists in the ability and willingness upon suitable occasions and in a good cause to expend one's wealth, talents or virtues lavishly and on a grand scale, using them according to the dictates of good judgement and right reason (*cf.*, Liberality).

MAGYAR. The language spoken by the people of Hungary. It is used liturgically by the Byzantine Catholics in that country.

MAJOR ORDERS. The sacred or major orders are the priesthood, diaconate and subdiaconate; when this last is received in the Western church a cleric is bound to celibacy and recitation of the Divine Office. The distinction between major and minor orders is not so clear in the East; *e.g.*, only the Gregorian Armenians among the dissidents count subdeacons as major clerics; other easterns, Catholic and dissident, count episcopacy as the third major order (*cf.*, Minor Orders).

MAJORDOMO. The official who formerly was head of the papal household in the Vatican. The office was abolished in 1929.

MALABAR, THE CHRISTIANS OF, the great majority of whom claim to be St. Thomas Christians (*q.v.*) in origin. They are now principally divided into: (*a*) Catholics of the Latin rite (about 500,000), mostly converts made by the Portuguese and Carmelite missionaries, those of the Syrian or Malabar rite, and the Malankarese (*qq.v.*). (*b*) The Nestorian party (Mellusians, *q.v.*). (*c*) The Jacobites, so called because when they went into schism in 1653, apparently being repulsed by or prevented from approaching the Nestorians, they eventually got an episcopate through the Jacobite patriarch of Antioch. They number about 363,000. About 1909 there arose a dispute among them about the nature of the jurisdiction of the Jacobite patriarch. One party fully accepted the patriarch's claims and is known as the patriarch's party; the other separated itself from the patriarch's obedience and placed itself under a *katholikos* chosen by themselves. It is doubtful if they really profess the monophysite heresy, but they certainly deny the primacy of the pope. Their orders and sacraments are valid. They use the West Syrian Rite. They have suffered much from quarrels and since 1816 from Protestant influence, so that there are also the Reformed Jacobites or Syrians (120,000). Under the influence of Anglican missionaries the worship of the latter has been "reformed" and the whole body is drifting towards Protestantism. They particularly arrogate to themselves the name of Mar Thomas Christians. There are several Protestant sects.

MALABAR RITE, The (better called Syro-Malabar). The system and forms of worship and administration of the sacraments used by the eastern Catholics of Malabar (*q.v.*) are according to the Chaldean rite (*q.v.*) as modified by the Synod of Diamper in 1599 and subsequently. The Syriac language and main lines of the Liturgy are preserved, but it is considerably latinized: Roman vestments, unleavened bread and communion in one kind are used and it has only one *anaphora*. The Divine Office was rearranged (the Psalter is spread over a fortnight, interspersed with hymns and prayers) and printed in 1875. The sacraments are now administered, with very slight changes, according to the Goan edition of the Roman "Rituale" translated into Syro-Chaldaic. The clergy dress as in the West and all the Western devotions (Benediction, rosary, scapulars, etc.) are popular. Leo XIII's prayers are said after low Mass. Their calendar is now that of the Roman church. The churches hardly differ from those of the Latin rite, but the older buildings have a style all their own.

MALABAR RITE, THE CATHOLICS OF THE, represent the true native church of south-west India, the St. Thomas Christians (*q.v.*). Whether or no they had ever embraced and renounced Nestorianism before the Synod of Diamper (*q.v.*), it is certain that they accepted the jurisdiction of the Latin archbishop of Goa, and thus came directly under the pope in 1599. A great schism occurred in 1653, largely due to the unreasonable efforts of the Portuguese to replace native customs and usages by those of Rome; it was somewhat repaired, but still remains (see *c* above). The Catholics number 928,000. They are now organized under the native archbishop of Ernakulam with three suffragans. The secular clergy are bound to celibacy; there is a congregation of native Carmelite regular tertiaries and congregations of native nuns with numerous convents. The faithful are divided into Norddists and Suddists (*q.v.*) and live mostly in Travancore and Cochin. Alone among Catholics of Eastern rites, the Malabarese (and now the Malankarese as well, *q.v.*) are able to do mission work among their non-Christian neighbours on a large scale.

MALABAR RITES, to be distinguished from the above, is the name given to a series of Hindu observances from which arose a controversy which had to do with the inland districts of Madura, Mysore and the Carnatic and not with the Malabar coast. The Jesuit missionaries of the 17th and 18th centuries, following the example of Fr. de Nobili (1577-1656), permitted their converts to retain certain Brahmin and Hindu customs, which they alleged had no religious significance or had been adapted to Christianity, but which others said were superstitious and idolatrous. Among these customs was the observance of caste (at one time there were distinct Brahmin and pariah missionaries); the Jesuits themselves lived as Indians; and their methods were exceedingly successful. The controversy as to their legality was carried on at intervals until the suppression of the Jesuits in 1773; on the whole, the Holy See was not unfavourable, though insisting on modification of certain practices (*cf.,* Chinese Rites).

MALACHIAS. The Greek form of the name *Malachi* (messenger of Yahveh), the last in order of time of the minor prophets and the last of the prophetical books of the Old Testament. He prophesied about 420 B.C., reproving the priesthood and the frequency of mixed marriages and divorces, announcing the coming of Christ to purify them, and warning unrepentant sinners; i, 10-11, are generally interpreted to refer to the eucharistic sacrifice. Malachias is named in the Roman Martyrology on Jan. 14.

MALANKARESE, The (*Malankara,* the old name of Malabar). A small but growing body (50,000 in 1946) of Indian Catholics of the West Syrian rite (*q.v.*) in Malabar. They date from 1930, when an archbishop, Mar Ivanios, and a bishop, Mar Theophilos, previously of the Malabar (*q.v. c*) Jacobite Church, came into communion with Rome with a number of their flock. They form an archdiocese (Trivandrum), with a suffragan diocese (Tiruvalla).

MALAYA, THE CHURCH IN. In the Malay states, Straits Settlements and adjoining areas there are about 6 million people, mostly Mohammedan, with about 100,000 Catholics. The mission of Malacca was founded by St. Francis Xavier, and is now a diocese (suffragan of Pondicherry in India), with its see at Singapore. North Borneo and Sarawak are prefectures apostolic.

MALAYALAM. A Dravidian language, closely related to Tamil, spoken by the people of Malabar. It is practically the sole liturgical language of the Malankarese (*q.v.*).

MALICE. The evil quality of an act by which it is opposed to the dictates of right reason. Malice may be found in any one of the three conditions for a human act, *i.e.,* in the purpose for which the act is performed, in the act itself, or in the circumstances in which the act takes place.

MALINES CONVERSATIONS, The. A series of conferences held at Malines between 1921-26 for the discussion of matters at issue between the Catholic Church and the Church of England. The conferences were private and quite unofficial, but were held with the approval of the Holy See and of the Anglican primate. Cardinal Mercier was the chairman and Viscount Halifax the principal Anglican concerned. After the death of Cardinal Mercier and the Abbé Portal in 1926 a report was drawn up and published (under Anglican auspices) and the conversations were not resumed.

MALTHUSIANISM. A term used, sometimes with the prefix *neo-,* for the theory that population tends to outstrip the means of subsistence and the corollary that some form of birth prevention (usually artificial) is necessary. It is derived from the name of Thomas Malthus (1766-1835) whose "Essay on the Principle of Population" popularized these ideas; he himself advocated "moral restraint" as the chief remedy.

MAMMON (Aramaic *mamon,* riches). Wealth regarded as a source of evil (*cf.,* Matt. vi, 24; Luke xvi, 9-13).

MAN. A rational creature composed of a body and a soul. The soul (*q.v.*), a spiritual substance, is united to the body as its substantial form (q.v.). Man's last end is happiness (q.v.).

MANDATUM, The. A Maundy Thursday observance, formerly confined to cathedral and monastic churches, but now extended to parish churches (if desired), when the bishop or other priest washes the feet of twelve men. It is in connexion with the celebration of the institution of the Holy Eucharist, referring to John xiii, 4-17. The name is from the first word of the initial antiphon *Mandatum novum do vobis* (A new commandment I give you). After the gospel of the Mass, the priest washes the feet while the choir sings certain antiphons; afterwards the priest says the Lord's Prayer silently, some versicles, and concludes with a prayer "that as here the outward stains are washed away for us and by us, so the inward sins of us all may be washed away by thee."

MANDEYLION, THE HOLY. An image of our Lord, impressed on a cloth according to the Armenian legend, painted by one Hannan according to the Syrian, and sent by our Lord with a letter (of which the text became a veritable charm all over Christendom in the middle ages) to King Abgar the Black at Edessa. The story is no longer believed, but whatever its origin, the picture was certainly there in 544 and its translation to Constantinople in 944 is commemorated by a feast on Aug. 16 in the Byzantine rite. It was stolen by Crusaders in 1207 and is now venerated in the church of S. Silvestro-in-Capite at Rome, though in the east is said to be only a copy and the original to have been lost at sea. There are copies of it in the Vatican, at Genoa in the church of St. Bartholomew-of-the-Armenians, and at the Mekhitarist monastery of St. Lazarus in Venice.

MANDYAS. i. A short black cloak, part of the habit of a Byzantine monk.
    ii. A large long mantle, blue or purple in colour, open in front but fastened at the neck and foot where it is ornamented with four squares of embroidery typifying the Scriptures, from which issue the streams of doctrine in the form of red and white horizontal stripes: it is the choir dress of a bishop in the Byzantine rite and is also worn in a modified form (black) by archimandrites.

MANICHÆISM. Doctrine of Manès (born and died in Persia, 3rd century) who taught a metaphysical and religious dualism. According to the doctrine there are two eternal first principles, God, the cause of all good, and matter, the cause of all evil; matter, or the Spirit of Evil, is also a god equal to the other. Manès, however, does not seem to have taught this doctrine formally; rather does his doctrine approach that of Plato and other ancient philosophers; but nevertheless he asserts that matter is not only the passive principle of evil but an active and very powerful principle. See EVIL. The Manichæans rejected the Old Testament, and admitted in the New Testament only what was in accordance with their opinions; the body being the work and effect of the Supreme Bad Principle all marriage is wrong and the begetting and bearing of children a crime (cf., Albigensianism, Catharism, etc.). In common speech Manichæism usually refers to the particular doctrine of the intrinsic evil of matter or at least to a supposed relative evil when compared with spirit.

MANIFESTATION OF CONSCIENCE. Laying open the whole state of one's spiritual life to another for guidance. Religious superiors are forbidden by canon law to induce their subjects to manifest their consciences to them; but subjects may spontaneously do so, and are generally recommended to if their superiors are priests.

MANIPLE (Lat. *manipulus*, a handful). A vestment worn at Mass by those in major orders, consisting of a band of silk of the colour of the day, worn over the left forearm, half on either side. Its modern pattern is about 3 ft. in length and 4¾ ins. wide, with splayed ends, often with a cross on each; a cross is prescribed only for the middle. The earlier form is longer and narrower, its edges parallel throughout. It was originally a linen handkerchief for use. The maniple is the distinctive badge of the subdeacon who is invested with it at ordination with the words, "Take the maniple, by which is meant the fruit of good works"; bishops when saying Mass do not put it on till after the *Confiteor*, except at a requiem. Professed Carthusian nuns are invested with a maniple when receiving the consecration of virgins (q.v.).

MANNA. i. The name given to the food with which the children of Israel were miraculously fed in the wilderness; it may have been a natural substance but what it was is not known. It is a special type of the Blessed Sacrament, the miraculous food given daily to sustain our souls (cf., John vi, 49-52).
    ii. Liquid exuding from the shrines or relics of certain saints is sometimes called manna, e.g., the *manna di Sant' Andrea* at Amalfi. See OIL OF SAINTS.

MANNERS. A code of rules governing external behaviour in social intercourse framed according to an accepted standard of propriety and good breeding. The learning and practice of this code is an important element in education. Nevertheless, a courteous bearing is not confined to the well educated and socially respectable; and good manners in a general sense are a fruit of Christian virtues, particularly of humility and charity.

MANRESA. A pilgrim shrine near Montserrat in Spain, being the place of the cave wherein St. Ignatius Loyola retired from the world and wrote his "Spiritual Exercises." The name is now often given to noviciates and retreat houses of the Society of Jesus, e.g., Manresa House, Roehampton.

MANSIONARIUS (Lat. *mansio,* a dwelling). A name now generally reserved for a cleric having a benefice in a cathedral or collegiate church and bound to reside there; a vicar choral.

MANSLAUGHTER. The name in English civil law for criminal homicide which lacks the malice aforethought (or intention) necessary to constitute murder. In Christian morals such manslaughter is not imputable to the agent if he did not advert to the danger of his action or if he reasonably supposed that no danger existed.

MANTELLATE, The. Formerly a common name in Italy for any tertiary sisters on account of the distinguishing dress which they wore. Now confined to and the usual name of the sisters of the Third Order Regular of the Servites, founded by St. Juliana Falconieri in 1305. They conduct schools, orphanages and similar works. The Divine Office or the Little Office B.V.M., is said in choir. Black habit and scapular.

MANTELLETTA (It.). A sleeveless outer garment, open in front but fastened at the neck, reaching nearly to the knees. It is worn by cardinals, bishops, abbots and certain prelates of the papal court. A bishop wears a purple (black or other colour if a regular) *mantelletta* over his rochet when present at a ceremony out of his diocese. The prelates *di mantelletta* are the superior prelates of the papal court (protonotaries apostolic, domestic prelates, etc., who form a college) who have the right to wear this garment (*cf., mantellone*).

MANTELLONE (It.). A purple cloak reaching to the ankles worn by inferior prelates of the papal court, the offices of many of whom cease with the death of the pope. They are called accordingly prelates *di mantellone* (*cf., mantelletta*).

MANTUM (Lat.). A cope, always either white or red in colour and with a short train, whose use is peculiar to the pope. When the liturgical colour is purple or black a red mantum is worn.

MANUAL MASSES. Those for which stipends are offered by the faithful, either of their own free will from time to time, or to satisfy an obligation attached to money inherited. Foundation Masses (*q.v.*) which cannot be said in the appointed place or by the appointed priest, and which have to be said elsewhere, are called manual Masses *ad instar.*

MANUAL OF PRAYERS, The. A book of prayers for congregational use in church

authorized by the English hierarchy in 1886. It contains morning and night prayers, preparation and thanksgiving for Mass, devotions "to the Unity and Trinity of God," to Jesus Christ, to the Blessed Sacrament, to the Sacred Heart, to the Holy Ghost, to the Blessed Virgin Mary, the *Bona Mors,* etc. "But while the use of popular devotions (*q.v.*) is warmly recommended, the difference between liturgical and extra-liturgical services must be borne in mind. . . ." (Preface).

MANUTERGE, -IUM. A towel for use in connexion with divine worship, e.g., the small linen used at the *lavabo.*

MAPPULA (late Lat., a small napkin). The linen gremial (*q.v.*) used by each of the three sacred ministers whenever they are seated at Mass in the Dominican rite.

ii. A portable canopy (*q.v.*) of honour.

MAR (Syriac, lord). A title given in all Syriac rites to saints and bishops, e.g., Mar Elias (the prophet), Mar Alexander (bishop of Kottayam). Mar is the masculine and Mart the feminine form, e.g., *Mart Mariam,* the Blessed Mary.

MARAN-ATHA in I. Cor. xvi, 22, is an Aramaic expression meaning "the Lord is near" or "O Lord, come." It is often confused with the curse conveyed in the previous word *anathema* (*q.v.*) and has so been incorporated into the most solemn form of excommunication.

MARAÑOS. Spanish Jews who, having received Baptism, relapsed into Judaism. The Spanish Inquisition proceeded against these but not against Jews as such.

MARCIONISM. A heresy, or series of heresies, taking its name from Bishop Marcion who seceded from the Church in 144: one of the many manifestations of Gnosticism and Manichæism (*qq.v.*). To the Marcionites our Lord was a manifestation (*cf.,* Docetism) of the Holy and Good God, who was opposed to the God of the Old Testament, the *Demiurge;* they therefore rejected those writings (together with all the New Testament except ten epistles of St. Paul and a mutilated gospel of St. Luke) as the revelation and law of an inferior, evil principle; matter being worthless, there would be no resurrection of the body, and Baptism was refused to those living in matrimony. Marcion's followers were highly organized and troubled the Church for 500 years, eventually being swallowed up in Manichæism (*cf.,* Paulicians).

MARIA MONK. An impostor who has given her name to a whole class of similar rogues who make money out of the gullibility of many people where the Catholic Church is concerned. She was a woman of very loose morals who falsely claimed to have been a nun in a Montreal convent and in 1835 published "Maria Monk's Awful Disclosures" wherein, *inter alia,* she gave an account of the murder of a nun by the bishop of Montreal and five priests. Her true history and the falsity of her allegations were made public several times in England and North America during the next few years, but her book still has a sale in pornographic book shops and there are still some who profess to believe in her integrity. She was mentally deranged and her stories were in part encouraged by unscrupulous persons. She died while in jail for pocket-picking in 1849.

MARIAMETTES *(Maryamat).* The Syrian Sisters of the Sacred Hearts of Jesus and Mary *(q.v.).*

MARIAN PRIESTS. Those priests in the reign of Queen Elizabeth who had been ordained in England, mostly in Mary's reign, as opposed to seminary priests, ordained abroad. They were excepted from the Act of 1585 which made it high treason for a priest to enter or remain in the country, but were required to take the oath of supremacy against the Holy See by the Act of 1559. A minority of them refused and lost their benefices. What happened to them is not known in detail; probably the majority simply vacated their cures when they saw what was coming and so were not expelled by process of law. But so late as 1593 over 40 Marian priests were ministering to the faithful in secret.

MARIANNHILL FATHERS, The. A small missionary congregation in South Africa, founded in 1882 by Dom Francis Pfanner, as a monastery of Cistercians, from whom they were separated in 1909. They have charge of the vicariates apostolic of Mariannhill and Umtata. Their official name is the Religious Missionaries of Mariannhill, which is in Natal.

MARIANOPOLITANUS. The Latin epithet for the archbishop of Montreal, formerly called Ville-Marie; also for the bishop of Sault Sainte Marie in the United States.

MARIANS, The. The Marian Clerks Regular of the Immaculate Conception were founded in Poland in 1673 by the Ven. Stanislaus Papczinski, for missionary and educational work among Poles, Lithuanians, Byelorussians, etc. Of their three provinces, one is in North America. Some of the members are of the Slav-Byzantine rite.

MARIAVITES, The. A sect in Poland originating in 1906 with a number of apostate clergy, associated with the Old Catholics *(q.v.)* since 1918. There are said to have been 100,000 Mariavites in 1939.

MARIOLATRY. Idolatrous worship of the Blessed Virgin Mary, with which Catholics have been, and by the ignorant still are, frequently charged. "It is forbidden to give divine honour or worship to the angels and saints [of whom Mary is one] for this belongs to God alone . . . we should pay to [them] an inferior honour or worship for this is due to them as the servants and special friends of God" ("The Penny Catechism"). See LATRIA; HYPERDULIA; DULIA.

MARIOLOGY. The study of the Blessed Virgin Mary and the body of theology, history, speculation, etc., concerning her, particularly her relationship with the Incarnation and Redemption.

MARISTS, The. i. The Society of Mary, a congregation of missionary priests founded in 1816 at Lyons by the Ven. John Claud Colin. They take the usual (simple) vows, with one of stability after ten years' profession. Their principal foreign missions are in the South Seas, but they also conduct home missions and boys' schools. There is an Anglo-Irish province, and provinces in the United States, New Zealand and elsewhere.
    ii. The Little Brothers of Mary or Marist Brothers of the Schools. An institute of teaching brothers founded by the Ven. Benedict Marcellinus Champagnat in 1817, with schools throughout the world. In Oceania and elsewhere they work in cooperation with the Marist fathers (above).
    iii. Sisters of the Holy Name of Mary, founded by Father Colin to teach girls and to care for orphans.
    iv. Missionary Sisters of the Society of Mary, who assist the Marist fathers in their foreign missions.

MARK, ST. i. Evangelist, whose feast is observed throughout the Church, nearly everywhere on April 25. He is supposed to be the young man who ran away naked at the taking of Jesus (Mark xiv, 51-52); he was certainly with St. Paul on his first mission and at other times; he probably founded the church of Alexandria and was martyred there about the year 74.
    ii. His gospel. This was written in Greek, probably for Roman readers, some time before the year 70. It is generally accepted that Mark's knowledge was derived from the preaching of St. Peter, and he emphasizes Jesus Christ as the Son of God incarnate, demonstrating by his miracles his power over the Father's creation. In 1913 the Biblical Commission *(q.v.)* affirmed the soundness of the arguments for the authorship by Mark, disciple and interpreter of St. Peter, of the gospel which bears his name. Further, it rejected the attempts of certain critics to prove the unauthenticity of the last twelve verses of chapter xvi. See also the SYNOPTIC PROBLEM.

MARKS OF THE CHURCH, The, *i.e.,* her notes or characteristics, are unity, holiness, catholicity and apostolicity *(qq.v.).* These four essential characteristics, proper to the

Catholic Church alone, visibly manifest to the world that she is the true Church of Christ.

MARONITE RITE, The. The system and forms of worship and administration of the sacraments used by the Maronites; the only Eastern rite used by Catholics only. The eucharistic liturgy is the Syrian St. James, in Syriac and Arabic, much modified, especially by way of "latinization." Maronite churches are in appearance indistinguishable from those of the West, and Roman vestments slightly modified (*e.g.*, "cuffs" instead of maniple) are worn by priests; bishops, lower clergy and servers have Syrian garments. The Liturgy begins with the preparation of the elements (unleavened bread) and a sort of *Confiteor;* a server reads the epistle which, with the gospel, is in Arabic; there are eight printed anaphoras; the words of consecration are said aloud, the people answering "Amen"; the ancient *epiklesis* is reduced to a prayer for the communicants; there is an elevation of each species, with genuflexions, before the priest's communion; the communion of the people is in one kind; the Liturgy ends with a long blessing. The prayers prescribed for the West by Pope Leo XIII are said after low Mass, and the "sanctus bell" is used. There is a regular equivalent to low Mass, but at which incense is normally used; the people kneel throughout the Liturgy. The Divine Office, founded on that of the Syrian rite, consists of seven "hours", with relatively few psalms but a large number of hymns. Baptism is by infusion as in the West. Confirmation is administered only by a bishop or his delegate; the indicative form of absolution is used; there are three minor orders, singer, reader and subdeacon. Parts of the "Rituale Romanum". are used in Syriac and Arabic with but little alteration. General Western feasts (*e.g.*, Corpus Christi) and Benediction, rosary, stations of the cross, devotion to the Sacred Heart, etc., are more in use than among any other Catholics of Eastern rite except the Malabarese.

MARONITES, The. A nation and church of Arabic-speaking Syrians living chiefly in the Lebanon. They are all Catholics, with their own proper rite and canon law. Their name is derived from Bait-Marun, a monastery founded at the shrine of St. Maro (d.433), on the river Orontes. Their later history begins at the time of the Crusades, and the Holy See recognized their chief bishop as a patriarch in 1254. They are now organized under their patriarch ("of Antioch") at Bekerke, who at one time was also temporal head of his people. There are nine other dioceses. There is a college for their secular clergy at Rome; married men may receive holy orders. There is a considerable number of Maronite monks (Antonians, *q.v.*) and a congregation of missionary priests, as well as houses of contemplative nuns and other convents. There are about 350,000 Maronites in Syria, Palestine, Egypt and Cyprus, and over 50,000 in the U.S.A., Australia and elsewhere. Those in the U.S.A. are subject to the Latin ordinaries, who must administer Maronite canon law in their respect; this is principally determined by the decrees of the Council of Dair Saïdat al-Luaizeh (Convent of Our Lady of the Almond Trees) in 1736. The Maronites, like other Syrians, are notable for their number of scholars, of whom the best known is Joseph Simeon Assemani (al-Sam'ani), 1687-1768. The three brothers Massabki, Francis, Abdulmuti and Raphael, all laymen martyred by Moslems in 1860, were beatified in 1926 and the causes of two monks and a nun, confessors, have been introduced.

MARQUISES OF THE CANOPY. The heads of the four houses of Patrizi, Sacchetti, Theodoli and Costaguti who formerly had the hereditary right to carry the canopy over the pope in solemn ceremonies. They have various privileges which otherwise appertain only to Roman princes and dukes. Their office is now discharged by notaries of the Signatura or other prelates.

MARRIAGE. The contract between a man and a woman by which they are associated and united with one another as a common principle for the generation of children and for their upbringing and education. Its basis is the mutual consent of the parties, and its essential properties are unity and indissolubility (*qq.v.*). The matrimonial contract between baptized persons is a sacrament of which the contracting parties are the ministers; the marriages of the unbaptized are not sacramental; but in either case the essential properties, rights and duties are the same. See MATRIMONY, SACRAMENT OF.

MARRIAGE BY PROXY is under certain circumstances lawful, under the conditions and with the safeguards laid down in the Code of Canon Law.

MARRIAGE, CONDITIONAL. If marriage is contracted with a lawful condition regarding the future, its validity is suspended until the fulfilment of the condition. If the condition is unlawful and contrary to the substance of marriage, the marriage is invalid; if unlawful, but not contrary to the substance of marriage, or if impossible, the marriage is valid, and the condition is to be ignored. A condition referring to the past or present makes the marriage valid or void according as the condition is already verified or not.

MARRIAGE, SPIRITUAL. The ultimate term of the mystic union (*q.v.*), called also Transforming Union, the seventh and last mansion of St. Teresa's "Interior Castle." To the closeness and intimacy of the soul's union with God, "like the raindrops that fall into the river," is due the name of this last degree of prayer. It is a practically indissoluble state, in which the consciousness of the presence of God in the soul, hitherto intermittent, becomes clear and abiding. Its effects are complete surrender into the hands of God, a thirst to suffer for him, and a most ardent zeal for souls. Ecstasies in this state are very rare. It is preceded by the "spiritual betrothal," in which in a vision, generally intellectual, Christ promises to unite the soul to himself in an indissoluble union. The spiritual marriage is not such an absorption of the soul in God that the two become actually one: God and his creatures always remain irrevocably distinct.

MARRIAGE, INDISSOLUBILITY OF. A consummated sacramental marriage can be dissolved only by death. One *ratum non consummatum* (*q.v.*) may be dissolved by the Holy See for a grave reason or by the taking of solemn religious vows; and a non-sacramental marriage by exercise of the Pauline privilege (*q.v.*). This indissolubility is of natural law (*Syllabus* of Pius IX, n. 67), the children's good requiring the permanent union of the parents, special cases to the contrary notwithstanding; these are provided for by separation (*q.v.*) "from bed and board." The indissolubility of marriage is upheld by the civil law of Italy, Spain and Malta (where the states accept the matrimonial provisions of canon law in their entirety), Ireland, Monaco, the Argentine, Peru, Cuba, Brazil, Colombia and Paraguay.

MARRIAGE, UNITY OF. The principle that no man can have more than one wife at the same time (*cf.*, polygamy), and no woman more than one husband (*cf.*, polyandry). This principle of the natural law in the first case provides for the mutual faith which must subsist between husband and wife; in the second for the good of the offspring (otherwise paternity is indeterminate, etc.). One whose partner dies is at perfect liberty to take another, and so on without restriction of number; but a twice-married man is irregular (*q.v.*) for reception of holy orders; and in the Eastern churches a third or subsequent marriage is looked on with considerable disfavour.

MARRIAGE CEREMONIES. The ritual of marriage is the least uniform of any in the Church. A simple and short rite (including the ancient "hand-fast") is given in the "Rituale Romanum" but every country may use its own form, that of Great Britain being a modification of the use of Sarum (*q.v.*). After having expressed their consent the bride and groom plight troth in a formula common to both and the priest declares them married. He then blesses gold, silver and a ring and the groom gives the gold and silver to the bride saying: "With this ring I thee wed; this gold and silver I thee give; with my body I thee worship; and with all my worldly goods I thee endow. In the name of the Father (here he puts the ring on the bride's thumb), and of the Son (here on the first finger) and of the Holy Ghost (here on the second finger), Amen." He puts it on the third finger and there leaves it. Then follow *Kyrie eleison*, the Our Father silently, some versicles and a final prayer by the priest. The bride and groom are themselves the ministers of the sacrament, which has its essence or "proximate matter" in the mutual promise with which the rite begins; the priest's function is to express the blessing of the Church. Note that the bride makes no promise of obedience; this is understood, and sufficiently expressed in the nuptial Mass (especially its epistle) which should follow the above ceremony. The most notable characteristic of marriage ceremonies in all Eastern churches is the crowning of the parties by the priest, which sometimes gives its name to the whole rite; but all countries and peoples have their own customs, as in the West.

MARRIAGE OF CLERGY. The marriage of a priest, whether bachelor or widower, must be distinguished from the ordination to the priesthood of a married man. The first is forbidden throughout the Catholic Church and by the canons of all the other ancient churches since at least the 4th century. See CELIBACY.

MARRIAGE OF CONSCIENCE, or secret marriage, is one celebrated without banns before a priest and witnesses who are bound to secrecy. For such the bishop's permission is necessary; in an urgent case, at a deathbed to regularize a union or for other grave reason, his permission may be assumed.

MARRIAGE OF THE UNBAPTIZED. The Church has no power to deal with the marriages of unbaptized persons contracting between themselves, except to interpret authoritatively the natural and divine law which binds all mankind. The state has the power to regulate such marriages, even making conditions for their validity. Marriages between baptized and unbaptized fall under the jurisdiction of the Church, even if the baptized persons are non-Catholics. Marriages between Catholics and unbaptized are invalid without a dispensation; not so those between baptized non-Catholics and unbaptized (since the Code of 1918). The marriages of unbaptized persons are indissoluble by divine law, except for the Pauline privilege (*q.v.*); nevertheless they are not sacramental, because the unbaptized are not capable of receiving other sacraments; upon the baptism of both parties the marriage becomes sacramental without renewal of consent, but not upon the baptism of one party only.

MARTINMAS. An old English name for the feast of St. Martin of Tours, Nov. 11. The name St. Martin's Summer for fine weather about this time refers to the same feast.

MARTYR (Gr. μάρτυς, later μάρτυρ, a witness). i. One who suffers martyrdom (*q.v.*).

ii. The Martyrs usually refers to those of the first three centuries of the Church, victims of Roman persecution; *cf.*, the Era of the Martyrs dating from Aug. 29, 284 (persecution of Diocletian), the Acts of the Martyrs etc. They it was who were first regarded as saints, their relics venerated and churches dedicated in their honour.

iii. Up to about the middle of the 3rd century the name was also given to those who suffered for or were notable confessors of the faith, irrespective of actual death.

MARTYRS OF THE COMMUNE, The. Mgr. Darboy, archbishop of Paris, and a number of clergy and laymen murdered by soldiers and others of the Commune in Paris on May 24, 25 and 26, 1871.

MARTYRS OF COMPIÈGNE, The. Sixteen sisters of the Carmel of Compiègne (10 choir nuns, 1 novice, 3 lay-sisters, 2 extern-sisters), put to death by the guillotine in Paris in 1794 for leading the religious life contrary to the laws of the Revolution. They were beatified in 1906 and their feast is kept by the Carmelites and in certain dioceses on July 24.

MARTYRS OF DAMASCUS, The. Eight Friars Minor and three Maronite laymen put to death by Mohammedans during the Lebanon massacre of 1860. Beatified by Pope Pius XI in 1926.

MARTYRS OF EGYPT, The. Numerous members of the church of Alexandria who gave their lives for Christ under the Roman emperors, in the Arian and Eutychian controversies, and under the Moslems. Several groups are named in the Roman Martyrology under various dates. The native Christians of Egypt (Copts) reckon their years from the persecution of Diocletian.

MARTYRS OF JAPAN, The. Numerous sufferers for the faith in Japan in the 16th, 17th, 18th and 19th centuries (over 100,000 in all) but particularly the 28 missionaries and converts in 1597 canonized by Pope Pius IX in 1862, whose feast-day is Feb. 5. Others have since been beatified.

MARTYRS OF NORTH AMERICA, The. Six Jesuits and 2 laymen who were martyred by Indians at various dates and places between 1642 and 1649, and were canonized in 1930. They were SS. John Brébeuf, Isaac Jogues, René Goupil, John Lalande, Antony Daniel, Gabriel Lalemant, Charles Garnier and Noel Chabanel. Their feast is kept on March 16 and September 26.

MARTYRS OF OXFORD UNIVERSITY, The. Those of the English martyrs (*q.v.*) who were members of that university; they have a special feast in the archdiocese of Birmingham on Dec. 1.

MARTYRS OF PERSIA, The. Numerous sufferers in Persia between 339 and 628, especially those mentioned in the Roman Martyrology on April 22.

MARTYRS OF SEPTEMBER, OR DES CARMES, The. One hundred and ninety-one clerics, secular and regular, including three bishops, put to death in hatred of the Faith by revolutionaries at the Carmelite church and elsewhere in Paris, Sept. 2 and 5, 1792. Beatified by Pope Pius XI in 1926

MARTYRS OF TYRE, THE INNUMER. ABLE. "Blessed martyrs whose number the wisdom of God alone can tell, who were slain by Veturius, the commander of the troops, under the emperor Diocletian, by many kinds of torment in turn succeeding each other" (The Roman Martyrology). A feast in their honour is observed in some places on Feb. 20.

MARTYRS OF UGANDA, The. About a hundred Africans who were killed by their king, Mwanga, in 1886, in an attempt to stamp out Christianity, partly because it interfered with his own vicious habits. Charles Lwanga, Matthias Marumba and twenty others were beatified in 1920.

MARTYRDOM. The voluntary endurance of death for the Catholic faith, or for any article therof, or for the preservation of some Christian virtue, or for some other act of virtue relating to God. To be a martyr one must actually be put to death or die as a direct result of one's sufferings. The unbaptized who suffer martyrdom thereby become justified and attain Heaven (baptism of blood; Matt. x, 32, 39) whether they are infants or adults, provided in the case of adults that they have attrition for their sins; therefore the Church never prays for the repose of the souls of martyrs. According to Pope Benedict XIV, a heretic or schismatic in good faith who dies for a point of the true faith is a martyr in the eyes of God (*coram Deo*) but not *coram Ecclesia;* and he did not deny the possibility that the same was true of one who died for an erroneous assertion, believing it to be of the faith. Of martyrdom in a vulgar use of the word St. Thomas says: "The truth of other sciences has no connexion with the worship of the Godhead; hence it is not called truth according to godliness and consequently the confession thereof cannot be said to be the direct cause of martyrdom" (II-II, cxiv, 5).

MARTYRION. A primitive name for the place of burial of a martyr, for a church built over a martyr's tomb, and then for any church; in particular, the basilica built by

Constantine to the east of Calvary, enclosing the cistern wherein the True Cross had been found.

MARTYROLOGY. A list for every day of the year of martyrs and other saints whose feasts or commemorations occur on each day, generally with a brief note about each individual. It may be local and proper to a district or religious order or it may aim at being general by the combination and collation of several local martyrologies: such is the Roman Martyrology (*q.v.*). Feasts of our Lord and of our Lady are also included. See SYNAXARION.

MARTYROLOGY, THE ROMAN, though to a considerable extent general in scope, is confined in use to the Western church. It makes no claim to be exhaustive; it contains over 5,000 entries, but the early martyrs (and some others) often appear in groups, with only one or some of their names recorded; the names of newly canonized saints are added to it. Some religious orders insert their own *beati* and other special feasts into the Roman Martyrology (*e.g.*, the Franciscans, Jesuits, Servites); others have a proper Martyrology of their own (*e.g.*, the Dominicans). "The Roman Martyrology" is a liturgical book and when the Divine Office is said in choir (the rubric says, "This may fittingly be also done in private"), a lesson therefrom is read daily (except on the last three days of Holy Week) at the end of Prime; this lesson consists of the entries for the following day, the feast whose office is observed being read first. (In monasteries this takes place in the chapter-house.) An historical statement in the "Martyrology" as such has no authority; its objective truth (except where it is a subject of the Church's definitions) must be tested by the ordinary scientific methods. A number of entries in the Roman Martyrology are found to be unsatisfactory when so tested.

MARY (Aramaic *Maryam* for Heb. *Miryam;* Gr. Μαριάμ; Lat. *Maria;* Irish *Muire,* when the Mother of God is referred to, all other Marys are *Moira;* Welsh *Mair;* Scots *Maire*). The derivation and meaning of the name of our Lady are uncertain, but it may mean "wished-for child"; it seems certainly to have nothing to do with "bitterness," "the sea," or "a star." It is now the commonest of all baptismal names; in several religious orders of both sexes it is customary to add it to the name taken at profession. A feast of the Holy Name of Mary is observed by the Western church, on Sept. 12; it bears the same relation to that of the Holy Name of Jesus as the feast of her Immaculate Heart bears to that of his Sacred Heart.

MARY, THE BLESSED VIRGIN. A Jewish maiden of the house of David, whose parents are commonly referred to as Joachim and Anne; at her conception she was preserved by God from all stain of original sin (the Immaculate Conception, *q.v.*); she was betrothed to a carpenter, Joseph; at the Annunciation (*q.v.*) the second Person of the Blessed Trinity took flesh in her womb by the power of the Holy Ghost, but her marriage to Joseph took place (Matt. i, 19-24); in due course she gave birth at Bethlehem to Jesus, the God-man. Both before and after her miraculous childbearing she was a virgin and so remained all her days, according to the unanimous and perpetual tradition and teaching of the Church. After her death her body was taken up into Heaven (the Assumption, *q.v.*). Mary is the mother of Jesus, Jesus is God, therefore she is the mother of God; the denial of this was condemned by the 3rd general council at Ephesus in 431; and that she remained for her whole life absolutely sinless is affirmed by the Council of Trent. As the "second Eve" Mary is the spiritual mother of all living; Catholics venerate her with an honour above that accorded to other saints (*hyperdulia, q.v.*), but different from the divine worship given to God only; they pray to her, and she in Heaven intercedes with her son, God the Son, for them. Recognizing that Mary is a creature and that all her dignity comes from God, devotion to her is far removed from the idolatry which prejudice has sometimes associated with it. It is a link binding men to God, based on the fact that she is mother of God. It has been a characteristic of Catholics from the earliest times, as is evident from monuments and from the writings of the Fathers. Her principal feast throughout the Church is that of her Assumption (Aug. 15).

MARY, SATURDAY OFFICE OF THE BLESSED VIRGIN. On all Saturdays of the year, except those of Advent, Lent, ember-times, vigils, and feasts above the rank of simple, the Divine Office is of our Lady, for which a proper office (*in Sabbato*) is provided in the Breviary. When this office displaces a simple feast a commemoration thereof is made at Vespers and Lauds.

MARYHELP ABBEY. See BELMONT.

MARYKNOLL FATHERS, The. A congregation of priests for the foreign missions, founded at the Maryknoll seminary, New York, in 1911 by Bishop J. A. Walsh and the Rev. T. F. Price. The members, over 200 in number, have charge of certain missionary areas in China.

MASCOT (from Provençal *masco*, a witch). Any object that is believed to bring luck. Such a belief is superstitious and therefore forbidden to Catholics, even though the object is a religious one.

MASS. i. See SACRIFICE OF THE MASS.

ii. The English form of Latin *Missa*, the official name of the eucharistic sacrifice, and of its liturgy of prayers and ceremonies, throughout the Western church and not properly used of any but the Latin liturgies (but *cf.*, Sacrifice of the Mass). The derivation of the word has been much discussed; it appears certainly to be from *missio*, meaning dismissal, having reference to the dismissal of the catechumens, public penitents and energumens before the offertory, and that of the faithful at the end (where we still have the words *Ite missa est*). Why and how the name of a part, and this particular part, of the Liturgy came to be used for the whole can only be explained by a reference to the growth of similar usages, *e.g.*, Maundy Thursday (*q.v.*). Before the 6th century the Mass was called *oblatio* (offering), *sacrificium* (sacrifice), *mysterium* (mystery), etc. The word has been naturalized in most European languages (*e.g.*, Fr. *messe*; Ger. *Messe*; Ital. *messa*; Span. *misa*), but not in the Celtic tongues; Welsh, *yr offeren*, Cornish, *an offeren*, Irish, *an t-aifreann*, Scots, *an aifrionn*, all mean simply, The Offering.

iii. There are four distinct types of the celebration of Mass, each one of which is an equally true and proper offering of the sacrifice; they are Pontifical Mass (of which Papal Mass is a special form), High or Solemn Mass, Sung Mass, and Low Mass (*qq.v.*). Masses are also differentiated in other ways, *e.g.*, according to their function in the life of the Church (parochial Mass, conventual Mass), according to their object or occasion (requiem Mass), etc.; these are explained herein under their separate names; each one may be celebrated in any one of the above four ways.

iv. Though it is the usual custom, priests are not bound to celebrate Mass every day; but all are bound to do so several times a year and their bishops are directed to see that they say Mass at least on all Sundays and holidays of obligation, on which days the faithful are bound to assist thereat. Except on Christmas day and All Souls, priests are forbidden to celebrate more than once in a day (but see DUPLICATION). Mass may be said on every day of the year except Good Friday; low Mass is forbidden on Maundy Thursday and Holy Saturday, except by leave of the bishop on the former. The general law at present is that Mass may not be begun before one hour before dawn nor after 1 p.m.

v. Musically (*e.g.*, Mass no. IX, *Cum iubilo*), the word Mass denotes a musical setting of the common parts that are sung (*Kyrie, Gloria, Credo, Sanctus, Agnus Dei*). Liturgically (*e.g.*, the Mass of St. Joseph), on the contrary, it means the parts proper (*q.v.*) to a particular feast or day.

MASS, APPLICATION OF. The Mass being an impetratory and propitiatory sacrifice, as well as one of worship and thanksgiving, can be offered or applied for the living and the dead, and for any good end. The fruit of the Mass is threefold: general, which accrues to all mankind, and especially to those participating; special or ministerial, which benefits the person or object for which it is expressly applied; and personal, which belongs to the celebrant himself. The application of Mass means its being offered to gain the second of these fruits. It is for the celebrant alone to determine the application, which he may do freely, except when bound by law (*e.g.*, Mass for the people) or contract (*e.g.*, from stipends) or promise. Mass may not be applied publicly for excommunicated persons; it may be applied to them privately, but in the case of a *vitandus* for his conversion only (*cf.*, Fruits of the Mass).

MASS, EVENING, and nocturnal, was forbidden from the 11th century till recently; but it persisted in some places, which may account for the reference thereto in *Romeo and Juliet* (iv, 1), though this more likely refers to Vespers which was sometimes loosely called Evening Mass. During world-war II celebration of Mass at any time after noon was allowed to military chaplains, and since then evening Mass, at the discretion of the bishop, has become common in various circumstances. It has proved one of the most fruitful of recent reforms.

MASS, MIDNIGHT. The first of the three Masses of Christmas day, which begins at midnight; except by apostolic indult, only a conventual or parochial celebration is allowed at this hour. The celebrant usually fasts the previous six hours, not in virtue of any law, but because of its becomingness; lay people who are going to receive holy communion are likewise not bound to any fast, but to do so from 9 p.m. is a common practice. Midnight Mass is by no means a universal custom, but is usual in England; where it can be done it should be preceded by Matins and followed by Lauds. Its liturgy has particular reference to the birth of Jesus in the flesh and its proper is taken from the Messianic Psalms 2 and 109.

MASS, THE LITURGY OF THE, ordinarily consists of the following parts; those here printed in italics vary according to the day or feast which is being celebrated: the preparation, the incensing of the altar (at high Mass), *introit*, Kyrie eleison, the Gloria in excelsis on feasts, and Sundays outside Advent, Septuagesima and Lent, *collect(s)*, *epistle*, *gradual* (followed in only five Masses by a *sequence*), *gospel* (followed by the sermon if there is one; it is no part of the Mass), the Nicene Creed (only on Sundays and chief feasts), *offertory-verse*, offertory of bread and wine, incensing of altar, offerings and all present (at high Mass), lavabo, prayer to the Holy Trinity, *secret*, *preface*, sanctus, the canon wherein takes place the consecration, the Our Father with its embolism, breaking of the Host, Agnus Dei, three prayers preparatory to communion (including at high Mass the kiss of peace), communion of the celebrant and then of the people, ablutions, *communion-verse, post-communion prayer(s)*, the dismissal, blessing, last gospel (*qq.v.*). All this is said and done by the celebrant at the middle of the altar with his back to the people, except the gospel and last gospel, said at the gospel side, and the introit, collects, epistle, gradual, preparation of the chalice, lavabo, ablutions, communion-verse and post-communion, at the epistle side. The liturgy of the Mass to-day is substantially as it was at the beginning of the 7th century; in particular, the canon is practically unchanged since the alterations of Pope St. Gregory the Great. The beginnings of a fixed liturgy are made clear by St. Clement in 96, and by the middle of the 2nd century its outline as we know it is clearly recognizable.

MASS OF THE CATECHUMENS. That part of the Mass, from the beginning until the offertory, at which, in primitive times, catechumens, public penitents, and energumens were allowed to be present, being excluded from the sacrifice proper in accordance with the discipline of the secret (*q.v.*). It may originally have been a separate service, and even now its construction of litanies, chants, Scripture lessons and prayers is notably different from the rest—a difference emphasized at a pontifical Mass, when it takes place at the throne and not at the altar. In the Liturgy of St. John Chrysostom (and some others) the catechumens are still dismissed by the deacon before the *Cherubikon*, "All the catechumens go out . . .," but of course they do not go now.

MASS OF THE DEAD. See REQUIEM MASS.

MASS OF THE FAITHFUL. That part of the Mass from the offertory to the end, the sacrifice proper, comprising the offering, immolation and communion, to which in primitive times only the baptized faithful were admitted.

MASS OF OBLIGATION. Every Catholic is bound to assist at Mass once on every Sunday and holiday of obligation (*q.v.*), unless prevented by sickness, distance, urgent duties or the requirements of charity. The obligation may be fulfilled in any public church or semi-public oratory, and the Mass need not be of one's own rite; *e.g.*, a Latin may fulfil his duty in a Catholic Eastern church and *vice versa*. One must be present at the very least from the offertory till after the communion; if one involuntarily misses a considerable part, there is an obligation to hear the corresponding part of another Mass if possible: the intention of the Church is that the worshipper should be present throughout the whole service. There must be the intention of assisting at the sacrifice

and at the very least external attention (*q.v.*) is required, though the Church strongly urges that we should attend with devotion and intelligence. The distance from church which excuses from this obligation depends on age, facilities for transit, etc.

MASS FOR THE PEOPLE. A Mass which canon law requires to be applied by pastors for the faithful under their care. Diocesan bishops and rectors of parishes and some others are bound to apply Mass for the people on all Sundays and holydays (including suppressed feasts, *i.e.*, feasts of devotion). They must celebrate the Mass personally, unless legitimately impeded. No stipend may be received for this Mass. Missionaries are bound by the law on a few days only.

MASS OF A SAINT. One celebrated in honour of a saint, in thankfulness for his triumph and to obtain his intercession in Heaven. The proper of the Mass has reference, direct or indirect, to the life of the saint, and is generally said on his feast-day (*i.e.*, the anniversary of his death). But it must be clearly understood that the Mass is, and can be, addressed and offered to God alone.

MASS AT SEA. Mass may not be said on a ship at sea, except by cardinals and bishops, unless the priest has a special indult so to do; and even so not unless the sea be calm and the place of celebration decent and respectable.

MASS OFFERING. See STIPEND.

MASS-PENNY. The money offered at the altar rails at the offertory of the Mass in the middle ages, a contribution to the cost of the bread, wine, candles, etc., required for the sacrifice and taking the place of offerings in kind.

MASS-PRIEST. An Old English term for one in priest's orders, to distinguish him from minor clerics who were then also called priests; afterwards used for a secular priest as opposed to a regular; and in the 16th century as a term of opprobrium by Protestants.

MASSES OF CHRISTMAS, The. It is permitted to a priest to say three Masses on Christmas day and each one has a different and appropriate proper. The first is of midnight, the second of dawn (*Aurora*), and the third (*qq.v.*) is in daylight.

MASSACRE OF THE INNOCENTS, The. The murder of the male babies of Bethlehem (the Holy Innocents, *q.v.*) by order of Herod as recorded in Matt. ii. 16-18. The phrase has been taken over into English parliamentary slang to signify the abandonment of measures at the end of a session for want of time, and into ordinary facetious speech for the infliction of misfortune, etc., on a number of helpless people or harmless things.

MASSACRE OF ST. BARTHOLOMEW, The. A massacre of Huguenots carried out by Catholics, beginning at Paris on Aug. 24, 1572, and spreading to Lyons, Rouen, Toulouse, Bordeaux, and elsewhere. The death of Admiral Coligny was desired by the Duke of Guise for personal reasons, and by the queen mother, Catherine de' Medici, and others for political ones; after much difficulty the king, Charles IX, gave his consent, and in an access of rage and fear probably ordered a more extensive slaughter. The murder of Coligny was carried out and at once precipitated an outburst of popular fury against the Huguenots which was the principal agency of the massacre. The pope, Gregory XIII, was informed that Charles and the royal family had been the objects of a plot of assassination by the heretics, that in dealing with this many of them had been killed, the king was saved, and the heretical power broken. The pope ordered a *Te Deum* and other marks of gratitude, granted an indulgence and struck a commemorative medal. The whole affair, including the action of the pope, was in origin predominantly a political business, inexcusable to all concerned.

MASSORAH, MASORA. The traditional Jewish comments on the text of the Hebrew Bible, preserved by careful copying of the text itself, with marginal textual notes.

MASTER. The academic degree next above that of Bachelor in the faculty of arts. Originally it implied a qualification to teach and was equivalent to Doctor (*q.v.*); it is used in that sense in the theological faculties of some universities, and the Dominican degree *Sacræ Theologiæ Magister* is the highest degree in the Church; it is not conferred until after 13 years of teaching theology, and until an examination of 100 theses in philosophy and theology is passed.

MASTER OF CEREMONIES. He whose business it is to see that a religious rite is properly carried out; besides supervising others, he has numerous duties to perform himself. He has complete authority within the limits of his office, and during its discharge is dressed in cassock and surplice. Ordinarily the duties are discharged by a layman. According to the "Cæremoniale Episcoporum" a bishop should have two masters of ceremonies, one a priest and the other at least a subdeacon.

MASTER OF THE CHAMBER, The. See MAESTRO DI CAMERA.

MASTER OF NOVICES. A novice master or mistress is an experienced religious appointed by the superior of a monastery or institute to supervise the training of the novices. He has sole charge of and control over them, subject to the superior, and lives in the noviciate.

MASTER OF THE SACRED PALACE, The. The pope's personal theologian and canonist; the office was first held by St. Dominic, its holder always belongs to his order, and has included a doctor of the Church, St. Albert the Great. Until 1917 his principal regular duty was to grant or to withhold permission for the printing and publication of books in Rome, all of which had to bear his *imprimatur*. He selects those who are to preach before the pope and examines their sermons, and is a palatine prelate, living in the Vatican.

MASTER OF THE SENTENCES, The. Peter Lombard (*c.* 1100-*c.* 1160), a theologian so called as author of the four Books of the Sentences (*q.v.*).

MASTER GENERAL. The head of the order of Friars Preachers. He is elected by the priors provincial and the diffinitors of each province for a period of twelve years. The friars' professions are all received in his name. He has the curious distinction for a mendicant friar of ranking as a grandee in Spain with the right to remain covered before his Catholic Majesty (when there is one). The head of the Mercedarians is also called master general.

MATERIA PRIMA. Prime matter (*q.v.*).

MATERIAL ELEMENTS. The material elements used for spiritual ends in the worship of the Church are principally air, ashes, bread, fire, incense, oil, palms, salt, water and wine (*qq.v.*). Man is not only sovereign of created nature, he is also its priest, and in the exercise of his priesthood he takes natural elements and offers them to Almighty God as a tribute and in testimony of his submission. Moreover, man is not pure spirit; a material body, whether in this life or after the resurrection, is an inalienable part of him, and so "at all times man has attached a symbolical significance, a significance in accordance with its natural use, to the great phenomena of nature and to those of its products that have a universal usefulness" (Abbot Cabrol). In accordance with this, these elements, when used liturgically, must be pure natural and not artificial products: fire is produced by cotton wick and the wax of bees, incense from vegetable gums, wine made from the juice of grapes, and not by a mixture of chemicals, etc.

MATERIALISM. i. A false theory which teaches that we can know nothing but matter, and that there is no ground for supposing the human mind to be anything more than a function or a phase of an organized material substance; it denies the existence of God and the reality and immortality of the human soul. Communist "dialectical materialism" derives from Marx's economic interpretation of history. He saw the neglected importance of economic factors in determining historical events, and he made them everything: for him history is in the long run wholly determined by the interplay of economic forces, and human society at each point of time reflects nothing but the stage of material development reached in the external world.

ii. In its modified and common sense materialism denotes an excessive concern for material development and comfort, in varying degrees to that stage where they are made the first consideration in life, which is quite incompatible with the profession of Christianity and is in effect a practical application of the false philosophy defined above.

MATERIALLY. Word applied to the aspect of a thing as the subject recipient of a perfection, or to the consideration of a subject without thought of its actual possession of a form or perfection. Opposed to formally (q.v.). See also SIN, MATERIAL.

MATHUSALA or METHUSELAH. The eighth antediluvian patriarch, who is said to have lived to the age of 720 (Septuagint) or 969 (Hebrew and Samaritan) years (Gen. v). The tradition of the longevity of the first men is very widespread. But the genealogies are not complete and continuous and offer no basis for a chronology of the human race, and there is no official decision of the Church settling the interpretation of this section of Scripture.

MATINS (Lat. *Matutinum* [*tempus*], the morning [time]). The principal and longest hour of the Divine Office, forming the night office thereof; it is usually joined to Lauds, whether said overnight or early in the morning. It begins with the invitatory (q.v.) and its psalm, followed by a hymn; then, if it is a feast of nine lessons, come the three nocturns (q.v.): otherwise there are nine psalms followed by three lessons (q.v., ii); if Lauds does not follow immediately, the office is concluded with a collect and versicles as usual. *Te Deum* is sung at the end of the 3rd nocturn on certain days, and in the Monastic Office the gospel of the day is here read. Matins is the most ancient of the offices and represents the Vigils service of primitive times. The equivalent office of the Byzantine rite is called *Mesonyktikon* (q.v.).

MATRIMONY, THE SACRAMENT OF, is a contract between a man and a woman both of whom are baptized and free to enter into the contract, to live together for the purpose of begetting and rearing children and of cherishing one another in a common life. The ends of matrimony are therefore, primarily, the procreation and bringing-up of children; secondarily, mutual support and affection and the satisfaction of desire. But in a wider sense, the "mutual inward formation of husband and wife, the determined endeavour to perfect one another, can in a real sense, as the Roman Catechism teaches, be said to be the chief reason and purpose of marriage when marriage is looked at more widely as the blending of life as a whole, the mutual interchange and sharing thereof, and not in the restricted sense as instituted for the begetting and bringing up of children" (Pope Pius XI in *Casti connubii*). Nevertheless, these words of the pope must not be taken as supporting certain so-called personalist views of marriage, which have been condemned by the Holy Office. The essential properties of marriage are unity and indissolubility (qq.v.). Those circumstances which make a marriage invalid or illegal are called impediments (q.v.). The efficient cause of the contract is the mutual consent of the parties who minister the sacrament to one another, therefore the marriages of baptized non-Catholics are valid; but since the Council of Trent the presence of a priest and witnesses is ordinarily necessary for its validity when the parties, or either one, are Catholics (cf., Clandestinity, *Tametsi* and *Ne temere*). The matter and form of the sacrament are the mutual offer and acceptance of matrimonial rights (the remote matter). Married people ought to live together as man and wife, unless there is good reason for a separation (q.v.). It is of faith that our Lord raised marriage to be a sacrament, conferring grace *ex opere operato*, and anything which invalidates the contract invalidates also the sacrament. That the sacrament is only an adjunct of the contract and separable from it, the sacrament itself consisting in the nuptial blessing alone, was a proposition condemned by Pope Pius IX (Syllabus, n. 66). But the Church expressly provides that the state may make binding legislation governing the civil effects of marriage (cf., canon 1016). A wife may join her husband's rite at marriage or any time after, and the wedding should take place according to his rite; but at his death she is free to return to her own. The marriages of the unbaptized (q.v.) are not sacramental; whether a baptized person who marries one non-baptized or, in a marriage of the unbaptized, one of the parties who is subsequently baptized, receives the sacrament, is undecided. Marriage is a type of the union between Christ and his mystical Bride the Church, and of Christ with the individual soul; in the outrage of these symbols lies some of the chiefest malice of sins against this sacrament; "for a type is a protestation of the truth, and therefore can never be detracted from in the slightest degree" (St. Thomas).

MATTER. See PRIME MATTER.

MATTER OF THE SACRAMENTS, The. The sensible things, substances or acts, which, in themselves indeterminate and capable of a variety of meanings, receive their definite sacramental significance from the accompanying words (the form, *q.v.*). Thus, in Baptism, the matter is water, which might be used for cleansing or cooling, but which here signifies cleansing from sin, as is clear from the form, "I baptize thee," etc. The matter may be remote, *i.e.*, the things of sense themselves, the water in Baptism; or proximate, *i.e.*, the application of the remote matter, the pouring of the water.

MATTHEW, ST. i. Apostle and evangelist, whose feast is kept by the Western church on Sept. 21. Beyond his business of tax-collecting and the authorship of the gospel which bears his name, nothing is known of him, not even that he suffered martyrdom. He is named in the canon of the Mass.
ii. His gospel. This was written in Aramaic to demonstrate to his fellow-Jews that Jesus was the Messias, but of this original we have no trace; the gospel we have is in Greek, probably a translation of the Aramaic made at an early date. The original was written about the year 50 or even earlier. Certain of the parables, miracles and events connected with our Lord's passion are recorded only in this gospel. See also the SYNOPTIC PROBLEM.

MATTHIAS, ST. The apostle chosen from among the 72 disciples to take the place of Judas Iscariot. His feast is kept in the Western church on Feb. 24, and in the East on Aug. 9, and he is named in the canon of the Mass; but of his life and death nothing is certainly known.

MAUNDY THURSDAY. The English name for *feria quinta in Cæna Domini* (Thursday of the Lord's Supper), *i.e.*, the Thursday in Holy Week; it is corrupted from the word *Mandatum*. On this day the institution of the Blessed Sacrament is celebrated. Only one Mass is offered in each church, and that in the evening; at *Gloria in excelsis* the organ is played and bells rung, after which they are silent until the Easter vigil Mass. After Mass the Blessed Sacrament for the morrow's communion is carried to the altar of repose (*q.v.*); afterwards the altars are stripped of everything but cross and candlesticks, and holy water stoups emptied. In cathedral-churches the holy oils (*q.v.*) are blessed, in many churches the *Mandatum* (*q.v.*) takes place, and in some the ceremonial washing of the altar. The reconciliation of penitents is found in the "Pontificale Romanum," but has now gone out of use. In some Byzantine churches the oil of the sick is blessed by 3, 5 or 7 priests, all present being anointed on the forehead. The Liturgy of St. Basil is sung. One hour after sunset is the office of the Passion: this consists principally of the reading of twelve passages from the gospels, and the veneration of the crucifix before the holy doors ("The Taking of Christ").

MAURISTS, The. A French Benedictine congregation (of St. Maur) founded under the auspices of Cardinal Richelieu, in 1618, and lasting till the Revolution; in 1700 it had 180 houses. Each monk was professed not for his own house but for the congregation, and the uniformity was rigid; but otherwise the observance of the rule of St. Benedict (*q.v.*) was strict (manual labour, night office, perpetual abstinence, etc.). Later it was relaxed and many monks were infected with Jansenism. The principal and famous work of the congregation was erudite studies; among its scholars were Mabillon, Montfaucon, d'Achery, Martène and Durand; they were backed by the corporate labours of numerous nameless workers. It also conducted a number of secular colleges.

MAY DEVOTIONS. The custom of dedicating the month of May in honour of our Lady, setting up a shrine, having processions, and meeting together daily in church for prayers and hymns. It is said to have originated in the Franciscan church of St. Clare at Naples about the end of the 16th century, though some investigators do not recognize it before 1815, in Rome; it was introduced into England by Father Aloysius Gentili about 1840. Pope Pius VII approved and indulgenced it. The word May is derived from Maia, a Roman goddess, and there is no traditional connexion between our Lady and this month; the May Queen and Maypole are in origin unrelated to her, and only one feast of our Lady, as Help of Christians, occurs at this time, on May 24.

MAY LAWS. Laws passed by the Prussian Landtag in May, 1873, and aimed at the detaching of the Church in Germany from Rome and the bringing of it entirely under the control of the state. They and subsequent related laws made ecclesiastical appointments depend on the state and on state examination; German authorities alone were to exercise ecclesiastical discipline; civil marriages were legalized; all temporalities were to be withheld from those clergy who refused to undertake in writing to obey these laws; all religious communities, other than those engaged in nursing, were suppressed; the state took over the administration of vacant sees and of all ecclesiastical property. This effort became known as the *Kulturkampf* (*q.v.*), and the ensuing struggle did not end until the laws (also known as Falk laws) were substantially modified in 1883-87.

MAYNOOTH. The Irish national seminary of St. Patrick in the archdiocese of Dublin, founded in 1795 by consent of King George III, and with an annual subsidy granted by the Irish parliament. On the disestablishment of the Protestant Church of Ireland in 1869 the annual grant was compounded for a capital sum. The average number of students is about 500. A society of missionaries, "of St. Columbanus," for work in China was founded at Maynooth in 1916 and has missions in that country.

MEAT. The meat forbidden to be eaten on certain days by the law of abstinence (*q.v.*) includes the flesh of all breathing animals and birds born upon land and soup made therefrom; but not eggs, milk, cheese or condiments made from animal fat. Suet may be used as an ingredient, *e.g.*, of puddings.

MEATH (*Midensis*). An Irish see, suffragan of Armagh, formed by the union of several ancient dioceses in 1172. It now comprises most of Meath, Westmeath and Offaly with parts of Longford, Louth, Dublin and Cavan; it is the largest episcopal diocese in Ireland and has precedence over all other episcopal sees in the country. Meath is a district, not a city: the bishop's residence, cathedral and diocesan seminary are at Mullingar. The patron of the diocese is our Lady Immaculate, under whose name the cathedral is dedicated. Irish name: An Mhidhe.

MECHANICISM. In philosophy, a system which explains all corporal changes by mechanical actions. Thus the mechanicism of Descartes was an endeavour to explain the corporal world and the human body by extension and movement. It is opposed to Dynamism (*q.v.*).

MEDAL. A flat metal disk bearing a religious image, of our Lord, our Lady or one of the other saints, a shrine, a mystery of religion, etc. They are worn on the person as one carries about a photograph or other relic of one dear, and must be regarded in the same way as any other image: they are mere signs of the prototypes to which due honour is accorded; in themselves they can have no efficacy, to look on them as mascots is superstitious. The efficacy consists in the blessing of the Church calling down the goodness of God on the wearer, and sometimes in indulgences attached thereto. There are innumerable different medals; the chief are the medal of St. Benedict, the scapular medal, and the Miraculous medal (*qq.v.*).

MEDAL OF ST. BENEDICT. A medal having on the one side a cross and on the other an image with the words, "*Eius in obitu nostro præsentia muniamur*" (May we be strengthened by his presence at the hour of our death). It also bears the following initials, CSPB (*Crux Sancti Patris Benedicti,* Cross of the Holy Father Benedict), CSSML (*Crux Sacra sit mihi Lux,* May the Holy Cross be my Light), NDSMD (*Non Draco sit mihi Dux,* Let not the Devil be my guide), VRS, NSMV, SMQL, IVB (*Vade retro Satanas, numquam suade mihi vana, sunt mala quæ libas, ipse venena bibas,* Begone, Satan, never suggest vain things to me; what thou offerest is evil, drink thou thine own poison). This last refers to the attempt to poison the saint. The medal must be blessed by a Benedictine or by a priest having the necessary faculty.

MEDIÆVALISM. i. As applied to the Catholic Church, her teaching and institutions, as a term of abuse, this word defies definition. It has been used of St. Paul's instructions to wives (1st century) and of probabilism (17th century), of the use of ceremonies and of the principle of religious authority. It can only be said that the middle ages had their part like any other in the development of the Church, and that the most conspicuous mediæval force in the Church to-day is the philosophical and theological synthesis of St. Thomas Aquinas—in the revival of the appreciation of which non-Catholics have taken a considerable part.

ii. Some Catholics desiderate the restoration of certain mediæval religious and quasi-religious institutions and customs with their accompanying economic conditions. With such aspirations the Church as such has nothing to do; but in so far as mediæval life was governed by religious principles which are now lost to many individuals and most nations, she works and prays for the recovery of such principles. That is the extent of her mediævalism.

MEDIATOR. One who intervenes between two persons or parties at variance, in order to reconcile them.

i. So the name is applied pre-eminently to Christ, who as God-man died to reconcile men to his Father "and who through the Church which he founded leads them in the way to Heaven": "For there is one God and one mediator of God and men, the man Christ Jesus" (1 Tim. ii, 5).

ii. But this does not militate against an analogous use of the term for the saints who intercede for us. The Council of Trent declares (sess. xxv) that "the saints reigning with Christ offer their prayers to God for men, and it is good and useful to invoke them, and to resort to their aid and help on account of the benefits to be begged from God through his Son Jesus Christ our Lord, who alone is our redeemer and saviour."

MEDIATRESS OF ALL GRACES (Lat. *mediatrix*). The Blessed Virgin Mary in her aspect of dispenser of the graces bestowed on human kind by the Holy Ghost through the merits of the crucified Christ. Having co-operated in the Incarnation and the Redemption by her motherhood and by her sufferings at the foot of the cross, our Lady merits to co-operate as channel for the graces flowing therefrom. In 1921 Pope Benedict XV granted to the dioceses of Belgium, and to any other diocese asking for it, permission to celebrate a Mass in honour of our Lady under this title.

MEDIOBURGENSIS. The adjectival form of the name of the see of Middlesbrough (*q.v.*) used in the designation of its bishop in Latin documents. Noun: *Medioburgum.*

MEDITATION. The lowest kind of mental prayer, called also discursive prayer. It consists of reflections on a given subject with the practical aim of stirring the will to make acts of faith, love, humility, etc., and to form resolutions. In recent centuries it has become common to have systematized methods of meditation, in order to give direction to one's reflections and ensure more deliberate and determined effort on the part of the will. There are many varieties of such methods, but the two chief are that of St. Ignatius, to be found in his "Spiritual Exercises," and the method of St. Sulpice. Benedictine prayer dispenses with such precise methods, and preserves the ancient traditional ways of meditation, in which the soul feeds on the Scriptures and the teaching of the sacred Liturgy. Meditation is the prayer of beginners in the spiritual life and is proper to the purgative way (*q.v.*). It grows gradually into affective prayer, in which the will requires less assistance from the reflections of the mind, but almost at once begins to make acts of love, humility, etc. Finally, there may come a time when, through no fault of her own, the soul can neither reflect nor make acts. She has fallen into aridity (*q.v.*). Yet she truly desires union with God. She is ripe for the prayer of simplicity (*q.v.*), and should be guided into it. St. John-of-the-Cross speaks severely of directors who in such circumstances would still force the soul to meditate.

MEEKNESS. A virtue allied to temperance, restraining anger under offence and resentment under rebuke. It must be distinguished from mean-spiritedness or pusillanimity.

MEGALOSKHEMOS (Gr., literally "a great habiter"). The highest rank of Byzantine monk, who wears the full or great habit, to which only a small proportion are admitted and those of considerable age and experience. They live a semi-eremitical and very penitential life.

MEGILLOTH (Heb., plural of *megilloh*, a roll, volume). One of the divisions of the Hagiographa of the Hebrew Bible, namely, Canticle of Canticles, Ruth, Lamentations, Ecclesiastes and Esther, each of which is written on a separate roll for use in the synagogue.

MEKHITARISTS, The. An order of monks of the Armenian rite professing the Rule of St. Benedict, founded by the Ven. Mekhitar, in 1702. They are engaged in mission work among their own countrymen, education and works of erudition: from the press at the abbey of San Lazzaro at Venice books are sent throughout the world. There are two congregations, of Venice and Vienna, totalling over 100 monks. Their habit is black, with wide sleeves, cloak and hood; beard.

MELCHISEDECH (Heb., King of Righteousness). King of Salem and priest of the most high God (Gen. xiv, 18-20). He was a type of Christ by reason of his combined kingship and priesthood and in other ways set out by St. Paul in Heb. vi, 20, vii, 1-8; (*cf.,* Ps. cix, 4). Melchisedech's sacrifice of bread and wine is a type of the Eucharist.

MELETIAN SCHISM, The. i. A schism raised against St. Peter, archbishop of Alexandria, by Meletius, bishop of Lycopolis. The Council of Nicaea made vain efforts to end the trouble by conciliatory methods, and the schism persisted till the middle of the 5th century.
ii. A name given to the disagreements and disturbances, arising from Arianism (*q.v.*), in the province of Antioch during the episcopate of St. Meletius (360-381).

MELKITE RITE. The Melkites have no distinct rite, though such is sometimes implied. They use the Byzantine rite, sometimes in Greek but usually in Arabic or with the lessons, ekphoneseis, etc., only in Greek, with minor modifications such as are found in all Byzantine churches. See below.

MELKITES, The (Syriac *malkâ*, emperor). i. Originally the name in Syria and Egypt for those Christians who followed the emperor and accepted the Council of Chalcedon, as opposed to the monophysites. Therefore, strictly speaking, all Byzantines, Catholic or dissident, in those parts are Melkites; but the term generally now indicates (and is so used herein)—
ii. The Arabic-speaking Catholics of the Byzantine rite in Syria, Palestine, Egypt and elsewhere. They were organized from 1724, when a Catholic, Cyril Tanas, became patriarch of Antioch. They number 200,000 in the above countries, under their patriarch of Antioch (who has vicars at Alexandria, Jerusalem and elsewhere), divided into 12 eparchies; and about 20,000 in the United States with a dozen priests, subject to the Latin ordinaries. Half the secular clergy is unmarried, largely owing to the influence of their seminary of St. Anne, conducted by the White Fathers at Jerusalem. There are three congregations of Basilian (*q.v.*) religious with over 300 hieromonks, of whom two-thirds administer parishes, and seven convents of contemplative nuns. Baptism is by semi-immersion with infusion; the use of the spoon in giving communion is being abandoned in favour of intinction (*q.v.*). The Melkites have had the feast of Corpus Christi since before 1700 and Benediction is according to a very impressive rite of their own. The codification of their canon law was begun by Dimitrios Kadi (patriarch 1861-1925) and is still in progress.

MELLUSIANS. A sect in Malabar, having its origin in a schism from the native Catholics organized by Bishop Mellos, in 1874. On the death of his successor, the schismatics got a bishop from the katholikos of the Nestorians, but their Nestorianism (*q.v.*) is nominal. They number a few thousand with headquarters at Trichur.

MEMENTO OF THE DEAD, The, or commemoration, is made soon after the consecration at Mass. The celebrant prays "Be mindful also, O Lord, of thy servants and handmaids who are gone before us with the sign of faith and sleep in the sleep of peace (here he names whom he wills). To these, O Lord, and to all that rest in Christ grant, we beseech thee, a place of refreshment, light and peace."

MEMENTO OF THE LIVING, The, or commemoration, is made at Mass at the beginning of the canon. The celebrant prays for the pope and his bishop by name and "all true believers and professors of the Catholic and Apostolic Faith"; then in the prayer *Memento* he names whom he wills and specially refers to those present. He then proceeds to the commemoration of the Church triumphant in the prayer *Communicantes* (*q.v.*).

MEMORARE, The. A popular prayer to our Lady, attributed to St. Bernard of Clairvaux, so called from its first word in Latin. Its use was greatly popularized by a French secular priest, Claude Bernard, in the early 17th century.

MEMORIA. Commemoration, the lowest rank of feast in the Dominican and Benedictine calendars.

MEMORIALE RITUUM (Lat., the Memorial of Rites). A liturgical book compiled in 1725 for use in parish churches wherein, on account of lack of sacred ministers, certain rites cannot be carried out according to the rubrics: namely, those of Candlemas, Ash Wednesday, Palm Sunday and the last three days of Holy Week.

MEMORY. The faculty of retaining, reproducing and recognizing representations of past experiences. The greater portion of our mental possessions lie below the surface of our consciousness; it is the power of recalling and recognizing these dormant cognitions which completes and perfects this instrument of knowledge. Memory, the passive faculty of retention, is radically distinct from reminiscence, or the power of active search or recall. The latter involves volitional and rational activity and is proper to man, whilst memory is common to brutes. There is intellectual memory and sensitive memory, the latter being one of the four internal senses common to man and brutes. The activity of the fingers when playing some well-known piece of music, the attention of the player being elsewhere, is an example of sensitive memory.

MENAION (Gr. μήν, month). A liturgical book of the Byzantine rite in 12 or 6 volumes, one for each month or two months, beginning with September. It contains the proper parts of the Divine Office for all immovable feasts; the *menaia* therefore corresponds roughly to the "proper of the saints" in Western breviaries.

MENDICANT FRIARS, ORDERS. Those orders of friars, namely, Dominican, Franciscan, Carmelite and Augustinian, of which the members by their constitutions were forbidden to possess property not merely personally but even in common; they, therefore, had to subsist by begging. The necessities of the times caused the Council of Trent to modify this prescription (except for the Friars Minor and the Capuchins), but the name has persisted and is now accorded to the Trinitarians, Mercedarians, Servites, Minims, Brothers of St. John-of-God and Order of Penitence as well. A notable Christian poverty is still a characteristic of friars.

MENEVIA (*Menevensis*; Menevia is the mediæval form of the Latin *Menapia;* Welsh, *Mynyw*, an alternative name for Saint Davids). A Welsh see founded about the end of the 6th century; in abeyance from 1559; revived as a title in 1850 and as a diocese in 1898. Suffragan of Cardiff. It comprises all Wales except Glamorgan and Monmouth, formerly divided between Bangor, St. Asaph and St. Davids or Menevia. Holywell and Talacre were mission centres all through penal times and the Brecon mission was established in 1642 or before. The bishop's residence and pro-cathedral of our Lady of Sorrows are at Wrexham. The patrons of the diocese are our Lady Help of Christians, St. David and St. Winefride (born at Holywell).

MENNONITES, The. Baptist sects originating in the Netherlands in the early 16th century, one of their leaders being Menno Simons, an apostate priest. The name is popular in the United States, where they have a small following; in Holland they are called simply *Doopers*, Baptists.

MENOLOGY, -OGION (Gr., month account). i. A name used in the West for several classes of unofficial martyrology, *e.g.*, any ecclesiastical calendar arranged according to months and days, a local register of saints with brief notices of each one (*cf.*, Stanton's "Menology for England and Wales"), a similar register of all persons of distinction in a religious order.

ii. In the East the word has several meanings also: the ecclesiastical calendar, divided into months; the historical notices of saints extracted from the *Menaia;* collections of lives of the saints in their daily order throughout the year.

MENSA (Lat., a table). i. The flat stone top of a fixed or consecrated altar; in an unconsecrated altar the portable altar-stone inserted thereon is properly and alone both *mensa* and altar, but for convenience the whole structure is called altar and its whole top *mensa*. See ALTAR-STONE.

ii. Mensal fund (*q.v.*).

MENSAL FUND. i. The division of the revenue of a church set apart for the support of its prelate or other person serving it, particularly that part of a cathedral's revenue reserved for the maintenance of the bishop. As secular canons no longer live in common, the capitular mensal fund (when there is one) is divided into personal shares called prebends. Mensal income is personal and has not to be accounted for; but the alienation of mensal property is strictly forbidden except by permission of the Holy See.

ii. In some dioceses (*e.g.*, of England) the mensal fund is a capital sum subscribed and invested for the express purpose of the bishop's maintenance.

MENSAL PARISH. One whose revenues are applied to the support of a bishop or other prelate, the parish being administered by a vicar.

MENTAL RESERVATION. The introduction of a tacit limitation in making a statement, taking an oath, etc., when it is thought inconvenient or unnecessary to speak openly. If the qualification can be perceived neither from the statement itself nor from the speaker's circumstances, this is strict mental reservation. If either the statement itself or circumstances show that a sense other than the obvious may be signified, this is broad mental reservation. Strict mental reservation is a form of lying and consequently sinful. But broad mental reservation is sometimes justifiable, *e.g.*, if it is a necessary means to preserve secrecy (*q.v.*).

MERCEDARIANS, The. The Glorious, Royal and Military Order of Our Lady of Mercy or Ransom, said to have been founded by St. Peter Nolasco in 1225, for the ransom of captives, particularly among the Moors; now a mendicant order engaged in hospital work, preaching, etc., though the fourth vow, to become a hostage among the infidels if required, is still taken. There are also nuns, both contemplative and active, chiefly in Spain and South America. The habit is tunic, belt, scapular and hood, all white, and a white cloak for outdoors; a badge is worn round the neck; some are discalced.

MERCY. A moral virtue prompting its possessor to have compassion for and to succour those in spiritual or temporal want. The performance of spiritual and corporal works of mercy is enjoined by the precept of charity (*q.v.*). In its special sense it means not to enforce the requirements of strict justice, a tempering of the rigour of the law, which is properly called clemency.

MERCY, ORDER OF OUR LADY OF. The Mercedarians (*q.v.*).

MERIDIAN (Lat. *meridies*, midday). An hour's rest taken at noon or soon after in many monasteries, especially in hot countries and when the night is broken by the Office.

MERIT. i. The right to reward due to a work freely done to gratify another.

ii. More particularly, as supernatural merit, the right to reward, which by divine ordinance is due to a good and supernatural work done freely for God's sake. Such a work must be supernatural (*q.v.*) in its source (*i.e.*, a faculty under the influence of grace) and in its object or end. The right must depend on divine ordinance, for a creature of itself can have no rights against its creator.

MESONYKTIKON (Gr., midnight). The night office of the Byzantine rite. In its ordinary form it consists of a prayer to the Holy Ghost, the *trisagion*, then Our Father and invitatory; then psalms with certain prayers, and the Nicene creed, three *troparia* (*q.v.*), and more prayers and psalms, four *troparia* for the dead, *Kyrie eleison* twelve times, and a prayer for the dead. The office is concluded by three more *troparia*, to which the Melkites, Slavs and Rumanians add a special litany.

MESSALIANISM. The doctrine and following of the Messalians (Aramaic: praying ones), also called Adelphians, after their first leader, Adelphius, and Euchites. They taught that prayer alone gives grace, that sacraments and other observances are unnecessary, and that every man has an interior devil who can be ousted by the personal indwelling of the Holy Ghost; this devil they seem to have allowed to enjoy a good deal of influence and they were known in Armenia as "the foul ones" in consequence. They were condemned by several eastern synods of the 4th and 5th centuries, but revived in a developed form as the Bogomili (*q.v.*). There was an obscure pagan sect of the same name.

MESSIAS, -IAH (Heb., anointed), commonly used of kings and especially of the great Davidic king who was to come to save his people Israel. Greek-speaking Christians translated the Hebrew word by *Christos*, the Greek equivalent. Jews retained the Hebrew form. Messianic prophecies are the indications of the great deliverance to come, spread through almost every book of the Old Testament, beginning with the promise of a redeemer after the Fall and found in Malachias, the last of the prophets.

METANY (Gr. μετάνοια, penance). A form of reverence in the Byzantine rite. (*a*) The "salutation" is an inclination of the head and shoulders; (*b*) the lesser metany, or simply metany, is a bow sufficiently low to bring the right hand level with the knees, followed by the sign of the cross and accompanied by the words, "O God, be merciful to me, a sinner, and have pity on me": it is frequently prescribed in the liturgy; (c) the greater metany is a complete prostration, the forehead, hands and feet only touching the ground: monks make a certain number of these daily according to their rank. The lesser metany, made several times, takes the place of the Western genuflexion among laypeople. The name is sometimes given to the Byzantine form of rosary (q.v., ii).

METAPHYSICS (Gr. μετὰ τὰ φυσικά, after physical things; originally the title given to those treatises of Aristotle placed after those on physics). That part of philosophy which treats of real being. It has two parts: (a) General, sometimes called Ontology (q.v.), and treats of being as such and the transcendentals (being something, unity, truth, goodness); of the Categories or supreme *genera* (substances, accidents; quality, quantity, relation, etc.); of causes (material, formal, efficient, final). (b) Special, called applied metaphysics, which treats of Cosmology (the world), Psychology (the soul), Theodicy (God).

METEMPSYCHOSIS (Gr. μετὰ, after; ἔμψυχος, living). Theory of the transmigration of souls from one body to another. Held by Indian philosophers and by Plato and his followers, and in our day by theosophists. It has been held by certain heretical Christian sects, e.g., the Manichæans and Albigensians, but it is quite incompatible with Christianity and the doctrine of the Redemption.

METHOD OF ST. SULPICE, The. The method of meditation taught in seminaries directed by the Sulpician fathers. It consists of a preparation, the meditation and the conclusion. The meditation itself must be simple and practical; reasoning and speculating are discouraged, all must be directed towards kindling the affections by considering the subject in relation to our Lord and eliciting acts of charity by considering its practical importance for the individual. This method of prayer has greatly assisted in the maintenance of the simple, solidly dutiful type of priest characteristic of St. Sulpice.

METHODIST. A name originally applied in contempt to the followers of John Wesley and assumed by them as a title of honour, cf., "The Rules of the Society of the People called Methodists," put forward by John and Charles Wesley in 1743. The Welsh Calvinistic Methodist sect had no right to take the name, as its members were not and are not subject to the doctrine and discipline of Wesleyanism (q.v.); it is a Presbyterian Calvinist body deriving from the preaching of Griffith Jones (d. 1761) and Howell Harris

of Trefecca (d. 1773), and declared a separate body under Thomas Charles in 1811.

METROPOLITAN. i. In the Western church the title and rank added to that of an archbishop who presides over a province and consequently has suffragan sees under him, e.g., the archbishop of Liverpool is a metropolitan, the archbishop of Winnipeg is not. The powers of a metropolitan are now greatly reduced: see ARCHBISHOP, i.

ii. In the Eastern churches, both Catholic and dissident, the title metropolitan, or metropolite, is distinct from that of archbishop but tends to oust it altogether, and this although there are numerous archbishops with no provinces or metropolitical rights. Metropolitan is added to the titles of those archbishops who have a primatial jurisdiction (e.g., Alba Julia in Rumania). See ARCHBISHOP, ii.

METROPOLITAN CHURCH, SEE, Etc. The cathedral, the see, etc., of an archbishop who is also metropolitan; simple, primatial or patriarchal according to the rank of the see.

METROPOLITICUM. The rights and duties of a metropolitan in respect of his province (q.v.) as distinct from his episcopal see.

MEXICO, THE CHURCH IN. The population of Mexico (about 20 million, of whom 5 million are native Indians) is nominally 90 per cent Catholic. In 1857 and subsequent years Church and State were separated, religious orders suppressed, ecclesiastical property confiscated; these and similar antireligious laws were not enforced from 1877 to 1910. The constitution of 1917 enacted further repressive measures which were strictly enforced; in 1926 President Calles ordered all churches to be closed and, all priests who would not regard themselves as government agents to be banished. With the approval of the Holy See, public religious worship was discontinued; the government conducted a direct persecution and clergy, men and women were put to death or imprisoned for resistance. In 1929 President Portes Gil agreed with the delegate apostolic for the bishops to name priests to be registered, to return a number of church buildings for worship and instruction, and to permit episcopal efforts to amend the constitution; this "armistice" is still in force, and during recent years a good deal of normal religious life has been restored on sufferance. Catholic Action is strong and well-organized, but there is a very serious shortage of clergy; a big seminary exists in New Mexico, U. S. A. The Archbishop of Mexico is primate; his province has 4 suffragan sees; there are 7 other archdioceses and 21 dioceses, with a vicariate apostolic for the Indians of Lower California.

MI-CARÊME (Fr.). Mid-Lent or *Lætare* Sunday.

MICAH. The Hebrew form of the name of the prophet Micheas.

MICHAELMAS. An archaic English name for the feast of the Dedication of the Church of St. Michael the Archangel kept on Sept. 29; now one of the legal quarter days in England. It is the principal feast of St. Michael in the West and was formerly much more popular. Michaelmas goose is the roast proper to the feast, being in its prime at this time.

MICHEAS (Heb. *Micah*, Who is like Jahveh?). A prophetical book of the Old Testament written, by him whose name it bears, in the 8th century B.C., contemporary with Isaias. He prophesies the ruin and desolation of Israel and Juda for their wickedness (contrasting it with God's mercy), the conversion of the Gentiles and the birth of our Lord at Bethlehem. He is named in the Roman Martyrology on Jan. 15.

MIDDLE AGES, The. A term commonly used to denote the period of European history from the end of the 10th to the end of the 15th century; more accurately, they began earlier. They are often considered to begin with the coronation of Charlemagne in 800 and to end with the invasion of Italy by King Charles VIII in 1494. Also called the Ages of Faith (*q.v.*).

MIDDLESBROUGH (*Medioburgensis*). An English see formed in 1878 at the suppression of Beverley and now suffragan to Liverpool; it includes the North and East Ridings of Yorkshire and part of York, formerly under the jurisdiction of York. In many places, *e.g.*, Everingham, the faith has survived since before the Reformation, and 18 parishes were first established in the 16th and 17th centuries. Its patrons are our Lady of Perpetual Succour, St. Wilfrid (bishop of York) and St. John (monk of Beverley); the cathedral is St. Mary's.

MIDENSIS. The adjectival form of the name of the see of Meath (*q.v.*) used in the designation of its bishop in Latin documents. Noun: *Midae*.

MIDRASH (Heb., study; plural, *midrashim*). An ancient Jewish commentary on and explanation of the Hebrew Scriptures, of which there are several collections in use by scholars.

MILANESE RITE, The. The Ambrosian rite (*q.v.*) in use in the province of Milan.

MILDNESS. Gentleness, but not involving softness or "slop": a fruit of the Holy Ghost (*q.v.*).

MILDNESS, DEFECT OF. An irregularity (*q.v.*) for holy orders incurred by those who, *e.g.*, as judges pass sentence of death, perform or assist immediately at an execution, as soldiers take part in an unjust war.

MILITARISM. Preponderance of the military spirit and glorification of war for its own sake, whether arising from or resulting in such doctrines as that of the omnipotence of the state, "biological necessity" of war, war necessary to human progress, etc. The Church condemns such militarism and correlative doctrines as the very negation of justice and Christian teaching.

MILITARY ORDERS. An institution, arising out of the Crusades, wherein it was attempted to combine monastic status with military life, for the defence of Christendom, the protection of pilgrims, etc. The principal orders of this kind were the Templars, the Hospitallers of St. John, the Knights of Alcantara and of Calatrava, the Teutonic Knights and the Mercedarians (*qq.v.*), no one of which survives in its full mediæval form; there were many lesser ones. The knights took the vows of religion, were bound to the Office and other religious obligations, and they and their houses had the ecclesiastical status, rights, and duties of monks and monasteries; there was a second combatant rank of brethren-at-arms. The military orders failed as a permanent institution because of the inordinate power conferred on them by the holding of huge amounts of property in common, and the almost impossibility of keeping to monastic vows men daily engaged in worldly pursuits. The name military order is now loosely extended also to certain lay orders, chiefly honorific, such as the Pontifical Order of Christ, the English Order of the Garter, the Spanish Order of the Golden Fleece, and the Italian Order of the Annunziata.

MILITARY SERVICE. By canon law all clerics, *i.e.*, those who have received the tonsure, are exempt from military service and are forbidden to undertake it unless compelled. Where civil law requires such service, the reception of orders must be postponed until after its completion.

MILITIA OF JESUS CHRIST, The. A military order (*q.v.*) founded early in the 13th century to combat the Albigensians and to defend ecclesiastical property and liberty. It soon coalesced with an order of penance and thus formed what is now known as the Third Order (*q.v.*) of St. Dominic.

MILL HILL FATHERS, The. The Society of St. Joseph for foreign missions founded by the Reverend (afterwards Cardinal) Herbert Vaughan at Mill Hill, in 1866. All these priests are either British or Dutch, and go to missions in Egypt, Borneo, Africa, Philippines, etc. They are trained in colleges at Mill Hill, Freshfield, Burn Hall and Roosendaal.

MILLENNIUM, The. Christ's reign of a thousand years on earth, described in the Apocalypse xx. Catholics take the number one thousand to designate an indefinite period of considerable length, and refer the reign of Christ to his spiritual reign in the Church on earth. A few early Fathers, mostly Greek, understood this chapter as referring to a temporal and visible reign of Christ of ten centuries' duration previous to the general resurrection. Adherents to this opinion were termed Millenarians or Chiliasts (Lat. *mille*, Gr. χίλια, a thousand); this error, never extensively held, has been revived by some Christian sects since the 16th century.

MINCHEN. An Old English word for a nun, now obsolete except in place-names such as Minchinhampton, Mincing Lane (referring to the Benedictine nuns of St. Helen's, Bishopsgate), etc.

MIND. In strict language mind designates the animating principle as the subject of consciousness, whereas soul refers to it as the root of all forms of vital activity. Spirit is of still narrower extension than mind, meaning a being capable of a higher, rational or intellectual, order of conscious life. See INTELLECT.

MIND OF THE CHURCH. The general belief of the Church in matters not defined to be of faith; the general practice of the Church where specific direction is lacking; the intention lying behind pronouncements of the highest authorities but not explicitly set out therein; directions of the same authorities that are intended to be more than merely opportune but are not binding under pain of sin. It is imprudent in any Catholic to disregard or oppose the known mind of the Church; but he is at perfect liberty in good faith to question whether a given statement really represents that mind; and her authorities are notably lenient in enforcing the mind of the Church (as defined above), looking rather to the good will and good sense of the faithful to conform thereto.

MINERVA, The. The church of Santa Maria sopra Minerva, so called because built on the site of a temple of that goddess; it is the only authentic gothic church in Rome. It belongs to the Dominicans, who have a priory and noviciate of their Roman province adjoining.

MINIMS, The. The Minim Hermits of St. Francis of Paola, a mendicant order founded by that saint in 1436, their name (Lat. *minimus*, the least) showing their abasement even below that of the Franciscan Friars Minor. They now number only a few hundred religious, in monasteries of which only one is outside Italy. The rule, founded on that of St. Francis of Assisi, is very penitential and includes a fourth vow, of perpetual abstinence from flesh-meat. They are principally engaged in giving missions and retreats to the poor and neglected. The order is governed by a corrector general, with correctors provincial and a corrector for each friary. The habit is a wide-sleeved tunic of black or natural wool, girdled with a cord, and a cape with hood of the same material. There are contemplative nuns and tertiaries of the order, which was formerly widely spread but was never established in Great Britain or Ireland.

MINISTER (Lat., a servant). i. The word *minister* to indicate an ordained cleric is not in use among Catholics except in a very general way (*e.g.*, the priests and ministers of a church) and as iii (below), and not at all specifically to indicate a parish priest (*cf.*, Anglican Book of Common Prayer and Nonconformist usage). Formerly it referred particularly to deacons (*cf.*, Fourth Council of Carthage, canon 4).

ii. The general and provincial superiors of the three branches of the Franciscans, the Order of Penance and the Trinitarians, and among the Jesuits the second-in-command of each house, are called minister. The prior of La Grande Chartreuse is *ex officio* minister general of the Carthusians, and is elected or re-elected annually by his community.

iii. Sacred ministers are those clerics taking part in a religious rite, particularly and usually the deacon and subdeacon attending the celebrant at a high Mass.

iv. Minister of a sacrament. Our Lord himself is the principal minister of all the sacraments, they deriving their efficacy from his sacrifice of himself on Calvary. In his name and by his authority certain men make (confect) and administer them as secondary ministers; to do so validly they must use the appropriate matter and form (*qq.v.*) and have the intention (*q.v.*) of doing what the Church does. It is of faith that the efficacy of the sacraments is independent of the good or bad dispositions of the minister, but a cleric sins who administers a sacrament solemnly, knowing himself to be in mortal sin. See under each sacrament for the respective ordinary ministers.

MINISTERS OF THE SICK, The, or Camillians. An order of priests and brothers (clerks regular) founded by St. Camillus of Lellis in 1582 to serve the sick in hospitals. They are not bound to office in choir or to the monastic fasts on account of the nature of their work. They number about 700 religious of whom about half are priests. Their dress is the ordinary cassock and cloak with a brown cross on each.

MINISTERIUM (Lat. *minister*, a servant). The group of ordained officers of the Church who have the duty of governing, teaching and sanctifying (by administering the sacraments, offering sacrifice, etc.); the ministry.

MINISTRATIONS OF NON-CATHOLICS. Just as he may not join in the worship, so a Catholic may not receive the religious ministrations of non-Catholic Christians. Each sect embraces some truth, "grace overflows its banks," and their "sacraments" and ordinances may be the occasion of religious efficacy for those who believe in them; but they refuse the full teaching of the Christian faith and maintain errors opposed thereto and so as bodies are outside the Church of Christ. For a Catholic therefore to, *e.g.*, knowingly go to confession to a Church of England minister would be an open defiance of the teaching of the Church, a taking part in erroneous worship, and a sealing of his action by an act of great religious significance—a most grave sin against faith. This does not mean that a Catholic may not prudently listen to and profit by the words of a non-Catholic who, in ordinary private intercourse, speaks wisely of God and the soul; such an one may well be a divine instrument. But *cf.*, Absolution i.

MINISTRY. The collective name for all those who hold governing and teaching office in the Church, who administer sacraments, or who in virtue of sacramental orders assist at their administration: pope, bishops, priests, deacons, etc.

MINOR CLERKS REGULAR. A congregation founded at Naples, in 1588, by St. Francis Caracciolo and the Ven. Augustine Adorno. Its members add perpetual adoration (*q.v.*) to their pastoral work and take a vow not to accept ecclesiastical dignities. It is now practically extinct.

MINOR ORDERS. The lower ranks of the clergy, through which all aspirants to the priesthood must pass. i. In the Western church they are door-keeper, lector, exorcist and acolyte (*qq.v.*), but these are now only stepping-stones to the priesthood, their duties being obsolete or performed by laymen (acolyte) or the higher clergy (exorcist). These minor orders, with the subdiaconate, are not of divine origin and so are not sacramental; the matter of the ordinations is the handing over of the symbols of office and the accompanying words constitute the form. Clerics in minor orders have all ecclesiastical privileges but are free to return to the lay state at will; they are also free to marry, but by so doing they lose all clerical status and any benefice they may hold. In case of need one may supply the place of a subdeacon at high Mass, singing the epistle and vested in a tunicle (but not a maniple). The ordinary minister of these orders is a bishop but they may be conferred on their own subjects by cardinals, prelates-*nullius* and abbots; they are usually conferred with very short intervals (interstices, *q.v.*).

ii. In the Eastern churches, Catholic and dissident, the minor orders have evolved differently. The Byzantines and Chaldeans have only subdeacon and lector (*qq.v.*); the Armenians and Malabarese just as in the West; the Copts, Syrians and Maronites have singer, lector and subdeacon. Except among the Armenians and Malabarese, the terminology major and minor is not used.

MINORITES, The. An archaic name for the Franciscan Friars Minor. The nuns were called Minoresses, hence the street called the Minories in the City of London where they formerly had a convent.

MINSTER (Old Eng. *mynster*, from Lat. *monasterium*, a monastery). An obsolete name for a conventual church of monks or nuns (*cf.*, Westminster, Minster-in-Sheppey). The two principal churches in England at York and Beverley to which the name is still popularly applied were both in fact formerly served by secular canons, though the second was founded for Benedictines.

MIRACLE. An effect wrought in nature directly by God. It is not necessarily a breach of the laws of nature, or even a suspension of these laws, but an effect wrought independently of natural powers and laws and of such a character that man reasonably concludes that God himself, who alone is above and beyond nature, is the immediate and direct cause of the effect, without having acted as normally through the series of intermediate causes we call Nature. Belief in miracles is based on the conviction of the uniformity and the ascertainable limits of the workings of nature, and the rational conviction that when a fact does not fall within this uniformity and this limitation, it can only be due directly to God. Christ promised the continuance of miracles in his church and the Catholic Church has always and does now display them and will always do so. Though a Catholic is bound to accept this principle as a matter of faith, the miraculous character of each individual occurrence must be settled by the evidence. Hence no individual miracles, except those mentioned in holy Scripture, are of faith. Christ left the gift of miracles not as a part of the functions of the office-bearers in the Church but as signs which follow those that believe (Mark xvi, 17-18). They are sometimes granted through the prayers and agency of saintly persons, who are called *thaumaturgi* or wonderworkers, but more frequently directly in response to petition. Christ promised that even greater things than he did should be done by believers, and church history shows that his word was true.

ii. As a motive of credibility. "If anyone should say that no miracles can be performed . . . or that they can never be known with certainty, or that by them the divine origin of the Christian religion cannot be rightly proved, let him be anathema" (Vatican Council, sess. iii, canon 3, 4). A miracle must be evident to the senses and therein lies its power; "it is natural to man to arrive at the intelligible truth through its sensible effects. Wherefore . . . he is brought to a certain degree of supernatural knowledge of the objects of faith by certain supernatural effects which are called miracles" (St. Thomas, II-II, clxxviii, 1; *cf.*, Mark xvl, 20; John x, 38).

iii. In canonization. Ordinarily at least two miracles must now be proved to have been performed by Almighty God through the person concerned, either during his life-time or by intercession after death, before beatification, and two more between that and canonization. Nevertheless, "it is a far bet-ter thing to convert a sinner than to restore a dead man to life" (St. Augustine) and the Bollandists, among others, have pointed out that many great saints worked few, if any, miracles, *e.g.*, St. Augustine himself, St. Athanasius, St. Gregory of Nyssa, St. Ignatius Loyola. For the canonization of Thomas More and John Fisher in 1935 the require-ment of miracles was waived.

MIRACLES OF CHRIST, The. The miracles done by Jesus Christ are one piece of evi-dence for the truth of the doctrine of his divinity (which is believed by Catholics on the authority of the teaching Church), for God alone can work miracles. "Reasoning is peculiar to man; therefore when anybody reasons, on whatever it may be, it is clear that he is a man. So, since God alone can of his own power work miracles, any single miracle done by Christ *by his own power* is a sufficient proof that he is God" (St. Thomas, III, xliii, 4 ad 3). The miracles commonly said to be performed by saints, relics, etc., are not done by their own power but by that of God alone. The gospels record certain miracles of our Lord and state that he did many others; of those recorded, three were of raising the dead, twenty were of healing, seven were of the possessed, and nine were "nature miracles" (*e.g.*, that at Cana). There is another class of event which on the evi-dence is not so certainly miraculous (*e.g.*, John viii, 20), but in Luke iv, 30, "to stand in the midst of these conspirators and not be taken was a glorious proof of his divinity" (St. John Chrysostom).

MIRACLE PLAY. A popular religious play of the middle ages, also called a Mystery. Miracles are sometimes distinguished from Mysteries as dealing with the life of a saint or other historical event, as opposed to the representation of a mystery of the faith or other matter from the Sacred Scriptures: or, again, as belonging to the earlier drama preceding the great efflorescence of Mysteries in the 15th century. They were usually per-formed out-of-doors on temporary fixed or wheeled stages. The most famous English Miracles are those contained in the Towneley or Wakefield, York, Chester and Coventry

collections or cycles. They were a character-istic product of the Christian life of those times, primarily a work and concern of the common people, folk drama in fact. There is nothing analogous to them in these days and all attempts at artificial revival have failed. Biblical plays are at least as old as the days of St. Gregory Nazianzen (*cf.*, Passion Play).

MIRACULOUS MEDAL, The. An oval medal bearing on one side an image of our Lady standing on a globe with rays of light coming from her hands, surrounded by the words: "O Mary conceived without sin! Pray for us who have recourse to thee"; on the re-verse, a cross, the initial M, and a representa-tion of the hearts of Jesus and his mother. This design is said to have been revealed to St. Catherine Labouré, a Sister of Charity of St. Vincent de Paul, who had three visions of our Lady in 1830. Its name appears to be due to the circumstances of its origin rather than to miracles connected with its pious use. It is worn on a blue ribbon as the badge of the Children of Mary. The Lazarists and some dioceses keep a feast of the Manifestation of the Miraculous Medal by our Lady Immaculate on Nov. 27, the date of the event.

MIRARI VOS. An encyclical letter, whereby in 1832 Pope Gregory XVI implicitly con-demned the journal *L'Avenir*, conducted by the Abbé de Lamennais, Lacordaire, and the Comte de Montalembert, which had clam-oured for a "huge liberty" in which religious and political right would assert itself. The extent of this liberty and the paper's en-thusiasm for revolt were deemed dangerous to religion and favourable to ultimate in-differentism.

MIRROR OF CREATION, The. A refer-ence to 1 Cor. xiii, 12. "The whole of creation is a mirror to us because we come to a knowledge of the divine wisdom, beauty and surpassing excellence from the harmony, beauty and splendour which God has pro-duced in his creation" (St. Thomas Aquinas).

MISERERE, The. Used without qualifica-tion, Ps. 1 is indicated, this being the first word in Latin: *Miserere mei Deus, secundum magnam misericordiam tuam* (Have mercy on me, O God, according to thy great mercy). It is the fourth of the Penitential Psalms and is of frequent use in the liturgy; *e.g.*, at Lauds (*ad Laudes*, II), at the end of *Tenebræ*, in the consecration of a church (with the antiphon *Asperges me* after every three verses) and of an altar, at burials, in bless-ing a church, cemetery or bell, in reconcil-ing a profaned church, and on other occa-sions. It is recited in monasteries when the discipline (*q.v.*) is taken, and has at all times been considered the psalm of penitence *par excellence.*

MISERICORD (Lat., compassion). A narrow ledge on the under side of the hinged seat of a choir stall; when the seat is turned up it allows one standing to recline against it. In many monasteries these are still used to support the person (instead of sitting) during the singing of the psalms of the Divine Office and certain of the chants at Mass. Such seats are often improperly called *misereres*.

MISERICORDIA, CONFRATERNITÀ DELLA (It., Confraternity of Pity). A generic name for societies of laymen who bind themselves together to assist the injured, sick and dying and arrange and attend funerals. Their robe of office is a black gown completely covering the body from crown to heels, with two eye-holes, girdled with a rope. The best known of these confraternities, common in Italy and Spain, is that of Florence, founded in 1244.

MISHNA, The (Heb., repetition). The oral law of the Jewish synagogue, collected by the rabbi Judah the Prince about (A.D.) 180 and codified into six orders (*seders*) according to subject matter. It covers civil and criminal law, social relations, liturgy, etc., and forms one part of the Talmud, the *Mishna* being the text upon which the Talmud enlarges.

MISSA DE ANGELIS (Lat., Mass of the Angels). The votive Mass of the Holy Angels, assigned to Tuesdays; but more usually the music of plainchant Mass no. VIII is meant.

MISSA CANTATA (Lat.). Sung Mass (*q.v.*).

MISSA PAPÆ MARCELLI (Lat., The Mass of Pope Marcellus). The most famous of all polyphonic compositions of music for the Mass, written in 1565 by Palestrina in 6 parts and edited by Anerio in 4.

MISSA PRO POPULO. Mass for the People (*q.v.*).

MISSA RECITATA. Dialogue Mass (*q.v.*).

MISSA SICCA. Dry Mass (*q.v.*).

MISSA SOLEMNIS. High Mass (*q.v.*).

MISSA SOLITARIA. A Mass said without server or congregation; normally such is forbidden.

MISSAL. The liturgical book which contains all the prayers necessary to enable a priest to celebrate Mass throughout the year; each use of Latin rite has its own proper missal, the "Missale Romanum" (*q.v.*) being easily the most widely used. The missal contains a calendar, minute and exhaustive rubrics, and private prayers for the use of the celebrant; the proper of the season (including the fixed feasts of Christmas time) beginning with the first Sunday in Advent, the proper of the saints (beginning at Nov.

29), the common of the saints, the votive Masses and divers prayers, the Masses for the dead (*qq.v.*); certain blessings connected with the Mass (*e.g.*, of holy water, of Easter eggs); some Masses proper to certain places or religious orders, and a local supplement. The ordinary and canon (*qq.v.*) of the Mass are printed for convenience immediately after the proper of Holy Saturday near the middle of the volume. The variable parts of the Mass printed or indicated in the propers, common, etc., are the introit, collect, epistle, gradual and alleluia or tract, gospel, offertory, secret, communion and post-communion (*qq.v.*) and such unusual additions as a sequence (*q.v.*): but the proper prefaces are all grouped together in the ordinary. The missal properly contains all the chant required by the priest at the altar. The only Eastern rites having a book corresponding entirely to the Latin missal are the Maronite and Malabarese; the name is sometimes erroneously given to *Euchologia*.

MISSAL-STAND. A small desk of metal or wood to support the missal on the altar during the celebration of Mass. A cushion is permissible for the purpose (indeed, is stipulated by the rubrics) and is always used by the Carthusians.

MISSALE ROMANUM. "The Roman Missal," that is, according to the general use of the Western church, published in its present form by St. Pius V in 1570, revised by Clement VIII, Urban VIII, Leo XIII and Pius X. At a time when very many dioceses had their own missals, the early Franciscans did much to spread the use of that of the church of Rome (see RITE). "Missale ad usum Fratrum Carmelitorum," as used by the Calced Carmelites; "Missale mistum secundum regulam Beati Isidori dictum Mozarabes," the Mozarabic Missal; "Missale Romanum in cuo antiqui ritus Lugdunenses serventur," as used at Lyons; "Missale ad usum insignis et præclaræ ecclesiæ Sarum," the former missal of Salisbury and south England, etc. The first printed missal was dated 1474.

MISSION. i. A missionary district which has not received any definite canonical organization or of which the organization is in abeyance; it is administered by a priest appointed by the Congregation of Propaganda.

ii. Quasi-parish. The division of a vicariate or prefecture apostolic, corresponding to a parish as the division of a diocese. The rector of a mission is called a *quasi-parochus*. He has all the rights and duties of a rector of a parish.

iii. The name given to the parochial divisions of England and Wales until they received canonical status upon its ceasing to be a missionary country, in the technical sense, in 1908. The expression "on the mission" used of a priest engaged in parochial work is still heard.

iv. Of a Divine Person. This involves a double notion: (*a*) that of a procession, a going forth, of the person sent from the sender, and this is eternal; and (*b*) a new mode of being in something external, and this is temporal. It is a substantial mission (as is a bud from a branch), but by way of origin implying no diminution in the person sent. Thus the Holy Ghost has a mission from the Father and the Son to take up his abode in the souls of the just, and the Son is sent from the Father to be incarnate.

MISSION, CONGREGATION OF PRIESTS OF THE. The Lazarists (*q.v.*).

MISSION SISTERS OF THE PRECIOUS BLOOD, The. A congregation founded by Dom Francis Pfanner in 1885 for missionary work among women and children in South Africa; they are associated with the Mariannhill Fathers (*q.v.*).

MISSIONS, FOREIGN, are missions to the heathen and Moslems as opposed to popular missions (*q.v.*) and the care of the faithful in predominantly non-Catholic countries. They are under the direction of the Congregation of Propaganda, and missionaries from among the secular clergy are supplied by special colleges in all parts of the world (*e.g.*, in England, at Mill Hill; in the U.S.A., the Josephinum at Columbus and Maryknoll). Most of the old religious orders do some foreign missionary work, particularly the Dominicans and Franciscans, and the Benedictines have a congregation, that of St. Ottilia, devoted entirely to it. More recent congregations, such as the Jesuits, Redemptorists, Passionists, Lazarists, have large foreign missions; others, *e.g.*, the White Fathers (Africa), Scheut Fathers (China and Africa), Society of Lyons (Africa), of Milan, of Paris, of the Consolata of Turin, of the Divine Saviour, the Holy Ghost Fathers, were founded particularly for this purpose. Missionary territories are normally organized as missions, prefectures and vicariates apostolic (*qq.v.*); the aim of the Church is to form an indigenous clergy, and in the fulness of time to organize them into a local hierarchy with native bishops, as has been done in parts of India, China and elsewhere. The object of foreign missions is the conversion of the heathen to the faith of Christ and their incorporation in his Church, the appointed means of salvation. Medical missions, schools, material relief, etc., are the corporal works of mercy which necessarily accompany the Christian missionary; but his job requires of him no other intervention in native affairs, except it be for the express purpose of saving souls or imparting that minimum of education which should enable them to improve themselves from within and in their own way. The missionary is an emissary of Christ, not of a continent, a country, a culture or of commerce. At the time of the last statistical survey before 1939 there were 489 missionary ecclesiastical divisions in 78 countries; these were served by 352 bishops and 137 other ordinaries (24 of them being "natives"), 17000 priests (4800 natives), 6180 brothers (2150 natives), 47,000 nuns (16,700 natives), and 74,000 native catechists, representing 56 nationalities; 720 hospitals, with 33,000 beds, treated over 11 million people; nearly 37,000 schools had 2¼ million pupils; 1900 orphanages sheltered 111,000 children; 17,500 old people were looked after in 417 homes. The missionaries ran 171 printing-presses, among whose productions were 320 periodicals. The number of baptized Catholics in these missions was 18 million, and 2½ million more were catechumens. The Russian Orthodox in the days of its imperial ascendancy was the only dissident Eastern church to preach to the heathen on any big scale in recent times (*e.g.*, in Tibet, Japan and China).

MISSIONS, POPULAR. A popular mission is a series of sermons or instructions with other religious exercises, continuing over a certain number of days and conducted by one or more missionary priests who visit the parish for the purpose. Such a mission is designed as a spiritual tonic to confirm the fervent, rouse the slack, instruct the ignorant and convert sinners and is commonly concluded by a renewal of baptismal vows. These missions originated with the Dominican and Franciscan friars, who still conduct them; but in modern times the work is particularly associated with the Jesuits, Redemptorists, Passionists and Lazarists who lay themselves out specially for it. Many parishes have a week or fortnight's mission every year. In 1896 Germanos Mu'akkad, ex-metropolitan of Baalbek, founded the Congregation of Missionaries of St. Paul to give missions on European lines among the Melkites of Syria.

MISSIONARY APOSTOLIC. An honorary title conferred by the Holy See on certain distinguished missioners in foreign missions.

MISSIONARY COUNTRY. A territory not subject to the common law of the Western church but under the jurisdiction of the Congregation of Propaganda, either as a mission, prefecture or vicariate apostolic. A few countries with ordinary hierarchies (*e.g.*, Australia, India, New Zealand) are so subject. Districts of Eastern rite are not missionary strictly speaking as in no circumstances do they come under Western common law or Propaganda but the jurisdiction of the Eastern Congregation, which is personal rather than territorial.

MISSIONARY RECTOR. A title with the status of irremovability, formerly conferred on the priests in charge of certain important missions or quasi-parishes in England until it ceased to be a missionary country in 1908.

MISSIONARY SISTERS OF THE SACRED HEART. A congregation founded by St. Frances Xavier Cabrini at Codogno in Italy in 1880. At the suggestion of Pope Leo XIII she led her sisters to the help of Italian immigrants in the U.S.A. Before her death in 1917 she had established over 70 convents and institutions, with hundreds of sisters, in North and South America and elsewhere, including the Columbus Hospitals in New York and Chicago; among the other works are schools and orphanages, and the giving of religious instruction.

MITRE (Gr. μίτρα, a turban). The liturgical head-dress proper to bishops of the Latin rite. It originated as a low, soft cap and has evolved through numerous forms into a high stiff hat consisting of two similar parts, back and front, with bulging sides which curve back to the top; the sides are joined with a head-band at the bottom and have soft material between enabling them to be folded together; two fringed lappets (*infulæ*) hang down behind. In western Europe the mediæval form, lower, softer and with straight sides, has again come into considerable use. In the consecration of a bishop the mitre is considered symbolically as the helmet of salvation. It is always taken off when the celebrant prays, *e.g.*, at the collects, during the canon, etc. Mitres are of three kinds, precious, golden and simple (*qq.v.*). Other prelates who have the use of *pontificalia* (*e.g.*, cardinals, abbots, protonotaries apostolic) wear the mitre, and a right to wear the simple mitre has been given to several cathedral chapters of canons, *e.g.*, at Lucca, Siena, Bamberg, Ravenna, Benevento, Urbino, Turin, Lisbon, Lyons. The Western mitre is worn by Catholic bishops of all the Eastern rites except the Byzantine, and by dissident Armenians; the dissident Malabarese have evolved a pattern of their own. The ordinary Eastern episcopal head-dress is the crown (*q.v.*).

MITRE, GOLDEN (Lat. *mitra auriphrygiata*). A mitre made of plain cloth-of-gold, to be worn during Advent and Lent and at other penitential times and occasions, and when during a sacred ceremony the bishop has to sit down for some time.

MITRE, PRECIOUS (Lat. *mitra pretiosa*). A mitre adorned with gold, precious stones, etc., worn by those who have the right thereto when they have occasion to officiate on any feast, on ferias in paschal-time and on Sundays outside of Advent, Septuagesima and Lent.

MITRE, SIMPLE. One made of plain white silk or linen. It is worn by cardinals, bishops and abbots at funerals, on Good Friday,

when blessing the candles on Candlemas, and when in solemn attendance on the pope. Inferior prelates (*e.g.*, protonotaries apostolic supernumerary and *ad instar*) who are granted the use of the mitre are usually restricted to the white linen one.

MIXED CHALICE. See WATER, i.

MIXED LIFE. The highest form of the spiritual life in which the active life is superadded to the contemplative. "One kind of active life is that which flows from the fulness of contemplation, as teaching or preaching. . . . And this is superior to simple contemplation. For just as it is a better thing to illuminate than merely to shine, so it is better to impart to others the things contemplated than merely to contemplate them. . . . So, therefore, among religious institutes those hold the highest place which are ordained to teaching and preaching, since they come nearest to the perfection of the episcopate" (St. Thomas, II-II, clxxxviii, 6).

MIXED MARRIAGE. A marriage between a Catholic and a non-Catholic. Mixed marriages are forbidden by ecclesiastical law, while if there is danger to the faith of the Catholic or the children, divine law itself forbids them. Though in some cases a dispensation may be obtained on certain conditions, the Church never approves of such marriages. Sacred rites, such as nuptial Mass and Blessing, are prohibited, and the banns are not published, but the ordinary may permit some ceremonial. If the non-Catholic is baptized the impediment is called Mixed Religion, and the marriage is unlawful but not invalid. If the non-Catholic is unbaptized the impediment is called Disparity (or Difference) of Worship, and the marriage is both unlawful and invalid. The conditions necessary for a dispensation in either case are: (*a*) a grave cause; (*b*) a written promise of the non-Catholic not to interfere with the religion of the Catholic, and of both parties to have all children baptized and educated as Catholics; and (*c*) moral certainty that the promises will be fulfilled. The Catholic is bound to try prudently to convert the non-Catholic. The parties must on no account go through a form of marriage also before a non-Catholic minister of religion, unless this is required by civil law to obtain the civil effects and it is clearly understood that it is purely a civil act. Anyone who contracts marriage before a non-Catholic minister, or who marries with an explicit or implicit agreement to bring up any child as a non-Catholic, incurs *ipso facto* excommunication reserved to the ordinary.* Catholics who contract a mixed marriage without a dispensation are *ipso facto* excluded from legitimate ecclesiastical acts and sacramentals (*e.g.*, churching after childbirth) till dispensed by the ordinary. Marriage between two non-Catholics, one baptized and

---

* These acts no longer carry the penalty of *ipso facto* excommunication. A Catholic may obtain a dispensation by which he can contract a valid marriage before a non-Catholic clergyman, but without such a dispensation he sins gravely and the union is invalid. Entering marriage with an intention not to raise a child as a Catholic is a grave sin.—*Publisher*, 1997.

the other unbaptized, is no longer invalid since the Code of Canon Law came into force in 1918. The Church's strict legislation in the matter of mixed marriages is due simply to her concern for the welfare of the Catholic party; there is always an element of danger to his faith and to that of the children, and loss of faith is a harm done to the whole Church, the Mystical Body of Christ, as well as to the party concerned. Moreover experience has shown that mixed marriages are undesirable on natural grounds, being a fruitful source of marital unhappiness and strife.

MIXED RELIGION. A prohibiting impediment (*q.v.*) of marriage which arises when one party is a Catholic and the other a baptized non-Catholic. It must be distinguished from difference of worship (*q.v.*) though both alike are commonly referred to as a mixed marriage. A dispensation for such a marriage may be obtained for good reasons and provided the non-Catholic party makes certain promises, for which see MIXED MARRIAGE.

MODE (Lat. *modus*, measure, manner). i. A determination (*q.v.*) of being. (*a*) Substantial, determines the substance in itself, as existence, subsistence, personality, suppositality, etc.; (*b*) accidental, the determination of an accident or of a substance by an accident, as place, roundness, redness, etc.

ii. In plainchant any note from *re* to *do*, except *si*, can be taken as the tonic of a distinct scale; a melody written in any such scale is said to be in such and such a mode or tone. The modes in which the compass is from the tonic to the octave above are termed authentic; when it is from the 4th below the tonic to the 5th above, they are plagal. The chief plainchant modes are eight in number, the tonic scales of *re*, *mi*, *fa* and *sol*, each in two positions; these, the so-called Gregorian Modes, are distinguished by numbers, thus: 1st *re* authentic, 2nd *re* plagal, and so on; to them are allied the four modes composed on the tonics *la* and *do*. It must be clearly understood that there is nothing distinctively ecclesiastical about this musical system; it is derived from the scales of the Graeco-Roman *citharodi*, and was common to all the music of western Europe until, about the beginning of the 17th century, it was superseded by the modern system wherein all the so-called scales can be reduced to two separate modes, *do* (major) and *la* (minor).

MODERNISM is described in the encyclical *Pascendi* (Sept. 7, 1907) of Pope Pius X as a "synthesis of all heresies." It appeared about the beginning of the 20th century, grew insidiously among clergy and laity (many of them of blameless life), and was destroyed by the energetic action of Pope Pius X.* Its foundation is in agnosticism (the teaching that God can in no way be the object of certain knowledge) and in Immanence (*q.v.*, the teaching that foundation of faith must be sought in an internal sense which arises from man's need of God). From these principles, allied with various evolutionary doctrines, Modernism tended to demolish dogmas (which it called variable symbols), sacraments (which it reduced to faith-nourishing signs), the authenticity and genuineness of the Scriptures, the Church, and ecclesiastical authority and discipline. It would reduce Christ to human dimensions, and make inspiration a common gift of mankind.

MODESTY. The virtue which enables a man to observe moderation in all things; *e.g.*, in estimating his own worth, in seeking after knowledge, in deportment and in dress. It will thus be seen that modesty in its commonest sense, with reference to deportment and dress, is a relative thing, varying from place to place and from age to age. Actions and words lawful and praiseworthy in the married are immodest for the single; social customs recognized in England are immodest in Spain; the dress of a Connemara fishing-girl is immodest in a drawing-room; the requirements of modesty in the Vatican or in church are more rigorous than those of Samoa or when sea-bathing. Modesty is allied to temperance and resides precisely in moderation according to the circumstances as recognized by a thoughtful mind and approved by a pure heart.**

MOHAMMEDANISM. A common name for the religion of Islam (*q.v.*), misleading because Moslems do not regard Mohammed as its founder but trace it back through the prophets (Noe, Abraham, Moses, etc.) to God's revelation to Adam.

MOHATRA (Span.). A contract for a fictitious sale and repurchase whereby money-dealers evaded ecclesiastical laws against usury. The conditions in which it might be morally justified were the subject of much discussion among casuists.

MOLINISM. The system proposed by Luis de Molina (1535-1600), and developed by other Jesuit theologians, to solve the problem of reconciling the freedom of man's will with the efficacy of divine grace. Molinism states that while grace prompts and assists the will, it neither physically nor morally coerces it to one course of action; the free consent of the will is a necessary condition for grace to produce its effect. A modified form of Molinism is preferred by many theologians to-day (*vide* Congruism); Dominican and many other theologians reject every form of Molinism.

MOMONA. The Latin name of the see of Cloyne (*q.v.*). Adjective: *Cloynensis*.

MONACHISM (Lat. *monachus*, a monk). See MONASTICISM.

---

* Modernism was driven underground, not destroyed; it resurfaced in the mid 1960's.—*Publisher*, 1997.
** Modesty is a moral virtue which guards chastity. Although its requirements are somewhat elastic, proper guidelines for modesty cannot be derived from persons or societies which do not accept the strict standards of chastity taught by Our Lord and the Catholic Church.—*Publisher*, 1997.

MONARCHIANISM (Gr. μο ναρχία, absolute rule). i. A name inaccurately given to the belief of a 3rd century sect, followers of one Theodotius, who taught that our Lord was simply a man in whom the Holy Ghost (The Christ) dwelt after his baptism.

ii. Another name for Sabellianism (q.v.).

MONASTERY (Gr. μοναστήριον, the dwelling of a solitary). The fixed abode of a community of monks, canons regular or nuns; the name is extended to include houses of friars and of certain more recent congregations, e.g., Passionists, Redemptorists, but never of Jesuits. See also CONVENT; DOUBLE MONASTERY. Normally it consists principally of a church, chapter-house, cloisters, refectory, cells or common dormitory, the superior's apartments, library and work-rooms, guest quarters, parlour for visitors. For the canonical erection of a monastery with enclosure (q.v.) the permission of the bishop is always required and in certain countries of the Holy See as well; normally at least twelve religious must live in it. A monastery is generally an abbey or a priory (qq.v.).

MONASTIC BREVIARY, The. See OFFICE, MONASTIC.

MONASTICISM. The essence of monasticism, strictly so called, is the formation of "a community of monks, bound to live together until death, under rule, in common life, in the monastery of their profession, as a religious family, leading a life not of marked austerity but devoted to the service of God" (Abbot Butler, O.S.B.). It must be distinguished from the community life of canons regular and the mendicant life of friars, both of which are monastic only to a certain extent and incidentally, and still more from the organized activity of later orders and congregations. See RELIGIOUS LIFE. Monasticism is known in all the great religions, e.g., Moslem, Confucian, Buddhist, with the notable exception of Judaism.

MONASTICISM, CELTIC. The life of the great monasteries of the Celtic church (q.v.) in Ireland and Wales was sui generis, an almost entirely indigenous growth, owing nothing to St. Augustine of Hippo or to St. Benedict. No connexion with the Egyptian system has been satisfactorily established, but there was strong Gallic influence. In its most rudimentary form the Celtic monastery was really a religious settlement of clerics and lay folk (Welsh llan, Cornish lan, Breton lann). Monastic life when properly established was so penitential as to be comparable with that of the hermits of Egypt; the Divine Office (in Latin, as all Celtic services) was exceedingly long in some monasteries; e.g., at Lauds, a minimum of 24 psalms and on Saturdays and Sundays from November to March a maximum of 75. The greatest monasteries were Clonard, Clonfert, Clonmac-

noise, Lismore and Glendalough in Ireland; Iona in Scotland; Bangor Iscoed and Llanilltyd Fawr in Wales; Dòl, Alet, Tréguier Landevenec, Redon and Saint Méen in Brittany; Luxeuil and Bobbio, founded by the Irish St. Columban, in central Europe. At Saint Gall (not founded by the saint of that name) Irish influence was not so strong.

MONASTICISM, EASTERN. i. The life of Orthodox (Byzantine) monks is substantially the same as in the 4th century; they follow no rule as understood in the West and though they are often distinguished as Basilians (q.v.) the name is wrong and misleading. A monk is just a monk, and his life is "the Angelic Life." Monasteries are divided into cœnobia and idiorrhythmic (qq.v.) and each is independent unless it is a kellion (q.v.) but is subject to the bishop, unless exempt (a stauropegion). There are three categories of monk, rasophore, staurophore and megaloskhemos (qq.v.). Their life is entirely given up to the singing of the Divine Office and work within the monastery, with long fasts, abstinence from meat, and other austerities. In Orthodox churches of recent years the monastic life has much decayed and there have been agitations for monks to abandon their vocation in favour of active work. Mount Athos (q.v.) has been since the 10th century the centre and head of Orthodox monachism.

ii. Non-Orthodox Eastern monachism is of the same kind as the Byzantine but even less organized and very decayed. Monks are most numerous among the Ethiopians; Armenian monks take no vows and the monasteries are more like communities of secular priests: they are training-grounds for the higher clergy; there are seven important ancient houses of men in Egypt; among the Nestorians the religious life is extinct and with the Jacobites nearly so.

iii. For Catholic Eastern monachism, see ANTONIANS; BASILIANS; MEKHITARISTS, etc.

MONASTICISM, WESTERN. All Western monasticism now derives from St. Benedict of Nursia (c. 480-547), who in his Rule (q.v.) adapted the life and ideas of the Fathers of the Desert, of St. Basil and of St. John Cassian to the needs and circumstances of European life. He legislated for independent, autocephalous families of men not in holy orders, whose spiritual life should be centred in the singing of the Divine Office and daily work the labour of their hands, under discipline and a moderate degree of austerity (see CONTEMPLATIVE LIFE). By the year 1000 it had become the regular thing for a monk to be ordained, paid servants were doing the manual work, choir duties had multiplied, many monks had become missionaries and scholars. The congregation of Cluny (q.v.) innovated the centralized control of a number of monasteries, and increased liturgical splendour. The Camaldolese, Vallombrosans, Grandmontines and Carthusians (qq.v.) reacted towards a more individual and enclosed life; the Cistercians (q.v.) returned to a more literal interpretation of St. Benedict's Rule and continue to this day a more primitive form of monastic life. The rise of the friars and general decline of feudal monasticism produced three principal further varieties of Benedictinism, the Sylvestrines, Celestines and Olivetans (qq.v.), but they remained local. After the Reformation, and again after the French Revolution, the parent Benedictine body and its chief limb, the Cistercian, revived: the latter confirming its strict programme of prayer and manual work, the former developing the numerous new forms and activities displayed by Benedictines (q.v.) to-day: in particular, the education of youth and the pursuance of learned studies combined with that attention to public worship to which St. Benedict of Aniane in the 8th century gave a great impetus. A monastery still aims at St. Benedict's ideal, "a school of the Lord's service, in the setting forth of which we hope to order nothing that is harsh or rigorous."

MONEYLESS ONES, HOLY (Gr. ἀνάργυροι). Certain saints who were physicians and treated the poor without payment are so called in the East, particularly Cosmas and Damian and Cyrus and John. They are greatly venerated by the Greeks, Copts and Syrians and the first two are named in the canon of the Mass.

MONISM (Gr. μόνος, alone). A materialist system, according to which all things proceed from one only principle, viz. matter, by way of evolution; it is opposed to the Dualism (q.v. ii) of matter and spirit. Generally speaking, the name Monism is given to all systems which reduce all beings to one and the same essential principle, whether matter or spirit.

MONITA SECRETA (Lat., secret orders). A forged code of instructions in which Aquaviva, fifth provost general of the Society of Jesus, is made to enjoin upon the superiors of the Society every disreputable means of increasing its wealth and influence; published in 1612, a year after its true author, Zahorowski, had been dismissed from the Society; now recognized as a forgery by all reputable writers.

MONK (Gr. μοναχός, a solitary). One who by taking the vows of religion binds himself to the monastic life (see MONASTICISM) in its integrity. In the Eastern churches all religious are monks; in the Western church, only the members of the following orders: the Benedictine, Camaldolese, Vallombrosan, Sylvestrine, Olivetan, Cistercian and Carthusian. Canons regular (q.v.) are sometimes classed as monks; but the distinction between a monk and a friar (q.v.) is very sharp, both in law and in fact.

MONKS OF UNION, The. A quasi-congregation of Benedictines formed, in 1924 at the request of Pope Pius XI to work for the reunion with the Catholic Church of the Russian and other dissident Slav churches. Until 1939 their chief establishment was the priory of Amay-sur-Meuse in Belgium; in that year they moved to Chevetogne in the same country. The community consists of two groups, one of the Latin, the other of the Byzantine rite; each group has its proper chapel, but on greater feasts all assist at the Byzantine liturgy, which is used in Greek and Slavonic in alternate weeks. The monks are of several nationalities, and follow the Rule of St. Benedict adapted to the requirements of their work and life. They publish a valuable oriental review, *Irenikon,* in French.

MONOGRAM, SACRED. This term usually indicates the letters IHS, a monogram of the Holy Name in Greek 'ΙΗσοῦΣ. It owes its modern popularity partly to the devotion to the Holy Name popularized by St. Bernardine of Siena and partly to its adoption as the badge of the Jesuits. Several fanciful interpretations of the letters are current.

MONOPHYSISM, MONOPHYSITISM (Gr. μονή φύσις, one nature). The heresy that there is only one nature in Jesus Christ, his humanity being entirely absorbed in his divinity, and his body not of one substance with ours. It was an extreme reaction from Nestorianism (q.v.) and logically involved a denial of Christ's humanity, rendering his earthly life nugatory. The archimandrite Eutyches brought Monophysism into prominence (448), but Dioscoros, patriarch of Alexandria, was its chief champion; it was eventually condemned by the Council of Chalcedon (q.v.), which defined the Catholic doctrine. Those who rejected this council are known to-day as the dissident Coptic, Ethiopian, Syrian and Malabar Jacobite and Armenian churches (qq.v.). They are consequently in communion neither with the Catholics nor the Orthodox, and are commonly called the Monophysite Churches. But in fact they all repudiated the teaching of Eutyches and what religious (as distinct from political) considerations led them to reject Chalcedon is a difficult question. Today their alleged heresy is less certainly a theological conviction than a national, sectarian, traditional shibboleth.

MONOPOLY. The exclusive possession of the trade in some commodity, whether conferred as a privilege by the state or obtained accidentally or deliberately by means of business dealings; that degree of control over the supply of a commodity which enables the possessor to limit the supply and fix its price. A monopoly is not in itself unlawful, but is subject to the ordinary moral law of the just price (q.v.) and other obligations affecting traders and employers. Nevertheless, such are the opportunities for unjust dealing and oppression enjoyed by unscrupulous men who possess a monopoly that moralists regard it as the duty of the state to prohibit unnecessary monopolies and strictly to control those that are allowed.

MONOTHEISM. The belief in the unity of God. There is but one God, who is the personal creator, preserver and ruler of the universe. This belief is opposed to Atheism, Pantheism, Deism (*qq.v.*). It is antecedent to belief in the Trinity and is held by many, *e.g.*, Mohammedans, who do not believe in the Trinity.

MONOTHELISM, MONOTHELITISM (Gr. μόνον θέλημα, one will.) A heresy arising out of efforts to reconcile the monophysites in the 7th century. It consisted in the affirmation of one single will and one operation (or energy) in the person of Jesus Christ. The third council of Constantinople (680) condemned it by defining the Catholic doctrine that Christ has "two natural wills, without division, change, partition or confusion: not contrary to one another but the human will following and subject to the divine"; he had "one will" only in the sense that the two wills were always in harmony. The condemnation of Pope Honorius (*q.v.*) arose out of the monothelite controversy; and the heresy is said to have been professed by and to have lingered on among the Maronites (*q.v.*) until the 12th century: but this is disputed.

MONS PIETATIS (Lat., heap [of money] of piety). A pawnshop conducted with the object of making small loans to the poor, upon pledged objects and at a low rate of interest, as a charitable work and not for profit. Many such *montes* were established in Italy in the 15th century by the Franciscans; they were challenged on the ground of the unlawfulness of usury, but were sanctioned by the fifth Lateran Council and spread to the Low Countries, France, Spain and the Germanies. They have mostly now ceased to be semi-ecclesiastical charitable institutions and are become municipal pawnshops.

MONSIGNOR, -E (It., my lord, but without any feudal connotation; pl., *monsignori*). A title pertaining to all prelates of the Western church by virtue of their office; a man, then, is not "made a monsignor" any more than he can be "made a lord." The title is generally used for the prelates of the Roman court, active and honorary, but in some countries it is the common title of bishops (*e.g.*, France, in the form of *Monseigneur*); this usage does away with the English habit of speaking and writing of "Bishop So-and-so," as who should speak of "Duke Churchill," meaning the Duke of Marlborough.

MONSTRANCE (Lat. *monstrare*, to show). A vessel in which the Blessed Sacrament is exposed to the view of the people at Benediction and Exposition and carried in procession on Corpus Christi. It consists of a broad base, a stem with a knop, and receptacle, closed with glass or crystal, within which the Host in its lunette is fixed, and which is usually surrounded by metal rays; these should be at least of silver and surmounted by a cross.

MONSTROSITIES, in the sense of unnatural offspring, must always be baptized, at least conditionally. In doubt whether there is one or more persons, one is to be baptized absolutely, the others conditionally.

MONTANISM. A schism of the 2nd century, named from a Phrygian, Montanus, who with Maximilla and Prisca and other followers claimed a gift of prophecy which involved direct inspiration by the Holy Ghost and a new revelation. They preached the imminency of the Second Coming, forbade remarriage to the widowed and flight from persecution, and imposed new and rigorous fasts; moreover, they denied the power of the Church to forgive sins. This last was apparently the only dogmatic error which they professed as a body. Tertullian, a convert first to the faith and then to the schism, was the only famous Montanist. The sect lingered for about 200 years.

MONTE CASSINO. An archabbey in the province of Frosinone, Italy: the cradle of Western monachism, where St. Benedict (*d.c.* 547) organized a community and wrote the Holy Rule after leaving Subiaco. It has been an abbey *nullius* (*q.v.*) since 1367. Its abbot is a bishop, with jurisdiction over a large area. When in 1860 its archives were threatened with removal by the Italian government they were saved for the monastery by the personal intervention of the British prime minister, Mr. Gladstone; but during world-war II nobody was able to save the buildings (some very ancient, but mostly of the 16th and 17th centuries), and they were destroyed by the bombs and shells of the allied armies. Monte Cassino gives its name to the Cassinese (*q.v.* i.) Benedictine congregation.

MONTFORT FATHERS, The. The Company of Mary (*q.v.*).

MONTH OF MARY. See MAY DEVOTIONS.

MONTH'S MIND. The Mass of requiem said on the 30th day after a death or burial. The expression is still in use for a corresponding memorial service among Protestants in remote parts of England and Wales.

MONTREAL (*Marianopolitanus*). The second diocese of Canada, erected in 1836. Montreal was originally called Ville-Marie (hence its Latin name), and was founded in 1642; the first clergy there belonged to the Society of St. Sulpice. Its first bishop was J. J. Lartigue, of that society. The see was made metropolitan in 1886, its suffragan dioceses being Joliette, Saint-Hyacinthe, Saint John-in-Quebec, Sherbrooke, and Valleyfield. Montreal cathedral, which is a minor basilica (q.v.), is one of the 3 in North America that have chapters of canons (The other 2 are its suffragans Joliette and Saint-Hyacinthe).

MORAL PERSON. A juridical entity other than a physical human being to which personality is attributed by public authority. Moral persons in the Church are either collegiate, as chapters, religious orders, or non-collegiate, as churches, benefices, seminaries. A collegiate moral person must consist of at least three physical persons. In law moral persons count as minors. A moral person is of its nature perpetual and continues until legitimately suppressed, or until it has ceased de facto for 100 years. A moral person may be the rector of a parish, in which case the duties are carried out by a vicar.

MORAL PHILOSOPHY. The science of human acts considered as they bear on happiness and duty; it is divided into Ethics, Deontology and Natural Law and must be distinguished from Moral Theology (qq.v.).

MORAL SENSE. Catholic philosophy does not recognize any moral sense as a special faculty distinct from intellect; but teaches that primary moral principles are self-evident, arising in the intellect in the same way as speculative first principles, being equally necessary truths. The current popular notion of a moral sense (which some wayward folk may have been conveniently born without) is founded in an unwillingness to submit emotional moral judgements to the discipline of reason and knowledge and to give up the principle of the infallibility of the individual conscience. The name "moral sense" is sometimes given to the notion of right and wrong which is native to every man, enlightened by instruction and developed by conduct, found in its perfection in the judgements of a correct conscience (cf., Synderesis).

MORALITY. That quality of an act which characterizes it as good or bad i.e., as keeping or breaking the law of God as taught by the conscience. The morality of an act depends not only on the nature of the act itself but also on the end desired and the accompanying circumstances (q.v.).

MORALITY PLAY. A form of the religious drama very popular in the 15th and 16th centuries wherein was set forth the struggle between virtue and vice; such as "Everyman" and "The Pride of Life." Artists may, but moralists need not, regret its disappearance; its function was taken over by the old popular melodrama and now, less adequately because less dogmatically and less

well done, by a large class of cinematograph-films (cf., Miracle Play).

MORAVIANS, MORAVIAN BRETHREN. A Protestant sect deriving from the Hussites in the mid-15th century, re-formed and separated from the Lutherans by Count Zinzendorf in 1735; now divided into the provinces of Great Britain, North America, South America and Germany. The Bible is their rule of faith, but their dogmas are very loosely defined; they acknowledge as sacraments Baptism and the Lord's Supper; human nature is "totally depraved," but they profess Universalism (q.v.). They are very zealous propagandists of their sect. Also known as Unitas Fratrum and Bohemian Brethren.

MORGANATIC MARRIAGE (Old High Ger., morgangeba, customary gift from husband to wife on the morning after marriage, the only claim which a morganatic wife has on her husband's property; cf., the cowyll of Welsh law). A marriage between a man of exalted rank and a woman of lower rank upon the agreement that she retains her station and that the children have no right of succession to their father's titles or possessions. Ecclesiastically this does not differ in any way from any other marriage. The expression is often misused and misunderstood because in practice princes tend to take another "wife" of their own rank and to regard the true wife as a mistress, hence morganatic wife is sometimes wrongly assumed to be synonymous with mistress.

MORISCOS. Moorish converts to Christianity in Spain, many of whom apostatized and were proceeded against by the Inquisition.

MORNING STAR (Lat. Stella matutina). A title given to our Lady in the litany of Loreto, first used by St. Peter Damian and St. Simon Stock.

MOROCCO, THE CHURCH IN. The sultanate of Moghrab al-Aksa, "the Farthest West," has an estimated population of 7½ million, solidly Mohammedan except for Jews and aboriginal Berbers. The first Christian mission to Morocco was in 1234 and there was a bishop there in 1566; the mission was revived by a Franciscan martyr, Bd. John of Prado, in 1631. The 110,000 Catholics are in large proportion foreigners living in the European spheres of influence. The mission is still in charge of the Friars Minor, and forms 2 vicariates apostolic.

MORSE (Lat. morsus, a buckle). A metal ornament worn on the fastening of the cope by cardinals and bishops. The name was originally applied to the fastening itself, which from being lappets of fabric, as they are now again, became a brooch or clasp of metal. Also called fibula, formale, pectorale.

MORTALIUM ANIMOS. An encyclical letter of Pope Pius XI, in 1928, on fostering true religious unity among Christians; it is a guide for all concerned with healing the wounds of Christendom, which must remain their charter and direction-post for so long as conditions remain as they are today, while its underlying principles are valid for all time. It is, on the one hand, a warning against rash, ill-considered or definitely illicit methods of trying to restore Christian unity; on the other, it is a call for mutual love, forbearance and prayer. *Mortalium animos* was followed in the same year by a letter specifically concerned with the Eastern churches, *Rerum orientalium.*

MORTIFICATION. The performance of acts of self-discipline; the acts themselves. Mortification is a practice of asceticism (*q.v.*) either spiritual by internal curbing and killing love of self in all its manifestations by denying it even blameless action; or physical, by means of self-inflicted bodily austerity (*q.v.*). Ascetically considered, this is only an auxiliary of spiritual mortification, but it is also practised for the motive of expiation of past sins, whether of oneself or of others.

MORTMAIN (Old Fr. *morte meyn*, dead hand, *i.e.*, impersonal ownership). The condition of land or other real property held in perpetual tenure by any corporation, that is, an undying body, but especially by an ecclesiastical corporation aggregate, such as an abbey, or a corporation sole, such as a bishop. There have been numerous enactments of English law to restrain alienation in mortmain, in the interests of the king and other superior landlords who were otherwise deprived of their reliefs, fines on marriage, wardships, escheats, and other feudal rights at the death of an owner or tenant, and sometimes of their military service. Many of the early acts were directed against ecclesiastical corporations (*e.g.*, in 1279; the first act was 9 Hen. III, c. 32, 1224); later they were in the general interests of the state rather than of feudal lords. Up to the Reformation the Crown granted licences to alienate and hold land in mortmain. The law in England is now that of the Mortmain and Charitable Uses Act, 1888, and its amendments.

MORTUARY CHAPEL. A chapel built specially to shelter the dead; a private or public chapel built in a cemetery or other burying place and used only for funeral purposes. Requiem Masses only may be celebrated therein. The chancel of the now Anglican parish church of Arundel is still the mortuary chapel of the Catholic dukes of Norfolk.

MOSAIC LAW, The. The legislation contained in the books of Exodus, Leviticus, Numbers and Deuteronomy, binding on the Jews and fulfilled by Christ, in part by confirmation (*e.g.*, the Ten Commandments), in part by abrogation (*e.g.*, legal uncleanness and purification).

MOSLEM, MUSLIM. The participle of the verb from which Islam (*q.v.*) is derived, signifying an adherent of that religion; more commonly called a Mohammedan in English.

MOST REVEREND. The style given to archbishops in English-speaking countries ("the Most Reverend X . . . Y . . . , Archbishop of Z . . .") and in Ireland extended to bishops as well. It is part of the official form of address of a cardinal and of certain Roman prelates, and is accorded to the heads of some religious orders, *e.g.*, the Abbot Primate of the Benedictines, the Master General of the Dominicans, the Custodian of the Holy Land, the Prior General of the Servites.

MOTET (dim. of Fr. *mot*, word). A short vocal composition in harmony, to Latin words usually taken from the Sacred Scriptures; an anthem. A motet is sometimes sung by the choir after the offertory-verse at high Mass, and one in honour of the Blessed Sacrament is permitted after the *Benedictus.*

MOTHER-CHURCH. i. The cathedral church of a diocese.
  ii. A parish church having chapels-of-ease (*q.v.*) for the convenience of the faithful. Ordinarily the mother-church reserves the right of baptizing, marrying and burying. In canon law it is called *ecclesia matrix*, its mothership is *matricitas* and the dependent churches are *filiales.*

MOTHER-HOUSE. i. A self-governing monastery which has planted out one or more conventual colonies (daughter-houses), retaining jurisdiction and authority over them and appointing the superior.
  ii. The convent wherein resides the mother general of a congregation of nuns.

MOTHER OF GOD, The. Mary is the mother of Jesus Christ, who is God and man. She is therefore the mother of God. This is a dogma of the faith accepted as such from the earliest times, as is evident from countless expressions of the Fathers, and it was defined by the Council of Ephesus in 431. It does not mean, of course, that Mary generated the Godhead, any more than an ordinary mother generates her son's soul. It means simply that she is the mother of a Person who is God. This is her fundamental dignity, and the origin and justification of all the honour which Catholics pay to her.

MOTHERING SUNDAY. The fourth Sunday of Lent, so called perhaps with reference to the epistle at Mass and to the former custom of visiting the cathedral or mother-church on this day. The name has been preserved in some parts of England, and has recently been revived in order to establish the observance of a visit to one's mother in the flesh on this day.

MOTION. i. In a wide sense, motion embraces all change, every passage from potency to act, etc.; in this sense God is immutable yet moving all creatures. In a particular sense it is the act of a being in potency (q.v.), which does not thereby cease to be in potency.

ii. The Argument from Motion. See EXISTENCE, i.

MOTIVE. Whatever attracts the will; an end (q.v.) apprehended as desirable; the cause or set of causes which of itself is sufficient to move one to rational action. The perfect motive for doing good and refraining from evil is desire to do the will of God, and the Catholic Church never ceases to hold this motive before the eyes of her children. But the weakness and variousness of man is such that for many this motive is not sufficiently impelling and they must be moved by hope of reward or fear of punishment; and these motives, though imperfect, are sufficient (cf., the act of perfect contrition made for love of God and of imperfect contrition made for fear of Hell). The Church reprobates the attitude of those "superior" persons who look down on the imperfect motives as "unworthy." A good motive makes good and a bad one makes bad any act which in the abstract is indifferent. But a good motive cannot make a bad action good (i.e., evil must not be done that good may come of it), though if the doer is ignorant of its unlawfulness the wrong is not imputable to him. Distinguish from intention.

MOTIVES OF CREDIBILITY. Sure signs by which revealed religion is made evidently believable by divine faith. They are: internal: the experience of profound personal peace and the fulfilment of the aspirations of the human race for God and his justice; external: "the Church herself, on account of her wonderful propagation, extraordinary sanctity, inexhaustible fruitfulness in all good things, her catholic unity and invincible stability, is a certain great and perpetual motive of credibility and irrefutable testimony of her own divine mission" (Vatican Council, sess. iii, cap. 3). *Motives of credibility are necessary for an act of faith; "in order that the homage of our faith may be in harmony with reason, God has willed to add to the interior aids of the Holy Ghost exterior proofs of his revelation," etc. (loc. cit.). So reason precedes faith, but does not produce it; the grace of God moves man inwardly to assent, but leaves his will free; "the act of believing is an act of the intellect assenting to the divine truth at the command of the will moved by the grace of God, so that it is subject to the free will in relation to God; and consequently the act of faith can be meritorious" (St. Thomas, II-II, ii, 9).

MOTIVE OF FAITH. The "reason why" we believe, namely, the authority of God revealing. It is preceded by motives of credibility (q.v.) having which we know that certain truths are believable because they are confirmed by signs which show that they are proposed on the authority of God. But God's knowledge is infinite and his truthfulness absolute. Therefore we believe these truths on this authority, moved thereto by the grace of God, but by a free act of the will.

MOTTO. Practically every institution within the Catholic Church has its appropriate motto, of which certain ones among the religious orders have become synonymous with their institutes. Such are Pax, Peace (the Benedictines); Stat Crux dum volvitur Orbis, The world changes but the Cross remains (the Carthusians); Veritas, Truth (the Dominicans); Deus meus et Omnia, My God and my all (the Franciscans); Ad majorem Dei gloriam, For the greater glory of God (the Jesuits).

MOTU PROPRIO (Lat., of his own accord). A rescript drawn up and issued by the pope on his own initiative, without the advice of others, and personally signed by him.

MOTU PROPRIO OF PIUS X, The. This almost invariably refers to the instruction on sacred music issued by that pope on Nov. 22, 1903, wherein he summed up the principles governing the music of public worship. It dealt with the various kinds of sacred music, the liturgical text, the external form and length of the music, the singers, the organ and other instruments, and the means of procuring good sacred music. It aimed principally at the abolition of camouflaged concerts in church, the revival of congregational singing, and the restoration of the use of Gregorian chant; polyphonic music of the classical school was not forbidden, but recommended for great churches. This instruction has the force of law as a canonical code concerning church music (q.v.).

MOUNT ATHOS. The principal centre of Byzantine monasticism and one of the strongholds of the Orthodox Eastern Church, a monastic republic situated on a steep promontory of the peninsula of Chalcidice in the Ægean Sea. There are 20 principal monasteries (17 Greek, 1 Russian, 1 Serbian, 1 Bulgarian) with 12 lesser ones, 200 kellia (cells) and over 400 hermitages depending on them, housing 4,858 monks in all (1928). In numbers, property and influence the Greeks easily preponderate. The federation is governed by a council of 20 members, one delegate from each of the great monasteries. Ecclesiastically the Holy Mountain is subject to the patriarch of Constantinople and the civil power is represented by a Greek governor at Karyes. There was an abbey of the Latin rite during the 11th-12th centuries,

---

* The external motives of credibility include miracles and prophecies of Christ and His followers. Miracles and prophecies are "the surest signs of divine revelation." (Vatican I). See MIRACLE; MIRACLES OF CHRIST.—*Publisher*, 1997.

peopled by Amalfitans, whose archives are in existence but still unstudied; the senior monastery, Lavra, was founded in 960.

MOUNT MELLERAY. A Cistercian abbey at Cappoquin, co. Waterford. It was founded by Irish monks from Melleraie Abbey in Brittany in 1832. It has a large community, and a boys' school as well as agriculture is carried on. Three other abbeys have been founded from Mount Melleray, viz., Mount St. Bernard's (q.v.), New Melleray in Iowa, U. S. A. (1848) and Mount St. Joseph's, Roscrea, co. Tipperary (1878).

MOUNT ST. BERNARD'S. A Cistercian abbey near Coalville in Leicestershire, founded in 1835 by Ambrose Phillipps de Lisle, with monks from Mount Melleray (q.v.) and Melleraie. It was erected into an abbey in 1848, and so is the senior abbey of Great Britain.

MOVABLE FEASTS. Easter, whose date depends on the paschal moon, and those other feasts whose date depends on that of Easter, namely, the Ascension, Pentecost, the Holy Trinity and Corpus Christi. In cathedral and other great churches the dates of these and of Septuagesima, Ash Wednesday and the first Sunday of Advent for the coming year are solemnly announced in a special chant by the deacon after the gospel at high Mass on the Epiphany. Another class of feast whose date is movable is formed of those reckoned from a certain Sunday, e.g., the Holy Name (q.v.), Christ the King (last Sunday in October). The Armenian and Chaldean calendars consist almost entirely of movable feasts, which fall on a certain weekday after a Sunday determined by the date of Easter.

MOZARABIC RITE, The (Span. Mozárabe corruption of Arabic mustarib, an arabized person, a Christian living in the Moorish parts of Spain), better called the Rite of Toledo or the Visigothic. A Latin liturgy of the Gallican family formerly in use throughout the Iberian peninsula but now preserved only in a chapel at the cathedral of Toledo, served by a special chapter of canons. The Mass differs greatly from the Roman, e.g., the bread and wine are prepared between the preliminary prayers and the introit, there is an Old Testament lesson before the epistle, the priest sings the gospel, a far greater proportion of the service is variable, and there are numerous proper prefaces. The Divine Office is also very different: it abounds in hymns and responsories and the hours as a rule have fixed psalms not based on a regular recitation of the Psalter; there is an extra "little hour" after Lauds. The other offices of this rite are no longer used, being supplied when required from the Roman books. At Toledo the rite is in ordinary daily use, and there are a number of families in the city who belong to

it canonically and by inheritance; at marriages a large veil or pall is held over bride and groom and they are tied together by a "yoke" of coloured ribbons. This was once, with local variations, the liturgy of all Gaul and Spain, and the Celtic rite (q.v.) was related to it. The Mozarabic marriage rite is used in Spanish South America.

MOZZETTA (It. mozzo, shortened). A cape reaching to the elbows, closed with buttons in front, and with a rudimentary hood behind, made of silk or wool. It signifies jurisdiction and is worn over the rochet by cardinals, bishops in their own dioceses, abbots in their abbeys, certain Roman prelates and other dignitaries by way of privilege (e.g., canons in England). It may be a descendant of the mediæval almuce (q.v.) or a shortened form of the cappa magna; it is worn at functions whereat the prelate is present officially but is not officiating. The pope's mozzetta is red (white in Easter week), a cardinal's red (purple in penitential times), a bishop's etc., purple, or black or other colour according to his habit if a religious. The similar short cape of certain monastic habits (e.g., Dominican, Trinitarian) is sometimes called a mozzetta.

MURATORIAN CANON, FRAGMENT, The. The oldest known list of books of the New Testament, with notes thereon, compiled at the end of the 2nd century, known from a fragmentary 8th-century MS. discovered by Muratori (d. 1750).

MURDER. The direct and wilful killing of an innocent person, contrary to the divine command, "The innocent and just person thou shalt not put to death" (Exod. xxiii, 7). When a death follows indirectly and according to the principle of double effect (q.v.), it is no murder, e.g., in defending oneself against an aggressor (cf., Abortion, Capital Punishment, Craniotomy, Euthanasia). Killing in a just war (q.v.) is indirect killing, and justified as self-defence against an unjust aggressor. A just war is essentially a defensive operation and in self-defence a man has the right to prevent his enemy from injuring him, though he must do that with a minimum of injury compatible with effectiveness. In war he sets out not to kill, but to put the enemy out of action. But a soldier cannot pause for any nice discrimination in the matter and therefore he does kill. His object is not directly to do so (else would the killing of wounded and prisoners be justifiable). Moreover, the only enemies it is lawful to attack (and therefore to kill indirectly) are actual participants in the hostilities, i.e., combatants, directors of operations, munition-workers, and the like. This, of course, does not mean that defended cities must not be attacked, even though it is known that non-combatants will be killed as a result of the attack: this is an accidental outcome of the operation, removed even a stage further from the intention to kill which would make the act justifiable.

MUSIC, CHURCH. Music has "the first place amongst those things which are most closely connected with the sacred liturgy and increase its splendour and efficacy" (Preface, Vatican "Graduale"). In the Western church sacred music is governed mainly by the *motu proprio* of Pope Pius X (*q.v.*). In this it is reiterated that the only official liturgical music of the Latin rite is plainsong (*q.v.*) in its various authentic forms, Vatican, Ambrosian, etc.; polyphonic music (*e.g.*, that of Palestrina, Anerio, Vittoria, Tallis, Byrd) is recommended where the choir can manage it; more modern music is allowed provided it has the requirements set out in the instruction. The music and its execution must be subordinate to the liturgical text, and musical instruments (*q.v.*) must be kept in subjection: "the proper music of the Church is only vocal . . . the music is really only a part of the liturgy and its humble handmaid" (Pius X). This was emphasized by Pope Pius XI in the constitution *Divini Cultus* in 1929: "We declare that accompanied singing is in no way considered by the Church to be a more perfect form of music or one more suitable for sacred purposes; indeed, it is fitting that the voice itself, rather than instruments, should sound in sacred buildings." In the Eastern rites the use of their own ecclesiastical chant is usual, and is governed by tradition; since the 17th century harmonized chant and polyphony influenced by Italian composers has been general in Russia, and in the Greek and other Byzantine churches of Europe contrapuntal music is increasingly heard.

MUSICAL INSTRUMENTS. The music of worship is essentially vocal and its decadence was greatly hastened by the introduction of orchestral instruments. In the Western Church to-day the organ (*q.v.*) is permitted, except at Office and Mass of the Dead and on ferias of Advent and Lent; on special occasions other instruments are allowed by particular leave of the bishop. Pianos, drums, cymbals, etc., and full bands are forbidden in church. Organs are absolutely forbidden in all Eastern rites, but, outside the Byzantine, it is common to use bells, drums, cymbals, and such-like on big occasions; and in some churches organs are now occasionally found.

MUTILATION OF SELF. The action of depriving oneself of any bodily organ or of its use. Since man is not the owner of his body but only its custodian, self-mutilation is gravely illicit save when necessary to preserve health or life.

MUTUUM, CONTRACT OF. A loan of a fungible commodity (*q.v.*) for a definite period, sometimes called a loan for consumption, as opposed to a loan for use. Upon such a loan it is unlawful to exact any interest when the goods are only useful for consumption, when the lender does not require their use himself within the stated time, when the loan is secured or otherwise made without risk, and when the lender by lending is not depriving himself of an opportunity of lawful gain.

MYRON (sweet oil). The Greek name for the holy Chrism (*q.v.*) which is consecrated only by the heads of churches. The patriarch of Constantinople consecrates it about every ten years, for several churches besides his own, *e.g.*, Jerusalem, Greece. The name is sometimes referred to the sacrament of Confirmation; *cf.*, the Italian *cresima*.

MYSTERIUM FIDEI. Words pronounced by the celebrant during the consecration of the wine in the Latin Mass; the origin of their insertion at this point is much disputed. They are borrowed from 1 Tim. iii, 9, and perhaps were originally an announcement by the deacon ("The Mystery of Faith!") of the completed consecration, taken over by the priest when low Mass began to be customary. The phrase is now often used to indicate the mystery of the sacrificial nature of the Mass, from the name of a treatise thereon by Père de la Taille, S. J.

MYSTERY (Gr., μυστήριον, something closed, a secret). i. Anything hidden from the scrutiny of our mind, either in its existence or in its nature, though its existence may be discovered later and even its nature, *e.g.*, the existence of an unknown element, the nature of telepathy. This is "natural" mystery.

ii. A rite or doctrine held secret from the intrusion of the uninitiated, *e.g.*, the Eleusinian mysteries.

iii. In theological use, we have: (*a*) Mystery of the second order, a truth whose existence is inaccessible to unaided created intelligence, but which, once known, is easily comprehensible, *e.g.*, the creation of the world in time, the institution of the Sabbath. This is supernatural mystery in the broad sense, or, better, preternatural. (*b*) Mystery properly so called. This is a truth which, though it is not *against* reason, so far transcends it that no created intelligence could ever discover it, and which, even when it is revealed, is in its nature impenetrable by any created intelligence. Its existence is therefore known only by faith; its nature is never completely known. Yet it is not without spiritual profit, for some knowledge of it is available by analogy with things of sense and by the light of faith. Such is the mystery of the Trinity. This is a strict supernatural mystery.

iv. In the primitive Church "mystery," in the sense of a profound spiritual truth and act, was the word used for what we now call a sacrament (*cf.*, Ephesians v, 32, where St. Paul wrote "mystery" and the Douay version translates "sacrament"); this is still the usage of the East, where they speak of, *e.g.*, The Seven Mysteries. In the West the expression The Holy Mysteries, for a celebration of the Eucharist, has not gone entirely out of use, and "mysteries" for the Eucharist is of frequent occurrence in the Latin liturgy.

v. One of the fifteen mysteries of the faith, meditations on which form the principal part of the rosary devotion. They are grouped into the joyful, sorrowful and glorious mysteries (*qq.v.*).

vi. A religious play. See MIRACLE.

MYSTERY OF FAITH. i. A truth the nature of which we cannot understand even when we know of its existence through revelation; that there are such mysteries was defined by the Vatican Council. Two examples are the mystery of the Blessed Trinity, the mystery of the Incarnation. See iii (*b*) above.

ii. A name frequently reserved to the mystery of the Holy Eucharist; the words "*Mysterium fidei*" occur in the form of consecration at Mass. See above.

MYSTICAL BODY OF CHRIST, The. The members of the Church are bound together and to Christ, their head, into a spiritual though real Body by the supernatural life of grace received in Baptism; each member has his proper function to fulfil and the graces necessary to fulfil it under the direction of the Head. Membership is necessary for salvation, since only through his Mystical Body are Christ's merits applied. Thus it is not the individual bishop who baptizes, preaches, governs, but Christ through him; Christ and the Church sacrifice with the priest; the individual Christian prays not alone, but Christ and the Church pray in his person (and, in liturgical prayer, hardly ever in the singular number). Nor is the Mystical Body confined to the Church visible on earth; it includes the redeemed in Heaven and the suffering in Purgatory and all those who by any means are said to belong to the Church invisibly. The Mystical Body was the subject of an encyclical of Pope Pius XII, *Mystici Corporis Christi* (*q.v.*). See COMMUNION OF SAINTS, "SOUL OF THE CHURCH," UNANSWERED PRAYER, MINISTER, iv.

MYSTICAL INTERPRETATION. i. That interpretation of Holy Scripture in which a person (*e.g.*, David), or a thing (*e.g.*, manna), or an event (*e.g.*, the story of Hagar) is ordained by God to typify some future person, thing or event, God's intention being revealed in Scripture or Tradition.

ii. Sometimes the equivalent of allegorical meaning (*q.v.*).

MYSTICAL ROSE (Lat. *Rosa mystica*). A title given to our Lady in the litany of Loreto (*cf.*, Ecclus. xxiv, 18; xxxix, 17).

MYSTICAL UNION. The union of the soul with God in contemplation. Its great characteristic is that the presence of God is felt in a spiritual touch, without images, as a direct experience, obscure and partly incomprehensible. Its effect is a large increase of charity, humility and self-sacrificing devotion: also, not infrequently, the perfecting of the natural powers of the contemplative. The grades of mystic union are the prayer of quiet, full union, in which the soul is more conscious and more certain of God's presence within it, ecstatic union or ecstasy, and the spiritual marriage (*qq.v.*).

MYSTICI CORPORIS CHRISTI. An encyclical letter issued by Pope Pius XII in 1943 on the Mystical Body of Christ and our union with Christ therein. It sets forth in some detail this concept of the Church and our Lord as her head, upholder and saviour; the nature of the union of the faithful in and with Christ, rejecting certain current errors; and ends with an exhortation to love the Church as Christ loves her, and an appeal to non-Catholics and to civil rulers.

MYSTICISM (Gr. μυστικός, connected with the secret things). i. A modern name for mystical theology.

ii. Experimental knowledge of God's presence, in which the soul has, as a great reality, a sense of contact with him. It is the same as passive contemplation or mystical union. It does not necessarily involve psycho-physical phenomena, such as visions or ecstasies; the great Western mystics, until the middle ages, seem rarely, if ever, to have experienced such things. It must be accepted as genuine, because it is unanimously attested by all the mystics of east and west and showed itself wonderfully operative of good in their lives. There is no reason for denying that God sometimes grants the experience in some degree to non-Catholic Christians and others who are in good faith: but most of the natural mysticism found in China, India, Persia and among the Neo-Platonists, although it bears resemblance to Christian, is wrong in both its aim and method: it is pantheistic, striving for fusion with divinity, and it is achieved either by the efforts of the mystic himself or in a quietistic way. But it can hardly be denied that there have been true mystics, in the above sense, *e.g.*, in Islam.*

iii. In a more general sense he may be called a mystic who is contemplative in any religious sense (see CONTEMPLATIVE LIFE), an acute "awareness" of God and his activities and manifestations being of the essence of mysticism. But beyond that limit the use of the word can hardly be pushed without falling into the current absurdities of identifying mysticism with esoteric occultism, the use of allegory and symbol, mysteriousness, pretty fancifulness, ineffectual idealism, "see-

---

* When speaking of "non-Catholic mystics" it must be borne in mind that any graces God gives, He gives spiritually through the Catholic Church, even if the Church's role in a particular case may not be visible.—*Publisher*, 1997.

ing things," second sight, anything "vast, vague and sentimental": usages which have added to the difficulties of a complex subject and brought a useful word, and even the noble thing which it expresses, into disrepute. A "practical" character and an "objective" cast of mind are characteristic marks of the Christian mystic.

N

NAG'S HEAD FABLE, The. The allegation that Parker, first Protestant archbishop of Canterbury, from whom Anglican orders (*q.v.*) derive, received episcopal consecration at the Nag's Head tavern, in Cheapside, by the laying-on of a Bible by Scory, who had been deprived of the see of Chichester in Mary's reign. This story was disproved in the 17th century, and the Catholic rejection of the validity of Anglican orders is not based on it in any degree whatsoever.

NAHUM (Heb., Comforter). A prophetical book of the Old Testament written by him whose name it bears. Both as a warning and as a consolation to Israel he denounces the Assyrian Ninive and prophesies its fall; it was in fact captured and destroyed by Cyaxares the Mede about 606 B.C. Nahum is named in the Roman Martyrology on Dec. 1.

NAILS, THE HOLY, with which our Lord was crucified are said to have been found with the True Cross by St. Helen. There are numerous alleged relics of them, principally in the Iron Crown of Lombardy at Monza, and at Santa Croce in Rome, but the authenticity of none of them is established. A feast of the Holy Lance and Nails is kept in some places on the second Friday in Lent.

NAME. i. Personal. In addition to the baptismal name (*q.v.*), it is the usual practice, but not obligatory, to take the name of a saint at Confirmation. The names of feasts and mysteries, *e.g.*, Hallows (Toussaint), Sorrows (Dolores), Assumption (Assunta), though very popular in some countries, are not encouraged by the Church; Jesus is a common name in Spanish-speaking countries, and W. H. Hudson met a Paraguayan youth called Circumcision.
ii. In religion. In all the old orders and most of the other religious institutes, the novice receives a new name at clothing by which he (she) is in future known. Some, *e.g.*, Carmelites, Passionists, Trinitarians, add thereto the name of a mystery, etc., as John-of-the-Cross, Frances-of-Jesus; others, both men and women, always add Mary to the new name, *e.g.*, the Servites. A regular priest should be addressed in the second person by his religious name, *e.g.*, Father Edward, and not by his family name, the use of which is abandoned entirely by Friars Minor, Passionists, Carmelites, Trinitarians, and Capuchins; the last are distinguished by the name of their place of origin, *e.g.*, Fr. Pius of Chester. Nuns often receive the names of male saints. Lay tertiaries also receive a religious name at clothing which they are at liberty to use to the exclusion of other personal names. In some parts of the East a new name is taken for use at every change of ecclesiastical status; *e.g.*, one baptized Leo became Dominic at ordination, and is now Theophilus, archbishop of Aleppo of the Syrian rite.
iii. See IN NOMINE PATRIS.

NAME-DAY. The celebration of the feast-day of the saint of one's name instead of, or in addition to, one's own proper birthday. The custom is usual in religious orders and certain countries of the world.

NARTHEX. The west end of the interior of a church of the Byzantine rite, parted from the nave by a wall or screen, with the royal doors in the middle and others on either side. In it is the font, and sometimes stalls, and in some Catholic churches confessionals and a holy water stoup; monks sing part of the Office here. It is exactly the *narthex* of the early Christian basilicas in which the catechumens, penitents and energumens (*qq.v.*) were accommodated. The name cannot properly be given to any form of western porch or ante-chapel in later churches of the West.

NATALITIA (Lat. *dies natalis*, birthday, anniversary). A word used in Latin liturgies for the day on which a saint's feast is kept, the anniversary of his death.

NATHANAEL, ST. See BARTHOLOMEW.

NATIONAL CATHOLIC WELFARE CONFERENCE. An organization of the Church in the United States for the unifying, coordinating and organizing of the Catholics of that country in works of education, social welfare, immigrant aid, good citizenship, etc. It was established in 1919 by a brief, *Communes*, of Pope Benedict XV. Every bishop of the United States and its territories is *ex officio* a member of the conference, which is administered by a board of 10 bishops elected annually by their confrères. The conference is not a canonical council or legislative assembly, and its resolutions do not have the force of law. Among its departments are those for education, the press, social action, youth, lay organizations, missions, and Near-East welfare. The headquarters of the conference is in Washington.*

NATIONALISM. The term is sometimes used as synonymous with patriotism (*q.v.*), but more often and conveniently (as by Pope Pius XI in his Christmas address of 1930) to distinguish an undue particularism in favour of one's own country. Nationalism in this sense amounts to a religion, in so far as it produces a like degree of enthusiasm and devotion and makes of the nation and its interests an end in itself. To this Catholicism is opposed as to any other false religion. Moreover, it is not in accordance with the Church's teaching on the solidarity of the human race and its oneness in Christ, and its fruits are opposed to justice and charity, as in policies affecting the rights and legitimate interests of other peoples, the fomenting of national hatred, the prosecution of unjust wars, the popularizing of the sentiment "My country, right or wrong." The extent to which in a given case the virtue of patriotism has been contaminated by Nationalism may be measured (other things being equal) by the degree to which passion and prejudice endure in the peoples of formerly combatant nations after a war is over. It is to be noted also that Nationalism, though commonly opposed to Socialism and Communism, equally with these upholds the false doctrine of the omnipotent state: *cf.*, fascism in Italy with sovietism in Russia. A most dangerous by-product of nationalism is the use of missions to the heathen to further the interests, political and economic, of a particular state, the imposition of foreign culture and language on natives, and the consequent association in the native mind of Catholicism not merely with Europe but with a particular country and with trade and politics. See also CHURCH, NATIONAL, ii.

NATIVE CLERGY. Clergy ordained from among the indigenous inhabitants of missionary countries outside of Europe and "European" America. The marked encouragement given by the Holy See of late years to the formation of native clergy is sometimes referred to as "papal policy" in this regard. The phrase is misleading. From the earliest times the Church, as missionary, ordained bishops and priests among her neophytes and entrusted her institutions to them at the earliest possible moment ·as a matter of course; it was hardly until the growth of European imperialisms in the 16th century that an indefinite state of tutelage for "native" converts became common (Pope Innocent XI recalled earlier practice in a forcible sentence, "I would rather see you ordain one indigenous priest than baptize fifty thousand heathen"). The task of the missionary is to break ground, to prepare the way: "Wherever there is a native clergy, adequate in number and training and worthy of its calling, there the missionary's

work may be considered to have been brought to a happy end; there the Church is founded" (Pope Benedict XV in *Maximum illud*). Native clergy are most numerous in China (including a cardinal and about 30 bishops), India (10 bishops), Indo-China, and some of the White Fathers' missions in Central Africa. See MISSIONS, FOREIGN.

NATIVITY (Lat. *nativitas*) or, as we should say, birthday, is the name of three feasts: of our Lord (Dec. 25), of our Lady (Sept. 8), and of St. John the Baptist (June 24). These are the only actual birthdays kept by the Church.

NATIVITY, THE FEAST OF THE, of Jesus Christ, called in England Christmas Day, celebrated on Dec. 25, though for what reason that date was selected is not known for certain. The Nativity was not observed separately from the Epiphany (Jan. 6) until the 4th century (the dissident Armenians still keep them together on that day), and the octave of the Epiphany is privileged above that of Christmas. Every priest may say Mass thrice on this day, and three different Masses are provided in the missal (Midnight, Dawn, the Third, *qq.v.*); this custom arose from the night vigil Mass at the chapel of the Crib in St. Mary Major's and the stational Mass at the same church or St. Peter's, between which the popes used to sing a Mass at the Byzantine imperial church of St. Anastasia. The feast is thus explained in the proper preface of the Mass: "By the mystery of the word made flesh the light of thy glory hath shone anew upon the eyes of our mind; so that while we acknowledge him God seen by men, we may be drawn by him to the love of things unseen."

NATIVITY, THE VIGIL OF THE. Christmas eve, a major vigil (*q.v.*), with a proper office; if it falls on a Sunday, the Sunday is only commemorated at Mass. The Martyrology is sung with extra solemnity at Prime, all kneeling during the recital of our Lord's birth. It is a day of fasting and abstinence.

NATIVITY OF OUR LADY, The. A feast kept throughout the Church, on Sept. 8 in the Latin and Byzantine rites, and on other dates elsewhere. As on the Immaculate Conception the epistle of the proper Mass applies to Mary the attributes of wisdom (Prov. viii, 22-35); the gospel appropriately recites her genealogy (Matt. i, 1-16).

NATURALISM. A system of philosophy that admits nothing but nature itself. There are two principal species: the one rejects God, whom it confounds with nature—this is Pantheism (*q.v.*); the other rejects revelation only.

NATURE (Lat. *natura*, from *nasci*, to be born). i. Essence understood as a principle of action. There is an opposition between

---

* The National Catholic Welfare Conference is now called the United States Catholic Conference (USCC).— *Publisher*, 1997.

nature and grace, the latter of which is added to nature and constitutes the supernatural order. Nature is also opposed to art, natural to artificial.

ii. The universe as a whole in so far as all things within it are endowed with certain powers and are capable of producing certain effects. Nature has its laws, that is, it acts in a constant and uniform manner. This constancy, uniformity and regularity of action is called the order of nature.

NAVE (Lat. *navis*, a ship, from its shape). That part, the body of a church west of the sanctuary and choir, reserved for the accommodation of the people. It may be flanked by one or more aisles which actually, but not architecturally, are considered as part of the nave. In Western churches seats for the laity are commonly provided in the nave, but generally speaking the further south one goes the more indifferent are people to comfort in church; such seats are still exceptional in Eastern rites.

NAZARENE. i. A native of Nazareth. The Nazarene is a name applied to Jesus Christ.
ii. A name, usually contemptuous, among Jews and Moslems for a Christian (*cf.*, Acts xxiv, 5).
iii. A member of a judaizing sect akin to the Ebionites (*q.v.*), but apparently orthodox.

NAZARETH HOUSE. The name given to every convent of Sisters of Nazareth (*q.v.*), each of which has a home for the aged poor.

NAZARITE (Heb. *nazir*, separated). A devout Jew leading the consecrated life legislated for in Num. vi, 1-21, prominent among the observances being abstention from wine and the barber. Some led this life continuously, being perhaps devoted thereto in infancy; such were Samson, Samuel and John the Baptist: others followed it for a limited time (*cf.*, Acts xxi, 22-27).

NE TEMERE. The opening words of a decree of the Congregation of the Council, issued in 1907, extending the provisions of the decree *Tametsi*, in a modified form, to those countries where it had not hitherto been in force, *i.e.*, Great Britain, U. S. A. The principal effect of this was that thereafter throughout the world the marriages of Catholics, and of a Catholic and a baptized non-Catholic ("mixed marriage"; "Catholic" includes apostates), must in order to be valid take place before the qualified parish priest or his delegate and two witnesses. Subsequently mixed marriages in Germany, Hungary and Yugoslavia were exempted for local reasons from this decree, but only in respect of natives of those countries living therein. See CLANDESTINITY.

NECESSARIANISM. The same as Fatalism, the doctrine which asserts that all things come to be of necessity.

NECESSARY, NECESSITY. That which cannot not be. Opposed to contingency and liberty; when opposed to liberty it is called Determinism (*q.v.*). There are three kinds of necessity, metaphysical, physical and moral, corresponding to metaphysical, physical and moral impossibility. In connexion with free-will there is an antecedent and a consequent necessity: the first precedes the act, thus destroying the freedom of the act; the latter accompanies or follows upon the act and in no way prejudices freedom. All contingent being (*q.v.*) presupposes the necessary and ultimately the absolute necessary, which is God. Theologians distinguish between necessity of means (absolute or relative) and necessity of precept. Thus faith and baptism of water are necessary to salvation (*q.v.*) by a necessity of means, absolutely and relatively respectively, and even their inculpable omission deprives of salvation; but holy communion is a necessity of precept, and its omission, if blameless, does not deprive of salvation.

NECESSARY TO SALVATION. Two conditions are indicated in our Lord's own words as being necessary to salvation: "He that believeth and is baptized shall be saved" (Mark xvi, 16). Baptism and Faith, therefore, are necessary for all. Further, the soul must at the moment of death be united to God by charity (*q.v.*), *i.e.*, it must be in a state of grace. Catholics, as such, fulfil the first two conditions, so for them the question of salvation turns on their freedom from mortal sin. Non-Catholics must be baptized in some way (by water, blood, or desire), and they must believe. The matter of that belief is (*a*) quite essentially, God who is a rewarder; (*b*) if they can learn such truths, the Trinity and Incarnation. Further, all are under obligation to join the Church, which is the one ark of salvation, and only invincible ignorance (*q.v.*) will excuse from the fulfilment of this precept. * And, of course, as for Catholics, the state of grace is necessary for all.

NECROMANCY (Gr. νεκρός, dead; μαντεία' divination). Attempting to get into communication with the spirits of the dead by evocation. The modern form of necromancy is Spiritism (*q.v.*); it is a grave sin of superstition.

NEGATION. The contrary of affirmation, and also the opposite of positive and real (*q.v.*). Negation is distinct from privation, since whilst the former signifies a simple absence, the latter signifies the absence of something that is due. Thus is evil a privation and not a simple negation.

NEGLIGENCE. A defect against prudence, a failing on the part of the intellect to arouse and direct the will or other faculties to perform what is right.

---

* Furthermore, the Catholic Church is the *necessary means* of salvation for *all.* (See NECESSARY, NECESSITY.) All who are saved are in the Catholic Church at the moment of their death, although in some cases, they may be in her invisibly.—*Publisher*, 1997.

NEGRO MISSIONS. This expression often refers to Catholic missions among the coloured people of the United States. These number some 15 million, of whom about half a million are Catholics. The annual number of conversions (mostly from city parishes in the north) is considerable. The Josephite fathers, Mother Drexel's Sisters of the Blessed Sacrament, and the Sisters of the Holy Family of New Orleans are outstanding workers among the coloured people.

NEHEMIAH (Heb., Jahveh comforts). The Hebrew form of the name Nehemias, author of the book of the Bible commonly called the Second Book of Esdras. He was cup-bearer to one of the Persian kings Artaxerxes and sent by him to rebuild the walls of Jerusalem.

NEO-EBORACENSIS. The Latin epithet for the archbishop of New York. *Eburacum* was the Roman name of the present English city of York; New York is not, however, named from this city but for James, duke of York (afterwards King James II).

NEO-PLATONISM. The philosophy of the School of Alexandria. Its masters assumed the name of Eclectics, since they chose from all ancient systems what to them seemed the best and endeavoured to co-ordinate the chosen doctrines into a corporate teaching. Because these philosophers received their greatest inspiration from Plato they are called Neo-platonists.

NEO-SCHOLASTICISM. The name assumed by certain contemporary scholastic philosophers among whom are to be numbered professors of the Institut Supérieur de Philosophie of Louvain, who publish the *Revue Neo-Scholastique*. Their aim is to bring scholastic philosophy up to date, or rather to keep it in touch with contemporary scientific research.

NEOPHYTE (Gr. νεόφυτος, newly-grown).
i. A newly-baptized convert in the early Church or from heathenism to-day.
ii. A postulant or novice in a religious order or anyone beginning his studies for the priesthood.

NEPOTISM (It. *nipote,* nephew). The undue exercise of public or official influence in favour of relatives, particularly and originally by certain popes (*e.g.,* Sixtus IV, Julius III, Urban VIII, Alexander VI, VII and VIII), whose *nipoti* were sometimes their children. Many popes legislated against nepotism and it was finally sternly repressed by a bull of Innocent XII in 1692. For the avoidance of undue favour or influence in the Sacred College and at the Roman Court those are not eligible for the cardinalitial dignity who have a living legitimate child or grandchild, or who are related by blood in the first or second degree to any living cardinal.

NESCIENCE. A state of mind which implies lack of knowledge, which knowledge a person is not bound to have. Opposed to Ignorance.

NESTORIAN CHURCH, The. The body of Christians adhering to Nestorianism (*q.v.*). They call themselves simply Syrians, though others often call them, inaccurately, Assyrians. Christianity is alleged to have been first preached in Mesopotamia, Chaldea and Persia by St. Thomas the Apostle, followed by SS. Addai and Mari; the Church was well established there in the 3rd century and in the 4th suffered tremendous persecution from the Persians. Nestorianism became influential through the theological school at Nisibis, and from the end of the 5th century the local church was committed to the heresy. Until the ravages of Timur Leng, in the 14th century, it was flourishing, extending to China and India. Since then it has dwindled to about 35,000 members. The Nestorians seem to have abandoned their heresy, a good effect of the work of Anglicans among them; but they admit only the first two œcumenical councils, claim that the *epiklesis* (*q.v.*) in the Liturgy consecrates, do not use confession, confirmation and anointing, admit divorce for adultery and the remarriage of widower priests. They use the same liturgy as the Catholic Chaldeans (*q.v.*), and their orders are valid. They are governed by the Patriarch-Katholikos of the East, whose office is hereditary, passing from uncle to nephew, and five bishops, who also belong to "episcopal families"; there are no monasteries. The Nestorians suffered greatly during and after World War I, and are now scattered in Irak, Syria and elsewhere, including the United States, whither their patriarch went in 1940. There is a Nestorian diocese in Malabar which had its origin in the 19th century (Mellusians, *q.v.*).

NESTORIAN MONUMENT, The. A stone monument discovered by Jesuit missionaries at Hsi-an-fu or Si-ngan-fu in Middle China, in 1625. It bears an inscription in Chinese and Syriac, and was set up by "King-tsing, priest of the Syrian Church," to commemorate the introduction 146 years earlier of the Illustrious Religion, *i.e.,* Christianity, of which it gives an account. It is dated "the second year of the period Kien-chung," *i.e.,* A.D. 781, and records a flourishing local church at that date. At one time the Jesuits were accused of having forged the monument, but it is now admitted by all to be genuine; the activities commemorated were almost certainly those of Nestorians, who were great missionaries, and known to have preached in China at an early date.

NESTORIAN RITE, The. The East Syrian rite used by the Nestorians is more conveniently called the Chaldean rite (*q.v.*), as its use is shared by the Catholic Chaldeans.

NESTORIANISM. The heresy of Nestorius, bishop of Constantinople (*d. c.* 451), who received it from Diodoros of Tarsus and Theodore of Mopsuestia. It consists in the doctrine that in Jesus Christ were two persons joined together, namely, God the Son (the Word) and the man Jesus; Jesus was the dwelling-place or vesture of the Word, he alone was born of our Lady, he only, not the Word, died on the cross: whereas the Catholic teaching was and is that from its first moment Christ's human nature existed as the human nature of the Word and never as a single, independently existing nature; God and man is one Christ, one person in two natures. The controversy raged round the representative word *theotokos* (θεοτόκος), Mother of God, a title which the Nestorians, of course, refused to our Lady. Nestorius was condemned by Pope St. Celestine I, but he continued to argue. The third œcumenical council therefore met at Ephesus in 431 and repeated the condemnation which was confirmed at the Council of Chalcedon. The errors of Nestorius were adopted by the Christians of Persia who, once mighty, still exist as the tiny Nestorian Church (*q.v.*).

NEUM (Gr. νεῦμα, a sign). In plainchant, a group of notes sung to a single syllable. A series of neums sung in one breath is sometimes distinguished as a *neuma*. Thus Dom Pothier in "Mélodies Grégoriennes" speaks of *le neum* and *le neume* or *jubilus* (*q.v.*); *e.g.*, the *podatus* and the *clivis* are neums, but the *jubilus* is a neuma.

NEW COVENANT, DISPENSATION, LAW. The law and dispensation of Jesus Christ as opposed to the old covenant of Moses, which it infinitely surpassed and superseded and yet fulfilled (*cf.* Matt. v, 17-18; 2 Cor. iii; Gal. iv; Heb. viii-x).

NEW FIRE, THE BLESSING OF THE. The first of the rites of Holy Saturday (*q.v.*), which takes place outside or in the porch of the Church. Fire is struck from a flint and fuel kindled, which is blessed; the paschal candle is then blessed, and lit from the fire. The candle is then taken into the church, borne by a deacon, the people following. They make three genuflexions, the first when the deacon has passed the door, the second in the nave and the third in the sanctuary; the deacon each time sings *Lumen Christi* (The Light of Christ), all answering *Deo Gratias* (Thanks be to God). Then the deacon sings the *Exsultet* (*q.v.*). The lessons or prophecies (*q.v.*) follow, during which in former times those about to be baptized were catechized and prepared. These observances have been much simplified from the former somewhat confused rites. The paschal new fire must be distinguished from the so-called Holy Fire (*q.v.*).

NEW LEARNING, The. The revival of Greek and Latin classical learning during the 15th and 16th centuries, together with a strong reaction against the spirit of the middle ages. It was the chief motive of the Renaissance, and was at its zenith from the fall of Constantinople in 1453 to the sack of Rome in 1527. Encouraged by many popes and adopted by scholars all over Europe, it developed along two distinct lines: the adoption of pleasure instead of duty as the law of life, unlimited "freedom of thought," scandalous laxity of morals, leading to the Reformation; and the assimilation of pagan culture without its grossness, leading to the educational system of the Jesuits. The name "new learning" was also sometimes applied, in derision or praise, to the teachings of the Protestant reformers.

NEW NORCIA, or Nursia. A Benedictine monastery in Western Australia founded in 1846 by Dom Rudesind Salvado and Dom Joseph Serra for missionary work among the aborigines. It was made an abbey *nullius* (*q.v.*) in 1867, and the monks have charge of a huge territory, including the Drisdale River mission. Among its institutions are boys' and girls' colleges. The great up-builder of this mission was Bishop-Abbot Fulgentius Torres, who died in 1914. The abbey belongs to the Spanish province of the Cassinese Congregation of Primitive Observance.

NEW ORLEANS (*Novae Aureliae, q.v.*). The second oldest diocese of the United States. The area was originally under the jurisdiction of the bishop of Quebec; in 1772 it became an organized mission territory, and in 1793 a diocese. The first bishop was Luis Peñalver y Cárdenas. New Orleans was made a metropolitan see in 1850; its suffragan dioceses are Alexandria, Lafayette, Little Rock, Mobile, and Natchez. The first convent of nuns (Ursulines) in what is now the United States was established at New Orleans in 1727, as was the first congregation of coloured nuns, in 1842. Until 1850 the see was called Saint Louis of New Orleans; the city takes its name from Orleans in France.

NEW STYLE, usually represented by the abbreviation N.S. with a date, indicates that it is reckoned according to the Gregorian calendar (*q.v.*), beginning the year on Jan. 1.

NEW YORK (*Neo-Eboracensis, q.v.*). One of the early dioceses of the United States. Although religious liberty was enacted in 1683, the first permanent Catholic church in the state of New York was not built till 1786, St. Peter's at Barclay and Church Streets. The see was erected in 1808, the first resident bishop being Friar John Connolly, O.P. In 1850 it was made metropolitan, the suffragan dioceses now being Albany, Brooklyn, Buffalo, Ogdensburg, Rochester, and Syracuse. Chief among New York's archbishops have been John Hughes, Cardinal John McCloskey (the first American cardinal), Cardinal John Farley and Cardinal Patrick Hayes. St. Patrick's cathedral on Fifth Avenue is one of the dozen largest churches in the world. Outstanding among New York's Catholic educational institutions are Fordham University, directed by the Jesuit fathers, and the Sacred Heart nuns' Manhattanville College for girls.

NEW ZEALAND, THE CHURCH IN. New Zealand, being a distinct dominion of the British Commonwealth, is organized ecclesiastically separately from Australia. Mass was first said there in 1838; it became a vicariate apostolic in 1842, and the country now forms one province with the metropolitan see at Wellington and three episcopal sees. The Catholic population numbers 225,000 (of whom 10,000 are native Maoris), in a total of 1¾ million. All religions are equal before the law but the state system of education is entirely secular.

NEWFOUNDLAND, THE CHURCH IN. Mass was probably first celebrated here at the end of the 15th century but there was no considerable body of Catholics till the end of the 18th. There is now one metropolitan see, Saint John's, with two suffragan bishops. Catholics are the largest body, numbering 111,000, over one-third of the population. In 1949, Newfoundland became the tenth province of the dominion of Canada, having previously been a separate state.

NEWPORT AND MENEVIA. A Welsh see erected in 1850; divided in 1895 into the diocese of Newport and the vicariate apostolic of Wales, which were made into the archdiocese of Cardiff in 1916 and the diocese of Menevia in 1898 respectively (*qq.v.*). From 1858 until its suppression the diocese of Newport had its pro-cathedral at Belmont Priory, Hereford, and its chapter of canons were Benedictine monks; the monastery was a cathedral priory (*q.v.*) with a mitred prior.

NICÆA, THE COUNCILS OF. The *First* Council of Nicæa was the first œcumenical council, convened by the Emperor Constantine with the sanction of Pope Silvester I, consisting of over 300 bishops, mostly Eastern, under the presidency of Hosius of Cordova and two Roman priests, legates of the Holy See, in 325. Its principal work was the condemnation of Arianism (*q.v.*), in the following terms: "The Catholic Church anathematizes those who say that there was a time when the Son of God was not, and that he was not before he was begotten, and that he was made out of nothing; or who assert that he is of other essense or substance than the Father, or that he was created, is alterable or is subject to change." It defined the true Catholic doctrine in a formula which was later expanded into the "Nicene

Creed" (*q.v.*), wherein our Lord was said to be "of the substance of the Father . . . begotten, not made, of the same substance with the Father." The day on which Easter should be celebrated was fixed by this council, which is commemorated by a feast in the Armenian, Coptic and Syrian rites. The *Second* was the seventh œcumenical council, held in 787, composed principally of bishops of the patriarchate of Constantinople, papal legates being present; it condemned Iconoclasm (*q.v.*), ordered the restoration of the holy images in churches, and passed a number of disciplinary canons. The Byzantine rite keeps a feast in honour of the Fathers of this council.

NICARAGUA, THE CHURCH IN. The ¾ million inhabitants, nearly all Indians and half-castes, are predominantly Catholic and the country forms an ecclesiastical province (the see of Managua was erected in 1531) with 3 suffragan sees, and a vicariate apostolic. A concordat was entered into with the Holy See in 1861, but from time to time legislation tends to be anti-religious; nevertheless the state contributes to certain church-run schools and colleges, and diplomatic relations are maintained with the Holy See.

NICENE CREED, The. The profession of faith commonly called by this name is the formula drawn up at the first Council of Nicæa as modified and expanded at the first Council of Constantinople, when it received practically its present form. The only subsequent alteration of any importance was the addition of *Filioque* (*q.v.*) in the West, which became and remains one of the stumbling blocks between the Catholic Church and the Eastern Orthodox. With this and minor verbal differences it is used in all the ancient churches and is accepted (with very varying interpretations) by many Protestant bodies. See CREED IN THE LITURGY.

NIGHT OFFICE. i. The office of Matins, normally said at midnight or in the very early morning; in practice, Lauds is usually joined to it.
    ii. The practice in stricter monasteries of singing Matins (and Lauds) some time between midnight and about 4 a.m., as opposed to the evening before or later in the morning.

NIHIL OBSTAT [QUOMINUS IMPRIMATUR] (Lat., Nothing hinders [it from being printed]). The words by which the censor of books (*q.v.*) certifies that he has inspected a given work and finds therein nothing contrary to faith or good morals.

NIMBUS (Lat., cloud). See HALO.

NINE CHOIRS, The. See CELESTIAL HIERARCHY.

NINE FRIDAYS, The. Among the promises said to have been made by our Lord to St. Margaret-Mary Alacoque was the following:

"In the greatness of the mercy of my heart its all-powerful love will give to all those who receive communion on the first Friday of every month, for nine consecutive months, the grace of full repentance, that they shall not die under my displeasure nor without receiving the sacraments, and that my heart shall be their sure refuge at that last hour." Catholics are not bound to believe that this promise was given and in this form, but there is nothing rash or imprudent in believing it; and it has in fact been preached and acted on, to the manifest good of many souls. The faithful, however, are warned by the Church against attaching any superstitious importance to the doing of an act a certain number of times or on certain days; and the receiving of holy communion in the right dispositions is not more efficacious for the salvation of the individual on one day than on another.

NINIVE, NINEVEH, THE FAST OF. A fast of some days, a short time before Lent, in remembrance of the penance of the Ninivites at the preaching of Jonas, observed in all Eastern rites except the Byzantine.

NOAH. The Hebrew form of the name of the patriarch Noe.

NOBIS QUOQUE PECCATORIBUS (Lat., And to us sinners). The opening of the prayer commemorating the Church Militant and Triumphant and the only words spoken aloud in the canon of the Latin Mass.

NOBLE ECCLESIASTICS, THE ACADEMY OF. A Roman college (founded in 1701) for men of good birth, other than Romans, with courses in ecclesiastical history, political economy, international law, modern languages, etc., and granting degrees in canon and civil law and theology. Its studies are particularly directed to training students for the ecclesiastical diplomatic service.

NOBLE GUARD, The. A bodyguard of gentlemen, of which a detachment is on duty whenever the pope attends a public function. The commandant is always a Roman prince, decorated with the Order of Christ, and every member must be of a family which has borne 16 quarterings of nobility for not less than 60 years and must have a certain income and stature, as well as unimpeachable health and character. Their uniform is ordinarily a cuirassier's helmet with plume, tunic and belts, trousers and sabre, but on special occasions a bearskin, white breeches and top-boots are worn. Established in 1801.

NOCTURN. The office of Matins consists principally of three divisions, called Nocturns. Each nocturn consists of three psalms with their antiphons, versicle and response, the Our Father, an absolution, a blessing, three lessons (q.v.) and a responsory; if *Te Deum* is to be said it takes the place of the last responsory. On simple feasts and ferias there is only one nocturn, which is similar in form but has nine psalms and three lessons. In the Monastic Office there are four lessons to each nocturn. *Nocturns* or a similar term was formerly often applied to the whole night-office (*cf.*, Rule of St. Benedict, caps. xv, xvii, and in the Celtic rite).

NOE. The Greek and Latin form of the Hebrew name Noah, used in the Rheims-Douay and other versions of the Bible.

NOMINALISM (Lat. *nomen*, a name). A system of philosophy which denies the reality of universals (*q.v.*) seeing in them nothing more than names or words, or at best ideas or concepts.

NOMOCANON (Gr. νόμος, law; κάνων, rule). A compendium of Eastern church law consisting of canons of councils and pertinent civil legislation, the texts arranged alphabetically. There are several such extant.

NON-CATHOLIC (Lat. *Acatholicus*). Technically, one who has been baptized but is not a Catholic (*cf.*, Infidelity, Heathen). Such are regarded as being within the jurisdiction of the Church and subject to canon law except in so far as they have been pronounced exempt from it, *e.g.*, the *Ne temere* (*q.v.*) legislation. In common speech the term is often applied to all those whatsoever who are not Catholics or to those who, whether baptized or no, accept some erroneous form of Christianity as a divine revelation.

NON-CATHOLIC SERVICES. See COMMUNICATIO IN SACRIS.

NON EXPEDIT (Lat., it is not expedient). The words of the Holy See's injunction to Italian Catholics to abstain from parliamentary elections either as electors or candidates; the injunction itself. It came into force during the strife between Italy and the States of the Church. It was subsequently modified and finally abolished by Pope Pius X.

NONCONFORMITY. A term now confined to the principles and practice of those Protestants in England and Wales who are members of religious bodies other than the Anglican, and to those people themselves as a body: also called Dissenters. As dissenting from the Established church, English Catholics are noncomformists, but the term is never applied to them. The principal Nonconformist denominations are the Baptists, Congregationalism and Wesleyanism or Methodism (*qq.v.*), and there are numerous smaller sects. Modernism and a religious pragmatism are increasingly common among them, but popular Nonconformity is still evangelical (*q.v.*) and its presentation and application of some of the fundamentals of Christianity closely approximate to Catholic dogmatic and moral teaching. Indeed, in traditional Nonconformity, *e.g.*, among the Methodists, the doctrines of the Holy Trinity, the Incarnation, the Atonement, the Passion and Resurrection are assumed and taken for granted; the religious "experience" to which they so often advert depends on the fullest conviction of the truth of these doctrines, and without them there is no meaning in any of the things which English Dissenters have particularly emphasized. Congregationalism and Presbyterianism (q.v.) represent Calvin's doctrine of the Church organized outside the Establishment in England when it became clear that it could not be dominant inside; the second is the centralized form of that doctrine, the first the decentralized form. Calvinism saved for them the idea of the Church at a time when it was being lost in the triumph of the secular state.

NONE (Lat. *nona* [*hora*], ninth [hour]). The hour of the Divine Office appointed to be said at the ninth hour, *i.e.*, between noon and 3 p.m. In practice it is said earlier; in cathedral, collegiate and conventual churches it is sung with Sext after the community Mass, or after dinner. It begins with *Deus in adiutorium*, etc., and an invariable hymn, *Rerum Deus tenax vigor;* three psalms according to the day of the week (on certain feasts the Sunday psalms are always said); variable little chapter and short responsory; collect of the day; and usual ending. The office commemorates the death of our Lord, which took place at this time of day and to which reference is made in the hymn.

NONES. The ninth day before the ides (*q.v.*), *i.e.*, 7th of Mar., May, July, Oct.; the 5th of other months. Part of the old Roman method of reckoning, still sometimes used in ecclesiastical documents.

NORBERTINES, The. The Premonstratensian (*q.v.*) canons regular, founded by St. Norbert.

NORDDISTS, NORTHISTS. The more numerous of the two sections of the Syro-Malabar Christians (*q.v.*). The division is a merely social one and affects both Catholics and Jacobites. Malabar tradition is unanimous in tracing the origin of the division to the coming of Syrian immigrants under Thomas Cana in 345. One party of the colonists lived to the north of Cranganore (the Muzires of older geographers) and were called Northerners or Norddists, the others lived to the south and were called Southerners or Suddists. As to the cause of the division, tradition is not unanimous. One version says that Thomas Cana (not St. Thomas the Apostle) had two wives, and that the descendants of the two wives formed the two divisions. A more critical version assigns the division to the two social classes among the immigrants. In course of time they mixed with the indigenous Christians. The Norddists claim that they are the exclusive descendants of the nobler section among

the immigrants who mixed with high-caste St. Thomas Christians; they are twelve times as numerous as the Suddists. The Catholics among the latter are all under the personal jurisdiction of the bishop of Kottayam.

NORMAL (Lat. *norma,* a carpenter's square). In accordance with a standard or rule. The normal is not necessarily the usual: it is "what ought to be", which is not always the same as "what is". For example: To preach the word of God at the principal Mass on Sundays is both normal and usual; to abstain from flesh-meat on Fridays is normal, but it has not been usual in several European countries since 1939; Vespers or Compline is the normal Sunday evening service, but neither is usual, or even frequent, in Great Britain, Ireland or the United States.

NORMAN. The English name for the variant of romanesque (*q.v.*) building used by the Normans in Great Britain and northern France, *e.g.*, Durham cathedral nave, St. Bartholomew's church in Smithfield, Barfreston in Kent, Abbaye aux Dames at Caen, Jumièges, St. Georges de Boscherville, Dunfermline abbey, Kirkwall cathedral.

NORTHAMPTON (*Northantoniensis*). An English see, suffragan of Westminster, erected in 1850. It covers the counties of Northampton, Bedford, Buckingham, Cambridge, Huntingdon, Norfolk and Suffolk, a large and almost entirely agricultural area with, therefore, a small and scattered Catholic population; before the Reformation it was divided between the then dioceses of Ely, Lincoln and Norwich. The missions of Costessey and Norwich were established in the 18th century; St. John's church at Northampton is pre-Reformation. The pilgrim shrine of Walsingham is in this diocese. The patrons of the diocese are our Lady Immaculate and St. Thomas Becket, in whose honour the cathedral is dedicated, his final stand against King Henry II having begun at Northampton.

NORTHERN BRETHREN'S FUND, The. A fund for the relief of the aged and infirm secular clergy of the diocese of Hexham and Newcastle, established in the 17th century.

NORWAY, THE CHURCH IN. The Church was dead in Norway from the middle of the 16th century until the 19th. In 1845 the penal laws were abolished; Lutheranism is the state religion, but Catholics are not taxed for its support. The country forms one diocese, with a vicariate and a prefecture, with about 3,500 Catholics out of over 3 million people. The episcopal see is at Oslo; Trondheim was the old chief see.

NOTARY (Lat. *notarius,* secretary, one who takes notes). An official appointed to draw up documents for certain Roman congregations and offices, dioceses, religious houses, etc., and to record the proceedings, evidence, etc., in cases in the Rota, diocesan courts, and other ecclesiastical tribunals. This work is often entrusted to laymen. See also PROTONOTARIES.

NOTATION, MUSICAL. Plainchant is written or printed upon a staff of four lines in square and diamond notes (*puncta*), without bars, and according to a system set out in the pertinent books. The sign **C** or **⁴C** at the beginning of a melody signifies that every note occurring on the line so marked is to be reckoned as *do* or *fa* respectively. This system is the right and proper way in which to write down plainsong, and its use is in no sense an archaic survival, for this music cannot be properly rendered into five-line notation; *e.g.*, the use of bars is not consonant with its rhythm, for whereas measure in modern music is based on the division of time into equal parts so that syllables must be adapted to the musical notes, the value of the notes in syllabic passages of plainchant depends on the value and place of the syllables; and moreover, the stress of the voice (*thesis*) is not regularly strong, but strong or weak as required by the melody; arrangements of minims, crotchets, quavers, etc., are misleading for they suggest strict proportional time.

NOTES OF THE CHURCH (Lat. *nota*, a mark). See MARKS OF THE CHURCH.

NOTION. An idea considered as objective, or the knowledge itself of a thing. First notions are the same, the most general ideas. The mind's knowledge starts from the most general and at the same time the most confused notions of things.

NOTORIOUS (Lat., *notus*, known). Acts or facts are said to be notorious when they are so public and manifest as to require no proof in law. Certain penalties are incurred only if the crimes are notorious, *e.g.*, deprivation of ecclesiastical burial for apostasy and heresy.

NOTRE DAME (Fr., Our Lady). Without any other words, except sometimes the name of the place, a common French name for a church dedicated in honour of the Blessed Virgin, *e.g.*, Notre Dame de Paris, usually the principal church of a town (*cf.*, Frauenkirche, Mariakirche). Its use for a shrine, picture, etc., is the same as in English.

NOTRE DAME NUNS. This name is given to several congregations which conduct schools and training colleges. The principal one in Great Britain is that of the Sisters of Notre Dame of Namur, founded by Bd. Julia Billiart in 1803. Others are the Daughters of Notre Dame (founded 1607; enclosed) and the School Sisters of Notre Dame.

NOTRE DAME UNIVERSITY. Properly the University of Notre Dame du Lac, in Indiana, founded in 1842 by Father Edward Sorin, of the Congregation of Holy Cross, which directs the university; it received its state charter two years later. It has faculties of arts and letters, law, natural science, engineering and commerce. The great success of the university as an educational institution has been equalled by the fame of its football team.

NOTTINGHAM (*Nottinghamensis*). An English see, suffragan of Westminster, erected in 1850. It includes the counties of Nottingham, Derby, Leicester, Lincoln and Rutland, most of which country was in the pre-Reformation diocese of Lincoln, but part in York. Three missions, Worksop, Spink Hill and Husbands Bosworth were founded in the 17th century and seven in the 18th. The patrons of the diocese are our Lady Immaculate and St. Hugh of Lincoln, and the cathedral is dedicated in honour of St. Barnabas the Apostle.

NOVAE AURELIAE. Genitive (in the archbishop's title) of *Nova Aurelia*, Latin form of the name of the see of New Orleans, La. Orleans in France was named from the emperor Marcus Aurelius.

NOVARCENSIS. The Latin epithet for the archbishop of Newark, N. J.

NOVATIANISM. The schism and heresy of Novatian, the first anti-pope, who in the middle of the 3rd century set himself up against Pope St. Cornelius. He denied the Church's power to absolve those who had lapsed into idolatry. His followers called themselves καθαροί (the pure), and further refused absolution to murderers, adulterers, fornicators and those "guilty" of a second marriage. The sect persisted until the 7th century.

NOVENA (fem. of Latin. *novenus*, ninth, consisting of nine). A prayer for some special object or occasion extended over a period of nine days. It may be carried on in common in church but is often private. A number of novenas, chiefly in preparation for various feasts, have been approved and indulgenced by the Holy See, the principal being that before Pentecost which alone must be observed in all parochial churches. In its earliest form the novena was for the repose of a person deceased. Various contributory causes are alleged for the choice of nine days, but at root the number seems to have been taken over from Roman paganism.

NOVENA, POPE'S. Nine consecutive days of Masses and prayers for a dead person. In the case of a pope it forms part of the official and formal mourning of his court.

NOVICE (Lat. *novicius*, new [slave]). One undergoing a period of probation, not less than one year, with the object of testing fitness for profession (*q.v.*) in a religious order or congregation of men or women. He is generally previously a postulant (*q.v.*) and becomes a novice by clothing with the habit of the order, which cannot take place till he has completed his 15th year. Certain conditions normally disable one from becoming a novice: *e.g.*, a subsisting marriage, parentage with dependent children or *vice-versa*, lack of free consent, involvedness in secular affairs which cannot be avoided. A novice may freely leave or be dismissed without reason given at any time; at the end of his canonical period he must be professed, dismissed or may have a further trial up to six months. A novice may not renounce his property or any part of it, either in favour of his own monastery, order or anybody else, nor ordinarily does he defray the cost of his noviciate even if unsuccessful. A female novice must be specially examined by the bishop or his delegate as to her free consent, etc., before profession.

NOVICIATE. i. The period or condition of being a novice. It is followed by profession in temporary vows.

ii. The separate house or apartments in a monastery set apart for the use of novices. They must be entirely cut off from those of the professed religious, and choir and lay-novices must occupy separate noviciates.

NULLITY OF MARRIAGE results from the presence of a diriment impediment (*q.v.*) of natural, divine or ecclesiastical law, or from the absence of true matrimonial consent, or from the omission of the form of celebration required for validity. The result of this is that a given union, whether or not it was entered into in good faith by both or one of the parties, is in fact no true marriage. Such a union, upon becoming known to the parties, must either be dissolved upon proof of its nullity by judicial process or be regularized by revalidation (*q.v.*). The most common reason for nullity of a marriage is the absence of consent on account of *vis et metus* (*q.v.*), a ground of nullity recognized also by the civil law of states. In 1945 the tribunal of the Rota (*q.v.*) made 35 definitive declarations of nullity, referred to it from all parts of the world; 40 other appeals for such a declaration were dismissed. The so-called divorce of King Henry VIII was in fact a petition for a declaration of nullity on the ground that his marriage with Catherine of Aragon was entered into by virtue of a dispensation from certain impediments, which dispensation he pretended to have been obtained on false pretences and therefore void.

NUMBER OF THE BEAST, The (Apoc. xiii, 18) has not been explained with certainty, but by far the best suggestion is that referring it to Neron Cæsar, which in Hebrew characters with numerical value gives 666,

whereas Nero, without the final "n" as in Latin, gives 616 (n = 50), the number given in many early MSS., according to Irenæus. See ANTICHRIST.

NUMBERS. The fourth book of the Old Testament, so called because it begins with the numbering of the people of Israel. It continues and concludes the history of their forty years' wandering, when they reached the plain of Moab on the east side of Jordan. In Hebrew it is called by its first word *Vaiedabber*. Its author was Moses (see PENTATEUCH).

NUN (late Lat. *nonna*, feminine of *nonnus*, old man [*cf. kalogeros*]). A member of a religious order or congregation of women. Canon law distinguishes between *moniales* (nuns strictly so-called) belonging to institutes having solemn vows, and *sorores* (sisters) who have only simple vows. Nuns may also be divided according to the nature of their life into contemplative and active (*qq.v.*). Generally speaking, widows are received to monastic profession by way of dispensation. Penitents are eligible; but for the Carthusians complete bodily integrity is required.

NUNC DIMITTIS, The. The song of Simeon (Luke ii, 29-32) from its opening words in Latin *Nunc dimittis servum tuum* (Now dost thou let thy servant go), said daily at Compline. It is recited or sung standing, the words being those of the Gospel, and where it is the custom the sign of the cross is made at the first verse. It is not sung in the Monastic Office. It is also sung during the distribution of candles on the feast of the Purification, farced with its own last verse, and when that feast occurs after Septuagesima it is the tract of the Mass. In the Byzantine rite it is sung at *Hesperinos* (Vespers).

NUNC PRO TUNC (Lat., now for then). An action performed of which the intended effect is to take place at some future time, near or distant, is done *nunc pro tunc; e.g.,* the plenary indulgence attached to the "last blessing" (*q.v.*) is not gained until the sick person is actually at the point of death.

NUNCIO, APOSTOLIC (It., from Lat. *nuntius*, a messenger). A legate of the Holy See sent as ambassador to a foreign court as the permanent diplomatic agent of the pope and accredited accordingly to the civil government. He also has the duty of watching over the welfare of the Church within the country of his mission. There are nunciatures in most of the principal countries of Europe and the Americas, excepting Great Britain, U. S. S. R., and U. S. A. See LEGATE; DELEGATE; DIPLOMATIC CORPS.

NUNNERY. A community of nuns and the house in which they live. The word is now rarely used by Catholics, having been superseded by the less definite term convent (*q.v.*). It is possible that by mistaken analogy with the word "monkery" and because of its use by low controversialists it may have acquired a slightly contemptuous sound to the public ear.

NUPTIAL BLESSING. The solemnization, as distinguished from the celebration, of marriage consists in the pronouncing of the solemn nuptial blessing over the bride and groom. This may not be given: (*a*) during the forbidden times (*q.v.*), (*b*) if either of the parties is not a Catholic, (*c*) if either of them has received it in a previous marriage, (*d*) except during a nuptial Mass or one taking its place, (*e*) if both parties are not present. *a* and *d* are sometimes dispensed and also *c* if it is the groom who has received it before. This blessing may and should be given to all those married couples who for any reason have not received it before, however long they have been married, provided any disability (*e.g.*, *b* above) has been overcome. The blessing is pronounced from the epistle-side of the altar after the Our Father of the Mass. It consists of a short general prayer and a long one in which, after references to the ordinance of marriage (" . . . in the covenant of marriage thou wouldst signify the sacrament of Christ and his Church . . ."), the bride is particularly prayed for, "may she be loving to her husband like Rachel, wise like Rebecca, long-lived and faithful like Sarah," etc. Again before the ordinary final blessing the celebrant says a special prayer over the couple.

NUPTIAL MASS. The wedding Mass for a bride and bridegroom may be celebrated, outside of "forbidden times" (*q.v.*), on any day except Sundays, holidays of obligation, double feasts of the first and second class, and certain others. On these days the three prayers of the nuptial blessing are interpolated into the Mass of the day and a commemoration (*q.v.*) of the nuptial Mass is made. The proper of this Mass all has direct reference to its subject; the epistle is St. Paul's instruction (Eph. v, 22-33) and the gospel Matt. xix, 3-6.

O

O ANTIPHONS, The. The Greater Antiphons (*q.v.*).

O SALUTARIS. The first words of a hymn, consisting of the last two verses of the hymn *Verbum supernum* sung at Lauds of Corpus Christi. In English-speaking countries it is invariably sung when the Host is exposed for Benediction.

O SAPIENTIA (Lat., O Wisdom). The opening words of the first of the greater antiphons (*q.v.*) preparatory for Christmas; the day on which it is solemnly sung in choir, Dec. 17.

OATES PLOT, The. An imaginary Catholic plot against King Charles II and the kingdom of England, invented and exposed for his own advancement by Titus Oates, a fugitive from justice, who said that poverty left him only the alternatives of becoming "a Jesuit or a Judas." The law was put into motion and between August, 1678, and July, 1681, sixteen priests and laymen were put to death for alleged complicity, and eight for being priests, including Bl. Oliver Plunket, archbishop of Armagh, and Viscount Stafford. In 1685 Oates was convicted of perjury and imprisoned for life, but was released and pardoned under William III.

OATH. An invocation of the divine Name as witness to the truth of a statement. It is an act of the virtue of religion and, if the statement is in the form of an undertaking, its fulfilment is binding under the obligation of religion. An oath required or sanctioned by law must be taken in person and not by proxy. An oath extorted by force or grave fear is valid, but can be relaxed by ecclesiastical authority. A promissory oath follows the nature of the act to which it is attached, and does not make lawful what is otherwise unlawful. Oaths may in certain circumstances be invalidated, dispensed or commuted by the competent authority. For the English coronation oath, see the ROYAL DECLARATION.

OATH AGAINST MODERNISM. Before clerics can be promoted to certain offices they are required to take a prescribed form of oath against Modernist errors, in addition to the usual profession of faith. This is a temporary requirement, and is not incorporated in the Code of Canon Law.

OBADIAH. One of the minor prophets, called Abdias in the Vulgate and Rheims-Douay versions of the Bible.

OBEDIENCE. i. A moral virtue which enables one to recognize the authority of his legitimate superior and to carry out his orders accordingly; the superior may be God, a parent, a husband, a public authority, an employer, etc. The virtue inclines one to carry out the known will of the superior, without waiting to be told. But a command to do an act certainly known to be sinful may never be obeyed, however high or fundamental the authority may be, and this no matter whether obedience be due by vow (*e.g.*, from a religious), by contract (*e.g.*, from a servant), by piety (*e.g.*, from a son or a soldier) or in any other way.

ii. An evangelical counsel. The free renunciation, in whole or in part, ot one's general independence of external action the better to follow Christ; a remedy against the dangers of self-love, self-esteem and the pride of life. The practice of the counsel may be given stability by a vow of obedience made to one's spiritual director or, more usually, to one's superiors in a religious order.

iii. Vow of obedience. The act by which a religious (*q.v.*) binds himself by the virtue of religion to submit to the direction of his superiors according to the rule and constitutions of the society. The vow of obedience is an essential element of the religious state. "The necessity which is consequent upon religious obedience is not a necessity of coercion but of free will, inasmuch as a man, although perhaps he would not be willing to do the thing commanded considered in itself, nevertheless wills to obey . . . and for this very reason that which he does is more acceptable to God" (St. Thomas II-II, clxxxvi, 5, ad 5).

iv. Marital. Though there is no explicit promise of obedience in the Catholic marriage service (*q.v.*), it is nevertheless the teaching of the Church that a woman is bound to obey the reasonable commands of her husband. This obedience is due not on account of any superior excellence of man as man or the worth of an individual, but because he is by the nature of things the senior partner in the matrimonial partnership. But though the wife must obey, the husband "is not commanded to rule, nor instructed how, nor bidden to exact obedience, or to defend his privilege; all his duty is signified by love." See also WIFE, HUSBAND.

OBEDIENTARY. The former common name, still occasionally used, for a permanent administrative official of a monastery. Those found in most monasteries are: the cellarer, bursar or procurator, the novice-master, the guest-master, master of the lay brothers, the infirmarian, the sacristan, the cantor or precentor, and the secretary (*qq.v.*). These are appointed by the superior and serve during his pleasure. Others take weekly turns according to a roster, *e.g.*, the hebdomadary (*q.v.*), the reader and servers at meals.

OBIT (Lat. *obitus*, death). An obsolete term for an anniversary Mass for the repose of the soul of one dead.

OBJECT. That which confronts the senses or the mind or any other faculty. Opposed to subject, which perceives or knows an object. The great problem of philosophy is to discover how the subject can know an object. There is an important distinction between material object and formal object; the first is the object in itself as receptive of a form or perfection; the second, the precise reason in the object which permits of its being perceived by some particular power. Thus in regard to the faculty of sight—a wall is the material object but colour is the formal object or the precise reason whereby the eye sees the wall. It is an axiom that powers, habits, sciences are specified by their formal objects. Objectivity is the character of that which is objective, real, existing independently of the subject.

OBLATE (Lat. *oblatus*, offered). i. The name given to members of certain religious congregations who have offered themselves to the service of God. See below.

ii. A child offered to God in accordance with the Rule of St. Benedict, cap. lix. This custom has been forbidden since the 7th century, but cf., *alumnus*.. Such *oblati* must be distinguished from ordinary oblates of St. Benedict.

OBLATE OF ST. BENEDICT. i. A lay person of either sex who, because of devotion or some personal relationship, is invested with a scapular and enrolled as an oblate of some particular Benedictine monastery. He becomes a partaker in the good works and satisfactions of the monastery, and by a decree of Pope Leo XIII, in 1898, is granted not only all the indulgences, graces and privileges belonging to oblates of other Benedictine congregations but also those common to secular tertiaries (*q.v.*). There is however no third order (*q.v.*) of St. Benedict and an oblate is not a member of the order; but if he wishes to join a third order he must withdraw his oblation. The obligations of an oblate vary, but they necessarily involve "conversion of manners," daily vocal prayer (Little Office B.V.M., or otherwise) and the wearing of a black scapular (*q.v.* ii) beneath the clothing. Some oblates reside permanently in a monastery upon conditions arranged with the superior. See CONFRATER.

ii. There is a congregation of Oblates Regular of St. Benedict who are bound by simple vows, and care for the sick poor in their own homes. The Australian active Sisters of the Good Samaritan have the anomalous name of Tertiaries Regular of St. Benedict. See also OBLATES OF ST. FRANCES.

OBLATE SISTERS OF THE ASSUMPTION, The. A congregation of nuns, founded in 1866 to do active work in the missions of the Augustinians of the Assumption (*q.v.*).

OBLATES OF MARY IMMACULATE, The. A congregation of priests and lay-brothers under simple vows, founded by Bishop C. J. E. de Mazenod, in 1816. It conducts seminaries, schools and colleges (including the University of Ottawa), missions in Canada (particularly the far north), Ceylon and Australia, and does pastoral work in connexion with all its establishments.

OBLATES OF ST. CHARLES, The. A society of secular priests without vows who live in common and undertake any work which their bishop may require; they were founded by Don G. M. Martinelli, in collaboration with St. Charles Borromeo, at Milan, in 1578, to raise the standard of the secular clergy. The English society was founded by Cardinal Wiseman and the Rev. H. E. Manning (afterwards cardinal).

OBLATES OF ST. FRANCES OF ROME, The, were founded by her in 1433. An association of women of good birth who live in community in Rome under an adaptation of the Rule of St. Benedict, working for the sick and poor. They take no vows but make a revocable promise of obedience to the superior, who is called the Mother President; they retain their property and private incomes and are not bound by enclosure. *Cf.,* Pallium.

OBLATES OF ST. FRANCIS DE SALES, The. A congregation of priests with simple vows engaged in teaching and pastoral work, founded by the Abbé Louis Brisson in 1871 and now having four provinces, with a mission in Africa.

OBLATION. An offering, particularly the act by which the victim of a sacrifice is offered to God. Some theologians hold that in the oblation lies the essence of a sacrifice, because by it man refers himself and all creation to God as his final end.

OBLIGATION. The moral necessity imposed by law of doing or omitting to do something. A negative law binds "always and for always," *i.e.,* it may never be broken; a positive law binds "always not for always," *i.e.,* it binds only when the occasion presents itself. A merely penal law (*q.v.*) imposes no moral obligation beyond that of submitting to the penalty imposed for infringement. Where there is a right (*q.v.*) there is a corresponding obligation or duty, but a duty does not necessarily involve someone else's right to its discharge, though they may claim it in charity; moreover, one may have a right and also a duty (*e.g.,* in charity) not to use it. Obligation or duty in its highest sense is the necessity of submission to the laws of God, determined by him for the welfare of his creatures and in accordance with their nature. God himself has no duties.

OBREPTION (in canon law; from Lat. *obrepere,* to deceive). The obtaining or attempting to obtain a papal rescript or dispensation (*q.v.*) by a statement which contains a lie.

OBSCURANTISM. Opposition to or prevention of free enquiry; the suppression of unpleasant truths or awkward facts; the unreasonable withholding of knowledge from people lest it should do them harm. Obscurantism is a vicious exaggeration of the virtue of prudence; those who accuse others of it have often insufficiently considered the virtue. Pope Leo XIII warned against it in 1883 when he opened the Vatican archives to the public and affirmed that the Church needs only the truth.

OBSECRATION (Lat. *obsecrare,* to implore). A prayer in the form of an appeal to sacred things, as in the second part of the litany of the Saints: "By thy nativity, deliver us, O Lord."

OBSERVANCE. The rule and constitutions of a religious order and the degree of strictness with which they are interpreted or kept. The adjective "Observant" always indicates a stricter observance, but common or relaxed observance is not a term of reproach: a lower standard well maintained is better than a higher standard badly maintained (*cf.,* Cassinese Benedictines of the Primitive Observance, Cistercians of the Common Observance). See REFORM.

OBSERVANTS, OBSERVANTINES. Those members of the Franciscan order who maintained the primitive rule of St. Francis against the mitigations of the Conventuals (*q.v.*). The differences of the two bodies were a source of dissension in the order up to the 16th century. In the course of time various bodies appeared among the Observants with the ideal of further austerities; such were the Reformed, Recollects, Alcantarines, etc. None of these bodies were autonomous, all being subject to the minister general of the Observants or Friars Minor. In 1897 Pope Leo XIII, by the bull *Felicitate quadam,* abolished all these differences in the practice of the rule and abrogated the name Observants, giving the order once more its simple appellation of Friars Minor.

OBSESSION. i. The state of one who is the unconscious or unwilling victim of fixed ideas or sentiments such as fear, love, aversion; the cause is sometimes ill-health.

ii. The state of one who suffers more or less continual molestation or even actual possession by the Devil.

OBSTINACY IN SIN. Shutting the heart to all promptings of grace and refusing to be moved to repentance by circumstances no matter how favourable. It implies grievous malice and is one of the sins against the Holy Ghost.

OCCASION (Lat. *occasio,* from *occidere,* to fall). The juncture suitable for the production of some effect; it is distinct from cause from which there is a real influx for the production of an effect. Thus the cause of wood burning is fire, the occasion is proximity to the fire.

OCCASION OF SIN. Any person, place or thing which allures a man to sin. It is narrower in meaning than "danger of sin." The latter indicates propensity to sin within the agent; the former denotes extrinsic enticement.

OCCULT (Lat. *occultus,* hidden) acts or facts are those for which evidence cannot be produced in the external forum (*q.v.*), *e.g.,* occult impediments to marriage, or which are not publicly known or likely to become known, *e.g.,* occult crimes. In canon law special provision is often made for occult cases.

OCCULT COMPENSATION. The act by which a creditor pays himself from the goods of the debtor without the latter's knowledge. For such compensation to be just and licit it is necessary that the debt be one of strict justice and quite certain, that no other means of redress be possible, and that injury to the debtor be avoided.

OCCULTISM. The principles or practice of knowledge which is held to involve the use of hidden and mysterious powers, *e.g.,* magic, divination, astrology (*qq.v.*).

OCCURRENCE of feasts is when two or more offices fall on the same day. In such cases the feast or office of the higher liturgical rank prevails and is celebrated; the other is transferred, has a commemoration (*q.v.*), or is left out altogether; *e.g.,* if the Annunciation falls in Holy Week, it is transferred to after Easter; if an ordinary saint's day (greater double, double, semi-double, *qq.v.*) falls on an ordinary Sunday, it is commemorated in the Sunday office; if an ordinary saint's day falls on a great feast of our Lord (*e.g.,* Pentecost) it is not observed at all that year. When an occurrence takes place, the procedure to be followed is given in the current *Ordo* (*q.v.*) (*cf.,* Concurrence).

OCTAVE (Lat. *octava* [*dies*], eighth [day]). The commemoration of a feast over a period of eight days, counting the feast itself; the final day of such a commemoration. Days in between are "within the octave." Only Easter, Pentecost and Christmas now have an octave; Epiphany has an octave-day only, commemorating the Lord's baptism in Jordan. The octaves of Easter and Pentecost are of the 1st rank, which means that throughout the week no other feast whatever may be celebrated. The equivalent in the Byzantine rite is called an *apodosis* (*q.v.*).

ODE. i. In the Byzantine rite, one of the nine scriptural canticles (*q.v.*).
ii. A series of *troparia* (*q.v.*) having relation to the theme of one of the above. Nine odes (sometimes less; in Lent three) form a *kanon,* sung at *Orthros.*

ODIUM THEOLOGICUM (Lat., theological hate). Ill-feeling on account of differences in religious belief. When the proper hatred of what is, or is thought to be, erroneous is carried over as hostility against those who profess the errors, it is none the less unlawful because the errors pertain to religion. The expression *odium theologicum* more generally designates that bitterness or prejudice which is too often apparent in those who engage in theological controversy.

ŒCONOMUS (Gr. οἶκος, house; νέμειν, to manage; *cf.* economy). i. In the Orthodox Eastern church, and particularly at patriarchal courts, the archdeacon or priest who has charge of the episcopal finance and sometimes administers the eparchy during a vacancy.
ii. Any official who looks after finance may be called an œconomus. Catholic bishops sometimes appoint one and may choose a qualified layman; chapters are bound to appoint an œconomus during an episcopal vacancy.

ŒCUMENICAL (Gr. ἡ οἰκουμένη, the inhabited [world]). Pertaining to or representing the whole world or Church, used especially of a general council (*q.v.*).

ŒCUMENICAL PATRIARCH. A title assumed to himself and his successors by John IV the Faster, patriarch of Constantinople (582-95), and still in use. It is not known quite what he meant it to signify. There cannot in fact be such a thing as an "œcumenical patriarch"; the Holy See has never used or formally recognized such a title. See SERVUS SERVORUM DEI.

OF FAITH. A thing is said to be of faith when a Catholic cannot withhold his belief therefrom without thereby severing himself from the Church.

OFFENSIVE TO PIOUS EARS (Lat. *piarum aurium offensiva*). See EVIL SOUNDING.

OFFERING[S], The. i. The Mass (*q.v.* ii) or Eucharistic Liturgy (*q.v.*).
ii. The bread and wine for the use of the celebrant in this.
iii. Bread, wine, candles, etc., formerly offered in kind by the people.
iv. The offertory (*q.v.* i).
v. A Mass stipend or stole fee (*qq.v.*) is frequently referred to as an offering, and the word exactly expresses the nature of these things, as voluntary gifts in acknowledgement of duties performed on our behalf; nor is this nature altered by the fact that local custom or law may fix a minimum amount for such offering.

OFFERING OF HOLY COMMUNION. A common practice among Catholics anxious to help the living or dead. *Ex opere operato* the sacrament benefits only the receiver; but *ex opere operantis* it can be of value to others, inasmuch as the receiver uses the time of his intimate union with Christ to pray for them and offers his prayer in union with the prayer of Christ. Moreover, to go to holy communion is an exalted religious act, and as such can be offered for the benefit of others. Hence a book of Théophile Renaud was condemned for belittling the practice as a pious fraud.

OFFERTORY. i. The offering of the bread and wine to God by the celebrant at Mass after the gospel or *Credo*. In the Roman rite the priest says the offertory verse (see ii) and offers up the bread on the paten with the prayer *Suscipe, sancte Pater . . . hanc immaculatam hostiam* (Receive, O holy Father . . . this spotless host); he receives wine from the server and pours it into the chalice followed by a few drops of water which he first blesses, saying a prayer referring to the divine (wine) and human (water) natures of Christ (this mingling also represents the union of Christ with his people); he then offers up the chalice with the prayer *Offerimus tibi, Domine, calicem salutaris* (We offer to thee, O Lord, the chalice of salvation); then, after two short prayers, he proceeds to the lavabo (*q.v.*), followed by another prayer of offering, *Suscipe*. At high Mass the celebrant is assisted at the offertory by deacon and subdeacon and the offerings, altar, etc., are incensed. The Carthusians, Carmelites and Dominicans offer chalice and host together, as was done in the pre-Reformation English uses.

ii. The offertory-verse is variable and consists of one verse of a psalm or otherwise sung by the choir in sung Mass, the relic of a whole psalm and antiphon (*cf.*, this verse at a requiem Mass), which were formerly sung while the people made their offerings in kind. This custom is preserved in the cathedral of Milan, and at ordination the candidates offer candles and at consecration the bishop elect offers bread, wine and candles at this point. These offerings were discontinued about the 11th century; to a certain extent the collection has taken their place, but more particularly Mass-stipends.

OFFICE (Lat. *officium*, a service, duty). i. The Divine Office (*q.v.*) or any part thereof, *e.g.*, the office of the day, of a saint.

ii. Other similar services of prayer, *e.g.*, the Little Office B.V.M. (*q.v.*).

iii. The prayers and ceremonies for some particular purpose, *e.g.*, the office of Burial of the Dead.

iv. The Church's services in general, *e.g.*, the day's office, meaning Divine Office, Mass and any other observances for a particular day.

v. The name of the introit in the Mozarabic, Carmelite, Carthusian and the Dominican rites and in all old English uses.

OFFICE, THE MONASTIC, contained in the "Breviarium Monasticum" and used by Benedictines and other monks and nuns, is an important variation of the Roman office, based on the directions contained in the Rule of St. Benedict caps. viii-xviii, and excluded from the reforms of Popes St. Pius V and Urban VIII. It differs in its distribution of the Psalter, number of lessons, etc. The Cistercians and Carthusians use variants of it, that of the latter being contained in a number of choir-books after the earlier fashion, the "Breviarium Carthusiense" being only for the use of the sick, etc.

OFFICE OF THE DEAD, The. An office for the repose of the souls of the dead, consisting of (First) Vespers (Ps. cxiv, cxix, cxx, cxxix, cxxxvii, the *Magnificat*, Our Father silently, Ps. cxlv, one or more collects), Matins (invitatory, three nocturns each of three psalms and three lessons from the book of Job), and Lauds (Ps. l, lxiv, lxii, canticle of Ezechias, Ps. cl, the *Benedictus*, Our Father silently, Ps. cxxix, collect). The recitation of this office is obligatory only on All Souls' day, when special lessons are appointed for Matins and psalms, etc., for Compline and the little hours; there is no second Vespers. The office as above is sung or said in choir on the day of death, of burial, and at other times according to custom and requirement. In certain religious orders its recitation is prescribed once a month or more frequently, and sometimes with a special rite, *e.g.*, the Dominican.

OFFICIAL. Formerly the name for what is now called a vicar general (*q.v.*), and still sometimes used in that sense; a diocesan judge acting for the bishop. In those dioceses where more than one vicar general is authorized, that one having charge of contentious business, *e.g.*, marriage and criminal causes, is distinguished as the official.

OIL. The use of oil for anointing is an apostolic injunction (James v, 14) and from the Jewish and primitive Church it has stood for strength, sweetness and spiritual activity, the ointment for the limbs of the athletes of the Lord. Pure olive oil is used for the oil of catechumens and of the sick, and is an ingredient of holy chrism (*qq.v.*). It is also prescribed to be burnt in sanctuary lamps, but if it cannot be had permission may be given for the use of other, preferably vegetable, oils.

OIL OF CATECHUMENS. Olive oil blessed by a bishop on Maundy Thursday. Used in the blessing of the font on Holy Saturday and the vigil of Pentecost, also in solemn Baptism, at the ordination of priests, consecration of altars and coronation of sovereigns. The infant or catechumen is anointed on the chest and between the shoulders, the priest on the palms of his hands, kings and queens on the right arm and between the shoulders. This oil symbolizes the priestly and royal power of Christ in which the baptized participate, the "royal priesthood" of 1 Pet. ii, 9.

OIL OF SAINTS. Oily and other liquids exuded from the shrine or relics of certain saints (*e.g.*, of St. Walburga, at Heidenheim, "the manna of St. Nicholas" at Bari, the water of St. Donatus at Concordia Veneta); oil blessed in honour of some saint (*e.g.*, of St. Serapion, in the "Rituale Romanum"). These are used for anointing with prayer and faith in God for health of soul and body.

OIL OF THE SICK. Olive oil blessed by a bishop on Maundy Thursday, and used in the administration of Extreme Unction (of which sacrament it is the matter), and at the blessing of church bells.

OLD BELIEVERS, The. Russian sectaries who repudiated the reforms of the Patriarch Nikon (*d.* 1681), calling themselves *Starovery.* They were cruelly persecuted and flourished in consequence, some keeping to their Orthodoxy, others taking up the wildest excesses of religious mania. It is noteworthy that those who remained Orthodox formally admit the immaculate conception of our Lady. With other sects (called in general *Raskolniky*) they numbered perhaps 30 millions in 1917.

OLD BROTHERHOOD OF THE SECULAR CLERGY, The. A body of 24 English secular priests under the presidency of one of their number, having organic continuity with the Old Chapter (*q.v.*) which ceased to function in 1850. It is a purely philanthropic and social society, but maintains a living link with penal times. It meets every six months and allocates its funds to charity; vacancies are filled by election of the members.

OLD CATHOLICS, The. A sect arising from the refusal of Dr. Döllinger and other German theologians and canonists to accept the definition of Papal Infallibility in 1870. A hierarchy was obtained through the Jansenist bishop of Deventer. They profess adherence to the first seven œcumenical councils and the Nicene creed, but confession, fasting, etc., are optional, the pastors are elected by their congregations, and so on. They are loosely organized into national churches of fluctuating numbers and are found in Germany, Central Europe and the U.S.A., about 50,000 in all. The Jansenist Church of Holland (*q.v.*) is now reckoned an Old Catholic church. Their orders and sacraments are valid.

OLD CHAPTER, The. An uncanonical chapter of 24 members, established in 1623 by William Bishop, first vicar apostolic for England, as part of his organization for ecclesiastical government. It functioned with the tacit approval of the Holy See and from

1655 to 1685 administered the Church in this country. It ceased to act after the establishment of four vicariates in 1688 but continued to exist, and 35 of its members became bishops; at the re-establishment of the hierarchy in 1850 it was reorganized as the Old Brotherhood of the Secular Clergy (*q.v.*).

OLD CHRISTMAS DAY. Jan. 6, according to the computation of the Julian calendar at the time it was superseded by the Gregorian in Great Britain. Certain Christmas and other celebrations are still observed locally on this date, which is also known as Twelfth Day.

OLD COVENANT, DISPENSATION, LAW. The law and covenant of Moses as opposed to the new covenant, of Jesus Christ, which in part fulfilled and in part superseded it (*cf.*, Matt. v, 17-18; Heb. viii, 7-13).

OLD HALL. The college of St. Edmund of Canterbury at Old Hall Green, near Ware; one of the two organic descendants of the English College at Douay (*q.v.*). A school for small boys, founded under Bishop Challoner in 1749 at Standon Lordship, was moved to Old Hall in 1769 and refounded and reorganized with students from Douay in 1793. It is now both the seminary for the archdiocese of Westminster and a boys' school.

OLD LATIN VERSION. A translation of the Bible made into Latin from the Septuagint in the 2nd century. There were several texts, some of which may have been independent versions, of which one is called *Itala Vetus* (*q.v.*), a name sometimes given to any Latin text which antedates the Vulgate (*q.v.*).

OLD STYLE, usually represented by the abbreviation O.S. with a date, indicates that it is reckoned according to the Julian calendar (*q.v.*), beginning the year on March 25 in England.

OLD TESTAMENT. Those books of the Bible (*q.v.*) written before the coming of Jesus Christ and, for the most part, accepted as canonical by the Hebrews. Though the word of God and inspired equally with the New Testament, it is not claimed that their moral teaching is other than far below the sublimity of Christian ethics, or that they display or forecast clearly and unmistakably the dogmatic teaching of Christianity. And this from the nature of the case. For God provided the Old Testament in the first place for the instruction of the Jewish church which, precisely because Christ had not yet come, was not fit or able to receive the full content of God's revelation for the faith and conduct of man (*cf.*, Matt. xix, 8).

OLD TESTAMENT SAINTS. The only holy ones of the Old Dispensation honoured liturgically throughout the Western church are the Holy Machabees (*q.v.*), though others are named in the Roman Martyrology (Abraham, Moses, David, Jeremias, etc.), and the Carmelites have feasts of Elias and Eliseus. Abel and Abraham are invoked in the litany for the dying, and the second of these, "patriarch and father of all believers," is frequently referred to. In the Eastern rites they are more common: *e.g.*, feasts of the Ancestors of the Messias, the Just or the Ancient Law, Joseph, David, Job the Great Athlete, Isaias and other prophets, the Three Children, and others, in the Byzantine rite.

OLIVETANS, The. An independent branch of the Benedictines founded by Bd. Bernard Tolomeo in 1313 and named after their abbey-*nullius* at Monte Oliveto near Siena. They are organized under an abbot general, and follow a strict interpretation of the Holy Rule. They have only about a dozen monasteries. They wear the ordinary Benedictine habit, but white. There are also nuns of the order.

OMBRELLINO (It., a little umbrella). A small flat canopy with one staff borne over the Blessed Sacrament when it is carried from its own altar to another for exposition, etc., and, in some countries, when it is taken to the sick.

OMEN. A chance word or event taken as foretelling the future or as a guide to conduct. Seriously to pay attention to omens and act on them in matters of weight is sinful (*cf.*, Divination).

OMNIPOTENCE OF GOD, The. God's infinite power to do all things, without the aid of any matter or instrument, and without fatigue, change, or diminution of capacity. It is no limitation of God's omnipotence to say that he cannot do that which is intrinsically impossible, for to assert that he could would be a contradiction in terms. But as St. Thomas remarks (I, xxv, 3), "It is better to say that impossibles cannot be done than that God cannot do them."

OMNIPRESENCE OF GOD. God's presence in every place. God's essence is uncircumscribed by any limits, and as it has no parts (for he is simple, *q.v.*) he is wholly everywhere. But also he is present in all his creatures by his knowledge: "From him, no creature can be hidden; everything lies bare, everything is brought face to face with him" (Heb. iv, 13). And, further, he is present by his power: his wisdom "reacheth from end to end mightily and ordereth all things sweetly" (Wisdom viii, 1).

OMNIS UTRIUSQUE SEXUS. Cap. 21 of the Fourth Lateran Council (1215), which confirmed the obligation on all who had attained years of discretion of making confession of one's sins at least once a year and of receiving holy communion about Easter. It also warned priests against betraying a confession by word or deed on pain of degradation and confinement. Canon 859 explains years of discretion as use of reason, *i.e.*, from about seven years old.

OMNISCIENCE OF GOD. God's knowledge (*q.v.*) of all things, even our most secret thoughts.

OMOPHORION (Gr.). A band of silk or velvet about ten inches wide twisted loosely round the neck so that one end passes over the left shoulder in front and the other reaches nearly to the ground behind, embroidered with crosses. It is worn over the *sakkos* by bishops of the Byzantine rite, and corresponds to the Latin *pallium*, which Catholic patriarchs sometimes wear over it. At certain parts of the liturgy a smaller one is worn for convenience. The *omophorion* is worn also by bishops of the Armenian, Coptic and (in a different form) Syrian rites.

ONANISM. A technical name for that form of "birth-control" (*q.v.*) practised by Onan (Gen. xxxviii, 8-10), which the Scripture calls "a detestable thing." The term is sometimes erroneously used to mean solitary self-abuse.

ONTOLOGISM. A philosophic system (Malebranche, Gioberti, Ubaghs, etc.) according to which God is the principle and the means of all our knowledge. God infuses the idea of being into the mind which is naught other than God himself. Hence the saying of the Ontologists: *Primum logicum est primum ontologicum:* "The first thought is the First Being (God)."

ONTOLOGY (Gr. ὄντος, of being, λόγος, science). The science which treats of being in general; also called general metaphysics.

OPERA CARDINAL FERRARI. See COMPANY OF ST. PAUL.

OPERATION. See ACT.

OPINION. An adhesion of the mind to one of two opposite statements with a certain fear lest the other alternative be true; it is distinct from certainty, ignorance, doubt (*qq.v.*).

OPPOSITION. A repugnance between two things, one of which excludes the other from the same subject at the same time and under the same aspect. There are four species: (*a*) *Contradictory*, as man and not man; (*b*) *Privative*, as vision and blindness; (*c*) *Contrary*, as virtue and vice; (*d*) *Relative*, as father and son.

OPPRESSION OF THE POOR. A sin which cries to Heaven for vengeance (*cf.*, Exod. ii, 23), since it is often in vain that the poor look to the rich and powerful for protection against their oppressors.

OPTIMISM. The view that good must ultimately prevail over evil in the universe. Leibniz, pushing his idea of the principle of sufficient reason to extremes, had perforce to conclude that the actual world is the best of all possible worlds; it is opposed to Pessimism, which maintains that evil prevails in the world, and, in the opinion of some extremists, that all is evil.

OPUS ANGLICANUM (Lat., English work). Name given to English embroidery of a characteristic type during the middle ages. Examples of it are the Syon cope (South Kensington Museum), the Steeple Aston cope, and a cope in the Anglican church at Skenfrith, orphreys on modern vestments in the Catholic churches at Abergavenny, Usk, Monmouth, and Marnhull, copes at St. John Lateran, Ascoli-Piceno, and Salzburg, chasubles at Stonyhurst, Ushaw, and elsewhere.

OPUS DEI (Lat., the Work of God). St. Benedict's name for the Divine Office, to which, in cap. xliii of his rule, he said his monks were to prefer nothing; that is, its celebration was to be the most important thing, *sine qua non*, of the monastic life, but not its only activity.

OPUS OPERATUM, OPERANTIS. See EX OPERE.

ORANGEISM. An anti-Catholic movement having its origin in northern Ireland and the activities of the 18th century Peep-o'-Day Boys, having for its object Protestant supremacy in Ireland, and spreading thence to Great Britain, the U.S.A., Canada and Australia. It is organized in lodges, the first of which was founded in 1795, with secret oaths, titles, ceremonies and regalia, and has always been distinguished for its violence, lawlessness and bigotry. The Orange Society was suppressed by Parliament from 1813 to 1828 and was the subject of official investigation in 1835 and later; it was adjudged an illegal body in Canada in 1882. Of late years Orangeism has been less active and noisy. The name refers to King William III, of Orange, whose "glorious, pious and immortal memory" is cherished by the society.

ORANS, ORANTE (Lat., It., pl. *orantes, oranti*). A figure praying with outstretched arms, found many times depicted in the catacombs. They are said to represent the souls of deceased persons.

ORARION (Gr.). The deacon's stole (*q.v.*) in the Byzantine rite. It is a narrow band of silk about 4 yds. long, with Ἅγιος (Holy) embroidered on it thrice. It is worn over the left shoulder, by the Greeks and Melkites with the back end hanging to the ground, the front carried under the right arm and over the left shoulder; by others, hanging down back and front. Gestures are made with the front end held between three fingers of the right hand. From the Lord's Prayer to after communion it is crossed over his back and chest, so as not to hamper his movements. All deacons of Eastern rites wear a similar stole; it is their distinguishing

ornament, and is imposed at ordination. Subdeacons and, by abuse in some places, other minor clerics wear a sort of short *orarion* round the middle and crossed over the shoulders. A stole falling back and front over the left shoulder is worn by the deacon in the Carthusian rite.

ORATE FRATRES (Lat., Pray, brethren). Words addressed by the celebrant to the people at Mass preparatory to the preface to the canon: "Pray, brethren, that my sacrifice and yours may be acceptable to God the Father Almighty"; to which in the Roman rite the people, server or ministers respond, "May the Lord receive the sacrifice at thy hands, to the praise and glory of his name and to the benefit of us and all his holy Church." Herein is emphasized the unity of the congregation, priest and Church in offering the sacrifice. There is an analogous feature in the Maronite Liturgy.

ORATIO (Lat., pl. *orationes*). i. A prayer, particularly the short liturgical prayers usually called collects (*q.v.*).
ii. A discourse.

ORATIO IMPERATA (Lat., ordered prayer). A collect ordered by the pope or bishop to be added to the others at Mass on a particular day or during a period of time, for some special object; *e.g.*, during the years 1939-45 the collect "for peace" was an *oratio imperata*. Such prayers are never said on Christmas, Epiphany, Maundy Thursday, Holy Saturday, Easter, Ascension, Pentecost, Trinity Sunday or Corpus Christi, nor, unless it is prescribed *pro re gravi* (*q.v.*), on feasts of the first and second class and a number of other days.

ORATIO SUPER OBLATA (Lat.). The prayer over the offerings, *i.e.*, the secret (*q.v.*, ii) said when the bread and wine have been offered on the altar.

ORATIO SUPER POPULUM (Lat., prayer over the people). A prayer added after the post-communions in ferial Masses of Lent, introduced by the words, "Bow down your heads before God"; it is always repeated as the collect at Vespers on the same day. Such a prayer for a blessing was formerly said here on other days.

ORATIONES DIVERSÆ (Lat., various prayers). A section of the missal containing thirty-three sets of collects, secrets and post-communions for insertion on special occasions into the Mass and most apt for general use as well. They are directed to obtaining spiritual and temporal needs of all kinds.

ORATORIANS, The. Members of the Congregation of the Oratory (*q.v.*) of St. Philip Neri.

ORATORIO. A musical composition on a religious theme, usually a biblical story, performed by soloists, chorus, and orchestra or organ, in a semi-dramatic way but without action, scenery or costume. It developed out of the popular evening services held by St. Philip Neri (1515-95) in his oratory at Rome: hence its name. Like some other distinctively Catholic inventions (*e.g.*, the Three Hours) its associations in the English popular mind are purely non-Catholic—in this case, with Anglican cathedrals, the Albert Hall, *etc.*

ORATORY. i. *Oratorium* (Lat. *orare*, to pray) is the technical name at canon law for a distinct class of building (*cf.*, church); divided into public, semi-public and private oratories (*qq.v.*), set apart for divine worship, not intended primarily for the general public but for a community, school, family or individual. It may be any size.

ii. An establishment of the Congregation of the Oratory (*q.v.*) and particularly its church.

iii. In common speech, a small chapel in a private house.

ORATORY, THE CONGREGATION OF THE. i. Of St. Philip Neri, founded by him in 1564, and taking its name from his oratory in the church of San Girolamo at Rome, where the first meetings took place. It consists of societies of secular priests living in community under obedience but without vows; every member should normally have private means to support himself. By the rule of St. Philip each house or congregation is independent, but this principle was altered for the French Oratory (*q.v.*, below). The institute's object is the salvation of souls by prayer, preaching and pastoral activity; there is a service with sermon every week-day evening except Saturday in all Oratory churches. The society is now established in the United States. In England there are two Oratories (Brompton in London, and Birmingham, founded by Cardinal Newman, who first brought the Oratory to England in 1849). Associated with the Birmingham Oratory is a school for boys at Caversham Park, near Reading. Attached to every Oratory is the Little Oratory (*q.v.*).

ii. The French Oratory is a congregation founded on the lines of St. Philip's by Cardinal Peter de Bérulle in 1611, but it is a distinct institution under its own superior general. It was suppressed at the Revolution, but reconstituted in 1852 by the Abbé Pétetot with the name of the Oratory of Jesus and Mary.

ORATORY, PRIVATE OR DOMESTIC, is a chapel in a private house for the sole use of an individual, his family, and their servants. If it is required for Mass to be said more than occasionally, a papal indult must be obtained, and only those persons referred to therein can fulfil their obligation of Sunday Mass in the chapel. A private mortuary chapel in a cemetery is a private oratory.

ORATORY, PUBLIC. An oratory (*q.v.*) erected for the benefit of a community or corporation (*e.g.*, of monks or nuns) or family, but to which all the faithful have a canonical right of access at least during service times. Such an one may be consecrated and have a title (*q.v.*).

ORATORY, SEMI-PUBLIC. An oratory (*q.v.*) erected for the benefit of a community, etc., as above, there being no habitual and indiscriminate right of the general public to make use of it. Such are usually the churches and chapels of schools, colleges, barracks, prisons, hospitals, many convents of nuns, etc. Such may be consecrated and have a title (*q.v.*). The private chapels in the houses of cardinals and bishops have all the rights and privileges of semi-public oratories.

ORDEAL. A legal practice formerly common in Teutonic countries, of deciding a suspect's innocence or guilt by application of a physical test, *e.g.*, handling red-hot metal, safe endurance of which was taken as a sign of divine acquittal. Trials by single combat (duel) first came under the ban of the Church in the 9th century, and all ordeals were condemned out of hand by the Fourth Lateran Council (1215) as superstitious and "tempting God." Nevertheless, they continued with local ecclesiastical approval in certain places down to the end of the 15th century.

ORDER. A happy disposition of things; it implies a multitude reduced in some wise to unity.

ORDER, THE SACRAMENT OF HOLY (Lat. *ordo*, rank). A sacrament of the New Law instituted by Christ, by which spiritual power is handed on and grace is conferred for the confection of the sacraments, especially of the Eucharist (and therefore for offering sacrifice) and for the proper carrying out of other ecclesiastical duties. It confers a character (*q.v.*) so that it cannot be repeated for the same grade. The minister of Holy Order is a bishop, who alone can confer the priesthood and episcopate. Vicars and prefects apostolic and abbots and prelates *nullius* even though not bishops can confer minor orders (*q.v.*) on those subject to them or having dimissorial letters (*q.v.*), as can any abbot of a monastery on those monks subject to him. The Holy See could delegate any priest to confer orders up to, and probably including the diaconate. Imposition of hands alone is the matter of the diaconate, priesthood and episcopate, and the form of the sacrament is the pertinent prayer. The sacraments of Baptism and Confirmation confer on every Christian a real participation in the priesthood of Christ, but the holy order of priesthood differs from these specifically in imparting its own particular indelible character and the power to minister divine grace to the faithful both by the sacraments and by the word.

ORDER, RELIGIOUS. i. Canon law reserves this name to the religious institutes (*q.v.*) in which the members take solemn vows. They consist principally of all the "old orders" (of canons regular, monks, nuns and friars) and the Jesuits.

ii. Historically, a society of persons united for religious ends, bound by vows, and organized ultimately under the authority of a "superior general." The word Order was first thus used in 1119 in the Charter of Charity (*q.v.*). In so far as the Benedictines formerly consisted of entirely independent and autocephalous monasteries (and still do to a considerable extent in both theory and practice), they did not form an order in this sense; but in both law and fact they are now recognized as the chief of the religious orders (see CONGREGATIONS O.S.B.).

iii. In common speech, any of the societies which canon law calls religious institutes (*q.v.*).

ORDER OF ST. AUGUSTINE, The. The Hermits of St. Augustine (*q.v.*).

ORDER OF ST. BENEDICT, The. The Benedictines (*q.v.*).

ORDER OF CHIVALRY. See MILITARY ORDER.

ORDER OF CHRIST, SUPREME. A military order founded in Portugal in 1319 on the ruins of the Knights Templars. After the 15th century the order declined and from 1832 membership was merely a titular honour conferred by the kings of Portugal. It has a separate survival in Rome, where it is the supreme pontifical order of knighthood; it is the highest secular decoration granted by the Holy See and is conferred very seldom. The uniform is a scarlet coat with white breeches and stockings.

ORDER, MILITIA, OF THE GOLDEN SPUR. A pontifical order of knighthood refounded and limited to one hundred members by Pope Pius X. It is awarded to those whose work in any sphere is notably illustrious and may be conferred on non-Catholics and even non-Christians. The uniform is red with black trousers.

ORDER OF ST. GREGORY THE GREAT. A pontifical order of knighthood founded by Pope Gregory XVI, in 1831. There are civil and military divisions, and each is ranked into grand-cross knights of the first and second class, commanders, and knights. This order is the one most commonly bestowed in recognition of distinguished services to the Church. The uniform is green with white trousers.

ORDER OF KNIGHTHOOD, PONTIFICAL. One with which the sovereign pontiff honours laymen of distinction. They are, in order of precedence, the orders of Christ, of the Golden Spur, of Pius, of St. Gregory the Great, of St. Silvester and of the Holy Sepulchre (*qq.v.*). These are all confined to Catholic laymen, except the second and third, which may be conferred on non-Catholics and the last, on clerics and women. The orders are purely honorary and in English-speaking countries have no title attached to them; in Italy their members are called *commendatore* or *cavaliere*, in France *chevalier*. Each order has its distinctive decoration, cross or star, and a uniform of dress coat and trousers in various colours, adorned with gold braid, etc., cocked hat and court sword. A British subject must have the permission of the king of Great Britain and the British Dominions to accept a pontifical title (or any other granted by a foreign sovereign).

ORDER OF ST. LAZARUS OF JERUSALEM. A lesser military order of knights who were originally hospitallers for the care of lepers. It was an offshoot of the Hospitallers and Templars, and had a few houses in England, *e.g.*, at Locko in Derbyshire, It still exists (*a*) as an order of merit (of SS. Maurice and Lazarus) conferred by the royal House of Savoy, (*b*) as an order of knighthood in France. This last, like the knights of St. John, still has a practical purpose for its existence, namely, to uphold the faith in Palestine and the Near East, particularly by working for the return to unity of the Orthodox of those parts.

ORDER OF PENANCE, PENITENCE. i. Groups of lay people in the early 13th century who banded themselves together to promote Christian life by preaching and penance, but without abandoning the lay state. The movement had its origin in the 12th century (Vaudois, Humiliati, *qq.v.*), but is assigned chiefly to St. Francis of Assisi, who gave a rule to some members in 1221 and so initiated his third order (*q.v.*); others, with the Militia of Christ (*q.v.*), formed the third order of St. Dominic; others, the Penitents of Blessed Mary Magdalene (1225), of Jesus Christ (1245), and others now extinct.

ii. The *Scalzetti* (*q.v.*).

ORDER OF PIUS, The. A pontifical order of knighthood, first founded by Pope Pius IV, and restored by Pius IX in 1847, as an honour to be bestowed upon worthy men, whether Catholics or not. It has three ranks, grand-cross, knight commander (three grades) and knight, of which the first is hereditary. The uniform is dark blue with white trousers.

ORDER OF PREACHERS, The. The Dominicans (*q.v.*).

ORDER OF THE HOLY SEPULCHRE, The. A pontifical order of knighthood restored by Pope Alexander VI in 1496, but having its origins in the crusades. Membership is conferred by the Latin Patriarch of Jerusalem, *ex officio* rector and perpetual administrator of the order for the Holy See. It is divided into three ranks, grand-cross knights, commanders and knights, and may be bestowed also upon clerics and women (dames). The uniform is dress coat, trousers and cloak, all white. Those who receive the order in Jerusalem are invested with ancient gold spurs and a sword said to have belonged to Godefroi de Bouillon, preserved in the church of the Holy Sepulchre. In 1928 Pope Pius XI commended the work of spreading the faith in Palestine by prayer and alms to the active attention of this order, and a council of its noble dames was at once set up to undertake it.

ORDER OF SERVANTS OF MARY, The. The Servites (*q.v.*).

ORDER OF ST. SILVESTER, The. The oldest pontifical order of knighthood, fabled to have originated with Pope St. Silvester I, called the Militia of the Golden Spur until its reconstitution by Pope Gregory XVI, in 1841. It has three classes and a black uniform.

ORDERS, NUMBER OF. There are seven separate degrees of holy orders in the Western church. Minor: doorkeeper or porter, lector or reader, exorcist, and acolyte; and major or sacred: subdeacon, deacon, priest (*qq.v.*). Tonsure (*q.v.*) is not an order. Bishops have the plenitude of the priestly power; archbishop, patriarch and pope are degrees within the episcopate. The cardinalate is an office, not an order, as are abbacy, canonry and other prelatures. In the East the number and reckoning of both major and minor orders (*qq.v.*) varies in the different churches.

ORDINAL. A form of prayers and ceremonies for the conferring of holy orders.

ORDINARIATE. A district wherein the faithful of an Eastern rite are subject to a prelate, usually a titular bishop, of their rite who has ordinary powers and duties in their regard, so his jurisdiction is personal rather than territorial; now usually called an exarchate. See EXARCH.

ORDINARY. i. Local. A cleric with ordinary jurisdiction (*q.v.*) in the external forum over a specified territory. The following are local ordinaries: the pope universally, residential bishops in their dioceses, abbots and prelates-*nullius*, vicars general, administrators, vicars and prefects apostolic, vicars capitular. The expression "the ordinary" generally indicates the bishop of the diocese.
ii. The Ordinary of the Mass (*Ordinarium*

Missæ) is that unchangeable, or practically unchangeable, part of the Mass into which the proper (*q.v.*) is fitted as into a framework, consisting principally of the preparatory prayers, *Kyrie, Gloria, Credo,* offertory prayers, preface, *Sanctus,* canon, *Paternoster,* fraction, *Agnus Dei,* communion prayers, conclusion and last gospel (*qq.v.*).
iii. A division of the Roman Breviary containing the unchangeable parts of the Office other than the psalms.

ORDINATION. The conferring and reception of any of the holy orders. The making of a bishop is called his consecration. "If anyone say that orders or sacred ordination is not truly a sacrament instituted by Christ the Lord . . . or that it is merely a kind of rite for choosing ministers . . . or that he who has once been made a priest can again become a layman: let him be anathema" (Council of Trent, sess. xxxiii, canons 3, 4).

ORDINATION, CONDITIONAL. Ordination may be repeated conditionally if there is a grave and positive doubt whether it has been validly administered.

ORDINATION, THE RITE OF. Holy orders are conferred by the handing to the cleric, with the appropriate words, of his symbols of office; but for deacons, priests and bishops it is by an imposition of hands. When priests are to be ordained, the bishop, after the gradual of the Mass, charges the people to denounce any unworthy candidates and then admonishes the deacons themselves; they then lie prostrate and the litany of the Saints is sung; afterwards the bishop and all priests present lay on their hands; then, after a preface reciting the dignity of priesthood, the bishop invests each deacon with a chasuble, says a prayer invoking the blessing of God, and *Veni, Creator Spiritus* is sung, during which the bishop anoints the hands of the ordinands with oil of catechumens and delivers to each a chalice and paten with the words, "Receive the power to offer sacrifice to God and to celebrate Mass both for the living and the dead in the name of the Lord." Mass is then resumed. At the offertory each ordinand presents a lighted candle to the bishop and from then onwards they all say the prayers of the Mass aloud with the bishop; after his communion each new priest takes a draught of wine. After the ablutions they recite the Apostles' Creed together, and then the bishop again lays on his hands saying, "Receive the Holy Ghost. Whose sins you shall forgive . . . ," etc.; each priest makes a promise of obedience, and the bishop solemnly blesses them together. In all Eastern rites ordination is by imposition of hands; Byzantine and Armenian bishops lay on the right hand only and deliver the chalice, etc., to the ordinand. The Orthodox ordain only one deacon, priest or bishop, at a time.

ORDO. i. Abbreviation for "Ordo Divini Officii Recitandi Sacrique Peragendi" or ". . . Persolvendi Missæque Celebrandæ" (The Order for the Recitation of the Divine Office and the Celebration of Mass). An annual calendar containing directions for the Mass and Office to be said on every day throughout the year. Every diocese, religious order and congregation has its own edition, or at least a supplement to that of the Roman church, providing for its own special feasts and observances. It is indispensable to every priest and to those who recite the Divine Office daily. It is drawn up throughout in Latin and has numerous abbreviations of which some of the principal are noted in the table of abbreviations at the end of this volume.

ii. *Ordo administrandi sacramenta et alia quaedam officia peragendi.* The book of the ritual for the administering of the sacraments and certain other offices (*Rituale*) authorized and recommended for the use of the clergy in England and Wales. Except in the marriage ceremony it conforms to the *Rituale Romanum* practically throughout, but has some additional matter.

ORDO MISSÆ. The section of the Missal comprising the ordinary and canon of the Mass (*qq.v.*).

ORDO ROMANUS. One of fifteen collections of rubrics and directions for the carrying out of sacred ceremonies according to the use of the Roman church. They are distinguished from one another numerically, "Primus," "Secundus," etc., and are contemporary descriptions of usages from the 7th to the 15th century.

OREMUS (Lat., Let us pray). An invitation said in all Latin liturgies except the Mozarabic before collects, post-communions and other prayers, several of which are sometimes joined together under one *oremus* and with one termination (*Per Dominum* . . . etc.). The *oremus* said before the offertory-verse at Mass was formerly followed by the "prayers of the Faithful," which have now disappeared. The word originally had reference not to the prayers which now follow but to the named object of the prayer, "Let us pray for . . ." (*cf.*, Good Friday Office). It stresses the unity of priest and people in divine worship.

ORGAN (Gr. ὄργανον, an instrument). The use of the organ at liturgical services can hardly be said to be more than tolerated by the Church, although such use is general in the West. It is absolutely forbidden from after the *Gloria* on Maundy Thursday until the same on Holy Saturday, and throughout Lent and Advent may at the most only be used to sustain the voices, except on solemn feasts: the accompaniment of the preface (*q.v.*) is prohibited at all times. Carthusians and Cistercians do not have organs in their churches, nor Capuchin friars, unless it be a parochial church. The Sistine choir always sings unaccompanied. On the other hand, the organ is allowed to be played by the rubrics of the "Pontificale" and the "Cæremoniale Episcoporum"; and the Roman "Ordo" expressly orders it on *Gaudete* and *Lætare* Sundays and on Maundy Thursday till the end of *Gloria in excelsis*, and also on Holy Saturday from the beginning of the *Gloria* (*cf.*, Music).

ORIENTAL. See under EASTERN.

ORIENTALIUM DIGNITAS. A constitution published by Pope Leo XIII in 1894 defining the relations and making laws for the intercourse between Catholics of Western and Eastern rites, of which one of the most important is that, "Any Latin missionary, secular or regular, who by his advice or influence shall have persuaded any Eastern Christian to adopt the Latin rite shall by that very fact incur suspension from his sacred offices" and other penalties.

ORIENTATION. The building of a church east and west, with its altar at the east end, because there lay man's first home, there our Lord lived and suffered, from thence he shall come again, and other symbolisms: perhaps also with a memory of sun-worship. Great importance was attached to this at one time, and it is still considered desirable, but no more. Many churches of Celtic foundation are said to be built on the line of the sun's rising on the feast day of the saint in whose honour it was dedicated. The altar end of a church is always referred to as its east end, whatever the actual direction. Bodies should be buried east and west, of a priest with his head and of a layman with his feet to the east, reproducing the relative position of priest and people, face to face with one another.

ORIGENISM. The system of erroneous teaching, rightly or wrongly attributed to Origen (*c.* 185-254). It is summed up in the following propositions: that there is an inequality among the divine persons; that human souls existed before Adam; that Christ's soul thus pre-existed; that there will be nothing material about the body after the resurrection; that there is no eternal punishment; that all intelligences tend to reabsorption in the one Fount of beauty; that the allegorical sense of Scripture is the one supreme and essential sense. Origen was one of the most brilliant of the early Christian apologists, and he died as the result of severe torture endured for the faith; the extent to which he taught these errors was, and still is, a matter of dispute, but he certainly seems to have been Greek rather than Christian in his attitude towards history and cosmology. The kingdom of God, for example, he understood in a metaphysical sense as the realm of spiritual reality, thus tending to make the historical facts of Christianity no more than symbols of immaterial realities; the history of mankind from Adam's sin to Christ's redemption became in his views a cosmic drama of spirit and matter on the gnostic pattern.

ORIGIN OF SPECIES. The much discussed source of the differentiation of the various types of animal and vegetable life. According to the theory of Creationism (*q.v.*) these were separately created by God to remain fixed for all time; according to Evolution (*q.v.*) in its various forms, they are the result of continuous minute modifications of an originally plastic organism, the common ancestor.

ORMENSIS, Sanctae Mariae. The Latin epithet for the bishop of Sault-Sainte-Marie in Canada. Greek *horme* = violent forward movement = rapids or waterfall = French *sault, saut.* Cf., Grand Rapids, Mich., *Grandormensis;* Fall River, Mass., *Riverormensis;* Great Falls, Mont., *Greatormensis;* Sioux Falls, S. Dak., *Siuxormensis.* But Rapid City, S. Dak., is *Rapidopolitanus,* and Sault Sainte Marie, Mich., is *Marianopolitanus.*

ORNAMENTS (Lat. *ornamentum,* equipment). The vesture proper to an ecclesiastical person or place during divine worship; the material accessories of worship. Of these the Pontifical Commission for Sacred Art says: "Riches and pomp are never necessary, and sobriety—even a decent poverty— is not unworthy of the house of God. . . . It should never be forgotten that the dignity and decorum of the church and its altars demand the removal of all useless artificial ornaments [paper flowers, aspidistras, coloured tin, etc.], the putting of alms boxes in suitable places, the very rare use of pictures on an altar, the gradual elimination of those coloured plaster images and oleographs which are often exposed for the veneration of the faithful, and a prudent judgement and moderation in the arrangement and decoration of electric-lighting, whether used for the illumination of the church or for throwing light on altars or shrines" (General Instructions, 1924).

ORNAMENTS OF THE ALTAR. In churches of the Latin rite a high altar should have a crucifix, six candlesticks, three white cloths, a frontal and be covered by a ciborium or other canopy (*qq.v.*). A side altar requires only a crucifix, two candlesticks and the three cloths. On more solemn days relics and images of saints and vases of flowers may be placed between the candlesticks. In the Byzantine rite the altar is surmounted by a ciborium; at each cornei is a piece of stuff with the name of an evangelist or his symbol on it; the topmost cloth may be of silk and coloured, and on it is the *antimension* wrapped in the *eileton* with the book of the gospels reposing on

them; between two or more candlesticks is the crucifix, and *ripidia* are ranged behind (*qq.v.*).

ORPHREY. (Old Fr. *orfreis,* from Lat. *auriphrygium,* gold Phrygian embroidery). The embroidered "pillar" or cross on the back and front of a chasuble and the wide border around the opening of a cope. These were in origin probably devices to cover the seams but have now long been only conventional ornaments, not at all essential to the garments. The *clavi* of the dalmatic and tunicle have a different origin and are a necessary part of those vestments.

ORTHODOX (Gr. ὀρθόδοξος, right believer). i. In common speech, *orthodox* as an adjective is used of those who profess true doctrine in all its integrity in reference to some standard, named or implied. In this sense the word is used by the Catholic Church in official pronouncements (*e.g.,* in the oath against Modernism) and the liturgy (*e.g.,* in the prayer *Te igitur* of the Mass) in reference to the true faith of the Church, and it is so used by religious writers, *e.g.,* St. Ignatius in the "Spiritual Exercises."

ii. In its technical historical sense, orthodox is as a noun and adjective aplied to those Christians who accept and hold the definitions of the Council of Chalcedon, namely, Catholics and "Greeks" as against monophysites and Nestorians. In the course of time it has become the distinguishing epithet of the "Greeks" (Orthodox Eastern Church, *q.v.*) and Catholics acknowledge their right to the name in this sense. If it is understood in sense i, we must use it of them only by courtesy, just as the Orthodox call us Catholics though claiming true catholicity for themselves alone (*cf.,* Catholic-Orthodox). The name is sometimes given by English writers to other Eastern dissidents (Armenians, Jacobites, Copts). This is absurd, both in historical fact and according to the usage of those concerned, who would vehemently repudiate the epithet in this sense; but the Copts not infrequently use it for themselves, apparently as part of their general imitation of their Byzantine neighbours, as do the Malabar Jacobites.

ORTHODOX EASTERN CHURCH, The. The Patriarchates of Constantinople, Alexandria, Antioch and Jerusalem with their associated churches which gradually severed themselves from the Holy See after 1054. See CERULARIUS, SCHISM OF. It now consists of the four independent churches governed by patriarchs of those places and the following other autocephalous churches, namely, of Cyprus, Russia, Georgia, Sinai, Greece, Bulgaria, Serbia, Rumania, Finland, Albania, Poland and Japan. The patriarch of Constantinople has only a primacy of honour; the chiefs of all these churches govern under the control of a holy synod (*q.v.,* ii). The Byzantine rite (*q.v.*), in many languages, is common to all. Their orders and sacraments are valid. The parochial clergy are usually married, and bishops are chosen from among the monks, formerly very numerous. In theory there is complete unity, in fact a substantial agreement touching faith and morals. The Catholic Church regards these churches as being only in schism, but certain dogmatic differences are maintained by many eminent Orthodox theologians. They teach that the infallible Church has no visible head and speaks through the voice of the bishops as a body; the primacy (except of honour) and infallibility of the Holy See are rejected and only the first seven councils recognized as œcumenical. They reject the *Filioque* (*q.v.*), teach that our Lady was purified from original sin at the Annunciation (*cf.*, Immaculate Conception) and are confused in their doctrine of Purgatory (*q.v.*, ii). Their teaching on the Real Presence seems indistinguishable from Transubstantiation, but like all dissident orientals they believe that consecration requires the *epiklesis* (*q.v.*). They reject indulgences, alleging that sacramental absolution remits all temporal punishment. The practice of admitting divorce for adultery and in other circumstances is spreading. Many of the clergy of these churches are most inadequately trained; the people are exceedingly devout and attached to their liturgies, but the use of the sacraments is far from general or even common, and their practice accordingly lags behind their external piety. Devotion to our Lady and other saints, and to their images and relics, is very strong. The Orthodox are the second largest Christian body, numbering some 40 millions (excluding the large but uncertain number in U.S.S.R.), and found by emigration in most parts of the world; but except by Russians in the middle and far East they have been able to do practically no foreign missionary work. There are two Orthodox churches in London (Greek and Russian) and one each in Manchester, Liverpool and Cardiff, and many in North and South America.

ORTHODOXY, THE FEAST OF. An important feast of the Byzantine rite kept on the first Sunday of Lent to celebrate the restoration of the *icons* to the churches in 842, and the triumph of orthodoxy over Iconoclasm (*q.v.*) and other heresies.

ORTHROS (Gr., daybreak). The office of the Byzantine rite corresponding to Matins and Lauds. It consists principally of six psalms, namely, iii, xxxvii, lxii, lxxxvii, cii and cxlii, a litany, *troparia*, a *kathisma* of psalms, a gospel on Sundays and feasts, a *kanon*, a reading of the *synaxarion* (*qq.v.*) for the day and other psalms, with *Gloria in excelsis* and the *Magnificat*.

OSCOTT. The College of St. Mary at Oscott near Birmingham, founded as a lay and clerical school in 1793, and intimately connected with the Catholic revival in England. It began at Oscott ("Maryvale") near Great Barr in Staffordshire and was later transferred to New Oscott near Sutton Coldfield. After the restoration of the hierarchy the first three synods of Westminster (whose province then covered the whole country) were held there in 1852, 1855 and 1859. In 1889 it was closed as a school and reopened at once as the seminary of the diocese of Birmingham, which it still is. Under the influence of Pugin and of the 16th Earl of Shrewsbury, Oscott was one of the nurseries of the gothic revival.

OSCULA SOLITA (Lat., the usual kisses), given to the hand of the celebrant and any object presented to or received from him during the course of divine worship. All such are omitted in requiem Masses and when the Blessed Sacrament is exposed.

OSCULATORIUM (Lat. *osculum*, a kiss). Another name for the *pax* (*q.v.*, ii).

OSEE (Heb. *Hosea*, Salvation). A prophetical book of the Old Testament, named after its author, who was a contemporary of Isaias in the 8th century B.C., and the first of the minor prophets. It begins with an account of his marriage to an adulteress (whether this is fact or figure is disputed), which leads up to the unfaithfulness of Israel and prevision of her afflictions, notably illustrated by reference to domestic and social life.

OSSERVATORE ROMANO, The (It., *Roman Observer*). An evening newspaper printed and published daily in the City of the Vatican. It was founded in 1860 by a group of Italians with no special connexion with the Holy See; it was later acquired by Pope Leo XIII. It is issued under the oversight of the papal secretariate of state, but it is only a semi-official organ and only the column headed *Nostre informazioni*, recording chiefly certain current Vatican events and occasional comments, is actually supplied by the secretary of state. The editor is a layman. Nevertheless, it accurately reflects the views of the Holy See and its communications are often "inspired"; the popes sometimes publicly refer to the columns of the *Osservatore* for a statement of their attitude on a given matter.

OSSORY (*Ossoriensis*). An Irish see, suffragan of Dublin. It covers the county of Kilkenny, and parts of Leix and Offaly. Since the end of the 12th century the bishop's see has been in Kilkenny city, where is now the episcopal residence, cathedral and college. The patron of the diocese is St. Kieran (Mar. 5), its apostle; the cathedral is dedicated in honour of our Lady. Irish name: Osraighe.

OSTIARIUS. A doorkeeper (*q.v.*), the lowest of the minor orders.

OSTRICH EGGS. The custom so common in churches of Eastern rites of using ostrich eggs as a decoration has been explained by an oriental writer thus: that the female ostrich is peculiar among birds in that she does not sit on her eggs, which are fertilized by the male and female birds looking at them until they hatch out. This stare must not be intermitted for a second or the egg will addle. Just so the Christian must fix his entire attention on God when at prayer or it will be fruitless. This pleasant explanation leaves a suspicion that it post-dates the beginning of the custom, as do so many symbolical meanings in the West. In fact they were probably first used to prevent rats and mice crawling down the chains to get at the oil in the lamps.

OUR FATHER, The. The Lord's Prayer, taught by him to his apostles (Matt. vi, 9-13; Luke xi, 2-4). The English version used by Catholics is the same as that of Protestants, with the trifling variations of "who art" and "on earth," and the invariable omission of the doxology (*q.v.*) in the West. The form "which art" was in use by Catholics until Challoner altered it in the middle of the 18th century. The Lord's Prayer occurs repeatedly in the Latin liturgies; *e.g.*, it is sung or said by the celebrant at Mass after the little elevation; at each nocturne of Matins, in the *preces* (*q.v.*), and on other occasions the first two words and last two clauses are sung or said aloud, the remainder said inaudibly. The people join with the celebrant in saying this prayer at the Good Friday communion; and they say it aloud in the vernacular at the renewal of baptismal promises in the Easter vigil. In the Monastic Office it is sung at Lauds and Vespers and said inaudibly after the little chapter of all the little hours and Compline (*cf.*, Rule of St. Benedict, cap. xiii). It is sung in all Eastern Liturgies, and usually has the doxology; the Copts add "through Jesus Christ our Lord." As the pattern of all prayers, given by our Lord himself, this prayer is honoured, loved and used above all others by Catholic and Protestant alike.

OUR LADY. The most usual expression in English, when speaking or writing informally, for the Blessed Virgin Mary. Its first recorded use in our tongue was by Cynewulf, in his poem called "Christ," written in the 8th century; but for long its ordinary form was Our Lady Saint Mary. It is used in many languages, but not so commonly as in English. It is often associated with an epithet indicating some particular association or attribute: Our Lady Immaculate, of Fair Love, Help of Christians, of Perpetual Succour (from a picture), of the Stump (a shrine at Antwerp), of Lourdes, of Walsingham, of Madhu, of Tong-lu (from shrines at those places). Our Lady of Pity was once a common name for her in England; this was a translation of *B.V.M. de Mercede* (of Ransom) or *de Pietate* (of Mercy) and did not refer to her sorrows.

OUR LADY IN HARVEST. An old English term for the feast of the Assumption (Aug. 15).

OUR LADY IN LENT. An old English term for the feast of the Annunciation (March 25).

OUR LADY OF MOUNT CARMEL. A feast kept by the Western church and by some orientals, on July 16. It was at first proper to the Carmelite order, to celebrate its approbation at Rome and St. Simon Stock's alleged vision of our Lady and the brown scapular (*q.v.*); it is in its latter aspect that it has obtained a wider observance (*cf.*, the collect and post-communion of the proper Mass).

OUR LADY OF RANSOM. A feast kept by the Western church, on September 24. It was originally proper to the Mercedarians (*q.v.*), celebrating their foundation, and is particularly concerned with the ransoming of the faithful from the bonds of sin. Our Lady is particularly invoked under this title for the conversion of the English from religious error.

OUR LADY OF THE SNOW. The name of the feast of the dedication (*q.v.*, i) of the basilica of St. Mary Major kept by the Western church on Aug. 5; so called on account of the legend of the miraculous fall of snow in August by which its site was indicated. The story is now discredited and in some calendars the name has been altered back to The Dedication of St. Mary.

OUR LADY'S BANDS (*i.e.*, bonds). An old English term for pregnancy.

OUR LORD. An abbreviation of Our Lord Jesus Christ, commonly used when speaking or writing informally. Its first recorded use in English is in the 12th century. "The Lord," however, more usually stands for the word "God" (see ADONAI).

OXFORD MOVEMENT, The. A successful effort to revive the Christian spirit in the Church of England after a long period of inertia, indifference and liberalism, by means of insistence on its alleged Catholic character and the resulting necessity for a reformation in its faith and worship; in its essential character the movement was a vindication of the supernatural character of Christianity. It was begun at Oxford by Dr. Keble, in 1833, and carried on there by J. H. Newman, Hurrell Froude, Pusey, Isaac Williams, Charles Marriott, Faber, Dalgairns and W. G. Ward, principally by means of "Tracts for the

Times" (*q.v.*). In 1841 Newman's Tract 90 (*q.v.*) was censured, and in 1845 Ward's book, "The Ideal of a Christian Church," was condemned and he himself deprived of his status by Convocation of the University. Shortly afterwards both became Catholics and were followed by numerous others, many of distinction, and the movement as such may be said to have then ended. But its results were very great; on the one hand the Church of England was transformed, its life re-newed, and an "Anglo-Catholic" party of power definitely established; on the other, the country at large became more familiar-ized with Catholic doctrine and practice, and numerous submissions to the Holy See were thus indirectly brought about. Both directly and indirectly the Catholic Church in Eng-land was affected by the Oxford Movement only less than the Established Church itself. The later "Oxford Groups" have nothing whatever to do with the Oxford Movement.

P

PACHOMIANS, The. The followers of St. Pachomius who in south Egypt about the year 318 established the first *cœnobium* or monastery for life in common as we now understand it.

PACHOMIUS, ST., THE RULE OF. The first rule written for monks living together in common, provided for the monasteries founded by Pachomius in Egypt between 318 and 346. Each monk had to attain a certain standard of education; manual work was an integral part of the life; the monasteries were large and divided into semi-independent sec-tions under provosts; the discipline strict and of a military pattern. Pachomian influence may still be seen in the Coptic monasteries of Egypt.

PACIFIC ISLANDS, THE CHURCH IN THE. The American, British, Dutch and French possessions in the islands that lie be-tween the west coast of America and a line drawn roughly north-east and south-west between New Guinea and the Moluccas have a total population of nearly 4½ million; of these, some 450,000 are Catholics. The territory is divided ecclesiastically into a score of vicariates apostolic, in the charge of various missionary congregations; except Hawaii, which is a suffragan diocese of San Francisco.

PACIFISM. In its first meaning, the doc-trine that the abolition of war is desirable, every Catholic not only may but must be a pacifist. Its more usual meaning is the doc-trine that war has and can have no lawful function and must be avoided at all costs. This the Church denies (see WAR).

PADROADO (Port., patronage). An ancient privilege of the crown of Portugal of nam-ing bishops for vacant sees in certain mis-sionary countries wherein Portuguese sub-jects were settled. In western India par-ticularly this led to conflict between the mis-sionaries of *Propaganda* and the Portuguese clergy and civil authorities. When the In-dian hierarchy was established in 1886 a sys-tem of double jurisdiction between Portu-guese and other bishops was established in the Bombay Presidency and other places. This "double jurisdiction" was abolished by an agreement between the Holy See and Portugal in 1928.

PÆNULA. A chasuble; the ample Roman cloak from which it is derived.

PAGAN CUSTOMS. Nothing but error and sin being foreign to Catholicism, the Church has ever sought to "baptize" rather than to destroy the customs, institutions and native life of those to whom her missionaries are sent. Thus wrote Pope St. Gregory the Great to St. Augustine: "The temples of the idols in that nation [of the English] ought not to be destroyed but let the idols that are in them be cast down; let water be blessed and sprinkled in the said temples and let altars be built and relics placed therein. For if those temples be well built, it is meet that they be converted from the worship of devils to the service of the true God. And because they are used to slay many oxen in that worship, some solemnity must be provided in exchange. . . . For without doubt it is impossible to cut off everything at once from their rude natures" (Bede, "Eccl. Hist.," i, 30). Latterly this policy has been hampered and diverted by the overweening self-assurance of European and American civilization and by the arro-gance of nationalist political interest which now so surely follow the missionary. Pope Pius XI in his encyclical *Rerum Ecclesiæ* pointed the way to a return to normal practice.

PAGANISM (Lat. *paganus*, "civilian," as op-posed to the Christian, an "enrolled soldier," *miles*, of Christ). In the widest sense this term comprises all religions other than that revealed by God in Christ; in a narrower sense it includes all except Christianity, Judaism and Islam. It is also used loosely of those who, though conscious of the Chris-tian revelation, reject or are indifferent to it and draw their beliefs and moral standard from purely natural sources. In paganism, especially before the Christian revelation, the Church has always recognized the existence of natural goodness and truth, the seeds of which the Fathers declare are to be found everywhere. All that is wise and true in the philosophies of antiquity, of Plato, of Plotinus, especially of Aristotle, has been incorporated in the Catholic system; all that is good and beautiful in their literature, arts and culture, whether of Hellas or Honolulu, is welcome to the Catholic mind. See also above (*cf.*, Heathen, Infidelity, non-Catholic, "After-Christian").

PAIN BÉNIT (Fr., blessed bread). Bread blessed during or after the parochial Mass with one of the forms in the "Rituale Romanum" and distributed to the people to be eaten as a sacramental with lively faith for the health of soul and body. It differs from *antidoron* in that the bread is not eucharistic bread surplus to the requirements of the celebrant, but ordinary household bread usually provided by members of the congregation in turn. The custom, formerly common (*e.g.*, in Wales from the 10th to the 14th century), survives in many churches of France and is met with occasionally in Switzerland and French Canada. Mistress Margaret Odom, at the end of the 15th century, bequeathed property to a gild at Bury Saint Edmunds that a priest might "say Mass in the chapel of the jail before the prisoners there, giving them holy water and *holy bread* every Sunday."

PAIN OF LOSS, OF SENSE. The two pains of Hell (*q.v.*), respectively the loss of the Beatific Vision and the presence of a pain tormenting to both soul and body (*cf.*, Matt. ix, 43). "In every sin there is a turning away from the Unchangeable Good which is infinite: whence sin itself is infinite; there is also a turning to changeable good things: whence sin is finite. . . . To the first responds the pain of loss which is itself infinite since it means the loss of the Infinite Good—God; to the latter responds the pain of sense which is finite" (St. Thomas, I-II, lxxxvii, 4).

PALATINE (adjective). i. Having to do with the Sacred Apostolic Palace of the Vatican.

ii. Having to do with the (Rhenish) Palatinate, a German electorate of the Holy Roman Empire.

iii. In general, appertaining to a territory whereof the earl or count had sovereign jurisdiction, *e.g.*, the former county palatine of Durham, formed out of the prince-bishopric.

PALATINE CARDINALS, PRELATES, are the Cardinal Secretary of State, the Cardinal Datary, the Maestro di Camera, the Master of the Sacred Palace, the Vice-Prefect of the Apostolic Palaces, and the Auditor of his Holiness (*qq.v.*). They are called palatine because they are personally attached to the pope and, except the Datary, live in the Vatican.

PALATINE GUARD OF HONOUR. A corps of papal volunteers, recruited from Roman citizens, established in 1850. They attend in the Antecamera, at processions and in solemn papal functions. They wear a dark blue uniform and a round busby with a plume in front.

PALATINE SECRETARIATES. Three offices standing in close relation to the pontifical court, namely the Secretariate of State, with its two departments, the Secretariates of Briefs to Princes and of Latin Letters (*qq.v.*).

PALESTINE, THE CHURCH IN. The population of Palestine and Transjordania is nearly 2¼ million, of whom over 1½ million are Mohammedans and over ½ million Jews (most of them Zionist immigrants). There are 45,000 members of the Orthodox Church, forming their patriarchate of Jerusalem, and 50,000 Protestants and others. Catholics number about 55,000, mostly Melkites (*q.v.*), who have 2 dioceses, and those of Latin rite, who form 1 diocese with the patriarchal title of Jerusalem. From the 13th century until 1847 the Latins of Palestine were under the jurisdiction of the Franciscan Custodian of the Holy Land, and the Friars Minor are still the official Catholic representatives in the church of the Holy Sepulchre and other Holy Places (*qq.v.*) and minister in a number of parishes. After 1917 all religions were of equal standing before the mandatory power, but Great Britain in most respects maintained the juridical privileges which various bodies acquired under Turkish domination.

PALL. i. A piece of stiff linen, or cardboard covered with linen, about 4 ins. square which covers the chalice at Mass to preserve the contents from flies, dust, etc. The upper side may be ornamented, the lower side must be plain. Its service was performed up to about the 12th century by folding over the big corporal, as is still done by the Carthusians, and in the Lyons rite at high Mass.

ii. A large cloth, which may be ornamented but must be substantially black in colour, spread over the coffin at funerals and over the catafalque at requiem Masses when the body is not present.

iii. A veil formerly held over bride and groom during the nuptial blessing in many local uses (*e.g.*, in England, Ireland and France); it is still used in the Mozarabic wedding ritual. It was probably associated with the bride's wedding veil (*q.v.* ii) and like it, was carried over by analogy to the profession of nuns; the symbolic association of this last use with ii above is quite arbitrary.

PALLIUM. i. A circular band of white wool 2 ins. wide ornamented with six crosses and having a pendent strip before and behind; it is worn on the shoulders by the pope and archbishops. It is the symbol of the fulness of the episcopal power enjoyed by the pope and shared in by archbishops who, before asking for (postulating) and receiving it from the Holy See, may not exercise metropolitan jurisdiction or those episcopal powers which require its liturgical use (*e.g.*, ordination). It is worn only on the occasions laid down in the "Pontificale." Its significance is both personal and territorial, so that an archbishop on being transferred to another residential see must ask for a new *pallium;* it is not conferred on non-residential titular archbishops. The *pallia* are made by the Oblates of St. Frances of Rome, of the wool of two lambs blessed in the church of St. Agnes on her feast; when made they are blessed by the pope on the feast of SS. Peter & Paul and stored in a casket in the *Confessio* of St. Peter. The *pallium* is occasionally granted to bishops as a purely honorary adornment; in the Eastern rites, only patriarchs are invested with it, certain of whom wear it but seldom. It is an outward sign of union with the Holy See, and was part of the coat of arms of the see of Canterbury, still used by the Anglican archbishops.

ii. The frontal (*q.v.*) of an altar.

PALLOTTINE FATHERS, The. The Pious Society of Missions, a religious institute founded by the Ven. Vincent Pallotti in Rome in 1835 to work especially for the preservation of the faith among emigrants and on foreign missions. The German and Italian churches in London and the English church in Rome are served by these priests. The Pallottine sisters help the fathers in their work, as catechists, teachers, etc.

PALM. i. The "branches of palm and olive" blessed on Palm Sunday are now generally the dried leaves of one or other of the trees of the palm family twisted into the form of a cross. But in many places and churches the older and more graceful custom is preserved of using whatever evergreen or other suitable shrub is locally available, *e.g.*, box, willow, yew, cypress.

ii. The emblem of victory (*cf.*, pagan practice, and Ps. xci, 13; Apoc. vii, 9), particularly of victory by martyrdom.

PALM SUNDAY. The Sunday next before Easter, on which is commemorated our Lord's entry into Jerusalem by the blessing and procession of palms (*q.v.*) before Mass. The Mass itself is entirely devoted to the Passion, which was to take place five days later and of which the tract (Ps. xxi) is a prophecy; the passion according to St. Matthew is read or sung by three deacons, during which the palms are held in the hand as a gesture of faith and acclamation. In the Byzantine rite a procession follows the Liturgy, the celebrant carrying the *icon* of the day.

PALMS, PROCESSION OF, takes place before Mass on Palm Sunday (called officially the Second Sunday of Passiontide). The palms ("palmorum, *seu* olivarum, *aut* aliarum arborum ramos"; any living greenery) are blessed in a brief rite and given out to the people, while parts of Psalm xxiii are sung, interspersed with the antiphon *Pueri Hebraeorum;* a gospel is then sung, Matt. xxi, 1-9. The procession takes place if possible outside the church; the palms may be blessed at a secondary church or chapel; and the procession made to the principal church. All carry green branches: the hymn to Christ the King, *Gloria, laus et honor tibi sit, Rex Christe Redemptor* ("All glory, laud and honour to thee, Redeemer King"), is sung, with Psalm cxliii, antiphons and other suitable pieces. On re-entering the church the antiphon *Ingrediente* is sung, "As the Lord entered the holy city . . . the people went to meet him, carrying palm branches and crying, Hosanna in the highest!" The procession ends with a collect asking that, wherever the branches shall be brought, they who dwell there may be blessed. This whole observance originated in Jerusalem itself in the 4th century.

PALMER. The mediæval name for a pilgrim from the Holy Land who wore a palm leaf as a badge (*cf.*, roamer, perhaps from Low Lat., *romeus*, one who had been to Rome on pilgrimage).

PANAGIA. i. "All holy," the ordinary Greek name for our Lady, short for ἡ παναγία Θεοτόκος, the all holy Mother of God.

ii. Another name for the *enkolpion* (*q.v.*).

PANAMA, THE CHURCH IN. Population about 610,000, of whom 80 per cent profess Catholicism. Government and public education tend to be secularist. The country forms 1 archbishopric (Panama, founded *c.* 1520), with a vicariate apostolic at Darien. The Canal Zone is under the civil jurisdiction of the United States, and there the faithful are cared for by American Lazarists. Nearly a dozen nationalities are represented among the Panamanian clergy.

PANCAKE. A thin flat batter fried in a pan, the traditional dish for Shrove Tuesday. This arose from the necessity in the past, when conditions of fasting were more strict, of using up eggs and fat before the beginning of Lent.

PANCHRISTIANITY (Gr. πᾶν, all). The doctrine that the church of Christ consists of a loose federation of bodies and individuals united in spirit but with no unity of faith, morals or organization; and that the disunion among Christians can be repaired by the coming together of existing sects in mutual amiability and tolerance, with a certain amount of doctrinal compromise and concession and a maximum collaboration in social work. In his encyclical *Mortalium animos*, of 1928, Pope Pius XI reiterated that for Catholics there can be no compromise on dogma and no Christian unity apart from communion with the Apostolic See; and Catholics were warned against taking part in Panchristian congresses, etc.

PANTHEISM (Gr. πᾶν, all; Θεός, God). A false philosophy which consists in confounding God with the world. According to some the world is absorbed by God (Indian pantheists, Spinoza); others teach that God is absorbed by the world of which he is the force and the life (Goethe). Some look upon the world as a real outpouring of the divine substance; others, with Spinoza, say the universe is a totality of modes of which the substance is God: others, with Hegel, confound finite with infinite, being with nothing, the *ego* with *non-ego*. But all seek to establish an identity of substance between God and the world.

PANTOKRATOR (Gr., all mighty). An image of our Lord ruling from Heaven.

PAPABILE. An Italian colloquial noun and adjective for one who, during a vacancy of the Holy See, is popularly fancied for the papacy or considered eminently fitted therefor.

PAPACY (Low Lat. *papa*, pope; late Lat. from Gk. *pappas*, father). i. The office of pope (*q.v.*).
ii. The system of ecclesiastical government in which supreme authority is vested in the pope.
iii. The series of popes taken collectively.
iv. The period of office of any one pope.

PAPAL. See also PONTIFICAL.

"PAPAL AGGRESSION AGITATION." The phrase used specifically generally refers to the outbreak of Protestant indignation at the restoration of the English Catholic episcopal hierarchy by Pope Pius IX in 1850, the signal for which was a letter of protest written by the prime minister, Lord John Russell, to the Anglican Bishop of Durham. It was modified by Cardinal Wiseman's "Appeal to the English People," and subsided with the passing of the Ecclesiastical Titles Act (*q.v.*) in 1851.

PAPAL CHOIR, The. The Sistine Choir (*q.v.*).

PAPAL MASS. A pontifical high Mass sung by the pope; a Mass celebrated by him in any other way is not a papal Mass in the technical sense. The most notable peculiarities are that the epistle and gospel are sung in Greek as well as in Latin, at the elevation both Host and Chalice are moved in a half-circle from left to right as though to show them to the whole world, and the pope receives holy communion standing at his

throne, the Precious Blood through a gold tube; the deacon and subdeacon receive holy communion in both kinds.

PAPAL STATES, The. The States of the Church (*q.v.*).

PAPIST (Lat. *papa*, pope). A term of contempt and hostility for a Catholic; its first known use is an attribution of it by St. John Fisher to Luther in 1521. In conversation, Catholics now sometimes use it of themselves as a term of honour. The words of O'Connell in 1814, "I am sincerely a Catholic, but I am not a Papist. I deny the doctrine that the pope has any temporal authority, directly or indirectly, in Ireland," show a specialized meaning formerly attached to the word. A similar word has sometimes been used by controversialists of the Orthodox Eastern Church in their less polite moments; *e.g.*, ἡ ἐκκλησία παπική ("the papic church") by their patriarch of Constantinople in a manifesto in 1895.

PARABLE. A story of human life, usually fictitious, used to illustrate a religious or moral truth. Over thirty parables are recorded in the gospels as having been spoken by our Lord; it is notable that the expounding of them was done privately to his immediate followers and not publicly to the multitude (*cf.*, Matt. xiii, 10-17). They are all susceptible of two lines of interpretation: with reference to the circumstances in which they were spoken and in reference to Christianity at large.

PARABOLANI (Gr., exposers of their lives). A brotherhood in the Eastern church in the 4th-6th centuries founded for the care of the sick. They degenerated into bodies of roughs, as when they murdered Hypatia in 415 and terrorized the "robber synod" at Ephesus in 449.

PARACLETE (Gr. παράκλητος, advocate). The first meaning is one called in to aid, an advocate, and the name is thus applied to Christ in 1 John ii, 1: "We have an advocate with the Father, Jesus Christ the just." But a very early derived meaning is that of comforter. Christ speaks of the Holy Ghost as "another paraclete" (John xiv, 16), whose function (*cf.*, John xvi, 7-10) is to teach, to bear witness, to take Christ's place among the Apostles, and "to convince the world of sin." The word is now only used of the Holy Ghost.

PARADISE (Gr. παράδεισος, from Old Persian *pairidaeza*, a royal park). i. A synonym for Heaven, "that spiritual paradise in which all are said to be who enjoy the glory of God."
ii. A place or state of bliss short of actual Heaven or the possession of the Beatific Vision. Thus used by our Lord to the penitent thief (Luke xxiii, 43) referring to Limbo (*q.v.* i; *cf.*, John xx, 17); by St. Paul of his state of

ecstasy when he was raised to the third heaven, and in the Old Testament an expression for the Garden of Eden or Terrestrial Paradise.

PARAGUAY, THE CHURCH IN. Population about 1 million, nine-tenths Catholic, at least nominally. All faiths may be freely exercised, but Catholicism is officially the religion of the state. Divorce *a vinculo* is not recognized, clergy are exempt from military service, and the state pays a salary to the archbishop; public lands for the establishment of missions to the Indians may be granted to any Christian body. Paraguay forms an ecclesiastical province, with 2 suffragan dioceses; the see of Asuncion was established in 1547. Until 1929 the whole country formed a diocese of the Church in the Argentine. See also REDUCTIONS.

PARALIPOMENON (Gr., of things left out). The name given in the Vulgate and Catholic vernacular translations to the two books of the Bible known to Protestants as 1 and 2 Chronicles. The name means either that they supplement the books of Kings (which they hardly do) or that many things are left out of them. They are called in Hebrew *Dibre hayyamim*, the "Words of the Days" or Chronicles, and may have been abridged from the "Book of the Words of the Days of the Kings of Israel" (referred to in 3 Kings xiv, 19 and elsewhere) by the priest Esdras. Certainly they were written after the return from Babylon by permission of Cyrus, and recapitulate principally the religious history of the Jews from Adam till that event.

PARAMENTS (Late Lat. *paramenta*). Vestments and other sacred ornaments.

PARASCEVE, The (Gr., preparation). The name given by Hellenistic Jews to the day of preparation for the Sabbath, *i.e.*, Friday. The liturgical name for Good Friday is *feria sexta in parasceve,* which may also be referred to the preparation for the day of resurrection.

PARAY-LE-MONIAL. A pilgrim shrine in the department of Saône-et-Loire, France, on account of the chapel of the convent of the Visitation wherein the visions and revelations to St. Margaret Mary relating to the Sacred Heart took place; her body is also enshrined there.

PARCLOSE (Old Fr. *parclore,* from Lat. *claudere,* to shut). A screen, of metal, stone or wood, dividing a chapel from the main body of a church or the choir from the choir aisles.

PARDON (Old Fr. *pardun,* remission). i. The word used in pre-Reformation England to translate *indulgentia,* which we now do by "indulgence." There is a tendency to restore this use of the word, which has received

high ecclesiastical encouragement: for pardon expresses more exactly what is meant by an indulgence and is less open to misunderstanding by non-Catholics.

ii. A religious festival in connexion with the feast of the patron saints of certain churches, places or pilgrimages, especially in Britanny. To those who assist and perform the prescribed works an indulgence is granted, whence the name pardon for the whole observance. The chief Breton pardons are those of Ste. Anne d'Auray, La Troménie de S. Ronan at Lacronan, S. Jeandu-Doigt, S. Yves at Tréguier, Le Folgoët, Rumengol and Ste. Anne de la Palude. The most popular is the first, though it is also one of the more recent, beginning only in the 17th century. Each pardon has an individual history, but the origins of most are obscure; a fair is often held on the same day. To the pardon of Chaumont (Haute Marne) Pope Sixtus IV granted the jubilee indulgence each year the birthday of St. John Baptist falls on a Sunday.

PARDONER. One licensed to preach and collect money for a specified object (*e.g.,* to finance a crusade or build a certain church or bridge), for contributing to which an indulgence was attached. The institution was grossly abused (*cf.,* Prologue, "Canterbury Tales," 669-714) and was abolished in session xxv of the Council of Trent.

PAREKKLESIA (Gr., beside church). According to Byzantine canon law there should be no more than one altar in each church. In large churches necessity is provided for by having one or more side chapels, with an altar, *prothesis,* and *diakonikon,* screened off by an *iconostasis,* and so in effect a separate church; such is a *parekklesia.*

PARENTS, DUTIES OF. Parents must love their children, show no unreasonable preference for one at the expense of others, provide for their upkeep and health, show them a good example, guard them from occasions of sin, and secure for them sound Christian instruction and suitable education. Serious neglect of any of these duties is gravely sinful. "Every head of a household," says St. Augustine, "should recognize that he owes a debt of fatherly love towards it. For the sake of Christ and of life everlasting he is to teach, encourage, reprove those who are his. . . . In this way he will discharge towards them the duties of a pastor, you might almost say of a bishop, and become such a servant of Christ as shall be with Christ for ever." See AUTHORITY OF PARENTS, ETC.

PARIS MISSIONS, The. The priests of the Paris society for foreign missions, founded in 1658. It has over 1,000 French missionaries and 1,500 native priests. Its missions are principally in the Far East. These fathers are responsible for numerous schools, orphanages and hostels, workshops and dispensaries, hospitals and lazar-houses.

PARISH. A defined territorial district, with a church and congregation, in charge of a priest who has cure of souls therein. Every diocese must be parcelled out into parishes; its boundaries, etc., may be altered for a canonical reason at the discretion of the bishop. The divisions of missionary countries, even of those few which have an ordinary hierarchy, are not parishes in the strict sense. Parishes are the ordinary charge of the secular clergy; regulars may be appointed to them, but they are removable at the will of the bishop or their religious superior (cf., Rector). The former close association between the parish and those having a domicile therein is now much relaxed; but it is still considered desirable, if not of obligation, that the Easter communion be made in one's own parish, and certain rites must take place therein unless the permission of the parish priest or ordinary is obtained (cf., Parish Church).

PARISH CHURCH. Canon law requires that in each parish a particular church must be designated in which the rector is to carry out the parochial offices, the celebration of Mass and administration of the sacraments, for the benefit of the parishioners. Parish churches must be consecrated wherever possible. The churches of religious men may be parish churches, but not those of nuns. The rector must live close to the parish church, and certain rites must take place in it, viz., baptisms, marriages and funeral services, preaching and catechizing, and normally Easter communion. Each parish church must have a baptismal font, and should also have its own cemetery attached, unless the ordinary allows one to be common to several parishes. The obligation of repairing the parish church is incumbent in the following order on (a) the fabrica (q.v.), (b) the patron, (c) those who derive revenue from the church according to the bishop's assessment, (d) the parishioners. In certain countries the bond between people and their own parish church has become rather attenuated; this state of affairs is contrary to the mind of the Church, to the definite prescriptions of canon law and to common sense.

PARISH PRIEST. A priest having cure of souls in a parish or quasi-parish under the authority of the local ordinary. In England this term has supplanted the old name of "parson" (q.v.). His assistant is a curate. See RECTOR; PASTOR.

PARKMINSTER. The Charterhouse of St. Hugh, near Horsham, a Carthusian monastery founded from the Grande Chartreuse in 1873, the community being formed from various houses of the order. It is the largest charterhouse in the world, having accommo-

dation for 96 monks; the present community totals about half that number.

PAROCHIAL MASS. The principal Mass said every Sunday, holiday and feast of devotion in each parish church. It should be a sung or high Mass, but if this is impossible at least some outward solemnity should be added to it, e.g., by the lighting of six candles on the altar and having two servers. On Sundays it is preceded by the Asperges and a sermon, generally on the day's gospel, is preached; the vernacular prayers after Mass are not said at the end.

PAROISSIEN. The most widely used form of French popular prayer book. It contains much liturgical matter, such as Mass and Vespers for Sunday in Latin and French, as well as the usual popular devotions, etc.

PAROUSIA. The Second Coming (q.v.) of our Lord. The word is a Greek term for the advent of a royal personage and is so carried over to refer to Christ.

PARSON (Lat. persona [ecclesiæ], personage [of the church]). In mediæval England a usual and one of the legal names for a priest who was a rector of a parish (cf., prologue to "Canterbury Tales," 477 ff.). Its use is now confined to ministers of the Church of England, especially such as are beneficed; it is erroneous to apply it to Nonconformist ministers.

PARTAKERS OF THE DIVINE NATURE. This mysterious expression is taken from 2 Peter i, 4. Of course it does not mean that we are one in substance with God. It means that the just man has received supernatural gifts by which he may share those activities which are characteristic of the divine nature, i.e., he can know God and love him supernaturally.*

PARTICLE. A consecrated Host of the small size distributed in holy communion.

PARVIS (through Old Fr. from Lat. paradisus, the name given to the atrium of old St. Peter's). An enclosed space or open porch at the entrance to a church, sometimes wrongly applied to a room over a porch.

PASCENDI. An encyclical letter of Pope Pius X in 1907 in which he demonstrated that the errors of Modernism (q.v.), due to curiosity, pride and ignorance of philosophy, attacked the supremacy of the supernatural order and threatened the teaching authority of the Church, the integrity of the Scriptures and the stability of dogma, and accordingly condemned it root and branch in all its forms, theological, philosophical, biblical, historical and social. Disciplinary measures were also taken; any cleric maintaining Modernism by writing or teaching was ipso facto suspended, and in 1910 an oath condemning the errors was imposed on all becoming priests, professors, etc. The "synthesis of all

---

* Moreover, through Sanctifying Grace a person also receives a created sharing in the divine nature, as well as being enabled to act in a manner characteristic of the divine nature.—Publisher, 1997.

the heresies," which had made great way among Catholics, thus received its death-blow.*

PASCH, The (Gr. form of Heb. *pesakh*, passover). i. The Jewish feast of the Passover (*q.v.*).

ii. The Christian feast of the Resurrection, especially as embracing the whole octave. The word has been naturalized as the name for Easter in nearly all European languages except English and High German. In Roman and most Latin liturgical books the feast is the Sunday of Resurrection, but the days following are "of the Pasch" and the Sundays up to Whitsun "after the Pasch"; the Ambrosian and Byzantine books refer also to the feast-day itself as the Pasch (*cf.*, Passover).

PASCHAL CANDLE. A large candle lighted at the beginning of the Easter vigil on Holy Saturday. It stands in a special candlestick at the gospel-side of the altar. It is lighted at high Mass and parochial or conventual Mass, and solemn Vespers on Sunday, Monday, Tuesday and Saturday of Easter Week and on all Sundays until Ascension day, when it is finally put out after the gospel at Mass. The candle symbolizes Christ as the light of the world, and formerly (and now again) particularly as the enlightener of those who have just received Baptism; the wax of bees has always been regarded as a type of the pure flesh of Jesus.

PASCHAL LAMB, The. i. The lamb eaten ritually by the Jews at the Passover festival.

ii. As antitype of the above, our Lord as victim both on the cross and on the altar.

iii. The lamb blessed in some places to be eaten on Easter day. Lambs are also blessed on St. Agnes's day at the Lateran, but this has no paschal reference; see PALLIUM.

PASCHAL PRECEPT. The obligation of receiving holy communion at about Easter. See EASTER DUTIES.

PASCHAL TIME extends for 56 days, from Holy Saturday until Vespers on the Saturday after Whitsunday, and principally corresponds to the period of rejoicing during which the risen Christ was again with his followers. The chief liturgical observances of this period of joy are that white vestments are used, and the *Gloria* is said at ferial Masses, two alleluias are added to each introit, one to each offertory and communion-verse, and the alleluiatic-verse replaces the gradual, *Te Deum* is said daily at Matins, *Vidi aquam* is sung instead of *Asperges me*, and *Regina Cœli* said instead of the *Angelus*. During the first week the holy doors remain open during the Liturgy in Byzantine churches, and Melkites and Armenians neither fast nor abstain from meat or other food during the eight weeks.

PASSION (Lat. *passio*, from *pati*, to suffer).

i. An accident (*q.v.*) opposed to action, the two corresponding as effect and cause.

ii. A movement of the sensitive appetite (*q.v.*) accompanied by some bodily alteration. A passion therefore resides not in the will nor in any physical power, but in the sensitive appetite. The will, however, can direct or subject a passion and also combat it. The passions are divided into concupiscible and irascible in so far as a sensible good is easy or difficult of attainment. Those passions in the concupiscible part of the sensitive appetite are: Love, hatred, desire, aversion, joy, sadness; in the irascible part: hope, despair, courage, fear, anger.

iii. Passion and Habit. Passion is an act of a faculty. Of its nature it is involuntary, and the will can only exert its influence over it indirectly. A habit is the result of constant repetition of acts to which consent is given; thus the free will is a cause of a good or bad habit, of a virtue or of a vice.

iv. Of our Lord. The sufferings of Jesus Christ which had their culmination in his death on the cross. By these was the redemption (*q.v.*) of man effected.

v. Of a martyr. The sufferings and death of one who laid down his life for the faith; a written account of them.

vi. Liturgical. The accounts of the Lord's passion from the gospels, sung at Mass on Palm Sunday, Tuesday, Wednesday and Friday of Holy Week respectively by three deacons, who may be assisted by the choir. Each passion is divided into three parts: the narrative (*chronista*), the words of our Lord (*Christus*), other spoken words (*synagoga*). When there are no deacons, it is usual in some countries (*e.g.*, England) for a layman to read the passion aloud in the vernacular, the priest reading it inaudibly.

PASSION, FEASTS OF THE. Certain special feasts with their proper Mass and Office peculiar to the Passionists, whose use is granted to some other congregations and dioceses. They are: the Prayer of Our Lord; commemoration of the Passion; the Pillar of Scourging (Tuesdays after Septuagesima, Sexagesima and Quinquagesima); the Crown of Thorns; the Lance and Nails; the Holy Winding-Sheet; the Five Wounds; the Precious Blood (the Fridays in Lent respectively). The last is in addition to the feast of July 1. There are also votive offices of the Cross and of the Passion which may be used on Fridays.

PASSION PLAY. A dramatized representation of the passion of our Lord performed primarily for its own sake or with reference to a spiritual end. Passion plays as known to-day at Oberammergau and elsewhere (*e.g.*, Exl, in the Tirol), though prompted by a similar spirit, have little else in common with the mystery plays of the middle ages. That of Oberammergau, for example, is now a literary drama, with appropriate music, archæologically accurate costumes and setting, and

---

* With hindsight it is apparent that Pope St. Pius X's attempted death-blow to Modernism was only a temporary suppression, for the heresy broke out again with new virulence in the second half of the 20th century.—*Publisher*, 1997.

naturalistic acting, though its origin was before the 17th century, as a decennial act of thanksgiving for deliverance from plague.

PASSION SUNDAY. The fifth Sunday of Lent, so called because it is the beginning of Passiontide when the mind of the Church is directed entirely to the sufferings and death of Christ. It is marked by the veiling of images (*q.v.*), at Mass, the psalm *Judica* is not said (possibly because the introit is taken therefrom), and *Gloria Patria* is omitted from the *Asperges* and elsewhere; the preface is of the Cross.

PASSIONISTS, The. The Congregation of Barefooted Clerks of the Most Holy Cross and Passion of our Lord Jesus Christ was founded in 1720 by St. Paul-of-the-Cross, to keep alive in the minds of men the memory of our Lord's sufferings and death on the cross. The object of the congregation is striven to be attained by missions and retreats to which, in non-Catholic countries, parish work is added, when so desired by the bishops, and it conducts foreign missions in China and elsewhere. The rule imposes the recitation of the Divine Office in choir, Matins and Lauds being said at 2 a.m.; it also prescribes three fast-days a week and other bodily austerities. Their vows are simple and their religious houses are called retreats. The English province was founded by the Ven. Dominic (Barberi), in 1842, and they were the first religious to wear their habit in public in post-Reformation England. Ireland is a separate province; there are two provinces in the U.S.A. and one in Australia. The habit consists of a coarse black tunic and mantle, leather belt, sandals and biretta. The tunic and mantle have a heart-shaped badge, known as the Sign, bearing a white cross and three nails with the words *Jesu Xpi Passio:* "the Passion of Jesus Christ." The Passionist nuns are contemplative.

PASSIONTIDE. The period from Passion Sunday to Holy Saturday morning. The whole liturgy is given up to the sufferings of our Lord and the peculiarities of Passion Sunday are preserved throughout except on any great feast, *e.g.*, the Annunciation, occurring: but even then the images remain veiled. Passion Week in the East signifies Holy Week (*q.v.*), but in the West only the first week of Passiontide.

PASSOVER, The (called in the Douay O. T., the *Phase* or passage). The first of the great feasts of the Jewish dispensation, commemorating "the passage of the Lord, when he *passed over* the houses of the children of Israel in Egypt, striking the Egyptians and saving our houses" (Ex. xii, 27); it is kept on the 14th of the lunar month Nisan. The word is also used figuratively for the paschal lamb slain for the festival, or for our Lord himself (1 Cor. v, 7). The celebration of the passion, death and resurrection of our Lord,

whereby the human race was redeemed from sin, is the Christian Passover: "Christ is the true lamb who has taken away the sins of the world, who by dying has overcome our death and by rising again has restored our life" (preface of the Easter Mass). (*Cf.,* Pasch).

PASTOR (Lat., shepherd). i. A priest who has cure of souls, whatever the canonical position of his parish or district may be. The term is in common use in the U.S.A. and Holland; in Great Britain and Ireland he is called simply the parish priest, in French-speaking countries the *curé, pfarrer* in Germany and Austria; *parocco* in Italy, *párroco* in Spanish lands.

ii. The bishop is the pastor *par excellence,* for to him belongs in a special way the duty of caring for a flock, teaching, sanctifying and ruling it; the liturgy refers to our Lord as "the eternal pastor" and to the pope as "pastor of the Church." But except adjectivally the term is not commonly used of any of these.

PASTOR ÆTERNUS. The constitution of the Vatican Council (sess. iv) dealing with the primacy and infallibility of the Roman pontiff.

PASTORAL EPISTLES, The. St. Paul's two letters to Timothy and one to Titus, so called because they instruct two young bishops how properly to discharge the pastoral office.

PASTORAL LETTER. One addressed by a bishop to all the faithful, clergy and laity, within his diocese. Such a letter is usually called simply a pastoral, and generally every diocesan bishop publishes one at the beginning of Advent and another at the beginning of Lent. They may deal with any matter whatsoever affecting in any way the spiritual life of the people and may be hortative, explanatory or disciplinary. They are made public by being read at the parochial Mass on Sunday.

PASTORAL OFFICES. Those offices to which the cure of souls is attached, namely, the papacy universally and the episcopal and parochial offices for their respective territories.

PASTORAL STAFF or CROSIER. A staff made of metal or carved wood, about 6 ft. 6 ins. long, with a curved top, often highly ornamented, and pointed foot. It is a symbol of episcopal office and jurisdiction, representing both the rod of correction and the crook of pastoral care, and is carried by bishops whenever they officiate pontifically. Since the 11th century the pope, alone among bishops, has ceased to use it; the reason is not known. Cardinals and abbots use the crosier, as may abbesses (other than Franciscan); their crosiers differ not at all from those of archbishops and bishops. The

Roman crosier has been adopted by some Catholic bishops of Eastern rites (as also by dissident Armenians). But the Byzantines use a somewhat shorter staff with a top formed of two serpents (symbolizing prudence), head to head, with their bodies bent outwards; Catholic Syrian and Coptic bishops also use this form. A similar staff is carried by regular archimandrites and by Armenian *vartapeds*.

PATEN (Lat. *patena*, a dish). A thin circular plate of metal, sufficiently large to rest on top of the chalice, which holds the Host at Mass. Its concave surface must be at least gilt, and it must be consecrated by a bishop. At high Mass, from the offertory till after the *Paternoster*, it is held, enveloped in a humeral-veil, by the subdeacon: this has been explained as a survival of holding the *Sancta* (*q.v.*) until it was required at the altar.

PATERNOSTER, The. i. The Lord's Prayer, from its first two words in the Latin version which runs: *Pater noster, qui es in cœlis, sanctificetur nomen tuum. Adveniat regnum tuum. Fiat voluntas tua, sicut in cœlo et in terra. Panem nostrum quotidianum da nobis hodie. Et dimitte nobis debita nostra, sicut et nos dimittimus debitoribus nostris. Et ne nos inducas in tentationem: sed libera nos a malo. Amen.* See OUR FATHER.

ii. A common name in the middle ages for a rosary or other string of beads used in repeating a set number of prayers, whether Our Fathers or others.

PATIENCE. A fruit of the Holy Ghost which strengthens the soul to bear the trials of this life with resignation to God's will, instead of giving way to sadness. In its common sense of patience between man and man it partakes also of the nature of meekness (*q.v.*).

PATRIARCH (Gr., ruler of a family). i. A bishop who holds the highest rank, after the pope, in the hierarchy of jurisdiction (*q.v.*). He is major or minor accordingly as he does or does not hold the see or title of one of the five great patriarchates (*q.v.*); of more importance, he either rules with patriarchal jurisdiction or is only titular (see below). Those with jurisdiction are the Patriarch of the West (the pope), the Coptic Patriarch of Alexandria, the Melkite, Syrian and Maronite Patriarchs of Antioch, the Armenian Patriarch of Cilicia and the Chaldean Patriarch of Babylon (*qq.v.*). Since the schism of the East, the power and importance of patriarchs (other than the Roman) have very greatly diminished, but they are still independent of any ecclesiastical authority other than that of the pope and his delegates. They are subject to him as Supreme Pontiff, it being the essence of the patriarchal office not to be subject to other patriarchal authority. Except the Coptic, who is appointed directly by the Holy See, they are elected by their bishops, the pope confirming the choice. They have the right to ordain all bishops of their patriarchate (after election has been confirmed at Rome, except among the Melkites); they alone may consecrate the holy chrism; they send the *omophorion* to their metropolitans (*cf.*, Pallium); summon synods, whose acts must be ratified by the Holy See; hear appeals from lower courts; and otherwise act as supreme rulers of their churches, saving the authority of the pope.

ii. Non-Catholic patriarchs are: Orthodox: of Constantinople, Alexandria, Antioch, Jerusalem, with the later autonomies of Moscow (Russia), Serbia, and Rumania; of the first four, the first, second and fourth represent the historical lines of these ancient sees. Coptic: of Alexandria. Syrian Jacobite: of Antioch. Nestorian: of the East (in Irak). Armenian: of All the Armenians (in U.S.S.R.), of Constantinople, of Sis, of Jerusalem. Their rights and authorities vary; but the activities of the Byzantine patriarchs are all curbed by a holy synod (*q.v.*).

iii. Biblical. The term patriarch is commonly applied to Abraham, Isaac and Jacob, and to their progenitors before the Flood, and sometimes to the sons of Jacob; Abraham is referred to as "our patriarch" in the canon of the Mass.

iv. The founders of the older religious orders are sometimes referred to as patriarch, *e.g.*, St. Dominic. St. Benedict is the patriarch of Western monks, St. Basil of Eastern monks.

PATRIARCH, TITULAR. A bishop of the Latin rite having the title of patriarch with none of the authority attaching to the office. There are eight such, of Constantinople, Alexandria, Antioch, Jerusalem, Venice, West Indies, East Indies and Lisbon (*qq.v.*). The first four are survivals of the Latin patriarchates set up in the near East during the Crusades, and the first three are purely titular, the holders residing in Rome attached to the papal court. Patriarch of the West Indies is a title formerly attached to the see of Toledo, but now used by the bishop of Madrid or other Spanish prelate. The others are in effect ruling archbishops, of Jerusalem (for Latin Catholics in Palestine and Cyprus), Venice, Goa and Lisbon respectively, who have only metropolitan powers but to whose sees the title of patriarch and certain corresponding honours have been granted for historical reasons and to add dignity thereto.

PATRIARCH OF THE WEST, The. The pope in his capacity of ruler of the Roman patriarchate (*q.v.*), as distinguished from his higher office as Supreme Pontiff and his lower offices in relation to the Church in Italy. His patriarchal activity is chiefly manifested in legislation which applies to Catholics of the Latin rite only; *e.g.*, in such matters as fasting and abstinence, matrimony, reception of the sacraments, devotional observances and liturgical ritual or questions of local Western importance. The promulgation of the Code of Canon Law in 1917 was such an act. It is thus seen that many of the most common relationships of Catholics in, e.g., England, with the Holy See are in its patriarchal and not its papal capacity. As patriarch the pope has the right of consecrating all bishops of the Latin rite, a right which for obvious reasons he rarely exercises.

PATRIARCHATE. The territory ruled ecclesiastically by a patriarch (q.v.). The first broad territorial divisions of the Church had their centres, civil and religious, at Rome, Alexandria and Antioch, their bishops having a primacy over all others. By the 6th century these had developed into the five great historical patriarchates, of Rome (comprising roughly all land west of a line drawn from Denmark to Salonika, including the coast of North Africa), Constantinople (all Europe east of that line, with Asia Minor), Alexandria (Egypt), Antioch (Syria, Mesopotamia, Georgia and Armenia) and Jerusalem (Palestine, Transjordania and the Sinai Peninsula). The patriarchs were independent of one another and equal in authority, but that he of Rome or the West exercised the primacy of honour and jurisdiction. The Eastern patriarchates early suffered from the defection of the Nestorians and the monophysites (q.v.); and they themselves, after the schism of Cerularius (q.v.), fell away definitively from Catholic unity after 1472, continuing to exist as non-Catholic patriarchates. The patriarchate of the West or Western church (qq.v.) alone retained territorial integrity; the other Catholic patriarchates have been in part revived (see PATRIARCH, i) in the form of organizations of Catholics of the different Eastern rites (qq.v.) wherever found, by whose names they are more usually called, so that as a territorial division the patriarchate has practically fallen into desuetude. The original Eastern patriarchates, now represented by the loose federation of Orthodox Churches (q.v.), have also been greatly modified (see PATRIARCH, ii). Catholic patriarchates are united in faith, morals and the communion of the Holy See; in canon law, liturgies and customs they differ according to the rites which they use.

PATRIARCHATE OF THE WEST, The (now better called the Roman patriarchate, also referred to as the Western or Latin church or Latin rite). All that part of the Catholic Church whose members are bound by the Roman Code of Canon Law, who use the Latin rite of worship in any of its forms, and are subject to the pope as patriarch. Originally this was a territorial division (middle and western Europe), but owing to its missionary activities, political aggression by Spain and other civil powers in newly discovered lands, and emigration (especially from Ireland and Italy), Catholics of the patriarchate with their ecclesiastical hierarchies may now be found in any part of the world. The continued schism of the East so far further increases the majority of western Catholics that they outnumber all others by 40 to 1, and in consequence are erroneously supposed by most people to constitute the whole Church. Notable characteristics of the Western patriarchate are its law of clerical celibacy and of communion in one kind for the laity and not-celebrating clergy, its Latin liturgies, and its highly efficient organization; the pope being their patriarch, Western Catholics have always been in closer touch with the Holy See than those of the Eastern patriarchates.

PATRICK, THE BROTHERS OF ST. A congregation of teaching brothers founded in 1808 in Ireland by Daniel Delany, bishop of Kildare & Leighlin. They conduct a number of schools in Ireland, Australia and India.

PATRIMONY. A title of ordination (q.v.) admitted by canon law for secular priests who are not ordained on the title of a benefice, provided the patrimony is secure and adequate for life.

PATRIMONY OF ST. CUTHBERT, The. The lands attached to the see of Durham, in England, which developed into the independent prince-bishopric.

PATRIMONY OF ST. PETER, The. The land and other property with which the see of Rome was endowed after the Peace of Constantine. After the States of the Church (q.v.) were definitely established in the 8th century, the name was sometimes applied to them in general, and to the duchy of Rome, conterminous with the province of Latio and the last territory left to Pope Pius IX up to 1870, in particular.

PATRIMONY OF THE POOR, The. A quarter part of episcopal revenues which from the 4th century was set aside for the relief of the poor. It gave place in time to a charge on rectorial tithes and the charities of the monasteries.

PATRIOTISM. The love of one's country. This is enjoined by the natural law; a good man will not hesitate to face death for the true welfare of his country, i.e., the human society of which he is a part. National interests are, however, subject to morality, and in the relations between nation and nation or between nation and super-national Church, no violation of justice or charity can be condoned on patriotic grounds. Patriotism is brotherhood among fellow citizens, that is, a special love for some men, not an opposition to other men ("foreigners"), an extension of human love, not a limitation of it. "We must love all men, and no man is a foreigner to a true Christian, so there is all the more reason for loving our fellow citizens. A man's love for himself, for his family, for his friends—all are united in his love for his country" (Bossuet). See NATIONALISM; CIVIL ALLEGIANCE.

PATRIPASSIANISM (Lat. *pater*, father; *passio*, suffering). The doctrine that God the Father suffered on the cross. See SABELLIANISM.

PATRISTICS, PATROLOGY. The study of the writings of the Fathers of the Church (*q.v.*) and the science of their contents.

PATRON SAINT. One chosen as its special advocate with God and to receive special honour by a place (country, diocese, province, city, village) or by an association, religious or lay, in accordance with Catholic teaching that angels and saints have special spheres of activity and tasks of love. The choice must be confirmed by the Holy See, whose special indult is required to choose one who is only beatified; there may be a principal and a lesser patron, but a mystery of religion cannot be a patron in the proper sense. Trades, professions, occupations, states of life, etc., also have their patron saint, usually by ancient tradition, as are those of places in old Christian countries. It is a common practice for an individual to take as patron the saint whose name is assumed at Confirmation; he puts himself under his protection, studies his life and seeks to profit by his example. The patron saint of a church gives his name thereto, whence he is technically called its titular (*q.v.*). See below.

PATRON SAINTS OF PLACES. The principal patrons of countries, not always distinguished from their apostles (*q.v.*), are: England, George; Scotland, Andrew the Apostle; Wales, David; Ireland, Patrick; France, Joan of Arc; Spain, James the Greater; Portugal, Vincent of Saragossa; Belgium, Joseph; Holland, Willibrord; Denmark, Anscar; Norway, Olaf; Sweden, Bridget; Poland, Stanislaus of Cracow; Czechoslovakia, Wenceslas; Lithuania, Casimir; Germany, Boniface; Italy, Francis of Assisi and Catherine of Siena; Switzerland, Nicholas of Flüe; Hungary, Stephen the King; Russia, Andrew; Greece and Sicily, Nicholas of Myra; the Southern Slavs, Cyril and Methodius; Brittany and Canada, Anne; the United States, Our Lady Immaculate; Chili, James the Greater; Mexico, Our Lady of Guadelupe; the Americas, Rose of Lima; Malabar, Thomas the Apostle; West Indies, Gertrude; Australia, New Zealand and China, Francis Xavier. The principal patron of dioceses of England and Wales is named under each diocese herein; most of them add thereto, either as another principal or as lesser patrons, other saints of local historical significance. Among saints honoured liturgically as the patrons of *cities* are St. Peter and St. Edward (Westminster),

St. Thomas Becket (Portsmouth) and St. Frideswide (Oxford).

PATRON SAINTS OF TRADES, Etc., include SS. Andrew, fishermen; Anne, housewives and miners; Barbara, gunners; Camillus of Lellis, nurses; Catherine of Alexandria, wheelwrights, philosophers and women students; Cecily, musicians; Christopher, bookbinders, travellers and sailors; Luke, Cosmas and Damian, physicians; Crispin and Crispinian, shoemakers; Eustace, huntsmen; Francis de Sales, journalists; Eligius (Eloi), blacksmiths and other metalworkers; George, soldiers; Joseph, carpenters; Joseph of Arimathea, tinners; Luke, painters; our Lady of Loreto, airmen; Nicholas of Myra, merchants, bakers, and all children; Raymund Nonnatus, midwives; Stephen, masons and Mass servers; Thomas Aquinas, all places of learning; Vincent de Paul, all societies for corporal works of mercy; Vitus, actors; Yves, lawyers ("Sanctus Ivo erat Brito, advocatus sed non latro—res miranda populo!"); Aloysius, young men; Antony the Abbot, cattle-farmers; Bernard of Menthon, mountaineers; Boniface of Crediton, brewers and tailors; Dorothy, gardeners; Francis Xavier and Teresa of Lisieux, foreign missions; Ignatius Loyola, retreats; Jerome Æmilian, orphans and deserted children; John Baptist Vianney, secular clergy; John of God, hospitals and the dying; Jude, tanners; Julian, innkeepers; Leonard of Port Maurice, home missions; Maurice d'Agaune, weavers and dyers; Peter Claver, Negro missions; Pascal Baylon, eucharistic congresses and societies; Zita, domestic servants. Against certain ills are or were invoked: SS. Antony of Padua, loss of material goods; Anne and John of Bridlington, in childbirth; Maurice, cramp, gout, etc.: Sebastian, plague; Scholastica, convulsions in children, and rain (both ways); Theodore the Great Martyr, tempests; Ubald, evil spirits; Agatha, diseases of the breast; Apollonia, toothache and lightning; Blaise, diseases of the throat; Benedict, poison; Dismas, on the scaffold; Hubert, hydrophobia; Roch, skin diseases; Vitus, epilepsy; our Lady of Lourdes, all sickness and bodily hurts. St. Joseph is the patron of the Universal Church. Most of the above are very ancient and were chosen on account of some event in the life of the saint, the circumstances of martyrdom, or obvious fitness (*e.g.*, particularly, airmen!); only some of them, including the one just referred to, are officially recognized by the Church.

PATRONAGE. i. The sum of privileges and obligations belonging to the founders of a church, chapel or benefice, and to their legitimate successors. The Code of Canon Law enacts that no patronage can validly arise in future, and patrons are to be exhorted to have their present patronage commuted into spiritual privileges. Patronage is real or personal, ecclesiastical or lay, hereditary, or restricted to a family or group of families. The chief privilege of patrons is that of presenting a cleric to the vacant church or benefice, their chief obligation that of contributing to its maintenance and repair.

ii. The position officially accorded by the Church to certain saints as patrons or protectors of communities, nations, churches, etc., sometimes with a special feast attached. The feast, then, of, e.g., the Patronage of our Lady of Help in Guatemala envisages her in her aspect of protector by her intercession.

PAUL, ST. The Apostle of the Gentiles, a tent-maker by trade, whose life is related in the Acts of the Apostles and doctrine set forth in his Epistles (q.v.). His principal feast is with that of St. Peter (q.v.). In the Western church it is followed on the next day by a special office in his honour called his Commemoration, and the feast of his Conversion (Acts ix) is celebrated on Jan. 25.

PAULICIANS, The. A sect, the origin of whose name is not known, which existed in the East from about 650 till the 11th century. They professed a manichæan dualism (q.v.), distinguishing between a God who made created souls, and a power of evil (Demiurge) who made human bodies and matter in general; our Lord was an angel who brought his body with him from Heaven; all the Old Testament and some of the New was rejected; the sacraments and holy images came under the ban of all material things; bishops and monks were particularly obnoxious to them; sin being natural to the evil body, it was inculpable and Paulician morals were not in accord with their idea of a purely spiritual Christianity (cf., Albigensianism, Marcionism).

PAULINE PRIVILEGE, The. If of two unbaptized persons united in a consummated marriage one is converted to the faith and the other will neither be converted nor live in peace with the Christian, the marriage may be completely dissolved. This is not done automatically by the fact of Baptism, but by the Christian (the other having been examined by the bishop as to the circumstances) entering into another marriage with a Christian partner. Before the dissolution can take effect, the required interpellations (q.v.) must be made, unless these are dispensed. The convert can validly and lawfully contract a new marriage if the answers to the interpellations are in the negative, unless the convert after baptism gives the other a just cause of separation. The privilege can be used even if cohabitation has taken place after baptism. The former marriage is dissolved only when the new marriage is validly contracted. The privilege enjoys in law the benefit of the doubt, and the only ecclesiastical authority competent to deal with it, judicially or otherwise, is the Holy Office. This proceeding is in accordance with the words of St. Paul in 1 Cor. vii, 12-17; whence its name.

PAULISTS, The. The Missionary Society of St. Paul the Apostle, founded in New York, in 1858, by Fr. I. T. Hecker, with four other priests. Their particular work is the conversion of non-Catholics by missions, writing, and otherwise. Their rule is founded on that of the Redemptorists, to which congregation the founders originally belonged, but they give a solemn undertaking instead of taking the usual vows. They have now over 150 priest members. All their activities are in the United States, except for establishments in Toronto and Johannesburg. The mother house is in New York, and they have a residence and house of studies with the church of Santa Susanna in Rome.

PAULITES, The. The monks of St. Paul the Hermit, once an important congregation; founded in 1225 in Hungary by Bl. Eusebius of Gran. It now numbers only a few members. The monks, governed by a prior general, are engaged in pastoral work and have charge of the shrine of our Lady of Czenstochowa in Poland. Habit: tunic, girdle, scapular and hood, cloak in choir, all white.

PAX. i. The kiss of peace (q.v.).

ii. A tablet or disc of metal, ivory, etc., bearing a holy image and furnished at the back with a handle. It was in use in Western Europe during the middle ages for conveying the kiss of peace from the celebrant to the people, it being handed to each member of the congregation in turn. It is still used to convey the kiss to a bishop assisting at low Mass, to a sovereign or other privileged lay person, among the Carthusians and Dominicans, and at a conventual low Mass. Also called the osculatorium or instrumentum pacis, and in England "pax-brede" or "pax-board."

PAX DEI, The. A perpetual immunity from the ravages of private warfare declared in favour of clerics, religious and non-combatants, inviolability of churches, monasteries, etc., and a truce on Sundays, declared by certain local French synods and confirmed by Pope John XIX, in 1030. The penalty for non-observance was interdict, and leagues for the maintenance of peace were set up with a militia and tribunals to enforce the peace (cf., Truce of God).

PAX ROMANA. i. The period of the rule of the emperors Nerva, Trajan, Hadrian and Antoninus Pius, 96-161, during which the Roman empire enjoyed peace.

ii. An international confederation of societies of Catholic university undergraduates whose object is the promotion of international understanding and appreciation, and so of peace.

PAX VOBIS (Lat., Peace be with you). The greeting given by a bishop at Mass (instead of the priest's *Dominus vobiscum*) after the *Gloria in excelsis*, but not when that hymn is omitted; it has reference to the words "et in terra pax" in the Gloria.

PAYMENT for Indulgences, Masses, etc. See SALE OF . . .

PEACE. i. One of the twelve fruits of the Holy Ghost enumerated by St. Paul in Gal. v, 22, which keeps the mind untroubled in the face of spiritual or temporal trials. It refers to *acts* of peace done by men under the influence of grace, and as a "fruit" it is filled with the sweet savour arising from the performance of a good work. It is the outcome of charity (*q.v.*) which establishes peace between man and God and between man and his neighbour. It is compatible with a state of suffering or of war, but not with sin or personal enmity.

ii. Among nations. Christianity has always recognized that peace should be a characteristic of Christian states, but also that it is a gift of God and so not obtainable by purely natural means alone (limitation of armaments, societies of nations, arbitration). The will to peace, and that for supernatural motives, must exist in individuals and through them inform the nations which they compose, so that there may be due subordination of international relations to moral law and of national to international interests; and a people that has thus purged its patriotism of false nationalism (*qq.v.*) may be trusted to demand and to exercise a direct control over foreign policy. Love between men can be maintained only by developing in them sensibility for abstract man, from whom the idea of God is properly inseparable, and opposing in them the interest for concrete man, *i.e.*, "the world" or humanism; national or racial hatred, held as a sentiment independent of any sanction beyond that of nationalism, is a consequence of the humanistic belief in man's self-sufficiency. "It is not from outward pressure, it is not from the sword that deliverance comes to nations; the sword cannot breed peace, it can only impose forms of peace. The forces, the influences, that are to renew the face of the earth must spring from men's hearts" (Pope Pius XII).

PEACE OF THE CHURCH, The. i. Of Constantine. The granting of toleration to Christians by the Emperor Constantine in 313, which was immediately followed by the bestowal of privileges on the Church: immunity of the clergy from taxation and public offices of obligation, recognition of ecclesiastical courts, right to hold property and to free slaves, etc. The freedom and expansion of Christianity dates from this time; it was established as the religion of the Empire in 380. The Peace of the Church is celebrated by a feast in some Eastern rites on June 10.

ii. The *Pax Dei* (*q.v.*).

PECULIAR (Lat. *peculiaris*, of private property). A parish or church exempt from the jurisdiction of the bishop in whose diocese it is situated. Such before the Reformation was the church of St. Mary-le-Bow in Cheapside, and numerous monastic churches all over the land. In the Anglican system a peculiar is generally the indication of a former monastic church, *e.g.*, Westminster Abbey, Davington Priory (Kent). The position brought about by its being a peculiar was the occasion of the submission to the Holy See of the Anglican monks of Caldey Island in 1913.

PECULIUM (Lat., property). An allowance of money made by a superior in a religious order or congregation to one of his subjects for legitimate expenditure at his discretion (but without withdrawing the money from the power of the superior, for that would be contrary to the vow of poverty). Under contemporary conditions such a system of allowances is often absolutely necessary, but it is only tolerated and with definite limitations and safeguards; the Church continually aims at "the perfect common life" for all religious.

PEDOBAPTISM. Infant baptism (*q.v.*).

PEERAGE, PAPAL. A pontifical title of nobility (*q.v.*) conferred not merely personally but with right of hereditary descent by primogeniture in tail male. Only those are elevated to the pontifical peerage whose faith and public and private life are beyond suspicion and whose family and associates have blameless reputation; whose social position is good and profession neither lowly nor undignified; and whose lineage and material circumstances are such as to enable him and his family to maintain a style of life suitable to exalted rank.

PELAGIA LEGEND, The. The series of pious romances centering round the idea of a penitent courtesan who disguised herself as a man and became a monk, associated with the names of Marina, Margaret, Euphrosyne, Theodora and others. The starting-point seems to have been the fictitious story of a certain Pelagia of Antioch, in the 4th century.

PELAGIANISM. The heretical doctrine of Pelagius (*c.* 400), a native of Britain. Its principal tenets were: rejection of original sin (*q.v.*); that death is not due to original sin, but is a law of human nature; that Baptism is not necessary for blotting out original sin, but is merely a title of admission to the kingdom of Heaven; that grace is not necessary for salvation. There was much wobbling over the last point: the necessity of external grace (*q.v.*) was first admitted, then that of natural grace (*q.v.*) for greater ease. These doctrines were condemned by the synods of Milevis and Carthage (416), and when these findings were ratified by the pope, St. Augustine uttered the famous phrase, *Causa finita est*, which later developed into the adage, "Rome has spoken, the case is ended."

PELICAN IN HER PIETY, or vulning herself. The heraldic way of expressing an image of a pelican wounding herself with her beak in order to feed her young with her blood, used in Christian symbolism to typify the Atonement and our Lord as redeemer and giver of the Blessed Sacrament (*cf.*, the 6th stanza of *Adoro te devote*).

PENAL TIMES, The. The period from 1559 until 1829 during which the Catholics of Great Britain and Ireland were subject to the Penal Laws (*q.v.*, ii). Up to 1700 was a time of active, intermittent persecution, after that date of negative repression and gradual relaxation. From 1598 to 1621 the Catholics of England were officially under an archpriest; from 1623 to 1688 (with a break of 30 years during which the Old Chapter, *q.v.*, assumed jurisdiction) under a vicar apostolic. Then four districts, London, Midland, Northern and Western, were created, each with a vicar apostolic (who was a titular bishop) and this arrangement lasted until 1840, when eight vicariates were formed. In 1850 the hierarchy was restored. The exterior history of the Church in England during this time is the history of the Penal Laws and of their repeal. In 1780 Dr. Berington estimated the Catholic population of England at 60,000; there were 30 chapels: the great increase at the time of Emancipation (*q.v.*) was largely a result of Irish immigration and the influence of the French *émigrés*.

PENALTIES, ECCLESIASTICAL, are deposition, degradation, and deprivation of Christian burial (*qq.v.*). See also CENSURE. It should be noted that penalties and censures are frequently incurred not on account of the intrinsic wickedness of the action but because of the circumstances attending it and serious consequences involved.

PENANCE (Old Fr., from Lat. *pænitentia,* regret, repentance). i. Penitence, or repentance, a virtue disposing a sinner to hatred of his own sin because it is an offence against God and prompting him to a firm purpose of amendment. The motive must be supernatural, consideration of the goodness of God and love for him, to distinguish it from natural remorse or fear. It is a necessary condition for forgiveness.*
ii. Public. The penitential discipline of the early Church, relaxed before the 11th century, in respect of notorious and grave sinners, especially idolaters, murderers and adulterers. The lifting of the penalty of

excommunication and admission to the ranks of the penitents was for long a privilege not easily to be obtained. In certain parts of the Church such penitents were marshalled into four degrees, through each of which they normally had to pass, namely, weepers, who were excluded from divine service; hearers, who attended the Liturgy of the catechumens; kneelers, who knelt apart, and standers, who were excluded from holy communion and the offertory (*q.v.*, ii). Such penance with its attendant austerities and disabilities sometimes lasted for life; in any case it was imposed for a period of years; the terms (of years and days) in which indulgences are now granted bear reference to this practice. In Great Britain, Ireland and elsewhere modified and unofficial forms of public penance were imposed and performed until well into the 18th century and in isolated instances even later; in some missions to the heathen such modified forms are still in full force.
iii. Canonical. Prayers and good works, *e.g.*, fasting, almsgiving, pilgrimage, retreat, imposed by ecclesiastical authority on those guilty of offences against canon law, either instead of, or to obtain release from, a penalty. Public penances may not be imposed for occult (*q.v.*) offences. A penance is imposed when heretics are reconciled to the Church.
iv. Sacramental. After hearing a penitent's confession and before giving him absolution a confessor must impose a penance. While such a penance rarely nowadays bears any real relation to the gravity of the sins confessed, it must be in some sense proportionate thereto. The penance may take the form of alms-giving or similar good work, but is usually the devout recitation of some certain prayers; such must be articulated with the lips, reading with the eyes or saying them in the mind is not sufficient. If the penitent in good faith forgets to perform his penance or forgets what it was, he is excused; in the second case it is a pious act to do some other work at one's discretion but it is not and cannot be a true substitute for the penance. See also SATISFACTION.
v. Any prayer, mortification, or other good work, imposed either on oneself or by a lawful superior, performed in a spirit of penitence for sin.

PENANCE, THE SACRAMENT OF. A sacrament of the New Law instituted by Christ in which by the absolution of a priest, acting as judge, sins committed after Baptism are forgiven to a person who confesses them with sorrow and a purpose of amendment. The sacrament is in the nature of a judgement, in which the priest is the judge and the penitent is the accused and self-accuser. It is an article of faith that this power was given to the Church in the circumstances related in John xx, 21-23: "If anyone shall say that those words of the Lord our Saviour, 'Re-

---

* See also CONTRITION (Perfect and Imperfect).—*Publisher*, 1997.

ceive ye the Holy Ghost: whose sins you shall forgive, they are forgiven them; and whose sins you shall retain, they are retained," are not to be understood of the power of forgiving and retaining sins in the sacrament of Penance, as the Catholic Church from the beginning has always understood; but shall distort [these words] against the institution of this sacrament to the authority to preach the gospel, let him be anathema" (Council of Trent, sess, xiv, can. 3). The matter of the sacrament are the sins (remote) and the contrition, confession and satisfaction (proximate) of the penitent, and its form is the words of absolution; only a priest or bishop can minister this sacrament.

PENITENCE. The virtue of penance (q.v., i).

PENITENTIAL CANONS. Various sets of rules of the early Church, laid down by councils and bishops, regulating the kind and period of penance to be done for different sins. The granting of indulgences in terms of periods of time is a survival of this penitential system.

PENITENTIAL PSALMS, THE SEVEN. Pss. vi, xxxi, xxxvii, l, ci, cxxix and cxlii, wherein penitence for sin and desire for pardon are expressed.

PENITENTIARIA, SACRED APOSTOLIC. The Roman tribunal dealing with matters of the internal forum (q.v.), granting absolutions and dispensations, deciding cases of conscience and dealing with the whole matter of indulgences on their practical side. It is a "court of mercy," conducted in strict secrecy and without fees; any Catholic is at liberty to approach the Cardinal Penitentiary by means of a letter, in any language, wherein he states his case; fictitious names should be used, any correct name and address being added for the receipt of the reply; but such applications are usually made by one's confessor.

PENITENTIARY. i. The Grand Penitentiary is the cardinal-priest presiding over the Sacred Penitentiaria. On four days of Holy Week and during the Holy Year he attends with his principal assistants at St. Peter's, St. John Lateran and St. Mary Major in order that all who wish may go to confession to one of them and, as an act of humility, kneel before him and receive a light blow on the head from his wand (ferula), by this public act acknowledging themselves to be sinners (c.f., the Roman legal process for the freeing of slaves by the prætor).

ii. The above three basilicas and that of Loreto have each a college of minor penitentiaries drawn from the mendicant orders, who may hear the confession of anyone at any time and have wide powers to absolve from reserved sins; they also receive the above act of public accusation.

PENTATEUCH, The (Gr.; literally meaning five cases, with reference to the boxes in which the rolls were kept). The first five books of the Bible: Genesis, Exodus, Leviticus, Numbers, Deuteronomy. The Biblical Commission (q.v.) issued a declaration, in 1906, against theories that these books are a compilation made in the 5th century B.C. of material the bulk of which does not reach back further than the 9th century, and with which Moses in the 14th or 15th century had nothing whatever to do, beyond possibly the text of the Decalogue and some other small fragments. It states that the arguments brought in support of these theories are not conclusive against Mosaic authorship. This does not necessarily mean that Moses wrote or dictated the whole present text; he may have committed the work conceived by him under divine inspiration to one or more other writers, who faithfully rendered his thoughts and neither wrote nor omitted anything against his will, and he may have approved and published the work thus compiled under his name. He may have utilized written or oral sources, from which he borrowed, either word for word or in substance, either abbreviating or amplifying his sources, thus carrying out his purpose under divine inspiration. Moreover, during the course of the centuries after Moses's death additions may have been made by some other inspired author; glosses and explanations may have been added to the text, antiquated terms and forms of speech may have been replaced by more recent ones, and faulty readings introduced by careless copyists. The attack on its Mosaic authorship outside the Catholic Church has weakened, so that common opinion is coming round to a position hardly distinguishable from that of the Roman decree. In the Bible the Pentateuch is referred to as one book, the "Book of the Law of Moses," "The Law," etc., and is the Book of the Law put by Moses into the Ark of the Covenant.

PENTECOST (Gr., fiftieth [day]). i. The feast on which is commemorated the visible coming-down of the Holy Ghost upon the Apostles and the establishment of the Church founded by our Lord on St. Peter, usually called Whit-sunday (q.v.) in English. It occurs fifty days after Easter and alone ranks with that feast; the two following days are doubles of the 1st class (q.v.), and no feast is allowed during the octave, but the ember days are observed. At Mass the sequence Veni, sancte Spiritus is sung and the vestments are red, as always in reference to the Holy Ghost, perhaps symbolizing the tongues of fire. At Terce Veni Creator is sung instead of the usual hymn, because it was at the third hour that the Spirit descended. The Sundays between this feast and Advent are reckoned as "after Pentecost" almost universally in the Western church. The coming of the Holy Ghost is the complement of the Redemption (John xvi, 13; Luke xxiv, 49), and on this feast a new lawgiver, the Spirit of God, comes into the hearts of men.

ii. The second in importance of the Jewish feasts, originally the harvest festival and the end of Passover-time, but now a commemoration of the giving of the law on Mount Sinai. The descent of the Holy Ghost happened during the Jewish Pentecost.

PENTECOST, THE VIGIL OF, or Whitsun eve, is a greater vigil (q.v.), and a day of fasting and abstinence. Although a vigil, red vestments are worn at Mass.

PENTECOSTARION. A liturgical book of the Byzantine rite, containing the proper office for the period from Easter to the Sunday after Pentecost (All Saints in the Byzantine calendar). The corresponding book for the ten weeks up to Easter, covering Lent, is the *Triodion. Cf.* Liturgical Books, ii.

PER ACCIDENS. That which is not from the nature of a thing as such, but which is from some adjunct. Thus a man is learned, not by his very nature but by his accumulation of knowledge; I go a walk and find sixpence—the finding of the sixpence is a *per accidens* effect of the walk.

PER DOMINUM. The indication in liturgical books of the following conclusion to a collect: *Per Dominum nostrum Jesum Christum filium tuum, qui tecum vivit et regnat in unitate Spiritus Sancti, Deus, per omnia sæcula sæculorum. Amen.* (Through our Lord Jesus Christ thy Son, who liveth and reigneth with thee in the unity of the Holy Ghost, one God, world without end); always used at the collect of the day when it is addressed to God the Father. If God the Son has been named at its beginning, *eumdem Dominum* (same Lord), is said: if near the end, the conclusion begins at *qui tecum.* If God the Holy Ghost has been named, *eiusdem Spiritus* (of the same Spirit) is said. If the collect is addressed to God the Son, it is ended: *Qui vivis et regnas cum Deo Patre in unitate Spiritus Sancti, Deus, per omnia sæcula sæculorum. Amen* (Who livest and reignest with God the Father, etc.). Certain collects have a short ending: *Per Christum Dominum nostrum* or *Qui vivis et regnas in sæcula sæculorum.* When several collects are said consecutively only the first and last have a conclusion and *Amen.* These conclusions are to relate the prayers to the other persons of the Blessed Trinity beside the one to whom they are addressed, so that the Church may always pray to God in all his persons.

PER MODUM SUFFRAGII (Lat., by way of suffrage). See SUFFRAGE.

PER SE. That which is from the nature of a thing as such. Thus, to be able to learn belongs to man *per se.*

PEREGRINUS (Lat., a stranger). In canon law, a person who is staying temporarily outside the place of his domicile or quasi-domicile. Although retaining his proper domicile, he is bound by the general ecclesiastical laws of the place where he actually is.

PERFECTION. i. The relatively perfect union with God which is possible in this world, consisting in and proportional to the degree of charity (q.v.) possessed and exercised; it is therefore compatible with venial sin, but not with mortal sin. "The perfection of a Christian life consists essentially in charity (q.v.), primarily in loving God, secondarily in loving one's neighbour" (St. Thomas, II-II, clxxxiv, 3). When a man loves God with his whole heart, soul, mind and strength, and his neighbour as himself for God's sake, then is he perfect. The perfection attainable in this life is only relative and progressive; absolute and ultimate perfection belongs to the next life, when the creature will have definitely gained his last end, God himself, in the Beatific Vision. The attachment to God by love which perfection demands involves as its counterpart detachment from all that hinders or diminishes that love. Hence the way of perfection is a way of renunciation and mortification. Perfection is open to all, because the full love of God is possible in any walk of life; and all are called to it, at least remotely, in the words of Jesus Christ: "You are to be perfect, as your heavenly Father is perfect" (Matt. v. 48)—the calendar of saints includes men and women of all types and all stations. But the religious life (q.v.) is more conducive to perfection than life in the world, because it concentrates definitely on this aim by means of the vows of religion and organized prayer and asceticism. Perfection demands the observance of the precepts and of such counsels as apply to one's state of life. The essence of perfection, therefore, does not consist in a multiplicity of devotions, confraternities, etc.: nor even in austerity (q.v.), solitude, silence, and virtuous exercises. All these are means of acquiring perfection, or are manifestations of its presence.

ii. Religious. The perfection peculiar to the religious state, as distinct from the clerical or the secular. All perfection is the heroic exercise of the virtue of supernatural charity but it may be achieved by different methods according to the vocation of each soul. Religious perfection is obtained by means of the vows of religion (q.v.), and the due observance of the rules and constitutions of a particular order or community (cf., State of Perfection).

PERFECTION, COUNSELS OF. Principles of conduct for those who, not content with "making sure of salvation," aim at higher and even the highest moral perfection, adopting means by which they may overcome obstacles to perfection and so resemble Christ more closely. The chief hindrances are riches, bodily pleasures and honours, which, innocent in themselves, easily lead to sins of self-indulgence and pride. Hence the chief counsels are those according to which voluntary renunciation of even innocent indulgence is made, namely, the three Evangelical Counsels—voluntary poverty, perpetual chastity, entire obedience.

PERFECTION, DIVINE. God is infinite perfection, the limitless sum of all perfection of being. We can attribute to God any simple perfection, as long as we recognize that in him it is unlimited; but when it is a question of those perfections which imply some imperfection and are opposed to greater perfection (*e.g.*, reasoning as opposed to intuitive understanding), we must recognize that these are in God in a higher way which does not imply imperfection. All perfections of creatures are mere analogues of the perfections of God.

PERICOPE (Gr., literally, a cutting round). A passage of the Holy Scriptures appointed for reading in the liturgy; a lesson (*q.v.*).

PERJURY. The confirming by an oath of a statement which the swearer knows to be false. When committed with full deliberation and knowledge it is always a mortal sin against the virtue of religion. Anyone giving perjured evidence before an ecclesiastical court incurs suspension if he is a cleric and a personal interdict (*q.v.*) if a layman.

PERPETUAL ADORATION. Worship of the Blessed Sacrament, either in the tabernacle but more usually exposed in a monstrance, continued by day and night without intermission. The practice developed in France during the 17th century out of the Forty Hours devotion (*q.v.*), and is now followed by a number of congregations of nuns; the watchers usually take one-hour turns by day, singly or in pairs. Certain congregations of men, such as the Picpus Fathers and the Society of the Most Blessed Sacrament, also maintain perpetual adoration as part of their work. The cathedral of Lugo in Spain is the only one having perpetual adoration, by an extraordinary privilege of some antiquity.

PERPETUAL SUCCOUR, OUR LADY OF. A 13th-century Byzantine picture of our Lady and the holy Child, brought to Rome in the 15th century and now venerated there in the church of the Redemptorists. It is one of the best known and most popular pictures of our Lady; but in many reproductions of it unwarrantable liberties have been taken with the design to make a less violent contrast with the productions of modern commercial ecclesiastical art; there is a faithful copy in the Redemptorist church at Clapham, and it may be seen in others in England. A feast of our Lady under this title on June 27 was established in 1876, and is observed, *e.g.*, in the dioceses of Leeds and Middlesbrough, of which she is the patron. It may be suggested that "of Unfailing Help" is a more graceful name in English.

PERSECUTION. The attempt to enforce religious conformity or the penalizing of religious dissent by the infliction of penalties. In Christian history persecution has been extensively used by both Catholics and Protestants and by others: but the Catholic Church as such has never approved strict persecution. St. Thomas Aquinas lays it down that "Unbelievers who have never received the faith, such as Jews and others, are in no way to be forced to believe . . . for belief is of the will" (II-II, x, 8), and canon law expressly prohibits the use of force in matters of faith (canon 1351). St. Thomas defended the punishment of heretics as a danger to social order and of apostates to compel them to keep their promises; and churchmen, or civil authorities supported by churchmen, have made much use of such punishment in the past. The Church today is opposed to all forms of persecution. See CONVERSION iii.

PERSEVERANCE. i. A moral virtue, annexed to fortitude, disposing one to continue in any good work, whether spiritual or corporal, sacred or secular, without being daunted by besetting difficulties and discouragement.
ii. Final. The grace (*q.v.*) of persevering to the end in a state of grace (*q.v.*) not necessarily from the beginning, but for a time from the last conversion to death; or, in the extreme case of a death-bed conversion, the grace of dying in a state of grace. This supreme and critical grace is not the object of condign merit (*q.v.*), but it can be deserved as a favour granted (not infallibly) to repeated prayers. No one can secure it once for all, so as to leave the subject in a state of certainty regarding his future.

PERSIA, THE CHURCH IN. Persia (formerly call Iran) has an estimated population of 15 million, solidly Mohammedan of the Shi'ah tradition. Since 1907 the small Christian minority has liberty of worship, and where their number warrants it they have the protection of a special magistrate who deals with their affairs. The ancient Nestorian (*q.v.*) Church of Persia was finally swept away by the Mongols at the end of the 14th century (there are a few thousand Nestorians there today); from that time on Western missionaries have worked in the country from time to time, but Catholics number only some 8,000, very few of whom are Persians. There are 2 Chaldean (q.v.) dioceses; 1 diocese of Armenians; and an archbishopric without suffragans (Isfahan, founded in 1629) of the Latin rite.

PERSON, PERSONALITY. i. The individual substance of a rational nature (Boethius). An unfolding of this definition is this: A substance perfectly subsistent, master of its own acts, and incommunicable. The human person is thus neither the body nor the soul, but the rational being arising out of the substantial union of both. Personality, the abstract of person, is the perfection whereby a substance becomes *sui juris* and incommunicable. "Supposit" is used instead of the word "person" when applied to non-rational and inanimate beings. A person must be an individual able to direct itself by its intelligence and will (so a brute is not a person), and accordingly the disposer of its own activities and the proper object of attribution of its acts. It is the person who eats, walks, thinks, speaks, loves. A valuable distinction is now often made between the human being as an individual—a fragment of society—and as a person—man considered in the totality of his being, whose end is ordained to God. In virtue of that end, a person must not be used as a mere instrument or means, and must not use other persons as such; the dignity and integrity of the human person must be upheld, and the autonomy of his regulation of his moral activity and inner life respected; a person is superior to the order of society, which exists to help him in the attainment of his end. But for that very reason, in accordance with his nature as a social being, there is a certain subordination of the person to society, he must submit himself to the common good. "As the person necessarily aspires to complete perfection, he tends, in virtue of his social nature, to pursue it in society. Society, in turn, must envisage the common good as embracing complete human perfection. For every common good worthy of the name is, in the last analysis, a good of persons" (J. A. Creaven). This is true humanism (q.v.). Hence the movement called Personalism is radically opposed to that self-affirmation of the individual called Individualism.

ii. Of the Holy Trinity. This perfection of personality, like all perfections, must be attributed in some way to God. But whereas in creatures, person and nature are so intimately united that the multiplication of the person involves multiplication of the nature, it is not so in God. In him there is but one nature, but there are three distinct persons, the most Holy and Undivided Trinity. These persons are three "subsistent relations." In creatures relation is an accident (q.v.), but there is nothing accidental in God. Hence they are *subsistent* relations, so that they can act, and to them actions can be

attributed. Therefore we say that the Father generates the Son, that the Son became man, that the Holy Ghost proceeds from the Father and the Son, etc. This is the most sublime of mysteries (q.v.).

iii. Ecclesiastical. The Church consists of physical and moral persons. Physical personality is obtained by baptism. A person attains his majority on completing 21 years of age; those under this age are minors. Male persons become adults on completing 14 years of age, females on completing 12 years, but in all that pertains to baptism adults of either sex are those over 7 years of age. Persons are considered in law to have attained the use of reason on completing 7 years of age; below that age they are counted infants. By divine institution there are in the Church clerics, distinct from lay persons, although not all clerics are of divine institution; either clerics or lay persons may be religious (q.v.).

PERU, THE CHURCH IN. The population of Peru is over 7 million, of whom three-quarters are Indian or mixed, nearly all Catholics by repute except for a number of Indians. Catholicism is officially the state religion, but any other is freely exercised. Places of worship are exempt from taxation and clergy from military service; the state makes a small annual grant for the missions and other church purposes; and there is no divorce *a vinculo*. The president has certain powers over the appointment of bishops and other dignitaries. The influence of secularist policies tends to increase. The country forms four metropolitan provinces, with seven suffragan dioceses; the so-called primatial see, Lima, was founded in 1543, and 4 others before 1620; there are also 4 Indian mission vicariates apostolic.

PESHITTO (Syriac, simple). A Syriac version of the Bible made between the 2nd and 5th centuries, the Old Testament being the first translation made for the use of Christians and second in importance only to the Septuagint (q.v.). It is still in use in all the Syrian churches; a new edition was issued by the Dominicans from their Chaldean seminary at Mosul in 1891.

PESSIMISM. See OPTIMISM.

PETER, SAINT. i. The name and figure of Peter is frequently used, both in words and pictorial symbolism, as a personification of the Church, the pope, the see of Rome, etc.; he being the first pope and bishop of Rome, prince of the Apostles, vicar of Jesus Christ, and human foundation of the Church. Peter's primacy (q.v.) of jurisdiction, carried on by every pope since, is an article of faith. His chief feast kept universally with that of St. Paul is on June 29, probably the day of the translation of their relics; traditionally they both suffered in Rome on the same day, probably Aug. 1, about the year 67 in the persecution of Nero, Peter being crucified head downwards in the circus of Nero on the Vatican Hill, Paul being slain by the sword at Tre Fontane, near the Ostian Way; Peter's body lies in the basilica of his name, Paul's in St. Paul's-outside-the-Walls. For his other feasts see below. In every office of St. Peter a commemoration is made of St. Paul, and *vice-versa,* and they are twice named together in the canon of the Mass.

ii. His epistles. Two letters written by Peter to the Christians of various provinces in Asia Minor are included in the canon of Holy Scripture. The general intention of both was the strengthening of faith, encouragement of virtue and comfort in distress; the second, like St. Paul's 2 Timothy, was written in view of the writer's approaching end.

PETER'S CHAINS, ST. A feast observed on Aug. 1 (Lammas day, *q.v.*) in the Western church, being the day of the dedication of the basilica of St. Peter-in-Chains, so called because there were (and are) preserved relics of the chains with which he was confined in prison. The Mass is that of the feast of SS. Peter and Paul (June 29) with a proper collect, gradual, secret and post-communion; after the commemoration (*q.v.*) of St. Paul, there is one of the Holy Machabees. The Veneration of the Precious Chain of the Holy and Illustrious Apostle Peter is celebrated in the Byzantine rite on Jan. 16.

PETER'S CHAIR, ST. The Western church celebrates two feasts of this name, "at Rome" on Jan. 18, and "at Antioch" on Feb. 22, commemorating the taking up by St. Peter of the episcopal office in these cities respectively (see CATHEDRA). Both feasts originally referred to Rome, and they are observed as one on Feb. 22 by the Benedictines. The Copts and Abyssinians, dissidents as well as Catholics, have this feast under the title of the Primacy of Peter on July 31. In a bronze monument above the altar in the apse of St. Peter's basilica is a chair which is said to have been used by him as bishop.

PETER'S PENCE. Voluntary contributions of any amount made by Catholics in all parts of the world towards the expenses of the Holy See. It is transmitted by the local bishops and is a considerable source of income, being administered by a special commission of cardinals. The name originated in the early middle ages for a tax of a penny on every household.

PETITIONS TO THE POPE. Any Catholic may present a petition to the Holy See on any matter at any time, and in judicial causes, whether civil or criminal, may have recourse to Rome at any stage of the trial. But, except in the case of legitimate appeal, the jurisdiction of the ordinary or inferior court is not suspended, unless the Holy See

signifies that the matter is to be reserved to itself. Petitions to the pope should be addressed to the particular department of the Roman Curia competent to deal with the matter, and should begin: *Beatissime Pater* (Most Holy Father).

PETRICULANUS. The Latin epithet for the bishop of Little Rock, Arkansas.

PEW. Originally that part of a church appropriated to the use of a particular family. The word is now used to designate seating accommodation for the laity in church consisting of fixed rows of undivided benches with backs, as opposed to rows of chairs. The pew is a purely Western arrangement, commonest in northern Europe and the United States. The word is the Middle English *puwe,* probably derived through Old French and Latin from Gr. ποδεῖον, pedestal.

PHANAR, The. The Greek quarter of Constantinople and the seat of the court of the Orthodox patriarch, the centre of Greek Orthodoxy. The name is used for this court and its authority, much as The Vatican is used for the Holy See. Its residents are Phanariots.

PHANTASM. An object represented in the imagination, which is one of the internal senses. A phantasm is therefore always of the sensuous order, and is wholly distinct from an idea. Whatever we imagine must have some definite size, colour, shape, etc., whereas an idea represents something universal and spiritual.

PHARISEES, The (Heb., *parush,* separated). The party among the Jews of our Lord's day who separated themselves from all intercourse with the Gentiles. They held to a minutely literal interpretation of the Law and the prophets and were scrupulous observers of tradition and ceremonial. Their power brought degeneration and they became exclusive, formal, proud and self-righteous, thus provoking the indignation of our Lord (*e.g.,* Matt. xxiii, 1–7, 13–36).

PHELONION, PHENOLION. The topmost and chief vestment of a priest of the Byzantine rite. Its origin and use are the same as those of the Western chasuble (*q.v.*), but it is also used as a cope; a bishop wears the *sakkos* (*q.v.*) instead. In form, the *phelonion* is an ample cloak of soft material, of no fixed colour, reaching nearly to the ground at the back and sides; the front may be long too, but is often cut away as high as the chest; there is an opening for the head. The eucharistic vestment proper to each Eastern rite resembles the *phelonion* more or less.

PHENOMENON (Gr., appearance). The appearance which an object presents to the mind from without. It is opposed to *nou-*

men, a term used by Kant to denote a thing-in-itself lying beyond the range of cognition.

PHILADELPHIA (*Philadelphiensis*). One of the early dioceses of the United States. In consequence of William Penn's ordinance of religious liberty Philadelphia early had a Catholic population, which at first was under the jurisdiction of the vicar apostolic of the London district in England; then they came under the bishop of Baltimore, and in 1808 were organized in a separate diocese, which now includes the city and several adjoining counties. The see became metropolitan in 1875, the suffragan dioceses being Altoona, Erie, Harrisburg, Pittsburgh, Scranton, and Youngstown. The first bishop was Friar Michael Egan, O.S.F., and among its other bishops were F. P. Kenrick and Cardinal Dennis Dougherty. Philadelphia is the residence also of the episcopal ordinary (exarch) for the Ukrainians in the United States. The city's name is Greek, and means "brotherly love"; the original Philadelphia in Asia Minor was one of the Seven Churches (*q.v.* i).

PHILEMON, THE EPISTLE TO. A short letter of St. Paul included in the canon of Holy Scripture. It refers to Onesimus, a runaway slave who had been converted by St. Paul; his master was a friend of Paul, who sent Onesimus back with this letter, asking Philemon to treat the bearer as he would the writer.

PHILIP AND JAMES, SS. i. Apostles, whose joint feast was kept by the Western church on May 1, the day of the dedication, in 561, of the church of the Holy Apostles at Rome; but it is now kept on May 11. Philip, one of the first of the apostles, may have preached the gospel in Asia Minor and have suffered death by crucifixion at Hierapolis. James, known as the Less and the Just, the son of Alpheus, was probably identical with one of the brethren of the Lord (*q.v.*) and the first bishop of Jerusalem; his epistle is a canonical book of the Bible; he was martyred, perhaps, by being thrown from the walls of the temple. They are named together in the canon of the Mass and are commemorated in the Byzantine rite, Philip on Nov. 14, James on Oct. 9; but in the East James the Bishop is regarded as a distinct person and has a separate feast on Oct. 23.
ii. Epistle of St. James. A letter written by James to Christian Jews outside of Palestine, probably a particular congregation, is included in the canon of holy Scripture. It encourages them to fervent faith and good works in the face of oppression. On account of its clear statement of the doctrine of the necessity of good works to salvation (ii, 14–26), this epistle had the distinction of being discarded by Luther as one "of straw."

PHILIPPIANS, THE EPISTLE TO THE. An intimate letter of exhortation and encouragement written by St. Paul to the Christians of Philippi, who had sent one Epaphroditus to look after him while in prison in Rome; a canonical book of Holy Scripture.

PHILIPPINES, THE CHURCH IN THE. The Filipinos were evangelized from 1564, principally by Augustinian, Dominican, and Franciscan friars, and today 70 per cent of the 15¾ million Filipinos are Catholic by profession. When the Spanish clergy were driven out in the revolt of 1898 there were so few indigenous clergy that the Church was in imminent danger of complete ruin. Under American administration the situation was saved and the proper training of Filipino clergy undertaken; over half the bishops and other clergy are now native Filipinos, but there is still a great shortage of priests. In recent years secularist influence has been strong in the government, and no clergyman may teach or lecture in the state university. The see of Manila was established in 1585; there is now another archbishopric, 13 bishoprics, and 3 missionary prefectures.

PHILOCALIAN CALENDAR, The. The earliest known list of feasts of martyrs kept by the Roman church, named after its compiler, Philocalus. It is also called "Depositio Martyrum" and the Liberian Calendar, as being compiled under Pope Liberius about 354. It was not an official calendar but formed part of a private collection of records of dates and festivals.

PHILOSOPHER. i. A master or student of philosophy.
ii. An aspirant to the priesthood who is engaged on the philosophical studies which precede those of theology.
iii. The Philosopher = Aristotle.

PHILOSOPHY (Gr., love of wisdom). A science (that is, a certain and evident knowledge) acquired by natural reason which is concerned with the highest of ultimate causes of things. There are three main divisions: Logic, which treats of the principles of knowledge and of the order among ideas; Metaphysics, which treats of real being and of the order among things; and Ethics, which treats of the principles of good behaviour.

PHOS HILARON (Gr., gladdening light). The most ancient and famous hymn of the Byzantine liturgy, sung at *Hesperinos;* it is a thanksgiving towards which all the other prayers converge and on feast days is sung solemnly in front of the holy doors. An English translation by Keble, with a good melody, is in "Hymns Ancient and Modern," No. 18. Its authorship is attributed by St. Basil to St. Athenogenes the Martyr, whose date is not known.

PHOTIUS, THE SCHISM OF. In 857 Photius was intruded into the patriarchal see of Constantinople; he was excommunicated therefor by Pope Nicholas I, and declared a state of schism by impugning Roman orthodoxy in respect of five customs of their patriarchate (the *Filioque* was the most important, *q.v.*). Photius was extruded by the eighth œcumenical council at Constantinople; but on the death of the patriarch Ignatius in 877 he was elected in his place and recognized at Rome; he then repudiated the council and reopened the schism, whereupon he was solemnly excommunicated by Pope John VIII, and in that state died. That is in brief outline the hitherto accepted story. Recent research seems to make it clear that (a) Photius was legitimately patriarch from the beginning; (b) the story of the œcumenical council needs revision; (c) an alleged forgery of papal letters by Photius is untrue; (d) his second schism and the excommunication by John VIII never took place. It has always been known that Photius was a man of great learning and irreproachable private life; and it looks now as if he was not an archschismatic and did not in fact play a decisive part in helping to range the church of the East against the church of the West.

PHYLACTERIES (Matt. xxiii, 5). Slips of parchment, bearing a summary of the moral law, worn in leather cylinders, one on the forehead, the other on the back of the right hand (*cf.*, Deut. vi, 9). They are still worn by some Jews in their houses. The fringes referred to (*loc. cit.*) are now worn on the *tallith* or prayer shawl.

PHYLETISM (Gr. φυλή, a tribe). The name by which a synod at the Phanar (*q.v.*) in 1872 condemned excessive nationalism of autonomous churches within the Orthodox Church. The condemnation was particularly aimed at the desire of the Bulgars to form a national church.

PIANO (ABITO) (It.). The ordinary everyday dress of prelates; a black cassock with red piping, buttons and sash for cardinals; purple for bishops and other prelates. It originated with the prelates of the Gaeta district and was extended by Pope Pius IX to the whole Western church, whence the name *abito piano* (Pian dress). In Rome it is worn on semi-state occasions, prelates at other times being distinguished only by a coloured stock.

PIARISTS, The. The Clerks Regular of the Religious Schools, a teaching congregation founded by St. Joseph Calasanctius in 1597. They have schools (free for the poor) and colleges in Italy, Spain and Central Europe.

PICKETING by strikers in a just cause in order to induce others to strike or to refuse work is lawful but only so long as it is "peaceful." It is a sin against justice to use threats, violence or other coercion, and those so doing are bound to restitution for damage caused to another thereby.

PICPUS FATHERS, The. The popular name, from their former headquarters in the rue de Picpus, at Paris, of the Congregation of the Sacred Hearts of Jesus and Mary, founded by Père Joseph Coudrin in 1800. The members have missions in the South Sea islands and elsewhere; they combine home and foreign missionary work with perpetual adoration. Fr. Damien of Molokai belonged to this congregation.

PIE, The. That is, the "parti-coloured." The name given in the Sarum liturgical books to the general rubrics, they being printed in red and black.

PIETÀ (It., *cf.*, piety). An image, generally carved in stone or cast in metal, of the dead body of our Lord lying in the arms of his mother.

PIETISM. A movement of some Protestants of the 17th and 18th centuries, originating among German Lutherans, towards a more devout daily life and stricter morality; there were strong mystical and pseudo-mystical elements in Pietism, of which the excesses caused the name to be used contemptuously, implying exaggeration or affectation. Their meetings were called Fellowships of Piety, whence the nickname.

PIETY (Lat. *pietas*, affectionate dutifulness). i. The gift of the Holy Ghost, which makes us duly affectionate and grateful to our parents, relatives and country in particular, and to all men, but especially the saints, in so far as they belong to God.

ii. A term loosely used to indicate fervour in fulfilling the duties of religion. Piousness is sometimes opposed to it, as an aggressively external or doubtfully genuine fervour. "Piosity" is a word invented for a superfluous or excessive observance or for an article of piety more notable for its commercial or emotional attractiveness than for its intrinsic worth.

iii. Article, object, of piety. An expression, apparently of commercial origin, to designate such things as crucifixes, rosaries, statues, medals, etc., which are intended for personal or domestic as opposed to liturgical or public use. They should always be blessed by a priest before use.

PILGRIMAGE (Old Fr. *pelerinage*, from Lat. *peregrinus*, a stranger). A journey to a sacred place undertaken as an act of religious devotion, either simply in order to venerate it or to ask the fulfilment of some need or as an act of penance or thanksgiving, or a combination of these. After the 8th century they were often imposed in substitution for public penance (*q.v.* ii). Contrary to some common notions, a pilgrimage is not necessarily penitential, it need not be performed under conditions of physical discomfort or with great solemnity, nor are ordinary means of travel, *e.g.*, by train or motor-car, essentially out of harmony with it. The principal places to which pilgrimages are made to-day are Rome, Jerusalem and the Holy Places, Lourdes, Bruges (the Holy Blood), the Holy House at Loreto, our Lady's shrines at Einsiedeln (Switzerland), Genazzano (Italy), La Salette (France), Vailankanni (Madras), Oostacker (Belgium) and Montserrat (Spain), Ste. Anne de Beaupré at Quebec, Ste. Anne d'Auray and Paray-le-Monial (France), Croagh Patrick, St. Patrick's Purgatory in Lough Derg (Ireland). Local to Great Britain are the tomb of St. Edward in Westminster Abbey, Holywell in North Wales, and the shrine of our Lady of Lourdes at Carfin near Glasgow; some of the old centres are not entirely neglected, *e.g.*, Canterbury, Glastonbury, Saint Albans and Walsingham.

PILGRIMAGE OF GRACE, The. A rising of the commons in the north of England, in 1536, to demand the re-establishment of the monasteries, the deprivation of Thomas Cromwell and heretical bishops, etc. Robert Aske of Aughton led over 30,000 insurgents in the field at Doncaster; he was tricked into dispersing them, executed with other gentry and four abbots, and the rising was crushed. The standard of this rising was the badge of the Five Wounds.

PILLAR SAINT, or Stylite (Gk. στῦλος, pillar). A solitary who lived on the top of a pillar or tower. Such were found in the East from the 4th to the 10th centuries, in Syria till the 14th, and spasmodically even later; this extreme form of mortification balanced the extreme sensuality of the people among whom they lived. Seraphin of Sarov, the Russian *starets* (d. 1833), lived for three years as a stylite in a forest, leaving an elevated rock only for his meals. Ordinarily the pillar was crowned with a platform on which the hermit had a tiny hut, nor was the pillar necessarily more than a few feet high; others were rather column-shaped cells in which the holy man lived. The chief stylite saints were the Simeons, the older and the younger, Daniel (these three are mentioned in the Roman Martyrology), Alipius and Luke.

PILLAR OF SCOURGING, The. i. A piece of porphyry pillar, about 3 ft. high, preserved in the Franciscan chapel in the church of the Holy Sepulchre, is said to be part of that to which our Lord was bound and beaten during his passion. (Another relic of the same name is in the church of Santa Prassede at Rome.)

ii. A piece of a column on which he is said to have sat in the house of Caiphas (Matt. xxvi, 57-68) is in the Armenian church of St. Peter in Jerusalem. Both these relics have been known since the 4th century.

iii. A feast of the Passion under this name

is celebrated in some places on the Tuesday after Quinquagesima.

PIOUS BELIEF. A belief which, while it lays no claim to be an element of infallible teaching, is nevertheless backed by good authority (*e.g.*, by individual theologians of merit), which does not run counter to any infallible teaching, and which is in harmony with the common sense (*q.v.*) of the faithful.

PIOUS UNION. An association of lay-people for the promotion of works of devotion or charity, and subject to canon law. They are numerous throughout the Church; some aim at the sanctification of their members by general means (*e.g.*, the Knights of the Blessed Sacrament, the Children of Mary); some adopt particular devotional practices (*e.g.*, the Scapular and Rosary Confraternities); others are for the encouragement of particular spiritual and corporal good works, *e.g.*, temperance in the use of alcoholic drink, raising funds for the spread of the faith, instructing the young in Christian doctrine. There are also special confraternities for the clergy, such as the Priests' Eucharistic League and the Apostolic Union of Secular Priests.

PISAN POPES, The. Two claimants to the papal throne elected as a result of the Council of Pisa in an effort to heal the Schism of the West (*q.v.*). Their names are often included in the lists of popes (Alexander V, 1409; John XXIII, 1410), but they seem now to be officially looked on as antipopes.

PISCINA (Lat., a basin). An aperture in the wall on the epistle side of an altar, provided with a shelf to accommodate the cruets at Mass and a drain (*sacrarium*), connected with the earth, for the disposal of water, etc., which has been used for some sacred purpose and is no longer required. Its place is often taken by a credence table (*q.v.*), the *sacrarium* then being in the sacristy.

PISTOIA, SYNOD OF. A local council held by Bishop Ricci of Pistoia in Tuscany, in 1786, which attempted to introduce Jansenism, Josephinism and other errors into Italy. It called forth the constitution *Auctorem Fidei* from Pope Pius VI, in which 85 propositions touching faith, morals, worship and discipline were condemned.

PLACEAT. The first word of a prayer to the Holy Trinity, said after the *Ite missa est* at Mass. It is a personal prayer of the celebrant asking that the sacrifice may be acceptable; it was added, with the blessing which now follows it, in the 11th century.

PLACEBO (Lat., I will please), the first word of the first antiphon at Vespers of the Office of the Dead, formerly used to stand for a recitation of the whole hour or office (*cf.*, Dirge).

PLAINSONG, PLAINCHANT. Unisonous vocal music; rhythmic, not metrical—an extension of speech rather than of verse. In its ecclesiastical form (plainchant) it is the normal music of the Latin liturgy. The modes (or scales) of the chant are confined to the natural intervals of the human voice and the melodies to its natural compass. In addition to the major scale (do—do) and the minor scale (la—la) there are naturally the scales re—re, mi—mi, fa—fa, sol—sol and si—si; there is no chromatic scale or chromatic progression and, normally, no modulation from one mode to another in the same melody. Individual notes are generally equal in time length but the speed of singing may be fast or slow according to the will of the singers. It is a characteristic of the chant that the "leading note" is generally avoided. Other characteristics are the use of two choirs singing the same melody alternately and the use of a reciting note upon which short melodies frequently repeated are dependent (e.g., in the psalm tones). The beauty of this music is that of pure melody and depends upon voice quality and rhythmical subtlety. See MODE. ii.

PLANETA. The ordinary Roman name for a chasuble, probably from *planare,* to wander, with reference to its origin as an outdoor garment. *Planeta plicata* is the folded chasuble (q.v.).

PLATONISM. The doctrine of Plato (427-347 B.C.). In the course of time it has been much modified by various schools according to their own diverse systems; Theosophists and Idealists interpreted Plato to suit their own ideas. Platonism and Aristotelianism do not go hand in hand; the aspirations of Plato are more noble, but the doctrine of the latter is more exact, and on the face of it more true. The first Christian philosophers, and even the Fathers of the Church, get their inspiration from the writings of Plato, whereas the Scholastics for preference derive their philosophy from Aristotle. Plato's speculations are so elevated that he loses touch with this world and does not take into account sufficiently the data of experimental knowledge. The object of scientific knowledge is the world of ideas, immutable and necessary, of which mundane things are participations; he refuses to see the necessary and universal realized in things individual (see UNIVERSALS) and that scientific knowledge can attain to both worlds, one through the other. Thus does Plato open the way to Ontologism (q.v.). In his philosophy of nature the world was matter, eternal and necessary, which is the passive element in things and the reason of the existence of evil in nature; this doctrine is analogous to that of the Persians and Manichæans (q.v.). In theodicy, he teaches with all his power the existence of God, sovereignly good, absolutely distinct from the material world—the source of all truth, good and beauty. God's wisdom and providence are manifested in all things. In psychology, the soul pre-existed before its union with the body, which union was the result of offences committed in its former state—and thus is the soul's union with the body a punishment. Moreover this union is merely accidental. All human knowledge is reminiscence, the body being the occasion of the soul's recalling actively something of its former knowledge possessed before union with the body. In the "Republic" Plato puts himself forward as the patron of communism the most absolute: wealth, family, children belong entirely to the state. In ethics, there are gaps which are the outcome of Greek paganism; Plato shut his eyes to certain vices against nature which at times he seems even to encourage. Slavery is not only tolerated, but deemed to be necessary.

PLEASURE. An agreeable feeling (q.v.) which is a positive resulting or concomitant quality of the free and vigorous exercise of some vital energy. To each faculty, whether sensuous or intellectual, belongs an appropriate pleasure. Pleasure in its ordinary acceptation is synonymous with sensuous enjoyment (cf., HAPPINESS).

PLENARY INDULGENCE. An indulgence (q.v.) which remits the whole of the temporal punishment which has been incurred by a sinner according to the justice of God. Unless the contrary is stated, all plenary indulgences may be applied for the benefit of the souls, or of an individual soul, in Purgatory, but the degree of its acceptance depends on the will of God, so that there is no certainty that the penalty of these souls is fully remitted. If gained for the living (i.e., oneself), there follows the complete remission of temporal punishment in this world and the next; but as we can never be certain of the perfection of our own dispositions, neither can we ever be absolutely certain of having profited to the full by a particular plenary indulgence (cf., toties quoties). A plenary indulgence cannot be gained more than once on the same day except when the contrary is expressly stated (e.g., the Portiuncula, q.v. ii). Attachment to a single venial sin prevents the gaining to the full of a plenary indulgence, but it is then efficacious to the extent of one's good dispositions.

PLURALISM. i. The illegal holding of more than one benefice by the same man. The Council of Trent decreed that no cleric of whatever rank should be appointed to more than one benefice unless that which he held was insufficient for his support; in which case he might receive a second provided it be not incompatible with the first, e.g., by involving the necessity of residing in two different places at once. Benefices, whether titular or commendatory, are incompatible if one of them alone is sufficient to provide a reasonable maintenance.

ii. The philosophical system that recognizes more than one ultimate principle, while denying the original unity of all things in God (*cf.*, Monism).

PLUVIALE (Lat. *pluvius*, rain). A cope, from its original use as a cloak for wet weather. *Pluvialistæ:* cantors and other assistants at solemn services dressed in copes.

PLYMOUTH (*Plymuthensis*). An English see, suffragan to Birmingham, erected in 1850. It is made up of the counties of Devon, Dorset and Cornwall and the Scilly Islands, formerly in the dioceses of Salisbury and Exeter. At Chideock, Lulworth, Ugbrooke, Lanherne, Stapehill, Marnhull, and elsewhere the faith, under the protection of the Welds, Cliffords, Arundells and others, has never died out and missions were established at all these places in the 17th and 18th centuries. The Lateran canons have their noviciate at Bodmin and serve 7 parishes. The Carmelite convent at Lanherne was founded in the 17th century at Antwerp. The patron of the diocese is St. Boniface (born at Crediton) and the cathedral is dedicated in honour of him and of St. Mary.

PLYMOUTH BRETHREN. A Protestant sect which received its name about 1830 from a congregation meeting in Plymouth and has since spread, especially in the U.S.A. They believe that the Christian church is only for the justified and an ordained and separate ministry is particularly obnoxious to them; the "breaking of bread" takes place weekly and is of obligation; they have strongly Calvinistic doctrines of predestination and justification; and a most remarkable eschatology. The Brethren, who have always been of a very separatist character, in spite of their original protest against Protestant divisions, have now broken up into further sects. They are a simple and devout people.

PODIUM (Lat., a platform) or **Talamo.** A portable platform upon which the pope is carried when he officiates at a procession of the Blessed Sacrament. To it is fixed a faldstool at which he sits or kneels and to which the monstrance containing the Sacred Host is attached.

POLAND, THE CHURCH IN. In 1939 the population was 33½ million, of whom three-quarters were Catholics; the rest were principally dissident Orthodox and Jews. Their primate was the archbishop of Gniezno-Poznan, with 5 other metropolitan sees and 18 bishoprics (including 1 archbishopric and 2 suffragan dioceses of Slav-Byzantine rite, and a diocese of Armenian rite). As a result of world-war II, the territory covered by western Poland has been increased, at the expense of Germany (*q.v.*); but in the east whole dioceses, comprising some 7 million

faithful and including practically all the Byzantine Ukrainians, have been transferred to the U.S.S.R. Those dioceses principally affected are Lvov (3 sees), Peremysl (2 sees), Stanislavov, Luck, Pinsk and Vilna. The future not only of these areas but of the whole church in Poland is a matter of very grave concern. In 1946 it was computed that it would take 15 years to replace the clergy killed or otherwise dead since 1939. The present population is estimated at 22 million. Warsaw is now the primatial see. There is still a small autonomous Orthodox Church.

POLEMICS (Gr. πόλεμος, war). Theological controversy.

POLITICS AND RELIGION. Because the Church is universal and has members in every country, even though it be pagan or non-Catholic, she finds it advisable to come to some agreement with the governments of countries to ensure liberty of worship for her members. Hence she arranges concordats, receives diplomatic representatives from various countries, sends legates and nuncios (*qq.v.*) to deal with foreign governments on her behalf. The Church does not interfere with the private political views of Catholics, who are consequently free to choose any political party whose tenets or activities are not contrary to Christian doctrine. The dictum that "The Church should not interfere in politics" is an easy and quite misleading phrase. Politics is bound up with human acts, with which the Church is very much concerned; she is therefore liable to have to interfere in politics at any time, not politically but morally. The agitation against "Political Catholicism" in certain countries is partly a dishonest opposition to this concern for good morals; but partly also it has been provoked by the political activities of Catholic individuals and parties improperly claiming to act in the Church's name. An extremely vicious form of "Political Catholicism" consists in "looking upon pure politics, social politics, national politics, not only as something wholly independent of religion, but as being the standard by which we should determine the degree to which Catholic Christianity may be utilized in public life" (Weiss).

POLYANDRY, the having by one wife of more than one husband at the same time, is contrary to a primary precept (*q.v.*) of the natural law, for by making parentage uncertain and in other ways it is fundamentally incompatible with the institution of marriage.

POLYGAMY, the having by one husband of more than one wife at the same time, is contrary to divine law and probably also to a secondary precept (*q.v.*) of the natural law, being opposed to, but not absolutely and essentially incompatible with, the good estate of marriage. In the age of the Jewish patriarchs the state of humanity was such that the prohibition of polygamy was suspended and was tolerated by the Mosaic law. Only the first marriage of a polygamist can be valid. But it may be that none of the marriages is valid, *viz.*, if indissolubility has been expressly excluded. In any case a polygamist convert may profit by the Pauline Privilege (*q.v.*) and the pope may, for a grave reason, especially in case of doubt, use his supreme power and dissolve whichever marriage was the valid one.

POLYPHONY. Music in which one or more melodies are added as accompaniment to a given melody; counterpoint. In the classical period of polyphonic writing (*c.* 1450-1650) are found the resources of fugue and free imitation developed within the limitations of the modes, a growing tendency towards the use of accidentals (particularly in the final cadence of a minor mode) and the dawning of the dominant seventh, etc., leading to the developments which characterize the music of the later time (1600-1700). See PLAINSONG; MUSIC.

POLYTHEISM. The belief in and worship of more than one God. Certain heretics, *e.g.*, some of the monophysites, fell into tritheism by regarding the Blessed Trinity as three Gods, and an accusation of this error is often made against all Christians by Moslems.

PONENTE (It., proposer). One who submits and reports on a case for a Roman congregation, particularly the cardinal appointed to take charge of a cause for beatification.

PONTIFEX MAXIMUS (Lat., the Supreme Pontiff). i. A title of the pope asserting his supremacy and sovereignty over the whole Church. It is related to the High Priest of the Jews and to ii below.

ii. A title of the emperors as heads of the principal college of priests in pagan Rome. It was abandoned to the pope in the West by Gratian, in 375, but survived at Constantinople till the 5th century.

PONTIFF (Lat., *pontifex*, a high-priest). Any bishop. *Supreme, Sovereign Pontiff:* the pope. This word is commonly derived from *facere*, to make, and *pontem*, a bridge (between the gods and men), but the first syllable may be from Oscan-Umbrian *puntis*, sacrifice.

PONTIFICAL. See also PAPAL.

PONTIFICAL CHAPEL, The (It. *Cappella Pontificia*). Those persons and bodies who attend officially on the pope at certain solemn functions, such as consistories. They are principally, as they enter in order of precedence before the pope, the preacher and confessor apostolic, procurators of mendicant orders, private chaplains and clerics, consistorial advocates, privy chamberlains, nota-

ries of the Signatura, clerks of the Camera Apostolica, auditors of the Rota and the Master of the Sacred Palace, the Master of the Sacred Hospice, the penitentiaries of St. Peter's, mitred abbots and the Commendatore S. Spirito, bishops and archbishops, ditto assistant at the Throne, the College of Cardinals, the Vice-chamberlain, the prince assistant at the Throne and the Governor of the Vatican City; after the Pope: the Dean of the Rota, protonotaries apostolic, generals of religious orders, the chapter of canons of St. Peter's.

PONTIFICAL FAMILY, The (It. *Famiglia Pontificia*). All those persons who are in the immediate service of the pope and fulfil duties in his household. They are principally the palatine cardinals and prelates, ten privy chamberlains (participants), the parish priest and sacristan of the household (always an Augustinian friar), the confessor (a Servite), the master of the hospice and the marshal of the conclave (both Roman princes). In a more extended sense the Family includes all domestic prelates, chamberlains, lay and clerical, the various guards, etc.

PONTIFICAL GENDARMERIE. The Corps of Pontifical Gendarmes, established by Pope Pius VII in 1816, polices the palace and city of the Vatican.

PONTIFICAL MASS. i. At the throne. A high Mass solemnly sung by a cardinal, by a bishop in his own diocese, or an abbot in his own abbey (elsewhere by permission). In addition to the usual ministers there are an assistant priest, two assistant deacons and at least nine acolytes; a seventh candle is lit on the altar. During the singing of Terce the bishop is vested from the altar, either where he is going to celebrate or in a side chapel. He begins the Mass at the usual place but continues from the introit to the offertory at his throne (*q.v.*); the rest takes place at the altar as usual, except that the bishop washes his hands after the cleansing of the chalice, sings the blessing with three signs of the cross, and says the last gospel as he goes back to his throne or to where he is to unvest.

ii. Bishops outside their dioceses, titular bishops and certain other prelates may sing pontifical Mass at the faldstool. There is only one extra minister, an assistant priest; the celebrant may vest and unvest at the faldstool, which is placed towards the epistle-side and where he says the first part of the Mass.

PONTIFICAL SERVICES. Services, usually Mass, Vespers or Benediction, celebrated solemnly by a bishop, or by a cardinal, abbot or other prelate with the right to wear *pontificalia* thereat.

PONTIFICALS, ALIA. The ceremonial ornaments proper to a bishop. The name is ordinarily confined to the pectoral cross and ring (worn always), mitre and pastoral staff (used whenever pontificating) and, at pontifical Mass, buskins, sandals, gloves, tunicle and dalmatic (the last two worn under the chasuble). The throne (*q.v.*) is also included among the *pontificalia*. Cardinals have the right to them and they are granted to abbots, and also to most protonotaries apostolic (without the pastoral staff and throne). Other prelates to whom certain pontificals are conceded are the Guardian of the Holy Land, the heads of the collegiate chapters of Carignano and our Lady of Help in Genoa, the cathedral canons of Bari, Benevento, Lucca, Ravenna and others. In the past they were also worn by the English cathedral priors (*q.v.*).

PONTIFICALE ROMANUM (Lat., The Roman Pontifical). A liturgical book containing the prayers and ceremonies of certain rites ordinarily reserved to a bishop. The first part is concerned with persons and provides for the administration of Confirmation and Holy Orders, consecration of a bishop, conferring the *pallium*, blessing of an abbot or abbess, consecration of a virgin, blessing and coronation of a sovereign, blessing of a knight and the reception of a member of a military order. Part II is concerned with things: the consecration of a church, altar, cemetery, chalice, the blessing of a bell, laying the foundation-stone of a church, reconciliation of a church, etc., and certain obsolete blessings. The third part provides for the announcement of movable feasts on the Epiphany, the expulsion of penitents on Ash Wednesday and their reconciliation on Maundy Thursday, blessing of the holy oils, order of a diocesan synod, the solemn degradation of a cleric, the visitation of a parish, the reception of a legate and of a sovereign prince and the absolutions for the dead.

PONTIFICATE, TO. To celebrate Mass or otherwise officiate solemnly, wearing *pontificalia*.

POOR CATHOLICS, The. A religious society of lay-preachers authorized by Pope Innocent III, in 1208, to preach against the Albigensians and Waldensians (*qq.v.*), the second of whom were sometimes called by the same name. They were not a success and gave place to preaching friars of St. Dominic.

POOR CLARES, The. Nuns of the second order of St. Francis of Assisi, founded by him and St. Clare in 1212. There are two branches. The Colettines are strictly enclosed; they rise for night office at midnight, and again at 5 a.m.; fasting and abstinence are perpetual; the Divine Office is recited, not sung; 6 hours of work a day; one hour's recreation; bed at 8 p.m. They may possess no property, even in common. The habit is brown and they go barefoot except out of

doors when they wear sandals. The Urbanists follow a modification of this rule, first approved by Pope Urban IV in 1263, and some of their convents undertake external work. There are convents, of both branches in Great Britain, Ireland and North America. See also CAPUCHINESSES.

POOR HANDMAIDS OF JESUS, The. An unenclosed congregation, founded in 1851, working for the sick and orphans. Black habit, girdled with cord.

POOR MEN OF LYONS, The. The name under which the Waldensians (*q.v.*) were condemned by Pope Lucius III in 1184. The *Humiliati* (*q.v.*) were known as the Poor Men of Lombardy.

POOR SERVANTS OF THE MOTHER OF GOD AND THE POOR, The. An unenclosed congregation of sisters, founded in London by Mother Mary Taylor, in 1868, for work amongst the poor and outcast, conducting refuges for penitents, dispensaries, etc. No lay-sisters. Numerous establishments in the British Isles, and a few abroad. Black tunic and veil, dark blue scapular. A somewhat similar Polish institute of the same name was founded in 1845.

POPE (Gr. πάππας, father). i. Title. Since the 11th century this has been the distinguishing title of the bishop of Rome as the supreme pontiff of the Catholic Church, and is used of no one else in the West; the first known example of this use is in the writings of St. Ennodius (*d.* 521). The title is complete in itself, without the addition of the words "of Rome"; the pope signs himself *Pius Papa XII*. In the East, it is a title of the Orthodox patriarch of Alexandria and is the name for all Greek-speaking priests; but to use it for a Russian, Rumanian or Serbian priest (*pop*), though common, is considered wanting in respect. An Italo-Greek priest also is *papàs*. The pope's full designation is: Bishop of Rome, Vicar of Jesus Christ, Successor of the Prince of the Apostles, Supreme Pontiff of the Universal Church, Patriarch of the West, Primate of Italy, Archbishop and Metropolitan of the Roman Province, and Sovereign of the State of the City of the Vatican.
ii. Office. The pope, as bishop of Rome, is the successor of St. Peter, and therefore the visible head of the Church on earth, the vicegerent of Christ, and the supreme ruler of all Christians. Christ commanded Peter to "feed my lambs, feed my sheep" (John xxi, 16, 17), which meant that he was to rule and govern the faithful and their pastors. He is therefore the supreme judge in all matters of faith and morals, in pronouncing upon which he may exercise infallibility (*q.v.*). He also exercises supreme jurisdiction and may legislate for the whole Church and dispense from canonical law. He alone can erect, suppress, or otherwise modify

dioceses and mission territories; confirm the election of bishops or translate or depose them; and fully approve new religious institutes. He reserves to himself the beatification and canonization of saints and the absolution of certain sins, and judges appeals from all lower authorities. But he cannot alter the faith once delivered to the saints or suppress or modify any essential rites or dispense from the divine law. Much of the papal power may be and is delegated, *e.g.*, to the Roman congregations, delegates apostolic, and others.

iii. The number of popes since St. Peter is not certain; there are 262 commonly enumerated. Of these, 105 were Romans, 77 other Italians, 15 Frenchmen, 14 Greeks, 7 Syrians, 4 Tuscans, 4 Germans, 3 Spaniards, 2 Africans, 2 Dalmatians, 2 Lombards, 2 Sardinians, and one each Alsatian, Burgundian, Calabrian Greek, Dutch, English (Adrian IV, 1154-59), Lorrainer, Ostrogoth, Samnite, Sicilian, Sicilian Greek, Umbrian and Galilean Jew. Some of these are uncertain, and a dozen are definitely unknown. 41 belonged to religious orders: 25 Benedictines, 5 Franciscans, 4 Dominicans, 3 Cistercians, 2 Canons Regular, 1 Augustinian friar, 1 Theatine and 1 Byzantine monk. 76 are venerated as saints, 7 beatified, and the cause of Pius X is begun. So far, the last canonized pope is Pius V (*d.* 1572) and the last non-Italian the Dutch Adrian VI (*d.* 1523). See Appendix III.

POPE, ABDICATION OF A. The pope validly abdicates his office without requiring the consent of the cardinals or of any other body in the Church. It is for the pope alone to judge whether such abdication is lawful and expedient. The classic example of the abdication of a pope is that of St. Celestine V in 1294.

POPE, AUTHORITY OF THE. Although elected by the college of cardinals, the pope's authority is not derived from them, but is given by God directly. He exercises it *de iure divino* (by divine right) as successor of St. Peter. He is infallible (*q.v.*) in teaching, and he has full and supreme power of jurisdiction (*q.v.*) over the whole Church, and directly and immediately over every Catholic, and all this in virtue of his office and permanently.

POPE, DEPOSITION OF A. A pope can only be deposed for heresy, expressed or implied, and then only by a general council. It is not strictly deposition, but a declaration of fact, since by his heresy he has already ceased to be head of the Church. This has never occurred; the deposition of antipopes was a different matter, for these had never in fact been pope. The case of John XXIII at the Council of Constance (1415) was a combination of deposition and forced resignation, and in any case his election was doubtfully valid.

POPE, ELECTION OF A. When a vacancy occurs, a new pope is elected by the votes of the cardinals (*q.v.*) meeting in conclave (*q.v.*).

POPE, PRIMACY OF. This is a primacy not merely of honour but of jurisdiction (*q.v.*), comprising the power of legislating, of judging and of securing obedience and submission by appropriate sanctions. Like all the pope's authority it is universal (*i.e.*, it is over all Christians), it is ordinary (*i.e.*, *ex officio* and permanent), it comes directly from Christ and is exercised immediately (not necessarily through bishops) over the faithful. It is independent of the civil authority. Thus it comes about that the pope is the centre of unity and communion, and communion with the pope is the hallmark of Catholic orthodoxy. None is exempt from this primacy and nothing is lacking to it which is necessary for the teaching, ruling and governing of the flock. There is no appeal from it, not even to an œcumenical council.

"POPE JOAN." That a female called Joanna at one time occupied the Holy See disguised as a man, and was betrayed by giving birth to a child, was recorded and believed by several responsible chroniclers between the 13th and the 16th centuries. It is now amply demonstrated that the story is a myth; how it arose is still in dispute.

POPERY. The first recorded use of this pejorative expression for the Catholic Church and Faith was in 1534. The adjective "popish" was known in 1528.

PORT ROYAL. A convent of the French Bernardine congregation of Cistercian nuns, Port Royal de Paris, brought thither by its abbess, Mère Angélique Arnauld, in 1626, and an establishment outside the city, Port Royal des Champs, which was a centre for priests and laymen. Some of these, the "solitaries of Port Royal," conducted schools for boys. Port Royal had profound influence on the intellectual and religious life of 17th-century France, both on account of the gifts and character of its members and of the new educational methods of the *petites écoles*, some of whose effects may be seen in the *lycées* of to-day. But Port Royal was also a centre of Jansenism (*q.v.*) and for 50 years stood out against ecclesiastical authority; the Port Royalists were "pure as angels but proud as devils" and it was suppressed by Pope Clement IX in 1713. Pascal's attack on the Jesuits in his *Provincial Letters* was an effect of this dispute.

PORTABLE ALTAR. A square or oblong piece of natural stone, about 1 in. thick and large enough to allow the Host and chalice to rest on it. It is consecrated by a bishop with the same ceremonies as for a fixed altar, and relics of martyrs are sealed in the cavity provided. This stone is used (a) to be inserted in the top of an unconsecrated altar structure in a church so that Mass may be said thereon; (b) to be laid in any place, e.g., on a table in a room, for the purpose of saying Mass there. The "privilege of a portable altar," granted by law to all bishops and by apostolic indult to others, is the permission to say Mass on one of these stones in any decent and respectable place, except at sea (cf., altar, altar-stone, antimension).

PORTER. The lowest of the minor orders; doorkeeper (q.v.).

PORTIUNCULA, The (Old It., the little piece). i. A ruined chapel near Assisi, given by Cluniac monks to St. Francis, who rebuilt it and made it the birthplace of his order. It is now enclosed within the basilica of S. Maria degli Angeli. It gives its name to:
ii. The Portiuncula Indulgence or Pardon of Assisi. This is a plenary indulgence (q.v.) which may be gained for the dead as often as one visits the chapel during the day of Aug. 2. In the course of time it was extended, for the same date, to all churches belonging in any way to the Franciscan order and since then, on other dates, to the principal churches of some other orders, e.g., the Dominicans, Carmelites, Servites, Minims, Benedictines. To gain the indulgence the usual conditions (q.v.) must be observed and at every visit to the church Our Father, Hail Mary and Gloria Patri must be said at least six times for the pope's intention. The origin of this pardon is a subject of dispute.

PORTSMOUTH (Portusmuthensis). An English see, suffragan of Westminster, formed in 1882 by the separation from Southwark of Hampshire, Berkshire, the Wight and Channel Islands, which before the Reformation belonged to the dioceses of Winchester, Salisbury and Coutances. On the estates of Tichborne of Tichborne and Easton of East Hendred the faith was preserved through penal times, the parish of Winchester was established as a mission in 1674, and six others date from the 18th century. There are four Benedictine abbeys in this diocese (Douay, Farnborough, Quarr and Ryde). The patrons of the diocese are our Lady Immaculate and St. Edmund of Canterbury (born at Abingdon), and the cathedral is dedicated in honour of St. John the Divine.

PORTUGAL, THE CHURCH IN. The revolution of 1910 repudiated the concordat of 1886 with the Holy See, separated church and state, expelled religious orders, and confiscated ecclesiastical property. Subsequent civil upheavals brought about a modification of governmental attitude and in 1918 diplomatic relations with the Holy See were resumed, the former embassy being replaced by a legation: an apostolic nuncio resides in Lisbon. Practically all the people of the country, numbering 6¼ millions, are Catholics. There are 3 metropolitan sees (the archbishop of Lisbon has the title and precedence of patriarch) and 12 suffragan dioceses. The Portuguese government entered into a new concordat with the Holy See in 1932.

PORTUGUESE HYMN, The. The hymn Adeste fideles, whose words and air were probably written by John F. Wade at Douay, c. 1740. The above name is usually ascribed to its having been first sung in England at the Portuguese embassy chapel in London; it is said that the tune is heard, sung to Portuguese words, among Goanese seamen.

PORTUS MAGNI. See PORTUSMUTHENSIS.

PORTUSMUTHENSIS. The adjectival form of the name of the see of Portsmouth (q.v.) used in the designation of its bishop in Latin documents. Noun: Portusmutum or Portus Magnus.

POSITIVISM (from its recognition of positive facts only). A system of philosophy that rejects all metaphysics. It has taken various forms, that of Spencer affirming absolutely an unknowable, differing from that of Comte, who asserts that supra-sensible realities, if there are any such, are outside the reach of his particular method or system, which he believes perfect.

POSSESSION, DEMONIACAL. The Church has always acknowledged the possibility of demonic possession and instituted the order of exorcist (q.v.) to combat it. At present priests alone are allowed to exorcise demoniacs and that only with express permission of the bishop. In countries where the bulk of the people is baptized diabolical possession is apparently rare. Possession is not necessarily a token of the sinfulness of the person possessed, for God seems sometimes for some hidden reason to allow even the innocent to be exposed to the physical violence of the Devil. Possession is of different degrees and often intermittent. It manifests itself by the inward control of human limbs and organs by an agent distinct from their owner.

POSSIBLE, POSSIBILITY. The possible is that which may be. There is an absolute possible and a relative: the first implies mere non-repugnance as regards existence, as "another world like ours"; the second is that which can be produced by some indicated cause, as the carving of a horse from a block of marble by an artist. The possible is opposed to the impossible, which is metaphysical (a square circle), physical (to jump over the moon) and moral (to avoid all venial sin).

POSTCOMMUNION. A final prayer or prayers, corresponding in form and number to the collects, said or sung after the communion-verse at Mass. It is a petition for profit from the fruits of the mysteries celebrated and often contains a reference to the feast of the day. On ferias of Lent it is followed by the *oratio super populum* (*q.v.*).

POSTULANT (Lat. *postulare*, to ask for). One preparing to be clothed as a novice in a religious house by means of a preliminary experience of the life. He wears lay clothes, or a cassock, and follows the usual community exercises under the novice-master. The period of postulancy varies in different congregations, rarely exceeding six months; but for all women and lay-brother postulants for orders with solemn vows it must be at least that period.

POSTULATE THE PALLIUM, TO. Within three months of his appointment every archbishop of the Latin rite must postulate, *i.e.*, ask the Holy See for a pallium (*q.v.*), which he does three times, "earnestly," "more earnestly," "most earnestly." He receives it from the hands of a bishop delegated by the pope to confer it and to accept his oath of obedience. Until this is done his metropolitan powers and privileges are in abeyance.

POSTULATOR. The official who prosecutes, either in his own name or in that of others, the cause of beatification of a servant of God, or canonization of a *beatus*, before the Congregation of Rites or other competent tribunal. He must be a priest, and have a fixed residence in Rome. He may appoint assistants, who are called vice-postulators.

POTENCY, POTENTIA, POTENTIALITY. An aptitude for doing or receiving something; correlative of act (*q.v.*, i). Active potency, which is a species of quality, is synonymous with a faculty or a power, such as the will; passive potency is an aptitude susceptive of something—as a piece of wax is susceptive of roundness. Passive potency may be objective, subjective or obediential, according as the potency is a pure possibility, *e.g.*, another world like the present one; or is in a subject already existing, as roundness in wax which is square; or is susceptive of a perfection beyond its natural capacity, as the soul's aptitude to have grace.

POVERELLO, IL (It., the little poor one). St. Francis of Assisi.

POVERTY. i. Social students mean by poverty the condition of those who have not in food, clothing, shelter and recreation what is necessary to keep them up to the normal standard of health and well-being proper to human creatures. Many a man is poor through his own fault; in great measure, however, social and economic conditions are responsible. The problem resolves itself into finding work for all those whose sole capital is their capacity for work, and distributing

wealth produced more fairly, *i.e.*, getting rid of the two harmful extremes, destitution of the many and the great wealth of the few. The poverty praised by Christianity is not the destitution or indigence connoted by the term as used above, and the Church has always striven to ameliorate the condition of the poor, so that they may reach a level of reasonable comfort. That poverty which Christianity holds up as an ideal for its followers is a matter of spirit and degree, a reasonable sufficiency of goods for decent human life, without superfluity. It is Christian poverty to go without, to give up, to lose rather than to gain, to give rather than to receive, to have little rather than much. And it is only in love that this poverty can be embraced.

ii. As an evangelical counsel. The free renunciation, in whole or in part, of the use or ownership or both use and ownership of one's temporal goods to follow Christ; recommended by Christ as a remedy against the dangers to which the possession of riches gives rise, such as greed, vainglory, and excessive solicitude. The practice of the counsel is usually given stability by a vow of poverty taken either by a person living in the world, or more usually, by one in religion. The vow of poverty varies in its range in the different religious orders from a limited renunciation of the use of worldly goods without leave to the complete and perpetual renunciation of dominion over them.

POVERTY, MONASTIC, consists in the holding of property in common by those who are individually bound by vow to have no personal possessions. There is no limit to the amount which may be held in common, but luxury, ostentation or mere accumulation of capital is not in accordance with the spirit of the religious state and denotes a relaxed monastic observance. The mendicant orders (*q.v.*) repudiated even property in common, but the Council of Trent (on account of the growing inconveniences and the abuses of scandal and inefficiency liable to arise from such a system) allowed them to hold sufficient property to ensure an adequate income; but the Friars Minor and Capuchins conform to the stricter discipline (*cf.*, Rule of St. Francis). The Passionists are allowed no endowments, but the congregation may own its monasteries and the necessary land attached.

POVERTY, VOW OF. This vow taken by a monk, nun, friar, etc., at profession involves the complete renunciation of all personal property. At simple profession the religious by this vow gives up his right to use any property he may have or acquire but retains the possession thereof (nor can his superior deprive him of it); he makes what arrangement he pleases for its administration and the disposal of income. At solemn profession he must dispose of its possession (not necessarily in favour of his monastery or order);

his use of common property or disposal of what may come to him by inheritance, etc., is at the discretion and will of his superior, according to the rules and customs of his order. The Fathers of Charity always retain the legal title to their personal property, but entirely give up the use of it; a solemnly professed Jesuit, Friar Minor or Capuchin may not receive a legacy or inheritance and dispose thereof in favour of the order: instead it passes to his next-of-kin.

POWER OF THE KEYS, The. An expression, derived from Matt. xvi, 19, denoting the complete ecclesiastical authority of orders, jurisdiction and doctrine conferred by our Lord in the first place on St. Peter and his successors and then on the other members of the hierarchy in their degree. Popularly and in the writings of many of the Fathers and other theologians it refers only to the power of binding and loosing exercised in the sacrament of Penance.

POWERS (1 Pet. iii, 22, etc.). One of the choirs of the celestial hierarchy (*q.v.*).

PRACTISING CATHOLIC. A loose non-technical term applied to a Catholic who accepts all Catholic teaching, avails himself of the sacraments of the Church, worships at Mass on Sundays at least, and in general endeavours to live according to the teaching of his religion.

PRÆCONIUM PASCHALE (Lat. Easter proclamation). Another name for the *Exsultet* (*q.v.*).

PRÆMUNIRE. The name given to an English statute, from the writ of its process, of Edward III, re-enacted in 1393 (16 Ric. II, c. 5), which was designed to enforce the statute of Provisors (*q.v.*). It forbade the admission and execution of papal instruments within the realm and the carrying of any suit (*e.g.*, in the matter of a benefice) to the papal court when the courts of the realm had cognizance therein; the penalty was outlawry, forfeiture of lands and other properties to the crown, and arrest. After the Reformation these penalties were invoked in several of the penal laws (*q.v.*) against Catholics.

PRÆTERMISSI (Lat., the omitted). Those sufferers whose claim to be martyrs was deferred at the time of the first and second beatifications of English martyrs. Their cause continues to be examined at Rome. They number 116, namely, 39 secular priests, 48 religious and 29 laymen, of whom some died in prison and others on the scaffold.

PRAGMATIC SANCTION (Lat. *pragmatica sanctio*, a term for certain fundamental laws ordained by the Roman emperors). The name given to several imperial and royal decrees; the one of chief ecclesiastical importance was that issued by King Charles VII at Bourges in 1438 limiting the rights of the Holy See in nominations to bishoprics and abbacies, in collecting revenues, in matters of appeal, interdict, etc. This Gallican act was suppressed in theory by Louis XI, but remained in force till 1516. The so-called Pragmatic Sanction of St. Louis was a 15th-century forgery.

PRAGMATISM (Gr. πρᾶγμα, work, action, result, end). A system which consists in proving the truth of a proposition or even of a metaphysical system by its practical results. Thus the good and the true are manifested by the useful. The Pragmatism of William James and the Humanism of Schiller differ only in name, and assert the pre-eminence of the practical over the speculative, of will over mind; they have their origin in the philosophy of Kant. The true doctrine holds the pre-eminence of the speculative over the practical. The Decalogue is not true just because it happens to work well or is the best for the individual and the society—it is true in itself. Pragmatism judges of the truth of metaphysical principles by their moral consequences— this is the topsy-turvydom of ethics.

PRAYER. i. The "raising of the mind and heart to God" (St. John Damascene). It is, after devotion (*q.v.*), the highest exercise of the virtue of religion, and includes worship, praise, thanksgiving, sorrow, reparation, and petition. It may be mental or vocal. It is to God primarily that we pray, because he is the source of all our good; but we ought to pray also to the saints, especially to our Blessed Lady, in order that through their prayers and merits God may deign to hear us. It is of faith that prayer is necessary for salvation, at least with the necessity of precept. Therefore it is to be made frequently during life. Good works, since they have an impetratory value, are called virtual prayer, and the man of prayer is not necessarily he who spends most time in its formal vocal or mental exercise; prayer is by definition an attitude of mind. It is a common error to suppose that prayer necessarily involves petition, but this is only one aspect of prayer: the highest form is that of adoration or worship. But the prayer of asking must not be despised (*cf.*, the Lord's Prayer, and 1 Tim. ii, 1), and all prayer (of adoration, thanksgiving, etc.) at least implicitly asks for God's graces, and obtains them. See UN-ANSWERED PRAYER. "Although public prayer, as proceeding from the Church herself, excels any other . . . nevertheless all prayers, even those made in the most private way, have their dignity and their efficacy and are of great benefit to the whole Mystical Body: for in that body there can be no good and virtuous deed done by an individual member which does not, through the communion of saints, redound to the welfare of all" (Pope Pius XII).

ii. A collect (*q.v.*).

PRAYER, ATTITUDE OF. i. Private. The position of the body is a matter of indifference when one is specifically engaged in prayer (as distinct from when the mind is engaged in prayer and the body concerned with other matters, *e.g.*, riding a bicycle), but it is nevertheless universally recognized that a bodily attitude of attention is most desirable. Probably most Christians nowadays prefer to kneel with clasped hands, the body partly supported against a *prie-dieu* or other thing. Many find that to stand erect, facing a crucifix or other image, is less conducive to slackening and inattention. But any attitude, pacing up and down, sitting, lying at length, is permissible, provided that any position of ease is not adopted through laziness, but on account of fatigue, ill-health, and so forth.

ii. In public prayer the attitude of the body is more important because here the whole congregation is united in a common act of worship of which the outward manifestation is an integral part. So far as the laity are concerned, there are no definite rules laid down, but rubricians are substantially agreed as to what these attitudes should be, though they may be reasonably modified by local custom. These is no doubt that standing is the normal position at Christian public prayer; the celebrant stands throughout at low Mass, as do those assisting at the Divine Office, except during the lessons at Matins and the psalms, when sitting is conceded. "Those who assist at low Mass kneel always . . . except while the gospel is read" (General Rubric, xvii, 2), but at all other liturgical services kneeling is abnormal—it is a penitential sign of Advent and Lent. Particularly during the singing of the collects, the preface and the post-communions at a sung or high Mass is standing the proper attitude; during these and the canon the celebrant prays with outstretched hands.

iii. There is no direction in the Roman Missal for a prostration throughout the consecration. On the contrary, Pius X granted an indulgence of seven years and seven quarantines each time and a plenary indulgence once a week to all who should gaze on the Blessed Sacrament at the moment of elevation, saying with devotion the words, "My Lord and my God"; and the thurifer is ordered to incense the Host from the epistle-side presumably in order not to obscure it from the people.

PRAYER, DISCURSIVE. Mental prayer in which reasoning or reflection is used in order to rouse the will to spiritual endeavour. It is the same as meditation (*q.v.*).

PRAYER, MENTAL. All kinds of prayer other than vocal; prayer which is directly an exercise of the mind and will, and for which the use of the organs of speech is not essential. It includes meditation (*q.v.*) and affective prayer, into which meditation normally develops, and contemplation (*q.v.*). All who

are striving to attain a substantial degree of holiness are urged to devote an allotted portion of time each day to mental prayer: hence it forms part of the daily routine for priests and for religious. It is supremely important for those engaged in the apostolate, that they may not be "as sounding brass or a tinkling cymbal."

PRAYER, VOCAL. Prayer in which the use of the organs of speech is essential (in this it differs from mental prayer) and which often, though not necessarily, consists in the repetition or reading of a set formula, *e.g.*, a psalm. It is an act of worship of the whole man, soul and body, and all public prayer or other prayer in common is necessarily vocal. The supreme form of vocal prayer is the liturgy, which is the voice of the Bride of Christ, and this fact alone is sufficient warning against any tendency to regard vocal prayer as something inferior to mental prayer. "And if thou by the prayer get devotion, look then that this devotion be only in affection—that is to say, in great desire of God with spiritual delight. Hold fast thy saying and break not lightly off; for oft it falleth that praying with the mouth getteth and keepeth devotion, and if a man cease saying, devotion vanisheth away" (Walter Hilton).

PRAYER-BOOK. A book of prayers for private use, as opposed to the official liturgical books of the Church or special editions of them for the use of lay-people. They usually contain one or more "methods of hearing Mass"; preparation and examination of conscience before confession; prayers for morning and evening and before and after holy communion, and a varied selection of devotions to our Lord, in honour of our Lady and the saints, and for particular occasions. The most widely used English prayer book is "The Garden of the Soul" (*q.v.*). The Catholic Church has no book corresponding to the Anglican "Book of Common Prayer" (*cf.*, Book of Hours, Primer).

PRAYER OF CHRIST, The. A feast observed in some places on the Tuesday after Septuagesima, wherein is honoured, not the Lord's Prayer or "Our Father," but the agony of Jesus Christ in the garden of Gethsemani (Matt. xxvi, 36-46).

PRAYER FOR ENGLAND, The. i. A prayer for the intercession of our Lady on behalf of England beginning, "O blessed Virgin Mary, Mother of God and our most gentle queen and mother," recited in the vernacular by the priest at Sunday Benediction in England. A similar but different prayer is in use in Wales.

ii. A prayer to God, asking for the intercession of the saints and invoking by name the memory of Eleutherius, Celestine, Gregory, Augustine, Columba, Aidan, Alban and Thomas Becket, on behalf of England: "Let not their memory perish from before thee, O

Lord." It is recited by the priest in the vernacular when Benediction is offered specifically for the conversion of England. This prayer forms part of a daily office of prayers written in Latin by Cardinal Wiseman in 1839 for the English College at Rome and still in use there.

PRAYER OF JESUS, The. "Lord Jesus Christ, Son of God, have mercy on me, a sinner." This prayer, said frequently and accompanied by a metany (*q.v.*), is of common use among Byzantine Christians, especially the Orthodox of Russia. It is associated with their devotion to the Holy Name.

PRAYER OF MANASSES, The. The prayer of penitence commonly thus called has no authentic connexion with that referred to in II Paralipomenon xxxiii, 18-19. It is first found in the "Apostolic Constitutions"; its text is printed at the end of the Latin Vulgate with III and IV Esdras and in the Greek *Euchologion* and translations are sometimes found in popular prayer books.

PRAYER OVER THE PEOPLE. See ORATIO SUPER POPULUM.

PRAYER OF QUIET. The first stage of the mystical union (*q.v.*) is called the state of quietude. Its characteristic prayer is the prayer of quiet. This prayer begins in passive recollection, when the eyes close, the ears cease to attend to outward objects (although they still hear them) and the body remains perfectly still. The imagination, however, is restless and wandering. Then God makes himself felt by the soul in an obscure way as a great Reality or Presence, and the heart reposes in tranquil love of him and is gently permeated with spiritual sweetness, to which sensible devotion (*q.v.*) bears no comparison. Such delightful prayer is at first of very brief duration, and the habitual condition of the soul is one of arid contemplation. Later, however, it lasts longer until, towards the end of the state of quietude, it becomes in a modified form habitual.

PRAYER OF SIMPLICITY. Called also, of faith, of simple regard, or of loving attention. It is the first contemplative prayer. "Meditation (*q.v.*) is very good in its time, and very useful at the beginning of the spiritual life, but one must not stop there; for by fidelity to mortification and recollection the soul ordinarily receives a purer and more intimate prayer, which may be called prayer of simplicity and consists in a simple look, regard or loving attention directed towards God himself or one of his mysteries or some other Christian truth. The soul ceases to reason and employs a sweet contemplation which keeps it peaceful, attentive to and susceptible of the divine operations and impressions which the Holy Ghost communicates to it" (Bossuet). Those who distinguish two kinds of contemplation (*q.v.*) call this ac-

quired contemplation, and teach that it is the ultimate term of the natural development of the spiritual life: it brings the soul to the borders of mysticism (*q.v.*).

PRAYER OF UNION. Contemplation (*q.v.*) in all its grades, except the prayer of simplicity (*q.v.*). It is also called mystical union (*q.v.*).

PRAYER FOR WALES, The. A prayer for the conversion of the Welsh people said, generally in English but sometimes in Welsh, by priest and people in the dioceses of Cardiff and Menevia at Benediction and on other occasions; it is followed by invocations of our Lady Help of Christians, St. David and St. Winefride.

PRAYERS AFTER LOW MASS. Hail Mary (thrice), *Salve Regina,* a prayer for sinners and the liberty of the Church, and a prayer for the intercession of St. Michael, prescribed to be said, in Latin (as in Italy) or the vernacular, by priest and people after every private Mass, by Pope Leo XIII in 1884. They are not said after a conventual or parochial Mass or at any other low Mass which has some special external solemnity (*e.g.,* at a wedding) and on some other occasions. In Ireland *De profundis* is added for the souls of the victims of religious persecution, and of those whose provisions for posthumous remembrance were destroyed during penal times. These prayers are said only by the Maronites and Malabarese in the East. They were originally appointed to be said for the solution of the Roman Question (*q.v.*); they are now offered for the people of Russia.

PRAYING TO SAINTS. See INVOCATION.

PRE-ADAMITES. The existence on earth of human beings, *i.e.,* beings with an animal body and a rational soul, previous to the appearance on earth of Adam and Eve and extinct at the time of that appearance, is an idle guess unsupported by natural science, and contrary to the tenor of Holy Scripture.

PREACHER, The. The name sometimes used for the book of Ecclesiastes; its author, the preacher, is by tradition King Solomon.

PREACHER APOSTOLIC. An office, always held by a Capuchin friar, whose duty it is to preach to the pope and his court on certain feasts in Advent and every week in Lent. The holder is a palatine prelate and member of the Pontifical Family.

PREACHER GENERAL. A degree conferred by the master general on Dominican friars distinguished for their assiduous labours in preaching over a long period. Such an one is addressed as "The Venerable and Very Reverend Father N . . ."

PREACHERESSES, The. Nuns (*moniales*) of the Order of Preachers, formerly called "of the Second Order" though in fact St. Dominic's first foundation (at Prouille, 1206). They are strictly enclosed, with solemn vows, and engaged in the singing of the Divine Office (Matins and Lauds at midnight) and manual labour, and have perpetual abstinence. They are a very integral part of the order and their prayers, fasts and disciplines are aimed at the salvation of souls and the strengthening of the friars in their work. They have two convents in England, at Carisbrooke (founded 1661 in Holland) and Old Headington (all other Dominican nuns in Great Britain are sisters of the third order (*q.v.*) regular). Habit: white tunic and scapular, linen wimple and fillet, black veil, black *cappa* in choir.

PREACHERS, THE ORDER OF. The Dominicans (*q.v.*).

PREACHING. The object of preaching is to instruct people in the Christian faith in order that they may know and love God and his revelation and lead a virtuous and charitable life; it is addressed both to the understanding and to the heart. The Council of Trent confirmed the doctrine that preaching is a principal office of bishops and ordered that their deputies, the priests of parishes, should preach at least on Sundays and holidays. This sermon is usually a discourse on the gospel of the day at the parochial Mass. Secular priests from outside the diocese and any religious may not preach in a public church without the bishop's permission. A deacon may be deputed to preach, but never a layman or a woman, even if a religious. Since the 17th century the importance of preaching has been more and more recognized, but at no time has it been other than auxiliary to public worship; popular preachers, especially at missions, can draw a great crowd, but extravagant cult of individual preachers or of exhortation for its own sake is practically unknown among Catholics.

PREBEND (Low Lat. *præbenda*, a pension). The stipend due to a canon from the revenues of a cathedral. Each canon is therefore a prebendary, but this name is often reserved for others, not members of the chapter, who are entitled to a share of the revenue (also called a *portionarius*); such a part-share or semi-prebend is a canonical benefice. Canons in Great Britain and Ireland have no prebends; for this and other reasons they do not reside at the cathedral and conduct divine service therein, but administer important parishes in the diocese.

PRECEDENCE is the right marshalling of people according to their rank, office, seniority, etc., for whatever ·purpose may be required, and an individual's or corporation's right to priority therein. In ecclesiastical precedence the pope always has first place and then the cardinals, even before other patriarchs; then bishops and other prelates, according to their rank, date of consecration and promotion determining the order amongst themselves. The Archbishop of Westminster always has precedence in England and Wales, and the Archbishop of Baltimore in the U.S.A. Secular clergy take precedence of regulars, among whom the order is canons regular, monks, friars, clerks regular; third orders come before confraternities, men before women. In processions precedence is to some extent governed by local custom. The Latin rite has no priority; precedence is settled without any reference to rite.

PRECENTOR (Lat., one who sings first). The master of the choir of a cathedral, collegiate or monastic church; a chief cantor (*q.v.*); the cantor who pre-intones the antiphons. As a dignitary the precentor no longer exists, except as a titular of honour in some cathedral chapters (*e.g.*, in Ireland), but the cleric in charge of the arrangements for divine worship may be so called.

PRECEPT, as distinct from a law, is a command given to a single person by his ecclesiastical superior. Unlike a law, it binds the person everywhere, even outside the territory of the superior. But it cannot be enforced judicially, and it ceases with the authority of the superior, unless imposed by a legal document or in the presence of two witnesses. See also COUNSELS AND PRECEPTS.

PRECEPTS OF CHARITY. The two great commandments given by Christ, "Thou shalt love the Lord thy God with thy whole heart and with thy whole soul, and with thy whole mind and with thy whole strength," and "Thou shalt love thy neighbour as thyself." The Ten Commandments given to Moses are comprised in these two. See LOVE OF GOD; LOVE OF OUR NEIGHBOUR.

PRECEPTS OF NATURAL LAW, The, are divided into primary and secondary. Primary are those the transgression of which entirely frustrates and does away with the object and end of a natural institution or law, *e.g.*, the artificial prevention of conception; these are absolutely unchangeable. Those are secondary whose transgression involves the hindering or making more difficult of the purpose of nature but does not absolutely nullify it. "Human nature is changeable, and therefore that which is natural to man may sometimes fail to hold good" (St. Thomas, II-II, lvii, 2, ad 1) and these secondary precepts in times and places God has dispensed for the hardness of men's hearts (*cf.*, Polygamy); but Christianity is the fulfilment of the law.

PRECEPTS OF THE CHURCH. The commandments of the Church (*q.v.*).

PRECEPTIVE. Imposing an obligation of observance, as opposed to directive, having the force only of an official recommendation.

PRECEPTORY. See COMMANDERY.

PRECES [FERIALES] (Lat., ferial prayers). A litany of versicles and responses, beginning with *Kyrie eleison* and the Lord's Prayer, said kneeling at all hours of the Divine Office, except Matins, Prime and Compline, on certain days. Those of Lauds and Vespers are the longest and are the same; the shorter form is common to the other hours. They are said immediately before the collect in the ferial office of Advent and Lent; but at Lauds and Vespers only on Wednesdays and Fridays of those seasons, and on ember days when the office is ferial. *Preces Dominicales,* a shortened form of the *feriales* said at Prime and Compline, are now abolished.

PRECIOUS BLOOD, The, of our Lord has been used from the time of the apostles as a synonym for the Redemption, and its outpouring as a symbol of the whole sacrifice of Calvary. In the Blessed Sacrament the Precious Blood is received under the species of bread equally with the Body, Soul and Divinity (and *vice versa*) by virtue of the indivisibility of Christ's glorified humanity and of the hypostatic union (*q.v.*). For the same reason the Blood actually shed at the Passion was reassumed by his body at the Resurrection and, according to St. Thomas, no alleged relic of the Holy Blood (*q.v.*) could possibly be genuine. On the other hand, Pope Benedict XIV taught that it was possible for such relics to exist disunited from the Godhead. A feast of the Most Precious Blood is kept by the Western church on July 1 (by the Passionists and others on the Friday after *Lætare* Sunday as well).

PRECONIZATION (Lat. *præconizare,* to announce publicly). The solemn confirmation given by the pope in consistory to appointments already made to episcopal sees and other consistorial offices.

PRECURSOR, The (Lat., forerunner). St. John the Baptist.

PREDELLA (It., a stool). i. The foot-pace (*q.v.*).
ii. A gradine (*q.v.*), and particularly a carving or painting on the vertical face thereof, whence
iii. The lowest and subsidiary compartment of a picture.

PREDESTINARIANISM. The heresy which, denying that God has a true will to save all mankind and not merely the elect (*q.v.*), declares that salvation or damnation depends on the will of God alone, irrespective of the action of the free will of the saved or damned, or of their foreseen merits or de-merits. Thus, according to this teaching, Predestination (*q.v.*) to glory or torment (Reprobation, *q.v.*) is based on an eternal decree of God, in which is comprised "irresistible grace" (*q.v.*) in the first case, and, in the second, a refusal of such grace and an impulsion of the will to sin. The heresy appeared shortly after the death of St. Augustine, and was rampant in the Reformation period; it received its clearest expression from Calvin.

PREDESTINATION. The act of foreordaining by which from eternity God decrees whatever he will do in time. The term particularly refers to the act of his providence (*q.v.*) which destines certain human beings for salvation. God knows from all eternity whether or not an individual will be saved, and from eternity he has decreed those graces by which a person is saved, including the grace of final perseverance. But man is free whether he does good or evil. God does not positively predestine anybody to Hell or to sin (which is the teaching of Predestinarianism, *q.v.*). He has foreseen the wickedness of the damned and has foreordained their punishment, but, none the less, he has a real will for their salvation, and he offers them the grace of conversion which they freely reject. Since God knows whether an individual will be saved or not, there is objective certainty about the fact. But man can never (except by a rare private revelation) be subjectively certain of his predestination, though he should have a very sure hope in God's mercy.

PREDETERMINATION, or Premotio Physica. The doctrine held by the Thomists concerning the divine activity and the activity of creatures, and in particular that of the free will. It teaches, in virtue of the primal causality of God, that God moves all created powers to their actions, not excepting free will. To move is of necessity to pre-move, to pre-move is of necessity to pre-determine. It is physical or real, or efficient, because God's motion really or efficiently (as opposed to morally) applies a created power to its act. The freedom of the will is in no wise prejudiced, seeing that the omnipotent God moves each thing according to its nature, necessary agents necessarily, free agents freely. The doctrine is based upon the real distinction between potency and act, and upon the metaphysical truth that whatever is in potency cannot pass from that state unless it be moved by something already in act. In accordance with this doctrine the Thomists teach the *intrinsic* efficacity of divine grace.

PRE-ESTABLISHED HARMONY. A false theory of Leibniz, according to which there is a parallel development of soul and body without any reciprocal action, in virtue of a harmony pre-established by God. He applies this theory to all things within the universe.

This theory is false because God would be the only cause: this is refuted by St. Thomas (*Cont. Gent.* c. 69; *Summa* I, cv, 5; *de Pot.* III, a7)—creatures are true causes.

PREFACE (Lat. *praefatio*, a saying beforehand). A prayer of thanksgiving occurring in all eucharistic Liturgies as a solemn introduction to the canon or *anaphora* (of which it is a part), preceded by versicles and responses inviting to give thanks and ending in the praise of the *Sanctus* (*q.v.*). In the Roman Mass there are 16 alternative prefaces: for Christmas and certain other feasts, for the Epiphany, for Lent, for Masses of the Passion and the Cross, for Eastertide, for Ascensiontide, for Whitsuntide, for the Holy Trinity and Sundays, for Masses of our Lady, of St. Joseph and of the Apostles, for the feasts of Christ the King and the Sacred Heart, for requiem Mass, for the Mass of the blessing of the holy oils, and a common preface for other feasts and ferias; some religious orders have special prefaces for their founder, *e.g.*, St. Augustine, St. Benedict, St. Francis, and the Carmelites have one for St. Teresa: Eastern Liturgies have only one preface. In the Latin rite it is said or sung aloud by the celebrant; in all others it is said silently with an *ekphonesis* before the *Sanctus*. Prayers in the form of a preface, and sung to the same tones, occur in the ordination of deacons, priests and bishops, the second part of the *Exsultet* (*q.v.*) is in preface form, etc. It is strictly forbidden ever to accompany the singing of the preface by playing an organ or other instrument.

PREFECT (Lat. *præfectus*, one set over). i. The president of a Roman congregation; the pope himself is prefect of those of the Holy Office, Consistorial and Eastern Church.
ii. Of the Apostolic Palaces. An office attached to that of the Secretary of State, having the administration and care of the papal residences, their accounts, up-keep, etc. The vice-prefect is also a palatine prelate.
iii. Apostolic, the head òf a prefecture apostolic (*q.v.*).
iv. The name is in frequent use for a minor superior, or one exercising delegated authority of a strictly limited scope, *e.g.*, the prefect of studies in a college.

PREFECTURE APOSTOLIC. The first stage in the ecclesiastical organization of a missionary territory, such being immediately subject to the Holy See and depending on the Congregation of Propaganda. A prefect apostolic is not usually a bishop, but has wide powers: he may administer Confirmation, confer minor orders, consecrate chalices and portable altars, absolve from censures and, in some reserved cases, dispense from marriage impediments, and has a limited use of *pontificalia*. The number of prefectures is constantly changing; they are mostly in Asia and Africa. The Church in Scotland

was governed by prefects apostolic from 1653 to 1694.

PRE-INTONING. When a prelate or other dignified person has to intone (or give out) an antiphon or hymn at a solemn service, a cantor first softly sings the opening phrase: accompanied by a master of ceremonies he approaches him who is to intone the antiphon, bows, sings the first few words in a low voice, bows again and retires. The custom dates from the time when only the precentor possessed a book of the antiphons. At pontifical Lauds and Vespers there is a special minister, the subdeacon of the antiphons, whose duty it is to pre-intone.

PRELATE (Lat. *prælatus*, one set before). i. A dignitary having jurisdiction in the external forum (*q.v.*) by right of his office. The principal prelates are the bishops; others are vicars and prefects apostolic, abbots and other major superiors of religious orders, and the higher officials of the Roman *curia*.
ii. There is a very large class of prelates who receive that name and rank without any office, duties or emoluments attached, as a mark of papal recognition of their services to the Church. All prelates, whether real or titular, have the title Monsignor(e), and have a special dress according to their rank and office; in choir they wear a rochet and *mantelletta*.

PRELATE, DOMESTIC (*Antistes urbanus*). An honorary distinction conferred by the pope on priests as a recognition of merit; they are accounted members of the papal household even though not resident in Rome and are said to have the same origin as protonotaries apostolic. Their dress is very similar to that of a bishop, with a purple cloak but a black biretta; they have no pontifical insignia except the *bugia* at Mass. Their form of address is "The Right Reverend Monsignor N . . ." In a wider sense, members of the colleges of assistants at the Pontifical Throne, protonotaries apostolic, and others are also domestic prelates.

PRELATE NULLIUS [DIŒCESIS] (Lat., of no diocese). One having independent jurisdiction over a district not under the authority of a diocesan bishop. He is usually a titular bishop but, even if he is not, he has the same ordinary powers and obligations as a bishop-in-ordinary. He may administer Confirmation, confer minor orders, consecrate churches, chalices, etc., grant indulgences of 50 days, give dimissorial letters, vote at an œcumenical council (if summoned thereto) and officiate pontifically (*cf.*, Abbot Nullius, Prefect and Vicar Apostolic). There are over 20 such prelatures in Brazil, depending on local metropolitans; the others, immediately subject to the Holy See, include Altamura, declared an independent archipresbyterate in 1248, and the Priory of the United Military

Orders of Spain, covering the province of Ciudad Real.

PRELATES DI FIOCCHETTI. The three chief prelates of the Roman *curia*, so called because their distinguishing badge is ten purple tassels (It. *fiocchetti*), instead of the usual six of prelates. They are the Vice-Chamberlain of the Church, the Auditor-General of the Apostolic Camera, and the Treasurer-General.

PRELATICAL DRESS. The costume proper to prelates present in choir and on other state and ceremonial occasions. It consists of biretta, cassock with short train, cincture with tassels, rochet and *mantelletta*. The colour and details of this dress vary according to the rank of the prelate and the nature of his prelacy.

PRELATURE NULLIUS. See PRELATE NULLIUS.

PREMISE. Either of the two propositions used in a syllogism (*q.v.*), from which a third proposition or conclusion is drawn.

PREMONSTRATENSIANS, The. The Canons Regular of Prémontré (*q.v.*).

PREPARATION AT MASS. i. Those prayers said at the foot of the altar steps, now part of, but once the celebrant's private preparation for, Mass. In the Roman Mass they begin with the sign of the cross and *In nomine . . .*, then Ps. xlii said alternately with the server, with the antiphon "I will go to the altar of God . . ."; *Confiteor* and *Misereatur* by both celebrant and server, *Indulgentiam*, versicles and responses; then the celebrant goes up to the altar, says two prayers for worthiness, kisses it (and incenses it at high Mass) and begins the Mass proper with the introit. There are variations: *e.g.*, instead of Ps. xlii, Dominicans and priests of the Ambrosian rite say ver. 1 of Ps. cxvii and Carthusians ver. 3 of Ps. cxl; religious orders use their proper versions of the *Confiteor*, the short prayers at the altar differ, etc.

ii. The preparation of the offering is made in the Roman Mass immediately after the offertory-verse: see OFFERTORY i. At low Mass of the Mozarabic, Braga, Carthusian, Carmelite and Dominican uses, the offerings are prepared before the Mass begins, as is done in Eastern liturgies (*cf.*, Proskomide).

PRESANCTIFIED [GIFTS], LITURGY OF THE. A eucharistic service in which there is no offering or consecration, hosts already consecrated being given in communion. It is therefore not a celebration of the Mass or eucharistic Liturgy at all.

i. The Mass of the Presanctified is the name given to a former observance of the Latin rite on Good Friday, when the celebrant alone communicated with the reserved host. In 1956, this was superseded by a short general communion-service, in accordance with earlier custom. After the veneration of the cross, the Blessed Sacrament is brought from the altar of repose by the deacon, while three antiphons are sung. Priest and people then say the Lord's Prayer together in Latin; after the prayer *Libera nos* aloud, the people answering Amen, the priest says *Perceptio corporis tui . . ., Domine, non sum dignus . . .*, and *Corpus Domini nostri . . .*, and communicates himself, and then the people, in the usual way; Psalm xxi may be sung meanwhile. The service ends with three prayers, the people responding Amen.

ii. The Liturgy of the Presanctified, called "of St. Gregory Dialogos" or Homiliastes (*i.e.*, Pope St. Gregory the Great), in the Byzantine rite is for use on every day in Lent except Saturday and Sunday (in practice usually only on Wednesday and Friday). In its general lines this service follows the Liturgy of St. John Chrysostom, but the first part is bound up with *Hesperinos;* there is no epistle or gospel unless it is a feast day; the great entrance is a sort of procession of the Blessed Sacrament; the whole *anaphora* is left out; the Host, which was dipped in the Precious Blood at the previous Liturgy, is immersed in unconsecrated wine before the communion at which lay people as well as clergy may partake. Other Eastern rites (except the Armenian, Coptic and Ethiopic) have Liturgies of the Presanctified for use in Lent; the Maronites and Malabarese use theirs only on Good Friday.

PRESANCTIFIED HOST. A Host consecrated at one Liturgy and put aside to be consumed at a later one in which there will be no consecration. See above.

PRESBYTER (Gr. πρεσβύτερος, elder). A priest, especially as distinguished from a bishop; the word is used in the Pastoral Epistles to distinguish the priests of the New Law from those of the Old, who are called ἱερεῖς, *hiereis.*

PRESBYTERIANISM. A system of church government based on the equal rank of all ordained ministers and the right of a congregation to choose its own pastor, lay elders and deacons; the pastors and lay elders of a district form a presbytery, several presbyteries a local synod, and there is a general assembly of delegates. Each of these "councils" is presided over by a temporary president (moderator). The system is therefore opposed both to episcopalianism and congregationalism. Presbyterianism was adopted principally by the followers of Calvin, but its Calvinism is now greatly modified; it uses as sacraments Baptism and the Eucharist; there is no official liturgy. The Westminster Confession, drawn up in 1643 and adopted by the Church of Scotland in 1689, is still the confession of faith to which

Presbyterian ministers must subscribe. The chief Presbyterian churches are the United Church of Scotland (including the established church and the United Free church), and they are numerous in the U.S.A. The Welsh Calvinistic Methodists are also Presbyterian. *Cf.,* Nonconformity.

PRESBYTERY. i. A term sometimes applied to the whole choir of a large church, but usually confined to the space between the choir-stalls and the altar steps. In a Roman basilica or Byzantine church the presbytery is between the altar and the bishop's throne in the apse.

ii. A body or council of priests (no longer in use except among some Protestant bodies).

iii. A priest's dwelling-house. In this sense the word is derived directly from Old Fr. *presbyterie,* which meant the same thing.

PRESCRIPTION (legal Lat. *præscribere,* to bring an exception against). The uninterrupted use or possession of rights or property over a period of time fixed by law, giving a good title or right thereto. The Church follows the civil legislation in regard to prescription obtaining in individual countries, with certain reservations. Some properties and rights are by canon law imprescriptible, *e.g.,* Mass stipends, benefices, clerical privileges. For prescription to be valid, good faith is necessary, not only at the beginning of the time necessary for prescription, but throughout the whole period.

PRESENCE OF GOD, PRACTICE OF THE. The effort to realize God dwelling within our souls as our friend. To achieve it, silence and solitude must be practised, motives purified outside the time of formal prayer by offering what is done to him for his glory, and frequently turning to him by ejaculations *(q.v.).* The growth of the spiritual life carries with it an increasing realization of God's presence, and perfection, as Cassian says, is the constant practice of that presence.

PRESENTATION, The. A feast celebrating the presentation of our Lady in the Temple but upon what occasion is uncertain. It has been kept throughout the Western church (now on Nov. 21) only since the 16th century, but in the East for twice as long, on the same date. In the Byzantine rite the "Entrance of the All-Holy Mother of God into the Temple at Jerusalem" is a feast of 5 days.

PRESENTATION, RIGHT OF, is the right of an individual or corporation, clerical or lay, to nominate an incumbent to a benefice of which the presenter has the patronage *(q.v.).* In the case of a lay person presentation is usually in respect of a church which he or his ancestor has built and endowed. Women may present equally with men. Upon presentation, the bishop must collate the beneficiary unless he discovers him to be an unfit person.

PRESENTATION BROTHERS, The. A teaching institute founded in Dublin by Edmund Ignatius Rice in 1802. It has schools in Ireland, England and Canada. The generalate is at Cork.

PRESENTATION NUNS, The. The Order of the Presentation of Our Lady, founded in 1777 by Nano Nagle in Cork, to conduct schools, orphanages and training-centres, especially for Irish children; since spread to other countries. Enclosed, with solemn vows. Black habit. Several other congregations have the title of the Presentation.

PRESTER JOHN (Old Fr. *prestre,* priest). A legendary potentate, sovereign and chief priest of a Christian kingdom in Asia, of whom much was heard in Europe in the middle ages *(cf.,* Marco Polo's travels, caps. xliv, liv, lv). The story probably had its origin in the existence of a province of Nestorians in the district south of Lake Baikal whose Christian prince lived in the city of Karakorum and bore the hereditary name and title of Owang Khan. Later versions of the story put the priest-king in Abyssinia.

PRESUMPTION. i. A vice opposed to hope *(q.v.),* whereby a man expects to gain eternal life by his own strength or without merits, or to obtain pardon without repentance. Of itself, presumption is a mortal sin; but in its usual form, *sc.,* so acting as to appear presumptuous, it may be venial.

ii. In law. A presumption of law, *i.e.,* one admitted by the law itself, frees the person whom it favours from the burden of proof, which falls on his opponent; and if he fails to disprove the presumption it stands as conclusive. Presumption of death with a view to a second marriage is not admitted in canon law: positive proof is required inducing moral certainty.

PRETERNATURAL GIFT. A favour granted by God which is above and beside the powers, exigencies, or capacities of the nature which enjoys it, but which is not beyond those of all created nature. It perfects the nature, but does not carry it beyond the limits of created nature. Such were the gifts of integrity, immortality and impassibility *(qq.v.)* in Adam and Eve. Sometimes called "relatively supernatural gift."

PRETIOSA. An addition to the office of Prime immediately after the Martyrology, named from the first word of the versicle "Precious in the sight of God." R̠. "Is the death of his saints," with which it begins. It consists of a prayer, *Kyrie,* Our Father, versicles and responses and another prayer, for the sanctification of the works of the coming day; in churches where the office is said in choir, it ends with a short lesson from the Holy Scriptures.

PRE-URBANITE HYMNS. Hymns of the Divine Office in their original forms before the "reform" of Pope Urban VIII (*q.v.*).

PREVIOUS MARRIAGE SUBSISTING is a diriment impediment (*q.v.*) to contracting another marriage and cannot be dispensed. It is an impediment by the law of nature and of positive divine law, so that for no one, either Christian or not, is it lawful to attempt a second marriage without certain proof of the death of the first partner. But *cf.*, Pauline Privilege.

PRICKSONG. An archaic name for contrapuntal music as opposed to plainsong— the melodies were pricked opposite one another; counterpoint, *contra punctum*, means pricked opposite. Pricksong was practised in England from the 13th century till Tudor times; King Henry VIII was expert in singing and writing it.

PRIDE. A capital vice opposed to humility (*q.v.*), consisting in excessive love of one's own excellence, exhibited in three ways: (*a*) contempt for lawful authority—a mortal sin; (*b*) contempt for equals and inferiors—mortal or venial according to the depth of the contempt; (*c*) desire to surpass one's equals— a venial sin. St. Thomas and many other spiritual writers put pride in a class by itself as the most deadly and devastating of all vices, which has its part in every sin, of whatever sort, that is committed; for every sin is in its degree a contempt of God and often of our superior or neighbour as well. Pride feeds and thrives on itself, continually stirring up the mind and will of man to rebellion against the moral law and against his lawful and qualified teachers, whether religious or civil. Ambition, presumption and vainglory (*qq.v.*) are among the more immediate handmaids of pride.

PRIE-DIEU (Fr., pray God). A small low desk with a ledge for kneeling thereat, or a low-seated chair with a high back for the same purpose.

PRIEST (Old Eng. *préost*, from Gr. πρεσβύτερος, elder). The minister of divine worship, especially in its highest act, sacrifice. Since a sacrifice is offered in the name of a whole religious society, its minister must be appointed by public authority. Priest and sacrifice are correlative terms. Christian priests are of two grades: (*a*) Priests of the second order by their ordination to the priesthood are given power to offer the sacrifice of the Mass, to baptize solemnly, and to administer Extreme Unction, but need jurisdiction (*q.v.*) for the valid administration of the sacrament of Penance and for valid assistance at the sacrament of Matrimony, and an indult for the valid administration of Confirmation. (*b*) Priests of the first order, *i.e.*, bishops, possess the additional power of administering the sacraments of Confirmation and Holy Order.

"PRIESTCRAFT." A charge of using cunning and oppressive dealing in order to bring and keep people at large under their control, made by unfriendly critics against the ministers of many religions, but those of the Catholic Church particularly. That in individual cases unworthy and unscrupulous priests may use their sacerdotal influence for personal or improper ends needs no demonstration. But with what object and for what personal advantage a world-wide body of clergy, or those of a district, or the prelates who compose the Roman *curia* should seek to impose themselves upon a people and keep them in intellectual, political and social subjection has never yet been ascertained.

PRIESTHOOD. i. The priestly office, character or dignity.

ii. The character imprinted on the soul by the valid reception of the sacrament of Holy Order.

iii. The aggregate of those of priestly rank, *e.g.*, in the Catholic Church, priests, bishops and the pope at their head. The existence of the Christian priesthood is the outcome of the institution of the sacrifice of the Mass by Christ and of his command that this sacrifice should be repeated in his commemoration.

iv. Of Jesus Christ. By his incarnation Jesus offered as a sacrifice to the Father all the acts of his will and body; on the cross he united all these mortal acts into one supreme sacrifice by which he became the mediator, priest and pontiff of the human race. As priest he worships, praises and thanks the divine Majesty in his own name and that of all people; he intercedes before the throne of the Father for us; and sends down therefrom the blessings of Heaven. This priesthood of our Lord is the one and only fundamental priesthood in the Church; it manifests itself visibly and in a special manner in the priesthood of Holy Order (above), whereby some are set apart for the offering of the eucharistic sacrifice, the ministering of the sacraments, and the teaching office.

v. Of the laity. By the Incarnation God the Son became united not only with a particular human body but with all mankind. Every Christian therefore becomes by Baptism a participator in the priesthood of Jesus Christ, a participation strengthened and extended by the holy Eucharist and Confirmation, an objective relationship distinct from the personal relationship that subsists between each soul and her Lord; "the sacramental characters (*q.v.*) are nothing else than certain sharings of the priesthood of Christ, derived from Christ himself" (St. Thomas, III, lxiii, 3). (*Cf.*, the Mystical Body.)

PRIMA-PRIMARIA is an archsodality which enjoys the privilege of being able to affiliate other sodalities not otherwise directly associated with it. The Prima-Primaria Sodality of the Blessed Virgin Mary can associate to itself, with communication of indulgences, etc., any approved pious confraternity, whatever its particular purpose, provided that it is placed under the patronage of our Lady.

PRIMACY. The jurisdiction of a bishop (e.g., a patriarch) over all the metropolitans and bishops of a given district, country or church, himself being subject only to the Holy See. In the case of the pope (q.v.) primacy is supreme and universal.

PRIMACY OF HONOUR. A priority of precedence and respect, but with no jurisdiction or legal authority in respect thereof. The dissident patriarch of Constantinople has such a primacy over the whole body of Orthodox churches. All the dissident Eastern churches seem to recognize a universal primacy of honour in the pope (as high-church Anglicans do), but of course deny a corresponding jurisdiction.

PRIMACY OF PETER IN THE N.T., The, is chiefly testified to by the following passages: Matt. xvi, 15-19 (see also ROCK; cf., Mark iii, 16, Luke xxii, 31-2, John i, 42); John xxi, 15-17; Acts ii, 14, iii, 12 and iv, 8, where he is the spokesman of the apostles; Mark xvi, 7, where he is singled out by name (cf., i, 36); 1 Cor. xv, 5, where his witness is named independently; Gal. ii, 7, recognized as head of the Christian Jews, but not of them only, Acts xv, 7-11; Gal. i, 18-19, Peter is the man who must be met. Paul's withstanding of Peter, recorded in Gal. ii, 11-15, refers to a matter of missionary expediency, not to a question of doctrine, and is perfectly reconcilable with the acknowledgement of Peter's superiority: open rebuke of the conduct of a superior is sometimes justifiable or even required of one. The fact of Paul's use of the title *Kephas*, or Rockman, for Simon Barjonah is an indication of his acknowledgement of Simon's position.

PRIMATE. A bishop who, without the rank of patriarch, exercises jurisdiction over all the metropolitans and bishops of a given district or country, himself being subject only to the Holy See. Such a position is no longer recognized by canon law, but numerous archbishops retain the title, which in a few cases carries with it precedence outside the local hierarchy. Many of these titles are of importance historically; the titles are the primates of Italy (the pope), Hungary (the archbishop of Esztergom), All Ireland (Armagh), Ireland (Dublin), Dalmatia (Antivari and Venice), Aquitaine (Bourges and Bordeaux), Portugal (Braga), Brazil (Bahia), Poland (Gniezno-Poznan and Warsaw), Gallia Belgica (Reims), Belgium (Malines), Lorraine (Nancy), Bohemia (Prague), Spain (Toledo), Germany (Salzburg), Corsica and Sardinia (Pisa), of the Gauls (Lyons), Mexico (Mexico City), Gaul and Germany (Sens), Normandy (Rouen), Africa (Carthage), of the East (Goa), Galicia and Lodomeria (Ruthenian see of Lvov), Colombia (Bogotá), and Peru (Lima). The metropolitan of the former archdiocese of Vienne was Primate of Primates as one of his suffragans was also a primate. Until recently the title was unknown in the East (cf., Exarch), its first use being in 1872, when the Orthodox eparchy of Bucarest was declared the primatial see of Rumania (it is now patriarchal).

PRIME. That portion of the Divine Office assigned to the first hour (*prima hora*), i.e., about 6 a.m., the approximate time of its recital in monastic churches. After the usual opening, it consists of an invariable hymn *Jam lucis orto sidere*), three psalms according to the day of the week or feast, little chapter, short responsory, *preces* (q.v.) on certain days, a variable short lesson and an invariable collect; then follows the reading of the Martyrology and *Pretiosa* (qq.v.) which in monasteries takes place in the chapter-house. On Trinity and certain other Sundays the Athanasian Creed is said after the third psalm in the Roman office. Prime is the morning prayer of the Western church, and the coming of a new day is particularly adverted to in the hymn and collect.

PRIME MATTER (*Materia prima*). That of which a thing is made. *Materia prima* is distinct from *materia secunda*. The latter is determined by an accidental form (roundness, squareness, or other qualities), and is therefore an already constituted body. The former is determined by the substantial form, e.g., as, according to the commonly received opinion, prime matter in man (wrongly called the body) is determined by the rational soul. Aristotle defines it, "matter is not being or quantity or quality or any of those things which determine or actuate being." It is the first subject of all corporal change and is the principle of extension and quantity. Prime matter is therefore related to form in that the latter determines it, from which it receives its specification and actualization, and through which alone it can be known.

PRIMER, The, or **PRYMER.** The generic name for a type of prayer book in ordinary use by the laity in England before the Reformation; its derivation is uncertain, but probably connected with the use of the book for teaching purposes. The contents of these books varied, but they always contained as a nucleus the Little Office of Our Lady, Office of the Dead, Penitential and Gradual Psalms, *Pater, Ave, Credo*, and Litany (these always in Latin), from which it will be observed that our forefathers had no need of a "liturgical movement" (q.v.). Numerous editions of the Primer were printed both in England and abroad during penal times, but the only recent edition (1923), containing the traditional matter, was not a success.

PRIMICER (Lat. *primus in cera,* first [name] on a wax tablet, *i.e.,* list). The name given to the superior or sub-superior of some chapters of canons, *e.g.,* of S. Giovanni Maggiore at Naples.

PRINCE. In its technical sense, the supreme ruler or governing body in civil society. Since supreme civil authority is given him for the prosecution of the common good, he is obliged to know in what that good consists and to avoid, so far as possible, all that would hinder it (*e.g.,* foreign and civil war) and to suppress anti-social organizations. He is further bound to ensure that public offices are filled by worthy and capable persons, to administer justice impartially, and to foster good relations with the Church.

PRINCE-BISHOP. One who in addition to his see ruled a territory as temporal prince; such were common in the middle ages, especially within the borders of the Holy Roman Empire. Such, for example, was the bishop of Durham in England; in his diocese the "bishop's writ" was issued against disturbers of the "bishop's peace," he minted coin, had civil and criminal courts with complete jurisdiction, could be the object of treason, could grant charters of incorporation, markets, etc., and all land was held mediately or immediately of him. Such palatinates no longer exist, but their memory is preserved in the prefix "prince" added to the episcopal title of certain dioceses, *e.g.,* the archdioceses of Gorizia, Olomuc, Prague, and Salzburg, the dioceses of Breslau, Brixen, Cracow, Gurk, Maribor, Seckau, Trent, Vienna, Liubliana. Other bishops were formerly princes of the Empire, but have dropped the title, *e.g.,* Cologne, Florence; among temporal titles retained are Count of Lyons (Lyons), Count of Turicchi (Fiesole), Chief Notary of Léon (Compostella), Prince of Conflans (Tarentaise). The bishop of Urgel (Spain) has the title of Sovereign Prince of Andorra and shares with France nominal lordship over the republic, which is an archipresbyterate of the diocese.

PRINCE OF THE APOSTLES, The. St. Peter. The word "prince" is here an inappropriate rendering of Latin *princeps,* chief, leader.

PRINCE OF THE CHURCH. A cardinal, who as such ranks after princes of the blood of reigning houses, as is recognized, *e.g.,* in Italy and Spain.

PRINCE ASSISTANT AT THE THRONE. The highest lay dignity of the Roman *curia,* vested in the families of Orsini and Colonna. Their office is purely ceremonial and includes ministering at the *Lavabo* in a solemn papal Mass.

PRINCIPALITIES (Eph. i, 21; Col. i, 16). One of the choirs of the celestial hierarchy (*q.v.*).

PRINCIPLE. That from which something flows in any way whatsoever. Distinct from Cause, since every cause is a principle, but not the converse.

PRINKNASH (pronounced *Prinnige*). A Benedictine abbey near Gloucester, of the Cassinese congregation of Primitive Observance. This community had its origin in a body of Anglican Benedictines founded in 1895. In 1913, while living on Caldey Island (*q.v.*), they submitted to the Holy See and were, in 1914, canonically erected as a Benedictine monastery. In 1928 they migrated to Prinknash Park, a former grange of St. Peter's Abbey at Gloucester. The life of the monks is purely contemplative.

PRIOR (Lat., elder, superior). A monastic superior or sub-superior, usually holding office temporarily for a fixed period. The superiors of colleges of secular canons are sometimes called prior, *e.g.,* at Roncesvalles, Pescia, and S. Maria in Trastevere at Rome. See below.

PRIOR, CATHEDRAL. The ruler of a cathedral-priory (*q.v.*). The office was peculiar to England and is now extinct. A cathedral prior had all the duties, powers and privileges of an abbot, and was more powerful and important than most English abbots.

PRIOR, CLAUSTRAL. The second-in-command of an abbey of monks or canons, regular, sometimes (*e.g.,* at Einsiedeln Abbey) called the dean. He holds his appointment at the will of the abbot and is usually assisted by a sub-prior.

PRIOR, CONVENTUAL. i. The superior of a monastery of Carthusians, Dominicans, Augustinian friars, Carmelites, Servites or Hospitallers of St. John, or of an independent house of Benedictines, Cistercians or canons regular which has not been erected into an abbey. They are either elected by the professed religious of the monastery, or more commonly are appointed by the provincial chapter or other higher authority. The office is usually held among the monks and canons for life, among the friars for a term of years; a Carthusian prior resigns every year but may be re-elected.

ii. Simple or obedientiary prior. The superior of a house of monks or canons regular which is dependent on an abbey; he is appointed by the abbot and is removable at will.

PRIOR, TITULAR. One having the title and precedence of a prior but with no corresponding office or duties. See CATHEDRAL-PRIORY.

PRIOR GENERAL. The head of the orders of Augustinian, Calced Carmelite and Servite friars, and the Hospitallers of St. John. They are elected and serve according to the constitutions of their order for a term of years.

PRIOR PROVINCIAL. The head of a local or national group of priories of Augustinian, Carmelite, Dominican or Servite friars or of Hospitallers of St. John. They are elected and serve according to the constitution of the order, *e.g.*, the Dominican is elected by the votes of the priors of the province and one other representative from each house and holds his position for three years; his election must be confirmed by the master general (*q.v.*).

PRIORESS. All convents of nuns having solemn vows, and some others, have a prioress, either as assistant to an abbess or governing as superior. Other convents are ruled by a mother superior.

PRIORY. Any monastery of men or women governed by a prior or prioress. A priory may be independent (conventual) or dependent upon an abbey or mother house (obedientiary).

PRISCILLIANISTS, The. A gnostic-manichæan sect in Spain in the 4th-6th centuries, named after its first leader, Priscillian, bishop of Avila. His condemnation and execution by a civil court, at the instance of Ithacius, bishop of Ossanova, was protested against by Pope St. Siricius, St. Martin of Tours and St. Ambrose.

"PRISONER OF THE VATICAN, The." A picturesque name given to the popes from the capture of Rome by the Piedmontese troops in 1870 until the Treaty of the Lateran in 1929, during which time they did not leave the precincts of the Vatican palace. This imprisonment was not contemplated by the Italian government nor maintained by physical force; but it was recognized on both sides that the emergence of the pope into territory violently wrenched from him would be an acknowledgement of his recognition of the *de facto* government and of himself as a subject thereof. His seclusion was therefore morally enforced.

PRIVATE MASS (Lat. *Missa privata*). A low Mass; more accurately, a low Mass celebrated out of devotion and not to answer the needs of a congregation (even though in fact a congregation be present). The term is used in several senses.

PRIVATION. A vindicative penalty by which a cleric is deprived of an ecclesiastical right, dignity, office, benefice or its fruit for certain serious crimes specified in law.

PRIVILEGE. i. In canon law. Privilege can be acquired, not only by concession of authority, but also by custom or prescription. Privileges are held to be perpetual, unless the contrary is proved. Privileges lawfully acquired from the Holy See before the Code of Canon Law (1918) are not abrogated by the contrary provisions of the code, or by any general law to the contrary, unless this is expressly stated; but the privileges granted by the code are revoked by a general law to the contrary. No one is bound to use a privilege acquired except in the case of certain faculties granted for the benefit of others.

ii. Of the clergy. Clerics alone can validly and lawfully exercise the power of holy orders and of jurisdiction, and obtain ecclesiastical offices. Reverence is due to them from all the faithful, and it is sacrilege to do them real injury. Clerics are exempt from military service and from civil duties unbefitting the clerical state. Clerics who have to satisfy their creditors should not be so deprived of maintenance as to be forced to live in a manner unbecoming their dignity. Clerics also enjoy the privilege of the Forum (*q.v.*). They cannot renounce their privileges, but lose them if reduced to lay estate.

PRO ALIQUIBUS LOCIS (Lat., for some places). The section of the Missal and Breviary containing some of the Masses and Offices used only in certain dioceses or religious orders, such as the Passion offices and those for the Flight into Egypt, the Maternity of Our Lady, All Holy Relics, etc.

PRO ARMENIS, DECREE. An important instruction on the seven sacraments contained in the bull *Exultate Deo* addressed by Pope Eugene IV to the Armenians, in 1439.

PRO-CATHEDRAL. A church used by a bishop as his cathedral until a more worthy one can be built. There are three pro-cathedrals in Great Britain: of the Apostles, Clifton; St. Nicholas's, Liverpool; St. Mary's, Wrexham (for Menevia). The Pro-cathedral, or "the old Pro," to Londoners meant the church of our Lady of Victories in Kensington, which served the purpose from the sale in 1867 of the old Moorfields church by Cardinal Manning until the opening of Westminster Cathedral in 1903.

PRO RE GRAVI (Lat., for an important object). A collect prescribed by a bishop to be said at Mass (*oratio imperata*) *pro re gravi* is omitted only on feasts of the first class and a few other days or, if so stated, on nine chief feasts only. A solemn votive Mass *pro re gravi* may be ordered or permitted by the bishop. *Res gravis* is such a matter as drought, pestilence, war, illness of the pope, bishop or sovereign.

PROBABILIORISM (Lat. *probabilior*, more probable). A system in moral theology which tries to solve the problem how to act when in doubt whether a law is or is not binding in given circumstances, by insisting that the law must be obeyed unless the opinion favouring liberty be *more* probable than that favouring the law (cf., Probabilism).

PROBABILISM. A system in moral theology which attempts to solve the problem: "If of two opinions one insists that in certain circumstances a law binds, while the other holds that in those circumstances it does not, when is it permissible and therefore safe to follow the opinion which favours liberty?" Probabilism replies that one is allowed to follow an opinion favouring liberty provided it be truly and solidly probable (*q.v.*), even though the opinion favouring the law be more probable. But Probabilism applies only to cases in which the lawfulness of an act is in question, and not its validity as, for example, in conferring the sacraments; in these latter cases the safer course must always be followed. Though we may follow a truly and solidly probable opinion, we are not bound to do so. Probabilism is primarily a principle for the moral theologian, not an ideal of Christian life, and often the more perfect and therefore more desirable course of action is to follow the more probable opinion according to which the law is binding.

PROBABLE. As used in theology, this word means "possible" rather than "probable" in the ordinary sense. That is to say, an opinion is "probable" if it has some solid reasons in its favour and is taught by some respectable theologians.

PROBATICA POOL, The (John v, 2). The Sheep Pool or, more probably, the Pool in the Sheep Market (Gr. πρόβατον, sheep), now identified with a pond by the church of St. Anne, near the Bab Sitti Maryam in Jerusalem.

PROCESS. In general, the cause, stages and modes of procedure in the beatification and canonization (*qq.v.*) of a saint. The ordinary process is conducted by the local bishop, and if and when his findings are approved by the Congregation of Rites the cause (*q.v.*) is introduced and the apostolic process begins.

PROCESSION. In common with all the great religions, Christianity makes use of processions of rejoicing, supplication, etc., in divine worship. They may be divided into four classes. (*a*) Those involved by the necessity of a number of people getting from one place to another with decency and good order. Such are the processions to the altar before high Mass, to the altar of repose on Maundy Thursday and from thence on Good Friday, and the great and little entrances of the Byzantine Liturgies. (*b*) Those directed to be held in accordance with liturgical observance, seven in number: of candles on Candlemas, of palms on Palm Sunday, of the Greater Litanies and of three rogation days (in expiation and for a blessing on the crops), and of the Blessed Sacrament at Corpus Christi. (*c*) Extra-ordinary processions, such as those for which the order and prayers are laid down in the "Rituale Romanum," namely, for rain, for fine weather, against tempests, famine, plague and war, in any great distress, of thanksgiving and at the translation of relics. (*d*) Processions of devotion, *e.g.*, of the Blessed Sacrament at the Forty Hours, of Our Lady, or with the statue or relics of a saint, usually in connexion with Sunday evening services. For the order of processions in general the "Rituale" lays down that they should be preceded by a cross, that those taking part shall be ranked two by two, the clergy separate from the laity and men from women, and that they shall proceed without chattering, laughter or looking about.

PROCESSION OF THE HOLY GHOST (Lat. *procedere*, to go forth). The mode in which the third Person of the Trinity has his origin from the other two as from a single principle of spiration (a word which indicates the act of loving, and denies the procession by generation which is proper to the Son). It is of the Catholic faith that the Holy Ghost proceeds from the Father and the Son. The 1st œcumenical Council of Constantinople (381) declared that the Holy Ghost proceeds from the Father, as it was at that time necessary to defend the divinity of the Holy Ghost against the Macedonians. This formula was subsequently misinterpreted as meaning from the Father only, and so the *Filioque* (*q.v.*) was inserted in the Nicene Creed.

PROCOPIUS LEGEND, The. The classical example of how lives of the saints have often been corrupted and overlaid with baseless popular accretions. A contemporary account records that St. Procopius was the first victim of the Diocletian persecution in Palestine; from this seed grew legends in the course of whose development Procopius was split up into three different people, none of whom remotely resembled the real martyr.

PROCURATOR (Lat. *procurare*, to look after). i. The representative of a religious order permanently residing in Rome.

ii. The official in a monastery (or convent, seminary or similar establishment) who has charge of the victualling, clothing, and, in general, the more domestic temporal affairs of the house. He is the modern equivalent of the cellarer, of whom the Rule of St. Benedict says that he must be "a man wise and of mature character, temperate, not a great eater, not haughty or headstrong or arrogant, not slothful or wasteful, but a God-fearing man who may be like a father to the whole community. Let him have the care of everything but do nothing without leave of the abbot" (cap. xxxi).

iii. Any person lawfully appointed to act for another, *e.g.*, a proxy for a sponsor at baptism.

PROFANATION of a church is its deliberate and lawful turning-over to decent non-religious use; for the reduction (*q.v.*) of its altars special procedure is laid down.

PROFANE (Lat. *profanus*, not sacred; literally, outside the temple) in common speech means irreverent or blasphemous, but ecclesiastically the word is used in its more exact sense to indicate secular as opposed to sacred: profane uses means simply not-religious uses; this sense implies no reproach whatsoever.

PROFANITY. The use of such expressions as "My God," "Hell," "damn," "bloody." However vulgar and unbecoming they may be and as such to be avoided, their use, if no definite blasphemous meaning or uncharitable intention is attached to them, is at most a venial sin.

PROFESSED. Those members of a religious institute (*q.v.*) who have been admitted to vows, whether simple or solemn; opposed to novices. The word is generally used only in the plural, but in the singular adjectivally, *e.g.*, a professed monk of St. Benedict.

PROFESSION, RELIGIOUS. A contract whereby a novice (*q.v.*) freely gives himself, by the taking of vows, to the religious life (*q.v.*) in a community approved by the Church. It may be solemn or simple, and this latter temporary or perpetual. Solemn profession is that which the Church recognizes as such and is always perpetual: any other profession is simple. Perpetual profession is not allowed except after simple temporary profession. The professed religious (*q.v.*) binds himself to tend to perfection by observing the evangelical counsels and obeying the rules and constitutions of his order. He must lead the life of the community and persevere in his state unless a just cause, approved by his superiors, obliges him to return to the world. He shares in all the indulgences, privileges and favours granted to his community. Dispensation from religious vows, solemn or simple, is reserved to the Holy See, but superiors general can generally release from simple vows religious whom they dismiss, provided such religious are not in major orders. Solemn vows are rarely dispensed.

PROFESSION OF FAITH. This is obligatory on all who take part in councils and synods, on those who are created cardinals or appointed bishops, abbots and prelates *nullius*, vicars and prefects apostolic, vicars capitular, dignitaries and canons, diocesan consultors, vicars general, rectors of parishes, beneficed clergy, seminary professors and religious superiors. It must be made in person, not by proxy, before the competent superior. The usual form is the Creed of Pope Pius IV, with later additions. Those who neglect to make the profession of faith,

if contumacious, are to be punished, even by the deprivation of their office.

PROHIBITED DEGREES. Degrees of relationship within which valid marriage is impossible, except by dispensation in those relationships wherein the Church is wont to dispense. The forbidden degrees are any degree of consanguinity or affinity (*qq.v.*) in the direct line; in the collateral line, up to the third degree inclusive in consanguinity, and up to the second in affinity.

PROHIBITED OCCUPATIONS. The practice of medicine or surgery, civil and military service, public and political offices, lay administration, legal practice in civil courts, membership of parliaments, trading and business, and also certain unsuitable recreations, as hunting, games of chance, dances, theatres, etc., are prohibited to clerics.

"PROHIBITION." The prohibition by the state of the manufacture, sale or consumption of intoxicants. The use of intoxicating drinks is not evil in itself and is not forbidden by the law of God or of the Church; hence prohibition is permissible only when the abuse of intoxicants seriously menaces the well-being of the state and no cure which would safeguard the freedom of the individual can be found. The argument of the arbitrary prohibitionists was already met by St. John Chrysostom in the 4th century: "I hear many cry when these deplorable excesses happen—'Would there were no wine!' What folly! What madness! When men sin you find fault with the gifts of God! What lunacy this is. Is it the wine that causes this abuse? No, it is the intemperance of those who take a wrong delight in it. Cry rather—'Would to God there were no drunkenness or luxury'; for if you shout 'Would there were no wine,' you should add 'Would there were no iron,' because of the murderers; 'Would there were no light," because of the thieves. . . . Thus could you destroy everything . . . it is a satanical way of arguing. . . . Wine was given us that it might produce a sweet joy, not that we might dishonour ourselves."

PROHIBITION OF MARRIAGE in the sense of a prohibiting impediment may be (*a*) a general prohibition of the Church, *e.g.*, mixed religion, without banns, etc.; (*b*) a special prohibition of the Church, as when a bishop in a particular case forbids a marriage for a just cause, *e.g.*, on account of some scandal or the suspicion of a concealed impediment: this prohibition lasts only so long as its cause and is binding under penalty of sin but not of invalidity; (*c*) parental prohibition. Consent of parents to marriage is required for its lawfulness according to the civil law of England in the case of a person under 21 years of age. It is recommended but not required by canon law, though no priest may assist at the marriage of a minor in face of parental prohibition unless he has the consent of his bishop.

PROHIBITING IMPEDIMENTS are circumstances in which a marriage is illicit (*q.v.*) but valid. They are principally: previous betrothal subsisting, forbidden times, simple vows, and mixed religion (*qq.v.*). They may all be dispensed for good reasons (*cf.,* Prohibition of Marriage).

PROLETARIAT (Lat. *proletarius,* one who serves the state by means of his offspring, *proles*). Those members of the community who are entirely dependent for their subsistence on the sale of their labour, especially the labour of their hands. The existence of a large and partially submerged class of manual labourers of this sort is a feature of industrialism (*q.v.*). According to the doctrine of St. Thomas and the common meaning of the word, the proletarian is in a modified state of slavery; for servitude is the condition of being under the dominion of another, not for the good of the servant or for the common good, but for the sake of that other's private interest. See also RESPONSIBILITY.

PROMISE. A mutual promise, or one given for a consideration, or one the breaking of which would do notable harm to the other party, is binding in justice and to break it is a sin according to the matter involved. Simple promises proposed and accepted, other than these, bind under pain of venial sin only unless the person promising intended to bind himself in justice; but they cease to bind at all if the circumstances in which they were made alter subsequently. A promise must be distinguished from a mere expression of intention to do something. See also under MIXED MARRIAGE and BETROTHAL.

PROMOTER OF THE FAITH, The (Lat. *Promotor Fidei*), commonly called the Devil's Advocate, is an official of the Congregation of Rites whose business it is scrupulously to examine all evidence both of miracles and virtue in the processes of beatification and canonization, in order that no person may, through human enthusiasm or error, receive the highest honours of the Church unless in every way worthy thereof. Every objection must be satisfactorily answered before the case is allowed to proceed.

PROMOTER OF JUSTICE. An official appointed by a bishop to act as judge in the diocesan court; he must therefore be of mature age and learned in the law. He forms one tribunal with the bishop so that there is no appeal from one to the other. The office is in many dioceses discharged by the vicar general.

PROMULGATION (Lat. *promulgare,* to make known). The public announcement of a law, before which it is not binding. Legislation of the Holy See is officially promulgated by publication in the "Acta Apostolicæ Sedis," but the pope is at liberty to do it in other ways in special cases.

PRONE (Fr.). An exhortation to pray for all sorts and conditions of men, living and dead, pronounced before the sermon at Sunday Mass in French and Belgian churches. The term is often extended to the sermon itself (*cf.,* Bidding-prayer).

PROOF. Evidence sufficing or helping to establish a fact. Direct or positive proof shows that a thing is so; indirect or negative shows the impossibility of any other alternative (*cf.,* Demonstration).

"PROPAGANDA." The Sacred Congregation *de Propaganda Fide* (for the Spreading of the Faith) is a Roman congregation (*q.v.*) established by Pope Gregory XV in 1622 and is concerned with all matters concerning missions of the Western church throughout the world. It has jurisdiction over all such missionary countries and districts, which are ordinarily organized into prefectures and vicariates apostolic (*qq.v.*) but some (*e.g.,* India, Japan) have regular hierarchies; Great Britain and the United States were taken from the jurisdiction of Propaganda to that of ordinary ecclesiastical government in 1908. The Urban College for training missionaries of all races is attached to the congregation and other missionary colleges in Europe are subject to it. The common word "propaganda" is derived from the name of this congregation: thus do the connotations of words degenerate.

PROPAGATION OF THE FAITH, THE ASSOCIATION FOR THE. A world-wide society of the faithful to further the evangelization of the world by united prayer and the collection of alms for distribution to the missions. Its headquarters are at Rome under the direction of the Congregation *de Propaganda Fide*.

PROPER OF THE MASS. Those parts of the liturgy of the Mass which are variable according to the day or feast which is being observed, namely the introit, collects, epistle, gradual and alleluia or their substitutes, gospel, offertory-verse, secret, communion-verse, post-communion prayers; often there is also a proper preface and occasionally a sequence (*qq.v.*). When the Mass is sung, the introit, gradual, etc., sequence, offertory and communion verses (as well as being said by the celebrant) are sung, or at least recited on a note, by the choir, nor must they or any part of them be on any account omitted by the singers. The "proper Mass of N . . ." are these parts proper to the Mass of such and such a feast, saint or day.

PROPER OF THE SAINTS, The. The division of the Missal and the Breviary in which is given those parts of the Mass and Office proper to certain feasts of our Lord and of our Lady and of the saints. It begins on Nov. 29 (vigil of St. Andrew), as being about the beginning of Advent (*cf.*, Common of Saints).

PROPER OF THE SEASON, The. The division of the Missal and the Breviary in which is given those parts of the Mass and office proper to the Sundays and other days of Advent, Christmas time, Septuagesima, Lent, Paschal time, Pentecost and the Sundays following; it begins with the first Sunday of Advent and includes the proper of those saints whose feasts are observed during the octave of Christmas (SS. Stephen, John, Innocents, Thomas Becket, Silvester).

PROPERTY, DEFENCE OF. Violence may be used to defend one's own or another's property provided it bear some proportion to the damage threatened (*e.g.*, if the danger would be averted by knocking the aggressor down, no more than the violence requisite for this should be used). Should the death of the aggressor ensue, this is not murder but justifiable homicide (*q.v.*), since his death is not intended as such but is the unfortunate effect of repelling the aggression.

PROPERTY, ECCLESIASTICAL. The Church as a perfect society (*q.v.*) has the right to own and administer property for her own purposes, independently of the civil power, and to exact from her members the material and temporal means to attain her spiritual end. The Church acquires property by the same just and lawful means as other persons, physical and moral, *e.g.*, by occupation, invention, accession, industry, contract, inheritance, prescription, etc. The Church's right to property is juridically equal to that of the state, but not so extensive, her need of material things being less. By art. 28 of the concordat between the Holy See and Italy, in 1929, the Holy See, in order to quieten consciences, accorded full and free title to all those who were in possession of ecclesiastical property as a result of previous spoliation of the Church by the Italian state.

PROPERTY, PRIVATE. The general right of using anything as one's own. This right has its basis in the law of nature which bestows on man the right to all means necessary for the purposes of life. Several of these, *e.g.*, exclusion of others from the use of things he now needs, provision for times of illness, for old age, and for future family needs, would be impossible to compass without the possession of at least some private property. Thus the right of private ownership is innate to each man and must be respected by his fellows. Nevertheless, this general right has three important limitations: (*a*) Before the right can be exercised, a just title to possession must be acquired in accordance with the conditions laid down by right reason or approved by custom and confirmed by state legislation; (*b*) the inviolabil-

ity of a man's private property ceases in his neighbour's extreme necessity; (*c*) although, in general, state control over private property stops at laying down conditions of tenure, the public welfare may call for a limited expropriation by the state; in such cases, however, commutative justice (*q.v.*) demands that full compensation should be made. A man's right to private property is therefore neither absolute nor unlimited (*cf.*, Wealth, Land).

PROPHECIES, The. Four (formerly twelve) readings from the Old Testament before the blessing of the font on Holy Saturday, now called "lessons." Each is followed by a collect and after three of them a short canticle is sung. They are Gen. i, 1-31, ii, 1-2; Exod. xiv, 24-31, xv, 1; Is. iv, 2-6; Deut. xxxi, 22-30, and originally were particularly directed to the instruction of those about to be baptized. The present lessons refer to man's first condition, the prophetic saving and cleansing of God's people, and Moses' warning against infidelity applied to Christians.

PROPHECIES OF ST. MALACHY, The. Spurious prophecies attributed to St. Maolmhaodhog, archbishop of Armagh (1094-1148), discovered at Rome in 1590. They consist of the attribution of certain conditions and characteristics to the popes, from the time of Celestine II (1143-44) until the end of the world under Peter the Roman, under the form of symbolical titles. Many of these cannot be verified without much ingenuity and distortion of meaning, but those of the last six popes are remarkably fitting without undue stretching of their application: Pius IX was *Crux de cruce*, a cross from a cross (the badge of the house of Savoy); Leo XIII, *Lumen in cœlo*, a light in the sky; Pius X, *Ignis ardens*, a glowing fire; Benedict XV, *Religio depopulata*, religion desolate; Pius XI, *Fides intrepida*, faith undaunted; Pius XII, *Papa angelicus*, angelic father. On the other hand St. Pius V was a "woodland angel" and Benedict XIV a "rustic animal." They are forgeries made at the end of the sixteenth century.*

PROPHECY is the certain foretelling of future events which cannot be known by natural means; theologically, God's teaching and will as delivered to men in the name and authority of God. It is a gift of God, an extraordinary grace which may be bestowed upon anybody. The only prophecies which the Church teaches to be divinely inspired are those of the Bible, ending with St. John's prophecy of the Church of the Risen Christ in its conflict with Satan, in the Apocalypse; those prophecies which foreshadowed the coming of Christ were "messianic." Subsequent prophecies are judged on their human merits, chiefly of course by whether they have been fulfilled or no (*cf.*, Private Revelation).

---

* This is one opinion. There are many who hold the other view, that the prophecies were indeed made by St. Malachy in the 12th century.—*Publisher*, 1997.

PROPHETS, The. A prophet among the Jews was a messenger of God and a preacher, secondarily a foreteller of the future; the name is particularly reserved to Isaias, Jeremias, Ezechiel and Daniel (the major prophets, because of the greater length of their works), Osee, Joel, Amos, Abdias, Jonas, Micheas, Nahum, Habacuc, Sophonias, Aggeus, Zacharias and Malachias (the minor prophets).

PROPITIATION (Lat. *propitiare,* to appease) is prayer appealing for the mercy of God on us sinners and for mitigation of punishment justly incurred. Distinguish from Impetration (*q.v.*).

PROPOSITIONS, THE CONDEMNED. By this term are sometimes indicated the 80 propositions condemned by Pope Pius IX in the syllabus attached to the bull *Quanta cura,* in 1864. But they are far from being the only propositions the Church has condemned. See SYLLABUS.

PROPRIUM DE TEMPORE. The proper of the season (*q.v.*).

PROPRIUM SANCTORUM. The proper of the saints (*q.v.*).

PROSE. Another name for a sequence (*q.v.*) from the earlier ones being written in measured prose rather than verse.

PROSELYTE (Gr. προσήλυτος, one who has come). A Gentile converted to Judaism, hence any convert from one religion to another. To proselytize, meaning to make converts, is generally used in a pejorative sense, either because one's own religion is the loser or as implying unscrupulous methods, *e.g.,* "souperism."

PROSKOMIDE (Gr., preparation). The rite which precedes the celebration of the Liturgies of St. John Chrysostom and of St. Basil. After prayers before the *iconostasis* the priest and deacon vest at the *diakonikon* with the appointed prayers; then at the *prothesis* the deacon pours wine and water into the chalice and the priest with the holy lance cuts up the *prosphora,* the seal for our Lord ("the Lamb") and the other parts in honour of our Lady and the saints and with prayers for the bishop, clergy and people, dead and living, and arranges them on the *diskos* (*qq.v.*). The *prothesis,* altar and whole church are incensed by the deacon, who then says "It is time to sacrifice to the Lord . . ." and goes to his place before the doors and the priest to the altar. The whole rite is accompanied by prayers and the last steps are marked by the deacon's requests to the priest: *e.g.,* "Sir, give the blessing," "Sir, make beautiful," "Sir, shelter," etc. In all Eastern Liturgies this preparation is made at the beginning (but, except by the Armenians, at the altar) and with forms resembling the Byzantine in varying degrees, but much shorter.

PROSPHORA (Gr., oblation). The altar-bread of the Byzantine rite. It is a round cake of leavened bread. It is stamped with one or more seals, with a cross between the letters IC XC NI KA (Jesus Christ conquers); on the left is a square with a triangle, the "all holy," because it is set aside as a commemoration of our Lady; on the right is a square with nine small triangles, in three rows of three, in commemoration of the choirs of angels and the saints.

PROSTRATION, in the sense of lying flat on the ground or kneeling so that the head touches it, is now confined to the ordinands during the singing of the litany at the ordination of subdeacons, deacons, priests and bishops, and to religious at profession and in the solemn consecration of a virgin. Members of some religious orders prostrate on other occasions, *e.g.,* the Carthusians; *cf.,* Metany (*c*).

PROTECTOR OF THE KINGDOM, The. The title and office of St. George the Martyr, more commonly called the patron saint of England; the title was given by Pope Benedict XIV in 1750.

PROTESTANT. An adherent of any one of the religious bodies detached from the Catholic Church at the time of the Reformation or of any sect deriving from them; one who professes the doctrines of those reformers. The name was first applied to and accepted by those Lutherans who *protested* against the decree of the second Diet of Speyer (1529) which ordained that in those states where the new religion had got a hold Catholic doctrine should not be attacked nor the celebration of Mass interfered with, pending the decisions of a council of the Empire. Its use afterwards spread to all reformers and is now generally interpreted as a "protest against the errors of the Church of Rome." It is a gross and misleading mistake to apply the name to members of the dissident Eastern churches, or to "after-Christians" (*q.v.*) who repudiate Protestantism equally (or nearly equally) with Catholicism.

PROTESTANTISM. A generic name for those forms of Christianity derived from the teachings of those who revolted from the Catholic Church in the 16th century and for the principles characteristic of them. These were chiefly the sufficiency and supremacy of the Bible as the rule of faith; the total corruption and depravity of human nature by the Fall; the dependence of salvation solely on the merits of Christ (justification by faith, *q.v.*); predestination to Heaven or Hell; the universal priesthood of all believers interpreted as an opposition to the divine appointment of an ordained priesthood and as a right to private interpretation (*q.v.*) of doctrine in general and the Bible in particular. The Hebrew Scriptures had a sudden and new importance; in particular, Calvinism, in its ultimate analysis, was an enlarged Judaism, and Hebraism (for example, the idea that prosperity and success are tokens by which election can be recognized) is still a characteristic of much Protestantism, even when it has to a considerable extent repudiated the Old Testament. There followed from these the rejection of papal (and in some cases of episcopal) authority and the doctrines of the Mass as a sacrifice, the Real Presence, confession and penance, Purgatory, indulgences, the intercession of the saints, the meritoriousness and necessity of good works for salvation, etc. The principle which became ruling was that of private judgement and free choice which is supreme in popular Protestantism to-day: the latest and most devastating development is "Modernism," which in effect adopts historical statements of doctrines in faith and morals and chooses the interpretation to be put on them according to the ideas and taste of the individual concerned. In accordance with the spirit of the times, Protestantism is now pragmatist, ethical and naturalistic, and less and less upholds a divine revelation of absolute truth. The primary forms from which Protestantism derives are Lutheranism, Calvinism, Zwinglianism and Anglicanism (*qq.v.*).

PROTESTING CATHOLIC DISSENTERS. A name suggested to be given to English Catholics who should sign a protest against principles erroneously attributed to them (as opposed to the rest, if any, who would be "papists"), proposed by a relief bill drafted in 1789 under the auspices of the Catholic Committee, who accepted the name. It was dropped when the bill was eventually passed in 1791.

PROTHESIS (Gr., ante-deposition). The part of the sanctuary of a church of the Byzantine rite to the north of the altar, and the table therein at which takes place the office of the *Prothesis* or *proskomide* (*q.v.*). It balances the *diakonikon* (*q.v.*).

PROTO- A prefix from the Gr. πρῶτος, first.

PROTOCANONICAL BOOKS. Those books of the Bible which have always been received without any contention as part of the canon of Scripture. (*Cf.*, Deuterocanonical.)

PROTOEVANGELIUM OF JAMES, The, or The Gospel of the Infancy. The oldest of the extant apocryphal gospels, dating in part from the 2nd century but attributed to St. James the Less. It is important as an early witness to the *cultus* of our Lady. Certain passages suggest that it had an Ebionite and docetic origin.

PROTOMARTYR. The first martyr to give his life for Christ was St. Stephen the Deacon (Acts vii, 54-9). Other protomartys are: St. Alban, of Britain (*c.* 304), St. Fidelis of Sigmaringen, of the missionaries of the *Propaganda* congregation (1622); Bl. Cuthbert Mayne, of the seminary priests in England (1577); Juan de Padilla, O.F.M., and his companions, of America (1549); Bl. Richard Gwyn, of Wales (1584); Bl. John Houghton and his companions, of the English Reformation (1535).

PROTONOTARY APOSTOLIC. A member of the first college of prelates of the Roman *curia,* said to originate in the 1st century with the seven notaries appointed by Pope St. Clement to collect the acts of the martyrs. They are divided into four classes: (*a*) *de numero participantium,* seven in number, who have certain duties in connexion with canonization and beatification in accordance with this origin; (*b*) supernumerary, an honorary distinction reserved to the canons of the patriarchal basilicas and to the chapters of eight Italian cathedrals; (*c*) *ad instar participantium,* an honorary distinction reserved to the members of certain other chapters of canons and to individuals; (*d*) titular, an honorary distinction conferred on ecclesiastics throughout the world (these are diocesan, not domestic, prelates and do not belong to the Pontifical Family). Each class has certain privileges of dress and precedence and the first three have a limited use of *pontificalia.*

PROTOPOPE, -PRESBYTER, -PRIEST. See ARCHPRIEST.

PROTOTYPE. The authentic and eternal image of all things in the mind of God.

PROVERBS. A book of the Old Testament, containing principally a large number of proverbial sayings, maxims and moral sentences, with instructions on wisdom and ending with a description of the "valiant woman." In Hebrew they are in poetic form and are called *Mishle Shelomoh,* the Proverbs of Solomon; it is likely that he wrote the greater part of the book, but not all, *e.g.,* the last chapter.

PROVIDENCE, DIVINE. St. Thomas teaches (I, xxii, 1) that the ordering of things to an end is in God called Providence. The end may be natural or supernatural. It is by his providence that God watches over and governs all that he had made: "reaching from end to end mightily and ordering all things sweetly" (Wisd. viii, 1). The presence of evil (*q.v.*) in the world is no conclusive argument against divine providence. Circumstances which are adverse to individuals are often for the common good; or they may be the punishment of sin or the testing of the just. Moreover, the world is not a place of rest, but one of trial, a place in which we have to win eternity.

PROVIDENCE ROW. A refuge, now at Crispin Street in east London, founded in 1860 by Mgr. Provost Gilbert. It has over 200 beds for men, women and children, gives food and shelter to the homeless poor (without distinction of creed), and conducts three hostels, for boys, women and business girls, and a home of rest for women at Saint Albans. Its headquarters were destroyed by enemy action in world-war II.

PROVIDENTISSIMUS DEUS. An encyclical letter of Pope Leo XIII in 1893 on the study of the Bible in general, and containing a doctrinal exposition of the concept of inspiration (q.v.), a landmark in the development of doctrine on this point. Though perhaps not infallible in mode of utterance, this encyclical as addressed to the whole Catholic world and accepted by it as decisive on a dogmatic question, embodies the voice of the ordinary *magisterium* of the Church and is invested with all its authority.

PROVINCE. i. The territory over which an archbishop exercises metropolitan (q.v.) jurisdiction, namely his own archdiocese and at least one suffragan diocese.

ii. The division of a religious order comprising all its houses and members in a given district; its territorial boundaries are often but not necessarily conterminous with those of a civil state.

PROVINCIAL. The superior of a province (q.v., ii) of a religious order. Provincial is often added to some other title, e.g., prior, vicar, minister. He is always elected for a term of years by the votes of a provincial chapter, but a Jesuit provincial is appointed by the general. The provincial is responsible to his superior general (q.v.) for the administration of his province and for the maintenance of religion therein, chiefly by means of visitations. He convenes the provincial chapter and is a member of the general chapter.

PROVISION, CANONICAL. The provision of a cleric to a benefice by due appointment, institution and induction (qq.v.).

PROVISORS. A statute of King Edward III, in 1351, which declared invalid all provisions (i.e., appointments) to English benefices and dignities made by the Holy See at the expense of the rights of the patron or chapter. The act, though unjustifiable canonically, was provoked by the abuse of their power by certain of the popes, especially John XXII, and was not directed against the Holy See as such. The bishops protested, and the act, though enforced by *Præmunire* (q.v.), was frequently disregarded. Abuses, direct or indirect, of the pope's right of provision were recognized and condemned by the Council of Trent, sess. xxiv, cap. 19.

PROVOST (Lat. *præpositus*, one placed before). i. The chief dignitary of a cathedral or collegiate chapter in certain countries (e.g., England, Scotland, Austria, Poland); sometimes the second dignitary under a dean. His duties are similar to those of a dean (q.v.).

ii. Provost General. The head of certain religious orders and congregations, e.g., Jesuits, Passionists, Fathers of Charity. The superior of the Discalced Carmelites is Provost General and Prior of the Holy Mountain, i.e., Carmel, but he lives in Rome, and Carmel is governed by a vicar.

PROXIMATE TO HERESY, ERROR (Lat. *hæresi, errori proxima*). A proposition is said to be proximate to heresy if the matter it contradicts is commonly accepted as revealed, though not actually defined, e.g., the Assumption;* to error, if it contradicts a proposition deduced with great probability from principles of faith.

PROXIMATE OCCASION. An occasion of sin (q.v.) in which a person always or nearly always falls. If in a given set of circumstances a man usually sins, those circumstances constitute for him a proximate occasion of sin. There is a grave obligation to avoid such occasion. If, however, duty places a person in proximate occasion, he must take measures to make the occasion of sin remote.

PRUDENCE. The right reason of doing or of behaviour, whereas art (q.v.) is the right reason of making or of production. In its essence it is an intellectual virtue, residing in the understanding, but as a cardinal moral virtue its office is to point out the golden mean between excess and defect in the matter of the other cardinal virtues (q.v.). It is the first of the cardinal virtues, enabling the intellect to see what is virtuous and what is not, how to do the one and avoid the other, and prompting the will to act accordingly. Prudence implies memory of the past, understanding of the present, docility, shrewdness, reasoning, foresight, circumspection and precaution; it is a habit of intellectual discernment which indicates to the will how the other moral virtues should be applied. This philosophical and theological signification of prudence must be carefully distinguished from the often rather "stuffy" use of the word in common speech.

PSALM (Gr. ψαλμός, song to be sung to a stringed instrument). One of the 150 such songs contained in the Biblical book of Psalms or Psalter. They have always been looked on as the incomparable expression of prayer and they form the basis of the Divine Office in all the old Christian churches, whether Catholic or not. In the Latin rite they are the principal part of the office and are so arranged that all should be sung during the course of every week, but in practice this is upset by the occurrence of the feasts and consequent offices of saints; but Ambrosian usage (which has a special version

---

* Since this was written, the Assumption of the Blessed Virgin Mary was defined as a dogma by Pope Pius XII in 1950.—*Publisher*, 1997.

of the psalms) spreads them over a fortnight and the Mozarabic alone of Latin offices does not use them all. The Byzantine and Armenian offices spread them over the week, the new Malabarese office over two weeks; in other Eastern rites the whole psalter is not used, at any rate in practice. Catholic psalters (q.v.) and bibles follow the order of the Septuagint (but omitting Ps. 151 as uncanonical), counting the Hebrew 9 and 10 as 9, 114 and 115 as 113, 116 as 114 and 115, and 147 as 146 and 147. Therefore Ps. 10-113 and 116-146 inclusive are one behind those numerations which follow the Hebrew. e.g., those in the Authorized Version of the Bible and the Book of Common Prayer.

PSALM-TONE. A chant to be employed in the singing of a psalm or canticle. They are eight in number, formed on the Gregorian modes (q.v.) with a special one (*Tonus Peregrinus*) usually reserved to Ps. cxiii, and with alternative mediations and endings. Each chant consists of two parts, corresponding to the two parts of the verse; the first part is monotonic with an inflected intonation and mediation, the second part monotonic with an inflected ending or cadence; between them is a pause of a length usually represented by the words "Ave Maria."

PSALMS, THE BOOK OF. A book of the Old Testament containing 150 songs in poetic form, called in Hebrew *Tehillim*, songs of praise. They are commonly called the Psalms of David and he probably wrote most, but not all, of them. Most psalms have a separate title, found either in the Hebrew or Greek versions; the signification of many of these titles is uncertain; others refer to the author, the occasion, the characteristics, etc. The psalms form a commentary upon a thousand years of the history of the Chosen People and in parts undeniably look forward to the coming of the Messias. The sublimity of their theological and ascetical teaching, as well as their familiarity to Jewish converts, caused them to be taken over into Christian worship from the Temple and synagogue. See above.

PSALMI IDIOTICI (Lat., private person's psalms). Psalms or hymns composed during the early Christian centuries, as opposed to those of the Bible. The only ones still in use are the *Te Deum, Gloria in excelsis,* and the *Phos hilaron* (qq.v.).

PSALMODY (Gr., singing to the harp). The singing of psalms in divine worship. The practice was carried over from the Jewish to the Christian liturgy and so has been in the Church from the very beginning.

PSALTER (Gr. ψαλτήριον, instrument played by plucking). i. The psalms.

ii. A book containing the psalms in numerical order.

iii. That portion of the Breviary which contains the psalms arranged as they are to be said in the Divine Office during the course of the week.

iv. The "psalter of our Lady" is the rosary (150 *Aves*). See JESU'S PSALTER.

PSALTER, THE GALLICAN. The second revision of the psalms made by St. Jerome and the one now in use in the Vulgate, the Divine Office, etc., Called Gallican, because said to have been introduced into Gaul by St. Gregory of Tours, to distinguish it from Jerome's first revision, or Roman Psalter. *Cf.,* Vatican Psalter.

PSALTER, THE ROMAN. See ITALA VETUS.

PSALTER, THE VATICAN. A new Latin translation of the Book of Psalms, prepared at the Biblical Institute at Rome, and published in 1945. It was made principally from the Hebrew Masoretic text; hardly a verse remains unchanged from the current version, and the gain in intelligibility is tremendous. Pope Pius XII at once gave permission for the optional use of this version in the recitation of the Divine Office, whether in private or in public.

PSEUDO-AREOPAGITE, The, or the Pseudo-Dionysius. An unknown mystical writer whose works enjoyed great authority during the middle ages. For long they were attributed to Dionysius the Areopagite (Acts xvii, 34); they were in fact written between 490 and 520.

PSEUDO-ISIDORE. The collection of false decretals (q.v.) ascribed to one Isidore Mercator.

PSEUDO-MATTHEW. An apocryphal gospel of the 5th century professing to be a translation by St. Jerome of a Hebrew work by St. Matthew. Popular stories of the flight to and sojourn in Egypt of the Holy Family are derived from it. Another form, ending with the birth of our Lord, is called "The Nativity of Mary."

PSYCHOANALYSIS. A means of discovering motives and springs of action which do not ordinarily come into consciousness. Material for the analysis is furnished either by the patient's unreserved account of his psychic life, or by his statements under hypnosis, or by more or less conjectural interpretations of his dreams. "Suppressed" and "unconscious" experiences and motives, the existence of which consciousness refuses to recognize, are said to result in a "psychosis," to bring about a disorganization of the conscious life-attitude. The aim of psychoanalysis is to remedy this psychosis by bringing the contents of the "unconscious" to the full conscious notice of the individual. The use of psychoanalysis demands extreme caution; it should never be employed except under expert advice, and then only by highly skilled practitioners of unimpeachable moral character.

PSYCHOLOGY (Gr. Ψυχή, soul: λόγος, science). i. Experimental. The investigation of those phenomena called sensations, perceptions, thoughts, volitions and emotions; by an analysis of these an endeavour is made to classify them and to reduce them to the smallest number of fundamental activities so that their chief and characteristic features may accurately be enunciated in a body of general truths.

ii. Rational. But psychology does not stop at the above investigation, it seeks to enquire into the inner nature and constitution of the root and subject of the above phenomena; it ascends from the knowledge of the effect to that of the cause. Hence rational or inferential psychology treats of the soul and of its simplicity, spirituality, immortality, origin, union with the body, etc.

PUBERTY. At canon law puberty is presumed to be reached at 14 full years of age in males, 12 in females, as at English common law, but marriages below 16 and 14 respectively are invalid.

PUBLIC DECENCY, HONESTY, PROPRIETY. A diriment (q.v.), but dispensable impediment to marriage arising from an invalid marriage or public or notorious concubinage. It annuls marriage in the first and second degree of the direct line between the one and the blood relations of the other partner. For the purposes of this impediment a civil marriage is equivalent to public concubinage.

PUBLIC AND OFFICIAL WORSHIP, as opposed to popular devotions (q.v.), is the liturgical worship (q.v.) of the Church.

PUBLICANS, The (Lat. publicanus, a tax-collector). Jews who farmed the taxes from the Romans of the equestrian order who, in their turn, farmed them from the imperial treasury. The average publican was both an extortioner and an upholder of the subjection of his people; so he was an outcast and the presence of one in a family prevented a Jew from marrying into it.

"PUGIN." An epithet used, sometimes with unnecessary contempt, of a certain type of building, ornament, and other work, characterized by a careful imitation of gothic forms combined with a tendency to skimpiness and penury of materials. The term is from Augustus Welby Pugin (1812-52), who was a leader of the Gothic Revival (q.v.) and architect of over twenty-five Catholic churches, including the cathedrals of Birmingham, Nottingham and Southwark and the monasteries at Mount St. Bernard's and Ramsgate.

PULPIT (Lat. pulpitum, a platform). The raised place enclosed by a low wall or parti-tion for the accommodation of the preacher; except in cathedral-churches, it should be on the gospel-side of the nave. Unless the church is too large, a bishop preaches sitting on a faldstool at the altar or choir gates, reminiscent of the primitive custom of preaching from his throne. Normally there are no pulpits in churches of Eastern rites; the preacher stands before the iconostasis or at the entrance to the sanctuary.

PULPITUM (Lat.). Another name for the choir-screen (q.v.); a lectern.

PUNISHMENT. i. Suffering inflicted for wrong done. It is retrospective or retributive if it is inflicted with a view to restoring the balance of justice disturbed by the evil-doer, prospective if it looks to the amendment of the offender (remedial, medicinal) and the encouragement of others not to imitate him (deterrent). In a well-ordered society the punishments imposed on law-breakers partake of the nature of all three kinds, according to the offence, the offender and other circumstances. According to St. Thomas, the remedial effect must be foremost in the legislator's mind. The philosophers of Utilitarianism (q.v.) and even more the Humanitarians who followed them, deny that retributive punishment is defensible in ethics; they are confuted by the universal judgement of mankind, which in all times and places has required that one of the functions of punishment shall be to punish; and the Christian knows that Almighty God himself inflicts retributive punishment on those who wilfully and maliciously disobey him.

ii. In canon law. The Church has the right, independent of any human authority, to punish her subjects guilty of offences with both spiritual and temporal penalties. In practice the Church rarely uses temporal penalties. The right to punish belongs to the pope universally and to ordinaries locally. The chief forms of punishment in use in the Church are censures, vindicative penalties, penal remedies and penances. Canonists and theologians are divided on the question whether the Church has the power of the sword, i.e., the right to inflict the death penalty. History gives many instances of popes using this power as the secular rulers of the Papal States, many again of the Church handing over to the secular arm (i.e., the state) criminals whom she has convicted of heresy, etc., for execution according to the current civil law; but no instance is known of the Church as a religious society wielding the sword. Her canon law has always forbidden clerics to shed human blood.

PUNISHMENT, CAPITAL. The right of the state to inflict the punishment of death as the penalty for grave crimes against society is necessary to its well-being, not only as a vindicative punishment (q.v.), but also as a salutary deterrent. The experiment has been made by several states of substituting life-imprisonment for the death penalty, but it is difficult to draw any useful conclusions from the results. According to St. Thomas this penalty is lawful not only because the criminal has by his crime become a destroyer of the common good but also because, by choosing to fall from the order of reason, he partakes in some measure of the state of slavery of the lower animals which are ordered only for the use of others. So the punishment of death, by giving him an opportunity to restore the order of reason in himself by an act of conversion to his last end, enables him to recover his dignity as a human being. See also PUNISHMENT, ii.

PUNISHMENT, MEDICINAL. An ecclesiastical penalty inflicted for an external and wilful violation of law, intended directly to procure the correction of the delinquent. Censures (q.v.) constitute this type of punishment and are withdrawn when the culprit ceases to be contumacious.

PUNISHMENT, VICARIOUS. The penalty due to an offence paid by some other than the actual offender; a misnomer, since, strictly speaking, a penalty becomes a punishment only when paid by the guilty one. Hence, strictly speaking, Christ was not *punished* for our sins; rather he voluntarily paid on our behalf the penalty due to them, though he did not undergo the precise penalties which we had deserved.

PUNISHMENT, VINDICATIVE. An ecclesiastical penalty inflicted for an external and wilful crime with a view to expiating the crime. Degradation and deposition (qq.v.) are forms of this punishment.

PURE ACT. That in which there is absolutely no admixture of potentiality whatsoever. Pure Act is therefore the absolute perfect in every order of perfection. Pure Act is synonymous with God.

PURE NATURE. The condition in which man would be had God never given him any gifts beyond those due to human nature; enjoying his natural powers of soul and body, intellect, free will, subject to the moral law, guided by conscience: but without original sin and sanctifying grace, destined neither to Heaven nor Hell, but to an eternity of natural happiness or natural misery. To Adam were gratuitously given the preternatural gifts (q.v.) which, along with sanctifying grace gratuitously bestowed, constituted him in the state of original justice (q.v.).

PURGATIVE WAY, The. The state of beginners in the spiritual life. "First, indeed, the principal effort incumbent on a man is to quit sin and resist his concupiscences, which tend to destroy charity; and this is proper to beginners, in whom charity is to be nourished and fostered lest it be destroyed" (St. Thomas II-II, xxiv, 9). The soul is still in its spiritual infancy, its charity is weak, and the main effort, therefore, must be the negative one of warding off the things that would kill it. Meditation (q.v.) is the prayer proper to this way, beginning with meditation on the four last things. It is the time to initiate mortification (q.v.), especially the essential mortification of keeping the commandments and fulfilling the duties of one's state of life. It is to be noted that St. Thomas says that purgation is the principal aim here; therefore it is not the only one. The doctrine of the three ways, purgative, illuminative and unitive, is traditional in mystical theology, in East and West, from very early times. They are really three stages of spiritual growth, corresponding to the quite natural division of souls into beginners, proficients and the fully developed, and the labels affixed to them denote the outstanding, not the only, feature of that part of the spiritual course. They are not rigidly divided one from the other, and a soul may be in a true sense in all three at once. Thus the way of union, for example, includes the fierce purgation of the dark night of the spirit (q.v.), and many graces of illumination that perfect the soul as a follower of Christ.

PURGATORY. i. The place and state in which souls suffer for a while and are purged after death, before they go to Heaven, on account of their sins. Venial (q.v.) sins, which have never in life been remitted by an act of repentance or love or by good deeds, and grave sins, the guilt of which with its eternal punishment has indeed been removed by God after an act of repentance but for which there is still left a debt of temporal punishment due to his justice on account of the imperfection of that repentance, must be purged away after death by the pain of intense longing for God, whose blissful vision is delayed, and also, as is commonly taught, by some pain of sense, inflicted probably by material fire. It is of faith that those in Purgatory can be helped by the prayers and sacrifices of the faithful on earth and especially by the acceptable Sacrifice of the Altar. Though there is no ecclesiastical decision in the matter, it is a common custom to pray *to* the souls in Purgatory that they will intercede for us with God. "I do not believe it would be possible to find any joy comparable to that of a soul in Purgatory, except the joy of the Blessed in Paradise. For every sight, however little, that can be gained of God exceeds every pain and every joy that man can conceive without it" (St. Catherine of Genoa).*

ii. Eastern doctrine. The state of departed souls is often stated to be a point at issue between the Catholic Church and dissident Eastern churches. They all offer the holy Sacrifice and pray for the dead, but Orthodox theologians frequently say that they deny the doctrine of Purgatory. Their doctrine is

---

* St. Catherine of Genoa also states that the Poor Souls' "joy in God" does not diminish their great pain. The sight of God which she speaks of is a seeing of "all things . . . as they are in God." (*Treatise on Purgatory*, Chaps. XVI, XII).—*Publisher*, 1997.

certainly less developed, and set out in different terms, but it is substantially the same as that of the Catholic Church; they strenuously deny any element of material fire, but neither does the Church impose this. The position of the other dissident Eastern churches is similar. The Greek Orthodox English catechism appears to contradict itself in this matter, seeming to contain both an assertion and a denial of the particular judgement at death.

PURIFICATION, The. A feast of our Lady (Feb. 2), commemorating her ritual purification in the Temple after childbirth, according to the Jewish law. It is accompanied by the blessing, distribution and procession with candles, whence the English name Candlemas (cf., Hypapante, Unclean).

PURIFICATOR. A small piece of linen used to dry the chalice and the celebrant's fingers when they have been cleansed with wine after the communion. In the Byzantine rite a small sponge is used for equivalent purposes. Used purificators, as well as corporals and palls (qq.v.), must not be handled by lay-people until they have been washed out once by a major cleric.

PURITANISM. i. Historically, a diffused movement, rather than a party, in English history, active and powerful from the reign of Elizabeth till the Restoration in 1660. It regarded the English Reformation as incomplete, reprobated all ritual and religious holidays whatsoever, practised a morality of great strictness, and condemned dancing, fine clothes, etc., as ungodly and sinful.

ii. An exaggerated rigorism which sees in remote or no occasions of sin proximate occasions, and in proximate occasions actual sin: condemning the use of fermented liquors, betting and gambling, Sunday games, dancing and noisy amusements, uneuphemistic speech, images of nudity, and so on, as bad in themselves. In its worst forms it is found among some English-speaking non-Catholics and is a heritage from i above, buttressed by a philosophy sometimes admittedly manichæan. Among individual Catholics rigorism or scrupulosity sometimes results in a kind of Jansenistic puritanism.

iii. Among the irreligious or indifferent is sometimes observed a sort of puritanism which fears the censure of society on what may be deemed unusual or contrary to custom or etiquette. This is more properly conventionalism or prudery.

PURITY. That condition of innocence which is preserved by abstinence from sin and especially by the observance of continence and chastity according to one's state of life; freedom from stain, defilement, adulteration; hence purity of soul, heart, conscience, motive, or intention. Purity in its ordinary sense of chastity according to one's state is a peculiarly sacred precept. "Certain actions are wrong, because in them some type is violated, some sacred symbolism outraged, and the dishonour done to the type redounds upon the antitype or thing typified. Such I conceive to be the radical reason of the grievousness of sins against purity. . . . The mischief and malice of such a life is not simply its unhealthiness, nor its undoing of character, nor even its uselessness and injury to the soul, but its offending against the symbolism of things mighty and holy" (Rickaby, S. J. Cf., Matrimony.)

PURPLE. i. The liturgical colour of vestments used on Sundays and ferias in Septuagesima, Lent and Advent, on rogation and ember days (except at Whitsun) and on vigils (except Epiphany, Ascension, white, and Pentecost, red at Mass, white at office, purple at prophecies, etc.). It is also used at the blessing of candles and other occasions, and for votive Masses of penitence and the Passion and the feast of Holy Innocents on a week-day.

ii. Purple is the colour proper to prelates of the Western church, and their birettas, cassocks, mozzette, etc., are of that colour unless they belong to a religious order. A priest is said to be "raised to the sacred purple" when he becomes a cardinal, though the cardinalitial colour is actually scarlet. Roman purple is reddish in shade.

PUSEYISM. An obsolete name for the activities and principles of the Oxford Movement (q.v.), from E. B. Pusey (1800-82), one of its leaders.

PUSILLANIMITY (Lat. pusillus, petty; animus, spirit). Mean-spiritedness: the vicious exaggeration of the virtue of humility. In his absolute and unreasoning contempt for himself and his abilities, the pusillanimous man lacks in respect for God who made him and endowed him with powers, and in his refusal of the more favourable estimates of his fellow men he fails in deference towards the opinions of others perhaps better able to judge.

PUTATIVE MARRIAGE (Lat. putativus, supposed). A marriage which is invalid, but has been contracted in good faith by at least one party. Such marriage remains putative until both parties have certain knowledge of its nullity. The children of a putative marriage are legitimate, and children born out of wedlock are legitimatized even by a putative marriage.

PYX (Gr. πυξίς, box). i. A small round metal vessel in which the Blessed Sacrament is carried to the sick when this has to be done privately. It is enclosed in a silk bag and hung round the neck by a cord.

ii. A ciborium (q.v. i).

iii. A vessel, often in the shape of a dove (at Durham, a pelican), in which the Blessed Sacrament was formerly ordinarily reserved, covered by a veil and suspended above the altar. This is now only permitted by very special privilege, e.g., at Amiens cathedral and at Valoires in the same diocese. Its use in England did not survive Queen Mary's reign. A similar form is still used in some churches of Eastern rite: e.g., at the Melkite church in Paris the Blessed Sacrament is enclosed in a dove which is hung under a small dome on the altar; the same is suspended from the *ciborium* of the altar at S. Atanasio in Rome (*cf.*, Artophorion).

Q

Q, the first letter of the Ger. *Quelle* (source), is the *siglum* adopted to designate the document supposed to have been used by the authors of our first and third gospels, in addition to the text of the gospel of St. Mark, to compile our extant St. Matthew and St. Luke. The existence of such a document and the offered solution of the Synoptic Problem (*q.v.*) rest on inconclusive arguments.

QUADRAGESIMA [DIES], *i.e.*, the fortieth (fasting) day before Easter, a term which has become the liturgical name for the whole of the Lent season in Latin liturgical books.

QUADRAGESIMO ANNO. An encyclical letter on repairing and improving the social order in accordance with the Gospel, published by Pope Pius XI in 1931 on the 40th anniversary of *Rerum novarum* (*q.v.*): perhaps the most important and certainly the most discussed of all Pius XI's utterances. Of *Rerum novarum* he wrote, "The high and noble teaching of Leo XIII, which was new and strange to worldly ears, was looked on with suspicion by some, even among Catholics, and gave offence to others": this was at least equally true of *Quadragesimo anno*. The encyclical makes a masterly analysis of contemporary industry and its results, speaking particularly strongly of the economic despotism of the few, "a natural result of limitless free competition"; and it gives no less masterly direction where to look for remedies, notably in the principle of the just wage and the enabling of "propertyless wage-earners" to acquire "a certain moderate ownership" of property.

QUADRIVIUM (Lat., crossroads, *i.e.*, four ways). See ARTS, LIBERAL.

QUÆSTOR (Lat., a seeker). A preacher appointed to collect alms for public purposes, *e.g.*, the building of a cathedral, furnishing a crusade; indulgences were usually attached to contributing. The system gave rise to many and great abuses and was abolished by the Council of Trent (*cf.*, Pardoner).

QUAKERS, The. A name, originally contemptuous, for members of the Society of Friends (*q.v.*); it originated in the 17th century with reference to their supposed "quaking at the word of the Lord."

QUAM OBLATIONEM. The first words of a prayer in the canon of the Mass, asking God unreservedly to bless the offering, and leading up to the words of institution. It is accompanied by three signs of the cross over the offerings, and one each over bread and wine separately. Some scholars see in it a mutilated *epiklesis*.

QUAM SINGULARI. A decree of the Congregation of the Sacraments in 1910 restoring the custom of receiving children at holy communion at an early age, which had fallen into disuse. It directed that a child should be prepared and brought to confession and communion so soon as it begins to use reason and can tell right from wrong (roughly about 7 years of age); it is sufficient that it should have an elementary idea of God, the Incarnation and the Redemption, that it should know the difference between the sacred Host and common bread, and appreciate the necessity of receiving it in a state of grace. This decree has to be read to the people in all public churches once every year, about Easter time.

QUANTA CURA. An encyclical of Pope Pius IX, in 1864, to which was attached a syllabus of errors (*q.v.*). It particularly refers to the "impious, absurd and calamitous" teaching that the government of society should be undertaken without reference to religion, true or false, that the family derives the reason for its existence from the requirements of civil law, and that the same law can deprive parents of their right to bring up their own children.

QUARANT' ORE (It., forty hours). The Forty Hours' exposition of the Blessed Sacrament (*q.v.*).

QUARANTINE (It. *quaranta*, forty). A period of 40 days. The term is frequently used in the granting of indulgences, *e.g.*, "7 years and 7 quarantines," 40 days of penance (*i.e.*, a Lent) having been a common ecclesiastical penalty in the early Church. It therefore represents the remittance of an amount of temporal punishment equivalent to that remitted by doing that penance.

QUARR. A Benedictine abbey of the congregation of France, near Ryde in the Isle of Wight. When the monks of Solesmes, not willing to ask the authorization to continue from the infidel French government, voluntarily left their home in 1901 they went to Appuldurcombe, near Wroxall; they moved to Quarr in 1908. On their return to France after the first Great War a community was left at Quarr. The buildings adjoin a former Cistercian abbey. The monks of this monastery are noted for the perfection of their carrying out of the sacred liturgy.

QUARTER TENSE (Old Fr. *quatre tens,* four times). An old term for the ember days (*q.v.*) still used in Ireland and elsewhere.

QUARTODECIMAN CONTROVERSY, The. The first of several disputes about the date on which Easter should be kept. The Quartodecimans (Lat. *quattuordecima,* fourteen) observed it on the same day as the Pasch of the Jews, 14 Nisan, on whatever day of the week it fell. The present practice was imposed by the Council of Nicæa in 325.

QUASI-DOMICILE. Residence begun in a parish or quasi-parish (parochial quasi-domicile), or at least in a diocese, vicariate or prefecture (diocesan quasi-domicile), together with the intention of remaining there for more than six months, if nothing calls one away, or together with actual residence continued for more than six months, but without the intention of remaining permanently. A quasi-domicile is retained until actual departure takes place with the intention of not returning. Minors and wives can acquire a quasi-domicile of their own, though not a domicile. A quasi-domicile makes one subject to the laws of the place where it is situated, if one is actually residing there. It also makes one a subject of the local ordinary and a parishioner of the local rector. It constitutes sufficient residence for licit celebration of marriage by the rector (*cf.,* Domicile).

QUASI-INSPIRATION. See ACCLAMATION, i.

QUASIMODO SUNDAY. Low Sunday (*q.v.*), from the first word of the introit.

QUASI-PARISH. See MISSION, ii.

QUEBEC (*Quebecensis*). The oldest diocese in North America. In 1632 the archbishop of Rouen claimed jurisdiction over the territory of New France; 27 years later it was made a vicariate apostolic; and in 1674 the diocese of Quebec was established. Its first bishop was Francis de Montmorency Laval, after whom Laval University (*q.v.*) is named. In 1844 the see became metropolitan, its suffragan dioceses now being Amos, Chicoutimi, Gaspé, Nicolet, Rimouski, and Trois-Rivières. As these names suggest, the inhabitants of Quebec province are mostly French-Canadians. The cathedral, which is a minor basilica (*q.v.*), is the successor, on the same site, of the first parish-church of Quebec, built in 1647.

QUEEN'S DAUGHTERS, The. The Daughters of the Queen of Heaven, an association of American lay-women founded at Saint Louis, in 1889, to supplement the charitable works of the Society of St. Vincent de Paul. The society works to a certain extent in collaboration with certain religious congregations and has branches in many parts of the U.S.A.

QUEST (sometimes in French, *quête*). The begging for alms undertaken by lay-brothers and extern sisters of the mendicant Friars Minor, Capuchins and Poor Clares, who are allowed by rule to possess no property of their own; the daily expedition of the Sisters of Nazareth and Little Sisters of the Poor to collect food, clothing, etc., for their indigent and aged dependents.

QUICUMQUE VULT, The. The opening words of the Athanasian creed (*q.v.*) in Latin used for the whole: "Whoever wishes. . . ."

QUIDDITY (Lat. *quid,* what). A word coined to mean the essence (*q.v.*) of a thing. The answer to the question "What is it?" tells us the essence or the quiddity or whatness of the thing.

QUIETISM. The false mystical teaching of Michel de Molinos (1640-96), who held that perfection consisted in the complete passivity of the soul. "Let God act" was his motto. Once the soul has made the act of full passivity, which she could do quite early in the spiritual life, she must make no other act of any virtue, nor even resist temptations. The gravest sins in such a soul were merely the work of the Devil and must not be heeded. This teaching was condemned by Pope Innocent XI in 1687. A mitigated quietism was taught by Mme. Guyon (1648-1717) and the great Fénelon (1651-1715): it has none of the immoral consequences of pure quietism, but it teaches the possibility of a pure love of God in which the soul can be indifferent to salvation (hence hope is not a virtue of the perfect) and can even make an absolute surrender of eternal happiness. Pope Innocent XII condemned twenty-three propositions of Fénelon in 1699.

QUIGNON BREVIARY, The. The most important of several attempts entirely to refashion the Divine Office of the Roman church, made by Cardinal Quiñonez (*d.* 1540). Among many innovations, he provided for the omission of all hymns, antiphons, responsories, etc., when the Office was said privately, a rigidly fixed arrangement of the psalms and the reading of the whole of Holy Scripture spread over the year. It was authorized for private use for some time but entirely rejected by Pope Paul IV in 1558. Cranmer made use of it in drawing up the Anglican Book of Common Prayer.

QUINQUAGESIMA (Lat., the fiftieth [day before Easter]). The Sunday next before the beginning of Lent (*cf.*, Septuagesima).

QUIRE. An archaic but not obsolete spelling of *choir* (*q.v.*). It is sometimes convenient to use it to distinguish the part of a church from the body of singers therein.

QUIRINAL, The. A palace on the Quirinal hill at Rome, built by Pope Gregory XIII, in 1580, and a papal residence till 1870, when it was seized by the Italian government. Since then it has been the palace of the kings of Italy. In times past The Quirinal was spoken of as a power in opposition to The Vatican.

QUOTATIONS, TACIT, in the Bible. The Biblical Commission in 1905 issued two warnings concerned with the interpretation of historical books of Holy Scripture: the first, against admitting in books any so-called tacit ·quotations from uninspired authors for the truth of which the inspired author does not vouch and which in consequence might be erroneous; the second, against departing from the literal sense in such books without cogent reason. The possibility of such quotations and such not strictly historical passages is not rejected in principle, but overwhelmingly solid proof is demanded in every case.

R

RABAT (Fr. *rabattu*, turned down). Part of the dress of the French secular clergy, consisting of a small piece of black material attached to a rudimentary collar and falling on the chest; it is divided lengthways into two rectangular parts, joined together and edged with white. It is now nearly superseded by the Roman collar. A white *rabat* is worn by the Brothers of Christian Doctrine, university professors, magistrates, barristers and attorneys, and is simply a survival of the turning-down of the neck of the linen shirt (*collet*), afterwards made detachable for cleanliness and worn by clerics and laymen alike. *Cf.*, the white "bands" worn by barristers, solicitors and other men-of-law in Great Britain.

RABBI (Heb., my master). i. The spiritual head and legal authority of a Jewish community. The rabbinate is conferred by a board of examiners. He gives rulings on matters of law and custom, family or business disputes, the ritual purity or otherwise of food or vessels, etc. The head of a less important synagogue is simply a "minister."
ii. The stock (*q.v.*, ii), corrupted from *rabat*, above.

RACCOLTA (It., collection). A book containing all the prayers, exercises, etc., to which indulgences have been attached and are still in force, with particulars of the indulgences. An official edition is published by the Congregation of the Holy Office, and translations are published locally for the use of the faithful.

RAMSGATE (St. Augustine's Abbey). The first house of the English province of the Cassinese Congregation of the Primitive Observance O.S.B. It was founded in 1856, when some English youths, who had undergone their training at Subiaco, returned to their native land to revive the Benedictine life near the spot where it had first been planted by St. Augustine. The house became an abbey in 1896. The monks conduct a large preparatory school, and have the charge of parishes incorporated with the monastery.

RANK OF FEAST. To arrive at the relative degree of solemnity with which they shall be observed, and to assist in the solution of difficulties arising from concurrence and occurrence (*qq.v.*), a liturgical rank is attached to every feast. These are, in ascending order, simple (*simplex*), double (*duplex*, *q.v.*), greater double (*duplex maior*), double of the 2nd class, double of the 1st class (*duplex secundae*, *primae*, *classis*). Feasts are by no means everywhere of the same class (except the greatest ones), *e.g.*, in the general calendar (*q.v.*) of the Roman church, ordinary Sundays and most saints' days are doubles, whereas in the Benedictine calendar they are both greater doubles; a feast has a higher rank in a place where it is proper (*q.v.*) than where it is not. The Ambrosian and other uses of the Latin rite have their own special classification, *e.g.*, the Dominican is: whole double, double, semi-double, simple, 3 lessons, commemoration (*cf.*, Feast, Feria). In Eastern rites the relative importance of feasts is differentiated in quite different ways; the Sunday office is never wholly superseded.

RAPHOE (*Rapotensis*). An Irish see, suffragan of Armagh; it was vacant for long periods between 1610 and 1725. It includes practically the whole of Donegal. The bishop's residence, cathedral and college are at Letterkenny. The patrons of the diocese and titulars of the cathedral are St. Eunan (Adamnan, Sept. 23) and St. Colmcille (Columba, June 9). Irish name: Ráth-bhoth.

RAPOTENSIS. The adjectival form of the see of Raphoe (*q.v.*) used in the designation of its bishop in Latin documents. Noun: *Rapotum*.

RAPTURE (Lat. *raptus*, seized). Sometimes used as a synonym for ecstasy (*q.v.*). But St. Teresa distinguishes it as a special kind of ecstasy, sudden in its onset, whereas ordinary ecstasy is quiet. She compares it to a "strong giant," or "a whirlwind carrying everything away." A more developed form of it, of special intensity, is called "flight of the spirit." In this the soul seems to leave the body and fly towards heaven (*cf.*, St. Paul's rapture, described in 2 Cor. xii, 2 *seq.*). The body is sometimes carried from the earth by the soul's vehemence, which is the phenomenon of levitation (*q.v.*).

RAPTUS (Lat., seizure, ravishment). i. See ECSTASY, and above.

ii. The Raptus of St. Elias is a feast of the Carmelite order on June 17, commemorating the assumption of the prophet (4 Kings, ii, 11).

iii. The impediment of abduction (*q.v.*).

RASH (Lat. *temeraria*). A proposition is censured as rash or temerarious when it is overbold in its contrariety from the common opinion current in the Church on a matter of faith or morals.

RASON. The outer garment of everyday dress proper to clergy of Eastern rite. It is a long loose black gown with wide sleeves, something like a Benedictine choir cowl but open down the front. It is also part of the monastic habit. The Ruthenian and some other Catholic clergy have given up the *rason*.

RASOPHORE (Gr., *rason*-wearer). A monk of the Byzantine rite in the lowest grade of monastic life, so called because he wears a *rason* over his tunic. Many continue in it for life, and may be elected abbot etc.

RATIFIED MARRIAGE. See RATUM below.

RATIO STUDIORUM. Abbreviation of "Ratio atque Institutio Studiorum Societatis Iesu" (The Method and System of Studies of the Society of Jesus), first published in 1599, revised in 1832, and still in some provinces the pedagogical norm in Jesuit schools and colleges. In practice the "Ratio" is modified by the demand for "scientific" or modern-side education, and its efficiency in attaining its prime object, the training of the mind, is somewhat impaired by the necessity of teaching with a view to success in public examinations.

RATIONAL SOUL. The substantial form (*q.v.*) of the human body; distinct from mind, which is a power through which the soul understands.

RATIONALE. An episcopal ornament, approximating to the *pallium*, worn formerly by a number of bishops of the Empire, but now only by those of Cracow, Eichstätt, Paderborn and Nancy (representing Toul), when they pontificate. It is in the form of a flat collar with metal appendages back and front.

RATIONALISM. The error of those who reject all revelation and give assent to nothing but what can be attained by the natural power of their own reason.

RATISBON CHANT. A debased version of Gregorian chant taking its name from its issue by the Ratisbon school of music in the middle of the 19th century. It is now definitely set aside and superseded by the Vatican edition (*q.v.*). It was a complete reprint of the ill-conceived Medicean edition of 1614-15. It included the Graduale as represented by Iginio to have been "corrected" by his father, Giovanni Pierluigi da Palestrina. It has since been shown by Mgr. R. Casimiri that Palestrina never completed the work of correction and moreover that by tearing the MS. in two he had signified his unwillingness to publish it. The Medicean edition was based on the current Venetian practice of plainsong.

RATUM NON CONSUMMATUM, MARRIAGE (Lat., ratified but not consummated). A valid sacramental contract which has been made, with the usual ceremony before a priest or otherwise, between a Christian man and woman, but has not yet been consummated by bodily union. Such an uncompleted marriage may be entirely dissolved (*a*) by dispensation of the Holy See for a grave reason, *e.g.*, a probable suspicion of impotence in either party, and (*b*) by the solemn religious profession of either party. The last is a state of affairs very unlikely to arise, for a religious profession is invalid unless preceded by a canonical noviciate, and such noviciate cannot be made by a person whose marriage subsists, except by dispensation of the Holy See.

RAYAH (Ar. *ra'iyyah*, herd). A Christian subject of the former Turkish empire.

READER. See LECTOR.

REAL PRESENCE. The doctrine that "in the Sacrament of the Eucharist the body and blood of our Lord Jesus Christ together with his soul and divinity are contained truly, really and substantially, and not merely in sign, figure or virtue" (Council of Trent, sess. xiii, can. 1). This statement condemns the error of Zwingli that the body of Christ is only representatively there; the error of Calvin that it is only virtually present by the effects of the sacrament; and the very common modern error that it is only there ideally by apprehension and faith. The Real Presence is effected by Transubstantiation (*q.v.*). Both doctrines are of faith, but they are not to be confused.

REALISM. This term signifies (*a*) the doctrine of a real extramental world, and (*b*) as opposed to Nominalism (*q.v.*) and Conceptualism (*q.v.*) to denote the theories according to which universal ideas are objective or real. Exaggerated realism teaches that these ideas, as such, exist outside the mind (Plato). It is, however, untenable that the universals (*q.v.*), as such, are individual and subsistent. Individuality and universality are mutually exclusive; and only individuals exist. The universal *as universal* is in the mind only, but the *foundation* of the universal is real and is *in* the individual, for it is nought else than the real essence in the individual; this is *Moderate* realism.

REALITY. That which has or can have existence. Actual reality is that which exists; possible reality that which can exist. Reality is distinct from mental being (*ens rationis*) which is in, and wholly dependent on, the mind, *e.g.*, "subject" and "predicate" as such.

REASON. This term is used sometimes to signify the total aggregate of spiritual powers possessed by man, and in this sense reason is said to separate man from the brute; sometimes it is used to mean simply the intellectual power of understanding, and sometimes to express the particular exercise of the understanding involved in the process of ratiocination, or reasoning. Reasoning and understanding, however, do not pertain to different faculties: the former is but a series of applications, a continuous exercise of the latter. Reason, speculative and practical, means the same intellectual power under different aspects. Viewed as apprehending truth or reality, the intellect is termed speculative; as cognizing the relation of action to an end, it is called practical. Conscience is thus described as an exercise of the practical reason.

REASON, PRINCIPLE OF SUFFICIENT. The same as the principle of causality, understood in its most universal sense. Everything that begins to be has not only an efficient cause (*q.v.*) but also a final and a formal and in certain cases also a material cause. From this principle Leibniz vainly endeavoured to establish his Optimism (*q.v.*).

REASON AND FEELING. In the doctrine of the schoolmen conscience or the moral faculty is simply the intellect directed towards the moral aspects of action, and was called by them the Practical or Moral Reason; it is not distinct from the Speculative Reason. By the latter the mind discerns truth and falsity, by the former the rightness and wrongness of conduct. On the other hand, in the false theory of a separate Moral Sense (*q.v.*) conscience is described as a special aptitude of the mind capable of feeling the moral quality of actions. Hume resolved the moral sense into Reason and Feeling; the first assists in ascertaining the useful and harmful consequence of different acts—but the chief element in conscience is sentiment or feeling. Such confusion between the in-

tellectual, emotional and appetitive elements in the exercise of the moral faculty has been the cause of much error, and these factors must be carefully distinguished, as follows: Moral Intuition is the percipient act by which the truth of a self-evident moral principle is immediately cognized. The name is also applied to the discernment of the moral quality of a particular action; this exertion of the practical reason, as well as moral decisions based on it, may be best called the Moral Judgement. Moral Sentiment is not an ethical cognition, but the attendant emotion—the feeling of satisfaction or remorse, of approval or disapproval, excited by the consideration of a good or bad action. Moral Instinct denotes a native disposition towards certain socially useful acts, *e.g.*, gratitude, generosity. Moral Habits, that is, dispositions acquired by intelligent free exercise, are moral in the fullest sence.

REASONING. The process whereby the mind from a known thing proceeds to the knowledge of an unknown thing. See SYLLOGISM; DEDUCTION; INDUCTION.

REASONS, SEMINAL. A theory of St. Augustine according to which God placed in matter certain active forces, seminal reasons or principles, whose germination, given the realization of appropriate circumstances, produced all individual beings. For each species there is supposed to be a distinct germ. It is likewise supposed that these seminal reasons were first of all impressed on, or passed through, the minds of the angels to matter; by these impressions angels know material and individual things.

REBAPTISM. Baptism is a sacrament which confers a character (*q.v.*) and therefore it cannot be repeated when it has once been validly received. The attempt to rebaptize is a grievous sin. But if there is a prudent doubt concerning the fact or validity of a previous baptism, conditional baptism (*q.v.*) must be administered. The rebaptism of converts from heresy was the subject of much controversy in the 3rd century; St. Cyprian approved of it, but Pope Stephen I condemned it and threatened to excommunicate all who persisted in the practice.

REBELLION. An armed aggression of citizens against their government which has offered no adequate provocation for such an attack. It is gravely unlawful as being directed against the general good of the community; "to despise legitimate authority in whomsoever vested is unlawful as a rebellion against the Divine Will" (Pope Leo XIII). From rebellion it is necessary to distinguish resistance, even armed, of citizens against tyranny. This is an act of self-defence against an unjust aggressor, and is justifiable under certain conditions (*cf.*, Tyrannicide, Revolution).

RECEIVED TEACHING. See ACCEPTED TEACHING.

RECEPTIONISM. The doctrine held by some Protestants, especially Lutherans, that Christ is present in the Eucharist only at the moment of its worthy reception by a devout Christian.

RECIDIVISM (Lat. *recidere,* to fall back). Falling into the same sin after many confessions thereof and showing little or no improvement. Absolution is not refused on this account (though as a matter of discipline it may be deferred) even though the confessor expects him to sin again, unless he judges that the offender is nursing affection for the sin and has not here and now a firm purpose of amendment.

RECOLLECTION (Lat. *recolligere,* to draw together). i. The endeavour to live in the presence of God by maintaining peace of soul, curbing the tendency to seek dissipation and pleasure, practising solitude and silence and striving to keep supernatural motives in view in one's conduct. It is very necessary in the spiritual life.
ii. Two grades of prayer. The first, or active recollection, is the same as the prayer of simplicity (*q.v.*), and is so called because the soul endeavours to still her faculties in order to concentrate on God with a simple regard. The second, or passive recollection, is the beginning of the prayer of quiet (*q.v.*), the faculties are quieted, not now by their own effort, but by the gentle action of divine grace.

RECOLLECTS. i. Franciscan. A family of the strictly observant branch of the Franciscans started in France at the end of the 16th century. See OBSERVANTS.
ii. See HERMITS OF ST. AUGUSTINE, iii.

RECONCILIATION. i. Of a church. A consecrated church which has been subjected to violation (*q.v.*) must, before it can be used for sacred purposes, be reconciled by the bishop or his deputy with the form provided in the "Pontificale," Gregorian water (*q.v.*) being specially blessed for the purpose. If the church was only blessed, it can be reconciled by the parish priest, or another, using ordinary holy water. A violated church need not be reconsecrated unless desecration (*q.v.*) has also occurred.
ii. Of penitents. This formerly took place solemnly on Maundy Thursday, the bishop having expelled the penitents from the church on Ash Wednesday. Both forms are still printed in the "Pontificale" but have been disused since the 12th century. This reconciliation of penitents gave rise to the solemn papal blessing with plenary indulgence from St. Peter's on Maundy Thursday (afterwards extended to other days and basilicas, *cf.,* apostolic benediction), which then

was not strictly *urbi et orbi* but rather particularly for those present.

RECTOR (Lat., a ruler). A priest legitimately appointed as the ruling head of a church (parish or otherwise), college (*e.g.,* seminary) or institution (*e.g.,* university). The superior general of the Redemptorists is called the Rector Major. A rector differs from a chaplain in having the whole management and not merely the spiritual duties. The rector of a parish (*parochus*) is a priest or moral person (*q.v.*) to whom a parish is committed *in titulum,* with the cure of souls to be exercised under the authority of the local ordinary (*q.v.*). Some rectors are irremovable, others removable, according to the procedure required to remove them from office. They are appointed by the local ordinary, but not by the vicar general without a special mandate. Priests who are religious may be appointed removable rectors. A priest may not be rector of more than one parish at the same time. Certain functions are reserved to the rector, *e.g.,* to administer solemn Baptism and Extreme Unction, to assist at marriages and give the nuptial blessing, to take holy Communion and Viaticum publicly to the sick, to conduct funerals and perform certain ceremonies of Holy Week; and also certain fees. He is bound to reside in the presbytery close to the parish church. He is bound to apply Mass for the people on the prescribed days, and he is allowed two months' absence in each year, which the ordinary may lengthen or shorten for a grave cause.

RECTOR, PROFESSOR, EMERITUS (Lat., honourably discharged). A title of honour sometimes conferred on a retired rector or professor of a university, seminary, etc.

RECTOR MAGNIFICUS (Lat., eminent). The title by which the governing rectors of some universities are distinguished, *e.g.,* Louvain.

RECUSANT (Lat. *recusare,* to refuse). One who was convicted of not attending and refusing to attend service in a church of the Church of England. Others besides Catholics were from time to time recusants, but the word nearly always indicates a Catholic; they were specifically indicated in several statutes. Several Acts against recusancy were passed between 1558 and 1627, and an Act of 1714 provided that anyone refusing the oath of allegiance and supremacy when lawfully tendered became subject to the penalties of a "popish recusant convict": these were fixed by the Act of 1593 at a monthly fine of £20 with various civil disabilities; failure to abjure the realm on nonpayment was a capital felony. These laws were not enforced with uniform strictness at all times but were far from being neglected; certain returns for 23 counties in the reign of Charles II give a total of 10,236 convicted recusants, mostly of the lower classes, over half of them in Lancashire. See PENAL LAW.

RED. i. The liturgical colour of vestments used on the vigil and feast of Pentecost and its octave, for Masses of the Cross and the Precious Blood and on the feasts of martyrs; it is used also for the octave-day of the Holy Innocents and on the feast itself when it falls on a Sunday, and by the pope when he sings a requiem Mass.

ii. Red is the colour proper to cardinals (though it is called "the sacred purple") and their birettas, *cappæ magnæ*, etc., are a bright scarlet. For everyday use the cassock has a red cincture and buttons. Red has been the papal colour since the Emperor Justin granted the use of imperial robes to Pope St. John I (*d.* 526).

RED HAT. A broad-brimmed, flat-crowned scarlet hat with two clusters of 15 tassels, distinctive of a cardinal; the expression "the red hat" is frequently used for the cardinalitial rank and office. It is imposed by the pope on a new cardinal at the first public consistory after his appointment and is not thereafter used until it is hung above his tomb, as may be seen in the Vaughan chantry in Westminster Cathedral. The red biretta is imposed on the day before the public consistory, if in Rome; if abroad, by the pope's delegate or, in Spain and France, by the civil head of the state.

RED MASS. A votive Mass of the Holy Ghost; in England, particularly one celebrated for the benefit of the judges, counsel and solicitors of the Supreme Court of Judicature at the beginning of the legal year or Michaelmas Term.

"RED POPE, The." A nick-name for the cardinal prefect of the Congregation of *Propaganda* (*q.v.*) given to him on account of the importance and widespread jurisdiction of that congregation; red, because that is the colour distinctive both of cardinals and missionaries.

REDEEMER, OUR HOLY. i. See REDEMPTION.

ii. A feast of our Lord under this title is kept in certain places on the 3rd Sunday of July, or on Oct. 23.

REDEMPTION, The. Man having been created in a state of original justice (*q.v.*) by his sin forfeited the friendship of God and became enslaved to the Devil. Christ by his death on the cross, in which he became a substitutional victim for the human race, paid the price of our redemption (buying back); by his satisfactions he blotted out our sin, and by his merits (*q.v.*) he won for us the restoration to the grace and friendship of God. This doctrine of the redemption of the human race therefore comprises the elements of an initial loss and a restoration at a price paid by Christ.

REDEMPTORISTINES, The. The nuns of the Order of the Holy Redeemer, founded in 1731. They are a strictly contemplative, enclosed and penitential order, singing the Divine Office and interceding especially for the conversion of sinners and the works of the Redemptorist fathers. Habit: dark red with blue scapular, blue choir-cloak, sandals, and ring.

REDEMPTORISTS, The. The Congregation of the Most Holy Redeemer, founded by St. Alphonsus Liguori, in 1732. It is devoted to giving missions and retreats, anywhere and everywhere, but particularly to the poor; when not engaged in this work the members live a strict community life, reciting the Divine Office in choir where possible. Perpetual simple vows are taken. The congregation has two provinces in the United States, one for Ireland, and one for Great Britain (which also has mission stations in South Africa). The priests of the Ukrainian vice-province are of the Byzantine rite and have a mission in Canada for the Ruthenian emigrants. Habit: a black cassock with cloth belt and crucifix, white collar, rosary, black cloak, biretta.

REDUCTION (of an altar). The ceremonies and procedure to be followed with respect to the altars of a church which is to be handed over to profane use. It includes the removal and taking away of the whole *mensa* if it is a fixed, and of the small stone if it is an unconsecrated, altar.

REDUCTIONS OF PARAGUAY, The. Indian mission territories administered by the Spanish Jesuits from 1607 for 160 years. "When the Paraguayan missions left the hands of the Jesuits in 1768 they had arrived at what is perhaps the highest degree of civilization to which it is possible to lead a young people. . . . Laws were there respected, morals were pure, a happy brotherhood bound men together, the useful arts and even some of the more pleasing sciences flourished; there was abundance everywhere" (Voltaire). The Jesuit administration was based on the principle that they were the guardians and trustees of the welfare of the Indians, not as a subject or lower race, but as untutored children of God; they had no contempt for their civilization and life; and their enemies failed to produce evidence for the assertion that the missionaries anticipated "the white man's burden" of exploitation. Their opposition to Spanish imperialism, to slavery by colonists, and to the Inquisition, wrought their downfall. In 1767 King Charles III suppressed the Jesuits in the Spanish dominions, and in the following year those of Paraguay unresistingly gave up their 30 missions and another Arcadia came to an end. Of the Reductions only ruins and memories are left.

REFECTORY (Lat. *reficere*, to refresh). The dining-hall of a monastery of men or women. All meals are taken therein, in silence; dinner and supper are accompanied by reading aloud, first a short passage from the rule or the holy Scriptures, then from a more general work such as the life of a saint. Carthusians feed together in the refectory only on Sundays and great feasts.

REFLEXION. An action of mind whereby attention is directed to our own states. This operation constitutes the exercise of self-consciousness, which may be defined as the knowledge which the mind has of its acts as its own.

REFORM. i. Of an Order. The bringing back of a religious order to its primitive austerity and observance of rule when it has become relaxed either through slackness or by lawful and authorized mitigation. This may be done either by a gradual process throughout the whole order, *e.g.*, the Dominicans in the 19th century, or by the creation of a new reformed branch, *e.g.*, the Capuchin Franciscans, the Cluniacs. The Carthusian order alone has never stood in need of a reform, but the existence of an unreformed, mitigated or common observance branch of an order, *e.g.*, the Calced Carmelites, Conventual Franciscans, Cistercians of Common Observance, involves no reproach to its members, their modified rule being necessitated by their work or the requirements of individuals and approved by the Holy See.

ii. Liturgical. (a). Of Pius V. The revisions of the Breviary and Missal published in 1568 and 1570 respectively by Pope St. Pius V and imposed on all dioceses and orders of the Latin rite not having their own use of at least 200 years' antiquity. Thus the Milanese province and the Carthusians, Carmelites, Dominicans and others were enabled to retain theirs and many French dioceses did not finally adopt the new books till the 19th century.

(b). Of Pius X. See DIVINO AFFLATU and his MOTU PROPRIO.

(c) Of Urban VIII. A correction of the Breviary and Missal issued in 1634, only important because of alterations in the text of the office-hymns, the barbarisms and false quantities of Prudentius, Venantius Fortunatus, St. Ambrose and others being offensive to the refined and Ciceronian scholarship of Renaissance Rome. "That those who were responsible outran their commissions and, under pretext of restoring the language of the hymns in accordance with the rules of metre and good grammar, deformed the works of Christian antiquity, is now an established fact" (Chevalier); the older versions, which are still used by the Carthusians, etc., are not merely old, they are better hymns (*cf.*, *Cœlestis urbs Ierusalem* (Roman Breviary) with *Urbs Ierusalem beata* (Monastic Breviary). In the "Vatican Antiphoner" of Pius X the untampered hymns with their melodies are printed in an appendix, for those churches which have permission to use them.

REFORMATION, THE PROTESTANT. The revolt from the Catholic Church in Western Europe begun and carried to its height in the 16th century. It differed from all previous heretical movements in that it was not concerned with one or a few definite points of doctrine but was directed against the whole complex and system of Christianity as then understood; it gave licence to the human self in the spiritual and religious order. Its principal causes were: the excessive temporal power, wealth and privilege which had accrued to the higher clergy, the wicked, worldly and careless lives of many of the clergy, secular and regular, and the decay of philosophy and theology (these resulted partly from the Renaissance, *q.v.*), with consequent low standard of spiritual life among the people generally; the weakening of the authority of the Holy See, following the Great Schism (*q.v.*), increased by the humanistic corruption of the papal court; the parallel insurgence of secular princes. Its principal motives were: desire for the purity of religion and godliness of life which, from the state of the clergy, precipitated a violent and unreasoning anti-clericalism which degenerated into contempt for all spiritual authority; the national ambitions of secular princes which flourished in the break-up of the Catholic integrity of Europe; an appetite for spoil and, as in England, fear of having to give up looted ecclesiastical wealth; in some, a hatred of the Church and Faith which can be attributed only to the direct working of the Devil. The principal results of the Reformation were: the true reform of the Church "in head and members" effected by the Council of Trent and the revivification of Catholicism so thoroughly achieved that it remains vital to this day (the Counter-reformation, *q.v.*); the putting of countless souls, notably in Great Britain, Scandinavia and the German parts of the Empire, in enmity to the Church and consequently outside those means provided by Christ for man to know and attain to God; the disappearance of any "higher unity" holding together the diverse peoples and nations of Europe; the inoculation of men with naturalistic and humanitarian (as opposed to theocentric) philosophy which is now the chiefest enemy of Christianity.

REFORMED, The. An expression commonly used on the continent of Europe, originating in 1561 at Poissy, to distinguish Calvinistic Protestants and their organizations from Lutherans: *e.g.*, the Dutch Reformed Church.

REFRESHMENT SUNDAY. The fourth Sunday of Lent (*Lætare*), with reference to the miracle of the five loaves read at the gospel and the general rejoicing of mid-Lent.

REGALE. An assumed right of sovereigns, often exercised during the middle ages and up to the 18th century, to receive the revenues of episcopal sees during a vacancy and to appoint to certain benefices therein.

REGENT (Lat., *regere*, to rule). A director, *e.g.*, regent of studies.

REGINA CŒLI (Lat., Queen of Heaven). The opening words of the fourth of the antiphons of our Lady (*q.v.*) said or sung standing at the end of the Divine Office from Holy Saturday until after Compline of the Friday after Pentecost. During the same period it is said standing instead of the *Angelus*.

REGISTERS, PAROCHIAL. Canon law requires that every parish priest should keep five registers, of baptisms, confirmations, marriages, deaths and the spiritual state of his people. Marriages of conscience and other private matters are recorded in a separate and secret volume. Subsequent confirmation, marriage, ordination to the subdiaconate or religious profession as they occur must be noted against the name of each baptized person and appear on any baptismal certificate.

REGIUM PLACET (Lat., royal assent). A name sometimes given to that aspect of *Exequatur* (*q.v.*) which requires the approval of the civil power before a newly appointed bishop takes office. For the avoidance of greater evils, *e.g.*, the protracted vacancy of a see, the Holy See sometimes concedes this, or, in a modified and safeguarded form, as a privilege.

REGNANS IN EXCELSIS. The bull by which Pope St. Pius V, in 1570, deposed Queen Elizabeth and absolved her subjects from allegiance.

REGULAR CLERGY, REGULARS. In its strict sense, the priests and other professed members, male and female, of any religious institute (*q.v.*) having solemn vows. In its common sense, those clerics who are bound by vows and live in community according to a rule (*regula*), as opposed to those, seculars, who do not so live, *i.e.*, the ordinary parochial clergy.

REINCARNATION Metempsychosis (*q.v.*).

RELATION. The way one thing holds itself in regard to another. It implies three elements: that which is related, that to which it is related and that whereby the relation is constituted. The first is the subject, the second the term and the third the foundation of the relation, thus: "Father" is the subject, "Son" the term, "Generation" the foundation of the relation. Real relation is the way one thing is ordered to another independently of thought, both terms and the foundation are real; mental relation is dependent upon

thought, which is capable of doubling a real term, *e.g.*, the relation between subject and predicate or between *genus* and species, etc.

RELATIONS, THE JESUIT. Series of letters written by the earliest Jesuit missionaries in foreign countries to their superiors and others in Europe. Selections of these were published annually from 1581 to 1654. Those written by the French pioneers in North America were intended for general circulation in book form and were so published from 1632 till 1673; they are the prime source for the early Christian history of the United States and Canada and of knowledge of the Red Indians of the country. A similar custom prevails among missionaries trained by the Urban College at Rome, every one of whom writes an annual letter to the cardinal prefect of Propaganda giving an account of his work.

RELATIONSHIP in canon law is either natural (by blood, consanguinity, or by marriage, affinity, *qq.v.*), legal (from adoption, *q.v.*), or spiritual. Spiritual relationship is that arising from Baptism and Confirmation, and is contracted by the baptized person with the person baptizing and with the godparents, and by the person confirmed with the sponsor. The relationship involves certain duties on the part of the sponsors (*q.v.*), and that arising from Baptism constitutes a diriment impediment of marriage, which may sometimes be dispensed.

RELIC (Lat., *reliquiæ*, remains). The corpse of a saint or any part thereof; any part of his clothing; any thing intimately connected with him. The veneration of Christian relics (see below) can be traced at least to the middle of the 2nd century and was regulated by the Council of Trent, which directed that no new relics should be admitted without episcopal authentication (*q.v.*). Honour may, and ought, to be paid to those relics whose genuineness is morally certain, but the question of their authenticity is one of fact, to be determined by the evidence, and the Church does not guarantee the genuineness of a single specific relic. The authorization of a Mass and Office (*e.g.*, of the Holy House of Loreto) is not to the contrary; at the time when such is granted the evidence for authenticity is deemed to be sufficient to justify veneration, and so the relic is made the occasion of a new act of worship, which is unaffected by the genuineness or otherwise of the relic: subsequent research may damage the reputation of the relic but cannot invalidate the worship of which it is the occasion. Many famous relics are almost certainly spurious, but there is no need to assume deliberate fraud. Honour given in good faith to a false relic is nevertheless profitable to the worshipper and in no way dishonours the saint; but relics proven and known to be false must be withheld from the people.

Those who make or knowingly sell, distribute or display false relics for veneration incur *ipso facto* excommunication reserved to the bishop. Relics in their cases may be exposed on an altar during sacred ceremonies, presented to the people for veneration, carried in procession, and blessing given therewith; those of the Cross (*q.v.*) are treated with particular reverence. But only those may be publicly honoured for which a proper authentication is held. It is forbidden to buy or sell relics. It is necessary for the valid consecration of an altar, whether fixed or portable, that it contain, sealed into the sepulchre (*q.v.*), relics of at least one martyr; the primitive custom of offering the holy Sacrifice over the tombs of the martyrs is thus perpetuated.

RELICS, DUPLICATION OF, may be accounted for in other ways besides fraud and fabrication, namely, by division: *e.g.*, the three pillars of scourging, at Jerusalem, at Rome and Constantinople, are actually three pieces of pillar; two or more parts of the same skull preserved in different places may each be "the head of St. N . . ."; filings from St. Peter's chains are magnified into a whole manacle through being enclosed in such; by association: something, such as a copy of it, which has touched a certain relic, comes to be regarded as the relic itself; and by other *bona-fide* errors and confusions: *e.g.*, the milk of our Lady, actually pieces of the white rock of the Moghâret as-Sitti Maryam, called the Milk Grotto, at Bethlehem, powdered into water.

RELICS, FEAST OF. Two proper Masses are given in the supplement *pro aliquibus locis* of the Missal, for a feast of all holy Relics on Nov. 5 and, for those churches which have notable relics, a feast in commemoration of the saints whose relics are preserved in the church (no fixed date). The first of these is observed in several English dioceses.

RELICS, THE VENERATION OF, is permitted and encouraged by the Church out of honour for the bodies of the saints, which were temples of the Holy Ghost and will be raised to eternal glory, and to satisfy the universal instinct of mankind to treat with affection and reverence the material souvenirs of those whom we love. Like holy images, sacred relics can neither see, hear nor help us and to give them divine worship would be idolatry; the honour given to them is a relative *dulia* (*q.v.*) or veneration which passes over to those saints with which they are connected (*cf.*, Idolatry); the mind of the Church in this matter is expressed by the prayer said when a relic is presented to be kissed: "May the Lord grant you salvation and peace through the merits and intercession of the holy N . . ." No Catholic is formally bound to the positive veneration of relics, but is forbidden by the Council of Trent to say that such veneration ought not to be given. See AUTHENTICATION.

RELIGION (Lat. *religio*, probably from *relegere*, to treat with care; its connexion with *religare*, to bind, *i.e.*, man and God, is inexact but expressive). i. "Religion is a virtue (*q.v.*) by which men give due worship and reverence to God" (St. Thomas, II-II, lxxxi, 1), as the creator and supreme ruler of all things, and to acknowledge his dependence on God by rendering him a due and fitting worship both interior (*e.g.*, by acts of devotion, reverence, thanksgiving, etc.) and exterior (*e.g.*, by external reverence, liturgical acts, etc.). This virtue can be sinned against by idolatry, superstition, false worship, sacrilege, blasphemy, etc. (*qq.v.*).

ii. A system of beliefs and practices having reference to man's relation with God, *e.g.*, the Catholic religion, the religion of Islam, the Bantu religion: "the sum-total of beliefs, sentiments and practices, individual or social, which have for their object a power which man recognizes as supreme, on which he depends, and with which he can enter, or has entered, into relation" (Grandmaison, S.J.). The first business of religion is to answer the questions: Who and what is God? Why and how are we here? Whither do we go?— and then to direct and help man to the attainment of the end put before him.

iii. In its colloquial general sense among Christians religion is by no means restricted to external or even internal acts of devotion or the cultivation of a feeling of awe in regard to God, as is sometimes supposed. Religion requires that the whole man worship with all his faculties and acts: praise, thanksgiving and petition are only part of the duties of religious worship; the intellect must believe that which is true concerning God (faith) and the will be directed to those actions which are right and the avoidance of those which are wrong (morals).

iv. An archaic and technical name for what is now called a religious institute (*q.v.*), the religion of St. Benedict, of St. Francis, etc., and for the state of those living in such an order. This use survives in the expression "to go into religion," meaning to enter a monastery or convent and in the technical terms "religious" and "religious life" (*qq.v.*).

RELIGION, NATURAL. Those relations between man and God which exist in the nature of things and are recognized by man antecedently to and independently of any divine revelation, real or supposed. The existence (*q.v.*) of God is the primary fact of natural religion, and the Vatican Council defined, against Traditionalism (*q.v.*) and other errors, that "God, the beginning and end of all, can be known with certainty from the works of creation by the natural light of human reason."

RELIGIOSITY (Lat. *-osus,* abounding in). A term generally used in a pejorative sense (*cf.,* piosity—not a dictionary word) to indicate religion held as a sentiment without intellectual or spiritual basis; a morbid and fussy addiction to pious practices; churchiness.

RELIGIOUS. Any person, clerical or lay, male or female, who is a member of a religious institute (*q.v.*). "A name common to many things is sometimes appropriated to that one to which it belongs in an eminent degree. . . . Now, religion is the virtue by which a man does something for the service and worship of God. And so by a transference of epithet, they are said to be religious who have devoted themselves entirely to the service of God" (St. Thomas Aquinas, I-II, clxxxvi, 1). Therefore, from the use of this word and such associated terms as "religious life," "religious house," it must by no means be inferred that the Church exalts the monastic and regulated life as the only really Christian life and monks and nuns as the only religious people; she merely says that, in the abstract, such life is the highest of many forms of truly Christian life.

RELIGIOUS, THE SACRED CONGREGATION OF. A Roman congregation (*q.v.*) having jurisdiction over all that concerns religious of either sex. It regulates matters between bishops and religious and amongst religious themselves, including those who live in community without vows and secular tertiaries.

RELIGIOUS HOUSE. One occupied by religious, as above; a monastery or convent.

RELIGIOUS LIFE. "A stable mode of life in community, whereby the faithful undertake to observe, not only the general precepts, but also the evangelical counsels by means of the vows of obedience, chastity and poverty" (*Code of Canon Law,* canon 487). Religious are in a state of perfection (*q.v.*), and are bound to tend to perfection by practising the counsels and submitting to the rules and constitutions of their order or congregation. They are to be content with the common life, even in the matter of food, clothing and furniture. Superiors must see to it that their subjects make an annual retreat, devote some time to meditation each day, unless lawfully hindered, and carefully attend to the other exercises of religion prescribed by rule, assist at Mass daily, go frequently or daily to communion, and weekly, at least, to confession. They have all the obligations and privileges of clerics that are applicable to them. When not occupied in any outside work that may be entrusted to him, a religious lives in community with his brethren; this is one of the chief external differences between the regular and secular clergy. Among the dissident orientals, especially where regular monasticism is moribund or dead, there are quasi-religious who take vows of poverty and chastity and continue to live in their own homes, according to the practice of the primitive Church; a number of Catholic Ethiopian and Chinese women do this.

RELIGIOUS OF ST. ANDREW, The. i. This congregation of nuns originated in a hospital at Tournai founded in 1230; it became an enclosed convent in 1611 and in 1857 was approved as an institute for teaching girls, providing retreats and other works of charity. Habit: black, with small cape and white collar and cap. The nuns are called "Madame."

ii. The congregation of Daughters of the Cross, founded by St. Andrew Fournet and St. Elizabeth Bichier des Ages at Maillé in France in 1807, are sometimes colloquially called Sisters of St. Andrew.

RELIGIOUS OF THE SACRED HEART, The. A congregation founded by St. Madeleine Sophie Barat and Fr. Joseph Varin, S.J., in 1800, for the education of girls, especially the daughters of the well-to-do. Its rule and constitutions are based on those of the Society of Jesus. This institute has spread to all parts of the world and has over 6,000 religious. Black habit, with white frilled cap.

RELIQUARY. Any vessel in which relics are sealed and kept. Reliquaries vary according to requirements from a simple box or casket to a metal model of the kind of relic enclosed, *e.g.,* an arm, a head, a cross. Most small relics are kept in a round case having a stem and stand, resembling a small monstrance; or in a sort of tiny pyx (*q.v.* i) which may be carried about the person. Relics may not be exposed for public veneration unless enclosed in reliquaries.

REMARRIAGE. A repetition of the sacrament of matrimony. The two parties to a consummated valid marriage may never remarry as long as both parties are alive. A widower or widow can, of course, marry again. True divorce is not tolerated by the Catholic Church, because it is against the law of God. But a marriage invalid on account of a diriment (*q.v.*) impediment can be declared null by the competent ecclesiastical authority, and then the parties are free to "remarry." Also the parties to a valid marriage that has not yet been consummated can for good reason be dispensed from their marriage vows, and thus be free to marry again. See RATUM NON CONSUMMATUM.

REMINISCERE SUNDAY. The second Sunday in Lent, from the first word of the introit at Mass.

REMISSION. i. Of sins. The forgiveness of sins which implies a complete blotting out of the guilt and stain, and consequent reconciliation with God. Sins are remitted by Baptism (all actual sin for which there is sorrow, and original sin), by Penance (post-baptismal sins) and by an act of perfect contrition (*qq.v.*). Venial sin (*q.v.*) may be remitted by prayer and other good works.

ii. Of temporal punishment (*q.v.*). See INDULGENCE.

REMOVAL FROM OFFICE. Holders of ecclesiastical offices are either removable or irremovable. The former can be removed by the ordinary (*q.v.*) for any just cause, and no special procedure is required, except in the case of removable rectors of parishes. Irremovable holders of offices cannot be removed except by judicial procedure in the ecclesiastical court. This normally requires a canonical crime, but irremovable rectors of parishes can be removed for economic reasons by special procedure.

RENAISSANCE, The (rebirth; first used in its present sense by Michelet). i. A change in the intellectual, moral and spiritual outlook of Western Christendom, becoming noticeable in Italy in the 14th century, reaching a height of ferment in that country in the 15th-16th, in England at the end of the 16th, and in France during the 17th. It arose from a gradual realization of continuity with and appreciation of the culture of Greek and Roman antiquity, and its heart was for long in Rome itself, where the glories of material achievement and the corruption of the papal court obscured its danger; the pontificates of Alexander VI and Leo X were melancholy examples of what may happen when Christianity cooperates with the spirit of the times. It was the precursor and then the support of the Reformation, giving licence to the human self in its natural and sensible activities as Protestantism did in the spiritual order: man's eyes were turned from God to man. By its rejection of scholastic Aristotelianism in favour of Platonism it helped to create the artificial rift between philosophy and physical science which still subsists to the harm of both and the confusion of men's minds; and its spirit ruled the intellectual world until the strong reactions of Romanticism, Physical Science and neo-Thomism in the 19th century. The name Renaissance is sometimes improperly narrowed to mean only its symptom, the revival of Humanism (*q.v.*), which received great impetus from the westward flight of scholars after the fall of Constantinople in 1453.

ii. The name Renaissance or Classical is given to that manner of building and style of ornament which is an adaptation of the models of ancient Greece and Rome, whether built during the Renaissance (*e.g.*, St. Peter's at Rome) or in our own time (*e.g.*, the Brompton Oratory in London, the cathedral at Baltimore).

RENEWAL OF CONSENT is required in canon law for the revalidation of a marriage. If marriage is invalid owing to defect of form or public impediment, consent must be renewed in the usual form of celebration; if invalid owing to an occult (*q.v.*) impediment, it is sufficient that the party aware of the impediment renews consent privately. Marriage invalid owing to defect of consent is revalidated by such consent being given, internally, privately or publicly, according as the defect was internal, occult or public. The pope has power to dispense from renewal of consent by a *sanatio in radice* (*q.v.*) if the marriage is invalid for any cause other than lack of consent. But the validity of the marriage will always depend on the condition that the party who gave consent has not since revoked it.

RENUNCIATION. i. The promises made, personally or by sponsor, at Baptism, in reply to the questions, "N . . ., dost thou renounce Satan?" "And all his works?" "And all his pomps?" These promises made by a godparent on behalf of a child relate to what every human being is morally bound to do in any case, and so in no way can be said to compromise the infant's adult liberty.

ii. The renunciation of a right, so that the action of another contrary thereto is no longer a violation of justice. But certain rights are inalienable and so cannot be renounced in this sense, *e.g.*, one's right to life or the mutual rights of husband and wife, the exercise of which may be foregone but which cannot be ceded to a third party.

REORDINATION. The sacrament of Holy Order confers a character (*q.v.*) and therefore it cannot be repeated for the same grade. But the sacrament is conferred successively for the successive grades of deacon, priest and bishop. This, however, is not the usual sense of Reordination, which means the first valid ordination of one who has received invalid orders, *e.g.*, a convert Anglican clergyman who is ordained priest. Also it may be used of the unlawful attempt to repeat a valid ordination in the same grade.

REPARATION. Making amends for a wrong wilfully done to another by homicide, contumely, detraction, adultery, fornication, scandal (*qq̄.v.*) or wrong advice. For reparation of harm caused by theft or damage to another's property or person, see RESTITUTION. The obligation is one of justice, and is grave when the harm caused is grave.

REPENTANCE. See CONTRITION; PENANCE, i.

REPROACHES, The. See IMPROPERIA.

REPROBATION. Literally, rejection by God, the state of the damned or of those whom God knows will be damned. Reprobation may be taken actively as the rejection by God, in which case it must be very carefully stated to remain within the ambit of Catholic teaching; or it may be taken passively as the state of the damned who as a matter of fact are rejected by God. It is

Catholic doctrine that God foreknows the damnation of those who will die in sin and preordains their punishment. It is the heresy of Predestinarianism (q.v.) to say that he has unconditionally and positively decreed from eternity that they shall sin and go to Hell as a result of their sin (cf., Eternal Punishment).

REPUTATION. The esteem in which others hold one's character and behaviour. To despoil a man of this unjustly is a sin of injustice, grave or venial according to the harm done, and involving the obligation of making due restitution (q.v.) so far as possible.

REQUIEM æternam dona eis, Domine, et lux perpetua luceat eis (Eternal rest give to them, O Lord, and let everlasting light shine on them). This prayer is an adaptation of vers. 34-5 of 4 Esdras ii (cf., Is. lviii, 11), which is not a canonical book of holy Scripture; it is used with vers. 1 and 2 of Psalm lxiv as the introit of Masses for the dead and is repeated in different forms elsewhere in that Mass and occurs frequently in the Office of the Dead. A *Requiem* means a Mass for the dead.

REQUIEM MASS (from the first word of the introit, see above). A Mass for the dead, appointed to be celebrated on All Souls' day, on the day of a death, burial, the 3rd (in memory of the Resurrection), 7th and 30th day after death and the annual anniversary, and on any other day when the rubrics permit and the celebrant wishes or is asked to pray for the dead in particular. There are four Masses provided in the Missal for this purpose: (a) a group of three for All Souls' day, (b) for the day of death and proximate anniversaries, (c) for the annual anniversary and (d) the common or ordinary Mass for the dead to be said on other occasions. The text of the proper parts sung by the choir are the same in all requiem Masses and include the sequence *Dies iræ* (q.v.); the collects, secrets, postcommunions, epistle and gospel vary, and there are a number of special collects for a deceased pope, priest, parents, benefactors, layman, woman, etc. This Mass is very ancient; *Iudica, Gloria* and Creed, being indicative of joy, are not said, the altar is not incensed at the introit nor the deacon and others at the offertory, lights are not carried nor a blessing given at the gospel, there are no *oscula solita* or kiss of peace, and omitted are all words and actions which indicate the participation of the living in the fruits of the sacrifice, e.g., "have mercy on us" at the *Agnus Dei* is altered to "give them rest," and there is no final blessing; the vestments are black. The proper parts of the Mass all refer to death and judgement, resurrection and life.

REQUIESCA(N)T IN PACE (Lat., May he [they] rest in peace). Words substituted for *Ite missa est* at the end of a requiem **Mass**, the server replying "Amen," and of common use in the Church's prayers for the dead.

REREDOS (Old Fr. *arere*, behind; *dos*, back). A carved or otherwise ornamented screen of wood or stone at the back of an altar; a painting in the same position; a combination of the two. The reredos may be separate or structurally part of the altar; the exuberant reredoses of the 17th and 18th century often made the altar to appear merely part of the reredos. The painting is often called an altar-piece. If the most prominent object in a reredos is an image of the Crucifixion, the crucifix on the altar may be dispensed with.

RERUM NOVARUM. The encyclical letter published by Pope Leo XIII in 1891 on the condition of the working classes, wherein he "identified the Church with the masses, not only collectively but also individually" (Parkinson). After stating the problem, he examined the transfer of ownership to the state as a remedy and rejected it on human, philosophical and religious grounds. He then set out the true remedy by action of the Church, of the state and of employers and employed. The encyclical maintained the priority of man and his family over the state, man's right by nature to possess property of his own in permanent possession, that the not-well-off should not be envious, that all have a natural right to a living wage and reasonable comfort and should be enabled to acquire private property, and that the rich had in effect enslaved the poor.[*]

RESCRIPT, PAPAL. The reply of the Holy See or a Roman congregation to a question or request submitted to them. A rescript usually only affects the person to whom it is addressed, but sometimes has the force of a general law. Papal dispensations are granted by rescript.

RESERVATION of the Blessed Sacrament. The preservation of particles of the Blessed Sacrament under the species of bread outside of Mass for the communion of the sick and others who for good cause cannot receive it during Mass: a custom going back at least to the beginning of the 2nd century; reservation in church itself to about the 7th.

i. Latin rite. Since the 11th century a subsidiary purpose of making the reserved Host a centre for private and public devotion (see EUCHARISTIC ADORATION) has continually gained in prominence in the Western Church, but this aspect of reservation is accidental: "We do not reserve in order to adore, but we adore because we reserve." Accordingly, the Blessed Sacrament must be reserved in all churches whose rectors have cure of souls, but in other churches and chapels only by episcopal or papal permission. It is kept in a ciborium within a tabernacle (qq.v.) on one altar (and no more),

---

[*] See LIVING WAGE for what is probably the most famous statement in this encyclical.—*Publisher*, 1997.

which is not necessarily the high altar (in cathedral and other churches where the Divine Office is celebrated the use of a worthy side-altar is usual), and is renewed at least every two weeks.

ii. Eastern rites. In all Catholic churches of Eastern rites the Sacrament is reserved and most of them have eucharistic devotions on Western lines; in certain places these are regarded as unnecessary innovations and have not been adopted. In no dissident Eastern church is any such worship given to the reserved Sacrament, which is kept solely for the sick, and Abyssinians, Copts, Syrians and Nestorians have given up the practice altogether. The Byzantines and Armenians dip the holy Bread into the precious Blood and reserve it in a receptacle on or above the altar or in any convenient place in the church. Normally the Orthodox consecrate for reservation only on Maundy Thursday and holy communion is not given from the reserved Sacrament (which is immersed in unconsecrated wine before administration) except as *viaticum*.

RESERVED CASE. A sin or censure the absolution of which is reserved to a certain superior. Reservation of censures usually involves indirectly the reservation of the sins to which the censures are attached, but some sins are reserved directly as such. Only one sin as such is reserved to the Holy See, namely, false denunciation of a priest for solicitation in confession. Local ordinaries are permitted to reserve three or four sins only. Reservation of sins ceases in the case of Easter communion, at parochial missions and for sick persons unable to go out. A censure *ab homine* is reserved to the authority inflicting it. Censures *latæ sententiæ* (*q.v.*) are not reserved, unless expressly so stated. Other censures *a jure* are reserved either to the Holy See (*simpliciter*, simply, *speciali modo*, specially, or *specialissimo modo*, very specially) or to the ordinary. In danger of death and certain emergencies any confessor can absolve from all censures and sins, under conditions specified in law.

RESIDENCE. To live in their own diocese is obligatory on all clerics. Those bound by the law of residence in the place of their office are cardinals in *curia*, diocesan bishops, religious superiors, canons, rectors of parishes and their assistants. Residence of canons is reckoned by presence in choir. The period of absence allowed for all the above is specified in law. The penalty for non-residence is loss of revenue for the period of unlawful absence. Offenders, if contumacious, are to be deprived of their office according to special procedure.

RESIGNATION to the will of God in Christian asceticism must be distinguished from the state of mind called Fatalism. Such resignation is not a passive acquiescence in the inevitable but an active co-operation in whatever may be prudently judged to be in accordance with divine intention. Nor is it to be assumed that such and such is God's will merely and *ipso facto* on the ground that it is unpleasant or adverse from our own desires; nor that Christian resignation precludes or excuses from effort to alter given circumstances or to attain a wished-for end. That God knows best what is for our good does not mean that he never gives us the light to make that judgement correctly for ourselves.

RESISTING EVIL. The doctrine of non-resistance to evil and renunciation of self-defence, founded on Matt. v, 38-48, xxvi, 52, Apoc. xiii, 10, etc., a doctrine which necessarily involves the unlawfulness of war: professed by Quakers and other extreme "pacifists." The Church denies any such wholesale interpretation of these and similar injunctions. As regards the individual, she teaches that they inculcate a higher and voluntary good, especially with reference to persecution and martyrdom: as a matter of personal vocation a man may bind himself to resist evil by non-violent means only, just as he may voluntarily bind himself to celibacy or poverty. As for the state, the injunctions were not addressed to it at all, for the state exists only for the welfare of its members and is bound to maintain their rights. St. Thomas says: "Not to resist evil may be understood in two ways: first, in the sense of forgiving wrong done to oneself, and this may pertain to perfection . . . secondly, in the sense of tolerating without protest wrongs done to others, and this pertains to imperfection or even to vice, if one be able to resist the wrongdoer in a suitable way" (II-II, clxxxviii, 3, ad i). And St. Augustine: "He who is overcoming evil by good submits patiently to the loss of temporal advantages that he may show how those things, through excessive love of which the other is made wicked, deserve to be despised when compared with faith and righteousness" (*Ep. ad Marcellinum*).

RESISTING KNOWN TRUTH. One of the sins against the Holy Ghost (*q.v.*), which are said to be without forgiveness. It implies a clear-eyed malice in refusing to accept truth known to come from God. One in such obstinate blindness would need an extraordinary grace before he could repent, and this, though possible, cannot be expected in the ordinary course of God's dispensation. If, however, he were to repent he would obtain forgiveness.

RESPONSE. Words said or sung by the server, choir or people in response or conclusion to a versicle, greeting, prayer, etc., of the celebrant or hebdomadary in many parts of the liturgy.

RESPONSIBILITY. The position or state accredited to a person on account of his voluntary action. He is held responsible for the evil effect of his action whenever the effect is itself intended, or even whenever the effect was not intended provided he foresaw this effect and could have prevented it and, at the same time, ought not to have taken action at all lest this effect should follow. In this case he is held responsible not because the effect follows, but because his will embraces it in making its choice (see WILL AND INTENTION; ACT, ii). It is of the essence of Catholic moral teaching that a man should be responsible, not for some, but for all of his human acts (*q.v.*) and their willed effects; any exterior influence militating against such responsibility is inimical to the full development of religion in the man concerned. Wherefore St. Thomas says: "The highest manifestation of life consists in this— that a being governs its own actions. That which is always subject to the direction of another is somewhat of a dead thing. Now a slave does not govern his own actions, but rather are they governed for him. Hence a man in so far as he is a slave is a very image of death" (Op. xvii, c. 14).

RESPONSORIAL CHANTS, The. See ANTIPHONAL CHANTS.

RESPONSORY, -ORIUM, RESPOND. i. At Matins. A series of versicles and responses, usually from the Bible with the first verse of *Gloria Patri* added, sung after each lesson. Their text varies with the office.

ii. Short responsory. A series of versicles and responses as above, sung after the little chapter of the little hours and Compline. It has slight variations in Passiontide and Paschal-time and on certain feasts. In the Monastic Office it occurs at Lauds and Vespers but not at the other hours.

RESTITUTION. i. Restoration of property, whether found or stolen, to its rightful owner. See THEFT, etc.

ii. Compensation for damage inflicted on another's property or person; obligatory if the offender's action was deliberate, was the real cause and not merely the occasion of the damage, and its evil effects were in some way foreseen. The obligation is one of justice, and is grave when the value involved would constitute a mortal sin of theft. A civil sentence in these matters is binding in conscience.

RESTORATION OF THE HIERARCHY, The. The re-establishment, in 1850, by letter apostolic of Pope Pius IX *Universalis Ecclesiæ* of a hierarchy of bishops-in-ordinary in the kingdom of England. There was then one metropolitan see, Westminster, with 12 suffragan sees: Beverley, Birmingham, Clifton, Hexham, Liverpool, Northampton, Nottingham, Plymouth, Salford, Shrewsbury, Southwark, and Newport & Menevia. This arrangement has since been much altered (see ENGLAND, CHURCH IN). The restoration was followed by a violent "papal aggression" agitation (*q.v.*). A hierarchy with two archbishops and four bishops was restored to Scotland (*q.v.*) in 1878. The Irish hierarchy was never allowed to die out.

RESURRECTION, CHURCH OF THE. Popularly known as the church of the Holy Sepulchre at Jerusalem. The anniversary of its consecration is celebrated in the Byzantine rite on Sept. 13.

RESURRECTION OF THE BODY. The reanimation of the bodies of all men, whether saved or lost, on the last day. Catholics are bound to believe in the identity of the resurrection-body with that possessed on earth, but since the principle of the identity of our bodies even during our mortal life is differently explained, it is no article of faith that the same particles of matter which were possessed at the moment of death will be reassumed at the moment of resurrection (see BODY, GLORIFIED). The truth of the resurrection of the body has always been affirmed by Christianity in accordance with divine revelation. There can be no resurrection of the soul, for the soul does not die. Moreover, "it is contrary to the nature of the soul to be without the body, and, since nothing that is contrary to nature can endure, the soul will not be forever without the body. Now the soul lasts for ever, and so it must be conjoined again with the body. That is the resurrection. . . . Man will rise again without any defect of human nature, for as God made his nature without defect so will he restore it . . . human nature will be brought by the resurrection to its state of ultimate perfection, in that youthful age at which the movement of growth has ceased and the movement of decay has not yet begun. . . . Whatever belongs to the integrity of the human nature of those who have part in the resurrection will rise again" (St. Thomas, III, lxxx).

RESURRECTION OF CHRIST, The. The reanimation of the body in the tomb by the soul of Christ on the morning of the third day after his death. Christ's body, though it has entered a glorified existence, for ever remains a true, material, physical human body, numerically identical with the body crucified on Calvary. So-called discrepancies in accounts of the Resurrection are only apparent and are owing to our lack of information enabling us to reconcile statements of independent veracious witnesses. Christ's resurrection is the fundamental argument for the Christian religion: "If Christ has not risen again, then our preaching is groundless, and your faith, too, is groundless" (1 Cor. xv, 14).

RESURRECTIONISTS, The. The Priests of the Resurrection, a congregation founded by two Poles, Bogdan Janski, a layman, and Fr. Peter Semenenko, in 1836, to minister to their countrymen. Members may be of the Latin or Byzantine rite. Not less than 6 priests form a community. Their habit is the dress of secular clergy with a black woollen girdle.

RETABLE. An altar-piece or reredos; the word is often used for a gradine (*q.v.*), especially one forming part of a reredos.

RETRAITE NUNS, The. The Dames de la Retraite du Sacré Cœur, founded at Quimper, in 1678, to provide retreats for women and schools for girls. Unenclosed; Little Office B.V.M. in choir. Black habit.

RETREAT. i. A period of time, short or long, during which a person withdraws from his ordinary life and occupations in order to pray, meditate and receive instruction in the spiritual life. A retreat is usually passed at a religious house or at one specially set apart for the purpose, and may be spent alone or in company with others; except for recreations and necessity, silence is observed. The clergy of every diocese meet in retreat once a year. All monasteries in England give retreats to individuals and some of them to parties; the Jesuits, who have been the modern pioneers of retreats for laymen, conduct special retreat houses, *e.g.*, at Rainhill and Craighead, and the nuns of our Lady of the Retreat in the Cenacle give facilities to women and children. The Redemptorists and others give parochial quasi-retreats for the benefit of people who are unable to leave their work.

ii. The name given to a monastery of Passionists, *e.g.*, St. Joseph's Retreat at Highgate.

RETRIBUTION. i. Reward of virtue granted by God: it is part of the hundredfold promised, even in this life, by Christ to his followers.

ii. Punishment inflicted by God on the sinner in the form of suffering or misfortune. If patiently borne it may cleanse the soul from all the effects of sin and so take the place of Purgatory. According to St. Thomas "the punishments of this life are medicinal rather than retributive" (II-II, lxvi, 6).

REUNION OF THE CHURCHES. The healing of the divisions among Christians by uniting in the communion of the one visible Catholic Church, under the supreme jurisdiction of the Sovereign Pontiff, the ancient churches of the East and all other non-Catholic people who profess and call themselves Christians. This object must be distinguished from the movement towards some sort of Christian unity advocated under varying conditions by different non-Catholic individuals and bodies. The Catholic Church displays complete and perfect Christian unity in itself; therefore non-Catholics, whether in schism or heresy, individuals or bodies, can only partake of that unity by the acceptance of the dogmatic and moral teaching of the Catholic Church in its entirety and the communion with the Holy see which it involves: this is outside of any possibility of bargaining or concession, being concerned with matters of absolute truth. But in matters of discipline and worship (*e.g.*, ordination of married men, vernacular liturgies) an ancient Eastern church would on return to unity keep its own customs; and it is not impossible that, in order to facilitate the conversion of a large organized body of Protestants, they might receive concessions in similar matters. Catholics are forbidden to take part in any public meeting or congress to discuss reunion on other than these conditions; but are exhorted to make every effort to understand and sympathize with the views and difficulties of non-Catholics.

REUNION, CORPORATE. The reconciliation with the Holy See of a whole church, or of a considerable body of clergy and laity, hitherto separated from Catholic unity, and their reception as a body, with their own dioceses and other institutions intact. This can take place just like that only in cases where the orders of the clergy concerned are valid; and in fact it has happened a number of times in respect of bodies reconciled from the dissident Eastern churches. "Corporate reunion" is sometimes opposed to "individual reconciliation"; but there need be no opposition: corporate reunion is a legitimate and praiseworthy object of reunionist work and is encouraged by the Holy See, provided no obstacle be put in the way of those persons who wish to be reconciled as individuals apart from groups. For some time the expression "corporate reunion" was in somewhat bad odour owing to the imprudences of certain enthusiasts towards the end of the last century who hoped to bring about the reconciliation of the Church of England in a body.

REUNION COUNCILS, The. Three councils which were concerned with healing the breach between East and West, namely, of Bari, in 1098, which prevented the Italo-Greeks going into schism, the second of Lyons, and of Florence (*qq.v.*), which both effected temporary reunion.

REVALIDATION, more correctly called validation, is necessary to regularize a putative marriage (*q.v.*). It is of two kinds, simple revalidation and *sanatio in radice* (*q.v.*). Simple revalidation consists in the cessation of the impediment on dispensation and renewal of consent (*q.v.*).

REVELATION (Lat. *revelare*, to unveil). i. The less proper use of the term signifies the manifestation of divine truths obtained by the use of our natural faculties alone. This is called natural Revelation.

ii. Strict supernatural Revelation means the removal of the veils which shroud the hidden things of God from man's enquiring mind. It may be immediate (private, *q.v.*), when God enlightens man directly or by an angel (*cf.*, Matt. xvi, 18); or, more commonly, mediate, when it is made through the instrumentality of men by Scripture and Tradition. That God has made such a revelation, first to a chosen people, the Jews, and then to the world by Jesus Christ, is the basis of the Christian religion; and the Catholic Church is the sole divinely authorized repository and exponent of that revelation.

REVELATION, THE BOOK OF. See APOCALYPSE.

REVELATION, PRIVATE. A revelation given by God to an individual for his own benefit or for the benefit of other individuals or a class of persons, as opposed to the universal revelation for all men given to Israel and the Apostles. If the people concerned are reasonably certain that such a revelation has been made, they should believe and act on it, as may outsiders who hear of it and are equally certain; but such certitude is not easily attained and should be submitted to the opinion of a prudent priest. The occurrence of manifest errors in non-essential matters does not prove the falsity or worthlessness of a revelation; such may be due to human misunderstanding or other causes. Some private revelations (*e.g.*, of SS. Bridget of Sweden and Joan of Arc) have been approved by the Church: this only means that they contain nothing contrary to faith and morals and that in addition there is sufficient evidence to justify belief in their authenticity; she does not, and cannot, impose belief in a private revelation and its contents, either on an individual or on the faithful at large. "Even though many of these revelations have been approved, we cannot and we ought not to give them the assent of divine faith, but only that of human faith, according to the dictates of prudence whenever these dictates enable us to decide that they are probable and worthy of pious credence" (Pope Benedict XIV).

REVENGE. The desire to inflict just punishment for an offence committed is quite lawful. The sin of revenge is committed when the desire is to inflict punishment beyond what is deserved, or on the wrong person, or from a motive of hate instead of justice. It is a sin against charity and justice, and consequently mortal unless the vengeance desired is light (*cf.*, Anger). "Do not avenge yourselves, beloved; allow retribution to run its course; so we read in scripture, Vengeance is for me, I will repay, says the Lord. Rather feed thy enemy if he is hungry, give him drink if he is thirsty; by doing this, thou wilt heap coals of fire upon his head. Do not be disarmed by malice; disarm malice with kindness" (Rom. xii, 19-21).

REVERENCE is the honour given to creatures, whether the special sort (veneration, *q.v.*) accorded to the saints or that degree of respect given to religious persons, to parents, to great men, to places of religious or historical importance, etc. In common speech it is often used as synonymous with its exterior manifestations: bowings, genuflections, tip-toeing, a chastened voice, kissing of rings, removal of the hat or putting it on, and the like. These are purely arbitrary and easily over-emphasized: the Western Catholic genuflects before the Blessed Sacrament, the Byzantine Catholic bows; it is deemed irreverent to applaud in church in England, but not so in Rome; some dutiful sons call their father "sir," others, equally dutiful, "old thing"; reverence is an attitude of the mind, but again must not be confused with that emotion which causes some people to assume a forbidding expression of face when confronted by something impressive, *e.g.*, the nave of Winchester cathedral.

REVERENCES, CEREMONIAL, ordinarily in use in the Catholic Church are bowing, the genuflexion and the metany (*qq.v.*).

REVEREND, The (Lat. *reverendus*, worthy of respect). The ordinary form of written address in English of a secular priest: "The Reverend A . . . B . . ."; if a religious, "Father" or his special title is added: "The Rev. Dom C . . . D . . ., C.R.L.," "The Rev. Father E . . ., O.D.C." Courtesy extends its use to tonsured and minor clerics, to choir-nuns and all nuns who have the title of "Mother." Higher ranks of clergy are "Very," "Right" and "Most Reverend" (*qq.v.*). Carthusians reserve the title "Reverend Father" for their prior general; the others are "Venerable Father."

REVERSURUS. A bull of Pope Pius IX in 1867 regulating the manner of electing the Armenian patriarch and bishops and forbidding the interference of lay-people in the government of that church. It was extended to the Chaldeans, and was the occasion of the schism of Mgr. Malachy Ormanian and the Armenian Antonians.

REVISED VERSION. An English version of the Bible, being a revision of the Protestant Authorized Version (*q.v.*), published in 1885. It is generally more accurate and less archaic in diction, but it is used chiefly for purposes of study.

REVOLUTION by resisting the civil power. It is lawful for the people to rise against their lawful rulers if their government has become gravely tyrannical and directed to private ends rather than the common good. But peaceful means must first be attempted, there must be reasonable hope of success and improvement, and the need and prudence of resistance must be the opinion of the majority or at least of the better part of the people. In his encyclical *Quod apostolici* in 1878 Pope Leo XIII warned against the unlawfulness of such insurgence on the part of mere parties or individuals in the state.

REVOLUTION, The, without qualification, means the French Revolution of 1789 and following years; in English history, the seizing of the throne by William of Orange in 1688.

RHEIMS-DOUAY BIBLE. The English translation of the Bible made by Dr. Gregory Martin and others at Rheims and Douay, and published, the New Testament in 1582, the Old shortly afterwards. It was based on the Vulgate, for reasons set out in the preface, and among subsidiary versions used was Coverdale's edition of the Vulgate New Testament (Paris, 1538). The translators kept very close not only to the sense but also to the words and phrases of the Latin, and their literalness often results in obscurity. A number of words were in this version first introduced into the English Bible and are now in common use through being adopted in the Authorized Version, whose debt to Rheims is hardly less than that to the previous Protestant versions on which it was supposed to be based. As an exercise in English prose it is far inferior to the Authorized Version, but the latter has familiarized Protestants with some of Dr. Martin's best passages. The version was armed with explanatory and controversial notes by Dr. Richard Bristow and, of course, included the deutero-canonical books (*q.v.*). For the so-called Douay Bible at present used by English Catholics, see CHALLONER'S BIBLE.

RHETORIC. The art of persuasion; the effective presentation of a case by clearness of statement and reasoning. The wordy appeals to the emotions commonly associated with rhetoric are really foreign to it—emotion properly follows from the conviction of the audience of the truth of the matter presented to it. As one of the seven liberal arts, rhetoric formed part of the *trivium* course of Christian education, and it is still the name of the middle range of studies in Jesuit schools.

RHYTHM OF ST. BERNARD, The. The office hymn for the feast of the Holy Name, *Iesu dulcis memoria,* usually attributed to St. Bernard of Clairvaux. The form with 50 stanzas was at one time used as a sort of rosary, in 5 decades. The first English translation known is of 24 verses in an office of the Eternal Wisdom compiled by Bl. Henry Suso, O.P., published at Douay in 1580 under the title: "Certayne sweete Prayers of the glorious name of Iesus, commonly called Iesus Mattens, with the howers thereto belonging"; it begins, "O Iesu meeke, the sweetest thought." The most widely used

translation is that of Fr. E. Caswell, "Jesu, the very thought of thee."

RHYTHMICAL OFFICE. An hour of the Divine Office in which the antiphons, responsories, etc., are all written in metre or rime. They were very popular in the middle ages and have left traces in the Roman Breviary (*e.g.,* antiphons at Vespers and Matins in the office of Trinity Sunday, invitatory and sixth responsory at Matins of the Holy Lance and Nails); in the mediæval Breviaries they are of course more common (*cf.,* the office of St. Antony of Padua in the Franciscan, of St. Dominic in the Dominican, and the Little Office of Our Lady of the same rite wherein, *inter alia,* the three lessons at Matins are in rime).

RHYTHMICAL SIGNS. Directions arranged and popularized by the monks of Solesmes to facilitate the accurate singing of Gregorian chant and added to some editions of the liturgical books. They consist of two signs of length and five of rhythmical division; to these are added a *comma* to indicate a place for breathing taken from the duration of the preceding note. The doubt as to whether these signs might be added to the Vatican edition of the chant was set at rest by a decree of the S.R.C. of Feb. 14, 1906. The idea of rhythmical signs was derived from those signs found in MSS. of the schools of St. Gall, Metz, Chartres and others, all of Roman origin. From these signs the transverse *episema* is directly taken; the dot or *moravocis* is expressive of the general teaching of all the ancient exponents of plainsong concerning the *mora vocis*.

RHYTHMUS SANCTI THOMÆ. The hymn of St. Thomas or his Prayer before the Body of Christ written by St. Thomas Aquinas about 1260, beginning with the line *Adoro te devote, latens Deitas.* It forms part of the thanksgiving prayers after Mass in the Missal and is often sung at Benediction or Exposition of the Blessed Sacrament.

RIDDELS (Fr. *rideau,* curtain). Curtains hung at the sides of an altar.

RIFORMATI, The (It., reformed). A strictly observant branch of the Franciscans formed in Italy in the 16th century. See OBSERVANTS.

RIGHT. The word "right" may be used in the sense of a law, or of an object to which one has a claim, or, thirdly, of a moral power. This third sense is the more usual, and a right is defined as a moral power vested in a person owing to which the holder of the power may claim something as due to him or as belonging to him or demand of others that they perform some acts or abstain from them. It is said to be moral because it does not depend on might or physical force and because deprivation of it is an offence against justice (*q.v.*); a right must be distinguished from that to which one has a claim on some other ground, *e.g.*, charity. There are positive or acquired rights, and natural rights. The former may have as immediate source the state; the latter, which are those usually understood by the term Rights of Man, are inherent in the human personality, and are ordinarily inalienable. Their source is the Eternal Law. They arise because the duties imposed on the creature by the Creator involve as correlatives rights to enable those duties to be fulfilled. Thus every man has the right to life, liberty and the pursuit of happiness, to develop himself according to his circumstances, and to the exercise of his faculties, providing such exercise does not violate the equal right of others. He has the right to enter into private associations for lawful purposes, the right, therefore, to marry and to found a family, whence flow further rights regarding his children and their education. These rights may be for just causes restricted or even abrogated; but man's spiritual rights, concerned with the eternal destiny of his soul and his relations with his Creator, are entirely indefeasible; the right to know God and to follow his conscience cannot be interfered with. Human rights may be divided into three categories. (1) Of the human person as such. The rights to life, to personal freedom under God and the just law, to the free quest of perfection, following of conscience, and religious activity,* to marry freely, to family independence, to reasonable private property, and to be treated not as a thing but as a person (*q.v.*), as an end, not a means. (2) Of the civic person. The rights to equal suffrage and participation in politics, to political self-determination and the forming of parties, to free investigation and discussion, to equal rights before the law, and to equal opportunity for equal ability. (3) Of the social and working person. The rights to choose one's work, to organize in unions and associations, to have free action in groups, to receive just wages, to a job of work, to share when possible in management and ownership, and to have social security by sharing in the elementary goods, both material and spiritual, of civilization. The correlative of right is duty (*q.v.*). In common speech right is used as an adjective for that which is just, lawful, good, and so opposed to wrong.

RIGHT REVEREND. The style given in English-speaking countries to bishops ("Most Reverend" in Ireland), abbots, abbesses (except Franciscan), vicars general, protonotaries apostolic, and domestic prelates.

RIGHT OF SUCCESSION, WITH. An auxiliary or coadjutor (*qq.v.*) bishop is occasionally appointed *cum iure successionis*. Upon the death, resignation or removal of the prelate whom he is assisting or understudying he automatically succeeds to the see and is enthroned upon confirmation by the Holy See.

RIGHTS OF ANIMALS. A loose expression for that in animals which corresponds to man's duties towards them. Strictly speaking, no animal has any rights, for only a person, *i.e.*, a being possessed of reason and free will, has rights. "Obligations and duties are between moral persons, and therefore the lower animals are not susceptible of the moral obligations which we owe to one another; but we owe a seven-fold obligation to the Creator of those animals. Our obligation and moral duty is to him who made them: and if we wish to know the limit and the broad outline of our obligation, I say at once it is his nature and his perfections, and among these perfections one is, most profoundly, that of Eternal Mercy. And although a poor mule or a poor horse is not, indeed, a moral person, yet the Lord and Maker of the mule or the horse is the highest Lawgiver and his nature is a law unto himself. And in giving dominion over his creatures to man, he gave it subject to the condition that it should be used in conformity to his perfections, which is his own law and therefore our law" (Cardinal Manning). See CRUELTY, ii.

RIGHTS OF WOMEN. See WOMAN; FEMINISM; WIFE, etc.

RIGHTEOUSNESS (Old English *rihtwisnisse*, right-wiseness). Goodness, virtuousness, uprightness, sinlessness; the perfection of God; and historically, man's state of justification through the Redemption. This word, one of the most noble in the English language, has with its derivatives gone out of use to a considerable extent among Catholics. The reason for this is that the translators of the Rheims-Douay Bible (*q.v.*) preferred the terms "justice" (*q.v.* iv), "just," "justly," *e.g.*, in Matt. v, 20, vi, 33, xiii, 17; Rom. iv, 6; Jam. v, 16; Tit. ii, 12 and very many other places. Some more recent translators (*e.g.*, Father Francis Spencer, the Westminister version) have used "righteousness" etc.

RIGORISM. A system in moral theology which tries to solve the problem how to act when in doubt whether a law is or is not binding in given circumstances, by insisting that the law must be obeyed unless the opinion favouring liberty be certain. Rigorism was condemned by Alexander VIII in 1690 (*cf.*, Probabilism).

RING. A gold ring with a stone worn upon the third finger of the right hand is part of the *insignia* of office of cardinals, bishops and abbots, and is kissed as a sign of respect by a cleric of lower rank or lay person when meeting one of these prelates. Such a ring is also worn by others having a right to *pontificalia* (*q.v.*), and by some abbesses. Rings

---

* For an additional explanation of religious rights, see FREEDOM OF WORSHIP.—*Publisher*, 1997.

are not worn by dissident Eastern bishops—some of them think it highly improper to do so. At the consecration of a virgin a plain ring is conferred and worn on the right hand, as is done at the solemn profession of many nuns, *e.g.*, Benedictines, Cistercians, Redemptoristines. The ring conferred on doctors in theology and canon law is not a liturgical ornament and may not be worn when celebrating Mass. There is no rule as to the stone of the ring: on ordinary occasions the pope generally has a cameo, emerald or ruby; cardinals, a sapphire; bishops and abbots, an amethyst. The episcopal ring signifies the seal of faith and the marriage which a bishop contracts with his diocese. The wearing of a wedding-ring by married women is now universal in Christian countries, but the custom varies greatly in detail; it appears to have originated in the betrothal rings given as a secular pledge by the Romans. In some countries rings are exchanged between bride and groom; in others one is put on by the priest; in others it is worn on the right hand: this last was the custom in England till the end of the 16th century and among Catholics till much later (*cf.*, Marriage Ceremonies).

RING OF THE FISHERMAN, The. A sealing-ring with which the pope is invested at his election and used only for sealing papal briefs; it is officially broken up at his death by the Chamberlain of the Roman Church. Its device is that of St. Peter fishing from a boat.

RIPIDION (Gr., fan). A flat metal disk representing a cherub's head surrounded by six wings, sometimes furnished with tiny bells, mounted upright on a shaft in such a manner that it can be made to revolve; used in the Byzantine, Armenian, Coptic, Maronite and Syrian rites. Its original purpose was to keep away flies from the holy Gifts during the *anaphora*, but a veil is often now waved instead. In the Byzantine rite there are often two *ripidia* behind the altar which are carried at the great and little entrances and other processions. It is the characteristic instrument of the deacon and is handed to him at ordination. *Ripidia* were formerly in use in the West and are now represented by the papal *flabella* (*q.v.*). Also called *hexapterygon*.

RISEN BODY. See BODY, GLORIFIED.

RISING OF THE NORTH, The. A rising (to be distinguished from the pilgrimage of Grace, *q.v.*) in 1569, led by the earl of Northumberland, in favour of Mary of Scotland as next heir to the throne and in order "to restore the Crown, the nobility, and the worship of God to their former estate." Durham was occupied and Mass sung in the cathedral, as well as in the parish-churches of Bishop Auckland, Darlington, Ripon and Staindrop, and probably Stokesby and Whitby. The effort speedily collapsed and fierce vengeance was taken on the rebels.

RISING IN THE WEST, The. A rising of the men of Devon and Cornwall under Humphrey Arundel on the imposition of the new English liturgy in 1549. They demanded among other things the restoration of at least two monasteries in each county and of the ancient rites of worship: "We will not receive the new service, because it is but like a Christmas game. We will have our old service of Matins, Mass, Evensong and Procession as it was before; and we the Cornish, whereof certain of us understand no English, do utterly refuse the new service." Ten thousand insurgents marched towards London, laid siege to Exeter; but it was raised, and they were again beaten at Callington Down and Bridgwater; 4,000 men died in the field or were executed.

RISORGIMENTO (It., resurrection). The nationalist and unifying movement among the kingdoms and other states of the Italian peninsula which became strong during the second quarter of the 19th century; it culminated in 1861 with the establishment of the Kingdom of Italy under the House of Savoy and was completed in 1870 by the seizure of Rome from the Holy See. Of all the countries of the world only Ecuador officially protested against this lawless act.

RITE (Lat., *ritus,* the form and manner of a religious observance). i. The words to be said and actions to be done in performing a given act of religion, *e.g.*, the rite of burial, of consecrating a bishop.

ii. A whole and complete system of forms, ceremonies and prayers to be used in the worship of God, the administration of the sacraments, and minor ecclesiastical occasions. The Catholic Church recognizes nine rites, each one of which has its own right and proper way of doing things, from celebrating the Holy Eucharist downwards; they are: the Latin (including variants), Byzantine, Armenian, Chaldean, Coptic, Ethiopic, Malabar, Maronite and Syrian rites. All these except the Latin and the Maronite are also used by numbers of Christians who are no longer Catholics. It should be noted that all rites are local in origin; historical events have extended their use to whole churches. Liturgically and scientifically the above rites are classified thus: Latin (or Roman), Byzantine, Alexandrian (Coptic and Ethiopic), Antiochene (Syrian and Maronite), Armenian, Chaldean (Chaldean and Malabarese).

iii. The organized body or bodies, Catholic or not, and their members, who use any one of the above-mentioned rites. In this sense it is equivalent to "church," and includes the manner of organization, proper canon law, customs, etc. To speak therefore of a Catholic of the Armenian rite means more than that he hears Mass said and is absolved in

Classical Armenian. Every child of Catholic parents belongs *de facto* and *de iure*, and every child of baptized non-Catholic parents belongs *de facto* or *de iure*, to one or other of the rites. See RITE, DETERMINATION OF.

iv. The word is sometimes used for rank or degree of solemnity of a feast, *e.g.*, the feast of the Presentation is of greater double rite.

v. The word is used with varying degrees of accuracy for certain variant forms of some of the rites named in ii, *e.g.*, Dominican and Ruthenian, whose rites, in the sense of iii, belong to the Latin and Byzantine rites respectively. The usage is clumsy and confusing, but usual, and is therefore followed in this work (*cf.*, Use).

RITE, CHANGE OF. Every Catholic takes the rite (Latin or Byzantine or Maronite, etc). of his parents even if, through error or emergency, he is baptized by a priest and with the forms of another rite. Except at matrimony (*q.v.*) under certain circumstances, one cannot change one's rite, except for a good reason and by permission of the Holy See. But any Eastern Catholic who has "turned Latin" is free to return to his own rite, and in certain cases must do so. Schismatics who become Catholics must keep their own rite (*e.g.*, an heretical Copt must become a Catholic Copt, not a Melkite or Latin); any Western priest inducing any Eastern Christian to embrace the Latin rite incurs suspension and other penalties. The rules governing change of rite were laid down by Pope Leo XIII in the constitution *Orientalium dignitas* of 1894; they are greatly neglected in certain places.

RITE, DETERMINATION OF. Except in a few special cases, all children of Catholic parents belong to the rite of their father, whatever that of the mother may be; nor is this altered by the child's being baptized, either accidentally or deliberately, by a priest and with the ceremonies of another rite. If only one of the parents is a Catholic, then the child follows that one's rite. In so far as it is applicable, this is also the law for non-Catholics who are reconciled; but in certain circumstances such have some power of choice. English-speaking Anglicans and other Western Protestants upon conversion belong to the Latin rite of their Catholic forefathers, England and America and their colonies belonging to the Western church (*cf.*, Change of Rite, above).

RITES, THE CONGREGATION OF SACRED. A Roman congregation (*q.v.*) erected by Pope Sixtus V in 1588 to supervise all that concerns the public worship of the Latin rite; it also deals with the beatification and canonization of saints, and everything relating to holy relics. Pope Pius IX gave authority to this congregation to make laws in liturgical matters of the Latin rite,

and its general decrees therefore bind the whole Western church. It is nearly always cited in English as the Sacred Congregation of Rites, but it often calls itself *Sacrorum Rituum Congregatio*.

RITUAL, -E. i. A book containing the prayers and ceremonies for the administration of the sacraments, blessings, etc. Many countries, dioceses and religious orders have their own proper Rituals, approximating closely to the "Rituale Romanum" (*q.v.*). *Cf.*, *ordo* ii.

ii. The approved order of religious ceremony (*q.v.*)

RITUAL MURDER. The killing of a Christian child in fulfilment of some rite, a slanderous and unfounded accusation made against the Jews for many centuries. It was condemned as false by the Holy See twice in the 13th century and again by Pope Clement XIV in 1756, while he was still a consultor of the Holy Office. Those young victims of Jews whose local *cultus* as martyrs the Church has approved (*e.g.*, Little St. Hugh of Lincoln, St. William of Norwich, St. Andrew of Rinn) are regarded as having been put to death out of hatred of the faith by individual Jews and not in pursuance of any Jewish rite.

RITUALE ROMANUM (The Roman Ritual). A liturgical book containing all that a priest requires in addition to the Missal and Breviary. It includes principally: all the rubrics and texts required for the administration of the sacraments of Baptism, Penance, Matrimony, Extreme Unction and the Eucharist out of Mass, for ministering to the dying and for burying the dead, for the churching of women, for exorcizing those possessed, and for conducting processions; and has several sections of very various blessings, namely, those which can be conferred by any priest, those reserved to a bishop or a priest with special faculties, and those reserved to a member of a particular religious order or other priest with special faculties; these blessings are constantly being added to.

RITUALISM. A name formerly extensively used, often contemptuously or in a hostile sense, for the principles of the "high-church" party in Anglicanism (*qq.v.*), on account of their ceremonial innovations, mostly borrowed from Catholic usage. It is now rarely used on account of the development of the party and the growth of understanding among Catholics and Protestants that its basis is a more serious one than a mere "taste for ecclesiastical millinery."

RITUS SERVANDUS. i. An abbreviation of the long name of a book authorized for the use of the clergy in England and Wales containing the order and prayers for Benediction of the Blessed Sacrament and other non-liturgical services. The corresponding book in Ireland is known as the *Benedictionale*.

ii. The section of the rubrics of the Missal containing detailed directions for the celebration of Mass.

ROBBER SYNOD, The, or *Latrocinium.* A council held at Ephesus (not to be confused with the 3rd œcumenical council) in 449, presided over by Dioscoros, monophysite patriarch of Alexandria, assisted by his bodyguard of roughs. It was terrorized into reversing the condemnation of Eutyches pronounced by Flavian, bishop of Constantinople, and the latter died from rough handling by the soldiers. Pope St. Leo I protested, and agreed to the summoning of an œcumenical council (at Chalcedon, 451).

ROBBERY is distinguished from theft (*q.v.*). in Christian morals by the use of violence in depriving another of his property.

ROCHET (cognate with Ger. *rock*, coat). A narrow-sleeved garment reaching to the knees, made of white linen, the lower part being lace. It is worn under the *mozzetta* as part of the choir-dress of bishops, abbots and prelates not members of religious orders. To wear it not covered by a *mantelletta* is a mark of jurisdiction. The right to its use (under a *mozzetta*) is granted to many chapters of cathedral canons, *e.g.*, in England, and an uncovered rochet is part of the religious habit of canons and canonesses regular (*cf.*, Surplice).

ROCK. "Thou art Peter and upon this rock . . ." (St. Matt. xvi, 18). The significance of this passage is lost in English, and to a considerable extent in Greek where the word πέτρα (rock) has to receive a masculine suffix in order to be made into a man's name, πέτρος. But in the Aramaic of our Lord the identity of the words is clear: "Thou art Kepha (Peter), and upon this kepha (rock) . . ."

ROCOCO (Fr. *rocaille*, pebble-work). An exaggerated form of baroque architecture (*q.v.*) marked by a profuse use of what was regarded in 18th-century France and Germany as the last word in elegant decoration; *e.g.*, the abbey church at Einsiedeln, St. John at Munich, the collegiate church at Neresheim, the cathedral of Versailles.

ROFFENSIS in America. The Latin epithet for the bishop of Rochester, N. Y., from *Hrofesceaster,* the early form of the name of Rochester in England.

ROGATION DAYS (Lat. *rogatio*, entreaty), also called Lesser Litanies. Monday, Tuesday and Wednesday before Ascension Day, specially set apart to supplicate the mercy of God and his blessings upon mankind. They are the Christian substitute for the old Roman Ambarvalia. The liturgical observances are the same as those for the Greater Litanies (*q.v.*), which is also a rogation day but not usually so called.

ROMAN CATHOLIC. A name used by many English-speaking non-Catholics for members of the Catholic Church, as a qualification of their exclusive right to be called Catholics, and the term recognized for use in official and legal documents. As every Catholic, of whatever rite, looks to Rome as the centre of the Church and the seat of her supreme pontiff and head, the expression in itself is unobjectionable and is in fact sometimes employed by them, especially in certain countries of Europe. But its use by Catholics is unnecessary and, having regard to its connotation for many non-Catholics, sometimes to be avoided.

ROMAN CATHOLIC RELIEF ACT. Five parliamentary measures, whereby the Penal Laws (*q.v.*, ii) were done away with, bear this name, passed in 1778, 1791, 1793, 1829 and 1926. See EMANCIPATION.

ROMAN CHURCH, THE HOLY. i. Strictly, the diocese of Rome, *e.g.*, in the expression Cardinal of the Holy Roman Church, cardinals being the councillors of the Bishop of Rome and Supreme Pontiff.

ii. By extension, synonymous with Latin rite and Western church (*qq.v.*), *e.g.*, as on the title-page of the "Graduale Romanum," "Gradual of the Most Holy Roman Church. . . ."

iii. By further extension, the whole Catholic Church as having its head at Rome. This sense is often used in a semi-hostile way by non-Catholics (*cf.*, Roman Catholic). For Caholics it is in effect an abbreviation of the "Holy Catholic Apostolic Roman Church" used by the Vatican Council (sess. iii, cap. 1).

ROMAN COLLAR. An upright collar of white linen, starched stiff and fastened at the back of the neck. It is worn by nearly all secular clerics, and in some places is the only remnant of distinctively ecclesiastical outdoor dress prescribed by "the lawful customs of the place and the precepts of the local ordinary" (canon 136). It is the only part of their uniform that secular priests are nowhere dispensed from wearing in public under ordinary circumstances; but having been adopted by many Protestant ministers it is no longer distinguishing.

ROMAN COLLEGE, The. The Gregorian University (*q.v.*).

ROMAN EMPIRE, THE HOLY (often referred to simply as The Empire). The old Roman Empire was divided into Eastern and Western parts by Arcadius and Honorius in 395. The Eastern empire ceased to exist when Constantinople was taken by the Turks, in 1453. The Western empire was dismembered, the last emperor being deposed in 476. The Holy Roman Empire began in 800 with the attempted restoration by the papacy of the Roman empire in the West, effected by the coronation of Charlemagne by Pope Leo III. Under his successors it consisted of the kingdoms of France, Germany, Italy and Lorraine, and afterwards of Burgundy (Switzerland, Provence and Savoy); France separated in 887. The sovereign of one of these was emperor and nominally had suzerainty over the others, but his real power was practically confined to his own hereditary dominions, the kingdoms being subdivided into virtually independent states. Pope John XII crowned Otto I, king of Germany, as emperor in 962, and henceforth the kingdoms of Germany and Italy remained united until the 16th century. The imperial crown was elective, the electors being the princes, secular and ecclesiastical; but from 1437 onwards only two emperors were not of the house of Habsburg. From 1530 the popes ceased even to crown the emperors, and Protestantism hastened the disruption. Ferdinand II attempted consolidation (the Thirty Years' War, 1619-48) and was frustrated through the efforts of Cardinal Richelieu who allied himself politically with the Protestants. It was finally abolished in 1806 by Napoleon I; the emperor-elect, Francis II, took the title of Emperor of Austria. Though of tremendous importance in the development of Europe, the theory of the Holy Roman Empire, as the temporal protector of the Church with the kings of the earth ruling as vicegerents of the emperor, was never much more than a theory. It was not holy and was in frequent collision with the Church; it was not Roman but Teutonic, having its chief power beyond the borders of the old Empire; and it was hardly an empire after the death of Frederick Barbarossa in 1190. Certain titles of the Empire are still in existence, e.g., the duke of Marlborough is a prince thereof, and Barons Arundell of Wardour and Clifford of Chudleigh, counts.

ROMAN PATRIARCHATE, The. More commonly called the Patriarchate of the West (q.v.).

ROMAN QUESTION, The. The matters at issue between the Holy See and the civil government of Italy consequent upon the seizure of Rome by the Piedmontese in 1870. The principal difficulty was as to the position of the popes who, as independent sovereign persons forcibly deprived of their territory, confined themselves within the Vatican; the civil power regarded them as Italian subjects with statutory privileges and immunities (cf., the Law of Guarantees). The Roman Question was settled by the Treaty of the Lateran in 1929.

ROMAN RITE, The. The typical and authentic form or use of the Latin rite (q.v.,

i), as opposed to such variants thereof as the Ambrosian, Mozarabic, Carmelite, Carthusian, Dominican (qq.v.); it is the most widely used of all liturgies, whether Latin or Eastern, being universal in its distribution. The term is very often used instead of "Latin rite" in both senses ii and iii of "rite" (q.v.); neither usage is quite accurate.

ROMAN SEMINARY, The. See COLLEGES, ROMAN.

ROMANS, THE EPISTLE TO THE. A letter written by St. Paul to the Church in Rome, about the year 57. It is a canonical book of Holy Scripture. It was preparatory for his visit to the city and sought to confirm their faith (and especially that of Jewish converts) by an exposition of the relations of faith, in Christ and his teaching, and of works, whether of the natural or Mosaic law, respectively, to the fundamental fact of justification.

ROMANESQUE. The methods of building and forms of ornament in use in romanized Europe which evolved from the basilican and early-Christian forms and developed into gothic (q.v.) building; e.g., the cathedrals of Perigueux, Cremona, Mainz and Speyer, St. Trophimus at Arles, St. Sernin at Toulouse, Vézelay, Maria Laach, Toro.

ROMANISM. A pejorative name for the faith and practice of the Roman Catholic Church. Its first recorded use was in 1674, but Romanist was a term of abuse in 1523, and earlier in Germany (cf., Romish).

ROMANOS PONTIFICES. A constitution of Pope Leo XIII, in 1881, regulating the relations between bishops and regular clergy in Great Britain; it was afterwards extended to North America and other parts of the world.

ROME. i. The City, the metropolis of the world. "To manifest his power still more effectively, [Christ] ordained that the head of his Church should be in Rome itself, the capital of the world, as a sign of his complete victory and that thence faith should spread to the whole world" (St. Thomas Aquinas, III, xxxv, 7, ad 3). That St. Peter, the first pope, set up his episcopal chair and was martyred and buried in Rome is historically established beyond a doubt, and since then, except for the Avignon Popes (q.v.), the popes have never abandoned the city. From 800 till 1870 they were sovereigns (but not always undisputed masters) of the city; it then became the de facto capital of united Italy, a state of affairs confirmed by Pope Pius XI in 1929, when the independent Vatican City State was carved out of it.

ii. Figuratively: the Holy See, the Catholic Church.

iii. "New Rome." Constantinople (Byzantium) which the Emperor Constantine made the new capital of the Roman Empire.

iv. "The Third Rome." A name given to

Moscow by Russian politicians and churchmen after the fall of Constantinople, the "Second Rome," in 1453.

ROMISH. This inelegant synonym for the adjective Catholic was used so early as 1531 by Tyndale. It was used in 1562 in the 22nd of the Thirty-Nine Articles of the Church of England to qualify the doctrines of Purgatory, indulgences, invocation of the saints, etc.

ROOD (Old Eng. *ród*, a cross). i. A large crucifix, often with statues of our Lady and St. John, especially one beneath a chancel-arch, either suspended, standing on a screen or supported by a beam.
ii. The True Cross (archaic use).

ROOD-BEAM. A beam across a chancel-arch supporting a crucifix, either separate or in association with a screen.

ROOD-LOFT. A gallery along the top of a rood- or choir-screen, very common in the middle ages. Its uses are uncertain, but it was probably sometimes used as an *ambo* (*q.v.*) and for the accommodation of singers; the present choir-gallery of St. Etheldreda's church at Ely Place in London exactly reproduces a rood-loft thus used, but at the other end of the church. Some lofts it is certain had altars on them.

ROOD-SCREEN. A semi-open screen of stone or wood, carved and painted, across the chancel opening of a church, generally with a gallery along the top and surmounted by a rood standing either directly on the screen or upon a separate beam. The screens were a product of the middle ages in Western Europe and have no connexion with the early sanctuary railings, such as those in Santa Maria-in-Cosmedin in Rome and in the church at Torcello, or with the Byzantine *iconostasis*. Large conventual churches often had a rood screen or beam as well as, and west of, the choir-screen (*q.v.*). Rood-screens are sometimes put into modern churches.

ROOD OF BOXLEY, The, or **Rood of Grace.** A crucifix from the Cistercian abbey of Boxley near Maidstone, displayed at St. Paul's Cross in 1538 as an example of monastic fraud and cunning, because it was "made with divers (de)vices to move the eyes and lips." It appears to have originally been treasured as a piece of ingenious mechanism, and perhaps used for deposition in the Easter sepulchre (*q.v.*), and then as an object of devotion and pilgrimage because of the graces associated therewith. There is no evidence that the image was used in a fraudulent way to impose on and cozen the common people.

RORATE SUNDAY. The 4th Sunday of Advent, from the first word of the introit at Mass.

ROSARY (Lat. *rosarium*, a rose-garden, whence, a wreath, or garland). i. A string of beads consisting of five sets (decades) each of ten small and one larger bead (a crucifix with two large and three small beads is ordinarily added); the prayers said on these beads. Each decade is associated with a mystery (*q.v.*) of the faith and these mysteries number fifteen, so that a full rosary consists of this number of decades and corresponding prayers, but these are rarely met with. The method of saying the rosary, in public or private, is to recite an Our Father (large bead), ten Hail Marys (small beads), and Glory be to the Father (large bead), while meditating on the appropriate mystery; the essence of the devotion consists in a loving and intelligent meditation and not a mechanical repetition of the prayers. The beads (*q.v.*) are simply a device for keeping count. The tradition that the rosary was revealed by our Lady to St. Dominic is unproven; but the devotion has been particularly associated with his order for over 400 years. The feast of the Most Holy Rosary is now celebrated on Oct. 7 (first Sunday of October with the Dominicans) and is "the commemoration of St. Mary of Victory which Pope Pius V ordained to be observed yearly in memory of the great victory gained on this same day by the Christians over the Turks, in a naval battle [Lepanto, 1571], by the help of the said Mother of God" (Roman Martyrology).
ii. Other devotions in which beads are employed are mentioned under that word; they are sometimes called rosaries. Among the Orthodox the rosary (*konbologion, chotki, metany*) is a purely monastic practice, consisting of 100 beads on each of which the same short prayer is said, followed by a lesser or greater metany (*q.v.*). This Byzantine rosary is also used by some Catholic monks of the rite, but not by lay-people; the Italo-Greeks, Ruthenians and Rumanians use the Dominican rosary, which is common among Catholics of other Eastern rites.

ROSES, THE BLESSING OF, takes place in Dominican and other churches on the feast of the Holy Rosary, with a form provided in the "Rituale Romanum."

ROSE-WATER, or other perfumed water, is used in some ceremonies of the Byzantine rite, *e.g.*, to sprinkle the *epitaphion* at the Burial of Christ on Good Friday, and in the consecration of an altar. It was formerly used at Rome in the washing of the altar on Maundy Thursday.

ROSMINIANISM. The philosophic system of Antonio Rosmini-Serbati (1797–1885). His theory of knowledge, based on the innate idea of necessary, eternal, infinite essence of being, has been held to issue logically in Ontologism, and even Pantheism (*qq.v.*). He himself rejected such conclusions, but a decree of the Holy Office in 1887 condemned forty propositions taken from his works.

ROSMINIANS, The. The members of the Institute of Charity (*q.v.*), from the name of their founder, Antonio Rosmini-Serbati.

ROSS (*Rossensis*). i. An Irish see, suffragan of Cashel, entrusted to Cork *in commendam* in 1693, united to Cloyne in 1748, and made independent again in 1849. It covers part of county Cork. The bishop's residence and cathedral are at Skibbereen; there is no diocesan chapter. The patron of the diocese is St. Fachnan (Aug. 14) and the cathedral is dedicated in honour of St. Patrick. Irish name: Ros.
ii. A pre-reformation Scottish see whose territory is now included in the diocese of Aberdeen.

ROSY SEQUENCE, The. A sequence for the feast of the Holy Name, printed in the "Graduale" of the use of Sarum in 1527. It is a cento of the hymn *Iesu dulcis memoria;* Dr. J. M. Neale's translation is no. 238 in the "English Hymnal." See also the RHYTHM OF ST. BERNARD.

ROTA, THE SACRED ROMAN. A tribunal first set up in the 13th century and re-established by Pope Pius X in 1908. It is a court of first instance, appeal or final appeal, according to the origin and history of the case, for all contentious cases (except *causæ maiores, q.v.*) which require judicial action with trial and examination of evidence, and it is bound to give reasons for its decisions (unlike the Roman congregations, *q.v.*). It is best known as a court of appeal from diocesan courts in matrimonial cases. Its judges (auditors), doctors in theology and canon law, form a college of prelates with a dean at their head. Since 1929 it has also been the court of appeal from the civil and criminal tribunals of the Vatican City.

ROTARY CLUBS. A system of business and social societies originating in the United States and now found in other countries. The bishops of Spain (in 1929) and Mexico warned their flocks that international Rotary was under suspicion of professing secularism and religious indifference, and the movement was viewed with disfavour at Rome. But the apostolic delegate in the United States told American priest members that they need not resign, and it seems that membership is tolerated for Catholics in that country.

RUBRICS, The (Lat. *ruber*, red). Rules laid down for the conduct of the services of the Church and the carrying-out of any liturgical rite. Rubrics refer to the actions to be done and are often printed in red for the sake of clearness and distinction. Canon law requires strict observance of the rubrics in the liturgical books for the celebration of Mass, the recitation of the Divine Office and the administration of the sacraments. These rubrics are preceptive, *i.e.*, they impose an obligation of observance, the gravity of the obligation varying with the importance of the matter to which the rubric refers.

RULE, RELIGIOUS. The regulations of life and daily discipline under which a religious (*q.v.*) lives. These vary in every order and congregation, but in theory may each be reduced to one of four (the rules strictly so called), being differentiated by special constitutions supplementing or modifying it: the rule of St. Basil (all monks of the East), of St. Augustine (all canons regular, Dominicans, Austin friars, Servites, etc.), of St. Benedict (Benedictines proper, Cistercians, Vallombrosans, etc.) and of St. Francis (all friars minor, Poor Clares, etc., *qq.v.*). But the Carthusians, Carmelites and Jesuits stand outside these four, and numerous more recent institutes observe constitutions specially adapted to their particular object and circumstances. Generally speaking, the directions of a religious rule do not bind under pain of sin; but deliberate and flagrant disregard of them is a grave violation of that obedience which the religious has vowed.

RULE OF FAITH. The only direct rule at any given time is the actual teaching of the Church, whether expressed solemnly by pope or council or in the ordinary way by the instruction of her bishops and priests. The indirect or remote rule, *i.e.*, the source from which this teaching is taken, is twofold, the Scriptures and Apostolic Tradition. Many truths of Christianity are conveyed in the Bible, but other truths were not written down by the inspired writers and included in the sacred books. Such truths were conveyed from mouth to mouth, or committed to uninspired documents, and thus handed down throughout the centuries, their correctness being guaranteed by Christ's promise of indefectibility to his Church.

RUMANIA, THE CHURCH IN. Population about 16 million. Some 10 million of the people are Eastern Orthodox, and since 1925 have formed the Patriarchate of Rumania: until 1948 it was in practice treated as the national state church, though in legal theory regarded as only "predominant." There are important minorities of Protestants and Jews, and a number of Mohammedans. There are about 1½ million Catholics of Byzantine rite (nearly all in Transylvania) and another 1¼ million of Latin rite; the latter are mostly of foreign origin, chiefly Hungarian and German. The Catholic Byzantines also were considered as a "national church" and had a certain precedence over the Latins. There is a Byzantine metropolitan see of Fagaras and Alba Julia at Blaj, with 4 suffragan dioceses; the Latin archbishopric is at Bucarest, also with 4 suffragans. There is an ordinariate for the very old Armenian colony in Transylvania. The

Catholic Byzantines celebrate their liturgy in the vernacular tongue, and a majority of the parish clergy are married. In 1948 the communist government denounced the Rumanian concordat with the Holy See, and proceeded to deal with the Catholic Byzantine church on the same lines as the Ruthenians (q.v.) in Galicia, and with similar results. All the bishops and many clergy were imprisoned, monasteries, schools and hospitals suppressed, and churches handed over to the Orthodox (in 1949 over seventy Orthodox priests were imprisoned for refusing to take over Catholic churches). A similar persecution overtook Latin Catholics, though more slowly and somewhat less severely; it was met with equal firmness by the faithful.

RUSINS, The. A name given to those Ruthenians (q.v.) living in or coming from the Podkarpatska Rus, formerly part of Czechoslovakia and now of the U.S.S.R.

RUSSICUM, The. The Pontifical Russian College, of the Byzantine rite, at Rome, founded by Pope Pius XI in 1929, under the direction of Jesuit fathers. The students are trained for work among Russians but themselves are not restricted to that nationality.

RUTH. An historical book of the Old Testament which relates the story of a Moabitess who received the faith of God and married a Jew, Booz. It is a record of faith, patience, affection and the providence of God, and the last few verses show Ruth as great-grandmother of King David and thus an ancestress of Jesus Christ.

RUTHENIAN RITE, The. The Ruthenians have no distinct rite, though such is sometimes referred to. They use the Byzantine rite (q.v.) in Church Slavonic, but it has been subjected to certain modifications. See below.

RUTHENIANS, The. A Slavonic people, usually called Ukrainians, found in southwest Russia. Ecclesiastically the name is confined to those of them who are Catholics of the Byzantine rite (q.v.), fruit of the Union of Brest (q.v.). They are the largest single Catholic body of Eastern rite and num-

ber over 4 millions in Europe; the province of Galicia is governed by the archbishop of Lvov with 2 suffragans; they have two more dioceses in the Podkarpatska Rus; and there are some in the Bukovina. There are over ¾ million Ruthenians in North America, with 2 episcopal exarchs in the U.S.A. and 3 in Canada; and some 67,000 in Brazil and the Argentine. In Europe 80% of the secular clergy are married, but those ordained in America must be celibate; they have a college at Rome. In Galicia there were Studite monks and a congregation of Basilians (qq.v.), together with many nuns. After 1939 practically all of the Ruthenians, both the Ukrainians of Poland and the Rusins of Czechoslovakia, came under the rule of the U.S.S.R. All institutions under ecclesiastical control and all monastic establishments were dissolved, the bishops and many clergy were deported and interned in Russia, and every effort is made by pressure, coercion, and cajolery to bring the Ruthenians from communion with Rome to communion with the Orthodox church of Moscow. During 1946 a bogus "synod" at Lvov proclaimed that this had in fact been effected. The truth seems to be that the overwhelming majority of Ruthenians, both clergy and laity, are resisting the pressure to the best of their ability, but the material result of the situation over a period of time can hardly be in doubt. Byzantine usage is modified by the Ruthenians in the following, among other, matters: the Filioque is inserted in the Creed, the holy doors (q.v.) remain open throughout the Liturgy, the use of ripidia, zeon and antidoron is abandoned, the Roman sequence of liturgical colours is followed, some translated Latin formulas take the place of those in their own books, etc.; several Western feasts and popular devotions have been adopted. The secular clergy wear a plain cassock, with a round cap, and are clean shaven. The cathedral churches have chapters of canons, and the diaconate is no longer ever a permanent rank, but always leads to the priesthood. Ruthenians still observe the Julian calendar. The feast of the Ruthenian martyr St. Josaphat is kept by the whole Western church.

S

SABAOTH (Heb., armies). Part of a majestic title of God in the Old Testament (cf., Dominus Deus sabaoth, Lord God of Hosts, in the Sanctus and Te Deum, where the heavenly hosts of angelic spirits are referred to). The word has no connexion with Sabbath (q.v.).

SABBATARIANISM. i. The transference of the Jewish conception and law of the Sabbath

observance to the Christian Sunday, manifested by the prohibition of games, dancing, travelling, etc., on that day. But it should be noted that Jewish law was directed against secular activity in any form, whereas puritanism especially forbade recreation and pleasure.

ii. The observance of Saturday instead of Sunday as a day of rest, peculiar to certain

Protestant sects, *e.g.*, the Seventh-Day Adventists.

SABBATH (Heb., rest). The seventh day of the week, on which Jews must refrain from all work whatsoever and join in divine worship; appointed for the honour of God and the recreation of man. Among Christians it was superseded by the Lord's Day, the first of the week, to which many Protestants have given the name and attributes of the Jewish observance. Saturday is called the Sabbath (*Sabbatum*) in Latin Liturgical books.

SABBATINE PRIVILEGE, The. The pious belief, sanctioned by the Holy See, that those who have worn the brown scapular (*q.v.*) observed chastity according to their state, abstained from flesh meat on every Wednesday and Saturday or daily recited the Little Office B.V.M., or faithfully observed some other such work, and otherwise led a virtuous life will after death particularly profit by the intercession of our Lady. The "Sabbatine Bull" attributed to Pope John XXII in 1322 which expressed this privilege in a far more definite and imposing form is now judged to be certainly spurious.

SABBATUM IN ALBIS. The liturgical name of the Saturday next after Easter, so called because it formerly formed one occasion with the following day (*Dominica in albis, q.v.*).

SABELLIANISM. The doctrine of the followers of Sabellius (*fl.* c. 220), who first regarded God the Father and God the Son as one person and later interpreted the Blessed Trinity as one God in his three different relations (or as Modernists would now say, aspects) to man, as Creator, Incarnate Redeemer and Sanctifier. Sabellius was condemned by Pope St. Callistus I. The earlier form of the heresy was called Patripassianism (*q.v.*) and its followers nicknamed Monarchians.

SACRAMENT (Lat. *sacramentum*, a sacred pledge, the word used to translate Gr. μυστήριον, mystery, *q.v.*). A sacred sensible sign instituted by Christ in perpetuity to signify sanctifying grace and to confer that grace on the soul of the recipient. A sacrament is not fulfilled by the fact that one believes in it but by the fact that it is made. As sacraments cause grace it is obvious that they must depend on God for their institution, for grace is the gift of God alone. It is Catholic teaching that every one of the seven sacraments of the New Law was instituted by Christ. A sacrament consists essentially of three things, the matter, the form and the minister who makes the sacrament with the intention of doing what the Church does; if any of these be wanting, the sacrament is not made (confected).

SACRAMENT-HOUSE. A cupboard for the reservation of the Blessed Sacrament, usually on the gospel-side of and not far from the high altar. In many cases it was a separate erection, canopied and ornamented with carved stone, metal or wood, the canopy sometimes being of great height. This method of reservation was known in Scotland and was common in Switzerland, Belgium and Germany in the middle ages and in the last two countries persisted until it was finally forbidden in 1863.

SACRAMENT OF THE ALTAR, The. The Holy Eucharist and the Sacrifice of the Mass wherein this sacrament is confected.

SACRAMENTS, NON-CATHOLIC. In the dissident Eastern and other non-Catholic churches which have valid episcopal orders those sacraments which of their nature require only valid orders, and not power of jurisdiction as well, are also valid. (The Church by her practice recognizes the validity also of Penance and Confirmation administered by an Orthodox priest). They are also subjectively efficacious for sanctification and salvation, in accordance with Pope Clement XI's condemnation of the proposition that "outside the Church no grace is given." The "sacraments" of Christian bodies without valid orders, *e.g.*, the Anglican, may be the occasions of the conferring of divine grace but cannot be the vehicle of that grace, having no objective validity, except those of Baptism and Matrimony.

SACRAMENTS, THE SEVEN, are Baptism, Confirmation, the Holy Eucharist, Penance, Extreme Unction, Holy Orders and Matrimony (*qq.v.*). The Council of Trent defined it to be of faith that these sacraments were all instituted by Jesus Christ, that they confer grace on all who receive them worthily and with the right disposition, that Baptism, Confirmation and Orders imprint an indelible character (*q.v.*) on the soul and so cannot be repeated, and that the sacraments are necessary to salvation, though not all are necessary to every person. Baptism and Penance are sacraments of the dead because they are conferred on those who are spiritually dead in sin; the others are of the living and should be received in a state of grace. All dissident Eastern churches have and recognize these same seven sacraments, though in the lesser churches the use of some of them (particularly Penance) has practically or quite died out. See each sacrament.

SACRAMENTAL. An action or object which in its performance or use bears some resemblance to a sacrament. They are numerous and commonly divided into six classes: prayer, *e.g.*, the Our Father and liturgical prayers; dipping, *e.g.*, the use of holy water, various anointings, the *Mandatum;* eating, *e.g.*, of blessed bread; confession, *e.g.*, the *Confiteor;* giving, *e.g.*, alms bestowed in the name of the Church and not merely as a private deed; blessings, the largest class, including the consecration of kings, the blessing of abbots, churches, houses, bells, etc., the blessing and use of candles, palms and ashes, and of many other objects, medals, scapulars, images, etc. If used in accordance with the mind of the Church sacramentals are the means of receiving actual grace to do good and avoid evil, of protection of soul and body, and the remission of venial sin. These effects are entirely dependent upon the mercy of God who regards the prayers of the Church and the good dispositions of those who use them. They therefore differ from the sacraments both in operation and effect; but they are an extension of the sacramental principle of using material objects to signify spiritual truths and processes, and employing the unity in man of matter and spirit.

SACRAMENTAL SYSTEM, The. Dealing with creatures in a manner appropriate to their spiritual and corporal nature, God has appointed visible external acts by which certain graces are conferred on men and the merits of Christ's passion applied. Moreover, the sacraments in virtue of their institution by Christ confer the grace they signify by the very fact of being used, provided no obstacle is placed in the way of their efficacy. Nevertheless God can and does give grace without the use of external ceremonies.

SACRAMENTARY, or "Book of the Sacred Mysteries," the first complete liturgical book known in the Latin rite. It is one of the two or more books which went to make up the later Missal. It contained the celebrant's part of the Mass and also the services for other sacraments which are now in the "Rituale" and "Pontificale." The choir's part was in another book, often called the Antiphonary, which sometimes contained also the choir parts of what are now the Breviary offices. The epistles were usually in a Lectionary or Epistle Book, and the gospels were read from a book of the Four Gospels. The chief sacramentaries extant are those known as the Gelasian, Gregorian and Leonine (qq.v.); there are also Gallican sacramentaries, the most elaborate being the Mozarabic "Liber Sacramentorum." The book of the celebrant in Eastern liturgies (euchologion) is a sacramentary.

SACRAMENTINES, The. The Perpetual Adorers of the Blessed Sacrament, a congregation of sisters founded in Rome in 1807 for that purpose and still confined to Italy; also the Sisters of the Blessed Sacrament (q.v. i).

SACRARIUM. Another name for the piscina (q.v.).

SACRED HEART, The. i. A devotion to Jesus Christ consisting in the divine worship of his heart of flesh considered as united to his divinity and as the symbol of his love for us in dying for our redemption: particu-

larly in reparation for human ingratitude for his goodness and mercy. It must be noted that worship is not directed to his heart detached and distinct from him, but is essentially worship of Jesus himself; cf., the connotation of the popular expression "a broken heart," which does not mean a cardiac affliction. This devotion is the modern version of the ancient conception of Jesus as the Good Shepherd, and its popularity in its present form dates from the revelations given to St. Margaret Mary Alacoque in 1673-5; the devotion was first publicly preached in England, by Bl. Claud de la Colombière in 1676. It may be noted that Thomas Goodwin, Congregationalist chaplain to Oliver Cromwell, wrote a book entitled "The Heart of Christ in Heaven towards Sinners on Earth" which has remarkable affinities with the teaching of Bl. Claud. Images of the Sacred Heart intended to be set up for public veneration must show it in association with a representation of our Lord's person; images representing the heart alone are tolerated only for private devotion.

ii. A feast in honour of the Sacred Heart is observed on the Friday after the octave of Corpus Christi throughout the Western church, and by most of the Catholic orientals. The first petition addressed to the Holy See for the institution of this feast was from Queen Mary, consort of James II of England.

SACRED HEART NUNS. This name usually means Religious of the Society of the Sacred Heart (q.v.) but there are other congregations to which it may be applied.

"SACRED MAJESTY." A title used of, rather than by, the kings of Great Britain and Ireland during the 17th and 18th centuries. It is generally believed that its earliest known use is on the title-page of Εἰκών βασιλική in 1649 and that the title had no Catholic associations and was void of traditional support; but Lingard refers to its use in Parliament so early as the reign of Henry VIII.

SACRED ORDERS, The, are the three major orders, subdiaconate, diaconate and priesthood in the West.

SACRIFICE. The supreme public and external act of divine worship by which a sensible offering of a victim is made to God, by a legitimately appointed priest, in recognition of his supreme dominion over all creation, and, in the supposition of sin, to express consciousness of guilt and hope of pardon. "Every visible sacrifice which is offered to God by exterior acts is a sign of that invisible sacrifice whereby a man offers himself and all he has to the service of God" (St. Augustine). The Sacrifice of Calvary was the one universal and absolute sacrifice. Consequently, to have any efficacy, the sacrifices offered at the Last Supper and in the Mass must bear some essential relation to that of Calvary; and actually in all three sacrifices the Victim and the principal Offerer are the same, namely, Christ; the difference is in the manner of offering, *sc.* in a bloody manner on the Cross, in a bloodless manner at the Supper and in the Mass.

SACRIFICE OF THE CROSS. The free offering made by Christ of the shedding of his blood at the hands of his executioners in atonement for the sins of men; the one universal and absolute sacrifice by which the world was redeemed, so that every means of grace before or since Calvary derives its efficacy from the Sacrifice of the Cross.

SACRIFICE OF EXPIATION, OF IM-PETRATION. The Mass, from the point of view of its value as an act of propitiation and of impetration (*qq.v.*) respectively.

SACRIFICE OF THE MASS, The. The true sacrifice of the Body and Blood of Christ made present on the altar by the words of consecration; a representation and a renewal of the offering made on Calvary; "in this divine sacrifice the same Christ is present and immolated in a bloodless manner who once for all offered himself in a bloody manner on the altar of the cross; . . . only the manner of offering is different" (Trent, sess. xxii, cap. 2). The sacrificial action is held by the majority of theologians to be contained in the separate consecrations of the bread and wine. The sacrifice of the cross was the one universal and absolute sacrifice; from it consequently the Mass derives its efficacy, consisting in an application of its fruits. Thus the Mass gives supreme honour and glory to God and offers him thanks for his benefits, both in an infinite degree; moreover, it begs and obtains God's pardon for our sins and is effective in obtaining further graces and blessings, to an extent dependent on the worthiness and devotion of the priest saying the Mass, of the faithful assisting, and of the whole Church on earth. See also MASS, etc. The name Mass properly belongs only to the Latin eucharistic service, but for convenience, *e.g.*, as above and below, is sometimes extended to the Holy Sacrifice in all rites.

SACRIFICE OF THE NEW LAW. Since the Sacrifice of the Cross was the one universal and absolute sacrifice, every other sacrifice must thence derive whatever efficacy it has. Thus those of the Old Law were types of the supreme Sacrifice of Calvary; in it they were fulfilled, and by it abrogated. Similarly, the Sacrifice of the New Law is the Mass, one and the same sacrifice with that of the Cross, instituted by Christ to satisfy the needs of mankind for sacrifice and as the means whereby the fruits of the Redemption might be applied to men for the remission of their daily sins (*cf.*, Council of Trent, sess. xxiv, cap. 1).

SACRIFICE OF PRAISE. i. A sacrifice offered to God in worship and thanksgiving. The Council of Trent condemned the Reformers for holding that "the Mass is only a sacrifice of praise and thanksgiving . . . not a propitiatory sacrifice," *i.e.*, effectively imploring pardon and offering satisfaction for our sins (sess. xxii, can. 3).

ii. All acts of religion (and therefore of praise) may be described as sacrifices, inasmuch as the purpose of sacrifice is to manifest the interior worship of God externally; but a sacrifice strictly requires the offering of a victim by a priest for its external sign (*cf.*, Ps. l, 19).

SACRILEGE. The irreverent treatment of sacred things, persons or places, *i.e.*, those dedicated by God or the Church to sacred purposes. It is a sin against the virtue of religion, of its nature grave, but admitting smallness of matter. Sacrilege may be either personal, as when violence is done to a cleric or religious; local, as when certain crimes are committed or actions done in a church; real, as by the abuse of sacraments, the theft of sacred objects or their irreverent misuse, and the sin of simony (*q.v.*). These varieties of the sin differ specifically from one another.

SACRING (Lat. *sacer,* holy). An archaic word for the consecration at Mass and for the consecration of a sovereign or bishop. Sacring-bell and sanctus-bell (*q.v.*) are now interchangeable terms but the second was formerly distinguished as larger.

SACRIST, -AN. The person who has the daily charge of a church, especially the sacristy and its contents, prepares the altar for Mass, rings the bell, etc. He fulfils several functions formerly performed by the clerics with the orders of doorkeeper, exorcist and acolyte. In cathedral and other important churches the sacristan is a priest, who has lay assistants. The sacristan of the Vatican is always an Augustinian friar, a titular bishop and *ex officio* assistant at the throne.

SACRISTY. An apartment adjoining a church wherein are kept the sacred vessels, books, vestments and other accessories of divine worship and where the clergy vest for their office. In addition to the necessary cupboards, etc., every sacristy must have a crucifix displayed above the vesting table and a vessel with water for the celebrant's hands. Though usually structurally part thereof, the sacristy is not blessed or consecrated with the church and is therefore not technically a "sacred place"; that, however, does not relieve a layman of the obligation of respectful carriage therein.

SACRO SPECO, The (It., holy cave). The cave at Subiaco in which St. Benedict lived, first as a hermit and then with companions; "from whence issued, with the rule and institution of St. Benedict, the flower of Christian polity, the permanent triumph of spirit over matter, the intellectual emancipation of Europe . . ." (Montalembert).

SADDUCEES, The (probably from *Zadok*, a personal name). The rival party among the Jews to the Pharisees, denying the authority of all revelation and tradition subsequent to Moses, the immortality of the soul, resurrection of the body and the existence of angels. They accepted Hellenic cultures and were, in effect, free-thinkers.

SAGESSE, NUNS OF LA. The Daughters of Wisdom (*q.v.*), from the community room in their first convent called La Sagesse in reference to the divine folly of Calvary, a large cross being set therein.

SAINT (Lat. (*sanctus*, consecrated). i. One whose holiness of life and heroic virtue have been confirmed and recognized by the Church's official processes of beatification and canonization (*qq.v.*), or by the continued existence of an approved *cultus* and feast. To such only may public veneration and liturgical honour be given; but the Church also produces numerous other saints who remain unknown and unrecognized (*cf.*, the feast of All Saints, whereon these also are honoured). In the Catholic economy the departed saints have not simply ethical significance as patterns of virtuous life, but also religious significance as living and functioning members of the Mystical Body of Christ, who by prayer are in vital contact with the Church militant and suffering. The canonized saints form a microcosm of the Church; among them are to be found representatives of all forms of human life, activity and temperament. They manifest exteriorly the hidden life of our Lord whom they have hidden in their hearts; the inner man being filled with his spirit, exterior and corresponding action flows from it as from its true source. Nor are their activities and greatness directed in strictly religious channels only; besides so many priests and monks and nuns the Church has canonized emperors and kings and queens, soldiers, artizans, domestic-servants, beggars, housemaids, lawyers, merchants, society dames, farmers and their labourers, artists, physicians, a retired hangman—sanctity is an order for which all are eligible. It must not be supposed that the actions of a saint must always appear good to everyone; he is immune neither from faults nor from errors of judgement; moreover, the "ordinary person" may be the least good judge of a saint's actions. The Church does not officially honour the sanctity of those who in good faith are separated from her visible unity (*cf.*, *Martyrdom*.)

ii. The word "saint" is rarely used as a title in the liturgy, such being ordinarily referred to as "the blessed N. . . .," *e.g.*, in the collects. In the Byzantine rite it is "the holy father N. . . .," "the holy martyr M. . . .," "The holy, glorious and illustrious apostles, the princes and first leaders, Peter and Paul," etc One language, the Welsh, does not know this use at all except in the case of three saints, *Dewi Sant* (David), *Cynnwyll Sant* and *Ffraid Santes* (Brigid); others were and are referred to simply as *Illtyd*, *Gwenfrewi* (Winefride), *Elen* (Helen), *Ieuan Ebostol* (John the Apostle), *Mari Llwyd* (the blessed Mary,) etc. In the New Testament the word "saints" is often used to designate all Christians of a place, as we should say "the faithful."

SAINTS, INTERCESSION OF THE. See INVOCATION OF SAINTS.

SAINTS, VENERATION OF. The *cultus* of *dulia* (*q.v.*) is paid to the saints; that of *hyperdulia* (*q.v.*) to the Blessed Virgin. Public *cultus* (*q.v.*) is to be paid only to those canonized or beatified (or otherwise recognized by the Church); the former may be venerated anywhere; the latter only where permitted by the Holy See. Saints may be chosen as patrons of nations, dioceses, religious societies, etc., with the approval of the Holy See; not so those who are beatified only. A relative honour or worship is due to images and relics of the saints (*cf.*, Invocation of Saints, Relics, etc.).

SAINTS OF THE MASS. Those saints whose names are mentioned during the canon of the Mass, at the commemoration of the Church triumphant and in the prayer *Nobis quoque peccatoribus*. The first group consists of our Lady, the eleven apostles and Paul, five martyred popes (Linus, Cletus, Clement, Sixtus II, Cornelius) and seven male martyrs of the first three centuries of whom the last five were laymen (Cyprian, Lawrence, Chrysogonus, John and Paul Cosmas and Damian); the second of John the Baptist, Stephen, Matthias and Barnabas, a bishop (Ignatius), a pope (Alexander I), two priests (Peter and Marcellinus), and seven women martyrs (Felicity, Perpetua, Agatha, Lucy, Agnes, Cecily and Anastasia). The last five were added by Pope St. Gregory the Great (*c.* 600) since whom no other additions have been made; the occurrence of the name of St. Andrew in the prayer *Libera* is said to be due to the same pope's personal devotion. Other saints are named in the canon of local rites (*e.g.*, Ambrose, Sabina, Nabor, Felix and others in the Milanese) and in Eastern anaphoras.

SAINT ANDREWS AND EDINBURGH (*Sancti Andreæ at Edimburgensis*). A Scottish see first set up before the 10th century; made a metropolitan archdiocese with primacy of Scotland in 1472; vacant from 1571 till 1878, when "Edinburgh" was added to its title and it was made metropolitan for all Scotland except Glasgow, but the primacy not renewed. It comprises the counties of East,

West and Mid Lothian, Berwick, Peebles, Roxburgh, Selkirk, most of Stirling and part of Fife. The archbishop's residence and the cathedral of St. Mary are at Edinburgh. The patron of the archdiocese is St. Andrew. Gaelic name: Naomh Anndra.

SAINT ANDREW'S CROSS. The cross saltire (*q.v.*), upon which St. Andrew the Apostle is said to have been put to death.

SAINT ANTONY'S FIRE or **Ignis sacer.** A disease so called because St. Antony the Abbot was invoked against its ravages. It has been identified with erysipelas (called in Welsh *Y fendigaid,* "the blessed") but it appears originally to have been a far more virulent and contagious disorder, caused probably by the consumption of wheat damaged by ergot. An order of hospitallers, afterwards canons regular, of St. Antony was founded in the 11th century to look after sufferers therefrom; it is now extinct.

SAINT ELMO'S FIRE. The name given to the ball of electrical light sometimes seen above the masts of ships during a storm; also called *corpo-sant,* from Portuguese *corpo santo,* being fabled to be departed souls. The name is from St. Erasmus (June 2), an Italian bishop and martyr, who was popular in the past, under the name of Elmo, as a patron of seamen. Spanish sailors attribute the name Elmo to their patron, Bd. Peter Gonzales; it is sometimes written "San Telmo."

SAINT MARY MAJOR. The principal church of our Lady in Rome. See LIBERIAN BASILICA.

SAINT MEINRAD. The mother-house of the Swiss-American Benedictine congregation (*q.v.*) in Indiana. St. Meinrad's monastery was founded from Einsiedeln Abbey in Switzerland by Dom Ulrich Christen and Dom Bede O'Connor in 1854, and became an abbey in 1870. The monks conduct a senior and junior seminary, and do mission work among the Sioux Indians.

SAINT OMER. A college established near Calais by Fr. Robert Persons S.J., in 1592, for the education of the sons of English Catholics, which flourished there until the Jesuits were turned out of France in 1762. The college, but not under that name, continued in Belgium till the Revolution, when it was removed to Stonyhurst. The original buildings were colonized from Douay (*q.v.*) for a short time.

SAINT OTTILIA, CONGREGATION OF. Founded in 1884 as the Society of the Sacred Heart for Foreign Missions and became in 1904 a Benedictine congregation engaged in the same work. It has its headquarters at the archabbey of St. Ottilia in Bavaria.

SAINT PATRICK'S PURGATORY. A sanctuary on an island in Lough Derg, Pettigo, in the diocese of Clogher. It has been a place of pilgrimage almost without intermission for a thousand years. Its church is now a minor basilica (*q.v.*). It is essentially a penitential undertaking and the exercises of the pilgrims last three days. There are two hospices for their accommodation and they number several thousand every year, mostly between June 1 and Aug. 15. A notable by-product of this pilgrimage is said to be the large number of marriages that are arranged in the course of or as a result of it. St. Patrick used to retire to this island for solitude.

SAINT PETER OF MUENSTER. A Benedictine monastery of the American-Cassinese congregation, founded in Illinois in 1892, migrated to Saskatchewan, Canada, in 1903. It was made an abbey *nullius* (*q.v.*) in 1921, and the abbot has jurisdiction over 28 parishes.

SAINT PETER'S. The Patriarchal Basilica of St. Peter, adjoining the Vatican Palace at Rome. It is commonly regarded as the chief church of the world, but strictly speaking is second to St. John Lateran, the papal cathedral, and it has not a permanent episcopal throne; its importance was increased during the confinement of the popes to the Vatican (1870-1929). All functions of world-wide importance, canonizations, opening and closing of jubilees, etc., take place therein. It is served by a chapter of 30 canons and 67 other beneficiaries, presided over by a cardinal archpriest with a vicar; there is also attached a college of 10 penitentiaries who are members of the Conventual branch of the Franciscans. The first basilica here was built by Constantine and the present was building from 1506 till 1626. It is the largest church in the world and occupies part of the site of Nero's circus wherein St. Peter was crucified, head downwards; his body lies in a vault beneath the high altar, unopened for a thousand years.

SAINT SAVIOUR. The title given to some churches dedicated to God the Son as redeemer; the titular feast of such churches is observed on Aug. 6 (the Transfiguration) unless permission is given by indult for the feast of the Holy Redeemer.

SAINT SOPHIA. A barbarous name commonly given to the church of the Holy Wisdom (Gr. *Hagia Sophia, q.v.*) at Constantinople; it was dedicated not to the Holy Ghost but to Christ as the Word of God.

SAINT-SULPICE. A seminary founded at Vaugirard by M. Olier and transferred to near the church of St. Sulpice in Paris in 1642; from it the Sulpicians (*q.v.*) take their name. The buildings were confiscated by the state in 1906 and the seminary is now at Issy.

SAINT THOMAS CHRISTIANS. A generic name for all the Christians of Malabar (*q.v.*) in south-west India, who claim from time immemorial to be descended from Brahmans converted by St. Thomas the Apostle, who is said to have founded seven churches and to have been martyred at Mylapore. They probably were evangelized by the East Syrian church, whose liturgy they adopted, but there is no proof that they were ever Nestorian. King Alfred in 883 sent Sighelm, bishop of Sherborne, on a pilgrimage to Rome and "the church of the apostles Bartholomew and Thomas" in India in fulfilment of a vow. Their modern history begins with the coming of the Portuguese in 1498 and the Synod of Diamper (*q.v.*). *Mar Thomakkar* is the official name now arrogated to themselves by the "reformed" sect. The native Christians were formerly considered superior and given precedence by all Hindu castes.

ST. VINCENT'S ARCHABBEY. The motherhouse of the American-Cassinese Benedictine congregation (*q.v.*) at Beatty, Pennsylvania, founded by Dom Boniface Wimmer and other monks from Bavaria in 1846. It be-became an abbey in 1855, the first Benedictine abbey of the United States. The monks conduct a senior seminary, among other works, and the abbey has several dependent priories.

SAINT-VANNES. A Benedictine abbey of Lorraine which, in 1598, initiated a reform in observance which became the distinct Congregation of St. Vanne from which originated the Maurists (*q.v.*) It did not survive the Revolution.

SAINT VINCENT DE PAUL SOCIETY, The. An association founded in Paris in 1833 by Frédéric Ozanam and seven others, primarily to help young men to live better lives by visiting the poor in their homes to assist them spiritually and materially, then to instruct and care for children, distribute books, and undertake any other charitable work, no form of which is regarded as foreign to the society. Its work is done by voluntary laymen formed into conferences and councils; women are not admitted as active members. The active brothers number over 100,000 throughout the world and form one of the most effective of all charitable organizations. The society was introduced into England in 1844 and into the United States, at Saint Louis, in the following year.

SAINTE AMPOULE, LA. The phial containing chrism (said to have been delivered miraculously to St. Remi at the baptism of Clovis in 496) used in anointing the kings of France at their coronation from Philip Augustus to Charles X. It was publicly smashed at the Revolution, but some of the contents was saved.

SAINTE UNION NUNS. The Sœurs de la Sainte Union des Sacrés Cœurs, an educational congregation founded by the Abbé de Brabant at Douai in 1828.

SAKKOS (Gr., a sack). A short tunic with half-sleeves, very like a dalmatic, but fastened up the sides, richly embroidered. It is the sacrificial vestment of archbishops and metropolitans of the Byzantine rite, but is now worn instead of the *phelonion* by bishops as well. It originated in the imperial tunic.

SALE OF INDULGENCES. It is simony to buy or sell indulgences (*q.v.*), but it is lawful to make an offering on the occasion of receiving an indulgence, provided all danger or suspicion of simony is removed. Those who grant or publish indulgences for money, or otherwise traffic in them, incur excommunication reserved to the Holy See *simpliciter*. An object to the use of which an indulgence is attached (*e.g.*, a rosary) loses its indulgence if the object is sold.

SALE OF MASSES. To buy or sell or otherwise traffic in the celebration of Mass is a sin of simony. Nevertheless, an offering (*q.v.* v) of money or goods may be made to and accepted by a priest who undertakes to offer the Sacrifice for a specific intention. Such stipends (*q.v.*) take the place of the offerings of bread, wine, candles, etc., made in primitive times by the congregation at every Mass for use at the altar and what remained over for the priest. But it must be clearly understood that this is not meant to be, nor in fact is regarded as, the price of a Mass, but as a contribution for the priest's support or an alms.

SALESIANS, The. The Society of St. Francis of Sales, a congregation of priests, clerics and lay-brothers founded by St. John Bosco in Turin in 1854, its object being the Christian perfection of its members through the exercise of spiritual and corporal works of mercy especially among the young and the poor. The principal work of the society is education of all kinds—elementary, secondary, technical, agricultural and social. It also undertakes foreign missions (South America, India, Siam, China, Japan), and the society has spread all over the world, with hundreds of establishments and over 10,000 members of all grades.

SALFORD (*Salfordiensis*). An English see, suffragan of Liverpool, erected in 1850, covering the hundreds of Salford and Blackburn in the county of Lancaster, formerly in the diocese of Lichfield. The mission of Samlesbury was established in 1690 and 6 others in the 18th century. The bishop's residence is at Wardley Hall, near Manchester; the cathedral in Salford. The Jesuit school of Stonyhurst is near Blackburn. The patrons of the diocese are our Lady of Mount Carmel, St. Joseph, St. Augustine of England and St.

John the Divine, in whose honour the cathedral is dedicated.

SALOPIENSIS. The adjectival form of the name of the see of Shrewsbury (q.v.) used in the designation of its bishop in Latin documents. Noun: *Salopia*.

SALT, exorcized and blessed, is put on the tongue of the candidate at Baptism as a symbol of wisdom and incorruption. It is also used in the blessing of Gregorian water and of ordinary holy water (qq.v.), with reference to its health-giving properties. A little salt is mixed with the eucharistic bread by the Catholic Syrians and Chaldeans.

SALUT (Fr., salutation). Benediction of the Blessed Sacrament. This name appears to be a reminiscence of the practice of singing *Salve Regina* (q.v.) and other hymns to our Lady as an evening devotion, to which solemnity was afterwards added by exposing the Blessed Sacrament. From this custom Benediction has probably evolved.

SALVADOR, THE CHURCH IN. The population of the Republic of The Saviour, about 1¾ milion, is Indian and half-caste, and nominally all Catholic. A concordat was entered into with the Holy See, but it has not been well observed; from time to time the government shows hostility to the Church, but it maintains diplomatic relations with the Vatican. Salvador is a metropolitan province, with 3 suffragan sees.

SALVATION. i. The freeing of the soul from the bonds of sin and its consequences and the attainment of the everlasting vision of God in Heaven, not merely by way of reward but as the achievement of man's proper end. Salvation, though ultimately depending solely upon the love and mercy of God, is open to all by co-operation with divine grace according to the individual's knowledge and powers. The ordinary road to salvation is through visible membership of the Church; but "God gives light, sufficient for its salvation, to every soul that attains to the use of reason in this life" (de Lugo, *De fide*).
ii. Outside the Church. "Outside the Church, no salvation." This dogma refers to those who are outside the Church by their own fault. There is a command to enter the Church, which is the prescribed way to Heaven. He who refuses to join the Church which Christ founded, recognizing that Christ commanded adhesion to his Church, is in the way of perdition. But those who are in invincible ignorance (q.v.) will not be condemned merely on account of their ignorance. "It is to be held as of faith that none can be saved outside the Apostolic Roman Church . . . but nevertheless it is equally certain that those who are ignorant of the true religion, if that ignorance is invincible, will not be held guilty in the matter in the

eyes of the Lord" (Pius IX, allocution of Dec. 9, 1854). Those non-Catholics who are saved are in life outside the visible body of the Church, but are joined invisibly to the Church by charity and by that implicit desire of joining the Church which is inseparable from the explicit desire to do God's will.*

SALVATION ARMY, The. A Protestant sect founded and organized by William Booth between 1865 and 1880. Its outward characteristics are a military organization and nomenclature (without ordained ministry) and a mode of evangelization admirably calculated to appeal to the common people. The great achievements of the Army are a notable success in raising the standard of personal behaviour, and numerous benevolent works of great efficiency and worth throughout the world. Doctrinally the Bible is the sole rule of faith; it is thoroughly in accordance with the spirit of the Army that the predestinarianism of Calvinistic and Lutheran Protestantism is utterly rejected.

SALVATORIANS, The. i. A congregation of Melkite Basilian (q.v.) monks (founded in 1708), chiefly engaged in parochial work in Syria.
ii. The Society of the Divine Saviour, a religious congregation founded at Rome by the Rev. Francis Jordan in 1881. It undertakes any work for the advancement of religion, principally education, social work and foreign missions. The habit is a loose black cassock, girdle, cloak and biretta.

SALVE REGINA. The first words and title of the fourth of the antiphons of our Lady (q.v.) and the most widely used prayer to her after the Hail Mary (English version begins: "Hail, holy Queen"). It is said or sung after the Divine Office from first Vespers of the feast of the Holy Trinity until Advent begins. After Compline according to Dominican usage it is accompanied by a procession; in the Carmelite rite it is said at the altar steps before the last gospel at Mass, and before the blessing in the Mozarabic rite.

SAMARITANS, The. The inhabitants of Samaria (Sichem), descendants of the Israelites who intermarried with the pagan Assyrian colonists planted there by Salmanasar after 721 B.C. They evolved a variant of Judaism and built a rival temple on Mount Garizim, whence the bitter enmity between them and the pure orthodox Jews (cf., John iv, 9, 20). They were practically annihilated in A.D. 529, but a tiny colony (180 souls in 1947) still inhabits a corner of Nablus; they have an annual Passover on Garizim (Jabel at-Tur) and preserve in their synagogue a famous Pentateuch roll of unknown date.

SAMPIETRINI (It., Saint Peter's men). A permanent body of skilled workmen of all the necessary trades, with their assistants,

---

* See also NECESSARY TO SALVATION and NECESSARY, NECESSITY.—*Publisher*, 1997.

engaged on the structural and decorative maintenance of St. Peter's basilica at Rome.

SAMUEL, BOOKS OF. The name given in Hebrew and Protestant versions of the Old Testament to 1 and 2 Kings; it is used as a sub-title in the Vulgate and Catholic vernacular versions.

SAN FRANCISCO (*Sancti Francisci*). Though not among the older American archdioceses, the metropolitan see of San Francisco is remarkable for the extent of its province. It was founded as the diocese of Both Californias in 1840; in 1854 this was divided and San Francisco became metropolitan. It has 4 suffragan dioceses, Reno, Sacramento, Salt Lake and Honolulu. With the addition to these of the vicariate apostolic of Guam in 1947 the province of San Francisco attained borders more extensive than any other in the world. Until its disruption after 1917 the Russian metropolitan province of Mogilev was generally accounted the largest.

SANATIO IN RADICE (Lat., a healing at the root, *i.e.*, a complete cure). The revalidation (*q.v.*) of a marriage in such way that the impediment (if any) is dispensed, renewal of consent is not required, and canonical effects are, by a fiction of law, attributed to the marriage as if it were valid from the beginning. The Holy See alone has power to grant a *sanatio*, and it is given only when revalidation in the ordinary form is impossible or difficult. It cannot be given to a marriage null owing to defect of consent, except to take effect from the time such consent was supplied, nor to a marriage in which consent, given at first, has afterwards been withdrawn. It is not given to a marriage void owing to an impediment of natural or divine law, not even to take effect from the time such impediment ceased.

SANBENITO. A garment shaped like the scapular of St. Benedict's monks (Spanish: *San Benito*) worn by those condemned by the Spanish Inquisition; its painted pattern varied in accordance with the wearer's punishment.

SANCTA. One of the three portions broken from the Host at Mass in early times; it was reserved until the next Mass and then put into the Chalice by the archdeacon. Thus was emphasized the unity of the sacrifice in time (*cf.*, fermentum). As the bishop worshipped the reserved *Sancta* before beginning Mass, so a bishop still prays before the Blessed Sacrament immediately before celebrating pontifically. It is maintained by some that the solemn veiling and holding of the paten by the subdeacon during the canon also refers to the former *sancta*, which was thus held on the paten (originally by an acolyte) till the moment of putting it into the chalice.

SANCTA SANCTIS. Gr. Τὰ ἅγια τοῖς ἁγίοις, Holy things to the holy (*q.v.*).

SANCTI CLODOALDI. Genitive (in the bishop's title) of *Sanctus Clodoaldus*, Latin translation of the name of the see of Saint Cloud, Minnesota.

SANCTION. i. The consideration on account of which a law or rule of conduct is obeyed; the authority on which a judgement or opinion is formed.
ii. A law; the penalty for breaking a law (vindicatory or punitive sanction) or reward for its observance (remuneratory sanction); the act whereby a legislator imposes a law.

SANCTISSIMUM, The. The Most Holy Thing, *i.e.*, the Blessed Sacrament.

SANCTITY. An eminent degree of "charity, from a pure heart, and a good conscience, and an unfeigned faith" (1 Tim. i, v). See HOLINESS.

SANCTITY OF THE CHURCH. One of the marks of the Church (*q.v.*): that holiness which distinguishes the Church in her doctrines, her worship, her government, the means of holiness which she offers to all; also the distinguishing holiness which so many of her subjects, especially the saints, have attained by her ministrations.

SANCTORALE, The. The part of the Breviary or Missal containing the proper offices of the saints; the offices themselves.

SANCTUARY. i. That part of a church immediately surrounding the high altar, or, where there is no chancel or a small one, all that part within the altar-rails.
ii. A shrine (*q.v.*).
iii. A refuge, usually the precincts of a church, to which persons might have recourse when threatened with public justice or private vengeance; they were then held by law to be untouchable, permanently or for a time and in circumstances varying according to the local privilege. There were over a score of such special sanctuaries in England; that of Beverley enclosed a radius of a mile from the church (*cf.*, the space called Broad Sanctuary at the west end of Westminster Abbey). All ecclesiastical sanctuary ceased in England in the 16th century and is now maintained nowhere; but according to canon law those who take refuge in a church must not, except in cases of necessity, be removed without the permission of the bishop or pastor.

SANCTUS, The, also called the *Tersanctus* and the Hymn of Victory, consists of the words "Holy, holy, holy, Lord God of Hosts. Heaven and earth are full of thy glory" (Is. vi, 3) with the *Benedictus* (*q.v.* ii) added. It is derived from the worship of the synagogue and occurs in all Liturgies at the end of the preface as its culminating point. In the Latin Mass it is said with a moderate inclination by the celebrant and sung by choir and people. It is sometimes erroneously referred to as the *Trisagion* (*q.v.*). A musical setting of the same.

SANCTUS-BELL. The small bell (*q.v.*, ii) rung at various parts of the Mass, the first ringing being three times at the *Sanctus*, whence the name. Formerly it was larger, distinguished from the little or sacring-bell, and in England in the middle ages was sometimes hung in a bell-cote over the chancel or suspended on the rood-screen.

SANDALS. i. Sandals without stockings are worn by certain religious who are distinguished as discalced (*q.v.*) or barefooted from those who wear ordinary boots or shoes. They are principally the Friars Minor, Capuchins, Trinitarians, Discalced Carmelites and Augustinian Friars, Minims, Passionists, Antonian monks, and the corresponding nuns. It is an error to suppose that sandals are a distinctively monkish form of foot-gear; they are rather characteristic of friars, monks wearing whatever is customary in their time and country.

ii. The so-called episcopal sandals are embroidered silk slippers worn by cardinals and bishops over the buskins (*q.v.*) when celebrating pontifical Mass. They are the same colour as the vestments.

SANHEDRIN, The (Gr. συνέδριον, council). The supreme court of judicature and administrative assembly of the Jewish church at the time of Christ. It had the regulation of religious and civil observances, the enforcement of the law of Moses and the control of doctrinal teaching. There were 72 members (*cf.*, Ex. xviii, 13-26; Num. xi, 16).

SANT' ANSELMO DE URBE. The international college at Rome of the monks of St. Benedict. It was founded in 1621, re-established in 1887, and moved to the Aventine hill in 1896. The office of grand chancellor is filled by the Benedictine abbot primate (*q.v.*), who has his seat at Sant' Anselmo.

SANTA CLAUS (corruption of Dutch *Sint Klaes*, St. Nicholas). This form of the cult of St. Nicholas of Bari, patron saint of children, was popularized in America by the Dutch puritans of New Amsterdam who had disguised the popish saint as a nordic magician. It appears to have been introduced into England by Bret Harte.

SAPIENTI CONSILIO. A constitution of Pope Pius X in 1908, whereby Great Britain, Canada, the U.S.A., Holland and Luxemburg were removed from the jurisdiction of the Congregation of Propaganda and subjected to the common law of the Western church with dependence on the Consistorial Congregation; they therefore ceased to be missionary countries in the technical sense.

SAPIENTIAL BOOKS, The. The books of Proverbs, Ecclesiastes, the Canticle, Wisdom and Ecclesiasticus, written by, in the person of, or attributed to, Solomon and directed to the praise and inculcation of wisdom (Lat. *sapientia*).

SAPIENZA, The (It., wisdom). The name given in the 16th century to the University of Rome, founded by Pope Boniface VIII in 1303. Since 1870 it has been the University of Italy under the control of the civil government.

SARABITES (derivation uncertain). One of the four kinds of monk named by St. Benedict in his rule, the "third and most baneful kind . . . whatever they think fit or choose to do, that they call holy; and what they like not, that they consider unlawful." A general term for unworthy or relaxed monks.

SARDICA, THE SYNOD OF. A council held at Sofia in 343 chiefly notable because of its 3rd, 4th and 5th canons which provided for the appeal by a deposed bishop from the deposing bishops to the Holy See.

SARDINIAN CHAPEL, The. An embassy chapel (*q.v.*) near Lincoln's Inn Fields founded in 1648. It was taken over from the Sardinian ambassador by the vicar apostolic of the London district in 1799 and was in use till it was pulled down when Kingsway was built in 1909. It is now represented by the church of SS. Anselm and Cecilia near the site of the former chapel.

SARUM USE, The (corrupt abbreviation of Lat. *Sarisburia*, Salisbury). The form of the Latin rite codified by St. Osmund (*d.* 1099) for use in his diocese of Salisbury. It spread beyond those boundaries and became the most widespread use in England up to the Reformation; it was introduced into Ireland in 1172 and Scotland about 1250. It closely resembled the Dominican rite (*q.v.*) as used at the present day; but its most notable divergence from Roman usage was an excess of mere ceremoniousness. The marriage ceremonies (*q.v.*) peculiar to English Catholics have survived from the Sarum "Rituale." After its restoration under Queen Mary it was superseded by the reformed Roman rite of Pope St. Pius V: *e.g.*, at the English college at Douay in 1576.

SATAN (Heb., adversary). A proper name, used frequently in the New Testament, for Lucifer or the Devil (*qq.v.*).

SATANISM. The conscious worship of Satan by those banded together for the purpose. This worship finds expression in hideous and obscene ceremonies and in particular in a blasphemous parody of the Holy Sacrifice, the "Black Mass." Though probably there has been much exaggeration as to the prevalence of this diabolical cult, it can hardly be questioned that it was practised by such characters as Gilles de Rais, the Abbé Guibourg, and Mme. de Montespan, and that something of the sort persists in holes and corners to the present day. One of the principal objects of Satanists is to obtain possession of the consecrated Host in order to profane it.

SATISFACTION. i. The act by which the sinner endeavours to make reparation to God for offences committed against him by undergoing some form of punishment. The intention to make satisfaction and willingness to accept the penance (*q.v.*) given by the priest in confession is a necessary condition for the validity of sacramental absolution. The penance given by the confessor is not intended to be sufficient satisfaction for sins confessed, but the confessor is bound to impose a penance in some way proportionate to the sins, and the penitent is bound to accept and fulfil it. The effect of sacramental satisfaction is the remission *ex opere operato* of temporal punishment due to sin.

ii. In monasteries, satisfaction is the brief act of penance or humility performed immediately after a slight infraction of the rule, *e.g.*, being late for Office or meals, making a mistake in singing or a noise in the refectory It usually consists in kneeling down in one's place or in the middle of the choir or elsewhere until the superior signals to rise (*cf.*, the Rule of St. Benedict, caps. xliii, xliv, *e.a.*).

SATISFACTION, VICARIOUS. Reparation made for an offence not by the offender but on his behalf by a mediator, with the consent of the person offended. Of himself man cannot make adequate reparation for his offence against God by mortal sin; Christ made it for him through his passion. See SACRIFICE OF THE CROSS; VICARIOUS PUNISHMENT.

SATURDAY. The seventh day of the week, the Sabbath, no longer has any particular significance in the West except in so far as it is regarded as specially dedicated in honour of our Lady; her Saturday office (*Officium B.M.V. in Sabbato*) is said outside of Lent and Advent whenever a feast of double rank or higher does not occur. Most Easterns modify or dispense their fast on Saturday during Lent and other fasting seasons, apparently with reference to the holiday of the Old Law.

SATURDAY ABSTINENCE. It was formerly the law (greatly modified by indults) that Saturday as well as Friday should be observed as a day of abstinence; the law is now definitely abolished. This Saturday abstinence was a prolongation of that of Friday and was not, as is sometimes stated, in honour of our Lady; its history is obscure but the idea seems to have been to fast or abstain during the time that our Lord was dead.

SAVIGNY, THE ORDER OF. A reformed congregation of Benedictines founded by Bd. Vitalis of Mortain at Savigny near Coutances about 1105, affiliated to the Cistercians in 1147. Among its monasteries were La Trappe and Buckfast, in Devon.

SAVOURING OF HERESY, ERROR (Lat. *sapiens hæresim, errorem*). A proposition condemned in these terms is one which is patent of a true or harmless interpretation, but is judged in the circumstances to have an heretical or erroneous meaning.

SCALA SANCTA (Lat., the Holy Stairs). A flight of 28 marble steps, now covered with wood, leading to the papal chapel of the old Lateran palace. They are alleged to be the steps of Pilate's *prætorium* (John xviii, 28), brought to Rome by St. Helen. This staircase is ascended by the faithful on their knees as an act of penitence and devotion, and to do so Pope Pius IX made his last public appearance in Rome, Sept. 19, 1870; but the authenticity of the relic is by no means well established.

SCALZETTI, The (It., shoeless, though in fact they are no longer so). The Order of Penance of Jesus of Nazareth, a small congregation of mendicant friars founded in Spain by Fr. J. A. Varella Losada in 1752. They have houses only in Italy, and their life, habit and constitutions resemble those of the Friars Minor. They take a vow to defend the doctrine of the Immaculate Conception.

SCAMNUM (Lat., bench). The seat on the epistle-side of the altar occupied by the celebrant, deacon and subdeacon during the *Kyrie, Gloria* and *Credo* at high Mass, and at solemn Lauds and Vespers. According to the rubrics and decrees it should be a single bench, not divided into three seats, without arms or high back and not raised on more than one step. Its use has superseded that of the *sedilia* (*q.v.*) in western Europe.

SCANDAL (Gr. σκάνδαλον, snare, stumbling block). Active scandal is occasioning the sin of another by any word or deed which is or appears to be evil; passive scandal is the sin so committed by the other. The former is a sin against charity, mortal if the other is thereby put into a proximate occasion (*q.v.*) of mortal sin; should the other's sin be intended and not merely foreseen, that sin also is committed by the giver of scandal. An action which, though good, appears evil to the onlookers, should not be performed unless grave inconvenience would result from its omission. Scandal caused in another by a good action on account of his evil dispositions is "Pharisaical," and need not be considered. See REPARATION; SIN OF OTHERS; ADMIRATIO.

SCANDALOUS. A proposition so condemned is one calculated to be the occasion of wrong thinking or acting in others.

SCAPULAR (Lat. *scapula*, shoulder). i. A garment made of two strips of cloth put on over the head so that one falls in front and one behind; it is usually the width of the shoulders and reaches to the ankles, but this varies according to the order and religious status. It originated in the working frock of Benedictine monks, but is now regarded as the distinctively monastic part of many religious habits, symbolizing by its shape the yoke of Christ. It is worn over the tunic and sometimes has the hood attached (Benedictines), is confined by the belt (Cistercians, Camaldolese) and is a different colour from the tunic (Cistercians, Dominican laybrothers), but normally it hangs free and is the same colour. The Carthusian scapular is joined at each side by a narrow band.

ii. A similar but smaller garment worn under the ordinary clothes by secular tertiaries (*q.v.*), who are no longer allowed to wear their proper habit in public. They vary in size and colour; the Dominican's consists of two pieces of white woollen cloth, about 12 ins. by 9 ins., joined by a 1-in. band over each shoulder.

iii. Two pieces of cloth, about 3 in. by 2 in., joined by strings and worn back and front under the clothes. There are seventeen such scapulars recognized, each the badge of a confraternity, mostly connected with a religious institute and with indulgences attached to wearing them. The best known is the brown scapular (*q.v.*). Such badges are to be worn with confidence in the mercy and might of God whose blessings are invoked on the wearers by the prayers of the Church; the attribution of any virtue to the material object in itself is superstitious and forbidden.

SCAPULAR, BROWN, often called simply The Scapular (*q.v.* iii), is the badge of the Confraternity of our Lady of Mount Carmel, adopted on account of the traditional vision wherein, through St. Simon Stock, she added a scapular to the Carmelite habit. To this is attached the Sabbatine privilege (*q.v.*) and many indulgences. Its use has spread to the East, especially among the Catholic Malabarese. The Carmelites keep a feast of St. Simon Stock, confessor of the Order of our Lady of Mount Carmel, on May 16, and reference is made in the Martyrology on that day to his reception of the scapular at the hands of our Lady.

SCAPULAR MEDAL. A medal which may be worn instead of any or all of the small scapulars (*q.v.*, iii) upon receiving the corresponding blessings. It bears on the one side an image of the Sacred Heart and on the other one of our Lady.

"SCARLET WOMAN, The." The harlot clothed in gold and scarlet (Apoc. xvii) represents imperial Rome, also symbolized by the name "Babylon" (*cf.*, xii, 1, where another woman represents the Church). Some of the more extreme Protestant commentators have seen in the Scarlet Woman a graceful prefiguring of the Church of Rome.

SCEPTICISM. The system of those who think it is permitted to doubt scientifically of all. This absolute sceptism is self-contradictory since it holds as certain that all truths must be doubted. There is a relative scepticism, which limits its doubt, *e.g.*, to metaphysics, and there is hypothetical scepticism, which starts with universal doubt and then investigates each truth (Cartesianism, *q.v.*).

SCHEUT FATHERS, The. The Missionaries of the Immaculate Heart of Mary, a congregation of missioners for China and Central Africa, founded at Scheut, near Brussels, in 1862. They publish books and journals, religious and secular, in 7 languages and 21 dialects; eleven of their priests have been put to death in China out of hatred of the faith.

SCHISM (Gr. σχίσμα, split). The refusal to submit to the authority of the pope or to hold communion with members of the Church subject to him. It differs from apostasy and heresy (*qq.v.*), but schism very often leads to them. Anyone guilty of an *external* act of schism is *ipso facto* excommunicated; the conditions for absolution are the same as for heresy. The sacraments may not be administered to schismatics, even those in good faith. Cf., Schismatic.

SCHISM OF THE EAST, The. The estrangement and severance from the Holy See of what is now called the Orthodox Eastern Church (*q.v.*) was a gradual process extending over centuries. After a number of minor schisms the first serious, though short, break was that of Photius (*q.v.*); from then on tension between East and West increased, and the schism of Cerularius (*q.v.*) occurred in 1054. From then on the breach gradually widened and has been definitive since 1472. There was a formal union from the 2nd council of Lyons (*q.v.*) in 1274 until 1282, and a more promising one after the council of Florence (*q.v.*) from 1439 to 1472. After the capture of Constantinople it was in the Turkish interest to reopen and widen the breach with the powerful Roman church; the patriarchates of Alexandria, Antioch and Jerusalem were dragged into this policy, Russia and the Slav churches stood out the longest of any: none of these churches, except Constantinople itself in 1472, formally and definitely broke away from the unity of the Church. But in the course of centuries the schism has set and crystallized into a definite separation from the Holy See of many million people with a true priesthood and valid sacraments. The origins, causes and development of the schism are matters of much complication, still not fully unravelled.

SCHISM OF THE WEST, The, or **Great Schism,** was not strictly a schism at all but a conflict between two parties within the Church each claiming to support the true pope. Three months after the election of Urban VI, in 1378, the fifteen electing cardinals declared that they had appointed him only as a temporary vicar and that in any case the election was invalid as made under fear of violence from the Roman mob. Urban retorted by naming twenty-eight new cardinals, and the others at once proceeded to elect Cardinal Robert of Geneva as Pope Clement VII, who went to reside at Avignon. The quarrel was in its origin not a theological or religious one, but was caused by the ambition and jealousy of French influence, which was supported to some extent for political reasons by Spain, Naples, Provence, and Scotland; England, Germany, Scandinavia, Wales, Ireland, Portugal, Flanders and Hungary stood by what they believed to be the true pope at Rome. The Church was torn from top to bottom by the schism, both sides in good faith (it was impossible to know to whom allegiance was due), which lasted with its two lines of popes (and at one time three) till the election of Martin V in 1417. It is now regarded as practically certain that the Urbanist popes (*q.v.*) were the true ones and their names are included in semi-official lists; moreover, the ordinal numbers of the Clementine (*q.v.*) claimants (who, however, are not called anti-popes, *q.v.*) were adopted by subsequent popes of the same name.

SCHISMATIC. In its strict sense, one who voluntarily, knowingly and deliberately separates himself from the unity of the Church. Ordinarily one who is so separated is called a schismatic regardless of the circumstances, but "anyone born and brought up in a schismatic church and turned away in good faith from the Roman Church, not knowing her to be the one true church . . . is called by the epithet 'schismatic' only in an improper sense; he is not in fact a party to the sin of schism" (Jugie, *Theol. Dogm.,* I, p. 17). Such is apparently the state of the overwhelming majority of non-Catholic Christians to-day, but the fact of their good faith in their inherited errors does not relieve them of the obligation to examine the claims of the Catholic Church when brought to their notice. (*cf.,* Apostasy, Heresy, Schism).

SCHOLA CANTORUM (Lat., school of singers). **i.** Historically, a school of music attached to a cathedral, monastery or other great church, with the duty of providing a choir for its services. The term is now loosely applied to any body of trained singers responsible for the music in a church or to an institution for tuition in and study of ecclesiastical music.

ii. That part in front of the altar of a basilican church enclosed for the accommodation of singers, *e.g.*, at San Clemente and Santa Maria in Cosmedin at Rome.

SCHOLASTIC. i. Or Schoolman. A master or student of Scholasticism (*q.v.*).

ii. One who has completed his noviciate and taken simple perpetual vows in the Society of Jesus; he remains in this rank from ten to seventeen years, teaching in one of the society's colleges or studying philosophy and theology, during which he is ordained priest. If he were already a priest when he entered he would remain a scholastic priest for ten years. After his theology he does a year of special probation (tertianship).

SCHOLASTICISM. The philosophy that flourished during the middle ages and which is personified in the Dominican St. Thomas Aquinas. It is the philosophy of the Fathers reduced to a grand synthesis and presented in a didactic form. To give a precise definition of Scholasticism is difficult, but it would seem to be: a spirit whereby an endeavour is made (by the Fathers of the Church and their successors) to bring into harmony faith and reason; a didactic method, derived especially from Aristotle's philosophy, such as is necessary to establish the aforesaid harmony; a system, always susceptible of further development, the foundations of which are to be discovered in the works of St. Thomas. The name is derived from Lat. *scholasticus,* the title given to the masters of the Christian schools of the early middle ages.

SCHOOL. The Church maintains as a divine right and ineluctable duty both of herself and of parents to supervise the instruction and share the control of all schools in which their children are taught. This follows from her teaching that education (*q.v.*) is far more than a mere system for instilling knowledge or fitting the pupil to make a living. It is further maintained that no system of public elementary schools, resulting from the application of this religious principle, should be allowed by the state to impose a relatively greater financial obligation on its supporters (whether Catholics or of other denominations) than that borne by the supporters of undenominational schools.

SCHOOL, APOSTOLIC. A school for the preliminary training of aspirants to the foreign missions, having the same relation to the missionary colleges and congregations as the "little" to the "great" seminaries of the parochial clergy.

SCHOOL, SUNDAY, called by Catholic children simply "catechism," is an institution for the religious instruction of the young which in England is associated particularly with Victorian Sunday dinners, sound Protestantism and the worthy name of Robert Raikes. It had its origin over 200 years earlier in the Confraternity of Christian Doctrine established for the work in Milan by St. Charles Borromeo.

SCHOOLMEN, The. The masters of Scholasticism (*q.v.*) in the middle ages: St. Thomas Aquinas, St. Anselm, St. Bonaventure, St. Albert the Great, Alexander of Hales, Duns Scotus, Peter Abelard, etc.

SCIENCE (Lat. *scientia*, knowledge). A knowledge of things by their causes. The end of demonstration is science, which is a certain and evident knowledge of a truth arrived at by demonstration. It deals with conclusions, not with principles. In modern usage the word is, by a perversion of language, confined to physical science and "scientific" to that which is concerned with what only deserves the name in a secondary sense.

SCIENCE, PHYSICAL, AND RELIGION. The physical sciences deal with the natures and properties of things and the laws by which they are governed; religion deals with truths, both of the physical and of the moral order, which lead man to God. Hence there is no direct connexion between them. Apparent conflicts between physical science and religion arise from a misunderstanding of what either means, or from scientists or theologians stepping outside their own province.

SCOTISM. The system, named after Duns Scot the Franciscan (1270-1308), which in many ways is distinct from, and even opposed to, that of St. Thomas. In logic there is a suspicion of scepticism (due perhaps to an uncalled for subtlety in hair-splitting) which is probably the outcome of the doctrine of the preponderance of the will over mind. It regards the demonstration of the immortality of the soul as beyond the powers of natural reason: it holds the univocation of being attributed to God and creatures; the principle of individuation is a certain entity distinct both from form and matter. It holds that prime matter can, absolutely speaking, exist with a form; that there are two substantial forms in man: it denies the real distinction between the soul and its powers. In ethics it holds that the natural law is not absolutely unchangeable, depending not from the mind but from the will of God. Lastly it holds that the essence of supreme happiness is to be sought in the act of love for God and not, as says St. Thomas, in a vision of the mind.

SCOTLAND, THE CHURCH IN. Scotland was principally evangelized in the 5th and 6th centuries by SS. Ninian, Colmkille (Columba) and his Irish monks, and Kentigern (Mungo). At the time of the Reformation the church was weak with feeble religious teaching, evil living, the corruption of benefices held *in commendam* (*q.v.*) and consequent decay of religion. The hierarchy became extinct in 1603. At first Scotland was under English jurisdiction, but from 1623 till a prefect apostolic was appointed in 1653 the position is not clear. From 1694 the Catholics were governed by vicars apostolic and were reduced to 40,000 or less in number (in three Canadian dioceses alone there are over 85,000 Catholics descended from Scottish immigrants of this period). The establishment of the Presbyterian Church and the following penal times were as violent and oppressive in Scotland as in England, but less bloody; John Ogilvie, S. J., has been beatified. In 1878 the hierarchy was restored; archbishops were appointed to the old sees, vacant for 300 years, of Saint Andrews and Glasgow, and bishops to Aberdeen, Argyll & the Isles, Dunkeld, and Galloway (*qq.v.*); the other ancient sees were suppressed. The population of Scotland is under 5 millions, of whom one-eighth are Catholics, a proportion largely due to recent Irish immigration. But there have been Scots Catholics in the Isles and elsewhere since before the Reformation. The prevalent faith of the country is Presbyterianism (*q.v.*). From the point of view of civil law the position of Catholics in Scotland is the same as in England, but their ecclesiastical organization is distinct and independent.

SCOTS COLLEGES abroad for the training of candidates for the priesthood are at Rome (founded in 1600) and Valladolid (founded at Madrid, 1627; transferred 1771). The colleges at Paris and Douay no longer exist, but the French government compensates for their loss by allowing a number of Scots students to be educated at various seminaries in France.

SCREEN. See CHOIR-SCREEN; ICONOSTASIS; ROOD-SCREEN; PARCLOSE-SCREEN.

SCRIBES, The (Heb. *Sopherim*). A professional class of trained copyists and notaries who in the time of our Lord had become the interpreters of the law of Moses. In doctrine and practice they commonly favoured the Pharisees (*cf.*, Matt. xxiii, 2; Luke v, 30; Acts xxiii, 9).

SCRIPTORIUM (Lat. *scribere*, to write). The room in a monastery set apart for the work of copying books and documents, writing letters, painting and illuminating, and similar work.

SCRIPTURES, The. The holy or sacred Scriptures are that part of the divine revelation, or deposit of faith, which, as to the Old Testament, was already in writing at the time of the Apostles, and, as to the New Testament, was committed to writing by them; the rest of the revelation was preserved by the

Tradition of the Church. Both Scripture and Tradition are of equal divine authority. It is contained in the books which form the Old and New Testaments, the two together being the Holy Bible (*q.v.*). See below and also INSPIRATION, etc. In the New Testament the "scripture" or "scriptures" means the Jewish Bible, that is, the Old Testament as we know it but without the deutero-canonical books (*q.v.*).

SCRIPTURES, THE CHURCH AND THE. Holy Scripture is profitable "to instruct us, to expose our errors, to correct our faults, to educate us in holy living (2 Tim. iii, 16), but the reading of it is not necessary to salvation nor is it the only or the direct rule of a Christian's faith. The direct rule is the teaching of the living Church, and divine tradition is with Scripture the joint source of revelation. A Catholic dogma, therefore, does not need any scriptural text for its warrant; dogmas are believed not because they are contained in the Scriptures, but because they are taught by the Church. The inspiration of the Scriptures is itself a dogma resting on the authority of the Church, though their general historical trustworthiness is ascertainable by purely scientific methods. The Missal, the Divine Office and the "Rituale" are almost exclusively made up of Holy Scripture, so that in them the New Testament and a great part of the Old is read through once a year, much of it publicly, and the whole Psalter is recited every week. Bible-reading by the laity is encouraged and rewarded with spiritual privileges granted by the popes. See BIBLE-READING; VERNACULAR BIBLES.

SCRUPLES. i. A term originally used to denote small quantities; now frequently used to signify minute points of behaviour or duty—thus a man is said to be scrupulously clean, exact, conscientious.

ii. Doubts which arise in the mind as to the lawfulness of an act.

iii. The promptings of a conscience which is led by insufficient motives to imagine sin where none exists or to regard as mortal sin what is only venial. (This is the only use of the term recognized by spiritual writers and moral theologians.) Scruples have their use in inciting to greater care in the service of God, but they are dangerous to the health both of soul and body, especially in one who relies entirely on his own judgement. The best, and frequently the only, remedy is humble submission to the advice of one's confessor.

SCRUTINY (Lat. *scrutari*, to examine). i. The usual method of election to ecclesiastical office by secret or private ballot. This is the normal way in which a conclave (*q.v.*) elects a pope.

ii. The canonical examination of candidates for holy orders.

iii. A canonical examination, to several of which catechumens were formerly submitted at intervals before Baptism. These are now merged in the exorcisms, etc., of the first part of the rite of Baptism.

SEAL OF AN ALTAR. The relics and the sepulchre (*q.v.*) in which they are contained.

SEAL OF CONFESSION. The inviolable secrecy to be observed by the confessor and all who have knowledge of matter confessed in the sacrament of Penance. Direct revelation of such matter by a priest involves excommunication *ipso facto*, reserved to the pope in a very special manner. Confessors are forbidden to use information obtained through confession, even without revelation of matter, if this would cause any hurt or offence to the penitent. Superiors may not use confessional information of any kind in the external forum (*q.v.*), nor is such information admissible in a court of law. English civil judges have respected the seal, but the position of a priest who refuses to reveal confessional matter in a court of law is not certainly secure. In most states of the United States confession to a priest is recognized by law as a privileged communication.

SÉANCE (Fr., sitting). A meeting of votaries of Spiritism (*q.v.*) for the purpose of attempting to communicate with the dead. Catholics are forbidden to be present at such séances, however inoffensive the meeting may appear, whether a medium be present or not, and whatever form the communication may take; they may not even be spectators, even though they protest tacitly or explicitly that they will have nothing to do with evil spirits. The use of hypnotism (*q.v.*) for spiritistic purposes is, of course, equally forbidden.

SEAT OF WISDOM (Lat. *Sedes Sapientiæ*). A title given to our Lady in the litany of Loreto. It is first found in the writings of St. Anselm and St. Bernard (11th-12th centuries).

SECOND COMING, CHRIST'S. Our Lord repeatedly foretold his return "on the clouds of Heaven," but the modernist view that he thought that this return would take place immediately or soon after his death is rejected by the Church not only because it is incompatible with the inerrancy of Christ but also because it contradicts the evidence of the gospels. The coming of Christ into his kingdom which his own generation was to see was the establishment of his kingdom in the founding of the Catholic Church on Pentecost day and the passing away of the Jewish commonwealth by the destruction of Jerusalem. It is expressly and repeatedly stated in the New Testament that Christ gave no revelation of the time of his second coming (*e.g.*, Mark xiii, 32). In 1915 the Biblical Commission (*q.v.*) decided that it is not permissible to assert that difficulties in this matter occasioned by certain passages in the epistles may be overcome by attributing them to the human and erroneous views of the apostles. It maintained, moreover, that St. Paul wrote nothing incompatible with that ignorance of the time of the Second Coming which our Lord stated to be man's lot; and that it is unlawful to reject the traditional interpretation of 1 Thes. iv, 14-17, as referring to those who shall be alive at the time of his coming (cf., 2 Thes. ii, 2).

SECOND ORDER. A name sometimes given to those orders of nuns who have a common founder and spirit with and a modified form of the rule of a corresponding order of men. Thus, the rules and life of the Franciscan and Dominican friars are not compatible with female sex, so that Franciscan and Dominican nuns (Poor Clares and Preacheresses) follow modified rules; whereas Benedictine, Carmelite and Eastern nuns have exactly the same rule as the corresponding men. The term is not used in canon law, though "third order" is (cf., Third Order, ii).

SECRECY. The keeping of silence about matters which it is not permissible to reveal. The obligation to secrecy is grave in all professional secrets and whenever a grave breach of charity or justice would be the effect of revelation.

SECRECY OF CONFESSION. See SEAL OF CONFESSION.

SECRET. i. Moral. See SECRECY.

ii. A variable prayer or prayers in the form of a collect said after the offertory and before the preface at Mass, usually asking for God's acceptance of the gifts and the sanctification of the offerers. Every secret has a corresponding collect and post-communion. The reason for the name has been the subject of much discussion; there is nothing secret about the prayer except that it is said inaudibly, ending with an *ekphonesis* (*q.v.*), but then the whole canon is so said: but it is the only prayer in collect form that is not said or sung aloud. The name probably means the prayers said over the offerings, the things "set apart" (Latin *secernere* = to set apart).

"SECRET OF LA SALETTE, The." The communications alleged to have been made by our Lady at her appearing at La Salette (*q.v.*). A version was published on the authority of one of the children concerned, and after much discussion and excitement the Holy Office forbade any further publications on the subject. The contents of the supposed revelations were made known only to the then reigning pope, Pius IX.

SECRET SOCIETIES. Catholics are expressly warned in the Code of Canon Law (can. 684) against joining associations that are secret, or condemned, or seditious, or suspect, or which seek to withdraw them-

selves from the legitimate vigilance of the Church. Anyone belonging to societies that plot against Church or state incurs *ipso facto* excommunication, simply reserved to the pope. Notorious members of such societies are deprived of ecclesiastical burial and priests may not assist at their marriages without consulting the ordinary. See FREEMASONRY.

SECRETARIUM (Lat., a place set apart). The chapel in which a cardinal, bishop or abbot assists at Terce and is ceremonially vested before singing pontifical Mass; this sometimes takes place at the same altar at which he is to celebrate.

SECRETO. A prayer in the liturgy appointed to be said "secretly" must be said in so low a voice that it is inaudible to those around.

SECT (from Lat., *sequi*, to follow; *secta*, primarily meaning a "trodden path," was used to translate the Gk., *hairesis*, "choice." *Cf.* heresy). This word has no precise meaning. It is most commonly applied to the numerous bodies of nonconformists who have broken away from the principal and established Protestant denominations of the 16th century. It is a convenient term to designate these and similar bodies that professedly adhere to one particular teacher or isolated doctrine and are thereby set apart from their fellows. Catholics often refer to "the Protestant sects," meaning all Protestants from the Anglicans to the Shakers, using the word in its etymological sense, in which no contempt or abuse inheres (*cf.*, Denomination); but otherwise there is usually an at least slightly pejorative sense implied by it. This is definitely so with Sectarianism, a quality which manifests itself in the stressing of difference in non-essential matters rather than of agreement about religious truths, the minimizing of virtue outside one's own denomination, the praising of the work of one's co-religionists regardless of its merits, and similar behaviour.

SECULAR (Lat. *sæculum*, the world). i. As adjective (*a*) Temporal, as distinguished from spiritual, not sacred or ecclesiastical; (*b*) pertaining to the secular clergy (*q.v.*).

ii (*a*) A member of the secular clergy. (*b*) A lay person as opposed to a cleric.

SECULAR ARM, The. The civil power; the civil court to which a condemned prisoner was handed over by an ecclesiastical court for sentence when it was considered desirable that he should receive a more severe punishment than the ecclesiastical court could canonically inflict, *e.g.*, as in the case of St. Joan of Arc and of numerous persons put to death for heresy. The procedure was liable to much abuse, and is now obsolete.

SECULAR CLERGY. The ordinary clergy who pursue their work, principally parochial, living independently in the world, as opposed to the regular clergy (*q.v.*) who are bound by a rule and usually live in monasteries. The secular priest is the normal Christian cleric; he is bound by no vows except, in the West, by implication that of celibacy; he possesses and enjoys his own property and is his own master except for the canonical obedience he gives to his bishop; the episcopate properly appertains to the secular clergy, though for sufficient reasons regulars are often made bishops, especially in foreign missions. They take precedence of regulars of equal rank and are alone eligible for minor and titular prelatures, canonries, etc., in ordinary circumstances. Better referred to as the parochial clergy.

SECULAR CLERGY COMMON FUND, The. A fund started in 1701 for the support and relief of aged and infirm priests in the old London District and still carried on for the dioceses of Westminster, Southwark, Portsmouth and Brentwood, formerly comprised in that district. The revenues of the Catholic cemeteries at Leytonstone and Kensal Green belong to the fund. A separate "New Fund" was started in 1801 and also continues.

SECULARISM. The teaching that the foundation of morality, duty, and religion is to be sought in nature alone, and that, therefore, the teaching aids and sanctions of supernatural religion and the Church are of no account in human conduct. This doctrine was formulated and systematized in England by George Bradlaugh (1833-91) and George Jacob Holyoake (1817-1906).

SECULARIZATION. i. Of religious. The act by which a religious is permanently separated from his order or congregation and released from his religious vows. Secularization requires a papal indult except in the case of purely diocesan societies. Secularized religious are excluded by law from certain ecclesiastical offices, and those in sacred orders may not exercise their orders till accepted for a diocese by a bishop. If readmitted to their society by papal indult they must go through the noviciate again and make a new profession.
   ii. Of things. The forcible action of a civil power in depriving the Church or ecclesiastical institutions (*e.g.*, religious orders) of the possession and use of their property; the withdrawal of schools, hospitals, etc., from ecclesiastical control or administration; and similar activities tending towards the complete subordination of religion to the state. Where property is concerned the Holy See usually makes provision so that purchasers or other acquirers of ecclesiastical property seized by a government may hold it with a good conscience, *e.g.*, the monastic lands in England in 1554, in France in 1907, in Italy in 1929; nor is it to be supposed that

a church or other sacred thing cannot be legitimately handed over by the competent authority to profane uses.

SECUNDUM QUID (Lat., according to something), that is, not according to all. Opposed to absolutely, or simply: *e.g.*, being is good (*i.e.*, simply), the Devil is good *secundum quid* (*i.e.*, as regards *being*).

SEDE IMPEDITA. Lat., "The see being obstructed" by the fact that its bishop, for whatever cause, is unable to administer his diocese.

SEDE VACANTE. Lat., "The see being vacant," by the resignation, translation or death of its bishop.

SEDGLEY PARK. A school in Staffordshire opened by Mr. William Errington, a secular priest, under Bp. Challoner's direction in 1763, and the first school to be publicly conducted in defiance of the penal laws (*q.v.*). It was moved to Cotton Hall in the same county in 1873 and still flourishes.

SEDIA GESTATORIA (It., portable chair). A chair fastened to a small platform on which the pope is carried, by means of a pole on either side each supported on the shoulders of six men, at solemn entries into St. Peter's, the Sistine chapel, and elsewhere. The immediate entourage on more important occasions includes four Swiss guardsmen with double-handed swords, representing the four Catholic cantons of Switzerland, the two *flabella* (*q.v.*) carried by privy chamberlains, the commandant and officers of the Swiss Guard and the commandants of the Noble and Palatine Guards. The carriers, *sediarii*, are dressed in crimson damask.

SEDILIA (Lat. *sedile*, a seat). Seats formed in the thickness of the wall on the epistle side of an altar, generally three in number for the use of the celebrant and his ministers at high Mass. They were common in mediæval churches in England, but elsewhere a movable bench (*scamnum, q.v.*) was nearly always used, as now. Some gothic-revival churches are furnished with *sedilia*.

SEE (Old Fr., from Lat. *sedes*, a seat). The charge of a bishop, which in its territorial aspect is called a diocese, *e.g.*, the see of Plymouth, the archiepiscopal see of Dublin. The word has reference to the episcopal throne (*cathedra*) which is set up in the cathedral city. The Holy See is the see of Rome, the pope and his court. The See of Peter is the see of Rome of which St. Peter was the first bishop. In Latin documents the Roman Curia usually designates a bishop by an adjectival form of the name of his see, *e.g.*, *Episcopus Cliftoniensis*, the Cliftonian bishop; but when the diocese has a saint's name (and in a few other cases) it is simply put in the genitive, *e.g.*, *Episcopus Sancti*

Claudii, bishop of St. Claud, *Lacus Salsi,* of Salt Lake.

SELF-DEFENCE. Whatever violence is necessary may be used to defend oneself against an unjust attack here and now taking place with danger to life or limb or virtue. Should the death of the aggressor ensue, this is not murder but justifiable homicide, since his death is not intended as such but is an unavoidable consequence of repelling the aggression.

SEM. The Greek form of the name of the son of Noe, called Shem in some versions of the Bible; whence the name Semite for the races said to be descended from him, namely the Jews, Arabs, Syrians, Phœnicians, Assyrians.

SEMANTRON (Gr., signal). A device used by Eastern Christians to summon the faithful to worship, invented in the days when Moslem rulers would not permit the use of bells. It consists of a board of wood (sometimes iron), suspended or fixed in tension to give it resonance, which is struck rhythmically with a hammer. It is still in use instead of or in addition to bells, *e.g.,* at Mount Athos and elsewhere. Christian historians attribute its use to an edict of the Khalifa Omar, about 637, but Mohammedan fable says that it was invented by Noe to summon the workmen who were building the ark.

SEMI-ARIANISM. The very fluid and undecided doctrines of a court party which arose in the second half of the 4th century, whose leader was Acacius, bishop of Cæsarea. They were moderates who agreed to the condemnation of St. Athanasius but who also rejected Arianism (*q.v.*). The nearest thing to a formula that they had was *homoiousion* (*q.v.*). Later they rejected the divinity of the Holy Ghost.

SEMI-DOUBLE (Lat. *semiduplex*). A rank of feast (*q.v.*) that was abolished in 1956, when all semi-doubles were reduced to the rank of simple feasts.

SEMI-PELAGIANISM. An early modification of Pelagianism (*q.v.*). It maintained that though grace is necessary for the accomplishment of good works, it is not necessary for their initiation; that grace is granted by merit; and that perseverance in good can be obtained by merit. The teaching was attacked by St. Augustine, and condemned by the Second Council of Orange (529).

SEMINARY (Lat. *seminarium,* seed plot). A college exclusively devoted to the training of candidates for the priesthood. By law there should be one such in every diocese, but this is not always possible; in England there are diocesan seminaries for Birmingham (Oscott), Liverpool (Upholland) and Southwark (Wonersh); Ushaw is an inter-diocesan seminary for the north and has a lay school attached, as has Old Hall, the Westminster seminary; Oscott also receives the subjects of other dioceses. Glasgow has a seminary at Bearsden and the rest of Scotland one at Blairs (founded at Scalan in 1712). There are also national seminaries at Rome (colleges, *q.v.*). Seminaries are for the training of secular clergy (*q.v.*) only and are normally directed and staffed by them or by one of the congregations whose special business it is (*e.g.,* Lazarists, Sulpicians). The usual course is six years, two of philosophy, four of theology, during which the student receives minor and major orders; his training includes dogmatic, moral and pastoral theology, holy Scripture, apologetics, ecclesiastical history, canon law, liturgy, and sacred chant. The expenses of the student are borne by his diocese, even if he leaves the seminary, unless he is able and willing to pay for himself. Every student must enter with a good general education which may, but need not, have been received at the "little seminary" (as opposed to the above "great seminary"; "junior" and "senior" are better epithets). This is a school for the general education of boys from 12 to 18, who wish to test their vocation for the priesthood; one of these should be conducted as part of every diocesan seminary, but not necessarily on the same premises. The metropolitan seminaries of Spain have the title of "pontifical university," with papal constitutions and the power to grant degrees in theology and canon law.

SEMINARY PRIESTS. An historical and legal term to distinguish priests ordained abroad and elsewhere from those ordained in England before the accession of Queen Elizabeth (Marian priests, *q.v.*). Distinctions were made between the two classes in the penal laws (*q.v.*); after 1585 it was high treason for a seminary priest even to be in England.

SEMINARIES AND UNIVERSITIES OF STUDIES, The Sacred Congregation of. A Roman congregation (*q.v.*) having direction of the temporal administration and studies of seminaries and ecclesiastical universities; it grants power to confer degrees and otherwise supervises clerical training and ecclesiastical research.

SENSE, ACCOMMODATED. The sense given to a scriptural text other than that originally intended. To accommodate Scripture for purposes of illustration is quite licit (*cf.,* Christ's accommodation of Deut. viii, 3, in Matt. iv, 4); but no attempt may be made to prove points of doctrine by the use of texts in an accommodated sense.

SENSE OF THE SCRIPTURES. In the interpretation of the Bible the Church recognizes two senses: (*a*) the literal sense, which is the objective, actual and immediate truth which God prompted the writer to convey;

(b) the typical sense (also called mystical or spiritual, which is the truth intended by God to be expressed by means of a figure or type (*q.v.*) which itself must be a matter of historical fact; this must be distinguished from any subjective or symbolical sense. It is the office of the Church to declare the sense of any given scriptural passage; according to St. Thomas, the literal sense alone can be used for purpose of argument from the Scriptures.

SENSIBLE. Term applied to a material object which can be known by the senses. Opposed to intelligible (*q.v.*). Something felt, *e.g.,* sensible devotion.

SENSUALISM. i. Empiricism (*q.v.*), which consists in regarding the senses as the sufficient principle of all our ideas and knowledge.
  ii. Addiction to sins of the flesh; inordinate attachment to those pleasures of which the bodily senses are the vehicle. In common speech there is sometimes made a convenient distinction between sensual and sensuous indulgence, the latter indicating legitimate and orderly enjoyment of the pleasures of the senses.

SENTENCES, The (Lat. *sententia,* a proposition). "The Four Books of the Sentences," the standard theological textbook of the middle ages, compiled by Peter Lombard, the Master of the Sentences, and lectured and commented on by all the great scholastic theologians. "Sentences" was a common title for books of the sort.

SEPARATION. i. Of husband and wife. Married persons are bound to live together except for a just cause. If one party commits adultery, the other has the right to a separation for life (the bond remaining), unless he or she consented to the adultery, or was a cause of it, or expressly or tacitly condoned it, or committed the same crime. If one party joins a non-Catholic sect, or lives a criminal or infamous life, or gravely endangers the other's soul or body, or makes life unbearable, such and similar causes entitle the other to separate for a time on the authority of the local ordinary, or even without such authority if the cause is manifest and there is danger in delay. The parties must live together again when such cause ceases. Children are to be educated with the innocent party or in a mixed marriage with the Catholic party, according as the ordinary judges best in the interest of the children and their Catholic upbringing.
  ii. Of Church and State. See LAY STATE.

SEPTUAGESIMA (Lat., the seventieth). The third Sunday before Ash Wednesday. It is not the seventieth day before Easter and the reason for its name is uncertain; it may be by analogy from *Quadragesima* (*q.v.* and *cf.,* Sexagesima, Quinquagesima*). The whole period from this Sunday to Ash Wednesday is preparatory to Lent, and is so marked in the liturgical propers; *Gloria in excelsis,* Alleluia and *Te Deum* are not said in ferial offices and purple vestments are worn.

SEPTUAGINT, The (Lat. *septuaginta,* seventy). The first Greek version of the Hebrew Scriptures (Old Testament), made at Alexandria in the 3rd century B.C., traditionally by 70 translators. New Testament quotations from the O.T. are mostly taken from it and not from the Hebrew. It is often referred to as the LXX.

SEPULCHRE. i. Of an altar. The cavity in every altar-stone (*q.v.*) in which are contained the relics of martyrs. It is between the middle of the stone and the front edge and is sealed with stone or slate. In a fixed altar it may be between the table and its support. Upon mounting the steps of the altar at the beginning of Mass the celebrant at once kisses it, saying, "Through the merits of thy saints whose relics are here, and of all the saints, we pray thee, O Lord, that thou wilt forgive us all our sins."
  ii. Easter. The custom in the Sarum and other mediæval uses of reserving the Blessed Sacrament in a special place from Maundy Thursday till Easter to represent our Lord's body in the tomb. Recesses for this purpose are sometimes found on the north side of the chancel of old churches (*e.g.,* at Arnold and Hawton in Nottinghamshire). This must not be confused with the present usage of reserving at the altar of repose (*q.v.*) from Maundy Thursday to Good Friday, though it is the custom to call this the sepulchre in some parts, *e.g.,* of Italy and Spain. The mediæval custom as well is observed in parts of Germany, Poland and Switzerland (*e.g.,* at Einsiedeln Abbey), where a third Host, consecrated on Maundy Thursday, is reserved in a monstrance and on Holy Saturday evening is carried in a paschal procession.

SEQUENCE. A sort of hymn but in no regular metre (whence often called a *prose*) said or sung between the gradual and the gospel of certain Masses. They were very numerous in the middle ages but the Roman Missal now contains only five: for Easter (*Victimæ paschali*), Pentecost (*Veni Sancte Spiritus*), Corpus Christi (*Lauda Sion*), the Seven Sorrows of our Lady (*Stabat Mater*), and requiem Masses (*Dies Iræ*). Certain religious orders have special sequences: the Augustinians and Dominicans for St. Augustine and St. Dominic respectively, the Benedictines for St. Benedict and St. Scholastica, the Franciscans for St. Francis, the Holy Name and four others, etc. The rite of Lyons still has twenty sequences and there are yet others. These hymns originated in the 10th century in the fitting of words to the long-drawn-out series of notes which were sung on the final syllable of the last alleluia of the gradual (the *jubilus*). Probably called *sequence* because they followed this alleluia where formerly no words had been.

SERAPHIC. An epithet commonly associated with St. Francis of Assisi, the Seraphic Father, and his order, *e.g.*, the Seraphic Doctor (St. Bonaventure, O.F.M.), Seraphic Rosary (Franciscan Crown, *q.v.*), Seraphic Missal, college, etc.

SERAPHIC BLESSING, The. *Benedicat tibi Dominus et custodiat te. Ostendat faciem suam tibi et misereatur tui. Convertat vultum suum ad te et det tibi pacem. Dominus benedicat, F. LeTo te:* (May the Lord bless thee and keep thee. May he shew his face to thee and have mercy on thee. May he turn his countenance to thee and give thee peace. May the Lord bless thee, brother Leo.) Words written down by St. Francis at the request of Brother Leo during their sojourn on Mount Alverna during August and September 1224. The original is preserved by the Conventual friars at Assisi. For the wording, *cf.*, Num. vi, 24-26.

SERAPHIM (Heb., plural of *seraph*). The highest of the nine choirs or orders of angels (*q.v.*) described by Isaias in his vision, vi, 2-7, with which *cf.*, the preface of the Mass and v. 4 of the *Te Deum*.

SERMON (Lat. *sermo*, speech). i. A generic term applied to any sort of religious discourse. A sermon, usually an instruction on the day's gospel, follows the gospel at the parochial Mass (*cf.*, Preaching).
ii. A lesson from the second nocturn of Matins when it consists of a reading from a Father of the Church or other ecclesiastical writer.

SERVANTS, DUTIES OF. Persons employed in the capacity of servants, whether domestic, industrial or otherwise, are bound to render to their employers obedience, by carrying out honestly and fairly all equitable agreements freely entered into; reverence, by respecting the person and property of their master and by abstaining from violence in their own cause; and fidelity, by the avoidance of agitators, "men of evil principles, who work upon the people with cunning promises and excite foolish hopes which usually end in useless regrets, followed by insolency" (Pope Leo XIII, *Rerum novarum; cf.*, Employers, Living Wage).

SERVANTS OF MARY, The. The Servites (*q.v.*).

SERVANTS OF THE SACRED HEART, The. An unenclosed congregation of sisters founded in Paris by the Abbé Victor Braun in 1866 to work for the poor. No lay-sisters. Black habit, scapular and veil.

SERVER. One who ministers in the sanctuary, particularly to the celebrant at low Mass, discharging the functions of an acolyte (*q.v.*). In parochial churches these are laymen and boys who for this purpose are allowed to wear the corresponding ecclesiastical dress, *i.e.*, cassock and cotta or surplice. A server, even if dressed in lay clothes, receives holy communion immediately after the priest, except for those with a prior right, *e.g.*, a cleric, a sovereign prince, a bridal couple. The server's chief duties are to make the responses, to minister to the celebrant at the offertory, the *lavabo*, and the ablutions, to move the missal from side to side of the altar as required, and to ring the altar bell. Two servers are allowed only on a great feast, a special occasion or a parochial low Mass; these make the responses together and help each other at the above ministrations, the senior doing everything else. It is not more fitting that a small boy should serve the altar than an adult, but rather the contrary, for the duty properly pertains to clerics. No woman, whether lay or religious, may serve Mass; but in default of a male she may kneel at the altar rails and make the responses. The name server is often given to acolytes, torch-bearers, and such lay assistants in general at high Mass, Benediction, etc.

SERVILE WORK. So called as having been formerly the work of slaves, as opposed to liberal work, that of free men. Servile work consists of labour that is principally bodily, manual or mechanical, its actual denotation depending on traditional usage and the common estimation of men. Work which is principally liberal, artistic, or intellectual is not servile, even if it involves physical labour (*e.g.*, stone carving, mountaineering), nor does payment for work make it servile. Servile work is forbidden on Sundays and holidays of obligation. The direct service of religion, requirements of charity, or grave inconvenience to oneself or others, excuse from the law and certain kinds of work are permitted by custom, *e.g.*, domestic cooking and some housework. Servile work involved in catering for the Sunday public, providing entertainment, facilities for travel, etc., is permissible, but it should be kept within reasonable limits.

SERVITES, The, or Servants of Mary. (i) An order of mendicant friars founded by the Seven Holy Founders (*q.v.*) at Florence in 1233 with the rule of St. Augustine and special constitutions. They work for the sanctification of souls by preaching, parochial work, giving missions, etc., and by fostering devotion to our Lady especially in her sorrows; like other friars they are bound to the choral recitation of the Divine Office. They number about 1,500 religious, mostly in Italy; there is a province for the U.S.A. and one in England, where they were not established before the Reformation. Habit: tunic, belt, scapular and hood, long cloak, all black.

ii. Nuns. The second order in its present form dates from 1629. They are strictly enclosed and contemplative, singing the Divine Office in choir; some houses have perpetual adoration. Black tunic, scapular and veil; sandals.

SERVUS SERVORUM DEI (Lat., The Servant of the Servants of God). A phrase used in subscribing himself by Pope St. Gregory the Great in 591 when the archbishop of Constantinople had assumed the title of Œcumenical Patriarch (*q.v.*), and used ever since by the popes in certain official documents, such as bulls.

SESSORIAN BASILICA, The. The church of the Holy Cross-in-Jerusalem at Rome, founded by St. Helen in a place called the *Sessorium*, land belonging to the palace of Sessorius, and endowed with a relic of the True Cross. It was the stational church (*q.v.*) for Good Friday.

SEVEN APOSTOLIC HELPERS, The. The seven deacons appointed and ordained by the Apostles (Acts vi, 1-6).

SEVEN CHURCHES, The. i. Of Asia. The earliest Christian churches of Asia Minor to which St. John was directed in vision to write, namely: Ephesus (now Aya Salouk), Smyrna, Pergamum (Bergama), Thyatira (Ak-Hissar), Sardis (Sart), Philadelphia (Ala Shehir) and Laodicea (Eski Hissar). Smyrna is still a residential see; the others are now only titular.
ii. Of Rome. The basilicas of St. John Lateran, St. Peter, St. Mary Major, St. Paul-outside-the-Walls, St. Lawrence-outside-the Walls, St. Sebastian-outside-the-Walls, and Holy Cross-in-Jerusalem. Indulgences are granted for visits to them, a reminiscence of the days when they were the principal churches visited by penitential pilgrims.

SEVEN COUNCILS, The. The first seven œcumenical councils (*q.v.*), the acceptance of which, no more and no less, is the historical test of Christian orthodoxy for the Orthodox Eastern Church.

SEVEN HEAVENS, The. A sevenfold division of Heaven was a notion of pre-Christian times adopted by some Christian writers of the first centuries and to a limited extent favoured as a popular belief. It is by no means affirmed by the Church (*cf.*, Third Heaven).

SEVEN HOLY FOUNDERS, The. They were SS. Bonfilius Monaldi, John Buonagiunta, Benedict Antella, Bartholomew Amidei, Ricovero Uguccione, Gerard Sostegni and Alexis Falconieri, gentlemen of Florence. In consequence of a vision of our Lady they withdrew from the world and formed a community on Monte Senario. This was the beginning of the order of the Servants of Mary, commonly called the Servites (*q.v.*). The last survivor, St. Alexis, died in 1310.

SEVEN SAINTS OF BRITTANY, The. A popular pilgrimage in the province of Rennes to the churches of Dol (St. Samson), Saint Brieuc, Tréguier (St. Yves), Léon (St. Pol), Saint Malo, Quimper (St. Corentin) and Vannes (St. Anne).

SEVEN SLEEPERS OF EPHESUS, The. Seven martyrs, the heroes of an ancient and obscure legend bearing on the resurrection of the body, whose names are mentioned in the Roman Martyrology on July 27. They are commemorated in the Byzantine rite on Aug. 4, and the *Euchologion* has a prayer to them against sleeplessness.

SEVEN WORDS, The. The recorded utterances of our Lord from the cross; see Luke xxiii, 34, 43; John xix, 26-27; Mark xv, 34; John xix, 28, 30; Luke xxiii, 46.

"SEX EDUCATION." The Church teaches that children and youths of both sexes should be instructed in the facts of human generation according to their age and mental capacity. This instruction is a right and duty of their parents; failing them, it should be given by some other suitable and qualified person, not necessarily a school-teacher. But there is "no room to doubt that the Church is opposed to *collective* or *public* sex education with or without supposed 'safeguards' " (Joint Pastoral Letter of the Bishops of England and Wales, 1944).

SEXAGESIMA (Lat., the sixtieth). The second Sunday before Ash Wednesday (*cf.*, Septuagesima).

SEXT (Lat. *sexta* [*hora*], sixth [hour]). The hour of the Divine Office appointed to be said at the sixth hour, *i.e.*, about midday (*cf.*, the hymn). In practice it is said earlier and in churches where the office is sung in choir it usually follows the capitular or conventual Mass. It begins with *Deus in adiutorium*, etc., and an invariable hymn, *Rector potens verax Deus;* three psalms according to the days of the week (on certain feasts the Sunday psalms are always said); variable little chapter and short responsory; collect of the day; and usual ending.

SEXTON. A Middle-English corruption of sacristan (*q.v.*). The word is now used as equivalent to grave-digger.

"SHEPHERD, THE," OF HERMAS. A book written by an unknown author, probably during the 2nd century, and at one time regarded by some as a canonical book of Scripture. It consists chiefly of the relation of visions and parables with the object of bringing the reader to penance and right living.

SHORT LESSON, The (Lat. *Lectio brevis*). A variable verse of Scripture said at the end of the *Pretiosa* at Prime and an invariable verse (1 Peter v, 8-9) at the beginning of Compline, both vestiges of former readings from the Bible in monasteries, where these two offices were first used.

SHORT RESPONSORY, The. See RESPON-SORY, ii.

SHREWSBURY (*Salopiensis*). An English see, suffragan of Birmingham, erected in 1850. It includes Shropshire and Cheshire, formerly in the dioceses of Lichfield and Hereford. At Acton Burnell, Plowden, and elsewhere the faith has never died out, and six other missions were established during the 18th century. The patrons of the diocese are our Lady Help of Christians and St. Winefride (whose shrine was at Shrewsbury until the Reformation): the cathedral is dedicated in honour of Our Lady and St. Peter of Alcantara.

SHRINE (Lat. *scrinium,* a box for writing materials). i. A box-shaped reliquary (*q.v.*). This, the original meaning, is now rare.

ii. A sacred image in a church, dwelling-house or elsewhere, to which special devotion is accorded; it is usually decked with flowers and candles and has a lamp burning before it.

iii. Any holy place but particularly the tomb of a saint and one to which pilgrimages are made.

SHRINES OF OUR LADY mostly originate from an image which gives rise to great devotion and is sometimes wonder-working (*q.v.*) (*e.g.,* our Lady of Perpetual Help, of Good Counsel, of Czestochowa, of Guadalupe), but sometimes from visions accorded of her (*e.g.,* Lourdes, Fatima) or other reasons. The chief Marian shrines in the British Isles today are our Lady of West Grinstead, of Walsingham, of Willesden and at the Warwick Street church, London, in England; our Lady of Penrhys in Wales; at Carfin and our Lady of Aberdeen in Scotland; and at Knock and our Lady of Limerick in Ireland. Among those outstanding in the United States are our Lady of Prompt Succour at New Orleans (image crowned in 1894); the Sorrowful Mother at Chicago and at Portland, Ore.; our Lady of Starkenburg, Mo.; of Victory at Lackawanna, N. Y.; of Consolation at Carey, Ohio; of the Miraculous Medal at Germantown and of Perpetual Help at Uniontown, Pa.; of Good Help at New Franken and of the Holy Hill at Hubertus in Wisconsin. Canada has the important shrines of our Lady of the Cape, Trois-Rivières, and of St. Mary-among-the-Hurons, and others. The greatest Marian shrine in the world is undoubtedly Lourdes (*q.v.*).

SHRINES OF SAINTS. Any place which is known or reputed to be the tomb of a saint is referred to as his shrine, irrespective of the degree of devotion attaching to it: St. Peter's at Rome, St. Thomas's at Mylapore, St. Benedict's at Monte Cassino, St. Francis's at Assisi, St. Francis Xavier's at Goa, St. James's at Compostela, and the Three Kings at Cologne are among the principal pilgrim shrines of this sort. Small relics may be preserved in such a way as to constitute a shrine, *e.g.,* St. Thomas Becket's in the Catholic church at Canterbury. There are no notable ancient shrines of saints in Great Britain to-day except that of St. Edward the Confessor in Westminster Abbey. There are considerable relics of St. Chad in Birmingham cathedral; the tomb of Bl. Oliver Plunket is in Downside abbey-church, of Bl. John Southworth in Westminster cathedral, and of the Ven. Dominic Barberi at St. Anne's Retreat, Saint Helens; and the burying-places of some of the English martyrs are known and honoured; the body of St. Candida (of whom nothing is known) still lies in the (now Anglican) church of Whitchurch Canonicorum. The chief saints' shrines of the past were of SS. Thomas Becket (Canterbury), Alban (Saint Albans), Edward (Westminster), Cuthbert (Durham), and David (Saint Davids). At the Reformation the bodies of these and many other saints were destroyed or lost, except SS. Edward and Candida and the relics of St. Cuthbert; these last are said to be hidden in a place in Durham cathedral whose locality is only known to and handed on by four monks of the English congregation O.S.B. (*cf.,* Pilgrimage).

SHROUD OF CHRIST, The. See WINDING-SHEET.

SHROVETIDE (Old Eng. *scrifan,* to shrive, to hear or make confession). The few days before Ash Wednesday, particularly Shrove Tuesday, which were formerly a period particularly set aside for going to confession and also for lively recreation (*cf.,* Carnival). A few special customs survive in England, *e.g.,* the eating of pancakes (*q.v.*), the "pancake bell" at Olney and elsewhere, communal football in the streets at Ashbourne, Alnwick, Atherstone and Doncaster.

SHUWAIRITES, The (Ar. *Shuwairiyin*). Two congregations of Melkite Basilians (*q.v.*) originating at the monastery of Mar Hanna at Shuwair near Bairut, known respectively as Baladites and Aleppines. The name Shuwairite is now generally used only of the first of these. Also spelt Soarites, Chouerites, Chouarites, etc.

SIAM, THE CHURCH IN. Though missionary effort in Siam (Thailand) goes back to 1669 there are only about 40,000 Catholics among her 14½ million people, who are mostly Buddhists. They form 3 vicariates apostolic.

SIBYL, The. The mention of the sibyl in the third line of the first stanza of *Dies Iræ* refers to a poem in Book VIII of the Sibylline Oracles, attributed by Eusebius to the Sibyl of Erythræ, containing a lurid description of the Day of Judgement. The Jews of the 2nd century B.C. produced Sibylline oracles for propaganda purposes; these were taken over, adapted and greatly venerated by some of the early Christians, especially by the gnostics; many of them are extant.

SICILIAN HYMN, The. The hymn *O sanctissima, O purissima, dulcis Virgo Maria* (Ould's "Book of Hymns," no. 150), so called because of its popularity among Sicilian sailors.

SIGLUM (Low Lat., dim. of *signum*, a sign). A sign of abbreviation, especially in biblical criticism, *e.g.*, the letter Q (*q.v.*).

SIGN. That the perception of which leads to the perception of something else.

SIGN OF THE CROSS. A confession of faith in Christ crucified and an invocation of his blessing made by a cruciform gesture on one's body. By all Catholics except those of the Byzantine rite it is made by touching the forehead, breast, left and right shoulders, with the tips of the fingers and thumb of the right hand held together, and is usually accompanied by the words "In the name of the Father and of the Son and of the Holy Ghost." All Byzantines, whether Catholic or not, make the sign from right to left with the thumb and first two fingers held together. The occasions upon which the action is directed or recommended are innumerable: before and after all spiritual and many temporal works (*e.g.*, prayer, meals, sleep), when receiving a blessing, at times of temptation or danger, etc. Liturgically, it is made at *Deus in adiutorium* at the beginning of the hours of the Divine Office, at the first verse of the *Benedictus, Magnificat* and *Nunc dimittis*, etc., and at Mass with the celebrant at the beginning, *Adiutorium nostrum, Indulgentiam*, the introit, end of the *Gloria* and *Credo, Benedictus* and the blessing, and in the form of small crosses on the brow, lips and breast before the gospel and last gospel, etc. By orientals it is commonly made several times in succession and accompanied by metanies (*q.v.*). The sign of the cross is made on or over persons and things when absolving, anointing and blessing, and often over the gifts in the celebration of Mass. In Eastern rites it is often made over persons with a small cross in the hand. No magic power attaches to the sign of the cross; the action must correspond to a devoutness of heart and mind or it is a useless observance; this does not mean that the mind must necessarily and always advert to the action: it may well be done unconsciously by one habitually religious.

SIGNATURA, THE APOSTOLIC. The supreme tribunal of the Church which deals with appeals from the Rota (*q.v.*) and other matters arising from that court. It is also the court of appeal for the civil and criminal tribunals of the Vatican City.

SILENCE. Like solitude (*q.v.*), with which it is intimately connected, silence may be exterior or interior. Exterior, actual silence is the silence of monastic or eremitical life, and is both a mortification and a means of ensuring quiet of heart, recollection and intimacy with God. Interior silence is peace of soul, *i.e.*, the effort to control the passions, to restrain the wanderings of the imagination and to check anxiety, undue excitement or depression. Such peace must be practised by every soul seeking holiness: without it, there can be no habitual practice of the presence of God. It connotes a certain amount of actual silence as its safeguard. Solitude and silence necessarily develop with the growth of charity, and are perfect in the prayer of union (*q.v.*), which is a prayer of silence, made in the solitude of the heart where God alone dwells. One who never restrains his tongue will be guilty of many sins: "If anyone deludes himself by thinking he is serving God, when he has not learned to control his tongue, the service he gives is vain" (James i, 26).

SILK, or corresponding precious material, must be used in making the sacred vestments (except the amice, alb and girdle, which are linen) and not even the mendicant orders may now have them of linen, woollen, etc. But for personal ecclesiastical dress (cassock, etc.) silk is forbidden to all clerics, including bishops, except such prelates as are members of the Pontifical Family or of the college of Assistants at the Throne (*qq.v.*) living in Rome.

SILLON, THE (Fr. furrow). A Catholic social movement inaugurated in France by Marc Sangnier and Etienne Isabelle about the year 1894. It began as a literary group without fixed aim and then undertook the work of social reform, especially by means of popular education in study-circles. Its members manifested an exemplary piety, generosity and devotion to the weak and suffering; but their enthusiasm was ill-informed and badly ordered. Their conceptions of human dignity, of liberty, authority and obedience, were not in accordance with Catholic teaching; the establishment of greater justice between man and man was subordinated to their ideas of democracy and a plan of action purely secular and exclusive; and eventually the *Sillon* declared itself to be working not for Christ's Church and his gospel but for "humanity." Thereupon in 1910 Pope Pius X condemned their errors and insubordination and ordered that the *Sillon* be reorganized on diocesan lines under the bishops. M. Sangnier and the *Sillonists* at once submitted, but the movement instead of being reconstituted died a natural death.

SIMON AND JUDE, SS. Apostles whose feasts are celebrated together on Oct. 28 by the Western church. Of Simon, called "the Zealous," nothing is certainly known, nor of Jude, or Thaddeus, except that he was a brother of James the Less and wrote the canonical epistle which bears his name; they are said to have preached and been martyred together in Persia, and they are named together in the canon of the Mass. Simon (who in the East is identified with Nathanael, *cf.*, Bartholomew) is commemorated in the Byzantine rite on May 10 and Jude on June 19.

SIMONY (from Simon Magus, Acts viii, 18). The deliberate intention of buying and selling or otherwise trafficking in sacred things. It is of two kinds: simony of divine law is buying and selling things intrinsically spiritual, *e.g.*, indulgences, or temporal things inseparable from spiritual, *e.g.*, benefices; and simony of ecclesiastical law, which is buying and selling temporal things attached to spiritual, or exchanging spiritual things for spiritual, or even in certain circumstances temporal for temporal. Those guilty of simony in ecclesiastical offices incur *ipso facto* excommunication reserved to the pope *simpliciter*.

SIMPLE. i. That which has no parts, and is therefore indivisible; opposed to composite.

ii. *Simplex.* The lowest rank of feast (*q.v.*) in the Roman calendar. All feasts that were simples up to 1956 were in that year made commemorations, and semi-doubles were made simples.

SIMPLE VOWS. Public vows not recognized by the Church as solemn. Usually they render contrary acts unlawful but not invalid. Thus religious (*q.v.*) in simple vows retain ownership of property, and their marriages are valid, though illicit; but some simple vows render contrary acts invalid. They cannot be taken before the 16th year of age is completed if temporary and the 21st if perpetual. A religious society of simple vows is called a congregation, and religious women in simple vows are technically called sisters, as distinct from nuns in solemn vows (*moniales*) (*cf.*, Triennial Vows, Vows of Religion, Secularization, etc.).

SIMPLICITER. i. Absolutely: that which is said of something void of limitation, opposed to *secundum quid* (*q.v.*).

ii. Simply, *e.g.*, as of the third division of cases reserved (*q.v.*) to the Holy See.

SIMPLICITY OF GOD. The absence of any composition in God. God has no parts physical or metaphysical. A composite thing is one that is made up of several parts and can be resolved. Physical parts are those which can really be found in the thing, *e.g.*, the limbs of a man; body and soul. Metaphysical parts are those which do not exist in real distinction, but for whose distinction in the mind there is a foundation in fact. Now in God there is no composition. He is just infinite perfection. The fundamental reason of this is that his being and all that it means is wholly from himself. All the different perfections which we attribute to him are in him identical with his being. The simplicity of God is not opposed to the Trinity of persons.

SIMULATION is lying (*q.v.*) by means of an action, or performing an act deliberately to give a false impression.

SIN. "Any thought, word or deed against the law of God" (St. Augustine). Sin is essentially a deliberate rebellion against the authority of God; by it man prefers to choose some self-gratification in opposition to and in defiance of the law of God. Hence serious sin deprives man of God's friendship, and the sinner will receive due punishment either here on earth or in the future life. In the sacrament of Penance God has mercifully provided means by which man can be restored to his friendship and favour. Sin is mortal or venial; it may be actual, habitual, formal or material (see below); it is called of ignorance if the lack of knowledge is culpable, of infirmity if the result of sudden passion or a bad habit, and of malice if it is deliberate and calculated wickedness. The essentially evil quality of every sin is that it is an act of the human will in opposition to the Divine Will as interpreted by the conscience. For the commission of sin it is not necessary that all inclination to the contrary be excluded or that the evil itself be directly intended.

SIN, ACTUAL. Any act or omission against the law of God. It is opposed to habitual sin or the state of sin, which is the effect produced in the soul by actual sin. It is personal sin, arising from the sinner's own free will, as opposed to original sin (*q.v.*).

SIN, FORMAL. Sin in the true sense, *viz.*, a deliberate transgression of what conscience (*q.v.*) regards as the divine law, whether the supposed law exists or not (*cf.*, material sin).

SIN, HABITUAL. i. Strictly speaking, the state of a man who has sinned and not repented; this state of aversion from God continues until he is forgiven; it is imputable to the sinner, since the sin producing it was voluntary.

ii. A vicious habit. This is an incorrect use of the expression.

SIN, MATERIAL. A transgression of the divine law committed without knowledge of its sinfulness or without free consent; it is no true sin, since the act is not a wilful transgression, *e.g.*, taking the property of another in the belief that it is one's own.

SIN, MORTAL. A transgression of the moral law in a serious matter, committed with clear advertence to the grievous nature of the act and with full deliberation and consent on the part of the will. It is called mortal since it deprives the soul of its supernatural life of sanctifying grace (*q.v.*). It deserves eternal punishment, since the offence is a deliberate act of rebellion against the infinite majesty of God.

SIN, ORIGINAL. The primary and essential element of original sin is the privation of sanctifying grace from, the lack of supernatural life in, the soul of every human creature born into the world since the Fall (but *cf.*, Immaculate Conception); it is not an actual sin (*q.v.*) but a state of sin in which each individual is involved by virtue of the solidarity of the human race: the will of all humankind rebelled in Adam, the head, fountain and representative of the race, when he rejected God's gift of a supernatural life by disobedience (the Fall, *q.v.*). His sin was the sin of human nature (Rom. v. 12-21) and inheres as habitual (*q.v.*) sin in all who share in that nature by bodily generation. The effects of original sin are, firstly, its own essence, the loss of sanctifying grace; then, the loss of integrity (*q.v.*), resulting in concupiscence, *i.e.*, a general propensity towards an uncontrolled love of oneself and of creatures; and the loss of immortality and impassibility (*q.v.*). It must be noted that the Church repudiates and abhors the doctrine that concupiscence is itself original sin or that man is wicked by the very condition of his nature as such or that original sin is an essential corruption of the soul. Original sin is entirely remitted, not simply covered up by external imputation of the righteousness of Christ, by Baptism (*q.v.*), but concupiscence, the tendency to sin, and the physical disabilities of death and suffering remain. See UNBAPTIZED, FATE OF.

SIN, VENIAL. An offence against the law of God less grievous than mortal sin, not depriving the soul of sanctifying grace. A sin is venial either when the matter is not grave, or when, given grave matter, either full advertence to its gravity on the part of the intellect or full consent on the part of the will is wanting. Venial sins can be remitted by prayer or other good works.

SIN AGAINST THE HOLY GHOST. The six sins of despair, presumption, envy, obstinacy in sin, final impenitence (*qq.v.*) and in particular, deliberate resistance to the known truth, may be regarded as specially directed against the work of the Holy Ghost in the soul; generally, they so harden the soul to the inspirations of grace that repentance is unlikely.

SIN OF OMISSION. A deliberate failure to fulfil an obligation imposed by the divine or ecclesiastical law.

SIN OF OTHERS. Share in the guilt of another's sin may be incurred in various ways, *e.g.*, by command, by counsel, by a vote of consent (as a juryman, councillor, etc.), by praise of the evil about to be done, by being a partner in the sin, by receiving stolen goods, by giving the offender refuge from justice, by silence. See, too, SCANDAL; CO-OPERATION; REPARATION.

SIN BY SILENCE. Share in the guilt of another's sin, especially if it be a case of damage to property or of other injustice, may be incurred by not warning others of the sinner's evil intention or otherwise preventing its fulfilment, or by not denouncing the sinner to legitimate authority once the harm is done. See also CO-OPERATION.

SIN OF SODOM, The. An unnatural form of completed copulation, especially that of one male with another; it is one of the four sins crying to Heaven for vengeance.

SINS CRYING TO HEAVEN for vengeance are: wilful murder (Gen. iv, 10), the sin of Sodom (Gen. xvii, 20-21), oppression of the poor (Exod. ii, 23), and defrauding labourers of their wages (Jas. v, 4).

SINAI, THE CHURCH OF. An autocephalous unit of the Orthodox Eastern Church (*q.v.*), and the smallest self-governing church in the world, independent of the patriarch of Jerusalem since 1782. It consists only of the monastery of St. Katharine with 15 monks, 50 neighbouring lay people, and 10 or so more monks in a dozen "cells" (*metokhia*) in Egypt, Greece and elsewhere. It is governed by an abbot who is also archbishop, and its monks are Antonian rather than Basilian (*qq.v.*). Owing to the popularity of the God-trodden Mountain as a place of pilgrimage, it was very wealthy but has now lost most of its European properties; in its library was found the Codex Sinaiticus (*q.v.*).

SINDON (Gr., a linen cloth). The winding-sheet in which our Lord's body was wrapped; a liturgical term sometimes used for veils and cloths in general.

SINLESSNESS OF CHRIST. It is an article of faith (Council of Florence) that Christ was immune from all sin, original or actual. More than that, it is certain that he was impeccable, for every act of his was an act of God. Nor was there in him any concupiscence, for this is a result of original sin, and he had no moral imperfections.

SINLESSNESS OF OUR LADY. The Blessed Virgin Mary was free of all stain of original sin by virtue of her immaculate conception and she was also free of all actual sin, whether mortal or venial (*qq.v.*). "If any one say that once a man is justified he can throughout his life avoid all sin, even venial, except by a special privilege of God such as the Church holds regarding the Blessed Virgin, let him be anathema" (Council of Trent, sess. vi, can. 23, *de justificatione*).

SINUS VIRIDIS. Latin translation of the name of the see of Green Bay, Wis.

SIOPOLITANUS, or *Siouxensis.* The Latin epithet for the bishop of Sioux City, Iowa.

SISTERS OF THE ASSUMPTION, The. An enclosed congregation of nuns founded by Eugénie Milleret de Brou, in 1839, primarily for the education of girls of the professional class; some convents have added perpetual adoration (*q.v.*). Violet habit, white veil; ceremonial white cloak. Distinguish from the Little and Oblate Sisters of the Assumption (*qq.v.*).

SISTERS OF THE BLESSED SACRA-MENT, The. Several institutes have this name. The chief are:
i. An order with solemn vows founded by the Ven. Antony le Quien, O.P., in 1639. Enclosed and contemplative, with perpetual adoration for the conversion of unbelievers and sinners. Black tunic and scapular; white choir cloak.
ii. An unenclosed congregation founded in 1715 in France for school and hospital work. Black habit.

SISTERS OF CHARITY. There are numerous congregations of active unenclosed nuns bearing this name with distinguishing epithets added. The principal are:
i. Of St. Vincent de Paul, founded by him and Bl. Louise de Marillac in 1634 to seek out the poor, the sick and the needy and to undertake any charitable work whatsoever for them; "their chapel is the parish church, their cloister the streets of the city or wards of the hospitals." There are no lay-sisters. They number about 43,000 throughout the world, divided into provinces which are all subject to the mother house at Paris, which is under the jurisdiction of the superior general of the Lazarists; they have nearly 100 convents in Great Britain and Ireland alone. They form the biggest of all congregations of women, and their distinctive dress is known and respected everywhere. Habit: the dress of a French peasant; blue-grey gown with wide sleeves and apron, white linen cap and *cornette* ("wings").
ii. Of St. Paul the Apostle. Founded by Mgr. Maréchaux at Chartres, in 1704. The chief work of these sisters is the education of children. The English congregation is independent and has over 60 convents, many of which conduct elementary schools. Black habit.
iii. Of Jesus and Mary. An enclosed congregation founded near Ghent by Canon E. J. Triest, in 1803, for the conduct of schools,

colleges, orphanages, homes for incurables, etc. No lay-sisters; Little Office B.V.M. in choir. White tunic with black scapular and veil; white choir cowl.
iv. Irish, founded by Mary Aikenhead in Dublin in 1815 to minister to the sick poor. They also conduct schools, refuges, hospitals, etc. Houses in Ireland, Great Britain and Australia. Black habit and veil; white linen cap, apron and collar.
v. Of Our Lady, Mother of Mercy. Founded by Mgr. Zwissen, archbishop of Utrecht, in 1832, for the education of children and care of the sick. Black habit.
vi. Of St. Louis. Founded at Vannes, in 1803, by Mdme. Molé de Champlâtreux for the education of poor girls. They commonly have orphanges attached to their convents which since 1902 are chiefly in Canada. Black habit, veil and apron.

SISTERS OF THE CHRISTIAN RE-TREAT, The. Founded in 1789 at Fontenelle by the Abbé Receveur to provide retreats and teach the young. Perpetual adoration; no lay-sisters; solemn promise instead of vows. Two habits, white indoors, black out.

SISTERS OF THE CROSS, The. A teaching congregation founded in Picardy in 1625, reorganized in 1837. Enclosed; Little Office B.V.M. in choir. Black habit with cape, wide sleeves and veil; white cap and collar.

SISTERS OF THE CROSS & PASSION, The (to be distinguished from the Daughters of the Cross and Passion, or Passionist nuns). An unenclosed congregation founded in Manchester by FF. Gaudentius and Ignatius, C.P., and Mother Mary Prout in 1850. They conduct homes for factory and other working girls, teach, visit the sick and lapsed Catholics. No lay-sisters. They have numerous establishments in Great Britain, and some in Ireland and in the Americas. Black habit with Passionist badge.

SISTERS OF THE HOLY CHILD JESUS, The (to be distinguished from the Dames of St. Maur, *q.v.*). A teaching congregation founded at Derby in 1846 by Mrs. Cornelia Connelly and established in the U.S.A. in 1862. Unenclosed. Their convents in England include a house for women members of the University at Oxford. Black habit.

SISTERS OF THE HOLY FAITH, The. A congregation founded in 1857 at Dublin by the Rev. John Gowan and Margaret Aylward to combat "souperism" (*q.v.*) by caring for orphans and other destitute Catholic children. Numerous convents in Ireland only.

SISTERS OF THE HOLY FAMILY, The.
i. See ASSOCIATION OF THE HOLY FAMILY.
ii. A congregation of nuns of the Maronite rite founded in 1900 by their patriarch Elias Hoyek, for the education of girls and for nursing in hospitals.

SISTERS OF THE HOLY GHOST, The. See WHITE SISTERS.

SISTERS OF THE HOLY HEART OF MARY, The. i. An unenclosed congregation founded for the education of girls in 1802. Blue habit, black veil.
ii. Native Indian teaching nuns under the rule of the third order of St. Francis, founded at Pondicherry in 1844.

SISTERS OF THE IMMACULATE CONCEPTION. The name given to several congregations with the title "of the Immaculate Conception." The chief are:
i. The Sisters of . . . A branch of the Association of the Holy Family (*q.v.*), for the education of children of all classes. In England.
ii. The Congregation of . . , or Conceptionists. An enclosed and contemplative order founded as Cistercians, in 1484 at Toledo, by Bd. Beatrice da Silva. They are found only in Spain, France and Italy. They have had their own constitution since 1511.

SISTERS OF ST. JOSEPH, The. Many unenclosed congregations bear this name in one form or another, among them:
i. Of the Le Puy, founded in 1650 by Father J. P. Médaille, S.J., to undertake any works of mercy. After the French Revolution the congregation was restored by Mother St. John Fontbonne at Lyons, whence it has spread to Great Britain, India, the Near East and elsewhere, especially North America. Other daughter branches are those of Anneçy and Chambéry.
ii. Of Cluny. Founded in 1807. Asylums, schools, hospitals and work on foreign missions. Blue habit with black scapular.
iii. Of Peace. Founded in 1883, by Mgr. Bagshawe, bishop of Nottingham, primarily to train girls in domestic work. No lay-sisters; Little Office B.V.M. in choir. This institute has spread to the U.S.A. and Canada. Dark blue habit.
iv. Missionary Sisters. . . . Founded in 1883 by Cardinal Vaughan to help the priests from Mill Hill missionary college both at home and abroad. Rule of the Third Order of St. Francis.

SISTERS OF MARIE AUXILIATRICE, The. An unenclosed congregation founded in 1854 by the Abbé and Sophie de Soubiran to teach Christian doctrine, provide hostels for working girls and nurse the sick. Perpetual adoration and Little Office B.V.M. in choir. Black habit and scapular.

SISTERS OF MARIE RÉPARATRICE, The (Blue Nuns). A society founded in 1854 by the Baroness Emily d'Hooghvorst to make reparation for the sins of mankind, through our Lady, by daily adoration of the Blessed Sacrament exposed, and by giving retreats, teaching Christian doctrine or other suitable work. Enclosed; office in choir. White tunic, blue scapular, veil and girdle; white cloak and veil in choir.

SISTERS OF ST. MARY, The. An unenclosed congregation, founded at Namur in 1819 by the Abbé J. Minsart. Vestment-making; schools for all classes. Black habit.

SISTERS OF MERCY, The. Founded by Catherine McAuley in Dublin, in 1827, for the practice of all the works of mercy, spiritual and corporal, elementary, secondary and private schools, homes of rest for women, hostels for business girls and domestic servants, training homes for girls, night-refuges, hospitals. They have spread to all English-speaking countries, with over 100 establishments in Great Britain alone. Each convent is independent but they are sometimes grouped with a common noviciate. Little Office B.V.M. in choir. Black habit with train, to which the lay-sisters add an apron. There are several other congregations called Sœurs de la Miséricorde or its equivalent engaged in similar works.

SISTERS OF NAZARETH, THE POOR. An unenclosed congregation founded by Mother St. Basil Larmenier in London in 1851 to give homes to the aged poor and incurable children and training to orphans and to relieve the sick and hungry. They make daily collections of alms, particularly of broken food, for their establishments. They have houses in the British Isles, South Africa, New Zealand, Australia and America. No lay-sisters. Black habit with long cloak and blue edged veil for outdoors.

SISTERS OF OUR LADY OF CHARITY OF THE REFUGE, The. An enclosed order with solemn vows founded by St. John Eudes in 1641 for the restoration of penitent women and the protection of those in danger. Little Office B.V.M. in choir. White habit.

SISTERS OF OUR LADY OF MISSIONS, The. A congregation founded in 1861 by Euphrasie Barbier at Lyons to train religious for active work on foreign missions, especially the conduct of schools. Little Office B.V.M. in choir. Black habit and scapular, sleeves bound with blue.

SISTERS OF THE POOR CHILD JESUS, The. Founded at Aachen in 1844 by Mother Clare Fey and others for the education and care of destitute children, later extended to higher schools. Unenclosed. Black habit; white cloak.

SISTERS OF THE PRECIOUS BLOOD. There are several small congregations of women bearing this or similar names, *e.g.* the Mission Sisters (*q.v.*), the Sisters Adorers, the Daughters of the Precious Blood.

SISTERS OF PROVIDENCE, The. A number of congregations have this name. The principal are:

i. Of the Institute of Charity. These were founded by the Ven. J. M. Maye in 1762, but take their name from the institute of the Abate Rosmini, who rewrote their rule in 1833, to which many of their convents are auxiliary. Unenclosed and chiefly engaged in teaching; they were the first religious to teach in elementary schools in England (1844). Black habit and white veil.

ii. Of the Immaculate Conception. An unenclosed congregation founded by Canon Vinet in Belgium in 1833 to undertake the care of hospitals, schools and orphanages.

SISTERS OF THE SACRED HEARTS OF JESUS AND MARY, The. Several institutes have this name; the chief is the Picpus (*q.v.*) congregation, founded in 1797. The convents have both perpetual adoration and schools, and the religious are divided into choir, school, lay and oblate sisters. There are many houses in Great Britain, with homes for penitents, schools for feeble-minded, hospitals, etc. White tunic, cape and veil; white cloak for choir, red for adoration. A native Syrian congregation (Mariamettes) of various rites was founded by the Jesuits with this name in 1860; they have charge of parochial schools.

SISTERS OF THE TEMPLE. The Sisters of the Finding of Jesus in the Temple (better known as Blue Nuns) were established in London, by Cardinal Wiseman and the Abbé Roullin, in 1860 as a nursing community. They spread from England to Belgium and France, where their hospital at Paris is particularly well known.

SISTERS OF ZION, The. The Congregation of Our Lady of Zion, founded by FF. Theodore and Alphonse Ratisbonne, in 1843, to pray and work for the conversion of the Jews. Unenclosed; Little Office B.V.M. in choir. The institute is under the direction of the Fathers of Zion (*q.v.*).

SISTINE CHAPEL, The. The principal chapel of the Vatican Palace, begun by order of Pope Sixtus (Sistus) IV in 1473. All the chief papal observances take place therein (except those of a more public nature, *e.g.*, canonizations, which are in St. Peter's), instead of in the Roman basilicas as was the custom before the papal residence at Avignon. It is also used for the voting of the cardinals at the election of a new pope and their first fealty (*adoratio*) is paid therein.

SISTINE CHOIR, The. The choir of the Sistine chapel numbers 24 men and boys, lay or clerical, under the direction of a permanent *maestro di cappella*. It always sings unaccompanied by any instrument. It originated in the early papal *schola cantorum*, whose members formed a college and lived in community; its present form evolved during and after the exile at Avignon. At present the choir is not an organized body:

whenever its services are required, the best singers in Rome are called upon and these, for the moment, form the Sistine Choir.

SITIENTES SATURDAY. The Saturday before Passion Sunday, from the first word of the introit of the Mass. It is one of the days appointed for ordinations.

SKULL CAP (Lat. *pileolus*). A skull cap may be worn at Mass, up to the preface and after the communion, by the pope (white), cardinals (red) and bishops (purple). That of a cardinal is conferred on him at the same time as the red biretta. It evolved during the middle ages from a tight-fitting cap with flaps worn to keep the ears and shaved scalp warm.

SLANDER. See DETRACTION.

SLAV, SLAVONIC, RITE. An inaccurate name given to:

i. The use of the Byzantine rite in Church Slavonic by the Catholic and Orthodox Russians, Ruthenians, Bulgars and Serbs. Slavonic is the most widely used liturgical language of the Byzantine rite. Its use was first granted by Pope Adrian II to SS. Cyril and Methodius for Moravia and Pannonia when it was still a spoken tongue (*c.* 867); the liturgical books are printed in an alphabet said to have been invented by St. Cyril for the purpose.

ii. The use of the Roman rite in Old (Southern) Slavonic has been the custom in certain parts since the 11th-12th century, or earlier, and is still followed in certain Dalmatian dioceses. Pope Pius XI extended the privilege to any diocese of Yugoslavia at the discretion of the bishop in answer to a unanimous wish of the faithful, and also to a few churches in Czechoslovakia on certain days. The liturgical books are exact translations of the typical Roman editions, and up to 1927 were printed in the Glagolitic (*q.v.*) characters; the edition of the missal of that year is in western characters. Old and Church Slavonic are different dialects of the same tongue, and a good deal of them is intelligible to speakers of the modern Slavonic languages.

SLAVERY. A servitude by which the whole man becomes the private property of his master is essentially contrary to the natural law, which bestows on every man certain inalienable rights. Yet a man is at liberty to sell to another the labour of his whole life; hence such a modified slavery, whereby a man's personal rights remain inviolate, could be tolerated. Nevertheless, this would ill agree with his dignity as man and as Christian. Slavery was an essential part of the social structure of Greek and Roman civilization; the helots in Sparta and the slaves of Rome were the chattels of their masters, possessing no rights as men; at Athens the slaves could appeal to the magistrate against harsh treatment. Under the influence of the Church (but without direct legislation) complete slavery gradually disappeared in the West to revive in revolting fashion after the discovery of America. During the 19th century slavery was slowly abolished in the British and French colonies, in the U.S.A., and more recently in Brazil. It is still practised by the Arabs in parts of Africa (*cf.*, proletariat, responsibility).

SLOTH, one of the seven deadly sins, is commonly expressed in the phrase "It's too much trouble to be good." This is directly contrary to the first of the commandments (Mark xii, 30) and is a mortal sin if and when it results in the breaking of a grave precept. Physical laziness is also mortally sinful when it results in harm to others, *e.g.*, want in those who are dependent on us, and if given in to usually results in culpable deterioration of character. See ACCIDIE.

SOBRIETY. A moral virtue, subordinate to temperance, effecting moderation in drink; it does not inculcate total abstinence (still less a fanatical teetotalism, which is indeed opposed to the virtue by excess) unless in a particular case prudence recommends so heroic a measure.

SOCIALISM. A politico-economic system which, when the ownership of all income-bearing wealth has been vested in civil society, gives to this society the exclusive control over its production and distribution. The movement takes many forms, varying widely as regards both principles and methods. On the continent the tendency is towards the revolutionary type in conformity with the teaching of Karl Marx and Communism (*q.v.*). In England and elsewhere the word has been attached to more moderate reforming movements, such as the British Labour Party, and correctly in so far as such parties uphold the fundamental socialist policy of "the nationalization of the means of production, distribution and exchange." There is nothing intrinsically wrong (provided just compensation be made to the former owners) about measures of such nationalization if the state of a society calls for so drastic a remedy (if it be a remedy). Having some extreme examples right under his eyes, Pope Pius XI declared that Socialism "conceives human society in a way utterly alien to Christian truth"; but there are other forms to which this does not apply. The catch-phrase "A Catholic cannot be a socialist" is dangerously ambiguous; it is true only of those forms of Socialism which profess condemned principles or advocate condemned methods, in general all revolutionary Socialism, in particular notably Communism. When he declared that "No one can be at the same time a sincere Catholic and a *true* socialist" (italics added) Pius

XI made clear that these were what he meant by "true Socialism."

SOCIETY. The stable union of several persons working together for some common end. Societies may be artificial unions entered upon at the free will of their members, *e.g.*, industrial combines, scientific associations, or they may be universally imposed by the nature of man, *e.g.*, the family, the state. Yet, be the society artificial or natural, at its basis is the social nature of man, daily taught the need of co-operation by the exiguity of his own powers. Natural societies have their ends already determined by nature, and are accordingly endowed with all the means necessary for their attainment, dependently on others in the case of imperfect societies such as the family, independently in the case of the one perfect natural society, the state. Amongst supernatural societies, only the Church is a perfect society, since it alone is supreme and self-sufficing in its own sphere.

SOCIETY, PERFECT. That society is said to be perfect when it contains within itself all the means necessary to attain its end, and is therefore endowed with adequate authority for that purpose, *e.g.*, the Church, the state. An imperfect society depends on external aid to fulfil its functions, *e.g.*, a family on the tribe, a municipality on the state, a religious order on the Church. A perfect society has supreme authority, legislative, judicial and executive, over its members.

SOCIETY OF THE FAITHFUL VIRGIN, The. A congregation of women founded at La Delivrande in Normandy by Mother St. Mary le Forestier d'Osseville, in 1831. Its principal object is the education of the young, but other works of charity are undertaken. Unenclosed; simple vows; Little Office B.V.M. in choir (Divine Office on Sundays and feasts). Habit: white, with scapular and black veil; brown scapular for lay-sisters. Nuns of this congregation volunteered and accompanied to Skutari the Sisters of Mercy who assisted Florence Nightingale.

SOCIETY OF JESUS, The. The Jesuits (*q.v.*).

SOCINIANISM (from Lælius Socinus, a Sienese priest, 1525-62). The doctrine of a Protestant sect of which the distinguishing tenet was that Jesus Christ was not God but a deified man (who should be worshipped), miraculously born of a virgin to be the secondary cause of our salvation as mediator of God, of whom the Holy Ghost was merely an activity. They therefore denied the Trinity, but were not Unitarians in the ordinary sense. Socinianism had a controversial importance in England during the 17th century.

SODALITY (Lat. *sodalis,* a companion). An alternative name for a confraternity (*q.v.*); sometimes the one and sometimes the other is used in the official titles of these pious associations. Sodality is particularly associated with those of the Blessed Virgin Mary (Children of Mary, *q.v.*), frequently referred to as The Sodality.

SODOR AND MAN. A former see which comprised the Isle of Man and the western islands of Scotland. It was a suffragan of Trondhjem in Norway until the Isles became a Scottish diocese in the 14th century and Man a suffragan of York in 1458. Sodor comes from Old Norse *suthr [eyjar],* i.e., the South Islands, as opposed to the North Islands, Orkney and Shetland.

SOLEA (Gr., high, royal place). The semi-circular step or steps at the holy doors (*q.v.*) in a Byzantine church. Here the laity receive communion and the gospel is sung thereon if there is no ambo.

SOLEMN MASS (Lat. *Missa solemnis*). A Mass sung with the assistance of deacon and subdeacon, called in English a High Mass (*q.v.*). The epithet solemn is sometimes added to pontifical or papal Mass to indicate that it is sung as above, and not simply said, by a bishop or pope.

SOLEMN VESPERS. Vespers sung with a priest, deacon and subdeacon in the sanctuary, cantors in copes, incense, etc.

SOLEMN VOWS. Those recognized as such by the Church. They render contrary acts not only illicit but invalid: thus religious (*q.v.*) in solemn vows cannot own property or contract valid marriage. They cannot be validly taken before the age of 21. A religious society of solemn vows is called an order, and its members are regulars; religious women in solemn vows are technically termed *moniales,* i.e., nuns (*cf.,* simple vows, vows of religion, secularization, etc.).

SOLEMNITY. In general, a solemnity is any feast that is celebrated with as much liturgical observance and splendour as possible, whether universally or locally. Specially, it is the name given to the second feast of St. Joseph (Wednesday after 2nd Sunday after Easter) because celebrated with more solemnity than his primary feast (Mar. 19) in Lent will allow; in the same way the Benedictines have a Solemnity of St. Benedict on July 11 (primary feast, Mar. 21). The external solemnity observed in celebrating Mass may in the case of certain feasts (Corpus Christi, St. Joseph, the Holy Rosary, the titular of the church, etc.) be transferred to the following Sunday in order that the faithful may more easily be present.

SOLEMNIZATION of marriage with nuptial Mass and Blessing must be distinguished from the simple performance of the marriage ceremony. See FORBIDDEN TIMES.

SOLESMES. An abbey and mother-house which gives its name to the congregation of Benedictines of France revived by Dom Prosper Guéranger, in 1837. When used in connexion with church music it indicates the editions of the Gregorian chant prepared by these monks at the request of Pope Pius X, and now the only authentic version of the chant. Pope Gregory XVI conferred on the congregation of Solesmes all the privileges and honours of the extinct Cluniac, St. Vannes and Maurist congregations, whose successor it is. It has one monastery in England, Quarr, and one in Canada, St. Benedict-of-the-Lake. This congregation undertakes no work outside its monasteries.

SOLICITATION. In canon law, the crime of making the use of the sacrament of Penance an opportunity of directly or indirectly enticing another, whether by word, sign or writing, to a grievous sin against chastity. The person solicited is bound under pain of excommunication to report the crime, in person or by signed letter, to his or her bishop, or the bishop of the place where it occurred, and to abide by his decision. Falsely to accuse a priest of solicitation is a sin specially reserved to the jurisdiction of the pope.

SOLITARY. In the strict sense of one who lives entirely alone, usually in a remote place, seeking sanctification in that state, solitaries are now practically non-existent in the Catholic Church, though the solitary life in its canonical and regulated forms still flourishes. Whether in its exact or its canonical sense, the Church has always not merely approved the solitary life as the vocation of certain individuals but has exalted it as being, in the abstract, the most perfect form of human spiritual life: not as the specific end but as the higher limit of Christian social life. "The human city has produced its highest results when it is crowned by the contemplative solitude of a certain number of souls united to God, who in their turn, moved by love, intercede for the multitude, and whose wisdom guides the life of that multitude from above" (Maritain). See CONTEMPLATIVE LIFE; HERMIT.

SOLITUDE. Solitude may be exterior, *i.e.,* actual, or interior. The former implies living apart from the world, either as a complete solitary or hermit, or in a religious community. Interior solitude means recollection (*q.v.*), peace of soul and the practice of the presence of God, even in the midst of occupations, with a certain predilection for actual solitude. It has always been recognized as a principle of spirituality that true holiness is impossible without interior solitude. The benefit to the soul of periods of actual solitude and silence is the motive for retreats (q.v.).

SOLO. The *motu proprio* of Pope Pius X on sacred music states that solos are not entirely excluded from church singing, "but these must never take the chief place in a service or absorb the greater part of the liturgical text; they must rather be points of musical emphasis and accent bound up closely with the rest of the composition, which must remain strictly choral" (sect. v, par. 12). This relates to the liturgical text but does not seem to exclude a solo as part of a motet (q.v.); but a motet consisting wholly of a solo, especially if sung by a female voice, is not in accordance with the spirit of Christian tradition and worship.

SOMASCHI, The. An order of clerks regular under the rule of St. Augustine with solemn vows, founded by St. Jerome Æmiliani at Somascha in Lombardy in 1533. They conduct schools and orphanages in Italy.

SON OF GOD, The. i. The second Person of the Blessed Trinity, the Word, is the true consubstantial (q.v.) Son of God, begotten from eternity, the only begotten. He is not merely a son in name or an adopted son. The manner of his begetting is by the intellect: "The Word proceeds by way of intelligible activity, which is a vital action" (St. Thomas, I, xxvii, 2).

ii. Jesus Christ is the Son of God, for the twofold nature of God and man belongs to the one person of the Word. So Peter's confession, "Thou are the Christ the Son of the living God," was pronounced a revelation from the Father (Matt. xvi, 18) and Christ said, "I and my Father are one" (John x, 30).

iii. The name son of God is sometimes used of the angels (Job i, 6), of the Jews (the prophets in particular), and of Christians in a state of grace (q.v., Gal. iv, 6). But none of these usages implies true natural sonship.

SON OF MAN, The. A title of the Messias (cf., Dan. vii, 13) and a favourite title of our Lord for himself, which emphasizes his true human nature and his office as mediator (q.v.). He was born of a human mother, but of no human father. He "took birth from a woman" (Gal. iv, 4) by the power of the Holy Ghost who came upon her (Luke i, 35).

SONG OF SIMEON, The. The *Nunc Dimittis* (q.v.).

SONG OF THE III CHILDREN, The. The *Benedicite* (q.v.).

SOPHONIAS. The Gr. form of the Heb. name Zephaniah (Jahveh protects), author of a prophetical book of the Old Testament. It was written between 642 and 611 B.C., and was directed against Judah and Jerusalem and the surrounding nations, ending with a notably universal Messianic promise. Sophonias is named in the Roman Martyrology on Dec. 3.

SORBONNE, The. The theological college of Paris founded by Robert de Sorbon in 1257. It became practically the theological faculty of the University of Paris and flourished until the Revolution. It was revived in 1808 by Napoleon I as the theological faculty of the new university but was suppressed in 1882. Until the rise of Jansenism, in which controversy it played an ambiguous part, the Sorbonne was one of the most famous of theological schools.

SORROW FOR SIN is a hatred of and a turning away from those sins which one has committed; it is an act of the will made from supernatural motives founded on faith. It is "being sorry," and is quite independent of and does not require "feeling sorry"; feeling sorry may be, and often is, an emotional revulsion which leaves affection for sin unimpaired. See CONTRITION.

SORROWS OF OUR LADY, THE VII, popularized as a subject for spiritual meditation by the Servite order, are: the prophecy of Simeon (Luke ii, 15), the flight into Egypt, the three days' disappearance of her Son, his painful progress to Calvary, his crucifixion, the removal of his body from the cross and its entombment. There were other enumerations. In the general calendar of the Roman church there are two feasts in honour of these mysteries, on the Friday in Passion week and on September 15. The first of these particularly commemorates our Lady sorrowing at the foot of the cross and is still called her Compassion in some calendars.

SORROWFUL MYSTERIES, THE V, of the rosary (q.v.) are: the agony of our Lord in the garden, his scourging, his crowning with thorns, the carrying of his cross to Calvary, and the crucifixion.

SOTERIOLOGY (Gr. σωτήρ, a saviour). The theology of the work of Christ as redeemer, studied in his life, passion and death and in his intercession at the right hand of the Father in Heaven.

SOUL. The thinking principle; that by which we feel, know, will, and by which the body is animated. The root of all forms of vital activity. It is a substance or a being which exists *per se*; it is simple or unextended, *i.e.*, not composed of separate principles of any kind; it is spiritual, *i.e.*, its existence, and to some extent its operations, are independent of matter; it is immortal (q.v.). The soul is the substantial form (q.v.) of the body. There are three kinds of soul, vegetative, the root of vital activity in plants; sensitive, the root of vital activity in animals; intellectual, the root of vital activity in man. The last contains the other two virtually (q.v.); the sensitive contains the vegetative also virtually. The sensitive and vegatative soul are both simple but incomplete substances, incapable of existing apart from matter; they are therefore neither spiritual nor immortal. See also IMMORTALITY; INCORRUPTIBILITY; BODY AND SOUL, etc.

"SOUL OF THE CHURCH," The. The Holy Ghost is the soul of the mystical Body (q.v.) of Christ, the Church, as Pope Pius XII declares in *Mystici Corporis Christi* (q.v.). But the expression "soul of the Church" has often been used in a metaphorical sense to designate all those who actually are in a state of grace in dependence on the merits of Christ and the sanctifying action of the Holy Ghost; many of these are persons who are not seen to be members of the visible body of the Church. But to say that such persons belong to the "soul of the Church" is not altogether free from objection. It is better to say of the non-Catholic in good faith that "he belongs invisibly to the Church," as being "related to the mystical Body of the Redeemer by some unconscious reaching out and desire" (Pius XII). (*Cf.* Salvation ii; Visibility of the Church; Catholic ii.)

SOULS IN PURGATORY, The. See HOLY SOULS.

"SOUPERISM." A slang name for the activities of a certain class of relief workers in Ireland, especially during the famine years (1845-51), who made the profession of Protestantism a condition for the reception of free soup and other material benefits; particularly in Connemara and Achill the bribery was open and bare-faced. The term has been extended to any "welfare" activities which result, whether foreseen and intended or not, in the falling away of Catholics from the Church.

SOUTANE (French). The cassock (q.v.) worn by the secular clergy.

SOUTHWARK (*Southwarcensis*). An English see, suffragan of Westminster, erected in 1850, now including Kent, Surrey and Sussex with London south of the Thames, before the Reformation in the dioceses of Canterbury, Rochester, Winchester and Chichester. At Arundel, Midhurst and West Grinstead the faith persisted throughout penal times; six parishes were established as missions in the 18th century. The episcopal residence and cathedral are in the London borough of Southwark, and the diocesan seminary at Wonersh. The Isle of Thanet is served by Benedictines from Ramsgate Abbey. The patrons of the diocese are our Lady Immaculate and SS. Thomas and Augustine of Canterbury; the cathedral is dedicated in honour of St. George.

SPACE. The room which a material object fills, and not to be confused with the extension of a thing, which is the co-existence of its parts outside of each other. Space may be defined thus: "The superficies of the containing body considered as immovable and immediately contiguous to the body located" (Aristotle).

SPAIN, THE CHURCH IN. Most of the 26 million inhabitants of Spain profess the Catholic faith, which is officially the religion of the Spanish nation; with the exception of certain public manifestations, other cults may be freely exercised. Canon law and the disciplinary decrees of the Council of Trent are recognized by the state, which pays a moderate subsidy towards the support of the clergy. The wealth of the Spanish church today has been exaggerated by popular estimation. The civil courts grant divorce *a vinculo* when both parties are non-Catholics, but not when either party is a Catholic. The relations between church and state are regulated by a concordat with the Holy See, with which diplomatic relations are maintained. The hierarchical organization is 9 metropolitan sees (the archbishop of Toledo having the title of primate) with 47 suffragans and a priorate-*nullius*. The bishop of Urgel shares with France nominal lordship over the republic of *Andorra*, in whose diocese its 5,000 people are included.

SPANISH CHAPEL, The. An embassy chapel (q.v.) taken over from the Spanish ambassador in London in 1791. The chapel then built lasted until the present church of St. James in Spanish Place was built in 1890.

SPATIAMENTUM (Lat. *spatium*, a journey). The weekly walk of several hours' duration taken in community by Carthusian monks.

SPECIALI MODO. In an especial way, specially, as of the second division of cases reserved (q.v.) to the Holy See.

SPECIALISSIMO MODO. In a most special way, very specially, as of the first division of cases reserved (q.v.) to the Holy See.

SPECIES. i. In logic. One which is capable of being in many, numerically distinct, and univocally predicated of them essentially and completely.
ii. In biology. Collection of individuals like to each other, capable of begetting offspring.
iii. In metaphysics. The same as essence (q.v.); the essential constitutives of a thing.

SPECIES, EUCHARISTIC. The accidents (q.v.) of the bread and wine (colour, taste, smell, quantity, etc.) which remain after the substance has been converted into the Body and Blood of Christ in the sacrament of the Eucharist.

SPECIFIC, SPECIFICALLY. That which designates the whole essence, or an essential attribute, of a thing: *e.g.,* to know and to will are specific acts of the rational soul. Man, as man, reasons; to reason, therefore, is said to be attributed to man specifically.

SPECULATION, SPECULATIVE. By reason of its immediate end knowledge is speculative or practical; the first stops at knowledge, the second applies it to action or to conduct. Speculation rules practice: the latter is therefore subordinate to the former.

SPIRATION (Lat. *spirare,* to breathe). See PROCESSION OF THE HOLY GHOST.

SPIRIT. Spirit is of narrower extension than mind (*q.v.*), indicating properly a being capable of the intellectual order of life. Spirit is opposed to material, yet adds something to simple (for not all the simple is spirit); it has the capability of existing and in some ways of operating independently of matter. When opposed to soul (*e.g.,* Heb. iv, 12) it is so opposed as the intellectual faculties to the animating principle.

SPIRITISM (commonly called Spiritualism). A practice whereby one endeavours to get into communication with the souls of the dead or with other spirits. The apparently preternatural phenomena observed at spiritistic *séances* can often be attributed to fraud, to the use of which the methods adopted give every opportunity; frequently they are due to abnormal but natural psychic qualities possessed by the medium or by the observers; others, however, must be ascribed either to natural forces not yet fully investigated or, possibly, to the intervention of evil spirits. The moral and intellectual effects of frequent indulgence in Spiritism are at times disastrous. Since communication with the other world is dependent on God's good pleasure, not on an arbitrary use of mediums or of table-turning, Spiritism involves the sin of superstition (*q.v.*); attendance at spiritistic meetings is strictly forbidden by the Church.

SPIRITUAL EXERCISES. A systematic series of meditations on the fundamental truths of religion, meditations and contemplations on the life of Christ, together with other spiritual practices, aptly arranged so as to appeal forcibly to both intellect and sentiment, and thus exert a cumulative and lasting effect on the will of the exercitant. "The Spiritual Exercises," whether as a book or a method of meditation, indicates the book of that name by St. Ignatius Loyola.

SPIRITUAL FRIARS. The name popularly given to numbers of Franciscans of the 13th-14th century who advocated a most extreme rigorism in the observance of the poverty prescribed by the rule of St. Francis; also called *Zelanti.* They formed eventually a separate religious congregation called the *Clareni;* a number joined the *Fraticelli* (*q.v.*), whose schismatic tendencies they shared. The opposition between Spirituals and the Community or ordinary-observance friars foreshadowed the later division into Observants and Conventuals (*qq.v.*).

SPIRITUAL LIFE. The supernatural life, consisting of the infused theological and moral virtues, endowment of sanctifying grace, and the gifts of the Holy Ghost (*qq.v.*) which man receives at baptism, in order that he may use and develop them until he is "filled with all the completion God has to give" (Eph. iii, 19). This growth will be opposed by hostile factors, the Devil, the world, and the flesh, whose influence tends to impede it or destroy it. It is divided into three stages, called respectively the purgative, the illuminative, and the unitive ways (*qq.v.*). The spiritual life must not be conceived as a thing apart from and necessarily in opposition to ordinary life; ideally they are one, the spiritual informing the temporal, for only sin and error are incompatible with the spiritual life: to separate them in thought leads to a separation in practice, to a notion of religion as "A thing for Sundays." Human nature is imperfect and "the impulses of nature and the impulses of the spirit are at war with one another" (Gal. v, 17), but it is precisely for the removal of the contrarieties of the natural man ("flesh") and the elevation to, and the preservation in, the life of sanctifying grace (*q.v.*) of the whole man, body and soul, that the supernatural life is ordained.

SPIRITUAL READING. Any serious reading which brings the soul nearer to God, whether directly by exhortation, exposition, meditation and example or indirectly by extending one's knowledge of the faith and holy things. The Bible being the word of God, nothing can excel it for spiritual reading; after it are the works of the great masters of spiritual life, SS. Augustine, Teresa, John-of-the-Cross, Francis of Sales, Thomas à Kempis, Blosius, the English mystics (*q.v.*) and of many more recent writers; the lives of the saints; theological and philosophical works; and sacred history. But while it excludes merely frivolous works and those read for a pastime, curiosity, secular study, etc., spiritual reading need not be confined to the books and topics vulgarly looked on as religious; many other books, not excluding novels, read with prudence and spiritual attention, fulfil the function of spiritual reading. Especially for those whose lives are passed in active physical work and secular business, a brief daily space of such reading is almost indispensable for freedom of soul and health of mind.

SPIRITUAL VESSEL (Lat. *Vas spirituale*). A title given to our Lady in the litany of Loreto; friar Bernardine de Bustis (*d.* 1500) referred to her as Vessel of the Holy Spirit. *Vas honorabile* is an echo of the *Vas honoratum* of Epiphanius (d. 403). *Vas insigne devotionis* is often translated in prayer-books as "Vessel of singular devotion" (whatever that may mean); it signifies, "Glorious vessel of devotion." For this use of the word "vessel," see Acts ix, 15.

SPIRITUAL WORKS OF MERCY, The, are to convert sinners, to instruct the ignorant, to counsel the redeless, to comfort the sorrowing, to bear ills patiently, to forgive wrongs and to pray for the living and the dead.

SPIRITUALS, -ITIES. All those things which belong to the Church or to a cleric as such, whether ecclesiastical rights and duties or material emoluments (such as stole fees), as opposed to temporals (*q.v.*).

SPIRITUALISM. i. The philosophical doctrine that spirit exists in the universe as well as matter or that spirit or mind is the only reality (Idealism); both are opposed to Materialism (*q.v.*).

ii. More commonly and quite improperly, the doctrine and practice of those who believe that man can, does and may communicate with the souls of the dead. Spiritism (*q.v.*) is the proper term for this (*cf.*, French, German and Italian usage).

SPIRITUALITY. i. The property of a complete substance, such as the human soul, whereby it is capable of existing and of performing specific operations (understanding, willing) independently, subjectively speaking, of matter.

ii. The quality of spiritual-mindedness as opposed to materialism or secularism; supernatural as opposed to natural goodness; the ascetical system or spiritual teaching of a given person (*cf.*, spiritual life).

iii. In plural. See SPIRITUALS.

"SPOILED PRIEST." A colloquial term applied in Ireland to a seminarist who has for any reason given up his preparation for the priesthood to adopt another way of life. In some localities it carries a stigma which is wholly undeserved. This is a double evil: it may be unjust to the ex-seminarist, and it is apt to introduce an element of constraint into what should be a perfectly free choice of a state of life.

SPOILS, THE OFFICE OF. A Roman department attached to the Congregation of Propaganda dealing with such property of deceased clerics as has been derived from their benefices and not disposed of by will. Such property belongs by law to the Holy See, but the law hardly operates outside of Italy. Cardinal-bishops have to render an annual account of the revenues of their sees to this office.

SPONGE, LITURGICAL. A triangular piece of sponge, covered with silk, recalling the one offered to our Lord on the cross, is used in the Byzantine rite to wipe the fingers and palms of celebrant and deacon after communion, to convey the holy Bread from the *diskos* to the chalice, and similar purposes. It therefore somewhat corresponds to the Western purificator.

SPONSOR Lat. *spondere,* to promise. One who offers a person to be baptized or confirmed, and undertakes a certain responsibility for the faith of such person, thereby contracting spiritual relationship (*q.v.*): commonly called in England "godfather" or "godmother." For validity sponsors must be Catholics over seven, have the intention of undertaking the office, and touch the person in the act of baptism or confirmation. For Confirmation the sponsor must himself be confirmed. For licit sponsorship the age of 13 years completed and knowledge of the rudiments of the faith are required. In Baptism there may be one sponsor only (of either sex), or one of each sex. In Confirmation one sponsor only is allowed, who should be of the same sex as the person confirmed. There is no sponsor required for conditional baptism, unless it is the same person who was sponsor at the first and doubtful baptism. The duties of sponsors are to take a permanent interest in the spiritual welfare of their godchildren and, if necessary, to undertake their religious education as far as they are able.

SPONTANEOUS GENERATION. See ABIOGENESIS.

SPOON, LITURGICAL. i. A flattish spoon of gold or silver gilt with which holy communion in both kinds is given to the people in the Byzantine rite (Catholic and dissident). It is also used for the communion of the celebrant and of clerics assisting at the Liturgy by the Catholic Syrians.

ii. A tiny spoon which it is permissible to use when adding water to the wine at the offertory at Mass, to avoid an excess.

SPOUSE. In spite of its derivation through Fr. from Lat. *spondere* (to promise, betroth), this word has always in English primarily meant a husband or wife in relation to the partner. A secondary meaning of "one betrothed" is first recorded in 1553 (in the form *espouse* in 1475), and this use may be held to justify the translation of St. Joseph's title *Sponsus B.V.M.* as Spouse of our Lady, to emphasize him as the husband in an unconsummated marriage.

SPY WEDNESDAY. A name for the Wednesday in Holy Week, used in Ireland and spread from thence to the United States. The allusion seems to be to Judas Iscariot (in the passion read at Mass on that day) as traitor, "spy."

STABAT MATER. i. The name from its first words, *Stabat Mater dolorosa,* of the sequence (*q.v.*) for the feasts of the Seven Sorrows of our Lady, commonly ascribed to a Franciscan friar, Jacopone da Todi (1220-1306). Divided into three parts it provides the office hymns at Vespers, Matins and Lauds for the first of these feasts. It is also usually sung during the devotion of the stations of the Cross.

ii. A musical setting of the same.

iii. Rarely, a hymn paralleling the above but in honour of the birth of our Lord, *Stabat Mater speciosa*.

STABILITY. The characteristic and peculiar vow of Benedictine monks and nuns, contained in the traditional formula of profession, "I promise, before God and his saints, stability, conversion of manners (*q.v.*) and obedience according to the rule of our holy father Benedict." By it the monk registers his intention of persevering in community life, and that in the monastery of his profession, unless his superior shall send him elsewhere. The permission of the Holy See has to be obtained for a monk permanently to be transferred from one to another monastery.

STALLS. The fixed seats in the choir of a church for the accommodation of the canons, monks, nuns, singing men and boys, or whoever sing the office therein. They consist of one or more rows on either side of seats divided by arm-rests with a continuous bookrest in front (*cf.*, Misericord). In England they were commonly returned along the choir-screen at the west end to provide places for the dean, abbot, prior, etc., but on the continent the prelate sits nearest to the altar; the superior's place is on the epistle side (*cf.*, Decani, Cantoris). In Great Britain and the U.S.A., stalls are now usually found only in cathedral and conventual churches (*cf.*, choir). In the singular, "stall" is often used figuratively for the benefice or office of a canon. In Byzantine churches there are stalls before the *iconostasis* for the singers, behind the altar on either side of the episcopal throne, and around the walls of the nave and *narthex* for the people; they are called "standing-places" (*stasidia*), for they are rarely sat on.

STANBROOK. An abbey of Benedictine nuns of the English congregation, founded at Cambrai in 1625. In 1793 they were driven from France and settled in 1838 at Stanbrook, near Worcester. They are enclosed and contemplative, and are under the jurisdiction not of the bishop but of the abbot president of the congregation.

STANDING is the normal bodily posture at Christian public prayer, kneeling (*q.v.*) being a penitential practice. This is conserved for the celebrant, sacred ministers and choir, except where sitting is conceded to avoid weariness (*e.g.*, during the psalms of the Divine Office); for lay people in the West custom varies, but the liturgical books assume that they stand, except at low Mass. In the Eastern rites any other position is almost unknown, except where, as in North America, Western example has brought about local innovations (*cf.*, the attitude of prayer).

STAR OF BETHLEHEM, The, seen by the Magi either in the east (*i.e.*, Babylonia-Persia, where they came from) or at its rising. Scripture does not say that they saw it during their journey to Palestine, but they saw it again on leaving Jerusalem till it stood over where the Child was. Catholic exegesis has always accepted the objective reality of the phenomenon, but whether it was in itself miraculous or a natural phenomenon used by God as a sign, whether perhaps it consisted in a conjunction of stars which to the naked eye would appear as one great light, all this is open to discussion.

STAROSLAV. A name, often used in French, for the Church Slavonic language. See SLAV RITE, i.

STATE. The whole body of people united under one government: a natural society, and therefore established by God, fulfilling his purpose, wielding in its own sphere his authority; and a perfect society, *i.e.*, supreme and independent in its own sphere, self-contained as to the necessary means for accomplishing its end, the temporal welfare of man. Its subject matter consists of (*a*) human acts which affect man's temporal welfare yet are not in themselves immediately connected with his eternal welfare; (*b*) all persons and things in so far as involved in such acts. Consequently the state is limited by the natural and supernatural laws—it cannot lawfully invade man's natural rights, still less his supernatural rights. Moreover, "The Gospel has not one law of charity for individuals and another for states and nations—which are indeed but collections of individuals" (Pope Benedict XV, *Pacem Dei munus*). See CHURCH AND STATE, etc.

STATE, THE PAPAL SECRETARIATE OF. The department of the Vatican whose chief business it is to negotiate with civil rulers, either directly or through nuncios or special legates. Its three sections deal with extraordinary ecclesiastical affairs, in association with the congregation of that name; with ordinary matters of state, granting of honours, appointments to curial offices, etc.; and with the forwarding of apostolic briefs and letters from the various congregations. The Cardinal Secretary of State is the pope's personal confidential assistant; he therefore lives in the Vatican and vacates his office at the pope's death.

STATE OF GRACE. i. Another name for habitual grace (*q.v.*).

ii. The state of the soul which is free of original sin and actual mortal sin. Its negative aspect is this absence of sin; its positive aspect, the presence of sanctifying grace, with the virtues and gifts of the Holy Ghost (*qq.v.*), implying the friendship of God and the personal indwelling of the Holy Ghost.

STATE OF PERFECTION. A technical term in canon law, denoting that the Church officially recognizes certain modes of life as stable conditions in which perfection (*q.v.*) is either acquired or presupposed. The obligations of the state are undertaken with a certain solemnity. Two states of perfection are definitely admitted: the religious life (*q.v.*) and the episcopal office. "Bishops are those who make others perfect, religious are made perfect: in the one case, therefore, there is action, in the other reception. Hence it is clear that the state of perfection is more excellent in bishops than in religious" (St. Thomas, II-II, clxxiv, 7). The state of perfection is not perfection, because perfection is found in men who are outside the state of perfection and many in the state of perfection are not perfect.

STATES OF THE CHURCH, The. The territory ruled by the pope as temporal king. They began after the Peace of Constantine with the Patrimony of St. Peter (*q.v.*) and by agreement with Charlemagne the Papal States, consisting principally of the district round Rome, Romagna and the Pentapolis, were reorganized in 781. But the popes did not actively govern as well as reign in their states till the 15th century. At their greatest extent, at the beginning of the 16th century, they included the duchies of Parma, Piacenza, Modena, Romagna, Urbino, Spoleto and Castro, the March of Ancona, and the provinces of Bologna, Perugia and Orvieto. Previous to 1860 they covered 17,000 sq. miles with 3 million inhabitants (in this so-called theocracy less than 1.5 of the administrators were ecclesiastics); in that year Romagna, the March and Umbria were annexed to the new kingdom of Italy, leaving the pope only the city of Rome and the province of Latio, which in 1870 were seized by Italy and *de facto* the States of the Church ceased to exist. In 1929 the temporal sovereignty was recognized in respect of the Vatican City (*q.v.*) by the Treaty of the Lateran. The Comtat Venaissin, around Avignon, was a papal possession from 1273 till the Revolution, but not a state of the Church in the ordinary sense.

STATIO (Lat., a standing-still, an assembly). i. A Roman station (*q.v.*).
ii. Any place where the clergy assemble or processions are drawn up to proceed to divine worship.
iii. A pause at some place for prayer, *e.g.*, at a temporary altar for Benediction during a procession of the Blessed Sacrament.

STATIONS, THE ROMAN. The ancient custom whereby every day in Lent, on the ember days, Sundays in Advent, and certain vigils and chief feasts, 84 days in all, the clergy and people of Rome met at an appointed place and went in procession to the stational church where the pope or his representative sang Mass. The place of the station is still noted on the days concerned in the Roman Missal, *e.g.*, *Statio ad Sanctam Mariam Maiorem* (Station at St. Mary Major), on Easter day. Indulgences are now attached for going, either privately or in procession, from a neighbouring church to a given stational church, saying certain prayers before setting out, on the way, and on arrival. These indulgences can be gained elsewhere, *e.g.*, by a secular tertiary who on the station days marked in the Missal visits a church of his order or his own parish church and there prays for the good of the Church and the intentions of the pope. The chief stations are: 1st Sunday of Advent, St. Mary Major; Christmas day, St. Mary Major (1st and 3rd Mass), St. Anastasia (2nd Mass); Epiphany, St. Peter's; Ash Wednesday, Santa Sabina; Good Friday, Santa Croce; Holy Saturday, St. John Lateran; Easter day, St. Mary Major; Ascension and Pentecost, St. Peter's. There are now about 45 station churches, of which 35 have only Lenten stations; the others, namely, St. John Lateran, St. Peter's, St. Mary Major, Santa Croce, St. Paul's and St. Lawrence's-outside-the-Walls, the Holy Apostles, Santa Maria in Trastevere, St. Peter ad Vincula and Sant' Anastasia, have them also at other times.

STATIONS OF THE CROSS, The (also called the Way of the Cross). i. A devotion in honour of the passion of our Lord which consists in moving from one to another of 14 crosses and praying before each one (there are no set prayers) meditating upon the passion. It may be done alone, or in company with others, with a priest presiding. The custom originated with the Friars Minor in the 15th century.
ii. The 14 wooden crosses, or stations, canonically blessed and set up, are all that is required for this service, but they are now almost invariably accompanied by images, representing the events to be meditated on, namely: the condemnation of Jesus, he receives the cross and sets out for Calvary, he falls the first time, he meets his mother, Simon of Cyrene bears his cross, Veronica wipes his face, his second fall, he speaks to the women of Jerusalem, his third fall, he is stripped of his garments, is crucified, and dies, his body is taken down from the cross, and laid in the tomb. At times and in places these have varied both in number and subject. They are commonly found on the walls of all churches of the Latin rite and sometimes of the Eastern rites, and may be set up in cloisters, in the open air, and so on.
iii. The original stations at Jerusalem, from which the above practice derives, more

usually called the *Via Dolorosa*. Not all these 14 holy places, though pointed out, are historically and archæologically verifiable or supported by traditions of equal weight. The Friars Minor celebrate a feast of the Mysteries of the Way of the Cross on the 1st Friday in March, the Mass having a proper sequence.

STATISTICS. The numerical strength of the principal religions of the world is estimated as follows: Catholics, 425 million; Orthodox, 120 million (a mere guess, the Orthodox in U.S.S.R. being impossible to estimate; they were about 100 million before 1917); other non-Catholic Eastern Christians, 8 million; Anglicans (including daughter churches of the Church of England), 50 million (a very rough estimate); other Protestants, 141 million; Jews, 11 million; Mohammedans, 315 million; Hindus, 255 million; Buddhists, 150 million; Confucians, 300 million; Taoists, 50 million; Shintoists, 25 million; Animists, 121 million; other non-Christians, 387 million.

STAUROPEGION (Gr., setting-up of a cross). A monastery of the Byzantine rite directly subject to a patriarch. Eastern monasteries are usually under the jurisdiction of the metropolitan or bishop.

STAUROPHORE (Gr., cross-bearer). A monk of the Byzantine rite in the second grade, so called because he has a wooden cross as a badge; not all pass into this or into the third grade of *megaloschemos* (*q.v.*).

STERILITY. Incapacity to bear or to beget children but not involving incapacity for the marriage act, must be distinguished from impotence (*q.v.*). Sterility is not an impediment to marriage nor does it make the marriage act unlawful.

STERILIZATION. An operation rendering one incapable of producing offspring. It is licit when the purpose of the operation is to save the life or health of the patient. The comparative painlessness of the operation makes it useless as a deterrent from crime; as a punishment it is futile, since the only certain way of preventing the sterilized criminal from repeating his offence is to keep him in prison, where sterilization is unnecessary. Sterilization of the unfit must be condemned on the ground that it is an unjust violation of bodily integrity (see EUGENICS).

STICHARION. A Byzantine vestment corresponding to the Western alb, made of silk or linen. The priest's is white (often red in Lent and in Liturgies for the dead) with narrow sleeves; the deacon's has shorter and wider sleeves and is of the same colour and often the same material and decoration as the celebrating priest's *phelonion*. Deacons wear this garment without a girdle.

STIGMATA (Gr., marks). Wounds or scars, corresponding to those in the feet, hands, side and brow of the crucified Christ, imprinted in the flesh of a human being and accompanied by physical pain; they may be recurrent or permanent; sometimes there is the local suffering without visible marks. This phenomenon has been recorded of over 300 persons from the 13th century until today, of whom more than 95 per cent were women; about 50 of the cases are well attested, some of them explainable on natural grounds. With some few exceptions the best known *stigmatisés* were either friars, nuns or tertiaries of one or other of the mendicant orders. The first, most famous and one of the best substantiated cases of *stigmata* was that of St. Francis of Assisi and the happening is celebrated throughout the Western church by a feast of their Impression on Sept. 17; a similar feast is observed by the Dominicans in respect of the (invisible) *stigmata* of St. Catherine of Siena, on April 3. The fact of stigmatization has been demonstrated in many modern examples and no satisfactory natural explanation is forthcoming; the *stigmata* often bleed periodically, notably on Fridays, and in no recorded case do the wounds suppurate. It appears then that God singles out certain noble souls to be united more closely with the sufferings of his Son, souls who are willing in a peculiarly fitting way to expiate the sins of others.

STIGMATISÉ, -E. One marked with the stigmata (*q.v.*).

STIPEND, MASS. It is lawful for any priest celebrating and applying Mass to receive an offering or stipend, the amount to be determined by the local ordinary (*q.v.*) or legitimate custom. Masses for which stipends have been received must be applied for the intention of the donor under an obligation of justice and within a reasonable time, according to the rules laid down in canon law. All priests must keep a careful record of stipends received and intentions fulfilled. They may transmit stipends to other priests if no condition is made by the donor to the contrary. Masses for which stipends are received from endowments canonically established for this purpose are called foundation Masses; others are called manual Masses. Not more than one stipend may be received for the same Mass, or on one day (except Christmas Day) if two Masses are said. In the latter case, if one Mass has to be applied *ex justitia*, *e.g.*, Mass for the people, no stipend can be received for the other (*cf.*, Sale of Masses).

STIPES (Lat., a post). That part of an altar upon which the *mensa* is supported, which may be a solid mass, a central column, or several detached pillars. The *stipes* must be of natural stone and solidly cemented to the *mensa*.

STOCK. i. A small metal vessel in which the holy oils are kept; every church must have three, one for each oil.

ii. The piece of black (purple for prelates) material worn by clergy under the collar in the opening of the waistcoat.

STOLE (Gr., robe). A vestment consisting of a band of silk, whose colour varies with the other vestments or occasion, 4 ins. wide and 8 ft. long with the two ends splayed out, marked with a cross in the middle; the earlier form is longer and narrower, its edges parallel throughout. It is the distinctive garment of the deacon, conferred at ordination, and is worn over the left shoulder, the ends joined under the right arm; priests wear it round the neck, if over an alb the ends crossed at the girdle, otherwise hanging loose; bishops always have it uncrossed. It must be worn when the cleric exercises his order (celebrating or ministering Mass, administering a sacrament, etc.); the pope may wear it always and everywhere as a sign of his universal jurisdiction. A Carthusian nun wears a stole when singing the gospel at Matins. The origin of the stole is not certainly known: it may be descended from the official scarf (*lorum*) of the Roman magistrate; it now symbolizes hierarchical order and the immortality of which man is unworthy (*cf., Epitrachelion, Orarion*).

STOLE FEES. Offerings made to the clergy on the occasion of the administration of certain sacred rites, *e.g.*, baptisms, marriages, funerals. It is for the provincial council or meeting of bishops to fix the amount payable. The fees for parochial functions are due to the rector of the parish, even when performed by another priest. Stole fees are not to be exacted from poor persons. Stole fees and stipends are not a price paid for spiritual ministrations (if they were, to give or take them would be simony, *q.v.*); their payment is a special discharge, made upon an appropriate special occasion, of part of the layman's general duty of supporting his pastors, in accordance with the words of St. Paul, ". . . those who preside at the altar share the altar's offerings. And so it is that the Lord has bidden the heralds of the gospel live by preaching the gospel" (1 Cor. ix, 13-14).

STOLONE. The folded chasuble (*q.v*). in its strip form.

STONE OF DESTINY, The. Called in Irish *Lia Fail* and identified with the stone brought from Scone by King Edward I which is now enclosed in the coronation chair at Westminster Abbey. It purports to be the same stone upon which the patriarch Jacob at Bethel poured oil and drink offerings (Gen. xxxv, 14). Legend maintains that it was taken to Tara in Ireland, and thence was conveyed by the Scotti to northern Britain, where it was used in the primitive coronation rite of the early kings.

STONYHURST. A large school for boys conducted by the Jesuits, near Blackburn. Founded in 1592 by Fr. Robert Persons at Saint Omer; transferred to Bruges in 1762, Liége in 1773, and to Stonyhurst at the Revolution, in 1794. From it derive the schools at Beaumont, Mount St. Mary's and Clongowes Wood, and day schools in England and Scotland. An important astronomical observatory is attached.

STOUDION, The or Studium. A monastery at Constantinople founded by the consul Studius in 463 and one of the formative influences of Eastern monachism; its monks were known as Studites. It declined from the 11th century and was destroyed in 1453. In its own day it was apparently always known as "the monastery of Studius."

STOUP (Old Eng. *stéap*, a vessel for liquid). A receptacle for holy water, either fixed or portable, sometimes called a font. A stoup with water must be provided close to all doors of churches of the Latin rite.

STRIKE. The refusal of workmen to go on working in order to force an employer to accede to demands which he has refused. Such concerted action is lawful if the demands are just and reasonable; if peaceful methods of obtaining them have been tried and failed; if the advantage to be gained is commensurate with the damage inflicted by the means taken; if no violation of a just contract freely entered into is involved, and if the strikers have reasonable hope of substantial success.

STRIKING THE BREAST with the hand, an ancient sign of sorrow and penitence (*cf.,* Luke xviii, 13, xxiii, 48), survives as a liturgical gesture in the Latin rite; it is prescribed during the *Confiteor* (three times, at the words *mea culpa:* through my fault, etc.), and for the Mass celebrant three times at *Agnus Dei* and *Domine non sum dignus*, and once at *Nobis quoque peccatoribus.* In requiem Masses it is omitted at *Agnus Dei* because the prayer is altered to apply specifically to the dead. The gesture is in use also among some Catholic orientals.

STRIPPING THE ALTAR takes place after the Mass and Vespers of Maundy Thursday. The celebrant, in alb and purple stole and reciting Ps. xxi with an antiphon, removes from all altars the linens, frontal, etc., leaving them bare except for the cross and candlesticks; the door of the empty tabernacle is left open. Thus is signified the suspension of Mass and the stripping off of the garments of our Lord.

STUDITES, The. i. Monks of the Stoudion *(q.v.)*.

ii. A congregation of monks of the Slav-Byzantine rite founded in 1900 by Metropolitan Andrew Szepticky to revive traditional Eastern monasticism among the Ruthenians *(q.v.)*. They were engaged in public prayer, manual work and study. In 1939 they had a principal *laura* *(q.v.)* and 4 lesser monasteries, with 200 monks (20 heiromonks); there were also 3 houses of corresponding nuns, and the whole congregation was very flourishing. It was dispersed during world-war II, and their homeland, the Polish Ukraine, is now part of the U.S.S.R. *Cf.*, Basilians.

STYLITE (Gr. στῦλος, pillar). One who lived on top of a pillar. See PILLAR SAINT.

SUB-APOSTOLIC. Pertaining to the times between the death of the apostles and the death of those who had, or could have had, any personal relations with them: roughly from the years 75 to 150.

SUBCINCTORIUM or **SUCCINCTORIUM** (Lat., below the girdle). An ornament peculiar to the pope at solemn Mass, consisting of a piece of silk, the size of a large handkerchief, with an image of a lamb embroidered on one end and a cross on the other, worn pendent from the girdle on the right side. It is the Western version and survival of the *epigonation (q.v.)*.

SUBCONSCIOUSNESS. Term used of certain mental states which underlie the normal conscious state. The question has been raised whether there are any latent mental processes of the mind of which we are completely unconscious. That this must be so is evidenced (*a*) in order to account for memory, (*b*) by the reproduction in dreams and delirium of long-lost recollections, etc. Philosophically there seems no sufficient reason for denying the existence of certain processes of the soul which do not themselves rise into consciousness.

SUBDEACON. In the Western church the lowest of the major orders, a sacramental of ecclesiastical institution involving the obligation of perpetual celibacy and daily recitation of the Divine Office. The duties of the subdeacon are limited to ceremonies at high Mass (which in practice are usually performed by a priest), chiefly the singing of the epistle, bringing the vessels to the altar, holding the paten during the canon and giving the kiss of peace to the choir. The order is bestowed by delivery of a chalice and paten and book of the epistles, and he is vested with the maniple and tunicle, the vestments of the order. In the Eastern churches the subdiaconate is a minor order; but all dissidents have ceased to observe it except the Orthodox and Armenians. The Maronite and Malabarese are the only Liturgies in which he has a liturgical office; in all others the epistle is sung by a lector or a layman or by the deacon.

SUBIACO CONGREGATION, The. See CASSINESE, ii.

SUBJECT. i. In logic. That to which something is attributed.

ii. In metaphysics. That in which something is in any way whatsoever.

iii. In psychology. That which knows.

iv. In canon law. A person becomes the subject of the Church and of the common law by baptism; of particular law and local authorities by domicile or quasi-domicile *(q.v.)*, or by membership of a religious institute.

v. Of a sacrament. All may receive the sacraments who are not prohibited by law. Baptism is a necessity for the valid reception of all the others, and there must be actual sin committed after baptism before the sacrament of Penance can be received; men only can receive holy Orders. In the Western church those who are married cannot receive holy Orders (but see BACHELOR) and nowhere can those who have been ordained deacon or upwards receive Matrimony. Only human beings can validly receive a sacrament, and they must be living; nevertheless, as the exact moment at which the soul leaves the body is not known, it is held by some theologians that the last sacraments may be administered for some little time after apparent death. It is forbidden to administer them to those in heresy and schism, even those in good faith, unless they abjure their errors and are reconciled to the Church. Excommunicated persons cannot receive the sacraments, nor those under an interdict, according to the terms of the interdict.

SUBJECTIVE. Relative to the subject thinking, within the subject; opposed to objective.

SUBJECTIVISM. The philosophy which reduces every object of knowledge to the subject knowing, in such wise that the latter knows only himself, and projects out the object of his sensations and ideas (*cf.*, Phenomenalism).

SUBLIME, The. The sublime is the beautiful in its highest reach; not to be confounded with the grandiose or the colossal. It is the beautiful as exceeding thought and imagination; nature abounds in sublime things, but the most sublime things are certain most elevated thoughts and desires that come from the heart of man.

SUBORDINATIONISM. Any form of doctrine, *e.g.*, Arianism *(q.v.)*, which teaches that the Son is subordinate to the Father, or the Holy Ghost subordinate to either or both. The true doctrine is that the three Persons of the Blessed Trinity are equal, consubstantial, one God.

SUBPRIOR, -ESS. The assistant to the prior or prioress of a monastery, the second superior if it is a priory, third if an abbey. He is appointed by the abbot or prior and is removable from office at will.

SUBREPTION (Lat. *subreptio,* stealing). A canon law term for the obtaining or attempting to obtain a papal rescript or dispensation (*q.v.*) by a statement in which some part of the truth is suppressed or misrepresented.

SUBSTANCE. (*a*) That which exists *per se:* this is the essential notion and as such can be predicated of God. (*b*) That which exists *per se* and serves as a subject in which accidents inhere (created substances). The notion of substance is fundamental and primitive. We know it through accidents; there must ultimately be a subject which does not inhere in another but exists *per se.* By reason of its perfection a substance is complete or incomplete. Examples of the first are God and angels; of the second, the human soul and animal souls, but the latter are incomplete as regards substantiality, whereas the human soul is incomplete as regards species. From the point of view of unity, substance is simple or composite; examples of the first are God, angel, human soul; of the second, man, animal, plant.

SUBTLETY. One of the four qualities attributed to the risen body by scholastic theologians. It is the coming of the body into complete subjection to the soul and is taking on of a spiritual character without, however, ceasing to be a true body: a perfecting, not a deprivation, of bodily nature, the "spiritual body" of 1 Cor. xv, 44.

SUBUNISTS. Those Catholics of Bohemia who adhered to the practice of communion *sub una* (*specie*), under one kind, as against the Hussites and the orthodox Utraquists (*qq.v.*).

SUBURBICARIAN DIOCESES (Lat., *suburbicarius,* adjoining the city [of Rome]). The 7 cardinal sees (*q.v.*) occupied by the cardinal-bishops.

SUCCENTOR (Lat. *canere,* to sing, one who sings after). i. The assistant to a precentor or chief cantor; now obsolete, except as a title of honour in some cathedral chapters.
    ii. Another name for the *synagoga* (*q.v.*).

SUCCESSION. A series of things or events following one upon the other. The Positivists (*q.v.*) tried to show that it cannot be argued that one thing is the cause of another in the sense that one thing comes from or is produced by another; all that we perceive is one thing following upon another. Against this view it is urged that succession is all that can be perceived by the senses, but that the mind perceives that a thing can and does in many circumstances come from another. Suc-

cession is of the essence of time, but it is excluded from eternity (*qq.v.*).

SUCCURSAL (Lat. *succursus,* assistant). i. A chapel of ease (*q.v.*).
    ii. A French parish of which the priest is removable at the will of the bishop.

SUDARIUM (Lat. a napkin for wiping off sweat). i. The shroud of Christ (*cf.,* Victimæ Paschali, strophe 6).
    ii. The Veronica (*q.v.*).
    iii. A veil of silk attached to the upper part of the staff of a bishop's or abbot's crosier, for the purpose of keeping the hand dry. It is now rarely used in the West, but is still seen in Eastern rites. A similar veil is often fastened to the processional cross and *ripidia,* e.g., in the Byzantine and Armenian rites, and to the episcopal hand-cross (Syriac and Armenian rites). It is also called *fanon* (*cf.,* the maniple, which has been called by the same names).

SUDDISTS. See NORDDISTS.

SUFFICIENT REASON, PRINCIPLE OF. This metaphysical principle is formulated thus: "Nothing real can be as it is without a sufficient reason why it is so," or as applied to mental processes: "No judgement can be true without a sufficient reason for its truth."

SUFFRAGAN BISHOP (Lat. *suffragari,* to support). A diocesan bishop who is subject to an archbishop as metropolitan; normally every bishop's see is suffragan to a metropolitan but some are immediately subject to the Holy See. This must not be confused with the Anglican use of the word to mean an auxiliary bishop (*q.v.*); only the auxiliary of a suburbicarian see (*e.g.,* Sabina) is called suffragan in this sense, and such are governed by special legislation.

SUFFRAGE (Lat. *suffragium,* a recommendation). i. An intercessory prayer. An act done by way of suffrage (*per modum suffragii*) depends for its efficacy on God's response to the prayer which accompanies it, *e.g.,* the granting of a plenary indulgence (*q.v.*) in favour of the souls in Purgatory over whom the Church has no jurisdiction.
    ii. Of the Saints. The name given to the prayer *A cunctis* from the Missal, for the good estate of the Church, invoking the intercession of our Lady, St. Joseph, SS. Peter and Paul and the titular of the church (in England, St. George and in Wales, St. David is substituted), to which religious may add the name of their founder. The prayer was formerly added to some hours of the Divine Office on certain days. There is a feast of our Lady *de Suffragio* kept in some places: here the word simply means "of Help."

SUICIDE. The killing of one's self, death being the willed object or the inevitable and immediate result of a given action. If the doer was *felo de se, i.e.,* had reached the age of reason and was sane and otherwise responsible for his action, it is a mortal sin against the fifth commandment; suicide is an infringement of God's dominion over human life and is contrary to the nature of man. It is not unlawful but laudable to do something that may or will cause death, when a certain and great good will follow and death is not intended, *e.g.,* going into a burning building to save life, nursing the infectious sick. Suicide may be committed by deliberate neglect to take reasonable care of one's self, but one is not bound to take extraordinary care, *e.g.,* by undergoing a ruinously expensive or exceedingly painful surgical operation. A *felo de se* may not be given Christian burial unless he has given some sign of repentance before dying; in Great Britain the clergy usually accept the verdict of the coroner's jury as to sanity or otherwise without question, but a priest is not bound to do so if he has certain knowledge to the contrary.

SUISSE (Fr. Swiss). i. A member of the pope's Swiss Guard (*q.v.*).
　　ii. The beadle in a French church. He wears a uniform with a cocked hat and carries a halberd; both his dress and name have reference to a treaty of Louis XI in 1474 whereby the French kings could levy troops in Switzerland, which was in fact often done by succeeding kings. He represents an extinct royal authority.

SULPICIANS, The. A society of secular priests founded by the Abbé Olier in 1642 to undertake the direction of seminaries, named from their headquarters, the seminary of St. Sulpice in Paris (now at Issy). They have members in France, Canada and the United States.

SUMMA (Lat., a compendium, a whole). A name commonly given to textbooks of theology and philosophy in the middle ages, *cf.,* "The Sentences." "The Summa," without qualification, always means the "Summa Theologica" of St. Thomas Aquinas.

SUMMA CONTRA GENTILES. A complete theological treatise on God and his creatures written by St. Thomas Aquinas. It is sometimes most erroneously called the "Summa Philosophica." At the beginning of the second book, St. Thomas speaks precisely of the difference of method between philosophy and theology and asserts that his method of procedure in this book is that of the theologian.

SUMMA THEOLOGICA. The chief theological work of St. Thomas Aquinas (*q.v.*), the fruit of his mature theological speculations, unfortunately left unfinished. Therein, more than in his "Commentaries" or elsewhere, the personal and definitive doctrines of the

Master are to be found. His admirable teaching method is here to be seen in its perfection. He divides each treatise into a number of *Questions* beginning with those whose solution helps to the solution of those that succeed. Each question he divides into *Articles,* brought into their narrowest limits, always most precise and distributed always in the same fashion thus: each article has three parts: (*a*) objections; (*b*) the body of the article or the solution of the matter; (*c*) replies to the objections. For the doctrine of St. Thomas, see THOMISM.

SUNDAY (Lat. *Dominica,* The Lord's Day). The observance of the first day of the week as one consecrated in a special way to Christion worship has no intrinsic connexion with the Jewish Sabbath, the observance of which was abrogated by the New Law of Christ. It is an ecclesiastical institution, due to the Apostles themselves. The Church's law now involves the obligation of assisting at Mass (*q.v.*) and of resting from servile work (*q.v.*) on this day; over and above this the day should be kept holy by attending other church services, spiritual reading, etc. Games and recreation are a natural relaxation on this day of rest and only cease to be commendable when they interfere with divine worship and time which should be given directly to God. Nevertheless it is a mistake to suppose that the so-called "continental Sunday" is more in accordance with the mind of the Church than the so-called "English Sunday." Pope Pius XI on one occasion gave high praise to the tradition of Sunday observance as kept in England, and recommended it to his Italian audience. Sunday is a weekly commemoration of the Resurrection and is in a special manner dedicated to the Blessed Trinity (*cf.,* the preface of the Sunday Mass outside Lent and paschal time); it is never a fast day. Liturgically, Sundays are thus divided: greater of the first class, namely, those of Advent and Lent, Easter, Low and Whit Sundays, which are never displaced; greater of the second class (Septuagesima, Sexagesima and Quinquagesima), whose offices are displaced only by feasts that are doubles of the 1st class; ordinary Sundays which, though of only double rank, take precedence over all feasts except doubles of the 1st and 2nd class.

SUNG MASS (Lat. *Missa cantata*). The name usually given in English to that way of celebrating Mass that lies ceremonially between high and low Mass, approximating to the first, from which it differs in the following chief points: there is no deacon or subdeacon, so that the celebrant, in addition to his own part, sings that of the deacon and also recites the epistle if no cleric be present to do so; he is ministered to by one or more servers as at low Mass; incense is not used except by permission of the bishop.

The celebrant is forbidden merely to say any part that should be sung (*e.g.*, collects, preface) except the epistle, and the choir or people are forbidden to omit any part of the common or proper. Sung Mass is the normal way of celebrating the parochial Mass in a parish church.

SUPER OBLATA, POPULUM. See ORATIO.

SUPERIOR. i. Any one having authority over others by virtue of his ecclesiastical rank either in the Church or in some unit thereof, *e.g.*, a seminary or monastery.

ii. In religious institutes (other than those of monks, canons regular and some congregations of nuns, who are organized on a basis of independent houses) superiors are local, provincial and general. In the older orders they are called variously (guardian, prior provincial, master general, etc.), but in the more recent congregations (especially of nuns) the word is used as a title, *e.g.*, mother superior, superior general, and in these the appointments are usually for a term of years and not for life. In Ireland many superioresses of nuns, *e.g.*, Carmelite prioresses, are known as "Mrs. A. . . . B. . . .," a survival of the "Mistress" of earlier days."

SUPERNATURAL. That which is superadded to nature; it is therefore that which neither constitutes an essence nor is necessarily consequent upon it, nor is it that which an essence has need of lest its being and activity be frustrated, but it is a special participation of the Divine Goodness itself. It is opposed to Natural, which is whatever constitutes an essence, or flows from it, or is due to it for its activity; and to Preternatural, which neither constitutes an essence, nor necessarily follows upon it, nor of which the essence has need for its being and activity, but which does not go beyond the order of the whole of nature.

SUPERNATURAL GIFT. In general, a gift which is above and beyond the powers and exigencies or capacities of a nature. It may be (*a*) relatively supernatural, and then it is more properly called preternatural (*q.v.*); or (*b*) absolutely, or simply, supernatural, and then it is a gift which is above all created nature and which therefore involves special participation in a divine good, which belongs naturally and properly only to a divine person. Such is habitual grace (*q.v.*).

SUPERNATURAL ORDER. Order means the apt disposing of means to an end. The supernatural order is the state in which man elevated by sanctifying grace and the accompanying virtues and gifts of the Holy Ghost (*qq.v.*) exercises his faculties under the influence of actual grace for the attainment of his last end, which is the face-to-face vision of God and the corresponding love of God. His progress is directed by the natural law and the divine positive law.

SUPERNATURAL THEOLOGY. The science which treats of God under the guidance of revelation (*q.v.*).

SUPERSTITION (Lat. *superstare*, to stand above, *i.e.*, an excess). The generic term for any act or practice which gives false or superfluous worship to God or undue honours to creatures, from idolatry (*q.v.*) to those common practices named under vain observance (*q.v.*); superstition is a sin against the virtue of religion (*q.v.*), grave unless the dishonour shown to God is slight.

SUPERSUBSTANTIAL BREAD. Found in some English versions of the Lord's Prayer for the words usually translated "daily bread." The Greek word (ἐπιούσιον) is untranslatable: the Vulgate has *supersubstantialem* in Matt. vi, 11, and *quotidianum* in Luke xi, 3 (*cf.*, these in the "Douay" Bible); "for immediate need" seems to be the sense of it.

SUPPEDANEUM (Lat., a footstool). i. The platform of an altar, *predella*.

ii. The projection on a crucifix which supports the feet; it is doubtful if the cross of Christ had such a thing.

SUPPLICES. The first word of the third prayer after the consecration at Mass. It is probably the remnant of a former *epiklesis* (*q.v.*) at this point. Some modern theologians (*e.g.*, Père de la Taille) maintain that it is a true *epiklesis* even in its present form.

SUPPLIED CEREMONIES. In some cases unessential ceremonies that have been omitted from a rite on account of urgency or for other reason may and should be supplied later when it is possible; *e.g.*, if a priest baptize at home a child in danger of death, the ceremonies then omitted are supplied in the church if and when the child recovers.

SUPPORT OF PASTORS. The fifth commandment of the Church (*q.v.*) is that we should contribute towards the support of our pastors, who are put in charge of parishes for our benefit and have a right in justice to a decent maintenance from us. The degree of responsibility depends in every case on the needs of the priest and the means of the parishioner; the manner of its discharge varies in different places, but one's obligation is not necessarily limited by stole fees, an occasional Mass stipend and the Sunday collection.

SUPPOSIT. A non-rational substance *per se* subsistent, the master of its activities, and incommunicable; in rational and intellectual natures it is called person (*q.v.*).

SUPPRESSION, The, in reference to religious orders, refers to the dissolution (*q.v.*) of the monasteries in England by King Henry VIII.

SUPRA QUÆ. The first words of the second prayer after the consecration at Mass, wherein the celebrant prays that the sacrifice be accepted by God on account of the devotion of those that offer it, just as he accepted the sacrifices of the past, naming Abel, Abraham and Melchisedech.

SUPREMACY, ACT OF. i. 26 Henry VIII c. 1 (1534). The Act by which the king and his successors were declared to be "the only supreme head on earth of the Church of England, called *Anglicana Ecclesia* . . . and shall have . . . all honours, dignities . . . jurisdiction . . . to the said dignity belonging . . . and shall have full power . . . to visit, repress, redress . . . all such errors, heresies . . . which by any manner of spiritual authority or jurisdiction ought to or may lawfully be reformed," etc. It was prescribed that an oath should be taken affirming this royal supremacy. SS. Thomas More, Cardinal Fisher and the Carthusian martyrs were the first to die for refusing so to swear. Queen Mary I used the royal supremacy for silencing preachers, removing and restoring bishops, and generally for undoing the work of her brother's reign, until a parliament could be summoned to repeal the act of Henry VIII and to agree to reconciliation with the Holy See.
ii. 1 Eliz. c. 1 (1559). "An act restoring to the Crown the ancient jurisdiction over the State ecclesiastical and spiritual and abolishing all foreign power repugnant to the same," gave all the above powers to the queen as "only supreme governor of this realm as well in all spiritual and ecclesiastical things or causes as temporal," provided a formula for the oath, imposing it on all ecclesiastics and on laymen doing homage; refusal involved the penalties of high treason by 5 Eliz. c. 1.

SUPREMACY, PAPAL. See POPE, PRIMACY OF.

SURPLICE (Lat. *superpellicium*, over the fur coat [its original use]). A loose white linen garment with wide sleeves. It is the choir and processional dress of the secular clergy over the cassock and is worn when administering the sacraments and on other occasions when the alb is not prescribed; it is the distinctive garment of minor clerics and its use is extended to laymen acting as acolytes, etc. It has two forms: the older is very full, with wide long sleeves, and reaching to the knees; the modern, generally called a *cotta*, reaches not much beyond the hips, has short sleeves and is bordered with lace or crochet work.

SUSCIPE. The first word of the prayer with which the celebrant offers up the bread at Mass: "Receive . . . this spotless host. . . ."

SUSPECT OF HERESY. i. Those who in any way knowingly and wilfully help to propagate heresy, or who hold *communicatio in sacris* (*q.v.*) with heretics. Suspects after fruitless admonition are to be punished, and if after a further six months there is no amendment they are to be counted heretics and incur all penalties for heresy.
ii. A proposition or work condemned in these terms (*suspecta de hæresi* or *sapiens hæresim*, "savouring of heresy") is one which is orthodox in expression but which on account of the known opinions of its author or the circumstances of its publication or for similar reasons is judged to be intended to convey an heretical meaning.

SUSPENSION. An ecclesiastical censure (*q.v.*) by which a cleric is forbidden the exercise of his office, orders or jurisdiction or/and the enjoyment of his benefice.

SUSPICION. St. Thomas distinguishes three degrees of suspicion: when one begins to question another's goodness on slight grounds, usually a venial fault; when one thinks on slight grounds that another is certainly wicked, and this is mortal sin in a case of grave matter; and when one condemns another outright merely on suspicion, and this is a mortal sin against justice. "If we cannot avoid suspicion, because we are men, we should at least avoid judgements, that is, definite and positive opinions" (St. Augustine).

SWALLOWS OF GOD. A colloquial name in the east for the Sisters of Charity of St. Vincent (*cf.*, their headdress).

SWEARING. See CURSING; PROFANITY.

SWEDEN, THE CHURCH IN. The Catholic faith was proscribed in Sweden from 1591 until 1780; three years later a mission was established, but not till 1860 could a person abjure the state religion (Lutheranism) without losing civil rights. There are still a few disabilities. The country forms one diocese, with 20,000 Catholics, two-thirds of whom are Poles and other displaced persons.

SWEDENBORGIANISM. A religious system taking its name from Emanuel Swedenborg (1688-1772) and organized as a sect by Richard Hindmarsh in 1787, called the Church of the New Jerusalem. Swedenborg claimed a personal and final revelation through a new interpretation of the Bible: God is identified with love and wisdom and life, which only exists in and from him; Father, Son and Holy Ghost are not persons but manifestations and this trinity was incarnate in Jesus Christ; man was redeemed by the example of Christ; activity is exalted and contemplation decried; there is no resurrection of the body but the dead become angels in Heaven or Hell; there is exact correspondence between the physical and spiritual worlds. The sect is small, most of its members being in England and the U.S.A.

SWISS AMERICAN CONGREGATION, The. One of the 2 American Benedictine congregations (*q.v.* iv). It had its origin in the monastery of St. Meinrad (*q.v.*) in Indiana, founded from Switzerland in 1854. St. Meinrad's became an abbey in 1870, and the new congregation was formed in 1881. It now consists of the mother house, the abbeys of Conception, Mo., New Subiaco, Ark., St. Joseph, Covington, La., and St. Benedict, Mount Angel, Ore. The monks have charge of a number of parishes and Indian missions and conduct several schools and colleges.

SWISS GUARD, The. The corps of papal guards responsible for the custody of the outer doors and gates of the Vatican Palace and City and of the personal apartments of the pope, whom also they attend at all functions. It was established in 1505 and has a strength of 104 men and 6 officers, all of whom must be Swiss, Catholics and eligible for the army of their own country. The Swiss have two uniforms, one for undress and night duty, of blue tunic and breeches and black *béret;* the other, for parade, was designed by Michelangelo and consists of tunic, breeches and stockings of wide yellow, blue and red stripes, with white ruff and steel morion, to which a steel breastplate is added on state occasions. They are armed with halberds and swords.

SWITHIN'S DAY, ST. St. Swithin was a bishop of Winchester, who died in the year 862. July 15 was the date of the translation of his relics to a new shrine in Winchester cathedral in 1093. The origin of the popular weather superstition connected with that date is unknown.

SWITZERLAND, THE CHURCH IN. The population of the republic is 4¼ million, of whom 41 per cent are Catholics, predominating in the cantons of Fribourg, Lucerne, Ticino, Valais, and Unterwalden. In these no distinctions between religions are made, but in some cantons the Protestant faith is established and supported by the state; other cantons have other arrangements. According to federal law the Society of Jesus is forbidden in the country, and establishment of new monasteries and convents is prohibited. There are no metropolitan sees; the ecclesiastical division of the country is into 5 dioceses, all i.s.h.s., and 2 abbeys-*nullius*, one Benedictine and the other of Augustinian canons.

SYDNEY (*Sydneyensis*). The senior metropolitan see of the Church in Australia. In 1834 the whole continent formed the vicariate apostolic of New Holland; in 1842 3 dioceses were erected, with their seats at Sydney, Adelaide and Hobart, and in the following year the first named was made an archbishopric. Its suffragan dioceses are Armidale, Bathurst, Goulburn, Lismore, Wagga-Wagga, and Wilcannia-Forbes. The first bishop and archbishop of Sydney was Dome Bede Polding, O.S.B.; the third archbishop, Patrick Moran, was the first Australian cardinal.

SYLLABUS, The. i. Without qualification, refers to the schedule of errors attached to the encyclical *Quanta cura* of Pope Pius IX in 1864. It consists of 80 propositions condemned by that pope from time to time, with a reference to the instrument or occasion of the condemnation. They are divided into 10 sections dealing with: Pantheism, Naturalism and Absolute Rationalism; Moderate Rationalism; Indifferentism, Latitudinarianism; Socialism, Bible Societies, etc.; errors about the Church and her rights; errors about the State and its relation to the Church; errors about ethics; errors about Christian marriage; errors about the pope's temporal power; and errors in connexion with Liberalism. Each proposition is condemned as an universal negative; *e.g.,* "An unjust action, being successful, is not to the detriment of the sanctity of right" (no 61). In every case the proposition is condemned only in the sense intended by those who maintained its truth; not necessarily, therefore, in the sense attached to it by a person reading the syllabus. Every Catholic must give exterior and interior assent to this syllabus; but it is not certain that every proposition is condemned infallibly and therefore irreformably.

ii. Of Pope Pius X. See LAMENTABILI.

SYLLOGISM. A species of reasoning by which from the fact that something particular is seen to be comprehended under something more universal it is concluded that the predicate of the more universal agrees or does not agree with the particular. Thus:

> Every animal is sensitive;
> But man is an animal;
> Therefore man is sensitive.

The principles upon which the syllogism is founded are, "Said of all" and "Said of none."

SYLVESTRINES, The. An independent branch of the Benedictines (*q.v.*) founded by St. Sylvester Gozzolini in 1231; they follow the Rule of St. Benedict (*q.v.*) strictly, with particular stress on poverty, and have perpetual abstinence. The order is small, with 8 monasteries in Italy and missions in Ceylon and the United States. They wear the ordinary Benedictine habit but dark blue in colour.

SYMBOL (Gr. σύμβολον, token, watchword. A sign by which something is known. i. Rufinus in the 4th century, speaking of the Apostles' Creed as a joint work of the apostles, says "they for many just reasons decided that this rule of faith should be called the *Symbol*"; he took the Greek word to mean both a password by which Christians might recognize each other, and an offering made up of separate contributions. This Symbol of the Trinity is recognized by St. Firmilian (d. c. 269) as an integral part of the rite of Baptism. The Nicene creed is sometimes referred to as *Symbolum maius* and the Apostles' as *Symbolum minor*.

ii. In art. Since the 4th century direct representation has almost entirely taken the place of the symbolic representation of Christian persons and mysteries. But a few symbols are still in common use: *e.g.*, the cross for Christ and his faith in general, the dove for the Holy Spirit, the triangle for the Holy Trinity, the keys for St. Peter and the Holy See, and the symbols of the four evangelists, namely, a winged man for Matthew, a winged lion for Mark, a winged ox for Luke and an eagle for John. These last are an accommodation of the visions of Ezechiel (i, 5-10) and John (Apoc. iv, 7); they are also referred to the characteristics of the gospels, emphasizing the historical importance of the life of Christ, his kingly dignity, his sacrificial character and his divinity respectively.

SYMBOLISM. Giving to outward things or actions a more or less hidden meaning, particularly to express religious ideas. Religious worship in the Old Testament is full of symbolism and the Church claims no monopoly of what is in a greater or less degree essential to every kind of external worship; *e.g.*, the outward signs of the sacraments, washings, lights, incense, vestments, rites.

SYNAGOGA. i. The church of the Old Law as opposed to *Ecclesia*, the church of the New; a synagogue.

ii. The deacon who sings the spoken words (other than those of Christ) at the solemn singing of the passion during Holy Week; the words of the crowd are sometimes sung by a choir.

SYNAGOGUE (Gr. συναγωγή, assembly). i. A building in which the Jews meet together for public worship. There was only one temple of sacrifice, at Jerusalem, but at least ever since the captivity in Babylon there have been synagogues wherever there are Jews. It is a rectangular building; the Books of the Law (*Sepher Torah*) are contained in a curtained "ark" (*Aron*) raised up at the east end and in the middle is a platform (*Al Memar*) with a lectern; women are accommodated separately in galleries. The service consists of "blessings of God," prayers, readings from the Law and the Prophets, and exposition of the Scriptures.

ii. The Synagogue. The doctrine and system of Judaism, and those who profess it.

SYNAPTE (Gr., joined). In the Byzantine rite a litany consisting of a series of calls to prayer for various objects recited by the deacon, each one ending with "Let us pray to the Lord," the people replying "Lord, have mercy." The Great Synapte (or the *Eirenika*, prayers for peace) occurs at *Hesperinos, Orthros* and at the beginning of the Liturgy, followed by the Little Synapte, a prayer for protection, and by a commemoration of the Mother of God.

SYNAXARION (Gr., collection). i. In the Byzantine rite, a brief account of a saint or feast printed in the *Menaion* to be read during *Orthros* after the sixth ode of the canon on the corresponding feast. The Greek editions add a sort of daily martyrology.

ii. A collection of readings from the Bible, lives of the saints, etc.

SYNAXIS (Gr., assembly). i. Any gathering together for divine worship, but particularly that of the earliest Christians, whether for the Eucharist or for the prayers, praises and readings from which has developed the Divine Office, or both together.

ii. A feast in the Byzantine rite on which the people meet together (formerly in a given church cf., stations) to honour those saints connected with the mystery celebrated on the previous day; *e.g.*, the Synaxis of St. Joachim and Anne (Sept. 9), of the all holy Mother of God (Dec. 26), of all the Holy Apostles (June 30).

iii. The council of seniors who assist the abbot in a Byzantine monastery.

SYNDERESIS (Gr. συντήρησις, careful guarding or watching). The habitual knowledge possessed by man of the first general principles of moral action (*e.g.*, "Do good," "Avoid evil") applicable at the bidding of conscience (*q.v.*) to particular cases.

SYNDIC APOSTOLIC (Gr. σύνδικος, advocate). A lay official who, as delegate and representative of the Holy See, administers property on behalf of the Friars Minor and Capuchins. The rule of St. Francis requires that his followers shall hold no property, even in common; but the absolute necessities of a great organization and the changed requirements of later social conditions and legal systems caused the Holy See to constitute itself owner in trust of any property that accrues to these friars by gift, bequest or otherwise; every friary has a syndic who is in charge of and administers such goods. The syndic is a layman who is appointed by the minister general or provincial, and he with his family enjoys the privilege of affiliation to the Franciscan order.

SYNKELLOS (Gr. σύν, with; κέλλιον, cell). A former official in both Western and Eastern churches whose business it was continually to accompany a bishop by day and night as a witness to his behaviour. The title is still often given to the secretary of a Byzantine bishop, and among the Melkites and Syrians to any titular bishop.

SYNOD (Gr. σύνοδος, a meeting). An ecclesiastical council. Œcumenical, plenary, national, provincial and diocesan councils (*qq.v.*) are equally called synods, but the name is now frequently reserved for the last of these, which is not properly a council.

SYNOD, HOLY. The governing council of each autocephalous Orthodox Church, its members usually selected from among the bishops in turn or consisting of all of them under the presidency of the patriarch or other primate. They are charged with the conservation of the faith and discipline of their churches, maintaining unity with other Orthodox churches, and in general have administrative and executive powers in all spiritual and temporal matters affecting their church. They are relatively a recent institution and have much reduced the power of their patriarchs as well as laid themselves open to the control of civil authorities. The Holy Directing Synod of Russia, established by the emperor Peter the Great, in 1721, as an instrument for controlling the church and in full force up till 1917, was the prototype of these institutions.

SYNOD OF THE OAK, The. i. The conference between St. Augustine of Canterbury and the native Celtic bishops of Britain held, some say on College Green at Bristol, others at Malmesbury, or elsewhere, about 600. It was a fruitless attempt to settle the Easter Controversy (*q.v.*) and the misunderstanding and mistrust between the British and English Christians lasted for long afterwards.

ii. A synod held near Chalcedon in 403 at which St. John Chrysostom was illegally deposed from the see of Constantinople by Theophilus of Alexandria.

SYNODAL EXAMINERS. From four to twelve clerics approved in diocesan synod appointed by the bishop to examine the fitness of candidates for parochial benefices and of individual priests for the cure of souls generally.

SYNODAL JUDGES. From four to twelve clerics who are competent canonists approved in diocesan synod and appointed by the bishop to act as judges in ecclesiastical causes.

SYNOPTIC PROBLEM, The. The problem of the literary interdependence of the Gospels of SS. Matthew, Mark and Luke. The Biblical Commission (*q.v.*) in 1911 declared that St. Matthew himself wrote the First Gospel, that his gospel preceded the others, that it was written before the destruction of Jerusalem and before St. Paul's arrival in Rome, that it was written in his native tongue but that the Greek translation which we possess is substantially identical, that it does not modify the words and acts of Christ under the influence of Old Testament texts or later ecclesiastical speculation, and that Matthew was followed first by Mark and then

by Luke, which both preceded the destruction of Jerusalem. All this applies to the original Aramaic text of Matthew, for it may be held that the present Greek translation followed the composition of the other two gospels. This decree proscribes the theory, current outside the Church, that Mark was written first, that the First Gospel was an originally Greek production not written by Matthew, etc.

SYNOPTICS, The (Gr. σύνοψις, general view). The Gospels of SS. Matthew, Mark and Luke, so called because their authors, the Synoptists, look at the life of our Lord and their business of writing it down in much the same sort of way and give a general view of his life and teaching.

SYNTHESIS. A building up, a combination of ideas or parts into a whole; a method of procedure from parts to the whole, from causes to effects, from principles to conclusions, etc. The opposite of analysis which corresponds to induction whereas synthesis corresponds to deduction; analysis is principally a method of discovery; synthesis a method of teaching.

SYON ABBEY. The monastery of the Holy Saviour, Our Lady and St. Bridget of Syon, a house of Bridgettine nuns at South Brent in Devonshire. It is the only religious community in Great Britain having an unbroken organic identity with a pre-Reformation community. It was founded in 1415 by King Henry V at Isleworth in Middlesex, as a double monastery (*q.v.*). The nuns were expelled in 1539 and went abroad, eventually settling at Lisbon. They returned to England in 1861. The community still prays especially for its founder and his family and all the faithful departed, in accordance with the terms of its original charter.

SYRIA, THE CHURCH IN. The population of Syria and the Lebanon is nearly 4 million, of whom Mohammedans (with 54,-000 Druzes) make up three-quarters. The Orthodox patriarchate of Antioch has a $\frac{1}{4}$ million faithful; the principal other dissident Christians, about 100,000, are the Syrian Jacobites and Armenians, each with a patriarch. The 500,000 Catholics are of various Eastern rites, chiefly, in numerical order of importance, Maronites, Melkites, Syrians and Armenians (*qq.v*). The Melkites have one patriarchal see, of Antioch, and 10 others; the Syrians, 5 sees (1 patriarchal), the Maronites, 9 sees (1 patriarchal), and the Armenians their patriarchal see of Cilicia and 1 other. The few Catholics of Latin rite have had a vicariate apostolic, centered at Aleppo, since 1762. For centuries the Catholics of Syria have been under the protection of France, and the Society of Jesus has done a great work, especially through its university at Bairut. There has been an apostolic delegate in Syria since 1762, the oldest of such delegations.

SYRIAC. The chief form of the Aramaic (*q.v.*) language, now no longer spoken except in a corrupt form in a few villages of Syria and more generally in Mesopotamia and Kurdistan. It is the liturgical language of the Syrian, Maronite, Chaldean and Malabar rites, which are in consequence sometimes lumped together as the Syriac rites; the first two and last two are essentially the same, though they differ considerably.

SYRIAN CHURCH, EAST. i. The Chaldean Catholics (*q.v.*). ii. The Nestorian Church (*q.v.*).

SYRIAN JACOBITE CHURCH, The, is the common name for the native monophysite Christians of Syria and Mesopotamia (to whom since 1653 must be added an independent branch in Malabar), from Jacob al-Baradai who organized them in the 6th century; they call themselves simply *Suriân*, Syrians. Up to the 12th century they were numerous and flourishing; now they number only some 80,000, governed by their patriarch (of Antioch), who lives at Homs, and a few bishops; the secular clergy receive only a little training, but the laity are very faithful. They use the (West) Syrian rite (*q.v.*), a good deal of it in Arabic; their orders and sacraments are valid. In addition to a more or less nominal adherence to Monophysism (*q.v.*) they admit only the first three œcumenical councils, claim that the *epiklesis* (*q.v.*) in the Liturgy consecrates, and have confused ideas about Purgatory, which they deny, while praying for the dead and yet teaching that Heaven is closed (even to saints?), until the last Judgement. The patriarch's authority over the Jacobite Christisms of Malabar (*q.v. c*) is slight and variable. The Jacobites are in communion with the dissident Copts.

SYRIAN RITE, EAST. The Chaldean rite (*q.v.*).

SYRIAN RITE, The (West), is the system, and forms of worship and administration of the sacraments used by the Catholic Syrians and Malankarese (*q.v.*) and by the Jacobites of Syria and Malabar. The Liturgy, substantially that of Antioch in the 4th century, is called "of St. James," with a number of alternative *anaphoras*; its language is Syriac but both Catholics and Jacobites say parts in Arabic; the epistle is sung by the deacon, the gospel by the priest; the words of consecration are sung aloud; the great intercession is long and in an imposing form, reminiscent of a litany, though there are now no proper litanies in this rite; communion for all is in both kinds according to a rather complicated rite of fraction and commixture. Catholics have added *Filioque* to the creed. The Divine Office has seven hours, of which part is sung in the evening and the rest before the Liturgy; it consists chiefly of hymns and prayers; the psalms are few. Baptism is by immersion with infusion, followed by Confirmation and (among the dissidents) communion under the species of wine. Catholic Syrian churches have confessionals; Jacobites rarely go to confession: when they do they kneel before the priest at the church door. The strict fasts are observed very conscientiously. Extreme Unction is administered to Catholics with the Western form in Syriac. The altar is usually in full view but sometimes has an open screen, there are pictures but no statues. The vestments are much the same as the Byzantine, with a *phelonion* like a cope; bishops wear at all times a small hood, to which the Catholics add the Western mitre. They have also adopted several Western feasts and practices of devotion, *e.g.*, Corpus Christi, Benediction, the rosary. Counting the Malabar Jacobites, 20% of the users of this rite are Catholics; but in Syria and Iraq they are about 39%.

SYRIAN RITE, CATHOLICS OF THE. Catholics of Syria and Mesopotamia who use the Western Syrian rite and are subject to their own canon law; they were not properly organized till 1783. They number 50,000, governed by their patriarch of Antioch at Bairut, with six archbishops and bishops; there are small congregations in Australia, U.S.A., and elsewhere. Their secular clergy are chiefly trained at the seminary at Sharfeh in the Lebanon by the Cassinese Benedictines. Celibacy has been obligatory on them since 1888 but the obligation is dispensable and some priests are married. Monks of this rite are being formed by the Benedictines. The Syrians and Maronites represent the native Catholics of Syria and Palestine before they adopted the Byzantine rite and became hellenized; the Melkites, after that happening. The Syrian St. Ephrem was declared a doctor of the Church and his feast extended to the whole Latin rite in 1920. See also MALANKARESE.

SYRO-ANTIOCHENE RITE, The. The (West) Syrian Rite (*q.v.*).

SYRO-CHALDEAN RITE, The. The Chaldean Rite (*q.v.*).

SYRO-MALABAR RITE, The. The Malabar Rite (*q.v.*).

SYRO-MARONITE RITE, The. The Maronite Rite (*q.v.*).

TAB 487 TAX

T

TABERNACLE (Lat. *tabernaculum*, a tent). i. The box-like receptacle wherein the Blessed Sacrament is reserved on an altar. Its use is universal in the Latin rite and in some form or other by Catholics of the Eastern rites; it is also often used in Byzantine and Armenian churches of dissidents as well (*cf.*, *artophorion*, pyx iii). It is made of wood, stone or metal, polygonal, square or round, the top is preferably a dome or pyramid, and it is covered by a tabernacle-veil (*q.v.*). The interior is lined with silk, a corporal is folded on the floor, and the small Hosts for communion are in a *ciborium* (*q.v.* i), that for Benediction in a *capsula*. It is kept locked and the key is the charge of the responsible priest of the church.

ii. In the Old Testament, an oblong tent, a wooden frame covered with cloth and skins, used by the Jews as a movable place of worship and shelter for the Ark (*q.v.* ii) when wandering in the wilderness. When they settled in Canaan it was set up at Silo (Shiloh).

TABERNACLE-VEIL (Lat. *conopeum*). A veil, which may be of any material, completely covering the top and sides of the tabernacle (*q.v.*) and divided in front so that the door may be opened. It is probably not lawful to leave the door of the tabernacle uncovered, however precious or beautiful it may be, when the Blessed Sacrament is within. The veil may be always golden, silver or white or follow the liturgical colour of the day, except that black is forbidden, purple being used at requiems. Another veil or curtain of white silk may be hung inside the door.

TABERNACLES, THE FEAST OF. i. The third of the great feasts of the Old Law. It is held from the 15th to the 23rd Tishri (the last is the "great day" of St. John vii, 37), and commemorates chiefly the wanderings in the wilderness, wherefore "tents" of branches were formerly lived in during the feast. It is preceded by ten days of penitence, ending in the fast of the day of Atonement (*Yom Kippur*).

ii. In the Armenian rite, Epiphany (Christmas), Easter, the Transfiguration, the Assumption and the Exaltation of the Cross are called the feasts of Tabernacles. These are the usual times for confession and communion for all.

TABLE OF ALTAR. The top of an altar on which the sacrificial vessels are placed. See MENSA.

TABOOT, TABUT (Ge'ez ark). See ARK, iii.

TABORITES. An extreme party of the Hussites (*q.v.*), so called because their refuge was in the mountains. They became the Bohemian Brethren and ultimately the sect of Moravians (*q.v.*).

TALACRE. An abbey of Benedictine nuns near Prestatyn, in Flintshire. It took its rise in a community of contemplative sisters of the Church of England, founded at Feltham in 1868 and living according to the Rule of St. Benedict. In 1913, while living at St. Bride's Milford Haven, the community with its abbess, Scholastica Ewart, submitted to the Holy See at the same time as the Caldey monks (see PRINKNASH). In 1914 they were erected into an abbey; in 1920 they migrated to Talacre, the ancestral home of the Mostyns; and in 1921 were admitted to the English congregation. They are enclosed and contemplative.

TALMUD, The (Heb., instruction). The written record of Jewish canon and civil law not contained in the Pentateuch, consisting of the *Mishna* and *Gemara* (*qq.v.*): the "tradition of the ancients" of Matt. xv, 2, and Mark vii, 6. There are two such records, the Palestinian (or Jerusalem) compiled in the late 4th century A.D., and the Babylonian in the early 6th.

TAMETSI. The opening word of the decree of the Council of Trent (sess. xxiv) which dealt with clandestinity (*q.v.*) in marriages, chiefly by ruling that for the future a union contracted without the presence of the parish priest or his representative and two witnesses would be null as a marriage instead of only unlawful as hitherto. This decree was only published to have effect in certain countries; from time to time it was extended to others (Ireland in 1906) and in 1907 the decree *Ne temere* (*q.v.*) applied its provisions, considerably modified, to practically the whole world, including Great Britain and the U.S.A.

TANTUM ERGO. The opening words of a hymn prescribed to be sung at Benediction of the Blessed Sacrament; it consists of the last two verses of the hymn *Pange lingua* (Vespers of Corpus Christi). This hymn and the blessing with the Host are the only essential and prescribed parts of the service.

TARGUM (Heb., translation, pl., *targumim*). A paraphrase in Aramaic of the Hebrew Scriptures, made after the Captivity and finally edited in the 5th century A.D. and later. Ten of these are still extant, covering the whole Old Testament except the books 1 and 2 Esdras (Ezra and Nehemiah).

TAXATION. The state has the right (of legal, not commutative, justice, *q.v.*) to impose moderate taxes on its subjects and they are bound to pay their reasonable share of such taxes, not merely as payment for services rendered but as an obligatory contribution to the maintenance of the civil society. Most theologians hold that indirect taxes (*e.g.*, customs and excise) are purely penal (see LAW, PENAL), unless the civil authority has made clear its intention to bind the conscience; hence smuggling is not sinful in itself, unless engaged in on so large a scale as to constitute a menace to good government. Many hold the same view of direct taxes (*e.g.*, income-tax, rates), provided the citizen contributes in some way a moderate sum towards the state's expenses, but "there is no possible excuse for studied evasion of taxes. . . . No countenance can be given to fraud, deceit or lying in the matter of income-tax returns" (Davis, *Moral Theology*, Vol. II). So to make false returns or declarations is sinful; but a reasonable sum may be deducted to allow for immoderate exactions on the part of the civil authority. To expose oneself to the probable danger of incurring very heavy penalties by omitting to pay just taxes would be a sin against prudence, if not against justice. The Church has the right to tax her subjects and the faithful are bound to contribute to the material support of religion where this is not already otherwise provided for; however, the Church rarely, if ever, imposes determinate taxes (but *cf.*, *cathedraticum*).

TE DEUM. The name, from the opening words, of a psalm-like hymn sung instead of the last responsory at Matins on all feast days, on all Sundays except in Advent and from Septuagesima till Easter, and on ferias in paschal-time. It is also sung as a hymn of thanksgiving on occasions of public rejoicing, whether religious or secular. It is called the Ambrosian Hymn through being attributed to St. Ambrose, but it is now usually held to have been written by St. Niketas of Remesiana (d. *c.* 414).

TE IGITUR. The opening words of the first prayer of the canon of the Mass, leading to the memento of the living wherein the celebrant prays for the Church and people, the pope and bishop being named. A diocesan bishop does not name himself but says "and with me thine unworthy servant." When the sovereign is a Catholic, he also is named. The image of the crucifixion opposite the beginning of the canon is an enlargement of the initial T which, as a cross *tau*, was formerly kissed (as the altar still is) at this point.

TEACHING OFFICE. See MAGISTERIUM.

TEACHING ORDER. A religious institute (*q.v.*) founded for the education of youth. The principal are: of men, Brothers of the Christian Schools, Irish Christian Brothers, Marist Brothers, Piarists, Salesians and Xaverian Brothers; of women, Congregation of the Holy Child Jesus, Sisters of the Poor Child Jesus, Religious of the Sacred Heart, Institute of Mary, School Sisters of Notre Dame, Daughters of Notre Dame, and the Ursulines. There are many others, and nearly all religious institutes have at least some members engaged in teaching.

TEETOTALISM (originally a facetious emphasizing of the word Total). Total abstinence from alcoholic drink. Since not the use but only the abuse of alcoholic drink is morally bad, teetotalism in itself is neither moral nor immoral. To practise it from motives of temperance or asceticism is praiseworthy. A grave obligation to teetotalism would arise should experience prove to any particular person that he cannot drink in moderation.

TELEOLOGY (Gr., τέλος, end). Properly, the science of ends or final causes, but in use teleology is the doctrine that there is design in the universe and that no adequate account of it is possible without taking its design and final cause into consideration. The teleological argument for the existence of God is therefore the argument from design (*q.v.*).

TEMERARIOUS. See RASH.

TEMPERAMENT. That complexity of inclinations derived from heredity and a person's own organic and nervous system. These natural dispositions can be changed to some extent by education, by external circumstances and by a person's own endeavours —this is Character. By temperament and character the moral freedom of the will is often lessened but never altogether taken away; hence it is that a man can always successfully act against his evil inclinations.

TEMPERANCE. The virtue which enables a man to control his natural appetite for sensual pleasure. It includes the subsidiary virtues of modesty, chastity, and abstinence as opposed to gluttony and drunkenness.

TEMPLARS, The. The Poor Knights of the Temple, first and most powerful of the military orders (*q.v.*), founded in 1118 for defence of the Christian kingdom of Jerusalem; its headquarters were near the site of the Temple and the Rule of St. Benedict was adopted. The order became wealthy and powerful, with estates and castles in the Holy Land, Italy, France, Spain, Portugal, the Germanies, Cyprus and England (*cf.*, Middle Temple, etc., in London); pride, tyranny and luxury followed. At the instance of King Philip the Fair, Pope Clement V put the order and its members on trial for heresy and secret depravities, and in 1312 decreed its suppression. Most of the property and many of the knights passed to the Knights Hospitallers, and the grand master was burnt alive by order of Philip, who was responsible for great cruelty and injustice towards them. The truth of the charges against the order is involved in much mystery. There were grave abuses, but it seems certain that it was the greed of Philip IV (*cf.*, Henry VIII and the English monasteries) which was primarily responsible for its suppression. It had some 23 establishments (preceptories) in England, under the Master of the Temple in London, who was sometimes in his official capacity summoned to Parliament (*cf.*, the numerous Temple place-names).

TEMPLE (Lat., *templum,* a sacred enclosure). i. A place of worship, especially one wherein sacrifice is offered to God (from ii).

ii. The Temple. The centre of the worship of God according to the Old Law, where alone sacrifice might be offered; the first temple at Jerusalem was finished by Solomon about 1004 B.C., destroyed 588 B.C., rebuilt by Zorobabel 515 B.C., restored and enlarged by Herod 17 B.C.-A.D. 62 finally and for ever destroyed by the Emperor Titus in A.D. 70. Its site is now occupied by the Moslem *Haram-ash-Sharif* (The Noble Sanctuary) enclosing the Dome of the Rock (frequently miscalled the Mosque of Omar) over the threshing floor of Ornan (Araunah) and the rock of holocausts, and the Mosque *al-Aksa,* once the church of the Templars.

iii. In France, temple is the ordinary name for a Protestant meeting house or chapel.

TEMPORAL POWER, The. The power of the pope in the sense of sovereignty and dominion over territory, which is regarded as a practical necessity to secure his complete independence of the civil power, which belongs to him by divine right. It is now exercised only in respect of the Vatican City (*q.v.*).

TEMPORAL PUNISHMENT (*i.e.,* punishment for a time). This punishment often remains due to sin after the guilt has been forgiven and can be paid in this world by any satisfactory work, but if not sufficiently paid here will be exacted in full hereafter in Purgatory. The Church has power by divine right to remit temporal punishment out of the Treasury of Merits (*q.v.*); such remission is called an indulgence (*q.v.*).

TEMPORALS. i. Those things appertaining to secular affairs or this world, as opposed to sacred affairs and eternity.

ii. Temporalities (*q.v.*).

iii. Temporal good things. It is the teaching of Christianity that such things may be lawfully sought, but secondarily to the Kingdom of Heaven; for that is necessary for us, whereas temporal good things, though good for us, are not absolutely necessary. But "not all anxiety about temporal things is forbidden but only such as is inordinate and superfluous. For when the mind is occupied with temporal things and makes them its goal, then it is depressed by them; but when it makes use of them for the attain-

ment of everlasting happiness, then it is not depressed thereby but rather lifted up out of itself" (St. Thomas, II-II, lxxxiii, 6, ad 1).

TEMPORALITIES. The material possessions attached to an ecclesiastical office, including the revenues of the benefice, and sometimes also the fund of the *fabrica* (*q.v.*).

TEMPORARY VOWS. See TRIENNIAL VOWS.

TEMPTATION. An enticement to sin, either by something external or by that natural inclination to evil inherent in everyone as a result of Adam's fall. No matter how vehement the temptation may be, nor how protracted, there can be no sin unless and until consent is freely given. Since temptation, then, is a trial to virtue, it may be the occasion of great merit.

TEMPTING GOD. An action by which one endeavours to test some attribute of God, *e.g.,* to see whether he is omnipotent, omniscient, merciful, etc. This is a sin against faith and religion; it is always grave when accompanied by doubts about one of God's perfections; if no doubt is present, but one rashly demands the manifestation of a divine attribute, *e.g.,* the cure of an illness, the sin against faith and religion is grave or venial according to the degree of rashness shown.

TEN PERSECUTIONS, The. The chief persecutions of Christians in the Roman Empire up to the time of the Peace of the Church, namely, under the Emperor Nero, begun in 64, Domitian (94), Trajan (98), M. Aurelius (166), Severus (200), Maximinus (235), Decius (249), Valerian (257), Aurelian (275), Diocletian and Maximian (303-13).

TEN TRIBES, The. The patriarch Jacob's twelve sons were the ancestors of the tribes which bore their names and possessed definite territory in Palestine. As Levi became the priestly tribe and had no territory, the two sons of Joseph, Ephrem and Manasses, took his place. After the death of Solomon, two tribes, Judah and Benjamin, remained faithful to his son, the remainder forming an independent and often hostile state. This existed as a distinct political entity for about 300 years till it was destroyed by the Assyrians in 722 B.C. Many of its inhabitants were transported to distant places in the Assyrian empire. A number of these were absorbed by the native population of the land of their exile; others remained Jews but ceased to form tribal units. The bulk of the people remained on its ancestral soil and intermarried with Assyrian colonists. Hence the Ten Tribes are not lost in the sense that they somewhere still lead a hidden existence and might be discovered: they are only lost in the sense that the Angles, Jutes and Saxons are lost in England. No evidence whatsoever exists of any connexion between the English and the Ten Tribes.

TENEBRÆ (Lat., darkness). A name given to the special Matins and Lauds of Maundy Thursday, Good Friday and Holy Saturday on account of the way they are celebrated. Where they are to be said or sung in choir, it must be done on the previous evening. Matins has three nocturns, each of three psalms with antiphons and three lessons with responsories; the first nocturn lessons are all from the prophecy and lamentations of Jeremias; the psalms and antiphons of Lauds have reference to the Passion. The hearse (*q.v.* ii) with 15 lighted candles stands in the choir; one is put out after every psalm and others during the *Benedictus*, but the last is hidden behind the altar; Our Father, Ps. l (*Miserere*) and a prayer are then said in darkness, a commotion is made, the lighted candle is replaced, and all disperse in silence. The whole service is in the nature of a mourning; the final signal of the senior to disperse has now grown into a mild clapping and noise with the choir books, symbolizing the convulsion of Nature at the Crucifixion, and the single light is the Light of the World.

TER-SANCTUS, The (Lat., three times holy). The *Sanctus*, (*q.v.*).

TERCE (Lat., *tertia* [*hora*], third [hour]). The hour of the Divine Office appointed to be said at the third hour, *i.e.*, about 9 a.m. In cathedral and monastic churches it precedes the capitular or conventual Mass. It begins with the usual opening of the little hours and a hymn, *Nunc, sancte nobis Spiritus*, invariable except during the octave of Pentecost when *Veni Creator* is sung; three psalms according to the day of the week (on certain feasts the Sunday psalms are always said); variable little chapter and short responsory; collect of the day; and usual ending. The office commemorates the descent of the Holy Ghost on the Apostles (Acts ii, 15), to which direct reference is made in the hymn.

TERESIANS. Discalced Carmelites (*q.v.*), particularly nuns, as reformed by St. Teresa of Avila.

TERNA (Lat., *ternus*, triple). A list of three names, especially of priests recommended to the Holy See by a chapter of canons for filling a vacant see. The names are in descending order: "most worthy," "very worthy," "worthy."

TERTIAN. A Jesuit undergoing his third year of probation (over and above the two years of noviciate) after he is ordained priest and has completed his studies.

TERTIARY. A member of a third order (*q.v.*). A secular tertiary is a lay person living in the world; a regular tertiary is a religious living in community and bound by vows. Tertiary, without qualification, nearly always means secular tertiary.

TESTAMENT. i. The English form of the Latin *testamentum* (testimony, witness, will), a mistranslation of the Greek διαθήκη, which, though actually meaning disposition of property by will, was used in the Septuagint to render the Hebrew *berith*, covenant (cf., 1 Cor. xi, 25; 2 Cor. iii, 6, 14); hence used for each of the two divisions of the Bible, the one dealing with God's old covenant with Israel, the other with the new.

ii. See WILL AND TESTAMENT.

TESTAMENT OF THE LORD, The. A work, probably of the second part of the 4th century, describing as from the mouth of our Lord disciplinary and liturgical usages of the Church in Syria and Egypt at that time.

TESTEM BENEVOLENTIÆ. An apostolic letter addressed by Pope Leo XIII, in 1899, to Cardinal Gibbons, archbishop of Baltimore, condemning the opinions known as Americanism (*q.v.*).

TETRAGRAMMATON (Gr., four letter [word]). The letters J H V H, the name of God, the vowels being unwritten and unknown: *cf.*, the prayer of the Breaking in the Coptic Liturgy, "The angels . . . worship his great *and invisible* Name." See JAHVEH.

TEUTONIC KNIGHTS, The. A military order (*q.v.*), which originated from a tent-hospital before Acre in 1189, to serve the poor and sick, and to combat the enemies of Christendom. It was composed of German knights, priests and serving brothers. In the 13th century the centre of the order was transferred to Europe and it undertook to convert the pagan Prussians. The knights conquered the country and took possession of it with violence and cruelty. The period of their highest power was from 1351-82; they declined after 1400, through the opposition and hatred aroused by the worldly temper and unholy aggressiveness of the knights. The order was secularized in 1805. It was reorganized in Austria in 1834, returning more actively to the service of the sick, and now consists of professed knights, priests and sisters; headquarters in Czechoslovakia. It also exists as a noble order of honour.

TEXT OF SCRIPTURE. The Church, for the proper exercise of her duty of conserving the Scriptures for the use of Christian people and interpreting them infallibly, necessarily has a text of them which is substantially identical with the original and free from doctrinal error. This text is not found in any single document but the version of it provided for universal use is the Vulgate (*q.v.*), which, by decree of the Council of Trent, must be received as authentic (*q.v.*) and certain.

THADDEUS, ST. See SIMON AND JUDE. In the Byzantine rite Thaddeus is distinguished from Jude and has a separate feast on Aug. 21.

THAUMATURGUS (Gr., wonder-worker). A title given to those noted for miracles, particularly to St. Gregory, bishop of Neo-cæsarea (d. *c.* 270). Others are SS. Cosmas and Damian (297), Stephen (816), Achilles (330), Dimitrios (306), Nicholas of Bari (*c.* 350), Bessarion (450), Antony of Padua (1231), Vincent Ferrer (1419).

THEATINES, The. The Order of Clerks Regular (*q.v.*), the first of its kind, founded by St. Cajetan in 1524 and called Theatines after their co-founder John Peter Caraffa, bishop of Chieti (*Theate*), afterwards Pope Paul IV. Their object was to maintain the faith by fighting heresy without and evil-living within, and they subjected themselves to complete poverty. The order had a notable success and established missions in the East Indies and hither Asia, but declined during the 19th century. Thomas Goldwell, the last bishop of the old hierarchy of England (*d.* 1585) was a Theatine, but the order has never been established in that country, though it is in the United States. There are a few nuns of the order, some active and others (Hermitesses) strictly enclosed and penitential.

THEBAID, The. The valley of the Nile, from Hermopolis Magna (Ashmunein) to Syrene (Assuan) with the adjoining deserts as far down as Nitria, and the monks and hermits who lived there in the 4th and 5th centuries, the Fathers of the Desert (*q.v.*).

THEBAN LEGION, The. A legion of the Roman army which, with its leader Maurice, is said to have been massacred for its Christianity at Agaunum (now St. Maurice-en-Valais, Switzerland) at the end of the 3rd century. On Sept. 22 their feast is kept by the Western church, but their story is surrounded with great uncertainty.

THEFT. Taking away, keeping or using another's property when he is reasonably unwilling; the owner cannot be reasonably unwilling in a case of extreme necessity or of occult compensation (*q.v.*) though he should be consulted first if possible. Absolutely serious matter, *i.e.*, which it is always a mortal sin to steal, even from a millionaire, is estimated from the danger which would accrue to society could such a sum be stolen without serious guilt; relatively serious matter is estimated from the harm done by the theft to the owner, respect being had to his circumstances. A series of small thefts coalesce so as to constitute absolutely or relatively grave matter if such was the original intention or if the thefts occur at fairly short intervals.

THEISM. The system of those who admit the existence of the one God and at least the possibility of a divine revelation; it is thus distinct from Deism (*q.v.*). The theist admits an external religion and a public cult, whereas the deist to all intents and purposes admits no more than, and acts as, the atheist.

THEO- A prefix from Gr. θεός, God.

THEOCRACY (Gr. κράτος, power). Government, or a state governed, directly by God through his representatives, a priesthood or otherwise, who control the civil power or, more properly, religious and civil power not being distinguished from one another. The classic example, The Theocracy, is the Jewish nation until its break-up at the beginning of our era. Until recent times and the penetration of modern European ideas, Islam also was a theocracy, and so remains in certain places, *e.g.*, Saudi Arabia. Though there have been local examples of theocratic rule, *e.g.*, the Jesuit reductions (*q.v.*) in Paraguay, the monastic republic of Mount Athos, theocracy is no part of the Catholic system which has always distinguished the spiritual from the civil power and strictly delimited the control of the first over the second (*cf.*, Church and State), while teaching that princes must rule in accordance with the laws of God.

THEODICY (Gr. δίκη, vindication, judgement) is properly the justification of God in view of the existence of evil, and the word was so used by Leibniz in 1710. But its meaning now comprehends the knowledge of God through the exercise of human reason alone (or natural theology, *q.v.*), the possibility of which was solemnly affirmed by the Vatican Council and reiterated in the oath against Modernism.

THEOLOGIAN. i. A master or student of theology.
ii. An aspirant to the priesthood who has completed his philosophical course, and is studying theology, often called in England a "divine."

THEOLOGY. The science which treats of God and the things of God.

THEOLOGY, ASCETICAL. That branch of theology which treats of Christian virtues and perfection and the means by which they may be attained.

THEOLOGY, DOGMATIC. The science of Christian doctrine; the systematic presentation of the faith, establishing the Church as the depository of revealed truth, setting out the relations between faith and reason and between religion and philosophy. The subject matter of dogmatic theology may be found reduced to its bare bones in the "Penny Catechism"; its broad divisions are God, Creation and Redemption, the last including Christology, Soteriology, Mariology, Grace, the Sacraments, and the Last Things or Eschatology (*qq.v.*). It is a science both speculative and practical, but being ordered to God it is primarily speculative.

THEOLOGY, MORAL. The science of human acts considered in the light of man's supernatural destiny; consequently not only reason but also the light of faith is employed in establishing and applying the principles of the science.

THEOLOGY, MYSTICAL. In patristic and mediæval times this expression was synonymous with the science of the spiritual life, but is now confined to that branch of it which treats of passive contemplation or mysticism (*qq.v.*). It is thus the complement of ascetical theology, which deals with the growth of charity and prayer preceding contemplation. It is based on Sacred Scripture and Tradition, as is all theology, and in the light of revealed teaching reasons on the information recorded by the mystics of their experiences, and so traces scientifically the course of the mystical union (*q.v.*).

THEOLOGY, NATURAL. The science which has God for its object and is pursued by the natural light of human reason. It is distinct from supernatural theology which uses the aid of revelation in its search after the knowledge of God.

THEOLOGY, PASTORAL. That branch of theology which deals with the care of souls. It takes the teaching of dogmatic, moral and ascetical theology and the rules of canon law and applies them to the everyday work of the parochial clergy in all its aspects.

THEOLOGY, POSITIVE. That branch and method of supernatural theology which contents itself with deriving the truths of revelation and the dogmas of faith from the *loci theologici* (*q.v.*), without proceeding to the refutation of the adversaries of the faith.

THEOPASCHITES, The (Gr. πάσχειν, to suffer). A party of the monophysites who pushed their heresy to the extent of believing that God (and therefore the Holy Trinity) suffered and died upon the cross.

THEOPHANY (Gr. φανός, bright). A name given to various appearances of God to man recorded in the Old Testament, *e.g.*, to Adam (Gen. iii, 8), to Abram (Gen. xii, 7), to Isaac (Gen. xxvi, 2, 24), to Moses (Exod. iii, 2, xix, 20), to Gedeon (Judges vi, 2). It has been sometimes believed that these were manifestations of God the Son in the form of an angel but it is now generally held that they were not of God himself (who cannot be seen corporeally in any of his persons by man), but were angels representing God and speaking for him. The feast of the Epiphany is sometimes called Theophany.

THEOPHORE (Gr., God-bearer). The name of St. Ignatius of Antioch and a title given in the Byzantine rite to certain saints who bore witness to God notably, *e.g.*, Athanasius, Antony the Great, the Fathers of Chalcedon.

THEOSOPHY (Gr. σοφία, wisdom). The teaching that, by a divine illumination which arises from a natural union of the soul with the Godhead, man can arrive at the knowledge of God intuitively, *i.e.*, without having recourse to discursive reasoning. It is based upon a false mysticism, Brahminism, and Buddhism, and is closely allied to the Modernist immanence theory (*q.v.*). It has been rejected by the Church (*cf.*, "Acta Ap. Sedis," Aug. 1, 1919).

THEOTOKION. A *troparion* (*q.v.*) in honour of our Lady; one commemorating her sorrows at the foot of the cross, sung on Wednesday and Friday, is a *staurotheotokion*.

THEOTOKOS (Gr. τόκος, childbirth). The Mother of God, a common way of referring to our Lady in the East, especially in liturgical books. In *c.* 427 this term became the centre of dispute between orthodox Christians and the followers of Nestorius, for denial of our Lady's divine maternity was the form in which Nestorianism (*q.v.*) was commonly expressed. The 1st canon of the third Œcumenical Council at Ephesus in 431 declared: "If anyone does not acknowledge that Emmanuel is truly God and that therefore the holy Virgin is Mother of God, since she gave birth according to the flesh to the Word begotten of God the Father, let him be anathema." The Nestorians have ever since refused the expression Theotokos.

THESSALONIANS, THE EPISTLES TO THE. Two letters written by St. Paul from Corinth to the church at Salonika, and canonical books of holy Scripture. He exhorts them to clean living, brotherly love and honest work, and in both refers to the resurrection and to the second coming of Christ, anticipation of the imminence of which apparently tended to paralyse the normal Christian life of the Thessalonians.

THIRD HEAVEN. A term for the Heaven of God and his vision arising from the cosmological and philosophical speculations of the middle ages. The "third heaven" of St. Paul (2 Cor. xii, 2-4) is of uncertain meaning; St. Thomas interprets it as an unique vision of the truth and very essence of God.

THIRD MASS OF CHRISTMAS, The, is to be celebrated in full day. It has particular reference to the new-born Christ as bringer of the tidings of our adoption as sons of God and celebrates the dignity and eternal generation of the Word. As the gospel is John i, 1-14, that of the Mass of the Epiphany is said as the last gospel.

THIRD ORDER. i. Secular. A branch of a religious order, whose members are laymen and women, pursuing the ordinary avocations of secular life (*cf.*, second order). It is a true religious order, with noviciate, rule (which does not bind under pain of sin), office and habit (which must not be worn in public without permission of the bishop and the order: a scapular [*q.v.*, ii] is worn under the clothing); its members are brethren and share in the spiritual life of the first order. It takes precedence of all confraternities, etc., no one may belong to more than one at the same time, but may leave one at will and be admitted for a good reason to another. The general object of these third orders is to bring something of the religious spirit of the cloister into the world and to sanctify its members by a striving after greater perfection in union with the fathers and nuns of the first and second orders; they are organized into chapters under a priest, but there are numerous isolated tertiaries; they are not bound by any vow; they may gain many special indulgences and other privileges. Third orders arose in the 13th century; they now are the Augustinian, Carmelite, Dominican, Franciscan, Minim, Premonstratensian, Servite and Trinitarian. They vary according to the spirit and aims of the first order. The Dominicans, for example, lay stress on penance; their candidates must be at least 18 years old; the habit is a white tunic and hood, leather belt and black cloak; they must say daily the Little Office B.V.M. according to the Dominican rite or else a certain number of *Paters* and *Aves;* they have three extra fast days and are bound to certain suffrages for deceased members; and they may join in certain amusements (dances, theatres, etc.) only with great discretion. The most numerous third order is the Franciscan. A secular priest tertiary may obtain permission to use the Missal, Breviary and calendar of his first order.

ii. Regular. Those members of a third order who leave the world and follow their rule under the ordinary simple vows of religion in community are regular tertiaries. They are principally women. The most important are: The Third Order Regular of Carmelites, particularly those founded for work among the Malabarese who have numerous Indian priests and teaching nuns of the Syro-Malabar rite; Dominican sisters, who combine the contemplative with the active life, teaching school, nursing, etc.; Franciscans, priests, brothers and sisters, all engaged in active work; and Servites, the Indian congregation of which has convents of native nuns.

THIRTY-NINE ARTICLES, The. A formulation of the beliefs of the Church of England, drawn up in 1562 and imposed on its clergy as a profession of faith by an act of Parliament, in 1571. To them every Anglican clergyman must publicly assent, and every incumbent admitted to a benefice must read them before the congregation on the first Sunday he officiates. Certain canons of the Council of Trent were probably directed against these articles, *e.g.*, sess. xxiii, can. 3. See ANGLICANISM.

THOMAS, ST. The feast of the apostle, called Didymus, *i.e.*, the Twin, who doubted Christ's resurrection, is kept by the Western church on Dec. 21. There is a widespread and ancient but unverified tradition that he preached the gospel in India (*cf.*, St. Thomas Christians) and was put to death near Mylapore, which city bears his name and claims his relics, as does the cathedral of Ortona in Italy. He is named in the canon of the Mass.

THOMISM. The system of philosophy and theology of St. Thomas Aquinas (*q.v.*), held by numerous Catholic schools of thought and in particular by Dominicans, who take a vow to keep St. Thomas's doctrine faithfully. There can be no such thing as eclecticism in the Thomist system, otherwise the system as a system is ruined. The fundamental principle of Thomism is the real distinction between act and potency (*qq.v.*); an unfolding of this principle is thus expressed: "That which is in the state of potency cannot pass from that state except by the intervention of something which is in act." By the application of this fundamental principle to every section of philosophy and theology St. Thomas built up a system remarkable for its perfect harmony and solidarity of thought. By this principle is established the real distinction between essence and existence in created things, the real distinction between substance and accidents, the essence of dimensive quantity, the truth of the principle of causality, the soul as substantial form of the body, the real distinction of faculties from the soul, the premotion by God of the free act, the composite of body from matter and form, the existence of God from motion, the intrinsic efficacity of efficacious grace, etc. Pope Pius XI published his encyclical *Studiorum Ducem* on June 29, 1923. After speaking of St. Thomas's great virtues he speaks of the extraordinary excellence of his doctrine and the great authority it holds in the Church. "Our predecessors," he says, "as it were with unanimous utterance, have sounded its praises." He recalls Pope Leo XIII, who did so much to revive Thomistic studies (*Æterni Patris*); then Pius X who declared the splendour of St. Thomas's doctrine in his *motu proprio* "*Doctoris Angelici*"; then Benedict XV reiterating the same praises, who declared: "To desert Aquinas, especially in his metaphysical teachings, is to risk disaster." Pope Pius XI says: "The following canon of the Church's code should be held as a sacred command: In the study of rational philosophy and theology and in the instruction of students the professor should follow entirely the method, doctrine and principles of the Angelic Doctor, and hold them religiously" (canon 1366, § 2).

THREE CAPPADOCIANS, The. St. Basil the Great, St. Gregory Nazianzen (*qq.v.*) and St. Gregory of Nyssa, brother of Basil. They were all natives of Cappadocia, personal friends, and fathers of the Church, their theological writings and discourses being directed particularly against Arianism (*q.v.*).

THREE CHAPTERS, The. Three Nestorian documents, the writings of Theodore of Mopsuestia, of Theodoret of Cyrus against the Council of Ephesus, and a letter of one Ibas: condemned in 544 by the Eastern patriarchs and the emperor Justinian, with the object of reconciling the adherents of Monophysism (*q.v.*). The bishops of Africa, north Italy and Dalmatia objected on the ground that condemnation of these writings (though clearly heretical in parts) compromised the Council of Chalcedon. Pope Vigilius in 548 condemned the Three Chapters while confirming Chalcedon; then withdrew it; and finally in 554 was bullied by the emperor into confirming the acts of the council at Constantinople which had again condemned the writings. Several protesting Western archbishops went into schism, particularly the metropolitan of Illyricum whose province was not reconciled till 700 (hence arose the patriarchs of Aquileia, *q.v.*). It must be observed that the controversy was concerned not with any definition of faith but with the expediency and implications of the disputed condemnation.

THREE CHILDREN, The. The three children of Juda, Ananias, Misael, and Azarias (Sidrach, Misach and Abdenago, *cf.*, Dan. i, 6-7, iii, 8 *et seq.*). They are named in the Roman Martyrology of Dec. 16, and in the Byzantine rite have a feast with the prophet Daniel on the following day.

THREE COMPANIONS, The, of St. Francis of Assisi, namely, Angelo, Leo and Rufino, authors of the account of the saint called after them "Legenda Trium Sociorum."

THREE HEAVENLY WITNESSES, The. A controversy arising from the following italicized clause in 1 John v, 7-8, "Thus we have a three-fold warrant *in Heaven, the Father, the Word, and the Holy Ghost, three who are yet one; and we have a three-fold warrant on earth,* the Spirit, the water and the blood, three witnesses that conspire in one." Determined efforts have been made by Catholic biblical scholars to have these words removed from the text on the ground that they are uncanonical: they appear in only a few early Latin MSS. and in no good MSS. in other languages. It was decided by the Holy Office in 1897 that the authenticity of the words may not safely be called in doubt; but this does not preclude further prudent research and is by no means equivalent to a declaration of canonicity. The Holy Office explained on June 2, 1927, that the above

decree was not intended to prevent Catholic scholars from further investigating the question or even inclining to the opinion that the text is not genuine, provided they profess willingness to submit to the judgement of the Church.

THREE HOLY HIERARCHS, The. "Our blessed fathers and universal teachers, the three holy hierarchs, Basil the Great, Gregory the Theologian (Nazianzen) and John Chrysostom" (celebrated thus in the Byzantine rite on Jan. 30).

THREE HOURS, The. A popular devotion (*q.v.*) observed in some churches, especially those of the Jesuits, on Good Friday, during the time of our Lord's suffering, from noon till 3 p.m. It consists of seven discourses on the seven words of Christ from the cross, interspersed with meditations and appropriate hymns and prayers. The earthquake of 1687 prompted the Jesuits of Lima (Peru) to institute this service. It has become popular also amongst Anglicans, who are usually quite unaware of its origin.

THREE KINGS OF COLOGNE, The. The Magi (*q.v.*), whose alleged relics, supposed to have been brought to Europe by St. Helen, were carried off from Milan to Cologne in 1164, making it one of the chief pilgrimage cities of the middle ages. They are still enshrined in the cathedral.

THREE MARYS, The. Mary Magdalen, Mary Salome (Mark xv, 40; xvi, i), and Mary Cleophas (John xix, 25). The shrine of the *Saintes Maries de la Mer* in the Camargue displays three ancient tombs alleged to be theirs and the feast of the Three Marys is permitted there and elsewhere; but the story of them, Lazarus and others preaching the gospel in the south of France has been shown to be devoid of any probability.

THRONE. i. The name generally used in English for the seat of honour (*cathedra,* whence cathedral) occupied by a cardinal, diocesan bishop or abbot when not at the altar during a service at which he is pontificating. In cathedral and abbey churches the throne must be a permanent structure, an armed chair, with back and canopy, mounted on steps. In Roman basilicas it is situated in the apse behind the altar, and may be so in any church where the altar stands well out into the church; but its usual place is now before the altar on the gospel-side. Outside his own diocese or abbey a bishop or abbot may not pontificate at the throne without permission of the local bishop; *cf.*, pontifical Mass. In the Byzantine rite the throne is in the apse behind the altar, beneath a large icon; there is also an episcopal stall in front of the *iconostasis* on the south side. In other Eastern rites the throne is now usually before the altar.

ii. A small platform surmounted by a

canopy on which the monstrance is placed at Benediction and Exposition; it should be removable and not part of the reredos or the altar.

THRONES (Col. i, 16). One of the choirs of the celestial hierarchy (*q.v.*).

THURIBLE (Lat., *thus*, frankincense), or Censer. A vessel in which incense is burned for liturgical incensations. It consists of a metal body with separate lid enclosing a pan for the charcoal and incense; it is carried by three chains attached to the body, a fourth chain actuating the lid.

THURIFER. The acolyte who has charge of the thurible when incense is required at sacred ceremonies.

TIARA (Gr., from the Persian royal head-gear; formerly synonymous with *mitre*). A round bulbous hat, about 15 ins. high, made of cloth-of-silver, adorned with three gold coronets and with pendant *infulæ* (*q.v.*), the whole decorated with precious stones. It is the diadem peculiar to the pope, who wears it at his coronation and on other occasions of non-liturgical solemnity; when pontificating he wears a mitre, like any other bishop. Its origin is uncertain and its significance varied, *e.g.*, a symbol of the Church militant, suffering and triumphant, of the spiritual powers of teaching, ruling sanctify-ing, etc. It is imposed at his coronation with the words: "Receive this tiara adorned with three crowns and know that you are the father of princes and of kings, guide of the world and vicar upon earth of Christ Jesus our Saviour."

TIME. "The number of movement, esti-mated according to its before and after" (Aristotle). It is founded upon the real succession of events. Strictly speaking, time has no real parts, such as past, present and future. As the past is past and future yet future, neither of them is actual or real; the present only is actual. Time has no entity except according to the indivisible now. There is therefore no distinct entity called time just as there is no distinct entity called space; but nevertheless both have real foundations, one in the succession of events, and the other in the extension of bodies.

TIMOTHY AND TITUS, THE EPISTLES TO. Three canonical books of Holy Scrip-ture, being letters written by St. Paul and known as the Pastoral Epistles. They con-sist chiefly of advice and instruction ad-dressed to the newly-appointed bishops re-spectively of Ephesus and Crete; in 2 Timo-thy he reviews his own experience in the apostolate and in Titus gives the Cretans a thoroughly bad character and states what sort of men their bishops should be.

TIRON, THE ORDER OF. A reformed congregation of Benedictines founded by St. Bernard of Tiron (*d.* 1117) in Normandy. It subsisted until 1627 when the mother-house at Tiron became Maurist. It had an abbey at St. Dogmaels in Wales, with cells at Pill and Caldey Island, and four houses in Scotland.

TITHES (Old Eng. *teotha*, a tenth). The tenth part of the produce of land, or a com-mutation of this in money, allotted in certain countries for the maintenance of clergy or other church purposes. The Code of Canon Law enacts that the particular laws and cus-toms of each locality are to be observed.

TITLE. i. Of ordination. An assured means of subsistence, sufficient and permanent, re-quired for candidates for ordination to sacred orders and accepted as such by canon law. For the secular clergy the proper title is that of a benefice, failing which that of patrimony or pension is admitted. In certain countries the title of the service of the Church is accepted in lieu of benefice: in missionary countries the title is the Mission. For the regular clergy, see below.

ii. Of poverty. The title of ordination required by regulars, *i.e.*, religious of solemn vows, for admission to sacred orders; it is also called the title of Solemn Religious Profession. Other religious do not have the title of Poverty, but that of Common Table, Congregation, or a secular title.

iii. Of an altar, etc. The name by which an altar, church, etc., is known, being that of the saint or mystery of religion in whose honour it is dedicated.

iv. Cardinalitial. The title which a cardinal priest or deacon takes from one or other of the titular churches (*q.v.*) of Rome.

v. Of the cross. The placard bearing his name fastened on the cross of a crucified criminal. The words on that of our Lord are given by St. John xix, 19; on images of the Crucifixion in the Western church this is usually represented by the initials I(*esus*) N(*azarenus*) R(*ex*) I(*udæorum*). To trace these initials on the forehead, with the prayer "May Jesus of Nazareth, king of the Jews, preserve my soul from sudden and unprepared death," is a practice attributed originally to an Eng-lish saint, Edmund Rich, archbishop of Can-terbury (1180-1240). A feast of our Lord under the name of the Title of the Holy Cross is observed in some places on the 3rd Sunday in July.

TITLES OF HONOUR, PONTIFICAL, are both civil and ecclesiastical. The civil is a title of nobility (prince, duke, marquis, count or baron) which the pope confers as a tem-poral sovereign, the honour being personal or hereditary in tail male and the title pre-fixed to the family name. A British subject must have the permission of the King of Great Britain and Ireland before accepting such a title; that sovereign being the sole fount of honour in his own dominions

Ecclesiastical titles of honour for the clergy are principally Assistant at the Pontifical Throne, Protonotary Apostolic, Domestic Prelate, and Privy Chamberlain (*qq.v.*, all of whom are addressed as *Monsignore*); for the laity, Privy Chamberlain, and Chamberlain of Honour, of the Sword and Cape, and membership of the various pontifical orders (*qq.v.*, these are usually knights or commanders, but have no prefix in English-speaking countries). The Order of the Holy Sepulchre is open to clergy and laity, men and women.

TITULAR. i. Of a church, is the divine Person, mystery, sacred object or saint in whose name the church is blessed or consecrated and after whom it is called: if a saint, generally called its patron (but see that word). It is chosen by the clergy and people of the district, but if a *beatus* is selected an indult of the Holy See is required. The feast of the titular must be celebrated in its churches as a double of the first class with an octave; and the feast of the titular of a cathedral (as also the patron of a diocese) is observed in the same way throughout the diocese. See DEDICATIONS.

ii. Of an altar. Every fixed altar must have a title, which cannot be altered; that of the high altar should be the same as that of the church; without an apostolic indult an altar may not be consecrated in honour of one only *beatus*, nor may two altars in one church bear the same title.

TITULAR CHURCHES. The ancient churches of Rome, formerly presided over by the chief presbyters and deacons, with others now added, from which cardinal priests and deacons take their titles. Every cardinal upon appointment must take possession solemnly of his titular church, in which he has jurisdiction and the right to a throne. Among the titular churches are St. Anastasia, St. Bartholomew-on-the-Island, St. Bernard-in-the-Baths, St. Cecily, Holy Cross, SS. John & Paul, St. Marcellus, St. Mary "sopra Minerva," St. Pancras, St. Praxedis, St. Pudentiana, St. Sabina, St. Silvester "in Capite," St. Susanna (presbyteral), St. George "in Velabro," St. Mary "in Cosmedin," St. Mary in Broad Street, St. Mary-of-the-Staircase, and St. Nicholas-in-the-Jail-of-Tully (diaconal).

TITULAR DIGNITARY. One whose rank carries no office or jurisdiction with it, nor duties nor rights except ceremonial privileges of precedence, dress, etc. Such may be bestowed or confirmed by the Holy See as a mark of honour, or because the holder has retired from the active exercise of his functions, or because he holds some office which makes it desirable. But *cf.*, Canon, Titular.

TITULUS (Lat., a notice, label). i. One of the 25 quasi-parochial churches established in Rome in the 4th century, see above.

ii. The titular church of a cardinal, as above.

iii. The title or name of a church or altar.

iv. A heading or superscription.

TOBIAS (Tobit: "God is good"). A deutero-canonical (*q.v.*) book of the Old Testament. It is so called because it relates the story of Tobias, the son of Tobias; how by the help of God through the archangel Raphael he safely married a wife under discouraging circumstances, recovered some money owed to his father, and cured his blindness: the whole illustrating the need and the reward of trust in God's goodness.

TOLEDO, THE RITE OF. The Mozarabic rite (*q.v.*).

TOLERATION, RELIGIOUS. i. Indulgence towards a religion other than one's own; this is equivalent to religious indifference, *viz.*, thinking one religion to be as good or as bad as another. The Church has never hesitated to condemn the errors of other religions. Truth and error, good and evil, cannot be reconciled. Hence intolerance of what is in itself wrong or evil is a virtue; but charity forbids the extension of this intolerance to the authors of the error or evil. The principle of dogmatic intolerance is balanced by another, namely, that "no man should be compelled against his will to embrace the Catholic faith, because except he be willing man cannot believe" (Pope Leo XIII).

ii. Respect for another's religious convictions, prescribed by the law of charity. Every man must be regarded as acting in good faith (*q.v.*) until the contrary is proved.

iii. State-guarantee of freedom of faith and worship; a practical necessity in the modern state where several religions find adherents, since physical coercion of another's convictions is grievous tyranny. Yet no state may countenance any form of religion or irreligion which is a social danger or subversive of morals.

TOLETANUS in America. The Latin epithet for the bishop of Toledo (*Toletum*) in Ohio.

TOMB OF OUR LADY, The. The site of the traditional burying-place of the Blessed Virgin Mary, where her body lay for three days before her assumption into Heaven, adjoins the Garden of Gethsemane at Jerusalem. The tomb is first recorded in the 4th century, and there has been a church there since the 5th. The present church was built in the 12th century, and has been in the hands of the Orthodox since 1757. But some, notably Pope Benedict XIV, have maintained that our Lady died at Ephesus.

TOME OF ST. LEO, The. A "dogmatic letter" of Pope St. Leo I to Flavian, bishop of Constantinople, in 449, in which he states the Catholic faith as against Eutychianism and Monophysism, namely, that Jesus Christ is one person with two natures, divine and human, and that each nature is real, perfect and complete. This was acclaimed by the Council of Chalcedon as "the faith of the Apostles, Peter speaking through Leo."

TONE. i. See MODE.
ii. A chant.

TONGUES, THE GIFT OF. The gift, first bestowed by the Holy Ghost at Pentecost on those present in the Upper Room, of singing the praises of God in divers languages, at least fifteen, most of which must have been naturally unknown to the speakers. The gift was not used for the purposes of preaching, but of praising God. If the Apostles possessed later the gift of speaking the languages of the foreign nations they evangelized, the Scripture texts themselves never make reference to it. From the words of St. Paul (1 Cor. xii, 7-10) we conclude that speaking with languages was a gift given both to laity and religious leaders and consisted, not in addressing the faithful, but in praising God in an unknown tongue understood only by a person of that speech who happened to be present. The gift was common in the Church for over one hundred years, for St. Irenæus had known people who possessed it. Christ promised the continuance in the Church of this gift of "new tongues" (Mark xvi, 17). Some later saints are said to have had the gift of preaching "with tongues."

TONSURE (Lat. *tondere*, to shave). i. A complete shaving of part of the hair of the head which is prescribed by canon law for all clerics (except where, as in England and the U.S.A., it is not in accordance with the received manners of the people). The tonsure is the outward and visible sign of the clerical state and symbolizes Christ's crown of thorns. That of the secular clergy is a round space about the size of a half-crown at the crown of the head. There is much variety among religious: the Carthusians and Camaldolese shave the whole head except for a horizontal strip (*corona*) about a half-inch wide; the Friars Minor, Cistercians and some Benedictines the same but a wider *corona*: Dominicans shave the whole crown above the top of the ears, etc.; these are called the great tonsure. The tonsure of Eastern monks is a cruciform cutting of part of the hair.
ii. The rite by which a layman is made a cleric and prepared for the reception of minor and major orders; it is not itself an order. The bishop, or other prelate with delegated authority, cuts the hair of the candidate in front, behind, over each ear and on the crown and invests him with a surplice, according to the office in the "Pontificale." He who has thus received the tonsure is admitted to all the ecclesiastical privileges (*q.v.*) of clerics and may receive the first minor order at the bishop's discretion or may abandon his state at will.

iii. The Celtic tonsure, a factor in the Easter Controversy (*q.v.*), was made by cutting off all the hair in front of a line drawn over the head from ear to ear; it was thus worn in Celtic monasteries on the continent as well as by Celtic monks at home.

TONUS PEREGRINUS (Lat. the wandering tone). A psalm-tone sung chiefly to the words of Ps. cxiii, *In exitu Israel,* when it is sung at Sunday Vespers, and on certain occasions for Ps. cxii, *Laudate pueri;* it is occasionally appointed for other psalms and canticles, *e.g.,* the *Benedicite* on the feast of the Holy Name and in the common office of many martyrs. It is so called because it has two dominants or reciting notes, namely *la* for the mediant and *sol* for the final, thus giving the effect of a peregrination or wandering of the voice from the ordinary pitch of recitation.

TOPHETH (Heb., a place to be spat upon). The place in the valley of Hinnom (Gehenna, *q.v.*) where Moloch had been worshipped and where at the time of our Lord the refuse of Jerusalem was burnt.

TORAH (Heb., [God's] instruction). The whole revelation of God to Israel and body of Jewish theology, but particularly and commonly that contained in the Pentateuch (*q.v.*).

TOTIES QUOTIES (Lat., so often as). The gaining of a plenary indulgence (*q.v.*) *toties quoties,* so often as the prescribed conditions are fulfilled on one day, is attached to certain places and occasions, *e.g.,* the Portiuncula (*q.v.,* ii). These may, of course, be applied for the advantage of the souls in Purgatory. They may, however, also be applied to oneself; but as, having gained one plenary indulgence, there can be no object in trying to gain another unless and until one has again fallen into sin and been absolved, it would appear that by this permission the Church only means to increase the opportunities for the living to obtain this one.

TOURIÈRE. An extern sister (*q.v.*); so called because she attends at the revolving box (Fr., *tour*) by means of which parcels, etc., are conveyed into the convent enclosure.

TOUSSAINT (Fr.). All Saints' Day, Nov. 1.

TOWER OF DAVID, OF IVORY (*Turris Davidica, eburnea*). Titles given to our Lady in the litany of Loreto, referring to her Davidic descent and the beauty of her virginity; first used of her by Honorius of Autun (d. *c.* 1135), and *cf.,* Cant. iv, 4; vii, 4.

TRACT (so called because sung *in uno tractu,* in one movement, by one cantor originally, straight through without interruption). A penitential chant which follows the gradual (*q.v.*) instead of the Alleluia in

Masses from Septuagesima till Easter, on ember days, some vigils and in Masses for the dead. It was originally a complete psalm and still is on the 1st Sunday of Lent, Palm Sunday, Good Friday, Holy Saturday and vigil of Pentecost; at other times it is a few verses of holy Scripture, often from the psalms. On Mondays, Wednesdays and Fridays of Lent the tract is always the same, its penitential character very marked, and emphasized by a genuflection.

TRACT 90. The last and most famous of the Tracts for the Times, in which J. H. Newman (afterwards cardinal) sought to reconcile the Thirty-Nine Articles of the Church of England with the decrees of the Council of Trent.

TRACTS FOR THE TIMES. The series of tracts by which J. H. Newman and his fellows carried on the Oxford Movement (*q.v.*). They were designed to illustrate the essential idea of a teaching Church, the errors of contemporary churches and the Catholicity of the Anglican body. They began in 1833 and ended with Tract 90, in 1841.

TRACTARIANISM. The principles of the Oxford Movement (*q.v.*), so called from the above.

TRADE UNION. A continuous association of wage earners for the purpose of maintaining or improving the conditions of their employment. Unlike the mediæval gilds, their existence implies a division between the two classes of wage-receivers and wage-payers. The trade-unions seek to attain their end by the substitution of collective for individual bargaining, the weapon being the strike. Their activities, mainly directed towards the maintenance of a certain rate of pay as a minimum and a certain number of working hours as a maximum, also extend to providing a system of insurance against sickness, old age, death, accidents and unemployment. Their objects and methods are as subject to the duties of religion and morality as are the acts and aims of the individual. See ASSOCIATION, RIGHT OF.

TRADITIO SYMBOLI (Lat., the Handing-on of the Creed). In the early Church, the first recitation and explanation of the Apostles' Creed to a catechumen on Wednesday of the 4th week of Lent (*cf.*, references to Baptism in the Mass of that day). The *Redditio*, repetition, *Symboli* by the catechumen took place on Easter-eve before Baptism.

TRADITION (Lat. *traditio*, a giving-up, delivery). The sum of revealed doctrine which has not been committed to sacred Scripture (though it may have appeared in uninspired writing) but which has been handed down by a series of legitimate shepherds of the Church from age to age. As revelation it must have come to the Apostles directly from the lips of Christ or been handed down by the Apostles at the dictation of the Holy Ghost. More broadly the term is used for the sum of doctrine revealed either in Scripture or by word of mouth; so in 2 Thess. ii, 14: "Hold by the traditions you have learned, in word or in writing, from us."

TRADITION OF THE INSTRUMENTS, SYMBOLS. The giving to ordinands of the instruments or symbols of the grade of holy orders to which they are being admitted. This tradition is the matter of minor orders (*q.v.*) and of the subdiaconate (*cf.*, Holy Order).

TRADITIONALISM. i. In general, the transmission of facts or dogmas by a successive series of witnesses, whose testimony is contained in word or writing.

ii. The teaching of those who maintained that by reason alone man could not arrive at the truths of natural religion. Some, led by Huet, bishop of Avranches (1630-1721), taught that faith was a necessary supplement of reason in the attainment of certitude; these were called *Fideists* (Latin, *fides*, faith). Others, *e.g.*, Lammenais (*d.* 1854) and Bonald (*d.* 1840) insisted on the necessity of human tradition which should hand down the elements of an initial revelation by God. All this is false doctrine. The Vatican Council (sess. iii, can. 1, *de revelatione*) defined "If anyone say that the one true God, our Creator and Lord, cannot be known for certain by the light of reason through the things that are made, let him be anathema."

TRADITOR (Lat., one who gives up). A Christian who delivered up the sacred books or vessels of the Church, whether real or spurious, in accordance with the edict of the emperor Diocletian; hence arose a class of penitents who had done this, the *traditores*.

TRADUCIANISM (Lat. *tradux*, a vine shoot). The doctrine that human souls are in some way handed on to children from the parents. Some (*e.g.*, Tertullian) described the act as a material generation; others (among whom was St. Augustine for a period) as a spiritual generation. Rosmini argued that a sensitive soul was generated by the parents, and that God then changed this into a spiritual soul. The true doctrine is that every human soul is created immediately by God (Creationism, *q.v.*).

TRANSCENDENTALS. In scholastic philosophy those notions and realities which surpass and transcend all genera and categories are called transcendental, such as being, unity, truth, goodness.

TRANSFERENCE OF FEASTS. When there is occurrence (*q.v.*) of feasts, if the one that gives place is a double of the 1st or 2nd class it is celebrated on the next day that is free according to certain rules; it is never anticipated. This, and how a feast of lesser rank is to be dealt with, is noted in the *Ordo* (*q.v.*) for the year.

TRANSFIGURATION, The. i. The manifestation of the divinity of Jesus Christ vouchsafed to SS. Peter, James and John when he permitted the divine light momentarily to pass from his Godhead and his soul to his body and to become visible as an interior shining (Luke ix, 28-36, etc.). "It arose from the divine arrangement that the glory of Christ's soul did not, from the first moment of his conception, shine forth in his body, in order that he might work out the mystery of our redemption in a body capable of suffering. But this does not mean that Christ was deprived of the power to transmit the glory of his soul to his body; this indeed is what he did at his Transfiguration [when] shininess passed from his Godhead and his soul to his body, not as an indwelling quality affecting his body but rather as something passing, for example, like the atmosphere when lit up by the sun. Therefore the brilliance which then appeared in Christ's body was miraculous, just as when he walked on the waves of the sea" (St. Thomas, III, xlv, 2). According to tradition, the mountain on which this took place was Tabor in Galilee.

ii. A feast commemorating this event is kept on Aug. 6, but is of greater liturgical importance in the East than the West. It is the titular feast of churches dedicated to Saint Saviour, and in many places it is the custom to bless fruit thereon.

TRANSITUS (Lat., the passing over). i. A service peculiar to the three branches of the Franciscan order, commemorating the death of their holy founder and celebrated after either first or second Vespers of his feast.

ii. *Transitus Mariæ.* An obsolete name for the feast of the Assumption (*q.v.*). See also the FALLING ASLEEP OF MARY, ii.

iii. The word may express the death of anybody, particularly a saint.

TRANSLATION (Lat. *translatio*, a transference, removal). i. The transferring of a saint's relics to a more worthy shrine or their solemn removal from one place to another. Such an event has often been the occasion of a new liturgical feast. There is none such in the general calendar of the Roman church, but the feasts of some saints have been fixed on the date of the translation of their relics, the day of their death being impeded by another feast, *e.g.*, St. Edward the Confessor (Oct. 13), St. Romuald (Feb. 7). The following translations are kept in Great Britain: of St. Thomas Becket, in the city of Portsmouth, on July 7; of St. Chad, in the diocese of Birmingham; of St. Andrew, in Saint Andrews (May 9); of St. Cuthbert in Hexham (Sept. 4); of St. Edmund, in Brentwood and Portsmouth (June 9). There are also feasts of this sort in the Byzantine rite,

e.g., of St. John Chrysostom's relics (Jan. 27); of St. Ignatius of Antioch (Jan. 29). The feast of the Holy House of Loreto (*q.v.*) given in the supplement to the Missal *pro aliquibus locis* is called its *translation*.

ii. The word is also used of the transference of a bishop from one see to another, and of the transference of a feast.

TRANSMIGRATION OF SOULS. Metempsychosis (*q.v.*).

TRANSUBSTANTIATION. The mode by which, according to the infallible teaching of the Church, Christ's presence in the Eucharist is brought about. The word is defined by the Council of Trent as "the wonderful and singular conversion of the whole substance of the bread into the Body of Christ and of the whole substance of the wine into the Blood, the species (*q.v.*) of bread and wine alone remaining" (sess. xiii, can. 2). This means that both the matter and form (*qq.v.*) of the bread and wine cease to be; that the Body and Blood begin to be in a new way; and that the common bond between these two pairs of terms is the species. There is a "conversion" when hot water becomes cold; but this is a merely accidental change, a change in the accident of temperature. There is a substantial conversion when bread on being eaten becomes flesh; but here only one part of the substance, the form is changed, the prime matter (*q.v.*) remaining. The singularity of the eucharistic conversion lies in the change of the *whole* substance, matter and form, and to this there is no parallel in nature.

TRANSVERBERATION. This clumsy term, which simply means a piercing, is applied to the mystical experience of St. Teresa of Avila, described by herself in cap. xxix of her "Life," wherein an angel pierced her heart as with a dart and "left me wholly inflamed with a great love of God." The Carmelites commemorate this with a feast on Aug. 27, of which the proper of the Mass admirably illustrates the Church's attitude towards mystical phenomena of this sort (and may be contrasted with the naturalism of Bernini's statue of the same subject in the church of S. Maria della Vittoria at Rome).

TRAPPISTINES. A colloquial name for Cistercian nuns of the strict observance. See below.

TRAPPISTS. Those Cistercian monks who followed the constitutions of the abbey of La Trappe as reformed in 1664. They in a sense ceased to exist in 1892 when they were absorbed into the Cistercians (*q.v.*) of the More Strict Observance, to whom, however, the name "Trappist" is commonly and wrongly given.

TREASURY OF MERITS (sometimes called Treasury of Satisfactions or of the Church). The superabundant store of the merits and satisfactions of Christ, which were beyond the needs of our salvation, to which are added the excess of merits and satisfactions of our Lady and the saints. It is from this treasury that the Church grants indulgences (*q.v.*).

TREE OF LIFE, OF KNOWLEDGE (Gen. ii, 9, 17; iii, 22). These twain were in the midst of the paradise of Eden. If Adam had eaten of the Tree of Life he would have lived for ever. The tradition of Catholic exegesis is against regarding this as a mere allegory; however, all the details of Gen. i-iii need not be taken literally although the chapters as a whole must be regarded as real history. Adam fell through eating the fruit of the Tree of Knowledge of Good and Evil. Catholic exegetes explain the name in various ways, *e.g.*, "for God willed that by eating the forbidden fruit man should learn that obedience was good and disobedience evil" (Procopius of Gaza).

TRENT, THE COUNCIL OF. The 19th œcumenical council held at Trent in the Austrian Tyrol, 1545-63, summoned for the purpose of combating Protestantism and reforming the discipline of the Church; the longest and one of the most important of all general councils. It dealt in detail with the doctrinal innovations of the Reformers and with those gross abuses which gave them an opportunity to take root. It was one of the most important events of modern history and has had lasting effect. The principal dogmatic decisions were: the confirmation of the Nicene creed; the authenticity of the Latin Vulgate and the canonicity of all books contained therein and of them only; the definition of the doctrine of Original Sin; the precision of the doctrine of Justification, condemning justification by faith alone and imputation of grace; the condemnation of thirty errors about the sacraments; the definition of the Real Presence and of Transubstantiation as its mode: the precision of the doctrine of the sacraments of Penance and Extreme Unction; the declaration that holy communion in both kinds was not necessary for lay-people and clerics not celebrating, Christ being received whole and entire under either species; the precision of doctrine concerning the sacrifice of the Mass and the sacraments of holy Orders and Matrimony; the affirmation of the doctrines of Purgatory, of the invocation of saints and the veneration of them, their relics and images, and of Indulgences (*qq.v.*). Far-reaching decrees of reformation in discipline and morals were adopted involving many alterations of canon law, *e.g.*, the decree *Tametsi* (*q.v*). One English bishop, Goldwell of St. Asaph, and three Irish, o'Hart of Achonry, MacCongail of Raphoe, and o'Herlihy of Ross, took part in the council; and Cardinal Pole, afterwards of Canterbury, was a presiding legate at the opening.

TRENTAL (Fr., *trente*, thirty). A term for a series of thirty successive daily Masses for the repose of a soul.

TRIBUNAL, ROMAN. A court of law of the Roman Curia. There are three, the Penitentiaria, the Signatura and the Rota (*qq.v.*).

TRIDENTINE (adj., from med. Lat. *Tridentum*, Trent). Of or pertaining to the Council of Trent (*q.v.*).

TRIDUUM (Lat., a space of three days). A series of special services or private devotions or a retreat over this period usually preparatory to a great feast *e.g.*, of St. Joseph, in honour of the Blessed Sacrament (octave of Corpus Christi) or of the Holy Trinity (any time), or in preparation for first communion, or to celebrate a beatification or canonization, etc. *Triduum Sacrum* is the liturgical name for the last three days of Holy Week.

TRIENNIAL VOWS. Religious of perpetual vows, of either sex, are bound to make a preliminary profession of simple vows for three years only, after the completion of their noviciate which cannot be before the end of the 16th year. Triennial vows are not made in those congregations that have annual professions. They lapse automatically at the end of the period unless renewed or made perpetual.

TRIFLUVIANENSIS. The Latin epithet for the bishop of Trois-Rivières, Canada.

TRIKERION (Gr., three-candlestick). A candlestick similar to the *dikerion* (*q.v.*), but having three candles. It is held in the right hand and represents the three Persons of the Blessed Trinity. The two together are called the *dikerotrikera*.

TRINITARIANS, The. The Order of the Holy Trinity, said to have been founded in 1198 by St. John of Matha and St. Felix of Valois as canons regular under the rule of St. Augustine for the ransoming of Christian captives of the infidels; recognized as mendicant friars in 1609. Now engaged in teaching, nursing and similar work, with houses in Italy, Spain and the United States. They had eleven small monasteries in England before the Reformation. Habit: very similar to the Dominican, with a red and blue cross *flory* on scapular and *cappa;* in Spain the *cappa* is brown; discalced.

ii. Nuns of this name now have no connexion with the original order. They were founded in 1685, to undertake any works of mercy, but especially teaching and nursing. Unenclosed. Black tunic with red and blue cross on breast.

TRINITY, THE MOST HOLY AND UNDIVIDED. The three Persons (*q.v.* ii) in one God. God is one in nature but in that one God there are three distinct persons, the Father, the Son who proceeds from the Father by generation, and the Holy Ghost who proceeds from the Father and the Son, as from one principle, by spiration.

TRINITY SUNDAY. The feast of the Most Holy Trinity, observed by the Western church on the first Sunday after Pentecost. Every Sunday, and every day, being dedicated to God and therefore in a measure a feast of the Trinity, a special feast did not become general until the 14th century, and it is still unknown in most Eastern rites; it was first used in the church of Canterbury under St. Thomas Becket and spread from thence. In England before the Reformation, and among the Dominicans still, the Sundays after Pentecost are reckoned as such-and-such a Sunday after the octave of Trinity.

TRIPLE CANDLE. The threefold candle is no longer used after the blessing of the new fire on Holy Saturday. But for another such candle, see TRIKERION.

TRISAGION, The. The thrice-holy (τρίς ἅγιος) hymn, namely, the invocation, "Holy God, holy strong One, holy deathless One, have mercy on us," said in the Byzantine Liturgies by the deacon thrice at the *proskomide,* and sung four times by the choir with the doxology at the little entrance; it also occurs in the Divine Office. It is sung in all other Eastern Liturgies. In the Latin rite it is sung in Latin and Greek at the veneration of the cross on Good Friday, and in Latin only in the ferial prayers at Prime in penitential seasons. It must not be confused with the *Ter Sanctus,* to which in the Mozarabic rite a Greek "reminiscence" of the *Irisagion* is joined.

TRITHEISM. The dividing of the substance of the Blessed Trinity, so that the three Persons become three Gods. The first and principal of several obscure sects of Tritheists were the followers of John Philoponos, a monophysite philosopher of Antioch (*fl.* 560).

TRIVIUM (Lat., meeting place of three ways). See ARTS, LIBERAL.

TROPARION (Gr., a collection or series of tropes). A generic name for the short hymns of the Byzantine rite. Each strophe is properly a *troparion,* of which several make up an *ode,* the rhythm and melody following that of the first *troparion* (the *hirmos*); nine odes, having reference to the scriptural canticles, make a *kanon,* but the second is always omitted except in Lent when three odes only form the *kanon* (*triodion*). There are numerous classes of *troparia, e.g.,* a *theotokion* is in honour of our Lady, a *kontakion* refers to the feast of the day, an *oikos* expands the same, the *katabasia* is a *hirmos* repeated at the end of each ode on greater feasts, an *apolytikion* precedes the dismissal, etc. These hymns are composed of syllabic lines, based on the tonic accent, and are of frequent occurrence throughout the offices.

TROPE (Gr. τρόπος, a turn of speech). An antiphon, verse, etc., interpolated into a liturgical text according to mediæval custom. The book containing them was called a *troparium* or *troper.* Their use became an abuse and was done away with in the reform of Pope St. Pius V. See FARCING.

TROPOLOGY. The use of words figuratively; the interpretation of the figurative sense (*q.v.*) of the Holy Scriptures.

TRUCE OF GOD, The (Low Lat., *Treuga, Treva Dei*). A development of the *Pax Dei* (*q.v.*), which forbade every act of private warfare on certain days (*e.g.,* Lent, Advent, all Fridays) and which eventually covered three-quarters of the whole year. It was enforced by excommunication of those who broke the truce. It began in France in 1027 and was at its strongest in the 12th century when it had spread to Flanders, Italy and Germany and been confirmed by the first three councils of the Lateran. It was superseded by the increasing power of kings and the enlarged jurisdiction of their courts of law which enforced local peace.

TRUE CROSS, The. The cross upon which Jesus Christ died; the term is particularly applied to relics of this cross (*q.v.*).

TRULLO, COUNCILS IN (Gr. τροῦλλος, dome; from the roof of the hall in which they were held at Constantinople). i. The sixth œcumenical council (III Constantinople, *q.v.*) in 680-81.

ii. A synod held in 692, at the instance of the Emperor Justinian II which published 102 disciplinary canons, many of them directed against Roman practice. The bishops claimed to legislate for the whole Church but the Holy See refused to acknowledge the synod and only accepted the canons in so far as they were in accord with good morals and earlier canons and decrees; but the Orthodox Eastern Church regards it as a lawful continuation of the 5th and 6th œcumenical councils (which passed no disciplinary legislation), whence it is sometimes called the *Quinisextum,* but it is usually referred to as The Council *in Trullo.*

TRUTH. i. Logical, an adequation or agreement between the mind and a thing.

ii. Ontological, or truth of a thing, the adequation between a thing and the Divine Mind.

iii. Moral, the conformity of words or other signs with the conscience.

TRUTH, REVEALED. Any truth communicated by God to man by revelation (*q.v.*) and proposed for our acceptance by God's Church. Such a truth may be revealed formally and explicitly (*e.g.,* the articles of the Apostles' Creed) or formally and implicitly (*e.g.*, the Immaculate Conception). Concerning a third class of revealed truths, those "virtually revealed" (*e.g.*, the impeccability of Christ), the teachings of theologians differ as to whether, when they are infallibly defined by the Church, they become of divine faith or no. Formally revealed truths are of divine faith (*q.v.*).

TUAM (*Tuamensis*). An Irish archiepiscopal see; it was made metropolitan in 1152 and has 6 suffragans. It now covers half of counties Mayo and Galway and part of Roscommon. The patron of the diocese is St. Jarlath (June 6), and our Lady is the titular of the cathedral. The pilgrimage shrine of Croagh Patrick is within the archdiocese. Irish name: Tuaim.

TÜBINGEN SCHOOL, The. A group of German Protestant theologians and exegetes, followers of F. C. Baur (1792-1860), professor at the University of Tübingen. Their radical Biblical exegesis was based on minute and often fanciful criticism of the documents and on such false principles as a rivalry throughout the New Testament between St. Peter and St. Paul.

TUNIC, TUNICLE. i. The vestment proper to the subdiaconate and also worn by a cardinal, bishop or abbot under the dalmatic at pontifical Mass. It is now often indistinguishable from the dalmatic (*q.v.*) but should be shorter, with narrower sleeves and the *clavi* unjoined. The subdeacon is invested with it at ordination with the words, "May the Lord clothe thee with the garment of gladness and the vesture of joy"; it is worn whenever the dalmatic is worn.

ii. The chief and undermost garment of all religious habits of men and many of women, a loose gown put on over the head, reaching to the ankles and generally with narrow sleeves.

TUNICA TALARIS (Lat., a gown reaching to the ankles). Ecclesiastically, the alb or cassock.

TURKEY, THE CHURCH IN. The population of the country is 17 million, of whom only 1 million live in European Turkey. The Turks are solidly Mohammedan, but Islam ceased to be the state-established religion in 1928 and the government is secularist, with a special hostility towards foreign Christians. Constantinople is the seat of the Œcumenical Patriarch (*q.v.*), the chief hierarch of the Orthodox Church, but he has only some 100,000 subjects in Turkey. The massacres, deportations and famines after 1915 almost cleared Asiatic Turkey of Christians; 17 Catholic dioceses, 13 of them Armenian, were destroyed there by Turks and Kurds during world-war I. There are now about 63,000 Catholics (50,000 of Latin rite), most of them in and around Constantinople and Smyrna. The latter city is an archiepiscopal see (with 1 suffragan, in Greece) and there is a vicariate apostolic for Constantinople, where the Catholics of Armenian rite have an episcopal see and those of Byzantine rite an ordinariate. The few Melkites and Chaldeans (*qq.v.*) have patriarchal vicars. Christians in Turkey are subject to some tiresome restrictions, *e.g.*, concerning ecclesiastical dress.

TUTIORISM (Lat. *tutior*, more safe). A system in moral theology which tries to solve the problem how to act when in doubt whether a law is or is not binding in given circumstances by insisting that the law must be obeyed unless the opinion favouring liberty be most certain. Tutiorism was virtually condemned along with Rigorism (*q.v.*) by Pope Alexander VIII in 1690. See PROBABILISM.

TWELFTH DAY. The twelfth day after Christmas, namely, the feast of the Epiphany and Old Christmas Day (by the Julian calendar, *q.v.*). Many old popular customs are associated with this day and its vigil, of which the one now best known in England is the removal of Christmas decorations from house and church.

TWELVE APOSTLES, The. It is of faith that Christ gave the college of the Apostles the prerogative of infallibility (*q.v.*) in handing down his doctrine of faith and morals; also that he gave them authority to govern the Church. "You, therefore, must go out, making disciples of all nations . . . teaching them to observe all the commandments which I have given you. And behold I am with you all through the days that are coming. . . ." (Matt. xxviii, 18-20); "All that you bind on earth shall be bound in Heaven: and all that you loose on earth shall be loosed in Heaven" (Matt. xviii, 18). They all had universal jurisdiction, exercising their apostolate in any field that they chose, and they all had personal infallibility. Some of them wrote, and their message was inspired. It is held that after Pentecost they had received "confirmation in grace" (*q.v.*). They all had the *charismata* (*q.v.*).

TWENTY-EIGHTH CANON OF CHALCEDON, The. A canon adopted by a minority of the bishops at that council to the effect that the primacy and the highest honour being, in accordance with the canons, preserved to the most holy Archbishop of Rome, the most holy Archbishop of Constantinople, the new Rome, must enjoy the same privileges of honour and rank next after the Roman patriarch The legates of the Holy See condemned the canon as infringing the rights of Alexandria and Antioch laid down at the Council of Nicæa. Pope St. Leo the Great confirmed their condemnation and Anatolius of Constantinople submitted and cancelled the canon. It was revived by Photius and Cerularius, but Constantinople was not fully recognized by Rome as the second patriarchal see until the fourth Lateran Council in 1215.

TWO SWORDS, The. The doctrine of the relationship between religious and secular power as expressed in the bull *Unam sanctam (q.v.)*: "We are taught by the gospels that there are two swords in the hand of this power [St. Peter], the spiritual sword and the temporal sword . . . [which] are then in the Church's power: the one to be wielded by the Church, the other for the Church; the one by priests, the other by kings and soldiers, but by the will and permission of the priest. But the one sword must be under the other, and the temporal authority subject to the spiritual. . . . 'The spiritual man judgeth all things, but he is judged by no man' " (1 Cor. ii, 15). This is the idea at the bottom of the Holy Roman Empire *(q.v.)*, but it is not a definition that princes and states are subject to the Holy See in temporal matters (for that is not the teaching of the Church), except in so far as her universal jurisdiction in morals may require such subjection in particular cases (*cf.*, Church and State).

TYBURN NUNS, The. The name given to the Sisters Adorers of the Sacred Heart, who have a convent and shrine of the English martyrs near the site of Tyburn gallows (Marble Arch) where many of the martyrs suffered, and another at Royston. They follow the Rule of St. Benedict with perpetual adoration *(q.v.)*.

TYNDALE'S BIBLE. An English version of the New Testament (1526) and the Pentateuch (1530), made by William Tyndale, an apostate Franciscan, and published abroad.

TYPE (Gr. τύπος, model, impression). i. In ordinary language the type of a genus or a species is the ideal of the genus or species; also it means the individual which seems to realize this ideal. In the philosophy of Plato types (or archetypes, *q.v.*) are the exemplary ideas of things.

ii. In its biblical sense a type is a person, thing, action or event in the Old Testament which the Holy Ghost presents as a foreshadowing of the future. Thus Adam (Rom. v, 14), Melchisideck (as priest), Jonas ("resurrected" from the monster) are types of Jesus Christ, the antitype; Jerusalem or Zion is a type of the Heavenly City; the Flood, of Baptism; the paschal lamb, of the sacrifice of Calvary, etc. (*cf.*, sense of Scriptures). There are many other spiritual types, the lower being the figure of the higher, *e.g.*, human marriage is a type of the union of Christ with his Church or with the individual soul.

TYPICA [EDITIO]. The standard and official edition of a liturgical or other book, to the text of which other editions or excerpts must conform.

TYPIKON. i. A liturgical book of Byzantine rite containing a perpetual calendar and full instructions for the recitation of the Divine Office and carrying out of various offices. Each chief church has its own *typikon*, generally founded on those of Jerusalem (St. Sabas) and Constantinople: thus the Catholic Melkites use one composed by Archimandrite Kyril Reqz for the council of Ain Traz in 1909.

ii. Plural, *typika*. Ps. cii and cxlv, with antiphons and followed by the Beatitudes, sung in the first part of the Liturgy on Sundays and chief saints' days.

TYRANNICIDE. The killing of a tyrant. A tyrant by usurpation, *i.e.*, one who attempts to usurp the supreme government of a state, may not be killed by a private person unless he has a mandate to do so from legitimate authority. Once the usurper reigns peacefully, his just laws must be obeyed; but assistance may be given to the legitimate ruler should he attempt to re-establish his authority with some prospect of success. In the case of a tyrant by oppression, it is of Catholic faith (defined in the Council of Constance) that no private person may kill such a tyrant.

U

UBIQUITY OF GOD. The omnipresence of God *(q.v.)*.

UDINE, PATRIARCH OF. A title sometimes given to the patriarchs of Aquileia during their residence in Udine from 1348 till 1451. See GRADO.

UKRAINIANS, The. See RUTHENIANS.

ULTRAMONTANISM (Lat., *ultra*, beyond; *montes*, the mountains). A term invented by the Gallicans to describe the doctrines and

policies which upheld the full authority of the Holy See. With the noun and adjective *ultramontane* it was used down to the end of the 19th century (especially at the time of the Vatican Council), and still is sometimes, usually by non-Catholic controversialists, to describe a real or supposed exaggeration of papal prerogatives and those who supported them. In the middle ages *ultramontane* was used at Rome with an opposite (geographical) meaning, for anyone domiciled north of the Alps; *cf.*, Cisalpine Club.

UNAM SANCTAM. A bull of Pope Boniface VIII in 1302. After stating Catholic doctrine concerning the unity of the Church and the primacy of the Holy See, it defined that "to be subject to the Roman Pontiff is a necessity for salvation for every human being," whereby was meant that obedience due to him in religious but not in solely temporal matters (*cf.*, also, salvation outside the Church). The rest of the bull was concerned with an exposition of the relationship between religious and secular power, expressed in terms of "the two swords" (*q.v.*), in view of the conditions obtaining in Europe at that time.

UNANSWERED PRAYER. Prayer of petition in which the object of requests is not granted. This may be the fault of the person who prays, in that he does not bring the due dispositions to his prayer. On the other hand, God may be trying the faith and fortitude of his child by not acceding immediately, but only after insistent prayer; or he may be really refusing the request for the reason that he, who knows all things, knows that this particular favour would not be good for the soul. Thus requests for temporal favours may be refused, or for definite spiritual ones, *e.g.*, deliverance from a trial or temptation; or prayers for others, because of their lack of good dispositions. There is, however, a lurking untruth in the phrase, because no prayer is really unanswered. It may not attain the definite object of request: but every true prayer brings down God's graces on the petitioner and his fellow-members in the Mystical Body; "the Lord always gives more than he is asked" (St. Ambrose), and see Isaias xl, 31. "The Christian prayer is quite infallible because of its universality of purpose; none of the demands of the 'Our Father' are ever refused, because the Body of Christ, the people of God, are the direct objects of the divine favours asked for in it. ... Any Christian saying [it] does, in a way, a sacramental thing, a thing that works with absolute certainty, because whatever he asks for is granted to the people to which he belongs" (Vonier).

UNBAPTIZED, FATE OF THE. Baptism is necessary for salvation, but where baptism of water is impossible, the desire of it will fulfill the necessary condition. This desire is implicitly contained in an act of perfect contrition or of charity. Such an act fully disposes the soul for the reception of sanctifying grace and so for the remission of original sin and actual mortal sin. Thus he can be saved. Of course, martyrdom ensures the salvation of the unbaptized adult. See also INFANTS, UNBAPTIZED, and LIMBO, ii.

UNCLEAN, RITUALLY. The state of being ceremonially or legally tainted and in need of external purification without reference to the purity or otherwise of one's moral condi-tion. Such a state is absolutely unknown to Christianity (*cf.*, churching of women). It was a notable characteristic of the Mosaic law (Lev. xi-xv), abrogated by Christ, but alive in Islam to-day. Purification following the eating of certain meats, the use of marriage, childbirth, etc., originated as an hygienic prescription but was universally regarded as an act to avert the visitation of God, though without reference to the moral quality of the act performed.

UNCTION (Lat. *unguere*, to anoint). A word that has come into common ecclesiastical use to designate anointings with oil for religious purposes, *e.g.*, Extreme Unction, at Baptism, Confirmation, etc.

UNDE ET MEMORES. The first words of the prayer after the consecration at Mass, wherein the celebrant, in obedience to the command "Do this in remembrance of me," recalls the passion, resurrection and ascension of our Lord—the *anamnesis*. It emphasizes the part of the people, who participate in Christ's universal priesthood, in offering up the sacrifice with the priest.

UNDENOMINATIONALISM. i. The doctrine that there is a deposit of undefined truth, mostly ethical, underlying all churches, sects and denominations and transcending their differences, and that this deposit may and should be the ground for complete intercommunion among, and the spring of common religious and social action for, all who call themselves Christians. It is a form of Pan-christianity (*q.v.*) and is by some extended to non-Christians.

ii. The conduct of certain activities, *e.g.*, education, social work, *ex professo* without reference to the teaching of any religious body, with the idea of making it acceptable to all or any of them. The Catholic Church repudiates such working in so far as it is based on the principle that such things are independent of religion and in so far as it is in practice an anti-Catholic activity (as it sometimes is). But there is plenty of undenominational activity that does not come under these condemnations, and in many countries Catholics co-operate with non-Catholics in corporal good works, with the highest ecclesiastical encouragement and excellent results.

UNDERSTANDING. i. The term used to denote intellect as exercised in the act of simple judgement, and as such is opposed to Reason, which is used to designate intellectual activity exhibited in ratiocination. The habit of the prompt and easy use of the understanding is one of the intellectual virtues (*q.v.*). This faculty of the soul is variously referred to as intelligence, intellect, reason, critical faculty, etc. By it a man is enabled to form ideas, to make judgements and comparisons, to perceive the meanings of things and to estimate their value. By it man is distinguished from the brutes, which do not possess it.

ii. As a gift of the Holy Ghost, understanding helps towards a better understanding of the mysteries of religion and a consequent greater attachment thereto, especially when confronted by difficulties, as expressed by Cardinal Newman's phrase "Ten thousand difficulties do not make one doubt."

UNFIT, KILLING OF THE. The putting to death of the deformed, the mentally defective and those suffering from hereditary disease, on the plea that they are a burden to themselves and upon society. This is murder and, as Pope Pius XII wrote in his encyclical *Mystici Corporis Christi*, "an outrage upon the noblest instincts of mankind." For segregation and sterilization, see EUGENICS.

UNFROCKING. A popular term in English for degradation (*q.v.*).

UNIAT, -ATE. A Catholic belonging to one or other of the Eastern rites. The name derives from Latin *unio,* union, through the Polish *unia* (Russian *unija,* Greek *ounia*), words devised after 1596 to designate the Union of Brest (*q.v.*) in spite of the fact that union is ordinarily called *jednosc, soedinenie* and *enosis* respectively in those languages. For historical reasons, *uniate* is a term of contempt among the Russian and Greek Orthodox and its use is offensive to many of the Catholics to whom it is applied; moreover, it has no authority and is never used in official ecclesiastical acts in Rome or in such publications as the *Annuario Pontificio.* Its continued use in ordinary speech and writing in England, the U.S.A., and elsewhere is to be deplored: "Catholic of such and such an Eastern rite" is less convenient but is strictly accurate and void of offence or regrettable association.

UNIATISM. A term of reproach recently devised to designate the process by which Catholics of Eastern rites tend to become de-orientalized, neglecting the study of the oriental fathers and early councils, adopting Western disciplinary customs, forms of popular devotion and ascetical treatises, adapting themselves to an European outlook, and accepting liturgical hybridism (*q.v.*). Such inovations make the principal external difference between dissidents and Catholics of the same rite and so come to be improperly identified with Catholicism itself, which becomes in consequence in bad odour among the separated who are greatly attached to their own legitimate customs, and fear to lose them if they submit to the Holy See. This uniatism has grown up in spite of numerous contrary provisions of the Holy See; it is a grave stumbling-block to the reunion of the dissident Eastern churches; and it is not in accordance with that variety, inclusiveness and local perfection and fittingness which

are marks of the Church as the universal ark of salvation.

UNICITY, as in the phrase "unicity of the Church," meaning the state of there being only one Church. It is an ungraceful word: if "unity" be deemed ambiguous, "uniqueness" or "oneness" correctly expresses the idea.

UNIFORMITY. Outside the boundaries of defined faith and morals, which being matters of divine revelation and therefore infallibly true are necessarily the same always and everywhere, there is no principle of uniformity in the Catholic Church. This is sufficiently demonstrated by the variety of rites of worship, liturgical languages, canon law and custom found among different peoples, from the earliest times down to the present day. Already in the middle of the third century Firmilian, bishop of Caesarea in Cappadocia, remarked that the liturgical variety then existing made no difference to Catholic unity. Though they do not refer specifically to these matters, the words of Pope Pius XII in *Summi pontificatus* are apposite: "The Church aims at unity . . . she does not aim at a uniformity which would only be external in its effects, and would cramp the natural tendencies of the peoples concerned. Every nation has its own genius, its own qualities, springing from the hidden roots of its being."

UNIFORMITY, ACTS OF. Several acts of Parliament by which it was sought to impose the worship of the Church of England upon all the people of England and Wales. The chief were: (*a*) 5 and 6 Ed. VI, c. 1 (1551-2), which made attendance at church compulsory on Sundays and holy days and the use of any other book but that of Common Prayer, *i.e.,* the second of Edward VI, punishable by fine and imprisonment; (*b*) 1 Eliz. c. 2 (1559) revived the previous act, repealed under Mary, making it more stringent and severe, every absence from the Protestant service involving a fine of 12 pence; (*c*) 13 Chas. II, c. 4 (1662), which again restored the Prayer Book and required all ministers to be ordained by a bishop and afterwards to take an oath of non-resistance to the crown: this resulted in the deprivation of their livings of numerous nonconformist ministers.

UNIFORMITY OF NATURE, THE PRINCIPLE OF. The metaphysical principle that natural causes, *i.e.,* those operative in the physical universe apart from the free will of man, when they act in similar circumstances always and everywhere produce similar results.

UNIGENITUS. i. A jubilee bull of Pope Clement VI in 1343 in which the doctrine of the treasury of merits (*q.v.*) was authoritatively taught.

ii. A constitution of Pope Clement XI in

1713 which condemned *in globo* 101 propositions drawn from a book of moral reflections on the New Testament by Pasquier Quesnel, particularly that all love except the supernatural love of God is evil, that the prayer of a sinner is sinful, that the elect alone form the Church, that sinners should not assist at Mass or be absolved till their penance is performed, and other errors of Jansenism (*q.v.*). At a metropolitan council of Rome in 1725 this act was confirmed by Pope Benedict XIII and declared to be a rule of faith involving complete obedience.

UNION OF BREST, The. The withdrawal of the allegiance of the metropolitan of Kiev and the other bishops of southwest Russia and the adjoining parts from the Orthodox Church and their submission to the Holy See, made at Brest-Litovsky in Lithuania in 1595; it involved the return of over 10 million Christians of the Byzantine rite to the Catholic Church. After the partition of Poland, in persecutions under Catherine II, Nicholas I and Alexander II, Russia reaggregated by force millions of these Ruthenians to the Orthodox Church for political reasons. The existing Catholic Ruthenians (*q.v.*) of Galicia are those who came under the government of Austria in 1795.

UNION OF FLORENCE, The. The reunion between the Catholic Church and the dissident Eastern Churches effected in 1439 at the Council of Florence (*q.v.*).

UNITARIANISM. In general, the rejection by any monotheist of the doctrine of the Holy Trinity (*e.g.*, a Mohammedan is a Unitarian); in particular, the religious system of a loosely organized religious body founded in London in 1774. Its members reject belief in the Trinity, the divinity of Christ, the Atonement, the infallibility of the Bible, Hell and "other orthodox beliefs," and from the first their principles have been simply those adopted by individual members on the ground of natural reason; their opinions therefore vary, but they agree in the rejection of all theological doctrine. Their rationalist basis has hitherto been their strength, resulting in a keen intellectualism, strong natural virtue and simple piety. The Unitarian denomination is principally represented in Great Britain and the U.S.A.

UNITED GREEKS. A loose term sometimes used to designate Catholics of the Byzantine rite, irrespective of their nationality and liturgical language. It is both clumsy and inaccurate. The analogous expressions, United Armenians, United Syrians, etc., are less objectionable.

UNITED STATES, THE CHURCH IN THE. The first missionaries in North America were Franciscan friars who came to Lower California with Cortes in 1535; the first permanent Christian establishment was in 1565, when a Spanish colony was formed at Saint Augustine, in Florida, and a parish canonically erected. The early martyrs of North America at the hands of the Indians were canonized in 1930. The episcopal hierarchy was begun by the setting-up of the diocese of Baltimore in 1789, John Carroll being the first bishop; he was consecrated at Lulworth Castle in Dorsetshire by the senior vicar apostolic of England, Dom Charles Walmesley, O.S.B. The American federal constitution forbids any religious test as a qualification for public office and forbids the state establishment of or interference with the free exercise of any religion. The constitutions of each of the states of the Union have in the course of time all adopted the principle that no person shall be preferred or penalized on account of his religious convictions, "unless under colour of religion the preservation of equal liberty and the existence of the state are manifestly endangered." In most states confession to a priest is recognized by law as a privileged communication, and clergy are exempt from compulsory enlistment for military service; in some states testamentary bequests for the celebration of Mass are invalid. The population of the United States is estimated at 168 million (1956), of whom over 30½ million are Catholics, the largest single religious body. Like the people as a whole, European emigration has made the Church in the United States a pentecostal gathering of national origins, in which Irish, German, Italian and Polish are numerically outstanding; there are ¾ million Ruthenians, and over 75,000 others of Eastern rites; about 120,000 of the indigenous Indians are Catholics, and a few thousand Eskimos in Alaska, but only about ½ million of the 15 million Negroes. The Church in the United States is divided into 24 metropolitan provinces, namely, Baltimore (which always has precedence), Boston, Chicago, Cincinnati, Denver, Detroit, Dubuque, Indianapolis, Kansas City, Los Angeles, Louisville, Milwaukee, Newark, New Orleans, New York, Omaha, Philadelphia, Portland (Oregon), San Francisco, Saint Louis, Saint Paul, San Antonio, Santa Fe and Seattle. These have 101 suffragan bishoprics. Washington, D.C., is an archbishopric without suffragans. There are as well a Benedictine abbacy *nullius* (Belmont), a vicariate apostolic (Alaska), two exarchates for the Ukrainians and one for the Rusins. None of the bishops of the United States has a chapter of canons, but each is assisted by a board of diocesan consultors. The Holy See has a delegate apostolic at Washington.

UNITIVE WAY, The. This follows schematically on the illuminative way (*q.v.*), although it may partly synchronize with it. It is the highest state of the spiritual life, in which the soul progresses in union with God through Jesus Christ, and realizes St. Paul's state: "I am alive; or rather, not I; it is Christ that lives in me" (Gal. ii, 20). "The third effort of man is to give his principal attention to union with God and enjoyment of God; and this pertains to the perfect, who desire to be dissolved and to be with Christ" (St. Thomas, II-II, xxiv, 8). It is the life of passive contemplation or mystical union (*qq.v.*).

UNITY. i. The abstract of *one,* and is that whereby a thing is undivided in itself and divided from all else. Essential unity is that oneness resulting from a complete nature, as man; accidental unity is a oneness resulting from two or more complete natures, as a heap of stones; or resulting from a complete nature and an accident, as a white wall. Unity may be individual, specific or generic; just as Peter is one individually, all men are one species, all animals one genus.

ii. Mathematical unity is wholly distinct from the above transcendental or essential unity. Mathematical unity is an accident, and belongs to quantity, and is therefore not identical with being; it is the principle of number.

UNITY OF THE CHURCH. A mark (*q.v.*) of the Church. Christ established one, and only one, church; and this church is an organic whole. It is one society, external and visible, whose members profess the same faith, follow the same essential forms of worship, use the same sacraments, and submit to the one central authority, the pope; and it is the one prescribed way of salvation for all, so that it is said "Outside the Church no salvation" (*q.v.*). It is this visible unity which is the mark, and not the simply internal unity, grounded on union with Christ, which some non-Catholics claim to be the mark. This visible unity does not require or involve uniformity in non-essential matters. See UNIFORMITY.

UNITY OF GOD. There is question here not of mathematical but of transcendental unity (see above). This unity does not add anything to being except the negation of division. On the other hand, mathematical unity which is the principle of number is opposed to multitude as the measure to the measured and this unity is not predicated of God; but *transcendental* unity is opposed to the many by way of privation as the undivided to the divided, and in this wise God is not only one, but supereminently one; he is the greatest being because he is *Ipsum esse;* he is supremely undivided because he is both actually and potentially undivided, since he is most simple (*q.v.*).

UNITY OF THE HUMAN RACE. See BROTHERHOOD OF MAN.

UNIVERSALIS ECCLESIÆ. A letter apostolic of Pope Pius IX of Sept. 29, 1850, by which the restoration of a regular hierarchy of bishops to England and Wales was effected. The bull erecting the diocese of Brentwood in 1917 and the constitution erecting that of Lancaster in 1924 began with the same words.

UNIVERSALISM. The doctrine of the ultimate salvation of all men, commonly expressed in the phrase, "I don't believe in Hell" (*q.v.*). It has given its name to the American Unitarian sect of Universalists; but its distinguishing tenet is a commonplace of contemporary Protestantism.

UNIVERSALS (Lat. *universalis,* belonging to the whole, or all). Certain general ideas which are attributable to several subjects. There are five: genus, species, difference, property and accident. Thus a genus is common to many, specifically different, and can be predicated of them as belonging, in part, to their essence; thus animal is common to man and different species of brutes, and is predicated of man and brutes as part of their essence. And so with the remaining universals, they are conceived as *one* common, in varying ways, to many. The question of the universals was fiercely discussed in the middle ages and has been debated even in our own day under different names. The question is: Are universals mere concepts having no corresponding objective reality or are they truly objective, representing extramental reality? Exaggerated Realism holds that universals *as such* are extramental; Nominalism and Conceptualism hold that they are either mere names or mere ideas. The truth, held by Moderate Realism, is that precisely as universals they exist only in the mind, but they have a real foundation in things themselves. The idea "man," for instance, formally as such, does not exist: there is no man who is simply "man"; but Peter and Paul exist in whom "man" is realized, who of course really have not only the nature of man but also other qualities which characterize them. To deny the reality of universals in this sense is to open the way to subjectivism, to denaturalize language, and to destroy knowledge.

UNIVERSITY (Lat. *universitas,* the whole, entireness, with reference both to the corporation and to the scope of its studies). An educational institution for instructing, examining and conferring degrees in the more important branches of learning. The troubled times which followed the Reformation crippled the once flourishing universities of the middle ages in many parts of Europe; the recovery of the 18th and 19th centuries still continues. Most countries of importance to-day possess either Catholic universities complete with faculties of theology and canon law, or at least Catholic faculties attached to some of the state universities— England is a prominent exception. Until 1895 English Catholics were debarred from university education, but in that year Pope Leo XIII gave permission for them to attend the Universities of Oxford and Cambridge, due safeguards of faith and morals being provided by the English bishops. The principal universities of the middle ages were Bologna (constituted in 1111), Paris (1200), Toulouse (1223), Naples (1224), Padua (1228), Rome (1245), Oxford (University College, 1249), Cambridge (Peterhouse, 1257), Salamanca (1255), Saint Andrews (1410), Louvain (1426), Glasgow (1450). Among those universities to-day which are entirely under Catholic control and authorized by the Holy See are the Pontifical University at Rome (1552, 1929), Louvain (1426, 1833), Laval (1876), Bairut (1881), Freiburg (1889), of America (Washington, 1889), Ottawa (1889), Tokyo (1913), Milan (1921), Nymegan (Holland, 1923), Peking (1929), and São Paulo (Brazil). The establishment of a Catholic university with faculties of theology and canon law requires the approval of the Holy See but has complete autonomy when established.

UNIVERSITY, THE PONTIFICAL GREGORIAN. The central university for ecclesiastical studies at Rome also includes as autonomous bodies the Biblical Institute and the Oriental Institute (*qq.v.*). The Dominican Biblical School at Jerusalem is regarded as a branch of this university and is open to all its members. See GREGORIAN UNIVERSITY.

UNWORTHY LIFE is a prohibiting impediment (*q.v.*) by which is rendered unlawful (but not invalid) marriage between a Catholic and one who is an apostate, a notorious public sinner, under censure, etc. If the offender has joined an heretical sect the additional impediment of "mixed religion" arises.

URBAN COLLEGE (OF PROPAGANDA), The. Founded by Pope Urban VIII, in 1627, for the training of missionaries of all nationalities, and to receive seminarians from any country under the jurisdiction of the Congregation *de Propaganda Fide,* to which the college itself is subject.

URBANIST POPES, The. The popes who reigned at Rome during the Schism of the West (*q.v.*), namely Urban VI (1378), Boniface IX (1389), Innocent VII (1404) and Gregory XII (1406).

URBI ET ORBI (Lat., to the City and the World). A phrase applied to the solemn blessing publicly given by the pope from the balcony of St. Peter's on special occasions such as his election, enthronization, during years of jubilee, etc. This custom fell into abeyance after 1870, but at his election on Feb. 6, 1922, Pope Pius XI gave the blessing publicly again from the façade of St. Peter's. The phrase was also applied to the public apostolic benediction (*q.v.*), but inaccurately (*cf.*, Reconciliation, ii).

URSULINES, The. The name of several congregations of sisters, all engaged in education of girls. The principal one is that founded by St. Angela Merici in 1535, the Company of St. Ursula, the first authorized teaching-order for women. The Ursulines of the Roman Union are semi-cloistered nuns; solemn vows; office in choir. Full black habit, wide sleeves, black veil; train on occasions. The Ursulines of Jesus (Dames de Chavagnes), unenclosed, are also represented in Great Britain and North America.

URUGUAY, THE CHURCH IN. The population is over 2 million, practically all Catholics by profession. There is no state religion, and all faiths are equally free; but the civil power is unfriendly towards the Church, and sometimes definitely hostile. The country has one metropolitan see, Montevideo, with 2 suffragan bishoprics.

USE. The peculiar liturgical texts and customs, neither historically nor in practice amounting to a distinct rite, used by a diocese, province or religious order; they were very numerous in the middle ages but few survived the reform of Pope St. Pius V and the subsequent movement towards uniformity in the Western church. The liturgies of Sarum, York, Hereford and Bangor were, and those of the Carmelites, Carthusians, Dominicans, Lyons, Braga, etc., are, uses of the Roman rite, as that of the Ruthenians is of the Byzantine rite. Nowadays each set of special usages is commonly called a rite, irrespective of its history and liturgical significance (*cf.*, Rite, ii, v).

USE OF REASON. Children are presumed in canon law to come to the use of reason on completing seven years of age, unless the contrary is proved, and are presumed not to have the use of reason before that age. Adults without the use of reason (*e.g.*, the insane) are counted in law as infants (*q.v.*).

USHAW. The College of St. Cuthbert, near Durham, established in 1794 at Crook Hall for the northern students of the English College at Douay (*q.v.*) when that was broken up by the Revolution. It is the seminary for the northern dioceses and a school for lay boys.

U.S.S.R., THE CHURCH IN THE. i. The overwhelming majority of the people of the country now known as The Union of Soviet Socialist Republics belongs nominally to the Russian Orthodox (*q.v.*) Church. After the revolution of 1917 there began an *ex-professo* atheistic regime which followed a policy of religious persecution: one aspect of it was violent, and brutal and bloody in the extreme; this was sporadic: the other aspect was the nation-wide and detailed attempt to extirpate religion (not only Christianity) by means of atheistic education, propaganda and discrimination; this has been continuous. People were at all times free to attend divine worship, but every other possible hindrance and discouragement was put in the way of an open Christian life: all religious charitable, recreational, cultural and, especially, educational activity (including religious teaching of those under 18) was forbidden, seminaries and monasteries were closed, and all ecclesiastical property confiscated. The full effect of all this is not known; many Orthodox bishops, priests, monks and lay people resisted to the death, and many more were punished with forced labour in concentration camps and exile to remote parts; but quite certainly the aim of totally destroying the influence of the Russian Church was not achieved, for when the U.S.S.R. was invaded by the nazis in 1941 the soviet government took steps to placate its Christian subjects: among the concessions eventually made were to allow the appointment of a patriarch of Moscow (the chief see had been vacant since 1925) and provision for training clergy. This brought about an apparent *rapprochement* between church and state in the U.S.S.R.; but there is no reason to suppose that it is more than a policy of expedience on either side. Outside of Russia the *emigrés* suffer from ecclesiastical divisions: many look to the refugee bishops of the Synod of Munich (formerly of Karlovtsy in Serbia), who are implacably opposed to the soviet government and do not recognize the patriarch it sponsors.

ii. *The Catholic Church, 1917-1939.* When Poland and Lithuania became independent again after world-war I there were only about 2 million Catholics left in Russia, practically all foreigners or Byelorussians in the west and south-west. Their head was the archbishop of Mogilev, who had 4 suffragan sees. There was also a small group of Byzantine rite, with an exarch (See also GEORGIA). These suffered equally and in the same way with their Orthodox brethren: outstanding among the martyrs and confessors were Mgr. Budkiewicz, Bishops Sloskan and Malecky, and the Exarch Leonid Feodorov. The diocesan organizations gradually disappeared, and the faithful became the charge of a special commission at Rome, which could do little. By 1935 the 473 clergy of the Mogilev archdiocese had been reduced by execution, exile, privation, imprisonment and natural causes to 16; 5 years later there was apparently only 1 Catholic priest at liberty in all Russia.

iii. *The Catholic Church, after 1939.* During world-war II the U.S.S.R. annexed a number of European territories, some of which have large Catholic populations. Particulars of these can be found herein by reference to Latvia, Lithuania, Poland, and the Ruthenians. There are then today within the U.S.S.R. altogether some 18 Catholic dioceses, comprising over 10 million faithful (4 million of Slav-Byzantine rite). What will become of them is a matter for discouraging speculation. Outside, as inside, U.S.S.R. the number of Great Russians (*i.e,* Russians properly-speaking) who are Catholics is infinitesimal—a few tiny groups scattered about western Europe, the Far East and the United States; they have an ordaining bishop of Byzantine rite at Rome.

"USUAL CONDITIONS, ON THE." A plenary indulgence (*q.v.*) granted in these terms involves the necessity, in addition to doing the good works prescribed, of receiving the sacraments of Penance and the Eucharist and of praying for the intentions of the pope. These are ordinarily: the common good of the Church, the spread of the faith, conversion of sinners, heretics and schismatics, and peace; it is not necessary to advert to these in detail. Our Father, Hail Mary and Glory be, or similar prayers, will suffice. Any church may be visited unless one is specified. Confession may be made within eight days before or eight days after the day on which the indulgence is to be gained; communion received the day before or within eight days after. The habit of confession once a fortnight entitles a person to gain all indulgences for which confession is a required condition, even when such confession is actually omitted owing to a legitimate impediment. To gain any indulgence it is probably necessary to have at least an implicit intention to do so, and to have a contrite heart, *i.e.*, be in a state of grace. Moreover, if the prescribed good work is the recital of a prayer or other form of words, these words must be articulated with the lips (not necessarily said aloud); to read them with the eyes or say them in the mind is not sufficient. Whether or no one in mortal sin can gain an indulgence on behalf of the dead is a matter disputed among theologians.

USURY (Lat., *usura*, use of money lent). Usury is strictly speaking profit exacted on a loan of money just because it is a loan. This is unjust, because money as money has no value save in its use. But interest may be justly charged for reasons extrinsic to the loan itself, such as danger of non-repayment or loss of opportunities of other profit. In modern times this latter extrinsic title always exists owing to economic conditions. The amount of interest that may reasonably be charged is determined by the common estimation of intelligent men; in the sin of usury this amount is exceeded. It may be committed by moneylenders, pawnbrokers, and persons selling goods by the instalment system of payment, as well as others.

UTILITARIANISM. A system of ethics which, ignoring man's spiritual nature and his hopes of a better world, teaches that the last end and final good of man lies in this world, and consists in the greatest happiness of the greatest number of mankind, happiness meaning pleasure of sense and of mind such as can be had in this world, along with immunity from pain. It also holds that human acts are right or wrong according as they are useful or hurtful, that is according as their consequences make for or against the above-mentioned end of social happiness (thus Bentham, the two Mills, Austin, and George Grote).

UTRAQUISM. The heretical doctrine of the Hussites and Wycliffites (*qq.v.*) that holy communion, and that under both kinds (*sub utraque specie*), is necessary to salvation. But the name Utraquist (or Calixtine), used as an historical term, does not necessarily imply a Hussite heretic; it is also applied to those Catholics who took advantage of the permission of the Council of Basle for priests in Bohemia to administer the Chalice as well to those who asked for it: provided the recipient had subscribed to the Catholic teaching underlying the practice of communion in one kind (*q.v.*) and that communion, though a means of incalculable value, is not a necessary condition of salvation.

UTRECHT, THE SCHISM OF. The defection, at the beginning of the 18th century, of a number of prelates and their followers in Holland, who adhered to Jansenism and formed the Jansenist (*q.v.*). Church of Holland.

V

VACANCY. i. Liturgical. A day for which no feast or other proper office is assigned. When Christmas day or its octave or St. Stephen's, St. John's, Innocents' day, or the Epiphany falls on a Sunday, no reference is made to the Sunday in Mass or Office and it is therefore called vacant.

ii. Of a diocese. A diocese becomes vacant by the death, resignation, translation or deposition of its bishop. When a vacancy occurs its government devolves upon the cathedral chapter of canons which within 8 days must appoint a vicar capitular (*q.v.*). If there is no chapter an administrator is appointed, by the bishop himself before the vacancy occurs or after by the metropolitan or senior suffragan.

iii. Of the Holy See. Upon the death or resignation of a pope the government of the Church devolves upon the College of Cardinals under the leadership of the Cardinal Chamberlain, who is responsible for the due summoning of the conclave (*q.v.*) to elect a successor. During this time the Sacred College does not have papal jurisdiction nor can it perform specifically papal acts.

VAGUS (Lat., a wanderer). In canon law, a person who has no fixed abode and consequently no domicile or quasi-domicile; such are Gipsies, bargemen, tramps. The Code of Canon Law makes special provision for, *e.g.*, their marriages. They must be distinguished from *peregrini* (*q.v.*).

VAIN OBSERVANCE. The use of charms, etc., as a preservation from harm, belief in lucky or unlucky events, seasons, dreams, actions, numbers, etc., indulgence in witchcraft or magic, which are sins of superstition according to their object and to the degree of credence given to them. "Touching wood," avoiding a ladder, fear of hawthorn in the house or new shoes on a table, of brushing dust through an outside door or of burning mountain-ash, etc., when observed merely from habit or custom are harmless, but silly practices. To regard, *e.g.*, simply the physical wearing of a medal of St. Benedict as a specific against sudden death, without reference to the will of God, the intercession of the saint, the blessing of the Church or one's own prayers, would be a vain observance.

VAINGLORY. The inordinate love or desire for the praise and honour of men. Its inordinateness consists in seeking honour from unworthy men or which one does not deserve or letting praise obscure one's dependence on God. But the desire for and preservation of a good reputation according to one's deserts is neither vainglorious nor sinful; "a good name is better than great riches" (Prov. xxii, 1).

VALENTINE'S DAY, ST. Valentine was a priest and martyr who suffered in Rome about the year 270. Nothing is known of him—except that his life had nothing to do with the graceful and now obsolete custom of sending valentines on his festival. It arose from the mediæval belief that Feb. 14 was the day on which birds began to pair, and so a peculiarly suitable festival for lovers. The Puys d'Amour, a sort of *eisteddfod* for love-minstrels and troubadours, were held on this date in the 12th century; earlier still the festival of Juno Februata, when lots were drawn for lovers, was held on Feb. 15.

VALENTINIANISM. The religious system of Valentinian (*d. c.* 160), the most widespread and important of the sects of Gnosticism (*q.v.*). It was a mixture of Platonism and Christianity with an extravagant and complex cosmogony in which the spiritual or ideal world alone was real; Christ was a spiritual being, an "æon," with no real body yet with a real humanity; he redeemed man by freeing his psychic nature from its material bondage, but to the extent that some men only were capable of receiving the enlightenment whereby they should be saved.

VALID BUT ILLICIT. See ILLICIT.

VALIDITY OF MARRIAGE. This depends on three conditions, true consent, proper form of celebration, and absence of diriment impediments (*q.v.*). If any one of these conditions is unfulfilled, the marriage is invalid. In the case of baptized persons, as the contract is inseparable from the sacrament, a substantial defect in either invalidates the marriage. In case of doubt the validity of a marriage must be upheld.

VALLADOLID. The College of St. Alban, founded by Cardinal Allen in 1589 to train priests for the English mission; the Scots College founded in 1627 for the same purpose. Both colleges are still in being.

VALLUMBROSANS, The. An independent order of Benedictine monks founded by St. John Gualbert, about 1030. They follow the Rule of St. Benedict (*q.v.*) with additional austerities, but are strictly enclosed and do no manual work; among them the institution of lay-brothers was popularized and extended in the 11th century. The congregation now numbers only a few monks, with 7 monasteries in Italy. They wear the ordinary black Benedictine habit. Their name is derived from the mother-house near Florence, Vallombrosa (Lat. *vallis umbrosa*, the shady valley).

VARTAPED. A rank in the Armenian hierarchy, whether Catholic or dissident, conferred by a sort of ordination ceremony. The *vartapeds* are celibate secular priests of superior learning and ability who are put in charge of responsible posts and from among whom the bishops are recruited; they are divided into several classes and theoretically are the only authorized preachers; their badge of office is a staff similar to the pastoral-staff of Byzantine bishops and often a pectoral cross as well.

VATICAN, The. The official residence of the pope at Rome, so named from being built on the lower slopes of the Vatican Hill; figuratively, the name is used to signify the papal power and influence and, by extension, the whole Church. In addition to the papal apartments, those of the palatine prelates, officials, and staff, the apartments of state and the chapels (the Sistine, Pauline, papal private, of the Swiss Guards, etc.), the palace itself includes the chief library of the world, the archives of the Roman church, five museums of antiquities, two picture-galleries, and a polyglot printing-press; an astronomical observatory is attached. The apartments of state, etc., have been described as the most stately and least luxurious of any mansion of the world; the rest of the palace is one vast workshop. Since 1929 the palace with its gardens and other immediate surroundings has been recognized as a sovereign state. See below.

VATICAN, THE CITY OF THE. The area of Rome recognized by the Treaty of the Lateran (*q.v.*) as constituting the territorial extent of the temporal sovereignty of the Holy See. It includes principally the Vatican palace, its gardens and annexes, the basilica and piazza of St. Peter, and contiguous buildings, in all an area of just under one square mile. Its population is about 500 souls, of whom a number are clerics; all male adults are in the immediate service of the Church or its ministers; such employment is the ordinary qualification for residence, and residence for citizenship. The Sovereign Pontiff has the plenitude of legislative, executive and judicial powers, which during a vacancy belong to the College of Cardinals. For the immediate government of the state he deputes a governor (a layman), and there is a consultative council, all named by the pope. The governor is responsible for public order and safety, the protection of property and rights, of public health and morality. The code of law is the canon law, supplemented by regulations for the city and such laws of the kingdom of Italy as may be adopted (see Courts, ii). Children from 6 to 14 years must be adequately instructed in the primary schools or otherwise on pain of fine and imprisonment. The possession of weapons, commercial or professional business, printing and such-like reproduction, hawking, touting as a guide or interpreter, are among the activties forbidden unless with the governor's permission. Though not included in the state, the following are recognized as the absolute property of the Holy See: the basilicas and buildings attached to St. John Lateran, St. Mary Major, St. Paul-outside-the-Walls, and the Holy Apostles and the churches of Sant' Andrea-della-Valle and San Carlo-ai-Catarini, with all the buildings attached, the palace of San Callisto and the papal residence at Castel-Gandolfo (see also IMMUNITY, ii). The papal Sacristan (a titular bishop of the Augustinian order) is vicar-general for the city and the sub-sacristan parish priest; the parish church is St. Anne's. "It will, we hope, be clear that the Sovereign Pontiff has no more material territory than is indispensable for him if he is to exercise the spiritual power entrusted to him for the good of mankind . . . we are pleased that the material domain is reduced to so small an extent" (Pope Pius XI); (*cf.*, States of the Church).

VATICAN BASILICA, The. The collegiate church of St. Peter (*q.v.*) adjoining the Vatican Palace.

VATICAN CHANT. The melodies of Gregorian chant as revised in accordance with the instructions of Pope Pius X that they "were to be restored in their integrity and identity after the authority of the earliest manuscripts and in accordance with the legitimate tradition of past ages as well as with the actual use of the liturgy of to-day." The work was entrusted to the Benedictine monks of the Solesmes congregation and the resulting version is the authentic one which must be used in all churches of the Latin rite, except those that have an indult to use another or are served by a religious order (*e.g.*, the Dominicans, Carthusians, Cistercians) which has an authorized edition of its own.

VATICAN COUNCIL, The. The twentieth œcumenical council, opened on Dec. 8, 1869, adjourned one month after the Italians seized Rome from the pope, on Oct. 20, 1870, and still unfinished. It was held in St. Peter's; it was attended by over 600 cardinals, patriarchs, archbishops and bishops, abbots and generals of orders; the bishops of all the dissident Eastern Churches were invited to attend and Protestants were officially informed of the council (both without result). The 3rd session issued a constitution on the Catholic faith, dealing with natural religion, revelation, faith, and faith and reason, to which 18 canons whose denial incurs anathema were attached; the 4th session, caps. 1-3 dealt with the primacy of the pope; cap. 4 defined his infallibility (*q.v.*). On the first voting on the last doctrine 451 fathers voted *for*, 88 *against*, and 62 conditionally *for;* at the last vote, 433 fathers were *for* and 2 *against*, while 55 opposers did not vote. The opposition was principally directed, not against the doctrine itself, but against the opportuneness of its definition; every single bishop accepted the decree and published it in his diocese. This council foresaw the trend of the time away from Christianity altogether, much of its doctrinal matter being concerned with the very fundamentals and starting-points of the Christian religion; and it was happily free from the necessity to legislate rigorously for moral and disciplinary reform within the Church. That the council's deliberations were without constraint and conducted with due dignity has been amply demonstrated by Abbot Butler.*

"VATICANISM." A pejorative term expressing the supposedly mistaken or arrogant pretensions of the Holy See coined by W. E. Gladstone with reference to papal infallibility at the time of the Vatican Council (*cf.*, Ultramontanism).

VAUDOIS, The. See WALDENSIANISM.

VEIL (Lat. *velum*, a covering). i. A veil over the head and shoulders is part of the habit of all enclosed nuns and of most others; some active orders dispense with it altogether (*e.g.*, Sisters of Charity of St. Vincent, Daughters of Wisdom), others wear it only out of doors (*e.g.*, Helpers of the Holy Souls); in some cases a veil completely covers the face when in choir (*e.g.*, Sisters of Marie Réparatrice). The form and material of the veil are very varied; its colour is usually black for professed nuns and white for novices. Its use is derived directly from that of the veil of the married woman, the nun being the bride of Christ.

ii. Wedding. A veil of lace or similar material worn by the bride at the marriage ceremony is all that is left among most Western Christians of the distinctive veil of the married woman, common to many parts of the world and known long before Christianity. Such a head-veil still forms part of some "national costumes" and in Mohammedan countries Christian wives sometimes wear a similar face-covering to their neighbours. The Christian significance of the veil was as a practical safeguard for that marital fidelity of which it has become a symbol; its association with virginity was later and accidental (*cf.*, Pall, iii).

iii. See also AËR, CIBORIUM, CHALICE, GREMIAL, HUMERAL, IMAGES, LENTEN, SUDARIUM, TABERNACLE, VERONICA, VIMPA.

VEIL OF OUR LADY, The. Many churches have claimed to have relics of the clothing of our Lady, generally under the name of her veil. The most famous in the West is that given by Charlemagne to Aix la Chapelle and now in the cathedral of Chartres; in the East, the veil or girdle of Blachernæ at Constantinople, deposited there in 473. It is said that there is such a relic built into the top of the spire of the cathedral church of Salisbury.

VENERABILE, The. i. The Blessed Sacrament. But more usually is meant

ii. The English College (*q.v.*) at Rome, venerable for its age, dignity and history.

VENERABLE. i. The title accorded to a servant of God whose cause of beatification (*q.v.*) has reached the state where his heroic virtue or martyrdom has been proved and a solemn decree to that effect signed by the pope. But his public veneration is not thereby authorized.

ii. The style of an archdeacon in Ireland and Australia (The Venerable the Archdeacon of A. . . .), of a preacher general (Venerable and Very Reverend Father), and of a Carthusian monk (Venerable Father).

VENERABLE BROTHER. The ordinary form of address of the pope to a brother bishop in grace and communion with the Apostolic See.

VENERATION. The word commonly used to express in English that worship (*hyperdulia, dulia, qq.v.*) given to the saints (*q.v.*), either directly or through images or relics,

---

* The Vatican Council treated here is now called Vatican Council I. The Second Vatican Council—"Vatican II"—was held from 1962-1965.—*Publisher*, 1997.

which is different in kind from the divine worship (adoration, *latria, qq.v.*) given to God only.

VENEZUELA, THE CHURCH IN. The population of 3½ million is made up almost entirely of Indians and half-castes, mostly Catholics, at least in name. All faiths have freedom of exercise; but, though Catholicism is officially the religion of the country, difficulties between Church and state have at times been grave. The state repairs churches and gives a small subsidy for the maintenance of bishops and their chapters; but the right of the Church to receive property by gift or legacy is much curtailed by law. There are 2 archiepiscopal sees (Caracas was founded in 1530), with 8 suffragan dioceses and 2 mission territories.

VENI CREATOR SPIRITUS (Lat., Come creating Spirit). The opening words and name of a hymn invoking the aid of the Holy Ghost, probably written by Rabanus Maurus in the early 9th century, sung at Vespers and Terce during Pentecost, and its octave and on numerous occasions such as ordinations, consecration of a bishop, monastic clothing and profession, dedication of a church and before deliberations, such as a synod or election, etc. All kneel while the first verse is sung.

VENI SANCTE SPIRITUS (Lat., Come Holy Spirit). The opening words and name of the sequence (*q.v.*), praying for the indwelling of the Holy Ghost, said or sung at the Mass of Pentecost and during the octave. Its author is not certainly known; though it was probably written in the 12th century and was called in the middle ages the "Golden Sequence," it was not definitely adopted in the Missal until the reform of Pope St. Pius V in 1570.

VENIA (Lat., pardon, permission). The genuflection or similar action performed by a religious by way of satisfaction when he has committed a fault or received leave to do something for which the superior's permission is necessary.

VENICE, PATRIARCH OF. The official title given in 1751 to the bishops of Venice in perpetuation of the style of Patriarch of Aquileia and Grado (*q.v.*) which they had adopted when their diocese absorbed those territories; actually he is an ordinary metropolitan with nine suffragans.

VERGER (Lat. *virga,* a rod, from his symbol of office). A beadle; one appointed to keep order in church; a sacristan.

VERNACULAR (Lat. *vernaculus,* native). The common spoken language of a people as opposed to a court, official or liturgical language. In the early days of Christianity public worship was in the spoken tongue; but in the process of history Latin became the language of public worship throughout the Western church, and in the East large numbers of people came to be using other dead languages or obsolete forms of living ones. This practice is not a matter of principle in the Church, and vernacular in the liturgy has recently received a certain measure of encouragement. At the present day among Catholics the spoken tongue is used, nearly or quite exclusively, in all services (including the Eucharist) by the Byzantine Rumanians, Hungarians and Melkites, and by the Malankarese; a greater or less amount of vernacular is used in all services by the Syrians, Maronites and Copts. In the Western church the Mass is nowhere in the vernacular;* but approximations to a liturgical use of German at sung and high Mass have been the custom in certain dioceses of Austria and Germany for a long time. A complete vernacular *Rituale* has been approved for Croatia, and since 1947 many other countries have been given a Ritual (*q.v.*) in varying degrees of the spoken tongue; the most notable are those of Germany and the United States, which are used as patterns for others. Parts of the rites of Baptism and Marriage are carried out in the vernacular everywhere. See also LITURGICAL LANGUAGE, CHINESE RITES, etc.

VERNACULAR BIBLES. i. The Church has ever been at pains to provide versions of the Bible in the native tongue; the Latin, Syriac, Armenian, Sahidic, Bohairic, Gothic, Ethiopic and Saxon versions are early proofs of her activity. For many centuries, however, the Latin sufficed in Western Europe: first, because the neo-Latin peoples, Italians, French, Spaniards, Portuguese, and Walloons, retained for long sufficient Latin to understand it; secondly, because whoever could read at all could read Latin, for reading was not taught apart from Latin grammar. The first French translations date from the 12th century, Italian and Spanish from the 13th, German and English from the 14th. The printing-press multiplied especially German Bibles at an early date: seven folio editions in High German appeared before 1477 and four in Low German; a score of editions were current in Germany before Luther. Catholic Bibles in the vernacular exist to-day among all civilized nations. In the missions of Asia and Africa Catholic translations especially of the gospels, epistles and the psalms are continually being produced. The reading of the Bible in the vernacular was never unconditionally forbidden, though the reading of unauthorized versions was prohibited, and from 1564 to 1757 the reading of vernacular versions without permission of parish priest or confessor. This regulation, though technically withdrawn only in the latter year, had fallen into general desuetude for almost a century previ-

---

* This was written prior to the introduction of the *Novus Ordo Missae* in the Latin Rite in 1970; the Novus Ordo Mass is almost always celebrated in the vernacular. The traditional ("Tridentine") Mass is always celebrated in Latin.—*Publisher,* 1997.

ously, and had been limited by many local exemptions. Only in Spain did a decree of the Spanish Inquisition (q.v.) totally forbid Bible-reading in the vernacular; this decree was withdrawn in 1782.

ii. Sir Thomas More wrote in 1530: "The whole Bible was long before his [Wycliff's, d. 1384] days by virtuous and well-learned men translated into the English tongue and by good and goodly people . . . well and reverently read." Thomas Cranmer wrote: "It is not much above one hundred years ago [1450-1550] since Scripture hath not been accustomed to be read in the vulgar tongue within this realm. It was translated and read in the Saxon's tongue, and when this language waxed old, it was again translated into the newer language whereof yet also many copies remain." Foxe (the "Book of Martyrs" man) writes: "Both before the Conquest and after, as well before John Wickliffe was born as since, the whole body of the Scripture was by sundry men translated into our country tongue." England, in common with France, Germany, Holland, Italy and Bohemia, possessed Bibles in the native tongue before the Reformation.

VERNICLE (Old Eng. corruption of "Veronica"). The veil of Veronica (q.v.) or a representation of it.

VERONICA. i. The veil with which, according to a tradition, a compassionate woman wiped the face of our Lord when on his way to Calvary, an impression of his features remaining printed thereon. It is one of the greater relics (q.v.) preserved in St. Peter's at Rome and it may be handled and exposed for veneration only by a canon of the basilica. Its name may be from the combination of vera (Lat., true) and eikon (Gr., image), or a corruption of or play on the name Berenike (see iii). This veronica is to be distinguished from another "holy face," also said to be miraculous, which is preserved in the Lateran basilica; this can be traced back to 754.

ii. Any image of the Holy Face represented as dead or imprinted on a cloth, such as that at Alicante, especially if the image is claimed to have been made by contact with the body of Christ, as the holy shroud of Turin.

iii. The traditional name of the woman referred to in i above. Whether this name has been formed from the Greek name Berenike (victory-bringer) and transferred to the relic or formed from vera εἰκών and transferred to the woman is not known. St. Veronica is not mentioned in the Roman Martyrology; she is sometimes identified with the woman with an issue of blood (Mark v, 25-34), also said to have been the wife of a Roman officer.

VERSE. i. Biblical. The sub-division of the chapters of the Bible into verses as we now know them was first introduced into the

Greek New Testament printed by Robert Etienne in 1551; in 1555 it was applied to the Vulgate, and in 1560 to the English Protestant Geneva Bible (the first to be printed in Roman type). Challoner's Bible (q.v.) was the first English Catholic version in which each verse was printed separately.

ii. Liturgical. See VERSICLE.

VERSE OFFICE. A rhythmical office (q.v.).

VERSICLE (Lat. versiculus, a little verse). An exclamatory line, usually taken from a psalm, and followed by a response, said or sung frequently in the Latin liturgy, as after the psalms of each nocturn at Matins, after the antiphon of a commemoration, and extra-liturgically before certain prayers and collects (e.g., V. "Let my prayer be directed, O Lord." ℞. "As incense in thy sight," after the hymn of Sunday Vespers). The term is also applied to other short verses with a response, as "Deus in adiutorium," etc.

VERY REVEREND. The style accorded in English to prefects apostolic not in episcopal orders, archpriests, provosts, deans, vicars forane, cathedral canons, rectors of seminaries and colleges, privy chamberlains, provincial, claustral and conventual priors and their equivalents, prioresses, and religious superiors generally below the rank of abbot or abbess.

VESPERALE. i. A book containing the text and chant for the office of Vespers throughout the year.

ii. A vespers cloth (q.v.).

VESPERS (Lat. vesper, eventide). The evening hour of the divine office and, with Lauds, the most solemn; it is the normal evening service in churches of the Latin rite and in monastic, cathedral and collegiate churches is sung daily between 3 and 6 p.m. It consists of five psalms with their antiphons varying according to the day of the week or feast (Ps. cix, cx, cxi, cxii and cxiii on Sundays), followed by a little chapter, hymn and versicle, all variable; then the canticle Magnificat (q.v.) with its antiphon; preces (q.v.) on certain days, collect of the day, commemorations (if any), and conclusion. The text of Vespers is sometimes modified by the occurrence or concurrence (qq.v.) of feasts. To facilitate the use of this office in parish churches it is permitted always to sing the Vespers of the Blessed Sacrament or of our Lady or of any other appropriate feast, without reference to the office of the day, and it is now sometimes sung in the vernacular. Liturgically Vespers retains its characteristics as the great evening assembly, particularly in the ferial hymns, each of which refers, according to the day of the week, to the creation of the universe, light, animals, etc. The equivalent office of the Byzantine rite is called Hesperinos (q.v.).

VESPERS CLOTH. The dust cover laid over the altar cloths, so called because it is not always removed for Vespers but simply turned back when the altar is to be incensed.

VESSELS, SACRED, of the Latin rite are the chalice and paten (which must be consecrated by a bishop) the *ciborium* and pyx (blessed by a priest) and the capsula, lunette and monstrance (*qq.v.*). These must not be handled by a layman unless he is in charge of the sacristy. Other vessels used in divine worship are the cruets, thurible, boat and *aspergillum* (*qq.v.*).

VESTIS TALARIS. "A garment reaching to the ankles," *i.e.*, ecclesiastically, a cassock (*q.v.*).

VESTMENTS. The special garments worn by ecclesiastics in the exercise of divine worship and administering the sacraments. It is in accordance with right reason and the customs of mankind that a priest, especially when engaged on his business of sacrificing to God, should wear a distinguishing and hieratic dress. But the early Church had none such; vestments worn to-day in both Western and Eastern rites have for the most part developed from the everyday clothes of the Roman Empire which, through the setting aside of "best suits" for the service of the altar, survived the changes of the 6th-7th centuries and came to be regarded as a special priestly vesture. The middle ages, besides modifying the forms, provided the garments with symbolical significances, some of which have been adopted by the Church but must not be mistaken for the *raison d'etre* of ecclesiastical vestments.

i. The sacred vestments of the Latin rite worn at the celebration of Mass are: the amice, alb, girdle, and maniple (common to celebrant, deacon and subdeacon); to these the subdeacon adds the tunicle, the deacon the stole and dalmatic, the priest, the stole and chasuble, and a pontificating bishop all four and the mitre, gloves, buskins and sandals; other vestments used are the surplice, cope and pallium (*qq.v.*). Most of these are made in one of two broad divisions of shape, commonly distinguished as "Gothic" and "Roman" (*qq.v.*).

ii. Those of the Byzantine rite correspond with the above and have the same origin, but have evolved into dissimilar forms. Those of the deacon are: the *sticharion* (alb), *epimanikia* and *orarion* (stole); of the priest, the first two and the *epitrachelion* (stole), *zone* (girdle), and *phelonion* (chasuble); the bishop substitutes for the last the *sakkos* and adds the *epigonation* (maniple), *omophorion* (pallium) and crown (mitre); minor clerics wear the *kamision* (alb or surplice) (*qq.v.*). The vestments of other Eastern rites correspond with these and more or less closely resemble them in form.

VETO, RIGHT OF. The right claimed by some rulers of states to exclude from episcopal sees or other important offices ecclesiastics not acceptable to the government. Without admitting the right, the Church sometimes grants in concordats a modified form of veto, consistent with her liberty of appointment, as a privilege or as a concession to prevent greater evils. In the days preceding Catholic emancipation in Great Britain and Ireland the Holy See was prepared to make certain concessions in this matter, but emancipation was eventually won without any form of royal veto being conceded (*cf.*, Exclusion).

VEXILLUM (Lat., a standard). i. A processional banner.

ii. Another name for a *sudarium* (*q.v.*, iii).

VIA MEDIA, The. A theory taught by J. H. Newman in his Anglican days. The preservation of the apostolic body of Christian truth is the fundamental note of the true Church: and according to this theory, the Roman Catholic Church has added to this truth, Protestantism has subtracted from it, whereas the Church of England maintains the middle way (*via media*) of primitive and patristic orthodoxy. The upholders of this erroneous theory did not deny that the Church of England had compromised this orthodoxy by toleration of Protestant errors.

VIATICUM (Lat., provision for a journey). Holy communion given to those in danger of death. It may be received at any hour of the day or night, not fasting, and so often as may be required during the same illness. If it is given at the same time as Extreme Unction, its administration precedes that sacrament. It is given with the words, "Receive, brother, the viaticum of our Lord Jesus Christ, that he may preserve thee from the malignant enemy and bring thee to everlasting life. Amen." The same form is used when a soldier receives communion on or going to the battlefield.

VICAR (Lat., *vicarius*, a deputy). A cleric who takes the place of another in the exercise of an ecclesiastical office and acts in his name and with his authority, as determined by canon law, *e.g.*, cardinal vicar (of the bishop of Rome), vicar apostolic (of the pope in missionary countries), vicar capitular (of the chapter when a diocese is vacant), vicar general (of a bishop in his whole diocese), vicar forane (of the bishop in a deanery), parochial vicars (parish administrators, rector's assistants); all of which see. Among the Franciscans and others the vicar is equivalent to a sub-prior.

VICAR APOSTOLIC. A titular bishop (*q.v.*) who rules a territory called a vicariate apostolic (*q.v.*) as delegate of the Holy See. Vicars apostolic have no territorial diocese, cathedral church or chapter of canons and their name is not mentioned in the canon of the Mass; but they usually exercise by delegation the same powers as diocesan bishops. The Church in England and Wales from 1623 to 1850 and in Scotland from 1694 to 1878 was governed by vicars apostolic. They have the right to sit and vote in general councils of the Church.

VICAR CAPITULAR. A cleric appointed by a cathedral chapter to administer the diocese during a vacancy; the whole of the bishop's ordinary jurisdiction in spirituals and temporals, except as forbidden by law, passes when the vacancy occurs to the chapter, and from it to the vicar, who must be elected within eight days. He must administer the diocese without serious innovation, doing nothing to its prejudice or to that of the bishop.

VICAR CHORAL. A clerical or lay assistant in the choir of a cathedral or collegiate church. The title seems to be now extinct in the Catholic Church.

VICAR FORANE (Lat., *foraneus*, at a distance [from the episcopal city]). An experienced priest appointed by his bishop to exercise a limited jurisdiction over a definite district of the diocese. He superintends the discipline of the clergy, presides over their conferences, keeps an eye on ecclesiastical property and provides for the care of sick clergy. In general he is equivalent to a rural dean (*q.v.*, ii).

VICAR GENERAL. A deputy appointed by a bishop to assist him in the government of his diocese. He succeeds to the position and some of the powers of the mediæval archdeacon. He is delegated to exercise episcopal jurisdiction in spirituals and temporals on behalf of the bishop up to the extent of the bishop's reservations and those of law, but he must exercise it according to the mind of the bishop. He forms one tribunal with the bishop, so there can be no appeal from the sentence of one to the other. Even if a simple priest the vicar general takes precedence of all clergy of the diocese and is a prelate with the dress and privileges of a titular protonotary apostolic so long as he retains his office, which terminates at the will, death or translation of the bishop.

VICAR PATRIARCHAL. A local representative appointed by Catholic patriarchs, somewhat after the manner of a vicar apostolic; *e.g.*, the Melkite patriarch has vicars at Alexandria, Jerusalem, Cairo and Khartum.

VICAR OF JESUS CHRIST, The. The pope, who as visible head of the Church, the Mystical Body (*q.v.*) of Christ, represents Christ on earth, and is therefore supreme in authority.

VICARIATE. The office and sphere of work of a vicar, especially of a vicar apostolic (*qq.v.*). A vicariate apostolic is an ecclesiastical district in a missionary territory, immediately dependent on the Congregation of Propaganda. Missionary countries are divided into vicariates and/or prefectures as other countries into dioceses. Vicariates are subdivided into missions or quasi-parishes. The Holy See alone can erect, alter, divide, unite or suppress vicariates apostolic. There are over 300 such vicariates, mostly in Asia and Africa, but the number is constantly changing. The vicariates in England at the restoration of the ordinary hierarchy in 1850 were 8 in number, namely, the London, Western, Eastern, Central, Welsh, Lancashire, Yorkshire and Northern districts.

VICARIATE OF ROME, The. The diocese of Rome as administered on behalf of its bishop, the pope, by the cardinal vicar general as ordinary, assisted by a titular archbishop called the *Vicesgerens* (Italian, *Vicegerente*). Its extent is the City of Rome and the rural district called the Agro Romano. The administration is divided into four sections, each with its own officials, for worship and visitation, discipline, judicial business and general management.

VICE. Any habit which leads a man into sin, more usually into one of the seven deadly sins; strictly speaking the habit is acquired through reiterated sin, but a certain disposition or inclination to it may be inherited. Vice, used without qualification, usually refers to a habit of impurity or drunkenness; vicious is sometimes synonymous with revengeful.

VICEGERENT OF GOD (Lat. *vices gerere*, to represent). The pope is Vicar of Jesus Christ, who is God in virtue of the Hypostatic Union (*q.v.*). Hence the pope is called Vicegerent of God.

VICEGERENT OF ROME. A titular archbishop appointed by the pope to assist the cardinal vicar in the administration of the Vicariate of Rome; he is appointed for life but is removable. All ecclesiastical books printed in Rome must bear his *imprimatur*.

VICTIM (Lat. *victima*, an animal adorned for, or thing made holy by, sacrifice). That which is offered in sacrifice; usually something which has life itself or can sustain life in man. By the immolation and offering of such a victim in the typical sacrifices of the Old Law, man signified that he owed everything to God and had by his sins forfeited all claim to life. In the Sacrifice of the Cross which they foreshadowed, the victim was Christ, head and representative of the whole human race.

VICTIM SOUL. A soul, chosen by God and deliberately corresponding with the divine will, who freely sacrifices himself, his health, happiness, etc., and suffers, after the example of the crucified Christ, for the advantage of the Church and the good of others in general or of a particular person.

VICTIMÆ PASCHALI. The first words and name of the sequence (*q.v.*) sung at the Mass of Easter Sunday and during its octave. It was probably written in the 11th century but the author's name is not known for certain. It emphasizes the unity of our Lord's passion, death and resurrection into the Christian Pasch, and includes a passage of dialogue which was carried over bodily into the Easter mystery plays. It has one of the finest of all plainsong tunes.

VIDI AQUAM. The name, from its first words, given to the variation of the *Asperges* (*q.v.*) sung during paschal time. The antiphon "I saw water flowing from the right side of the temple, alleluia; and all to whom that water came were saved, and they shall say alleluia, alleluia" (*cf.*, Ezech. xlvii, 2) is followed by v. i of Ps. cxvii with *Gloria* and the antiphon repeated. The prayer and sprinkling with holy water are as usual.

VIENNE, THE COUNCIL OF. The fifteenth œcumenical council, in 1311-12. It ordered the suppression of the Templars (but without giving judgement on the terrific charges made against them); condemned the errors of the Béghards concerning perfection in this life and of Peter John Olivi concerning the Incarnation, the human soul and Baptism; legislated for the reform of the clergy (especially the black monks) and proclaimed a crusade (which never took place).

VIGIL (Lat. *vigilia*, a watching). The day preceding certain feasts (also called the eve), observed as a preparation therefor, with special offices and formerly always with a fast attached. In the general Western calendar the following feasts have vigils: Easter (in a class by itself), Christmas and Pentecost (greater vigils), our Lord's Ascension, our Lady's Assumption, St. John the Baptist, St. Laurence the Martyr, and SS. Peter and Paul (lesser vigils). The vigils of Pentecost, Assumption and Christmas are fast-days, except when either of the last two feasts falls on a Monday. Vigils, called *proeortia* (preparations) are also observed in the East: the Byzantine rite has four greater, which last several days, and ten lesser lasting one day; the fast-day before Christmas and Epiphany is the *paramone*, perseverance, *i.e.* in prayer. Vigils had their origin in over-night services preparatory to feasts (*cf.*, the revived Easter vigil service and the midnight Mass of Christmas), which became occasions of disorder and were gradually abolished or moved back to the daytime.

VIGIL LIGHT. A lamp, excluding that before the high altar or the Blessed Sacrament, perpetually burning before a shrine, image, etc. The use of the term seems to be peculiar to the United States.

VILLA BARBERINI. See CASTEL GANDOLFO.

VIMPA (Low Lat.). A silk veil worn over the shoulders and covering the hands of the acolytes who carry the mitre and pastoral staff at pontifical services; not to be confused with a humeral veil (*q.v.*).

VINCENTIAN CANON, The. A name given to the principle enunciated by St. Vincent of Lérins (*d. c.* 440) that "That must be regarded as true which all men have believed at all times and everywhere," *quod semper, quod ubique, quod ab omnibus*, when a new point arises in any matter of doctrine. The principle is true in what it affirms, but must not be taken in an exclusive sense so as to deny the divine origin of truths that have not always been in the explicit faith of the whole Church.

VINCENTIANS, The. The Lazarists (*q.v.*).

VIOLATION. A church or public oratory is violated by the occurrence in the body of the building of an act of voluntary homicide (even if death occurs elsewhere), by the malicious infliction of wounds causing any considerable effusion of blood, by impious or sordid uses, and by burial therein of an infidel or of one declared and condemned as excommunicate. Immediately after the occurrence the Blessed Sacrament is removed and the altars stripped and the church may not be used for divine service of any sort until it has been reconciled, by a priest if it was only blessed, by the bishop if consecrated. Private chapels are not subject to violation (*cf.*, Desecration).

VIOLET. The liturgical colour *violaceus*, usually referred to as purple.

VIRGIN, CONSECRATION OF A. This solemn consecration, common in the early Church for deaconesses and others, is now unknown, except among Carthusian nuns who receive it four years after profession. The rite, which must be performed by a bishop, is that contained in the *Pontificale Romanum*, approximating to the ordination of a deacon; the nun is invested with a plain wooden cross, crown, black veil, ring, stole and maniple, which she assumes again only on the 50th anniversary of her profession and for burial. She must be at least 25 years old. A few Benedictine houses are said also to have this privilege of consecration, but investment with stole and maniple is proper to the Carthusians.

VIRGIN BIRTH, The. It is a dogma of the Church that Christ was born of Mary, a virgin, without prejudice to her virginity. She was his only human parent. The Son of Man had no man for his father; he was conceived of the Holy Ghost. This is the doctrine of the Virgin Birth, which must be carefully distinguished from that of the Immaculate Conception (*q.v.*). It is also of Catholic faith that our Lady remained a virgin throughout her life, to which SS. Jerome, Augustine, Ambrose, John Chrysostom, and others bear witness.

VIRGINITY. Virginity in either sex implies (*a*) physically, bodily integrity, (*b*) morally, absence of complete voluntary sexual pleasure in the past and the resolution to abstain from all sexual pleasure in the future. Physical virginity may be lost by violation against one's will without the loss of moral virginity. That virginity is preferable in itself to the married state was taught by Christ (Matt. xix, 11) and defined by the Council of Trent (sess. xxiv, can. 10). There is no special virtue of virginity, and in a given case this state is preferable to that of marriage only if it is chosen directly for God's sake, and for no other reason, in order thereby to belong to him or to serve him in a special way.

VIRTUALLY. See EMINENTLY.

VIRTUE (Lat. *virtus*, manliness, power). The excellence or perfection of a thing. The chief exact meanings of the word are four.

i. For a habit (*q.v.*) operative of good, *i.e.*, for a lasting disposition of the soul's faculties, setting them towards good, and thus perfecting them by lifting their natural indetermination and substituting a definite tendency (but without constraint) to good rather than evil. Thus we speak of intellectual and moral virtues

ii. As opposed to vice: virtue being a good habit, vice a bad habit (note, habits, not acts; a virtuous man may do an evil act and *vice versa*).

iii. For any active quality, *e.g.*, the virtue of plants.

iv. In the phrase "in virtue of," meaning "by reason of" or "by the power of."

VIRTUE, INFUSED. A virtue (*q.v.*) or perfection of our natural faculties which does not arise from the repetition of acts or any merely human effort, but is given immediately by God. It is a principle of supernatural (*q.v.*) activity in the soul. Thus, charity perfects the will so as to enable it to produce supernatural acts of charity (*q.v.*). These virtues make supernatural acts possible; they do not necessarily make them easy, though they do contribute to this end by bestowing an inclination to the good. The man with an infused virtue of temperance may find it very hard to avoid the sin of drunkenness, but it is possible for him to produce supernatural acts of temperance; whereas the man who has not this virtue may not have the slightest inclination to enter a public-house, but he would be utterly unable to make a supernatural act of temperance. Infused virtues may be either theological or moral (*qq.v.*).

VIRTUE, HEROIC. The virtue of Christian heroes, of those who lived as saints or who achieved heroism in the moment of death by martyrdom. It implies an unusual control of the insurgent passions, and a promptitude and facility in well-doing which are above the common. According to Benedict XIV, for the manifestation of heroic virtue the matter must be difficult, so as to demand spiritual energy above the ordinary and the practice must be prompt, unhesitating, joyful, enthusiastic and habitual. St. Thomas brings the heroic virtues under the gifts of the Holy Ghost (*q.v.*).

VIRTUE, MORAL. A habit (*q.v.*) perfecting a man's will and lower appetites to dispose him to act in accordance with right reason in his dealings with God (*e.g.*, religion, *q.v.*), with others (*e.g.*, justice, *q.v.*), with himself (*e.g.*, temperance, *q.v.*). Moral virtues are either acquired by practice, with or without supernatural aid, or immediately infused by God along with sanctifying grace.

VIRTUE, NATURAL. A habit (*q.v.*) which disposes a man to act in accordance with right reason, not essentially connected with grace, and acquired by the repetition of suitable acts.

VIRTUES (1 Pet. iii, 22; Eph. i, 21). One of the choirs of the celestial hierarchy, (*q.v.*).

VIRTUES, THE INTELLECTUAL. Wisdom, understanding and knowledge, with reference to truth (speculative), prudence and art with reference to action (practical), these being the virtues which well dispose the intellect for its proper operations in reference to its object; they are seated in the understanding, which cannot act against itself. It is not the function of these virtues to produce "virtue" in its common sense, *i.e.*, moral righteousness, but to give a facility in doing a good act; moral virtue puts the facility to use.

VIRTUES, THE MORAL. The cardinal virtues, prudence, justice, fortitude and temperance (*qq.v.*) under one or other of which all the other moral virtues, purity, religion, etc., fall. They are concerned with our duties and relate to God only indirectly (*cf.*, the theological virtues), and reside in powers which can act against the commands of the understanding, namely, the will and the sensitive appetite. The moral virtues enable us to put into use the easiness in doing a good action which is conferred by the intellectual virtues (*q.v.*)

VIRTUES, THE SUPERNATURAL. The theological virtues, faith, hope and charity (*qq.v.*) and the infused moral virtues (*q.v.*). The virtues which are beyond the reach of man's natural powers and enable him to attain to a supernatural end.

VIRTUES, THE THEOLOGICAL. Supernatural gifts enabling man to attain his final destiny, so called because they have God—the object of our faith, in whom we hope, whom we love—for their immediate object; three in number: faith, hope, charity (*qq.v.*).

VIS ET METUS (Lat., violence and fear). Grave fear caused by extrinsic violence unjustly used by someone to force another into matrimony against his or her will is a diriment (*q.v.*) impediment of marriage at least by ecclesiastical law. This is the most common ground upon which an apparent marriage is declared to have been null from the beginning. *Metus reverentialis i.e.,* fear arising from reverence for parents or that of other superiors, is not grave unless when connected with some serious circumstances.

VISIBILITY OF THE CHURCH, The. It is Catholic doctrine that the Church, as founded by Jesus Christ, is not only materially but also essentially and formally visible, that is, that her material phenomena can not only be known but known to be true, and that without such visibility there is and can be no Church. It is the duty of every man who has it brought to his notice honestly to examine the claims of that Church and upon conviction of their truth to associate himself with its visible body. But this doctrine does not exclude the existence of people who are in fact united with the Church but not in a visible way; such are all non-Catholics who have received baptism in some way, are in good faith, and in the state of grace. This must be carefully distinguished from the false doctrines that there are two Churches, one visible and one invisible; or that there is one Church, and that invisible only; or that visible unity with the Church is unnecessary and may even be undesirable in some individual cases. *Cf.,* Salvation ii; "Soul of the Church."

VISIGOTHIC RITE, The. The Mozarabic (*q.v.*) rite, which was developed during the time of the ascendancy of the Visigoths in Spain, 450-710.

VISION. A supernatural perception. It may be: (*a*) A bodily or sensible vision, *i.e.,* an apparition, in which something naturally invisible is seen with the bodily eye; (*b*) an imaginative vision, produced in the imagination during sleep, or when awake; such was the angel who appeared to St. Joseph; (*c*) an intellectual vision in which the mind perceives a spiritual truth, without any sense image (*cf.,* St. Teresa's vision of the Holy Trinity). These extraordinary favours are not to be desired or asked for, because they are quite unnecessary for perfection. Imaginative and sensible visions may be counterfeited by the Devil or by hysteria. The distinctive characteristics and effects of true and false visions are similar to those of true and false locutions (*q.v.*).

VISIT AD LIMINA [APOSTOLORUM]. A visit "to the thresholds of the Apostles" Peter and Paul, *i.e.,* to their tombs and to their living representative, the pope, which must be made, personally if possible, by every archbishop and bishop-in-ordinary of the Latin rite, once every five years if from Europe and once every ten years if from elsewhere; the obligation extends to vicars apostolic and prelates-*nullius*. Each diocese, vicariate and prelature has fixed years for its visits, in rotation from 1911. Each visitor has to take with him a report of his diocese, according to a fixed syllabus of questions, which furnishes a most detailed statement of the spiritual state and observance of its clergy and people. and its condition canonically, intellectually, socially and materially, with the relevant statistics.

VISITANDINE. A nun of the Order of the Visitation (*q.v.*).

VISITATION, The. The visit paid by our Lady to her cousin St. Elizabeth at Ain Karim (St. John-in-the-Mountains), 4½ miles south-west of Jerusalem, as narrated in Luke i, 39-57. A feast in its commemoration is celebrated throughout the Western church on July 2, and has been adopted in some Eastern rites, *e.g.,* by the Melkites.

VISITATION. i. Canonical. The act of an ecclesiastical superior who visits persons and places subject to his jurisdiction, in order to safeguard faith and morals and to ensure the observance of canon law, or for some special purpose. The duty is incumbent specially on bishops and the chief superiors of religious. The pope sometimes appoints a visitor apostolic for a special mission.
ii. Episcopal. The pastoral visit of the bishop to the persons and places of the diocese. He must carry out this duty each year in such way as to complete the visitation of the whole diocese at least every five years. The bishop must visit the diocese personally, but if legitimately impeded he may depute the vicar general or other person. Provision is made in canon law for the metropolitan to visit the diocese if his suffragan neglects to do so. Exempt religious are not subject to the bishop's visitation except in cases specified in law.
iii. Of the sick. The "Rituale Romanum" provides for a more solemn visiting of the sick in addition to the ordinary calls incumbent on a pastor. After a psalm, the Our Father and three prayers for health of soul and body are said; to these may be added the reading of four gospels (Matt. viii, 5-13; Mark xvi, 14-18; Luke iv, 38-40; John v, 1-14), each followed by a prayer and a psalm (xv, xix, lxxxv, lxc) and after the last the priest prays, laying his hand on the head of the sick person (Mark xvi, 18; Acts xxviii, 8). The rite is concluded with the reading of John i, 1-14 and a blessing.

VISITATION NUNS, The. i. The Order of the Visitation B.V.M., founded in 1610 by St. Francis de Sales and St. Jane Frances de Chantal. It provides particularly for women of poor health and for widows. Solemn vows, enclosed and contemplative, though some convents have schools; Little Office B.V.M. in choir. Three classes: choir nuns, associate nuns (without choir obligation) and lay-sisters. Black habit with wide sleeves.

ii. The Sisters of the Visitation. An unenclosed teaching congregation founded in 1660, with constitutions brought into line with those of the above in 1826. Black habit, straight and double-breasted, and apron.

VISITOR APOSTOLIC. A legate of the Holy See specially deputed to carry out a visitation and report on the religious state of a given ecclesiastical district or of a house or province of a religious order.

VITALISM. The theory that there is some element in living things other than those elements known to chemistry and physics. This other element is the soul or principle of life; and this alone is capable of explaining the immanence (*q.v.*) of all vital functions.

VITANDUS (Lat. from *vitare*, to avoid). An excommunicated person so called as having to be specially shunned by the faithful. Those only are *vitandi* who are excommunicated expressly as such by name by the Holy See. Divine Service may not proceed if a *vitandus* is present. The faithful are not to hold communion with them even in secular matters, so far as it can be avoided, unless a parent, child, husband or wife, etc., is in question. A *vitandus* must not be buried in any sacred place, and if so buried the body is to be exhumed and deposited elsewhere.

VITUS'S DANCE, ST. Beyond the fact of his early martyrdom nothing is certainly known of Vitus. For some unknown reason he (whose name took the form of Guido in Italy and Guy in France and England) was invoked against the "falling sickness," epilepsy, whence the name of the associated disorder "St. Vitus's dance."

VIVISECTION. The dissection of an animal while still living, the better to study the phenomena of life; since the lower animals have no strict rights (*q.v.*), this is not immoral provided that torture is not inflicted for its own sake. In actual practice the animal, whenever it is possible, is previously anæsthetized. The valuable assistance given to physiology and pathology by the practice of vivisection completely outweighs the objections which are urged against it.

VOCATION (Lat. *vocare*, to call). i. A call given by God to a soul, and, in its general sense, it is applied by the Apostles to God's efficacious calling of souls to Christianity: "You are a chosen race . . . . it is yours to proclaim the exploits of God who has called you out of darkness into his marvellous light" (1 Pet. ii, 9). But it is not to be restricted to those only who accept the call, for all men are called to salvation, at least remotely, by receiving sufficient grace to be saved. Vocation is a prevenient grace (*q.v.*). In another general sense a man's vocation means the circumstances in which his life has to be passed, because our lives are under the care of God's providence; thus St. Paul exhorts his disciples: "Everyone has his own vocation, in which he has been called; let him keep to it" (1 Cor. vii, 20), and a secular vocation imposes a duty on the person called analogous to that of priestly and religious vocation (see ii). Nor is it to be supposed that any legitimate human activity, however humble or profane (*q.v.*), may not be the object of a divine call.

ii. Religious. A fitness in the subject to bear the burdens of the religious life (*q.v.*) and a right intention of serving God in that life. Nothing more is necessary, no vivid inspiration or distinct divine locution: because the elements enumerated are definitely due to God's action, the fitness being produced by natural causes under the guidance of divine Providence, and the generous will to quit the world and devote self to God being clearly the work of grace. Priestly vocation, which is higher than religious, demands the same qualities in the subject, with the addition of actual holiness of life. But here the qualities of the subject do not alone suffice. The priesthood belongs to the public order of the Church, and therefore external authority, in the person of the bishop, is the decisive factor in ecclesiastical vocation. It is the bishop's call that is the real manifestation of the divine vocation, for then, and not till then, is the candidate called by God as Aaron was. "It is better to go into religion with a view to testing oneself than not to go in at all, since this is the first step to stopping in it altogether. Nor may we say of a man who makes this experiment that he has 'looked back' (Luke ix, 62) unless he has drawn back from something to which he was bound" (St. Thomas).

VOLTO SANTO (It., holy face). The name given to certain images of the face or of the crucifixion of our Lord, particularly to a cedar wood crucifix, the "Sovereign Lord of Lucca," in the cathedral of that city; the body wears a long velvet garment and a crown which are removed only on Good Friday. Its history is said to be attested so far back as 797 and by the 11th century its veneration had spread all over Europe; it is mentioned by Langland in "Piers Plowman." The *volto santo* of Borgo San Sepolcro is a similar image (*cf.*, Holy Face, Veronica).

VOLUNTARY ACT. An act is voluntary when the will acts freely with knowledge of the end in view. Such an act differs from one that is forced, instinctive, or merely ineffectual wishing. An act is perfectly voluntary when full knowledge and consent are present.

VOTIVE MASS (Lat. *votum*, a wish). A Mass differing from that of the feast or office of the day, celebrated for a special intention as directed by authority or because the circumstances require it (*e.g.*, a nuptial or funeral Mass) or simply at the choice of the priest. The days on which the first two classes may or must be celebrated are governed by special rubrics; those of the third, private votive Masses, may be said at the discretion of the celebrant on any day below the rank of a double (*q.v.*), with certain exceptions. He may elect to say any Mass in the missal taken from those of our Lord, our Lady or the proper of saints, or of any saint named in the Roman Martyrology with a corresponding Mass taken from the common of the saints, or any one of the Masses called votive in that section of the missal. These last include special Masses assigned to each day of the week and others for the election of a pope, for the removal of schism, to implore a good death, for peace, for the sick, for the spread of the faith, for any need, etc.

VOTIVE OFFERING (Lat. *votum*, a vow). Anything offered to God or a saint, as a sign of gratitude or act of veneration, sometimes in discharge of a vow or promise. Such an offering is usually set up in or offered at a shrine or before an image and may be any object from a valuable jewel to a penny candle: for example, the candles in any church, the silver hearts in the church of the Assumption, London, the wedding-rings on the tabernacle-veil at Westminster Cathedral, the surgical instruments at the shrine at Lourdes, the model ships in Notre Dame de Boulogne (the last two having reference to the occasion of the offering). So to make offerings is one of the universal natural religious instincts of mankind and therefore has its place in the worship of the Catholic Church.

VOTIVE OFFICE. An office differing from the Divine Office proper to the day and said instead of it as a matter of privilege. Votive offices were abolished in 1911, except that of our Lady, to be said on Saturdays when no important feast occurs.

VOW. i. A solemn promise made to God freely and deliberately to perform some good work or to embrace a higher state of life. The fulfilment of a vow is an obligation of the virtue of religion (*q.v.*). Vows are public (*e.g.*, the vows of monks and nuns) or private, solemn or simple (*qq.v.*), personal or real. A vow binds no one but the vower, but the obligations of real vows, whereby property is dedicated to God, pass to heirs. Ordinaries can dispense or commute vows for a just cause, except those reserved to the pope. The only private vows reserved to the pope are those of perfect and perpetual chastity, and of entering a religious society of solemn vows. Vows pronounced under grave extrinsic fear unjustly inflicted are null and void (*cf.*, Triennial Vows, Profession, etc.).

ii. As impediment to marriage. The solemn vows taken by a religious, the vow of chastity taken implicitly on ordination to the subdiaconate, and by special privilege, the simple vows taken at first profession by a Jesuit, are diriment (*q.v.*) impediments to marriage, and are practically never dispensed. The simple religious and private vows of virginity, of perfect chastity, of celibacy, to receive holy orders and to enter a religious order or congregation are prohibiting (*q.v.*) impediments only. Those bound by solemn or perpetual simple vows who attempt marriage, and their partners if they are privy to the fact, *ipso facto* incur excommunication, simply reserved to the Holy See in the first case, to the ordinary in the second.

VOWS OF RELIGION. These are the three vows whereby the religious binds himself to practise the evangelical counsels of poverty, chastity and obedience, and thus use means of perfection wonderfully adapted to their end, because they combat the three great enemies of spiritual progress, the envy of the eyes, the desire of the flesh and the pride of life. St. Thomas shows that the vow of obedience is the greatest of the three, because by it a man offers to God, not just exterior goods, as by poverty, nor his body, as by chastity, but his will and himself, which is the hardest thing to surrender. The vows are taken at religious profession (*q.v.*). Some religious add to the usual three vows a fourth, for some special purpose.

VULGATE, The. i. The Latin version of the Bible in common use in the Catholic Church and declared authentic (*q.v.*) or authoritative by the Council of Trent. The New Testament is St. Jerome's revision of the Old Latin text (*Itala Vetus, q.v.*), made in 382 by command of Pope Damasus. The Psalter is his second revision of the Old Latin with the aid of Origen's "Hexapla" and the Hebrew text. Wisdom, Ecclesiasticus, Baruch and the two books of the Machabees are in the Old Latin version, untouched by Jerome. All other books are his translation straight from the Hebrew or Aramaic and, in the case of the deutero-canonical fragments, from the Greek. The authenticity, or authoritative character, of the Vulgate does not imply any preference of this version above the original text or above versions in other languages, but is a direction to regard it as authoritative among Latin translations; it involves the belief that the Vulgate substantially represents the original texts, and is free from doctrinal error. The present official edition is called the Clementine, having been issued under the auspices of Pope Clement VIII.

ii. Revision of the Vulgate. Pope Pius X, in 1907, entrusted to the Benedictine order the duty of restoring the original text of the Vulgate, which during the fifteen centuries of its use had become considerably modified and corrupted. This gigantic work, which involves the comparison of many hundreds of MSS., necessarily proceeds slowly and only the first eight books of the Old Testament have as yet appeared. The Commission has its seat in Rome, at the abbey of St. Jerome.*

W

WAFER BREAD. Altar breads (*q.v.*) made in the form of thin, flat, crisp disks, as used in the Latin, Armenian, Maronite and Malabarese rites of the Catholic Church. Bread in this form has no particular significance beyond being a matter of ancient custom and present discipline, but its use has been one of the subjects of dispute between "high" and "low" in the Protestant Church of England.

WAKE (Old Eng., *wacian*, watch). The custom, particularly as practised in Ireland, of passing the night preceding burial in the house where the dead body lay, either engaged in prayer or comforting the relatives of the deceased. Tending in later days to lose its religious significance and to give occasion at times to excess in drink and other abuses, the custom has to a large extent disappeared owing to regulations laid down by the ecclesiastical authorities. A similar custom with the same name was formerly observed on the vigil of the anniversary of the consecration of a church; its memory is preserved in the holidays called "wakes" in Lancashire.

WALDENSIANISM. A movement initiated at Lyons in the 12th century by Peter Waldo (Pierre Valdez) which began as an evangelical reaction against luxury and developed into heresy. The pope was repudiated; the Church should not have property; Purgatory was denied; to take oaths or to go to war was unlawful; righteous laymen could absolve and preach; evil priests could not minister validly, etc.; the sect was influenced by Albigensianism (*q.v.*) and adopted its organization of "perfects" and "believers." The Waldenses spread to Spain, Bohemia, Lombardy and elsewhere and, in spite of persecution, persisted till the 16th century, when they were resurrected by the reformers as a survival of primitive Christianity. They became completely protestantized in the 17th century and still survive in small numbers, chiefly in the Alps of Savoy.

WALES, THE CHURCH IN. So far as is known the Celtic church (*q.v.*) of Britain after the coming of the Saxons survived as an organization only in Wales, where it experienced a period of great monastic activity which had its centres at Bangor-is-Coed, Llancarfan, Llanilltyd Fawr, Llanelwy, Henllan, and Mynyw (Saint Davids). The church in Wales although it never had a metropolitan see, did not become part of the province of Canterbury till the 12th century. At the Reformation it had four sees, Bangor, Saint Asaph, Llandaff and Saint Davids or Menevia. The faith survived penal times in the districts of Holywell, Brecon, Monmouth and Abergavenny at least, and would have done so probably throughout the land had not the supply of Welsh-speaking priests failed in the 17th century. Fifteen of the beatified "English" martyrs were Welsh, and many more gave their lives for liberty. In 1850 the see of Menevia was revived with Newport added, and in 1916 Wales received from Pope Benedict XV its first archbishop when Cardiff was erected as a metropolitan see, with one suffragan, Menevia (*q.v.*). The population of Wales is 2½ million; only about 3.5% are Catholics, of whom Irish, English or other foreigners form a very large proportion.

WAR. The Church teaches that it is lawful to wage war in certain circumstances and under certain conditions. St. Thomas Aquinas, Suarez and other theologians summarize the conditions, all of which must be observed for a war to be just, as: that it shall be undertaken by the lawful authority; that it shall be undertaken for the vindication of an undoubted and proportionate right that has been certainly infringed; that it shall be a last resort, all peaceful means of settlement having been tried in vain; that the good to be achieved shall outweigh the evils that war will involve; that there shall be a reasonable hope of victory for justice (a war undertaken in face of certain failure is, however heroic, irrational and therefore indefensible); there must be a right intention, that is, to right the wrong and not simply to maintain national prestige and influence or to enlarge territory (Vittoria taught that extension of territory is not a just cause of war), nor may war be waged as part of a scheme for converting the heathen to Christianity; and the methods of warfare must be legitimate, *i.e.*, in accordance with international agreements, with our nature as rational beings and with

---

* A New Latin Vulgate Bible was promulgated by John Paul II in 1979 as *editio typica* (the official edition).—*Publisher*, 1997.

the moral teaching of Christianity. There is obviously room for much uncertainty and disagreement in any given example about the fulfilment or otherwise of these conditions; it has been argued by some that were they all observed a just war in contemporary conditions would be impossible. It is generally held that those who intend actively to take part in a war that has already broken out must first be morally certain of its justness; soldiers, etc., enlisted before the outbreak may take its justness for granted unless the contrary be apparent. In our own time, every pope, from Leo XIII's encouragement of disarmament in 1899 to Pius XII's *Summi pontificatus* and other efforts, has had the prevention of war among the first of his aims. Christian hatred of war is faithfully reflected in the Church's canonical forbiddance of all clerics and religious to bear arms. *Cf.*, RESISTING EVIL.

WARS OF RELIGION, The. A series of seven politico-religious wars in France beginning with the jealousy of the Chatillons, Condé and others, for the rising power of the Catholic Guises and lasting from the Protestant attempt to kidnap King Francis II in 1560 until the conversion to Catholicism of Henry of Navarre in 1593.

WASHING. i. Of altar. In the Roman basilicas (with particular solemnity at St. Peter's) and certain other churches, including Westminster Cathedral, after *Tenebræ* on Maundy Thursday the table of the high altar is ceremonially washed with water and wine. This ceremony was formerly more general.

ii. Of feet. See MANDATUM.

iii. Of hands. See LAVABO.

WATCHER. One who takes a turn of prayer before the Blessed Sacrament on the altar of repose (*q.v.*) during the Forty Hours' Prayer (*q.v.*), or at any other time when it is publicly exposed. The relays of watchers, generally two at a time, are so arranged that the Blessed Sacrament is never left unattended whether by day or by night.

WATER. i. In the chalice. The mingling of a few drops of water with the wine to be consecrated at Mass was observed from the beginning, possibly by our Lord, for the Jews took water with their wine; it also symbolizes the union of two natures in Christ, the unity of Christ and his people, and the water that came out with blood from his side. In the Latin rite the water, as symbolizing humanity, is blessed (except at requiem Masses), whereas the wine is not, the celebrant saying as he pours, "O God, who didst wonderfully make the dignity of human nature and still more wonderfully renew it, grant that by this mystery of water and wine we may be made partakers in the divinity of him who deigned to share in our humanity." This adding of water is used by all Christians, Catholic and dissident, of ancient rites

with the sole exception of the dissident Armenians (*cf.*, Zeon).

ii. Other liturgical uses of water are at Baptism, blessing bells, consecrating a church, *Lavabo*, *Mandatum*, the numerous uses of holy water, etc. (*qq.v.*). The Church regards the absolute necessity of water to human life, its part in human history (the Flood, the Red Sea, Jordan) and in particular the symbolic significance of its natural qualities: "The disposition of Heaven: water trodden by the feet of Jesus; you are surrounded by the mountains but not confined thereby, broken up by the rocks but at once reunited, spread out over the earth but not lost; you bear up the hills and are not crushed by them, you are contained in the depths of the sky, you are poured out everywhere, cleansing all things and being cleansed by none" (from the blessing of water at the consecration of a church).

WATER, THE BLESSING OF, is directed to take place before the principal Mass on Sundays. It consists of exorcisms of salt and of water, each followed by a prayer; salt is then put thrice into the water cross-wise; and there follows a prayer that "wherever it shall be sprinkled and thy holy name invoked in prayer, every assault of the unclean spirit may be baffled . . . and the presence of the Holy Spirit vouchsafed." The water is removed from all stoups during the last three days of Holy Week.

WATERFORD AND LISMORE (*Waterfordiensis et Lismoriensis*). An Irish see, suffragan of Cashel, formed by the union of the two older sees in 1363. It includes county Waterford and parts of Tipperary and Cork. The bishop's residence, cathedral and seminary are in the city of Waterford. The patron of Waterford is St. Otteran (Oct. 27) and of Lismore St. Carthage (May 14); the cathedral is dedicated to the Holy Trinity. Irish name: Portláirge.

WAX. The beeswax of which candles were made, as a pure and indestructible substance, mysteriously made, early came to be regarded as a symbol of the flesh of Christ. In our own day this is recognized (and also the principle that no artificial substance should be used in the service of the sanctuary so long as a natural substance is available, *cf.*, silk, olive oil) in the regulations that the paschal candle and Mass candles should be in their greater part of pure beeswax, and that other candles put upon the altar should be wax to at least a notable proportion.

WAY OF THE CROSS, The. The Stations of the Cross (*q.v.*).

WEALTH. Things having value in exchange; things for which people are willing to give money. Anything is wealth if anyone can be found to pay for it. Ability to labour is wealth and is the only wealth possessed by very large numbers of labourers to-day. Water is wealth in the Sahara but not in Wales; sand is wealth in Wales but not in Surrey; gold is wealth in London but not at the South Pole. Land is the most important form of wealth while air, though all men need it, being obtainable by all without payment, is wealth to nobody. Money is simply the medium of exchange: it may be in the form of metal coins, precious or not, of paper notes, of plugs of tobacco (as in New Guinea), or any other convenient thing.

WEALTH, OBLIGATIONS OF. The possession of wealth carries its responsibilities; its employment merely for the private advantage of the owner is an abuse. The Gospel bids the wealthy man regard himself as a steward who, after making due provision for his reasonable maintenance and for the upkeep of his business, should freely employ his wealth in promoting the welfare of his neighbour. St. Basil warns the rich man that his superfluous food and clothing belong to his hungry and naked neighbours; St. Ambrose says that the rich man who gives to the poor does not bestow an alms but pays a debt; from St. Paul (2 Cor. viii, 14) onwards Christian teaching has been that surplus wealth is a trust to be administered for the benefit of the poor.

WELL, HOLY. Wells and other waters have been regarded as sacred places always and everywhere; many of these places of religious association have been carried over into Christianity and "baptized" (e.g., the well in the crypt of Chartres cathedral) and new ones become popular (e.g., the spring at Lourdes). Usually the association is with some particular saint or event, with or without alleged curative power in the use of the water itself. There are numerous holy wells in Great Britain of which many are the subject of more or less incomplete and superstitious local beliefs and practices. The principal wells in the British Isles still the resort of genuine pilgrims among Catholics are St. Winefride's (q.v.) in Flintshire, and St. Brigid's at Faughart, in county Louth.

WESLEYANISM. The religious system, doctrine and organization of the followers of John Wesley (1703-91), who, after his death but in accordance with the trend of his actions, seceded from the Church of England and ultimately formed several sects of which the original and most important is that of the Wesleyan Methodists. Wesley preached the total depravity of man but that he becomes justified by his free will co-operating with the grace of God, and his righteousness is inherent, not merely imputed (the individual experience of present justification is called conversion); the Bible is the sole rule of faith, but he did not repudiate all tradition; the Trinity, the atonement, incarnation, passion and resurrection of our Lord

are fundamental truths, but these are now less explicitly emphasized than "personal intuition" of truth; his ethics are rigorist and puritan; presbyteral but not episcopal ordination was necessary to the ministry, but later Wesleyanism has been divided on the degree of ministerial authority and activity required. The weekly class-meeting of a dozen members under a leader whose office it is to exhort, reprove, entreat, rebuke is, or was, the classical and characteristic feature of Wesleyan organization. Wesley led a reaction towards traditional Christianity from Calvinism and his insistence on personal holiness was actually grounded on the "Imitation of Christ" of Thomas à Kempis. In the United States, more than in England, Wesleyanism becomes more and more undogmatic and as an organization for social work and "uplift", it played a considerable part in foisting Prohibition on the first-named country. Cf., Nonconformity.

WEST INDIES, THE CHURCH IN THE. The West Indies were discovered and evangelized by Spain in the 15th-16th centuries. Those of them now belonging to Great Britain are principally Trinidad and its islands, with an archbishopric, one suffragan diocese, and 300,000 Catholics, and the vicariate apostolic of Jamaica (63,000). In Trinidad Catholics are a majority of the population and the Church retains a somewhat privileged position inherited from before the surrender by Spain in 1797, the government contributing to the support of the clergy. Porto Rico has two dioceses i.s.h.s. (San Juan has been a bishopric since 1511) and 1¾ million Catholics. Guadaloupe and Martinique are dioceses i.s.h.s., Curaçao a vicariate and St. Pierre and Miquelon a prefecture, and practically all of their 550,000 inhabitants are Catholics. The few Catholics of the Bahamas are under the jurisdiction of a vicar apostolic. There is a delegate apostolic "for the Antilles" at Havana. See also CUBA, etc.

WEST INDIES, PATRIARCH OF THE. A purely honorary title made appurtenant to the Church in Spain by Pope Leo X in 1520. It is at present enjoyed by the bishop of Madrid.

WESTERN CHURCH, The. That part of the Catholic Church which is subject to the pope of Rome as patriarch (q.v.) as well as supreme pontiff. It is a convenient expression and commonly used but no longer accurate except in a limited sense; from being the peoples of those territories in Europe and Africa that depended immediately on the Roman patriarch and used the Latin rite it has now spread throughout the world and includes the great majority of all Catholics: so much so that the Western church is often assumed to be the whole Church. This historical development and preponderance is due to the separation of the churches of the east, to the colonization of the New World by western nations (*e.g.*, Spain in South America) and to the activity and zeal of the missionaries of the Western church in heathen lands. "Western church" is synonymous with "Latin church," Roman church (ii) and Patriarchate of the West (*q.v.*); see also LATIN RITE (*b*).

WESTMINSTER (*Westmonasteriensis*). The senior archiepiscopal see of the restored hierarchy of England and Wales, including London north of the Thames, Middlesex and Hertfordshire, formerly in the diocese of London. Its archbishop as ordinary is the successor of the last bishop of London, Edmund Bonner (*d.* in prison, 1569), and as metropolitan succeeds to the position of Cardinal Reginald Pole, last archbishop of Canterbury (*d.* 1558), for, though the see has no primacy, its seniority is perpetual and its archbishop (the first six of whom have all been made cardinals) represents the Church in England in dealing with the civil power; the see, therefore, legitimately represents Canterbury and has the same armorial device, but with different tinctures. In addition to the embassy chapels (*q.v.*) the principal old missions are Isleworth (1675), Moorfields (1710), Soho Square (1792), Somers Town (1798) and the diocesan seminary at St. Edmund's College, Old Hall, near Ware (1793); the Rosminian church of St. Etheldreda, Ely Place, off Holborn, was built in 1297. Its patrons are our Lady Immaculate, St. Joseph, St. Peter and St. Edward. The cathedral, wherein the whole Divine Office is celebrated daily in choir, is dedicated to the Precious Blood of our Lord and the feast of its consecration is on June 28. Westminster was first made a diocese during the schism of Henry VIII in 1540, but was suppressed in 1550.

WHITBY, THE SYNOD OF. An assembly held at St. Hilda's abbey in 663, at which St. Chad and King Oswy of Northumbria were prevailed on by St. Wilfrid to adopt the usages of the Roman church. This and the agreement thereto of St. Cuthbert was the beginning of the end of the Easter Controversy (*q.v.*). The opposing party was led by St. Colman, bishop of Lindisfarne, who afterwards retired with some of his monks to Ireland.

WHITE. The liturgical colour of vestments used on all feasts of our Lord (except those of his cross and passion), of our Lady, of confessors, of all women not martyrs, on Sundays and ferias in paschal-time and some other occasions. Since the reign of Pope St. Pius V (1566-72) white has also been the ordinary colour of papal garments.

WHITE CANONS. The Canons Regular of Prémontré (*q.v.*), from the colour of their habits.

WHITE FATHERS, The. The popular name of the Society of Missionaries of Africa founded by Cardinal C. M. A. Lavigerie, at Algiers, in 1868. It is a society of secular priests and brothers living in community, bound by oath to labour for the African missions; they live so far as possible in the same way as the natives and their dress is a white tunic (*gandura*) and an ample mantle (*burnus*). They are helped by the White Sisters (*q.v.*, i). They have numerous missions in north, north-west and central Africa, with 1½ million baptized Christians. They also conduct the Melkite seminary of St. Ann at Jerusalem. There are two missionary colleges and other important establishments of the White Fathers in Great Britain, and others in Canada.

WHITE FRIARS. The Carmelites (*q.v.*) from the colour of their cloaks.

WHITE GARMENT, ROBE, VEIL. See BAPTISMAL GARMENT.

WHITE LADIES, The. i. The Daughters of the Presentation, an order of teaching nuns founded in France in 1796 and now established in North America.
ii. A former name for Cistercian nuns, still surviving in the place-name Whiteladies, in Shropshire and elsewhere.

WHITE MONKS. The Cistercians (*q.v.*) from the colour of their tunics and cowls.

WHITE SISTERS, The. i. The Missionary Sisters of Our Lady of Africa founded by Cardinal Lavigerie in 1869 to help in the missions of the White Fathers, especially among Mohammedan women. They have many establishments in north, west and central Africa. In the equatorial regions they are helped by native nuns (*Bannabikira*, *q.v.*).
ii. The Sisters of the Holy Ghost, so called from their most becoming white habit, founded in Brittany in 1706 by Mgr. Angeuin and Madame Balaven for educational and other active works of charity. They are now found principally in Wales, Belgium and the U.S.A.

WHITSUNDAY (*i.e.*, White Sunday). The popular name in England, from at least the 12th century, for the feast of Pentecost (*q.v.*), so called because of the white coifs (*cf.*, baptismal garment) worn by the babies baptized at that time. Whitsun eve is, accordingly, the vigil of Pentecost.

WIDOWHOOD. The marriage of widows or widowers is lawful among Christians, nor is there any limit to the number of successive marriages that may be thus entered into. But the representation of the union of Christ with his Church is less perfect in second and subsequent marriages; *cf.*, Bigamy, i, Nuptial Blessing (3). The Orthodox forbid marriages after the third. In those churches, whether Catholic or dissident, in which married men may receive sacred orders, a deacon or priest whose wife dies is forbidden to marry again. A widower is not debarred from receiving sacred orders or from entering any religious order (but see BIGAMY, i); nearly all orders of nuns receive widows by dispensation (the Visitation Order is formally open to them). Widows are sometimes treated as a distinct class of the saints, but liturgically they are not distinguished from other holy women not virgins, except that there is an alternative epistle (1 Tim. v. 3-10) for the common Masses.

WIFE. i. Status. Though her husband's companion, the wife is subject to him as the head of the family, owing him love, reverence and obedience (Eph. v. 22-24). She would sin mortally by showing great contempt for his authority or by arrogating it to herself. She is her husband's equal in the rights and duties of marital intercourse. She has a right to support at his expense for herself and for her children, and may bequeath her separate property to whom she pleases and choose her own place of burial. (*cf.,* Husband).

ii. In canon law. A wife, not legally separated from her husband, has necessarily the domicile of her husband, and cannot establish her own. She may, however, acquire a quasidomicile, and if legally separated (*i.e.,* by the law of the Church) even a domicile. As regards the canonical effects of marriage, the wife shares her husband's status.

WILGEFORTIS LEGEND, The. Wilgefortis (also known as Liberata, Uncumber, Kummernis, Livrade) was the heroine of a pseudo-edifying romance of a girl who grew a beard so that she would not have to be married. This tale was widely spread in Europe in the middle ages, and wives oppressed by unsatisfactory husbands used to invoke "St. Wilgefortis."

WILL. The power which is capable of directing itself to a good apprehended by the mind; the intellectual appetite as opposed to the sensitive appetite which inclines to a good apprehended by the senses. The will is a blind faculty, in the sense that it depends upon intellectual cognition, whence the axiom *Nil volitum quin præcognitum:* "There can be no willing of an unknown thing." Now although the mind thus moves the will by presenting to it its object (called movement *quoad specificationem*), the will can move, or apply the mind to act (called movement *quoad exercitium*) just as it moves certain lower powers to act. The elicited acts of the will, *i.e.,* those which proceed immediately from it, can never suffer violence, whereas its imperated acts, *i.e.,* those commanded by the will to be done by some other faculty, can suffer violence. The will may be considered as a nature, or precisely

as will; in the first case its act is necessary and thus it seeks its appropriate good, but as will its acts are free for it can choose any means that lead to its appropriate good. "It is by our will that we employ whatever powers we may have. Hence a man is said to be good, not by his good understanding, but by his good will" (St. Thomas, I, v, 4 ad 3).

WILL, ACT OF THE. An act of the will is made whenever a man exercises his freedom of choice. The will may either act alone, as in an act of love or of hatred, or it may call upon other faculties, such as the intellect, whenever an act of faith is elicited.

WILL, DIVINE. That inclination which is in all things towards appropriate good is called appetite; it is called Will when the inclination is consequent upon intellectual cognition. Since then in God there is a mind, there is also a will. Now since God is an absolutely simple (*q.v.*) being, or Pure Act, his will is not a power distinct from the Divine Essence. The will of God primarily and necessarily wills his own Divine Essence since it is the Supreme Good, and secondarily and freely it wills things other than himself.

WILL AND TESTAMENT. In canon law, certain proof of a testator's intention is sufficient to make a testamentary disposition of property valid, *i.e.,* in practice, to involve a moral obligation on the part of heirs or others. There is a moral obligation on a testator to provide according to his means for those who have just claims on him; this can only be set aside for a just cause. A testamentary direction for cremation (*q.v.*) is void in canon law, and it and any other directions for the disposal of one's body are voidable at the discretion of the executor in the civil law of England. Bequests for Masses (*q.v.*) and other prayers, or for the benefit of religious orders, are now valid in Great Britain and Ireland. A beneficed cleric cannot dispose by will of property bought with the proceeds of his office. A novice in an order with solemn vows must, before simple profession, make a will disposing of his present and future property; it is forbidden subsequently to change the will if the effect of the change is to benefit his order to the extent of a notable part of the property.

WIMPLE (Old Eng., derivation uncertain). A close headdress of linen arranged in folds about the head, throat and neck and forming with a veil the head-covering of nearly all nuns. It was formerly common to other women.

WINDING SHEET, THE FEAST OF THE HOLY. A feast of the Passion observed in some places on Friday after the second Sunday in Lent; the offices assigned to it in the Roman Missal and Breviary are those granted to the diocese of Turin in reference to the alleged shroud of Christ preserved in the cathedral of that city. Half-a-dozen other places have similar relics, with proper offices for various days. It is practically certain that no one of these relics is genuine.*

WINE. i. Altar. Wine used in the Eucharistic Sacrifice must be pure grape juice naturally fermented; it may be white or red. A few drops of water (*q.v.* i) are added to it at the offertory, and in the Byzantine rite warm water as well just before the communion (*zeon, q.v.*). Wine made from raisins may be used in an emergency provided it be pure.

ii. Other liturgical uses. The pope at a solemn papal Mass and new priests at the Mass of their ordination immediately after receiving communion take a draught of ordinary wine from a chalice; the same is done by all communicants in some churches of the Byzantine rite. This was formerly a very common custom and is still prescribed in the "Cæremoniale Episcoporum" for the general communion on Easter day. It was intended for an ablution of the month (just as some people always drink water before eating after holy communion and as it is given by the priest to the sick), and had nothing to do with communion in one kind. Wine is also used in the ceremonial washing of an altar (*q.v.*), and in the consecration of an *antimension* and of a Byzantine altar. It formerly was a widespread custom to give a draught of unconsecrated wine from the chalice to sick persons, especially children and in cases of whooping-cough. This was done within living memory in England, *e.g.*, at Little Crosby in Lancashire.

WISDOM. i. As a gift of the Holy Ghost (*q.v.*), is a perfection of the understanding enabling the just man to judge of all things according to divine standards, to take "God's point of view." This does not imply any extraordinary mental analysis, but a contemplation (*q.v.*) of things in God. So it is that an uneducated person can often make (and even communicate) a judgement more in accordance with the mind of God than that of a trained mind which lacks the gift of wisdom.

ii. As an intellectual virtue, it is a habit (*q.v.*) perfecting the intellect and enabling it to pursue a speculative inquiry into the nature of truth, especially in the search after the first and supreme causes of things, such as their essence and last end. It is different from knowledge, which is the perfection of the intellect produced by the satisfactory result of the inquiry.

iii. The Book of. A deutero-canonical book of the Old Testament, written in the person of King Solomon, but by an unknown writer in Greek of a much later date. It exhorts princes and magistrates and others to all virtues under the general figures of

wisdom and justice, and reviews the history of Israel in the light of that teaching.

WITCHCRAFT. From the earliest recorded times the learned and experienced as well as the common people have believed in witchcraft (Pope Innocent VIII published a bull about it in 1484), but it was not until the 16th and 17th centuries that anything resembling a witch-mania broke out; this was a frenzy of fear, ignorance and superstition which was very widespread but particularly violent in the Protestant countries of northern Europe. The reaction from this disastrous panic has done away with any belief at all in witchcraft among most educated people, but "it must be steadily remembered that the most brilliant minds, the keenest intelligences, the most learned scholars, the noblest names, men who had heard the evidence at first hand, all firmly believed in witchcraft" (G. B. Harrison); and the experience of the Church in barbarian lands forbids her to deny the possibility, and indeed actual occurrence, of the exercise of preternatural powers possessed in virtue of an alliance with evil spirits, usually with the intention of injuring others.

WITNESS. Witnesses are required by canon law for the valid and licit performance of certain acts, *e.g.*, celebration of marriage (two), abjuration of heresy (two), etc.

WOMAN. i. Woman has a double life-task: as an individual, her moral perfection; as a member of society, in union with man to represent and develop humanity in all its aspects. As individuals, man and woman are morally equals. Since humanity is composed of male and female, each requires the other for its social complement; each has qualities lacking in the other. Since the completely developed feminine personality is found in motherhood (not necessarily restricted to its physiological aspect) all activities impairing woman's chief social duty, maternal influence whether in the spiritual or material sphere, are to be avoided. Christianity, in raising marriage to the dignity of a sacrament, raised woman from varying degrees of degradation to moral equality with man, and it taught the nobility of freely chosen virginity. This elevation of woman centres in the Blessed Virgin Mary: respect for woman rises and falls with that for her. The Christian view of woman's sphere is that her proper influence should extend to Church and state, provided her double life-task is not thereby impeded.

ii. In canon law. In many matters there is special legislation in canon law in regard to women. They cannot be members of confraternities properly so called, except to share in the spiritual benefits and indulgences. Their confessions are only to be heard in churches and in a properly appointed confessional. They are not allowed

* The most current research indicates that the Shroud of Turin is indeed genuine; any other "Shroud" relics would presumably be spurious.—*Publisher*, 1997.

to serve Mass at the altar, but if there is no man a woman is permitted to make the liturgical responses from outside the sanctuary. ". . . singers in church have a real liturgical office and therefore women, being incapable of such an office, cannot be admitted to the choir" (*motu proprio* of Pope Pius X on Church Music); but *cf.*, choir, iii. *Cf.*, Abbess, Wife, etc.

iii. In church. The Code of Canon Law lays down: "It is to be desired that in accordance with ancient discipline women in church should be separate from men" (canon 1262, § 1). This is now practically a dead letter in the Western church though still customary in certain places (women to the north, men to the south) and required by the "Rituale Romanum" and the Ceremonial of Bishops when it can be done without inconvenience. In the Eastern rites it is still usual, but is being modified in Europe and still more in America, except among the Ukrainians. See also HATS, ii; GYNACEUM.

WONDER-WORKING. An image, shrine, or relic is said to be wonder-working when God uses it as an instrument by means of which he performs a miracle ("The bodies of saints and martyrs . . . through which many benefits are bestowed by God on mankind," Council of Trent, sess. xxv) or as an occasion for wonders ("God fittingly does honour to such relics by performing miracles in their presence," St. Thomas). To do so has been God's pleasure from biblical times, *e.g.*, as recorded in Num. xxi, 8, 9; 4 (2) Kings xiii, 21; Acts xix, 12; John v, 2-4. No virtue, efficacy or power inheres in these objects themselves.

WORD, The. i. The term used by St. John to designate the second Person of the Blessed Trinity, God the Son. As the word is the utterance of the thought, and at the same time its representative and equivalent, and as it were its image projected beyond the speaker, it was an apt term for the Son of a purely spiritual Being, begotten and brought forth in a mental and incorporeal way as his own image. The Jews already used *Memra* (word, or utterance) as an alternative for the Divine Name, and the Greeks had used the Stoic term *Logos* (λόγος) since the 5th century B.C.; Platonists had used it for a divine emanation and Philo the Jew had combined Stoic and Platonic ideas in the use of the term: St. John therefore used an expression current in his day to describe a newly-revealed truth.

ii. The Holy Scriptures, which were so inspired by God that they are in very truth his written word. "The books of the Old and New Testaments . . . are to be received as sacred and canonical . . . because, having been written under the inspiration of the Holy Ghost, they have God for their author" (Council of Trent, sess. iii, c. 2). See BIBLE, INSPIRATION, etc.

WORDS OF INSTITUTION, The. The words reciting the institution of the Holy Eucharist said by the celebrant whereby the consecration of the bread and wine at Mass is effected. These words are taken from the gospels, 1 Cor. xi, 23-25 and apostolic tradition. They vary somewhat in different rites; those of the Latin Mass are: "Who, the day before he suffered, took bread into his holy and worshipful hands; and having lifted up his eyes to Heaven, to thee, God, his almighty Father, giving thanks to thee, he blessed, broke and gave to his disciples saying. Take and eat ye all of this, *for this is my Body*. In like manner after supper taking also this glorious chalice into his holy and worshipful hands and giving thanks to thee, he blessed and gave it to his disciples saying, Take and drink ye all of this, *for this is the chalice of my Blood, of the new and eternal testament, the mystery of faith, which shall be shed for you and for many for the forgiveness of sins*. So often as ye do these things, do them in remembrance of me"; in the Byzantine Liturgy of St. John Chrysostom: "Who . . . in the night in which he was betrayed, or rather surrendered himself for the life of the world, taking bread into his holy, pure and spotless hands, giving thanks, blessing, sanctifying and breaking, gave it to his holy disciples and apostles saying, *Take, eat, this is my Body broken for you for the forgiveness of sins*. [Amen]. In like manner the cup after he had supped, saying, *Drink ye all of this, this is my Blood, of the new testament, shed for you and for many for the forgiveness of sins*. [Amen]"; and so on. In all Liturgies except the Latin Mass these words are said or sung aloud, the people or assistants answering *Amen*. The present teaching of the dissident Eastern churches is that the words of institution (which of course they recite) alone do not effect consecration, but that the *epiklesis* (*q.v.*) is required as well.

WORK. Energy expended for a purpose. The normal state of man is that in which work is a pleasure and, in spite of "the curse of Adam" by which men must work whether they like it or not, this state of normality is common wherever the workman is a responsible person. In places where servile conditions of work prevail, that is where responsibility in work is denied or reduced, the workman's pleasure in work is generally destroyed and the quality of the work done degraded, unless it be purely mechanical. "I have found that nothing is better than for a man to rejoice in his work, and that this is his portion" (Eccl. iii, 22).

WORK OF GOD, The. See OPUS DEI.

WORLD, The. By the expression "the world" when spoken of by spiritual writers as in opposition to God, the Church, the individual soul, "the World, the Flesh, and the Devil," must be understood not the material universe or the natural order, but the world as ordered by man to his own ends without reference to God, the allurements of the visible creation in so far as they fill the human heart and draw it away from God, and the bad example and deceitful doctrines of wicked men (*cf.*, John xv, 19; 1 John v, 19). One who becomes a religious (*q.v.*) is said to have "left the world."

WORLDLINESS. Devotion to the things of the world and the pleasures accompanying them to the neglect of one's spiritual needs. "A man may be in the world in two ways: in the one by his bodily presence, in the other, by the cast of his mind" (St. Thomas).

WORSHIP. The unique adoration and reverence paid to God, called *latria* (*q.v.*); the word is sometimes used also for the honour paid to the saints (*dulia, q.v.*), but this is better distinguished by some such word as "veneration." To give worship to God on account of his infinite and uncreated excellence, as our first beginning and last end, is the highest duty of man, and the worship of Jesus Christ as God incarnate has ever been the mark of the Christian man. Worship is moral activity, and therefore must be first of all interior. But man is not a pure spirit: he is body as well as soul, and hence his interior worship expresses itself in bodily gestures or postures, as singing, prostrating, etc. He is also a social animal and must worship socially, and this is only possible by means of public exterior worship, expressive of the united will of the worshippers: hence rites and ceremonies, especially sacrifice (*q.v.*). Moreover, the Christian religion and the Catholic Church are of their nature such as to require public communal worship. Therefore all worship cannot be *only* in spirit and in truth, but without this interior spirit external service is worthless. Christian social and public worship is the Liturgy (*q.v.*), centring round the Sacrifice of the Mass (*q.v.*).

WREATH. i. The custom of covering the coffins of the dead at funerals with wreaths of flowers is not condemned by the Church, but while it is a laudable thing to show honour to the memory and the bodies of the dead, it is more necessary to remember their welfare, and the money expended on costly wreaths may more fittingly be offered for the celebration of Masses for the repose of their souls.

ii. See CROWN, MARRIAGE.

WYCLIFFITES, or Lollards. The followers of John Wyclif (1324-84), parish priest of Lutterworth, Leicestershire. His chief doctrines were: that "dominion (*q.v.*) is founded in grace," eucharistic companation (*q.v.*), the sufficiency of the Scriptures as a rule of life, the importance of preaching over Mass and the sacraments, and that the Holy See has no primacy of jurisdiction. He was condemned by local synods in England and posthumously by the Council of Constance. Lollardy as a general form of religious dissent persisted until the Reformation; but its real influence was through the Hussites (*q.v.*) of Bohemia who adopted its errors.

X

XAVERIAN BROTHERS, The. A congregation of laymen, bound by simple vows, for the conduct of schools, chiefly secondary, founded by Brother Francis-Xavier Ryken at Bruges in 1839. They have numerous establishments in Belgium and the U.S.A., and a few in England.

XYLOPOLITANUS. The Latin epithet for the bishop of Boise City, Idaho. Boise = French *bois* = wood = Greek *xulon*.

Y

Y.M.C.A. The initials of an international society called the Young Men's Christian Association, of which the religious basis is undenominationalism (*q.v.*, ii); membership, and co-operation except on strictly defined lines approved by ecclesiastical authority, is therefore debarred to Catholics. The philanthropic and social works of the Y.M.C.A. have in certain places a definitely proselytizing aspect towards members of the Catholic Church and other non-Protestant Christian bodies. On account of its activities in Italy it was distinguished by name in a letter of the Holy Office in 1920 warning bishops against certain such organizations. It was also condemned by the holy synod of the Orthodox Church of Bulgaria, in 1926 and again in 1928.

YAHWEH. See JAHVEH.

YEAR. The ecclesiastical year, during which are celebrated and spiritually renewed in due order the mysteries pertaining to man's salvation and the memory of the saints, begins in the Western church, since the 16th century, on the first Sunday of Advent, which is that which falls nearest to the feast of St. Andrew on Nov. 30. Its arrangement is not arbitrary but has grown up in the course of history. It is commonly divided into the Christmas cycle, which begins with the first Sunday of Advent, includes Christmas, the Circumcision, the Epiphany, and the Purification, and ends on the Saturday before Septuagesima; the Easter cycle, whose incidence depends on the date of Easter (*q.v.*) and includes Septuagesima-time, Lent, Holy Week, and paschal-time, with the Ascension and Pentecost; and the time after Pentecost, beginning on Trinity Sunday, during which many of the most important feasts of saints occur. The liturgy, with which the life of every Christian is meant to be intimately connected, thus celebrates in historical order the waiting for the Messias, his birth, childhood and the fast which prepared for his entry into public life, the last week of that life, his passion, death, resurrection and ascension, the Holy Ghost's confirmation of the Church at Pentecost, and the subsequent life of the Church brought into association with the earthly life of her Master. The year of the Byzantine rite begins on Sept. 1 and has no liturgical cycles corresponding to those of the West; but the period from three weeks before Lent to the Saturday after Whitsunday stands apart for importance. See also CALENDAR.

YELLOW. Formerly a liturgical colour (*e.g.*, for confessors in the Sarum use) but now forbidden. It is, however, sometimes seen as a substitute for white or masquerading as cloth of gold.

YORK, THE USE OF. The version of the Roman liturgy used in the diocese and province of York before the Reformation.

YUGOSLAVIA, THE CHURCH IN. The state of Yugoslavia was formed after world-war I by the union of Serbia, Croatia, Slovenia, Dalmatia, Montenegro, Bosnia and Herzegovina. The population in 1939 was 14¾ million, of whom 46 per cent (mostly Serbs) were dissident Orthodox, 33 per cent (mostly Croats and Slovenes) were Catholic, and 11 per cent (mostly Bosnians) Mohammedan. The hierarchical divisions, which the Holy See had not succeeded in reorganizing by 1939, were 2 metropolitan sees (Zagreb, Vrhbosna [Sarajevo]) with 5 suffragan dioceses, 2 archbishoprics without suffragans, and 9 bishoprics immediately subject to the Holy See. The diocese of Krizevci is of Slav-Byzantine rite. After 1944 the government was definitely hostile towards religion, and many clergy were imprisoned or executed. Religious instruction was abolished in the public schools. Since 1920 the dominant Orthodox church in Yugoslavia has formed a patriarchate of the dissident Orthodox Church, under the Serbian patriarch of Ipek (Péc); in 1945 its privileged position was abolished by the civil power. It is said that one-third of its clergy were killed during world-war II.

YULE. The Old English *geól*, at first the name of a pagan mid-winter feast. It is current in Scotland and northern England and in the term "yule-log," but otherwise its use is now a literary affectation.

Z

ZACHARIAS. i. The Greek form of the name of the prophet and his book contained in the Old Testament, called in Hebrew Zechariah (Remembered by Jahveh). He prophesied at the same time and upon the same occasion as Aggeus (*q.v.*), urging the Jews to the rebuilding of the Temple; the book has numerous allusions to the coming of Christ and is often quoted in the New Testament. Zacharias is named in the Roman Martyrology on Sept. 6.

ii. The priest and husband of St. Elizabeth (Luke i, 5), commonly called Zachary.

ZACHARY, THE CANTICLE OF. The *Benedictus* (*q.v.*, i).

ZEON (Gr., boiling). A small quantity of hot water (and also the vessel which contains it) poured into the Chalice immediately before the celebrant's communion in the Byzantine rite. It signifies the fervour of faith and fulness of the Holy Ghost communicated to the faithful by partaking of the Precious Blood; but its origin was probably practical, to prevent the contents of the cup freezing in cold climates. This usage has been abandoned by the Ruthenians.

ZEPHANIAH. The Hebrew form of the name of the prophet Sophonias.

ZIMARRA (It.). The black cassock worn ordinarily and in the house by bishops and other prelates, having a cape and purple sash, with purple buttons and piping. Sometimes anglicized as "simar."

ZION, SION, (Heb. *Tsiyon*, hill). That hill of Jerusalem whereon the city of David was built; according to traditional topography, the institution of the holy Eucharist and the descent of the Holy Ghost took place on Mount Sion. The name is used figuratively to mean the household of God, whether the Hebrew theocracy or the Christian church; but above all, with Jerusalem itself it appears in hymns, poems, sermons, mystical treatises, and the daily speech of Christians as the Celestial City, the Kingdom of Heaven.

ZIONISM. The policy of giving Jews a national home by colonizing Palestine with them, the colonization itself as carried out after 1918, and the more developed Zionist ambitions in this regard. For the Catholic the matter has no intrinsic religious aspect.

ZONE (Gr., girdle). The girdle worn by priests and bishops of the Byzantine rite when vested. It is a narrow band of material confining the *sticharion* and *epitrachelion*, either tied behind or fastened with a buckle in front.

ZOUAVES, PONTIFICAL (French military term for light-infantry, from the name of an Algerian tribe from which recruits were originally taken). A volunteer corps, forming the principal part of the pontifical military forces, raised at Rome in 1860 by General Louis Lamoricière. At first its members were chiefly French and Belgian, but in time other countries and all classes were represented: at the taking of Rome by the Piedmontese in 1870 they numbered 8,300, of whom two-thirds were Italians; England, Wales, Scotland, Ireland and Canada were represented (in spite of the Foreign Enlistment Act) and the ranks included a prince of the house of Bourbon and a convert Turk. They fought well under General Kantzler at Mentana (1867), at Spoleto, Ancona and elsewhere, and some were killed at the Porta Pia; afterwards they served France against Prussia. They were disbanded at the fall of Paris.

ZUCCHETTO (It., dim. of *zucca*, gourd, pate). The skull-cap (*q.v.*) of a prelate.

ZWINGLIANISM. The doctrines of Ulrich Zwingli (1484-1531), the first leader of Protestantism in Switzerland, particularly his teaching that the Eucharist conveys no grace and is merely figurative, a denial of the Real Presence, as against Luther, who taught such presence but by impanation and at the moment of reception only.

APPENDIX I

COMMON ECCLESIASTICAL ABBREVIATIONS

A

A.A.: *Augustinianus Assumptionis;* Augustinian of the Assumption (Assumptionist).

A.A.S.: *Acta Apostolicæ Sedis;* The Acts of the Apostolic See.

Ab.: *Abbas;* abbot.

Abp.: Archbishop.

abst.: abstinence day.

A.C. (N.): *Ante Christum (natum);* Before (the birth of) Christ.

Alb. or A.: *Albus;* white (vestments).

A.M.: *Anno Mundi;* in the year of the world (also *Artium magister;* Master of Arts).

A.M.D.G.: *Ad maiorem Dei gloriam;* For the greater glory of God.

ana or ant.: *antiphona;* antiphon.

And may God: May God enrich your Holiness with his gifts (in a petition).

Ap. (plural **App.**): *Apostolus;* apostle.

A.P.F.: The Association for the Propagation of the Faith.

Archieps.: *Archiepiscopus;* archbishop.

A.V.: Authorized Version (Anglican) of the Bible.

B

B. (plural **BB.**): *Beatus, -a (Beati, -ae);* The Blessed (title).

B.C.L.: *Baccalaureus Canonicæ* (sive *Civilis*) *Legis;* Bachelor of Canon (or Civil) Law.

B.D.: *Baccalaureus Divinitatis;* Bachelor of Divinity.

Bl.: The Blessed (title).

B.M.: Bishop and martyr.

Bp.: Bishop.

Br., Bro.: Brother.

B.M.V.: *Beata Maria Virgo;* Blessed Mary the Virgin.

B.U.J.: *Baccalaureus utriusque Juris;* Bachelor of Both (canon and civil) Laws.

B.V.M.: The Blessed Virgin Mary.

C

C. or Conf.: Confessor.

Can.: *Canonicus;* canon.

Cap.: *Capitulum;* little chapter, chapter.

C.C.: Catholic curate (Irish usage).

C.D. or Conf. Doct.: *Confessor et doctor;* Confessor and Doctor of the Church.

C.I.C.: *Codex Iuris Canonici;* The Code of Canon Law.

C.J.M.: *Congregatio Jesu et Mariæ;* The Congregation of Jesus and Mary (Eudists).

C.M.: *Congregatio Missionis;* The Congregation of the Mission (Lazarists).

Com. præc.: *Commemoratio præcedentis;* commemoration of the preceding (feast).

Com. seq.: *Commemoratio sequentis;* commemoration of the following (day's feast).

Compl.: *Completorium;* Compline.

Conf. (non) Pont.: *Confessor (non) pontifex;* Confessor and (not) bishop.

Cong. Orat.: *Congregatio Oratorii;* The Congregation of the Oratory (Oratorians).

C.P.: *Congregatio Passionis;* The Congregation of the Passion (Passionists).

Cr.: *Credo;* The Creed.

C.R.L: *Canonicus Regularis Lateranensis;* Canon Regular of the Lateran (Augustinian canon).

C.R.P.: *Canonicus Regularis Præmonstratensis;* Canon Regular of Premontré (Premonstratensian).

C.S.C.: *Congregatio Sanctæ Crucis;* The Congregation of the Holy Cross.

C.S.P.: *Congregatio Sancti Pauli;* The Congregation of St. Paul (Paulists).

C.S.Sp.: *Congregatio Sancti Spiritus;* The Congregation of the Holy Ghost.

C.SS.R.: *Congregatio Sanctissimi Redemptoris;* The Congregation of the Most Holy Redeemer (Redemptorists).

C.SS.S.: *Congregatio Sanctissimi Salvatoris;* The Congregation of the Most Holy Saviour (Bridgettines).

D

D. (plural **DD.**): *Dominus;* lord. Dom. Dame. Doctor of the Church.

d.: double (feast).

d.d.: *dono dedit;* gave as a gift.

d.d.d.: *dat, dicat, dedicat;* gives, devotes and dedicates.

D.C.L.: *Doctor Canonicæ* (sive *Civilis*) *Legis;* Doctor of Canon (or Civil) Law.

D.D.: *Divinitatis Doctor:* Doctor of Divinity.

de ea.: of this (weekday).

de oct.: of the octave.

de seq.: *de sequenti;* of the following (day's feast).

D.N.J.C.: *Dominus noster Jesus Christus;* Our Lord Jesus Christ.
Dnus.: *Dominus;* lord, master, sir.
Doct.: Doctor of the Church.
Dom.: *Dominica;* Sunday; see also within.
D.O.M.: *Deo optimo maximo;* To God, the best and greatest.
Dom. Prel.: Domestic Prelate.
dp. or dupl.: *duplex;* double (feast).
dp. 1(2)cl.: *duplex primæ (secundæ) classis;* double (feast) of the first (second) class.
dpm. or dupl. maj.: *duplex maius;* greater double (feast).
D.S.S.: *Doctor Sacræ Scripturæ;* Doctor of Holy Scripture.
D.V.: *Deo volente;* God willing.

E

E.M.: *Episcopus et martyr;* bishop and martyr.
Emus.: *Eminentissimus;* Most Eminent.
Ep., Epus.: *Episcopus;* bishop.
Ev. ult.: *Evangelium ultimum;* the Last Gospel.

F

F. or Fr. (plural **FF.**): Father. Friar. *Frater:* brother.
F.D. or Fest. Dev.: *Festum devotionis;* Feast of Devotion.
fer. 2, 3, 4, 5, 6: *feria secunda,* etc.; Monday, Tuesday, Wednesday, Thursday, Friday.
fl.: *floruit;* he flourished, i.e., lived.

G

Gl.: The *Gloria in excelsis* or *Gloria Patri.*
gr.d.: greater double (feast).

H

H.B.: His Beatitude or Blessedness.
H.E.: His Eminence.
H.H.: His Holiness.
H.O.: Holiday of Obligation.

I

I.C.: *Institutum Charitatis;* The Institute of Charity (Rosminians).
ICXC NIKA: A monogram from Greek letters, "Jesus Christ conquers."
IHS.: A monogram of the holy Name in Greek letters.
I.N.R.I.: *Iesus Nazarenus Rex Iudæorum;* Jesus of Nazareth, King of the Jews.
i.p.i.: *in partibus infidelium;* (an episcopal see) in heathen lands.
i.s.h.s.: immediately subject to the Holy See.

J

J.C.: *Jesus Christus;* Jesus Christ.
J.C.D.: *Juris Canonici* (sive *Civilis*) *Doctor;* Doctor of Canon (or Civil) Law.

J.C.L.: *Licentiatus,* Licentiate, etc., as above.
J.M.J.: Jesus, Mary, Joseph.

K

K.C., etc.: Knight Commander of any of the following.
K.H.S.: Knight of the Holy Sepulchre.
K.P.: Knight of Pius IX.
K.S.G.: Knight of St. Gregory.
K.S.S.: Knight of St. Silvester.

L

L.D.S.: *Laus Deo semper;* Praise be to God always.
L.S.: *Locus sigilli;* the place of the seal.
L.S.S.: *Licentiatus Sacræ Scripturæ;* Licentiate of Sacred Scripture.

M

M. (plural **MM.**) or **Mart.:** martyr.
M.C.: Master of Ceremonies.
Mgr. or Msgr.: Monsignor.
Miss.Ap.: *Missionarius Apostolicus;* Missionary Apostolic.
M.pro p.: *Missa pro populo;* Mass (said) for the people.
M.R.: *Missionarius rector;* Missionary rector.

N

n.: *natus;* born.
n.a.n.: *nisi aliter notetur;* unless otherwise noted.
N.C.W.C.: National Catholic Welfare Conference. (U.S.A.).
N.D.: *Notre Dame;* Our Lady.
Nigr. or N.: *Niger;* black (vestments).
N.S.: new style (in dates).
N.T.: New Testament.

O

O.: *Ordo;* the (religious) Order, as below. After a personal name: *Ordinis;* of the Order of . . . . .
ob.: *obiit;* died.
O.C.: *Ordo Cisterciensium;* The Cistercian Order.
O.Cart.: *Ordo Cartusiensis;* The Carthusian Order.
O.C.C.: *Ordo Carmelitarum Calceatarum;* The Order of Calced (Shod) Carmelites.
O.C.D. (and **O.D.C.**): *Ordo Carmelitarum Discalceatarum;* The Order of Discalced (Barefooted) Carmelites.
oct.: *octava;* octave.
O.F.M.: *Ordo Fratrum Minorum;* The Order of Friars Minor (Franciscans).
O.M.C.: *Ordo Minorum Conventualium;* The Order of Conventual (Friars) Minor (Conventual Franciscans).
O.M.Cap.: *Ordo Minorum Capuccinorum;* The Order of Capuchin (Friars) Minor (Capuchin Franciscans).

O.M.I.: *Oblatus Mariæ Immaculatæ;* Oblate of Mary Immaculate.

O.P.: *Ordo Prædicatorum;* The Order of Preachers (Dominicans).

or.: *oratio;* collect, prayer.

Ord. Præm.: *Ordo Præmonstratensium;* The Premonstratensian Order.

O.S.: old style (in dates).

O.S.A.: *Ordo Sancti Augustini;* The Order of St. Augustine (Augustinian friars or hermits).

O.S.B.: *Ordo Sancti Benedicti;* The Order of St. Benedict (Benedictines).

O.S.B.M.: *Ordo Sancti Basilii Magni;* The Order of St. Basil the Great (Basilians).

O.S.C.: *Oblatus Sancti Caroli;* Oblate of St. Charles.

O.S.D.: *Ordo Sancti Dominici;* The Order of St. Dominic (Dominicans, generally used for the third order).

O.S.F.: *Ordo Sancti Francisci;* The Order of St. Francis (Franciscans, now generally used for the third order).

O.S.F.C.: *Ordo Sancti Francisci Capuccinorum;* The Order of St. Francis of the Capuchins.

O.S.J.D.: *Ordo Sancti Joannis de Deo;* The Order of St. John of God (Brothers of Mercy).

O.S.M.: *Ordo Servorum Mariæ;* The Order of the Servants of Mary (Servites).

O.T.: Old Testament.

P

P.: *Pater;* father. *Papa;* pope.

P.A., or **Pref. Ap.:** Prefect Apostolic.

Ph.D.: *Philosophiæ Doctor;* Doctor of Philosophy.

P.G.: *Patrologiæ Græcæ (Cursus Completus);* Migne's "Greek Patrology"; Preacher General.

P.L.: *Patrologiæ Latinæ (Cursus Completus);* Migne's "Latin Patrology."

plen. ind.: plenary indulgence.

Pont.: *Pontifex;* bishop.

Pont. Max.: *Pontifex Maximus;* Supreme Pontiff.

PP., Pp.: *Papa;* pope.

P.P.: Parish-priest (Irish usage).

propr.: *proprium;* proper.

Prot. Ap.: Protonotary Apostolic.

P.S.M.: *Pia Societas Missionum;* The Religious Society of Missions (Pallottini).

Q

Quadrag.: *Quadragesima;* Lent.

R

℟.: response.

R.A.: *Reverendus admodum;* Very Reverend.

R.D.: Rural Dean. Reverend Dom. Rheims-Douay (version of the Bible).

R.I.P.: *Requiescat (-ant) in pace;* May he, she (they) rest in peace.

Rosac.: *Rosaceus;* rose-coloured (vestments).

R.P.: *Reverendus pater;* Reverend Father.

RR.: *Reverendissimus;* Most, Right Reverend

R.S.H.: Religious of the Sacred Heart.

Rub. or **R.:** *Ruber;* red (vestments).

R.V.: Revised Version (Anglican) of the Bible.

S

Sabb.: *Sabbatum;* Saturday.

S.C.: *Sacra Congregatio;* Sacred Congregation. *Salesianorum Congregatio;* The Salesian Congregation.

S.D.B.: Salesians of Don Bosco.

S.D.S.: *Societas Divini Salvatoris;* The Society of the Divine Saviour (Salvatorians).

sem., semid., sd.: *semiduplex;* semi-double (feast).

simpl. or **S.:** *simplex;* simple (feast).

S.J.: *Societas Jesu;* The Society of Jesus (Jesuits).

S.M.: *Societas Mariæ;* The Society of Mary (Marists).

Soc.: *Socius, -ii;* Companion, -s.

S.P.A.Mag.: *Sacri Palatii Apostolici Magister;* Master of the Sacred Apostolic Palace.

Sr.: *Soror;* Sister.

S.R.C.: *Sacrorum Rituum Congregatio;* Congregation of Sacred Rites.

S.R.E.: *Sancta Romana Ecclesia;* Holy Roman Church.

SS.D.N.: *Sanctissimus Dominus noster;* Our most holy Lord (the pope).

S.T.B.: *Sacræ Theologiæ Baccalaureus;* Bachelor of Sacred Theology.

S.T.D.: *Sacræ Theologiæ Doctor;* Doctor of Sacred Theology.

S.T.L.: *Sacræ Theologiæ Licentiatus (sive Lector);* Licentiate (or Lector) of Sacred Theology.

S.T.M.: *Sacræ Theologiæ Magister;* Master of Sacred Theology.

S.T.P.: *Sacræ Theologiæ Professor;* Professor of Sacred Theology.

suffr.: *suffragium;* the suffrage of the saints.

Sum. Theol.: The *Summa Theologica* of St. Thomas Aquinas; it is divided into three parts (the second subdivided into two), each part into questions, each question into articles which in turn contain objections and replies. It is therefore quoted, e.g., thus: II-II, lxxxiii, 6, ad1—the second division of the second part, question eighty-three, article six, the first answer.

S.V.P.: Society of St. Vincent de Paul.

T

tit.: titular.

T.O.S.D.: Tertiary of the Order of St. Dominic.

T.O.S.F.: Tertiary of the Order of St. Francis.

T.P.: *Tempore Paschali;* in paschal time.

U

U.I.O.G.D.: *Ut in omnibus glorificetur Deus;* That God may be glorified in all things.

V

V. (plural **VV.**) or **Ven.:** *Venerabilis, -es;* The Venerable. Virgin.

℣.: versicle.

V.A. or **Vic. Ap.:** *Vicarius apostolicus;* Vicar apostolic.

V.F.: *Vicarius foraneus;* Vicar forane.

V.G.: *Vicarius generalis;* Vicar general.

Vic. Cap.: *Vicarius capitularis;* Vicar capitular.

Vid.: *Vidua;* widow.

Viol. or **U.:** *Violaceus:* purple, violet (vestments).

Virg.: *Virgo:* virgin.

Vir., virid., or **V.:** *Viridis:* green (vestments).

Vp. a cap. seq. com. præc.: *Vesperae a capitulo sequentis, commemoratio præcedentis:* Vespers from the little chapter onwards of the following, with a commemoration of the preceding, feast.

W

W.: Widow.

W.F.: White Father.

APPENDIX II

THE GENERAL CALENDAR OF THE ROMAN CHURCH

With the exception of certain religious orders and a few places, this calendar, modified to meet the needs of particular countries, dioceses etc., is used throughout the Latin rite, and so may be said to merit the epithet "universal" often given to it (see within). There have, however, been added to it in the course of history some feasts whose inclusion in a universal calendar is difficult to justify, and so long ago as the middle of the 18th century Pope Benedict XV projected a most drastic reform, which he did not live to carry out. The Vatican Council again mooted a reform, and Pope Pius X took a step in this direction when he restored all Sundays and the weekdays of Lent to something of their former dignity. The new calendar approved by the Congregation of Sacred Rites in 1915 for the monks of St. Benedict shows the lines which a revised Roman calendar would be likely to take.

The First Sunday of Advent

November 29 The Vigil of St. Andrew. Com. of St. Saturninus
           30 St. Andrew the Apostle

December   2 St. Bibiana
            3 St. Francis Xavier
            4 St. Peter Chrysologus. Com. of St. Barbara
            5 Com. of St. Sabas
            6 St. Nicholas of Myra
            7 St. Ambrose
            8 The Immaculate Conception of the Blessed Virgin Mary
          10 Com. of St. Miltiades
          11 St. Damasus I
          13 St. Lucy
          15 Octave-day of the Immaculate Conception
          16 St. Eusebius of Vercelli
          21 St. Thomas the Apostle
          24 Christmas Eve
          25 THE BIRTHDAY OF OUR LORD JESUS CHRIST (Christmas)
          26 St. Stephen the First Martyr
          27 St. John the Evangelist
          28 The Holy Innocents
          29 St. Thomas of Canterbury
          31 St. Silvester I

January   1 The Circumcision of Our Lord Jesus Christ
            2 Octave-day of St. Stephen
            3 Octave-day of St. John
            4 Octave-day of the Innocents
            5 The vigil of the Epiphany. Com. of St. Telesphorus
            6 THE EPIPHANY OF OUR LORD JESUS CHRIST
          11 Com. of St. Hyginus
          13 Octave-day of the Epiphany
          14 St. Hilary of Poitiers. Com. of St. Felix of Nola
          15 St. Paul the Hermit. Com. of St. Maurus
          16 St. Marcellus I
          17 St. Antony the Abbot
          18 St. Peter's Chair at Rome. Com. of St. Paul and of St. Prisca
          19 St. Marius and his Fellow Martyrs. Com. of St. Canute
          20 SS. Fabian and Sebastian
          21 St. Agnes

Com. = Commemoration

536

22 SS. Vincent and Anastasius
23 St. Raymund of Peñafort. Com. of St. Emerentiana
24 St. Timothy
25 The Conversion of St. Paul
26 St. Polycarp
27 St. John Chrysostom
28 St. Peter Nolasco
29 St. Francis de Sales
30 St. Martina
31 St. John Bosco
Sunday between the Circumcision and the Epiphany: The Holy Name of Jesus
Sunday within the octave of the Epiphany: The Holy Family

February   1 St. Ignatius of Antioch
2 The Purification of the Blessed Virgin Mary (Candlemas)
3 St. Blaise
4 St. Andrew Corsini
5 St. Agatha
6 St. Titus. Com. of St. Dorothy
7 St. Romuald
8 St. John of Matha
9 St. Cyril of Alexandria. Com. of St. Apollonia
10 St. Scholastica
11 The Appearing of the Blessed Virgin Mary at Lourdes
12 The Seven Founders of the Servite Order
14 St. Valentine
15 SS. Faustinus and Jovita
18 St. Simeon
22 St. Peter's Chair at Antioch
23 St. Peter Damian
24 St. Matthias the Apostle
27 St. Gabriel Possenti

Between February 4 and March 10: Ash Wednesday

March   4 St. Casimir. Com. of St. Lucius
6 SS. Perpetua and Felicity
7 St. Thomas Aquinas
8 St. John of God
9 St. Frances the Roman
10 The XL Martyrs of Sebaste
12 St. Gregory the Great
17 St. Patrick
18 St. Cyril of Jerusalem
19 St. Joseph
21 St. Benedict
24 St. Gabriel the Archangel
25 The Annunciation of the Blessed Virgin Mary (Ladyday)
27 St. John of Damascus
28 St. John of Capistrano

Friday after Passion Sunday: The Compassion of the Blessed Virgin Mary
Between March 22 and April 25 inclusive: THE RESURRECTION OF OUR LORD
JESUS CHRIST (Easter)

April   2 St. Francis of Paula
4 St. Isidore of Seville
5 St. Vincent Ferrer
11 St. Leo the Great
13 St. Hermenegild
14 St. Justin. Com. of St. Tiburtius and his Fellow Martyrs
17 St. Anicetus
21 St. Anselm
22 SS. Soter and Caius
23 St. George
24 St. Fidelis of Sigmaringen
25 St. Mark the Evangelist
26 SS. Cletus and Marcellinus
27 St. Peter Canisius

28 St. Paul-of-the-Cross. Com. of St. Vitalis
29 St. Peter Martyr
30 St. Katharine of Siena

Third Wednesday after Easter: The Solemnity of St. Joseph

May

1 SS. Philip and James the Apostles
2 St. Athanasius
3 The Finding of the Holy Cross. Com. of St. Alexander and others
4 St. Monica
5 St. Pius V
6 St. John "before the Latin Gate"
7 St. Stanislaus
8 The Appearing of the Archangel Michael
9 St. Gregory Nazianzen
10 St. Antoninus. Com. of SS. Gordian and Epimachus
12 SS. Nereus, Achilleus, Domitilla and Pancras
13 St. Robert Bellarmine
14 St. Boniface
15 St. John-Baptist de la Salle
16 St. Ubald
17 St. Pascal Baylon
18 St. Venantius
19 St. Celestine V. Com. of St. Pudentiana
20 St. Bernardine of Siena
25 St. Gregory VII. Com. of St. Urban
26 St. Philip Neri. Com. of St. Eleutherius
27 St. Bede the Venerable. Com. of St. John I
28 St. Augustine (Austin) of Canterbury
29 St. Mary-Magdalen de'Pazzi
30 St. Felix I
31 St. Angela Merici. Com. of St. Petronilla

Forty days after Easter: The Ascension of our Lord Jesus Christ
Seven weeks after Easter: PENTECOST (Whitsunday)
The Sunday after Pentecost: The Most Holy Trinity
Thursday after Trinity Sunday: The Blessed Sacrament (Corpus Christi)
Second Friday after Corpus Christi: The Sacred Heart of Jesus

June

2 SS. Marcellinus, Peter and Erasmus
4 St. Francis Caracciolo
5 St. Boniface
6 St. Norbert
9 SS. Primus and Felician
10 St. Margaret of Scotland
11 St. Barnabas
12 St. John of Saint Facundo. Com. of St. Basilides and others
13 St. Antony of Padua
14 St. Basil the Great
15 SS. Vitus, Modestus and Crescentia
18 St. Ephrem the Syrian. Com. of SS. Mark and Marcellian
19 St. Juliana Falconieri. Com. of SS. Gervase and Protasius
20 St. Silverius
21 St. Aloysius Gonzaga
22 St. Paulinus of Nola
23 The Vigil of St. John
24 The Birthday of St. John the Baptist
25 St. William of Vercelli
26 SS. John and Paul
28 St. Irenaeus
29 St. Peter and St. Paul the Apostles
30 The Commemoration of St. Paul

July

1 The Precious Blood of our Lord Jesus Christ
2 The Visitation of the Blessed Virgin Mary. Com. of SS. Processus and Martinian
3 St. Leo II
5 St. Antony Zaccaria
6 Octave-day of SS. Peter and Paul
7 SS. Cyril and Methodius

8 St. Elizabeth of Portugal
10 The Seven Brothers, with SS. Rufina and **Secunda**
11 St. Pius I
12 St. John Gualbert. Com. of SS. Nabor and Felix
13 St. Anacletus
14 St. Bonaventure
15 St. Henry II (Emperor)
16 Our Lady of Mount Carmel
17 St. Alexis
18 St. Camillus of Lellis. Com. of St. Symphorosa and her **Sons**
19 St. Vincent de Paul
20 St. Jerome Emiliani. **Com.** of St. Margaret of Antioch
21 St. Praxedes
22 St. Mary Magdalen
23 St. Apollinaris. Com. of St. Liborius
24 Vigil of St. James. Com. of St. Christine
25 St. James the Elder the Apostle. Com. of St. **Christopher**
26 St. Ann
27 St. Pantaleon
28 SS. Nazarius and Celsus, Victor I and Innocent I
29 St. Martha. Com. of St. Felix II and others
30 SS. Abdon and Sennen
31 St. Ignatius Loyola

August
1 St. Peter in Chains. Com. of The Holy Machabees
2 St. Alphonsus Liguori. Com. of St. Stephen I
3 The Finding of St. Stephen's Body
4 St. Dominic
5 The Dedication of St. Mary Major ("Our Lady of the Snow")
6 The Transfiguration of our Lord Jesus Christ. **Com.** of St. Sixtus II and others
7 St. Cajetan. Com. of St. Donatus
8 SS. Cyriacus, Largus and Smaragdus
9 St. John Vianney. Com. of St. Romanus
10 St. Lawrence
11 St. Tiburtius and Susanna
12 St. Clare
13 SS. Hippolytus and Cassian
14 Vigil of the Assumption. Com. of St. Eusebius
15 The Assumption of the Blessed Virgin Mary
16 St. Joachim
17 St. Hyacinth
18 Com. of St. Agapitus
19 St. John Eudes
20 St. Bernard
21 St. Jane Frances de Chantal
22 The Immaculate Heart of Mary. **Com. of SS.** Timothy, Hippolytus and Symphorian
23 St. Philip Benizi
24 St. Bartholomew the **Apostle**
25 St. Lewis IX of France
26 St. Zephyrinus
27 St. Joseph Calasanctius
28 St. Augustine of Hippo. Com. of St. Hermes
29 The Beheading of St. John the Baptist. Com. of St. Sabina
30 St. Rose of Lima. Com. of SS. Felix and Adauctus
31 St. Raymund Nonnatus

September
1 St. Giles. Com. of The XII Brothers
2 St. Stephen of Hungary
5 St. Laurence Justinian
8 The Birthday of the Blessed Virgin Mary. **Com.** of St. Adrian
9 St. Gorgonius
10 St. Nicholas of Tolentino
11 SS. Protus and Hyacinth
12 The Holy Name of Mary
14 The Exaltation of the Holy Cross
15 The VII Sorrows of the Blessed Virgin Mary. Com. of St. Nicomedes.
16 SS. Cornelius and Cyprian. Com. of St. Euphemia and her Fellow Martyrs

17 The Imprinting of the Stigmata on St. Francis
18 St. Joseph of Cupertino
19 St. Januarius and his Fellow Martyrs
20 St. Eustace and his Fellow Martyrs
21 St. Matthew the Evangelist
22 St. Thomas of Villanova. Com. of St. Maurice and his Fellow Martyrs
23 St. Linus. Com. of St. Thecla
24 Our Lady of Ransom
26 SS. Cyprian and Justina
27 SS. Cosmas and Damian
28 St. Wenceslaus
29 St. Michael and All Angels (Michaelmas)
30 St. Jerome

October   1 St. Remigius
2 The Guardian Angels
3 St. Teresa of Lisieux
4 St. Francis of Assisi
5 St. Placid and his Fellow Martyrs
6 St. Bruno
7 The Rosary of the Blessed Virgin Mary. Com. of Pope St. Mark and others
8 St. Bridget of Sweden
9 St. John Leonardi. Com. of SS. Denis, Rusticus and Eleutherius
10 St. Francis Borgia
11 The Motherhood of the Blessed Virgin Mary
13 St. Edward the Confessor
14 St. Callistus I
15 St. Teresa of Avila
16 St. Hedwig
17 St. Margaret Mary
18 St. Luke the Evangelist
19 St. Peter of Alcantara
20 St. John of Kenty
21 St. Hilarion. Com. of St. Ursula and her Fellow Martyrs
24 St. Raphael the Archangel
25 SS. Chrysanthus and Daria
26 St. Evaristus
27 Vigil of SS. Simon and Jude
28 SS. Simon and Jude the Apostles
31 Vigil of All Saints

Last Sunday in October: Our Lord Jesus Christ the King

November 1 All Saints
2 The Commemoration of the Faithful Departed (All Souls' Day)
4 St. Charles Borromeo. Com. of SS. Vitalis and Agricola
8 Octave-day of All Saints. Com. of the IV Crowned Martyrs
9 The Dedication of the Archbasilica of the Saviour (St. John Lateran, the cathedral of Rome). Com. of St. Theodore
10 St. Andrew Avellino. Com. of SS. Tryphon, Respicius and Nympha
11 St. Martin of Tours. Com. of St. Menas
12 St. Martin I
13 St. Didacus
14 St. Josaphat Kuntsevich
15 St. Albert the Great
16 St. Gertrude
17 St. Gregory the Wonderworker
18 The Dedication of the Basilicas of St. Peter and of St. Paul
19 St. Elizabeth of Hungary. Com. of St. Pontian
20 St. Felix of Valois
21 The Presentation of the Blessed Virgin Mary
22 St. Cecily
23 St. Clement I. Com. of St. Felicity
24 St. John-of-the-Cross. Com. of St. Chrysogonus
25 St. Katharine of Alexandria
26 St. Silvester Gozzolini. Com. of St. Peter of Alexandria

APPENDIX II A

After the Roman and its variants the most widely used calendar is the Byzantine. It varies somewhat from place to place, especially in the saints commemorated in the Slav countries. The following is the usage of the Melkites, which with some variations is the calendar of the Church of Constantinople. The ecclesiastical year begins on 1 September. The lesser-known saints in this calendar can be identified from the Dictionaries of Saints of Holweck (Saint Louis, 1924) and Attwater (London, 1938).

September 1 The Miracle of the Mother of God at Miasene; St. Simeon the Stylite; and others
2 St. Mamas; St. John the Faster
3 St. Anthimus; St. Theoctistus of Pharan
4 St. Babylas; Moses the Prophet
5 St. Zachary
6 The Miracle of St. Michael at Colossæ
7 Vigil of the morrow's feast; St. Sozon
8 The Birthday of the Mother of God
9 Synaxis of SS. Joachim and Ann
10 SS. Menodora, Metrodora and Nymphodora
11 St. Theodora of Alexandria
12 End of the feast of Our Lady's Birthday
13 Vigil of the morrow's feast; Dedication of the Church of the Resurrection at Jerusalem
14 The Exaltation of the Life-giving Cross; St. John Chrysostom
15 St. Niketas
16 St. Euphemia
17 SS. Faith, Hope, Charity and Wisdom
18 St. Eumenius the Wonderworker
19 SS. Trophimus, Sabbatius and Dorymedon
20 SS. Eustathia and Theopistus and their Sons
21 End of the feast of the Cross; St. Codratus
22 St. Phocas
23 Conception of St. John the Forerunner
24 St. Thecla
25 St. Euphrosyne
26 St. John the Evangelist
27 St. Callistratus
28 St. Khariton
29 St. Cyriacus the Anchorite
30 St. Gregory of Armenia

October 1 St. Ananias; St. Romanus the Hymnwriter
2 SS. Cyprian and Justina
3 St. Dionysius the Areopagite
4 St. Hierotheus of Athens
5 St. Kharitina
6 St. Thomas the Apostle
7 SS. Sergius and Bacchus
8 St. Pelagia
9 St. James the Less
10 SS. Eulampius and Eulampia
11 St. Philip the Apostle; St. Theophanes the Hymnwriter; The Fathers of the Second Council of Nicæa
12 SS. Probus, Tarachus and Andronicus
13 St. Carpus and Other Martyrs
14 SS. Nazarius, Gervasius and Protasius; St. Cosmas the Poet
15 St. Lucian
16 St. Longinus

17 Hosea the Prophet; St. Andrew the Calybite
18 St. Luke the Evangelist
19 Joel the Prophet; St. Varus
20 St. Artemius
21 St. Hilarion
22 St. Abercius; The Seven Children of Ephesus
23 St. James the Greater
24 St. Arethas
25 SS. Marcian and Martyrius
26 St. Demetrius; The Earthquake of A.D. 740
27 St. Nestor
28 SS. Terentius and Neonilla; St. Stephen the Sabbaite; and others
29 St. Anastasia of Rome; St. Abramius
30 SS. Zenobius and Zenobia
31 SS. Stachys and others; St. Epimachus

November 1 SS. Cosmas and Damian
2 St. Acyndinus and his Fellow Martyrs
3 SS. Acepsimas, Joseph and Aithala; Dedication of the Church of St. George at Lydda
4 St. Joannicius; SS. Nicander and Ermeus
5 SS. Galaktion and Episteme
6 St. Paul the Confessor
7 St. Hieron and the Martyrs of Melitene; St. Lazarus the Wonderworker
8 Synaxis of the Archangels Michael and Gabriel and All the Heavenly Powers
9 SS. Onesiphorus and Porphyrus; St. Matrona; St. Theoctista of Lesbos
10 SS. Olympus, Rodion and their Fellow Disciples; St. Orestes
11 St. Menas of Cotiæum; St. Victor; St. Vincent; St. Stephanides; St. Theodore the Studite
12 St. John the Almsgiver; St. Nilus
13 St. John Chrysostom
14 St. Philip the Apostle
15 SS. Gurias and Samonas; St. Abibus
16 St. Matthew the Evangelist
17 St. Gregory the Wonderworker
18 St. Platon; St. Romanus
19 Abdias the Prophet; St. Barlaam
20 Vigil of the morrow's feast; St. Gregory the Decapolite; St. Proclus
21 The Entry of the Mother of God into the Temple (The Presentation)
22 St. Philemon and his Fellow Disciples; SS. Cecily, Valerian and Tiburtius
23 St. Amphilocius; St. Gregory of Agrigentum
24 Pope St. Clement I; St. Peter of Alexandria
25 End of the feast of our Lady's Entry; St. Katharine of Alexandria; St. Mercurius
26 St. Alypius the Stylite; St. Nicon
27 St. James Intercisus
28 St. Stephen the Younger; St. Irenarchus
29 St. Paramon; St. Philemon
30 St. Andrew the First Apostle

December 1 Nahum the Prophet
2 Habacuc the Prophet
3 Sophonias the Prophet
4 St. Barbara; St. John of Damascus
5 St. Sabas
6 St. Nicholas of Myra
7 St. Ambrose
8 Vigil of the morrow's feast; St. Patapius
9 The Child-begetting of the Mother of the Mother of God (The Immaculate Conception)
10 St. Menas the Eloquent and his Fellow Martyrs
11 St. Daniel the Stylite
12 St. Spyridon
13 St. Eustratius and his Fellow Martyrs; St. Lucy
14 St. Thyrsus, St. Philemon, and their Fellow Martyrs
15 St. Eleutherius; St. Paul the Hermit
16 Aggeus the Prophet
17 Daniel the Prophet and the Three Children

18 St. Sebastian and his Fellow Martyrs
19 St. Boniface
20 Beginning of the vigil of Christmas; St. Ignatius the God-bearer
21 St. Juliana
22 St. Anastasia
23 The X Martyrs of Crete
24 St. Eugenia
25 THE BIRTHDAY OF JESUS CHRIST, OUR LORD, OUR SAVIOUR AND OUR GOD
26 Synaxis of the Mother of God; St. Euthymius of Sardis
27 St. Stephen the First Martyr; St. Theodore the Writer
28 The Martyrs of Nicomedia in 303
29 The Holy Innocents; St. Marcellus Akimetes
30 St. Anysia
31 End of the feast of Christmas; St. Melania; St. Zoticus

On the 11th if a Sunday, or the Sunday following: The Ancestors of the Messias
On the Sunday before Christmas: The Fathers who have been Pleasing to God from Adam to St. Joseph

January 1 The Circumcision of our Lord Jesus Christ; St. Basil the Great
         2 Beginning of the vigil of the Epiphany; Pope St. Silvester I
         3 Malachy the Prophet; St. Gordian
         4 The LXX Disciples of the Lord; St. Theoctistus of Cucuma
         5 SS. Theopemptos and Theonas; St. Syncletica
         6 THE EPIPHANY (THEOPHANY) OF JESUS CHRIST, OUR LORD, OUR SAVIOUR AND OUR GOD (His Baptism)
         7 Synaxis of St. John the Forerunner
         8 St. George of Khoziba; St. Domnica; St. Æmilian
         9 St. Polyeuctes
        10 St. Gregory of Nyssa; St. Marcian; St. Dometian of Melitene
        11 St. Theodosius the Cenobiarch
        12 St. Tatiana
        13 SS. Hermylus and Stratonicus
        14 End of the feast of the Epiphany; The Martyrs of Sinai
        15 St. Paul the Theban; St. John Calbyites
        16 St. Peter's Chains
        17 St. Antony the Great
        18 St. Athanasius; St. Cyril of Alexandria
        19 St. Macarius the Egyptian; St. Arsenius of Corcyra
        20 St. Euthymius the Great
        21 St. Maximus the Confessor; St. Neophytus
        22 St. Timothy; St. Anastasius the Persian
        23 St. Clement of Ancyra; St. Agathangelus
        24 St. Xenia
        25 St. Gregory Nazianzen
        26 St. Xenophon
        27 Translation of the Relics of St. John Chrysostom
        28 St. Ephrem the Syrian
        29 Translation of the Relics of St. Ignatius the God-bearer
        30 The Three Holy Hierarchs; St. Hippolytus of Porto
        31 SS. Cyrus and John

February 1 Vigil of the Meeting; St. Tryphon
          2 The Meeting of our Lord Jesus Christ (Hypapante; the Presentation)
          3 Holy Simeon and Anna the Prophetess
          4 St. Isidore of Pelusium
          5 St. Agatha
          6 St. Bucolus; St. Julian of Emesa
          7 St. Parthenius; St. Luke the Hermit
          8 St. Theodore Stratelates; Zachary the Prophet
          9 End of the feast of the Meeting; St. Nicephorus of Antioch
         10 St. Charalampus
         11 St. Blaise
         12 St. Meletius of Antioch
         13 St. Martinian
         14 St. Auxentius the Hermit
         15 St. Onesimus

16 St. Pamphilus and his Fellow Martyrs
17 St. Theodore Tiro
18 Pope St. Leo I
19 St. Archippus
20 St. Leo of Catania
21 St. Timothy of Symbola; St. Eustathius of Antioch
22 The Finding of the Martyrs' Relics in 606
23 St. Polycarp
24 The Finding of the Head of St. John the Forerunner
25 St. Tarasius
26 St. Porphyry of Gaza
27 St. Procopius the Decapolite
28 St. Basil the Confessor
29 St. John Cassian

Tenth Sunday before Easter: Beginning of the triodion of Lent
Ninth Saturday before Easter: Commemoration of the Faithful Departed
Eighth Saturday before Easter: All Holy Ascetes
Seventh Monday before Easter: Great Lent begins
Sixth Sunday before Easter: The Feast of Orthodoxy
Fifth Sunday before Easter: All Holy Relics
Third Sunday before Easter: The Praises of the Mother of God (Akathistos)
Second Saturday before Easter: The Raising of Lazarus

March   1 St. Eudokia
          2 St. Theodotus of Kyrenia
          3 SS. Eutropius, Cleonicus and Basiliscus
          4 St. Gerasimus
          5 St. Conon
          6 The Martyrs of Amorium
          7 St. Ephrem and his Fellow Martyrs
          8 St. Theophylact
          9 The XL Martyrs of Sebaste
         10 St. Codratus of Corinth
         11 St. Sophronius
         12 St. Theophanes
         13 Translation of the Relics of St. Nicephorus of Constantinople
         14 St. Benedict; St. Alexander of Pydna
         15 St. Agapius
         16 St. Sabinus
         17 St. Alexis
         18 St. Cyril of Jerusalem
         19 SS. Chrysanthus and Daria
         20 The Martyrs of Mar Saba
         21 St. James the Confessor
         22 St. Basil of Ancyra
         23 St. Nicon
         24 Vigil of the Annunciation; St. Zachary the Recluse
         25 The Annunciation of the Mother of God
         26 Synaxis of the Archangel Gabriel
         27 St. Matrona of Salonika
         28 St. Stephen the Wonderworker; St. Hilarion the Younger
         29 St. Mark and his Fellow Martyrs; St. Jonas and his Fellow Martyrs
         30 St. John Climacus
         31 St. Hypatius

Between March 22 and April 25 inclusive (equivalent days in the Julian reckoning): THE
   RESURRECTION OF JESUS CHRIST, OUR LORD, OUR SAVIOUR AND OUR GOD
Friday after Easter: The Visitation of the Mother of God

April   1 St. Mary the Egyptian
          2 St. Titus the Wonderworker
          3 St. Niketas the Confessor
          4 SS. Theodulus and Agathopodes; St. George of Maleon; St. Joseph the Hymn-
            writer
          5 St. Claudius and his Fellow Martyrs
          6 St. Eutychius
          7 St. Calliopus; St. George of Melitene
          8 St. Herodion and his Fellow Disciples

9 St. Eupsychius
10 St. Terentius and his Fellow Martyrs
11 St. Antipas
12 St. Basil of Paros
13 Pope St. Martin I
14 St. Aristarchus and his Fellow Disciples
15 St. Crescentius
16 SS. Agape, Irene and Khionia
17 St. Simeon of Seleucia; St. Acacius of Melitene
18 St. John the Isaurian
19 St. Paphnutius the Martyr; St. John of Khariton
20 St. Theodore the Hairy
21 St. Januarius
22 St. Theodore of Sykeon
23 St. George the Victorious
24 St. Elizabeth the Wonderworker; St. Sabas the Martyr
25 St. Mark the Evangelist
26 St. Basil of Amasea
27 St. Simeon of Jerusalem
28 The Martyrs of Cyzicus; St. Memnon
29 SS. Jason and Sosipater; SS. Dadas, Maximus and Quintilian
30 St. James the Greater

May
1 Jeremy the Prophet
2 Translation of the Relics of St. Athanasius
3 SS. Timothy and Mauran
4 St. Pelagia
5 St. Irene
6 The Righteous Job
7 The Appearing of the Cross at Jerusalem in 351; SS. Acacius and Quadratus
8 St. John the Evangelist; St. Arsenius the Great
9 Isaias the Prophet; St. Christopher
10 St. Simon the Apostle
11 The Foundation of Constantinople in 330; St. Mucius
12 St. Epiphanius; St. Germanus of Constantinople
13 St. Glyceria
14 St. Isidore of Khios
15 St. Pachomius; St. Achilles
16 St. Theodore the Sanctified
17 SS. Andronicus and Junias
18 St. Peter and his Fellow Martyrs; St. Theodotus and his Fellow Martyrs
19 St. Patricius and his Fellow Martyrs
20 St. Thalalæus
21 SS. Constantine and Helen
22 St. Basiliscus
23 St. Michael of Synnada
24 St. Simeon Stylites the Younger
25 The Third Finding of the Head of St. John the Forerunner
26 St. Carpus
27 St. Helladius
28 St. Eutychius of Melitene
29 St. Theodosia
30 St. Isaac the Abbot
31 St. Hermes

Forty days after Easter: The Ascension of our Lord Jesus Christ
Sixth Sunday after Easter: The Fathers of the First Council of Nicæa
Seventh Saturday after Easter: Commemoration of the Faithful Departed
Seventh Sunday after Easter: THE FEAST OF PENTECOST (The Most Holy Trinity)
Monday after Pentecost: The Monday of the Holy Spirit
Saturday after Pentecost: The Leave-taking of Pentecost and the end of the triodion of Easter
Sunday after Pentecost: All Saints
Second Thursday after Pentecost: The Most Holy Mystery (Corpus Christi)

June
1 St. Justin the Philosopher
2 St. Nicephorus of Constantinople
3 SS. Lucillian and Paula and their Sons
4 St. Metrophanes

5 St. Dorotheus
6 St. Bessarion; St. Hilarion the Later
7 St. Theodotus of Ancyra
8 Translation of the Relics of St. Theodore Strateletes
9 St. Cyril of Alexandria
10 SS. Alexander and Antonina; St. Timothy of Brusa
11 St. Bartholomew the Apostle; St. Barnabas the Apostle
12 St. Onuphrius; St. Peter the Athonite
13 St. Aquilina; St. Tryphillius
14 Eliseus the Prophet; St. Methodius the Confessor
15 Amos the Prophet
16 St. Tychon the Wonderworker
17 SS. Manuel, Sabel and Ismael
18 SS. Leontius, Hypatius and Theodulus
19 St. Jude the Apostle
20 St. Methodius of Patara
21 St. Julian of Tarsus
22 St. Eusebius of Samosata
23 St. Agrippina
24 The Birthday of St. John the Baptizer and Forerunner
25 St. Febronia
26 St. David of Salonika
27 St. Samson the Hospitable
28 The Finding of the Relics of SS. Cyrus and John
29 St. Peter and St. Paul, Leaders of the Apostles
30 Synaxis of the Twelve Apostles

July
1 SS. Cosmas and Damian
2 The Garment of the Mother of God at Blachernae
3 St. Hyacinth; St. Anatolius
4 St. Andrew of Crete
5 St. Martha of Antioch; St. Athanasius the Athonite; St. Lampadus
6 St. Sisoes
7 St. Thomas of Maleon; St. Acacius the Sinaite; St. Cyriaca
8 St. Procopius
9 St. Pancras of Taormina
10 The Martyrs of Nicopolis
11 St. Euphemia
12 SS. Proclus and Hilarion
13 The Archangel Gabriel; St. Stephen the Wonderworker
14 St. Aquila; St. Joseph of Salonika
15 SS. Cyriacus and Julitta
16 St. Athenogenes
17 St. Marina
18 St. Æmilian
19 St. Macrina; St. Dios
20 Elias the Prophet
21 SS. John and Simeon Salus
22 St. Mary Magdalen
23 Translation of the Relics of St. Phocas; The Prophet Ezechiel; SS. Trophimus and Theophilus
24 St. Christine
25 St. Ann; SS. Olympias and Euphrasia
26 St. Hermolaus; St. Parasceve
27 St. Pantaleon
28 St. Prochorus and his Fellow Deacons
29 St. Callinicus; St. Theodota and her Children
30 St. Silas and his Fellow Disciples
31 St. Eudocimus; Vigil of the morrow's feast

On the 13th if a Sunday, or the Sunday following: The Fathers of the Council of Chalcedon and of the other first five oecumenical councils

August
1 The Procession of the Cross at Constantinople; The Holy Machabees
2 Translation of the Relics of St. Stephen
3 SS. Isaac, Dalmatius and Faustus
4 The Seven Children of Ephesus; Translation of the Relics of St. Eudokia
5 Vigil of the morrow's feast; St. Eusignius

6 The Transfiguration of our Lord Jesus Christ
7 St. Dometius
8 St. Æmilian of Cyzicus
9 St. Matthias the Apostle
10 SS. Lawrence, Pope Sixtus II and Hippolytus
11 St. Euplius
12 SS. Photius and Anicetus
13 End of the feast of the Transfiguration: Translation of the Relics of St. Maximus the Confessor
14 Vigil of the morrow's feast; Micheas the prophet
15 The Falling Asleep of the All-Holy Mother of God
16 The Translation of the Image of the Lord in 944; St. Diomedes
17 St. Myron
18 SS. Florus and Laurus
19 St. Andrew the Great Martyr
20 Samuel the Prophet
21 St. Thaddeus the Apostle
22 St. Agathonicus and his Fellow Martyrs
23 End of the feast of the Assumption; St. Lupus
24 St. Eutyches
25 Translation of the Relics of St. Bartholomew; St. Titus
26 SS. Adrian and Natalia
27 St. Poemen
28 St. Moses the Ethiopian
29 The Beheading of St. John the Forerunner
30 SS. Alexander, John III and Paul IV of Constantinople
31 The Putting of the Girdle of the Mother of God at Constantinople

APPENDIX III

THE BISHOPS OF ROME,
SUPREME PONTIFFS OF THE UNIVERSAL CHURCH

There are some discrepancies in the lists of popes, owing to conflicting records and the uncertain status of certain pontiffs; the following is an attempt to record historical probabilities. Family names, when known, are given in brackets, and the date of accession follows. The dates up to the third century are extremely uncertain.

ST. PETER (Simon bar-Jona)...after	A.D.43	ST. FELIX II (III)^A	483
ST. LINUS	c.67	ST. GELASIUS I	492
ST. CLETUS (or ANACLETUS)	c.79	ANASTASIUS II	496
ST. CLEMENT I	c.91	ST. SYMMACHUS	498
ST. EVARISTUS	c.99	ST. HORMISDAS	514
ST. ALEXANDER I	c.107	ST. JOHN I	523
ST. SIXTUS (XYSTUS) I	c.113	ST. FELIX III (IV)^A	526
ST. TELESPHORUS	c.126	BONIFACE II	530
ST. HYGINUS	c.136	JOHN II	533
ST. PIUS I	c.142	ST. AGAPITUS I	535
ST. ANICETUS	c.154	ST. SILVERIUS	536
ST. SOTER	c.165	VIGILIUS	c.537
ST. ELEUTHERIUS	c.174	PELAGIUS I	556
ST. VICTOR I	c.189	JOHN III	561
ST. ZEPHYRINUS	c.199	BENEDICT I	574
ST. CALLISTUS (CALIXTUS) I	c.217	PELAGIUS II	578
ST. URBAN I	c.222	ST. GREGORY I (probably of the gens	
ST. PONTIAN	c.230	Anicia)	590
ST. ANTHERUS	c.235	SABINIAN	604
ST. FABIAN	c.236	BONIFACE III	607
ST. CORNELIUS	251	ST. BONIFACE IV	608
ST. LUCIUS I	253	ST. DEUSDEDIT (or ADEODATUS I)	615
ST. STEPHEN I	254	BONIFACE V	619
ST. SIXTUS II	257	HONORIUS I	625
ST. DIONYSIUS	259	SEVERINUS	640
ST. FELIX I	c.269	JOHN IV	640
ST. EUTYCHIAN	c.275	THEODORE I	642
ST. CAIUS	283	ST. MARTIN I	649
ST. MARCELLINUS	296	ST. EUGENIUS I	c.655
ST. MARCELLUS I	308	ST. VITALIAN	657
ST. EUSEBIUS	310	ADEODATUS (II)	672
ST. MILTIADES (MELCHIADES)	311	DONUS (or DOMNUS)	676
ST. SILVESTER I	314	ST. AGATHO	678
ST. MARK	336	ST. LEO II	682
ST. JULIUS I	337	ST. BENEDICT II	684
LIBERIUS	352	JOHN V	685
ST. DAMASUS I	366	CONON	686
ST. SIRICIUS	384	ST. SERGIUS I	687
ST. ANASTASIUS I	399	JOHN VI	701
ST. INNOCENT I	401	JOHN VII	705
ST. ZOSIMUS	417	SISINNIUS	708
ST. BONIFACE I	418	CONSTANTINE	708
ST. CELESTINE I	422	ST. GREGORY II	715
ST. SIXTUS III	432	ST. GREGORY III	731
ST. LEO I	440	ST. ZACHARY	741
ST. HILARUS	461	STEPHEN II^B	752
ST. SIMPLICIUS	468	STEPHEN III (II)	752

MARTIN V (Odo Colonna) 1417
EUGENIUS IV (Gabriel Condolmieri).. 1431
NICHOLAS V (Thomas Parenturelli).. 1447
CALLISTUS III (Alfonso de Borja).... 1455
PIUS II (Aeneas Silvius Piccolomini) .. 1458
PAUL II (Peter Barbo) 1464
SIXTUS IV (Francis della Rovere) 1471
INNOCENT VIII (John-Baptist Cibò). 1484
ALEXANDER VI (Rodrigo Borgia) ... 1492
PIUS III (Francis Todeschini-Picco-
lomini) 1503
JULIUS II (Julian della Rovere) 1503
LEO X (John de'Medici) 1513
ADRIAN VI (Adrian Dedel)H 1522
CLEMENT VII (Julius de'Medici) 1523
PAUL III (Alexander Farnese) 1534
JULIUS III (John Ciocchi del Monte) . 1550
MARCELLUS II (Marcello Cervini) .. 1555
PAUL IV (John Peter Caraffa) 1555
PIUS IV (John Angelo Medici) 1559
ST. PIUS V (Michael Ghislieri) 1566
GREGORY XIII (Hugh Buoncompagni) 1572
SIXTUS V (Felix Peretti) 1585
URBAN VII (John-Baptist Castagna) .. 1590
GREGORY XIV (Nicholas Sfondrati) .. 1590
INNOCENT IX (John Facchinetti) 1591
CLEMENT VIII (Hippolytus Aldobran-
dini) 1592
LEO XI (Alexander de'Medici) 1605
PAUL V (Camillo Borghese) 1605
GREGORY XV (Alexander Ludovisi) .. 1621

URBAN VIII (Maffeo Barberini) 1623
INNOCENT X (John-Baptist Pamfili). 1644
ALEXANDER VII (Fabio Chigi) 1655
CLEMENT IX (Julius Rospigliosi) ... 1667
CLEMENT X (Emilio Altieri) 1670
INNOCENT XI (Benedict Odescalchi) . 1676
ALEXANDER VIII (Peter Ottoboni)... 1689
INNOCENT XII (Antony Pignatelli) .. 1691
CLEMENT XI (John Francis Albani).. 1700
INNOCENT XIII (Michelangelo dei
Conti) 1721
BENEDICT XIII (Peter Francis Orsini) 1724
CLEMENT XII (Laurence Corsini) ... 1730
BENEDICT XIV (Prosper Lambertini) 1740
CLEMENT XIII (Charles della Torre
Rezzonico) 1758
CLEMENT XIV (John Laurence
Ganganelli) 1769
PIUS VI (John Angelo Braschi)........ 1775
PIUS VII (Gregory Chiaramonti)...... 1800
LEO XII (Hannibal della Genga) 1823
PIUS VIII (Francis-Xavier Castiglione). 1829
GREGORY XVI (Maurus Bartholomew
Cappellari)I 1831
PIUS IX (John Mastai-Ferretti) 1846
LEO XIII (Joachim Pecci) 1878
* PIUS X (Joseph Sarto) 1903
BENEDICT XV (James della Chiesa).. 1914
PIUS XI (Achilles Ratti) 1922
PIUS XII (Eugene Pacelli) 1939

JOHN XXIII (Angelo Giuseppe Roncalli)
1958
PAUL VI (Giovanni Battista Montini) 1963.
JOHN PAUL I (Albino Luciani) 1978.
JOHN PAUL II (Karol Wojtyla) 1978.
BENEDICT XVI (Josef Ratzinger) 2005

NOTES

A These two popes are often numbered III and IV respectively, owing to the intrusion into ancient lists of a Felix II who was certainly an antipope, under Liberius.

B This pope died on the third day after his election before being consecrated bishop, and his name was therefore often omitted from some lists. This accounts for the alternative numeration of subsequent Stephens.

C The first pope of whom it is recorded that he took a new name upon election to the papacy, in his case out of respect to the memory of St. Peter.

D Lists differ in the numeration of the subsequent Johns. *Cf.* note to John XXI. John XVI was an antipope 997-8.

E He was really only the twentieth, but somewhere among his predecessors an error of enumeration had been made (Mgr. Duchesne attributes it to a doubling of John XIV).

F Really the second; *cf.* Marinus I and II.

G The last pope up to the present who was not a cardinal at the time of his election.

H Adrian VI, a Dutchman, was the last pope to date who was not a Roman or other Italian; but Sixtus V was an Italo-Slav and Clement XI was of Albanian descent.

I The last pope to date who was not already a bishop at the time of his election.

---

* Now ST. PIUS X since his canonization in 1954.—*Publisher*, 1997.

APPENDIX IV

ECCLESIASTICAL TITLES AND MODES OF ADDRESS

These vary considerably according to the country, but the following is good English usage for (1) addressing a letter, etc., (2) beginning a letter and in its body, (3) personal speech. Many of the forms are, of course, modified by the occasion and the degree of acquaintanceship.

The Pope. (1) His Holiness Pope N——. (2) Most Holy Father; your Holiness; Prostrate at the feet of your Holiness, I have the honour to profess myself with the most profound respect, your Holiness's most obedient and humble servant ——. (3) Your Holiness.

Cardinals. (1) His Eminence Cardinal N——. (2) My Lord Cardinal; your Eminence; I have the honour to be, with great respect, your Eminence's most obedient and humble servant——. (3) Your Eminence. *If he is an archbishop or bishop:* (1) His Eminence the Cardinal Archbishop of ——, *or* His Eminence Cardinal N——, Archbishop of ——. *The rest as above.*

Patriarchs, Eastern. (1) His Beatitude (or Blessedness) the Patriarch of ——, *or* His Beatitude the Lord (*Christian name*), Patriarch of ——. (2) Most Reverend Lord; your Beatitude; I have the honour to be your Beatitude's obedient servant ——. (3) Your Beatitude.

Patriarchs, Latin Titular, and Nuncios. (1) His Excellency the Patriarch (Archbishop) of ——, *or* His Excellency Monsignor N——, Patriarch (Archbishop) of ——. (2) My Lord Patriarch (Archbishop) *or* Most Reverend Excellency; your Excellency; I have the honour to be your Excellency's obedient servant ——. (3) Your Excellency.

Archbishops. (1) His Grace the Archbishop of ——, *or* The Most Reverend A—— B——, Archbishop of ——. (2) My Lord Archbishop *or* My Lord; your Grace; I have the honour to be your Grace's obedient servant ——. (3) Your Grace.

Bishops. (1) The Lord Bishop of ——, *or* The Right Reverend A—— B——, Bishop of ——. (2) My Lord Bishop *or* My Lord; your Lordship; I have the honour to be your Lordship's obedient servant ——. (3) My Lord.
 Bishops in Ireland are Most Reverend; the style Lord, Lordship, etc., is not generally used in the United States for archbishops, bishops, or abbots.

Titular Archbishops and Bishops. *These are best addressed in exactly the same way as diocesan prelates, but their office may be added, e.g.,* The Right Reverend A—— B——, Vicar Apostolic of ——.
 On the use of the title Monsignor (*to which all bishops are entitled*) *and of bishop as a prefix, see within under* Monsignor.

Abbots. (1) The Lord Abbot of —— *or* The Right Reverend Dom A—— B——, O.S.B. (*or otherwise*), Abbot of ——. (2) My Lord Abbot *or* Dear Father Abbot. (3) My Lord *or* Father Abbot. Abbesses *similarly, substituting* Lady Abbess, Dame and Mother.

Protonotaries Apostolic, Domestic Prelates, Vicars General. (1) The Right Reverend Monsignor A—— B——, Prot. Ap., *or* V.G. (2) Right Reverend Monsignor *or* Dear Monsignor N——. (3) Monsignor.

Provosts, Canons. (1) The Very Reverend Provost A—— B——. The Very Reverend Canon A—— B——. The Very Reverend A——, Canon B—— *is a common usage.* (2) Very Reverend Provost, Dear Canon N——. (3) Provost, Canon.

Papal Chamberlains. (1) The Very Reverend Monsignor A—— B——. (2) Very Reverend Monsignor *or* Dear Monsignor N——. (3) Monsignor.

Rectors of Seminaries, Heads of Colleges, etc., *are commonly addressed as* The Very Reverend A—— B——.

Provincials of Religious Orders. (1) The Very Reverend Father Provincial, O.F.M. (*or otherwise*), *or* The Very Reverend Father A—— B——, Provincial S.J. (2) Very Reverend Father *or* Dear Father Provincial. (3) Father Provincial.

Conventual Priors and their equivalents. (1) The Very Reverend the Prior of —— *or* The Very Reverend Father (*or* Dom, *see below*) A—— B—— O.P. (*or otherwise*), Prior of ——. The Very Reverend Father Guardian, O.F.M. (2) Very Reverend Father *or* Dear Father Prior. (3) Father Prior. Prioesses *similarly, substituting* Prioress, Mother, Dame (*if required*).

Claustral Priors. (1) The Very Reverend Dom A—— B——, O.C. (*or otherwise*) *or* The Very Reverend Father Prior, —— Abbey. (2) Very Reverend Father *or* Dear Father Prior. (3) Father Prior.

Archdeacons. (1) The Venerable the Archdeacon of —— *or* The Venerable A—— B——, Archdeacon of ——.
There are no archdeacons *and no* deans, *properly so called, in England.* Rural Deans *are addressed as* The Very Reverend A—— B——, R.D., *or* V.F.

Preachers General. (1) The Venerable and Very Reverend Father A—— B——, O.P., P.G.

Priests, Secular. (1) The Reverend A—— B——. (2) Reverend Sir *or* Dear Father N——. (3) Father. *For this usage of* Father, *see within under that word.*

Priests, Regular. (1) The Reverend Father A—— B——, O.S.M. (*or otherwise; and see below*). (2) Reverend Father *or* Dear Father N. (*Christian name*). (3) Father. *Benedictine and Cistercian monks and Canons Regular are addressed* Dom, *thus:* The Reverend Dom A—— B——, C.R.L. (*or otherwise*), *but in speech as* Father; *Carthusian monks as* The Venerable Father Dom A—— B——, O.Cart.

Clerics below the order of priesthood. (1) The Reverend A—— B——. (2) Reverend Sir *or* Dear Mr. N——. (3) Mr. N——. *The Style of* clerics who are members of religious orders *is modified according to their status in the order.*

If you have enjoyed this book, consider making your next selection from among the following . . .

Prices subject to change.

Prices subject to change.

Prices subject to change.

Prices subject to change.

At your Bookdealer or direct from the Publisher.

Toll-Free 1-800-437-5876   Fax 815-226-7770
Tel. 815-226-7777   www.tanbooks.com
Prices subject to change.